Baseball America®

2018
PROSPECT
HANDBOOK

BASEBALL AMERICA INC. DURHAM, N.C.

Baseball America

2018 PROSPECT HANDBOOK

Editors
J.J. COOPER, MATT EDDY AND KYLE GLASER

Assistant Editors
BEN BADLER, TEDDY CAHILL,
CARLOS COLLAZO, MICHAEL LANANNA,
JOSH NORRIS AND KEGAN LOWE

Database and Application Development
BRENT LEWIS

Contributing Writers
BILL BALLEW, MIKE BERARDINO,
MIKE DIGIOVANNA, DUSTIN DOPIRAK,
TOM HAUDRICOURT, STEVE KRONER,
JOHN MANUEL, JON MEOLI, BILL MITCHELL,
NICK PIECORO, ALEX SPEIER, TRACY RINGOLSBY
AND C. TRENT ROSECRANS

Photo Editor
BRENDAN NOLAN

Design & Production
JAMES ALWORTH, SARA HIATT MCDANIEL
AND LINWOOD WEBB

Cover Photo
VLADIMIR GUERRERO JR. BY CLIFF WELCH

FOR ADDITIONAL COPIES, VISIT OUR
WEBSITE AT BASEBALLAMERICA.COM OR
CALL 1-800-845-2726 TO ORDER.

US $32.95, PLUS SHIPPING AND HANDLING PER ORDER.
EXPEDITED SHIPPING AVAILABLE.

DISTRIBUTED BY SIMON & SCHUSTER
ISBN: 978-1-932391-76-3

STATISTICS PROVIDED BY MAJOR LEAGUE BASEBALL
ADVANCED MEDIA AND COMPILED BY
BASEBALL AMERICA.

Baseball America

ESTABLISHED 1981 • P.O. Box 12877, Durham, NC 27709 • Phone (919) 682-9635

EDITOR AND PUBLISHER	B.J. Schecter
EXECUTIVE EDITORS	J.J. Cooper, Matt Eddy
DIRECTOR OF BUSINESS DEVELOPMENT	Ben Leigh

EDITORIAL
ASSOCIATE EDITORS	Kegan Lowe @KeganLowe
	Josh Norris @jnorris427
SENIOR WRITER	Ben Badler @benbadler
NATIONAL WRITERS	Teddy Cahill @tedcahill
	Carlos Collazo @CarlosACollazo
	Kyle Glaser @KyleAGlaser
	Michael Lananna @mlananna
SPECIAL CONTRIBUTOR	Tim Newcomb

PRODUCTION
DESIGN & PRODUCTION DIRECTOR	Sara Hiatt McDaniel
MULTIMEDIA MANAGER	Linwood Webb
DESIGN ASSISTANT	James Alworth

ADVERTISING
ADVERTISING DIRECTOR	George Shelton
DIGITAL SALES MANAGER	Larry Sarzyniak

BUSINESS
DIRECTOR OF OPERATIONS	Hailey Carpenter
TECHNOLOGY MANAGER	Brent Lewis
CUSTOMER SERVICE	Jonathan Smith

STATISTICAL SERVICE
MAJOR LEAGUE BASEBALL ADVANCED MEDIA

BASEBALL AMERICA ENTERPRISES

Alliance
>>>> BASEBALL <<<<

CHAIRMAN & CEO	Gary Green
PRESIDENT	Larry Botel
GENERAL COUNSEL	Matthew Pace
DIRECTOR OF MARKETING	Amy Heart
INVESTOR RELATIONS	Michele Balfour
DIRECTOR OF OPERATIONS	Joan Disalvo
PARTNERS	Jon Ashley
	Stephen Alepa
	Martie Cordaro
	Brian Rothschild
	Andrew Fox
	Maurice Haroche
	Dan Waldman
	Sonny Kalsi
	Glenn Isaacson
	Robert Hernreich
	Craig Amazeen
	Peter Ruprecht
	Beryl Snyder
	Tom Steiglehner

3STEP

MANAGING PARTNER	David Geaslen
CHIEF CONTENT OFFICER	Jonathan Segal
CHIEF FINANCIAL OFFICER	Sue Murphy
DIRECTOR OF DIGITAL CONTENT	Tom Johnson
DIRECTOR OF OPERATIONS, DATABASE/VIDEO	Brendan Nolan

When the first Prospect Handbook was published in 2001, it seemed like an audacious idea. Under founder Allan Simpson's leadership, Baseball America had popularized organization Top 10 Prospects lists in the magazine, but the effort required to turn a Top 10 into a Top 30 for all 30 organizations required a massive amount of additional work.

But it was done. And what we found is that the reporting required to do a Top 30 not only gave fans a chance to read up on more of their team's future big leaguers, but it also improved out Top 10s. Every year since then, we have figured out ways to do this book a little better. The amount of information we gathered to produce the 2018 Prospect Handbook would have been beyond our imagination when we produced the first book in 2001.

Now we update our Top 100 and Top 10s at midseason. That idea seemed nearly impossible a decade ago, but now it's just a normal part of the Baseball America workflow.

We hope that the updates and tweaks we've made to this year's edition will make this the best Prospect Handbook you've ever purchased. Next year will surely bring some additional tweaks.

The Prospect Handbook is the biggest project the Baseball America staff undertakes each year. We're proud of that, and we want to make sure that it's well worth your purchase. We hope you enjoy it as much as we enjoyed spending the past year watching players, talking to scouts and writing up these 900-plus reports.

J.J. COOPER AND MATT EDDY
EXECUTIVE EDITORS, BASEBALL AMERICA

A NOTE ABOUT THIS EDITION

Baseball America introduced BA Grades in the 2012 edition of the Prospect Handbook. Now for the first time, we grade all tools for the 300 players who rank as Top 10 Prospects, providing an quick overview of each player's strengths and weaknesses. All grades are projected future grades.

We grade players' tools on the 20-80 scouting scale, where 50 is average. A key to the abbreviations:

Players		Pitchers*	
HIT	Ability to hit for average	**FB**	Fastball
POW	Power	**CB**	Curveball
SPD	Speed	**SL**	Slider
FLD	Fielding ability	**CHG**	Changeup
ARM	Throwing arm	**CTL**	Control

* Some pitchers receive a grade for OTH or "Other," which is typically a cutter or splitter. In the case of Rays righthander Brent Honeywell it's a screwball.

ALSO NEW IN THE 2018 EDITION:

• **POSITION RANKINGS:** Beginning on Page 13, we rank prospects at all eight field positions plus righthanded and lefthanded starting pitcher, all to at least 10 places. We know many fantasy and simulation league players make use of the Prospect Handbook to gain an edge, so we enhanced the book's utility by grading prospects at each position. The Position Rankings supplant the personal Top 50 Prospects from previous editions.

• **PROJECTED 2021 LINEUPS:** Our crystal ball now includes players' season ages in 2021. Find out if your team is building a dynasty.

• **MORE SPACE FOR REPORTS:** We budgeted an additional page for each chapter to give you more of what you value most: scouting reports. We also improved the readability of our reports by breaking them into the three familiar segments that appear in the magazine: Track Record, Scouting Report and The Future.

EDITOR'S NOTE: The transactions deadline for this book was Dec. 14, 2017. You can find players who changed organizations by using the handy index in the back.
>> For the purposes of this book, a prospect is any player who has not exceeded 50 innings, 30 relief appearances or 130 at-bats in the major leagues, regardless of major league service time. Finally, the grades attached to each team's draft class, as evaluated by Teddy Cahill, are based solely on the quality of the players signed, with no consideration given to any players acquired by trading those draft picks or for how many draft picks a team might have lost.

TABLE OF CONTENTS

CHICAGO WHITE SOX

STARTS ON PAGE 98

No. Player, Pos.	Grade/Risk	No. Player, Pos.	Grade/Risk	No. Player, Pos.	Grade/Risk
1. Eloy Jimenez, OF	70/H	11. Zack Burdi, RHP	55/X	21. Alex Call, OF	45/H
2. Michael Kopech, RHP	65/M	12. Spencer Adams, RHP	50/H	22. Ian Clarkin, LHP	45/H
3. Alec Hansen, RHP	55/H	13. Carson Fulmer, RHP	45/M	23. Ian Hamilton, RHP	45/H
4. Luis Robert, OF	60/X	14. Luis Gonzalez, OF	50/H	24. Tyler Johnson, RHP	45/H
5. Dane Dunning, RHP	55/H	15. A.J. Puckett, RHP	50/H	25. Jordan Guerrero, LHP	45/H
6. Zack Collins, C	55/H	16. Jordan Stephens, RHP	50/H	26. Bernardo Flores, LHP	40/H
7. Jake Burger, 3B	55/H	17. Micker Adolfo, OF	50/V	27. Tito Polo, OF	40/H
8. Blake Rutherford, OF	55/V	18. Luis Alex. Basabe, OF	50/V	28. Lenyn Sosa, SS	45/X
9. Gavin Sheets, 1B	50/H	19. Lincoln Henzman, RHP	50/V	29. Seby Zavala, C	40/H
10. Dylan Cease, RHP	50/H	20. Thyago Vieira, RHP	50/V	30. Connor Walsh, RHP	40/H

CINCINNATI REDS

STARTS ON PAGE 114

No. Player, Pos.	Grade/Risk	No. Player, Pos.	Grade/Risk	No. Player, Pos.	Grade/Risk
1. Nick Senzel, 3B	65/M	11. Jeter Downs, SS	50/X	21. Gavin LaValley, 1B	45/H
2. Hunter Greene, RHP	65/X	12. Jose Israel Garcia, SS	50/X	22. Keury Mella, RHP	45/H
3. Taylor Trammell, OF	60/H	13. Alfredo Rodriguez, SS	45/H	23. Nick Longhi, 1B	45/H
4. Tyler Mahle, RHP	50/M	14. Aristides Aquino, OF	45/H	24. Jackson Stephens, RHP	40/M
5. Jesse Winker, OF	50/M	15. Jacob Heatherly, LHP	50/X	25. Jose Lopez, RHP	40/M
6. Tony Santillan, RHP	50/H	16. Stuart Fairchild, OF	45/H	26. Miles Gordon, OF	45/H
7. Jose Siri, OF	50/H	17. T.J. Friedl, OF	45/H	27. Alex Blandino, 2B	40/M
8. Shed Long, 2B	50/H	18. Jimmy Herget, RHP	40/M	28. Packy Naughton, LHP	45/H
9. Vladimir Gutierrez, RHP	50/H	19. Phillip Ervin, OF	40/M	29. Scott Moss, LHP	45/H
10. Tyler Stephenson, C	50/V	20. Tanner Rainey, RHP	45/H	30. Nick Hanson, RHP	50/X

CLEVELAND INDIANS

STARTS ON PAGE 130

No. Player, Pos.	Grade/Risk	No. Player, Pos.	Grade/Risk	No. Player, Pos.	Grade/Risk
1. Francisco Mejia, C	60/H	11. Erik Gonzalez, SS/2B	40/L	21. Johnathan Rodriguez, OF	50/X
2. Triston McKenzie, RHP	60/H	12. Aaron Bracho, SS	55/X	22. Luis Oviedo, RHP	50/X
3. Bobby Bradley, 1B	55/V	13. Quentin Holmes, OF	55/X	23. Tyler Krieger, 2B	45/H
4. Nolan Jones, 3B	55/H	14. Aaron Civale, RHP	50/H	24. Ernie Clement, 2B/SS	45/H
5. Shane Bieber, RHP	50/H	15. Conner Capel, OF	50/H	25. Mark Mathias, 2B/3B	45/H
6. Yu-Cheng Chang, SS	50/H	16. Tyler Freeman, SS	55/X	26. Ryan Merritt, LHP	40/M
7. Willi Castro, SS	50/H	17. Julian Merryweather, RHP	50/H	27. Gavin Collins, 3B	45/H
8. Greg Allen, OF	45/H	18. Sam Hentges, LHP	50/V	28. Brady Aiken, LHP	50/X
9. George Valera, OF	55/X	19. Logan Ice, C	45/H	29. Eli Morgan, RHP	45/H
10. Will Benson, OF	55/X	20. Oscar Gonzalez, OF	50/V	30. Marcos Gonzalez, SS	50/X

COLORADO ROCKIES

STARTS ON PAGE 146

No. Player, Pos.	Grade/Risk	No. Player, Pos.	Grade/Risk	No. Player, Pos.	Grade/Risk
1. Brendan Rodgers, SS/2B	65/H	11. Sam Howard, LHP	45/M	21. Mike Nikorak, RHP	50/X
2. Ryan McMahon, 1B/2B	50/M	12. Tom Murphy, C	45/M	22. Harrison Musgrave, LHP	40/M
3. Riley Pint, RHP	60/X	13. Brian Mundell, 1B	50/H	23. Daniel Montano, OF	50/X
4. Colton Welker, 3B	50/H	14. Sam Hillard, OF	50/H	24. Yonathan Daza, OF	45/H
5. Peter Lambert, RHP	50/H	15. Jordan Patterson, OF/1B	40/L	25. Josh Fuentes, 3B	40/M
6. Ryan Castellani, RHP	50/H	16. Breiling Eusebio, LHP	50/V	26. Reid Humphreys, RHP	45/H
7. Yency Almonte, RHP	45/M	17. Jesus Tinoco, RHP	50/V	27. Vince Fernandez, OF	45/H
8. Garrett Thompson, 2B/SS	45/M	18. Forrest Wall, 2B/CF	45/H	28. Chad Spanberger, 1B	45/H
9. Ryan Vilade, SS	55/X	19. Will Gaddis, RHP	50/X	29. Dom Nunez, C	40/H
10. Tyler Nevin, 3B	50/H	20. Ben Bowden, LHP	45/H	30. Rayan Gonzalez, RHP	40/H

DETROIT TIGERS

STARTS ON PAGE 162

No. Player, Pos.	Grade/Risk	No. Player, Pos.	Grade/Risk	No. Player, Pos.	Grade/Risk
1. Franklin Perez, RHP	60/H	11. Kyle Funkhoser, RHP	50/H	21. Wladimir Pinto, RHP	50/X
2. Alex Faedo, RHP	60/H	12. Spencer Turnbill, RHP	50/H	22. Grayson Greiner, C	40/M
3. Matt Manning, RHP	60/V	13. John McMillan, C	50/H	23. Jason Foley, RHP	50/X
4. Beau Burrows, RHP	50/M	14. Mike Gerber, OF	45/M	24. Wenceel Perez, SS	50/X
5. Jake Rogers, C	50/H	15. Joe Jimenez, RHP	45/M	25. Victor Reyes, OF	40/M
6. Daz Cameron, OF	50/H	16. Bryan Garcia, RHP	45/H	26. Sergio Alcantara, SS	40/M
7. Isaac Paredes, 2B/SS	50/H	17. Jose King, SS	50/X	27. Troy Montogermy, OF	40/M
8. Dawel Lugo, 2B/3B	45/M	18. Gerson Moreno, RHP	45/H	28. Derek Hill, OF	40/M
9. Christin Stewart, OF	50/H	19. Anthony Castro, RHP	45/H	29. Austin Sodders, RHP	45/H
10. Gregory Soto, LHP	50/H	20. Wilkel Hernandez, RHP	50/X	30. Sandy Baez, RHP	45/H

TABLE OF CONTENTS

MILWAUKEE BREWERS

STARTS ON PAGE 258

No. Player, Pos.	Grade/Risk	No. Player, Pos.	Grade/Risk	No. Player, Pos.	Grade/Risk
1. Lewis Brinson, OF	60/M	11. Tristen Luiz, OF	55/X	21. Kodi Medeiros, LHP	45/H
2. Brandon Woodruff, RHP	55/M	12. Freddy Peralta, RHP	50/H	22. Marcos Diplan, RHP	45/H
3. Corbin Burnes, RHP	55/M	13. Mauricio Dubon, SS/2B	45/M	23. Jacob Nottingham, C	45/H
4. Keston Hiura, 2B	60/H	14. Jake Gatewood, 1B/3B	50/H	24. Caden Lemons, RHP	50/X
5. Monte Harrison, OF	60/V	15. Trent Grisham, OF	50/H	25. Trey Dupak, RHP	45/H
6. Luis Ortiz, RHP	55/H	16. K.J. Harrison, C	50/H	26. Carlos Herrera, RHP	45/H
7. Brett Phillips, OF	50/M	17. Phil Bickford, RHP	50/H	27. Nathan Kirby, LHP	50/X
8. Lucas Erceg, 3B	55/V	18. Cody Ponce, RHP	50/H	28. Payton Henry, C	45/X
9. Isan Diaz, 2B/SS	50/H	19. Josh Pennington, RHP	55/X	29. Antonio Pinero, SS	45/X
10. Corey Ray, OF	50/H	20. Mario Feliciano, C	45/H	30. Chad McClanahan, 3B/1B	45/X

MINNESOTA TWINS

STARTS ON PAGE 274

No. Player, Pos.	Grade/Risk	No. Player, Pos.	Grade/Risk	No. Player, Pos.	Grade/Risk
1. Royce Lewis, SS	65/V	11. Akil Baddoo, OF	50/H	21. John Curtiss, RHP	45/H
2. Wander Javier, SS	60/X	12. Felix Jorge, RHP	45/M	22. Jacob Pearson, OF	50/X
3. Alex Kirilloff, OF	60/X	13. Landon Leach, RHP	50/H	23. Mitch Garver, C	40/M
4. Stephen Gonsalves, LHP	50/M	14. Yunior Severino, 2B	55/X	24. Jose Miranda, 2B	50/X
5. Brusdar Graterol, RHP	60/X	15. Luis Arraez, 2B	50/H	25. Andrew Bechtold, 3B	50/X
6. Fernando Romero, RHP	55/H	16. Lewis Thorpe, LHP	50/H	26. Lewin Diaz, 1B	45/H
7. Brent Rooker, OF/1B	55/H	17. LaMonte Wade, OF	50/H	27. Zack Granite, OF	40/M
8. Nick Gordon, SS	50/M	18. Zack Littell, RHP	50/H	28. David Banuelos, C	45/H
9. Blayne Enlow, RHP	55/X	19. Aaron Whitefield, OF	50/V	29. Travis Blankenhorn, 2B	45/H
10. Tyler Jay, LHP	50/H	20. Tyler Watson, LHP	45/H	30. Kohl Stewart, RHP	45/V

NEW YORK METS

STARTS ON PAGE 290

No. Player, Pos.	Grade/Risk	No. Player, Pos.	Grade/Risk	No. Player, Pos.	Grade/Risk
1. Andres Gimenez, SS	55/H	11. Ronny Mauricio, SS	55/X	21. Adonis Uceta, RHP	45/H
2. David Peterson, LHP	55/H	12. Tomas Nido, C	45/M	22. Quinn Brodey, OF	50/V
3. Justin Dunn, RHP	55/V	13. Gavin Cecchini, 2B/SS	45/M	23. Jacob Rhame, RHP	45/H
4. Peter Alonso, 1B	50/H	14. Anthony Kay, LHP	55/X	24. P.J. Conlon, LHP	45/H
5. Thomas Szapucki, LHP	55/X	15. Jordan Humphreys, RHP	50/H	25. Gerson Bautista, RHP	45/H
6. Mark Vientos, SS/3B	55/X	16. Corey Oswalt, RHP	45/H	26. Luis Carpio, 2B/SS	50/X
7. Marcos Molina, RHP	50/H	17. Jamie Callahan, RHP	45/H	27. Ali Sanchez, C	50/X
8. Desmond Lindsay, OF	55/X	18. Patrick Mazeika, C/1B	45/H	28. Adrian Hernandez, OF	50/X
9. Chris Flexen, RHP	45/M	19. Ty Bashlor, RHP	45/H	29. David Thompson, 3B	45/H
10. Luis Guillorme, 2B/SS	45/M	20. Drew Smith, RHP	45/H	30. Christian James, RHP	50/X

NEW YORK YANKEES

STARTS ON PAGE 306

No. Player, Pos.	Grade/Risk	No. Player, Pos.	Grade/Risk	No. Player, Pos.	Grade/Risk
1. Gleyber Torres, SS/3B	65/M	11. Matt Sauer, RHP	55/X	21. Juan De Paula, RHP	50/H
2. Estevan Florial, OF	65/V	12. Nick Solak, 2B	50/H	22. Taylor Widener, RHP	50/H
3. Justus Sheffield, LHP	60/H	13. Freicer Perez, RHP	50/H	23. Billy McKinney, OF/1B	45/M
4. Chance Adams, RHP	55/M	14. Clarke Schmidt, RHP	55/X	24. Deivi Garcia, RHP	50/V
5. Miguel Andujar, 3B	55/M	15. Tyler Wade, SS/2B	45/M	25. Jonathan Loaisiga, RHP	50/V
6. Albert Abreu, RHP	60/H	16. Domingo German, RHP	50/H	26. Oswaldo Cabrera, SS/2B	45/H
7. Luis Medina, RHP	60/X	17. Juan Then, RHP	55/X	27. Diego Castillo, SS	50/X
8. Thairo Estrada, SS/2B	50/H	18. Trevor Stephan, RHP	50/H	28. Alexander Vargas, RHP	45/H
9. Domingo Acevedo, RHP	50/H	19. Glenn Otto, RHP	50/H	29. Rony Garcia, RHP	45/H
10. Dillon Tate, RHP	50/H	20. Dermis Garcia, 3B	50/H	30. Cody Carroll, RHP	45/H

OAKLAND ATHLETICS

STARTS ON PAGE 322

No. Player, Pos.	Grade/Risk	No. Player, Pos.	Grade/Risk	No. Player, Pos.	Grade/Risk
1. A.J. Puk, LHP	60/H	11. Greg Deichmann, OF	50/H	21. Frankie Montas, RHP	40/M
2. Franklin Barreto, SS	55/M	12. Grant Holmes, RHP	55/H	22. Alexander Campos, SS	50/X
3. Jorge Mateo, SS	55/H	13. Daulton Jeffries, RHP	55/X	23. Richie Martin, SS	40/H
4. Dustin Fowler, OF	55/H	14. Sheldon Neuse, 3B	50/H	24. B.J. Boyd, OF	40/H
5. Jesus Luzardo, LHP	60/X	15. Nick Allen, SS	50/X	25. Yerdel Vargas, SS	45/X
6. Austin Beck, OF	60/X	16. Kevin Merrell, SS	45/H	26. James Naile, RHP	40/H
7. Sean Murphy, C	50/H	17. Tyler Ramirez, OF	45/H	27. Casey Meisner, RHP	40/H
8. James Kaprielian, RHP	55/X	18. Heath Fillmyer, RHP	45/H	28. Marcos Brito, 2B	45/X
9. Lazaro Armentaros, OF	55/X	19. Will Toffey, 3B	45/H	29. Dakota Chalmers, RHP	40/H
10. Logan Shore, RHP	50/H	20. Renato Nunez, 3B/OF	40/M	30. Ramon Lauereano, OF	40/H

TABLE OF CONTENTS

SEATTLE MARINERS

STARTS ON PAGE 418

No.Player, Pos.	Grade/Risk	No.Player, Pos.	Grade/Risk	No.Player, Pos.	Grade/Risk
1. Kyle Lewis, OF	60/V	11. Wyatt Mills, RHP	45/H	21. Oliver Jaskie, LHP	45/H
2. Evan White, 1B	55/H	12. Dan Vogelbach, 1B	40/M	22. Mike Ford, 1B	40/H
3. Sam Carlson, RHP	55/X	13. Nick Rumbelow, RHP	40/M	23. Donnie Walton, SS	40/H
4. Julio Rodriguez, OF	55/X	14. Eric Filia, OF/1B	45/H	24. Luis Liberato, OF	40/H
5. Braden Bishop, OF	45/M	15. Rob Whalen, RHP	40/M	25. Joseph Rosa, 2B	45/X
6. Max Povse, RHP	45/M	16. Chase De Jong, RHP	40/M	26. Tommy Romero, RHP	45/X
7. Matt Festa, RHP	45/H	17. Seth Elledge, RHP	45/H	27. Bryson Brigman, 2B	40/H
8. Art Warren, RHP	45/H	18. Anthony Misiewicz, LHP	40/M	28. Johnny Adams, 3B	40/H
9. Joe Rizzo, 3B	50/V	19. Ian Miller, OF	40/M	29. Ronald Rosario, OF	45/X
10. Juan Querecuto, SS	50/X	20. Sam Moll, LHP	40/M	30. Jorge Benitez, LHP	45/X

TAMPA BAY RAYS

STARTS ON PAGE 434

No.Player, Pos.	Grade/Risk	No.Player, Pos.	Grade/Risk	No.Player, Pos.	Grade/Risk
1. Brent Honeywell, RHP	65/M	11. Josh Lowe, OF	55/X	21. Nick Ciuffo, C	40/M
2. Willy Adames, SS	60/M	12. Ronaldo Hernandez, C	55/X	22. Jake Cronenworth, SS	45/H
3. Brendan McKay, LHP/1B	60/H	13. Michael Mercado, RHP	55/X	23. Yonny Chirinos, RHP	40/M
4. Jake Bauers, 1B/OF	55/M	14. Genesis Cabrera, LHP	50/H	24. Resly Linares, RHP	50/X
5. Jesus Sanchez, OF	60/H	15. Tobias Myers, RHP	50/H	25. Jose De Leon, RHP	45/H
6. Wander Franco, SS	60/X	16. Brandon Lowe, 2B	45/M	26. Ryan Yarbrough, LHP	40/M
7. Lucius Fox, SS	50/H	17. Joe McCarthy, 1B/OF	45/M	27. Chih-Wei Hu, RHP	40/M
8. Justin Williams, OF	45/M	18. Ryan Boldt, OF	45/H	28. Jaime Schultz, RHP	45/H
9. Garrett Whitley, OF	50/H	19. Drew Strotman, RHP	50/H	29. Diego Castillo, RHP	40/M
10. Austin Franklin, RHP	55/X	20. Vidal Brujan, 2B	55/X	30. Ian Gibaut, RHP	45/H

TEXAS RANGERS

STARTS ON PAGE 450

No.Player, Pos.	Grade/Risk	No.Player, Pos.	Grade/Risk	No.Player, Pos.	Grade/Risk
1. Willie Calhoun, OF/2B	55/M	11. Joe Palumbo, LHP	55/X	21. Nick Gardewine, LHP	40/M
2. Leody Taveras, OF	60/V	12. Matt Whatley, C	50/H	22. Josh Morgan, SS/C	45/H
3. Hans Crouse, RHP	60/X	13. Carlos Tocci, OF	45/M	23. Yanio Perez, 3B/OF/1B	45/H
4. Cole Ragans, LHP	55/H	14. Drew Robinson, OF	40/L	24. Pedro Gonzalez, OF	50/X
5. Yohander Mendez, LHP	50/M	15. Tyreque Reed, 1B	50/X	25. A.J. Alexy, RHP	45/H
6. Ronald Guzman, 1B	45/M	16. David Garcia, C	50/X	26. Alex Speas, RHP	50/X
7. Kyle Cody, RHP	50/H	17. Johnathan Hernandez, RHP	45/H	27. Anderson Tejeda, SS	45/V
8. Miguel Aparicio, OF	50/H	18. Brett Martin, LHP	45/H	28. Jose Trevino, C	40/H
9. Bubba Thompson, OF	55/X	19. C.D. Pelham, LHP	45/H	29. Andy Ibanez, 2B/3B	40/H
10. Chris Seise, SS	55/X	20. Keyber Rodriguez, SS	50/X	30. Michael Matuella, RHP	45/X

TORONTO BLUE JAYS

STARTS ON PAGE 466

No.Player, Pos.	Grade/Risk	No.Player, Pos.	Grade/Risk	No.Player, Pos.	Grade/Risk
1. Vladimir Guerrero Jr., 3B	75/H	11. Sean Reid-Foley, RHP	50/H	21. Rowdy Tellez, 1B	40/M
2. Bo Bichette, SS	65/H	12. T.J. Zeuch, RHP	50/H	22. Harold Ramirez, OF	40/M
3. Anthony Alford, OF	50/M	13. Ryan Noda, RHP	50/V	23. Max Pentecost, C/1B	45/V
4. Nate Pearson, RHP	55/V	14. Edward Olivares, OF	50/V	24. Mc Gregory Contreras, OF	45/V
5. Lourdes Gurriel, SS/2B	55/V	15. Reese McGuire, C	45/H	25. Kevin Vicuna, SS	45/V
6. Eric Pardinho, RHP	55/X	16. Conner Greene, RHP	45/H	26. Kevin Smith, SS	45/V
7. Danny Jansen, C	50/H	17. Miguel Hiraldo, SS	50/X	27. Jordan Romano, RHP	40/H
8. Logan Warmoth, SS	50/H	18. Leonardo Jimenez, SS	50/X	28. Hagen Danner, C	45/X
9. Richard Urena, SS	45/M	19. Carlos Ramirez, RHP	40/M	29. Jon Harris, RHP	40/H
10. Ryan Borucki, LHP	45/M	20. Riley Adams, C	45/H	30. Yennsy Diaz, RHP	40/V

WASHINGTON NATIONALS

STARTS ON PAGE 482

No.Player, Pos.	Grade/Risk	No.Player, Pos.	Grade/Risk	No.Player, Pos.	Grade/Risk
1. Victor Robles, OF	65/M	11. Blake Perkins, OF	50/H	21. Nick Raquet, LHP	45/H
2. Juan Soto, OF	60/V	12. Kelvin Gutierrez, 3B	50/H	22. Kyle Johnston, RHP	45/H
3. Erick Fedde, RHP	50/M	13. Andrew Stevenson, OF	45/M	23. Jose Sanchez, SS	50/X
4. Carter Kieboom, SS	55/V	14. Pedro Severino, C	45/H	24. Jefry Rodriguez, RHP	50/X
5. Seth Romero, LHP	55/X	15. Rafael Bautista, OF	40/M	25. Telmito Agustin, OF	45/V
6. Luis Garcia, SS	55/X	16. Jackson Tetrault, RHP	45/H	26. Austin Voth, RHP	40/H
7. Wil Crowe, RHP	50/H	17. Brigham Hill, RHP	45/H	27. Joan Baez, RHP	45/X
8. Daniel Johnson, OF	50/H	18. Jose Marmolejos, 1B/OF	40/M	28. Anderson Franco, 3B	40/H
9. Raudy Reed, C	45/M	19. Drew Ward, 3B	45/H	29. Jakson Reetz, C	40/H
10. Yasel Antuna, SS/3B	55/X	20. Taylor Gushue, C	45/H	30. Osvaldo Abreu, SS	40/H

For the seventh year in a row, Baseball America has assigned Grades and Risk Factors for each of the 900 prospects in the Prospect Handbook. For the BA Grade, we used a 20-to-80 scale, similar to the scale scouts use, to keep it familiar. However, most major league clubs put an overall numerical grade on players, called the Overall Future Potential or OFP. Often the OFP is merely an average of the player's tools.

The BA Grade is not an OFP. It's a measure of a prospect's value, and it attempts to gauge the player's realistic ceiling. We've continued to adjust our grades to try to be more realistic, and less optimistic, and keep refining the grade vetting process. The majority of the players in this book rest in the 50 High/45 Medium range, because the vast majority of worthwhile prospects in the minors are players who either have a chance to be everyday regulars but are far from that possibility, or players who are closer to the majors but who are likely to be role players and useful contributors. Few future franchise players or perennial all-stars graduate from the minors in any given year. The goal of the Grade/Risk system is to allow readers to take a quick look at how strong their team's farm system is, and how much immediate help the big league club can expect from its prospect. Got a minor leaguer who was traded from one organization to the other after the book went to press? Use the player's Grade/Risk and see where he would rank in his new system.

BA GRADE	
50	Risk: High

It also helps with our Organization Rankings, but those will not simply flow, in formulaic fashion, from the Grade/Risk results as we incorporate a lot of factors into our talent rankings including the differences in risk between pitchers and hitters. Hitters have a lower injury risk and therefore are safer bets

BA Grade Scale

GRADE	HITTER ROLE	PITCHER ROLE	EXAMPLES
75-80	Franchise Player	No. 1 starter	Mike Trout, Kris Byrant, Clayton Kershaw
65-70	Perennial All-Star	No. 2 starter	Freddie Freeman, Mookie Betts, Zack Greinke
60	Occasional All-Star	No. 3 starter, Game's best reliever	Charlie Blackmon, Marcell Ozuna, Kenley Jansen
55	First-Division Regular	No. 3/No. 4 starter, Elite closer	Jean Segura, Lance Lynn, Zach Britton
50	Solid-Average Regular	No. 4 starter, Elite set-up reliever	Mike Leake, Mitch Moreland, Bryan Shaw
45	Second-Division Regular/Platoon	No. 5 starter, Lower-leverage reliever	Steve Pearce, Cory Spangenberg, Ricky Nolasco
40	Reserve	Fill-in starter, relief specialist	Andrew Romine, Craig Breslow, Chris Smith

RISK FACTORS

LOW: Likely to reach realistic ceiling, certain big league career barring injury.

MEDIUM: Some work left to refine their tools, but a polished player.

HIGH: Most top draft picks in their first seasons, players with plenty of projection left, players with a significant flaw left to correct or players whose injury history is worrisome.

VERY HIGH: Recent draft picks with a limited track record of success or injury issues.

EXTREME: Teenagers in Rookie ball, players with significant injury histories or players whose struggle with a key skill (especially control for pitchers or strikeout rate for hitters).

Explaining The 20-80 Scouting Scale

None of the authors of this book is a scout, but we all have spoken to plenty of scouts to report on the prospects and scouting reports enclosed in the Prospect Handbook. So we use their lingo, and the 20-80 scouting scale is part of that. Many of these grades are measurable data, such as fastball velocity and speed (usually timed from home to first or in workouts over 60 yards). A fastball grade doesn't stem solely from its velocity—command and life are crucial elements as well—but throwing 100 mph will earn a player an 80 grade. Secondary pitches are graded in a similar fashion. The more swings-and-misses a pitch induces from hitters and the sharper the bite of the movement, the better the grade.

Velocity steadily has increased over the past decade. Not all that long ago an 88-91 mph fastball was considered major league average, but current data shows it is now below-average. Big league starting pitchers now sit 92-93 mph on average. You can reduce the scale by 1 mph for lefthanders as they on average throw with slightly reduced velocity. Fastballs earn their grades based on the average range of the pitch over the course of a typical outing, not touching or bumping the peak velocity on occasion.

A move to the bullpen complicates in another direction. Pitchers airing it out for one inning should throw harder than someone trying to last six or seven innings, so add 1-2 mph for relievers. Yes, nowadays an 80 fastball for a reliever needs to sit at 98-99 mph with some movement and command.

Hitting ability is as much a skill as it is a tool, but the physical elements—hand-eye coordination, swing mechanics, bat speed—are key factors in the hit tool grade. Raw power generally is measured by how far a player can hit the ball, but game power is graded by how many home runs the hitter projects to hit in the majors, preferably an average over the course of a career. We have tweaked our power grades based on the recent rise in home run rates.

Arm strength can be evaluated by observing the velocity and carry of throws, measured in workouts with radar guns or measured in games for catchers with pop times—the time it takes from the pop of the ball in the catcher's mitt to the pop of the ball in the fielder's glove at second base. Defense takes different factors into account by position but starts with proper footwork and technique, incorporates physical attributes such as hands, short-area quickness and fluid actions, then adds subtle skills such as instincts and anticipation as a last layer.

Not every team uses the wording below. Some use a 2-to-8 scale without half-grades, and others use above-average and plus synonymously. But for the Handbook, consider this BA's 20-80 scale.

20: As bad as it gets for a big leaguer. Think R.A .Dickey's fastball or Dee Gordon's power.

30: Poor, but not unplayable, such as Coco Crisp's arm or Joe Mauer's power.

40: Below-average, such as Wilmer Flores' defense, or Zach Davies' fastball velocity.

45: Fringe-average. Mike Leake's fastball, Tanner Roark's control and Steven Vogt's defense qualify.

50: Major league average. Aaron Nola's fastball or Melky Cabrera's power.

55: Above-average. Russell Martin's power.

60: Plus. Joe Panik's defense or Jon Lester's control.

70: Plus-Plus. Among the best tools in the game, such as Corey Seager's arm, Felix Hernandez's changeup or Brandon Crawford's defense.

80: Top of the scale. Some scouts consider only one player's tool in all of the major leagues to be 80. Think Giancarlo Stanton's power tool, Byron Buxton's defense or Aroldis Chapman's fastball.

20-80 Measurables

SPEED 60-Yard Dash Times (In Seconds)	SPEED Home-First (In Secs.) RHH—LHH	POWER Grade Home Runs	FASTBALL Velocity (Starters) Grade Velocity	ARM STRENGTH Catcher: Pop Times To Second Base (In Seconds)
80 . . . . < 6.44	80 . . . . 4.00—3.90	80 . . . . 45+	80 . . . . . 97+ mph	80 . . . . < 1.74
70 . . . . . . 6.45-6.64	70 . . . . 4.10—4.00	70 35-44	70 96	70 . . . . . 1.75-1.84
60 . . . . . . 6.65-6.84	65 . . . . 4.15—4.05	65 30-34	65 95	60 . . . . . 1.85-1.94
50 . . . . . . 6.85-6.99	60 . . . . 4.20—4.10	60 25-29	60 94	50 . . . . . 1.95-2.04
40 . . . . . . 7.00-7.24	55 . . . . 4.25—4.15	55 21-24	55 93	40 . . . . . 2.05-2.14
30 . . . . . . 7.25-7.44	50 . . . . 4.30—4.20	50 18-20	50 91-92	30 . . . . . 2.15-2.24
20 . . . . > 7.45	45 . . . . 4.35—4.25	45 15-17	45 90	20 . . . . > 2.25
	40 . . . . 4.40—4.30	40 10-14	40 88-89	
	30 . . . . 4.50—4.40	30 5-9	30 86-87	
	20 . . . . 4.60—4.50	20 0-4	20 . . . . . 85 or less	

AN OVERVIEW

Another feature of the Prospect Handbook is a depth chart of every organization's minor league talent. This shows you at a glance what kind of talent a system has and provides even more prospects beyond the Top 30.

Players are usually listed on the depth charts where we think they'll ultimately end up. To help you better understand why players are slotted at particular positions, we show you here what scouts look for in the ideal candidate at each spot, with individual tools ranked in descending order.

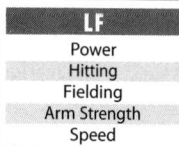

LF
Power
Hitting
Fielding
Arm Strength
Speed

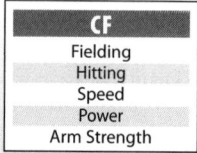

CF
Fielding
Hitting
Speed
Power
Arm Strength

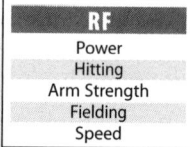

RF
Power
Hitting
Arm Strength
Fielding
Speed

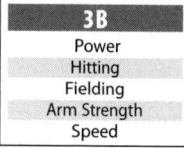

3B
Power
Hitting
Fielding
Arm Strength
Speed

SS
Fielding
Arm Strength
Hitting
Power
Speed

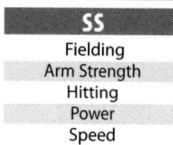

2B
Hitting
Fielding
Power
Speed
Arm Strength

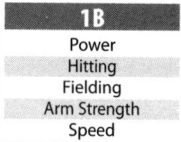

1B
Power
Hitting
Fielding
Arm Strength
Speed

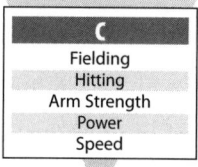

C
Fielding
Hitting
Arm Strength
Power
Speed

STARTING PITCHERS

No. 1 starter	No. 2 starter	No. 3 starter	No. 4-5 starters
• Two plus pitches	• Two plus pitches	• One plus pitch	• Command of two major league pitches
• Average third pitch	• Average third pitch	• Two average pitches	• Average velocity
• Plus-plus command	• Average command	• Average command	• Consistent breaking ball
• Plus makeup	• Average makeup	• Average makeup	• Decent changeup

CLOSER
• One dominant pitch
• Second plus pitch
• Plus command
• Plus-plus makeup

SETUP MAN
• Plus fastball
• Second above-average pitch
• Average command

For the first time in this edition of the Prospect Handbook—our 18th—we include position rankings for all eight field positions plus righthanded and lefthanded starting pitchers. The rankings go deeper at the glamor positions, i.e. shortstop, center field and righthanded starter.

We grade players' tools on the 20-80 scouting scale, where 50 is average. The tools listed for position players are ability to hit for average (HIT), power (POW), speed (SPD), fielding ability (FLD) and throwing arm (ARM). The tools listed for pitchers are fastball (FB), curveball (CB), slider (SL), changeup (CHG), other (OTH) and control (CTL). The "other" category can be a splitter, cutter or screwball.

Included as the final categories are BA Grades and Risk levels on a scale ranging from Low to Extreme.

CATCHER

No	Player	Org	HIT	POW	SPD	FLD	ARM	BA Grade	Risk
1.	Francisco Mejia	Indians	60	45	40	50	80	60	Medium
2.	Keibert Ruiz	Dodgers	60	45	40	55	50	60	High
3.	Carson Kelly	Cardinals	50	50	20	70	60	50	Low
4.	Chance Sisco	Orioles	60	45	40	50	50	50	Medium
5.	Zack Collins	White Sox	45	60	20	50	45	55	High
6.	Alex Jackson	Braves	40	60	40	45	60	55	High
7.	Sean Murphy	Athletics	45	50	30	55	70	50	High
8.	Danny Jansen	Blue Jays	55	40	30	45	50	50	High
9.	Will Smith	Dodgers	45	45	55	60	60	50	High
10.	Andrew Knizner	Cardinals	55	50	30	50	50	50	High

FIRST BASE

No	Player	Org	HIT	POW	SPD	FLD	ARM	BA Grade	Risk
1.	Jake Bauers	Rays	60	55	50	55	45	55	Medium
2.	Yordan Alvarez	Astros	55	60	50	50	45	60	High
3.	Ryan McMahon	Rockies	60	55	45	50	55	50	Medium
4.	Pavin Smith	D-backs	60	50	40	50	45	55	High
5.	Evan White	Mariners	60	50	60	70	60	55	High
6.	Bobby Bradley	Indians	50	70	20	45	50	55	Very High
7.	Nick Pratto	Royals	60	55	45	60	55	55	Extreme
8.	Peter Alonso	Mets	50	60	30	30	40	50	High
9.	Gavin Sheets	White Sox	50	60	30	50	50	50	High
10.	Brendan McKay	Rays	60	50	30	55	60	50	High

SECOND BASE

No	Player	Org	HIT	POW	SPD	FLD	ARM	BA Grade	Risk
1.	Scott Kingery	Phillies	60	55	60	50	45	60	Medium
2.	Luis Urias	Padres	70	40	50	60	55	55	Medium
3.	Keston Hiura	Brewers	60	55	45	45	45	60	High
4.	Isaac Paredes	Tigers	55	50	40	50	55	50	High
5.	Isan Diaz	Brewers	45	55	45	50	50	50	High
6.	Nick Solak	Yankees	55	45	55	50	45	50	High
7.	Shed Long	Reds	55	50	45	45	55	50	High
8.	Garrett Hampson	Rockies	55	40	60	55	50	45	Medium
9.	Max Schrock	Cardinals	55	40	50	50	45	45	Medium
10.	Marco Hernandez	Red Sox	50	40	60	50	50	45	Medium

THIRD BASE

No	Player	Org	HIT	POW	SPD	FLD	ARM	BA Grade	Risk
1.	Vladimir Guerrero Jr	Blue Jays	80	70	40	40	55	75	High
2.	Nick Senzel	Reds	60	60	55	60	60	65	Medium
3.	Austin Riley	Braves	50	60	40	55	70	55	Medium
4.	Miguel Andujar	Yankees	55	55	40	50	60	55	Medium
5.	Michael Chavis	Red Sox	50	60	45	45	55	55	Medium
6.	Ke'Bryan Hayes	Pirates	60	45	50	60	60	55	High
7.	Jake Burger	White Sox	50	60	30	45	55	55	High
8.	Lucas Erceg	Brewers	50	55	45	55	60	55	Very High
9.	Nolan Jones	Indians	55	60	50	50	60	55	Very High
10.	Colton Welker	Rockies	55	50	50	50	55	50	High

SHORTSTOP

No	Player	Org	HIT	POW	SPD	FLD	ARM	BA Grade	Risk
1.	Gleyber Torres	Yankees	60	55	40	60	60	65	Medium
2.	Fernando Tatis Jr.	Padres	60	60	50	55	60	65	High
3.	Bo Bichette	Blue Jays	70	60	50	45	60	65	High
4.	J.P. Crawford	Phillies	60	45	50	55	60	60	Medium
5.	Willy Adames	Rays	55	45	50	60	60	60	Medium
6.	Brendan Rodgers	Rockies	60	55	50	55	60	65	High
7.	Royce Lewis	Twins	60	55	60	60	55	65	Very High
8.	Franklin Barreto	Athletics	60	50	55	50	50	55	Medium
9.	Jorge Mateo	Athletics	50	45	80	50	55	55	High
10.	Nick Gordon	Twins	55	45	55	50	60	50	Medium
11.	Andres Gimenez	Mets	55	40	50	60	60	55	High
12.	Kevin Maitan	Angels	60	60	40	40	60	60	Extreme
13.	Wander Javier	Twins	50	50	60	55	70	60	Extreme
14.	Wander Franco	Rays	55	55	50	55	50	60	Extreme
15.	Carter Kieboom	Nationals	55	55	50	45	50	55	Very High
16.	Aramis Ademan	Cubs	55	50	50	55	50	55	Very High
17.	Kevin Newman	Pirates	60	30	55	50	50	45	Medium
18.	Jazz Chisholm	D-backs	50	45	55	55	60	55	Extreme
19.	Cole Tucker	Pirates	55	40	60	55	55	50	High
20.	Gabriel Arias	Padres	50	45	50	60	70	55	Extreme

CENTER FIELD

No	Player	Org	HIT	POW	SPD	FLD	ARM	BA Grade	Risk
1.	Ronald Acuna	Braves	60	70	70	70	60	70	Medium
2.	Victor Robles	Nationals	60	50	70	60	60	65	Medium
3.	Lewis Brinson	Brewers	55	60	60	55	60	60	Medium
4.	Estevan Florial	Yankees	50	55	70	60	70	65	Very High
5.	Alex Verdugo	Dodgers	60	50	50	55	70	55	Medium
6.	Austin Meadows	Pirates	60	55	60	60	50	60	High
7.	Anthony Alford	Blue Jays	50	50	60	60	40	55	Medium
8.	Monte Harrison	Brewers	50	55	60	55	60	60	Very High
9.	Leody Taveras	Rangers	55	50	60	60	60	60	Very High
10.	Jo Adell	Angels	60	70	70	55	60	60	Extreme
11.	Luis Robert	White Sox	55	60	70	50	60	60	Extreme
12.	Heliot Ramos	Giants	50	60	60	55	55	60	Extreme
13.	Brett Phillips	Brewers	50	55	60	60	80	50	Medium
14.	Dustin Fowler	Athletics	55	50	60	60	50	55	High
15.	Jahmai Jones	Angels	50	55	60	55	50	55	High
16.	Cristian Pache	Braves	50	40	80	70	55	55	High
17.	Jeren Kendall	Dodgers	50	50	70	70	60	55	Very High
18.	Magneuris Sierra	Marlins	50	30	70	60	60	50	High
19.	Daz Cameron	Tigers	45	50	55	55	50	50	High
20.	Mickey Moniak	Phillies	55	40	60	50	60	50	High

CORNER OUTFIELD

No	Player	Org	HIT	POW	SPD	FLD	ARM	BA Grade	Risk
1.	Eloy Jimenez	White Sox	60	70	45	50	45	70	High
2.	Kyle Tucker	Astros	60	60	50	55	50	60	Medium
3.	Austin Hays	Orioles	60	60	50	55	60	60	Medium
4.	Willie Calhoun	Rangers	60	70	30	30	40	55	Medium
5.	Taylor Trammell	Reds	55	60	60	55	40	60	High
6.	Jesus Sanchez	Rays	60	55	55	50	50	60	High
7.	Juan Soto	Nationals	60	60	50	55	50	60	Very High
8.	Kyle Lewis	Mariners	55	60	50	55	55	60	Very High
9.	Brent Rooker	Twins	50	60	50	50	50	55	High
10.	Tyler O'Neill	Cardinals	45	70	50	50	55	50	Medium

RIGHTHANDER

No	Pitcher	Team	FB	CB	SL	CHG	OTH	CTL	BA Grade	Risk
1.	Shohei Ohtani	Angels	80	45	60	—	70*	55	75	Medium
2.	Walker Buehler	Dodgers	70	60	60	40	—	55	65	Medium
3.	Michael Kopech	White Sox	80	—	60	50	—	45	65	Medium
4.	Mitch Keller	Pirates	70	60	—	50	—	60	65	Medium
5.	Alex Reyes	Cardinals	80	70	—	60	—	50	70	High
6.	Brent Honeywell	Rays	70	55	55	60	70^	60	65	Medium
7.	Forrest Whitley	Astros	70	60	60	55	50†	55	65	High
8.	Sixto Sanchez	Phillies	70	55	—	60	—	60	65	High
9.	Mike Soroka	Braves	60	—	60	55	—	60	60	Medium
10.	Kyle Wright	Braves	70	60	60	55	—	50	65	High
11.	Michel Baez	Padres	70	55	55	60	—	60	65	Extreme
12.	Hunter Greene	Reds	80	—	55	50	—	55	65	Extreme
13.	Cal Quantrill	Padres	60	45	50	70	—	50	60	High
14.	Triston McKenzie	Indians	60	60	—	55	—	55	60	High
15.	Franklin Perez	Tigers	60	60	45	50	—	60	60	High
16.	Ian Anderson	Braves	60	60	—	55	—	50	60	High
17.	Alex Faedo	Tigers	60	—	60	60	—	55	60	High
18.	Brandon Woodruff	Brewers	60	—	60	60	—	55	55	Medium
19.	Jack Flaherty	Cardinals	60	50	55	50	—	55	55	Medium
20.	Mitchell White	Dodgers	60	55	60	45	—	50	60	High
21.	Chance Adams	Yankees	60	45	60	45	—	50	55	Medium
22.	Albert Abreu	Yankees	70	60	—	55	—	50	60	High
23.	Sandy Alcantara	Marlins	70	50	50	40	—	45	55	Medium
24.	Corbin Burnes	Brewers	60	60	55	50	—	55	55	Medium
25.	Anderson Espinoza	Padres	70	55	—	70	—	50	65	Extreme
26.	Matt Manning	Tigers	60	60	—	60	—	45	60	Very High
27.	Jorge Guzman	Marlins	80	—	50	50	—	50	60	Very High
28.	Tyler Mahle	Reds	60	40	50	50	—	60	50	Medium
29.	Erick Fedde	Nationals	60	45	60	55	—	50	50	Medium
30.	Jon Duplantier	D-backs	60	55	60	50	—	60	55	High
31.	Alec Hansen	White Sox	70	55	40	55	—	45	55	High
32.	Yadier Alvarez	Dodgers	70	—	55	40	—	40	55	High
33.	Adonis Medina	Phillies	60	—	55	60	—	55	55	High
34.	Riley Pint	Rockies	70	60	50	60	—	45	60	Extreme
35.	Dane Dunning	White Sox	60	—	60	55	—	55	55	High
36.	Hunter Harvey	Orioles	70	60	—	50	—	50	60	Extreme
37.	Shane Baz	Pirates	70	55	55	50	—	50	60	Extreme
38.	Luis Ortiz	Brewers	60	—	60	50	—	50	55	High
39.	J.B. Bukauskas	Astros	60	—	70	40	—	50	55	High
40.	Hans Crouse	Rangers	70	—	60	45	—	60	60	Extreme

* Splitter. ^ Screwball. † Cutter.

LEFTHANDER

No	Pitcher	Team	FB	CB	SL	CHG	OTH	CTL	BA Grade	Risk
1.	Luiz Gohara	Braves	80	—	70	45	—	45	65	High
2.	MacKenzie Gore	Padres	60	60	55	60	—	60	65	Extreme
3.	A.J. Puk	Athletics	70	—	60	50	—	45	60	High
4.	Justus Sheffield	Yankees	70	—	55	55	—	50	60	High
5.	Kolby Allard	Braves	50	60	—	60	—	60	55	Medium
6.	Adrian Morejon	Padres	60	50	—	60	—	55	60	High
7.	Jay Groome	Red Sox	60	60	—	50	—	50	65	Extreme
8.	Brendan McKay	Rays	55	60	55	55	—	55	60	High
9.	Max Fried	Braves	60	60	—	45	—	45	60	Very High
10.	Anthony Banda	D-backs	60	55	—	55	—	50	50	Medium
11.	Trevor Rogers	Marlins	60	45	55	45	—	50	60	Extreme
12.	JoJo Romero	Phillies	55	55	45	55	—	60	55	High
13.	David Peterson	Mets	50	40	55	50	—	60	55	High
14.	Logan Allen	Padres	55	50	—	60	—	50	55	High
15.	Cole Ragans	Rangers	55	50	—	60	—	50	55	Very High

Team	2017	2016	2015	2014	2013
1. Atlanta Braves	1	3	29	26	21

New general manager Alex Anthopoulos inherits a farm system deep in pitching prospects and that has a nice mix of potential impact bats as well, led by center fielder Ronald Acuna. Not all the Braves' pitching prospects are going to pan out, but they have the numbers to make up for the expected attrition.

2. New York Yankees	3	16	19	18	11

It's hard to pull off a quick sell-off and rebuild better than the Yankees did. With a young core of talent in place in New York, the Yankees now have an incredibly deep and varied group of young players coming up behind them to fill out the lineup, rotation and bullpen as well as provide trade chips.

3. San Diego Padres	9	25	14	6	15

The Padres spent more to acquire their 2016 international signing class than they did to pay their actual big league roster in 2017. The payoff won't come for several years, but the Padres have more high-risk, high-upside prospects than anyone else, along with enviable depth.

4. Chicago White Sox	5	23	20	24	29

The White Sox executed a sell-off in 2016 that brought in a much-needed influx of talent. Yoan Moncada's graduation hurts their standing, but the system still has an impressive core of young talent. Chicago's depth of potential impact talent, though, is a bit short compared with other top farm systems.

5. Tampa Bay Rays	11	13	17	20	4

The Rays love to be patient in developing their top prospects. Righthander Brent Honeywell and shortstop Willy Adames got plenty of minor league seasoning, and the system has impressive depth beyond its top prospects.

6. Milwaukee Brewers	8	9	21	29	22

The Brewers graduated top pitching prospect Josh Hader during their surprising run at a playoff spot in 2017. An entire wave of prospects will follow him in 2018. The Milwaukee system is more impressive for its depth than for any one or two top prospects, but it has a lot of players with plausible paths to being big league regulars.

7. Philadelphia Phillies	6	8	22	22	23

Top 10 Prospects J.P. Crawford, Scott Kingery and Jorge Alfaro will likely step into significant big league roles at some point in 2018, and a number of talented pitchers have pooled at the lower levels of the system. What Philadelphia needs is for some of its young hitters, like Mickey Moniak and Adam Haseley, to take steps forward.

8. Toronto Blue Jays	20	24	9	15	12

Given a choice between depth or stars, teams would rather have stars, and few can match up with the Blue Jays' dynamic duo of Vladimir Guerrero Jr. and Bo Bichette. Those two give Toronto a pair of potential cornerstone bats to build around despite not having great depth throughout the system.

9. Los Angeles Dodgers	2	1	3	14	19

The Dodgers wrap up a fourth consecutive top 10 showing in our talent ranking as they continue to produce big league-ready prospects year after year. Corey Seager and Julio Urias were followed by Cody Bellinger and Austin Barnes, who will now be followed by Alex Verdugo and Walker Buehler.

10. Cincinnati Reds	13	12	16	16	14

Nick Senzel, Hunter Greene and Taylor Trammell is a trio of prospects any team would be proud to have at the top of its ranking. The graduation of righthander Luis Castillo keeps the Reds from ranking higher, but the team has a large number of high-upside players surrounded by safer, lower-ceiling bats.

11. Houston Astros	4	2	10	5	9

Even after trading away three notable prospects to land Justin Verlander, the World Series champs still have a system with elite prospects and plenty of depth, especially when it comes to young, projectable pitchers. Houston's deep big league roster makes it hard for a group of decent Triple-A prospects to break through, so the Astros also have some surplus to trade.

12. Minnesota Twins	22	10	2	3	10

Picking at the top of the draft has its benefits. Selecting prep shortstop Royce Lewis No. 1 overall was a big addition to a system that has a number of future big leaguers. Minnesota's best prospects are spread from Triple-A to the lowest levels of Rookie ball, so it's going to be a steady stream rather than one big wave of prospects arriving.

13. St. Louis Cardinals	12	14	15	7	1

Recent trades drop the Cardinals to a middle-of-the-pack ranking, but St. Louis still has exceptional depth of outfielders and righthanded pitchers. This is an unbalanced farm system with clear strengths and weaknesses. That's OK, because a few clever trades can quickly fill holes.

14. Los Angeles Angels	30	30	27	30	18

The signing of 23-year-old Japanese star Shohei Ohtani changed everything for an already-improving Angels system. The Angels haven't had a truly elite prospect since the days of Mike Trout. Ohtani changes that, while Jo Adell, Jahmai Jones and Brandon Marsh make for a high-upside outfield trio.

15. Washington Nationals	19	5	12	21	16

The Nationals had the prospect talent to acquire relievers to help fix their bullpen problems in 2017. They have the ammunition to make moves again in 2018, but Victor Robles and Juan Soto are the kind of prospects teams usually find a way to keep. A pitching-heavy 2017 draft helped add arms to a system in need of them.

Team	2017	2016	2015	2014	2013
16. Pittsburgh Pirates	7	11	7	1	8

Pittsburgh is truly at a crossroads. The big league club can't match the talent of the Cubs and others in the National League Central, but the farm system isn't as deep or strong as others, either. The Pirates need to spend to bulk up the big league team—or sell off and rebuild.

17. Baltimore Orioles	27	27	28	12	17

This is the first time the Orioles have cracked the top 20 since Dylan Bundy and Jonathan Schoop were top prospects heading into 2014. Outfielder Austin Hays' emergence was a huge boost, but recent pitching draftees, such as Cody Sedlock and Keegan Akin, need to take step forward in 2018.

18. Oakland Athletics	17	18	19	23	25

The A's could vastly exceed this ranking, but the riskiness of the system's prospects is significant. Most of Oakland's top prospects have high ceilings but also considerable drawbacks. For example, Dustin Fowler, Jesus Luzardo and James Kaprielian have had major injuries.

19. Colorado Rockies	10	6	8	11	20

The Rockies 10-spot drop in the ranking this year should be lauded. They saw four members of last year's Top 10 Prospects—Jeff Hoffman, German Marquez, Kyle Freeland and Antonio Senzatela—graduate to the rotation and help push Colorado to the playoffs. Even without those arms, Brendan Rodgers is a strong No. 1 prospect.

20. Detroit Tigers	25	26	30	28	27

The Tigers' rebuild sped up with the Justin Verlander trade that netted them three of their Top 10 Prospects—Franklin Perez, Jake Rogers and Daz Cameron. Detroit has a nice group of pitching prospects coming up through the minors, but it needs to add more position players who can be pencilled into a future big league lineup.

21. Cleveland Indians	18	17	23	17	24

The Indians have two top prospects in Francisco Mejia and Triston McKenzie, but after that there is a large group of good but not great talent. The Indians' excellent player development staff will likely help a few of them exceed expectations, a la Yan Gomes and Jose Ramirez.

22. Texas Rangers	23	7	11	9	3

Texas' attempts to stay in the playoff hunt in recent years understandably cost some prospects, but the Yu Darvish trade last year brought back new No. 1 prospect Willie Calhoun. Still, the Rangers don't have a lot left in their system as they try to keep up in a very competitive American League West.

23. Boston Red Sox	14	4	5	2	6

Year after year the Red Sox have produced big league regulars, which explains why they ranked in the top 10 in four of the past five years. That talent pipeline is starting to slow down with president of baseball operations Dave Dombrowski quite happy to trade prospects, even elite ones, for big leaguers.

24. Miami Marlins	29	29	25	27	5

The Marlins were in consideration for the bottom spot in this ranking when the offseason began. The Giancarlo Stanton, Marcell Ozuna and Dee Gordon trades helped turn what was a barren system into one with a respectable top 10 that still lacks in depth.

25. San Francisco Giants	24	19	26	19	28

The Giants usually have a number of unheralded prospects who end up putting together solid big league careers. That is still true, but it's hard to find impact big leaguers once you get past the very top of the list.

26. Arizona Diamondbacks	28	22	6	13	7

The D-backs were able to acquire impact bat J.D. Martinez at a modest price at the 2017 trade deadline. It shows they have the prospect ammunition to help the big league team, but there aren't many prospects on the farm right now who project as big league regulars in Phoenix any time soon.

27. New York Mets	15	15	4	10	26

It wasn't that long ago the Mets' system was filled with elite pitching prospects. That group helped them to a World Series appearance in 2015, but when the Mets need reinforcements now, they don't have much in the way of either position players or pitchers available to help.

28. Chicago Cubs	16	20	1	4	13

Just a few years ago, the Cubs had a farm system to envy, and that group of players has already led the Cubs to the 2016 World Series title and three straight seasons of 90 or more wins. But the system now is as fallow as it has been in years because of graduations and trades (Gleyber Torres, Eloy Jimenez) to keep the club rolling.

29. Kansas City Royals	26	21	13	8	18

Now the rebuild begins. After riding the "Blue Wave" to back-to-back World Series appearances and a 2015 title, the Royals have to start over. Right now they don't have a clear Top 100 Prospect, and a needed infusion of first-round draft picks will likely begin in 2018.

30. Seattle Mariners	21	28	24	25	2

The Mariners have traded Tyler O'Neill, Luiz Gohara, Nick Neidert and many others in the past year with little to show for it. The push to improve the big league club has left the farm system nearly desolate after its top three.

Arizona Diamondbacks

BY NICK PIECORO

When he landed the job in October 2016, new D-backs general manager Mike Hazen inherited one of the worst farm systems in baseball—a farm system that was ranked dead last by some publications. Rather than dispute it, Hazen owned it, and vowed that under his watch the organization needed to get better.

Hazen's first year on the job went exceedingly well at the big league level. The club won 93 games (and the Wild Card Game) and advanced to the postseason for the first time in six years, finishing as one of baseball's more pleasant surprises. A little more under-the-radar was how encouraging a year it was from a player development standpoint.

In addition to the three college bats they nabbed with their first three picks in the 2017 draft and the $2.5 million they spent in the international market on toolsy Bahamian slugger Kristian Robinson, the D-backs watched as several prospects began to blossom in their system.

Righthander Jon Duplantier showed the makings of a frontline starter. Outfielder Marcus Wilson converted his tools into performance. Righty Yoan Lopez emerged from oblivion to display late-inning potential. Little known outfielders Eduardo Diaz and Gabriel Maciel popped up. Righthander Sam McWilliams started to look like a future starter.

The D-backs system still has a ways to go, something Hazen continues to acknowledge, but it's no longer necessary to squint as hard in order to see contributors on the horizon.

In order to add to the big league roster before the trade deadline, Hazen peeled away from his farm system, but he managed to land slugger J.D. Martinez, utility infielder Adam Rosales and reliever David Hernandez without parting with his best prospects.

Scouting director Deric Ladnier survived the regime change, and with assistant GM Amiel Sawdaye and analytics director Mike Fitzgerald involved, the club began incorporating analytics in the draft in a far more significant way. Ladnier, who has overseen 11 drafts, the first eight coming with the Royals, called it the best and most comprehensive process he's ever been a part of.

In first baseman Pavin Smith (first round), third baseman Drew Ellis (second) and catcher Daulton Varsho (supplemental second), the D-backs' draft class produced three advanced college bats with the upside of everyday regulars. In third-round righthander Matt Tabor, they also landed a high school arm with rotation potential.

The D-backs remain in a tricky spot. They have

Paul Goldschmidt launched 36 home runs in 2017 to finish third in NL MVP balloting.

PROJECTED 2021 LINEUP

Catcher	Daulton Varsho (24)
First Base	Paul Goldschmidt (33)
Second Base	Brandon Drury (28)
Third Base	Jake Lamb (30)
Shortstop	Ketel Marte (27)
Left Field	Pavin Smith (25)
Center Field	A.J. Pollock (33)
Right Field	David Peralta (33)
No. 1 Starter	Zack Greinke (37)
No. 2 Starter	Robbie Ray (29)
No. 3 Starter	Taijuan Walker (28)
No. 4 Starter	Jon Duplantier (26)
No. 5 Starter	Anthony Banda (27)
Closer	Archie Bradley (28)

a roster built to win now. It's filled with prime-age players whose years of control are dwindling and whose salaries are rising. Paul Goldschmidt can become a free agent after 2019. A.J. Pollock and Patrick Corbin are free agents after 2018. Jake Lamb and Robbie Ray are just entering their arbitration years.

Below those players, the D-backs have a farm system with most of its impact players still several years away from maturation. They still need to bridge that gap between the current crop and the next one. For Hazen, Sawdaye and assistant GM Jared Porter, it will be a balancing act to keep the window of contention open without sacrificing long-term sustainability.

J. CHRISTIAN PETERSEN/GETTY IMAGES

ARIZONA DIAMONDBACKS

TOP 2018 ROOKIE: Jimmie Sherfy, RHP. The undersized but hard-throwing reliever has a leg up for a big league bullpen spot.

BREAKOUT PROSPECT: Sam McWilliams, RHP. Athletic and projectable, he flashes three plus pitches, and the 6-foot-7 righty started to find consistency in his delivery in 2017.

SLEEPER: Jordan Watson, LHP. The 2016 NAIA strikeout leader missed most of 2017 following Tommy John surgery. Now healthy, he has a fastball in the low 90s and a curveball that some scouts say is plus-plus.

SOURCE OF TOP 30 TALENT			
Homegrown	24	Acquired	6
College	10	Trade	6
Junior college	0	Rule 5 draft	0
High school	6	Independent league	0
Nondrafted free agent	0	Free agent/waivers	0
International	8		

LF
Kristian Robinson (11)
Gabriel Maciel (15)
Anfernee Grier

CF
Marcus Wilson (6)
Eduardo Diaz (7)
Jesus Marriaga
Tramayne Holmes
Wilderd Patino
Jorge Barrosa

RF
Socrates Brito (19)
Victor Reyes
Ben DeLuzio

3B
Drew Ellis (9)
Joey Rose (20)
Buddy Kennedy (27)

SS
Jazz Chisholm (4)
Jack Reinheimer
Geraldo Perdomo
Neyfy Castillo
Liover Peguero

2B
Domingo Leyba (12)
Ildemaro Vargas (24)
Eddie Hernandez
Keshawn Lynch
Jose Caballero

1B
Pavin Smith (3)
Kevin Cron (22)
Christian Walker (26)
Eudy Ramos

C
Daulton Varsho (5)
Andy Yerzy (16)
Michael Perez (30)
Jose Herrera
Sergio Gutierrez

LHP

LHSP	LHRP
Anthony Banda (2)	Jared Miller (17)
Mack Lemieux	Colin Poche (29)
Cody Reed	Jordan Watson
	Kirby Bellow
	Josh Taylor
	Gabe Speier

RHP

RHSP	RHRP
Jon Duplantier (1)	Jimmie Sherfy (14)
Taylor Clarke (8)	Yoan Lopez (18)
Matt Tabor (10)	Tommy Eveld (25)
Sam McWilliams (13)	Curtis Taylor
Jhoan Duran (21)	Joey Krehbiel
Jose Almonte (23)	Wei-Chieh Huang
Elvis Luciano (28)	Mason McCullough
Matt Koch	Erbert Gonzalez
Emilo Vargas	
Brian Shaffer	
Harrison Francis	
Ryan Atkinson	

DRAFT ANALYSIS

2017

BEST PURE HITTER: The D-backs loved 1B Pavin Smith's (1) ability to handle the bat at Virginia and took him with the seventh overall pick. He showed them what they expected in the short-season Northwest League, where he hit .318/.401/.415 with more walks (27) than strikeouts (24).
BEST POWER HITTER: Both 3B Drew Ellis (2) and C Daulton Varsho (2s) qualify. Ellis likely has more raw power than Varsho, but Varsho has gotten to his power more regularly thanks to a higher average and speed that allows him to hit for extra bases as well. He led the Northwest League with a .534 slugging percentage in his debut.
FASTEST RUNNER: OF Tra'Mayne Holmes (11) is a plus-plus runner. He went 59-for-69 in stolen base attempts at Faulkner (Ala.) this spring. He'll need to make some adjustments at the pro level, but still went 12-for-17 in his pro debut.
BEST DEFENSIVE PLAYER: Scouts had some doubts about Ellis as an amateur, but he impressed the D-backs with plus hands, instincts and arm strength. Club officials say he has largely avoided rushing on challenging plays.
BEST FASTBALL: RHP Matt Brill (12) has touched 99 mph regularly. The explosive pitch helped him strike out 25 batters in 20.1 relief innings in the short-season Northwest League. Other notable fastballs include RHP Matt Tabor (3), who touches 97, and RHP Brian Shaffer (6), whose low-90s fastball has great life.
BEST SECONDARY PITCH:, Tabor is in the conversation here with a plus changeup, but RHP Harrison Francis (4) tops him with a changeup of his own that is a plus-plus offering.
BEST PRO DEBUT: Varsho showed more power than Smith to earn the nod while hitting .311/.368/.534, ranking fifth in the NWL in batting and first in slugging. Brill posted a 0.89 ERA for short-season Hillsboro.
BEST ATHLETE: The D-backs are excited about the overall toolset that Holmes offers, but he'll have to figure out some of the intricacies of the game before he's able to make the most of them.

TOP DRAFT PICKS OF THE DECADE

Year	Player, Pos.	2017 Org
2008	Daniel Schlereth, LHP	Marlins
2009	Bobby Borchering, 3B	Did not play
2010	*Barret Loux, RHP	Did not play
2011	Trevor Bauer, RHP	Indians
2012	Stryker Trahan, C	Did not play
2013	Braden Shipley, RHP	D-backs
2014	Touki Toussaint, RHP	Braves
2015	Dansby Swanson, SS	Braves
2016	Anfernee Grier, OF (1st round supp.)	D-backs
2017	Pavin Smith, 1B	D-backs
* Did not sign		

The speed is obvious and gives him a chance to be an impact defender in center.
MOST INTRIGUING BACKGROUND: Varsho is the son of former big leaguer Gary Varsho, who played for the Cubs, Pirates, Reds and Phillies over an eight-year career. Ellis starred in the 2008 Little League World Series, primarily as a pitcher. Unsigned RHP Cole Percival (31) will play at UC Riverside for his father Troy Percival.
CLOSEST TO THE MAJORS: Even though the D-backs are set in the big leagues with Paul Goldschmidt at first, Smith has the offensive polish to make short work of the minor leagues.
BEST LATE-ROUND PICK: The D-backs were going to take C Dominic Miroglio (20) in the 2016 draft, but the Rays popped him in the 16th round. He didn't sign and Arizona was able to land him a year later. He hit .317/.384/.430 with 14 walks and eight strikeouts in his pro debut, though he was old for the Rookie-level Pioneer League. The D-backs see him as a leader with plus defensive skills who can catch and throw and potentially turn into an everyday player.
THE ONE WHO GOT AWAY: The D-backs liked LHP Tarik Skubal (29), but didn't have the cap room to keep him from returning to Seattle for his redshirt junior year as he bounces back from Tommy John surgery. Prior to his injury, Skubal had posted a 2.86 ERA in 126 innings for Seattle, with 118 strikeouts and 44 walks.

—CARLOS COLLAZO

2016

RHP Jon Duplantier (3) led the minor leagues in ERA in a strong first full professional season, but top pick OF Anfernee Grier (1s) struggled at low Class A. Prep hitters C Andy Yerzy (2) and 3B Joey Rose (5) showed some upside.

GRADE: C

2015

This draft will likely all come down to what SS Dansby Swanson (1) does in Atlanta and he's coming off a disappointing rookie season. RHP Taylor Clarke (3) is the D-backs best hope to get a contribution in Arizona out of the draft.

GRADE: B

2014

RHP Touki Toussaint (1) continues to matriculate in the Braves system. LHP Zac Curtis (6) gives the draft a big leaguer, though he is now on his third team. OF Marcus Wilson (3) remains raw, but had an encouraging season at low Class A.

GRADE: C

1 JON DUPLANTIER, RHP

Born: July 11, 1994. **B-T:** L-R. **Ht.:** 6-4. **Wt.:** 225. **Drafted:** Rice, 2016 (3rd round). **Signed by:** Rusty Pendergrass.

The D-backs couldn't be sure what they were getting when they drafted Duplantier in the third round in 2016. They weren't even sure when spring training began in 2017, before he ultimately turned in one of the best minor league pitching seasons in recent memory. He led the minors with a 1.39 ERA that trailed only Justin Verlander's 1.29 ERA in 2005 among qualified minor league starters since 1993. Duplantier put together an impressive junior year at Rice but had missed the previous season with a shoulder injury that did not require surgery. On top of that was the perception that Rice pitchers tend not to stay healthy once they turn professional. Duplantier's first impression wasn't great, either. In the summer after the draft, he logged only one inning before being shut down with an elbow issue, then missed instructional league with a hamstring injury. But he showed up at spring training with a delivery he smoothed out with rehab coordinator Brad Arnsberg, who helped him lower his arm angle.

Duplantier has an athletic build and a solid, sturdy frame with room to grow. His arm action is a bit funky because he extends his arm straight behind him just after separation, leading to a delivery that can appear stiff or robotic. But he repeats it well, and coaches say he makes adjustments quickly when he gets out of whack. Duplantier has the potential for a legitimate four-pitch mix. His fastball velocity fluctuated at times in 2017, but he sat mostly 90-94 mph. His stuff ticked up late in the season, when he sat 93-94 mph and topped out at 97. He throws both a four-seamer and a two-seamer and both pitches have armside run. His most consistent secondary pitch is a spike curveball, but coaches believe his new slider has the most upside. He also throws a changeup that generates average to above-average grades. Duplantier is proud that he was able to make all of his starts in 2017, saying he grew more confident in his health as the season progressed. Still, the D-backs proceeded cautiously by waiting until mid-June before promoting him from low Class A Kane County to high Class A Visalia.

Duplantier's late-season stuff indicates he has the potential to be a front-line starter. For some, though, his injury history and delivery mark him as a possible reliever. Another strong year in the rotation at Double-A Jackson will strengthen his starter case.

BILL MITCHELL

BA GRADE	SCOUTING GRADES
55 Risk: High	**FB:** 60. **CB:** 55. **SL:** 60. **CHG:** 50. **CTL:** 60.

Projected future grades on 20-80 scouting scale

TOP PROSPECTS OF THE DECADE

Year	Player, Pos.	2017 Org
2008	Carlos Gonzalez, OF	Rockies
2009	Jarrod Parker, RHP	Did not play
2010	Jarrod Parker, RHP	Did not play
2011	Jarrod Parker, RHP	Did not play
2012	Trevor Bauer, RHP	Indians
2013	Tyler Skaggs, LHP	Angels
2014	Archie Bradley, RHP	D-backs
2015	Archie Bradley, RHP	D-backs
2016	Dansby Swanson, SS	Braves
2017	Anthony Banda, LHP	D-backs

BEST TOOLS

Best Hitter for Average	Pavin Smith
Best Power Hitter	Kevin Cron
Best Strike-Zone Discipline	Marcus Wilson
Fastest Baserunner	Gabriel Maciel
Best Athlete	Daulton Varsho
Best Fastball	Yoan Lopez
Best Curveball	Jordan Watson
Best Slider	Jared Miller
Best Changeup	Matt Tabor
Best Control	Jon Duplantier
Best Defensive Catcher	Michael Perez
Best Defensive Infielder	Drew Ellis
Best Infield Arm	Jazz Chisholm
Best Defensive Outfielder	Eduardo Diaz
Best Outfield Arm	Juan Araujo

Year	Club (League)	Class	W	L	ERA	G	GS	CG	SV	IP	H	HR	BB	SO	K/9	WHIP	AVG
2016	Hillsboro (NWL)	SS	0	0	0.00	1	0	0	0	1	0	0	2	3	27.0	2.00	.000
2017	Kane County (MWL)	LoA	6	1	1.24	13	12	0	0	73	45	4	15	78	9.7	0.83	.180
	Visalia (CAL)	HiA	6	2	1.56	12	12	0	0	63	46	2	27	87	12.4	1.15	.204
Minor League Totals			12	3	1.38	26	24	0‡	0	137	91	6	44	168	11.0	0.99	.190

2 ANTHONY BANDA, LHP

Born: Aug. 10, 1993. **B-T:** L-L. **Ht:** 6-2. **Wt:** 190. **Drafted:** San Jacinto (Texas) JC, 2012 (10th round). **Signed by:** Brian Sankey (Brewers).

Despite some rough results at Triple-A Reno, Banda reached the big leagues in 2017, throwing well in two starts and struggling in two others before finishing the season in the bullpen as a September callup. Scouts say he continued to flash impressive stuff throughout the season but went through stretches where his command backed up.

Banda has gradually added velocity to his fastball and now sits 93-94 mph and touches 96. His breaking ball and changeup can both be inconsistent but have a chance to be above-average pitches. Scouts thought Banda left too many pitches over the plate in 2017, though pitching at hitter-friendly Reno didn't help. Some in the organization thought Banda's continued uptick in velocity might have played a part in his inconsistent command and the occasional lack of effectiveness of his secondary pitches.

Banda showed flashes of mid-rotation potential during his brief time with Arizona and dominated at times in relief. His future remains as a starter, but if the big league rotation remains crowded, he might have to wait for an opportunity.

BA GRADE
50 Risk: Medium
FB: 60. CB: 55.
CHG: 55.
CTL: 50.

Year	Club (League)	Class	W	L	ERA	G	GS	CG	SV	IP	H	HR	BB	SO	K/9	WHIP	AVG
2015	Visalia (CAL)	HiA	8	8	3.32	28	27	1	0	152	150	8	39	152	9.0	1.25	.260
2016	Mobile (SL)	AA	6	2	2.12	13	13	0	0	76	70	4	28	84	9.9	1.28	.241
	Reno (PCL)	AAA	4	4	3.67	13	13	0	0	74	73	6	27	68	8.3	1.36	.257
2017	Reno (PCL)	AAA	8	7	5.39	22	22	0	0	122	125	15	51	116	8.6	1.44	.266
	Arizona (NL)	MAJ	2	3	5.96	8	4	0	0	26	26	1	10	25	8.8	1.40	.255
Major League Totals			2	3	5.96	8	4	0	0	26	26	1	10	25	8.8	1.40	.255
Minor League Totals			40	34	3.83	130	113	1	2	645	652	49	239	625	8.7	1.38	.262

3 PAVIN SMITH, 1B

Born: Feb. 6, 1996. **B-T:** L-L. **Ht:** 6-2. **Wt:** 210. **Drafted:** Virginia, 2017 (1st round). **Signed by:** Rick Matsko.

The lefthanded-hitting Smith was one of the most well-regarded pure hitters in the 2017 draft because of his sweet swing, impressive contact ability and a solid statistical track record in the Atlantic Coast Conference. As a junior at Virginia, he hit .342/.427/.570 and homered (13) more times than he struck out (12). While that played well with the D-backs' beefed up analytics department, team officials say traditional scouting played a larger role in his selection.

Many D-backs scouts never saw Smith swing and miss, and the team believes that his power will develop last. His only professional home run came in short-season Hillsboro's final postseason game. Believers say the raw power is there, but it's a matter of Smith learning when to tap into it in game situations. No one doubts his ability to hit, with "advanced" and "special" used as descriptors by scouts, coaches and opposing managers. Smith doesn't run well, and though his arm and glove are fine at first base, scouts aren't sure he'd be an average defender in a corner outfield spot if he had to move.

Whether Smith's future is at first base or in the outfield depends on Paul Goldschmidt, who is signed through 2019.

BA GRADE
55 Risk: High
HIT: 60. POW: 50.
SPD: 40. FLD: 50.
ARM: 45.

Year	Club (League)	Class	AVG	G	AB	R	H	2B	3B	HR	RBI	BB	SO	SB	CS	OBP	SLG
2017	Hillsboro (NWL)	SS	.318	51	195	34	62	15	2	0	27	27	24	2	1	.401	.415
Minor League Totals			.318	51	195	34	62	15	2	0	27	27	24	2	1	.401	.415

4 JAZZ CHISHOLM, SS

Born: Feb. 1, 1998. **B-T:** L-R. **Ht:** 5-11. **Wt:** 165. **Signed:** Bahamas, 2015. **Signed by:** Craig Shipley.

The D-backs spotted Chisholm at a workout showcasing fellow Bahamas native Lucius Fox, his half-brother, and ultimately signed him for $200,000. That price now looks like a bargain, given how well regarded he is by rival scouts. Unfortunately, they did not have many chances to see Chisholm in 2017. He played just 29 games at low Class A Kane County before suffering a "bucket-handle" torn meniscus in his right knee.

Chisholm bats lefthanded and has big, strong hands and takes powerful, aggressive swings. His approach can get overly aggressive at times, leading to swings and misses, but he can also generate huge power. He led the organization's minor leaguers in home runs during spring training. An average runner, he can improve his raw speed as he builds his lower half. Chisholm has smooth, athletic actions at shortstop and a strong arm, but like a lot of young infielders needs to improve his consistency and focus in the field. He's confident, talkative, well liked by teammates and clearly enjoys playing the game.

Chisholm will look to make up for lost developmental time in 2018. He could open the season in high Class A Visalia.

BA GRADE
55 Risk: Extreme
HIT: 50. POW: 45.
SPD: 55. FLD: 55.
ARM: 60.

Year	Club (League)	Class	AVG	G	AB	R	H	2B	3B	HR	RBI	BB	SO	SB	CS	OBP	SLG
2016	Missoula (PIO)	R	.281	62	249	42	70	12	1	9	37	19	73	13	4	.333	.446
2017	Kane County (MWL)	LoA	.248	29	109	14	27	5	2	1	12	10	39	3	0	.325	.358
Minor League Totals			.271	91	358	56	97	17	3	10	49	29	112	16	4	.331	.419

5 DAULTON VARSHO, C

Born: July 2, 1996. **B-T:** L-R. **Ht:** 5-10. **Wt:** 190. **Drafted:** Wisconsin-Milwaukee, 2017 (2nd round supplemental). **Signed by:** Rick Short.

The son of big leaguer Gary Varsho and the namesake of his father's former teammate, Darren Daulton, Varsho came off a huge junior season at Wisconsin-Milwaukee when the D-backs selected him 68th overall in 2017. He led the Horizon League in batting average (.362), on-base percentage (.490) and slugging (.643), then in his pro debut led the short-season Northwest League with a .902 OPS.

Varsho has an unusual profile in that he's a catcher who runs better than he throws—but most believe he will hit. With short arms producing a compact lefthanded swing, he has a mature approach, a good feel for the strike zone and makes consistent loud contact, showing power to all fields. His lack of arm strength is a concern, but D-backs coaches clocked his pop times on throws to second base as low as 1.9 seconds. If catching doesn't pan out, Varsho runs well enough to be a solid left fielder, and he might even be an option in center field or at second base. He runs well enough that some scouts could envision him reaching 30 steals.

Some believe in Varsho's hitting potential to the extent that they might move him to a less grueling position to hasten his development. He has a chance to start at high Class A Visalia in 2018.

BA GRADE
50 Risk: High
HIT: 55. POW: 45.
SPD: 55. FLD: 55.
ARM: 45.

Year	Club (League)	Class	AVG	G	AB	R	H	2B	3B	HR	RBI	BB	SO	SB	CS	OBP	SLG
2017	Hillsboro (NWL)	SS	.311	50	193	36	60	16	3	7	39	17	30	7	2	.368	.534
Minor League Totals			.311	50	193	36	60	16	3	7	39	17	30	7	2	.368	.534

6 MARCUS WILSON, OF

Born: Aug. 15, 1996. **B-T:** R-R. **Ht:** 6-3. **Wt:** 175. **Drafted:** HS—Gardena, Calif., 2014 (2nd round supplemental). **Signed by:** Hal Kurtzman.

The D-backs believed Wilson was so raw when they selected him in 2014 they viewed him as a multi-year Rookie-level player. That's exactly how it played out, and after years of showing glimpses of his ability, particularly when it came to recognizing pitches, Wilson put things together in 2017, emerging as one of the organization's better position prospects. At low Class A Kane County he ranked third in the Midwest League in batting average (.295) and second in on-base percentage (.383).

Wilson has perhaps the best plate discipline in the organization, drawing rave reviews from coaches for his ability to wait out pitchers until he gets something he can handle. He has average power, with some seeing the potential for 15 homers. He hit eight of his nine homers before the MWL all-star break, with some believing he might have worn down in the second half. He runs well and has a chance to stay in center field, though some scouts think that once he adds strength to his thin frame he might fit better on a corner.

The D-backs were conservative with their promotions in 2017, so Wilson will get his first taste at high Class A Visalia in 2018.

BA GRADE	
50	**Risk:** High
HIT: 55. POW: 45.	
SPD: 60. FLD: 55.	
ARM: 60.	

Year	Club (League)	Class	AVG	G	AB	R	H	2B	3B	HR	RBI	BB	SO	SB	CS	OBP	SLG
2015	Missoula (PIO)	R	.258	57	213	42	55	12	1	1	22	33	61	7	4	.357	.338
2016	Hillsboro (NWL)	SS	.252	43	135	24	34	5	2	0	15	38	40	18	3	.418	.319
	Kane County (MWL)	LoA	.253	26	99	11	25	8	1	1	5	13	32	7	2	.357	.384
2017	Kane County (MWL)	LoA	.295	103	383	56	113	21	5	9	54	55	90	15	7	.383	.446
Minor League Totals			.264	268	961	148	254	48	11	12	118	155	263	51	18	.369	.375

7 EDUARDO DIAZ, OF

Born: July 19, 1997. **B-T:** R-R. **Ht:** 6-2. **Wt:** 175. **Signed:** Venezuela, 2015. **Signed by:** Gregorio Ramirez/Junior Noboa.

Just like shortstop Jazz Chisholm, Diaz was signed in 2015 while the D-backs were in the penalty for exceeding their international spending limit on Cuban right-hander Yoan Lopez in 2014. Diaz signed for just $10,000 but has quickly emerged as one of the system's most exciting position prospects. He jumped to Rookie-level Missoula in 2017 and delivered 30 extra-base hits in 57 games.

Diaz is a toolsy player whom scouts and coaches feel has a chance to grow into a power-speed center fielder. Everything about his game is built on aggressiveness—whether it's at the plate, on the bases or in the outfield—and sometimes it works against him. He gets himself out too often, especially on the first pitch he sees, and he needs to learn to better manage his at-bats. He hunts fastballs but could stand to improve his breaking ball recognition, as well as use the whole field more. He's not a pure power hitter but has the juice in his swing to drive pitches. Diaz is a plus runner who gets good jumps and takes good routes in the outfield. His arm strength is above-average. He has a wiry strong build that might add another 15 pounds.

Diaz is set for low Class A Kane County and his first taste of full-season ball in 2018.

BA GRADE	
55	**Risk:** Extreme
HIT: 55. POW: 50.	
SPD: 60. FLD: 60.	
ARM: 55.	

Year	Club (League)	Class	AVG	G	AB	R	H	2B	3B	HR	RBI	BB	SO	SB	CS	OBP	SLG
2016	D-backs (DSL)	R	.358	33	123	36	44	6	1	3	16	19	19	19	6	.449	.496
	Diamondbacks (AZL)	R	.229	26	96	7	22	2	1	0	7	10	24	4	2	.312	.271
	Missoula (PIO)	R	.000	3	2	0	0	0	0	0	0	0	1	0	0	.000	.000
2017	Missoula (PIO)	R	.312	57	247	58	77	18	5	7	44	11	47	11	2	.357	.510
Minor League Totals			.306	119	468	101	143	26	7	10	67	40	91	34	10	.372	.455

8 TAYLOR CLARKE, RHP

Born: May 13, 1993. **B-T:** R-R. **Ht:** 6-4. **Wt.:** 200. **Drafted:** College of Charleston, 2015 (3rd round). **Signed by:** George Swain.

Clarke didn't allow a run in his 2015 pro debut, then advanced to Double-A Jackson in his first full season in 2016. He then opened at Double-A in 2017 and served as the club's best starter before a promotion to Triple-A Reno, where he acquitted himself well in a challenging environment.

Nothing about Clarke overwhelms hitters. His fastball ranges from 89-94 mph and sits 92-93 with average life, good downhill angle and some deception from his high three-quarters release point. His solid-average slider is his best secondary pitch, and he's continuing to refine his changeup and curveball. Clarke is able to survive with four average pitches because of his consistent command and ability to repeat his delivery. Coaches rave about his mound presence and competitiveness. He can come across as quiet but he doesn't seem intimidated. His walk rate ticked up from 2016, but scouts continue to believe in his ability to command the ball and his overall pitching acumen.

Clarke will return to Reno to start 2018 while he waits for a need to arise at the big league level. Once Clarke gets there, he projects as a reliable and durable back-end starter.

BA GRADE
45 Risk: Medium
FB: 60. CB: 45.
SL: 50. CHG: 45.
CTL: 55.

Year	Club (League)	Class	W	L	ERA	G	GS	CG	SV	IP	H	HR	BB	SO	K/9	WHIP	AVG
2015	Hillsboro (NWL)	SS	0	0	0.00	13	0	0	3	21	8	0	4	27	11.6	0.57	.114
2016	Kane County (MWL)	LoA	3	2	2.83	6	6	0	0	29	24	1	5	24	7.5	1.01	.222
	Visalia (CAL)	HiA	1	1	2.74	4	4	0	0	23	19	3	7	22	8.6	1.13	.221
	Mobile (SL)	AA	8	6	3.59	17	17	0	0	98	99	9	21	72	6.6	1.23	.261
2017	Jackson (SL)	AA	9	7	2.91	21	21	0	0	111	94	7	39	107	8.6	1.19	.232
	Reno (PCL)	AAA	3	2	4.81	6	6	0	0	34	29	8	13	31	8.3	1.25	.225
Minor League Totals			24	18	3.11	67	54	0	3	315	273	28	89	283	8.1	1.15	.232

9 DREW ELLIS, 3B

Born: Dec. 1, 1995. **B-T:** R-R. **Ht:** 6-3. **Wt:** 210. **Drafted:** Louisville, 2017 (2nd round). **Signed by:** Nate Birtwell.

Starting at third base on the same team as No. 4 overall pick Brendan McKay, Ellis led Louisville in batting average (.355), slugging percentage (.701) and home runs (20) in 2017 and was drafted 44th overall by the D-backs. He signed for just over $1.5 million. Ellis' pro debut at short-season Hillsboro started well, but he tailed off as he wore down following a long college season.

Ellis generates plus power out of his athletic frame, but some scouts have questions about his balance and weight transfer, which leads to him getting out on his front foot and lunging too often. He often had a solid approach and managed at-bats well in college, but some of that backed up as he struggled in his pro debut. Viewed as a questionable third baseman defensively coming out of the draft, Ellis put some of those doubts to rest in pro ball. He lacks a certain amount of range

BA GRADE
50 Risk: High
HIT: 50. POW: 50.
SPD: 40. FLD: 55.
ARM: 55.

and quickness but makes up for it with good hands, solid footwork, an above-average arm and a steady heartbeat that helps him slow the game down.

Ellis struggled with wood bats in college summer leagues and did so again in his pro debut. He will seek a strong year from start to finish in 2018, perhaps at high Class A Visalia.

Year	Club (League)	Class	AVG	G	AB	R	H	2B	3B	HR	RBI	BB	SO	SB	CS	OBP	SLG
2017	Hillsboro (NWL)	SS	.227	48	181	35	41	8	0	8	23	24	45	3	1	.327	.403
Minor League Totals			.227	48	181	35	41	8	0	8	23	24	45	3	1	.327	.403

10 MATT TABOR, RHP

Born: July 14, 1998. **B-T:** R-R. **Ht:** 6-2. **Wt:** 175. **Drafted:** HS—Milton, Mass., 2017 (3rd round). **Signed by:** Dennis Sheehan.

Tabor added size and strength throughout his senior year of high school and jumped from 88-90 mph with his fastball to 90-94 mph. The huge improvement made him a third-round pick last spring, when he signed for $1 million and passed on a college commitment to Elon. Tabor signed later in the process and made just four appearances in the Rookie-level Arizona League in 2017.

Standing at just 5-foot-11 in the fall before his draft year, Tabor topped out at 91 mph before rapidly growing three inches and bumping 95 mph by the spring. He credits some of the velocity gain to a new long-tossing program he picked up in 2016. Tabor has a clean, athletic delivery that he repeats well and also has a lightning-quick arm. His changeup, which is his best secondary offering, draws comparisons with that of former D-backs righthander Chase Anderson. He threw a curveball in high school but he has since traded that for a slider upon turning pro, and the pitch flashes plus. He has good feel for pitching, sometimes even quick pitching or altering the tempo of his delivery to keep hitters off balance.

The D-backs are impressed with Tabor's polish and makeup and see a potential No. 3 starter. He likely will start 2018 in extended spring training before reporting to one of the club's short-season affiliates.

BILL MITCHELL

BA GRADE
55 Risk: Extreme
FB: 55. SL: 55.
CHG: 60.
CTL: 55

Year	Club (League)	Class	W	L	ERA	G	GS	CG	SV	IP	H	HR	BB	SO	K/9	WHIP	AVG
2017	Diamondbacks (AZL)	R	0	1	1.93	4	4	0	0	5	8	0	0	9	17.4	1.71	.348
Minor League Totals			0	1	1.93	4	4	0	0	5	8	0	0	9	17.4	1.71	.348

11 KRISTIAN ROBINSON, OF

BA GRADE
55 Risk: Extreme

Born: Dec. 11, 2000. **B-T:** R-R. **Ht.:** 6-3. **Wt.:** 190. **Signed:** Bahamas, 2017. **Signed by:** Cesar Geronimo/Craig Shipley.

The D-backs liked what they saw when they first laid eyes on Robinson during a 2015 showcase for fellow Bahamian Lucius Fox—the same workout they discovered shortstop Jazz Chisholm. Their conviction in Robinson grew after seeing him perform well the following year at the Perfect Game World Wood Bat Championship against players two years his senior. They wound up signing him for $2.5 million on July 2, the fourth-highest bonus in the 2017 class.

Robinson, a product of the Maximum Development academy in Nassau, has the size and strength to make him a physical specimen at any age, but especially at 16, and he has premium athleticism to go with it. It runs in his family, as his grand-uncle, Thomas Robinson, is a four-time track-and-field Olympian who has a stadium named after him in Nassau. Robinson has the potential to be a five-tool playe with plus raw power. He can handle velocity and the D-backs like the way he tracks offspeed pitches. He's a plus runner who has a chance to stay in center field, though his physical maturation could determine if he ends up in a corner.

Given that he's coming out of the Bahamas rather than, say, the Dominican Republic or Venezuela, many view Robinson's profile as even riskier than other teenage international signees. But no one denies the physical tools needed to potentially grow into a star.

Year	Club (League)	Class	AVG	G	AB	R	H	2B	3B	HR	RBI	BB	SO	SB	CS	OBP	SLG
2017	Did not play—Signed 2018 contract																

12 DOMINGO LEYBA, SS/2B

BA GRADE
45 Risk: Medium

Born: Sept. 11, 1995. **B-T:** B-R. **Ht.:** 5-11. **Wt.:** 160. **Signed:** Dominican Republic, 2012. **Signed by:** Miguel Rodriguez/Carlos Santana/Ramon Perez/Miguel Garcia (Tigers).

A sometimes forgotten part of the three-team deal that brought Robbie Ray to the D-backs and sent Didi Gregorius to the Yankees, Leyba had a rough 2017 season. He suffered a shoulder injury late in spring training and missed about two and a half months before ultimately needing surgery in July. Between a rehab assignment at short-season Hillsboro and his time at Double-A Jackson, Leyba played just 23 games in 2017.

In that brief snapshot, however, Leyba was able to show some of the same improvements he displayed in 2016, prior to his shoulder injury. Leyba improved his pitch selectivity and tapped into more power while at high Class A Visalia in 2016, all while bumping up both his walk rate and slugging percentage. He has a quick bat, strong hands and also shows an ability to find the barrel from both sides of the plate.

Defensively, most scouts seem to view him as more of a second baseman than a shortstop, mostly because his arm is a little short and not as strong as scouts would like. One scout compared his all-around game with Alberto Callaspo, who played in the big leagues for 10 years at third base and second base.

Leyba will look to bounce back from his shoulder injury and stay fully healthy in 2018, continuing to similar steps forward as he did in 2016.

Year	Club (League)	Class	AVG	G	AB	R	H	2B	3B	HR	RBI	BB	SO	SB	CS	OBP	SLG
2015	Visalia (CAL)	HiA	.237	124	514	60	122	21	5	2	43	26	90	10	6	.277	.309
2016	Visalia (CAL)	HiA	.294	86	340	48	100	25	1	6	40	29	62	5	1	.346	.426
	Mobile (SL)	AA	.301	44	156	21	47	7	1	4	20	17	22	4	2	.374	.436
2017	Hillsboro (NWL)	SS	.286	6	28	4	8	1	0	1	6	4	2	0	0	.375	.429
	Jackson (SL)	AA	.276	17	58	11	16	4	0	2	9	5	6	0	0	.344	.448
Minor League Totals			.287	401	1557	235	447	91	16	22	178	129	238	37	21	.343	.408

13 SAM McWILLIAMS, RHP

Born: Sept. 4, 1995. **B-T:** R-R. **Ht.:** 6-7. **Wt.:** 190. **Drafted:** HS—Hendersonville, Tenn., 2014 (8th round). **Signed by:** Nate Dion (Phillies).

BA GRADE
50 Risk: High

McWilliams was still raw and unrefined when the D-backs acquired him in the Jeremy Hellickson deal with the Phillies in November 2015, but he started rounding into form in 2017. During his senior year of high school, McWilliams was inconsistent with his stuff and command—some days throwing in the mid-80s, and other days topping out at 94 mph. The Phillies liked his arm speed, athleticism and his body projection and eventually selected him in the eighth round.

McWilliams got out of whack mechanically in 2016, during his first season with the D-backs, but started tapping into his athleticism while repeating a season in the low Class A Midwest League in 2017. McWilliams throws a 90-95 mph two-seamer with good life and downhill plane out of his 6-foot-7 frame and draws comparisons with Brandon McCarthy. His breaking ball, a slider, grades out as average and flashes plus, and he made strides with his changeup after going from a circle-change to a split-change grip. He averaged just 6.6 strikeouts per nine innings in 2017, but the D-backs don't mind because he induces so many ground balls.

Scouts who saw McWilliams at his best like him as much as any starting pitcher in the system and say he has the upside of a No. 3 starter.

Year	Club (League)	Class	W	L	ERA	G	GS	CG	SV	IP	H	HR	BB	SO	K/9	WHIP	AVG
2015	Phillies (GCL)	R	0	2	3.27	7	7	0	0	33	29	1	5	21	5.7	1.03	.232
2016	Kane County (MWL)	LoA	3	6	3.98	15	15	0	0	75	86	4	18	43	5.2	1.39	.292
2017	Kane County (MWL)	LoA	11	6	2.84	25	25	0	0	133	112	5	31	98	6.6	1.08	.231
Minor League Totals			16	17	3.46	56	52	0	0	266	255	11	60	172	5.8	1.19	.255

14 JIMMIE SHERFY, RHP

Born: Dec. 27, 1991. **B-T:** R-R. **Ht.:** 6-0. **Wt.:** 175. **Drafted:** Oregon, 2013 (10th round). **Signed by:** Donnie Reynolds.

BA GRADE
45 Risk: Medium

After hitting a speed bump in 2015, Sherfy got his career back on track with solid 2016 season and reached the majors in August 2017. He pitched so well down the stretch, in fact, that he earned himself a spot on the D-backs' postseason roster. Interestingly, his first big league manager with the D-backs, Torey Lovullo, is the father of Nick Lovullo, who was one of Sherfy's teammates at Newbury Park (Calif.) High.

Mechanical changes in his delivery in 2016 have helped Sherfy sit in the mid-90s with his fastball and touch the upper 90s. He has a curveball he uses as his out pitch to get swings-and-misses and also mixes in an occasional changeup to keep hitters off balance. His improved dedication to the game off the field has allowed him to maintain his stuff throughout the season. He didn't allow an earned run in the regular season during his brief stint in the majors and Lovullo gave him the ball with the lead late in games, even letting him get the final six outs for a save at Coors Field in September.

Sherfy showed he could pitch at the major league level in 2017 and figures to be in the mix for a prominent bullpen role when the D-backs open the regular season in 2018.

Year	Club (League)	Class	W	L	ERA	G	GS	CG	SV	IP	H	HR	BB	SO	K/9	WHIP	AVG
2015	Mobile (SL)	AA	1	6	6.52	44	0	0	2	50	50	3	28	50	9.1	1.57	.265
2016	Visalia (CAL)	HiA	0	0	0.00	12	0	0	8	12	5	0	6	21	15.3	0.89	.128
	Mobile (SL)	AA	2	0	0.46	16	0	0	10	20	6	1	5	31	14.2	0.56	.092
	Reno (PCL)	AAA	1	4	6.17	24	0	0	12	23	20	5	13	27	10.4	1.41	.240
2017	Reno (PCL)	AAA	2	1	3.12	44	0	0	20	49	37	6	10	61	11.2	0.96	.211
	Arizona (NL)	MAJ	2	0	0.00	11	0	0	1	11	5	0	2	9	7.6	0.66	.143
Major League Totals			2	0	0.00	11	0	0	1	11	5	0	2	9	7.6	0.66	.143
Minor League Totals			12	13	3.96	206	0	0	66	220	171	21	89	287	11.7	1.18	.216

15 GABRIEL MACIEL, OF

BA GRADE

50 Risk: Extreme

Born: Jan. 10, 1999. **B-T:** B-R. **Ht.:** 5-10. **Wt.:** 170. **Signed:** Brazil, 2015. **Signed by:** Kelvin Kondo/Mack Hayashi.

The D-backs made Maciel the second Brazilian-born player in club history, following righthander Bo Takahashi, when they signed him for $90,000 in October 2015. Maciel is from Londrina, a city known for its baseball history because of a heavy influx of Japanese settlers who brought the game with them. The D-backs first spotted him at a baseball academy in Brazil when he was either 12 or 13. He grew into a legit prospect by age 15, with his off-the-charts athleticism evident in how quickly he picked things up. He showed well at the 18U World Cup in Japan in 2015 and the D-backs signed him a month later.

Maciel has the tools to be a prototype leadoff man. He has some of the best strike-zone discipline in the organization, doesn't strike out much, has the feel to hit and even has some sneaky power that could grow into more when he learns to cut it loose in the right spots. He runs well but needs to work on his jumps. A switch-hitter, he's more confident from the right side but he has made improvements from the left. He's an above-average defender who scouts think has a chance to stick in center field, though he split time at Rookie-level Missoula with Eduardo Diaz, who most consider to be the better defender.

Maciel draws comparisons with Ender Inciarte and figures to get his first crack at full-season ball in 2018.

Year	Club (League)	Class	AVG	G	AB	R	H	2B	3B	HR	RBI	BB	SO	SB	CS	OBP	SLG
2016	Diamondbacks (AZL)	R	.289	37	149	28	43	3	0	0	10	12	22	11	4	.341	.309
	Missoula (PIO)	R	.266	23	79	15	21	2	0	0	4	5	19	11	1	.318	.291
2017	Missoula (PIO)	R	.323	52	217	40	70	14	1	3	25	24	34	9	8	.389	.438
Minor League Totals			.301	112	445	83	134	19	1	3	39	41	75	31	13	.361	.369

16 ANDY YERZY, C

BA GRADE

50 Risk: Extreme

Born: July 5, 1998. **B-T:** L-R. **Ht.:** 6-3. **Wt.:** 215. **Drafted:** HS—Toronto, 2016 (2nd round). **Signed by:** Dennis Sheehan.

Yerzy settled in during his second pro season and put together some of the more impressive offensive numbers in the system in 2017. The power bat the D-backs envisioned out of the draft began to emerge, as Yerzy began driving balls to the opposite field and also began to tap into more power to his pull side, as well.

By the end of the 2017 season, Yerzy controlled the zone and put together quality at-bats as well as anyone at Rookie-level Missoula. Questions still remain on the other side of the ball, however. Yerzy's receiving skills improved behind the plate but he still struggled at times on pitches with late life. His transfer is sound and his throws are mostly accurate, but his pop times on throws to second base were still below-average. His large 6-foot-3 frame will always pose a challenge when it comes to throwing, but scouts have concerns about his overall athleticism, as well. Still, Yerzy has made strides defensively and could continue to do so given how little experience he had catching high-caliber pitchers as an amateur.

Yerzy does not run well, leading some to believe he's a catcher or bust in terms of a long-term position. Others see a potentially special bat that could play at first base or as a DH—if traded to an American League club—if his catching doesn't continue to improve.

Year	Club (League)	Class	AVG	G	AB	R	H	2B	3B	HR	RBI	BB	SO	SB	CS	OBP	SLG
2016	Diamondbacks (AZL)	R	.196	27	102	5	20	3	0	1	15	4	22	0	0	.220	.255
	Missoula (PIO)	R	.250	18	60	2	15	2	0	0	1	0	16	0	1	.274	.283
2017	Missoula (PIO)	R	.298	54	225	36	67	12	0	13	45	24	45	0	0	.365	.524
Minor League Totals			.264	99	387	43	102	17	0	14	61	28	83	0	1	.314	.416

17 JARED MILLER, LHP

BA GRADE

40 Risk: Medium

Born: Aug. 21, 1993. **B-T:** L-L. **Ht.:** 6-7. **Wt.:** 240. **Drafted:** Vanderbilt, 2014 (11th round). **Signed by:** Nate Birtwell.

In the offseason following the 2015 season, Miller picked the brain of fellow lefthander and Vanderbilt product David Price and came away with a new weapon. Miller's newfound cutter was the pitch that pushed him over the top and helped him catapult onto the D-backs' prospect landscape with a dominant 2016. He then arrived at big league camp in 2017 but struggled with his command, which is an issue that carried over to the start of the Double-A season.

Coaches say Miller cleaned up the direction in his delivery and started mixing in more curveballs, and from May through the end of the season he posted a 1.69 ERA with 80 strikeouts in 58.2 innings. Miller uncorks his 6-foot-7 frame in a high-effort delivery, and all of his pitches, including a low- to mid-90s fastball, have good life. Opinions on Miller vary in the scouting community. Some scouts see a potential late-inning reliever and possible closer, while some see him as a left-on-left matchup type. Still, other scouts are concerned about Miller's command, noting that he seemed to struggle against lineups that waited him out.

On the heels of another impressive season, Miller could work his way to the big leagues in 2018, although a start at Triple-A Reno isn't out of the question.

Year	Club (League)	Class	W	L	ERA	G	GS	CG	SV	IP	H	HR	BB	SO	K/9	WHIP	AVG
2015	Hillsboro (NWL)	SS	7	2	1.81	9	9	1	0	60	42	2	12	57	8.6	0.91	.194
	Kane County (MWL)	LoA	4	5	5.88	13	12	0	0	60	69	5	31	42	6.3	1.68	.291
2016	Kane County (MWL)	LoA	0	0	0.00	9	0	0	2	14	4	0	5	21	13.2	0.63	.085
	Visalia (CAL)	HiA	0	1	1.88	12	0	0	1	14	9	0	3	20	12.6	0.84	.184
	Reno (PCL)	AAA	0	0	6.00	5	0	0	0	6	5	2	2	3	4.5	1.17	.238
	Mobile (SL)	AA	0	1	3.71	19	0	0	2	27	18	1	13	36	12.2	1.16	.188
2017	Jackson (SL)	AA	0	3	3.89	31	0	0	2	39	33	2	18	51	11.7	1.30	.222
	Reno (PCL)	AAA	3	3	1.72	22	0	0	1	31	16	2	10	43	12.6	0.83	.147
Minor League Totals			15	16	3.32	128	26	1	8	279	217	17	103	294	9.5	1.15	.211

18 YOAN LOPEZ, RHP

Born: Jan. 2, 1993. **B-T:** R-R. **Ht.:** 6-3. **Wt.:** 185. **Signed:** Cuba, 2015. **Signed by:** De Jon Watson.

The D-backs spent more than $16 million to sign Lopez, the total amount encompassing his $8.25 million signing bonus and a 100 percent overage penalty. After two seasons, the decision looked like a huge bust. But Lopez dominated the high Class A California League as a reliever in 2017, creating some optimism that he could one day be a big league contributor.

The D-backs viewed Lopez as a potential frontline starter when they signed him out of Cuba in January 2015, but for two years he not only did not throw well—he struggled to maintain his stuff from start to start—he also had issues off the field. Each of those years, he left his Double-A Mobile team without permission. He has never publicly discussed why, but he told team officials he was considering retirement the second time. Instead, he returned in 2017 and, after dealing with blister and shoulder issues in the first half, turned in two dominant months at Visalia. His fastball sat 95-98 mph touched 99 with late life up in the zone, and his slider was a wipeout pitch, with sharp, late action.

It's a red flag that his brief stint in the Arizona Fall League in 2017 ended with more shoulder issues, but if he's healthy he could pitch his way into the big league bullpen in 2018.

Year	Club (League)	Class	W	L	ERA	G	GS	CG	SV	IP	H	HR	BB	SO	K/9	WHIP	AVG
2015	Diamondbacks (AZL)	R	1	0	0.00	1	1	0	0	6	3	0	0	6	9.0	0.50	.158
	Mobile (SL)	AA	1	6	4.69	10	9	0	0	48	46	4	24	32	6.0	1.46	.261
2016	Mobile (SL)	AA	4	7	5.52	14	14	1	0	62	67	10	32	36	5.2	1.60	.277
	Diamondbacks (AZL)	R	0	0	0.00	2	2	0	0	3	3	0	0	4	12.0	1.00	.250
2017	Diamondbacks (AZL)	R	0	0	0.00	1	0	0	1	1	0	0	1	3	27.0	1.00	.000
	Visalia (CAL)	HiA	2	0	0.88	20	0	0	4	31	16	2	9	56	16.4	0.82	.152
Minor League Totals			8	13	3.94	48	26	1	5	151	135	16	66	137	8.2	1.33	.242

19 SOCRATES BRITO, OF

Born: Sept. 6, 1992. **B-T:** L-L. **Ht.:** 6-2. **Wt.:** 205. **Signed:** Dominican Republic, 2010. **Signed by:** Junior Noboa.

Coming off an injury-riddled 2016, Brito was bit by the injury bug again in 2017 while he repeated the Pacific Coast League at Triple-A Reno. In 2016, he suffered a fractured toe while with the big league team, then he fractured the hamate in his wrist while getting ready for winter ball in November. In 2017, he needed yet another surgery after severely dislocating his left ring finger on a headfirst slide into home plate during a game early in spring training.

The injury cost him two and a half months, impacting his standing on the organization's depth chart, and journeyman Jeremy Hazelbaker stepped into the fourth outfielder void. Brito, meanwhile, didn't play well enough at Reno to warrant even a September callup. Little has changed in terms of Brito's tools and upside, and he still gets high marks for his work ethic. Coaches say he might have become bogged down at the plate by mechanics, limiting his athleticism, and he still could use work on his approach. He runs well and can handle all three outfield positions, but he probably is best suited for a corner. Brito has handled righthanded pitchers better than lefthanders in his career, leading some scouts to view him as a potential platoon outfielder.

Brito will have to show he can stay healthy in order to reach even that ceiling as he fights for a spot with the D-backs out of spring training.

ARIZONA DIAMONDBACKS

Year	Club (League)	Class	AVG	G	AB	R	H	2B	3B	HR	RBI	BB	SO	SB	CS	OBP	SLG
2015	Mobile (SL)	AA	.300	129	490	70	147	17	15	9	57	29	84	20	6	.339	.451
	Arizona (NL)	MAJ	.303	18	33	5	10	3	1	0	1	1	7	1	0	.324	.455
2016	Diamondbacks (AZL)	R	.143	2	7	0	1	0	0	0	2	0	3	0	0	.143	.143
	Visalia (CAL)	HiA	.111	2	9	1	1	0	0	1	2	0	2	0	0	.111	.444
	Reno (PCL)	AAA	.294	73	303	46	89	10	8	6	39	13	60	7	6	.322	.439
	Arizona (NL)	MAJ	.179	40	95	10	17	3	1	4	12	2	23	2	0	.196	.358
2017	Reno (PCL)	AAA	.291	78	292	43	85	15	8	5	44	22	64	6	1	.336	.449
Major League Totals			.211	58	128	15	27	6	2	4	13	3	30	3	0	.229	.383
Minor League Totals			.288	687	2739	390	789	118	58	38	331	180	584	131	55	.331	.415

20 JOEY ROSE, 3B

BA GRADE
50 Risk: Extreme

Born: Jan. 20, 1998. **B-T:** R-R. **Ht.:** 6-1. **Wt.:** 205. **Drafted:** HS—Tom's River, N.J., 2016 (5th round). **Signed by:** Rick Matsko.

Drafted out of the same New Jersey town that produced Todd Frazier, Rose finished his 2016 debut season with a strong final month, then carried that success into his first full year as a pro. He put up a .907 OPS in the hitter-friendly Rookie-level Pioneer League in 2017, when he hit third all season for Missoula.

Scouts see the potential for plus power but they also saw swing-and-miss issues, leading many to believe he'll be a power-over-hit player. Coaches say Rose had a tendency to drop his back side in hopes of creating lift, an action that actually wound up leading to more ground balls. He struggled at times defensively at third base, making mistakes on routine plays and leading to speculation he took his at-bats with him into the field. But coaches say his defense improved as the season progressed, and that part of his game will need to remain a focus for him going forward in hopes of staving a move to a less demanding position. Rose is a below-average runner.

Rose likely will get his first crack at full-season ball in 2018, perhaps at low Class A Kane County.

Year	Club (League)	Class	AVG	G	AB	R	H	2B	3B	HR	RBI	BB	SO	SB	CS	OBP	SLG
2016	Diamondbacks (AZL)	R	.229	47	153	19	35	10	4	1	9	13	55	2	0	.310	.366
	Hillsboro (NWL)	SS	.000	2	2	0	0	0	0	0	0	0	1	0	0	.333	.000
2017	Missoula (PIO)	R	.312	49	199	32	62	15	2	9	39	13	56	2	0	.364	.543
Minor League Totals			.274	98	354	51	97	25	6	10	48	27	113	4	0	.340	.463

21 JHOAN DURAN, RHP

BA GRADE
50 Risk: Extreme

Born: Jan. 8, 1998. **B-T:** R-R. **Ht.:** 6-5. **Wt.:** 175. **Signed:** Dominican Republic, 2014. **Signed by:** Jose Ortiz/Junior Noboa.

Duran was skinny and throwing in the upper 80s when the D-backs signed him for $65,000 in December 2014, but he was bumping the upper 90s in 2017 and now represents one of the higher-upside arms in the system.

Duran already averages about 94 mph with his fastball, but with a 6-foot-5 frame that could still add significant weight, scouts see projection remaining. Duran has three pitches. He can vary speeds on his curveball to the point that some scouts identified it as a slider. It's considered an above-average to plus pitch. His changeup is still developing but flashes plus. D-backs coaches wanted to see him learn to handle adversity within his outings better, rather than losing confidence when opposing hitters had success. Scouts say Duran has control over command at this point, and some see a back-end reliever if his command doesn't improve enough.

If everything comes together, Duran has all the ingredients of a mid-rotation starter. He'll likely get his first crack at full-season ball at low Class A Kane County in 2018.

Year	Club (League)	Class	W	L	ERA	G	GS	CG	SV	IP	H	HR	BB	SO	K/9	WHIP	AVG
2015	D-backs (DSL)	R	4	1	3.25	12	12	0	0	64	62	1	22	44	6.2	1.32	.263
2016	Diamondbacks (AZL)	R	1	2	5.85	4	4	0	0	20	24	1	5	13	5.9	1.45	.312
	Missoula (PIO)	R	0	1	3.55	3	3	0	0	13	14	1	5	9	6.4	1.50	.250
2017	Diamondbacks (AZL)	R	0	2	7.15	3	3	0	0	11	19	0	4	13	10.3	2.03	.352
	Hillsboro (NWL)	SS	6	3	4.24	11	11	0	0	51	44	5	17	36	6.4	1.20	.228
Minor League Totals			11	9	4.20	33	33	0	0	159	163	8	53	115	6.5	1.36	.265

22 KEVIN CRON, 1B

BA GRADE
45 Risk: High

Born: Feb. 17, 1993. **B-T:** R-R. **Ht.:** 6-5. **Wt.:** 245. **Drafted:** Texas Christian, 2014 (14th round). **Signed by:** J.R. Salinas.

Cron registered his third consecutive season with 25 or more home runs in 2017, only this time he exhibited far better on-base skills. While repeating the Double-A Southern League, he led the circuit with 25 homers and 91 RBIs to earn MVP honors.

Cron's improvement represented an important step forward for the bat-only slugger. Cron comes from a baseball family. His father Chris played parts of two seasons in the majors and the D-backs currently employ him as minor league hitting coordinator. Kevin's older brother C.J. plays for the Angels. Kevin made big strides in his at-bat management in 2017, showing improvement in both his approach and pitch recognition. Scouts are split on his defensive ability, but his believers say he makes all the routine plays and he has improved his footwork He doesn't run well, though, so he is limited to first base.

Cron will have to hit to succeed in the majors, and next up is Triple-A Reno.

Year	Club (League)	Class	AVG	G	AB	R	H	2B	3B	HR	RBI	BB	SO	SB	CS	OBP	SLG
2015	Visalia (CAL)	HiA	.272	127	518	71	141	34	0	27	97	28	131	0	0	.314	.494
2016	Mobile (SL)	AA	.222	127	465	60	103	20	1	26	88	33	134	3	1	.278	.437
2017	Jackson (SL)	AA	.283	138	515	76	146	35	0	25	91	56	134	1	0	.357	.497
Minor League Totals			.265	456	1759	261	466	107	1	90	321	137	444	4	1	.324	.480

23 JOSE ALMONTE, RHP

BA GRADE
45 Risk: High

Born: Sept. 8, 1995. **B-T:** R-R. **Ht.:** 6-2. **Wt.:** 185. **Signed:** Dominican Republic, 2012. **Signed by:** Manny Nanita (Red Sox).

Acquired as part of the 2016 deadline deal that sent Brad Ziegler to the Red Sox, Almonte put together a solid first full season in the D-backs organization in 2017. He finished the year with the most strikeouts (162) and second-lowest ERA (3.55) in the high Class A California League.

Almonte's calling card is a fastball ranging from 88-94 mph with natural cutting action—a pitch that moves so much and acted so much like a slider that it left opposing hitters unsure of what type of pitch he was throwing. He also throws a true slider, curveball and changeup, and coaches like his ability to spin the ball. Almonte's fastball command needs to improve—he walked 4.3 batters per nine innings in 2017—as does his level of maturity on the mound—both in terms of controlling emotions and finishing hitters.

The D-backs believe the movement on his fastball gives him a weapon that would play at the big league level, perhaps in the bullpen if not as a back-of-rotation starter.

Year	Club (League)	Class	W	L	ERA	G	GS	CG	SV	IP	H	HR	BB	SO	K/9	WHIP	AVG
2015	Lowell (NYP)	SS	3	3	3.43	14	14	0	0	66	38	1	38	64	8.8	1.16	.171
2016	Greenville (SAL)	LoA	2	2	3.91	10	10	0	0	53	50	4	13	45	7.6	1.19	.249
	Kane County (MWL)	LoA	2	4	3.23	11	11	0	0	56	48	4	22	59	9.5	1.26	.234
2017	Visalia (CAL)	HiA	11	8	3.55	27	27	0	0	139	129	10	66	162	10.5	1.40	.243
Minor League Totals			23	23	3.34	85	82	0	0	412	349	23	178	406	8.9	1.28	.229

24 ILDEMARO VARGAS, SS/2B

BA GRADE
40 Risk: Medium

Born: July 16, 1991. **B-T:** B-R. **Ht.:** 6-0. **Wt.:** 170. **Signed:** Venezuela, 2007. **Signed by:** Jobel Jimenez (Cardinals).

Vargas became the fourth player in the past five years to reach the big leagues after being plucked out of independent ball by the D-backs.

Vargas has performed ever since, showing good bat-to-ball skills, a solid approach at the plate, above-average speed and the ability to play all over the infield. He even saw time in center field for Triple-A Reno in 2017. He probably fits best at second base. Vargas is not physical and has never hit for much power.

Vargas brings energy and an upbeat, infectious attitude to the park with him every day, which are good attributes for a player most scouts see as an utility infielder candidate.

Year	Club (League)	Class	AVG	G	AB	R	H	2B	3B	HR	RBI	BB	SO	SB	CS	OBP	SLG
2015	Bridgeport (ATL)	IND	.273	30	110	17	30	5	0	0	8	6	9	7	1	.316	.318
	Kane County (MWL)	LoA	.321	86	336	62	108	18	3	5	39	35	16	9	6	.385	.438
2016	Mobile (SL)	AA	.276	83	323	41	89	15	2	4	19	24	24	8	0	.325	.372
	Visalia (CAL)	HiA	.250	1	4	0	1	0	0	0	0	0	2	0	0	.250	.250
	Reno (PCL)	AAA	.354	49	198	35	70	13	0	2	18	20	13	13	1	.418	.449
2017	Diamondbacks (AZL)	R	.375	2	8	2	3	0	0	0	0	0	0	1	0	.375	.375
	Reno (PCL)	AAA	.314	113	487	87	153	35	4	10	65	30	40	8	3	.357	.464
	Arizona (NL)	MAJ	.308	12	13	4	4	1	0	0	4	0	3	0	0	.308	.385
Major League Totals			.308	12	13	4	4	1	0	0	4	0	3	0	0	.308	.385
Minor League Totals			.285	779	2909	437	829	156	22	29	300	231	284	72	35	.343	.384

25 TOMMY EVELD, RHP

Born: Dec. 30, 1993. **B-T:** R-R. **Ht.:** 6-5. **Wt.:** 195. **Drafted:** South Florida, 2016 (9th round). **Signed by:** Luke Wrenn.

BA GRADE
45 Risk: High

In a little more than two years, Eveld went from not having played baseball since his sophomore year of high school to showing some of the most electric stuff of any pitcher in the organization. He spent two seasons at South Florida as a quarterback but never played before tearing his ACL and needing knee surgery. That was the first of two ACL surgeries he had in college. In 2015, he walked on to the USF baseball team, and the D-backs drafted him as a righthander the following year.

Eveld has a fastball that can range from 92-97 mph and a power slider that sits around 89-91. He also showed improvement in 2017 with a curveball, a pitch he throws around 76-80 mph. He gave up only one earned run in 22 appearances at low Class A Kane County in 2017 before a promotion to high Class A Visalia, where he struggled for about two weeks after dealing with a left knee issue. Eveld has a sort of aggressive, football mentality on the mound—he comes out of the bullpen to the "Monday Night Football" theme—and the D-backs love his competitiveness.

Some believe he might have the best stuff in the organization and could move quickly in 2018.

Year	Club (League)	Class	W	L	ERA	G	GS	CG	SV	IP	H	HR	BB	SO	K/9	WHIP	AVG
2016	Hillsboro (NWL)	SS	2	1	1.86	24	0	0	2	29	17	0	8	31	9.6	0.86	.168
2017	Kane County (MWL)	LoA	1	0	0.33	22	0	0	14	28	10	0	8	33	10.7	0.65	.111
	Visalia (CAL)	HiA	0	5	5.73	19	0	0	2	22	22	1	11	26	10.6	1.50	.262
Minor League Totals			3	6	2.40	65	0	0	18	79	49	1	27	90	10.3	0.97	.178

26 CHRISTIAN WALKER, 1B

Born: March 28, 1991. **B-T:** R-R. **Ht.:** 6-0. **Wt.:** 220. **Drafted:** South Carolina, 2012 (4th round). **Signed by:** Chris Gale (Orioles).

BA GRADE
40 Risk: Medium

The D-backs were the third team to claim Walker on waivers prior to the 2017 season, doing so just days before the end of spring training. They ran him through waivers as well, and he cleared, allowing Arizona to outright him to Triple-A Reno. But Walker put together a huge offensive season and won the MVP award in the hitter-friendly Pacific Coast League, not only earning himself a spot back on the 40-man roster but finding his way on to the D-backs' Division Series roster against the Dodgers.

Walker said he made changes to his bat path that helped produce more contact, evident in a strikeout rate that went from 25 percent in 2016 to 18 percent in 2017. Coaches rave about his hitting acumen. Walker is a fringe-average defender at first. He also has some experience in left field over the past two seasons but is below-average there. He is blocked at first base in Arizona by Paul Goldschmidt and will be 27 in 2018 and some scouts aren't convinced he'll ever be more than a bench bat.

Still, Walker impressed the D-backs in 2017 with his power and approach, and he could be in the mix for a big league bench job.

Year	Club (League)	Class	AVG	G	AB	R	H	2B	3B	HR	RBI	BB	SO	SB	CS	OBP	SLG
2015	Norfolk (IL)	AAA	.257	138	534	68	137	33	1	18	74	49	136	1	3	.324	.423
	Baltimore (AL)	MAJ	.111	7	9	0	1	0	0	0	0	3	4	0	0	.333	.111
2016	Norfolk (IL)	AAA	.264	131	504	64	133	29	2	18	64	40	138	1	3	.321	.437
2017	Reno (PCL)	AAA	.309	133	514	104	159	34	9	32	114	61	104	4	2	.382	.597
	Arizona (NL)	MAJ	.250	11	12	2	3	1	0	2	2	1	5	0	0	.400	.833
Major League Totals			.179	24	39	3	7	2	0	3	3	5	18	0	0	.304	.462
Minor League Totals			.283	666	2558	372	723	153	14	107	413	250	591	12	13	.350	.479

27 BUDDY KENNEDY, 3B

Born: Oct. 5, 1998. **B-T:** R-R. **Ht.:** 5-11. **Wt.:** 215. **Drafted:** HS—Millville, N.J., 2017 (5th round). **Signed by:** Rick Matsko.

BA GRADE
45 Risk: Extreme

The D-backs made Kennedy the first player drafted out of Millville High since Mike Trout in 2009 then signed him for $550,000 to buy him out of a college commitment to North Carolina. While he doesn't have the same skill set as Trout, with whom he regularly works out in the offseason, he does have a lot of skills to like, most notably a knack for squaring up baseballs.

Kennedy has a short, compact swing that has a chance to produce above-average power. Though he didn't hit a home run in the Rookie-level Arizona League in his pro debut, he did collect 17 extra-base hits, including nine triples. His body—a stout, stocky frame—is a drawback for some scouts, who wonder about his athleticism. Others remain unconcerned, with one scout drawing a comparison with Jedd Gyorko—both for his physique and his ability to barrel balls. He's an above-average to plus runner, has good hands and has a plus arm that works at third base.

Kennedy will likely start 2018 in extended spring training before heading to Rookie-level Missoula.

Year	Club (League)	Class	AVG	G	AB	R	H	2B	3B	HR	RBI	BB	SO	SB	CS	OBP	SLG
2017	Diamondbacks (AZL)	R	.270	50	178	29	48	9	8	0	20	19	47	7	2	.343	.410
Minor League Totals			.270	50	178	29	48	9	8	0	20	19	47	7	2	.343	.410

28 ELVIS LUCIANO, RHP

BA GRADE 45 Risk: Extreme

Born: Feb. 15, 2000. **B-T:** R-R. **Ht.:** 6-2. **Wt.:** 184. **Signed:** Dominican Republic, 2016. **Signed by:** Junior Noboa.

The D-backs saw Luciano throw just twice before snapping him up for $85,000 in the fall of 2016. They liked his heavy fastball, the spin on his breaking ball and his feel for a changeup.

Luciano pitched in 2017 at the tender age of 17, but he is advanced beyond his years. He has an athletic delivery, a loose arm, a good feel for pitching and an unfazed demeanor on the mound. He began the year in the Dominican Summer League but moved to the Rookie-level Arizona League before finishing in the Rookie-level Pioneer League and getting a taste of the Pioneer League playoffs. He sits 91-93 mph with his fastball but the D-backs believe he has a chance to get up to the mid-90s. His changeup projects to be a plus pitch, and he shows feel to spin a curveball that has slurvy shape.

Luciano is years away from the big leagues but has the raw ingredients to be a big league starter.

Year	Club (League)	Class	W	L	ERA	G	GS	CG	SV	IP	H	HR	BB	SO	K/9	WHIP	AVG
2017	D-backs (DSL)	R	3	1	2.98	11	6	0	0	48	42	2	15	41	7.6	1.18	.236
	Diamondbacks (AZL)	R	1	0	2.76	4	2	0	1	16	16	0	3	9	5.0	1.16	.242
	Missoula (PIO)	R	0	0	0.00	1	0	0	0	2	0	0	0	2	9.0	0.00	.000
Minor League Totals			4	1	2.84	16	8	0	1	67	58	2	18	52	7.0	1.14	.232

29 COLIN POCHE, LHP

BA GRADE 40 Risk: High

Born: Jan. 17, 1994. **B-T:** L-L. **Ht.:** 6-3. **Wt.:** 185. **Drafted:** Dallas Baptist, 2016 (14th round). **Signed by:** J.R. Salinas.

Poche needed Tommy John surgery after his sophomore year at Arkansas and decided to transfer, since he wasn't totally happy with the Razorbacks. He landed at Dallas Baptist. The D-backs shifted him to a full-time relief role in 2017 after taking him in the 16th round in 2016 and he took off.

Poche's 1.25 ERA between low Class A Kane County and high Class A Visalia was the sixth-lowest among full-season minor league pitchers with at least 50 innings. He misses bats but doesn't do it in a traditionally overpowering way. His fastball sits in the low 90s, occasionally touching 95 mph, but he appears to hide the ball well and is said to get good extension from his over-the-top delivery. His slider is a little short but has late break and showed improvement as the year progressed.

Poche projects as a matchup reliever, but if his fastball develops, he could become more than that.

Year	Club (League)	Class	W	L	ERA	G	GS	CG	SV	IP	H	HR	BB	SO	K/9	WHIP	AVG
2016	Hillsboro (NWL)	SS	1	2	3.19	21	4	0	0	31	20	2	17	36	10.5	1.19	.194
2017	Kane County (MWL)	LoA	2	0	1.09	13	0	0	1	25	16	0	6	44	16.1	0.89	.186
	Visalia (CAL)	HiA	1	1	1.40	18	0	0	2	26	14	0	13	37	13.0	1.05	.163
Minor League Totals			4	3	1.99	52	4	0	3	81	50	2	36	117	12.9	1.06	.182

30 MICHAEL PEREZ, C

BA GRADE 40 Risk: High

Born: Aug. 7, 1992. **B-T:** L-R. **Ht.:** 5-11. **Wt.:** 180. **Drafted:** HS—San Juan, P.R., 2011 (5th round). **Signed by:** Frankie Thon Jr.

After a big season at Rookie-level Missoula in 2012, Perez's career seemed to stall, but he had a mild breakthrough in 2017, hitting .279/.365/.424 at Double-A Jackson.

Perez said a tip from former winter ball teammate Juan Ciriaco helped him stop being so pull-conscious. Coaches say he's also become far more selective at the plate. The adjustment led to fewer homers (six) but far more balls in the gap. For years, Perez has been regarded as a solid defensive catcher who throws and blocks well and calls a good game. He focused his efforts during the Arizona Fall League on improving his framing, particularly on pitches down in the strike zone.

Some view Perez as a potential big league backup, particularly because he's a lefthanded hitter.

Year	Club (League)	Class	AVG	G	AB	R	H	2B	3B	HR	RBI	BB	SO	SB	CS	OBP	SLG
2015	Visalia (CAL)	HiA	.188	34	117	15	22	6	0	3	20	9	37	1	0	.254	.316
	Kane County (MWL)	LoA	.224	55	183	18	41	9	0	1	26	20	31	4	3	.306	.290
2016	Mobile (SL)	AA	.205	39	122	7	25	4	1	3	10	7	29	0	1	.252	.328
	Visalia (CAL)	HiA	.256	47	156	17	40	10	2	1	19	15	33	1	0	.318	.365
2017	Jackson (SL)	AA	.279	80	262	29	73	23	0	5	39	35	61	0	2	.365	.424
	Reno (PCL)	AAA	.444	3	9	2	4	1	1	1	6	1	0	0	0	.500	1.111
Minor League Totals			.241	514	1757	230	423	113	15	42	256	196	498	9	11	.319	.394

Atlanta Braves

BY J.J. COOPER

As the Braves dismantled their team in 2014 and 2015, they did so with a long-term plan in place.

The rebuilt farm system would begin to produce big leaguers just as the team moved into its new ballpark in 2017. The team, freed of significant long-term contracts, would be able to add talent as needed on the free agent market in 2018. With the help of the increased revenue of the new ballpark, the team would contend by 2018, with a loaded farm system both producing big leaguers and trade assets.

This offseason didn't go according to plan.

The architects of that plan have been deposed.  The organization has been disgraced, and now the new leadership has to finish the rebuild after the most embarrassing offseason in Braves history. Major League Baseball discovered rampant cheating helped the Braves sign players on the international market and may have helped sign a draft pick as well.

The list of Braves violations is long and varied, stretching across the international signing market and the draft. The punishment commissioner Rob Manfred handed down was one of the harshest in baseball history. Twelve Braves players were declared free agents—including Venezuelan shortstop Kevin Maitan—and a 13th player's contract was not approved. The team also lost a 2018 third-round draft pick, and the team will face international signing sanctions for the rest of the decade.

General manager John Coppolella and international scouting director Gordon Blakeley were fired. Coppolella was permanently banned from baseball. President of baseball operations John Hart left voluntarily.

The Braves moved quickly to bring in experienced leadership, hiring former Blue Jays GM Alex Anthopoulos to try to carry the rebuild to fruition. He inherits a team well equipped to rebuild.

Atlanta opened its new ballpark, a suburban stadium that is part of a planned retail-residential development that should bolster revenue for decades, allowing the team to increase its payroll.

And there is a solid lineup core already in place, thanks to Freddie Freeman, Ender Inciarte and the young double-play combo of Ozzie Albies and Dansby Swanson. Outfielder Ronald Acuna, the Minor League Player of the Year, gives the team another potential cornerstone.

The front office turmoil does create an unusual dynamic. What Anthopoulos and his staff will have to do is figure out which of the team's many pitching prospects are big league starters, which are relievers and which ones are best traded elsewhere.

Second baseman Ozzie Albies gained traction in Atlanta during a strong rookie season.

PROJECTED 2021 LINEUP

Catcher	Alex Jackson (25)
First Base	Freddie Freeman (32)
Second Base	Ozzie Albies (25)
Third Base	Austin Riley (23)
Shortstop	Dansby Swanson (28)
Left Field	Ender Inciarte (31)
Center Field	Cristian Pache (22)
Right Field	Ronald Acuna (23)
No. 1 Starter	Luiz Gohara (25)
No. 2 Starter	Mike Soroka (24)
No. 3 Starter	Kyle Wright (25)
No. 4 Starter	Julio Teheran (31)
No. 5 Starter	Ian Anderson (23)
Closer	A.J. Minter (28)

Atlanta will likely begin the 2018 season with three first- or second-year big leaguers in its rotation. A full rotation of candidates—including Top 10 Prospects Luiz Gohara, Mike Soroka, Kyle Wright, Kolby Allard and Max Fried—will be lined up behind them at Double-A and Triple-A. If the team is going to contend by 2019, the new front office must sort through the arms quickly.

Anthopoulos' staff in Toronto did an excellent job of drafting and developing pitchers, though the Blue Jays did trade away some of the best of their arms, including righthanders Noah Syndergaard, Daniel Norris and Joe Musgrove. In Atlanta, he and his staff will have to get up to speed quickly on whom to keep and whom to trade.

DEPTH CHART

ATLANTA BRAVES

TOP 2018 ROOKIE: Ronald Acuna, OF. He's ready, and with Matt Kemp traded in the offseason he should have space to play soon in Atlanta.
BREAKOUT PROSPECT: William Contreras, C. The Braves are very deep at catcher, but Contreras' offensive ability stands out.
SLEEPER: Josh Graham, RHP. Thanks to a solid fastball-changeup combo, Graham isn't that far away from helping the big league bullpen.

SOURCE OF TOP 30 TALENT

Homegrown	23	**Acquired**	**7**
College	5	Trade	7
Junior college	1	Rule 5 draft	0
High school	9	Independent league	0
Nondrafted free agent	0	Free agent/waivers	0
International	8		

LF
Dustin Peterson (24)
Jeffrey Ramos (25)

CF
Ronald Acuna (1)
Cristian Pache (9)
Drew Waters (17)
Isranel Wilson (27)
Ray Patrick-Didder
Lane Adams
Anfernee Seymour

RF
Raysheandall Michel

3B
Austin Riley (6)
Jean Carlos Encarnacion (22)

SS
Derian Cruz

2B
Travis Demeritte
Luis Valenzuela

1B
Braxton Davidson
Tyler Neslony

C
Alex Jackson (10)
William Contreras (18)
Drew Lugbauer (28)
Kade Scivicque
Brett Cumberland
Lucas Herbert
Tanner Murphy

LHP

LHSP	LHRP
Luiz Gohara (2)	A.J. Minter (15)
Kolby Allard (7)	Phil Pfiefer (29)
Max Fried (8)	Thomas Burrows
Joey Wentz (11)	Tyler Pike
Tucker Davidson (13)	Miguel Jerez
Ricardo Sanchez (19)	
Kyle Muller (20)	
Drew Harrington	

RHP

RHSP	RHRP
Mike Soroka (3)	Huascar Ynoa (23)
Kyle Wright (4)	Josh Graham (30)
Ian Anderson (5)	Anyelo Gomez
Bryse Wilson (12)	Dan Winkler
Touki Toussaint (14)	Evan Phillips
Patrick Weigel (16)	Corbin Clouse
Freddy Tarnok (21)	Walter Borkovich
Jasseel de la Cruz (26)	Devan Watts

DRAFT ANALYSIS

2017

BEST PURE HITTER: Switch-hitting OF Drew Waters (2) has a sound approach and plenty of bat speed, and his plus speed should help him beat out the occasional infield hit as well. His swing is pretty similar from both sides of the plate.

BEST POWER HITTER: C/1B Drew Lugbauer (11) never hit for average at Michigan, but he always had power. After hitting 12 home runs for the Wolverines, he added 13 more in a half-season as a pro, several of the long and loud variety. His swing generates natural loft and leverage to go with solid-average bat speed.

FASTEST RUNNER: Waters is a 4.1-4.15 runner from home to first from the left side, giving him 60 grades on the 20-to-80 scouting scale. He's adept on the basepaths although he didn't show much basestealing aptitude in his pro debut.

BEST DEFENSIVE PLAYER: Waters' plus speed and plus arm should allow him to stay in center field long-term. INF Jordan Rodgers (6) adeptly handled the challenge of playing shortstop, second and third base in his pro debut.

BEST FASTBALL: RHP Kyle Wright (1) sits at 92-96 mph and touched 97-98 in his pro debut. It's a potential top-of-the-scale pitch with late life and excellent angle. RHP Freddy Tarnok (3) pitches at 92-94, touching 97 on his best days, although like many teenagers he has plenty of work to do on his consistency.

BEST SECONDARY PITCH: Wright's slider and curveball have both earned plus-plus grades at their best. The mid-80s slider has plenty of power while the slower curveball has good depth, but the quality of both varies from outing to outing.

BEST PRO DEBUT: Lugbauer hit .261/.352/.514 with 13 home runs in stops at Rookie-level Danville and low Class A Rome while also adapting to catching more than he did in college.

BEST ATHLETE: Waters' combination of speed and developing power stands out, but it's par for

the course in his very athletic family. His father was a Georgia Tech offensive lineman, his older brother played baseball at Georgia and his sister played soccer at Georgia as well.

MOST INTRIGUING BACKGROUND: RHP Jacob Belinda (10) is the nephew of former Pirates righthander Stan Belinda. C Justin Morhardt (22) is from a baseball family; his grandfather Moe briefly reached the major leagues in the early 1960s with the Cubs, and his father Greg is a Braves area scout and famously signed Mike Trout when he worked for the Angels.

CLOSEST TO THE MAJORS: Wright is a top-of-the-draft college righthander. Normally those are some of the fastest-moving draft picks in every draft class.

BEST LATE-ROUND PICK: Lugbauer was the only post-10th round pick to receive more than $125,000 (he counted $100 toward the Braves' bonus allotment). If he can develop his catching ability, he has a chance to be a find as a power bat who plays adequate defense.

THE ONE WHO GOT AWAY: RHP Cade Cavalli (29) barely pitched during his senior year of high school because of a back injury, but he pitched at 92-95 mph in the Oklahoma playoffs. He will compete for a spot in the Sooners' rotation instead.

—J.J. COOPER

TOP DRAFT PICKS OF THE DECADE

Year	Player, Pos.	2017 Org
2008	Brett DeVall, LHP (1st round supp.)	Did not play
2009	Mike Minor, LHP	Royals
2010	Matt Lipka, SS (1st round supplemental)	Rangers
2011	Sean Gilmartin, LHP	Cardinals
2012	Lucas Sims, RHP	Braves
2013	Jason Hursh, RHP	Braves
2014	Braxton Davidson, OF	Braves
2015	Kolby Allard, LHP	Braves
2016	Ian Anderson, RHP	Braves
2017	Kyle Wright, RHP	Braves

2016

The Braves loaded up on prep pitchers in 2016 and the early returns have been good. RHP Ian Anderson (1), LHP Joey Wentz (1s) and RHP Bryse Wilson (4) all found success as teammates in 2017.

GRADE: B

2015

With three of the first 41 picks, the Braves landed a trio of prep stars in LHP Kolby Allard (1), RHP Mike Soroka (1) and 3B Austin Riley (1s). The class has already produced a big leaguer in LHP A.J. Minter (2s).

GRADE: A

2014

RHP Max Povse (3) reached MLB with Seattle in 2017. Otherwise, this class has come up dry. OF Braxton Davidson (1) hasn't gotten out of A ball and RHP Garrett Fulenchek (2) is stuck in short-season ball.

GRADE: F

1 RONALD ACUNA, OF

Born: Dec. 18, 1997. **B-T:** R-R. **Ht.:** 6-0. **Wt.:** 180.
Signed: Venezuela, 2014. **Signed by:** Rolando Petit.

Acuna's father Ron was a long-time Mets minor leaguer. But from an early age, the elder Acuna knew that his son would likely end up the better player. Ronald signed for $100,000, choosing the Braves over the Royals, and was advanced enough to begin his pro career in the U.S. in 2015. Acuna missed much of 2016 with a thumb injury and began 2017 at high Class A Florida. The Braves were confident he was ready for an in-season promotion—and they were right. Acuna blitzed through Double-A Mississippi in just two months and was even better for Triple-A Gwinnett, earning Minor League Player of the Year honors. The Braves' experience with Andruw Jones, who similarly jumped three minor league levels in a POY season in 1996, influenced their decision to move Acuna aggressively. They quickly realized he thrived when challenged.

Acuna has a wide range of strengths and few glaring weaknesses. Multiple scouts predicted multiple all-star appearances in his future. He's the rare prospect who actually carries future 60 (or better) grades on the 20-80 scale for all five tools. Acuna is a 70 runner with 70 defense who has a 60 arm and 60 hit tool. Many scouts project him to future 70 power. He already uses the whole field, and he went deep six times in 2017 to right or right-center field. Acuna used the opposite field more often as the season progressed. Not coincidentally he became tougher to strike out. Scouts looking for flaws noted that his strong arm is sometimes inaccurate and he could sometimes be stymied by quality fastballs up and in. But he already shows an ability to lay off breaking balls and velocity out of the zone. When he gets a pitch to hit, Acuna has extremely fast hands with strong wrists that whip the bat through the zone with excellent bat speed. He already generates exceptional exit velocities, which should pay off with 25-30 home runs once he matures.

Even though he has fewer than 1,000 minor league at-bats, Acuna is big league ready and will head to spring training expected to play a significant role in 2018. With Ender Inciarte in center field, his initial role will be left or right fielder. The track record for 20-year-old big leaguers is spotty, but Acuna's defense and plate discipline should help ease his transition.

KARL L. MOORE

BA GRADE	SCOUTING GRADES	
70 Risk: Medium	**HIT:** 60. **POW:** 70. **SPD:** 70.	
	FLD: 70. **ARM:** 60.	

Projected future grades on 20-80 scouting scale

TOP PROSPECTS OF THE DECADE

Year	Player, Pos.	2017 Org
2008	Jordan Schafer, OF	Cardinals
2009	Tommy Hanson, RHP	Deceased
2010	Jason Heyward, OF	Cubs
2011	Julio Teheran, RHP	Braves
2012	Julio Teheran, RHP	Braves
2013	Julio Teheran, RHP	Braves
2014	Lucas Sims, RHP	Braves
2015	Jose Peraza, 2B	Reds
2016	Sean Newcomb, LHP	Braves
2017	Dansby Swanson, SS	Braves

BEST TOOLS

Best Hitter For Average	Ronald Acuna
Best Power Hitter	Ronald Acuna
Best Strike-Zone Discipline	Brett Cumberland
Fastest Baserunner	Cristian Pache
Best Athlete	Cristian Pache
Best Fastball	Luiz Gohara
Best Curveball	Max Fried
Best Slider	A.J. Minter
Best Changeup	Kolby Allard
Best Control	Mike Soroka
Best Defensive Catcher	Lucas Herbert
Best Defensive Infielder	Austin Riley
Best Infield Arm	Austin Riley
Best Defensive Outfielder	Cristian Pache
Best Outfield Arm	Ray Patrick-Didder

Year	Club (League)	Class	AVG	G	AB	R	H	2B	3B	HR	RBI	BB	SO	SB	CS	OBP	SLG
2015	Braves (GCL)	R	.258	37	132	31	34	9	2	3	11	18	23	11	3	.376	.424
	Danville (APP)	R	.290	18	69	10	20	5	2	1	7	10	19	5	1	.388	.464
2016	Braves (GCL)	R	.333	2	6	1	2	0	0	0	1	1	1	0	0	.500	.333
	Rome (SAL)	LoA	.311	40	148	27	46	2	2	4	18	18	28	14	7	.387	.432
2017	Florida (FSL)	HiA	.287	28	115	21	33	3	5	3	19	8	40	14	3	.336	.478
	Mississippi (SL)	AA	.326	57	221	29	72	14	1	9	30	18	56	19	11	.374	.520
	Gwinnett (IL)	AAA	.344	54	221	38	76	14	2	9	33	17	48	11	6	.393	.548
Minor League Totals			.310	236	912	157	283	47	14	29	119	90	215	74	31	.378	.488

2 LUIZ GOHARA, LHP

Born: July 31, 1996. **B-T:** L-L. **Ht.:** 6-3. **Wt.:** 215. **Signed:** Brazil, 2012. **Signed by:**
Emilio Carrasquel/Hide Sueyoshi (Mariners).

Coming into 2017, Gohara was largely seen as a high-ceiling tease. His development was slowed by disagreements with the Mariners front office over his conditioning. Traded to the Braves for righthander Shae Simmons and Mallex Smith
in January 2017, Gohara seemed to embrace the Braves' lighter touch, and he
advanced three minor league levels before reaching Atlanta in September.

BA GRADE
65 Risk: High
FB: 80. **SL:** 70.
CHG: 45.
CTL: 45.

Gohara's pure stuff compares favorably with anyone. In just 29 big league
innings, he threw more 98-plus mph fastballs than any other lefty starter. His 95-99
mph fastball generates top-of-the-scale grades and his 82-85 mph slider is equally
impressive because it looks like his fastball coming out of his hand before diving
with late tilt. He shows some feel for a changeup and throws hard enough that the
change of pace gives it some deception, but it lacks late fade and he struggles to
keep it on the edges of the plate. He will need to refine if it's going to be anything more than a show-me
pitch. Gohara's control is fringe-average at best, but he has made significant strides and should develop
average control.

Gohara's speedy climb in 2017 ensures he will go to spring training competing for a spot in the rotation. He has the potential to be a front-line starter, though his lack of a track record of durability is a
concern.

Year	Club (League)	Class	W	L	ERA	G	GS	CG	SV	IP	H	HR	BB	SO	K/9	WHIP	AVG
2015	Clinton (MWL)	LoA	0	1	1.86	2	2	0	0	10	10	0	6	5	4.7	1.66	.294
	Everett (NWL)	SS	3	7	6.20	14	14	0	0	54	67	4	32	62	10.4	1.84	.305
2016	Everett (NWL)	SS	2	0	1.76	3	3	0	0	15	13	1	3	21	12.3	1.04	.224
	Clinton (MWL)	LoA	5	2	1.82	10	10	0	0	54	44	1	20	60	9.9	1.18	.223
2017	Florida (FSL)	HiA	3	1	1.98	7	7	0	0	36	33	0	10	39	9.7	1.18	.243
	Mississippi (SL)	AA	2	1	2.60	12	11	0	0	52	42	2	18	60	10.4	1.15	.218
	Gwinnett (IL)	AAA	2	2	3.31	7	7	0	0	35	31	4	16	48	12.2	1.33	.230
	Atlanta (NL)	MAJ	1	3	4.91	5	5	0	0	29	32	2	8	31	9.5	1.36	.283
Major League Totals			1	3	4.91	5	5	0	0	29	32	2	8	31	9.5	1.36	.283
Minor League Totals			19	23	3.73	74	73	0	0	328	319	19	140	375	10.3	1.40	.253

3 MIKE SOROKA, RHP

Born: Aug. 4, 1997. **B-T:** R-R. **Ht.:** 6-4. **Wt.:** 195. **Drafted:** HS—Calgary, 2015 (1st
round). **Signed by:** Brent Evert.

The Braves skipped Soroka over high Class A in 2017 and made him the second-
youngest player in Double-A on Opening Day. He responded by finishing second
in the Southern League in ERA (2.75).

Soroka is a sinker/slider pitcher who touches 95 mph but lives at 90-93 mph
with his two-seamer. His delivery has a little crossfire action that adds deception
and has not affected his plus control. He started to throw his four-seamer more to
alter hitters' eye levels. Soroka's plus breaking ball is hard to classify. At it's best it's
an above-average 84-86 mph curveball because of 1-to-7 shape, but it's tighter and
has a sharper break than normal. When his adrenaline is flowing, it morphs into a

BA GRADE
60 Risk: Medium
FB: 60. **SL:** 60.
CHG: 55.
CTL: 60.

high-80s pitch with slider tilt. His changeup flashes above-average with some late
run but could use more consistency. It's vital for Soroka to handle lefties. His sinker
and breaking ball are good for righthanders, but those same offerings end up down and in where lefties can
feast, so his changeup must show run away from lefties.

Soroka's pure stuff doesn't match Kyle Wright, Luiz Gohara or Ian Anderson, but his exceptional
makeup, pitchability and athleticism make him a safe bet to be a mid-rotation starter.

Year	Club (League)	Class	W	L	ERA	G	GS	CG	SV	IP	H	HR	BB	SO	K/9	WHIP	AVG
2015	Braves (GCL)	R	0	0	1.80	4	3	0	0	10	5	0	1	11	9.9	0.60	.143
	Danville (APP)	R	0	2	3.75	6	6	0	0	24	28	0	4	26	9.8	1.33	.283
2016	Rome (SAL)	LoA	9	9	3.02	25	24	1	0	143	130	3	32	125	7.9	1.13	.244
2017	Mississippi (SL)	AA	11	8	2.75	26	26	0	0	154	133	10	34	125	7.3	1.09	.233
Minor League Totals			20	19	2.91	61	59	1	0	331	296	13	71	287	7.8	1.11	.239

4 KYLE WRIGHT, RHP

Born: Oct. 2, 1995. **B-T:** R-R. **Ht.:** 6-4. **Wt.:** 220. **Drafted:** Vanderbilt, 2017 (1st round). **Signed by:** Dustin Evans.

Wright traveled the typical Vanderbilt ace development track, going from dominating reliever as freshman to reliable starter as a sophomore and junior. The Braves went nearly $1.3 million over slot to sign Wright for $7 million as the fifth overall pick in 2017. He finished the year with six starts at high Class A Florida.

Wright's plus-plus fastball ranges from 92-98 mph, with late life at its best to go with excellent angle. His command is better when he's pitching in the lower registers of his velocity range. Wright's curveball and slider both generate potential plus grades, but he often shows a knack for locating one or the other, depending on the day. His curveball is a low-80s pitch with late break and good depth. His harder mid-80s slider has modest break but plenty of power. His mid-80s changeup is his fourth pitch for now but shows excellent fade and run when he's locked in.

CARL KLINE

BA GRADE
65 Risk: High
FB: 70. CB: 60.
SL: 60. CHG: 55.
CTL: 50.

Wright is still adjusting to the five-day schedule of pro ball, but in an organization that doesn't hesitate to challenge players, an Opening Day assignment to Double-A isn't out of the question. He has a chance to be a future top-of-the-rotation starter thanks to his varied repertoire, physicality and control.

Year	Club (League)	Class	W	L	ERA	G	GS	CG	SV	IP	H	HR	BB	SO	K/9	WHIP	AVG
2017	Braves (GCL)	R	0	0	1.59	3	3	0	0	6	3	0	2	8	12.7	0.88	.150
	Florida (FSL)	HiA	0	1	3.18	6	6	0	0	11	8	0	4	10	7.9	1.06	.205
Minor League Totals			0	1	2.65	9	9	0	0	17	11	0	6	18	9.5	1.00	.186

5 IAN ANDERSON, RHP

Born: May 2, 1998. **B-T:** R-R. **Ht.:** 6-3. **Wt.:** 170. **Drafted:** HS—Clifton Park, N.Y., 2016 (1st round). **Signed by:** Greg Morhardt.

Anderson was a victim of his own success in 2017. His success and efficiency in the first half meant he bumped up against his innings limit earlier than expected. Worried about overtaxing a cold-weather arm in his first full season, the Braves slammed the brakes on Anderson's pitch limits, holding him to just 17.2 innings in the final two months.

The Braves' initial point of emphasis with young pitchers is to teach them to throw a quality changeup. Anderson embraced the pitch, developing it from an afterthought to a pitch that flashes above-average in the span of a year. The improved change gives him a chance to end up with three above-average pitches. His 91-95 mph fastball touches 97, and he gets downhill thanks to his over-the-top delivery. As he worked on his change, Anderson relied less on his plus curveball with 12-to-6 action, but it's still his best secondary offering. His walk numbers would indicate otherwise, but scouts believe Anderson has advanced control and command for his age, despite his walk rate of 4.7 per nine innings.

BA GRADE
60 Risk: High
FB: 60. CB: 60.
CHG: 55.
CTL: 50.

Anderson projects as a future No. 2 or 3 starter, though he has to prove his durability and consistency. He will jump to high Class A Florida in 2018.

Year	Club (League)	Class	W	L	ERA	G	GS	CG	SV	IP	H	HR	BB	SO	K/9	WHIP	AVG
2016	Braves (GCL)	R	1	0	0.00	5	5	0	0	18	14	0	4	18	9.0	1.00	.222
	Danville (APP)	R	0	2	3.74	5	5	0	0	22	19	1	8	18	7.5	1.25	.244
2017	Rome (SAL)	LoA	4	5	3.14	20	20	0	0	83	69	0	43	101	11.0	1.35	.232
Minor League Totals			5	7	2.79	30	30	0	0	123	102	1	55	137	10.1	1.28	.232

6 AUSTIN RILEY, 3B

Born: April 2, 1997. **B-T:** R-R. **Ht.:** 6-2. **Wt.:** 220. **Drafted:** HS—Southaven, Miss., 2015 (1st round supplemental). **Signed by:** Don Thomas.

Many teams saw Riley as a better pitching prospect than hitter coming out of high school. The Braves disagreed, believing in Riley's power. He's rewarded their faith by hitting 20 home runs in each of his first two full seasons while advancing to Double-A Mississippi at age 20 in 2017.

Riley has embraced the Braves' focus on improving his nutritional habits. He appears slimmer, stronger and quicker than he was when drafted. He also has shortened his swing and improved his bat speed, helping him to more consistently get to his plus power potential and alleviating concerns about his now average hit tool. Riley's biggest improvement has come defensively. He has alleviated fears he would need to move to first base and is now an above-average third baseman. His plus-plus arm is still his calling card, but he also improved his first-step quickness.

BA GRADE
55 Risk: Medium
HIT: 50. POW: 60.
SPD: 40. FLD: 55.
ARM: 70.

Riley headed to the Arizona Fall League, which will help prepare him for a move to Triple-A Gwinnett in 2018. Unless blocked by a future trade or free agent acquisition, Riley is the Braves' third baseman of the not-too-distant future.

Year	Club (League)	Class	AVG	G	AB	R	H	2B	3B	HR	RBI	BB	SO	SB	CS	OBP	SLG
2015	Braves (GCL)	R	.255	30	106	18	27	5	0	7	21	12	37	2	1	.331	.500
	Danville (APP)	R	.351	30	111	18	39	9	1	5	19	14	28	0	1	.443	.586
2016	Rome (SAL)	LoA	.271	129	495	68	134	39	2	20	80	39	147	3	3	.324	.479
2017	Florida (FSL)	HiA	.252	81	306	43	77	10	1	12	47	23	74	0	2	.310	.408
	Mississippi (SL)	AA	.315	48	178	28	56	9	1	8	27	20	50	2	0	.389	.511
Minor League Totals			.278	318	1196	175	333	72	5	52	194	108	336	7	7	.343	.477

7 KOLBY ALLARD, LHP

Born: Aug. 13, 1997. **B-T:** L-L. **Ht.:** 6-1. **Wt.:** 180. **Drafted:** HS—San Clemente, Calif., 2015 (1st round). **Signed by:** Dan Cox.

The Braves challenged both Allard and Mike Soroka with a two-level jump to Double-A Mississippi in 2017. Allard handled it with few issues. The youngest player in Double-A at the start of the season, Allard worked five or more innings in 25 of 27 starts.

Allard is a nibbler by necessity. His average 88-92 mph fastball lacks the oomph and plane to consistently challenge hitters, but thanks to plus command, he largely avoids the heart of the plate. He can manipulate his fastball by cutting it to get in on hitters' hands. His changeup graded as consistently plus in 2017, while his curveball is plus at its best, but it wasn't as consistent. His lack of size limits his projection, but his preternatural polish and command give him a high likelihood of big league success.

BA GRADE
55 Risk: Medium
FB: 50. CB: 60.
CHG: 60.
CTL: 60.

Even as Allard earns comparisons with front-line Braves pitchers of the past, like Steve Avery, scouts consistently project him as a future No. 4 starter, with a few seeing a potential No. 3 and others saying No. 5. Allard is ready for Triple-A Gwinnett and could reach the majors as a 20-year-old in 2018.

Year	Club (League)	Class	W	L	ERA	G	GS	CG	SV	IP	H	HR	BB	SO	K/9	WHIP	AVG
2015	Braves (GCL)	R	0	0	0.00	3	3	0	0	6	1	0	0	12	18.0	0.17	.053
2016	Danville (APP)	R	3	0	1.32	5	5	0	0	27	18	0	5	33	10.9	0.84	.186
	Rome (SAL)	LoA	5	3	3.73	11	11	1	0	60	54	5	20	62	9.2	1.23	.244
2017	Mississippi (SL)	AA	8	11	3.18	27	27	2	0	150	146	11	45	129	7.7	1.27	.258
Minor League Totals			16	14	3.03	46	46	3	0	244	219	16	70	236	8.7	1.19	.243

8 MAX FRIED, LHP

Born: Jan. 19, 1994. **B-T:** L-L. **Ht.:** 6-4. **Wt.:** 200. **Drafted:** HS—Los Angeles, 2012 (1st round). **Signed by:** Brent Mayne (Padres).

The first high school pitcher drafted in 2012, Fried has endured Tommy John surgery, a trade and bouts of wildness. A blister issue helped ruin his first half in 2017, but he rebounded to make his big league debut in August.

Fried's fastball and curveball combo can be devastating when he's throwing strikes. His plus curve has long been his biggest weapon. He loosens it up as a 72-74 mph get-me-over pitch early in counts, but then tightens it into a harder 75-77 tight-breaking curve that generates swings and misses later in counts. Fried's 92-93 mph fastball touches 97 at its hottest. It is an above-average pitch, but his current below-average control limits its effectiveness. His fringe-average changeup is a usable pitch Fried unveils against righthanders. He fields his position well and has a dangerous pickoff move. He toys with hitters' timing by varying his time over the rubber in his delivery.

Fried lacks the polish and control of younger system-mates Mike Soroka or Kolby Allard, but he also has better pure stuff. As a member of the 40-man roster, he figures to see big league time in 2018, though his control could use further refinement up the road in Gwinnett.

BA GRADE
60 Risk: V. High
FB: 60. CB: 60.
CHG: 45.
CTL: 45.

Year	Club (League)	Class	W	L	ERA	G	GS	CG	SV	IP	H	HR	BB	SO	K/9	WHIP	AVG
2015	Did not play—Injured																
2016	Rome (SAL)	LoA	8	7	3.93	21	20	0	0	103	87	10	47	112	9.8	1.30	.236
2017	Mississippi (SL)	AA	2	11	5.92	19	19	0	0	87	88	8	43	85	8.8	1.51	.268
	Gwinnett (IL)	AAA	0	0	0.00	2	2	0	0	6	1	0	2	6	9.0	0.50	.056
	Atlanta (NL)	MAJ	1	1	3.81	9	4	0	0	26	30	3	12	22	7.6	1.62	.286
Major League Totals			1	1	3.81	9	4	0	0	26	30	3	12	22	7.6	1.62	.286
Minor League Totals			16	27	4.23	80	78	0	0	343	312	27	159	330	8.7	1.37	.249

9 CRISTIAN PACHE, OF

Born: Nov. 18, 1998. **B-T:** R-R. **Ht.:** 6-2. **Wt.:** 185. **Signed:** Dominican Republic, 2015. **Signed by:** Matias Laureano.

A top prospect in the 2015 international class, Pache has gotten better since he signed. An above-average runner then, he's now a top-of-the-scale runner. His glove work has similarly improved as he advanced to low Class A Rome in 2017.

Pache's aggressive, almost cocky center field defense will get him to the big leagues. He plays shallow, challenging hitters to hit it over his head. If they do, he proves he can track balls over his head with ease. He's one of the best defensive center fielders in the minors and has Gold Glove potential with an above-average arm. Pache's speed plays on the basepaths, too. At the plate, his swing has some length that leads scouts to see a future average hit tool, but he has shown improved strike-zone recognition and solid bat-to-ball skills. Scouts love his athleticism and believe that once he fills out he'll hit for at least average power, even though he has yet to homer as a pro.

Pache's bat will determine whether he becomes an impact regular or just a useful, speedy outfielder. He has plenty of time to develop power, which probably won't show up in the expansive parks of the high Class A Florida State League in 2018.

BA GRADE
55 Risk: High
HIT: 50. POW: 40.
SPD: 80. FLD: 70.
ARM: 55.

Year	Club (League)	Class	AVG	G	AB	R	H	2B	3B	HR	RBI	BB	SO	SB	CS	OBP	SLG
2016	Braves (GCL)	R	.283	27	106	16	30	2	4	0	11	6	11	7	3	.325	.377
	Danville (APP)	R	.333	30	114	12	38	2	3	0	10	7	13	4	2	.372	.404
2017	Rome (SAL)	LoA	.281	119	469	60	132	13	8	0	42	39	104	32	14	.335	.343
Minor League Totals			.290	176	689	88	200	17	15	0	63	52	128	43	19	.340	.358

10 ALEX JACKSON, C

Born: Dec. 25, 1995. **B-T:** R-R. **Ht.;** 6-2. **Wt.:** 215. **Drafted:** HS—Rancho Berando, Calif., 2014 (1st round). **Signed by:** Gary Patchett (Mariners).

Considered one of the best power hitters in the 2014 draft class, Jackson's pro career with the Mariners quickly fell apart. He proved to be a less accomplished hitter with less hand-eye coordination than projected and he battled injuries.

The Braves acquired Jackson after the 2016 season for Rob Whalen and Max Povse in a change-of-scenery trade and immediately moved him back to catcher, which he hadn't played since high school. It was a wise move, as Jackson's big power and hit tool concerns fit much better at catcher than as a below-average defender in right field. Understandably Jackson looked rusty and raw behind the plate, but he showed a willingness to work and improve and he has a plus arm (although poor footwork sometimes affects his accuracy). As a big bodied catcher, he's never going to be particularly agile, but scouts say he could work to be a fringe-average defender. At the plate, Jackson's plus-plus raw power came more into play in 2017. He's too aggressive and his power comes more from strength than bat speed, which makes him vulnerable to velocity, but he has 20-plus home run potential, even if it comes with .230-.240 batting averages.

Jackson needs a year or more of defensive work, and his glove will determine how quickly he advances from Double-A Mississippi.

BA GRADE
55 Risk: V. High
HIT: 40. POW: 60.
SPD: 40. FLD: 45.
ARM: 60.

Year	Club (League)	Class	AVG	G	AB	R	H	2B	3B	HR	RBI	BB	SO	SB	CS	OBP	SLG
2015	Clinton (MWL)	LoA	.157	28	108	10	17	6	0	0	13	6	35	1	1	.240	.213
	Everett (NWL)	SS	.239	48	163	31	39	11	1	8	25	21	61	2	4	.365	.466
2016	Clinton (MWL)	LoA	.243	92	333	43	81	20	1	11	55	34	103	2	1	.332	.408
2017	Florida (FSL)	HiA	.272	66	257	44	70	17	0	14	45	13	74	0	1	.333	.502
	Mississippi (SL)	AA	.255	30	110	12	28	4	0	5	20	10	32	0	0	.317	.427
Minor League Totals			.245	287	1053	151	258	64	4	40	174	93	329	5	8	.328	.427

11 JOEY WENTZ, LHP

BA GRADE
50 Risk: High

Born: Oct. 6, 1997. **B-T:** L-L. **Ht.:** 6-5. **Wt.:** 210. **Drafted:** HS—Shawnee Mission, Kan., 2016 (1st round supplemental). **Signed by:** Nate Dion.

A lanky, power-hitting first baseman who blossomed into one of the better lefthanders in the 2016 draft class with an outstanding senior season of high school, Wentz's first full pro season in 2017 was outstanding. He finished second in the South Atlantic League in strikeouts (152), third in opponent average (.209) and fourth in ERA (2.60).

Wentz's approach and stuff draws comparisons with Kolby Allard's, because both are lefties with 88-92 mph fastballs and above-average changeups. Wentz stuck his above-average curveball in his back pocket for some starts as he worked on refining his changeup, and the focus on his change did seem to lessen his feel for his curve. It paid off in the sense that his changeup has developed into a difference maker, but the hope in the long run is that he'll be throwing a pair of above-average offspeed pitches. Wentz's fastball is an average pitch right now, and he's touched 96 mph in the past, so some believe that the skinny lefty will add more velocity as he fills out. Scouts debate how much projection he has left.

If he adds another two or three ticks to his fastball, Wentz has the makings of a front-line starter, but any erosion of his current velocity would lead him into fringe territory.

Year	Club (League)	Class	W	L	ERA	G	GS	CG	SV	IP	H	HR	BB	SO	K/9	WHIP	AVG
2016	Braves (GCL)	R	0	0	0.00	4	4	0	0	12	3	0	5	18	13.5	0.67	.083
	Danville (APP)	R	1	4	5.06	8	8	0	0	32	31	0	20	35	9.8	1.59	.265
2017	Rome (SAL)	LoA	8	3	2.60	26	26	0	0	132	99	4	46	152	10.4	1.10	.209
Minor League Totals			9	7	2.87	38	38	0	0	176	133	4	71	205	10.5	1.16	.212

12 BRYSE WILSON, RHP

BA GRADE
55 Risk: Extreme

Born: Dec. 20, 1997. **B-T:** R-R. **Ht.:** 6-1. **Wt.:** 215. **Drafted:** HS—Hillsborough, N.C., 2016 (4th round). **Signed by:** Billy Best.

Football was always Wilson's second-best sport, but he still received scholarship offers from various Division I teams after they watched him excel as a quarterback, running back, wide receiver, linebacker and punter. Whenever there was an injury for his Orange High team, Wilson just slid to another spot and did the job. That same attitude is apparent on the mound.

The Braves believe Wilson has special makeup. He pitches off of his above-average 92-94 mph fastball, but it's the development of his changeup into an above-average pitch that has really helped him take a step forward. He was a fastball/slider pitcher before 2017, but his newly-refined changeup has surpassed his breaking ball already. Wilson's delivery has a lot of length in his takeaway and a wrap, which leads some scouts to worry that it will be difficult for him to ever consistently snap off his slider, but when it's on, it's an above-average pitch.

Wilson's potentially above-average control, strong frame and three-pitch mix gives him a shot to be a future mid-rotation starter. He's ready for high Class A Florida.

Year	Club (League)	Class	W	L	ERA	G	GS	CG	SV	IP	H	HR	BB	SO	K/9	WHIP	AVG
2016	Braves (GCL)	R	1	1	0.68	9	6	0	0	27	16	0	8	29	9.8	0.90	.172
2017	Rome (SAL)	LoA	10	7	2.50	26	26	1	0	137	105	8	37	139	9.1	1.04	.211
Minor League Totals			11	8	2.20	35	32	1	0	164	121	8	45	168	9.2	1.01	.205

13 TUCKER DAVIDSON, LHP

BA GRADE

50 Risk: High

Born: March 25, 1996. **B-T:** L-L. **Ht.:** 6-2. **Wt.:** 215. **Drafted:** Midland (Texas) JC, 2016 (19th round). **Signed by:** Nate Dion.

No player drafted out of Midland (Texas) JC ever has made the majors, but Davidson has a chance to become the first. He has proven to be an impressive scouting find.

Expected to be a useful organization reliever, Davidson showed up in 2017 in better shape than he'd been in his draft year, and his fastball took a step forward. After he blew 95-97 mph fastballs by Asheville hitters in a three-inning relief outing in June, the Braves decided to see how he handled starting. He survived an awful rotation debut, where he allowed seven unearned runs in 1.2 innings, to allow two runs or less in nine of his remaining 11 starts. As a starter, Davidson maintained a 90-95 mph fastball that earns plus grades thanks to its excellent finish. He also flashes a plus curveball and changeup. He has less track record, but Davidson's pure stuff is better than that of Joey Wentz or Kyle Muller.

On the other hand, Davidson has more effort to his delivery and is not as fluid an athlete, leading some scouts to expect he'll eventually return to the bullpen. He's ready to head to high Class A Florida.

Year	Club (League)	Class	W	L	ERA	G	GS	CG	SV	IP	H	HR	BB	SO	K/9	WHIP	AVG
2016	Braves (GCL)	R	0	3	1.52	11	1	0	0	30	32	1	4	32	9.7	1.21	.271
2017	Rome (SAL)	LoA	5	4	2.60	31	12	0	2	104	96	4	30	101	8.8	1.22	.248
Minor League Totals			5	7	2.36	42	13	0	2	133	128	5	34	133	9.0	1.22	.253

14 TOUKI TOUSSAINT, RHP

BA GRADE

55 Risk: Extreme

Born: June 26, 1996. **B-T:** R-R. **Ht.:** 6-3. **Wt.:** 185. **Drafted:** HS—Coral Springs, Fla. 2014 (1st round). **Signed by:** Frankie Thon Jr. (Diamondbacks).

Data demonstrates that first-round high school pitching prospects can take a while to develop. Toussaint is a prime example of that adage, because his minor league career has yet to match the expectations that come with his exceptional stuff.

Scouts who see Toussaint on a good night throw an easy plus grade on his 93-95 mph fastball and a plus-plus grade on his 12-to-6 hammer curveball. After tweaking his grip, his changeup has improved to become a useful, fringe-average third pitch that he can throw for strikes as well. It lacks late drop, but it has good deception and separation. He's an excellent athlete with long arms and a solid frame. But Toussaint has yet to develop the consistency to go with his stuff, and his fastball proves more hittable than its velocity (he can touch 98 mph) would indicate. Too often, his control wanders and he leaves hittable fastballs up in the zone. When he runs into trouble, he's yet to figure out how to limit the damage. With a long arm action, Toussaint has yet to show he can consistently repeat his delivery, leading to below-average control.

The pieces are there for Toussaint to be a solid mid-rotation starter, but he has plenty of work to do on control and consistency as he heads back to Double-A Mississippi.

Year	Club (League)	Class	W	L	ERA	G	GS	CG	SV	IP	H	HR	BB	SO	K/9	WHIP	AVG
2015	Kane County (MWL)	LoA	2	2	3.69	7	7	0	0	39	31	4	15	29	6.7	1.18	.218
	Rome (SAL)	LoA	3	5	5.73	10	10	1	0	49	40	6	33	38	7.0	1.50	.229
2016	Rome (SAL)	LoA	4	8	3.88	27	24	0	0	132	105	13	71	128	8.7	1.33	.217
2017	Florida (FSL)	HiA	3	9	5.04	19	19	0	0	105	101	8	42	123	10.5	1.36	.245
	Mississippi (SL)	AA	3	4	3.18	7	7	1	0	40	30	3	22	44	10.0	1.31	.207
Minor League Totals			17	32	4.66	82	77	2	0	394	345	39	201	394	9.0	1.39	.233

15 A.J. MINTER, LHP

BA GRADE

45 Risk: Medium

Born: Sept. 2, 1993. **B-T:** L-L. **Ht.:** 6-0. **Wt.:** 205. **Drafted:** Texas A&M, 2015 (2nd round supplemental). **Signed by:** Darin Vaughan.

If the Braves can keep Minter healthy, he will be a valuable piece of their bullpen. But much like Arodys Vizcaino, staying healthy has long been a problem for Minter.

Minter missed most of his freshman year at Texas A&M with thoracic outlet syndrome. He missed most of his junior season because of Tommy John surgery. He got off to a late start in 2017 because of elbow soreness, but once he returned, he rocketed to the big leagues, where he quickly proved to be one of the Braves' most effective relievers. Minter eats up lefties with a plus 94-98 mph fastball, an average cutter and a hard 88-91 mph plus slider. Minter's combo annihilates lefties (big leaguers hit .190/.227/.190 against him), but his slider isn't as effective against righthanders. Still, his cutter and velocity give him a chance to be more than a lefty matchup reliever.

Minter is big league ready and has late-inning stuff. He just has to stay off the disabled list.

Year	Club (League)	Class	W	L	ERA	G	GS	CG	SV	IP	H	HR	BB	SO	K/9	WHIP	AVG
2015	Did not play—Injured																
2016	Rome (SAL)	LoA	0	0	0.00	5	0	0	2	7	2	0	1	6	8.1	0.45	.091
	Carolina (CAR)	HiA	0	0	0.00	8	0	0	0	9	3	0	4	10	9.6	0.75	.100
	Mississippi (SL)	AA	1	0	2.41	18	0	0	0	19	13	0	6	31	14.9	1.02	.188
2017	Rome (SAL)	LoA	0	0	0.00	1	0	0	0	1	1	0	0	1	9.0	1.00	.333
	Florida (FSL)	HiA	0	0	1.80	5	0	0	0	5	3	1	0	9	16.2	0.60	.167
	Mississippi (SL)	AA	0	0	0.00	3	0	0	0	3	1	0	2	3	9.0	1.00	.111
	Gwinnett (IL)	AAA	1	2	4.70	17	0	0	0	15	15	1	10	17	10.0	1.63	.259
	Atlanta (NL)	MAJ	0	1	3.00	16	0	0	0	15	13	1	2	26	15.6	1.00	.224
Major League Totals			0	1	3.00	16	0	0	0	15	13	1	2	26	15.6	1.00	.224
Minor League Totals			2	2	2.14	57	0	0	2	59	38	2	23	77	11.7	1.03	.182

16 PATRICK WEIGEL, RHP

BA GRADE

55 Risk: Extreme

Born: July 8, 1994. **B-T:** R-R. **Ht.:** 6-6. **Wt.:** 230. **Drafted:** Houston, 2015 (7th round). **Signed by:** Darin Vaughn.

A steal of a seventh-round pick who quickly established himself as a hard-throwing starting pitching prospect as a pro, Weigel was putting himself in contention for a spot in Atlanta in 2017 when his season ended in mid-June with a torn elbow ligament. His final outing blew up his ERA as he labored through three innings, giving up nine runs.

Before he went down with the elbow injury, Weigel had been a dominating presence despite a delivery that seems better suited for 15-20-pitch stints out of the bullpen. He has a high back elbow in his delivery and his arm sometimes has to catch up to his lower half, but he generally makes it work because he's extremely strong. He has average control. Hitters get a good look at the ball thanks to Weigel's delivery and high slot, but they still have trouble catching up. Weigel has a power approach, attacking hitters with a 92-95 mph fastball. He'll mix a curveball and slider that trade back and forth as far as which is better. Both flash above-average on a good day, and he's comfortable using his slider to backdoor hitters or get them to chase away. Weigel's below-average changeup needs more separation.

Weigel will likely be ready for instructional league in 2018, but his next official outing may not be until 2019.

Year	Club (League)	Class	W	L	ERA	G	GS	CG	SV	IP	H	HR	BB	SO	K/9	WHIP	AVG
2015	Danville (APP)	R	0	3	4.53	14	14	0	0	52	53	2	26	49	8.5	1.53	.256
2016	Rome (SAL)	LoA	10	4	2.51	22	21	1	0	129	92	7	47	135	9.4	1.08	.203
	Mississippi (SL)	AA	1	2	2.18	3	3	0	0	21	9	2	8	17	7.4	0.82	.132
2017	Mississippi (SL)	AA	3	0	2.89	7	7	0	0	37	32	2	11	38	9.2	1.15	.234
	Gwinnett (IL)	AAA	3	2	5.27	8	8	0	0	41	42	5	17	30	6.6	1.44	.269
Minor League Totals			17	11	3.31	54	53	1	0	280	228	18	109	269	8.7	1.21	.223

17 DREW WATERS, OF

BA GRADE

55 Risk: Extreme

Born: Dec. 30, 1998. **B-T:** B-R. **Ht.:** 6-2. **Wt.:** 183. **Drafted:** HS—Woodstock, Ga., 2017 (2nd round). **Signed by:** Dustin Evans.

The Braves have long focused on drafting some of the top talents in the Atlanta area. Waters was the top hitter and athlete in the state of Georgia in 2017, making him a logical choice to be the Braves' second-round pick. He showed enough for the Braves to quickly move him to the Rookie-level Appalachian League, but a 36 percent strikeout rate was a sign of how much work Waters has left to do.

Scouts are divided on the switch-hitter's hitting potential. There are some who don't believe Waters' funky swing will work consistently, but other scouts see loose hands and an ability to whip the bat head through the zone that compensates for a noisy and high-maintenance swing. He's already toned down what was an exaggerated leg kick that messed with his timing. Scouts are more confident in the rest of his tools. He has an excellent frame and the strength to develop plus power by getting bigger and stronger over the next few years. He is a plus runner who plays an above-average center field, though he's a little too aggressive with his plus arm, making throws he should leave in his back pocket.

Waters will head to low Class A Rome in 2018.

Year	Club (League)	Class	AVG	G	AB	R	H	2B	3B	HR	RBI	BB	SO	SB	CS	OBP	SLG
2017	Braves (GCL)	R	.347	14	49	13	17	3	1	2	10	7	11	2	1	.448	.571
	Danville (APP)	R	.255	36	149	20	38	11	1	2	14	16	59	4	2	.331	.383
Minor League Totals			.278	50	198	33	55	14	2	4	24	23	70	6	3	.362	.429

18 WILLIAM CONTRERAS, C

BA GRADE 55 Risk: Extreme

Born: Dec. 24, 1997. **B-T:** R-R. **Ht.:** 6-0. **Wt.:** 180. **Signed:** Venezuela, 2015. **Signed by:** Rolando Petit.

The younger brother of Cubs catcher Willson Contreras, William was not a prominent prospect as an amateur, but he's shown a knack to hit that endears him to scouts.

Even as a teenager, Contreras has shown strength in his swing, but he's a hitter first, serving up line drives to right field more than he yanks the ball. Eventually, he should hit for average power as well, because he already lofts the ball with some thump from time to time. Contreras is undersized, but like his brother he has more athleticism than the average catcher. He has the building blocks to be a solid-average receiver with an above-average arm and a quick transfer, though he has further work to do on his game calling. In a system suddenly filled with catchers at the lower levels, Contreras' hitting ability and athleticism help him stand out as the most likely of the Braves' many young catchers to develop into a future big league regular.

Contreras is ready for low Class A Rome, where he'll catch a good staff that will challenge his ability to handle velocity.

Year	Club (League)	Class	AVG	G	AB	R	H	2B	3B	HR	RBI	BB	SO	SB	CS	OBP	SLG
2015	Braves (DSL)	R	.314	49	172	21	54	9	4	0	32	15	21	2	2	.370	.413
2016	Braves (GCL)	R	.264	30	72	8	19	5	0	1	8	7	15	0	1	.346	.375
2017	Danville (APP)	R	.290	45	169	29	49	10	1	4	25	24	30	1	0	.379	.432
Minor League Totals			.295	124	413	58	122	24	5	5	65	46	66	3	3	.370	.414

19 RICARDO SANCHEZ, LHP

BA GRADE 50 Risk: High

Born: April 11, 1997. **B-T:** L-L. **Ht.:** 5-11. **Wt.:** 170. **Signed:** Venezuela, 2014. **Signed by:** Lebi Ochoa/Carlos Ramirez/Mauro Zerpa (Angels).

The Braves acquired Sanchez in a 2015 trade that sent Kyle Kubitza and Nate Hyatt to the Angels. Hyatt retired and Kubitza hit .192 for the Angels, ending up back with the Braves when he hit waivers. Sanchez is the reason the trade could still avoid being irrelevant.

Sanchez has better pure stuff than any lefthanded starter in the Braves' system other than Luiz Gohara. He will show three plus pitches at his best, including a 91-94 mph fastball, as well as a changeup and curveball, but he's never been consistent enough to have real success. He's a short lefty whose size gets in the way when he lets his release point drop, causing his stuff to flatten out. But when he stays tall in his delivery, Sanchez can get swings and misses and also locates better. His curveball isn't as consistent as his changeup and his control is below-average. The lefty also hasn't yet figured out damage control.

Sanchez joined the 40-man roster in November and is headed to Double-A Mississippi. He's yet to put it together, but he'll be just 21 for the entire 2018 season.

Year	Club (League)	Class	W	L	ERA	G	GS	CG	SV	IP	H	HR	BB	SO	K/9	WHIP	AVG
2015	Rome (SAL)	LoA	1	6	5.45	10	10	0	0	40	37	3	21	31	7.0	1.46	.250
2016	Rome (SAL)	LoA	7	10	4.75	24	23	0	0	119	119	14	54	103	7.8	1.45	.268
2017	Florida (FSL)	HiA	4	12	4.86	22	21	0	0	100	116	10	46	101	9.1	1.62	.288
Minor League Totals			14	30	4.72	68	63	0	0	298	312	27	143	278	8.4	1.53	.271

20 KYLE MULLER, LHP

BA GRADE 55 Risk: Extreme

Born: Oct. 7, 1997. **B-T:** R-L. **Ht.:** 6-7. **Wt.:** 240. **Drafted:** HS—Dallas, 2016 (2nd round). **Signed by:** Nate Dion.

Muller's prospect stock soared when his velocity spiked as a senior and he dominated all comers on the Texas high school circuit. That stuff has taken a step back as a pro.

The Braves are an aggressive organization when it comes to minor league assignments, but with Muller, they hit the brakes. Unlike most every top prep pitching prospect Atlanta drafts, Muller didn't make it to low Class A in his first full season. Instead he spent the year at extended spring training and at Rookie-level Danville. He's shown a feel to pitch, but his fastball is more consistently 88-91 mph, touching 93, and not the 91-95 he showed on longer rest in high school. It does have angle and enough movement to avoid the sweet spot of bats, but he lacks deception. His curveball improved this year as it's showing a tighter break and late movement—some evaluators described it as a slider—giving it a chance to be an above-average pitch. He's still working on getting comfortable with his nascent changeup.

Muller's command and angle give him survival skills even with a fringe-average fastball, but for him to live up to expectations, he'll need more arm speed and velocity. He'll work on that at low Class A Rome in 2018.

Year	Club (League)	Class	W	L	ERA	G	GS	CG	SV	IP	H	HR	BB	SO	K/9	WHIP	AVG
2016	Braves (GCL)	R	1	0	0.65	10	9	0	0	28	14	0	12	38	12.4	0.94	.144
2017	Danville (APP)	R	1	1	4.15	11	11	0	0	48	43	5	18	49	9.3	1.28	.232
Minor League Totals			2	1	2.87	21	20	0	0	75	57	5	30	87	10.4	1.15	.202

21 ISRANEL WILSON, OF

BA GRADE

50 Risk: High

Born: March 6, 1998. **B-T:** L-R. **Ht.:** 6-3. **Wt.:** 185. **Signed:** Dominican Republic, 2014. **Signed by:** Luis Ortiz.

Wilson is one of the more athletic outfielders in the Braves' system. A shortstop as an amateur, Wilson immediately moved to the outfield in pro ball, where his plus speed is apparent and his 6-foot-3, 185-pound frame fits better.

As a lefthanded-hitting center fielder with an above-average arm that can handle right field, Wilson has the perfect fourth outfielder profile, though it's not hard to find scouts who think he'll develop into a regular. The Braves were happy to see the strides he took at the plate this year. He's still pull-happy and right field is still a no-fly zone for Wilson, but he started to use center field regularly in 2017. Wilson has the tools and the short, simple swing to be a plus hitter. He also can drop down a bunt and beat it out using his speed. He's too skinny as of yet to drive the ball consistently, but he has the frame to end up with average power if he fills out as expected.

Wilson likely returns to low Class A Rome to start 2018, but he could play his way to high Class A Florida before the season ends.

Year	Club (League)	Class	AVG	G	AB	R	H	2B	3B	HR	RBI	BB	SO	SB	CS	OBP	SLG
2015	Braves (GCL)	R	.222	48	144	29	32	5	1	10	22	26	56	3	4	.349	.479
2016	Danville (APP)	R	.192	38	130	19	25	8	1	2	12	14	51	6	2	.276	.315
2017	Danville (APP)	R	.250	17	68	11	17	2	3	4	12	9	18	2	0	.338	.544
	Rome (SAL)	LoA	.262	43	168	28	44	3	3	2	20	18	52	9	3	.340	.351
Minor League Totals			.231	146	510	87	118	18	8	18	66	67	177	20	9	.326	.404

22 DUSTIN PETERSON, OF

BA GRADE

45 Risk: Medium

Born: Sept. 10, 1994. **B-T:** R-R. **Ht.:** 6-3. **Wt.:** 210. **Drafted:** HS—Gilbert, Ariz., 2013 (2nd round). **Signed by:** Dave Lottsfeldt (Padres).

The younger brother of Mariners' 2013 first-round pick D.J. Peterson, Dustin was helped by D.J.'s well-timed college breakout season and went 31 rounds earlier than his brother did coming out of high school. The Padres drafted him but traded him to the Braves after the 2014 season in the Justin Upton deal.

Peterson's value, much like his brother's, is tied to his bat. A high school shortstop who immediately moved to third base as a pro, Peterson was quickly booted to left field, where he's perfectly adequate. He's a fringe-average runner with an average arm. If Peterson is going to be a big leaguer, it's going to be because he has above-average bat speed and above-average power. But a hamate injury cost him a month of the 2017 season and seemed to sap his power afterward. Peterson's modest power surge in 2016 seemed to show he was making progress toward being an above-average hitter with the above-average power he needs to be an everyday big leaguer. Now he has to prove that his 2017 power outage was injury-related.

The Braves left Peterson off the 40-man roster in 2017, making him Rule 5 eligible, and he was not picked. As a righthanded-hitting corner outfielder, he doesn't really fit as a backup. He's more of an up-and-down fill-in or a regular, with few in-between options.

Year	Club (League)	Class	AVG	G	AB	R	H	2B	3B	HR	RBI	BB	SO	SB	CS	OBP	SLG
2015	Carolina (CAR)	HiA	.251	118	446	58	112	15	2	8	62	44	91	6	3	.317	.348
2016	Mississippi (SL)	AA	.282	132	524	65	148	38	2	12	88	45	100	4	1	.343	.431
2017	Gwinnett (IL)	AAA	.248	87	314	35	78	17	1	1	30	27	78	1	2	.318	.318
Minor League Totals			.258	501	1968	242	507	109	8	31	277	150	439	15	9	.314	.368

23 FREDDY TARNOK, RHP

BA GRADE

50 Risk: Extreme

Born: Nov. 24, 1998. **B-T:** R-R. **Ht.:** 6-3. **Wt.:** 185. **Drafted:** HS—Riverview, Fla., 2017 (3rd round). **Signed by:** Rick Sellers.

Tarnok was a two-way prospect whose pitching took a big step forward during his senior year, launching him from being a guy for scouts to keep an eye on in three years to a third-round pick in 2017.

Tarnok is raw potential and power at this point. His fastball has loads of angle and sink and pops the mitt. He sits at 92-94 mph and touches 97 with room to add a little more velocity as he adds muscle and weight with maturity. He has also shown feel for spinning a 77-80 mph curveball that flashes at least average now, and he quickly picked up a changeup. He throws a typical Rookie-level Gulf Coast League changeup right now—which means for every good pitch, there are several poor ones—but he showed aptitude and some conviction throwing it. Tarnok has to work on his consistency and a lot of the little things—holding runners, time to the plate—but he has athleticism and poise.

With fewer innings on his résumé than most young pitchers, Tarnok may need a stop at Rookie-level Danville, but his stuff may force a jump to low Class A Rome instead.

Year	Club (League)	Class	W	L	ERA	G	GS	CG	SV	IP	H	HR	BB	SO	K/9	WHIP	AVG
2017	Braves (GCL)	R	0	3	2.57	9	9	0	0	14	11	0	3	10	6.4	1.00	.208
Minor League Totals			0	3	2.57	9	9	0	0	14	11	0	3	10	6.4	1.00	.208

24 JEAN CARLOS ENCARNACION, 3B

BA GRADE

50 Risk: Extreme

Born: Jan. 17, 1998. **B-T:** R-R. **Ht.:** 6-3. **Wt.:** 195. **Signed:** Dominican Republic, 2016. **Signed by:** Jonathan Cruz.

Encarnacion signed for a modest $10,000 bonus in 2016, but he's quickly proven to be one of the highest-ceilinged prospects in the organization thanks to a rare combination of speed, size and strength.

Encarnacion played shortstop in the Dominican Summer League in 2016 and first and third base in 2017. First base is a waste of his athleticism, so he played third base exclusively after being promoted to Rookie-level Danville. He has to improve his footwork and angles on balls, but with a plus arm, excellent range and adequate hands, he could end up as at least an average third baseman. Other scouts see a rangy outfielder. Encarnacion will turn plus times from home to first and has some of the best raw power in the organization. He'll have to get more selective, because he has a swing-at-everything approach right now. His strength and bat-to-ball skills have made him a career .298 hitter.

If Encarnacion heads to full-season ball in 2018, expect some initial struggles, but he has the tools to be worth plenty of patience.

Year	Club (League)	Class	AVG	G	AB	R	H	2B	3B	HR	RBI	BB	SO	SB	CS	OBP	SLG
2016	Braves (DSL)	R	.264	37	140	19	37	3	3	0	16	11	30	4	0	.340	.329
2017	Braves (GCL)	R	.350	27	103	16	36	8	4	2	16	4	22	4	2	.374	.563
	Danville (APP)	R	.290	23	93	14	27	3	0	1	6	3	21	3	5	.316	.355
Minor League Totals			.298	87	336	49	100	14	7	3	38	18	73	11	7	.343	.408

25 HUASCAR YNOA, RHP

BA GRADE

50 Risk: Extreme

Born: May 29, 1998. **B-T:** R-R. **Ht.:** 6-3. **Wt.:** 175. **Signed:** Dominican Republic, 2014. **Signed by:** Fred Guerrero (Twins).

Former Braves general manager John Coppolella added R.A. Dickey, Bartolo Colon and Jaime Garcia on short-term deals for the 2017 season with the hope of stabilizing the rotation and getting some prospects back in deadline deals. Dickey and Colon didn't work out, but Garcia was traded to the Twins for the high-ceiling, high-risk Ynoa.

Ynoa is the younger brother of Michael Ynoa, who set an international bonus record in 2009 when he signed with the Athletics for $4.25 million. The younger Ynoa signed for $800,000. Much as it was true when he signed, Ynoa has loads of potential, but is too inconsistent as of yet to dominate. He will sit 95-96 mph and touch 99 with a fastball that is hard to square up. He naturally cuts the ball and has shown an ability to spin a breaking ball, though his curveball and slider tend to merge into one pitch at times and are inconsistent. When he's on, Ynoa's slider shows plus potential with good depth. Ynoa's mechanics are rough. He yanks his fastball at times, doesn't always stay in line to the plate and needs to repeat everything more consistently to refine his control.

Ynoa has the foundation to be a mid-rotation starter or power reliever as he embarks on his first full-season assignment in 2018.

Year	Club (League)	Class	W	L	ERA	G	GS	CG	SV	IP	H	HR	BB	SO	K/9	WHIP	AVG
2015	Twins (DSL)	R	2	5	2.70	14	14	0	0	57	43	1	30	47	7.5	1.29	.207
2016	Twins (GCL)	R	3	5	3.18	11	11	0	0	51	44	1	12	51	9.0	1.10	.228
2017	Elizabethton (APP)	R	0	1	5.26	6	6	0	0	26	28	1	14	23	8.1	1.64	.277
	Danville (APP)	R	0	3	5.26	7	7	0	0	26	24	1	15	27	9.5	1.52	.238
Minor League Totals			5	14	3.68	38	38	0	0	159	139	4	71	148	8.4	1.32	.231

26 JEFFREY RAMOS, OF

BA GRADE
50 Risk: Extreme

Born: Feb. 10, 1999. **B-T:** R-R. **Ht.:** 6-1. **Wt.:** 185. **Signed:** Dominican Republic, 2016. **Signed by:** Jonathan Cruz.

Ramos is going to have to really hit because he's a left fielder who doesn't run all that well. As such, he's already on the wrong end of the defensive spectrum. Virtually all of his value at the big league level would come from his bat.

That's a good thing for Ramos because he has a very good chance to hit. Signed for $250,000 as an 18-year-old, Ramos led the Rookie-level Gulf Coast League Braves and finished third in the GCL with six home runs despite being promoted to the Rookie-level Appalachian League in early August. Because he's yet to even reach full-season ball, there's plenty of risk with Ramos, but scouts see a hitter who has a chance to hit for plus average and plus power. Defensively, he's a below-average runner. He's improved in the field, but he's a left fielder only thanks to a below-average arm, and he'll have to work to get to average defensively.

Because he is a late bloomer, Ramos has to move a little quicker than a 16-year-old signee, and he is ready for low Class A Rome.

Year	Club (League)	Class	AVG	G	AB	R	H	2B	3B	HR	RBI	BB	SO	SB	CS	OBP	SLG
2016	Braves (DSL)	R	.230	33	126	19	29	8	1	1	12	9	27	3	2	.283	.333
2017	Braves (GCL)	R	.325	30	117	22	38	7	1	6	30	8	27	1	0	.374	.556
	Danville (APP)	R	.278	20	72	7	20	6	0	1	8	3	15	0	0	.308	.403
Minor League Totals			.276	83	315	48	87	21	2	8	50	20	69	4	2	.323	.432

27 JASSEEL DE LA CRUZ, RHP

BA GRADE
50 Risk: Extreme

Born: June 26, 1997. **B-T:** R-R. **Ht.:** 6-1. **Wt.:** 175. **Signed:** Dominican Republic, 2015. **Signed by:** Matias Laureano.

The Braves snagged de la Cruz, a late-blooming 18-year-old, for a modest five-figure bonus in 2015 and quickly saw him blossom into a fire-balling righthander with two potential swing-and-miss offerings.

De la Cruz sits 90-96 mph with his fastball, though he struggles to maintain that velocity deeper into games. The velocity, life and control of his fastball all vary from pitch to pitch. His hard 85-88 mph slider gives him a second potentially plus pitch. It's not yet as consistent as it needs to be, but when he locks in, it's got late movement. His changeup will be a point of emphasis going forward, because currently it lacks deception and is too hard.

De la Cruz has room to fill out. He's all long, lanky arms and legs at this point.

Year	Club (League)	Class	W	L	ERA	G	GS	CG	SV	IP	H	HR	BB	SO	K/9	WHIP	AVG
2015	Braves (DSL)	R	0	1	7.11	7	0	0	0	6	6	0	8	6	8.5	2.21	.261
2016	Braves (DSL)	R	2	0	3.42	12	3	0	0	26	23	1	14	20	6.8	1.41	.247
	Braves (GCL)	R	2	0	0.00	6	0	0	0	15	4	0	1	12	7.2	0.33	.085
2017	Braves (GCL)	R	2	1	1.89	4	4	0	0	19	13	1	7	17	8.1	1.05	.188
	Danville (APP)	R	0	2	5.32	7	6	0	0	24	25	1	11	19	7.2	1.52	.260
Minor League Totals			6	4	3.29	36	13	0	0	90	71	3	41	74	7.4	1.24	.216

28 DREW LUGBAUER, C

BA GRADE
45 Risk: High

Born: Aug. 23, 1996. **B-T:** L-R. **Ht.:** 6-3. **Wt.:** 220. **Drafted:** Michigan, 2017 (11th round). **Signed by:** Rick Sellers.

Lugbauer's versatility was a blessing for Michigan. He played all over the diamond for the Wolverines while providing lefthanded power. Lugbauer continued to bounce around the diamond in his pro debut with the Braves, but his path to the majors involves a lot of squatting in his future.

Lugbauer's best assets are his strong frame and his plus lefthanded power. He hit 13 home runs in his pro debut. He produces power to his pull side more because of leverage and strength than bat speed, so he'll have to prove that he can catch up to better velocity. His ability to play first base and a below-average third base is a bonus, though he lacks range. The Braves understandably are trying to develop Lugbauer's catching. His hands work pretty well and he has an above-average arm, but he's big enough that there are some questions whether he can hold up and be nimble enough to stick behind the plate five nights a week.

As a big, strong-armed catcher with plus power, Lugbauer fits the backup catcher profile perfectly if he can refine his technique behind the plate.

Year	Club (League)	Class	AVG	G	AB	R	H	2B	3B	HR	RBI	BB	SO	SB	CS	OBP	SLG
2017	Danville (APP)	R	.243	29	103	23	25	4	0	10	27	19	30	0	0	.366	.573
	Rome (SAL)	LoA	.277	31	119	13	33	11	1	3	19	8	38	0	0	.338	.462
Minor League Totals			.261	60	222	36	58	15	1	13	46	27	68	0	0	.352	.514

29 PHIL PFEIFER, LHP

BA GRADE
40 Risk: Medium

Born: July 15, 1992. **B-T:** L-L. **Ht.:** 6-0. **Wt.:** 190. **Drafted:** Vanderbilt, 2015 (3rd round). **Signed by:** Marty Lamb (Dodgers).

Pfeifer holds the Tennessee high school record with 46 wins in his career at Knoxville's Farragut High, but his baseball career was almost derailed soon after. Drug and alcohol abuse slowed his career at Vanderbilt, eventually culminating in a wake-up call when he was suspended for the Commodores' 2014 national championship season.

Pfeifer sobered up, returned to the mound in 2015 and remade himself as a draft prospect. The Braves picked him up in a June 2016 trade that sent Bud Norris to the Dodgers. Pfeifer is a two-pitch lefty reliever, but those two pitches are good enough to get him to the big leagues. His above-average 93-95 mph fastball has played up in relief, but his strikeout pitch is a big downer curve. It's a big breaking pitch that hitters can pick up quickly, but his ability to locate it in any count makes it an above-average pitch. Lefties have been generally helpless against him, hitting .200 with just three extra-base hits (all doubles) in 130 pro at-bats. But Pfeifer's control is below-average, which limits his effectiveness.

Pfeifer will return to Triple-A Gwinnett to try to tame his control, but with even fringe-average control, he's a lefty matchup reliever.

Year	Club (League)	Class	W	L	ERA	G	GS	CG	SV	IP	H	HR	BB	SO	K/9	WHIP	AVG
2015	Ogden (PIO)	R	0	0	0.00	1	1	0	0	2	1	0	3	2	10.8	2.40	.167
2016	Great Lakes (MWL)	LoA	1	0	0.00	3	0	0	0	6	2	0	1	9	13.5	0.50	.100
	R. Cucamonga (CAL)	HiA	2	1	3.33	14	0	0	0	24	21	1	17	33	12.2	1.56	.241
	Carolina (CAR)	HiA	0	0	2.57	6	0	0	2	7	3	0	4	10	12.9	1.00	.130
	Mississippi (SL)	AA	1	0	4.35	11	0	0	0	10	9	0	6	8	7.0	1.45	.243
2017	Mississippi (SL)	AA	1	3	3.45	30	0	0	3	44	37	2	33	68	13.8	1.58	.227
	Gwinnett (IL)	AAA	0	2	3.60	11	1	0	1	15	10	0	9	9	5.4	1.27	.192
Minor League Totals			5	6	3.23	76	2	0	6	109	83	3	73	139	11.5	1.44	.214

30 JOSH GRAHAM, RHP

BA GRADE
45 Risk: High

Born: Oct. 14, 1993. **B-T:** R-R. **Ht.:** 6-1. **Wt.:** 215. **Drafted:** Oregon, 2015 (4th round). **Signed by:** Brett Evert.

Graham was drafted by the Twins in the 22nd round coming out of high school as a strong-armed catcher who also pitched. He was Oregon's starting catcher as a freshman, but he lost the job and became a backup as a sophomore. Buried on the bench, the Ducks let him go back to the mound and he quickly turned into one of their better pitchers.

Graham's catching roots are still apparent in his delivery. He cocks the ball near his ear in his setup, then begins with a plunge and speeds his arm through his delivery. It's not pretty, and it leads to fringy command and control. But Graham has a plus 93-96 mph fastball and a changeup that has developed into a weapon. It's a plus pitch with good velocity separation and late fade. His loopy slider is much less consistent. He'll tighten it up sporadically, but usually it's a loopy fringy pitch.

Graham got a quick taste at Double-A Mississippi to end the 2017 season. He'll head back there, but with further refinement, he could be yet another catcher-to-reliever success story.

Year	Club (League)	Class	W	L	ERA	G	GS	CG	SV	IP	H	HR	BB	SO	K/9	WHIP	AVG
2015	Danville (APP)	R	1	1	2.60	6	5	0	0	17	17	0	3	21	10.9	1.15	.239
2016	Rome (SAL)	LoA	1	2	3.40	35	0	0	6	42	35	4	12	50	10.6	1.11	.217
2017	Florida (FSL)	HiA	3	3	4.69	31	0	0	1	48	41	0	18	56	10.5	1.23	.228
	Mississippi (SL)	AA	0	1	1.38	10	0	0	2	13	10	0	9	10	6.9	1.46	.213
Minor League Totals			5	7	3.58	82	5	0	9	121	103	4	42	137	10.2	1.20	.224

Baltimore Orioles

BY JON MEOLI

After five years of winning baseball—timely power hitting, lockdown relief pitching, strong defense that delivered three playoff appearances and a division title against nearly all expectations—the 2017 Orioles saw the artifice fall and their flaws exposed in a major way.

Contenders into September in a crowded American League wild card race, the Orioles went 7-21 after Sept. 1 to finish in last place in the AL East and leave themselves with plenty of questions, both for 2018 and beyond.

While the offense lacked the consistency of recent years and all-star closer Zach Britton missed nearly half the year with a forearm strain, the organization's struggles with evaluating starting pitchers reared its head in 2017. Kevin Gausman and Dylan Bundy will be rotation fixtures for years to come. But as the Orioles were forced to hand 86 starts to Chris Tillman, Wade Miley, Ubaldo Jimenez and Jeremy Hellickson—all underperforming veterans set to leave in free agency—former Orioles farmhands Zach Davies, Parker Bridwell, Ariel Miranda, Eduardo Rodriguez and Jake Arrieta thrived in other teams' rotations. All were traded in the last five years, and their absences leaves the Orioles scrambling to fill the big league rotation in 2018.

Starting pitching will be the main question mark for a team that's expected to return most of its lineup and bullpen core for one final run in 2018. After next season, Britton, third baseman Manny Machado, center fielder Adam Jones and reliever Brad Brach are free agents, while the contracts of executive vice president Dan Duquette and manager Buck Showalter come up as well.

The Orioles have a strong core of position players to complement Machado and Jones. Second baseman Jonathan Schoop made his first all-star team. Rookie Trey Mancini learned left field in spring training and made himself an everyday player there, batting .293 with 24 home runs. And the acquisition of shortstop Tim Beckham on July 31 from the Rays was one of the year's best trades.

They were joined in September by top prospects Austin Hays and Chance Sisco, who will have the chance to compete for the starting right field and catching jobs in spring training. Rule 5 pick Anthony Santander could also make an impact in the outfield in 2018. The Orioles have in recent years done well to identify bats in the draft, such as Hays and third baseman Ryan Mountcastle, though their emphasis on hitters and ownership's strategic mandate not to invest heavily in international amateurs have left the system largely devoid of up-the-middle athletes to supplement their future boppers.

And though they're a few years away, the Orioles' 2016 and 2017 drafts have transformed the pitching ranks into something much more intriguing. Top picks Cody Sedlock and Keegan Akin from 2016 were challenged at high Class A Frederick in 2017, but they remain on track as future starters, while the top of the 2017 draft class featured high-upside lefthander D.L. Hall and impressive college arms Zac Lowther and Mike Baumann. With that group, and the return to health of 2013 first-rounder Hunter Harvey, the Orioles have done well to add pitching talent and depth to the low minors. The challenge, as ever, will be to get that talent to the majors.

MITCHELL LAYTON/GETTY IMAGES

Trey Mancini switched from first base to left field and bashed 24 home runs as a rookie.

PROJECTED 2021 LINEUP

Catcher	Chance Sisco (26)
First Base	Trey Mancini (29)
Second Base	Jonathan Schoop (29)
Third Base	Manny Machado (28)
Shortstop	Tim Beckham (31)
Left Field	Ryan Mountcastle (24)
Center Field	Cedric Mullins (26)
Right Field	Austin Hays (25)
Designated Hitter	Chris Davis (35)
No. 1 Starter	Kevin Gausman (30)
No. 2 Starter	Dylan Bundy (28)
No. 3 Starter	Hunter Harvey (26)
No. 4 Starter	D.L. Hall (22)
No. 5 Starter	Cody Sedlock (26)
Closer	Zach Britton (33)

DEPTH CHART

BALTIMORE ORIOLES

TOP 2018 ROOKIE: Austin Hays, OF. With an opening in right field, there should be plenty of opportunity to build on his outstanding 2017 and produce as an everyday player.

BREAKOUT PROSPECT: Brenan Hanifee, RHP. The 19-year-old's heavy fastball and projectable frame have scouts raving about his potential.

SLEEPER: Mason McCoy, SS. A senior sign from Iowa with an above-average glove, he hit .301 at short-season Aberdeen and seems poised to tear through the low minors.

SOURCE OF TOP 30 TALENT			
Homegrown	26	Acquired	4
College	12	Trade	2
Junior college	2	Rule 5 draft	1
High school	8	Independent league	0
Nondrafted free agent	0	Free agent/waivers	1
International	4		

LF
Ryan Mountcastle (2)
D.J. Stewart (16)
Mike Yastrzemski
Randolph Gassaway
Cole Billingsley
Gerrion Grim

CF
Cedric Mullins (9)
Lamar Sparks (25)
Ryan McKenna
Josh Hart

RF
Austin Hays (1)
Anthony Santander (8)
Ademar Rifaela (27)
Jake Ring

3B
Jomar Reyes (12)
Drew Dosch
Trevor Craport

SS
Adam Hall (18)
Erick Salcedo
Chris Clare
Irving Ortega
Milton Ramos
Mason McCoy

2B
Steve Wilkerson (30)
Luis Sardinas
Adrian Marin
Drew Turbin

1B
Preston Palmeiro

C
Chance Sisco (3)
Austin Wynns (29)
Ben Breazeale

LHP

LHSP	LHRP
D.L. Hall (5)	Tanner Scott (6)
Chris Lee (10)	Nestor Cortes
Keegan Akin (11)	Paul Fry
Alex Wells (13)	Luis Gonzalez
Zac Lowther (17)	Travis Seabrooke
Cameron Bishop (21)	Brandon Bonilla
Brian Gonzalez	

RHP

RHSP	RHRP
Hunter Harvey (4)	Jesus Liranzo (19)
Cody Sedlock (7)	Matthias Dietz (22)
Mike Baumann (14)	Jimmy Yacabonis (23)
David Hess (15)	Pedro Araujo
Brenan Hanifee (20)	Jose Mesa Jr.
Ofelky Peralta (24)	Lucas Long
Gray Fenter (26)	Matt Wotherspoon
Yefry Ramírez (27)	Tanner Chleborad

DRAFT ANALYSIS

2017

BEST PURE HITTER: Canada has a better track record of producing hitters than shortstops, but SS Adam Hall (2) could be both. He has excellent bat speed and quick hands and has seen plenty of quality pitching while playing for Canada's junior national program.

BEST POWER HITTER: In a pitcher-heavy O's class, C Ben Breazeale (7) has the best power potential. He heartened club officials with five homers in his .318/.428/.467 debut after having hit only one homer with wood in summer collegiate action previously.

FASTEST RUNNER: Hall turns in plus times, as has OF Lamar Sparks (5), who has a projectable 6-foot-2, 165-pound frame that could add strength while allowing him to maintain his speed.

BEST DEFENSIVE PLAYER: Sparks has the body and speed for center field and has shown the Orioles he has some baseball instincts as well. His arm also earns plus grades if he ever has to move to a corner, but they see him as a future asset in center field.

BEST ATHLETE: Hall and Sparks both have the athletic ability to potentially stay in the middle of the diamond.

BEST FASTBALL: LHP D.L. Hall (1), no relation to Canada's Hall, has a plus fastball from the left side, reaching 96-97 mph at his best but sitting comfortably at 92-95 when he's back in rhythm, which he was in instructional league after an inconsistent spring and pro debut. RHP Michael Baumann (3) also has reached 97, with natural late life.

BEST SECONDARY PITCH: Both Hall's curveball and changeup have plus potential, with the curveball earning consistently higher marks. If he commands his plus fastball, he has frontline starter stuff.

BEST PRO DEBUT: LHP Zac Lowther (2s) used his elite extension to baffle short-season New York-

TOP DRAFT PICKS OF THE DECADE

Year	Player, Pos.	2017 Org
2008	Brian Matusz, LHP	D-backs
2009	Matt Hobgood, RHP	Did not play
2010	Manny Machado, SS	Orioles
2011	Dylan Bundy, RHP	Orioles
2012	Kevin Gausman, RHP	Orioles
2013	Hunter Harvey, RHP	Orioles
2014	Brian Gonzalez, LHP (3rd round)	Orioles
2015	D.J. Stewart, OF	Orioles
2016	Cody Sedlock, RHP	Orioles
2017	D.L. Hall, LHP	Orioles

Penn League hitters, going 2-2, 1.66 with a 75-11 strikeout-to-walk ratio in 54.1 innings. Opponents hit .182 against him. Baumann (4-2, 1.31, 41/19 SO/BB in 41.1 IP) was wilder but nearly as good.

MOST INTRIGUING BACKGROUND: LHP Cameron Bishop (26) missed the spring for UC Irvine with a strained oblique but showed a 94 mph fastball and four-pitch mix in three Cape Cod League starts, and the Orioles signed him for a $605,00 bonus. Baumann was the second-straight Jacksonville Dolphin selected by the Orioles in the third round; Austin Hays—drafted in 2016—has already reached the major leagues.

CLOSEST TO THE MAJORS: If Lowther keeps getting awkward swings at his fastball, which can be 88-90 mph on bad days and 89-94 on good ones, he'll move quickly as a back-of-the-rotation starter.

BEST LATE-ROUND PICK: Bishop stands out, but RHP Reed Hayes (13) also stands out for raw arm strength. A former two-way player at Walters (Tenn.) State JC, he just pitched at Vanderbilt and is still inexperienced on the mound.

THE ONE WHO GOT AWAY: RHP Jack Conlon (4), who is good friends with Sparks, didn't pass his physical and was declared a free agent by the commissioner's office. He didn't pass a physical with the Giants, either, and wound up at Texas A&M.

—JOHN MANUEL

2016

OF Austin Hays (3) shot to the big leagues with a phenomenal first full pro season. The Orioles went heavy on pitching and RHP Cody Sedlock (1) and LHP Keegan Akin (2) are both off to solid starts.

GRADE: A

2015

OF D.J. Stewart (1) and 3B/SS Ryan Mountcastle (1) continue to do what they need to with the bats. RHP Gray Fenter (7) returned to action after surgery, and OF Cedric Mullins' (13) dynamism has emerged.

GRADE: C

2014

Baltimore had no pitcks in the first two rounds. Still, the class has a big leaguer in LHP Tanner Scott (6) and RHP David Hess (5) could soon join him. 2B Steve Wilkerson (8) is the best of the position players.

GRADE: D

1 AUSTIN HAYS, OF

Born: July 5, 1995. **B-T:** R-R. **Ht.:** 6-1. **Wt.:** 195.
Drafted: Jacksonville, 2016 (3rd round).
Signed by: Arthur McConnehead.

Hays' ascent from an unheralded and under-sized amateur player to becoming the first 2016 draftee to make the majors has been a testament to his dedication and the benefit of playing baseball regularly, no matter the level. A four-year starter at Spruce Creek High in Port Orange, Fla., Hays spent a year at Seminole State (Fla.) JC and was the team's MVP before transferring to Jacksonville. There, he blossomed into a star, posting a solid sophomore season before hitting 16 home runs and shooting up draft boards as a junior. The Orioles selected Hays in the third round in 2016, and despite him missing time with a wrist issue after the draft, he began 2017 at high Class A Frederick and reached the majors by mid-September. The power spike that began in college continued as a professional. He went from three home runs as a sophomore to 33 between Frederick, Double-A Bowie and Baltimore in 2017. The consistent success Hays showed in the minors indicated that he was steady enough to handle the majors.

A baseball rat who has endeared himself to the Orioles for a playing style that's energetic-bordering-on-reckless, Hays' compact swing and above-average bat speed help him attack the ball and drive it to all fields. He has proved to be particularly adept at hitting fastballs in any count. While he controls the barrel and can be a plus hitter with plus power, his aggression in attacking fastballs made him susceptible to major league secondary pitches, an issue that Hays and the Orioles knew of before his stint in the big leagues and believe can be improved with more experience. Hays can be an above-average right fielder thanks to a plus arm and good instincts in the field, and he has played some center field. Though he hasn't stolen many bases as a professional, he runs a tick above-average and always hustles out of the box.

Hays' overall package plays as an everyday regular who contributes in all phases of the game, and his solid-average to plus tools play up because of his effort and makeup. He will need to adapt his aggressive approach to major league secondary pitches, but his defense and ability to hit lefthanders could help him hold down a big league roster spot in 2018. He'll likely get a chance to earn the Orioles' vacant right field job in spring training.

RODGER WOOD

BA GRADE	SCOUTING GRADES
60 Risk: Medium	HIT: 60. POW: 60. SPD: 50. FLD: 55. ARM: 60.

Projected future grades on 20-80 scouting scale

TOP PROSPECTS OF THE DECADE

Year	Player, Pos.	2017 Org
2008	Matt Wieters, C	Nationals
2009	Matt Wieters, C	Nationals
2010	Brian Matusz, LHP	D-backs
2011	Manny Machado, SS	Orioles
2012	Dylan Bundy, RHP	Orioles
2013	Dylan Bundy, RHP	Orioles
2014	Dylan Bundy, RHP	Orioles
2015	Dylan Bundy, RHP	Orioles
2016	Dylan Bundy, RHP	Orioles
2017	Chance Sisco, C	Orioles

BEST TOOLS

Best Hitter for Average	Austin Hays
Best Power Hitter	Austin Hays
Best Strike-Zone Discipline	Chance Sisco
Fastest Baserunner	Cedric Mullins
Best Athlete	Cedric Mullins
Best Fastball	Tanner Scott
Best Curveball	Hunter Harvey
Best Slider	Tanner Scott
Best Changeup	Yefry Ramirez
Best Control	Alex Wells
Best Defensive Catcher	Austin Wynns
Best Defensive Infielder	Erick Salcedo
Best Infield Arm	Jomar Reyes
Best Defensive Outfielder	Cedric Mullins
Best Outfield Arm	Austin Hays

Year	Club (League)	Class	AVG	G	AB	R	H	2B	3B	HR	RBI	BB	SO	SB	CS	OBP	SLG
2016	Aberdeen (NYP)	SS	.336	38	140	14	47	9	2	4	21	11	32	4	3	.386	.514
2017	Frederick (CAR)	HiA	.324	64	262	42	85	15	3	16	41	12	40	4	6	.361	.588
	Bowie (EL)	AA	.330	64	261	39	86	17	2	16	54	13	45	1	1	.367	.594
	Baltimore (AL)	MAJ	.217	20	60	4	13	3	0	1	8	2	16	0	0	.238	.317
Major League Totals			.217	20	60	4	13	3	0	1	8	2	16	0	0	.238	.317
Minor League Totals			.329	166	663	95	218	41	7	36	116	36	117	9	10	.368	.575

2 RYAN MOUNTCASTLE, 3B/SS

Born: Feb. 18, 1997. **B-T:** R-R. **Ht.:** 6-3. **Wt.:** 195. **Drafted:** HS—Oviedo, Fla., 2015 (1st round). **Signed by:** Kelvin Colon.

Signed for a below-slot $1.3 million in 2013, Mountcastle has looked like a bargain because of his powerful bat. After hitting .281 with 10 home runs in his full-season debut at low Class A Delmarva in 2016, he won the Carolina League batting title (.314) at high Class A Frederick in 2017 with a minor league-leading 51 extra-base hits at the time of his promotion to Double-A Bowie.

Mountcastle shifted from shortstop—where he had committed 13 errors in 82 games and showed a well below-average arm—to third base when he joined Bowie. Early reports indicate the momentum taking him toward first base on most plays from the hot corner helps him arm tick up, although it will always limit him. Because of his lack of arm strength, many scouts believe he's eventually ticketed for left field

BA GRADE

55 Risk: High

HIT: 60. **POW:** 60.
SPD: 45. **FLD:** 45.
ARM: 30.

or first base. Mountcastle's plus raw power, advanced approach and plus hit tool will carry him, but he'll face added pressure because of his defensive profile. He gets good extension in his righthanded swing to attack the ball and hit with power to all fields, and he has shown ability to recognize spin and stay with pitches.

While Mountcastle's defensive future is in doubt, his above-average offensive potential makes him the most promising bat in the system, and he could become an everyday player, regardless of his position. He'll be back at Bowie to start 2018.

Year	Club (League)	Class	AVG	G	AB	R	H	2B	3B	HR	RBI	BB	SO	SB	CS	OBP	SLG
2015	Orioles (GCL)	R	.313	43	163	21	51	7	0	3	14	9	36	10	4	.349	.411
	Aberdeen (NYP)	SS	.212	10	33	2	7	0	0	1	5	0	10	0	1	.206	.303
2016	Delmarva (SAL)	LoA	.281	115	455	53	128	28	4	10	51	25	95	5	4	.319	.426
2017	Frederick (CAR)	HiA	.314	88	360	63	113	35	1	15	47	14	61	8	2	.343	.542
	Bowie (EL)	AA	.222	39	153	18	34	13	0	3	15	3	35	0	0	.239	.366
Minor League Totals			.286	295	1164	157	333	83	5	32	132	51	237	23	11	.317	.448

3 CHANCE SISCO, C

Born: Feb. 24, 1995. **B-T:** L-R. **Ht.:** 6-2. **Wt.:** 195. **Drafted:** HS—Corona, Calif., 2013 (2nd round). **Signed by:** Mark Ralston.

The Orioles saw in Sisco a natural hitter who had taken well to catching duties once he picked up the position as a senior in high school. They signed him to a $785,000 bonus, and they may now have their catcher of the future. A career .311 minor league hitter, he represented the Orioles in the last two Futures Games and made his big league debut in September 2017.

Sisco has a calm lefthanded swing with fluid hands, and he projects to be an above-average hitter with the potential for average power as he continues to add strength to his slight frame and improve on his gap power. While the Orioles tout improvement in all facets of his defensive game, including receiving, blocking and game-management, the running game has always challenged Sisco's average arm. He threw out 41 percent of basestealers in the second half of 2017 at Triple-A Norfolk,

BA GRADE

50 Risk: Medium

HIT: 60. **POW:** 45.
SPD: 40. **FLD:** 50.
ARM: 50.

but that only raised his season rate to 23 percent. He'll need to have perfect footwork and transfers to consistently lower his pop times to better than 2.0 seconds. The Orioles believe that Sisco is ready to contribute in the majors, though his defense will dictate how comfortable manager Buck Showalter is in using the 23-year-old catcher.

Average defense will make Sisco an everyday catcher due to his offensive abilities, especially against righthanded pitching, and he'll enter spring training with the chance to make the Opening Day roster.

Year	Club (League)	Class	AVG	G	AB	R	H	2B	3B	HR	RBI	BB	SO	SB	CS	OBP	SLG
2015	Frederick (CAR)	HiA	.308	75	263	30	81	12	3	4	26	33	41	8	1	.387	.422
	Bowie (EL)	AA	.257	20	74	9	19	4	0	2	8	9	14	0	1	.337	.392
2016	Bowie (EL)	AA	.319	111	407	51	130	28	1	4	44	58	82	2	2	.405	.423
	Norfolk (IL)	AAA	.250	4	16	4	4	0	0	2	7	2	5	0	0	.333	.625
2017	Norfolk (IL)	AAA	.267	97	344	47	92	23	0	7	47	32	99	2	2	.340	.395
	Baltimore (AL)	MAJ	.333	10	18	3	6	2	0	2	4	3	7	0	0	.455	.778
Major League Totals			.333	10	18	3	6	2	0	2	4	3	7	0	0	.455	.778
Minor League Totals			.311	454	1632	213	508	98	7	25	206	194	343	14	9	.389	.426

4 HUNTER HARVEY, RHP

Born: Dec. 9, 1994. **B-T:** R-R. **Ht.:** 6-3 **Wt.:** **175. Drafted:** HS—Catawba, N.C., 2013 (1st round). **Signed by:** Chris Gale.

Harvey is attempting to follow in his father's footsteps. Bryan Harvey made two all-star appearances and saved 177 games as a closer with the Angels and Marlins. The younger Harvey dazzled in his first year as a professional before elbow injuries derailed him. Two years of elbow soreness culminated in Tommy John surgery in June 2016. He also dealt with a shin fracture and a sports hernia in that span.

Harvey rehabbed to full strength by the end of 2017, allowing his first earned runs in his eighth and final rehab appearance to finish with a 2.08 ERA and 30 strikeouts in 18 innings. Most encouragingly, Harvey's stuff showed no ill effects from the long layoff. Harvey's 92-95 mph fastball reaches 97 and rates as an above-average pitch with downhill angle that he can command to both sides of the plate with armside run. His curveball slowly came back after the surgery but by the end of the season it was showing the sharp, two-plane break that made it a plus pitch pre-injury. He seldom throws his changeup in games, but the pitch has average potential. Harvey matured physically and grew into the wiry frame that initially led to durability concerns.

A healthy Harvey projects as a No. 3 starter, with the potential for high-leverage relief if his changeup doesn't develop or his crossfire delivery prevents him from gaining quality strikes with all three pitches. Baltimore added him to the 40-man roster during the offseason to protect him from the Rule 5 draft. The Orioles hope he can build up his innings in the minor leagues to provide a firm base for his future.

BA GRADE
60 Risk: Extreme
FB: 70. CB: 60.
CH: 50.
CTL: 50.

Year	Club (League)	Class	W	L	ERA	G	GS	CG	SV	IP	H	HR	BB	SO	K/9	WHIP	AVG
2015	Did not play—Injured																
2016	Orioles (GCL)	R	0	0	0.00	2	2	0	0	5	3	0	0	11	19.8	0.60	.167
	Aberdeen (NYP)	SS	0	1	3.52	3	3	0	0	8	9	0	6	7	8.2	1.96	.310
2017	Orioles (GCL)	R	0	0	0.00	3	3	0	0	5	6	0	0	6	10.8	1.20	.300
	Aberdeen (NYP)	SS	0	0	0.00	2	2	0	0	5	1	0	3	10	18.0	0.80	.063
	Delmarva (SAL)	LoA	0	1	2.08	3	3	0	0	9	4	0	3	14	14.5	0.81	.133
Minor League Totals			7	8	2.56	38	38	0	0	144	110	5	51	187	11.7	1.12	.210

5 D.L. HALL, LHP

Born: Sept. 19, 1998. **B-T:** L-L. **Ht.:** 6-0. **Wt.:** 180. **Drafted:** HS—Valdosta, Ga., 2017 (1st round). **Signed by:** Arthur McConnehead.

Hall helped lead Houston County High in Warner Robins, Ga., to a state baseball title as a junior. He then solidified his status on the national scene by striking out seven batters in three innings at the 2016 East Coast Pro Showcase. He also showed off his atheltism as an excellent basketball player, averaging nearly 20 points per game while showing an ability to throw down some impressive dunks. Even with an inconsistent 2017 at Valdosta (Ga.) High, the Orioles were convinced he would be gone by the time they picked at No. 21. When he was available, they pounced, signing him away from a Florida State commitment for an above-slot $3 million bonus.

Hall struggled in his pro debut, walking 10 in 10.1 innings in the Rookie-level Gulf Coast League, and ending with a 6.97 ERA but was one of the best pitchers at Orioles instructional league and impressed club officials with his consistent release point along with his pitchability. Even with expected physical maturation, his fastball already grades as plus at 92-95 mph, with the ability to throw inside to both lefties and righties. His 1-to-7 curveball projects as an above-average pitch, with his changeup presently below-average but with average potential.

Though far from the majors, Hall showed the best breaking ball among the high school class of 2017 and could blossom into a mid-rotation starter. He'll be ticketed for low Class A Delmarva to begin 2018 and will be further introduced to the professional game as a 19-year-old.

BA GRADE
55 Risk: Extreme
FB: 60. CB: 60.
CH: 50.
CTL: 50.

MIKE JANES

Year	Club (League)	Class	W	L	ERA	G	GS	CG	SV	IP	H	HR	BB	SO	K/9	WHIP	AVG
2017	Orioles (GCL)	R	0	0	6.97	5	5	0	0	10	10	1	10	12	10.5	1.94	.263
Minor League Totals			0	0	6.97	5	5	0	0	10	10	1	10	12	10.5	1.94	.263

6 TANNER SCOTT, LHP

Born: July 22, 1994. **B-T:** R-L. **Ht.:** 6-2. **Wt.:** 220. **Drafted:** Howard (Texas) JC, 2014 (6th round). **Signed by:** Thom Dreier.

A 2014 sixth-round pick who signed for an above-slot $600,000 bonus out of junior college, Scott showed himself to have one of the most electric (albeit wild) arms in the system.

After two years as a reliever, Scott moved to the rotation at Double-A Bowie in 2017, typically working three innings per start. This allowed him to hone his delivery and develop his secondary pitches, both in games and in between-start bullpen side sessions. Scott shows well above-average velocity with his fastball, which he can sink and run at 97-100 mph with deception. His slider went from average to above-average at 86-90 mph with tight break. While his command improved with extra work on his mechanics, his violent delivery precludes pinpoint command. So far, the Orioles are just trying to get him to fringe-average control. That could still prove effective because he's difficult to square up, even over the plate.

The Orioles haven't committed to using Scott as a starter long-term, but the initial plan is to keep Scott in a rotation spot for continued development in 2018. His changeup and control will need to improve for him to profile as even a back-end major league starter, but with his fastball-slider combination out of the bullpen, the Orioles see a possible future closer.

BA GRADE
50 Risk: High
FB: 80. SL: 50.
CH: 40.
CTL: 40.

Year	Club (League)	Class	W	L	ERA	G	GS	CG	SV	IP	H	HR	BB	SO	K/9	WHIP	AVG
2015	Aberdeen (NYP)	SS	4	0	3.38	9	1	0	0	21	16	0	12	31	13.1	1.31	.211
	Delmarva (SAL)	LoA	0	3	4.29	9	2	0	2	21	19	0	10	29	12.4	1.38	.247
2016	Frederick (CAR)	HiA	4	2	4.47	29	0	0	5	48	22	1	42	63	11.7	1.32	.133
	Bowie (EL)	AA	1	2	5.63	14	0	0	0	16	18	0	15	18	10.1	2.06	.305
2017	Bowie (EL)	AA	0	2	2.22	24	24	0	0	69	45	2	46	87	11.3	1.32	.188
	Baltimore (AL)	MAJ	0	0	10.80	2	0	0	0	2	2	0	2	2	10.8	2.40	.286
Major League Totals			0	0	10.80	2	0	0	0	2	2	0	2	2	10.8	2.40	.286
Minor League Totals			10	14	3.85	95	35	0	7	199	141	3	145	251	11.4	1.44	.200

7 CODY SEDLOCK, RHP

Born: June 19, 1995. **B-T:** R-R. **Ht.:** 6-3. **Wt.:** 190. **Drafted:** Illinois, 2016 (1st round). **Signed by:** Dan Durst.

Sedlock was the top player in an Orioles draft class that received high reviews, signing for a $2.097 million bonus. He earned Big Ten Conference pitcher of the year honors at Illinois and looked sharp at short-season Aberdeen in 2016, so the Orioles started him at high Class A Frederick in 2017. However, Sedlock struggled and later dealt with a strained flexor mass in his right elbow that shelved him on two occasions.

Sedlock's delivery gives scouts pause, as his arm stroke features a pronounced stab behind his body and a long arm action. His fastball was missing its high-end velocity in 2017 but remains a future plus pitch at 91-94 mph with hard run and late sink. His curveball and changeup both project as potentially above-average pitches, while he also throws a slider that could be an average pitch. He didn't pitch at instructional league but worked there to revert back to his delivery from 2016, which he had altered in an unsuccessful effort to add velocity.

The Orioles hope that Sedlock's old delivery allows him to command an arsenal that profiles as a No. 3 starter. If not, he could see his stuff play up in shorter bursts in relief, where repeating his delivery won't be as much of an issue. Sedlock could return to Frederick in 2018.

BA GRADE
50 Risk: High
FB: 60. CB: 55.
SL: 45. CH: 50.
CTL: 50.

Year	Club (League)	Class	W	L	ERA	G	GS	CG	SV	IP	H	HR	BB	SO	K/9	WHIP	AVG
2016	Aberdeen (NYP)	SS	0	1	3.00	9	9	0	0	27	16	1	13	25	8.3	1.07	.158
2017	Frederick (CAR)	HiA	4	5	5.90	20	20	0	0	90	119	11	36	69	6.9	1.72	.313
Minor League Totals			4	6	5.23	29	29	0	0	117	135	12	49	94	7.2	1.57	.281

8 ANTHONY SANTANDER, OF

Born: Oct. 19, 1994. **B-T:** B-R. **Ht.:** 6-2. **Wt.:** 190. **Signed:** Venezuela, 2011. **Signed by:** Ramon Pena/Antonio Caballeo (Indians).

The Orioles knew the risk in selecting Santander in the Rule 5 draft from the Indians after offseason shoulder surgery, but they were intrigued by his 2016 at high Class A Lynchburg, where he hit .290/.368/.494 with 20 home runs and 42 doubles. However, elbow issues emerged while he rehabbed in spring training, and Baltimore shut him down to ensure that he was fully healthy before they began their Rule 5 evaluation.

Santander didn't join the Orioles until mid-August, when he played sparingly, hitting .267 in 30 at-bats. A switch-hitter with fluid hands and above-average power from both sides, Santander has drawn Victor Martinez comparisons. He is a below-average runner with a fringe-average arm who needs experience to be a fringe-average corner outfielder, meaning his bat will have to carry him should he continue as a corner outfielder. However, that's a possibility, especially because of his traditional uppercut lefthanded swing that he's shown in the minors.

Because he spent just 46 days in the majors, Santander needs to accrue 44 more days in 2018 for the Orioles to keep his rights under the Rule 5 stipulations. If they accomplish that, the 23-year-old could benefit from his first substantial time in Double-A, where the Orioles hope he'll develop into a solid-average regular.

BA GRADE
50 Risk: High
HIT: 50. POW: 60.
SPD: 40. FLD: 45.
ARM: 50.

Year	Club (League)	Class	AVG	G	AB	R	H	2B	3B	HR	RBI	BB	SO	SB	CS	OBP	SLG
2015	Mahoning Valley (NYP)	SS	.419	8	31	6	13	6	0	3	9	4	8	0	0	.486	.903
	Lake County (MWL)	LoA	.278	64	248	46	69	16	0	10	42	18	53	4	2	.337	.464
2016	Lynchburg (CAR)	HiA	.290	128	500	90	145	42	0	20	95	54	118	10	5	.368	.494
2017	Bowie (EL)	AA	.380	15	50	13	19	5	0	5	14	7	9	0	0	.458	.780
	Frederick (CAR)	HiA	.400	1	5	0	2	0	0	0	0	0	1	0	0	.400	.400
	Baltimore (AL)	MAJ	.267	13	30	1	8	3	0	0	2	0	8	0	0	.258	.367
Major League Totals			.267	13	30	1	8	3	0	0	2	0	8	0	0	.258	.367
Minor League Totals			.276	363	1370	225	378	106	2	48	233	126	318	28	13	.347	.461

9 CEDRIC MULLINS, OF

Born: Oct. 1, 1994. **B-T:** B-L. **Ht.:** 5-8. **Wt.:** 175. **Drafted:** Campbell, 2015 (13th round). **Signed by:** Rich Morales.

Despite his 5-foot-8 frame and small-college pedigree out of Campbell, Mullins has been a dynamic presence in the Orioles' system since they selected him in the 13th round in 2015. He was one of eight minor leaguers to reach double digits in doubles, triples, home runs and stolen bases while hitting .273 for at low Class A Delmarva in 2016, and he jumped to Double-A Bowie in 2017, where hamstring issues led to two disabled list stints.

Mullins impressed the major league coaching staff in limited spring training looks with his calmness and range in the outfield, showing the ability to play solid-average defense in center field and above-average defense in left. His above-average speed is enough to cover ground at all three spots, but his below-average arm will limit him. At the plate, he's a switch-hitter with average potential and a line-drive swing from the left side who still is developing as a righthanded hitter. But his quick-twitch swing and reactions at the plate intrigue scouts.

With just 76 games at Double-A, Mullins could return there to start 2018, though he'll likely get a chance to make another impression in big league camp. His defensive profile and speed could grant him the opportunity to play in the big leagues as at least a fourth outfielder.

BA GRADE
50 Risk: High
HIT: 50. POW: 45.
SPD: 60. FLD: 60.
ARM: 40.

Year	Club (League)	Class	AVG	G	AB	R	H	2B	3B	HR	RBI	BB	SO	SB	CS	OBP	SLG
2015	Aberdeen (NYP)	SS	.264	68	277	34	73	15	5	2	32	22	33	17	4	.333	.375
2016	Delmarva (SAL)	LoA	.273	124	517	79	141	37	10	14	55	37	101	30	6	.321	.464
2017	Bowie (EL)	AA	.265	76	309	53	82	19	1	13	37	27	58	9	7	.319	.460
Minor League Totals			.268	268	1103	166	296	71	16	29	124	86	192	56	17	.323	.441

10 CHRIS LEE, LHP

Born: Aug. 17, 1992. **B-T:** L-L. **Ht.:** 6-3. **Wt.:** 180. **Drafted:** Santa Fe (Fla.) JC, 2011 (4th round). **Signed by:** Larry Pardo (Astros).

Given how the Orioles shuttle 40-man roster pitchers between the minors and the majors, it's a wonder that Lee has been on the 40-man for two seasons without a big league appearance. Added to the Orioles' 40-man roster after an impressive 2015 season that followed a trade for international bonus pool money from the Astros, Lee pitched just 51.1 innings in 2016 due to a lat strain in his left shoulder. He was challenged with an assignment to Triple-A Norfolk in 2017, where some of his best outings came later in the season as a piggyback starter.

Lee works from a fluid, athletic lefthanded delivery. He features a 91-95 mph fastball that sinks, a changeup with plus potential and a developing slider, though the pitch is currently below-average. Lee's secondary pitches, especially his slider, need to be more consistent in order to be swing-and-miss threats, though he's effective against lefthanders, and scouts believe his stuff would tick up in the bullpen.

For now, the Orioles' focus is on getting Lee as many innings as possible, and they're showing uncharacteristic patience with a young talent who at worst can be a late-inning relief arm if he doesn't reach his No. 4 starter ceiling. Lee will be in the mix for a major league role in spring training, but a return to Norfolk is more likely in 2018.

BA GRADE
45 Risk: Medium
FB: 55. SL: 40.
CH: 55.
CTL: 50.

Year	Club (League)	Class	W	L	ERA	G	GS	CG	SV	IP	H	HR	BB	SO	K/9	WHIP	AVG
2015	Quad Cities (MWL)	LoA	3	2	4.11	7	6	0	0	31	36	1	10	24	7.0	1.50	.283
	Frederick (CAR)	HiA	3	6	3.07	14	14	0	0	76	76	1	29	48	5.7	1.38	.266
	Bowie (EL)	AA	4	2	3.08	7	7	0	0	38	32	0	20	26	6.2	1.37	.232
2016	Bowie (EL)	AA	5	0	2.98	8	7	0	0	51	41	4	13	19	3.3	1.05	.222
2017	Norfolk (IL)	AAA	5	6	5.11	27	20	0	0	116	144	11	54	83	6.4	1.70	.302
Minor League Totals			32	31	4.02	120	96	0	0	532	552	32	237	385	6.5	1.48	.269

11 KEEGAN AKIN, LHP

BA GRADE
50 Risk: High

Born: April 1, 1995. **B-T:** L-L. **Ht.:** 6-0. **Wt.:** 225 **Drafted:** Western Michigan, 2016 (2nd round). **Signed by:** Dan Durst.

The Orioles drafted Akin 54th overall in 2016, signed him for $1.177 million and set him on a similar path to Cody Sedlock, his fellow 2016 top pick and teammate for Orleans in the Cape Cod League in the summer of 2015. After he finished strong in short-season ball in his debut, Akin went right to high Class A Frederick, where he struggled early and was skipped a turn in the rotation to work on his lower-half mechanics.

Akin returned to post a 2.97 ERA from the beginning of June until Aug. 4, when he was sidelined with an oblique injury. The Orioles were encouraged once Akin regained control of his solid-average 92-93 mph sinker, which he can locate inside to batters on either side of the plate. He also throws a solid-average changeup that's regularly in the 82-85 mph range. There's not much projection in his frame, but Akin holds velocity well and projects as a No. 4 starter if he remains in the rotation, though his stuff would likely play up in relief.

Akin was sent to regain some of his lost innings in the Arizona Fall League, but showed enough in Frederick to likely warrant an assignment to Double-A Bowie in 2018.

Year	Club (League)	Class	W	L	ERA	G	GS	CG	SV	IP	H	HR	BB	SO	K/9	WHIP	AVG
2016	Aberdeen (NYP)	SS	0	1	1.04	9	9	0	0	26	15	0	7	29	10.0	0.85	.161
2017	Frederick (CAR)	HiA	7	8	4.14	21	21	0	0	100	89	12	46	111	10.0	1.35	.240
Minor League Totals			7	9	3.50	30	30	0	0	126	104	12	53	140	10.0	1.25	.224

12 JOMAR REYES, 3B

BA GRADE
50 Risk: High

Born: Feb. 20, 1997. **B-T:** R-R. **Ht.:** 6-3. **Wt.:** 220. **Signed:** Dominican Republic, 2013. **Signed by:** Fred Ferreira/Calvin Maduro/Enrique Constante.

A hulking third baseman who represents a rare international expenditure for the Orioles—his $350,000 signing bonus in 2014 was the most the club has ever given to an amateur from the Dominican Republic—Reyes broke a finger on his right hand in April 2017 by punching a dugout wall at high Class A Frederick. He missed three months and ended up hitting .302/.333/.434 in 50 games, but missed a big opportunity to show that he had moved on from a disappointing 2016.

However, the club saw a mature player during instructional league, and believe that changes to Reyes' swing that get his bat into the zone earlier eliminate his severe timing issues and balance out his swing. That could help him tap into his well-above-average raw power, which sporadically shows in games. Reyes has plenty of arm for third base, and while he has improved defensively, his size and footwork could push him to first. That adds pressure on Reyes to put it together offensively, as his bat is his carrying tool going forward.

An overall consistent approach could elevate Reyes' tools to that of a solid-average regular. He'll head to Double-A Bowie in 2018.

Year	Club (League)	Class	AVG	G	AB	R	H	2B	3B	HR	RBI	BB	SO	SB	CS	OBP	SLG
2014	Orioles (GCL)	R	.285	53	186	23	53	10	2	4	29	15	38	1	0	.333	.425
2015	Orioles (GCL)	R	.250	5	16	2	4	2	0	0	4	2	5	1	0	.368	.375
	Delmarva (SAL)	LoA	.278	84	309	36	86	27	4	5	44	18	73	1	0	.334	.440
2016	Frederick (CAR)	HiA	.228	126	464	53	106	16	2	10	51	25	102	3	0	.271	.336
2017	Orioles (GCL)	R	.464	7	28	6	13	1	0	0	4	1	3	0	0	.484	.500
	Frederick (CAR)	HiA	.302	50	182	28	55	10	1	4	21	8	31	1	0	.333	.434
Minor League Totals			.268	325	1185	148	317	66	9	23	153	69	252	7	0	.314	.397

13 ALEX WELLS, LHP

BA GRADE

45 Risk: Medium

Born: Feb. 27, 1997 **B-T:** L-L. **Ht.:** 6-1. **Wt.:** 190. **Signed:** Australia, 2015. **Signed by:** Brett Ward/Mike Snyder.

Wells signed for $300,000 as an 18-year-old out of Australia in 2015, and has posted peerless results for the Orioles in his two seasons since coming to the United States. After pitching to a 2.15 ERA with a 0.91 WHIP in the short-season New York-Penn League in 2016, Wells had an identical 0.91 WHIP to go with a 2.38 ERA in 140 innings for low Class A Delmarva in 2017 and walked just 10 batters all season—including none in his last 68 innings.

Wells' WHIP was the lowest of any minor league pitcher with at least 20 starts, earning him the organization's Jim Palmer Minor League Pitcher of the Year Award. Wells succeeds with a fringe-average fastball that gets swings and misses at 87-92 mph, plus a curveball and changeup that could grade out as average pitches, Wells works quickly and hides the ball well from a smooth delivery that allows his arsenal to jump on hitters. His understanding of how to pitch, especially as someone frequently in the strike zone, improved demonstrably over the course of the season.

Wells is expected to bump up to high Class A Frederick, and he'll continue to have to prove it at every level to remain a starter.

Year	Club (League)	Class	W	L	ERA	G	GS	CG	SV	IP	H	HR	BB	SO	K/9	WHIP	AVG
2016	Aberdeen (NYP)	SS	4	5	2.15	13	13	0	0	63	48	1	9	50	7.2	0.91	.216
2017	Delmarva (SAL)	LoA	11	5	2.38	25	25	0	0	140	118	16	10	113	7.3	0.91	.222
Minor League Totals			15	10	2.31	38	38	0	0	203	166	17	19	163	7.2	0.91	.220

14 MICHAEL BAUMANN, RHP

BA GRADE

50 Risk: High

Born: Sept. 10, 1995. **B-T:** R-R. **Ht.:** 6-4. **Wt.:** 225. **Drafted:** Jacksonville, 2017 (3rd round). **Signed by:** Arthur McConnehead.

As with Austin Hays a year earlier, the Orioles are already thrilled with their third-round selection out of Jacksonville. A three-year starter there, Baumann was the Atlantic Sun Pitcher of the Year as a freshman in 2015 and struck out a career-high 97 batters in 87.1 innings with a 3.09 ERA and a 1.202 WHIP as a junior, despite an early-season bout with mononucleosis.

Baumann, a physical righthander with broad shoulders, throws downhill with a 91-94 mph fastball that touches 97 mph and projects as a plus pitch. He also features an above-average slider and a curveball, plus a developing changeup. With better command and development of his secondary pitches, Baumann could be a No. 4 starter.

While the Orioles have moved highly drafted college arms straight to high Class A Frederick for their first seasons recently, Baumann will likely be ticketed for low Class A Delmarva.

Year	Club (League)	Class	W	L	ERA	G	GS	CG	SV	IP	H	HR	BB	SO	K/9	WHIP	AVG
2017	Orioles (GCL)	R	0	0	0.00	1	1	0	0	1	2	0	0	2	18.0	2.00	.400
	Aberdeen (NYP)	SS	4	2	1.31	10	9	0	0	41	25	2	19	41	8.9	1.06	.168
Minor League Totals			4	2	1.28	11	10	0	0	42	27	2	19	43	9.1	1.09	.175

15 DAVID HESS, RHP

BA GRADE

45 Risk: Medium

Born: July 10, 1993. **B-T:** R-R. **Ht.:** 6-2. **Wt.:** 180. **Drafted:** Tennessee Tech, 2014 (5th round). **Signed by:** Adrian Dorsey.

Hess' second full season at Double-A Bowie was a marked improvement from his first, as he went 11-9, 3.73 and a 1.22 WHIP in 2017 after posting a 5.37 ERA and a 1.58 WHIP at the same level in 2016.

Hess is a four-pitch pitcher whose fastball sits 92-94 mph and reaches 96 mph, though there's more life to it when the velocity is lower. His slider profiles as above-average, and he also features a changeup and curveball from a smooth delivery with a high leg kick. Despite a high-effort delivery, Hess is able to maintain his fastball velocity deep into outings, and shows the pitchability to get through a lineup multiple times when he has all of his pitches.

Some scouts believe Hess could thrive as a reliever, with his fastball and slider playing up in short spurts, though the Orioles still view him as a starter. The makings are there for a No. 5 starting pitcher or a front-end reliever if he's able to translate his 2017 results to Triple-A Norfolk and beyond.

Year	Club (League)	Class	W	L	ERA	G	GS	CG	SV	IP	H	HR	BB	SO	K/9	WHIP	AVG
2015	Frederick (CAR)	HiA	9	4	3.58	26	25	1	0	133	112	8	53	110	7.4	1.24	.224
	Bowie (EL)	AA	1	1	4.50	2	2	0	0	10	10	0	4	12	10.8	1.40	.256
2016	Bowie (EL)	AA	5	13	5.37	25	24	1	0	127	162	19	39	85	6.0	1.58	.310
2017	Bowie (EL)	AA	11	9	3.73	27	26	0	0	154	136	16	53	123	7.2	1.22	.235
Minor League Totals			28	28	4.12	90	84	2	0	458	449	44	157	366	7.2	1.32	.255

16 D.J. STEWART, OF

BA GRADE
45 Risk: High

Born: Nov. 30, 1993. **B-T:** L-R. **Ht.:** 6-0. **Wt.:** 230. **Drafted:** Florida State, 2015 (1st round). **Signed by:** Arthur McConnehead.

Stewart's 2017 season calmed many concerns for the 2014 Atlantic Coast Conference Player of the Year at Florida State, who badly disappointed in his first year after being drafted 25th overall in 2015 and signing a $2,064,500 bonus. But after finishing strong in 2016 for high Class A Frederick and going to the Arizona Fall League, Stewart put together a solid all-around season at Double-A Bowie, batting .278 with an .859 OPS, 21 home runs and 20 steals.

Known as an amateur for hitting from a low crouch, Stewart and the Orioles got on the same page this season. Stewart raised his eye level, which combined with starting his swing earlier and changing his swing plane created more loft and unlocked above-average power potential. He already reads the strike zone well, and could be an average hitter for contact with his new swing. While his speed is fringe-average, Stewart runs the bases well, and he'll need more experience to become an average left fielder.

Stewart will have to continue to outperform his tools to be an everyday player. Stewart will likely begin 2018 at Triple-A Norfolk in an effort to continue his 2017 progress.

Year	Club (League)	Class	AVG	G	AB	R	H	2B	3B	HR	RBI	BB	SO	SB	CS	OBP	SLG
2015	Aberdeen (NYP)	SS	.218	62	238	25	52	8	2	6	24	23	52	4	1	.288	.345
2016	Delmarva (SAL)	LoA	.230	62	213	27	49	12	1	4	25	42	58	16	6	.366	.352
	Frederick (CAR)	HiA	.279	59	201	41	56	12	2	6	30	36	46	10	3	.389	.448
2017	Bowie (EL)	AA	.278	126	457	80	127	26	2	21	79	65	87	20	4	.378	.481
Minor League Totals			.256	309	1109	173	284	58	7	37	158	166	243	50	14	.359	.421

17 ZAC LOWTHER, LHP

BA GRADE
45 Risk: High

Born: April 30, 1996. **B-T:** L-L. **Ht.:** 6-2. **Wt.:** 235. **Drafted:** Xavier, 2017 (2nd round supplemental). **Signed by:** Adrian Dorsey.

When the Orioles selected Lowther 74th overall and signed him at slot for $779,500, they made him Xavier's highest draftee ever. His school-record 123 strikeouts as a junior helped him to a 2.92 ERA in 15 starts, while he ranked in the top five in the country in hits per nine innings (5.18, third overall) and strikeouts per nine (13.28, fourth overall).

That success carried over to short-season Aberdeen, where Lowther had a 1.66 ERA in 12 games with 12.42 strikeouts per nine innings and a 0.85 WHIP. He does it with below-average fastball velocity, sitting 88-92 mph, but his low, three-quarters delivery hides the ball well and keeps hitters off his fastball with above-average command. He throws his changeup with deceptive arm speed at 81-83 mph and it profiles as an average pitch. He also has a slurvy breaking ball with average potential. Lowther's elite extension off the mound helps his entire arsenal play up. His stuff might limit him to a No. 4 starter's role, but Lowther has a high floor and could easily be a swingman or lefty reliever with his current profile. An assignment to low Class A Delmarva to open 2018 is likely.

Year	Club (League)	Class	W	L	ERA	G	GS	CG	SV	IP	H	HR	BB	SO	K/9	WHIP	AVG
2017	Aberdeen (NYP)	SS	2	2	1.66	12	11	0	0	54	35	1	11	75	12.4	0.85	.182
Minor League Totals			2	2	1.66	12	11	0	0	54	35	1	11	75	12.4	0.85	.182

18 ADAM HALL, SS

BA GRADE

50 Risk: Extreme

Born: May 22, 199. **B-T:** R-R. **Ht.:** 6-0. **Wt.:** 170. **Drafted:** HS—London, Ont., 2017 (2nd round). **Signed by:** Chris Reitsma.

A rare shortstop prospect from Canada, Hall has long been on the amateur radar as one of his country's top prospects, and showed well during summer showcases in the United States to solidify his status.

The Orioles signed Hall away from a Texas A&M commitment with an above-slot $1.3 million bonus, and were impressed with his bat in two games in the rookie-level Gulf Coast League, where he had six hits and a stolen base before an oblique strain kept him out for the rest of the season. While still learning the intricacies of the game, Hall returned for instructional league and showed a smooth, righthanded swing with quick hands that's more contact-oriented at this point, with present gap power that could blossom into more as he develops. He made all the plays at shortstop, and could project as an average up-the-middle defender with range to both sides, showing an above-average arm and plus speed as an amateur and in his professional debut.

Hall may not make a full-season affiliate out of spring training in 2018 in order to maximize his development time before rookie ball begins in June.

Year	Club (League)	Class	AVG	G	AB	R	H	2B	3B	HR	RBI	BB	SO	SB	CS	OBP	SLG
2017	Orioles (GCL)	R	.667	2	9	4	6	1	1	0	2	0	2	1	0	.667	1.000
Minor League Totals			.667	2	9	4	6	1	1	0	2	0	2	1	0	.667	1.000

19 JESUS LIRANZO, RHP

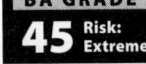

BA GRADE

45 Risk: Extreme

Born: March 7, 1995. **B-T:** R-R. **Ht.:** 6-2. **Wt.:** 175. **Signed:** Dominican Republic, 2012. **Signed by:** Matias Laureano Fortunato (Braves).

Atlanta released Liranzo in 2013, and the Orioles saw him take off after he recovered from 2014 elbow surgery. He was stateside by 2016, but because the team had to evaluate him for the 40-man roster ahead of the Rule 5 draft, he was pushed from low Class A Delmarva to Double-A Bowie and showed enough to be protected last winter.

After displaying uncharacteristically strong command in big league camp, Liranzo went back to Bowie for the 2017 season and struggled badly. Carrying a 6.85 ERA in early June, Liranzo got on the same schedule as Tanner Scott, which saw him make three-inning starts every fifth game to allow him to work on his mechanics between starts. That improved his results a bit, but his lack of control produced a career-high 5.95 walks per nine innings, even as he struck out 10.38 per nine. Liranzo has an electric arm with an above-average, mid-90s fastball, while featuring a slider and a splitter, but his arm lags behind his body in his delivery, causing his control to fail him.

Liranzo's velocity makes him an intriguing middle-inning bullpen piece if he can stay around the strike zone, but his inconsistency could prevent him from being anything more.

Year	Club (League)	Class	W	L	ERA	G	GS	CG	SV	IP	H	HR	BB	SO	K/9	WHIP	AVG
2015	Orioles1 (DSL)	R	3	2	2.35	23	0	0	0	38	28	0	19	46	10.8	1.23	.200
2016	Delmarva (SAL)	LoA	0	0	1.05	16	0	0	0	34	12	0	15	46	12.1	0.79	.109
	Bowie (EL)	AA	1	1	3.38	11	0	0	0	19	8	3	12	20	9.6	1.07	.127
2017	Bowie (EL)	AA	3	4	4.85	31	12	0	2	65	54	12	43	75	10.4	1.49	.224
Minor League Totals			7	8	3.71	91	15	0	2	170	119	17	103	202	10.7	1.31	.194

20 BRENAN HANIFEE, RHP

BA GRADE

50 Risk: Extreme

Born: May 29, 1998. **B-T:** R-R. **Ht.:** 6-5. **Wt.:** 180. **Drafted:** HS—Bridgewater, Va., 2016 (4th round). **Signed by:** Rich Morales.

A multi-sport athlete who pitched his way onto the MLB draft radar late in his senior year, Hanifee eschewed a commitment to East Carolina to sign with the Orioles for an above-slot $500,000 bonus, then flourished in a rotation full of more advanced college pitches for short season Aberdeen in 2017.

Hanifee didn't pitch in 2016, but went 7-3, 2.75 and a 1.12 WHIP in his professional debut, impressing scouts with a heavy sinker at 91-94 mph with a good feel for the strike zone. His youth and athleticism, plus his projectable frame, makes scouts dream on potential for added strength and velocity that could make his fastball a plus pitch going forward. He also features a slider and changeup that are still developing, which will be the keys to his progress, but the Orioles believe that as he gains more experience, those could develop enough to keep him as a starter.

Hanifee's frame and fastball suggest a mid-rotation starter at present, but Hanifee's youth means he's far from that. He'll open 2018 in low Class A Delmarva for his first full professional season.

Year	Club (League)	Class	W	L	ERA	G	GS	CG	SV	IP	H	HR	BB	SO	K/9	WHIP	AVG
2016	Did not play																
2017	Aberdeen (NYP)	SS	7	3	2.75	12	12	0	0	69	65	2	12	44	5.8	1.12	.249
Minor League Totals			7	3	2.75	12	12	0	0	69	65	2	12	44	5.8	1.12	.249

21 CAMERON BISHOP, LHP

BA GRADE

45 Risk: High

Born: Feb. 14, 1996. **B-T:** L-L. **Ht.:** 6-4. **Wt.:** 215. **Drafted:** UC Irvine, 2017 (26th round). **Signed by:** Mark Ralston.

After making 14 starts with a 4.61 ERA and a team-high 79 strikeouts as a sophomore at UC Irvine in 2016, Bishop was one of the top prospects in the West Coast League in 2016, and was projected to be the Anteaters' ace and pitch himself into the first day of the draft this spring.

However, Bishop strained his oblique the week before the season began, and didn't throw a pitch all year. The Orioles took a flier on him in the 26th round, and moved to sign him after three strong appearances in the Cape Cod League. A clerical error meant his signing for an above-slot $650,000 was announced a week after the July 15 deadline, though both sides showed that the agreement was reached in time. Bishop made one scoreless start in the Gulf Coast League before going to short-season Aberdeen, where he had a 0.78 ERA and a 1.07 WHIP in 34 innings, with 38 strikeouts and 16 walks. He has a low-90s fastball that reaches 95 mph, with a curveball/changeup/slider combination that is raw across the board.

Bishop will continue on a starter's track at low Class A Delmarva in 2018.

Year	Club (League)	Class	W	L	ERA	G	GS	CG	SV	IP	H	HR	BB	SO	K/9	WHIP	AVG
2017	Orioles (GCL)	R	0	0	0.00	1	1	0	0	3	1	0	0	1	3.0	0.33	.111
	Aberdeen (NYP)	SS	1	1	0.78	8	8	0	0	35	20	1	16	38	9.9	1.04	.165
Minor League Totals			1	1	0.72	9	9	0	0	38	21	1	16	39	9.3	0.98	.162

22 OFELKY PERALTA, RHP

BA GRADE

45 Risk: High

Born: April 20, 1997. **B-T:** R-R. **Ht.:** 6-5. **Wt.:** 195. **Signed:** Dominican Republic, 2013. **Signed by:** Fred Ferreira/Enrique Constante/Calvin Maduro/Joel Bradley.

Peralta, the recipient of the club's then-highest signing bonus to a Dominican player at $325,000 in 2013, has moved quickly since joining the organization and debuting stateside in 2015. He struck out nearly a batter per inning with a 4.01 ERA at low Class A Delmarva in 2016, but struggled in 2017 for high Class A Frederick, where he had a 5.33 ERA with 95 strikeouts and a Carolina League-high 86 walks in 101 innings.

Peralta, a tall, projectable righthander, features a live, loose arm with a 90-95 mph that's presently plus. While he shows feel for a future-average changeup, and is now throwing a slider as his breaking ball, all of his pitches suffer from the lack of a repeatable delivery and arm slot. If the Orioles and Peralta are able to find mechanical consistency and the control that comes with it, he could project as a No. 4 starter.

At age 20, there's no rush to move him off that track. Peralta is likely ticketed back to Frederick in hopes of finding that consistency in 2018.

Year	Club (League)	Class	W	L	ERA	G	GS	CG	SV	IP	H	HR	BB	SO	K/9	WHIP	AVG
2015	Orioles (GCL)	R	0	2	5.61	11	10	0	0	26	20	0	19	31	10.9	1.52	.202
2016	Delmarva (SAL)	LoA	8	5	4.01	23	23	1	0	103	87	3	60	101	8.8	1.42	.230
2017	Frederick (CAR)	HiA	2	10	5.33	26	26	0	0	105	109	8	86	95	8.2	1.86	.269
Minor League Totals			10	21	4.52	71	70	1	0	277	244	11	202	260	8.4	1.61	.236

23 JIMMY YACABONIS, RHP

BA GRADE

40 Risk: Medium

Born: Nov. 28, 1993. **B-T:** R-R. **Ht.:** 6-3. **Wt.:** 205. **Drafted:** St. Joseph's, 2013 (13th round). **Signed by:** Dean Albany.

After lowering his walk rate in 2016 and enjoying his best full season to date, Yacabonis went to the Arizona Fall League and solidified himself on the Orioles' major league radar. Though he didn't get invited to major league spring training in 2017, he impressed in six big league spring games and ultimately made his major league debut in May.

Overall, while Yacabonis had success at Triple-A Norfolk with a 1.32 ERA and a 0.95 WHIP in 61.1 innings, he struggled with his control both there and in the majors. He walked 14 in 20.2 major league innings with just eight strikeouts, and had a 4.35 ERA. With a max-effort delivery from the right side, Yacabonis' 94-96 mph fastball is a plus pitch with sink that tops out at 98 mph, and he features an average, 83-85 mph slider that he can struggle to command at times.

If Yacabonis can harnesses that control, he can ascend to a seventh-inning relief role. As it stands how, he'll likely split time in 2018 between Norfolk and Baltimore.

Year	Club (League)	Class	W	L	ERA	G	GS	CG	SV	IP	H	HR	BB	SO	K/9	WHIP	AVG
2015	Frederick (CAR)	HiA	3	3	4.02	43	0	0	2	63	74	3	33	66	9.5	1.71	.296
2016	Frederick (CAR)	HiA	0	2	3.98	16	0	0	5	20	17	2	6	21	9.3	1.13	.227
	Bowie (EL)	AA	2	2	2.03	34	0	0	6	44	34	2	14	46	9.3	1.08	.211
2017	Norfolk (IL)	AAA	4	0	1.32	41	0	0	11	61	30	0	28	48	7.0	0.95	.144
	Baltimore (AL)	MAJ	2	0	4.35	14	0	0	0	21	18	2	14	8	3.5	1.55	.247
Major League Totals			2	0	4.35	14	0	0	0	21	18	2	14	8	3.5	1.55	.247
Minor League Totals			13	13	3.01	190	0	0	42	272	213	9	138	263	8.7	1.29	.216

24 MATTHIAS DIETZ, RHP

BA GRADE 45 Risk: High

Born: Sept. 20, 1995. **B-T:** R-R. **Ht.:** 6-5. **Wt.:** 220. **Drafted:** John A. Logan (Ill.) JC, 2016 (2nd round). **Signed by:** Dan Durst.

A growth spurt between Dietz's freshman and sophomore seasons at John A. Logan (Ill.) JC made him the top junior college arm in the 2016 draft, and the Orioles' selected him in the second round and lured him away from a commitment to Texas Christian with a $1.5 million bonus.

Dietz stumbled at short-season Aberdeen in the New York-Penn League in his professional debut, pitching to a 4.82 ERA with an identical 4.82 walks per nine innings and a 1.71 WHIP. His assignment to low Class A Delmarva this year was a learning experience for a pitcher who's very young in baseball terms. His fastball, which projects to be a plus pitch at 92-96 mph with occasional armside run from a low three-quarters arm slot, can be erratic both in and out of the zone. His slider is the most advanced of his secondary pitches with average potential, while he also throws a firm changeup that is a below-average offering.

Dietz is still learning his delivery and all that comes with pitching, and a return to Delmarva in 2018 to reinforce those could be in play for the 22-year-old.

Year	Club (League)	Class	W	L	ERA	G	GS	CG	SV	IP	H	HR	BB	SO	K/9	WHIP	AVG
2016	Aberdeen (NYP)	SS	0	3	4.82	7	7	0	0	19	22	0	10	8	3.9	1.71	.306
2017	Delmarva (SAL)	LoA	3	10	4.93	26	26	0	0	130	144	6	50	92	6.4	1.50	.282
Minor League Totals			3	13	4.91	33	33	0	0	148	166	6	60	100	6.1	1.52	.285

25 LAMAR SPARKS, OF

BA GRADE 50 Risk: Extreme

Born: Sept. 26, 1998. **B-T:** R-R. **Ht.:** 6-2. **Wt.:** 170. **Drafted:** HS—Katy, Texas, 2017 (5th round). **Signed by:** Thom Dreier.

Despite his flying under the radar for most of his amateur career, the Orioles are intrigued by the upside of the athletic Sparks, whom they signed to a $304,800 signing bonus as their fifth-round selection in 2017.

A childhood friend of the Orioles' unsigned fourth-round pick, Texas prep righthander Jack Conlon, Sparks was also a pitcher in high school, but the team has worked him in the outfield as a professional. With a wiry, athletic frame and broad shoulders that suggest room for physical maturation, Sparks' right-handed swing can be a bit complicated, but at times he showed a plan at the plate and some pop in the rookie-level Gulf Coast League. He already possesses the athleticism and range to play center field, with his arm and speed both projecting as plus tools. As currently constituted, Sparks provides more value with his glove than bat, but the Orioles feel he can develop into an all-around up-the-middle talent.

Sparks is likely to get more work in extended spring training in 2018 before another rookie ball assignment.

Year	Club (League)	Class	AVG	G	AB	R	H	2B	3B	HR	RBI	BB	SO	SB	CS	OBP	SLG
2017	Orioles (GCL)	R	.241	42	145	31	35	7	2	0	9	33	39	11	3	.385	.317
Minor League Totals			.241	42	145	31	35	7	2	0	9	33	39	11	3	.385	.317

26 YEFRY RAMIREZ, RHP

BA GRADE 45 Risk: High

Born: Nov. 28, 1993. **B-T:** R-R. **Ht.:** 6-2. **Wt.:** 215. **Signed:** Dominican Republic, 2011. **Signed by:** Junior Noboa (Diamondbacks).

The Yankees acquired Ramírez, a converted position player from his time with the Arizona Diamondbacks, in the minor league Rule 5 draft and saw him flourish as a starting pitcher. They added him to the 40-man roster after a breakout 2016 season, and dealt him to the Orioles for international signing bonus slots in late July after a strong spell at Double-A Trenton.

Ramirez continued that progress with the Orioles, ending his season with a combined 15-3, 3.47 and a 1.19 WHIP in 24 starts. Ramírez has a starter's frame with a 91-95 mph fastball from a three-quarter slot with average life but poor command, while his 83-85 mph slider is inconsistent with vertical break. His changeup has above-average potential and is his out pitch, as he sets hitters up with his fastball and gets them out with his top offspeed pitch. The only thing keeping him from projecting as a starter is below-average control, but if that cleans up, he could be a No. 5 starter or a high-leverage reliever.

Ramirez will be a dark-horse candidate in the Orioles' rotation race in spring training, but is more likely ticketed for Triple-A Norfolk to open 2018.

Year	Club (League)	Class	W	L	ERA	G	GS	CG	SV	IP	H	HR	BB	SO	K/9	WHIP	AVG
2015	Missoula (PIO)	R	5	5	5.35	14	13	0	0	69	68	11	21	61	8.0	1.29	.259
2016	Charleston, SC (SAL)	LoA	4	2	2.80	11	11	0	0	61	48	4	14	66	9.7	1.02	.209
	Tampa (FSL)	HiA	3	7	2.84	11	11	0	0	63	34	5	18	66	9.4	0.82	.156
2017	Trenton (EL)	AA	10	3	3.41	18	18	2	0	92	78	9	38	91	8.9	1.26	.229
	Bowie (EL)	AA	5	0	3.66	6	6	1	0	32	27	6	11	26	7.3	1.19	.241
Minor League Totals			35	26	3.45	104	80	3	0	470	395	46	146	455	8.7	1.15	.226

27 ADEMAR RIFAELA, OF

BA GRADE

45 Risk: High

Born: Nov. 20, 1994. **B-T:** L-L. **Ht.:** 5-10. **Wt.:** 180. **Signed:** Curacao, 2013.
Signed by: Fred Ferreira/Ernst Meyer.

A native of Curacao, Rifaela's minor league breakout season in 2017 mirrored that of his mentor, fellow Curacaoan Jonathan Schoop. After he repeated low Class A Delmarva in 2016, Rifaela took advantage of regular playing time for the first time in years and hit a career-best .284/.358/.500 with 24 home runs and 23 doubles to earn the Carolina League most valuable player award.

Undersized but physically mature at a listed 5-foot-10, Rifaela generates above-average raw power from the left side and translated that into games in 2017, and has shown the ability to handle fastball velocity. That's fed by an overly aggressive approach, one that led to 124 strikeouts in 126 games in 2017. While he doesn't project to be more than an average outfielder and is a below-average runner, the quiet, assured way in which he went about his breakout season impressed the organization.

Rifaela could serve as a lefthanded platoon bat in the major leagues, but will be challenged by more advanced secondary pitches at Double-A Bowie in 2018 and beyond.

Year	Club (League)	Class	AVG	G	AB	R	H	2B	3B	HR	RBI	BB	SO	SB	CS	OBP	SLG
2015	Aberdeen (NYP)	SS	.200	7	30	3	6	2	0	0	1	3	4	0	1	.273	.267
	Delmarva (SAL)	LoA	.262	59	233	39	61	15	1	5	20	25	59	4	0	.341	.399
2016	Frederick (CAR)	HiA	.167	5	18	2	3	1	0	1	3	2	5	1	0	.250	.389
	Delmarva (SAL)	LoA	.239	92	343	41	82	14	6	12	45	27	97	2	3	.297	.420
2017	Frederick (CAR)	HiA	.284	126	450	73	128	23	1	24	78	41	124	7	5	.358	.500
Minor League Totals			.257	386	1394	213	358	70	13	46	176	153	354	18	21	.339	.425

28 GRAY FENTER, RHP

BA GRADE

45 Risk: High

Born: Jan. 25, 1996. **B-T:** R-R. **Ht.:** 6-0. **Wt.:** 200. **Drafted:** HS—West Memphis, Ark., 2015 (7th round). **Signed by:** Mike Boulanger/Nathan Showalter.

Signed to an above-slot $1 million bonus as a 2015 seventh-round pick out of high school in Arkansas, Fenter had Tommy John surgery in April 2016 and missed all of that season. Upon returning in 2017 for his rehab year, he made all but one of his 12 appearances in the rookie-level Gulf Coast League and eventually rounded into form, allowing two earned runs in 20 August innings.

Listed at 5-foot-11 and with a compact delivery, Fenter has a mature frame that lacks projection and draws comparisons to the sturdy build of Orioles starter Dylan Bundy. His size limits the downhill angle he can get on his fastball, but it's presently a plus pitch at 92-96 mph post-surgery. His curveball has above-average shape when he stays behind it, but his rehab restrictions limited him from throwing that or his changeup often this summer. Observers both inside and outside the organization regard him as a tremendous competitor who wants to improve.

With the development of a changeup, Fenter could project as a No. 4 starter, though his two-pitch mix and delivery make him a bullpen candidate. He should open 2018 with low Class A Delmarva.

Year	Club (League)	Class	W	L	ERA	G	GS	CG	SV	IP	H	HR	BB	SO	K/9	WHIP	AVG
2015	Orioles (GCL)	R	0	0	1.66	9	8	0	0	22	15	0	6	18	7.5	0.97	.200
2016	Did not play—Injured																
2017	Orioles (GCL)	R	0	1	3.45	11	11	0	0	29	17	0	10	33	10.4	0.94	.172
	Aberdeen (NYP)	SS	0	0	16.20	1	0	0	0	2	3	1	0	1	5.4	1.80	.375
Minor League Totals			0	1	3.12	21	19	0	0	52	35	1	16	52	9.0	0.98	.192

29 AUSTIN WYNNS, C

BA GRADE

45 Risk: High

Born: Dec. 10, 1990. **B-T:** R-R. **Ht.:** 6-2. **Wt.:** 205. **Drafted:** Fresno State, 2013 (10th round). **Signed by:** Rich Morales.

A senior sign in 2013 out of Fresno State, Wynns got an invitation to major league spring training in 2017 and has long been on the coaching staff's radar for his defensive abilities. He followed an eye-opening stint in the Arizona Fall League in 2016 with his best year as a pro. He threw out 38.2 percent of would-be basestealers in 2017 and was charged with just five passed balls in 781.1 innings for Double-A Bowie, career-bests in both categories.

Wynns has an above-average arm with consistent pop times around 2.0 seconds, and presents a good target for his pitchers behind the plate. His bat has also come around, to the tune of .281/.377/.419 with a career-high 10 home runs and 18 doubles. A prototypical catcher, Wynns could be a good long-term complement to Chance Sisco behind the plate.

He'll likely get another chance to make an impression in a crowded catching scene during major league camp in 2018, but could be the everyday catcher at Triple-A Norfolk if Sisco makes the big league club.

Year	Club (League)	Class	AVG	G	AB	R	H	2B	3B	HR	RBI	BB	SO	SB	CS	OBP	SLG
2015	Bowie (EL)	AA	.375	4	16	1	6	2	0	0	3	0	4	0	0	.375	.500
	Frederick (CAR)	HiA	.274	74	230	21	63	16	0	3	28	26	39	2	1	.347	.383
2016	Bowie (EL)	AA	.247	21	73	11	18	7	0	0	10	7	12	1	0	.309	.342
	Frederick (CAR)	HiA	.303	51	188	23	57	10	0	5	20	13	32	0	0	.351	.436
	Norfolk (IL)	AAA	.278	8	18	3	5	1	0	1	4	0	2	0	0	.278	.500
2017	Bowie (EL)	AA	.281	105	370	54	104	19	1	10	46	52	64	1	0	.377	.419
Minor League Totals			.269	407	1409	151	379	79	1	20	169	136	238	5	4	.336	.369

30 STEVE WILKERSON, 2B/3B

BA GRADE

45 Risk: High

Born: Jan. 11, 1992. **B-T:** S-R. **Ht.:** 6-1. **Wt.:** 195. **Drafted:** Clemson, 2014 (8th round). **Signed by:** Rich Morales.

A senior sign out of Clemson in 2014, Wilkerson broke out in 2017 between high Class A Frederick and Double-A Bowie. He hit .305/.375/.423 with 31 extra-base hits while playing all four infield positions and right field.

While shortstop may be a challenge long-term, his solid-average speed and versatility made him a frequent topic of conversation among the major league coaching staff as the team sought roster flexibility during the season. Wilkerson's ability to handle shortstop on a long-term basis will determine his value as a utility player, with second base and third base his best positions currently. He is a switch-hitter with speed who projects as a fringe-average bat with gap power from either side and can plug in anywhere on the diamond.

Wilkerson's audition in the Arizona Fall League was an audition for the 40-man roster with an eye toward replacing utilityman Ryan Flaherty on the major league roster in 2018. However he was not added to the 40-man roster as he was suspended for 50 games after testing positive for an amphetamine. The suspension will take him out of the competition for a big league job coming out of spring training. Instead, he will likely come off the suspension looking for consistent playing time at Double-A Bowie again.

Year	Club (League)	Class	AVG	G	AB	R	H	2B	3B	HR	RBI	BB	SO	SB	CS	OBP	SLG
2015	Delmarva (SAL)	LoA	.287	92	342	61	98	15	4	2	30	45	84	10	5	.376	.371
2016	Bowie (EL)	AA	.222	3	9	1	2	0	0	0	0	0	1	0	0	.222	.222
	Frederick (CAR)	HiA	.251	114	402	49	101	17	4	4	36	45	98	18	6	.334	.343
2017	Frederick (CAR)	HiA	.316	41	155	29	49	10	0	2	15	19	40	2	3	.401	.419
	Bowie (EL)	AA	.294	71	245	34	72	13	0	6	30	20	53	5	2	.354	.420
Minor League Totals			.266	381	1363	193	362	64	9	16	126	143	318	38	22	.343	.361

Boston Red Sox

BY ALEX SPEIER

On June 27, the Red Sox rolled the Twins, 9-2, to move a game ahead of the Yankees in the American League East. Yet that contest was significant beyond that small shift in the standings, in a season when the Red Sox went on to win their division for the second straight year.

That day, the Red Sox featured homegrown players at every defensive position. Third baseman Deven Marrero, shortstop Xander Bogaerts, second baseman Dustin Pedroia, and first baseman Sam Travis had all spent every day of their professional careers in the Red Sox organization. So had catcher Christian Vazquez and outfielders Andrew Benintendi, Jackie Bradley Jr., and Mookie Betts.

The sight of that positional group–backing a starting pitcher in Drew Pomeranz who'd been acquired a year earlier for another top prospect–in many ways represented the state of the club.

The 2017 Red Sox roster was shaped by the previous winter's blockbuster move to trade a four-prospect package headlined by Yoan Moncada and Michael Kopech to the White Sox to land Chris Sale. But that move was made only because the Red Sox were trying to supplement an elite core of homegrown position players–a group that was joined in 2017 by 20-year-old third base phenom Rafael Devers.

While the Red Sox' young big league position players largely took a step backwards in 2017 – with the somewhat disappointing years by Betts, Bogaerts, and Bradley contributing to the Red Sox' decision to fire manager John Farrell and replace him with former Astros bench coach Alex Cora–their group of homegrown position players remains one of the most talented and dynamic in the game.

Yet below the big league surface, the Red Sox organization has altered dramatically in the span of a few years. The team's best young prospects have now graduated to the big leagues. Beyond that group, numerous others (Moncada, Kopech, Manuel Margot, Anderson Espinoza, Mauricio Dubon, and others) have been dealt to build a pitching staff that in 2017 received just five starts from homegrown pitchers.

A farm system that had been one of the strongest in the game now largely has been drained in support of a championship window. While the Red Sox still feature some promising young talents in the minors, their affiliates no longer teem with players who combine shoot-the-moon ceilings with solid floors.

At the time of the Sale deal, Sox officials acknowledged the challenge that lies in front of their amateur scouting and player development

Red Sox rookie third baseman Rafael Devers should be a lineup fixture for many years.

PROJECTED 2021 LINEUP

Catcher	Christian Vazquez (30)
First Base	Michael Chavis (25)
Second Base	Dustin Pedroia (37)
Third Base	Rafael Devers (24)
Shortstop	Xander Bogaerts (28)
Left Field	Andrew Benintendi (26)
Center Field	Jackie Bradley (31)
Right Field	Mookie Betts (28)
Designated Hitter	Sam Travis (25)
No. 1 Starter	Chris Sale (32)
No. 2 Starter	David Price (35)
No. 3 Starter	Jay Groome (23)
No. 4 Starter	Tanner Houck (25)
No. 5 Starter	Bryan Mata (23)
Closer	Craig Kimbrel (33)

staffs as they try to refill their talent pipeline. Yet the organization remains aware that such an undertaking won't happen overnight, particularly after the first efforts to reload took a sudden and tragic turn when highly regarded international catching prospect Daniel Flores–who signed out of Venezuela in July for $3.1 million–passed away in November due to cancer.

As they look to 2018, the Red Sox remain in a championship contention window largely because of the recent successes of their scouting and player development efforts. How long they remain there will depend upon what transpires with some promising but raw talents in the lower levels of their system, and with the ongoing efforts by their amateur scouts to uncover a new group of standouts.

DEPTH CHART

BOSTON RED SOX

TOP 2018 ROOKIE: Marco Hernandez, 2B. The versatile, lefty-hitting infielder could see time at second base or shortstop as needed.

BREAKOUT PROSPECT: Danny Diaz, 3B. Diaz has the sort of projectable power that will command notice once the 2017 international free agent starts playing in games.

SLEEPER: Bobby Poyner, LHP. Poyner's light stuff caps his upside, but he's been a ridiculously strong performer over three years in the system and has a chance to find his way to the big leagues in 2018.

SOURCE OF TOP 30 TALENT

Homegrown	29	Acquired	1
College	12	Trade	1
Junior college	0	Rule 5 draft	0
High school	8	Independent league	0
Nondrafted free agent	0	Free agent/waivers	0
International	9		

LF
Tyler Esplin (28)
Bryce Brentz
Tyler Dearden
Danny Mars
Aneury Tavarez
Tyler Hill

CF
Cole Brannen (5)
Kervin Suarez (30)
Lorenzo Cedrola
Tate Matheny

RF
Pedro Castellanos
Yoan Aybar
Jeremy Barfield

3B
Michael Chavis (2)
Danny Diaz (14)
Bobby Dalbec (16)

SS
Antoni Flores (17)
C.J. Chatham (26)
Andre Colon
Denny Daza
Jeremy Rivera

2B
Marco Hernandez (10)
Brett Netzer (18)
Tzu-Wei Lin (21)
Chad De La Guerra (25)
Everlouis Lozada
Josh Tobias

1B
Sam Travis (7)
Josh Ockimey (12)

C
Roldani Baldiwn (15)
Austin Rei

LHP

LHSP	LHRP
Jay Groome (1)	Williams Jerez (27)
Darwinzon Hernandez (6)	Bobby Poyner
Jalen Beeks (11)	Trey Ball
Brian Johnson (23)	Brendan Nail
Dedgar Jimenez	
Jhonathan Diaz	

RHP

RHSP	RHRP
Tanner Houck (3)	Austin Maddox (19)
Bryan Mata (4)	Joan Martinez (24)
Mike Shawaryn (8)	Ty Buttrey
Alex Scherff (9)	Chandler Shepherd
Jake Thompson (13)	Ben Taylor
Hector Velazquez (20)	Jake Cosart
Travis Lakins (22)	Nick Duron
Roniel Raudes (29)	Kyle Martin
Hildemaro Requena	Trevor Kelley
Justin Haley	Juan Florentino
	Zach Schellenger
	Aaron Perry

DRAFT ANALYSIS

2017

BEST PURE HITTER: OF Cole Brannen (2) has to adjust to pro ball, but he's an advanced hitter for his age who uses the whole field, recognizes pitches and works counts. 2B Brett Netzer (3) is a more polished and advanced hitter right now and hit .286 in 182 pro at-bats.

BEST POWER HITTER: OF Tyler Esplin (7) shows plus raw power with the ability to hit the ball out to left or right field. The Red Sox were impressed with his ability to drive the ball the opposite way, a healthy indicator of future productive power.

FASTEST RUNNER: Brannen is at least a plus runner who will turn in times that rate as a 70 on the 20-to-80 scouting scale on his best days.

BEST DEFENSIVE PLAYER: Like many young outfielders, Brannen takes inconsistent routes and his reads should get better as he matures, but he's already a true center fielder with the speed to stay there. He's a potentially plus defender in center.

BEST FASTBALL: RHP Alex Scherff (5) can regularly get to 95-98 mph with a fastball that has plenty of life. RHP Tanner Houck (1) has also touched 98 and his fastball generates plenty of swings and misses.

BEST SECONDARY PITCH: RHP Zach Schellenger (6) gets plus grades for his low 80s slider because of a funky delivery, plus tilt and its hard and late movement.

BEST PRO DEBUT: Netzer hit .286/.350/.341 between short-season Lowell and low Class A Greenville. RHP Jake Thompson (4) impressed in his 11.1-innings stint as his fastball sat 94-95 mph. It touched higher and he showed improved command on his way to a 0-3, 3.18 stat line.

BEST ATHLETE: OF David Durden (20) was slated to head to Mercer to play wide receiver if he didn't sign with the Red Sox. He's an excellent

TOP DRAFT PICKS OF THE DECADE

Year	Player, Pos.	2017 Org
2008	Casey Kelly, RHP	Giants
2009	Reymond Fuentes, OF	Diamondbacks
2010	Kolbrin Vitek, 2B	Did not play
2011	Matt Barnes, RHP	Red Sox
2012	Deven Marrero, SS	Red Sox
2013	Trey Ball, LHP	Red Sox
2014	Michael Chavis, SS	Red Sox
2015	Andrew Benintendi, OF	Red Sox
2016	Jay Groome, LHP	Red Sox
2017	Tanner Houck, RHP	Red Sox

athlete with speed, strength and body control.

MOST INTRIGUING BACKGROUND: OF Jordan Wren (10) is the son of Red Sox vice president Frank Wren. LHP Rio Gomez (36) is the son of ESPN reporter Pedro Gomez.

CLOSEST TO THE MAJORS: Houck should move quickly as an experienced college pitcher with a track record of success and a plus fastball. The Red Sox watched his innings very carefully in his pro debut, but he will likely be moved aggressively in his first full pro season.

BEST LATE-ROUND PICK: Durden has a good swing to go with plenty of athleticism. He just needs time to catch up to more advanced pitchers. The Red Sox were happy to land NDFA Brendan Nail as they signed him after seeing him pitch effectively with a 91-93 mph fastball, plus breaking ball and a deceptive delivery in the Cape Cod League all-star game.

THE ONE WHO GOT AWAY: OF Marcus Ragan (15) is the only player the Red Sox failed to sign in the top 20 rounds. The athletic, speedy outfielder is expected to return to East Mississippi JC for his sophomore season.

—J.J. COOPER

2016

LHP Jay Groome (1) battled injuries in a tough first full season, but still offers significant upside. RHP Mike Shawaryn (5) led all Red Sox minor leaguers with 169 strikeouts. RHP Shaun Anderson (3) was part of the trade for Eduardo Nunez.

GRADE: B

2015

OF Andrew Benintendi (1) posted a 20-20 season in Boston and was the runner-up in the AL rookie of the year voting. RHP Ben Taylor (7) gives the draft a second big leaguer, and LHP Logan Allen (8) continues to progress in the Padres system.

GRADE: A

2014

Michael Kopech (1) was a part of the Chris Sale trade last winter and now is one of the best pitching prospects in the game. 3B Michael Chavis (1) made a jump in 2017, and 1B Sam Travis (2) made his big league debut.

GRADE: A

1 JAY GROOME, LHP

Born: Aug. 23, 1998. **B-T:** L-L. **Ht.:** 6-6. **Wt.:** 220.
Drafted: HS—Barnegat, N.J., 2016 (1st round).
Signed by: Ray Fagnant.

Groome was viewed as a potential No. 1 overall pick in the 2016 draft as a standout talent who as a teenager had a big league frame, low-effort velocity and a swing-and-miss curveball that made it easy to imagine an impact starter. He fell to No. 12 due to both signability and off-field concerns, but the Red Sox felt comfortable with his makeup and were thrilled at the chance to select someone with such a high ceiling, and they signed him for a just-above-slot $3.65 million. Groome's full-season debut in 2017 proved rocky. He left his first start at low Class A Greenville with an intercostal strain that sidelined him for two months and later experienced minor forearm soreness that ended his season in mid-August. During the season, his father was arrested on drug and weapons charges. In between those challenges, Groome showed inconsistent but promising flashes of the stuff.

With a tall, upright delivery and the ability to spin a hammer curveball to pair with elevated four-seam fastballs, Groome already harbors similarities with Drew Pomeranz. While he worked in the low 90s for most of his injury-riddled 2017, he's expected to gain velocity with more exposure to a professional conditioning program. He's still learning how best to employ a changeup, but evaluators believe that his natural ability to manipulate the ball will give him the ability to emerge with at least a solid-average pitch, while anticipating that his ability to spin the ball will allow him to develop a quality cutter. His cutter, in turn, could allow him to open the plate in a way that allows him to move beyond some of the pitch efficiency challenges he endured in 2017. His athleticism and easy ability to generate power from his delivery suggest that, despite walking 4.9 per nine innings in 2017, he has a chance to develop above-average control.

With Chris Sale reaching out to Groome to work out with him during the offseason, the Red Sox are optimistic that the young lefthander will be ready to hit the ground running in 2018. He should be able to gain momentum at Greenville before an in-season move to high Class A Salem. He'll be pitching nearly all of 2018 as a 19-year-old, suggesting little need to rush across levels. If he can remain healthy, his anticipated pitch development suggests a possibility of a No. 2 or No. 3 starter.

TOM PRIDDY

BA GRADE	SCOUTING GRADES
65 Risk: Extreme	**FB:** 60. **CB:** 60. **CHG:** 50. **CUTTER:** 55. **CTL:** 50.

Projected future grades on 20-80 scouting scale

TOP PROSPECTS OF THE DECADE

Year	Player, Pos.	2017 Org
2008	Clay Buchholz, RHP	Phillies
2009	Lars Anderson, 1B	Japanese indy league
2010	Ryan Westmoreland, OF	Did not play
2011	Jose Iglesias, SS	Tigers
2012	Will Middlebrooks, 3B	Rangers
2013	Xander Bogaerts, SS	Red Sox
2014	Xander Bogaerts, SS/3B	Red Sox
2015	Blake Swihart, C	Red Sox
2016	Yoan Moncada, 3B	White Sox
2017	Andrew Benintendi, OF	Red Sox

BEST TOOLS

Best Hitter for Average	Sam Travis
Best Power Hitter	Michael Chavis
Best Strike-Zone Discipline	Josh Ockimey
Fastest Baserunner	Cole Brannen
Best Athlete	Kervin Suarez
Best Fastball	Darwinzon Hernandez
Best Curveball	Jay Groome
Best Slider	Tanner Houck
Best Changeup	Ty Buttrey
Best Control	Bryan Mata
Best Defensive Catcher	Austin Rei
Best Defensive Infielder	Antoni Flores
Best Infield Arm	Bobby Dalbec
Best Defensive Outfielder	Tate Matheny
Best Outfield Arm	Yoan Aybar

Year	Club (League)	Class	W	L	ERA	G	GS	CG	SV	IP	H	HR	BB	SO	K/9	WHIP	AVG
2016	Red Sox (GCL)	R	0	0	2.25	2	2	0	0	4	3	0	0	8	18.0	0.75	.200
	Lowell (NYP)	SS	0	0	3.38	1	1	0	0	3	0	0	4	2	6.8	1.50	.000
2017	Lowell (NYP)	SS	0	2	1.64	3	3	0	0	11	5	0	5	14	11.5	0.91	.132
	Greenville (SAL)	LoA	3	7	6.70	11	11	0	0	44	44	6	25	58	11.8	1.56	.257
Minor League Totals			3	9	5.37	17	17	0	0	62	52	6	34	82	11.9	1.39	.223

2 MICHAEL CHAVIS, 3B

Born: Aug. 11, 1995. **B-T:** R-R. **Ht.:** 5-10. **Wt.:** 190. **Drafted:** HS—Marietta, Ga., 2014 (1st round). **Signed by:** Brian Moehler.

After struggling in 2015 and 2016 with a crude offensive approach and injuries, Chavis made a concerted effort to address those concerns in 2017. He took extensive notes about everything from his pregame routine and pitch-by-pitch sequences of his plate appearances, starting in spring training.

That meticulous approach set the stage for a breakout season in which Chavis blasted 31 homers to rank fifth in the minors) and 68 extra-base hits (third), marks that had several evaluators identifying him as the system's top prospect.Chavis uses phenomenal bat speed and a strong core to generate standout power from his compact frame. While he proved hyper-aggressive in his attempt to drive the ball 600 feet in previous years, he showed a greater commitment to maintain his balance, stay back and drive the ball to all fields in 2017, particularly at high Class A Salem.

BA GRADE

55 Risk: Medium

HIT: 50. **POW:** 60.
SPD: 45. **FLD:** 45.
ARM: 55.

That approach led to both a career-low 21.6 percent strikeout rate and impressive displays of in-game power. Defensively, Chavis likewise made significant improvements to the point that many evaluators now believe he can be playable at third base. Chavis has middle-of-the-order power, though his relatively low walk rates (7.4 percent in 2017) suggest more of a future No. 6 hitter in the mold of a Mike Moustakas than a No. 3 or 4 hitter. Even though he had balanced left/right splits in 2017, some evaluators wonder whether he'll end up being a platoon contributor.

With Rafael Devers at third base, the Red Sox exposed Chavis to first base in the Arizona Fall League, and he also has the potential to add left field and perhaps second base to the corner infield positions. His spring training will dictate whether he opens 2018 at Double-A Portland or Triple-A Pawtucket

Year	Club (League)	Class	AVG	G	AB	R	H	2B	3B	HR	RBI	BB	SO	SB	CS	OBP	SLG
2015	Greenville (SAL)	LoA	.223	109	435	56	97	29	1	16	58	29	144	8	5	.277	.405
2016	Greenville (SAL)	LoA	.244	74	279	30	68	11	3	8	35	22	74	3	1	.321	.391
	Salem (CAR)	HiA	.160	7	25	5	4	0	0	0	1	2	7	1	0	.222	.160
2017	Salem (CAR)	HiA	.323	59	223	50	72	18	2	17	56	19	57	1	0	.392	.650
	Portland (EL)	AA	.250	67	248	39	62	18	0	14	39	20	56	1	0	.310	.492
Minor League Totals			.252	355	1344	201	339	88	9	56	205	107	376	19	9	.318	.456

3 TANNER HOUCK, RHP

Born: June 29, 1996. **B-T:** R-R. **Ht.:** 6-5. **Wt.:** 220. **Drafted:** Missouri, 2017 (1st round). **Signed by:** Todd Gold.

After strong performances in his freshman and sophomore seasons as well as a solid showing for Team USA in 2016, Houck entered 2017 as a preseason All-American. Yet despite another solid year in the Southeastern Conference, his anticipated dominance as a junior didn't materialize, leaving a pitcher projected as a potential top-10 pick on the board for the Red Sox at No. 24, where the Red Sox jumped at a chance to take a pitcher who it saw as having potentially untapped upside.

BA GRADE

50 Risk: High

FB: 60. **SL:** 60.
CHG: 45. **CUT:** 45.
CTL: 45.

Houck features a low three-quarters arm slot and a cross-body delivery, with moving parts that create deception but also pose challenges for his mechanical consistency. While his velocity was down at the start of his junior year, he was once again sitting at 92-93 mph and topping out at 97 by the end of the year, with a nasty two-seamer that evoked comparisons with Jake Peavy and Kevin Brown. He also threw a slider that came on as a wipeout offering. The Red Sox believe that with his ability to spin the ball from a low arm slot, he has a chance to generate more swings and misses by using his slider off an elevated four-seamer. They also plan to introduce a cutter, changeup and two-seam fastball to the mix. Houck's fastball and slider offer a solid floor of a late-inning reliever, but if he can broaden his mix with the addition of a cutter and development of a changeup, he has mid-rotation potential.

After a pro debut that saw Houck acclimate to a five-day routine and incorporate a four-seamer, He will open his first full pro season in 2018 at one of the Class A affiliates.

Year	Club (League)	Class	W	L	ERA	G	GS	CG	SV	IP	H	HR	BB	SO	K/9	WHIP	AVG
2017	Lowell (NYP)	SS	0	3	3.63	10	10	0	0	22	21	0	8	25	10.1	1.30	.239
Minor League Totals			0	3	3.63	10	10	0	0	22	21	0	8	25	10.1	1.30	.239

4 BRYAN MATA, RHP

Born: May 3, 1999. **B-T:** R-R. **Ht.:** 6-3. **Wt.:** 160. **Signed:** Venezuela, 2016. **Signed by:** Alex Requena/Eddie Romero.

Signed for $25,000, Mata has stood out since entering the system for the maturity of both his stuff and demeanor, traits that earned him a late-May assignment at low Class A Greenville, making him the youngest pitcher in the South Atlantic League.

Mata's clean delivery allows him to attack the strike zone with a three-pitch mix anchored by a four-seamer that typically sits at 91-92 mph, tops out at 94 mph, and has a chance to gain additional ticks as he fills out. His arm speed and consistent release point create good sell on a changeup that has late fade, creating the potential for a plus offering that he uses for swings and misses. Though his 77-78 mph curveball hasn't been a swing-and-miss offering, it has depth and he can throw it for strikes., giving him a potential mix of three pitches that are average or better. Projected above-average command will allow his pitch mix to play up. As an 18-year-old, Mata showed the potential to advance quickly. If his breaking ball doesn't progress, then his future may be in the bullpen.

But if Mata gains more consistency with the pitch while gaining additional power on his fastball, he has the upside of a No. 3 or No. 4 starter.

BA GRADE

50 Risk: High

FB: 55. CB: 50.
CHG: 60.
CTL: 60.

Year	Club (League)	Class	W	L	ERA	G	GS	CG	SV	IP	H	HR	BB	SO	K/9	WHIP	AVG
2016	Red Sox2 (DSL)	R	4	4	2.80	14	14	0	0	61	54	2	19	61	9.0	1.20	.242
2017	Greenville (SAL)	LoA	5	6	3.74	17	17	1	0	77	75	3	26	74	8.6	1.31	.259
Minor League Totals			9	10	3.33	31	31	1	0	138	129	5	45	135	8.8	1.26	.251

5 COLE BRANNEN, OF

Born: Aug. 4, 1998. **B-T:** L-R. **Ht.:** 6-0. **Wt.:** 170. **Drafted:** HS—Perry, Ga., 2017 (2nd round). **Signed by:** Brian Moehler.

Brannen stood out in the showcases following his junior year of high school, offering glimpses of a potential five-tool talent with his move to the outfield. Surgery to repair a broken hamate prior to the start of his senior year contributed to a slow start.

Brannen fell to the second round of the 2017 draft, where but over the season he once again displayed the tools that had drawn the Sox to him entering the year, with the Red Sox signed him for an above-slot $1.3 million. He started well in the Rookie-level Gulf Coast League before hitting a wall in August as he wore down in the Florida humidity. Brannen possesses elite speed and athleticism that serve as the cornerstone of his projections, giving him a chance to be a true center fielder (once experience permits him to take cleaner routes to the ball) while also elevating his offensive impact. He's shown advanced plate discipline and solid bat-to-ball skills that suggest a top-of-the-order skill set of high averages and on-base percentages, strong stolen base totals, and the ability to take an extra base. He showed the ability to drive the ball to the opposite field as an amateur, but it remains to be seen whether his strength is playable or whether he's a line-drive hitter whose ability to use the opposite field would play well at Fenway Park.

Brannen will be a candidate to open 2018 at low Class A Greenville. He has one of the highest ceilings of any Red Sox position player and represents the system's best up-the-middle prospect in the U.S. While it will take years to get a read on how his offense plays against professionals, his tools permit the Sox to daydream.

BA GRADE

55 Risk: Extreme

HIT: 60. POW: 40.
SPD: 60. FLD: 55.
ARM: 50.

Year	Club (League)	Class	AVG	G	AB	R	H	2B	3B	HR	RBI	BB	SO	SB	CS	OBP	SLG
2017	Red Sox (GCL)	R	.231	39	134	23	31	2	0	0	7	30	37	9	1	.383	.246
	Lowell (NYP)	SS	.111	3	9	0	1	0	1	0	1	4	4	1	1	.385	.333
Minor League Totals			.224	42	143	23	32	2	1	0	8	34	41	10	2	.383	.252

6 DARWINZON HERNANDEZ, LHP

Born: Dec. 17, 1996. **B-T:** L-L. **Ht.:** 6-2. **Wt.:** 185. **Signed:** Venezuela, 2013. **Signed by:** Rolando Pino/Ramon Mora.

Signed out of Venezuela for $25,000, Hernandez has shown stuff matched by few others in the Red Sox system. He has struck out more than a batter per inning as a starter across three consecutive levels, including a strong performance at low Class A Greenville in 2017, where his success was a product of stuff, because his abilities remained relatively unrefined.

Hernandez makes hitters uncomfortable with his low three-quarters arm slot, coming at them aggressively with 93-96 mph fastballs that top out at 97. His fastball can be so overwhelming to lower-level hitters that it may have slowed the development of his secondary pitches. Though his primary breaking pitch has been a curveball, his arm slot has long seemed suited to a slider. He used the pitch sparingly for most of 2017 before, in his final outing, leaning heavily on it in a dominant performance. While his walk rate remains high (4.3 per nine innings in 2017), it represented a major improvement over 2016 (6.7). Poor control is a major stumbling block after walking 4.3 per nine innings in 2017.

Hernandez's fastball and slider give him the look of a pitcher with at least late-innings potential–lefties hit .134 with a 37 percent strikeout rate against him–and if he can improve his control, he has a chance to be a mid-rotation starter.

BA GRADE
50 Risk: High
FB: 60. CB: 50.
SL: 60. CHG: 40.
CTL: 45.

Year	Club (League)	Class	W	L	ERA	G	GS	CG	SV	IP	H	HR	BB	SO	K/9	WHIP	AVG
2015	Red Sox2 (DSL)	R	6	1	1.10	16	13	0	0	65	55	0	30	66	9.1	1.30	.227
2016	Lowell (NYP)	SS	3	5	4.10	14	14	0	0	48	39	1	36	58	10.8	1.55	.217
2017	Greenville (SAL)	LoA	4	5	4.01	23	23	0	0	103	85	8	49	116	10.1	1.30	.221
Minor League Totals			14	12	3.12	67	51	0	0	245	203	9	134	255	9.4	1.38	.223

7 SAM TRAVIS, 1B

Born: Aug. 27, 1993. **B-T:** R-R. **Ht.:** 6-0. **Wt.:** 205. **Drafted:** Indiana, 2014 (2nd round). **Signed by:** Blair Henry.

After his 2016 season was cut short by a blown out ACL in his knee, Travis got off to a strong start in spring training but endured an uneven season. At times, he looked like a hitter who controlled the strike zone and did a good job identifying pitches on which he could make hard contact, with a May surge at Triple-A Pawtucket setting the stage for his first big league callup. However, from that point, his year became disjointed, with occasional contributions as a big league platoon option but he provided little sustained impact.

Despite his 2017 inconsistencies, Travis still has the foundation of a strong offensive approach, with an ability to identify pitches he can hit hard and barreling them while limiting his swings and misses (10.8 percent walk rate, 16.7 percent strikeout rate)thanks to strong strikeout and walk rates. His flat-plane bat path, however, has

BA GRADE
45 Risk: Medium
HIT: 55. POW: 45.
SPD: 45. FLD: 50.
ARM: 50.

resulted in line drives rather than the power of a first base prototype, resulting in questions of whether he'll hit enough to be an everyday player or if he'll fall more into the mold of a platoon bat against lefthanders. (He pounded southpaws in Pawtucket and the big leagues.) Defensively, Travis made considerable progress at first base, and he also gained exposure to left field in the Dominican League. Most evaluators agree that Travis soon will be ready to help in the big leagues but remain divided on his potential role.

The 2018 season may be pivotal in shaping Travis' future. If he can make swing adjustments to turn raw strength into in-game power, he could carve out a big league role, but a return to Pawtucket is likely until he proves he has the power needed from a first baseman.

Year	Club (League)	Class	AVG	G	AB	R	H	2B	3B	HR	RBI	BB	SO	SB	CS	OBP	SLG
2015	Salem (CAR)	HiA	.313	66	246	35	77	15	4	5	40	26	43	10	6	.378	.467
	Portland (EL)	AA	.300	65	243	35	73	17	2	4	38	33	34	9	6	.384	.436
2016	Pawtucket (IL)	AAA	.272	47	173	26	47	10	0	6	29	15	40	1	0	.332	.434
2017	Pawtucket (IL)	AAA	.270	82	304	40	82	14	0	6	24	37	57	6	2	.351	.375
	Boston (AL)	MAJ	.263	33	76	13	20	6	0	0	1	6	23	1	0	.325	.342
Major League Totals			.263	33	76	13	20	6	0	0	1	6	23	1	0	.325	.342
Minor League Totals			.295	327	1238	176	365	72	8	28	175	122	206	31	16	.360	.434

8 MIKE SHAWARYN, RHP

Born: Sept. 17, 1994. **B-T:** R-R. **Ht.:** 6-2. **Wt.:** 200. **Drafted:** Maryland, 2016 (5th round). **Signed by:** Chris Calciano.

After a dominant sophomore year at Maryland (1.71 ERA, 10.7 strikeouts per nine innings), Shawaryn's draft stock slipped thanks to a less-impressive draft season. The Terrapins ace pitched more to contact as a junior. He went 6-4, 3.18 as a junior, while his strikeout rate dipped and his walk rate got worse.

The 2016 fifth-round pick elevated his strikeout rate in 2017, ranking 11th among full-season minor league starters with 11.3 strikeouts per nine innings at two Class A levels. Shawaryn has the frame and thick core of a starter. His low three-quarters release point, somewhat evocative of Max Scherzer, challenged hitters to recognize whether he was throwing his low-90s fastball or a slider that frequently became a chase pitch. In 2017, Shawaryn showed increasing comfort elevating a four-seamer, creating a greater vertical spread of his arsenal. He's working to add a changeup with depth that will give him greater freedom to attack both sides of the plate.

Shawaryn's swing-and-miss slider and fastball offer a floor of a reliever. If he can improve his changeup, he could be an innings-eating No. 4 starter. He'll likely open 2018 at Double-A Portland, but his ability to attack the strike zone with his pitch mix could allow him to move up during the season.

BA GRADE

50 **Risk:** High

FB: 55. SL: 60.
CHG: 45.
ARM: 50.

Year	Club (League)	Class	W	L	ERA	G	GS	CG	SV	IP	H	HR	BB	SO	K/9	WHIP	AVG
2016	Lowell (NYP)	SS	0	1	2.87	6	6	0	0	16	15	0	7	22	12.6	1.40	.254
2017	Greenville (SAL)	LoA	3	2	3.88	10	10	0	0	53	44	5	13	78	13.2	1.07	.222
	Salem (CAR)	HiA	5	5	3.76	16	16	0	0	81	71	10	35	91	10.1	1.30	.232
Minor League Totals			8	8	3.71	32	32	0	0	150	130	15	55	191	11.4	1.23	.231

9 ALEX SCHERFF, RHP

Born: Feb. 5, 1998. **B-T:** B-R. **Ht.:** 6-3. **Wt.:** 205. **Drafted:** HS—Colleyville, Texas, 2017 (5th round). **Signed by:** Brandon Agamennone.

A few years ago, Scherff was one of the hardest-throwing pitchers in the sophomore class as he could already get to 92-93 mph. But Scherff admits he wasn't mature enough to yet understand the work involved in keeping that velocity. He gained weight as the summer wore on and he wore down, losing 5-6 mph off his fastball. Scherff learned from the experience, upper his workout regime, dropped 40 pounds of bad weight, regained his velocity and turned himself into one of the better arms in the 2017 draft class.

MIKE JANES

BA GRADE

55 **Risk:** Extreme

FB: 60. CB: 45.
CHG: 60.
CTL: 45.

Scherff claimed Gatorade Texas player of the year honors in 2017 after going 8-0, 0.44 and striking out 89 in 48 innings as a senior at Colleyville (Texas) Heritage. His performance made him a consideration for the Red Sox with their first-round pick. While signability concerns pushed him into the fifth round, he passed on a scholarship at Texas A&M to sign for $700,000. He didn't pitch after signing, but the Red Sox said that he was healthy but with a heavy spring workload they kept him out of any official outings. Scherff, a former linebacker in football, has a number of delivery traits—size, strength, athleticism, repeatability—that suggest starter potential, and his command of a low- to mid-90s fastball that tops out around 97 mph is unusual for a high school pitcher. He shows some late fade on his changeup, which could become a swing-and-miss weapon. His curveball is inconsistent but flashes the potential to be a decent third pitch. That arsenal gives Scherff a chance to start, though his ability to generate tremendous arm speed from a relatively upright/low-extension delivery might eventually push him to the bullpen.

Scherff will have an opportunity to open at low Class A Greenville in 2018. If he solidifies a three-pitch mix anchored by an elite fastball, he has the ceiling of a No. 3 starter, though it's also easy to imagine him complementing his fastball with one swing-and-miss secondary option as a reliever, with a fallback option of two-pitch, late-game reliever.

Year	Club (League)	Class	W	L	ERA	G	GS	CG	SV	IP	H	HR	BB	SO	K/9	WHIP	AVG
2017	Did not play																

10 MARCO HERNANDEZ, SS/2B

Born: Sept. 6, 1992. **B-T:** L-R. **Ht.:** 6-0. **Wt.:** 170. **Signed:** Dominican Republic, 2009. **Signed by:** Jose Serra/Jose Estevez (Cubs).

Acquired from the Cubs for Felix Doubront in 2014, Hernandez stood out at times in 2015 and 2016 for the electricity of his tools. He opened 2017 in the big leagues as a utility infielder, though when given a chance to take over at third base, he struggled defensively while providing only modest offense.

Hernandez dealt with ongoing left shoulder subluxations that required season-ending surgery. Hernandez's quick-twitch athleticism and strong wrists help generate bat speed and frequent firm contact. His extremely aggressive approach and flat-plane swing limit his power and mean that much of his offensive value is built around his batting average and above-average speed–and on the latter front, his stolen-base figures don't align with his raw speed. Defensively, he's shown the potential for average to above-average defense at second base and playable defense at shortstop, though a player who struggles with his game clock he has yet to look comfortable at third base.

Hernandez's recovery from shoulder surgery serves as a wild card for 2018. With Dustin Pedroia out for at least the first two months of 2018, Hernandez will have a chance to claim playing time at second base. He has a chance to be a second-division starter at the position or a lefthanded-hitting utility infielder.

BA GRADE
45 Risk: Medium
HIT: 50. POW: 40.
SPD: 60. FLD: 50.
ARM: 50.

Year	Club (League)	Class	AVG	G	AB	R	H	2B	3B	HR	RBI	BB	SO	SB	CS	OBP	SLG
2015	Portland (EL)	AA	.326	68	282	30	92	21	4	5	31	9	49	4	2	.349	.482
	Pawtucket (IL)	AAA	.271	46	181	27	49	9	2	4	22	8	39	1	0	.300	.409
2016	Pawtucket (IL)	AAA	.309	57	223	26	69	7	4	5	29	12	51	4	2	.343	.444
	Boston (AL)	MAJ	.294	40	51	11	15	1	0	1	5	5	10	1	0	.357	.373
2017	Boston (AL)	MAJ	.276	21	58	7	16	3	0	0	2	1	15	0	1	.300	.328
Major League Totals			.284	61	109	18	31	4	0	1	7	6	25	1	1	.328	.349
Minor League Totals			.283	634	2435	316	688	118	33	31	284	131	433	93	42	.320	.396

11 JALEN BEEKS, LHP

BA GRADE
45 Risk: Medium

Born: July 10, 1993. **B-T:** L-L. **Ht.:** 5-11. **Wt.:** 195. **Drafted:** Arkansas, 2014 (12th round). **Signed by:** Chris Mears.

In his first two full pro seasons, Beeks flashed interesting components but did so in inconsistent fashion.

In 2017, however, he regained the impressive depth to his changeup that he showed in Greenville in 2015 while developing a cutter that he could use to get on the hands of righties, thus opening up the plate for a two-plane, low-90s fastball and an average curveball in a campaign that altered the view of his abilities. In his third straight season of making all 26 of his starts, Beeks saw his strikeout rate jump to 25.6 percent while seeing a healthy uptick in his groundball rate—a noteworthy development given concerns that as a shorter pitcher, he could be susceptible to fly balls and homers based on the plane of his pitches.

Beeks' four-pitch mix of solid average to slightly above-average pitches coupled with a high mound IQ and impressive competitiveness suggest a pitcher with a chance to contribute as a spot starter in 2018 with a chance to emerge as a solid No. 5 starter.

Year	Club (League)	Class	W	L	ERA	G	GS	CG	SV	IP	H	HR	BB	SO	K/9	WHIP	AVG
2015	Greenville (SAL)	LoA	9	7	4.32	26	26	0	0	146	156	17	28	100	6.2	1.26	.272
2016	Salem (CAR)	HiA	4	4	3.07	13	13	1	0	67	67	9	24	55	7.4	1.35	.259
	Portland (EL)	AA	5	4	4.68	13	13	0	0	65	72	6	28	56	7.7	1.53	.283
2017	Portland (EL)	AA	5	1	2.19	9	9	1	0	49	35	3	22	58	10.6	1.16	.199
	Pawtucket (IL)	AAA	6	7	3.86	17	17	0	0	96	86	10	33	97	9.1	1.24	.236
Minor League Totals			29	23	3.78	80	78	2	0	428	419	45	135	374	7.9	1.29	.255

12 JOSH OCKIMEY, 1B

BA GRADE
50 Risk: High

Born: Oct. 18, 1995. **B-T:** L-L. **Ht.:** 6-1. **Wt.:** 215. **Drafted:** HS—Philadelphia, 2014 (5th round). **Signed by:** Chris Calciano.

Ockimey continued to show impressive pole-to-pole raw power along with advanced plate discipline (his 83 walks ranked ninth in the minors) while posting a .274/.385/.436 line with 14 homers for high Class A Salem and Double-A Portland.

Ockimey features an open stance with little shorter stride and reduced lower body movement, instead relying on his hands and impressive core and upper body strength to drive the ball. It's an approach that also comes with plenty of swing-and-miss (he struck out in 26.1 percent of plate appearances) and raises questions about whether he'll be a low-average, three-true-outcomes hitter. Evaluators are split on whether he'll continue to make sufficient defensive improvements to stay at first base or if he'll need to DH.

There's also a concern among some that Ockimey might only be a platoon player. Still, there's enough power in the bat to give him opportunities, and his work ethic and makeup suggest that he'll maximize his talents.

Ockimey should return to Double-A to begin 2018, with a chance to move to Triple-A in the second half. If he succeeds at the upper levels, he'll do quite a bit toward improving his stock.

Year	Club (League)	Class	AVG	G	AB	R	H	2B	3B	HR	RBI	BB	SO	SB	CS	OBP	SLG
2015	Lowell (NYP)	SS	.266	56	199	30	53	13	3	4	38	25	78	2	2	.349	.422
2016	Greenville (SAL)	LoA	.226	117	407	60	92	25	1	18	62	88	129	3	1	.367	.425
2017	Salem (CAR)	HiA	.275	100	349	56	96	20	2	11	63	66	110	1	4	.388	.438
	Portland (EL)	AA	.272	31	103	12	28	7	0	3	11	17	33	0	0	.372	.427
Minor League Totals			.248	340	1170	175	290	68	7	36	184	210	387	7	7	.364	.410

13 JAKE THOMPSON, RHP

BA GRADE
50 Risk: High

Born: Sept. 22, 1994. **B-T:** R-R. **Ht.:** 6-1. **Wt.:** 200. **Drafted:** Oregon State, 2017 (4th round). **Signed by:** Justin Horowitz.

Thompson was one of the top college performers of 2017, going 14-1, 1.96 at Oregon State. However, his sinker/slider combination (which gained deception thanks to some herky-jerky funk in his delivery) seemed solid, perhaps the stuff of a depth starter or middle reliever.

Yet when Thompson joined the Sox, he informed team officials that he had a curveball and a changeup that he'd rarely used in college, and he also proved amenable to shifting to a four-seamer that topped out at 96 mph in seven outings of two or fewer innings with short-season Lowell in his pro debut. One Sox official after another who saw Thompson emerged raving about an explosive fastball he used to fill up the zone, accompanied by an ability to spin a slider, get action on his changeup, and mix in some solid curveballs.

In a brief glimpse, the Sox are hopeful that they may have found a sleeper with No. 4 or 5 potential. If Thompson doesn't stick in that role, his fastball and slider have late-innings potential. He'll get his first chance at full-season ball in 2018, likely with a trip to low Class A Greenville.

Year	Club (League)	Class	W	L	ERA	G	GS	CG	SV	IP	H	HR	BB	SO	K/9	WHIP	AVG
2017	Lowell (NYP)	SS	0	3	3.18	7	7	0	0	11	10	0	6	11	8.7	1.41	.238
Minor League Totals			0	3	3.18	7	7	0	0	11	10	0	6	11	8.7	1.41	.238

14 DANNY DIAZ, 3B

BA GRADE
55 Risk: Extreme

Born: Jan. 2, 2001. **B-T:** R-R. **Ht.:** 6-3. **Wt.:** 200. **Signed:** Venezuela, 2017. **Signed by:** Ernesto Gomez/Eddie Romero.

There's plenty of risk associated with a player who has yet to play an official game of pro ball, but Diaz showed tremendous size and strength as a 16-year-old July 2 signee by the Red Sox.

As an amateur, he was lauded as one of the best hitters in the class and ranked as the No. 7 international prospect in the 2017 class. While he's demonstrated standout power that runs from the left-field line to right-center, the Sox also saw an impressive feel to hit and an ability to impact the ball while generating loft. Diaz has above-average raw power and projects to have 60-grade raw poweronce he's fully developed. He gets in trouble when he hunts for home runs and lets his swing get long. Though scouted as a shortstop, the Sox moved Diaz to third once he entered their system, and the Red Sox believe he has the glove and the plus arm to make the hot corner his long-term home.

If that isn't the case, Diaz could move over to first base and have his bat profile at the position. He's posted average run times as an amateur, but could slow down as he gets older.

Year	Club (League)	Class	AVG	G	AB	R	H	2B	3B	HR	RBI	BB	SO	SB	CS	OBP	SLG
2017	Did not play—Signed 2018 contract																

15 ROLDANI BALDWIN, C

BA GRADE
50 Risk: High

Born: March 16, 1996. **B-T:** R-R. **Ht.:** 5-11. **Wt.:** 175. **Signed:** Dominican Republic, 2013. **Signed by:** Manny Nanita/Eddie Romero.

After he shuttled between catcher and third base in his early pro career, Baldwin flourished in his first everyday opportunity as a catcher in 2017. He performed solidly on offense with 14 home runs in 95 games, and scouts see a line-drive hitter who combines a slightly lofted bat path with a strong, powerful frame.

Baldwin does need to work to increase his 4.8 percent walk rate, though. Although he threw out 33 percent (41 of 124) of runners trying to steal, evaluators see a catcher with suspect footwork and inconsistent throws. Sometimes that footwork would lead to throws in the dirt before reaching the bag, while others would sail into center field. He needs work as a receiver, too. He stabs at balls when trying to frame and lets them travel too deep in the zone. Scouts also noticed that he had particular trouble handling sinkers to his gloveside.

Baldwin's future may be as a catcher/corner infielder, but given the lack of quality catching prospects in the minors, it would be smart for the Red Sox to continue giving him chances to stay behind the plate. Baldwin will likely head to high Class A Salem in 2018.

Year	Club (League)	Class	AVG	G	AB	R	H	2B	3B	HR	RBI	BB	SO	SB	CS	OBP	SLG
2015	Red Sox (GCL)	R	.288	47	156	18	45	8	0	3	25	14	19	1	1	.362	.397
	Lowell (NYP)	SS	.286	3	7	0	2	1	0	0	0	0	1	0	0	.286	.429
2016	Lowell (NYP)	SS	.305	25	95	10	29	8	1	0	14	6	21	0	0	.358	.442
	Greenville (SAL)	LoA	.249	61	225	26	56	12	0	3	23	9	57	1	1	.282	.342
2017	Greenville (SAL)	LoA	.274	95	368	45	101	35	1	14	66	19	73	1	0	.310	.489
Minor League Totals			.273	296	1093	135	298	74	5	25	170	75	212	6	3	.328	.418

16 BOBBY DALBEC, 3B

BA GRADE
50 Risk: High

Born: June 29, 1995. **B-T:** R-R. **Ht.:** 6-4. **Wt.:** 225. **Drafted:** Arizona, 2016 (4th round). **Signed by:** Vaughn Williams.

Though Dalbec propelled Arizona to the brink of a championship with his work on the mound in the 2016 College World Series, he remained resolute in his preference to pursue a career as a position player.

Dalbec made a spectacular short-season debut with Lowell that year, showing immense power and a better-than-expected offensive approach while hitting .386/.427/.674. But in 2017, a difficult start was quickly compounded by wrist soreness and a broken hamate, the latter of which required surgery. While injuries played a role in some of his approach challenges, Dalbec endured extreme difficulties making contact, striking out in a shocking 37.4 percent of plate appearances with low Class A Greenville while hitting .246/.345/.427. There were particular concerns about his inability to recognize breaking balls and a tendency to swing through hittable fastballs in the strike zone.

Those woes were sufficient to have some evaluators writing off Dalbec, but others remained convinced that injuries rendered the 2017 season insufficient to overlook Dalbec's top-of-the-charts raw power and potentially strong third base defense. He represents as much of a boom-or-bust prospect as the Red Sox have.

Year	Club (League)	Class	AVG	G	AB	R	H	2B	3B	HR	RBI	BB	SO	SB	CS	OBP	SLG
2016	Lowell (NYP)	SS	.386	34	132	25	51	13	2	7	33	9	33	2	2	.427	.674
2017	Red Sox (GCL)	R	.259	7	27	3	7	1	0	0	2	5	9	1	0	.375	.296
	Greenville (SAL)	LoA	.246	78	284	48	70	15	0	13	39	36	123	4	5	.345	.437
Minor League Totals			.289	119	443	76	128	29	2	20	74	50	165	7	7	.370	.499

17 ANTONI FLORES, SS

BA GRADE
55 Risk: Extreme

Born: Oct. 14, 2000. **B-T:** R-R. **Ht.:** 6-1. **Wt.:** 160. **Signed:** Venezuela, 2017. **Signed by:** Angel Escobar/Eddie Romero.

The Red Sox signed Flores for $1.4 million based on a diverse complement of tools, including a shortstop's athleticism and arm strength and an advanced feel to hit with potential doubles power. He's also been praised in the past for his knowledge of the game, which is advanced for a player his age.

Flores has a skinny frame now, but there's plenty of room for projection still. Some liken the wiry shortstop to a young Alcides Escobar, identifying a player whose future will be on the left side of the infield with enough offensive potential to give him a chance many years down the road of emerging as an everyday option. One minor ding scouts found was with Flores' throwing arm. Its overall strength was solid-average, but he tended to throw from a lower, less accurate slot.

The lack of power or elite speed limits Flores' upside, but his feel for the game gives him the potential to make the most of the tools that he does have and to emerge as a big league regular.

Year	Club (League)	Class	AVG	G	AB	R	H	2B	3B	HR	RBI	BB	SO	SB	CS	OBP	SLG
2017	Did not play—Signed 2018 contract																

18 BRETT NETZER, 2B

BA GRADE
50 Risk: High

Born: June 4, 1996. **B-T:** L-R. **Ht.:** 6-0. **Wt.:** 195. **Drafted:** Charlotte, 2017 (3rd round). **Signed by:** Pat Portugal.

Netzer showed a consistently sound offensive approach at Charlotte, posting a .342/.425/.509 line with more walks (29) than strikeouts (27) as a junior. He also got a bit of a boost from a pair of strong summers—first in the Ripken League in 2015 where he ranked as the No. 8 prospect, then in 2016 in the Cape Cod League.

Netzer makes steady, hard contact while controlling the strike zone, a combination that has tended to yield some undervalued college players in the draft. His hit tool is his calling card because of a strong knowledge of the strike zone and above-average bat speed. He projects to have gap power, or perhaps a tick better. Still, a hitter who seemingly represents a quality eight-hole option with a chance to move rapidly up the ladder stands out in a system that is short on middle-of-the-field players. He played to those expectations in his first pro summer, hitting .317/.376/.390 with short-season Lowell before moving up to low Class A Greenville, where he performed modestly in the final month of the regular season. His defense is closer to average or a tick below.

Netzer should return to Greenville to start the year with a chance to finish at high Class A Salem.

Year	Club (League)	Class	AVG	G	AB	R	H	2B	3B	HR	RBI	BB	SO	SB	CS	OBP	SLG
2017	Lowell (NYP)	SS	.317	22	82	11	26	6	0	0	14	9	20	0	3	.376	.390
	Greenville (SAL)	LoA	.260	26	100	15	26	4	0	0	13	9	24	5	1	.327	.300
Minor League Totals			.286	48	182	26	52	10	0	0	27	18	44	5	4	.350	.341

19 AUSTIN MADDOX, RHP

BA GRADE
45 Risk: Medium

Born: May 13, 1991. **B-T:** R-R. **Ht.:** 6-2. **Wt.:** 220. **Drafted:** Florida, 2012 (3rd round). **Signed by:** Anthony Turco.

Maddox endured an undistinguished first few years in the Red Sox's system, a period in which he didn't move beyond Class A while struggling on the field and missing time due to off-field issues.

But starting in 2016, Maddox's velocity—roughly 91-92 mph at the beginning of 2016—started to creep up, and he impressed as a non-roster invitee in spring training, becoming one of the final cups of camp. When he finally got his big league opportunity, he was determined to take advantage of it, attacking the strike zone with a four-seam fastball that sat at 93-96 mph with sink and tail, an offering he complemented with a changeup that showed enough depth to create an effective north-south mix against big league hitters. He also features an occasional slider that scouts think could be average in the future. The mix was enough to earn Maddox a surprise spot on Boston's playoff roster.

Maddox lacks a true plus out pitch that would give him a clear path to a setup role, but he showed the ability to be a useful big league bullpen piece in 2018 on the strength of his fastball.

Year	Club (League)	Class	W	L	ERA	G	GS	CG	SV	IP	H	HR	BB	SO	K/9	WHIP	AVG
2015	Salem (CAR)	HiA	1	4	3.71	20	0	0	10	27	24	2	5	22	7.4	1.09	.238
2016	Salem (CAR)	HiA	2	0	3.33	13	0	0	5	24	29	0	8	24	8.9	1.52	.290
	Portland (EL)	AA	2	3	3.96	23	2	0	0	39	29	3	16	38	8.8	1.16	.207
	Pawtucket (IL)	AAA	1	0	1.93	3	0	0	0	5	4	1	1	2	3.9	1.07	.222
2017	Portland (EL)	AA	0	1	1.35	10	0	0	2	13	9	0	5	8	5.4	1.05	.205
	Pawtucket (IL)	AAA	2	2	3.50	27	0	0	6	36	22	2	21	38	9.5	1.19	.176
	Boston (AL)	MAJ	0	0	0.52	13	0	0	0	17	13	1	2	14	7.3	0.87	.200
Major League Totals			0	0	0.52	13	0	0	0	17	13	1	2	14	7.3	0.87	.200
Minor League Totals			13	18	4.27	143	13	0	25	261	252	26	83	227	7.8	1.28	.250

20 HECTOR VELAZQUEZ, RHP

BA GRADE
40 Risk: Medium

Born: Nov. 26, 1988. **B-T:** R-R. **Ht.:** 6-0. **Wt.:** 180. **Signed:** Mexico, 2017. **Signed by:** Allard Baird/Jared Banner.

Velazquez represented a considerable success in the Sox's concerted effort to expand their scouting efforts in the Mexican League—the cost of acquiring prospects is less expensive for international slot bonus purposes because only the amount paid to the player counts toward the bonus slots, while the amount paid to the team does not. The Sox acquired Velazquez's rights from Campeche after a 2016 season that saw him win the league's pitcher of the year honors for the second time in his career, believing he could emerge as a solid rotation depth option despite a lack of knockout stuff.

Velazquez did just that, carving both sides of the strike zone with a sinking fastball that sat at 90 mph and topped out at 94, while mixing in enough split-changeups and sliders to stay off the barrels of hitters in both Triple-A and the big leagues. He also mixed in a cut fastball in the high-80s that scouts believe could be a tick above-average at its best. Velazquez has shown enough of a feel for pitching, command, deception, and guts to look like a solid depth starter who could emerge as No. 5 starter on some teams.

Velazquez is likely to return to Triple-A Pawtucket in 2018 but could make starts in the big leagues if needed.

Year	Club (League)	Class	W	L	ERA	G	GS	CG	SV	IP	H	HR	BB	SO	K/9	WHIP	AVG
2015	Campeche (MEX)	AAA	6	4	4.44	18	17	0	0	95	98	10	35	70	6.6	1.40	--
2016	Monclova (MEX)	AAA	5	1	2.47	22	22	1	0	131	115	8	16	120	8.2	1.00	--
2017	Pawtucket (IL)	AAA	8	4	2.21	19	19	0	0	102	78	7	24	79	7.0	1.00	.213
	Boston (AL)	MAJ	3	1	2.92	8	3	0	0	25	21	4	7	19	6.9	1.14	.236
Major League Totals			3	1	2.92	8	3	0	0	25	21	4	7	19	6.9	1.14	.236
Minor League Totals			51	33	3.56	155	139	2	0	789	778	74	237	607	6.9	1.29	.262

21 TZU-WEI LIN, SS/2B

BA GRADE
40 Risk: Medium

Born: Feb. 15, 1994. **B-T:** L-R. **Ht.:** 5-9. **Wt.:** 170. **Signed:** Taiwan, 2012. **Signed by:** Louie Lin/Jon Deeble/Eddie Romero.

Lin represented a player with a diverse skill set—the glove and arm to play shortstop, speed, and good bat-to-ball skills—that the Red Sox signed him out of Taiwan for a $2.05 million bonus in 2012. The on- and off-field cultural transition proved long and challenging, with Lin's offensive passivity holding back his progression through the system.

This spring, Sox officials challenged Lin to use some of the strength in his swing and to focus on hard contact even if it meant an uptick in swings and misses. The message took and set the stage for something of a revelation, with Lin earning a big league promotion after hitting .302/.379/.491 in 48 games to start the year in Double-A. He gave the Sox a midsummer spark, hitting .268/.369/.339 in 23 big league games before spending most of the season's remainder Triple-A Pawtucket.

Defensively, Lin added impressive work in centerfield to already solid defense at short, second, and third. That versatility, in combination with high contact rates, the ability to shoot gaps with his liners, and good baserunning speed suggest a player who could have a lengthy career as a valuable utility man.

Year	Club (League)	Class	AVG	G	AB	R	H	2B	3B	HR	RBI	BB	SO	SB	CS	OBP	SLG
2015	Salem (CAR)	HiA	.281	73	281	37	79	12	3	2	34	22	34	22	15	3	.331	.367
	Portland (EL)	AA	.202	46	173	21	35	5	3	0	14	16	27	8	3	.268	.266
2016	Portland (EL)	AA	.223	108	372	39	83	10	5	2	27	34	55	10	7	.287	.293
2017	Portland (EL)	AA	.302	48	159	31	48	9	3	5	19	20	27	8	2	.379	.491
	Pawtucket (IL)	AAA	.227	35	141	12	32	5	1	2	9	11	28	2	4	.283	.319
	Boston (AL)	MAJ	.268	25	56	7	15	0	2	0	2	9	17	1	1	.369	.339
Major League Totals			.268	25	56	7	15	0	2	0	2	9	17	1	1	.369	.339
Minor League Totals			.240	501	1868	250	449	77	19	13	181	201	330	69	32	.312	.323

22 TRAVIS LAKINS, RHP

BA GRADE
45 Risk: High

Born: June 29, 1994. **B-T:** R-R. **Ht.:** 6-1. **Wt.:** 180. **Drafted:** Ohio State, 2015 (6th round). **Signed by:** John Pyle.

After his 2016 season with high Class A Salem was halted by a stress fracture in his right elbow tip, Lakins returned to the Carolina League to open 2017 and looked as impressive as any pitcher in the Red Sox system.

Lakins improved his strike-throwing by moving from the first- to the third-base side of the rubber, and a tightened his slider into a swing-and-miss pitch that complemented a mid-90s fastball and a potentially above-average curveball and changeup. But after Lakins went 5-0 with a 2.61 ERA and 27.7 percent strikeout rate in seven starts in Salem, his season ground to a halt following a promotion to Double-A, where he went 0-4, 6.23 with a 13.8 percent strikeout rate in eight starts before getting shut down with a recurrence of his elbow stress fracture. Scouts also noted that Lakins needs to focus on keeping the ball down in the zone.

At his best, Lakins' four-pitch arsenal continues to show mid-rotation potential, and the Sox plan to continue his development as a starter, but some evaluators wonder whether narrowing his repertoire to a fastball/slider pairing as a reliever will become necessary to protect his elbow.

Year	Club (League)	Class	W	L	ERA	G	GS	CG	SV	IP	H	HR	BB	SO	K/9	WHIP	AVG
2015	Lowell (NYP)	SS	0	0	0.00	1	1	0	0	2	0	0	1	3	13.5	0.50	.000
2016	Salem (CAR)	HiA	6	3	5.93	19	18	0	0	91	111	8	36	79	7.8	1.62	.299
2017	Salem (CAR)	HiA	5	0	2.61	7	7	0	0	38	32	2	13	43	10.2	1.18	.225
	Portland (EL)	AA	0	4	6.23	8	8	0	0	30	34	2	21	19	5.6	1.81	.301
Minor League Totals			11	7	5.13	35	34	0	0	161	177	12	71	144	8.0	1.54	.280

23 BRIAN JOHNSON, LHP

BA GRADE

40 Risk: Medium

Born: Dec. 7, 1990. **B-T:** L-L. **Ht.:** 6-3. **Wt.:** 240. **Drafted:** Florida, 2012 (1st round). **Signed by:** Anthony Turco.

Once seemingly on the cusp of claiming a long-term spot in Boston's rotation, Johnson has endured a challenging three-year span in which he's been sidelined both while seeking treatment for anxiety and dealt with numerous injuries and that have led to a steady drop in his velocity and power.

A pitcher who worked at 88-92 mph in 2014, Johnson now typically sits at 87-89 mph while occasionally cracking 90-91 mph. Yet while that velocity gives him little margin for error, he understands how to mix with his fastball, still above-average to plus curveball, changeup, and slider, with pitchability that allowed the Sox to go 5-0 in his five big league spot starts in 2017. It's possible that Johnson could still see an uptick in velocity if he emphasizes explosiveness rather than a rocking-chair rhythm to his delivery, and Sox officials are hopeful that his planned exposure to the bullpen in spring training could aid that process.

Johnson's feel for pitching is good enough that even a small bump in the power of his stuff could allow him to realize his ceiling as a back-of-the-rotation starter or multi-innings reliever.

Year	Club (League)	Class	W	L	ERA	G	GS	CG	SV	IP	H	HR	BB	SO	K/9	WHIP	AVG
2015	Boston (AL)	MAJ	0	1	8.31	1	1	0	0	4	3	0	4	3	6.2	1.62	.214
	Pawtucket (IL)	AAA	9	6	2.53	18	18	1	0	96	74	6	32	90	8.4	1.10	.211
2016	Red Sox (GCL)	R	0	1	3.86	2	2	0	0	7	7	0	2	9	11.6	1.29	.259
	Lowell (NYP)	SS	0	0	0.00	2	2	0	0	11	7	0	2	11	9.0	0.82	.184
	Pawtucket (IL)	AAA	5	6	4.09	15	15	0	0	77	74	9	36	54	6.3	1.43	.258
2017	Lowell (NYP)	SS	0	0	3.38	1	1	0	0	3	2	0	2	4	13.5	1.50	.200
	Boston (AL)	MAJ	2	0	4.33	5	5	1	0	27	32	5	8	21	7.0	1.48	.283
	Pawtucket (IL)	AAA	3	4	3.09	17	17	0	0	90	82	10	28	70	7.0	1.22	.241
Major League Totals			2	1	4.88	6	6	1	0	31	35	5	12	24	6.9	1.50	.276
Minor League Totals			32	26	2.69	103	103	3	0	518	409	35	177	458	8.0	1.13	.216

24 JOAN MARTINEZ, RHP

BA GRADE

45 Risk: High

Born: Aug. 29, 1996. **B-T:** R-R. **Ht.:** 6-3. **Wt.:** 195. **Signed:** Dominican Republic, 2016. **Signed by:** Todd Claus/Michel DeJesus.

Martinez slipped through the scouting cracks, permitting the Red Sox to sign the wiry righty with intriguing arm speed to a bonus of just $5,000 as a 19-year-old in early 2016.

Martinez has done nothing but dominate while moving through the system in a late-innings role, combining standout velocity (96-98 mph) with a slider that was inconsistent but had moments that it could be evaluated as a potential plus pitch with plenty of refinement. Martinez forged a 1.11 ERA in 32.1 innings split between short-season Lowell and low Class A Greenville in 2017. He hasn't struck out as many batters (24.8 percent in 2017) as might be expected from the power of his fastball, but the arm-side action on the pitch has kept it off barrels and allowed him to pitch in to righthanders, making him a very uncomfortable at-bat. A number of mechanical improvements would also help Martinez's stock. Namely, he needs to add deception to his delivery, work to get over his front side more often and stay on line toward home plate.

If he can accomplish that, Martinez has back-end potential with a chance to move quickly as a strike-thrower on a straight relief track.

Year	Club (League)	Class	W	L	ERA	G	GS	CG	SV	IP	H	HR	BB	SO	K/9	WHIP	AVG
2016	Red Sox2 (DSL)	R	1	2	1.88	18	0	0	9	29	17	1	8	26	8.2	0.87	.175
2017	Lowell (NYP)	SS	0	2	1.56	11	0	0	1	17	12	0	4	13	6.8	0.92	.197
	Greenville (SAL)	LoA	1	0	0.60	8	0	0	1	15	7	0	5	18	10.8	0.80	.137
Minor League Totals			2	4	1.48	37	0	0	11	61	36	1	17	57	8.4	0.87	.172

25 CHAD DE LA GUERRA, SS/2B

BA GRADE

40 Risk: Medium

Born: Nov. 24, 1992. **B-T:** L-R. **Ht.:** 5-11. **Wt.:** 190. **Drafted:** Grand Canyon (Ariz.), 2015 (17th round). **Signed by:** Vaughn Williams.

De La Guerra immediately showed a surprising ability to hit after entering the Red Sox's system following a four-year college career, but with questions about whether he had the defensive ability to move up the ladder as a solid utility option.

In 2017, however, De La Guerra held his own in the field while playing mostly shortstop, and he showed likewise solid offensive ability at both high Class A and Double-A, posting a combined .283/.361/.437 line with 43 extra-base hits. One evaluator referred to him as an "intangibles giant" whose instincts permit him to play at a level beyond his tools. While second base is his best position, he now profiles as a reliable utility option who can play at shortstop or third base as well with more bat than is typically found in that role.

The Red Sox sent De La Guerra to the Arizona Fall League at season's end, and he saw time at mostly second and third base with one game of shortstop mixed in as well. He's not far from big league ready.

Year	Club (League)	Class	AVG	G	AB	R	H	2B	3B	HR	RBI	BB	SO	SB	CS	OBP	SLG
2015	Lowell (NYP)	SS	.265	58	223	28	59	14	3	2	29	21	46	4	3	.321	.381
2016	Greenville (SAL)	LoA	.250	66	240	40	60	8	4	1	20	31	57	7	2	.336	.329
2017	Salem (CAR)	HiA	.292	58	219	47	64	16	3	5	36	24	40	5	2	.364	.461
	Portland (EL)	AA	.270	52	196	34	53	15	0	4	23	23	48	2	1	.353	.408
Minor League Totals			.269	234	878	149	236	53	10	12	108	99	191	18	8	.343	.393

26 C.J. CHATHAM, SS

| BA GRADE |
| 50 Risk: Extreme |

Born: Dec. 22, 1994. **B-T:** R-R. **Ht.:** 6-4. **Wt.:** 185. **Drafted:** Florida Atlantic, 2016 (2nd round). **Signed by:** Willie Romay.

The Sox took Chatham out of Florida Atlantic as arguably the top college shortstop prospect in the 2016 draft and signed him to a slightly underslot bonus of $1.1 million. He's a player with the glove and arm for the position along with the power to elicit J.J. Hardy comps.

Chatham showed that power in his junior season with FAU when he led Conference USA with a 1.017 OPS. But near the end of spring training in 2017, Chatham felt a pop in his hamstring that required six weeks of rehab. When he finally got to low Class A Greenville, he re-aggravated the hamstring injury in his first game, essentially wiping out his first full pro season. This comes after he played through a bone chip in his right wrist during his draft year. Because he's so tall and rangy, there were questions coming out of the draft about whether he'd be able to stick at shortstop in the long-term.

Chatham's bat speed and defense suggest a player with the tools to profile as an everyday shortstop—particularly if the all-fields approach that he showed in spring training is sustainable—but it's hard to anticipate how he'll be impacted by the lost year of player development.

Year	Club (League)	Class	AVG	G	AB	R	H	2B	3B	HR	RBI	BB	SO	SB	CS	OBP	SLG
2016	Red Sox (GCL)	R	.167	8	24	2	4	2	0	1	2	0	7	0	0	.200	.375
	Lowell (NYP)	SS	.259	27	108	19	28	4	1	4	19	8	20	0	1	.319	.426
2017	Greenville (SAL)	LoA	.333	1	3	0	1	0	0	0	2	0	0	0	1	.333	.333
	Red Sox (GCL)	R	.313	6	16	5	5	0	0	1	3	2	1	0	0	.389	.500
Minor League Totals			.252	42	151	26	38	6	1	6	26	10	28	0	2	.309	.424

27 WILLIAMS JEREZ, LHP

| BA GRADE |
| 40 Risk: Medium |

Born: May 16, 1992. **B-T:** B-L. **Ht.:** 6-4. **Wt.:** 190. **Drafted:** HS—Brooklyn, 2011 (2nd round). **Signed by:** Ray Fagnant.

As a converted outfielder who is now four years into his career as a pitcher, it's not surprising to see Jerez continuing to develop as he moves through the upper levels. The 2017 season represented a sizable step forward for the lefthanded reliever.

Jerez has a heavy four-seam fastball that sits at 93-96 mph and a slider in the mid-to-high-80s that helped him hold lefties to a .182/.264/.221 with a 26.1 percent strikeout rate. He also developed a splitter this year that gave him a pitch that got righthanders off his fastball and helped him excel over a nearly two-month midsummer stretch in Portland and pave the way for both a season-ending promotion to Triple-A and a return to the Red Sox's 40-man roster. The final step for Jerez is to drive his pitches down in the zone consistently and work to not get his delivery out of sync to the point that he yanks his fastball out of the zone.

At the least, Jerez appears to have a good shot at emerging as a power left-on-left option, and if he can gain greater consistency with the splitter, he could emerge as a solid middle-innings contributor.

Year	Club (League)	Class	W	L	ERA	G	GS	CG	SV	IP	H	HR	BB	SO	K/9	WHIP	AVG
2015	Greenville (SAL)	LoA	3	1	2.06	14	0	0	3	39	43	3	10	43	9.8	1.35	.279
	Salem (CAR)	HiA	1	0	0.73	5	0	0	0	12	11	0	4	12	8.8	1.22	.234
	Portland (EL)	AA	1	2	3.65	22	0	0	1	37	34	2	17	31	7.5	1.38	.245
2016	Portland (EL)	AA	1	6	4.71	40	0	0	0	65	70	6	30	65	9.0	1.54	.282
2017	Portland (EL)	AA	2	0	3.33	29	0	0	4	51	50	3	17	47	8.2	1.31	.258
	Pawtucket (IL)	AAA	0	2	3.75	9	0	0	0	12	9	3	6	10	7.5	1.25	.209
Minor League Totals			12	13	3.37	133	0	0	9	251	250	17	95	248	8.9	1.37	.261

28 TYLER ESPLIN, OF

Born: July 6, 1999. **B-T:** L-R. **Ht.:** 6-4. **Wt.:** 225. **Drafted:** HS—Bradenton, Fla., 2017 (7th round). **Signed by:** Stephen Hargett.

BA GRADE

45 Risk: High

The Red Sox found Esplin at the prestigious IMG Academy in Bradenton, Fla., and liked his line-drive stroke and present strength and power. That was enough to take him in the seventh round.

Though Esplin features unusual size for a high schooler, the Sox were taken with the fact that despite standing at 6-foot-4, Esplin demonstrated balance at the plate, athleticism, excellent makeup, and an understanding of how to drive the ball in the air to all fields. In a pre-draft workout, Esplin showed the ability to clear the 40-foot left-field wall at the Red Sox's spring training facility, an almost unheard-of feat for a big league left-handed hitter, let alone a high schooler. Esplin didn't turn 18 until just after he'd started pro ball, suggesting plenty of time and room for development to build upon a promising debut in the Rookie-level Gulf Coast League. His hitting ability and projectable power give him a chance to rise rapidly in these rankings.

Esplin split his time between right and left field as a pro and projects as an average defender with an average arm. He's an average runner as well. His next stop should be low Class A Greenville.

Year	Club (League)	Class	AVG	G	AB	R	H	2B	3B	HR	RBI	BB	SO	SB	CS	OBP	SLG
2017	Red Sox (GCL)	R	.271	22	85	16	23	4	0	2	11	7	26	1	0	.340	.388
Minor League Totals			.271	22	85	16	23	4	0	2	11	7	26	1	0	.340	.388

29 RONIEL RAUDES, RHP

Born: Jan. 16, 1998. **B-T:** R-R. **Ht.:** 6-1. **Wt.:** 160. **Signed:** Nicaragua, 2014. **Signed by:** Eddie Romero/Rafael Mendoza.

BA GRADE

45 Risk: High

One year after Raudes excelled as a pitchability starter in low Class A Greenville at 18, the righthander failed to carry his performance forward to high Class A, going 4-7, 4.50 with a declining strikeout rate and a walk rate that ascended by 75 percent to 3.41 per nine innings.

Still extremely skinny, Raudes' average fastball velocity sat at 90 mph and peaked at 92. He added a slider to his mix in July and showed improvement over his final 10 outings. Raudes still throws strikes with a four-pitch mix, and he creates deception with his delivery, but his stuff will need to improve for him to advance as a starter. The closest he has to a plus pitch right now is his changeup, which features both fade and sink. He'll double or triple up on the pitch and isn't afraid to throw it to either right or lefthanders. His curveball is below-average because it lacks enough depth and bite get swings and misses.

Raudes could open 2018 back at Salem or with Double-A Portland.

Year	Club (League)	Class	W	L	ERA	G	GS	CG	SV	IP	H	HR	BB	SO	K/9	WHIP	AVG
2015	Red Sox (DSL)	R	4	3	3.52	11	10	0	0	54	46	3	3	63	10.6	0.91	.228
	Red Sox (GCL)	R	3	0	0.90	4	4	0	0	20	13	0	6	16	7.2	0.95	.191
2016	Greenville (SAL)	LoA	11	6	3.65	24	24	0	0	113	112	8	23	104	8.3	1.19	.260
2017	Salem (CAR)	HiA	4	7	4.50	23	23	0	0	116	134	14	44	95	7.4	1.53	.297
Minor League Totals			22	16	3.77	62	61	0	0	303	305	25	76	278	8.3	1.26	.265

30 KERVIN SUAREZ, 2B/CF

Born: Dec. 19, 1998. **B-T:** S-R. **Ht.:** 5-11. **Wt.:** 165. **Signed:** Venezuela, 2015. **Signed by:** Eddie Romero/Ernesto Gomez.

BA GRADE

45 Risk: High

Suarez stands out as arguably the best athlete in the Red Sox system, a player who one evaluator described as looking like a defensive back with plenty of quick-twitch and fluidity in his overall game.

Suarez started switch-hitting after entering the Sox's system, showing some intriguing pop from the left side while displaying greater refinement as a righthanded hitter (.322/.369/.407 in the GCL in 2017). Both of his swings have average or better bat speed with smoothness and rhythm. He's got average hands and range, which means he's probably more suited to second base than shortstop. His average speed with controlled aggression on the basepaths showed up in games, as he went 11-for-12 in stolen base attempts last year, adding to the impressions of a player who, though raw, has the diverse skill set to emerge as an everyday center fielder.

No matter where he plays, the next step is either at low Class A Greenville or a return to short-season Lowell after extended spring training.

Year	Club (League)	Class	AVG	G	AB	R	H	2B	3B	HR	RBI	BB	SO	SB	CS	OBP	SLG
2016	Red Sox (DSL)	R	.274	66	259	40	71	11	3	1	25	21	58	18	7	.345	.351
2017	Red Sox (GCL)	R	.274	47	190	33	52	9	1	2	13	17	47	11	1	.335	.363
	Lowell (NYP)	SS	.250	3	8	1	2	0	0	0	0	2	2	0	0	.400	.250
Minor League Totals			.274	116	457	74	125	20	4	3	38	40	107	29	8	.342	.354

Chicago Cubs

BY JOHN MANUEL

O nce upon a time, the 2017 season would have been good enough for most Cubs fans.

A 92-win season resulted in a second consecutive National League Central division title and third straight appearance in the NL Championship Series. Third baseman Kris Bryant and first baseman Anthony Rizzo turned in MVP-contending seasons as the Cubs made the playoffs for the third straight season. Only the 1906-08 Cubs have matched that in franchise history.

And yet, after winning the World Series in 2016 for the first time since 1908, the 2017 Cubs felt like a sequel that wasn't as fulfilling as the original, a "Temple Of Doom" to the "Raiders Of The Lost Ark." It wasn't as good, and it wasn't as fun.

The Cubs handled the doomed Nationals in a grueling five-game Division Series, but they were no match for the Dodgers in the NLCS, winning only once before Los Angeles wrapped up the series. The Cubs won 11 fewer games than the previous season, mostly thanks to a listless first half that finished with a 43-45 record, and they didn't put away the pesky Brewers—who swept them in a three-game September series in Wrigley Field—until a seven-game win streak that immediately followed the sweep.

Most organization still envy the Cubs' position depth. Their young position player core, for the most part, improved in 2017, with Javier Baez, rookies Albert Almora and Ian Happ and especially catcher Willson Contreras—all 25 or under at the start of the season—emerging as strong complements to Bryant and Rizzo, if not potential cornerstone pieces themselves.

Bigger questions lurk on the pitching staff and on the farm. Chicago traded its top remaining prospects, outfielder Eloy Jimenez and righthander Dylan Cease, to the White Sox for lefthander Jose Quintana, who at 28 is accomplished, durable and under club control through 2020. However, closer Wade Davis and mercurial starter Jake Arrieta could both depart as free agents; 38-year-old John Lackey, second on the team in innings, was expected to retire, and Jon Lester will be 34 in 2018 and is inching past his prime.

Moreover, Chicago has yet to develop a homegrown starter since president of baseball operations Theo Epstein, general manager Jed Hoyer and assistant GM Jason McLeod arrived in 2011. Of course, the group has delivered a World Series title, but to deliver another, the Cubs will have to figure out the pitching puzzle behind Lester, Quintana, Kyle Hendricks and Mike Montgomery.

Versatile rookie Ian Happ blasted 24 home runs while starting games at five positions.

PROJECTED 2021 LINEUP

Catcher	Willson Contreras (29)
First Base	Anthony Rizzo (31)
Second Base	Javier Baez (28)
Third Base	Kris Bryant (29)
Shortstop	Addison Russell (27)
Left Field	Kyle Schwarber (28)
Center Field	Albert Almora (27)
Right Field	Ian Happ (26)
No. 1 Starter	Jose Quintana (32)
No. 2 Starter	Jon Lester (37)
No. 3 Starter	Kyle Hendricks (31)
No. 4 Starter	Adbert Alzolay (26)
No. 5 Starter	Mike Montgomery (31)
Closer	Carl Edwards (29)

To that end, scouting director Matt Dorey and international director Louie Eljajua and their staffs have been aggressive and tried to be creative to find arms for the Cubs' pitching pipeline. Righthander Adbert Alzolay took a step forward in 2017 and finished the year in Double-A, but the Cubs' highest-ceiling arms are farther away, as is most of the system's top talent.

The Cubs may not have the ammunition to pull another trade the caliber of the Quintana deal, but they have the financial wherewithal—and the creative front office juice—to keep building on the best stretch in Cubs history. Chasing the Dodgers and winning another World Series shouldn't seem like such a Last Crusade.

CHICAGO CUBS

TOP 2018 ROOKIE: Victor Caratini, C/1B. His bat and ability to fill in at the infield corners should make him a valuable reserve.

BREAKOUT PROSPECT: Bryan Hudson, LHP. Tall pitchers take longer, and the 6-foot-8 lefty showed signs he was coming around in 2017.

SLEEPER: Carlos Sepulvida, 2B. He had a rough 2017, but the Cubs like the Mexican infielder's bat.

SOURCE OF TOP 30 TALENT

Homegrown	28	Acquired	2
College	10	Trades	2
Junior college	2	Rule 5 draft	0
High school	9	Independent leagues	0
Nondrafted free agents	0	Free agents/waivers	0
International	7		

LF
Mark Zagunis (20)
Charcer Burks (24)
Chris Pieters

CF
D.J. Wilson (11)
Luis Ayala
Chris Singleton

RF
Nelson Velazquez (10)
Jonathan Sierra
Eddy Martinez

3B
Jason Vosler (25)
Wladimir Galindo
Austin Filierre

SS
Aramis Ademan (1)
Luis Vazquez
Zack Short
Rafael Nera

2B
David Bote (12)
Chesny Young
Carlos Sepulvida
Vimael Machin
Yonathan Perlaza

1B
Austin Upshaw
Yasiel Balaguert
Ian Rice
Taylor Alamo

C
Victor Caratini (4)
Miguel Amaya (22)
P.J. Higgins
Michael Cruz
Taylor Davis

LHP

LHSP	LHRP
Brendon Little (7)	Rob Zastryzny
Bryan Hudson (13)	Randy Rosario
Justin Steele (18)	Wyatt Short
Manuel Rondon	Ricky Tyler Thomas
Jose Paulino	Ryan Kellogg
Braylin Marquez	

RHP

RHSP	RHRP
Adbert Alzolay (2)	Dillon Maples (15)
Jose Albertos (3)	Duane Underwood (19)
Alex Lange (5)	Dakota Mekkes (21)
Oscar de la Cruz (6)	Michael Rucker (26)
Thomas Hatch (8)	Jake Stinnett (30)
Jen-Ho Tseng (9)	Bailey Clark
Keegan Thompson (14)	Jake Steffens
Cory Abbott (16)	Yunior Perez
Trevor Clifton (17)	
Javier Assad (23)	
Erich Uelmen (27)	
Alec Mills (28)	
Jeremiah Estrada	
Erling Moreno	
Tyson Miller	
Ben Hecht	
Duncan Robinson	

DRAFT ANALYSIS

2017

BEST PURE HITTER: Lefthanded-swinging 1B Austin Upshaw (13) has a pretty swing and a track record of hitting for average, and played to the scouting report in his debut, batting .292/.337/.407, mostly in low Class A South Bend. The 6-foot, 195-pounder can pay second and third base in addition to his primary position, which would help as he lacks profile first-base power.

BEST POWER: The Cubs hired ex-big leaguer Edwards Guzman to scout Puerto Rico in recent years to help dig deeper on the island, so they were ready when OF Nelson Velazquez (5) came on late in the spring, especially with an explosive, toolsy performance in the Excellence Games. Velazquez puts on a show in batting practice, with easy plus raw power. He hit eight homers in just 110 at-bats in the Rookie-level Arizona League.

FASTEST RUNNER: Velazquez has plus raw speed and an explosive burst. OF Chris Singleton (19) lacks the burst but is close to a 70 runner underway, most evident in center field or when going first to third.

BEST DEFENSIVE PLAYER: SS Luis Vazquez (14), another Puerto Rico find, impressed the club's coaches with his flexibility, body control and soft hands. His plus arm also shined during instructional league.

BEST ATHLETE: Velazquez needs reps to polish his skills, but his raw tools are undeniable.

BEST FASTBALL: LHP Brendon Little (1), the club's first pick, reaches 96 mph and sits 93-94 mph at his best, though he wasn't there consistently after signing. RHP Erich Uelmen (4) was more consistent after the draft, pitching at 92-93 mph and touching 95 with plus life.

BEST SECONDARY PITCH: RHP Alex Lange (1), taken three spots after Little after a 30-9, 2.91 career at LSU, has more track record and a curveball that has earned 70 grades at its best. When he lands his curveball, it opens up his entire arsenal.

BEST PRO DEBUT: 3B Austin Filiere (8), the first player from M.I.T. drafted since 2000, has power that played even at short-season Eugene, batting .261/.392/.443 with six homers. RHP Ben Hecht (12) struck out 30 in 20 innings while posting a 2.70 ERA.

MOST INTRIGUING BACKGROUND: Singleton's mother Sharonda was murdered in the Charleston church shooting in 2015, and his father died in the spring as well. His toughness and grace inspire, and the Cubs like his tools as well, though he's raw for a college position player.

CLOSEST TO THE MAJORS: Southeastern Conference RHPs Lange and Keegan Thompson (3) are the main challengers. Thompson threw a lot of breaking balls in college, like Lange, and his curve is plus, but he has a bit more feel for pitching and a true four-pitch mix.

BEST LATE-ROUND PICK: Vazquez has room to grow with the bat but his glove could be special. RHP Jake Steffens (29), a fifth-year senior out of Santa Clara, has good sink on his 93 mph fastball.

THE ONE WHO GOT AWAY: The Cubs made runs at RHP Bryce Bonnin (26), a two-way player who wound up at Arkansas, and OF Kier Meredith (28), who's now at Clemson.

—JOHN MANUEL

TOP DRAFT PICKS OF THE DECADE

Year	Player, Pos.	2017 Org
2008	Andrew Cashner, RHP	Rangers
2009	Brett Jackson, OF	Did not play
2010	Hayden Simpson, RHP	Did not play
2011	Javier Baez, SS	Cubs
2012	Albert Almora, OF	Cubs
2013	Kris Bryant, 3B	Cubs
2014	Kyle Schwarber, C	Cubs
2015	Ian Happ, OF	Cubs
2016	Thomas Hatch, RHP (3rd round)	Cubs
2017	Brendon Little, LHP	Cubs

2016

With no picks in the first two rounds, RHP Thomas Hatch (3) became the Cubs' top selection. He's off to a solid start as a pro, but Chicago doesn't yet have much else to show in a class that focused on college pitching.

GRADE: D

2015

OF Ian Happ (1) became the latest college hitter to rocket to the big leagues for the Cubs. Preps LHP Bryan Hudson (3) and OF D.J. Wilson (4) are more developmental projects and have exciting raw tools.

GRADE: B

2014

OF Kyle Schwarber (1) hit 30 homers, but was otherwise disappointing as he returned from a knee injury. OF Mark Zagunis (3) joined him in Chicago and RHP Dylan Cease (6) was a part of the trade for Jose Quintana.

GRADE: B

1 ARAMIS ADEMAN, SS

Born: Sept. 13, 1998. **B-T:** L-R. **Ht.:** 5-11. **Wt.:** 160.
Signed: Dominican Republic, 2015. **Signed by:** Jose Estevez/Gian Guzman/Jose Serra/Louie Eljaua.

BILL MITCHELL

Ademan, who played for the Dominican Republic's 15U national team in 2013, trained with Amaurys Nina, and the Cubs have had success with Nina's players before, most notably Eloy Jimenez. The Cubs traded Jimenez to the White Sox in 2017 in the Jose Quintana deal, one of many trades that thinned the farm system considerably and made room at the top for Ademan, who signed in August 2015 for $2 million. He was considered a light-hitting yet smooth infielder when he signed, but he started to change perceptions in 2017, his first year in the U.S., by skipping Rookie ball and jumping straight to short-season Eugene. The Cubs kept pushing him with a promotion to low Class A South Bend for the final 29 games of the season, where he replaced Isaac Paredes after he was traded to the Tigers. Ademan has a high-waisted, projectable frame with solid athleticism, good body control and natural feel for the game. He plays under control and has savvy for his age, which is most evident offensively. He has surprising strength in his wiry frame and can drive balls to the gaps consistently and even over the fence. He has a feel for barreling the baseball, repeats his smooth swing and has shown some selectivity as well, allowing his average power to play. He should be a steady above-average hitter. Ademan is steady at shortstop with quick feet, excellent hands and a solid-average arm. He's still a teenager who makes some mistakes on routine plays, though scouts project him as an above-average defender, if not better, with time and experience. In 2017 he made 17 errors in 67 games at shortstop, 10 of them on throws. Ademan is an average runner with times in the range of 4.2 to 4.3 seconds to first base, though he will need to be a more selective basestealer at higher levels. Ademan has a high floor as a middle infielder who can hit, and he already has hopped on the fast track by reaching full-season ball. He'll have to gain strength and improve his ability to learn which plays he can make and which he cannot to be a future regular at shortstop. He likely will continue to move quickly because the Cubs need trade chips more than they need another middle infielder. Ademan should return to South Bend to start 2018, but if he heats up before July, his name will be involved in trade talks for pitchers.

BA GRADE	SCOUTING GRADES
55 Risk: Very High	HIT: 55. POW: 50. SPD: 50. FLD: 55. ARM: 50.

Projected future grades on 20-80 scouting scale

TOP PROSPECTS OF THE DECADE

Year	Player, Pos.	2017 Org
2008	Josh Vitters, 3B	American Assoc.
2009	Josh Vitters, 3B	American Assoc.
2010	Starlin Castro, SS	Yankees
2011	Chris Archer, RHP	Rays
2012	Brett Jackson, OF	Did not play
2013	Javier Baez, SS	Cubs
2014	Javier Baez, SS	Cubs
2015	Kris Bryant, 3B	Cubs
2016	Gleyber Torres, SS	Yankees
2017	Eloy Jimenez, OF	White Sox

BEST TOOLS

Best Hitter for Average	Victor Caratini
Best Power Hitter	Nelson Velazquez
Best Strike-Zone Discipline	Mark Zagunis
Fastest Baserunner	D.J. Wilson
Best Athlete	D.J. Wilson
Best Fastball	Dillon Maples
Best Curveball	Alex Lange
Best Slider	Dillon Maples
Best Changeup	Jose Albertos
Best Control	Jen-Ho Tseng
Best Defensive Catcher	P.J. Higgins
Best Defensive Infielder	Luis Vazquez
Best Infield Arm	Luis Vazquez
Best Defensive Outfielder	D.J. Wilson
Best Outfield Arm	Eddy Martinez

Year	Club (League)	Class	AVG	G	AB	R	H	2B	3B	HR	RBI	BB	SO	SB	CS	OBP	SLG
2016	Cubs2 (DSL)	R	.254	59	209	37	53	5	4	0	16	34	28	17	9	.366	.316
2017	Eugene (NWL)	SS	.286	39	161	23	46	9	4	4	27	14	30	10	6	.365	.466
	South Bend (MWL)	LoA	.244	29	127	13	31	6	1	3	15	4	24	4	2	.269	.378
Minor League Totals			.262	127	497	73	130	20	9	7	58	52	82	31	17	.342	.380

2 ADBERT ALZOLAY, RHP

Born: March 1, 1995. **B-T:** R-R. **Ht.:** 6-1. **Wt.:** 175. **Signed:** Dominican Republic, 2012. **Signed by:** Julio Figueroa/Hector Ortega.

Alzolay signed as a 17-year-old, and he's never been a priority prospect. He had his best year by far in 2017, finishing the year at Double-A Tennessee to emerge as the Cubs' most advanced pitcher with upside.

A better fastball—up to a consistent 93-95 mph and touching 96, up from 91-92 last year—made Alzolay a better pitcher and better prospect. It started with a greater commitment to the club's throwing program, then continued with an improved delivery, drawing more power from his lower half. Alzolay always had shown the athleticism to repeat his delivery and pound the strike zone, but now he was beating hitters with his plus heater thanks to both its velocity and his in-charge, up-tempo pitching style. He locates his average low-80s curveball well enough to throw it for strikes when behind in the count, keeping hitters off his fastball. The Cubs are focused on helping his below-average changeup make progress.

The lack of a second plus pitch to go with his fastball profiles Alzolay as a future No. 4 starter. A strong start would make him an early candidate for a 2018 callup if Chicago needs help either in the rotation or in the bullpen.

BA GRADE
50 Risk: High
FB: 60. CB: 55.
CHG: 40.
CTL: 45.

Year	Club (League)	Class	W	L	ERA	G	GS	CG	SV	IP	H	HR	BB	SO	K/9	WHIP	AVG
2015	Eugene (NWL)	SS	6	2	2.04	12	3	0	0	53	29	5	15	49	8.3	0.83	.159
2016	South Bend (MWL)	LoA	9	4	4.34	22	20	0	0	120	119	9	28	81	6.1	1.22	.260
2017	Myrtle Beach (CAR)	HiA	7	1	2.98	15	15	1	0	82	65	8	22	78	8.6	1.07	.217
	Tennessee (SL)	AA	0	3	3.03	7	7	0	0	33	27	0	12	30	8.3	1.19	.229
Minor League Totals			29	18	3.30	81	60	1	0	382	322	26	99	327	7.7	1.10	.227

3 JOSE ALBERTOS, RHP

Born: Nov. 7, 1998. **B-T:** R-R. **Ht.:** 6-1. **Wt.:** 185. **Signed:** Mexico, 2015. **Signed by:** Sergio Hernandez/Louie Eljaua.

Albertos had pitched just four innings as a pro thanks to forearm tightness in 2016, but the Cubs awaited his 2017 season as much as any of their minor leaguers. Signed for $1.5 million out of Mexico in the Cubs' loaded international class of 2015, Albertos made 12 starts overall, including in the short-season Northwest League playoffs, after one start in 2016.

A clean arm action, smooth delivery and athleticism helps produce the premium fastball velocity that Albertos has shown. He dialed back a bit to 93-94 mph for most of 2017, showing the ability to hit 97 when needed, and he's hit 99 in extended spring training. His fastball has solid life as well, and he has harnessed it more, improving his control and hinting at future command. His changeup earns some plus-plus grades from scouts thanks to its action and the arm speed he uses to sell the pitch. He pitches backward at times and locates his changeup; it's his best pitch, and he trusts his fastball-changeup combination. That has inhibited the progress of his slider. He can spin a breaking ball but doesn't throw it enough for it to play to its above-average potential.

Throwing his slider enough to improve his feel and consistency will be one key for Albertos in 2018. The other will be staying healthy again as he makes the jump to low Class A South Bend. He has a higher ceiling than any Cubs pitching prospect.

BA GRADE
55 Risk: Extreme
FB: 60. SL: 45.
CHG: 70.
CTL: 45.

Year	Club (League)	Class	W	L	ERA	G	GS	CG	SV	IP	H	HR	BB	SO	K/9	WHIP	AVG
2016	Cubs (AZL)	R	0	0	0.00	1	1	0	0	4	1	0	1	7	15.8	0.50	.077
2017	Cubs (AZL)	R	0	0	4.32	2	2	0	0	8	6	0	3	6	6.5	1.08	.200
	Eugene (NWL)	SS	2	1	2.86	8	8	0	0	35	24	0	14	42	10.9	1.10	.181
Minor League Totals			2	1	2.87	11	11	0	0	47	31	0	18	55	10.5	1.04	.176

4 VICTOR CARATINI, C

Born: Aug. 17, 1993. **B-T:** B-R. **Ht.:** 6-1. **Wt.:** 215. **Drafted:** Miami Dade JC, 2013 (2nd round). **Signed by:** Buddy Hernandez (Braves).

A Puerto Rico native who attended Southern and then Miami Dade JC, Caratini progressed from converted catcher to big leaguer by 2017, replacing Miguel Montero in late June when the Cubs designated the veteran for assignment. Caratini got sporadic playing time after Chicago traded for veteran Alex Avila in July.

A bat-first catcher, Caratini was hitting .343, ranking fourth in the Triple-A Pacific Coast League, when promoted. He repeats his short, strong swing from both sides of the plate and gained the confidence to hunt his pitch and get out front a bit more to produce improved power. He has modest bat speed but average raw power and a feel for hitting that allows the power to play. Caratini's arm plays average at third base but fringe-average behind the plate, where he has solid footwork to go with his soft hands. He's worked at refining his average receiving and blocking skills and at calling games, but the Cubs didn't think he was ready to carry the load when Willson Contreras was hurt.

Caratini's overall profile resembles that of Avila, an impending free agent whom Caratini could replace as the backup in Chicago in 2018.

BA GRADE

45 Risk: Medium

HIT: 55. POW: 45.
SPD: 40. FLD: 50.
ARM: 45.

Year	Club (League)	Class	AVG	G	AB	R	H	2B	3B	HR	RBI	BB	SO	SB	CS	OBP	SLG
2015	Myrtle Beach (CAR)	HiA	.257	112	393	39	101	31	1	4	53	49	75	0	0	.342	.372
2016	Tennessee (SL)	AA	.291	115	412	57	120	25	2	6	47	54	80	2	1	.375	.405
2017	Iowa (PCL)	AAA	.342	83	292	50	100	27	3	10	61	27	48	1	0	.393	.558
	Chicago (NL)	MAJ	.254	31	59	6	15	3	0	1	2	4	13	0	0	.333	.356
Major League Totals			.254	31	59	6	15	3	0	1	2	4	13	0	0	.333	.356
Minor League Totals			.289	469	1673	224	483	128	12	26	241	207	321	4	4	.369	.426

5 ALEX LANGE, RHP

Born: Oct. 2, 1995. **B-T:** R-R. **Ht.:** 6-3. **Wt.:** 197. **Drafted:** Louisiana State, 2017 (1st round). **Signed by:** Kevin Ellis.

A first-team All-American as a freshman in 2015, Lange went 30-9, 2.91 in three seasons at Louisiana State and helped the Tigers reach the 2017 College World Series finals. His heavy reliance on his curveball, one of the best in the 2017 draft class, dropped his stock a bit as a junior, and the Cubs got him with their second pick (30th overall). An undisclosed issue with his physical prompted him to sign a below-slot deal, at $1.925 million, the only first-round bonus below $2 million.

Lange earns plus-plus grades for his curveball from his admirers, and even skeptics grade his curve as plus. He spins it with mid-80s power at his best. When he locates his curveball and can throw it for strikes whenever he wants, it opens up his whole arsenal and increases his confidence in his fastball. Lange has sat 92-96 mph at his best, but he rarely if ever did that in 2017, instead pitching at 90-93 with some 94s mixed in. The Cubs will force Lange to throw his changeup as a pro more than he ever did in college and try to get him to pitch inside and up in the zone with his fastball to make him less predictable.

With his current two-pitch mix, Lange could move quickly as a closer, with one club official likening him to a more physical, better version of Justin Grimm. The Cubs will push the 22-year-old to high Class A Myrtle Beach to see if his competitiveness can help him learn a changeup quickly.

BA GRADE

50 Risk: High

FB: 55. CB: 70.
CHG: 50.
CTL: 45.

Year	Club (League)	Class	W	L	ERA	G	GS	CG	SV	IP	H	HR	BB	SO	K/9	WHIP	AVG
2017	Eugene (NWL)	SS	0	1	4.82	4	4	0	0	9	9	0	3	13	12.5	1.29	.243
Minor League Totals			0	1	4.82	4	4	0	0	9	9	0	3	13	12.5	1.29	.243

6 OSCAR DE LA CRUZ, RHP

Born: March 4, 1995. **B-T:** R-R. **Ht.:** 6-4. **Wt.:** 200. **Signed:** Dominican Republic, 2012. **Signed by:** Mario Encarnacion/Jose Serra.

An infielder before signing as a 17-year-old, de la Cruz shifted to the mound after signing with the Cubs for $85,000. He seemed poised to bust out after his 2015 U.S. debut with short-season Eugene, but he has pitched less than 100 innings the last two seasons with a variety of ailments, from forearm soreness to muscle pulls to oblique strains. In 2017 he missed nearly three months before returning to pitch in August, then was pulled from the Cubs' Arizona Fall League contingent.

At his best, de la Cruz features an athletic delivery with excellent extension that helps his 92-94 mph fastball pop, and he has touched 97 in the past. He can show above-average fastball life and downhill angle as well, eliciting weak contact. His curveball and changeup both have had their moments, with the curveball earning above-average grades. Its consistency is about as good as his health track record, and he hasn't had the reps to gain proper feel for his changeup.

It's all about staying healthy for de la Cruz, who rivals Albertos for ceiling in the system as a potential No. 2 or No. 3 starter. The Cubs won't waste his bullets in the minors; if he stays healthy, he'll zoom to Wrigley Field.

BA GRADE
55 Risk: Extreme
FB: 55. CB: 60.
CHG: 55.
CTL: 50.

Year	Club (League)	Class	W	L	ERA	G	GS	CG	SV	IP	H	HR	BB	SO	K/9	WHIP	AVG
2015	Eugene (NWL)	SS	6	3	2.84	13	13	0	0	73	56	4	17	73	9.0	1.00	.211
2016	Cubs (AZL)	R	0	1	6.00	1	1	0	0	3	3	1	1	2	6.0	1.33	.250
	Eugene (NWL)	SS	0	0	1.08	2	2	0	0	8	5	1	2	14	15.1	0.84	.167
	South Bend (MWL)	LoA	1	2	3.25	6	6	0	0	28	22	0	8	35	11.4	1.08	.218
2017	Cubs (AZL)	R	0	0	0.00	1	0	0	0	2	0	0	0	1	4.5	0.00	.000
	Myrtle Beach (CAR)	HiA	4	3	3.46	12	12	1	0	55	55	6	13	47	7.7	1.24	.263
Minor League Totals			20	10	2.83	53	49	1	0	255	213	16	65	248	8.8	1.09	.225

7 BRENDON LITTLE, LHP

Born: Aug. 11, 1996. **B-T:** L-L. **Ht.:** 6-1. **Wt.:** 195. **Drafted:** State JC of Florida, 2017 (1st round). **Signed by:** John Koronka.

A top 200 prospect out of a Pennsylvania high school, Little attended North Carolina as a freshman but decided to transfer after getting just four innings. He pitched very well in the Cape Cod League in 2016 and then pitched his way into the first round at State JC of Florida in the spring of 2017. He was the Cubs' first pick and struggled a bit after signing for $2.2 million.

A lefthander with two plus pitches, Little lacks precise command but can be effectively wild in the mold of Gio Gonzalez or Francisco Liriano. His fastball has above-average life even at high velocity, and he touched 96 mph in the spring. He pitches more at 90-94 mph, though he sat at the lower end of that register in his pro debut. His tight 12-6 curveball has firm upper-70s power and has flashed plus as a pro. His average changeup gives him a true third pitch and grants him some pitchability. His inconsistent delivery costs him command and can get choppy and robotic.

When Little's delivery stays athletic, he's a three-pitch lefty with plus stuff who projects as a mid-rotation starter. He's younger than fellow first-rounder Alex Lange but also less polished and should earn a spot at low Class A South Bend in 2018.

BA GRADE
50 Risk: High
FB: 55. CB: 55.
CHG: 50.
CTL: 40.

Year	Club (League)	Class	W	L	ERA	G	GS	CG	SV	IP	H	HR	BB	SO	K/9	WHIP	AVG
2017	Eugene (NWL)	SS	0	2	9.37	6	6	0	0	16	21	2	9	12	6.6	1.84	.300
Minor League Totals			0	2	9.37	6	6	0	0	16	21	2	9	12	6.6	1.84	.300

8 THOMAS HATCH, RHP

Born: Sept. 29, 1994. **B-T:** R-R. **Ht.:** 6-1. **Wt.:** 200. **Drafted:** Oklahoma State, 2016 (3rd round). **Signed by:** Ty Nichols.

Hatch had tremendous success as an amateur, first at Jenks (Okla.) High, then at Oklahoma State, where he missed a year with a strained ulnar collateral ligament. A platelet-rich injection helped him recover without surgery to lead Oklahoma State to the 2016 College World Series, and he made every start in 2017, his first as a pro, while ranking fifth in the high Class A Carolina League with 9.1 strikeouts per nine innings.

Hatch has diversified his sinker-slider repertoire as a pro by adding a four-seam fastball and throwing his average changeup much more often than he did in college. He can reach 95 mph with his four-seamer and is learning to work up in the zone, particularly against lefthanded hitters, to change their eye level. Improved pitch sequencing would help his whole arsenal play up. His low-90s sinker with plus life remains his bread and butter, and his above-average slider pairs with it to allow him to pitch to both sides of the plate. His pitch mix and late life in the zone helped him give up just two homers

Command was Hatch's bugaboo in 2017. The Cubs believe he's a good enough athlete, one who fields his position well and holds runners, to make the leap. He'll be tested at Double-A Tennessee in 2018 and profiles as a No. 3 or No. 4 starter.

BA GRADE
50 Risk: High
FB: 50. SL: 60.
CHG: 50.
CTL: 45.

Year	Club (League)	Class	W	L	ERA	G	GS	CG	SV	IP	H	HR	BB	SO	K/9	WHIP	AVG
2016	Did not play																
2017	Myrtle Beach (CAR)	HiA	5	11	4.04	26	26	0	0	125	126	2	50	126	9.1	1.41	.264
Minor League Totals			5	11	4.04	26	26	0	0	125	126	2	50	126	9.1	1.41	.264

9 JEN-HO TSENG, RHP

Born: Oct. 3, 1994. **B-T:** L-R. **Ht.:** 6-1. **Wt.:** 195. **Signed:** Taiwan, 2013. **Signed by:** Steve Wilson/Paul Weaver.

Signed for $1.625 million out of Taiwan, Tseng received the third-largest bonus in the Cubs' 2013 international class, behind Eloy Jimenez and Gleyber Torres. Tseng had made slow, steady progress since then, taking it one level at a time before repeating Double-A Tennessee in 2017. He earned organization pitcher of the year honors and made his first big league start against the Mets in September.

Tseng has the same stuff he has had, for the most part, since signing. His above-average changeup remains his best pitch. He locates his 90-93 mph fastball consistently to both sides of the plate. He's confident enough to throw his average curveball and cutter-type slider, a fringe-average pitch, in any count. Tseng trusted his catchers more and sequenced his pitches better in 2017, staying out of pitch patterns and using his offspeed stuff to different locations than he had in the past. Tseng's offseason preparation also was better, and he stayed strong throughout the season.

Tseng profiles as a back-of-the-rotation starter with durability a key attribute. After throwing more than 150 innings in 2017, he's the upper-level Cubs arm most likely to earn a big league rotation spot in 2018.

BA GRADE
45 Risk: Medium
FB: 45. CB: 50.
SL: 50. CHG: 55.
CTL: 55.

Year	Club (League)	Class	W	L	ERA	G	GS	CG	SV	IP	H	HR	BB	SO	K/9	WHIP	AVG
2015	Myrtle Beach (CAR)	HiA	7	7	3.55	22	22	0	0	119	115	5	30	87	6.6	1.22	.256
2016	Tennessee (SL)	AA	6	8	4.29	22	22	0	0	113	138	12	32	69	5.5	1.50	.308
2017	Tennessee (SL)	AA	7	3	2.99	15	15	0	0	90	79	7	24	83	8.3	1.14	.232
	Iowa (PCL)	AAA	6	1	1.80	9	9	0	0	55	48	5	14	39	6.4	1.13	.235
	Chicago (NL)	MAJ	1	0	7.50	2	1	0	0	6	5	2	2	8	12.0	1.17	.227
Major League Totals			1	0	7.50	2	1	0	0	6	5	2	2	8	12.0	1.17	.227
Minor League Totals			32	20	3.17	87	85	1	0	483	456	36	115	363	6.8	1.18	.251

10 NELSON VELAZQUEZ, OF

Born: Dec. 26, 1998. **B-T:** R-R. **Ht.:** 6-0. **Wt.:** 190. **Drafted:** HS—Carolina, P.R., 2017 (5th round). **Signed by:** Edwards Guzman.

BILL MITCHELL

BA GRADE

55 Risk: Extreme

HIT: 45. **POW:** 60.
SPD: 60. **FLD:** 50.
ARM: 55.

The Cubs invested in Puerto Rico by hiring former big leaguer Edwards Guzman as a scout focused on the island's prep talent. He gave the Cubs the information to crosscheck Velazquez early, so when he popped at May's Excellence Games event—Puerto Rico's top predraft showcase—the Cubs were ready and made him the first position player they drafted in 2017.

Velazquez showed some rust in his pro debut because he sat out about six weeks after the draft before playing in the Rookie-level Arizona League, but he showed electric tools once he played. His eight homers tied for third in the league, and he produces power with bat speed, present strength and more feel to hit than was expected. His plus-plus raw power grades above his hitting ability, but he has some natural feel for the barrel. His approach is raw, as are some aspects of his defense, but he's a plus runner if not better underway and has a solid-average arm.

With his power and athleticism, Velazquez likely will fit the right-field profile, though any outfield spot is possible. His aptitude will determine how quickly he moves, but he likely will be in extended spring training to start 2018.

Year	Club (League)	Class	AVG	G	AB	R	H	2B	3B	HR	RBI	BB	SO	SB	CS	OBP	SLG
2017	Cubs (AZL)	R	.236	32	110	26	26	5	2	8	17	15	39	5	2	.333	.536
Minor League Totals			.236	32	110	26	26	5	2	8	17	15	39	5	2	.333	.536

11 D.J. WILSON, OF

BA GRADE

50 Risk: High

Born: Oct. 8, 1996. **B-T:** L-L. **Ht.:** 5-9. **Wt.:** 177. **Drafted:** HS—Canton, Ohio, 2015 (4th round). **Signed by:** Daniel Carte.

A $1.3 million bonus swayed Wilson, a Vanderbilt commit, to sign in 2015; he remains the highest-drafted high school position player for the Cubs since 2012 first-rounder Albert Almora. He missed six weeks with low Class A South Bend due to a fractured fibula and performed better after returning.

Wilson has an explosive, athletic but smallish body and has earned comparisons to players from Adam Eaton (a fellow Ohio product) to 2017 first-rounder Jeren Kendall out of Vanderbilt. Wilson is a 70 runner, the fastest prospect in the system, with the potential to be a consistent plus defender in center field if not better. He's a playmaking defender and improving basestealer with power to the gaps. His above-average raw power plays in games more frequently when he slows the game down and stays with an all-fields approach. Wilson needs development time but is all over the Cubs' Best Tools chart. He has the upside to be a big league regular at a premium position.

Wilson likely is headed to high Class A Myrtle Beach thanks to his strong finish but will move slower than most Cubs hitting prospects.

Year	Club (League)	Class	AVG	G	AB	R	H	2B	3B	HR	RBI	BB	SO	SB	CS	OBP	SLG
2015	Cubs (AZL)	R	.266	22	79	12	21	3	2	0	6	6	15	5	1	.322	.354
2016	Eugene (NWL)	SS	.257	64	245	37	63	15	2	3	29	20	56	21	8	.320	.371
2017	Cubs (AZL)	R	.500	3	8	5	4	1	0	3	5	2	1	1	0	.583	1.750
	South Bend (MWL)	LoA	.229	88	310	56	71	16	8	9	45	33	89	15	7	.309	.419
Minor League Totals			.248	177	642	110	159	35	12	15	85	61	161	42	16	.319	.410

12 DAVID BOTE, 2B/3B

BA GRADE

45 Risk: Medium

Born: April 7, 1993. **B-T:** R-R. **Ht.:** 5-11. **Wt.:** 185. **Drafted:** Neosho County (Kan.) JC, 2012 (18th round). **Signed by:** Rick Schroeder.

Bote jumped into the Top 30 for the first time after the 2016 season, capitalizing on his first extended playing time, and earned a bigger challenge in 2017. He was an everyday player for the first time as a pro, hitting third for Double-A Tennessee most of the year and ranking fifth in the Southern League in total bases (206).

Bote has the makeup and baseball savvy—his dad and older brother both worked as amateur coaches—to get the most out of his tools, which grade out as average or fringe-average across the board. He has a simple swing with solid strength and average power that produces plenty of doubles and enough home runs even for this era. While some evaluators see some stiffness in his actions, he's worked hard to improve and earned Best Defensive Second Baseman honors from SL managers. He lacks the dynamism of Chicago's current batch of infielders and profiles better as an extra player or second-division regular in the Yangervis Solarte mold.

BaseballAmerica.com

Bote has shown defensive versatility throughout his career, playing the outfield and infield corners, and earned a 40-man roster spot in November.

Year	Club (League)	Class	AVG	G	AB	R	H	2B	3B	HR	RBI	BB	SO	SB	CS	OBP	SLG
2015	South Bend (MWL)	LoA	.253	97	312	45	79	20	2	6	41	28	60	5	3	.329	.388
2016	Iowa (PCL)	AAA	.364	12	22	4	8	0	0	1	3	2	5	0	0	.417	.500
	Tennessee (SL)	AA	.200	7	25	1	5	0	0	0	1	2	6	0	0	.259	.200
	Myrtle Beach (CAR)	HiA	.337	72	276	55	93	26	3	6	41	31	41	6	1	.410	.518
2017	Tennessee (SL)	AA	.270	127	470	65	127	30	3	14	59	49	101	5	2	.351	.436
Minor League Totals			.262	542	1852	279	485	117	11	39	237	210	392	40	21	.351	.400

13 BRYAN HUDSON, LHP

Born: May 8, 1997. **B-T:** L-L. **Ht.:** 6-8. **Wt.:** 220. **Drafted:** HS—Alton, Ill., 2015 (3rd round). **Signed by:** Stan Zielinski.

Hudson was raw when the Cubs signed him for $1.1 million in 2015 as the 82nd overall pick, but he made significant strides in 2017 and has evolved considerably as a pro. Hudson flashed one of the better breaking balls in the 2015 draft class, a low-80s power curveball that, along with his projectable 6-foot-8 frame, prompted the Cubs to buy him out of his Missouri commitment.

Hudson's gains as a pro started with stepping back to focus on fundamentals—fitness, a functional delivery and his fastball. His work ethic has improved as he's adapted to the rigors of pro ball, giving him the strength to stay tall in his delivery and drive the ball downhill. He used his angle to pitch off his 89-90 mph fastball in 2017, producing an extreme groundball rate, with more than three ground outs for every air out, and finished well, going 8-1, 3.69 in his last 13 starts. Hudson's curveball and changeup lack consistency at this point because he's focused so much on commanding his fastball. He's spun the curveball and has flashed 94-95 mph velocity in the past.

If Hudson can recapture his curve and improve the consistency of his velocity, he'll have two plus weapons to attack hitters, profiling as a mid-rotation starter. He's headed to high Class A in 2018.

Year	Club (League)	Class	W	L	ERA	G	GS	CG	SV	IP	H	HR	BB	SO	K/9	WHIP	AVG
2015	Cubs (AZL)	R	0	0	2.70	5	0	0	0	7	6	0	2	5	6.8	1.20	.222
2016	Eugene (NWL)	SS	5	4	5.06	13	13	0	0	59	56	4	41	41	6.3	1.65	.262
2017	South Bend (MWL)	LoA	9	3	3.91	24	24	0	0	124	128	10	52	81	5.9	1.45	.272
Minor League Totals			14	7	4.22	42	37	0	0	190	190	14	95	127	6.0	1.50	.267

14 KEEGAN THOMPSON, RHP

Born: March 13, 1995. **B-T:** R-R. **Ht.:** 6-0. **Wt.:** 193. **Drafted:** Auburn, 2017 (3rd round). **Signed by:** Alex McClure.

A decorated amateur, Thompson has the pitchability to move through the Cubs system quickly. He teamed with fellow Cubs farmhand Trevor Clifton to help USA Baseball's 16U national team win a world championship in 2011 and won gold again in 2012 with the 18U club. He wasn't drafted out of high school and spent four seasons at Auburn, missing a year due to Tommy John surgery but logging 252.2 innings and retaining excellent control after surgery (1.6 walks per nine innings in 2017).

Thompson could start or relieve with his aggressiveness and four-pitch mix. He had a plus curve before surgery, but some scouts like his slider better now. He's got two average or better, distinct breaking balls with a feel for locating his spin, and he pounds the zone and an out with an average 89-92 mph fastball that touched 94-95 in shorter bursts after signing. His changeup also earns average grades. Moreover, Thompson is advanced at setting hitters up, making the right pitch at the right time and never giving in. Scouts laud his competitiveness, and he has a professional routine.

Thompson will be 23 in 2018 and should be pushed, likely to high Class A Myrtle Beach.

Year	Club (League)	Class	W	L	ERA	G	GS	CG	SV	IP	H	HR	BB	SO	K/9	WHIP	AVG
2017	Eugene (NWL)	SS	1	2	2.37	7	1	0	0	19	15	1	4	23	10.9	1.00	.214
Minor League Totals			1	2	2.37	7	1	0	0	19	15	1	4	23	10.9	1.00	.214

15 DILLON MAPLES, RHP

Born: May 9, 1992. **B-T:** R-R. **Ht.:** 6-2. **Wt.:** 225. **Drafted:** HS—Southern Pines, N.C., 2011 (14th round). **Signed by:** Billy Swoope.

The 2011 draft was the last before the capped-draft era began, and Maples got $2.5 million, the 17th-highest in that entire draft even though he was the 429th pick. The only high school righthanders to get more were Archie Bradley, Dylan Bundy and Joe Ross, all of whom had broken through to the major leagues by 2017.

Maples entered the 2017 season ranked outside the Top 30, seemingly out of the Cubs' plans and with just 182.1 innings as a pro. However, he stayed free of the injuries that had interrupted past seasons—such as a UCL injury in his elbow, or the rib and oblique injuries of previous years—and added a cutter in offseason workouts. The cutter, a low-90s pitch that has enough break to pass for a slider, gave him a pitch he could throw for strikes consistently; an adjustment to make his delivery more compact improved his control. Suddenly, Maples had confidence to go with his power curveball, thrown in the mid-80s, and hitters couldn't sit on his mid-90s fastball. It's touching 100 mph now, and while he wasn't fine with it in the big leagues, Maples made it there, finally, in 2017.

Maples has below-average control; he walked 5.3 per nine innings even in his breakout season. But he also struck out more than 14 per nine and has the stuff to be a factor in the Cubs' bullpen in 2018.

Year	Club (League)	Class	W	L	ERA	G	GS	CG	SV	IP	H	HR	BB	SO	K/9	WHIP	AVG
2015	Eugene (NWL)	SS	0	1	7.20	3	0	0	0	5	7	0	1	8	14.4	1.60	.292
	South Bend (MWL)	LoA	1	1	4.15	15	0	0	1	30	28	2	12	19	5.6	1.32	.252
2016	Myrtle Beach (CAR)	HiA	0	1	7.71	9	0	0	0	7	9	0	7	6	7.7	2.29	.281
	South Bend (MWL)	LoA	1	2	3.24	19	0	0	9	25	18	1	10	17	6.1	1.12	.198
2017	Myrtle Beach (CAR)	HiA	4	0	2.01	21	0	0	3	31	21	2	15	44	12.6	1.15	.188
	Tennessee (SL)	AA	1	1	3.29	14	0	0	6	14	11	0	11	28	18.4	1.61	.212
	Iowa (PCL)	AAA	1	2	1.96	17	0	0	4	18	12	1	11	28	13.7	1.25	.185
	Chicago (NL)	MAJ	0	0	10.13	6	0	0	0	5	6	0	6	11	18.6	2.25	.286
Major League Totals			0	0	10.13	6	0	0	0	5	6	0	6	11	18.6	2.25	.286
Minor League Totals			13	17	4.54	135	30	0	24	246	217	7	153	260	9.5	1.51	.234

16 CORY ABBOTT, RHP

BA GRADE

50 Risk: High

Born: Sept. 20, 1995. **B-T:** R-R. **Ht.:** 6-2. **Wt.:** 210. **Drafted:** Loyola Marymount, 2017 (2nd round). **Signed by:** Tom Myers.

Abbott was a key recruit for Loyola Marymount and pitched regularly for the Lions for his first two seasons before having a first-team All-America season as a junior. In late March, he threw the first perfect game in school history en route to an 11-2, 1.74 season. He ranked 10th in the country in ERA and strikeouts (130 in 98.1 innings), and he was the 67th overall pick in the draft.

Abbott hadn't pitched for three weeks before signing and was slowly built up before his five short starts as a pro. He threw quality strikes with short-season Eugene, though he didn't have his sharp predraft stuff after his time off. Abbott took off this year after studying video of Noah Syndergaard, adopting his slider grip and suddenly throwing 85-88 mph sliders that earn average grades. He hides the ball in his delivery with a hip turn, and his slider and 89-93 mph fastball both play above-average with his deception and command. Abbott will have to throw his changeup more as a pro to gain conviction in it.

Old for his draft class, Abbott has the command to potentially earn a spot at high Class A Myrtle Beach.

Year	Club (League)	Class	W	L	ERA	G	GS	CG	SV	IP	H	HR	BB	SO	K/9	WHIP	AVG
2017	Eugene (NWL)	SS	0	0	3.86	5	5	0	0	14	14	1	3	18	11.6	1.21	.269
Minor League Totals			0	0	3.86	5	5	0	0	14	14	1	3	18	11.6	1.21	.269

17 TREVOR CLIFTON, RHP

BA GRADE

50 Risk: High

Born: May 11, 1995. **B-T:** R-R. **Ht.:** 6-4. **Wt.:** 220. **Drafted:** HS—Maryville, Tenn., 2013 (12th round). **Signed by:** Keith Rymon.

Clifton had his best season in 2016 and his worst in 2017, but it didn't start off that way. Coming off a strong offseason in which he got into good physical shape, Clifton had seemed to grow into his now 6-foot-4, 220-pound frame.

Clifton—who attended high school roughly 50 minutes from Tennessee Smokies Stadium—handled the jump to Double-A well, going 5-3, 2.84 in the first half, with 3.8 walks and 7.6 strikeouts per nine innings. But Clifton lost all five decisions after the break while posting a 9.89 ERA and .376 opponent average. His breaking balls went backward in 2017; his slider morphed into a cutter, which helped him at times, but he lost the feel for his curveball, and neither pitch was working. Clifton also fell into pitch patterns with his changeup, so soon he trusted none of his secondary pitches, relying on his above-average 90-94 mph fastball that touches 95. His response was to work harder, and he hit a physical wall, exacerbating the problem.

The Cubs shut Clifton down in late August 2017, hoping he can hit the reset button in the offseason.

Year	Club (League)	Class	W	L	ERA	G	GS	CG	SV	IP	H	HR	BB	SO	K/9	WHIP	AVG
2015	South Bend (MWL)	LoA	8	10	3.98	23	22	0	0	109	91	7	47	103	8.5	1.27	.230
2016	Myrtle Beach (CAR)	HiA	7	7	2.72	23	23	0	0	119	97	4	41	129	9.8	1.16	.225
2017	Tennessee (SL)	AA	5	8	5.20	21	21	0	0	100	112	8	45	86	7.7	1.56	.286
Minor League Totals			24	27	3.94	88	80	0	0	399	372	22	171	387	8.7	1.36	.250

18 JUSTIN STEELE, LHP

Born: July 11, 1995. **B-T:** L-L. **Ht.:** 6-2. **Wt.:** 195. **Drafted:** HS—Lucedale, Miss., 2014 (5th round). **Signed by:** J.P. Davis.

BA GRADE

50 Risk: V. High

Steele was having a breakthrough season, his best since signing for $1 million in 2014. Always highly regarded for his athleticism, Steele combined some twitchiness with improved aptitude to earn a mid-season all-star nod in the high Class A Carolina League, but he didn't make it all the way through the season. He left an Aug. 1 start in the third inning due to an elbow injury and wound up requiring Tommy John surgery.

Steele, when healthy, was pitching at 92 mph and hit 95 in short stints, harnessing his fastball more and throwing hard enough with ease to believe more was in the tank. He'd started learning to use the top and bottom of the zone in 2017, leading to fewer walks. His secondary pitches, a curveball with slurvy shape, earned above-average to plus grades, with a solid-average changeup that he was learning to trust more.

Steele likely won't return until instructional league or perhaps the Arizona Fall League in 2018.

Year	Club (League)	Class	W	L	ERA	G	GS	CG	SV	IP	H	HR	BB	SO	K/9	WHIP	AVG
2015	Eugene (NWL)	SS	3	1	2.66	10	10	0	0	41	38	0	15	38	8.4	1.30	.245
2016	South Bend (MWL)	LoA	5	7	5.00	19	19	0	0	77	93	3	39	76	8.8	1.71	.305
2017	Myrtle Beach (CAR)	HiA	6	7	2.92	20	20	0	0	99	100	6	36	82	7.5	1.38	.265
Minor League Totals			14	15	3.56	58	53	0	0	235	246	9	98	221	8.5	1.46	.271

19 DUANE UNDERWOOD, RHP

Born: July 20, 1994. **B-T:** R-R. **Ht.:** 6-2. **Wt.:** 210. **Drafted:** HS—Marietta, Ga., 2012 (2nd round). **Signed by:** Keith Lockhart.

BA GRADE

45 Risk: High

Underwood set several career highs in 2017, which was especially encouraging following two injury-interrupted seasons preceding it. Elbow soreness, forearm tightness and inflammation had plagued him previously, but he stayed healthy in 2017 and set career highs with 138 innings, 98 strikeouts, 13 victories and 24 starts, and did it all at Double-A Tennessee.

Underwood's fastball was better at full health; he showed some 97 mph readings and held his typical 92-95 velocity a bit better than before. He still lacks consistency with his fastball command, and the pitch has modest life, so it's not a big swing-and-miss fastball. His curveball and changeup have above-average moments; he still lacks the feel of how and when to use them to dominate minor league hitters. He made progress, though, and still has the three-pitch mix to start, if not the true pitchability.

Underwood's stuff likely would play up in relief, whether in short bursts such as Carl Edwards or one time through an order in a swing role. He's headed for Triple-A in 2018.

Year	Club (League)	Class	W	L	ERA	G	GS	CG	SV	IP	H	HR	BB	SO	K/9	WHIP	AVG
2015	Cubs (AZL)	R	0	0	0.00	2	2	0	0	5	3	0	0	6	10.8	0.60	.167
	Myrtle Beach (CAR)	HiA	6	3	2.58	14	14	0	0	73	52	6	24	48	5.9	1.04	.202
2016	Tennessee (SL)	AA	0	5	4.91	13	13	1	0	59	66	7	31	46	7.1	1.65	.280
	Cubs (AZL)	R	0	0	0.00	1	1	0	0	1	1	0	0	2	18.0	1.00	.250
	South Bend (MWL)	LoA	0	1	2.08	3	3	0	0	9	5	0	4	12	12.5	1.04	.172
	Myrtle Beach (CAR)	HiA	0	0	1.93	1	1	0	0	5	3	0	0	2	3.9	0.64	.176
2017	Tennessee (SL)	AA	13	7	4.43	25	24	0	0	138	130	13	50	98	6.4	1.30	.250
Minor League Totals			28	25	3.72	100	95	1	0	453	414	41	178	341	6.8	1.31	.242

20 MARK ZAGUNIS, OF

Born: Feb. 5, 1993. **B-T:** R-R. **Ht.:** 6-0. **Wt.:** 205. **Drafted:** Virginia Tech, 2014 (3rd round). **Signed by:** Billy Swoope.

BA GRADE

45 Risk: High

The Cubs had four hitters at higher levels who looked ready for the major leagues entering 2017. Ian Happ and since-traded Jeimer Candelario graduated to the majors, while Victor Caratini got his first callup and moved into the Top 10. Zagunis also earned his first callup as well, but it went poorly, with an 0-for-14 stretch in June that resulted in a return trip to Triple-A Iowa.

Zagunis' season ended early for the second straight year; in 2016 it was a broken big toe, while in 2017 he broke the hamate bone in his left hand. He has the best plate discipline in the system, with a .402 career on-base percentage in the minor leagues, to go with average power. He's still a solid athlete, an average runner who can steal a base. As he's slowed down, the former catcher has become a corner outfielder only, with average ability in either corner to go with an above-average arm. Zagunis lacks a plus tool or the defensive versatility to be a true fourth outfielder, limiting his options for the Cubs.

A perfect second-division regular profile, Zagunis is ticketed for a return to Iowa and will have to heat up fast if he gets another shot in the big leagues.

Year	Club (League)	Class	AVG	G	AB	R	H	2B	3B	HR	RBI	BB	SO	SB	CS	OBP	SLG
2015	Myrtle Beach (CAR)	HiA	.271	115	413	78	112	24	5	8	54	80	86	12	10	.406	.412
2016	Tennessee (SL)	AA	.302	51	179	30	54	13	1	4	24	30	36	1	2	.408	.453
	Iowa (PCL)	AAA	.274	50	179	31	49	12	4	6	25	22	42	4	0	.360	.486
2017	Chicago (NL)	MAJ	.000	7	14	0	0	0	0	0	1	4	6	2	0	.222	.000
	Iowa (PCL)	AAA	.267	97	330	59	88	21	1	13	55	70	93	4	3	.404	.455
Major League Totals			.000	7	14	0	0	0	0	0	1	4	6	2	0	.222	.000
Minor League Totals			.277	370	1313	242	364	86	14	33	190	244	299	37	17	.402	.439

21 DAKOTA MEKKES, RHP

BA GRADE

45 Risk: High

Born: Nov. 6, 1994. **B-T:** R-R. **Ht.:** 6-7. **Wt.:** 252. **Drafted:** Michigan State, 2016 (10th round). **Signed by:** Daniel Carte.

The massive Mekkes took a while to thrive, redshirting as a freshman at Michigan State and throwing just 12 innings the next spring. That summer, he starred in the Texas Collegiate League with 33 strikeouts in 26 innings. He had one of the best seasons of any college pitcher in 2016, leading the nation in most strikeouts (15.2) and fewest hits allowed (4.1) per nine innings.

Signed for $275,000, Mekkes hasn't quite maintained that strikeout ratio, but he had a tremendous first full season in 2017, again proving hard to square up. Opponents hit just .155 against him in two Class A stops. Mekkes has deception in his long-limbed delivery, and hitters just don't pick up his 90-92 mph fastball, which can touch 94, with any consistency. Cubs officials say Mekkes' ball moves late and jumps even when you're just playing catch with him, though the pitch lacks extraordinary spin rate. His average slider and changeup aren't extraordinary, but they come out of the same low three-quarters slot as his fastball and play off the pitch.

Mekkes' control actually has been better as a pro than it was in college, but Double-A will test if he can keep fooling hitters with his heater and pitch around the walks he does issue.

Year	Club (League)	Class	W	L	ERA	G	GS	CG	SV	IP	H	HR	BB	SO	K/9	WHIP	AVG
2016	Cubs (AZL)	R	0	0	0.00	2	0	0	0	3	1	0	0	6	18.0	0.33	.100
	Eugene (NWL)	SS	1	1	2.12	9	0	0	0	17	11	1	4	21	11.1	0.88	.186
2017	South Bend (MWL)	LoA	3	0	0.58	18	0	0	4	31	14	1	14	47	13.6	0.90	.133
	Myrtle Beach (CAR)	HiA	5	2	1.28	24	0	0	3	42	25	0	20	45	9.6	1.06	.171
Minor League Totals			9	3	1.16	53	0	0	7	93	51	2	38	119	11.5	0.95	.159

22 MIGUEL AMAYA, C/1B

BA GRADE

50 Risk: Extreme

Born: March 9, 1999. **B-T:** R-R. **Ht.:** 6-1. **Wt.:** 185. **Signed:** Panama, 2015. **Signed by:** Cirillo Cumberbatch/Hector Ortega/Louie Eljaua.

Amaya had a strong amateur track record, representing his native Panama in 15U tournaments in 2013-14. That helped convince the Cubs to sign him for $1 million in the 2015 class, and the club pushed him in 2017, promoting him to short-season Eugene for his U.S. debut.

Amaya's defense ranks ahead of his offense at this point, which helped him make such a jump as a teen catcher. His intangibles fit the position; he has leadership skills, plays with energy and has the desire to catch. He also has catch-and-throw skills, with soft hands and the agility to block balls in the dirt. His arm strength was just fringy when he signed but has improved to average with 2.0-second pop times, and he threw out 41 percent of basestealers. Amaya is more raw on the offensive side of the ball, but he's shown more raw power than expected, as his 14 doubles led Eugene. He's a bit of a free swinger at this point, but he has offensive upside.

A potential two-way catcher, Amaya is the best catching prospect in the system's lower levels and should advance to low Class A South Bend.

Year	Club (League)	Class	AVG	G	AB	R	H	2B	3B	HR	RBI	BB	SO	SB	CS	OBP	SLG
2016	Cubs2 (DSL)	R	.245	58	208	29	51	12	0	1	22	21	27	9	3	.344	.317
2017	Eugene (NWL)	SS	.228	58	228	21	52	14	1	3	26	11	49	1	0	.266	.338
Minor League Totals			.236	116	436	50	103	26	1	4	48	32	76	10	3	.305	.328

23 JAVIER ASSAD, RHP

BA GRADE

50 Risk: Extreme

Born: July 30, 1997. **B-T:** R-R. **Ht.:** 6-1. **Wt.:** 200. **Signed:** Mexico, 2015. **Signed by:** Sergio Hernandez/Louie Eljaua.

The Cubs' 2015 international class provides several key pieces of this year's Top 30, many of whom played together in the Dominican Summer League in 2016 and at short-season Eugene last summer. Assad, a $150,000 signee in July 2015, is in that group and made a big step forward with the Emeralds.

A bit older than other members of the class at 20, Assad isn't a power pitcher, projecting more as a back-of-the-rotation innings eater. Assad has a big frame and will have to maintain his conditioning to maintain his stuff. The more he worked, the better he pitched, capped by a strong six-inning outing in the Northwest League playoffs. Assad's fastball sits at 92-93 mph and can reach as high as 96, and he throws plenty of strikes with it to both sides of the plate. None of his secondary pitches grades as above-average; however, he's shown he can keep his slider and curveball against, as well as some feel for his solid-average changeup. One club official compared him to fellow farmhand Jen-Ho Tseng.

Assad figures to join fellow Mexican signee Jose Albertos again in 2018 in the low Class A South Bend rotation.

Year	Club (League)	Class	W	L	ERA	G	GS	CG	SV	IP	H	HR	BB	SO	K/9	WHIP	AVG
2016	Cubs (AZL)	R	2	2	2.87	10	7	0	1	38	39	1	13	42	10.0	1.38	.267
2017	Eugene (NWL)	SS	5	6	4.23	13	13	0	0	66	69	2	21	72	9.8	1.36	.275
Minor League Totals			7	8	3.73	23	20	0	1	104	108	3	34	114	9.9	1.37	.272

24 CHARCER BURKS, OF

BA GRADE

40 Risk: Medium

Born: March 9, 1995. **B-T:** R-R. **Ht.:** 6-0. **Wt.:** 170. **Drafted:** HS—Richmond, Texas, 2013 (9th round). **Signed by:** Trey Forkerway.

Not all players develop at the same speed, and Burks has needed time to come around. But come around he did in 2017, when he turned 22 and reached Double-A for the first time. He has been a regular for three straight seasons in the minors but profiles as a fourth outfielder in the big leagues.

A plus-plus runner when he signed, Burks has matured physically and slowed down as a pro, with above-average speed still being his best tool. He's fast enough to play center field and a better fit on the outfield corners, with a fringe-average arm. Burks' offensive approach has evolved; he works counts and grinds through at-bats well, making himself a tougher out, and he set the table well as a leadoff hitter for Double-A Tennessee. His natural power stroke is often to right-center field and he's shown fringy power to this point, playing more to the gaps.

To be a regular, Burks will have to hit for more power, keep hitting and keep drawing walks.

Year	Club (League)	Class	AVG	G	AB	R	H	2B	3B	HR	RBI	BB	SO	SB	CS	OBP	SLG
2015	South Bend (MWL)	LoA	.260	115	431	63	112	22	4	3	44	51	82	28	9	.342	.350
2016	Myrtle Beach (CAR)	HiA	.247	124	445	71	110	28	5	11	43	66	116	23	7	.356	.407
2017	Tennessee (SL)	AA	.270	121	456	67	123	21	3	10	40	69	107	16	12	.370	.395
Minor League Totals			.266	448	1633	253	434	84	15	25	164	220	388	86	33	.360	.382

25 JASON VOSLER, 3B

BA GRADE

40 Risk: Medium

Born: Sept. 6, 1993. **B-T:** L-R. **Ht.:** 6-1. **Wt.:** 190. **Drafted:** Northeastern, 2013 (16th round). **Signed by:** Matt Sherman.

A three-year starter at shortstop for Northeastern, Vosler hit only one home run as a junior, dropping his draft stock. The Cubs picked him up in the 16th round and moved him quickly to third base.

Vosler finally came into the power for his new position in 2017, tying for second in the Double-A Southern League with 21 homers for Tennessee. He set career highs for on-base percentage (.343) and slugging (.429), aided by some adjustments to his offensive approach. He's closer to the plate, changed his swing path to add more loft and traded some strikeouts for power. Vosler's swing remains somewhat rotational, but his path to the ball is shorter, and he's athletic enough to repeat his swing. Power is Vosler's best tool; he's average or fringy as a runner and defender, with an average arm. He doesn't have the bat speed or barrel feel to be an above-average hitter, and he struggles with big velocity.

Vosler profiles as a second-division regular and should move up to Triple-A in 2018.

Year	Club (League)	Class	AVG	G	AB	R	H	2B	3B	HR	RBI	BB	SO	SB	CS	OBP	SLG
2015	South Bend (MWL)	LoA	.235	69	255	26	60	11	2	4	20	15	34	3	4	.285	.341
	Myrtle Beach (CAR)	HiA	.244	38	127	19	31	7	0	6	20	26	27	0	0	.389	.441
2016	Myrtle Beach (CAR)	HiA	.254	93	334	32	85	25	2	2	39	33	52	1	2	.325	.359
	Tennessee (SL)	AA	.250	26	92	11	23	7	0	1	12	9	26	0	0	.314	.359
2017	Tennessee (SL)	AA	.241	129	452	70	109	18	2	21	81	53	120	1	1	.343	.429
Minor League Totals			.246	385	1354	171	333	69	9	35	183	148	275	5	9	.332	.388

26 MICHAEL RUCKER, RHP

BA GRADE
45 Risk: High

Born: April 27, 1994. **B-T:** R-R. **Ht.:** 6-1. **Wt.:** 185. **Drafted:** Brigham Young, 2016 (11th round). **Signed by:** Steve McFarland.

Like many pitchers who go to Brigham Young, Rucker was old for his draft class. However, it's not because he went on his Mormon mission trip. His career began at Gonzaga, but he transferred to BYU and converted from Catholicism to being Mormon after meeting his now-wife Sydney. Rucker sat out a year as a transfer, then thrived (11-1, 2.73) in 2016 in the West Coast Conference, which featured second-round picks A.J. Puckett and Mitch White and fourth-rounder Corbin Burnes as opposing Friday night starters.

Rucker fell to the 11th round but got an above-slot $180,000 bonus. The lower levels of the Cubs' system are crowded with pitchers, but in 2017 Rucker pitched his way from the low Class A South Bend bullpen to Myrtle Beach's rotation and was the Pelicans' first playoff starter. His fastball hits 96 mph when he relieves, sitting more in the 89-93 range as a starter. He can pitch to both sides of the plate with it and has excellent control, pounding the bottom of the strike zone. His ability to locate his slider and changeup helps them play up; both bump average, and he'll flip in a curveball as well.

Rucker may wind up in the bullpen but will get time to develop as a starter, heading to Double-A Tennessee to open 2018.

Year	Club (League)	Class	W	L	ERA	G	GS	CG	SV	IP	H	HR	BB	SO	K/9	WHIP	AVG
2016	Cubs (AZL)	R	3	0	0.00	5	0	0	0	9	4	0	1	11	11.4	0.58	.138
	Eugene (NWL)	SS	0	0	0.00	2	0	0	0	4	5	0	0	7	15.8	1.25	.313
2017	South Bend (MWL)	LoA	0	0	1.42	7	0	0	1	13	7	1	0	22	15.6	0.55	.156
	Myrtle Beach (CAR)	HiA	5	5	2.51	20	15	0	1	93	82	5	21	92	8.9	1.10	.235
Minor League Totals			8	5	2.12	34	15	0	2	119	98	6	22	132	10.0	1.01	.223

27 ERICH UELMEN, RHP

BA GRADE
45 Risk: High

Born: May 19, 1996. **B-T:** R-R. **Ht.:** 6-3. **Wt.:** 195. **Drafted:** Cal Poly, 2017 (4th round). **Signed by:** Tom Myers.

While Las Vegas is known as a baseball hotbed today, it's mostly for its hitters such as Kris Bryant, Joey Gallo and Bryce Harper. Uelmen has a chance to follow in the footsteps of Vegas big league pitchers such as Erick Fedde, Aaron Blair and Amir Garrett. He attended Cal Poly, teaming in the rotation in 2017 with second-rounder Spencer Howard (Phillies).

Uelmen surprised the Cubs with improved velocity after signing. He's more of a sinker/slider pitcher with a fast arm. His fastball was most notable before the draft for its heavy, plus life, with one club official giving it a 70 grade on the 20-80 scale, and he touched 95 mph in relief after signing, though the extra kick cost him some command. Uelmen's fastball is his lone plus pitch; his slider has some slurvy shape to it and earns average grades, while his changeup is in its nascent stages.

Uelmen, like Michael Rucker entering 2017, has a chance to earn his way into a 2018 rotation but may have to pitch in relief due to the crowded nature of the Cubs' lower minors staffs.

Year	Club (League)	Class	W	L	ERA	G	GS	CG	SV	IP	H	HR	BB	SO	K/9	WHIP	AVG
2017	Eugene (NWL)	SS	0	2	2.04	7	0	0	0	18	18	2	9	23	11.7	1.53	.265
Minor League Totals			0	2	2.04	7	0	0	0	18	18	2	9	23	11.7	1.53	.265

28 ALEC MILLS, RHP

BA GRADE
40 Risk: Medium

Born: Nov. 30, 1991. **B-T:** R-R. **Ht.:** 6-4. **Wt.:** 190. **Drafted:** Tennessee-Martin, 2012 (22nd round). **Signed by:** Sean Gibbs (Royals).

Mills walked on at Tennessee-Martin, a program that hasn't had a winning record since 1992, and became its first big league alumnus with a 2016 callup to the Royals. In February 2017, Kansas City traded him to the Cubs for outfielder Donnie Dewees.

Mills opened 2017 at Triple-A Iowa but missed most of the season with a left ankle injury, reported as a bruise, though there also were reports the Tommy John surgery alumnus had elbow issues. He didn't get back on the mound until late August and wound up with high Class A Myrtle Beach for its playoff run before reporting to the Arizona Fall League to get needed innings. Mills has made it this far based on command of a 90-93 mph sinker that can reach 95 when he's right, and his above-average changeup has similar sink. He throws both a curveball and a slider, though neither has elicited empty swings on a consistent basis, earning fringe-average grades at best. Control (1.9 walks per nine innings in the minors) stands out as his best attribute.

Mills is a depth arm for the 2018 Cubs, but only if he stays healthy.

Year	Club (League)	Class	W	L	ERA	G	GS	CG	SV	IP	H	HR	BB	SO	K/9	WHIP	AVG
2015	Wilmington (CAR)	HiA	7	7	3.02	21	21	1	0	113	122	3	14	111	8.8	1.20	.271
2016	NW Arkansas (TL)	AA	1	2	2.39	12	12	0	0	68	57	2	12	68	9.0	1.02	.234
	Omaha (PCL)	AAA	4	3	4.19	12	11	0	0	58	62	8	19	54	8.4	1.40	.272
	Kansas City (AL)	MAJ	0	0	13.50	3	0	0	0	3	3	0	5	4	10.8	2.40	.231
2017	Iowa (PCL)	AAA	2	0	3.21	3	3	0	0	14	12	0	3	7	4.5	1.07	.231
	Cubs (AZL)	R	0	0	0.00	2	2	0	0	5	2	0	1	6	10.8	0.60	.133
	Myrtle Beach (CAR)	HiA	0	1	3.00	2	2	0	0	9	8	0	1	7	7.0	1.00	.250
Major League Totals			0	0	13.50	3	0	0	0	3	3	0	5	4	10.8	2.40	.231
Minor League Totals			21	23	3.00	101	74	1	9	420	394	21	90	397	8.5	1.15	.248

29 JONATHAN SIERRA, OF

Born: Oct. 17, 1998. **B-T:** L-L. **Ht.:** 6-3. **Wt.:** 190. **Signed:** Dominican Republic, 2015. **Signed by:** Carlos Reyes/Jose Serra/Louie Eljaua).

BA GRADE
50 Risk: Extreme

Sierra did not rank among the top 30 prospects in the 2015 international signing class. However, the Cubs coveted the lean, athletic outfielder. Sierra signed for $2.5 million, the largest bonus the club handed out that year, $500,000 more than top prospect Aramis Ademan received.

Sierra has a body and raw tools for scouts to dream on, with hitting ability that is much more raw than other recent high-dollar Cubs signees. He may already be taller than his listed 6-foot-3 and has the above-average speed and plus arm to fit the right-field profile defensively, and his glove is ahead of his bat at this point. He has shown above-average raw power and hasn't been able to tap into it yet as a pro, even though the Cubs installed him as the No. 3 hitter in the Rookie-level Arizona League team in his 2017 U.S. debut. Sierra has some buggy-whip to his swing, and Cubs officials believe in his pitch recognition skills.

Sierra's learning curve to date has been slow, but he has athletic ability that stands out in the system. He likely will return to extended spring training to start 2018.

Year	Club (League)	Class	AVG	G	AB	R	H	2B	3B	HR	RBI	BB	SO	SB	CS	OBP	SLG
2016	Cubs (DSL)	R	.264	64	220	33	58	11	3	0	19	37	48	12	5	.384	.341
2017	Cubs (AZL)	R	.259	48	185	19	48	10	2	2	22	18	59	6	2	.332	.368
Minor League Totals			.262	112	405	52	106	21	5	2	41	55	107	18	7	.361	.353

30 JAKE STINNETT, RHP

Born: April 25, 1992. **B-T:** R-R. **Ht.:** 6-4. **Wt.:** 202. **Drafted:** Maryland, 2014 (2ns round). **Signed by:** Billy Swope.

BA GRADE
45 Risk: High

A converted third baseman who became Maryland's ace in 2014, Stinnett was the Cubs' second pick in 2014. He and top pick Kyle Schwarber signed below-slot deals that helped the club sign prep pitchers Justin Steele, Carson Sands and Dylan Cease to above-slot deals in what the club hoped would be a breakthrough pitcher class.

Stinnett's stuff in his first two full pro seasons never lived up to what he'd shown as an amateur, particularly his slider. A double-plus pitch at times at Maryland, it flattened out as a pro, and shoulder inflammation sidelined him for the first half of 2017. (He has a pin in his elbow from an injury in his youth.) When he returned with a rehabilitation stint in the Rookie-level Arizona League, it was as a reliever, not as a starter, and Stinnett finally started getting some of the swings and misses he did as an amateur. While his 83-84 mph slider isn't consistent yet, at times it has the power and depth of a plus pitch, and his fastball velocity kept climbing, as he sat 92-94 mph and hit 96 regularly in the Arizona Fall League.

Stinnett still throws a decent changeup, even in a relief role, and the Cubs hope his stuff continues to tick up in shorter relief stints.

Year	Club (League)	Class	W	L	ERA	G	GS	CG	SV	IP	H	HR	BB	SO	K/9	WHIP	AVG
2015	South Bend (MWL)	LoA	7	6	4.46	22	22	0	0	117	117	6	50	91	7.0	1.43	.267
2016	Myrtle Beach (CAR)	HiA	9	4	4.27	20	20	0	0	116	114	7	40	97	7.5	1.33	.263
2017	Cubs (AZL)	R	0	0	0.00	3	0	0	0	5	4	0	0	9	17.4	0.86	.222
	Myrtle Beach (CAR)	HiA	0	1	5.40	2	0	0	0	3	5	1	2	4	10.8	2.10	.385
	Tennessee (SL)	AA	0	1	0.61	9	0	0	0	15	6	0	6	14	8.6	0.82	.130
Minor League Totals			16	13	4.12	61	46	0	0	267	258	15	100	225	7.6	1.34	.260

Chicago White Sox

BY JOSH NORRIS

The story of the 2017 White Sox really began at the 2016 Winter Meetings. After realizing they were unlikely to be competitive with their current roster, management began a teardown in the hopes of turning their high-end, cost-effective major league talent into a slew of top prospects.

First, they dealt lefty Chris Sale to the Red Sox in exchange for a four-player package fronted by Yoan Moncada, the reigning Baseball America Minor League Player of the Year at the time. The return also included righthander Michael Kopech, who now ranks as the team's top pitching prospect.

They completed a 1-2 punch by dealing outfielder Adam Eaton to the Nationals for three high-end righthanders: Lucas Giolito, Reynaldo Lopez and Dane Dunning. All three look like big pieces of the White Sox's rebuild and Giolito and Lopez exhausted their rookie eligibility in 2017.

Then came the regular season. As predicted, the team was not particularly competitive. On July 13, a day before the team was to return from the all-star break and with a 38-49 record, Chicago made its next move. Lefthander Jose Quintana was sent to the crosstown Cubs for a four-player package led by outfielder Eloy Jimenez and righthander Dylan Cease.

Jimenez is one of the game's very best prospects, and he and Cease are both among the team's Top 10 prospects. Overall four of the White Sox's Top 10 prospects were acquired in megadeals consummated over a seven-month period. That also includes outfielder Blake Rutherford, the top talent acquired from the Yankees in exchange for third baseman Todd Frazier and relievers David Robertson and Tommy Kahnle.

The White Sox also made a splash by signing Cuban wunderkind Luis Robert to a $26 million deal. He immediately found a spot in the top part of their already-stacked system.

With most of the team's top talent traded away—though Jose Abreu and Avisail Garcia remain as possible targets—the next step is developing the next generation.

The White Sox got a glimpse of that future with Giolito, Lopez and Moncada, to mixed results. With Chicago, Moncada was allowed to focus on second base only instead of the utility role he was preparing for with the Red Sox. That made the developmental path a little less complicated, but there were still other dings. He struck out at a 28.6 percent clip with Triple-A and whiffed in 33 percent of his plate appearances with the big league

After struggling at Triple-A, Lucas Giolito recorded a 2.38 ERA in 45 big league innings.

PROJECTED 2021 LINEUP

Catcher	Zack Collins (26)
First Base	Gavin Sheets (24)
Second Base	Yoan Moncada (25)
Third Base	Jake Burger (24)
Shortstop	Tim Anderson (27)
Left Field	Eloy Jimenez (24)
Center Field	Luis Robert (23)
Right Field	Avisail Garcia (29)
Designated Hitter	Jose Abreu (34)
No. 1 Starter	Michael Kopech (24)
No. 2 Starter	Carlos Rodon (28)
No. 3 Starter	Lucas Giolito (26)
No. 4 Starter	Reynaldo Lopez (27)
No. 5 Starter	Alec Hansen (26)
Closer	Zack Burdi (26)

club. There were glimpses of his talent, but there's still plenty of development remaining before determining if he'll reach his ceiling.

Giolito started poorly at Triple-A but slowly made enough adjustments to earn a callup and pitch to a 2.38 ERA in the big leagues. Lopez was inconsistent at Triple-A, but still found his way to Chicago. He cut his walk rate significantly from his time in the majors with the Nationals, and also was used exclusively as a starter.

The top portion of their system is among the best in baseball, thanks to all the trades plus some smart draft choices. Abreu and Garcia still provide a little bit of veteran leadership, but the best is clearly yet to come in Chicago.

CHICAGO WHITE SOX

TOP 2018 ROOKIE: Michael Kopech, RHP. If he can command the ball at Triple-A, he should find his way to Chicago quickly.

BREAKOUT PROSPECT: Luis Alexander Basabe, OF. With a year of good health, he could blossom into his big-time potential.

SLEEPER: Jake Peter, 2B/OF. He might have a future as a utility player with a little bit of offensive upside.

SOURCE OF TOP 30 TALENT

Homegrown	20	Acquired	10
College	15	Trade	10
Junior college	0	Rule 5 draft	0
High school	2	Independent league	0
Nondrafted free agent	0	Free agent/waivers	0
International	3		

LF
Eloy Jimenez (1)
Blake Rutherford (8)
Alex Call (21)
Courtney Hawkins
Aaron Schnurbusch
Alex Destino

CF
Luis Robert (4)
Luis Gonzalez (14)
Jameson Fisher
Jacob May
Logan Taylor

RF
Micker Adolfo (17)
Tito Polo (27)
Ryan Cordell
Willy Garcia

3B
Jake Burger (7)
Trey Michalczewski
Patrick Leonard
Amado Nunez

SS
Yeyson Yrizarri
Tracy Hadley
Johan Cruz
Eddy Alvarez

2B
Lenyn Sosa (28)
Jake Peter
Ti'Quan Forbes
Bryant Flete
Danny Mendick
Sam Dexter
Luis Curbelo

1B
Gavin Sheets (9)
Daniel Palka
Casey Gillaspie
Matt Rose
Danny Hayes
Matt Skole

C
Zack Collins (6)
Seby Zavala (29)
Evan Skoug

LHP

LHSP	LHRP
Ian Clarkin (22)	Louie Lechich
Jordan Guerrero (25)	Aaron Bummer
Bernardo Flores (26)	

RHP

RHSP	RHRP
Michael Kopech (2)	Zack Burdi (11)
Alec Hansen (3)	Thyago Vieira (20)
Dane Dunning (5)	Ian Hamilton (23)
Dylan Cease (10)	Tyler Johnson (24)
Spencer Adams (12)	Connor Walsh (30)
Carson Fulmer (13)	Robinson Leyer
A.J. Puckett (15)	Brad Goldberg
Jordan Stephens (16)	Hunter Kiel
Lincoln Henzman (19)	Victor Diaz
Kade McClure	

DRAFT ANALYSIS

2017

BEST PURE HITTER: Because of his power production, hitting ability is not what comes to mind first regarding 3B Jake Burger (1). A career .339 hitter at Missouri State, he walked more than he struck out as a junior. He has fast hands and a good feel for the strike zone.

BEST POWER HITTER: Burger's back-to-back seasons of more than 20 home runs at Missouri State were no fluke. He produces plus power thanks to above-average bat speed and his strong frame. 1B Gavin Sheets (2) also offers plus raw power.

FASTEST RUNNER: OF Logan Taylor (16) has plus speed that plays well both on the basepaths and in the outfield, where he tracks down balls well.

BEST DEFENSIVE PLAYER: Taylor was a good enough defender in center field to often push 2016 Brewers first-rounder Corey Ray to a corner at Louisville. OF Luis Gonzalez (3) also earns praise for his play in center field.

BEST FASTBALL: RHP Tyler Johnson (5) is the prototypical power reliever and can reach 100 mph with his fastball. He routinely sits in the upper 90s in short stints.

BEST SECONDARY PITCH: RHP Lincoln Henzman (4) succeeded Zack Burdi as Louisville's closer and now joins him in the White Sox organization. Henzman's slider isn't as good as Burdi's, but it's still an above-average offering.

BEST PRO DEBUT: OF Craig Dedelow (9), 22, was old for the Rookie-level Pioneer League, but he excelled with Great Falls, earning a spot on the circuit's postseason all-star team and producing 36 extra-base hits. 3B Justin Yurchak (12) ranked fourth in the league in OBP during a .345/.448/.520 campaign for the Voyagers.

BEST ATHLETE: Dedelow and Taylor both have impressive athleticism. Taylor is a better runner, but Dedelow carries his 6-foot-4, 195-pound frame well, giving him a solid power-speed combination.

TOP DRAFT PICKS OF THE DECADE

Year	Player, Pos.	2017 Org
2008	Gordon Beckham, SS	Mariners
2009	Jared Mitchell, OF	Atlantic League
2010	Chris Sale, LHP	Red Sox
2011	Keenyn Walker, OF (1st round supp.)	Frontier Lge
2012	Courtney Hawkins, OF	White Sox
2013	Tim Anderson, SS	White Sox
2014	Carlos Rodon, LHP	White Sox
2015	Carson Fulmer, RHP	White Sox
2016	Zack Collins, C	White Sox
2017	Jake Burger, 3B	White Sox

MOST INTRIGUING BACKGROUND: 1B Sam Abbott (8) was a star water polo player in high school. He was named state MVP three times in the sport and was committed to play it at Long Beach State before the White Sox drafted him. He has athletic bloodlines as well, as his mother was an Olympic swimmer with the Russian national team. Sheets' father Larry hit 94 home runs in eight big league seasons, including 31 for the Orioles in 1987.

CLOSEST TO THE MAJORS: Burger is an advanced hitter, and his combination of hittability and power give him a chance to move quickly in the minor leagues.

BEST LATE-ROUND PICK: Yurchak proved his contact ability as a career .316 hitter in college and with a strong showing in the Cape Cod League. He has elite bat-to-ball skills and rarely strikes out, though there are some questions about how he profiles as a corner infielder.

THE ONE WHO GOT AWAY: The White Sox signed their first 34 picks and inked all but five of their selections. LHP Angelo Smith (40) is undersized at 5-foot-10, 155 pounds but could be the best of the small unsigned group. The Chicago native, who now attends Michigan, has a fast arm and an exciting fastball-curveball combination.

—TEDDY CAHILL

2016

RHP Alec Hansen (2) has made a leap and finished second in the minors in strikeouts. C Zack Collins (1) has moved quickly and showed big power, but still has rough edges. RHP Zack Burdi (1) is recovering from Tommy John surgery.

GRADE: B

2015

RHP Carson Fulmer (1) raced to the big leagues, but hasn't yet found a home on the staff. LHP Zack Erwin (4) was a part of the trade for Brett Lawrie, and RHP Jordan Stephens (5) is the class' next-best shot at producing a productive piece.

GRADE: D

2014

LHP Carlos Rodon (1) has become a rotation regular for the White Sox, but hasn't found the dominant form he showed in college. LHPs Jace Fry (3) and Aaron Bummer (19) made it a trio of lefties from the class to pitch in Chicago in 2017.

GRADE: C

1 ELOY JIMENEZ, OF

Born: Nov. 27, 1996. **B-T:** R-R. **Ht.:** 6-4. **Wt.:** 205.
Signed: Dominican Republic, 2013. **Signed by:**
Jose Serra/Carlos Reyes (Cubs).

The Cubs signed two of the best prospects in the 2013 international class in Jimenez and shortstop Gleyber Torres. Four years later, both have been traded away. The Cubs dealt Torres to the Yankees at the 2016 trade deadline in a package for closer Aroldis Chapman. Jimenez, who signed for $2.8 million, was sent to the White Sox in 2017 as the grand prize in a four-player package for lefthander Jose Quintana. Jimenez showed standout tools at every stop with the Cubs, played in two consecutive Futures Games and went viral on Twitter last season with a home run in the Carolina League all-star game home run derby that blasted a light tower in left field, a la Roy Hobbs in "The Natural." As far as games that counted, Jimenez missed time with shoulder and hamstring injuries at high Class A Beach but returned to star form after the mid-July trade to the White Sox.

Scouts who saw Jimenez last season used words like "manchild," "mutant" and "Superman." More specifically, Jimenez is an intimidating, strong-bodied prospect with a whip-quick bat capable of massive home runs. More than his raw power, which is borderline top of the scale, Jimenez is a diligent, dedicated worker. One manager recalled seeing Jimenez strike out multiple times during a game, then seeing him on the field early the next day for tracking drills. Rival managers lamented not being able to find many holes in his swing, even when they'd pitch him backward. And here's the scary part: He might not be done developing physically. Jimenez played all season at 20 years old, and still has room to sculpt his body and add more strength, possibly becoming a perennial 40-home run threat. Defensively, he's spent his career flopping back and forth between right and left field, with left his likely eventually home because of his below-average arm. He's also a tick below-average runner. Defense and speed were never expected to be selling points of his game, however. Jimenez is a hitter, period, with mix of power and the ability to get to it to change a game.

Jimenez will likely begin 2018 back at Double-A Birmingham. With a rare mix of above-average hitting ability, massive power potential and the work ethic to make it all click, Jimenez projects as foundational hitter in the middle of the White Sox's order for years to come.

BRIAN WESTERHOLZ/SPORTS ON FILM

BA GRADE	SCOUTING GRADES
70 Risk: High	HIT: 60. POW: 70. SPD: 40. FLD: 45. ARM: 45.

Projected future grades on 20-80 scouting scale

TOP PROSPECTS OF THE DECADE

Year	Player, Pos.	2017 Org
2008	Gio Gonzalez, LHP	Nationals
2009	Gordon Beckham, SS	Mariners
2010	Jared Mitchell, OF	Atlantic League
2011	Chris Sale, LHP	Red Sox
2012	Addison Reed, RHP	Red Sox
2013	Courtney Hawkins, OF	White Sox
2014	Jose Abreu, 1B	White Sox
2015	Carlos Rodon, LHP	White Sox
2016	Tim Anderson, SS	White Sox
2017	Yoan Moncada, 2B/3B	White Sox

BEST TOOLS

Best Hitter for Average	Eloy Jimenez
Best Power Hitter	Eloy Jimenez
Best Strike-Zone Discipline	Zack Collins
Fastest Baserunner	Logan Taylor
Best Athlete	Luis Robert
Best Fastball	Michael Kopech
Best Curveball	Alec Hansen
Best Slider	Zack Burdi
Best Changeup	A.J. Puckett
Best Control	Dane Dunning
Best Defensive Catcher	Nate Nolan
Best Defensive Infielder	Yeyson Yrizarri
Best Infield Arm	Zach Remillard
Best Defensive Outfielder	Luis Alexander Basabe
Best Outfield Arm	Micker Adolfo

Year	Club (League)	Class	AVG	G	AB	R	H	2B	3B	HR	RBI	BB	SO	SB	CS	OBP	SLG
2015	Eugene (NWL)	SS	.284	57	232	36	66	10	0	7	33	15	43	3	2	.328	.418
2016	South Bend (MWL)	LoA	.329	112	432	65	142	40	3	14	81	25	94	8	3	.369	.532
2017	Myrtle Beach (CAR)	HiA	.271	42	155	23	42	6	2	8	32	18	35	0	0	.351	.490
	Winston-Salem (CAR)	HiA	.345	29	110	20	38	11	1	8	26	12	21	0	2	.410	.682
	Birmingham (SL)	AA	.353	18	68	11	24	5	0	3	7	5	16	1	1	.397	.559
Minor League Totals			.302	300	1147	168	346	80	8	43	206	85	241	15	9	.350	.498

2 MICHAEL KOPECH, RHP

Born: April 30, 1996. **B-T:** R-R. **Ht.:** 6-3. **Wt.:** 205. **Drafted:** HS—Mount Pleasant, Texas, 2014 (1st round). **Signed by:** Tim Collinsworth (Red Sox).

Kopech has long reigned as one of the hardest-throwing starters in the minors, and the White Sox acquired him as part of the trade for Chris Sale at the 2016 Winter Meetings. Kopech had a couple of extracurricular incidents mar his development—a 50-game suspension for amphetamines and a broken hand sustained in a fight with a teammate—but he's still become an elite prospect and finished a dominant 2017 at Triple-A Charlotte.

Kopech's calling card is his top-of-the-scale fastball, which sits in the upper-90s and regularly touches 100 mph with armside run and downhill plane. It's an elite pitch, but he will overthrow it at times. The White Sox asked Kopech to add a two-seam fastball to induce more grounders and help teach him not to overthrow. Kopech boasts a slider that projects as a future plus pitch, as well as an average, low-90s changeup the White Sox encouraged him to throw more. Kopech still needs to iron out some inconsistencies in his delivery—particularly a tendency to fall off the rubber—in order to improve his below-average command and control.

Kopech is likely to begin 2018 back at Triple-A, with a good shot of making his major league debut during the year. If he can tame his arsenal a bit more, he can be a top-of-the-rotation starter.

BA GRADE

65 Risk: Medium

FB: 80. SL: 60.
CHG: 50.
CTL: 45.

Year	Club (League)	Class	W	L	ERA	G	GS	CG	SV	IP	H	HR	BB	SO	K/9	WHIP	AVG
2015	Greenville (SAL)	LoA	4	5	2.63	16	15	0	0	65	53	2	27	70	9.7	1.23	.228
2016	Lowell (NYP)	SS	0	0	0.00	1	1	0	0	4	4	0	4	4	8.3	1.85	.250
	Salem (CAR)	HiA	4	1	2.25	11	11	0	0	52	25	1	29	82	14.2	1.04	.147
2017	Birmingham (SL)	AA	8	7	2.87	22	22	0	0	119	77	6	60	155	11.7	1.15	.184
	Charlotte (IL)	AAA	1	1	3.00	3	3	0	0	15	15	0	5	17	10.2	1.33	.263
Minor League Totals			17	15	2.74	61	60	0	0	269	185	9	134	344	11.5	1.18	.196

3 ALEC HANSEN, RHP

Born: Oct. 10, 1994. **B-T:** R-R. **Ht.:** 6-7. **Wt.:** 235. **Drafted:** Oklahoma, 2016 (2nd round). **Signed by:** Clay Overcash.

Considered a candidate to go first overall in the 2016 draft, Hansen had a disastrous junior season at Oklahoma and got bumped from the starting rotation as well as the first round. The White Sox snatched him up in the second round and signed him for $1.2 million.

They started Hansen in Rookie-ball after signing to regain his confidence against less experienced hitters, and he came out in 2017 and finished second in the minors with 191 strikeouts, finishing in Double-A. Hansen starts his arsenal with a hard mid-90s fastball that peaks at 98 mph. He gets downward plane on the pitch, and the White Sox made mechanical tweaks—namely keeping his shoulders even throughout his delivery—to help keep his fastball life consistent. Hansen couples the pitch with a hard curveball that flashes plus potential. He's improved his changeup from a show-me pitch at Oklahoma to one with heavy sink and average potential. He's also working to develop a slider.

Hansen's imposing size at 6-foot-7, 235 pounds gives him an intimidation factor on the mound, but also contributes to inconsistent command and control. Hansen will return to Double-A to begin 2018. He has the ceiling of a No. 3 starter if everything clicks.

BA GRADE

55 Risk: High

FB: 70. CB: 55.
SL: 40. CHG: 55.
CTL: 45.

Year	Club (League)	Class	W	L	ERA	G	GS	CG	SV	IP	H	HR	BB	SO	K/9	WHIP	AVG
2016	White Sox (AZL)	R	0	0	0.00	3	3	0	0	7	1	0	4	11	14.1	0.71	.048
	Great Falls (PIO)	R	2	0	1.23	7	7	0	0	37	12	3	12	59	14.5	0.65	.102
	Kannapolis (SAL)	LoA	0	1	2.45	2	2	0	0	11	11	0	4	11	9.0	1.36	.262
2017	Kannapolis (SAL)	LoA	7	3	2.48	13	13	0	0	73	57	3	23	92	11.4	1.10	.207
	Winston-Salem (CAR)	HiA	4	5	2.93	11	11	1	0	58	42	5	25	82	12.7	1.15	.203
	Birmingham (SL)	AA	0	0	4.35	2	2	0	0	10	15	0	3	17	14.8	1.74	.333
Minor League Totals			13	9	2.39	38	38	1	0	196	138	11	71	272	12.5	1.07	.195

4 LUIS ROBERT, OF

BILL MITCHELL

Born: Aug. 3, 1997. **B-T:** R-R. **Ht.:** 6-3. **Wt.:** 185. **Signed:** Cuba, 2017. **Signed by:** Kenny Williams/Marco Paddy.

Robert built an impressive track record in Cuba, including posting an .895 OPS as a 15-year-old against older competition in the island's national 18U league. Robert had heaps of international success as well and signed with the White Sox for $26 million in May, a franchise record for an international signee.

Robert began in the Dominican Summer League and impressed despite missing time with a few nagging injuries. The White Sox's top prospect, Eloy Jimenez, is farther along, but Robert's tools are just as impressive. He boasts a strong, lean frame at 6-foot-3 and 220 pounds. His swing is compact and simple, and he produces well above-average bat speed. He's got plus raw power and slugged three homers in limited time in the DSL. He does swing and miss on elevated fastballs, but it's not a huge ding on his record. Robert was rated as a 55-60-grade runner as an amateur, but he has gotten faster as he matured and now earns plus-plus grades for his speed.

BA GRADE
60 Risk: Extreme
HIT: 55. **POW:** 60.
SPD: 70. **FLD:** 50.
ARM: 60.

Defensively the White Sox believe Robert will be able to maintain enough speed and range to stay in center field long-term. If that doesn't work out, his bat will more than play in a corner. After spending the summer in the DSL mainly for tax purposes, Robert is likely to join a crowded outfield in high Class A Winston-Salem in 2018.

Year	Club (League)	Class	AVG	G	AB	R	H	2B	3B	HR	RBI	BB	SO	SB	CS	OBP	SLG
2015	Ciego de Avila (CNS)	CNS	.305	68	269	68	82	10	2	5	29	32	46	8	2	.384	.413
2016	Ciego de Avila (CNS)	CNS	.401	53	182	51	73	12	2	12	40	38	30	11	6	.526	.687
	Cuban Team (C-A)	IND	.286	16	63	12	18	2	1	1	8	4	15	3	0	.319	.397
2017	White Sox (DSL)	R	.310	28	84	17	26	8	1	3	14	22	23	12	3	.491	.536
Minor League Totals			.310	28	84	17	26	8	1	3	14	22	23	12	3	.491	.536

5 DANE DUNNING, RHP

Born: Dec. 20, 1994. **B-T:** R-R. **Ht.:** 6-4. **Wt.:** 200. **Drafted:** Florida, 2016 (1st round). **Signed by:** Buddy Hernandez (Nationals).

The Florida Gators produce pro-ready pitchers at a prodigious rate. Dunning is yet another example of the team's pitching proclivity. He was used as a valuable reliever by the Gators, but was long targeted by pro scouts as a quality starting pitching prospect—he made more starts in 2017 in pro ball than he made in three seasons at Florida.

The White Sox targeted Dunning in the 2016 draft, but the Nationals took him at the end of the first round before they had a chance to grab him. Six months later, the White Sox acquired Dunning along with Reynaldo Lopez and Lucas Giolito for Adam Eaton from the Nationals. Dunning cruised through the Class A levels in his first full season, posting a combined 2.94 ERA. Dunning operates primarily with a sinker and a slider, and has a changeup as well. He sits in the low-to-mid-90s,

BA GRADE
55 Risk: High
FB: 60. **SL:** 60.
CHG: 55.
CTL: 55.

peaking at 96 mph. When his delivery is clicking, Dunning features heavy sink and will coax hitters into beating the ball into the ground. He struggled at times to get out over his front side, which had a flattening effect on his stuff and resulted in an elevated—and out of character—home run rate at high Class A Winston-Salem. Dunning's slider and changeup, both thrown in the low-to-mid-80s, have above-average or plus potential. To maintain consistency and crispness on his pitches, the White Sox have stressed to Dunning the need to stay tall through his delivery.

Dunning will likely join Alec Hansen atop a very talented rotation at Double-A Birmingham in 2018. With three quality pitches and a clean, repeatable delivery, he has a mid-rotation ceiling moving forward.

Year	Club (League)	Class	W	L	ERA	G	GS	CG	SV	IP	H	HR	BB	SO	K/9	WHIP	AVG
2016	Nationals (GCL)	R	0	0	0.00	1	1	0	0	2	0	0	0	3	13.5	0.00	.000
	Auburn (NYP)	SS	3	2	2.14	7	7	1	0	34	26	1	7	29	7.8	0.98	.208
2017	Kannapolis (SAL)	LoA	2	0	0.35	4	4	0	0	26	13	0	2	33	11.4	0.58	.143
	Winston-Salem (CAR)	HiA	6	8	3.51	22	22	2	0	118	114	15	36	135	10.3	1.27	.250
Minor League Totals			11	10	2.76	34	34	3	0	180	153	16	45	200	10.0	1.10	.226

6 ZACK COLLINS, C

Born: Feb. 6, 1995. **B-T:** L-R. **Ht.:** 6-3. **Wt.:** 220. **Drafted:** Miami, 2016 (1st round).
Signed by: Jose Ortega.

Collins earned a reputation as one of the best offensive catchers in the country at Miami and was drafted ninth overall by the White Sox in 2016. He signed for $3,380,600 and moved quickly in his first full season, reporting straight to high Class A Winston-Salem and finishing the year at Double-A Birmingham, posting a combined .816 OPS.

Collins is divisive, but everybody sees his nearly unmatched batting eye and pole-to-pole power. It's an excellent starting point, but not everyone is convinced he'll hit for average, especially after he hit .224 in his debut year. Collins has a bat tip at the beginning of his swing, which diminishes his ability to get to hard fastballs. He re-tooled his swing in the instructional league, making it quieter to get in a better position to hit. Collins worked diligently on his defense throughout the season and needs to continue. He struggles with velocity and presents pitches poorly, turning strikes into balls. He's improved with blocking but has work to do with his agility. Collins' arm ranges from average to plus on throws to second, and improved footwork would make his arm play up.

Collins will return to Double-A to start 2018 and continue working to improve his contact skills and defense. If it all comes together, he could be an offensive-minded everyday catcher.

BA GRADE
55 Risk: High
HIT: 40. POW: 60.
SPD: 20. FLD: 50.
ARM: 45.

Year	Club (League)	Class	AVG	G	AB	R	H	2B	3B	HR	RBI	BB	SO	SB	CS	OBP	SLG
2016	White Sox (AZL)	R	.091	3	11	1	1	0	0	0	0	0	7	0	0	.091	.091
	Winston-Salem (CAR)	HiA	.258	36	120	24	31	7	0	6	18	33	39	0	0	.418	.467
2017	Winston-Salem (CAR)	HiA	.223	101	341	63	76	18	3	17	48	76	118	0	2	.365	.443
	Birmingham (SL)	AA	.235	12	34	7	8	2	0	2	5	11	11	0	0	.422	.471
Minor League Totals			.229	152	506	95	116	27	3	25	71	120	175	0	2	.377	.443

7 JAKE BURGER, 3B

Born: April 10, 1996. **B-T:** R-R. **Ht.:** 6-2. **Wt.:** 210. **Drafted:** Missouri State, 2017 (1st round). **Signed by:** Clay Overcash.

Burger raked for three years at Missouri State and emerged as the top power prospect in the 2017 draft. He swatted 47 home runs his sophomore and junior seasons and while never batting below .328, earned a spot on the US Collegiate National Team and was First Team All-America as a junior.

The White Sox jumped on Burger with the 11th overall pick and signed him for $3.7 million. Burger's power is prodigious, and his leadership-oriented makeup is legendary, but scouts have concerns about his body. At 6-foot-2 and a thick, bottom-heavy 210 pounds, Burger stayed in Arizona over the winter to have access to the White Sox's complex and work on his conditioning. Scouts see a solid-average hitter with above-average power potential, and the plate discipline to get to it in games as a pro. Burger's body opens the door for questions about his defense, but he's worked hard to improve his footwork and range to stay at third base. He has more than enough arm strength to stay at the position and the power to profile there long-term. He's a well below-average runner.

Burger will head to high Class A Winston-Salem in 2018, where he'll get to show off his power in the hitter-friendly confines of BB&T Ballpark

BA GRADE
55 Risk: High
HIT: 50. POW: 60.
SPD: 30. FLD: 45.
ARM: 55.

Year	Club (League)	Class	AVG	G	AB	R	H	2B	3B	HR	RBI	BB	SO	SB	CS	OBP	SLG
2017	White Sox (AZL)	R	.154	4	13	4	2	1	0	1	2	1	2	0	0	.353	.462
	Kannapolis (SAL)	LoA	.271	47	181	21	49	9	2	4	27	13	28	0	1	.335	.409
Minor League Totals			.263	51	194	25	51	10	2	5	29	14	30	0	1	.336	.412

8 BLAKE RUTHERFORD, OF

Born: May 2, 1997. **B-T:** L-L. **Ht.:** 6-3. **Wt.:** 195. **Drafted:** HS—Canoga Park, Calif., 2016 (1st round). **Signed by:** Bobby DeJardin (Yankees).

The Yankees were ecstatic Rutherford fell to them at No. 18 in the 2016 draft and signed him for $3.282 million. But after a middling start to his first full professional season at low Class A Charleston, the Yankees traded Rutherford in mid-July to the White Sox as the headliner of a four-player package for relievers David Robertson and Tommy Kahnle and third baseman Todd Frazier.

Rutherford's sweet lefthanded swing, disciplined approach and the sound the ball makes off his bat makes scouts believe he'll be an above-average hitter in the future, but questions about his power potential have yet to be answered, especially after he hit just two homers in his full-season debut. Rutherford is likely to move off of center field, so the emergence of power will be key to his profile as a big leaguer. Evaluators with both of his employers saw average power potential so long as he works to add muscle, which was one of his goals this season. Because of his below-average footspeed and arm, Rutherford is likely to settle into left field.

BA GRADE
55 Risk: V. High
HIT: 55. POW: 50.
SPD: 45. FLD: 50.
ARM: 45.

Rutherford is likely to be part of a crowded outfield picture in high Class A Winston-Salem in 2018. He'll rotate between center and left field, and whether his power starts to play in games will be a key storyline.

Year	Club (League)	Class	AVG	G	AB	R	H	2B	3B	HR	RBI	BB	SO	SB	CS	OBP	SLG
2016	Yankees2 (GCL)	R	.240	8	25	3	6	1	0	1	3	4	6	0	0	.333	.400
	Pulaski (APP)	R	.382	25	89	13	34	7	4	2	9	9	24	0	2	.440	.618
2017	Charleston, SC (SAL)	LoA	.281	71	274	41	77	20	2	2	30	25	55	9	4	.342	.391
	Kannapolis (SAL)	LoA	.213	30	122	11	26	5	0	0	5	13	21	1	0	.289	.254
Minor League Totals			.280	134	510	68	143	33	6	5	47	51	106	10	6	.346	.398

9 GAVIN SHEETS, 1B

Born: April 23, 1996. **B-T:** L-L. **Ht.:** 6-4. **Wt.:** 230. **Drafted:** Wake Forest, 2017 (2nd round). **Signed by:** Abe Fernandez.

The son of former Orioles slugger Larry Sheets, Gavin Sheets hit 11 home runs combined during his first two seasons at Wake Forest but erupted for 21 homers as a junior in 2017. His power burst carried the Demon Deacons to the Super Regionals, and the White Sox grabbed him with their second-round pick, No. 49 overall, and signed him for $2 million.

After a long college season Sheets was a bit fatigued when he made his pro debut, mostly with low Class A Kannapolis, but still showed impressive hitting ability. Sheets has a leveraged swing with plus raw power, but evaluators note he will have to be more selective with pitches in the zone as a pro to find ways to do damage. He rarely chases out of the zone and posts promising strikeout-to-walk marks for a power hitter. Defensively, Sheets moves well for a big man and is a solid defender at first base with average range and an average throwing arm.

BA GRADE
50 Risk: High
HIT: 50. POW: 60.
SPD: 30. FLD: 50.
ARM: 50.

Some scouts see Sheets as a hitter in the mold of a Lucas Duda at the highest level. He will move to high Class A Winston-Salem in 2018 and try to continue slugging in one of the better hitters' parks in the country.

Year	Club (League)	Class	AVG	G	AB	R	H	2B	3B	HR	RBI	BB	SO	SB	CS	OBP	SLG
2017	White Sox (AZL)	R	.500	4	12	3	6	2	0	1	3	3	0	0	0	.625	.917
	Kannapolis (SAL)	LoA	.266	52	192	16	51	10	0	3	25	20	34	0	0	.346	.365
Minor League Totals			.279	56	204	19	57	12	0	4	28	23	34	0	0	.365	.397

10 DYLAN CEASE, RHP

Born: Dec. 28, 1995. **B-T:** R-R. **Ht.:** 6-2. **Wt.:** 190. **Drafted:** HS—Milton, Ga., 2014 (6th round). **Signed by:** Keith Lockhart (Cubs).

Cease had Tommy John surgery as a senior in high school, but the Cubs saw enough in his younger years to draft him in the sixth round in 2014 and sign him for $1.5 million. After he spent a year recovering, Cease debuted in 2015 and was steadily moving up the Cubs system when he was traded to the White Sox in July with Eloy Jimenez, Matt Rose and Bryant Flete for Jose Quintana.

Cease's best pitch is a hard, mid-90s fastball that reaches 98 mph and has tickled triple-digits in the past. It's elite velocity plays up with sink as well. Cease couples his fastball with a hard, 12-to-6 curveball that he uses to get swings-and-misses, and projects as a plus pitch. His changeup has made progress, but it's still a distant third pitch. Cease's below-average command and control have improved some, but he still walked 4.2 batters-per-nine innings across the Class A levels the past year. There's some thought, because of his two dominant pitches, Cease might have more success as a high-leverage reliever. It's too early for that move now and the White Sox will continue developing him as a starter.

Cease will head high Class A Winston-Salem in 2018. His main goals will be to sharpen his command and improve his secondary pitches.

BA GRADE
50 Risk: High
FB: 70. CB: 60.
CHG: 40.
CTL: 40.

Year	Club (League)	Class	W	L	ERA	G	GS	CG	SV	IP	H	HR	BB	SO	K/9	WHIP	AVG
2015	Cubs (AZL)	R	1	2	2.63	11	8	0	0	24	12	0	16	25	9.4	1.17	.145
2016	Eugene (NWL)	SS	2	0	2.22	12	12	0	0	45	27	1	25	66	13.3	1.16	.175
2017	South Bend (MWL)	LoA	1	2	2.79	13	13	0	0	52	39	2	26	74	12.9	1.26	.214
	Kannapolis (SAL)	LoA	0	8	3.89	9	9	0	0	42	35	1	18	52	11.2	1.27	.229
Minor League Totals			4	12	2.89	45	42	0	0	162	113	4	85	217	12.1	1.22	.198

11 ZACK BURDI, RHP

BA GRADE
55 Risk: Extreme

Born: March 9, 1995. **B-T:** R-R. **Ht.:** 6-3. **Wt.:** 205. **Drafted:** Louisville, 2016 (1st round). **Signed by:** Phil Gulley.

Burdi was one of the country's most dominant closers at Louisville, racking up 83 strikeouts in 70 collegiate innings and recording 20 career saves. The White Sox drafted him 26th overall in 2016 and signed him for $2,128,500. Burdi spent all but 22 innings of his pro career at Triple-A Charlotte, but his 2017 ended at midseason after he had Tommy John surgery. His brother Nick, a reliever in the Twins system, also went down with Tommy John surgery during the year.

When healthy, Burdi brings elite heat with a 98-102 mph fastball featuring with intense riding action borne of a high spin rate. He goes for strikeouts with his 86-89 mph slider, which can be inconsistent but projects as a plus pitch at its best. Burdi has a tendency to get quick in his delivery and get off line to home plate, leading to below-average command.

Burdi's stuff is that of a long-time closer, but he's been used just once in his pro career in back-to-back games, and he got shellacked in the second outing. There's also a chance the White Sox could utilize him as multi-inning "relief ace." Burdi is rehabbing from surgery and could return late in 2018.

Year	Club (League)	Class	W	L	ERA	G	GS	CG	SV	IP	H	HR	BB	SO	K/9	WHIP	AVG
2016	White Sox (AZL)	R	0	0	0.00	1	0	0	0	1	1	0	0	1	9.0	1.00	.250
	Winston-Salem (CAR)	HiA	0	0	5.40	4	0	0	0	5	6	1	0	4	7.2	1.20	.316
	Birmingham (SL)	AA	0	0	3.94	12	0	0	0	16	7	2	9	24	13.5	1.00	.132
	Charlotte (IL)	AAA	1	0	2.25	9	0	0	1	16	9	0	11	22	12.4	1.25	.161
2017	Charlotte (IL)	AAA	0	4	4.05	29	0	0	7	33	30	2	17	51	13.8	1.41	.231
Minor League Totals			1	4	3.66	55	0	0	8	71	53	5	37	102	12.9	1.26	.202

12 SPENCER ADAMS, RHP

BA GRADE
50 Risk: High

Born: April 13, 1996. **B-T:** R-R. **Ht.:** 6-3. **Wt.:** 171. **Drafted:** HS—Cleveland, Ga., 2014 (2nd round). **Signed by:** Kevin Burrell.

When the White Sox zeroed in on Adams in 2014, they saw an athletic pitcher with plenty of projectability. He starred as a basketball player in Georgia, and touched has high as 96 mph as an amateur. That was enough for the White Sox to take him in the second round and sign him for nearly $1.3 million.

Adams' velocity has taken a step back since he turned pro. He presently sits more in the 89-92 mph range with the fastball, albeit with above-average sink. He pairs his fastball with a slider that flashes above-average potential at its best, but sometimes morphs into a slurvier offering. The White Sox worked with Adams in 2017 at Double-A Birmingham to make that pitch more consistently crisp. His changeup has average potential, but needs to take a step forward with its consistency. Adams is a quick worker on the mound and is lauded for his willingness to attack the strike zone. He doesn't strike out a ton of hitters, but he doesn't walk many either.

Adams projects as a back-end type of starter with plenty of pitchability, though that could change if he matures physically and develops more velocity. He's slated for Triple-A Charlotte in 2018.

Year	Club (League)	Class	W	L	ERA	G	GS	CG	SV	IP	H	HR	BB	SO	K/9	WHIP	AVG
2015	Kannapolis (SAL)	LoA	9	5	3.24	19	19	1	0	100	111	7	11	73	6.6	1.22	.275
	Winston-Salem (CAR)	HiA	3	0	2.15	5	5	0	0	29	31	1	7	23	7.1	1.30	.267
2016	Winston-Salem (CAR)	HiA	8	7	4.01	18	18	1	0	108	120	7	21	74	6.2	1.31	.275
	Birmingham (SL)	AA	2	5	3.90	9	9	0	0	55	59	2	10	26	4.2	1.25	.274
2017	Birmingham (SL)	AA	7	15	4.42	26	26	2	0	153	171	19	40	113	6.7	1.38	.281
Minor League Totals			32	35	3.83	87	86	4	0	487	541	40	93	368	6.8	1.30	.277

13 CARSON FULMER, RHP

BA GRADE
45 Risk: Medium

Born: Dec. 13, 1993. **B-T:** R-R. **Ht.:** 6-0. **Wt.:** 195. **Drafted:** Vanderbilt, 2015 (1st round). **Signed by:** Phil Gulley.

Fulmer's highly successful college career at Vanderbilt included a College World Series championship in 2014 and First Team All-America selection in 2015. The White Sox used their first-round pick on him in 2015 and put him on a fast track to the major leagues. He made his big league debut on July 17, 2016, barely 13 months after he was drafted.

It's been a rocky road since then for Fulmer, who was used as both a reliever and a starter in the big leagues but pitched exclusively out of the rotation at Triple-A Charlotte in 2017. He's toned down his high-effort delivery since he turned pro, including reducing his hand pump and eliminating a stab in the back of his motion. It's still rushed, but less so than it was at Vanderbilt. Fulmer's fastball sat between 89-93 mph in 2017 with Charlotte, and he mixed in a heavy dose of cutters as well. He also showed an inconsistent but promising curveball and a below-average changeup.

Fulmer still has a chance to find a spot at the back of a rotation, but there's a better chance he winds up as a middle reliever. He'll have a chance to earn a place with the big club in spring training, but he could wind up back at Charlotte to start 2018.

Year	Club (League)	Class	W	L	ERA	G	GS	CG	SV	IP	H	HR	BB	SO	K/9	WHIP	AVG
2015	White Sox (AZL)	R	0	0	0.00	1	1	0	0	1	1	0	0	1	9.0	1.00	.333
	Winston-Salem (CAR)	HiA	0	0	2.05	8	8	0	0	22	16	2	9	25	10.2	1.14	.205
2016	Birmingham (SL)	AA	4	9	4.76	17	17	0	0	87	82	7	51	90	9.3	1.53	.248
	Chicago (AL)	MAJ	0	2	8.49	8	0	0	0	12	12	2	7	10	7.7	1.63	.273
	Charlotte (IL)	AAA	2	1	3.94	4	4	0	0	16	14	1	5	14	7.9	1.19	.233
2017	Charlotte (IL)	AAA	7	9	5.79	25	25	0	0	126	132	18	65	96	6.9	1.56	.268
	Chicago (AL)	MAJ	3	1	3.86	7	5	0	0	23	16	4	13	19	7.3	1.24	.188
Major League Totals			3	3	5.40	15	5	0	0	35	28	6	20	29	7.5	1.37	.217
Minor League Totals			13	19	4.96	55	55	0	0	252	245	28	130	226	8.1	1.49	.254

14 LUIS GONZALEZ, OF

BA GRADE
50 Risk: High

Born: Sept. 10, 1995. **B-T:** L-L. **Ht.:** 6-1. **Wt.:** 185. **Drafted:** New Mexico, 2017 (3rd round). **Signed by:** John Kazanas.

Brendan McKay was the headliner as far as college two-way players went in 2017, but Gonzalez deserved mention as well. Born in Sonora, Mexico, Gonzalez's pitching stats didn't jump off the page, but he started 22 games over three seasons at New Mexico and hit .361/.500/.589 in his junior year.

The industry much preferred Gonzalez as an outfielder, and the White Sox took him in the third round and signed him for $517,000. Though he was a little tired after his college season, Gonzalez made it to low Class A Kannapolis in his first try as a pro and immediately showed contact ability and strike-zone discipline. There are questions about Gonzalez's long-term power potential, though, the answer to which will determe his ceiling. The White Sox believe he'll have average to slightly better power. He's got enough speed and range to play center field, but he's likely to move around the outfield in 2018. His throwing arm is plus.

Gonzalez will start 2018 at either Kannapolis or at high Class A Winston-Salem, and his power output will be important to keep an eye on.

Year	Club (League)	Class	AVG	G	AB	R	H	2B	3B	HR	RBI	BB	SO	SB	CS	OBP	SLG
2017	Great Falls (PIO)	R	.118	4	17	3	2	1	0	0	3	4	3	0	0	.286	.176
	Kannapolis (SAL)	LoA	.245	63	233	26	57	13	4	2	12	38	50	2	3	.356	.361
Minor League Totals			.236	67	250	29	59	14	4	2	15	42	53	2	3	.351	.348

15 A.J. PUCKETT, RHP

Born: May 27, 1995. **B-T:** R-R. **Ht.:** 6-4. **Wt.:** 200. **Drafted:** Pepperdine, 2016 (2nd round). **Signed by:** Rich Amaral (Royals).

BA GRADE
50 Risk: High

Puckett, who was drafted by the Royals in the second round in 2016 and signed for $1.2 million, is lucky to be alive. He was placed in a medically-induced coma after a serious car accident in high school, which left him with plates in his head after surgery to repair a skull fracture. He was dealt to the White Sox at the 2017 trade deadline—along with lefthander Andre Davis—in exchange for outfielder Melky Cabrera.

Puckett missed time after the trade with a lat injury, but when he was on the mound showed the makings of a potential back-end starter with pitchability. Puckett's fastball typically parks in the 89-92 mph range and can either run or cut. He backs it up with a potentially plus changeup in the high-70s he throws with enough conviction to deceive hitters. He also throws a downer curveball in the 73-79 mph range that has improved since his early days in the Royals system.

Some scouts see a little bit more projection and velocity to come from Puckett, which would help improve his ceiling. He should start 2018 at either high Class A Winston-Salem or Double-A Birmingham.

Year	Club (League)	Class	W	L	ERA	G	GS	CG	SV	IP	H	HR	BB	SO	K/9	WHIP	AVG
2016	Royals (AZL)	R	0	1	3.86	2	2	0	0	7	8	1	0	8	10.3	1.14	.258
	Lexington (SAL)	LoA	2	3	3.66	11	11	0	0	52	42	4	15	37	6.4	1.10	.227
2017	Wilmington (CAR)	HiA	9	7	3.82	20	20	0	0	108	106	7	46	98	8.1	1.40	.257
	Winston-Salem (CAR)	HiA	1	0	4.28	5	5	0	0	27	35	2	5	21	6.9	1.46	.327
Minor League Totals			12	11	3.84	38	38	0	0	194	191	14	66	164	7.6	1.32	.260

16 JORDAN STEPHENS, RHP

Born: Sept. 12, 1992. **B-T:** R-R. **Ht.:** 6-1. **Wt.:** 190. **Drafted:** Rice, 2015 (5th round). **Signed by:** Chris Walker.

BA GRADE
50 Risk: High

Stephens stood out his sophomore year at Rice but had Tommy John surgery his junior year and took a medical redshirt. He rebounded the following year and the White Sox drafted him in the fifth round and signed him for $300,000. Stephens struck out a system-best 155 hitters in 141 innings in his first full year as a pro in 2016.

Stephens' stuff and results in 2017 at Double-A Birmingham were solid but not spectacular. Stephens typically sits in the low 90s with his four-seam fastball but can bump the mid-90s on his best days. His fastball isn't particularly lively, so he added a cutter in the high-80s to his arsenal. His primary offspeed pitch is an 11-to-5 curveball with average potential. He needs more consistency with it, as it was sometimes loopy out of his hand instead of the better, tighter offering. His sparsely-thrown changeup is below-average.

Some in the White Sox's organization believe Stephens' stuff might play better out of the pen, but he'll head to Triple-A Charlotte in 2018 as a starter to see if he can find more consistency.

Year	Club (League)	Class	W	L	ERA	G	GS	CG	SV	IP	H	HR	BB	SO	K/9	WHIP	AVG
2015	White Sox (AZL)	R	0	0	0.61	9	1	0	0	15	7	0	2	18	11.0	0.61	.140
	Great Falls (PIO)	R	0	0	0.00	2	0	0	0	3	2	0	1	3	9.0	1.00	.182
2016	Winston-Salem (CAR)	HiA	7	10	3.45	27	27	0	0	141	129	12	48	155	9.9	1.26	.243
2017	Birmingham (SL)	AA	3	7	3.14	16	16	0	0	92	84	4	35	83	8.1	1.30	.249
Minor League Totals			10	17	3.13	54	44	0	0	250	222	16	86	259	9.3	1.23	.239

17 MICKER ADOLFO, OF

Born: Sep. 11, 1996. **B-T:** R-R. **Ht.:** 6-3. **Wt.:** 200. **Signed:** Dominican Republic, 2013. **Signed by:** Marco Paddy.

BA GRADE
50 Risk: V. High

Adolfo, then known as Micker Zapata, ranked as one of the top international prospects in 2013 and received a $1.6 million bonus from the White Sox. After a few years of tantalizing tools with little production, Adolfo made strides with improved plate discipline and improved hitting mechanics in 2017 at low Class A Kannapolis, but his season ended in late August after he fractured his hand punching a wall.

Adolfo's improvements in the box yielded an OPS 125 points better than his previous career-high, and his 16 home runs were good for third in the South Atlantic League. He also managed to mostly banish the injury bug. He played in a career-high 112 games, besting his previous career-high of 69, before his self-inflicted, season-ending injury. Adolfo has power potential, but he needs to improve his plate discipline further and better determine which pitches he can drive and which will result in weak contact.

Adolfo's an average defender in right field with average range and a plus-plus arm that draws a few "80" grades on the 20-80 scouting scale. He turns in run times that are average or a tick better. Adolfo should graduate to high Class A Winston-Salem in 2018.

Year	Club (League)	Class	AVG	G	AB	R	H	2B	3B	HR	RBI	BB	SO	SB	CS	OBP	SLG
2015	White Sox (AZL)	R	.253	22	83	14	21	3	1	0	10	6	25	3	2	.323	.313
2016	White Sox (AZL)	R	.250	4	16	2	4	2	0	1	2	1	8	0	0	.333	.563
	Kannapolis (SAL)	LoA	.219	65	247	30	54	13	1	5	21	14	88	0	1	.269	.340
2017	Kannapolis (SAL)	LoA	.264	112	424	60	112	28	2	16	68	31	149	2	0	.331	.453
Minor League Totals			.242	249	949	133	230	56	6	27	122	66	355	5	3	.305	.399

18 LUIS ALEXANDER BASABE, OF

BA GRADE
50 Risk: V. High

Born: Aug. 26, 1996. **B-T:** S-R. **Ht.:** 6-0. **Wt.:** 160. **Signed:** Venezuela, 2012.
Signed by: Eddie Romero/Luis Segovia (Red Sox).

For a time, both Basabe and his identical twin brother Luis Alejandro Basabe were part of the Red Sox system. Luis Alejandro Basabe was dealt to the Diamondbacks for reliever Brad Ziegler in 2016, and Luis Alexander Basabe was shipped to the White Sox as part of the deal that brought ace Chris Sale to Boston.

At his best, Basabe's believers see a player with a chance to impact the game offensively and defensively. Problem was, Basabe was nowhere near his best for most of 2017. He hit .221/.320/.320 as he battled knee injuries all year. Eventually he had season-ending surgery to repair a torn left mensicus in August. When he was healthy, Basabe worked with the White Sox to become more consistent at the plate. In particular, they were adjusting his bat path to allow him to make more contact. Basabe has above-average to plus range in the outfield, and a strong throwing arm that could allow him to play in a corner if needed.

Basabe is expected to be ready in time for spring training and should return to high Class A Winston-Salem in 2018.

Year	Club (League)	Class	AVG	G	AB	R	H	2B	3B	HR	RBI	BB	SO	SB	CS	OBP	SLG
2015	Lowell (NYP)	SS	.243	56	222	36	54	8	3	7	23	32	67	15	4	.340	.401
2016	Greenville (SAL)	LoA	.258	105	403	61	104	24	8	12	52	40	116	25	5	.325	.447
	Salem (CAR)	HiA	.364	5	22	5	8	2	1	0	1	1	3	0	0	.391	.545
2017	Winston-Salem (CAR)	HiA	.221	107	375	52	83	12	5	5	36	49	104	17	6	.320	.320
Minor League Totals			.245	405	1484	256	364	71	30	26	170	214	407	90	26	.345	.386

19 LINCOLN HENZMAN, RHP

BA GRADE
50 Risk: V. High

Born: July 4, 1995. **B-T:** R-R. **Ht.:** 6-2. **Wt.:** 205. **Drafted:** Louisville, 2017 (4th round). **Signed by:** Phil Gulley.

Louisville used Henzman in a setup role for two seasons before moving him into the closer role in 2017, replacing White Sox organization-mate Zack Burdi.

Henzman went 3-0, 1.67 with 16 saves for a Cardinals club that made it to the College World Series, and the White Sox loaded up on Louisville players in the draft, taking Henzman as well as teammates Kade McClure and Logan Taylor. Henzman signed for $450,000 in the fourth round a year after turning down the Mariners in the 31st round. The White Sox plan to convert Henzman into a starter because he has three pitches, and he made nine starts at Rookie-level Great Falls after signing. Henzman starts his arsenal with a heavy low-to-mid-90s fastball and couples it with an average slider with varying bite in the mid-80s. His slider has flashed plus at its best. He's also got a split-type changeup as his third pitch with average potential.

Because of his age and college pedigree, Henzman should begin 2018 in the rotation at low Class A Kannapolis.

Year	Club (League)	Class	W	L	ERA	G	GS	CG	SV	IP	H	HR	BB	SO	K/9	WHIP	AVG
2017	White Sox (AZL)	R	0	0	0.00	1	0	0	0	1	0	0	0	1	9.0	0.00	.000
	Great Falls (PIO)	R	0	3	4.00	10	7	0	0	27	27	0	9	16	5.3	1.33	.270
Minor League Totals			0	3	3.86	11	7	0	0	28	27	0	9	17	5.5	1.29	.262

20 THYAGO VIEIRA, RHP

BA GRADE
50 Risk: V. High

Born: July 1, 1993. **B-T:** R-R. **Ht.:** 6-2. **Wt.:** 210. **Signed:** Brazil, 2010. **Signed by:** Emilio Carrasquel/Hide Sueyoshi (Mariners).

When the Mariners signed Vieira in 2010 as a 17-year-old for just $65,000, they saw a raw arm with the potential to light up radar guns as he matured. They were, in a word, right. Vieira became a must-see minor league who lit up radar guns as high as 104 mph and made his major league debut in August.

The Mariners dealt him to the White Sox after the season in exchange for international slot money to help the Seattle's unsuccessful pursuit of Japanese two-way star Shohei Ohtani. Vieira, along with

Michael Kopech and Zack Burdi, is part of a trio of White Sox prospects who have touched at least 102 mph with their fastballs. He couples the pitch, which typically sits in the 98-100 mph range, with a fringe-average slider and a developing changeup in the low-90s. He's also working on a split-fingered fastball. If that takes, he could quickly become a back-end of the bullpen stalwart.

Vieira, who has an effortful delivery, still needs to improve his command to up his odds of finding a spot as a high-leverage bullpen arm. He's likely to head to Triple-A Charlotte to begin the 2018 season.

Year	Club (League)	Class	W	L	ERA	G	GS	CG	SV	IP	H	HR	BB	SO	K/9	WHIP	AVG
2015	Clinton (MWL)	LoA	1	4	6.97	22	0	0	0	31	35	2	20	22	6.4	1.77	.287
2016	Bakersfield (CAL)	HiA	1	0	2.84	34	0	0	8	44	37	1	18	53	10.8	1.24	.222
2017	Arkansas (TL)	AA	2	3	3.72	29	0	0	2	36	30	1	15	35	8.7	1.24	.224
	Seattle (AL)	MAJ	0	0	0.00	1	0	0	0	1	0	0	0	1	9.0	0.00	.000
	Tacoma (PCL)	AAA	0	1	4.58	12	0	0	2	18	18	1	7	11	5.6	1.42	.261
Major League Totals			0	0	0.00	1	0	0	0	1	0	0	0	1	9.0	0.00	.000
Minor League Totals			14	19	4.58	149	28	0	13	291	283	10	147	238	7.4	1.48	.259

21 ALEX CALL, OF

BA GRADE
45 Risk: High

Born: Sept. 27, 1994. **B-T:** R-R. **Ht.:** 6-0. **Wt.:** 188. **Drafted:** Ball State, 2016 (3rd round). **Signed by:** Garrett Guest.

After Call hit .353/.425/.530 in three seasons at Ball State, the White Sox took him in the third round of the 2016 draft and signed him for $719,100. His first full season was limited to 38 games at low Class A Kannapolis (and another 13 rehabbing in the Rookie-level Arizona League) because of an intercostal strain and a small fracture to one of his ribs.

To make up for lost time he participated in fall instructional league in both Arizona and in the Dominican Republic. Call is a well-rounded player who doesn't have a plus tool, but doesn't have anything below-average, either. When healthy, Call's smooth swing allows him to hit for average with a little bit of power. He's a tick above-average runner, though he's slowed a little bit as he gained strength. He has average range in the outfield and an above-average arm, though those inside the organization believe he's likely to land in left field. It was a lost season for Call, who could get back on track with a strong year at high Class A Winston-Salem.

Call projects as an extra outfielder in the majors but could be more if he hits like he always has.

Year	Club (League)	Class	AVG	G	AB	R	H	2B	3B	HR	RBI	BB	SO	SB	CS	OBP	SLG
2016	Great Falls (PIO)	R	.308	27	107	19	33	3	1	3	17	19	18	4	4	.444	.439
	Kannapolis (SAL)	LoA	.308	46	185	23	57	17	0	3	18	15	40	10	2	.361	.449
2017	Winston-Salem (CAR)	HiA	.244	10	41	2	10	3	1	0	5	3	11	2	1	.311	.366
	White Sox (AZL)	R	.059	13	51	8	3	1	0	0	6	7	5	1	0	.180	.078
	Kannapolis (SAL)	LoA	.248	38	145	24	36	9	1	3	22	16	33	2	2	.333	.386
Minor League Totals			.263	134	529	76	139	33	3	9	68	60	107	19	9	.350	.388

22 IAN CLARKIN, LHP

BA GRADE
45 Risk: High

Born: Feb. 14, 1995. **B-T:** L-L. **Ht.:** 6-2. **Wt.:** 215. **Drafted:** HS—San Diego, 2013 (1st round). **Signed by:** Dave Keith (Yankees).

Clarkin was the third of the Yankees' three first-round picks in the 2013 draft, and was traded to the White Sox in the middle of 2017 as part of the package that sent third baseman Todd Frazier and relievers David Robertson and Tommy Kahnle to New York.

To this point, Clarkin's career has been stuttered by injuries. He missed all of 2015 with elbow inflammation before finally getting on the mound in the Arizona Fall League. He dealt with an oblique injury when he changed teams and missed a month after making his White Sox debut at high Class A Winston-Salem. Back at instructs, Clarkin showed a four-pitch mix fronted by an 86-88 mph fastball with tail and sink. He backed it with a potential plus curveball in the mid-70s, an average slider in the low-80s and a below-average changeup in the mid-80s. White Sox personnel note how driven he is off the field and how vocal he is about wanting to be part of the team's rebuild.

Clarkin largely projects to end up in situational relief role with his poor health track record and a curveball that will play against lefties.

Year	Club (League)	Class	W	L	ERA	G	GS	CG	SV	IP	H	HR	BB	SO	K/9	WHIP	AVG
2015	Did not play—Injured																
2016	Tampa (FSL)	HiA	6	9	3.31	18	18	2	0	98	100	4	30	72	6.6	1.33	.265
2017	Tampa (FSL)	HiA	4	5	2.62	15	14	0	0	76	70	4	25	58	6.9	1.26	.254
	Winston-Salem (CAR)	HiA	0	0	2.45	3	3	0	0	11	7	1	8	5	4.1	1.36	.194
Minor League Totals			14	19	3.16	56	54	2	0	265	253	17	90	214	7.3	1.30	.257

23 IAN HAMILTON, RHP

BA GRADE
45 Risk: High

Born: June 16, 1995. **B-T:** R-R. **Ht.:** 6-0. **Wt.:** 200. **Drafted:** Washington State, 2016 (11th round). **Signed by:** Robbie Cummings.

Hamilton relieved at Washington State his first two seasons before moving to the rotation in 2016. He was middling at best as a starter with the Cougars, and his stuff and his results backed up significantly. But the White Sox saw plenty of Hamilton out of the bullpen for the Cape Cod League's Wareham Gatemen in the summer of 2015 and believed in him enough as a reliever to take him with their 11th-round pick.

Hamilton has been a reliever only in pro ball and experienced quick success, reaching Double-A in his first full season. Hamilton's fastball hovers in the upper-90s and has touched 99 mph. He's also got a plus slider that works in the low-90s and gets swings-and-misses, as well as changeup that could be average in the future. He uses a high-effort delivery and is aggressive attacking the strike zone. The White Sox have encouraged Hamilton to continue to throw his changeup more often to help hasten its development.

Hamilton was roughed up toward the end of 2017 at Double-A Birmingham, and he'll return there to begin 2018.

Year	Club (League)	Class	W	L	ERA	G	GS	CG	SV	IP	H	HR	BB	SO	K/9	WHIP	AVG
2016	White Sox (AZL)	R	0	0	0.00	1	0	0	0	1	0	0	1	2	18.0	1.00	.000
	Kannapolis (SAL)	LoA	1	1	3.69	21	0	0	8	32	22	3	14	27	7.7	1.14	.202
2017	Birmingham (SL)	AA	1	3	5.50	13	0	0	1	18	24	0	8	21	10.5	1.78	.317
	Winston-Salem (CAR)	HiA	3	3	1.71	30	0	0	6	53	32	1	8	52	8.9	0.76	.179
Minor League Totals			5	7	2.96	65	0	0	15	103	78	4	31	102	8.9	1.05	.214

24 TYLER JOHNSON, RHP

BA GRADE
45 Risk: High

Born: Aug. 21, 1995. **B-T:** R-R. **Ht.:** 6-2. **Wt.:** 180. **Drafted:** South Carolina, 2017 (5th round). **Signed by:** Kevin Burrell.

A near-exclusive reliever at South Carolina, Johnson was taken in the fifth round in 2017 and signed to $390,000 bonus because of his supreme arm strength.

Johnson dealt with injuries in college, including a stress reaction in his humerus and inflammation in his biceps and triceps. Johnson baffled hitters in the Southeastern Conference with a fastball that sat in the 95-98 mph range and touched triple-digits on occasion. That velocity, plus downhill angle and armside life, helped him strike out 107 hitters in 86 innings for the Gamecocks. He's found the sledding a little bit tougher in pro ball, where he'll need to improve his mechanics and sharpen his offspeed pitches. The White Sox would like to see Johnson stay on line longer through his delivery and would also like to see him improve his slider, which is a below-average pitch right now. He needs to throw that pitch with more conviction moving forward and currently, his changeup is ahead of his slider.

Johnson should return to low Class A Kannapolis in 2018, and if everything goes well could become a fast-moving reliever.

Year	Club (League)	Class	W	L	ERA	G	GS	CG	SV	IP	H	HR	BB	SO	K/9	WHIP	AVG
2017	Great Falls (PIO)	R	1	1	0.90	8	0	0	0	10	7	0	7	16	14.4	1.40	.194
	Kannapolis (SAL)	LoA	0	0	5.74	14	0	0	2	16	19	0	12	21	12.1	1.98	.302
Minor League Totals			1	1	3.86	22	0	0	2	26	26	0	19	37	13.0	1.75	.263

25 JORDAN GUERRERO, LHP

BA GRADE
45 Risk: High

Born: May 31, 1994. **B-T:** L-L. **Ht.:** 6-3. **Wt.:** 190. **Drafted:** HS—Moorpark, Calif., 2012 (15th round). **Signed by:** Gary Woods.

When the White Sox drafted Guerrero in 2012, they saw a lefthander with present average fastball velocity as well as a feel for a pair of secondary pitches. His career stalled early after shoulder problems limited him to just 25 innings in 2012 and 2013. He was eased into the rotation toward the end of 2014 at low Class A Kannapolis, then became a full-time rotation piece upon his return there in 2015.

Guerrero spent the last two seasons at Double-A Birmingham, where he's struggled to overcome command issues. Guerrero cut his walks roughly in half from 2016 to 2017, but the White Sox would like to see further improvement. That's particularly true when it comes to repeating his arm slot. He brings his fastball between 91-93 mph and has touched 94. He backs it with a plus changeup, but needs to continue to improve his fringy curveball and slider. The White Sox also noted an improved effort on Guerrero's part to be more physically prepared every time he took the mound.

Guerrero was left off the 40-man roster and was not picked in the Rule 5 draft, an indicator of how he has further work to do to be big league ready. He'll turn 24 this year and will likely move up to Triple-A Charlotte.

Year	Club (League)	Class	W	L	ERA	G	GS	CG	SV	IP	H	HR	BB	SO	K/9	WHIP	AVG
2015	Kannapolis (SAL)	LoA	6	1	2.28	9	9	0	0	55	42	1	10	60	9.8	0.94	.214
	Winston-Salem (CAR)	HiA	7	3	3.56	16	16	0	0	94	82	6	21	88	8.5	1.10	.240
2016	Birmingham (SL)	AA	7	8	4.83	25	25	0	0	136	133	13	73	108	7.1	1.51	.260
2017	Birmingham (SL)	AA	7	12	4.18	25	25	2	0	146	150	8	43	136	8.4	1.32	.270
Minor League Totals			33	30	3.92	114	89	2	0	544	529	37	183	493	8.2	1.31	.259

26 BERNARDO FLORES, LHP

BA GRADE
40 Risk: High

Born: Aug. 25, 1995. **B-T:** L-L. **Ht.:** 6-3. **Wt.:** 170. **Drafted:** Southern California, 2016 (7th round). **Signed by:** Kenny Williams Jr.

Just as his stock was rising at Southern California, Flores lost the strike zone in his junior year and saw his ERA jump from 3.38 to 6.70. Nevertheless, the White Sox liked the ease with which his left arm produced low-to-mid 90s fastballs and popped him in the seventh round.

He performed well at low Class A Kannapolis in 2017 to begin first full pro season, then jumped to high Class A Winston-Salem. His fastball took a step back this year, sitting in the 89-91 mph range as opposed to the version that had touched as high as 94 in the past. He paired it with an average changeup in the mid-70s and a below-average curveball in the 69-71 mph range. He's also added a cutter-slider hybrid to his mix, but that pitch is still in the developmental stages. Flores doesn't have a putaway pitch right now, but the White Sox are hoping his stuff will return once he adds enough strength to his frame to sustain a full-season's workload.

Flores is likely to return to Winston-Salem in 2018.

Year	Club (League)	Class	W	L	ERA	G	GS	CG	SV	IP	H	HR	BB	SO	K/9	WHIP	AVG
2016	White Sox (AZL)	R	0	1	1.50	3	0	0	0	6	4	0	0	7	10.5	0.67	.174
	Great Falls (PIO)	R	6	1	3.66	11	11	0	0	59	63	4	12	45	6.9	1.27	.280
2017	Kannapolis (SAL)	LoA	8	4	3.00	14	14	0	0	78	73	5	13	70	8.1	1.10	.251
	Winston-Salem (CAR)	HiA	2	3	4.24	9	9	0	0	40	43	5	19	33	7.4	1.54	.267
Minor League Totals			16	9	3.44	37	34	0	0	183	183	14	44	155	7.6	1.24	.261

27 TITO POLO, OF

BA GRADE
40 Risk: High

Born: Aug. 23, 1994. **B-T:** R-R. **Ht.:** 5-10. **Wt.:** 195. **Signed:** Colombia, 2012. **Signed by:** Rene Gayo/Orlando Covo (Pirates).

Polo has been a traveling man the last couple of seasons. The Pirates traded him and lefthander Stephen Tarpley in the summer of 2016 to the Yankees in the deal that brought Ivan Nova to Pittsburgh. A year later, the Yankees sent him to the White Sox in the deal that sent Todd Frazier, Tommy Kahnle and David Robertson to New York.

In between, Polo played for Team Colombia in the World Baseball Classic. At 5-foot-10 and 195 pounds, Polo possess a strong, compact build and enough power and speed to slash and burn his way around the bases. He's a well above-average runner whose speed is ranked by some as a 70 on the 20-to-80 scouting scale as well as an adept base stealer who was successful in 34 of 44 tries. That speed serves him well in the outfield, where he has enough range to play center field and enough arm to fit in either corner.

Polo is an exciting player who has a ceiling of an extra outfielder with benefits on both sides of the ball. He's slated to return to Double-A Birmingham in 2018.

Year	Club (League)	Class	AVG	G	AB	R	H	2B	3B	HR	RBI	BB	SO	SB	CS	OBP	SLG
2015	West Virginia (SAL)	LoA	.236	102	360	51	85	20	2	3	26	28	77	46	13	.313	.328
2016	West Virginia (SAL)	LoA	.302	54	225	46	68	14	3	12	37	13	47	20	10	.368	.551
	Bradenton (FSL)	HiA	.276	55	214	40	59	3	0	4	28	21	51	17	7	.351	.346
	Tampa (FSL)	HiA	.250	2	8	2	2	0	0	0	1	1	0	0	0	.333	.250
2017	Tampa (FSL)	HiA	.289	60	235	42	68	10	6	4	20	16	62	20	6	.346	.434
	Trenton (EL)	AA	.382	14	55	14	21	4	1	1	17	6	8	7	1	.460	.545
	Birmingham (SL)	AA	.278	21	72	10	20	4	2	0	7	5	15	7	3	.342	.389
Minor League Totals			.278	452	1619	291	450	73	24	31	203	138	363	164	56	.355	.410

28 LENYN SOSA, SS

BA GRADE

45 Risk: Extreme

Born: Jan. 25, 2000. **B-T:** R-R. **Ht.:** 6-0. **Wt.:** 180. **Signed:** Venezuela, 2016.
Signed by: Amador Arias.

Sosa, who signed with the White Sox on July 2, 2016, was considered one of the best hitting shortstops out of Venezuela in that year's international class and received a $350,000 bonus. As an amateur, he showed coordination, bat-to-ball skills and a touch of gap power as well.

The White Sox challenged Sosa by sending him to the Rookie-level Arizona League. He rewarded their confidence. Sosa has a simple, fluid swing that should allow him to continue to hit for average as he matures. Though evaluators believe he will eventually move off of shortstop as he gets bigger and stronger—they note he's already a below-average runner—he has above-average or better hands and average arm strength. If Sosa gains power he'll also profile better offensively at third.

The White Sox may continue their aggressive path with Sosa and move him to low Class A Kannapolis as an 18-year-old at some point in 2018.

Year	Club (League)	Class	AVG	G	AB	R	H	2B	3B	HR	RBI	BB	SO	SB	CS	OBP	SLG
2017	White Sox (AZL)	R	.270	42	159	19	43	4	2	2	23	14	24	3	4	.330	.358
Minor League Totals			.270	42	159	19	43	4	2	2	23	14	24	3	4	.330	.358

29 SEBY ZAVALA, C

BA GRADE

40 Risk: High

Born: Aug. 28, 1993. **B-T:** R-R. **Ht.:** 5-11. **Wt.:** 205. **Drafted:** San Diego State, 2015 (12th round). **Signed by:** George Kachigian.

After hitting two home runs over his first two seasons at San Diego State, Zavala missed his junior year after having Tommy John surgery. He returned for his senior season as a left fielder and saw his power break out. He hit 14 home runs that year and was selected in the 12th round by the White Sox.

As a pro, that theme seems to have repeated itself. After hitting just seven home runs in his first full season in 2016 at low Class A Kannapolis, Zavala tripled that total between both levels of A-ball in 2017. In fact, his 21 home runs were most in the White Sox system. The team worked with him to find a diet that helped him maintain strength throughout the course of the season, and he altered his swing path to get a higher launch angle. Combine the power with an all-fields approach and fringy but playable defensive ability with a fringe-average arm, a ceiling as a major league backup catcher starts to come into focus.

Zavala will try to continue to get to his power at Double-A Birmingham in 2018.

Year	Club (League)	Class	AVG	G	AB	R	H	2B	3B	HR	RBI	BB	SO	SB	CS	OBP	SLG
2015	White Sox (AZL)	R	.326	35	129	33	42	17	5	4	35	15	27	2	0	.401	.628
2016	Kannapolis (SAL)	LoA	.253	93	360	40	91	19	3	7	49	35	108	1	1	.330	.381
2017	Kannapolis (SAL)	LoA	.259	52	185	32	48	8	0	13	34	13	52	0	0	.327	.514
	Winston-Salem (CAR)	HiA	.302	55	202	31	61	13	0	8	38	24	52	1	0	.376	.485
Minor League Totals			.276	235	876	136	242	57	8	32	156	87	239	4	1	.351	.469

30 CONNOR WALSH, RHP

BA GRADE

40 Risk: High

Born: Oct. 18, 1992. **B-T:** L-R. **Ht.:** 6-2. **Wt.:** 180. **Drafted:** Cincinnati, 2014 (12th round). **Signed by:** Phil Gulley.

After missing his freshman season at Cincinnati due to Tommy John surgery, Walsh became a part of the Bearcats' rotation the next two seasons. The White Sox have used him exclusively in relief in pro ball and he reached Triple-A Charlotte in 2017.

Walsh's calling card is his premium arm strength, which allows him to pump fastballs consistently in the mid-to-upper 90s. He pairs the fastball with a mid-80s curveball that can be devastating when it's on. At its best it is a plus pitch that gets swings-and-misses. Those numbers dipped some during a stint at Triple-A toward the end of the year, and he got hammered in the Arizona Fall League. Walsh's command is well below average right now, but his raw stuff is still plenty intriguing. If he can smooth out his high-effort delivery and improve the command, he could find a spot as a big league reliever.

Walsh will head back to Triple-A Charlotte in 2018.

Year	Club (League)	Class	W	L	ERA	G	GS	CG	SV	IP	H	HR	BB	SO	K/9	WHIP	AVG
2015	Kannapolis (SAL)	LoA	2	3	4.92	29	0	0	0	53	39	3	44	79	13.4	1.57	.201
2016	White Sox (AZL)	R	0	0	0.00	1	0	0	0	1	0	0	0	3	27.0	0.00	.000
	Winston-Salem (CAR)	HiA	2	2	3.40	25	0	0	5	40	28	1	19	41	9.3	1.18	.207
	Birmingham (SL)	AA	0	0	4.70	6	0	0	0	8	7	0	5	7	8.2	1.57	.233
2017	Birmingham (SL)	AA	2	2	3.19	27	0	0	3	42	24	1	27	50	10.6	1.20	.166
	Charlotte (IL)	AAA	1	1	3.86	12	0	0	0	14	16	0	6	13	8.4	1.57	.308
Minor League Totals			9	9	4.00	119	0	0	10	185	139	5	117	222	10.8	1.39	.210

Cincinnati Reds

BY C. TRENT ROSECRANS

A total of 17 players made their major league debut for the Reds in 2017, and 29 over the last two seasons, both the highest numbers in the big leagues. If anything, there's been no shortage of opportunity over the last two seasons in Cincinnati. The question has been: Who has stepped up to take advantage of that?

While the Reds' rebuild only started in earnest at the All-Star break of 2015, many of those trades have shown modest results, and the draft classes from back-to-back seasons in the second slot are still working their way through the system.

While some of the team's heralded pitching prospects took steps forward beyond simply making their debut in 2017, only one, Luis Castillo, cemented his place in the 2018 rotation. Castillo, 24, was acquired in January along with reliever Austin Brice and outfielder Zeke White, in exchange for Dan Straily. The righthanded Straily, who was the team's pitcher of the year in 2016, was picked up off of waivers from the Padres just days before Opening Day in 2016 and flipped for a package that included one of the Marlins' top arms, and Castillo exceeded even the Reds' lofty expectations.

A total of 10 rookies made starts for the Reds in 2017, and nine rookies made a combined 33 starts in the team's final 40 games of the season. When that many auditions are given, you'd hope to have more callbacks.

Lefthander Amir Garrett started out strong, but struggled after being sent back to the minors in mid-May, in part to keep his service time down. He also dealt with nagging injuries and never performed the way he did in his first six starts of the season (3-2, 4.25 ERA). Righthanders Rookie Davis and Sal Romano started the season in the Reds' rotation and were quickly demoted. Davis ended the year with hip surgery, while Romano finished strong down the stretch after improving his changeup as a third offering. Robert Stephenson started in the big league bullpen, and finished strong down the stretch, giving the Reds hope for his future in the rotation. Lefty Cody Reed continued to show disappointing results that belie his overall talent in what was something of a lost season in the Reds' bullpen and in the Triple-A rotation.

Like Castillo, righthander Tyler Mahle started the season in Double-A and ended it in the big leagues with a leg up on the competition for the 2018 rotation.

Dick Williams is entering his third year as the team's general manager, but just his second as the team's primary decision maker. In the last interna-

Rookie Luis Castillo emerged as a potential front-of-the-rotation option for the Reds.

JOE ROBBINS/GETTY IMAGES

PROJECTED 2021 LINEUP

Catcher	Tucker Barnhart (30)
First Base	Joey Votto (37)
Second Base	Eugenio Suarez (29)
Third Base	Nick Senzel (26)
Shortstop	Jose Peraza (27)
Left Field	Taylor Trammell (23)
Center Field	Billy Hamilton (30)
Right Field	Jesse Winker (27)
No. 1 Starter	Hunter Greene (21)
No. 2 Starter	Luis Castillo (28)
No. 3 Starter	Tyler Mahle (26)
No. 4 Starter	Robert Stephenson (28)
No. 5 Starter	Amir Garrett (29)
Closer	Raisel Iglesias (31)

tional signing season, the Reds blew past the team's international pool limit, spending more than $30 million overall, including penalties. That netted a trio of Cubans, a market that the Reds have mined before, for shortstops Alfredo Rodriguez and Jose Israel Garcia and righthander Vladimir Gutierrez.

The system has also been bolstered by two strong drafts while picking in the second spot. Both third baseman Nick Senzel and righthander Hunter Greene are considered to be the top picks in those drafts, while the team has added other high-profile pieces the last two Junes, such as outfielder Taylor Trammell and shortstop Jeter Downs. The Reds continue to build depth, but producing stars is the next step.

DEPTH CHART

CINCINNATI REDS

TOP 2018 ROOKIE: Nick Senzel, 3B. The No. 2 overall pick in 2016 began to exercise more power in the second half of 2017 and should spend most of 2018 in Cincinnati.

BREAKOUT PROSPECT: Nick Hanson, RHP. Coming off Tommy John surgery, a healthy Hanson could shoot up the charts.

SLEEPER: Victor Ruiz, C. Signed out of Mexico, Ruiz showed potential as a 17-year-old playing in the Rookie-level Arizona League.

SOURCE OF TOP 30 TALENT			
Homegrown	28	Acquired	2
College	9	Trade	2
Junior college	0	Rule 5 draft	0
High school	13	Independent league	0
Nondrafted free agent	1	Free agent/waivers	0
International	5		

LF
Taylor Trammell (3)
Jesse Winker (5)
Phillip Ervin (19)

CF

Jose Siri (7)
Stuart Fairchild (16)
T.J. Friedl (17)
Miles Gordon

RF
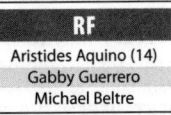
Aristides Aquino (14)
Gabby Guerrero
Michael Beltre

3B
Nick Senzel (1)
Brandon Dixon

SS
Jeter Downs (11)
Jose Israel Garcia (12)
Alfredo Rodriguez (13)
Blake Trahan
Zach Vincej

2B
Shed Long (8)
Alex Blandino
Juan Perez

1B
Gavin LaValley (21)
Nick Longhi (23)
Montrell Marshall

C
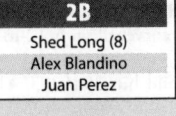
Tyler Stephenson (10)
Stuart Turner
Chris Okey
Victor Ruiz
Henrik Clementina

LHP

LHSP	LHRP
Jacob Heatherly (15)	Ismael Guillon
Packy Naughton (28)	Joel Bender
Scott Moss (29)	
Wennington Romero	

RHP

RHSP	RHRP
Hunter Greene (2)	Jimmy Herget (18)
Tyler Mahle (4)	Tanner Rainey (20)
Tony Santillan (6)	Keury Mella (22)
Vladimir Gutierrez (9)	Ariel Hernandez
Jackson Stephens (24)	Kevin Shackelford
Jose Lopez (25)	Zach Weiss
Nick Hanson (30)	Ryan Hendrix
	Moises Nova

DRAFT ANALYSIS

2017

BEST PURE HITTER: SS Jeter Downs (1s) catches up to good fastballs, stays balanced at the plate, uses the whole field and smirks at sliders in the dirt like a three-year-old looking at a brussel sprouts. Scouts are pretty confident that he will be an above-average hitter.

BEST POWER HITTER: RHP Hunter Greene (1) will put away his bat and focus on pitching fulltime, but if he had remained a position player he had some of the best power in the class as scouts saw 30-plus home run potential thanks to his near top-of-the-scale raw power.

FASTEST RUNNER: OF Stuart Fairchild (2) is a plus runner who turns in times of 4.1 seconds from home to first.

BEST DEFENSIVE PLAYER: Fairchild's speed also plays well in the outfield, He's projected as an above-average to plus defender in center field.

BEST FASTBALL: Greene has one of the best fastballs in draft history. He touched 102 mph in his first pro outing and sat 97-100 mph during the high school season.

BEST SECONDARY PITCH: LHP Jacob Heatherly (3) has a plus 77-82 mph curveball with 12-to-6 downer action.

BEST PRO DEBUT: Fairchild hit .304/.393/.412 for Rookie-level Billings. Downs' season was not as impressive statistically, but considering he was fresh out of high school, the shortstop's .267/.370/.424 season was equally impressive.

BEST ATHLETE: Greene was a first-round talent as a shortstop as well. His only lacking tool is his first speed. Fairchild is an impressive athlete with

TOP DRAFT PICKS OF THE DECADE

Year	Player, Pos.	2017 Org
2008	Yonder Alonso, 1B	Mariners
2009	Mike Leake, RHP	Mariners
2010	Yasmani Grandal, C	Dodgers
2011	Robert Stephenson, RHP	Reds
2012	Nick Travieso, RHP	Reds
2013	Phillip Ervin, OF	Reds
2014	Nick Howard, RHP	Reds
2015	Tyler Stephenson, C	Reds
2016	Nick Senzel, 3B	Reds
2017	Hunter Greene, RHP	Reds

plenty of speed and burst.

MOST INTRIGUING BACKGROUND: Greene's father is a high-powered Los Angeles private investigator who has worked with A-level Hollywood stars. RHP Tyler Buffet (6) is cousins with famed billionare Warren Buffet. RHP Mac Sceroler (5) counts among his uncles ex-big league RHPs Brett Laxton and Ben McDonald, the No. 1 overall pick in 1989.

CLOSEST TO THE MAJORS: Greene should move fast for a high school pitcher thanks to his fastball and consistent delivery.

BEST LATE-ROUND PICK: RHP John Ghyzel (18) is a promsing reliever with a 94-97 mph fastball and a useful slider.

THE ONE WHO GOT AWAY: The Reds would have loved to have signed RHP Tommy Mace (12). Instead he'll head to Florida where he has a good chance to blossom into a top-three round pick in a few years.

—J.J. COOPER

2016

3B Nick Senzel (1) proved to be the advanced college bat he was expected to be, excelling in his first full professional season and reaching Double-A. OF Taylor Trammell (1s) has also hit the ground running, giving the Reds two stars in the class.

GRADE: A

2015

C Tyler Stephenson (1) and RHP Tony Santillan (2) have made slow progress, but both flash their potential. RHPs Tanner Rainey (2s) and Jimmy Herget (6) could both join the Cincinnati bullpen as soon as 2018.

GRADE: C

2014

2B Alex Blandino (1) got to the cusp of the big leagues with his best pro season, but is unlikely to be a regular. RHP Nick Howard (1) missed the season following shoulder surgery and 3B Taylor Sparks (2) was also limited by injury.

GRADE: F

1 NICK SENZEL, 3B

Born: June 29, 1995. **B-T:** R-R. **Ht.:** 6-1. **Wt.:** 205.
Drafted: Tennessee, 2016 (1st round).
Signed by: Brad Meador.

CLIFF WELCH

High expectations follow players drafted second overall, like Senzel, but even by those standards he has overachieved in his brief pro career. After a good start at low Class A Dayton in 2016, he jumped to high Class A Daytona in 2017 and earned a midseason promotion to Double-A Pensacola. Senzel performed better in the Southern League than he had in the Florida State League, particularly in terms of power production. He hit .340/.413/.560 with 10 home runs for the Blue Wahoos in 235 plate appearances. He finished the season on the disabled list with a bout of vertigo, but he reportedly began to feel better after returning home and resting.

Scouts see plenty to like about Senzel from a tools standpoint, but those who have seen him time and again like the intangibles just as much. He runs hard, grinds out at-bats, takes extra bases, plays smart in the field and leads his team. He's not only the best player on the field but plays the hardest. That mentality is coupled with a good approach at the plate and a short, compact swing with good balance and bat speed, leading to high exit velocity off the bat. Opponents say they rarely see him get fooled, and he constantly barrels balls. While many questioned his power coming out of college, he has shown the ability to drive the ball to all fields. Among his 10 Double-A homers were multiple shots to center field and the opposite field. Though not a prototypical burner, he still shows above-average speed to go with good instincts on the bases. Defensively, Senzel has shown the potential to be a plus defender at third with a strong, accurate arm that he has shown he can use on the run. He played shortstop and second base in addition to third base in college, but he has proven to be a quick study at third, working on his footwork with Pensacola bench coach Dick Schofield.

With the emergence of Eugenio Suarez at third base in Cincinnati, the Reds don't feel rushed to promote Senzel to the big leagues. Still, they expect to have to make tough decisions in 2018, when Senzel will likely reach the big leagues. Both he and Suarez have shown defensive ability at third, but barring a trade, one of them could move to either second or a corner outfield spot. Senzel's versatility gives the Reds multiple options. Senzel will likely start 2018 at Triple-A Louisville, but he shouldn't be there too long.

BA GRADE	SCOUTING GRADES
65 Risk: Medium	HIT: 70. POW: 60. SPD: 55. FLD: 60. ARM: 60.

Projected future grades on 20-80 scouting scale

TOP PROSPECTS OF THE DECADE

Year	Player, Pos.	2017 Org
2008	Jay Bruce, OF	Indians
2009	Yonder Alonso, 1B	Mariners
2010	Todd Frazier, 3B	Yankees
2011	Aroldis Chapman, LHP	Yankees
2012	Devin Mesoraco, C	Reds
2013	Billy Hamilton, OF	Reds
2014	Robert Stephenson, RHP	Reds
2015	Robert Stephenson, RHP	Reds
2016	Robert Stephenson, RHP	Reds
2017	Nick Senzel, 3B	Reds

BEST TOOLS

Best Hitter for Average	Nick Senzel
Best Power Hitter	Jose Siri
Best Strike-Zone Discipline	Jesse Winker
Fastest Baserunner	Jose Siri
Best Athlete	Jose Siri
Best Fastball	Hunter Greene
Best Curveball	Ariel Hernandez
Best Slider	Jimmy Herget
Best Changeup	Tony Santillan
Best Control	Tyler Mahle
Best Defensive Catcher	Chris Okey
Best Defensive Infielder	Alfredo Rodriguez
Best Infield Arm	Nick Senzel
Best Defensive Outfielder	Stuart Fairchild
Best Outfield Arm	Jose Siri

Year	Club (League)	Class	AVG	G	AB	R	H	2B	3B	HR	RBI	BB	SO	SB	CS	OBP	SLG
2016	Billings (PIO)	R	.152	10	33	3	5	1	0	0	4	6	5	3	0	.293	.182
	Dayton (MWL)	LoA	.329	58	210	38	69	23	3	7	36	32	49	15	7	.415	.567
2017	Daytona (FSL)	HiA	.305	62	246	41	75	26	2	4	31	23	54	9	2	.371	.476
	Pensacola (SL)	AA	.340	57	209	40	71	14	1	10	34	26	43	5	4	.413	.560
Minor League Totals			.315	187	698	122	220	64	6	21	105	87	151	32	13	.393	.514

2 HUNTER GREENE, RHP

Born: Aug. 6, 1999. **B-T:** R-R. **Ht.:** 6-4. **Wt.:** 197. **Drafted:** HS—Sherman Oaks, Calif., 2017 (1st round). **Signed by:** Rick Ingalls.

The Reds were ecstatic when Greene "fell" to them as the second pick in the draft and paid him a $7.23 million bonus that is a record for the current draft format. The prep righthander was not only touted as the best player in the draft, but he also offered pro potential as both a power-hitting shortstop and a pitcher. Some scouts said he had the strongest and easiest arm they had ever seen in a shortstop.

The Reds drafted Greene as a pitcher and let him DH at Rookie-level Billings as he built up his arm, but his days of playing shortstop are behind him. Greene said he's a full-time pitcher going forward. Greene pitches at 98-100 mph and touches 102 with a top-of-the-scale fastball. What's most notable is how easy he gets to triple-digit velocity. His slider flashes plus and his changeup has been more consistently plus, but he still is inconsistent with both of them—they were a little sharper in the summer before his senior year than they were in the leadup to the draft. He commands his fastball well, even when nearing the century mark, although scouts looking for nits to pick note that hitters seem to see the ball well coming out of Greene's hand, which helps explain why he gave up a .400 average against in Billings in his brief debut. At the plate he's shown raw power, but scouts worried about his hit tool. A steady glove at shortstop, he also has an obvious top-of-the-scale arm.

The Reds will ease Greene into his first full year of pro ball, likely starting out at low Class A Dayton on tight pitch counts.

BA GRADE

65 Risk: Extreme

FB: 80. SL: 55.
CHG: 50.
CTL: 55.

Year	Club (League)	Class	W	L	ERA	G	GS	CG	SV	IP	H	HR	BB	SO	K/9	WHIP	AVG
2017	Billings (PIO)	R	0	1	12.46	3	3	0	0	4	8	0	1	6	12.5	2.08	.400
Minor League Totals			0	1	12.46	3	3	0	0	4	8	0	1	6	12.5	2.08	.400

Year	Club (League)	Class	AVG	G	AB	R	H	2B	3B	HR	RBI	BB	SO	SB	CS	OBP	SLG
2017	Billings (PIO)	R	.233	7	30	1	7	2	1	0	3	0	8	0	0	.233	.367
Minor League Totals			.233	7	30	1	7	2	1	0	3	0	8	0	0	.233	.367

3 TAYLOR TRAMMELL, OF

Born: Sept. 13, 1997. **B-T:** L-L. **Ht.:** 6-2. **Wt.:** 195. **Drafted:** HS—Kennesaw, Ga., 2016 (1st round supplemental). **Signed by:** Jon Poloni.

A record-breaking high school running back in Georgia who was his classification's player of the year, Trammell's multi-sport background kept him from playing baseball year-round. After drafting him 35th overall in 2016, the Reds signed Trammell for a well above-slot $3.2 million to woo him from his college football commitment at Georgia Tech—he was a top student with a 4.0 grade-point average. At low Class A Dayton in 2017, he ranked among the Midwest League top 10 in on-base percentage and slugging percentage.

A gifted athlete, Trammell showed improved plate discipline, even if that's the area of his game that needs the most work. He has a feel to hit that should help him be an above-average to plus hitter. His bat has untapped power that should come as his body fills out. There are evaluators who believe he'll carry 20 more pounds on his athletic frame when he fully matures. If he fills out as expected he could blossom into a 20-25 home run hitter. Trammell's plus-plus speed helps cover poor jumps in the field. He projects as an average defender in center field, but his below-average arm could limit him to left field, especially if he slows down as expected as he gains size and strength. His speed also helps him on the bases where he has shown good instincts. There's an expectation that Trammell will trade some of that speed for increased power over the next five years.

Trammell turned 20 after the season and should start 2018 at high Class A Daytona. He has the potential to develop into a first-division corner outfielder, particularly if his power continues to grow.

BA GRADE

60 Risk: High

HIT: 55. POW: 60.
SPD: 60. FLD: 55.
ARM: 40.

Year	Club (League)	Class	AVG	G	AB	R	H	2B	3B	HR	RBI	BB	SO	SB	CS	OBP	SLG
2016	Billings (PIO)	R	.303	61	228	39	69	9	6	2	34	23	57	24	7	.374	.421
2017	Dayton (MWL)	LoA	.281	129	491	80	138	24	10	13	77	71	123	41	12	.368	.450
Minor League Totals			.288	190	719	119	207	33	16	15	111	94	180	65	19	.370	.441

4 TYLER MAHLE, RHP

Born: Sept. 29, 1994. **B-T:** R-R. **Ht.:** 6-4. **Wt.:** 200. **Drafted:** HS—Westminster, Calif., 2013 (7th round). **Signed by:** Mike Musuraca.

The younger brother of the Angels' Greg Mahle, Tyler became the second member of his family to reach the big leagues with a late-August callup in 2017. In previous years, Mahle had struggled to get settled in after a promotion, but in 2017 he performed right away at Triple-A Louisville and the big leagues. In April, he threw a perfect game for Double-A Pensacola. It was his second no-hitter in two seasons.

Mahle has a skinny build and lacks the frontline stuff of some of the Reds' other pitching prospects, but his plus command and control allows him to succeed. He has an ability to mess with hitters' timing in a way few young pitchers can. While command will always be Mahle's calling card, he's hardly a soft-tosser. He sits in the low 90s but runs his fastball up to the mid 90s, and the final pitch of his April perfect game read 99 mph. Mahle likes to toy with hitters timing by intentionally varying the speed of his fastball, making it harder to time him. His slider and changeup are both potentially average offerings, with his slider flashing above-average. His below-average curveball is simply a get-over pitch. Mahle finished the season in Cincinnati by making four starts, and he will enter spring training with a chance to join the Opening Day rotaton. Ultimately, he profiles as a No. 4 starter.

BA GRADE
50 Risk: Medium
FB: 60. CB: 40.
SL: 50. CHG: 50.
CTL: 60.

Year	Club (League)	Class	W	L	ERA	G	GS	CG	SV	IP	H	HR	BB	SO	K/9	WHIP	AVG
2015	Dayton (MWL)	LoA	13	8	2.43	27	26	0	0	152	145	7	25	135	8.0	1.12	.252
2016	Daytona (FSL)	HiA	8	3	2.50	13	13	1	0	79	58	6	17	76	8.6	0.95	.206
	Pensacola (SL)	AA	6	3	4.92	14	14	0	0	71	78	12	20	65	8.2	1.37	.281
2017	Pensacola (SL)	AA	7	3	1.59	14	14	1	0	85	57	5	17	87	9.2	0.87	.190
	Louisville (IL)	AAA	3	4	2.73	10	10	0	0	59	52	4	13	51	7.7	1.10	.233
	Cincinnati (NL)	MAJ	1	2	2.70	4	4	0	0	20	19	0	11	14	6.3	1.50	.253
Major League Totals			1	2	2.70	4	4	0	0	20	19	0	11	14	6.3	1.50	.253
Minor League Totals			43	28	2.85	105	96	4	0	558	502	39	115	515	8.3	1.11	.239

5 JESSE WINKER, OF

Born: Aug. 17, 1993. **B-T:** L-L. **Ht.:** 6-3. **Wt.:** 210. **Drafted:** HS—Orlando, 2012 (1st round supplemental). **Signed by:** Greg Zunino.

Winker was the best hitter in every lineup he appeared until he played with Joey Votto. He has hit at every level, including at Triple-A Louisville, where he started for the second straight season in 2017. The Reds called him up three separate times, and he performed in the big leagues just as he had in the minors.

Scouts don't question Winker's ability to hit, but as a corner outfielder, his power potential has long been questioned by scouts. He can put on a batting practice show and won the Midwest League all-star game home run derby several years ago, but his game power was lacking until he reached the big leagues. Winker hit seven home runs in 121 at-bats—or as many as he hit in the minors in 2016-17 combined. Winker has had a series of wrist injuries that did play a part in his limited power production–he broke his wrist diving for a ball in 2015 and the injury also affected him in 2016. Opinions on his fielding ability range from below-average to average in either corner outfield spot. Few players benefit from Great American Ball Park and its small outfield dimensions as much as Winker. It helps boost his potentially average power and aid his defense.

General manager Dick Williams has already said Winker has nothing left to prove at Triple-A. At the very least, he will be a member of a big-league outfield rotation in 2018.

BA GRADE
50 Risk: Medium
HIT: 60. POW: 45.
SPD: 45. FLD: 40.
ARM: 40.

Year	Club (League)	Class	AVG	G	AB	R	H	2B	3B	HR	RBI	BB	SO	SB	CS	OBP	SLG
2015	Pensacola (SL)	AA	.282	123	443	69	125	24	2	13	55	74	83	8	4	.390	.433
2016	Reds (AZL)	R	.462	4	13	6	6	0	0	2	6	2	4	0	0	.533	.923
	Louisville (IL)	AAA	.303	106	380	39	115	22	0	3	45	59	59	0	0	.397	.384
2017	Louisville (IL)	AAA	.314	85	299	33	94	22	0	2	41	38	46	2	4	.395	.408
	Cincinnati (NL)	MAJ	.298	47	121	21	36	7	0	7	15	15	24	1	1	.375	.529
Major League Totals			.298	47	121	21	36	7	0	7	15	15	24	1	1	.375	.529
Minor League Totals			.298	566	2062	319	615	122	10	56	315	330	385	22	13	.398	.449

6 TONY SANTILLAN, RHP

Born: April 15, 1997. **B-T:** R-R. **Ht.:** 6-3. **Wt.:** 240. **Drafted:** HS—Arlington, Texas, 2015 (2nd round). **Signed by:** Byron Ewing.

Even as a prep pitcher in Texas, Santillan looked like he would fit in with the Reds' recent infatuation with physical pitchers such as Sal Romano, Rookie Davis and Nick Travieso. In high school, he had a big fastball to go with a big body. Though he struggled in his first go-round in the Midwest League, he comported himself much better in 2017, ranking third in opponent average (.222), fourth in strikeouts (128) and fifth in ERA (3.38).

Santillan has long had a near-top-of-the-scale fastball, but he refined his 88-91 mph changeup to be a potentially plus offering in 2017. His 90-91 mph slider is a work in progress that flashes plus with good tilt and depth, though he has shown little consistency with any of his pitches. His delivery has little deception, but he throws 96-98 mph with movement. He's not consistent with his delivery yet, which is why his velocity will vary pretty dramatically as he'll follow up a 92 mph fastball with a 100 mph one, and it's not always intentional. He pitches from the stretch at all times, which simplifies what he has to work on. His delivery is very uptempo and energetic and he's a fast worker. His ability to start depends on developing even fringe-average control.

Right now Santillan's control and stuff varies widely, but at his best, he can dominate. With his talent, Santillan could move quickly if he can improve the consistency of his delivery and control. He will begin 2018 at high Class A Daytona, but he could continue climbing and reach Double-A Pensacola.

BA GRADE

50 Risk: High

FB: 70. SL: 50.
CHG: 50.
CTL: 40.

Year	Club (League)	Class	W	L	ERA	G	GS	CG	SV	IP	H	HR	BB	SO	K/9	WHIP	AVG
2015	Reds (AZL)	R	0	2	5.03	8	7	0	0	20	15	1	11	19	8.7	1.32	.217
2016	Billings (PIO)	R	1	0	3.92	8	8	0	0	39	32	4	16	46	10.6	1.23	.221
	Dayton (MWL)	LoA	2	3	6.82	7	7	0	0	30	27	3	24	38	11.3	1.68	.245
2017	Dayton (MWL)	LoA	9	8	3.38	25	24	0	0	128	104	9	56	128	9.0	1.25	.222
Minor League Totals			12	13	4.11	48	46	0	0	217	178	17	107	231	9.6	1.31	.224

7 JOSE SIRI, OF

Born: July 22, 1995. **B-T:** R-R. **Ht.:** 6-2. **Wt.:** 175. **Signed:** Dominican Republic, 2012. **Signed by:** Richard Jimenez.

Siri's second go-round at low Class A Dayton went much better than his first. He hit just .145 in 27 games there in 2016 before being demoted to Rookie-level Billings, where he finished 2015. At Dayton in 2017, Siri not only led the Midwest League with 46 stolen bases and finished second in homers with 24. He also set a league record with a 39-game hitting streak.

Siri's tools can make any scout drool–he is an 80 runner with plus raw power, arm strength and range in center field–but there is still a genuine concern about his hitting approach and makeup. Siri swings and misses frequently but impacts the ball when he connects. The Reds left him in low Class A all year despite his age (he's the same age as Senzel) because they wanted him to have success to build on. His agressiveness at the plate will be tested as he climbs the minor league ladder.

Regardless, Siri has genuine power-speed potential and is a true center fielder, which makes him a high-risk, but high-reward prospect. If it all comes together, Siri is an excellent defender who could hit 25 home runs or more while stealing bases and hitting for modest average. Siri turns 23 during the 2018 season, which he should begin at high Class A Daytona. Ideally, he'll play well enough to move up to Double-A Pensacola or higher during the season to speed up his development.

BA GRADE

50 Risk: High

HIT: 40. POW: 55.
SPD: 70. FLD: 70.
ARM: 60.

Year	Club (League)	Class	AVG	G	AB	R	H	2B	3B	HR	RBI	BB	SO	SB	CS	OBP	SLG
2015	Reds (AZL)	R	.246	43	171	34	42	7	9	3	19	3	64	9	2	.259	.444
	Billings (PIO)	R	.200	3	5	1	1	0	0	0	0	1	1	2	0	.333	.200
2016	Dayton (MWL)	LoA	.145	27	83	5	12	3	0	0	3	2	34	3	2	.163	.181
	Billings (PIO)	R	.320	59	241	52	77	12	8	10	35	8	66	17	4	.348	.560
2017	Dayton (MWL)	LoA	.293	126	498	92	146	24	11	24	76	33	130	46	12	.341	.530
Minor League Totals			.279	367	1393	255	389	62	41	44	174	77	387	106	32	.322	.477

8 SHED LONG, 2B

Born: Aug. 22, 1995. **B-T:** L-R. **Ht.:** 5-8. **Wt.:** 180. **Drafted:** HS—Jacksonville, Ala., 2013 (12th round). **Signed by:** Ben Jones.

Drafted as a catcher in the 12th round in 2013, Long moved to second base in 2015 to take advantage of his bat. He started slowly at high Class A Daytona in 2017 before catching fire and earning a starting nod in the Florida State League all-star game. He hit 13 homers in 62 games before being moving up to Double-A Pensacola, where a wrist injury sidelined him for three weeks in the final month of the season.

BA GRADE

50 Risk: High

HIT: 55. POW: 55. SPD: 45. FLD: 45. ARM: 55.

Long's 5-foot-8 stature belies his power. He has a quick, strong wrists that produce thunder in his bat. He has a solid approach, even if he's not looking to walk. and has shown the ability to hit for average thanks in part to his short stroke. Defensively, Long has improved at second base to become a fringe-average, though his bat will always be his calling card. While not a burner, Long has the savvy to steal bases.

Long's background behind the plate is a plus that can add flexibility as an emergency catcher, and that skill could be a tiebreaker as the Reds fill out their bench. Long will get another chance at Double-A in 2018 after struggling there in 2017. Though the Reds have plenty of options at second base, Long could work his way into the big league picture soon as he had more offensive potential than any of the Reds other second base candidates.

Year	Club (League)	Class	AVG	G	AB	R	H	2B	3B	HR	RBI	BB	SO	SB	CS	OBP	SLG
2015	Dayton (MWL)	LoA	.283	42	152	22	43	7	2	6	16	18	31	2	3	.363	.474
2016	Dayton (MWL)	LoA	.281	94	335	47	94	24	1	11	45	44	85	16	3	.371	.457
	Daytona (FSL)	HiA	.322	38	143	22	46	6	4	4	30	10	35	5	1	.371	.503
2017	Daytona (FSL)	HiA	.312	62	247	37	77	16	1	13	36	27	63	6	3	.380	.543
	Pensacola (SL)	AA	.227	42	141	13	32	6	2	3	14	19	31	3	1	.319	.362
Minor League Totals			.276	331	1183	156	327	64	10	38	155	131	280	35	13	.353	.444

9 VLADIMIR GUTIERREZ, RHP

Born: Sept. 18, 1995. **B-T:** R-R. **Ht.:** 6-1. **Wt.:** 172. **Signed:** Cuba, 2016. **Signed by:** Tony Arias/Chris Buckley.

The Reds have been as aggressive as any team in terms of signing Cuban players. It started with Aroldis Chapman and continued with Raisel Iglesias and now includes Guerrero and shortstops Alfredo Rodriguez and Jose Israel Garcia. The Reds have a lot of confidence in their ability to both scout players coming out of Cuba and their ability to help Cuban players acclimate to playing in the States. Gutierrez, signed with the Reds for $4.75 million in August 2016.

BA GRADE

50 Risk: High

FB: 60. CB: 45. SL: 55. CHG: 50. CTL: 50.

Shaking off the rust of a long layoff, he pitched for high Class A Daytona in 2017 and performed well before tiring near the end of the season and sitting out August. Like Iglesias, Gutierrez worked as a reliever in Cuba, and because he's less athletic than Iglesias, he could be destined for the bullpen eventually. He has flashed a plus fastball, a changeup and a pair of breaking balls, including a slider that is generally better than his curve. Gutierrez has gone back and forth over the years over which breaking ball he emphasizes. His curveball was better when he was in Cuba, then he shelved it for the slider which has been more consistent recently. At some point he may need to choose one because on some nights the two end up blending together. His fastball ranges from 90-97 mph depending on the night.

Gutierrez attended instructional league and participated in drills but did not compete in games. Gutierrez should start 2018 at Double-A Pensacola, where the Reds hope he can pitch a full season. He was in big league camp in 2017, often paired in throwing groups with Iglesias, and he could do the same again in 2018.

Year	Club (League)	Class	W	L	ERA	G	GS	CG	SV	IP	H	HR	BB	SO	K/9	WHIP	AVG
2015	Did not play																
2016	Did not play																
2017	Daytona (FSL)	HiA	7	8	4.46	19	19	0	0	103	108	10	19	94	8.2	1.23	.267
Minor League Totals			7	8	4.46	19	19	0	0	103	108	10	19	94	8.2	1.23	.267

10 TYLER STEPHENSON, C

Born: Oct. 16, 1996. **B-T:** R-R. **Ht.:** 6-4. **Wt.:** 225. **Drafted:** HS—Kennesaw, Ga., 2015 (1st round). **Signed by:** John Poloni.

Stephenson's second full season ended the same as his first on the disabled list at low Class A Dayton. In 2016, he suffered a concussion that caused him to miss time and then a right wrist injury that required surgery. Stephenson's 2017 season ended prematurely with a thumb injury suffered while sliding into second base. He returned in time for instructional league, giving the Reds a sense of optimism going forward.

While Stephenson struggled in his first full year, he showed a better eye at the plate in his return to Dayton. His plus power potential is real, even if he hasn't put up eye-popping home run totals so far. His large frame oozes power potential that could only be bolstered once he reaches Great American Ball Park. The development timetable for catchers takes longer, and Stephenson's injuries have slowed him even more. He shows plus arm strength but his throwing mechanics need work, which help explain why he threw out just 21 percent of basestealers in 2017.

As a long-limbed catcher, Stephenson has to work to maintain the flexibility to be an adequate receiver and there are scouts who worry that he'll simply be too big and too inflexible to handle it long-term. The most important thing Stephenson has to show is that he can stay on the field as he advances to high Class A Daytona in 2018.

BA GRADE

50 Risk: V. High

HIT: 45. POW: 55.
SPD: 40. FLD: 50.
ARM: 55.

Year	Club (League)	Class	AVG	G	AB	R	H	2B	3B	HR	RBI	BB	SO	SB	CS	OBP	SLG
2015	Billings (PIO)	R	.268	54	194	28	52	15	0	1	16	22	42	0	2	.352	.361
2016	Reds (AZL)	R	.250	5	20	4	5	1	0	1	2	2	7	0	0	.348	.450
	Dayton (MWL)	LoA	.216	39	139	17	30	4	1	3	16	12	45	0	0	.278	.324
2017	Dayton (MWL)	LoA	.278	80	295	39	82	22	0	6	50	44	58	2	1	.374	.414
Minor League Totals			.261	178	648	88	169	42	1	11	84	80	152	2	3	.347	.380

11 JETER DOWNS, SS

BA GRADE

50 Risk: Extreme

Born: July 27, 1998. **B-T:** R-R. **Ht.:** 5-11. **Wt.:** 180. **Drafted:** HS—Miami Gardens, Fla., 2017 (1st round supplemental). **Signed by:** Hector Otero.

Jeter Downs' mother was so impressed with the way a young Yankees shortstop played that she named her second son after Derek Jeter. Nearly 20 years later, he was drafted by one of the teams that passed on the future Hall of Famer in the 1993 draft. Downs' father played professionally in Colombia, and his older brother, Jerry, is a first baseman in the Red Sox organization.

A Miami commitment, Downs passed on playing for the Hurricanes when the Reds took him 33rd overall. His potentially plus bat is his best tool, with gap-to-gap power. Downs started in rookie ball at Billings and showed a good approach with quality at-bats. He put up a .370 on-base percentage with the Mustangs, with 27 walks to 32 strikeouts in 50 games. He has good motions and hands at shortstop, with enough arm to stick there.

Some evaluators wonder if Downs will be better suited at second base long-term, but the Reds will give him every chance to show that he can be an every-day shortstop. He'll likely start 2018 at low-Class A Dayton.

Year	Club (League)	Class	AVG	G	AB	R	H	2B	3B	HR	RBI	BB	SO	SB	CS	OBP	SLG
2017	Billings (PIO)	R	.267	50	172	31	46	3	3	6	29	27	32	8	5	.370	.424
Minor League Totals			.267	50	172	31	46	3	3	6	29	27	32	8	5	.370	.424

12 JOSE ISRAEL GARCIA, SS

BA GRADE

50 Risk: Extreme

Born: April 5, 1998. **B-T:** R-R. **Ht.:** 6-2. **Wt.:** 175. **Signed:** Cuba, 2017. **Signed by:** Chris Buckley/Tony Arias/Miguel Machado/Jim Stoeckel/Bob Engle/Hector Otero.

The Reds spent more than $30 million in the international signing period, including penalties, with Garcia representing the final splash, signing for a nearly $5 million bonus. The Reds followed him for years with the Cuban junior national team, where he played second base. The Reds believed that he could play shortstop, and that's where he'll start with them. He has the athleticism to move back to second, or even center field.

The Reds liked not Garcia's athleticism and his energy and enthusiasm, as well as his smooth movements in the field, with the arm, range and feet to play shortstop. At the plate, he has shown an advanced approach for his age, using all fields. A righthanded hitter, he has a long swing, but does a good job of hitting balls on the outer third to the opposite field. He showed plus speed in his workouts before signing, increased from what he had shown in international competition.

Working in the Reds' Dominican instructional league, he has started to fill out his large, projectable frame. Garcia will turn 20 as the 2018 season begins, so he'll move quicker than the typical first-year player and his feel for the game gives him a chance to handle more aggressive assignments.

Year	Club (League)	Class	AVG	G	AB	R	H	2B	3B	HR	RBI	BB	SO	SB	CS	OBP	SLG
2017	Did not play—Signed 2018 contract																

13 ALFREDO RODRIGUEZ, SS

BA GRADE
45 Risk: High

Born: June 17, 1994. **B-T:** R-R. **Ht.:** 6-0. **Wt.:** 190. **Signed:** Cuba, 2016. **Signed by:** Tony Arias/Chris Buckley.

The Reds started their Cuban spending spree in the 2016-17 international signing period by inking the slick-fielding Rodriguez to a $7 million signing bonus. A former rookie of the year in Cuba's Serie Nacional, he was also voted the league's best defensive shortstop, and that glove has done nothing to disappoint in his time in the U.S.

Rodriguez spent all of the 2017 season at High-Class A Daytona, where he showed off his defensive prowess. The bat, though, has always been the question, and it will continue to be one. While Rodriguez has big league quality defense right now, the Reds have continued to be the biggest believer in his bat, something that so far has not played out statistically. In his first year in the U.S., he hit .253/.294/.294. Rodriguez will never have much power, but can add strength. In the first half, he hit an encouraging .272/.316/.315, but tired over the second half in his first full season. Most of all, he needs to improve his on-base skills to be a big league player.

Rodriguez doesn't have to be a plus hitter to be a big leaguer, but even with his defense he has to provide some sort of offensive value, which means he needs to add strength and a little more plate discipline. He's similar to fellow Cuban shortstops Adeiny Hechavarria and Jose Iglesias, both of whom did show some offensive improvement after slow starts in the minors.

Year	Club (League)	Class	AVG	G	AB	R	H	2B	3B	HR	RBI	BB	SO	SB	CS	OBP	SLG
2016	Reds (DSL)	R	.234	22	77	12	18	5	0	0	8	9	16	9	0	.333	.299
2017	Daytona (FSL)	HiA	.253	118	483	52	122	14	0	2	36	25	79	11	9	.294	.294
Minor League Totals			.250	140	560	64	140	19	0	2	44	34	95	20	9	.300	.295

14 ARISTIDES AQUINO, OF

BA GRADE
45 Risk: High

Born: April 22, 1994. **B-T:** R-R. **Ht.:** 6-4. **Wt.:** 220. **Signed:** Dominican Republic, 2011. **Signed by:** Richard Jimenez.

Aquino won the Reds' minor league player of the year award in 2016, and followed that with a flop in his first season in Double-A. After an impressive .273/.327/.519 showing in High A Daytona in 2016, he hit just .216/.282/.397 for the Blue Wahoos, but still managed 17 home runs. With 20 doubles and six triples, nearly half of his 99 hits went for extra bases.

When Aquino does make contact, he's adept at using the entire field, and can drive the ball to any part of the park. Aquino has all the tools you could hope for–he's tall and powerfully built. He has both strength in his bat and in his arm. He's an excellent defender in right field, with good speed and a great arm. The hit tool is the biggest question. Against the advanced pitchers in Double-A, he struggled laying off pitches, especially breaking balls out of the zone. Until he develops some ability to take a late-strike breaking ball out of the zone, pitchers have zero reason to work in the zone. But challenge him with a fastball and he'll live up to his "Punisher" nickname.

Aquino will likely repeat Double-A in 2018. His power is real, but he doesn't really fit as a backup outfielder, so he needs to show he can hit enough to play everyday.

Year	Club (League)	Class	AVG	G	AB	R	H	2B	3B	HR	RBI	BB	SO	SB	CS	OBP	SLG
2015	Billings (PIO)	R	.308	13	52	7	16	1	3	2	13	2	9	0	1	.333	.558
	Dayton (MWL)	LoA	.234	61	231	25	54	9	3	5	27	11	53	6	1	.281	.364
2016	Daytona (FSL)	HiA	.273	125	484	69	132	26	12	23	79	34	104	11	7	.327	.519
2017	Pensacola (SL)	AA	.216	131	459	54	99	20	6	17	56	39	145	9	3	.282	.397
Minor League Totals			.243	587	2211	308	537	110	40	76	334	158	567	61	39	.302	.432

15 JACOB HEATHERLY, LHP

BA GRADE

50 Risk: Extreme

Born: May 20, 1998. **B-T:** L-L. **Ht.:** 6-2. **Wt.:** 208. **Drafted:** HS—Cullman, Ala., 2017 (3rd round). **Signed by:** Jim Moran.

Projected as a first-rounder headed into his senior season of high school, Heatherly fell to the second day of the draft, where the Reds pounced on him with the 77th overall pick. Cincinnati actually considered taking him in the second round, but passed in favor of Wake Forest center fielder Stuart Fairchild. The Reds still paid him second-round money, giving him a $1 million bonus to sign and forgo his commitment to Alabama.

Once in the system, Heatherly pitched well in the Arizona League before earning a late-season callup to rookie league Billings, where he struggled in three appearances. The lefty sits in the 91-93 mph range with his fastball. His filled-out body belies his age; he's big and throws with a good downward plane. Despite his age, he has good pitchability and the presence on the mound of a more experienced player. He's working on his changeup and curveball, both of which have the makings of being above-average pitches, but neither is close to being consistently above-average yet.

While the raw talent is there, Heatherly still needs time to develop in pro ball to get to his projection as a back-of-the-rotation starter with a chance for more. He will head to spring training competing to earn a spot in low Class A Dayton.

Year	Club (League)	Class	W	L	ERA	G	GS	CG	SV	IP	H	HR	BB	SO	K/9	WHIP	AVG
2017	Reds (AZL)	R	2	1	2.93	9	6	0	0	31	26	3	16	26	7.6	1.37	.224
	Billings (PIO)	R	0	1	12.00	3	3	0	0	9	17	0	4	5	5.0	2.33	.405
Minor League Totals			2	2	4.99	12	9	0	0	40	43	3	20	31	7.0	1.59	.272

16 STUART FAIRCHILD, OF

BA GRADE

45 Risk: High

Born: March 17, 1996. **B-T:** R-R. **Ht.:** 6-0. **Wt.:** 190. **Drafted:** Wake Forest, 2017 (2nd round). **Signed by:** Perry Smith.

The Reds took Fairchild with the 38th overall pick, and see him as a true center fielder who could be in the big leagues within three years. The biggest part of that is his defense and speed. He covers plenty of ground in the field and has good instincts, making up for an average arm. Although he struggled in the Cape Cod League before his junior year, he had a solid debut with the wood bat in rookie ball, hitting .302/.393/.412 in Billings.

Fairchild has a short, compact swing and a short stride, playing to his speed. He has shown the ability to let balls get in deep, and has a late trigger with a line-drive approach and good bat speed. His power developed in his junior year for the Demon Deacons, hitting five home runs in each of his first two seasons before hitting 17 as a junior. It's not a sure bet that power will translate to wood bats as Wake Forest's Gene Hooks Field is considered a great park for power. In Billings, he showed the power in batting practice, but it didn't necessarily translate into game situations. Scouts see him as having 10-15 home run power, but not the plus power his college stats might indicate.

Fairchild will likely begin the season at low Class A Dayton, but there's a good chance he won't end the year there.

Year	Club (League)	Class	AVG	G	AB	R	H	2B	3B	HR	RBI	BB	SO	SB	CS	OBP	SLG
2017	Billings (PIO)	R	.304	56	204	36	62	5	4	3	23	19	35	12	4	.393	.412
Minor League Totals			.304	56	204	36	62	5	4	3	23	19	35	12	4	.393	.412

17 T.J. FRIEDL, OF

BA GRADE

45 Risk: High

Born: Aug. 14, 1995. **B-T:** L-L. **Ht.:** 5-10. **Wt.:** 170. **Signed:** Nevada, 2016 (NDFA). **Signed by:** Rich Bordi/Sam Grossman.

Friedl had one of the most engaging stories in 2016, when the Reds gave him $735,000, the highest-ever bonus for a non-drafted free agent. He was a redshirt sophomore at Nevada, and several area scouts didn't know that he was draft eligible while other scouts who did know he was draft eligible were worried about his somewhat slight frame. So he went unselected despite hitting .401 for the Wolf Pack. After he had a strong summer with USA Baseball's collegiate national team where he hit .290/.362/.452, the Reds won a bidding war for his services.

Friedel's unique story may have brought him more notoriety than his actual skills. After hitting .284/.378/.472 at Low-A Dayton, he struggled to a .257/.313/.346 slash line in High-A Daytona, where he'll likely start 2018. Friedl has solid all-around tools, but no true plus skill. He's a good defender with a good enough arm to play all three spots. He makes contact at the plate and is a good bunter. He actually has a little more power than his slight frame would suggest, but neither his hit tool or power projects as better than fringe-average.

Friedl projects as a fourth outfielder that would have to make serious strides at the plate to become an everyday regular. Still, he brings value off the bench, particularly with his defense and speed.

Year	Club (League)	Class	AVG	G	AB	R	H	2B	3B	HR	RBI	BB	SO	SB	CS	OBP	SLG
2016	Billings (PIO)	R	.347	29	121	24	42	11	2	3	17	13	25	7	2	.423	.545
2017	Dayton (MWL)	LoA	.284	66	250	47	71	20	6	5	25	29	46	14	7	.378	.472
	Daytona (FSL)	HiA	.257	48	179	15	46	6	2	2	13	10	39	2	1	.313	.346
Minor League Totals			.289	143	550	86	159	37	10	10	55	52	110	23	10	.368	.447

18 JIMMY HERGET, RHP

BA GRADE

40 Risk: Medium

Born: Sept. 9, 1993. **B-T:** R-R. **Ht.:** 6-3. **Wt.:** 170. **Drafted:** South Florida, 2015 (6th round). **Signed by:** Greg Zunino.

Cincinnati hasn't produced anyone with this much funk since Parliament Funkadelic bassist Bootsy Collins. A starter out of South Florida, the Reds have had Herget in the bullpen from Day 1 and he's generally dominated, posting a lot of strikeouts while hitters rarely square him up.

Herget comes at batters from several different angles, with elbows and knees flying and a mid-90s fastball, power sinker and a tight, sweeping slider. His mix of velocity, command and deception makes him death on righthanded hitters. He throws with no fear of using any pitch in any count. Herget does a good job of changing velocities and arm angles and he tries to mess with hitters timing as well, but his fringy changeup needs to improve to get lefties out. Against lefthanders, he tends to throw more from a three-quarters arm slot than a true sidearm. Herget had 25 saves between Double-A Pensacola and Triple-A Louisville, holding hitters to a .226 batting average against.

Herget was the only reliever on the U.S. roster for the Futures Game, throwing a scoreless inning in Miami. He should debut in the majors in 2018 and has a good shot at the Opening Day roster.

Year	Club (League)	Class	W	L	ERA	G	GS	CG	SV	IP	H	HR	BB	SO	K/9	WHIP	AVG
2015	Billings (PIO)	R	3	0	3.20	24	0	0	15	25	16	1	11	26	9.2	1.07	.188
2016	Daytona (FSL)	HiA	4	4	1.78	50	0	0	24	61	47	3	22	83	12.3	1.14	.208
2017	Pensacola (SL)	AA	1	3	2.73	24	0	0	16	30	22	1	12	44	13.3	1.15	.202
	Louisville (IL)	AAA	3	1	3.06	28	0	0	9	32	30	4	9	28	7.8	1.21	.248
Minor League Totals			11	8	2.49	126	0	0	64	148	115	9	54	181	11.0	1.14	.213

19 PHILLIP ERVIN, OF

BA GRADE

40 Risk: Medium

Born: July 15, 1992. **B-T:** R-R. **Ht.:** 5-10. **Wt.:** 207. **Drafted:** Samford, 2013 (1st round). **Signed by:** Ben Jones.

The Reds' first-rounder in 2013, Ervin made his major league debut in 2017, earning a pair of callups during the season. He played well in his brief big league time, including three home runs in his 64 plate appearances.

A toolsy player, Ervin projects as an extra outfielder, but with more seasoning in the minors, has a shot to be more, although it's hard to see his path to being a first-division regular unless he revamps his approach and lays off more pitches off the outer half of the strike zone. He's struggled to hit for average in the minors, he has gotten on base at a decent clip because he will take a walk. There are holes in his swing and he can be beaten on the outside corner. He has a pull approach and his home run power is largely limited to left field, but with a tardy bat, he will wear out the opposite field for singles and doubles. He runs well in the field and on the bases, swiping 23 bags in 99 games in Triple-A. He has an above-average arm.

While he is unlikely to be a star, Ervin's skillset projects to a be a bench outfielder capable of playing all three spots, which he did in the big leagues, with the ability to steal a base as a pinch-runner with above-average speed.

Year	Club (League)	Class	AVG	G	AB	R	H	2B	3B	HR	RBI	BB	SO	SB	CS	OBP	SLG
2015	Daytona (FSL)	HiA	.242	109	405	68	98	18	0	12	63	53	83	30	7	.338	.375
	Pensacola (SL)	AA	.235	17	51	7	12	3	0	2	8	13	15	4	3	.409	.412
2016	Pensacola (SL)	AA	.239	123	419	71	100	22	3	13	45	65	88	36	10	.362	.399
2017	Louisville (IL)	AAA	.256	99	363	46	93	20	2	7	40	37	83	23	6	.328	.380
	Cincinnati (NL)	MAJ	.259	28	58	8	15	2	0	3	10	4	15	4	1	.317	.448
Major League Totals			.259	28	58	8	15	2	0	3	10	4	15	4	1	.317	.448
Minor League Totals			.251	526	1908	294	478	108	13	50	259	239	413	137	32	.343	.399

20 TANNER RAINEY, RHP

Born: Dec. 25, 1992. **B-T:** R-R. **Ht.:** 6-2. **Wt.:** 235. **Drafted:** West Alabama, 2015 (2nd round supplemental). **Signed by:** Ben Jones.

BA GRADE
45 Risk: High

There's never been much doubt that Rainey would end up in the bullpen, and in 2017 he pitched exclusively as a reliever for the first time. He's big and throws hard—really hard. The Reds had him clocked as high as 102 mph in 2017. He spent time between high Class A and Double-A, striking out 104 batters in just 62 innings.

Rainey's below-average command and his control still must improve, but if it does, he's got a shot to be a big league closer thanks to his top-of-the-scale fastball. Rainey already has the look of a big league closer, with intimidating size, Jonathan Broxton-size thighs and a light-em-up fastball. He can throw that fastball up in the zone, above the hitting plane and hitters can't get comfortable because every now and then, one gets away from him. His slider, like his fastball, is hard as it will touch 90 mph. It can be an above-average pitch if he commands it more, but even when he buries it, the power of it makes it hard for hitters to adjust to it. He has thrown a changeup in the past, but hasn't developed it. Now that he's working in the bullpen he has less in-game opportunities to work on it and less need to as well.

If Rainey throws strikes, he could find himself in the big leagues in 2018. His delivery has a little effort, but there's not an glaring red flags, so there's hope he'll clean it up.

Year	Club (League)	Class	W	L	ERA	G	GS	CG	SV	IP	H	HR	BB	SO	K/9	WHIP	AVG
2015	Billings (PIO)	R	2	2	4.27	15	15	0	0	59	58	2	28	57	8.7	1.46	.258
2016	Dayton (MWL)	LoA	5	10	5.57	29	20	0	1	103	109	9	66	113	9.8	1.69	.273
2017	Daytona (FSL)	HiA	2	2	3.80	39	0	0	9	45	21	4	22	77	15.4	0.96	.136
	Pensacola (SL)	AA	1	1	1.59	14	0	0	4	17	8	2	11	27	14.3	1.12	.146
Minor League Totals			10	15	4.57	97	35	0	14	224	196	17	127	274	11.0	1.44	.235

21 GAVIN LAVALLEY, 1B

Born: Dec. 28, 1994. **B-T:** R-R. **Ht.:** 6-3. **Wt.:** 235. **Drafted:** HS—Midwest City, Okla., 2014 (4th round). **Signed by:** Mike Keenan.

BA GRADE
45 Risk: High

An offensive lineman in high school with a chance to play college football, LaValley has always had projected power, but only in 2017 did that carry over to games.

LaValley had as many home runs in the first half of the season (15) as he did in his first two years of full-season ball combined. At the time of his promotion to Double-A, he led the Florida State League with those 15 home runs, not including a pair of homers he hit in the FSL All-Star Game en route to being named the game's MVP. Those homers dried up, though, in Double-A, where he hit just three in 67 games. LaValley struggled against more advanced pitching, and needs to improve his ability to recognize the breaking ball. He has played some third base in the past, but projects as a first baseman. He's a better athlete than many would suspect upon first glance, but it may not be enough to allow him to play in the outfield.

LaValley played alongside Nick Senzel at High-A Daytona and Double-A Pensacola this season, limiting his time at third base to just four innings in one game.

Year	Club (League)	Class	AVG	G	AB	R	H	2B	3B	HR	RBI	BB	SO	SB	CS	OBP	SLG
2015	Dayton (MWL)	LoA	.267	125	469	52	125	29	1	4	53	50	114	4	1	.343	.358
2016	Dayton (MWL)	LoA	.211	5	19	2	4	1	0	0	0	3	7	0	0	.318	.263
	Daytona (FSL)	HiA	.275	92	338	50	93	29	2	11	61	29	72	0	0	.334	.470
2017	Daytona (FSL)	HiA	.288	61	236	38	68	14	0	15	45	15	49	0	0	.332	.538
	Pensacola (SL)	AA	.251	67	247	24	62	16	0	3	34	19	67	0	0	.305	.352
Minor League Totals			.270	409	1519	197	410	99	5	39	225	142	363	7	1	.336	.419

22 KEURY MELLA, RHP

Born: Aug. 2, 1993. **B-T:** R-R. **Ht.:** 6-2. **Wt.:** 200. **Signed:** Dominican Republic, 2011. **Signed by:** Pablo Peguero (Giants).

BA GRADE
45 Risk: High

Mella was thought to be the main piece in the Reds' deadline deal that sent righthander Mike Leake to the Giants in 2015. That deal also netted outfielder Adam Duvall who has proven to be the headliner in return, as he was an all-star in 2016. Mella made his big league debut in 2017, pitching in two games for the Reds following the end of his season at Double-A Pensacola.

Mella has been inconsistent, looking great for some periods and terrible in others. In 2016, he was called up from high Class A to Triple-A to make an emergency start for the Bats, and allowed one run on three hits in seven innings to end the season. Primarily a starter in the minors, Mella projects as a reliever in the big leagues. Scouts have projected him to relieve for years, but starting has allowed him to develop his pitches. Out of the bullpen, Mella's fastball ramped up to 95-97 mph, and he has an above-average changeup which comes in about 10 mph slower than his fastball with similar arm speed and deception. His power slider is a developing pitch which needs more depth.

The Reds will likely give him every opportunity to continue to start, but few scouts think he will end up there. He projects as a setup man.

Year	Club (League)	Class	W	L	ERA	G	GS	CG	SV	IP	H	HR	BB	SO	K/9	WHIP	AVG
2015	San Jose (CAL)	HiA	5	3	3.31	16	16	0	0	82	66	5	26	83	9.1	1.13	.216
	Daytona (FSL)	HiA	3	1	2.95	4	4	0	0	21	11	2	15	23	9.7	1.22	.151
2016	Daytona (FSL)	HiA	8	9	3.90	25	24	0	0	132	150	7	56	95	6.5	1.56	.290
	Louisville (IL)	AAA	1	0	1.29	1	1	0	0	7	3	1	1	6	7.7	0.57	.130
2017	Pensacola (SL)	AA	4	10	4.30	27	26	1	1	134	135	14	43	109	7.3	1.33	.260
	Cincinnati (NL)	MAJ	0	0	6.75	2	0	0	0	4	5	1	2	1	2.3	1.75	.294
Major League Totals			0	0	6.75	2	0	0	0	4	5	1	2	1	2.3	1.75	.294
Minor League Totals			31	32	3.49	115	112	2	1	567	543	33	199	515	8.2	1.31	.251

23 NICK LONGHI, 1B

BA GRADE
45 Risk: High

Born: Aug. 16, 1995. **B-T:** R-L. **Ht.:** 6-2. **Wt.:** 205. **Drafted:** HS—Venice, Fla., 2013 (30th round). **Signed by:** Willie Romay (Red Sox).

A two-way star in high school that was a viable prospect as a pitcher, Longhi played in just seven games for the Reds' Double-A team before he blew out his left elbow, requiring Tommy John surgery. He was off to a promising start with the team, going 6-for-19 with a home run and seven RBIs in those seven games. Cincinnati acquired him from Boston in exchange for $2.75 million in international bonus pool space.

A righthanded hitter, Longhi was touted as one of the best pure hitters in Boston's system. He was a 30th-round pick by the Red Sox in 2013 and was signed to play at Louisiana State before getting $440,000 from Boston. Longhi has a flat bat plane that allows him to use the entire field. He hit just two home runs in all of 2016, and bounced back with six in 62 games at Double-A Portland before being traded to the Reds. A lefthanded thrower, he's limited to first base and corner outfield spots. Despite the surgery, he's expected to be ready for spring training.

Longhi needs to develop more power to profile at power-oriented positions and his swing as of yet hasn't really allowed him to tap into his strength as he's geared to hit line drives more than lofting the ball.

Year	Club (League)	Class	AVG	G	AB	R	H	2B	3B	HR	RBI	BB	SO	SB	CS	OBP	SLG
2015	Greenville (SAL)	LoA	.281	115	442	52	124	27	3	7	62	34	88	2	0	.338	.403
2016	Salem (CAR)	HiA	.282	124	471	56	133	40	3	2	77	50	106	2	3	.349	.393
2017	Portland (EL)	AA	.262	62	237	26	62	15	0	6	33	13	40	0	1	.306	.401
	Pensacola (SL)	AA	.316	7	19	2	6	1	0	1	7	3	5	0	0	.409	.526
Minor League Totals			.279	354	1323	159	369	98	7	17	193	114	273	5	7	.339	.402

24 JACKSON STEPHENS, RHP

BA GRADE
40 Risk: Medium

Born: May 11, 1994. **B-T:** R-R. **Ht.:** 6-2. **Wt.:** 220. **Drafted:** HS—Oxford, Ala., 2012 (18th round). **Signed by:** Ben Jones.

Of the 10 rookies to start for the Reds in 2017, only Tyler Mahle was younger than Stephens, who made four starts and three relief appearances in the big leagues. He went five innings and picked up the win against the Cubs in his debut before heading back down to Triple-A Louisville.

Stephens was as notable in high school as a quarterback and a third baseman as he was for pitching. And he would have been a two-way player for Alabama had he not signed with the Reds. Another of the Reds' big righthanders, Stephens has a four-pitch mix with his above-average fastball sitting around the 90-92 mph area, but was able to dial it up to 97 in the big leagues. He has good spin on his average curveball, while his slider is more of a show-me below-average pitch. The changeup is average. Stephens may lack a true plus pitch, but his feel for pitching and ability to mix a wide assortment of pitches gives him survival skills.

He'll likely start 2018 in Triple-A and get a chance at the big league level throughout the season. His ceiling is probably a back-end-of-the-rotation starter, but he could also be useful out of the bullpen or as a swing man.

Year	Club (League)	Class	W	L	ERA	G	GS	CG	SV	IP	H	HR	BB	SO	K/9	WHIP	AVG
2015	Daytona (FSL)	HiA	12	7	2.97	26	26	0	0	145	157	11	30	97	6.0	1.29	.276
2016	Pensacola (SL)	AA	8	11	3.33	27	26	1	0	151	148	7	41	131	7.8	1.25	.254
2017	Louisville (IL)	AAA	7	10	4.92	26	25	1	0	139	156	16	51	110	7.1	1.49	.281
	Cincinnati (NL)	MAJ	2	1	4.68	7	4	0	0	25	19	6	9	21	7.6	1.12	.209
Major League Totals			2	1	4.68	7	4	0	0	25	19	6	9	21	7.6	1.12	.209
Minor League Totals			33	43	3.97	127	97	2	3	589	633	50	165	469	7.2	1.35	.275

25 JOSE LOPEZ, RHP

BA GRADE

40 Risk: Medium

Born: Sept. 1, 1993. **B-T:** R-R. **Ht.:** 6-1. **Wt.:** 185. **Drafted:** Seton Hall, 2014 (6th round). **Signed by:** Lee Saras.

The Reds took Lopez in the sixth round of the 2014 draft despite the fact that he missed his entire junior year at Seton Hall after having Tommy John surgery. Lopez reached high Class A Daytona in 2016 and started at that level again in 2017. The Reds promoted him after nine starts with Daytona. He was even better in Pensacola.

Lopez worked six or more innings in 10 consecutive Double-A starts despite being limited to less than 100 pitches per start. Lopez pitches in the low 90s, but can get up to 95 mph. He has an above-average slider that he can throw for strikes, while his below-average changeup is still a work in progress. Pensacola pitching coach Danny Darwin raves about Lopez's competitiveness and pitchability.

Because of the stockpile of arms in Triple-A, Lopez will probably start 2018 in Double-A again, but should move up sometime in the season and could even find himself in the big leagues before the end of the year.

Year	Club (League)	Class	W	L	ERA	G	GS	CG	SV	IP	H	HR	BB	SO	K/9	WHIP	AVG
2015	Billings (PIO)	R	3	2	3.16	15	14	0	0	57	53	4	19	67	10.6	1.26	.248
2016	Dayton (MWL)	LoA	6	9	3.97	21	21	0	0	113	118	2	32	113	9.0	1.32	.262
	Daytona (FSL)	HiA	0	3	4.41	6	5	0	0	35	29	3	10	34	8.8	1.13	.227
2017	Daytona (FSL)	HiA	2	4	2.84	9	9	0	0	51	50	3	14	48	8.5	1.26	.262
	Pensacola (SL)	AA	7	2	2.43	17	15	1	0	96	64	9	35	95	8.9	1.03	.189
Minor League Totals			18	20	3.30	68	64	1	0	352	314	21	110	357	9.1	1.20	.238

26 MILES GORDON, OF

BA GRADE

45 Risk: High

Born: Dec. 3, 1997. **B-T:** L-R. **Ht.:** 6-1. **Wt.:** 175. **Drafted:** HS—Oakville, Ont., 2015 (4th round). **Signed by:** Billy Byckowski.

Gordon was a hockey player in 2015. Just two years later, the Canadian outfielder was a fourth-round pick, helping validate his decision to focus on the summer sport.

Gordon was back at rookie league Billings in 2017, repeating the level after his 2016 stint there was cut to 22 games because of a shoulder injury. Still just 19, Gordon was the Mustangs' best player at the plate, hitting .319/.389/.538 with 28 of his 74 hits going for extra bases, including eight home runs. With Stuart Fairchild in center, Gordon mostly played right, though he has the speed and ability to play at least an average center field. He is starting to develop some power as he has grown into his projectable frame. He's strong, but can get stronger. Scouts project him as having average power potential. There are questions if his swing will translate at higher levels and if he can continue to hit for average, but he does have a relatively short stroke and above-average bat speed.

Gordon is ready to head to low Class A Dayton and his first taste of full-season ball.

Year	Club (League)	Class	AVG	G	AB	R	H	2B	3B	HR	RBI	BB	SO	SB	CS	OBP	SLG
2015	Reds (AZL)	R	.220	31	118	15	26	4	3	0	12	7	26	5	3	.262	.305
2016	Billings (PIO)	R	.262	22	65	11	17	3	2	0	11	11	14	3	2	.372	.369
2017	Billings (PIO)	R	.319	61	232	40	74	15	5	8	37	27	55	7	3	.389	.530
Minor League Totals			.282	114	415	66	117	22	10	8	60	45	95	15	8	.352	.441

27 ALEX BLANDINO, 2B/3B

BA GRADE

40 Risk: Medium

Born: Nov. 6, 1992. **B-T:** R-R. **Ht.:** 6-0. **Wt.:** 190. **Drafted:** Stanford, 2014 (1st round). **Signed by:** Rich Bordi.

A first-rounder in 2014, Blandino put up arguably his best season as a pro, hitting better once he moved up to Triple-A Louisville, where he put up a .270/.390/.444 slash line in 63 games after hitting .259/.374/.462 at Double-A. With Louisville, he had 32 walks to just 37 strikeouts. It was a very good bounce-back season after an injury-plagued 2016 when hamstring injuries ruined his season.

There's not a loud tool in Blandino's bag, although he has shown the ability to put up good at-bats, a valuable quality to be sure, but nothing that jumps off a page. He started his career with the Reds at shortstop, but he's below-average there and has largely stopped playing there. He's average at second or third base with good hands and an above-average arm. Blandino has the ability to put up double-digit homers in a full season, but is hardly a slugger. He plays with a coolness that's off-putting to some observers.Blandino is an average runner at best and was caught stealing more than he was successful in 2017.

Blandino projects as a potential utility infielder who could end up as a second-division regular.

Year	Club (League)	Class	AVG	G	AB	R	H	2B	3B	HR	RBI	BB	SO	SB	CS	OBP	SLG
2015	Daytona (FSL)	HiA	.294	80	299	46	88	18	2	7	35	31	56	7	10	.370	.438
	Pensacola (SL)	AA	.235	30	115	15	27	7	0	3	18	18	21	2	2	.350	.374
2016	Pensacola (SL)	AA	.232	113	401	52	93	18	0	8	37	55	114	14	5	.333	.337
2017	Pensacola (SL)	AA	.259	62	197	31	51	22	0	6	31	32	49	3	4	.374	.462
	Louisville (IL)	AAA	.270	63	196	29	53	14	1	6	20	32	37	1	3	.390	.444
Minor League Totals			.262	411	1452	213	381	99	5	38	173	197	337	34	29	.361	.416

28 PACKY NAUGHTON, LHP

BA GRADE 45 Risk: High

Born: April 6, 1996. **B-T:** R-L. **Ht.:** 6-2. **Wt.:** 195. **Drafted:** Virginia Tech, 2017 (9th round). **Signed by:** Jeff Brookens.

There was nothing in Naughton's statistics at Virginia Tech that indicated he would be drafted. Despite a 2-6 record and 6.24 ERA for the Hokies, the Reds liked what they saw.

Naughton throws his fastball in the 92-94 mph range with an easy delivery. At Billings, he went 3-3 with a 3.15 ERA in 14 appearances, including 12 starts. He throws a slider, curveball and changeup in addition to a plus fastball. He'll throw his slider from a three-quarters arm angle and then drop a true curveball. He has a good changeup that he throws in the low 80s. The Boston native throws all four pitches for strikes and competes well.

Naughton has a strange pitching motion with some funk, but is able to repeat it, adding some deception to the delivery. He'll start for now as his feel for pitching gives him survival skills.

Year	Club (League)	Class	W	L	ERA	G	GS	CG	SV	IP	H	HR	BB	SO	K/9	WHIP	AVG
2017	Billings (PIO)	R	3	3	3.15	14	12	0	0	60	58	5	20	63	9.5	1.30	.256
Minor League Totals			3	3	3.15	14	12	0	0	60	58	5	20	63	9.5	1.30	.256

29 SCOTT MOSS, LHP

BA GRADE 45 Risk: High

Born: Oct. 6, 1994. **B-T:** L-L. **Ht.:** 6-5. **Wt.:** 215. **Drafted:** Florida, 2016 (4th round). **Signed by:** Greg Zunino.

Moss was limited to one year at Florida after Tommy John surgery, and he was limited to mid-week starting duties and relief on the weekends. The Reds thought Moss was similar to Anthony DeSclafani, another pitcher who was buried on the Gators' depth chart before becoming a big leaguer.

Moss' average fastball sits in the 88-93 mph range and also has a potentially average slider and changeup. He has a bit of a herky-jerky motion and wraps his wrist, but is able to repeat the delivery and some of that funkiness adds deception to stuff that can only be described as average. He has plus command and control, which helped him against young hitters in the Midwest League.

Moss could be a back-of-the-rotation starter or a matchup guy in the big leagues.

Year	Club (League)	Class	W	L	ERA	G	GS	CG	SV	IP	H	HR	BB	SO	K/9	WHIP	AVG
2016	Billings (PIO)	R	3	1	2.35	10	10	0	0	38	35	2	14	29	6.8	1.28	.241
2017	Dayton (MWL)	LoA	13	6	3.45	26	26	0	0	136	114	11	48	156	10.3	1.19	.224
Minor League Totals			16	7	3.21	36	36	0	0	174	149	13	62	185	9.6	1.21	.227

30 NICK HANSON, RHP

BA GRADE 50 Risk: Extreme

Born: June 10, 1998. **B-T:** R-R. **Ht.:** 6-5. **Wt.:** 205. **Drafted:** HS—Savage, Minn., 2016 (3rd round). **Signed by:** Andy Stack.

Hanson was already a little behind because he came from a cold weather state in Minnesota, but then he had Tommy John surgery in 2017, costing him another year of development. Still, he has a big arm to go with a spindly, 6-foot-5 frame that can add plenty of bulk as he matures.

Hanson had signed to play baseball at Kentucky, but a $925,000 bonus changed his mind and convinced him to try to go up Interstate 71 to Cincinnati. Before surgery, the righthander struggled to keep his mechanics in sync. He would often overthrow and spike his curveball. That curveball nonetheless flashes as a plus pitch when he stays in sync, he just has to show he can do that much more consistently. His fastball sat at 91-95 mph before his injury. If it returns, he has a chance to develop two plus pitches.

Still 19, Hanson will likely start 2018 at Rookie-level Billings, and the Reds will keep it slow with him. He's a lottery ticket that if he hits, could move up quickly.

Year	Club (League)	Class	W	L	ERA	G	GS	CG	SV	IP	H	HR	BB	SO	K/9	WHIP	AVG
2016	Reds (AZL)	R	0	2	9.18	8	8	0	0	17	25	1	15	15	8.1	2.40	.352
2017	Did not play—Injured																
Minor League Totals			0	2	9.18	8	8	0	0	17	25	1	15	15	8.1	2.40	.352

Cleveland Indians

BY TEDDY CAHILL

The Indians entered the 2017 season as the American League favorites following their heartbreaking loss to the Cubs in the 2016 World Series. Their young core returned intact, buttressed by the signing of Edwin Encarnacion to a $60 million deal, the largest free agent contract in franchise history.

Cleveland largely lived up to its preseason promise. The Tribe won 102 games, the second-most in club history, and won the AL Central again, giving it back-to-back division titles for the first time this century. The season was highlighted by their 22-game winning streak in late-August and September, breaking the American League-record 20-game streak set by the Athletics in 2002.

But the same fate befell the Indians as the Moneyball A's, and they lost in the division series. The Tribe took a 2-0 lead on the Yankees at home, but was unable to close out the series. The playoff loss again brought the season to a frustrating end.

The Indians' future remains bright, however. The same young core that returned in 2017 is set for another campaign in 2018, and perhaps looks even better now. Shortstop Francisco Lindor, who will play 2018 as a 24-year-old, and righthander Corey Kluber, the AL Cy Young winner, remain focal points, and they have been joined by infielder Jose Ramirez, who finished third in AL MVP voting after an impressive breakout season, and center fielder Bradley Zimmer, who graduated to the big leagues.

The Tribe's farm system has been strengthened over the last year as well. Club president Chris Antonetti, the 2016 Executive of the Year, and general manager Mike Chernoff made deals to improve the big league club in 2017 without trading any of the team's top prospects. And while signing Encarnacion cost them their first-round pick in 2017, the Indians made a heavy commitment in the international market under Paul Gillespie, who was promoted to international scouting director during the offseason.

The Tribe signed two of the top 20 players in the international class, showing an increased financial commitment to the market.

The Indians' have increased their spending in other areas, as well. They set a franchise record in 2017 with an Opening Day payroll of nearly $125 million and should be able to again support a large payroll in 2018 after drawing more than two million fans for the first time in a decade.

The Indians also had a productive season down on the farm. Catcher Francisco Mejia, the team's No. 1 prospect the last two years, made his major

Rookie power-speed threat Bradley Zimmer established himself as an outfield regular.

DUANE BURLESON/GETTY IMAGES

PROJECTED 2021 LINEUP

Catcher	Francisco Mejia (25)
First Base	Bobby Bradley (24)
Second Base	Jose Ramirez (28)
Third Base	Nolan Jones (22)
Shortstop	Francisco Lindor (27)
Left Field	Tyler Naquin (29)
Center Field	Greg Allen (28)
Right Field	Bradley Zimmer (28)
Designated Hitter	Yu-Cheng Chang (25)
No. 1 Starter	Corey Kluber (34)
No. 2 Starter	Triston McKenzie (23)
No. 3 Starter	Trevor Bauer (30)
No. 4 Starter	Mike Clevinger (30)
No. 5 Starter	Shane Bieber (25)
Closer	Cody Allen (32)

league debut in September after a solid season in Double-A. Righthander Triston McKenzie was named Carolina League pitcher of the year and ranked second in the minor leagues in strikeouts as he helped high Class A Lynchburg to a share of the league title. Third baseman Nolan Jones and righthander Shane Bieber, both 2016 draftees, had outstanding first full professional seasons, raising their profiles.

Cleveland has the longest championship drought in the sport, which now stretches to 70 years. But with a strong, young core and a stable, successful front office, the Indians look poised to soon end that streak.

CLEVELAND INDIANS

TOP 2018 ROOKIE: Greg Allen, OF. After making his big league debut in September and earning a spot on the playoff roster, Allen could take on a regular role in 2018.

BREAKOUT PROSPECT: Luis Oviedo, RHP. The Venezuelan's stuff impressed during his U.S. debut in 2017 and he could make another jump as he continues to fill out his 6-foot-5 frame.

SOURCE OF TOP 30 TALENT			
Homegrown	30	Acquired	0
College	10	Trades	0
Junior college	2	Rule 5 draft	0
High school	9	Independent leagues	0
Nondrafted free agents	0	Free agents/waivers	0
International	9		

SLEEPER: Austen Wade, OF. Texas Christian's leading hitter in 2017 as a junior, Wade has excellent on-base skills and can play all three outfield positions thanks to his above-average speed and instincts.

LF
George Valera (9)
Oscar Gonzalez (20)
Andrew Calica
Richie Shaffer
Mitch Longo

CF
Greg Allen (8)
Quentin Holmes (13)
Austen Wade
Ka'ai Tom
Gabriel Mejia

RF
Will Benson (10)
Conner Capel (15)
Johnathan Rodriguez (21)
Mike Papi
Alexfri Pena

3B
Nolan Jones (4)
Gavin Collins (27)
Henry Pujols

SS
Yu-Cheng Chang (6)
Willi Castro (7)
Erik Gonzalez (11)
Tyler Freeman (16)
Marcos Gonzalez (30)
Luke Wakamatsu
Jesse Berardi
Eric Stamets

2B
Aaron Bracho (12)
Tyler Krieger (23)
Ernie Clement (24)
Mark Mathias (25)
Jose Fermin

1B
Bobby Bradley (3)
Nellie Rodriguez
Ulysses Cantu
Emmanuel Tapia

C
Francisco Mejia (1)
Logan Ice (19)
Eric Haase
Mike Rivera

LHP

LHSP	LHRP
Sam Hentges (18)	Kyle Nelson
Ryan Merritt (26)	Tanner Tully
Brady Aiken (28)	Billy Strode
Shawn Morimando	Ben Krauth
Juan Hillman	
Matt Turner	
Kirk McCarty	
Rob Kaminsky	
Sean Brady	

RHP

RHSP	RHRP
Triston McKenzie (2)	Dylan Baker
Shane Bieber (5)	Leandro Linares
Aaron Civale (14)	Dalbert Siri
Julian Merrywather (17)	Jonathan Teaney
Luis Oviedo (22)	Cameron Hill
Eli Morgan (29)	Josh Martin
Victor Soteldo	Tommy DeJuneas
Roberto Hernandez	Argenis Angulo
Grant Hockin	
Zach Plesac	
Matt Esparza	
Adam Plutko	
James Karinchak	
Shao-Ching Chiang	
Micah Miniard	

DRAFT ANALYSIS

2017

BEST PURE HITTER: Many of the position players the Indians drafted with their first six picks stand out for their pure hitting ability, but SS Tyler Freeman (2s) is the best of the bunch. He handles the barrel well and has a quick, direct swing that creates consistent, hard contact.

BEST POWER HITTER: OF Johnathan Rodriguez (3) was one of the youngest players in the class and is still physically maturing, but he has plus raw power and profiles as a prototypical right fielder.

FASTEST RUNNER: OF Quentin Holmes (2) is a top-of-the-scale runner and clocked a 6.15 second 60-yard dash at Perfect Game National in 2016, one of the fastest in the event's history. 2B/SS Ernie Clement (4) and OF Clark Scolamiero (22) are plus runners.

BEST DEFENSIVE PLAYER: C Mike Rivera (6) was one of the best defensive catchers in the country throughout his college career at Florida. He has an above-average arm, is a solid receiver who has handled velocity on high-profile teams for years and earns praise for his leadership behind the plate.

BEST FASTBALL: The Indians didn't draft a pitcher until the seventh round, and when they did start selecting pitchers, few were power arms. RHPs Jonathan Teaney (20) and Tommy DeJuneas (26) were the exceptions. Both throw in the mid-90s and could add more velocity in pro ball with more consistent work.

BEST SECONDARY PITCH: RHP Eli Morgan (8) ranked eighth in the country in strikeouts in 2017 at Gonzaga in large part because of his plus changeup, which one area scout before the draft called the best college changeup he'd ever seen. LHP Kyle Nelson (15) has a plus slider that he can consistently throw for strikes.

BEST PRO DEBUT: Morgan looked every bit the part of polished college pitcher in the New York-Penn League, where went 3-2, 1.03 and struck out 58 batters in 35 innings. Teaney struck out 51 in 30.1 innings for the same Mahoning Valley team while posting a 2.08 ERA.

BEST ATHLETE: Holmes' athleticism goes hand-in-hand with his elite speed. He is a toolsy, twitchy player which gives him a high ceiling on the diamond.

MOST INTRIGUING BACKGROUND: LHP Kirk McCarty (7) had a prolific high school athletics career and won state titles in both baseball and football. His offensive coordinator at Oak Grove High in Hattiesburg, Miss., was Brett Favre, and under his tutelage McCarty threw for more than 4,000 yards and 44 touchdowns during his senior year.

CLOSEST TO THE MAJORS: Morgan's exceptional pro debut could put him on the fast track to the big leagues. Other polished college pitchers like McCarty and Nelson could also move quickly.

BEST LATE-ROUND PICK: Listed at 6-foot-4, 180 pounds, LHP Matt Turner (11) is lanky and projectable. He has a good feel for pitching and an effective three-pitch mix, with an upper-80s fastball and a changeup and slider that both have the makings of becoming above-average.

THE ONE WHO GOT AWAY: SS Oscar Serratos (14) is a steady defender with promising offensive potential, but the Indians were unable to sign him away from his commitment to Georgia Tech. Cleveland also took late-round fliers on OF Cole Turney (34, Arkansas), RHP Spencer Strider (35, Clemson) and SS Austin Martin (37, Vanderbilt), who all have the tools to develop into stars in college.

—TEDDY CAHILL

TOP DRAFT PICKS OF THE DECADE

Year	Player, Pos.	2017 Org
2008	Lonnie Chisenhall, 3B	Indians
2009	Alex White, RHP	American Association
2010	Drew Pomeranz, LHP	Red Sox
2011	Francisco Lindor, SS	Indians
2012	Tyler Naquin, OF	Indians
2013	Clint Frazier, OF	Yankees
2014	Bradley Zimmer, OF	Indians
2015	Brady Aiken, LHP	Indians
2016	Will Benson, OF	Indians
2017	Quentin Holmes, OF (2nd round)	Indians

2016

Prep hitters OF Will Benson (1), 3B Nolan Jones (2) and OF Conner Capel (5) all impressed in their first full professional seasons. RHP Shane Bieber (4) made a leap forward thanks to improved stuff and the best walk-rate in full-season ball.

GRADE: B

2015

RHP Triston McKenzie (1s) was named Carolina League pitcher of the year, continuing his outstanding start to his career. LHPs Brady Aiken (1) and Juan Hillman (2) suffered through down campaigns in their first year of full-season ball.

GRADE: B

2014

OF Bradley Zimmer (1) graduated to MLB. LHP Justus Sheffield (1), who was dealt to the Yankees in 2016, and 1B Bobby Bradley (3) continue to look like Top 100 prospects. OF Greg Allen (6) made the Tribe's playoff roster after a solid debut.

GRADE: A

1 FRANCISCO MEJIA, C

Born: Oct. 27, 1995. **B-T:** B-R. **Ht.:** 5-10. **Wt.:** 175.
Signed: Dominican Republic, 2012.
Signed by: Ramon Pena.

BILL MITCHELL

Mejia's precocious talent has been apparent since the Indians signed him out of the Dominican Republic in 2012 and sent him to make his professional debut in the Rookie-level Arizona League the following season. He had an eventful path through the minor leagues that included a historic hitting streak and nearly being included in a blockbuster trade before making his major league debut in September as a 21-year-old. Mejia broke out in 2016 and authored a 50-game hitting streak that is the longest in the modern era of the minor leagues (dating to 1963). Mejia kept hitting in 2017 as he advanced to Double-A Akron. He finished the year in the Arizona Fall League, where he was one of the circuit's leading hitters.

Mejia has long been known for his hitting ability and the switch-hitter consistently makes hard contact from both sides of the plate. He has matured as a hitter to use the whole field to hit, instead of the pull-oriented approach he had when he was younger. His bat speed gives him more raw power than his lean, 5-foot-10 frame would suggest, but he more typically drives balls into the gaps than over the fence. He has an aggressive approach and doesn't walk much, but his excellent feel for the barrel means he also doesn't strike out much and is comfortable working behind in the count. Mejia has made strides defensively and has elite arm strength and has become a good receiver. He has gotten comfortable speaking English, a key skill for him to work with his pitchers, and has developed more consistency behind the plate. For all his progress defensively, however, Mejia's bat remains ahead of his glove. Because he isn't far off from being ready for the big leagues offensively and because the Indians have a pair of excellent defensive catchers in Cleveland, Mejia went to the AFL to get experience at third base. He is naturally still learning the position, but he will continue to see action at the hot corner in 2018.

Mejia will open 2018 with Triple-A Columbus, and if he continues to hit the way he has throughout his career he will find his way into the big league lineup sometime during the summer. His long-term future remains behind the plate, but his added defensive versatility will help him as he breaks into the major leagues.

BA GRADE	SCOUTING GRADES
60 Risk: Medium	HIT: 60. POW: 45. SPD: 40.
	FLD: 50. ARM: 80.

Projected future grades on 20-80 scouting scale

TOP PROSPECTS OF THE DECADE

Year	Player, Pos.	2017 Org
2008	Adam Miller, RHP	Did not play
2009	Carlos Santana, C	Indians
2010	Carlos Santana, C	Indians
2011	Lonnie Chisenhall, 3B	Indians
2012	Francisco Lindor, SS	Indians
2013	Francisco Lindor, SS	Indians
2014	Francisco Lindor, SS	Indians
2015	Francisco Lindor, SS	Indians
2016	Bradley Zimmer, OF	Indians
2017	Francisco Mejia, C	Indians

BEST TOOLS

Best Hitter for Average	Francisco Mejia
Best Power Hitter	Bobby Bradley
Best Strike-Zone Discipline	Nolan Jones
Fastest Baserunner	Quentin Holmes
Best Athlete	Will Benson
Best Fastball	Julian Merryweather
Best Curveball	Triston McKenzie
Best Slider	Aaron Civale
Best Changeup	Eli Morgan
Best Control	Shane Bieber
Best Defensive Catcher	Logan Ice
Best Defensive Infielder	Erik Gonzalez
Best Infield Arm	Nolan Jones
Best Defensive Outfielder	Greg Allen
Best Outfield Arm	Jonathan Rodriguez

Year	Club (League)	Class	AVG	G	AB	R	H	2B	3B	HR	RBI	BB	SO	SB	CS	OBP	SLG
2015	Lake County (MWL)	LoA	.243	109	391	45	95	13	0	9	53	38	78	4	1	.324	.345
2016	Lake County (MWL)	LoA	.347	60	239	41	83	17	3	7	51	15	39	1	0	.384	.531
	Lynchburg (CAR)	HiA	.333	42	168	22	56	12	1	4	29	13	24	1	2	.380	.488
2017	Akron (EL)	AA	.297	92	347	52	103	21	2	14	52	24	53	7	2	.346	.490
	Cleveland (AL)	MAJ	.154	11	13	1	2	0	0	0	1	1	3	0	0	.214	.154
Major League Totals			.154	11	13	1	2	0	0	0	1	1	3	0	0	.214	.154
Minor League Totals			.293	399	1498	208	439	89	11	40	245	113	259	18	10	.349	.447x

2 TRISTON McKENZIE, RHP

Born: Aug. 2, 1997. **B-T:** R-R. **Ht.:** 6-5. **Wt.:** 165. **Drafted:** HS—Royal Palm Beach, Fla., 2015 (1st round supplemental). **Signed by:** Juan Alvarez.

McKenzie continued to build on his outstanding track record of success in 2017. He was named Carolina League pitcher of the year, pitched for the U.S. team in the Futures Game and ranked second among all minor leaguers with 186 strikeouts. He did it all while pitching nearly the whole season as a 19-year-old, making him one of the youngest players in the CL.

McKenzie also presents the same challenge to evaluators today that he did as an amateur: His track record is unimpeachable and he has impressive present stuff, but he is listed at a rail-thin 6-foot-5, 165 pounds. McKenzie's fastball can get up to 95 mph and it averaged about 92 mph in 2017. He held that velocity throughout the season and while it would dip during starts, he also showed the ability to reach back for more and finish strong at the end of his outings. His fastball plays up and gets swings and misses thanks to his delivery's extension and the high spin rate at which he throws it. He also has a good feel for spinning his curveball and gets good depth on the offering, which can be an out pitch. His changeup isn't as advanced as his other two pitches, but continues to develop and has the potential to be an above-average offering. He commands the ball well and earns praise for his makeup and understanding of his craft. McKenzie's biggest area for development remains improving his physique to allow him to manage a starter's workload, and he made important strides to that end with Lynchburg.

McKenzie is speeding toward the big leagues and has the upside to be a frontline starter. He'll advance to Double-A Akron in 2018 for his first taste of the upper minors.

BA GRADE

60 Risk: High

FB: 60. CB: 60.
CHG: 55.
CTL: 55.

Year	Club (League)	Class	W	L	ERA	G	GS	CG	SV	IP	H	HR	BB	SO	K/9	WHIP	AVG
2015	Indians (AZL)	R	1	1	0.75	4	3	0	0	12	4	0	3	17	12.8	0.58	.100
2016	Mahoning Valley (NYP)	SS	4	3	0.55	9	9	1	0	49	31	2	16	55	10.0	0.95	.180
	Lake County (MWL)	LoA	2	2	3.18	6	6	0	0	34	27	2	6	49	13.0	0.97	.214
2017	Lynchburg (CAR)	HiA	12	6	3.46	25	25	0	0	143	105	14	45	186	11.7	1.05	.204
Minor League Totals			19	12	2.68	44	43	1	0	238	167	18	70	307	11.6	0.99	.196

3 BOBBY BRADLEY, 1B

Born: May 29, 1996. **B-T:** L-R. **Ht.:** 6-1. **Wt.:** 225. **Drafted:** HS—Gulfport, Miss., 2014 (3rd round). **Signed by:** Mike Bradford.

Bradley has been one of the most productive players in the Indians' farm system since they drafted him in 2014. He won the Rookie-level Arizona League triple crown that summer by hitting .361 with eight home runs and 50 RBIs. He led the Midwest League with 27 home runs in 2015 and the Carolina League with 29 home runs in 2016, while also collecting MVP honors.

Bradley fell short of making four straight home run crowns, however, ranking sixth in the Eastern League with 23 homers in 2017 as the third youngest player on the circuit on Opening Day. Bradley's raw power is the best in the system and he has shown he is adept at getting to it in games. He has a strong, physical frame and creates excellent bat speed that allows him to drive the ball out to all fields. That power comes with a lot of swing and miss, but he cut his strikeout rate in 2017 from 29 percent to a much more manageable 22 percent, his lowest in full-season ball. Bradley is a well-below average runner with an average arm, limiting him to first base.

Bradley will advance to Triple-A Columbus in 2018, where he could take advantage of Huntington Park's hitter-friendly dimensions to again post some big power numbers. He has the potential to become a middle-of-the-order hitter in the major leagues before too long.

BA GRADE

55 Risk: V. High

HIT: 45. POW: 70.
SPD: 20. FLD: 45.
ARM: 50.

Year	Club (League)	Class	AVG	G	AB	R	H	2B	3B	HR	RBI	BB	SO	SB	CS	OBP	SLG
2015	Lake County (MWL)	LoA	.269	108	401	62	108	15	4	27	92	56	148	3	0	.361	.529
	Lynchburg (CAR)	HiA	.000	2	8	0	0	0	0	0	0	1	2	0	0	.111	.000
2016	Lynchburg (CAR)	HiA	.235	131	485	82	114	23	1	29	102	75	170	3	0	.344	.466
2017	Akron (EL)	AA	.251	131	467	66	117	25	3	23	89	55	122	3	3	.331	.465
Minor League Totals			.261	411	1516	249	395	76	12	87	333	203	478	12	3	.352	.499

4 NOLAN JONES, 3B

Born: May 7, 1998. **B-T:** L-L. **Ht.:** 6-3. **Wt.:** 195. **Drafted:** HS—Bensalem, Pa., 2016 (2nd round). **Signed by:** Mike Kanen.

Jones was regarded as one of the best prep hitters in the 2016 draft class, but he slipped to the second round, where the Indians were happy to take him at No. 55 overall. After a very modest debut in the rookie-level Arizona League in 2016, Jones got back to his elite hitting ways in 2017 with short-season Mahoning Valley, where he led the New York-Penn League in OPS (.912) as a 19-year-old.

Jones has an easy lefthanded swing and uses the whole field to hit. He is a patient hitter and led the NYPL in walks (43). He significantly cut down on his strikeout rate from his pro debut in 2016, but his patience means he works in many deep counts and will always strike out a fair amount as a result. He has proven to be an advanced hitter, but also has above-average raw power that he is still learning to get to consistently in games. As he physically matures, he projects to hit for plus power.

BA GRADE
55 Risk: V. High
HIT: 55. POW: 60.
SPD: 50. FLD: 50.
ARM: 60.

Jones fits the third base profile, but he still has work to do to ensure he can stick at the hot corner. He has plus arm strength, but needs to improve his glove-work and infield actions. If he did need to move, his athleticism and average speed would play in right field.

Jones' first full professional season was very encouraging for the Indians and he provides plenty of upside. He'll get his first taste of full-season ball in 2018 when he opens the year with low Class A Lake County.

Year	Club (League)	Class	AVG	G	AB	R	H	2B	3B	HR	RBI	BB	SO	SB	CS	OBP	SLG
2016	Indians (AZL)	R	.257	32	109	10	28	5	2	0	9	23	49	3	1	.388	.339
2017	Mahoning Valley (NYP)	SS	.317	62	218	41	69	18	3	4	33	43	60	1	0	.430	.482
Minor League Totals			.297	94	327	51	97	23	5	4	42	66	109	4	1	.416	.434

5 SHANE BIEBER, RHP

Born: May 31, 1995. **B-T:** R-R. **Ht.:** 6-3. **Wt.:** 195. **Drafted:** UC Santa Barbara, 2016 (4th round). **Signed by:** Carlos Muniz.

Bieber took over as UC Santa Barbara's ace in 2016 and led the Gauchos to their first-ever appearance in the College World Series. He made a smooth transition to the minor leagues and excelled in his first full professional season, reaching Double-A Akron almost exactly a year after his pro debut.

Bieber came into pro ball with a reputation as relying more on his command than his stuff to succeed. He has continued to show above-average control as a professional and his 0.5 walks per nine innings in 2017 led all full-season minor leaguers. He's one of those rare players whose control and command are big league ready from day one. But Bieber is starting to outgrow the command-and-control label, as his stuff made a jump in 2017. His fastball, which sat around 90 mph at UCSB, now sits 92-94 and touched 96 mph. His curveball got sharper and more

BA GRADE
50 Risk: High
FB: 55. CB: 55.
SL: 50. CHG: 50.
CTL: 70.

consistent, developing into his best secondary pitch. He also throws a slider and changeup, which both can be average offerings. He has a clean, easy delivery and has shown he can handle a heavy workload–his 173.1 innings led all minor leaguers in 2017.

Bieber made one of the biggest jumps in 2017 of any player in the Indians' system and now profiles as a potential mid-rotation starter. He will advance to Triple-A Columbus in 2018 and could pitch his way into the big league mix.

Year	Club (League)	Class	W	L	ERA	G	GS	CG	SV	IP	H	HR	BB	SO	K/9	WHIP	AVG
2016	Mahoning Valley (NYP)	SS	0	0	0.38	9	8	0	0	24	10	0	2	21	7.9	0.50	.122
2017	Lake County (MWL)	LoA	2	3	3.10	5	5	0	0	29	34	1	1	31	9.6	1.21	.291
	Lynchburg (CAR)	HiA	6	1	3.10	14	14	0	0	90	95	5	4	82	8.2	1.10	.275
	Akron (EL)	AA	2	1	2.32	9	9	0	0	54	56	2	5	49	8.1	1.12	.264
Minor League Totals			10	5	2.55	37	36	0	0	197	195	8	12	183	8.3	1.05	.258

6 YU-CHENG CHANG, SS

Born: Aug. 18, 1995. **B-T:** R-R. **Ht.:** 6-1. **Wt.:** 175. **Signed:** Taiwan, 2013. **Signed by:** Allen Lin/Jayson Lynn.

Chang was a prominent prep player in Taiwan and was one of the top amateur free agents to sign out of Asia in 2013. His profile has risen in the last two years as his power has developed and he has reportedly received heavy interest in trade talks. Chang has solid all-around offensive tools and is now better at tapping into his raw power.

Chang has produced 104 extra-base hits in the last two years, more than half his total hits (205) in that time. His swing is still geared for hitting line drives, but he has done a better job of incorporating his lower half into his swing and understanding what pitches he can drive. He is a patient hitter, but his willingness to work deep in counts leads to an elevated strikeout rate, which spiked to a career-high 26 percent in 2017. Chang's tools are good enough to play at shortstop, though his future as an everyday player may be elsewhere in the infield. He is an average defender with average or better speed and arm strength. Chang has exclusively played shortstop in full-season ball, but that will almost certainly change when he advances to Triple-A Columbus in 2018.

The Indians have held off playing Chang at other positions as long as possible, but with Francisco Lindor holding down shortstop in Cleveland for the foreseeable future and the Tribe's predilection for versatility, Chang will likely start getting exposed to other infield positions.

BA GRADE
50 Risk: High
HIT: 45. POW: 55.
SPD: 55. FLD: 50.
ARM: 55.

Year	Club (League)	Class	AVG	G	AB	R	H	2B	3B	HR	RBI	BB	SO	SB	CS	OBP	SLG
2015	Lake County (MWL)	LoA	.232	105	393	52	91	16	4	9	52	27	103	5	6	.293	.361
2016	Lynchburg (CAR)	HiA	.259	109	417	78	108	30	8	13	70	45	110	11	3	.332	.463
2017	Akron (EL)	AA	.220	126	440	72	97	24	5	24	66	52	134	11	4	.312	.461
Minor League Totals			.249	382	1409	241	351	79	21	52	213	142	375	33	14	.325	.446

7 WILLI CASTRO, SS

Born: April 24, 1997. **B-T:** B-R. **Ht.:** 6-1. **Wt.:** 165. **Signed:** Dominican Republic, 2013. **Signed by:** Ramon Pena/Felix Nivar.

The Indians have aggressively pushed Castro since signing him out of the Dominican Republic in 2013 and he had been the youngest player on his team at every stop of his pro career until 2017, when he was edged by Triston McKenzie and had to settle for being the youngest position player at high Class A Lynchburg.

Despite his youth, Castro has held his own at every level and had a breakout season with Lynchburg, earning a spot on the Carolina League's postseason all-star team. A switch-hitter, Castro sprays line drives from both sides of the plate. He started coming into his power more in 2017, when he hit 11 home runs to more than double his career total. He is an aggressive hitter, limiting his walks, but controls the strike zone well and makes a lot of contact. He has above-average speed and is a threat on the bases. Defensively, he has an above-average arm, good hands and

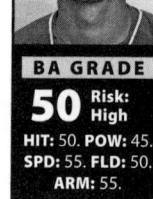

BA GRADE
50 Risk: High
HIT: 50. POW: 45.
SPD: 55. FLD: 50.
ARM: 55.

infield actions at shortstop. He still has to work on his consistency after making 25 errors in each of the last two years, but his tools and instincts give him a good chance to stay at shortstop.

Castro is a confident player and his approach to the game has matured in the last year. He will advance to Double-A Akron to start 2018.

Year	Club (League)	Class	AVG	G	AB	R	H	2B	3B	HR	RBI	BB	SO	SB	CS	OBP	SLG
2015	Mahoning Valley (NYP)	SS	.264	67	273	34	72	9	3	1	25	10	31	20	7	.304	.330
2016	Lake County (MWL)	LoA	.259	123	518	68	134	21	8	7	49	19	96	16	11	.286	.371
	Lynchburg (CAR)	HiA	.222	3	9	0	2	0	0	0	0	0	2	0	1	.222	.222
2017	Lynchburg (CAR)	HiA	.291	123	468	69	136	24	3	11	58	28	90	19	9	.337	.425
Minor League Totals			.268	359	1423	202	381	59	17	21	143	63	252	64	32	.306	.377

8 GREG ALLEN, OF

Born: March 15, 1993. **B-T:** B-R. **Ht.:** 6-0. **Wt.:** 175. **Drafted:** San Diego State, 2014 (6th round). **Signed by:** Ryan Thompson.

Allen got off to a strong start to the 2017 with Double-A Akron before breaking the hamate bone in his right hand. The injury sidelined him for two months, but he played well enough upon his return to get called up to Cleveland when rosters expanded in September to make his major league debut. He then made the playoff roster as a pinch runner/defensive replacement and appeared in two games.

Allen's game is built around his plus speed. He has good on-base skills, is a disciplined hitter and has walked about as often as he has struck out in his career. His approach at the plate is geared toward making contact, limiting his power potential and some of his offensive impact. He is a good baserunner and is always a threat to steal when he gets on base. Allen's speed also plays well in the outfield, where he is a plus defender. He takes good routes, has an above-average arm and the speed to cover plenty of ground. Allen doesn't fit the typical corner outfield profile, but with Bradley Zimmer set to man center field in Cleveland, that may be where the Indians ask him to play.

Allen will either open 2018 in the big leagues or with Triple-A Columbus, depending how the offseason plays out in Cleveland. His lack of power limits his everyday regular potential, but he does enough things well to have a lengthy big league career.

BA GRADE
45 Risk: Medium
HIT: 50. POW: 20.
SPD: 60. FLD: 60.
ARM: 55.

Year	Club (League)	Class	AVG	G	AB	R	H	2B	3B	HR	RBI	BB	SO	SB	CS	OBP	SLG
2016	Lynchburg (CAR)	HiA	.298	92	346	93	103	16	4	4	31	58	51	38	7	.424	.402
	Akron (EL)	AA	.290	37	145	26	42	7	3	3	13	19	27	7	6	.399	.441
2017	Indians (AZL)	R	.333	5	15	3	5	0	0	0	2	0	1	3	0	.353	.333
	Akron (EL)	AA	.264	71	258	37	68	16	1	2	24	22	55	21	2	.344	.357
	Cleveland (AL)	MAJ	.229	25	35	7	8	1	0	1	6	2	8	1	0	.282	.343
Major League Totals			.229	25	35	7	8	1	0	1	6	2	8	1	0	.282	.343
Minor League Totals			.274	388	1481	290	406	75	12	16	134	181	220	145	36	.379	.373

9 GEORGE VALERA, OF

Born: Nov. 13, 2000. **B-T:** L-L. **Ht.:** 5-10. **Wt.:** 160. **Signed:** Dominican Republic, 2017. **Signed by:** Jhonathan Leyba/Domingo Toribio.

The Indians took advantage of their recently revamped international scouting department and the rule changes in the latest Collective Bargaining Agreement to make a splash on the international market in 2017. Valera, the fifth-ranked player in the class, was their top signing, inking a deal worth $1.3 million.

Valera was born in New York and lived there until his family moved to the Dominican Republic when he was 13. Valera was one of the best hitters in the international class and drew comparisons to Nationals prospect Juan Soto. Valera has a loose, compact swing and keeps his bat in the zone for a long time. His feel for the barrel, bat-to-ball skills, pitch recognition and discipline all help him to make consistent, hard contact and give him the kind of hittability the Indians look for. He has above-average raw power and gets to it in games well, though he has more of a hit-over-power profile. Valera profiles as a corner outfielder with average speed and arm strength.

Valera will make his professional debut in the Dominican Summer League in 2018 as he begins his path to reaching his considerable ceiling.

BILL MITCHELL

BA GRADE
55 Risk: Extreme
HIT: 55. POW: 50.
SPD: 50. FLD: 50.
ARM: 50.

Year	Club (League)	Class	AVG	G	AB	R	H	2B	3B	HR	RBI	BB	SO	SB	CS	OBP	SLG
2017	Did not play—Signed 2018 contract																

10 WILL BENSON, OF

Born: June 16, 1998. **B-T:** L-L. **Ht.:** 6-5. **Wt.:** 215. **Drafted:** HS—Atlanta, 2016 (1st round). **Signed by:** C.T. Bradford.

Benson was a two-sport star in high school and, as a senior, was a member of the USA Baseball team that won the 2016 18U World Cup in Japan and earned second-team all-state honors in basketball. On the diamond, he developed a reputation as a toolsy, athletic player, which he has lived up to thus far as a professional.

Benson produces elite bat speed thanks to his strength and quick hands, and turns that bat speed into tremendous lefthanded raw power, rivaling Bobby Bradley for the best in the system. He is learning to get to that power more consistently and this season led the New York-Penn League in home runs (10) and ranked second in isolated power (.237). His power comes with a lot of swing-and-miss, however, and he has struck out in a third of his plate appearances as a pro. He has frequently tinkered with his swing in the past, but seemed to hit on a comfortable swing in the

BA GRADE
55 Risk: Extreme
HIT: 45. POW: 60.
SPD: 55. FLD: 55.
ARM: 60.

second half of the season. Those adjustments, as well as his ability to work a walk, leads to some optimism that he'll be able to cut down his strikeouts as he continues to develop. He is an excellent athlete and runs well for his size, particularly once he is underway. He has a plus arm and is a solid defender in right field. As a big, athletic, lefthanded-hitting outfielder from Atlanta,

Benson is often compared with Jason Heyward, who was also the 14th overall pick in the draft. Benson has a long way to go to reach that ceiling and will advance to full-season ball for the first time when he opens 2018 with low Class A Lake County.

Year	Club (League)	Class	AVG	G	AB	R	H	2B	3B	HR	RBI	BB	SO	SB	CS	OBP	SLG
2016	Indians (AZL)	R	.215	44	158	31	34	10	3	6	27	22	60	10	2	.326	.430
2017	Mahoning Valley (NYP)	SS	.238	56	202	29	48	8	5	10	36	31	80	7	1	.347	.475
Minor League Totals			.228	100	360	60	82	18	8	16	63	53	140	17	3	.338	.456

11 ERIK GONZALEZ, SS/2B

BA GRADE
40 Risk: Low

Born: Aug. 31, 1991. **B-T:** R-R. **Ht.:** 6-3. **Wt.:** 195. **Signed:** Dominican Republic, 2008. **Signed by:** Andres Garcia.

Gonzalez spent much of 2017 serving as the Indians' utility infielder, a position in which he has plenty of experience. He played every position but pitcher and catcher early in his professional career before settling in at shortstop in 2013 and eventually getting the opportunity to fill in at shortstop for Francisco Lindor after a midseason promotion.

But in the Indians' crowded big league infield, Gonzalez has returned to his utility roots, appearing at five positions in 81 games. He has some intriguing offensive tools, including above-average speed and surprising pop stemming from his wiry strength and bat speed. He is an aggressive hitter and rarely walks, limiting his chances as a top-of-the-order hitter. Defensively, Gonzalez stands out for his quickness and above-average arm strength. He can produce highlight-reel plays, but has also been prone to making mental mistakes. He is versatile enough to play anywhere in the infield and has gotten some work in the outfield corners as well.

Gonzalez will play 2018 as a 26-year-old and will have a difficult challenge to win a starting spot in the Indians' infield. He could still become an everyday player, but he is more likely to return to his utility role in Cleveland, where his versatility is an asset.

Year	Club (League)	Class	AVG	G	AB	R	H	2B	3B	HR	RBI	BB	SO	SB	CS	OBP	SLG
2015	Akron (EL)	AA	.280	72	311	38	87	18	4	6	46	11	56	10	5	.304	.421
	Columbus (IL)	AAA	.223	65	238	32	53	6	3	3	23	15	47	8	2	.277	.311
2016	Columbus (IL)	AAA	.296	104	429	62	127	31	1	11	53	19	88	12	10	.329	.450
	Cleveland (AL)	MAJ	.313	21	16	2	5	0	0	0	0	1	8	0	1	.353	.313
2017	Columbus (IL)	AAA	.256	40	160	21	41	4	3	6	13	7	53	5	1	.286	.431
	Cleveland (AL)	MAJ	.255	60	110	18	28	6	0	4	11	3	37	1	2	.272	.418
Major League Totals			.262	81	126	20	33	6	0	4	11	4	45	1	3	.282	.405
Minor League Totals			.273	744	2930	422	801	149	41	44	359	163	577	104	39	.314	.397

12 AARON BRACHO, SS

BA GRADE
55 Risk: Extreme

Born: April 24, 2001. **B-T:** B-R. **Ht.:** 5-11. **Wt.:** 175. **Signed:** Venezuela, 2017. **Signed by:** Hernan Albornoz/Rafael Cariel.

Bracho joined George Valera in headlining the Indians' 2017 international signing class. Bracho, a Venezuelan native, was the 17th-ranked player in the class. Bracho stood out for his offensive performance in game action before signing.

Bracho is a switch-hitter with a mature approach and a smooth, compact swing from both sides of the plate. He has plenty of bat speed, helping him produce a surprising amount of power for his size that could develop into average pop. Bracho was signed as a shortstop and will get a chance to develop there, but many scouts are not convinced he will stay at the position. He is an above-average runner and has good hands, but his infield actions and arm strength will likely profile better at second base.

Bracho will make his professional debut in 2018 in the Dominican Summer League.

Year	Club (League)	Class	AVG	G	AB	R	H	2B	3B	HR	RBI	BB	SO	SB	CS	OBP	SLG
2017	Did not play—Signed 2018 contract																

13 QUENTIN HOLMES, OF

BA GRADE
55 Risk: Extreme

Born: July 7, 1999. **B-T:** R-R. **Ht.:** 6-3. **Wt.:** 175. **Drafted:** HS—East Elmhurst, N.Y., 2017 (2nd round). **Signed by:** Mike Kanen.

Holmes starred on the showcase circuit in the summer of 2016, establishing himself as one of the best athletes in the draft class and earning a spot on the USA Baseball 18U team that won gold at the Pan Am Championships that fall. But Holmes remains raw on the diamond and his solid but unspectacular senior season helped drop him to the back of the second round, where the Indians were happy to take a player with his upside.

Holmes' game is geared around his top-of-the-scale speed. He mostly looks to shoot balls into the gaps to let his speed play and his feel for the barrel helps him do so. But he also generates above-average bat speed and can hit for power, especially when he turns on the ball. He is an aggressive hitter and often hunts fastballs early in the count, and will need to improve his pitch recognition as he advances in the minor leagues. His speed helps him cover lots of ground in center field, where he could develop into a plus defender. As a New York prep product, Holmes remains raw in nearly every aspect of his game, which showed in a tough professional debut in the Rookie-level Arizona League. But he was young for the class (he was still 17 on draft day) and figures to make a jump once he gets used to facing advanced competition.

Holmes' rawness and age mean he will likely open 2018 back in Arizona, with a chance to advance to short-season Mahoning Valley sometime during the summer.

Year	Club (League)	Class	AVG	G	AB	R	H	2B	3B	HR	RBI	BB	SO	SB	CS	OBP	SLG
2017	Indians (AZL)	R	.182	41	159	22	29	5	3	2	15	8	61	5	4	.220	.289
Minor League Totals			.182	41	159	22	29	5	3	2	15	8	61	5	4	.220	.289

14 AARON CIVALE, RHP

BA GRADE
50 Risk: High

Born: June 12, 1995. **B-T:** R-R. **Ht.:** 6-2. **Wt.:** 215. **Drafted:** Northeastern, 2016 (3rd round). **Signed by:** Mike Kanen.

Civale moved to the rotation as a junior at Northeastern and delivered phenomenal results in 2016, ranking in the top 15 nationally in ERA (1.73), strikeouts (121) and WHIP (0.93).

Civale built on that success in his first full professional season, and his above-average command helped him rank third among all qualified minor league starters in walks per nine innings (0.8). Civale's pinpoint control is his best tool, but he also mixes in solid stuff. His fastball sits in the low 90s and his feel for spin enables him to throw a cutter, slider and curveball. His slider is the best of the group, but they all work well in concert to give the effect of an above-average breaking ball that changes angles and power. Civale worked in 2017 to improve his changeup after never needing it as an amateur. His stuff, size and makeup give him a chance to stay in the rotation in the long run.

Civale will face a challenge in 2018 as he advances for the first time to the upper levels of the minor leagues.

Year	Club (League)	Class	W	L	ERA	G	GS	CG	SV	IP	H	HR	BB	SO	K/9	WHIP	AVG
2016	Mahoning Valley (NYP)	SS	0	2	1.67	13	13	0	0	38	23	0	8	28	6.7	0.82	.180
2017	Lake County (MWL)	LoA	2	4	4.58	10	10	0	0	57	64	2	5	53	8.4	1.21	.284
	Lynchburg (CAR)	HiA	11	2	2.59	17	17	0	0	108	96	11	9	88	7.4	0.98	.238
Minor League Totals			13	8	2.98	40	40	0	0	202	183	13	22	169	7.5	1.01	.242

15 CONNER CAPEL, OF

BA GRADE

50 Risk: High

Born: May 19, 1997. **B-T:** R-R. **Ht.:** 6-1. **Wt.:** 185. **Drafted:** HS—Katy, Texas, 2016 (5th round). **Signed by:** Kyle Van Hook.

Capel was set to follow in the footsteps of his father, former big leaguer Mike Capel, to Texas before the Indians drafted him in the fifth round in 2016 and signed him for slot. He was assigned to low Class A Lake County for his first full professional season and he excelled in the Midwest League, where he ranked third in home runs (22) and fifth in slugging percentage (.482).

One of the knocks on Capel before the draft was that his swing didn't produce enough loft to get to his above-average raw power. He has since made some swing adjustments to allow him to tap into his pop without sacrificing his ability to make consistent contact. He did strike out more often in 2017, but he cut his strikeout rate in the second half of the season and his discipline at the plate should help him further cut down his strikeouts as he continues to develop. Capel is an above-average runner, but doesn't have blazing speed. He has an above-average arm and played all three outfield positions in 2017, seeing most of his time in right field. That may be where he profiles best, but he has a chance to end up in center field.

Capel earns praise for his makeup and hard-nosed style of play. He will advance to high Class A Lynchburg in 2018.

Year	Club (League)	Class	AVG	G	AB	R	H	2B	3B	HR	RBI	BB	SO	SB	CS	OBP	SLG
2016	Indians (AZL)	R	.210	35	138	22	29	5	3	0	13	11	20	10	3	.270	.290
2017	Lake County (MWL)	LoA	.249	119	438	73	109	22	7	22	61	43	107	15	10	.319	.482
Minor League Totals			.240	154	576	95	138	27	10	22	74	54	127	25	13	.307	.436

16 TYLER FREEMAN, SS

BA GRADE

55 Risk: Extreme

Born: May 21, 1999. **B-T:** R-R. **Ht.:** 6-0. **Wt.:** 170. **Drafted:** HS—Rancho Cucamonga, Calif., 2017 (2nd round supplemental). **Signed by:** Mike Bradford.

Freeman had a dominant senior season in Southern California, hitting .526/.638/.814 and helping his high school to its first sectional title. He carried that performance over to the rookie-level Arizona League, where he had a solid debut.

Freeman stands out most for his hittability and feel for the barrel. He makes consistent hard contact, is difficult to strike out and has a direct swing. He has some power, mostly when he can turn on the ball, but power is not expected to be a large part of his game. Freeman was drafted as a shortstop, but questions remain about his chances to stay at the position. He has an average arm and is an average runner, making a move across the bag to second base a possibility down the line. For now, however, the Indians will develop Freeman as a shortstop.

Freeman is lauded for his makeup and instincts, which help his tools play up and will serve him well in his first full professional season, likely with short-season Mahoning Valley.

Year	Club (League)	Class	AVG	G	AB	R	H	2B	3B	HR	RBI	BB	SO	SB	CS	OBP	SLG
2017	Indians (AZL)	R	.297	36	128	19	38	9	0	2	14	7	12	5	1	.364	.414
Minor League Totals			.297	36	128	19	38	9	0	2	14	7	12	5	1	.364	.414

17 JULIAN MERRYWEATHER, RHP

BA GRADE

50 Risk: High

Born: Oct. 14, 1991. **B-T:** R-R. **Ht.:** 6-4. **Wt.:** 200. **Drafted:** Oklahoma Baptist, 2014 (5th round). **Signed by:** Mark Allen.

Following a breakout 2016 season, Merryweather carried that momentum into 2017. After a strong start to the season with Double-A Akron, he was promoted to Triple-A at the end of May. While Merryweather's results suffered down the stretch with the Clippers, his stuff and peripherals remained strong.

Merryweather has the stuff to start, but still is learning some of the finer points of pitching. His fastball sits in the mid 90s and regularly reaches 97 mph. His changeup can be an above-average pitch with fading action, but he will need to tighten the pitch up to get hitters to chase it more often. He throws both a curveball and a slider, which can be average offerings. He does a good job of using his 6-foot-4 frame to his advantage and works well down in the strike zone to create groundouts. He throws a lot of strikes and repeats his delivery well.

Merryweather has the potential to be a starter in the big leagues, but he will be 26 on Opening Day and breaking into the Indians' already crowded rotation is no easy task. He'll start 2018 back at Columbus and have a chance to pitch his way into the mix in Cleveland.

Year	Club (League)	Class	W	L	ERA	G	GS	CG	SV	IP	H	HR	BB	SO	K/9	WHIP	AVG
2015	Lake County (MWL)	LoA	2	3	4.08	21	4	0	1	71	89	6	12	69	8.8	1.43	.299
2016	Lynchburg (CAR)	HiA	8	2	1.03	11	11	0	0	61	47	4	15	58	8.6	1.02	.210
	Akron (EL)	AA	5	4	3.89	13	13	0	0	74	75	6	17	61	7.4	1.24	.255
2017	Akron (EL)	AA	4	2	3.38	9	9	0	0	51	37	3	10	52	9.2	0.93	.196
	Columbus (IL)	AAA	3	7	6.58	16	16	0	0	78	105	13	25	76	8.8	1.67	.327
Minor League Totals			23	20	3.92	83	65	0	1	381	400	34	92	351	8.3	1.29	.265

18 SAM HENTGES, LHP

BA GRADE 50 Risk: V. High

Born: July 18, 1996. **B-T:** R-R. **Ht.:** 6-6. **Wt.:** 245. **Drafted:** HS—Arden Hills, Minn., 2014 (4th round). **Signed by:** Les Pajari.

Hentges was raw even for a prep player from Minnesota when the Indians drafted him in 2014. He was one of the youngest players in the draft class and didn't pitch much until late in his junior year of high school. He has come along slowly in the minor leagues, in part because he needed Tommy John surgery during the 2016 season.

Hentges returned to the mound in 2017 and finished the season strong at short-season Mahoning Valley. During his rehab, he improved his physique and filled out his big, physical frame. He has a quick arm and his fastball sits at 92-95 mph. His best secondary pitch is his curveball, which is a plus pitch at its best. His changeup is still developing, but shows promise. He has gotten better in pro ball at repeating his delivery and returned from injury throwing more strikes.

Hentges will still be just 21 years old on Opening Day 2018 and has significant upside. He will likely start the season at low Class A Lake County.

Year	Club (League)	Class	W	L	ERA	G	GS	CG	SV	IP	H	HR	BB	SO	K/9	WHIP	AVG
2015	Indians (AZL)	R	3	3	3.10	11	9	0	0	49	49	4	19	59	10.8	1.38	.254
	Mahoning Valley (NYP)	SS	0	2	14.21	2	2	0	0	6	13	0	8	2	2.8	3.32	.433
2016	Lake County (MWL)	LoA	2	4	6.12	14	14	0	0	60	71	8	29	73	10.9	1.66	.296
2017	Indians (AZL)	R	0	3	4.85	6	6	0	0	13	16	2	3	18	12.5	1.46	.296
	Mahoning Valley (NYP)	SS	0	1	2.04	5	5	0	0	18	5	1	12	23	11.7	0.96	.088
Minor League Totals			6	13	4.51	46	36	0	0	160	158	15	76	185	10.4	1.47	.256

19 LOGAN ICE, C

BA GRADE 45 Risk: High

Born: May 27, 1995. **B-T:** B-R. **Ht.:** 5-10. **Wt.:** 195. **Drafted:** Oregon State, 2016 (2nd round supplemental). **Signed by:** Conor Glassey.

Ice broke out offensively in 2016 during his junior season at Oregon State and the Indians made him a supplemental second round pick, the highest they have drafted a catcher since 2003.

Ice hasn't carried that offensive momentum into pro ball, but continues to stand out for his defensive ability. He blocks balls well, is a solid receiver and earns praise for his ability to handle the pitching staff. He has an accurate, average arm. A switch-hitter, Ice has a patient approach at the plate. He produces hard contact, but that hasn't translated into much power yet, partially due to a wrist injury that sidelined him for about two weeks in the first half of 2017.

Thanks to his defensive ability, Ice won't have to hit much to become a big league contributor. And while he hasn't made quick work of the low minors, he was young for his draft class and will still be 22 when he opens the 2018 season with high Class A Lynchburg.

Year	Club (League)	Class	AVG	G	AB	R	H	2B	3B	HR	RBI	BB	SO	SB	CS	OBP	SLG
2016	Mahoning Valley (NYP)	SS	.198	39	126	13	25	7	0	2	8	23	38	0	0	.329	.302
2017	Lake County (MWL)	LoA	.228	93	316	38	72	10	1	11	42	42	74	1	1	.320	.370
Minor League Totals			.219	132	442	51	97	17	1	13	50	65	112	1	1	.322	.351

20 OSCAR GONZALEZ, OF

BA GRADE 50 Risk: V. High

Born: Jan. 10, 1998. **B-T:** R-R. **Ht.:** 6-2. **Wt.:** 180. **Signed:** Dominican Republic, 2014. **Signed by:** Ramon Pena/Felix Nivar.

Gonzalez, the Indians' top target in the 2014 international class, made a resounding U.S. debut in 2016, when he won MVP honors in the Rookie-level Arizona League. He moved up in 2017 to the New York-Penn League as a 19-year-old. While he wasn't as productive at the plate while facing older competition, he still excited evaluators with his raw skill set.

Gonzalez stands out most for his well above-average raw power, and he does a good job of getting to it in games. His approach at the plate is still crude and he'll need to improve his plate discipline as he faces more advanced pitchers. But he produces plenty of bat speed and has better bat-to-ball skills than his strikeout rate (24.7 percent) indicates. Gonzalez is an average runner and has plus arm strength, giving him a chance to play right field, though he has mostly played left field the last two seasons.

Wherever he ends up defensively, the onus will be on his bat to push him through the minor leagues. He will advance to low Class A Lake County in 2018.

Year	Club (League)	Class	AVG	G	AB	R	H	2B	3B	HR	RBI	BB	SO	SB	CS	OBP	SLG
2015	Indians (DSL)	R	.203	70	256	25	52	17	1	4	38	19	65	1	3	.262	.324
2016	Indians (AZL)	R	.303	40	145	30	44	10	2	8	26	8	57	4	0	.342	.566
	Mahoning Valley (NYP)	SS	.000	1	3	0	0	0	0	0	0	1	1	0	0	.250	.000
2017	Mahoning Valley (NYP)	SS	.283	55	237	20	67	16	0	3	34	5	61	0	0	.301	.388
Minor League Totals			.254	166	641	75	163	43	3	15	98	33	184	5	3	.294	.401

21 JOHNATHAN RODRIGUEZ, OF

Born: Nov. 4, 1999. **B-T:** B-R. **Ht.:** 6-3. **Wt.:** 180. **Drafted:** HS—Florida, P.R., 2017 (3rd round). **Signed by:** Juan Alvarez.

Rodriguez was one of the youngest players in the 2017 draft class and didn't turn 18 until November. He is more of a long-term developmental bet, but the product of the Beltran Baseball Academy in Puerto Rico adjusted faster to professional baseball than some had expected, debuting with a solid summer in the Arizona League.

Rodriguez, a switch hitter, has a smooth swing and showed he has some feel for the strike zone. He has above-average raw power and projects to hit for power as he fills out his projectable frame. Rodriguez has below-average speed, but his plus arm plays well in right field, where he can be a solid defender. Rodriguez's age means the Indians won't feel any need to rush him, and he'll likely start 2018 back in Arizona.

Rodriguez is raw, but he has the tools and work ethic to develop into a prototypical right fielder with time.

Year	Club (League)	Class	AVG	G	AB	R	H	2B	3B	HR	RBI	BB	SO	SB	CS	OBP	SLG
2017	Indians (AZL)	R	.250	31	96	13	24	4	2	0	11	21	23	0	1	.381	.333
Minor League Totals			.250	31	96	13	24	4	2	0	11	21	23	0	1	.381	.333

22 LUIS OVIEDO, RHP

Born: May 15, 1999. **B-T:** R-R. **Ht.:** 6-4. **Wt.:** 170. **Signed:** Venezuela, 2015. **Signed by:** Koby Perez/Luis Camacho.

Oviedo, the top pitcher in the Indians' 2015 international signing class, made his U.S. debut in the Rookie-level Arizona League in 2017. And while his 7.14 ERA was unsightly, he still stood out for his stuff as an 18-year-old in the league.

Oviedo has continued to grow since he signed and his velocity has grown with him. He now throws in the mid 90s after sitting in the upper 80s when he signed, and he could add still more velocity as he continues to mature. This past year he scrapped his big curveball in favor of a slider that he picked up well. He also has good feel for his changeup, which is advanced for his age. He produced a lot of ground balls, which led to a high batting average on balls in play in Arizona, but will serve him well as he advances in the minor leagues. He has a solid delivery and does a good job of throwing strikes.

Like many young pitchers, Oviedo is still learning to harness his stuff and will need to improve his consistency. He will likely advance to short-season Mahoning Valley in 2018.

Year	Club (League)	Class	W	L	ERA	G	GS	CG	SV	IP	H	HR	BB	SO	K/9	WHIP	AVG
2016	Indians (DSL)	R	2	8	4.00	14	14	0	0	63	67	1	17	56	8.0	1.33	.276
2017	Indians (AZL)	R	4	2	7.14	14	7	0	0	52	62	2	22	70	12.2	1.63	.286
Minor League Totals			6	10	5.42	28	21	0	0	115	129	3	39	126	9.9	1.47	.280

23 TYLER KRIEGER, 2B

Born: Jan. 16, 1994. **B-T:** B-R. **Ht.:** 6-2. **Wt.:** 170. **Drafted:** Clemson, 2015 (4th round). **Signed by:** Brad Tyler.

Coming into 2017, Krieger had not advanced past Class A. He got plenty of experience against upper-level competition during the year, however. He started the year playing for Team Israel in the World Baseball Class, helping the team on its Cinderella run, and then spent the season with Double-A Akron.

Krieger struggled at the plate as he worked through some adjustments. He is at his best when he focuses on spraying line drives to all fields and takes advantage of his above-average feel for the barrel. That approach doesn't lead to much power, but his above-average speed helps him produce extra-base hits when he drives the ball to the gaps. Defensively, Krieger has been limited to second base since suffering a shoulder injury during his sophomore year of college that required labrum surgery to repair.

Kreiger is a solid defender at his new position, but there is now more pressure on his bat, particularly given his below-average power. He'll look to get back on track at the plate in 2018 as he advances to Triple-A Columbus.

Year	Club (League)	Class	AVG	G	AB	R	H	2B	3B	HR	RBI	BB	SO	SB	CS	OBP	SLG
2015	Did not play—Injured																
2016	Lake County (MWL)	LoA	.313	69	262	51	82	13	4	3	35	29	66	15	8	.385	.427
	Lynchburg (CAR)	HiA	.282	59	220	33	62	13	4	2	23	28	52	6	7	.369	.405
2017	Akron (EL)	AA	.225	119	418	55	94	25	2	6	43	42	107	12	6	.303	.337
Minor League Totals			.264	247	900	139	238	51	10	11	101	99	225	33	21	.343	.380

24 ERNIE CLEMENT, 2B/SS

BA GRADE
45 Risk: High

Born: March 22, 1996. **B-T:** R-R. **Ht.:** 6-0. **Wt.:** 170. **Drafted:** Virginia, 2017 (4th round). **Signed by:** Bob Mayer.

Largely overlooked coming out of the New York prep ranks in 2014, Clement developed a reputation as a pure hitter during college. He was a career .306 hitter at Virginia and whiffed just 31 times in three seasons with the Cavaliers. He also found success with a wood bat, earning MVP honors in the Cape Cod League in 2016 after leading the circuit in hits and stolen bases.

Clement embodies the saying, "Good things happen when you put the ball in play." He has an aggressive approach and an uncanny knack for putting the bat on the ball. He has minimal power and instead sprays the ball all over the field and takes advantage of his plus speed to get on base. Clement also offers versatility defensively. He moved to shortstop in 2017 after mostly playing second base his first two years of college, with action in center field also mixed in. He has average arm strength and likely won't ever be an everyday shortstop, but his overall skill set gives him a chance at the position.

Clement is most likely to end up a super-utility player, and his speed, instincts and bat-to-ball skills help that profile. He could move quickly in the minor leagues and he could open his first full professional season with high Class A Lynchburg.

Year	Club (League)	Class	AVG	G	AB	R	H	2B	3B	HR	RBI	BB	SO	SB	CS	OBP	SLG
2017	Mahoning Valley (NYP)	SS	.280	45	175	32	49	9	1	0	13	6	12	6	2	.315	.343
Minor League Totals			.280	45	175	32	49	9	1	0	13	6	12	6	2	.315	.343

25 MARK MATHIAS, 2B/3B

BA GRADE
45 Risk: High

Born: Aug. 2, 1994. **B-T:** R-R. **Ht.:** 6-0. **Wt.:** 200. **Drafted:** Cal Poly, 2015 (3rd round). **Signed by:** Carlos Muniz.

Since winning the Big West Conference batting title as a Cal Poly sophomore in 2014, Mathias has battled injuries to stay on the field. He injured the labrum in his right shoulder while playing for USA Baseball's Collegiate National Team in the summer of 2014 and was limited the next year as he recovered from surgery. He had a healthy first full professional season, reaching Double-A Akron, but was again bothered by shoulder injuries in 2017.

Mathias missed the first month of the season after dislocating his left shoulder in spring training and landed back on the disabled list later in the season with more shoulder trouble. When healthy, Mathias has lived up to his reputation as a pure hitter. He has one of the best approaches in the organization because he controls the barrel well and is a patient, disciplined hitter. He has below-average power, but does a good job of driving the balls in gaps. Mathias was drafted as a second baseman, but offers defensive versatility. He mostly played third base during his abbreviated 2017 and has also seen some time at shortstop.

As an everyday player, Mathias profiles best at second base, but his average arm and speed give him a chance to be a utility infielder. First, however, he needs to show he can stay healthy. He'll return to Double-A Akron in 2018.

Year	Club (League)	Class	AVG	G	AB	R	H	2B	3B	HR	RBI	BB	SO	SB	CS	OBP	SLG
2015	Mahoning Valley (NYP)	SS	.282	67	245	38	69	19	3	2	32	35	36	5	4	.382	.408
2016	Lynchburg (CAR)	HiA	.274	115	427	70	117	39	1	5	60	48	87	9	1	.359	.405
	Akron (EL)	AA	.067	5	15	1	1	1	0	0	1	1	6	0	0	.125	.133
2017	Akron (EL)	AA	.212	35	104	17	22	5	1	1	13	13	34	4	0	.328	.308
Minor League Totals			.264	222	791	126	209	64	5	8	106	97	163	18	5	.358	.388

26 RYAN MERRITT, LHP

BA GRADE
40 Risk: Medium

Born: Feb. 21, 1992. **B-T:** L-L. **Ht.:** 6-0. **Wt.:** 180. **Drafted:** McLennan (Texas) JC, 2011 (16th round). **Signed by:** Kevin Cullen.

Merritt wrote himself into the club's postseason lore in 2016. Having made just four career big league appearances (one start), he was pressed into action as the Indians' starter in Game Five of the AL Championship Series and threw 4.1 scoreless innings to help send Cleveland to the World Series for the first time since 1997.

Before that game, he had mostly been known for his incredible minor league walk rate, and returned to that identity in 2017, sprinkling a few spot starts for the Indians into a solid campaign with Triple-A Columbus. Merritt doesn't have overpowering stuff, instead relying on his command and feel for pitching to get outs. His fastball sits in the upper 80s, occasionally touching 91 mph, and he knows how to add or subtract velocity as necessary. His above-average changeup is his best pitch, and he also has both a curveball and a cutter that can be effective offerings. All of his stuff plays up thanks to his plus control. Merritt's ceiling is as a back-end starter, and he will always have to be fine with his command to succeed.

Merritt was one of just seven pitchers to start a game for the Indians in 2017, but breaking into the rotation full time will be difficult. He could find a spot in the bullpen, but is more likely to start 2018 back at Columbus.

Year	Club (League)	Class	W	L	ERA	G	GS	CG	SV	IP	H	HR	BB	SO	K/9	WHIP	AVG
2015	Akron (EL)	AA	10	7	3.51	22	22	2	0	141	145	8	16	89	5.7	1.14	.269
	Columbus (IL)	AAA	2	0	4.20	5	5	0	0	30	38	1	6	16	4.8	1.47	.309
2016	Columbus (IL)	AAA	11	8	3.70	24	24	2	0	143	156	15	23	92	5.8	1.25	.279
	Cleveland (AL)	MAJ	1	0	1.64	4	1	0	0	11	6	0	0	6	4.9	0.55	.167
2017	Lake County (MWL)	LoA	1	0	2.57	1	1	0	0	7	7	0	1	4	5.1	1.14	.269
	Columbus (IL)	AAA	10	5	3.03	19	18	1	0	116	116	19	25	85	6.6	1.22	.263
	Cleveland (AL)	MAJ	2	0	1.74	5	4	0	0	21	26	0	4	7	3.0	1.45	.310
Major League Totals			3	0	1.71	9	5	0	0	32	32	0	4	13	3.7	1.14	.267
Minor League Totals			56	36	3.33	140	134	7	1	807	831	69	134	560	6.2	1.20	.267

27 GAVIN COLLINS, 3B

BA GRADE
45 Risk: High

Born: July 17, 1995. **B-T:** R-R. **Ht.:** 5-11. **Wt.:** 205. **Drafted:** Mississippi State, 2016 (13th round). **Signed by:** Chuck Bartlett.

Collins was hampered by hand injuries during his junior year at Mississippi State, but still helped the Bulldogs to the Southeastern Conference title and was drafted in the 13th round by the Indians. He got back to health in 2017 and broke out at the plate, raising his stature in the process.

Collins has above-average power and does a good job of getting to it. He has good plate discipline, though his strikeout rate did jump after his midseason promotion to high Class A Lynchburg. Collins was the first Mississippi State player to earn SEC all-freshman honors as a catcher, but injuries have severely limited his time behind the plate in the last two years. The Indians have not ruled out him catching going forward, but it will be tough for him to do so in a regular role. He has an average arm and primarily played third base the last two seasons, and may end up at first base due to his below-average hands and athleticism. No matter where he ends up defensively, it will be up to Collins' bat to carry him through the minor leagues.

Collins will advance to Double-A Akron in 2018 for his first taste of upper-level pitching.

Year	Club (League)	Class	AVG	G	AB	R	H	2B	3B	HR	RBI	BB	SO	SB	CS	OBP	SLG
2016	Mahoning Valley (NYP)	SS	.260	48	173	19	45	8	1	0	19	22	28	0	0	.348	.318
2017	Lake County (MWL)	LoA	.270	40	141	23	38	5	1	8	19	14	30	0	0	.340	.489
	Lynchburg (CAR)	HiA	.275	40	142	18	39	16	0	4	35	13	45	1	1	.340	.472
Minor League Totals			.268	128	456	60	122	29	2	12	73	49	103	1	1	.343	.419

28 BRADY AIKEN, LHP

BA GRADE
50 Risk: Extreme

Born: Aug. 16, 1996. **B-T:** L-L. **Ht.:** 6-4. **Wt.:** 205. **Drafted:** HS—Bradenton, Fla., 2015 (1st round). **Signed by:** Mike Soper.

Aiken emerged during his senior year of high school as the best player in the 2014 draft class and the Astros made him the No. 1 overall pick. A series of ill-fated events for him has followed. First, when a post-draft physical revealed an elbow issue, the Astros withdrew the $6.5 million offer they had agreed to. Aiken ultimately turned down a reported $5 million offer and chose to pitch for IMG Academy's postgrad team in 2015. He left his first start of the year injured and required Tommy John surgery. The Indians selected him 17th overall in 2015 and he finally made his pro debut the next year.

Aiken has struggled in pro ball, especially in 2017, when he ranked second among all minor leaguers with 101 walks in 132 innings with low Class A Lake County. The gap between what evaluators saw from

Aiken leading up to the 2014 draft and what they saw in 2017 was striking. His velocity has not returned since having surgery and his fastball sat in the upper 80s and touched 91 with Lake County, down from his prep days when he touched 97 mph and sat in the low 90s. More worryingly, Aiken's control abandoned him in 2017 and he struggled to locate his fastball. His secondary stuff, however, remained solid and helped him battle through many tough outings. His curveball can be a plus offering and his changeup gives him another advanced pitch.

Aiken may be able to correct some of his struggles if he gets stronger and more athletic, which would likely help his velocity and consistency. He will enter a critical point in his development in 2018 and there is still optimism that he can bounce back.

Year	Club (League)	Class	W	L	ERA	G	GS	CG	SV	IP	H	HR	BB	SO	K/9	WHIP	AVG
2015	Did not play—Injured																
2016	Indians (AZL)	R	0	4	7.13	9	8	0	0	24	32	1	13	35	13.1	1.88	.308
	Mahoning Valley (NYP)	SS	2	1	4.43	5	5	0	0	22	20	3	8	22	8.9	1.25	.233
2017	Lake County (MWL)	LoA	5	13	4.77	27	27	0	0	132	134	12	101	89	6.1	1.78	.277
Minor League Totals			7	18	5.05	41	40	0	0	178	186	16	122	146	7.4	1.73	.276

29 ELI MORGAN, RHP

BA GRADE 45 Risk: High

Born: May 13, 1996. **B-T:** R-R. **Ht.:** 5-10. **Wt.:** 190. **Drafted:** Gonzaga, 2017 (8th round). **Signed by:** Conor Glassey.

Despite capping his college career with a strong junior season in which he ranked in the top 10 nationally in strikeouts (138) and strikeouts per nine innings (12.34), Morgan lasted until the eighth round in the draft due to his stature and below-average fastball velocity. But his outstanding professional debut in the New York-Penn League showed there may be more than meets the eye.

Morgan threw a bit harder in pro ball, running his fastball up to 93 mph. His fastball is just good enough to allow his changeup, which was one of the best secondary pitches in the draft class, to be effective. His changeup has fading action, and he locates and sells the pitch well. He also throws a slurvy slider, which he will need to tighten up to give him a better third pitch. Morgan has a nontraditional profile as a short righthander whose primary offspeed pitch is his changeup. He has a starter's mentality and the Indians will develop him as one, believing he could move quickly in the minor leagues.

Morgan is advanced enough to handle an assignment to high Class A Lynchburg in 2018.

Year	Club (League)	Class	W	L	ERA	G	GS	CG	SV	IP	H	HR	BB	SO	K/9	WHIP	AVG
2017	Mahoning Valley (NYP)	SS	3	2	1.03	13	5	0	0	35	24	0	9	58	14.9	0.94	.188
Minor League Totals			3	2	1.03	13	5	0	0	35	24	0	9	58	14.9	0.94	.188

30 MARCOS GONZALEZ, SS

BA GRADE 50 Risk: Extreme

Born: Oct. 22, 1999. **B-T:** R-R. **Ht.:** 6-0. **Wt.:** 160. **Signed:** Dominican Republic, 2016. **Signed by:** Koby Perez/Felix Nivar/Marcelino Vallejo.

Gonzalez, ranked No. 27 in the 2016 international signing class, was one of the top performers in the Dominican Prospect League in the year leading up to his signing with the Indians for $250,000. He carried that performance over to 2017 during his professional debut in the Dominican Summer League.

Gonzalez has a chance to have about average tools across the board, and gets the most out of his tools thanks to his steady play and advanced baseball IQ. He has a good feel for the barrel and does a good job of controlling the strike zone, even drawing more walks than strikeouts during his debut. His swing is more geared toward hitting line drives in the gaps, but he has a chance to grow into more power as he physically matures. He has average speed and above-average arm strength.

Gonzalez already has good defensive instincts and soft hands, giving him a good chance to stick at shortstop. Gonzalez is on track to make his U.S. debut in 2018 in the Arizona League.

Year	Club (League)	Class	AVG	G	AB	R	H	2B	3B	HR	RBI	BB	SO	SB	CS	OBP	SLG
2017	Indians (DSL)	R	.274	56	215	31	59	7	0	1	24	31	28	13	4	.371	.321
Minor League Totals			.274	56	215	31	59	7	0	1	24	31	28	13	4	.371	.321

Colorado Rockies

BY TRACY RINGOLSBY

Over the years the Rockies have made their bold moves on the free agent market in hopes of finding help for their rotation. It never worked.

They tried with Bill Swift and Mike Hampton and Denny Neagle and Darryl Kile. All of them welcomed the challenge at the time of signing their contracts, but in the end, despite their track records in other venues, the veterans struggled with the adjustment to altitude.

What works, however, has been to develop starting pitchers from within, which was underscored by the Rockies success in 2017, when seven of the eight starters they used had spent time in the Rockies farm system. That total included four rookies, two of whom—righthander German Marquez and lefthander Kyle Freeland—received Rookie of the Year votes.

With Mark Wiley overseeing the pitching in the organization, and sharing the belief with pitching coach Steve Foster and bullpen coach Darren Holmes that the curveball is a critical pitch, the Rockies are suddenly turning scouting director Bill Schmidt's draft choices into a formidable rotation.

The influx of homegrown pitchers took an unexpected major step forward in 2017 because of a series of injuries that began with Chad Bettis being diagnosed with a recurrence of testicular cancer in spring training. As a result, the Rockies integrated four rookies in their rotation by June, though all four had ranked in the organization's Top 10 Prospects in the preseason.

And nobody was complaining. The Rockies, after all, got off to the best start in franchise history over the first 11 weeks of the season, and they overcame a midseason struggle to advance to the postseason for just the fourth time in franchise history.

After the emergence of righthander Jon Gray and lefthander Tyler Anderson in 2016, the Rockies brought in Freeland and Marquez as well as righthanders Antonio Senzatela and Jeff Hoffman in 2017. Marquez and Hoffman came to the Rockies via trades but did spend time in the farm system before claiming a spot on the big league roster.

It's not a new phenomenon. Seven of the 10 lowest single-season ERAs in Rockies history have been compiled by pitchers whom they signed as amateurs. Never did they have the concentration of homegrown pitchers like they did in 2017.

The impact of the Rockies' six young pitchers over the past two seasons has become a rallying point for the farm system, where the young pitchers see not only the opportunity to get to the big

A two-time all-star, Charlie Blackmon led the NL in batting (.331), hits (213) and runs (137).

PROJECTED 2021 LINEUP

Catcher	Tom Murphy (30)
First Base	Ryan McMahon (26)
Second Base	Brendan Rodgers (24)
Third Base	Nolan Arenado (30)
Shortstop	Trevor Story (28)
Left Field	Raimel Tapia (27)
Center Field	David Dahl (27)
Right Field	Charlie Blackmon (34)
No. 1 Starter	Jon Gray (29)
No. 2 Starter	Kyle Freeland (28)
No. 3 Starter	German Marquez (26)
No. 4 Starter	Antonio Senzatela (26)
No. 5 Starter	Tyler Anderson (31)
Closer	Riley Pint (23)

leagues but the opportunity to succeed.

And those free agents? Swift, Hampton, Neagle and Kile were a combined 75-91 in their Rockies career, and combined for a 5.69 ERA.

The Rockies graduated five members of their preseason Top 10 Prospects list in 2017—Hoffman (No. 3), outfielder Raimel Tapia (No. 4), Marquez (No. 5), Freeland (No. 8) and Senzatela (No. 10)—and only the Yankees, led by Aaron Judge, received more value from prospects during the season. The rash of prospect graduations has led to great turnover at the top of the Rockies' prospects list, however, where shortstop Brendan Rodgers still ranks No. 1, though his supporting cast has thinned.

DEPTH CHART

COLORADO ROCKIES

TOP 2018 ROOKIE: Ryan McMahon, 1B. He made quick adjustments at Double-A and Triple-A in 2017 to earn his first big league callup.
BREAKOUT PROSPECT: Jesus Tinoco, RHP. He belatedly is beginning to reach his potential.
SLEEPER: Wes Rogers, OF. He has speed that can change a game, offensively and defensively.

SOURCE OF TOP 30 TALENT			
Homegrown	28	Acquired	2
College	13	Trade	2
Junior college	0	Rule 5 draft	0
High school	11	Independent league	0
Nondrafted free agent	1	Free agent/waivers	0
International	3		

LF
Daniel Montano (23)
Vince Fernandez (27)
Noel Cuevas

CF
Yonathan Daza (24)
Wes Rogers

RF
Sam Hilliard (14)
Mike Tauchman
Willie Abreu
Ramon Marcelino

3B
Colton Welker (4)
Ryan Vilade (9)
Tyler Nevin (10)
Josh Fuentes (25)

SS
Brendan Rodgers (1)
Daniel Castro

2B
Garrett Hampson (8)
Forrest Wall (18)
Brett Boswell
Shael Mendoza

1B
Ryan McMahon (2)
Brian Mundell (13)
Jordan Patterson (15)
Chad Spanberger (28)

C
Tom Murphy (12)
Dom Nunez (29)

LHP
LHSP
Sam Howard (11)
Breiling Eusebio (16)
Harrison Musgrave (22)

LHRP
Ben Bowden (20)
Jerry Vasto

RHP
RHSP
Riley Pint (3)
Peter Lambert (5)
Ryan Castellani (6)
Yench Almonte (7)
Jesus Tinoco (17)
Will Gaddis (19)
Mike Nikorak (21)
Robert Tyler
Zach Jemiola
Parker French

RHRP
Reid Humphreys (26)
Rayan Gonzalez (30)
James Farris
Jair Diaz
Justin Lawrence
Salvador Just

DRAFT ANALYSIS

2017

BEST PURE HITTER: SS Ryan Vilade (2), Colorado's top pick, grew up around the game, has a long track record for hitting as an amateur—often hitting third for USA Baseball's 18U national team in 2016—and has shown the ability to make adjustments.

BEST POWER: 1B Chad Spanberger (6) turned on his power at the right time, first in the Southeastern Conference tournament (five homers), and then with 19 homers in the Rookie-level Pioneer League. He's got plenty of swing-and-miss to go with his plus power, as does OF Casey Golden (20).

FASTEST RUNNER: Vilade can turn in above-average to plus run times, closing in on 4.2 seconds to first base. He worked hard on it in his last high school year with a conditioning program to improve his running form. OF Joey Bartosic (19) also runs well and is George Washington's career stolen-bases leader with 84.

BEST DEFENSIVE PLAYER: The Rockies will let Vilade play his way off shortstop. He may slow down as he grows into his listed 6-foot-2, 194-pound frame, but he has the above-average arm to handle third base.

BEST ATHLETE: Vilade also checks in here in a college-heavy class; he's the only high school player the Rockies signed.

BEST FASTBALL: RHP Will Gaddis (3) has touched 95 but pitches in the low 90s with plus life and solid fastball command when he's going right. RHP Tommy Doyle (2.5), the club's second pick, has touched 96 and could go higher as he throws more fastballs in pro ball.

BEST SECONDARY PITCH: LHP Nick Kennedy (5), an eligible sophomore, has a good 90-94 mph fastball but a better slider with finish and low-80s power. He has a fresh arm, having thrown just 70 innings in two seasons at Texas and shifted into a

TOP DRAFT PICKS OF THE DECADE

Year	Player, Pos.	2017 Org
2008	Christian Friedrich, LHP	Padres
2009	Tyler Matzek, LHP	Did not play
2010	Kyle Parker, OF	Did not play
2011	Tyler Anderson, LHP	Rockies
2012	David Dahl, OF	Rockies
2013	Jon Gray, RHP	Rockies
2014	Kyle Freeland, LHP	Rockies
2015	Brendan Rodgers, SS	Rockies
2016	Riley Pint, RHP	Rockies
2017	Ryan Vilade, 3B (2nd round)	Rockies

starting role full-time after signing.

BEST PRO DEBUT: Golden and Spanberger did their jobs with Rookie-level Grand Junction, protecting Vilade in the lineup. Golden led the league with 20 homers while Spanberger tied for second with 19; Golden hit .288/.372/.654 while Spanberger batted .294/.368/.617.

MOST INTRIGUING BACKGROUND: RHP Moises Ceja (32) has an older brother, Nestor, who has reached Double-A as an umpire. Kennedy's father Dave is the head strength and conditioning coach for the Tampa Bay Buccaneers; he's also done that for powerhouse college programs at Nebraska, Ohio State, Pittsburgh and Texas A&M.

CLOSEST TO THE MAJORS: Gaddis' fastball command should help him move quickly; he walked just seven in 44.1 innings in his debut, though he was eminently hittable at Grand Junction.

BEST LATE-ROUND PICK: LHP Hunter Williams (11) had his moments at North Carolina, with a 2.43 ERA in 77.2 innings in two seasons before failing out of the program. He pitched in indy ball in 2017 prior to the draft and still has arm strength, striking out 30 in 27 innings for Grand Junction. Golden's power also gives him a chance.

—JOHN MANUEL

2016

RHP Riley Pint (1) has struggled with his control as a pro, but his stuff remains electric. 3B Colton Welker (4) had a breakout year, despite a second-half injury. SS Garrett Hampson (3) led the minors in runs.

GRADE: B

2015

SS Brendan Rodgers (1) has developed into one of the game's most promising prospects. RHP Peter Lambert (2) has succeeded in hitter friendly parks and 3B Tyler Nevin (1s) got back on track following injury.

GRADE: A

2014

LHP Kyle Freeland (1) took over a spot in Colorado's rotation and earned rookie of the year votes. RHP Ryan Castellani (2) and LHP Sam Howard (3) have become workhorse starters and are nearing the big leagues.

GRADE: B

1 BRENDAN RODGERS, SS/2B

Born: Aug. 6, 1996. **B-T:** R-R. **Ht.:** 6-0. **Wt.:** 185.
Drafted: HS—Lake Mary, Fla., 2015 (1st round).
Signed by: John Cedarburg.

BILL MITCHELL

The Rockies made Rodgers the No. 3 overall pick in the 2015 draft, behind fellow shortstops Dansby Swanson and Alex Bregman, and signed him to a franchise-record $5.5 million bonus. Rodgers worked with former big leaguers Dante Bichette and Tom Gordon during his high school days, and has proven at ease in the professional environment since signing. He played only 89 games in 2017 due to a hand injury and quad strain, but shined when he was on the field. He flirted with .400 at high Class A Lancaster during the first half of the year and made his way to Double-A Hartford at the minor league all-star break.

Rodgers' calling card is his smooth, controlled swing that bodes well for him to hit for average and power. He possesses the bat speed to handle any velocity and the balance and pitch recognition to barrel breaking balls. At times Rodgers becomes too pull-happy, but he has shown he has the strength to drive the ball the other way. Rodgers rarely walks, but knows how to work a count and doesn't miss the pitch he wants. Evaluators nearly universally regard him as a future plus hitter with enough power to impact a game. A natural shortstop, Rodgers has also seen time at second and third base with the Rockies' approach of having players work at multiple positions in the minors. Rodgers has the reliable hands, quick release and plus arm strength to play shortstop, but his fringy foot speed could be a deciding factor in an eventual move to second base. Rodgers makes up for his lack of natural range by positioning himself well and showing advanced instincts, enough that some evaluators give him a chance to stay at shortstop and possibly be an average defender there, although not all are convinced.

The idea of having a middle infielder with an impact bat is exciting, which is why Rodgers isn't likely to end up at third base. How Rodgers' body changes over time, particularly if he gets bigger and loses a step, will determine whether he stays at shortstop or makes the move to second base. Even if he does end up at second, he can be an impact player along the lines of Bobby Grich or Ryne Sandberg. The Rockies have brought Rodgers along slowly, but it is not out of the question for him to be in the big leagues at some point after the 2018 all-star break.

BA GRADE	SCOUTING GRADES
65 Risk: High	HIT: 60. POW: 55. SPD: 50. FLD: 55. ARM: 60.

Projected future grades on 20-80 scouting scale

TOP PROSPECTS OF THE DECADE

Year	Player, Pos.	2017 Org
2008	Franklin Morales, LHP	Mexican League
2009	Dexter Fowler, OF	Cardinals
2010	Tyler Matzek, LHP	Did not play
2011	Tyler Matzek, LHP	Did not play
2012	Drew Pomeranz, LHP	Red Sox
2013	Nolan Arenado, 3B	Rockies
2014	Jon Gray, RHP	Rockies
2015	David Dahl, OF	Rockies
2016	Jon Gray, RHP	Rockies
2017	Brendan Rodgers, SS	Rockies

BEST TOOLS

Best Hitter for Average	Brendan Rogers
Best Power Hitter	Ryan Vilade
Best Strike-Zone Discipline	Garrett Hampson
Fastest Baserunner	Wes Rogers
Best Athlete	Ryan McMahon
Best Fastball	Riley Pint
Best Curveball	Jesus Tinoco
Best Slider	Riley Pint
Best Changeup	Peter Lambert
Best Control	Peter Lambert
Best Defensive Catcher	Dom Nunez
Best Defensive Infielder	Garrett Hampson
Best Infield Arm	Brendan Rodgers
Best Defensive Outfielder	Yonathan Daza
Best Outfield Arm	Sam Hilliard

Year	Club (League)	Class	AVG	G	AB	R	H	2B	3B	HR	RBI	BB	SO	SB	CS	OBP	SLG
2015	Grand Junction (PIO)	R	.273	37	143	22	39	8	2	3	20	15	37	4	3	.340	.420
2016	Asheville (SAL)	LoA	.281	110	442	73	124	31	0	19	73	35	98	6	3	.342	.480
2017	Hartford (EL)	AA	.260	38	150	20	39	5	0	6	17	8	36	0	2	.323	.413
	Lancaster (CAL)	HiA	.383	51	222	44	85	21	3	12	46	6	35	2	1	.403	.667
Minor League Totals			.300	236	957	159	287	65	5	40	156	64	206	12	9	.352	.504

2 RYAN McMAHON, 1B/2B

Born: Dec. 14, 1994. **B-T:** L-R. **Ht.:** 6-2. **Wt.:** 185. **Drafted:** HS—Santa Ana, Calif., 2013 (2nd round). **Signed by:** Jon Lukens.

A third baseman in high school, McMahon added first base to his resume in 2016 and began playing second base in 2017. After a down year offensively in 2016 he rebounded in 2017, batting a combined .355 between Double-A and Triple-A. He made his major league debut on Aug. 12.

McMahon possesses soft hands and a strong arm, but his reaction time was a concern at third base. He handled the move to first base well and, while physically large for second base, impressed the Rockies with how he adapted to the position, although opposing scouts are less convinced. Offensively, McMahon has a consistent, short stroke and uses the whole field. He sits fastball and takes advantage of mistakes, with the strength to produce above-average power in Coors Field. Strikeouts were an issue in the past, but McMahon significantly improved his approach and plate discipline and struck out just 97 times in 2017, compared to an average of 153 strikeouts his first three seasons.

> **BA GRADE**
> **50** Risk: Medium
> **HIT:** 60. **POW:** 55.
> **SPD:** 45. **FLD:** 50.
> **ARM:** 55.

McMahon's positional versatility gives the Rockies options. Wherever he plays, the Rockies envision his bat making a significant everyday contribution.

Year	Club (League)	Class	AVG	G	AB	R	H	2B	3B	HR	RBI	BB	SO	SB	CS	OBP	SLG
2015	Modesto (CAL)	HiA	.300	132	496	85	149	43	6	18	75	49	153	6	13	.372	.520
2016	Hartford (EL)	AA	.242	133	466	49	113	27	5	12	75	55	161	11	6	.325	.399
2017	Hartford (EL)	AA	.326	49	181	28	59	16	2	6	32	20	39	7	0	.390	.536
	Albuquerque (PCL)	AAA	.374	70	289	46	108	23	2	14	56	21	53	4	3	.411	.612
	Colorado (NL)	MAJ	.158	17	19	2	3	1	0	0	1	5	5	0	0	.333	.211
Major League Totals			.158	17	19	2	3	1	0	0	1	5	5	0	0	.333	.211
Minor League Totals			.298	569	2132	343	635	173	21	79	392	227	608	40	33	.368	.510

3 RILEY PINT, RHP

Born: Nov. 6, 1997. **B-T:** R-R. **Ht.:** 6-4. **Wt.:** 195. **Drafted:** HS—Overland Park, Kan., 2016 (1st round). **Signed by:** Bret Baldwin.

Pint touched 100 mph in high school and the Rockies drafted him with the fourth overall pick in 2016, signing him for $4.8 million. His big velocity has not translated to professional success, however. After a poor 2017 at low Class A Asheville, Pint is 3-16, 5.40 with 82 walks, 14 hit batters and 34 wild pitches in 130 professional innings, to go along with 115 strikeouts.

Pint simply overpowered high school hitters, which covered up mechanical shortcomings that have hampered him in pro ball. His fastball ranges anywhere from 93-98 mph and touches 102 but plays down due to poor command and control—the result of a delivery he doesn't repeat even though it is clean. He pulls off of pitches and misses the zone, and isn't much better with his secondaries. His slider flashes above-average and his curveball and changeup flash average potential,

> **BA GRADE**
> **60** Risk: Extreme
> **FB:** 70. **CB:** 60.
> **SL:** 50. **CHG:** 60.
> **CTL:** 45.

but he doesn't have consistent control of any of them. The Rockies have taken a cautious approach with Pint, limiting his innings and adjusting his mechanics slowly.

Scouts remain bullish on Pint because of his premium stuff and clean delivery, but his lack of strike-throwing ability is alarming. High Class A Lancaster is likely next in 2018.

Year	Club (League)	Class	W	L	ERA	G	GS	CG	SV	IP	H	HR	BB	SO	K/9	WHIP	AVG
2016	Grand Junction (PIO)	R	1	5	5.35	11	11	0	0	37	43	2	23	36	8.8	1.78	.307
2017	Asheville (SAL)	LoA	2	11	5.42	22	22	0	0	93	96	3	59	79	7.6	1.67	.264
Minor League Totals			3	16	5.40	33	33	0	0	130	139	5	82	115	8.0	1.70	.276

4 COLTON WELKER, 3B

TONY FARLOW

Born: Oct. 9, 1997. **B-T:** R-R. **Ht.:** 6-2. **Wt.:** 195. **Drafted:** HS—Parkland, Fla., 2016 (4th round). **Signed by:** Rafael Reyes.

Welker led Douglas High in Parkland, Fla., to its first state championship in 2016 and a No. 1 ranking in BA's final national high school poll. The Rockies drafted him in the fourth round and signed him for $855,000. Welker impressed immediately and was en route to the South Atlantic League batting title in his first full season, but an abdominal strain shelved him for two months and cost him the necessary at-bats.

Welker's bat is his best asset. He has impressive knowledge of the strike zone, particularly for a young power hitter, and makes full use of the entire field. His swing has some length to it and a bit of a hitch, but he makes up for it with advanced feel to hit, above-average power potential and limited swing-and-miss. A high school shortstop, Welker moved to third base as a pro and has shown above-average potential there. He has a good first step, is quick on his feet and possesses a plus, accurate arm, although his below-average speed and fringy athleticism cuts into his range.

Nolan Arenado is a free agent after 2019, and Welker is in line to be Arenado's eventual replacement if the Rockies are unable to resign him. For now, Welker will head to high Class A Lancaster.

	BA GRADE
50	Risk: High

HIT: 55. POW: 55.
SPD: 50. FLD: 50.
ARM: 55.

Year	Club (League)	Class	AVG	G	AB	R	H	2B	3B	HR	RBI	BB	SO	SB	CS	OBP	SLG
2016	Grand Junction (PIO)	R	.329	51	210	38	69	15	2	5	36	13	28	6	4	.366	.490
2017	Asheville (SAL)	LoA	.350	67	254	32	89	18	1	6	33	18	42	5	7	.401	.500
Minor League Totals			.341	118	464	70	158	33	3	11	69	31	70	11	11	.385	.496

5 PETER LAMBERT, RHP

Born: May 28, 1997. **B-T:** R-R. **Ht.:** 6-2. **Wt.:** 185. **Drafted:** HS—San Dimas, Calif., 2015 (2nd round). **Signed by:** Jon Lukens.

The Rockies took advantage of four early picks in the 2015 draft and landed Lambert at No. 44 overall. Lambert didn't overpower and there were questions about his thin frame, but the Rockies saw a highly successful teen with a live arm, room to fill out and a desirable competitive streak.

Lambert's poise and fearless mentality have helped him conquer three of the most hitter-friendly environments in baseball in Rookie-level Grand Junction, low Class A Asheville and class High A Lancaster during his first three seasons. The expected physical gains have come too. Lambert now sits 91-93 mph and touches 95 with his fastball, dialing it up and down as necessary. The pitch plays up even further because of excellent control and sink, as well. Both his biting 78-82 mph curveball and mid-80s changeup consistently project above-average-to-plus, with the best of his swing-and-miss curveballs drawing plus-plus grades. Lambert throws everything for strikes and keeps the ball down, a critical factor in his success pitching in environments similar to Coors Field.

Lambert has all the components of a quality mid- to back-of-the-rotation starter, and could be more if he continues to add fastball velocity.

	BA GRADE
50	Risk: High

FB: 55. CB: 55.
CHG: 60.
CTL: 55.

Year	Club (League)	Class	W	L	ERA	G	GS	CG	SV	IP	H	HR	BB	SO	K/9	WHIP	AVG
2015	Grand Junction (PIO)	R	0	4	3.45	8	8	0	0	31	29	3	11	26	7.5	1.28	.227
2016	Asheville (SAL)	LoA	5	8	3.93	26	26	0	0	126	125	7	33	108	7.7	1.25	.264
2017	Lancaster (CAL)	HiA	9	8	4.17	26	26	0	0	142	147	18	30	131	8.3	1.24	.267
Minor League Totals			14	20	3.99	60	60	0	0	300	301	28	74	265	8.0	1.25	.262

6 RYAN CASTELLANI, RHP

Born: April 1, 1996. **B-T:** R-R. **Ht.:** 6-3. **Wt.:** 190. **Drafted:** HS—Phoenix, 2014 (2nd round). **Signed by:** Chris Forbes.

The Rockies signed Castellani for $1.1 million out of high school in 2014 and were protective of him early, limiting him to 150 innings in his first two seasons combined. They then bulked him up and turned him loose, and he's been exceptionally durable since. Castellani led the high Class A California League in innings pitched in 2016, and did the same in the Double-A Eastern League in 2017.

Castellani works with a three-pitch mix with sinking action. His fastball holds serve at a steady 93 mph, and he has shown the ability to touch 97. His best secondary is a hard slider, and he also mixes in a usable changeup. All three pitches have flashed above-average at one point or another, but he runs into trouble when he isn't keeping the ball down. When right, Castellani commands both sides of the plate in the bottom half of the zone, and his strong lower half allows him to hold his stuff late in games. He is cerebral with a feel for the game that helps his stuff play up.

Castellani projects as a potential workhorse in the middle-to-back of a rotation as long as he keeps the ball down. His ability to do that will be tested at Triple-A Albuquerque to open the 2018 season.

BA GRADE
50 Risk: High
FB: 60. SL: 55.
CHG: 55.
CTL: 50.

Year	Club (League)	Class	W	L	ERA	G	GS	CG	SV	IP	H	HR	BB	SO	K/9	WHIP	AVG
2015	Asheville (SAL)	LoA	2	7	4.45	27	27	0	0	113	134	5	29	94	7.5	1.44	.291
2016	Modesto (CAL)	HiA	7	8	3.81	26	26	1	0	168	156	8	50	142	7.6	1.23	.248
2017	Hartford (EL)	AA	9	12	4.81	27	27	1	0	157	163	16	47	132	7.6	1.33	.264
Minor League Totals			19	29	4.28	90	90	2	0	475	488	31	135	393	7.4	1.31	.264

7 YENCY ALMONTE, RHP

Born: June 4, 1994. **B-T:** B-R. **Ht.:** 6-3. **Wt.:** 205. **Drafted:** HS—Miami, 2012 (17th round). **Signed by:** Ralph Reyes (Angels).

Traded from the Angels to the White Sox and then to the Rockies as a prospect, the hard-throwing Almonte has blossomed in Colorado's system. He posted a 2.00 ERA at Double-A and rose to Triple-A in 2017 despite separate disabled list stints for arm fatigue and knee soreness.

Almonte gained 25 pounds since turning pro, which has led to a fastball that topped out at 92 mph in high school now sitting 93-96 mph and touching 98 with hard sink as a starter. Almonte also has a two-seamer he likes to use to further induce ground balls, and his main secondary is an 86-88 mph slider that is consistently above-average and flashes plus. He flashes a usable changeup but it is not consistent, although he still kept lefthanded hitters in check with a .217/.319/.310 slash line in 2017. Almonte's control is lacking at times, the result of an arm action evaluators fear may hamper his ability to throw consistent strikes.

Almonte's lack of a changeup and inconsistent control lessen his chance to start, but it's not out of the question. As a fallback, his hard sinker-slider combination would play extremely well in late relief. He will begin 2018 back at Triple-A.

BA GRADE
45 Risk: Medium
FB: 60. SL: 55.
CHG: 55.
CTL: 50.

Year	Club (League)	Class	W	L	ERA	G	GS	CG	SV	IP	H	HR	BB	SO	K/9	WHIP	AVG
2015	Kannapolis (SAL)	LoA	8	4	3.88	17	16	0	0	93	92	8	26	71	6.9	1.27	.256
	Winston-Salem (CAR)	HiA	3	3	2.42	7	6	0	0	45	28	1	12	39	7.9	0.90	.179
2016	Modesto (CAL)	HiA	8	9	3.71	22	22	1	0	138	124	14	39	134	8.7	1.18	.237
	Hartford (EL)	AA	3	1	3.00	5	5	1	0	30	22	4	16	22	6.6	1.27	.204
2017	Hartford (EL)	AA	5	3	2.00	14	14	0	0	76	58	4	31	71	8.4	1.17	.213
	Albuquerque (PCL)	AAA	3	1	4.89	8	7	0	0	35	41	7	21	22	5.7	1.77	.315
Minor League Totals			35	30	3.95	100	92	2	0	519	483	48	182	431	7.5	1.28	.247

8 GARRETT HAMPSON, 2B/SS

Born: Oct. 10, 1994. **B-T:** R-R. **Ht.:** 5-11. **Wt.:** 185. **Drafted:** Long Beach State, 2016 (3rd round). **Signed by:** Matt Hattabaugh.

Hampson is next in a long line of Long Beach State shortstops in the big leagues, headed by Bobby Crosby, Troy Tulowitzki, Danny Espinosa and Matt Duffy. Drafted in the third round and signed for $750,000 in 2016, Hampson led the minors with 113 runs and finished fourth with 51 steals in his first full season at high Class A Lancaster.

A top-of-the-lineup catalyst, Hampson is an undersized plus-plus runer who plays at full speed all the time. He keeps the ball on the ground or strokes it on a line to let his speed play, and he shows hints of power, although that will never be his game. His plate discipline is improving, allowing him to project as an above-average hitter with a lot of steals. Hampson gets too big in his swing sometimes, but generally self-corrects. Drafted as a shortstop, Hampson's arm is a bit short for the position, but his exemplary hands, quick-first step and top-notch reaction times fit at second base, where he shows flashes of being a plus defender. He also got some exposure to center field last year.

Most evaluators see Hampson as a future super utility player, but a few see enough for him to start at second base. Double-A Hartford is next in 2018.

BA GRADE
45 Risk: Medium
HIT: 55. POW: 40.
SPD: 60. FLD: 55.
ARM: 50.

Year	Club (League)	Class	AVG	G	AB	R	H	2B	3B	HR	RBI	BB	SO	SB	CS	OBP	SLG
2016	Boise (NWL)	SS	.301	68	256	43	77	14	8	2	44	48	56	36	4	.404	.441
2017	Lancaster (CAL)	HiA	.326	127	533	113	174	24	12	8	70	56	77	50	14	.387	.462
Minor League Totals			.318	195	789	156	251	38	20	10	114	104	133	86	18	.393	.455

9 RYAN VILADE, SS

Born: Feb. 18, 1999. **B-T:** R-R. **Ht.:** 6-2. **Wt.:** 194. **Drafted:** HS—Stillwater, Okla., 2017 (2nd round). **Signed by:** Jesse Retzlaf.

Vilade's father, James, is an assistant coach at Oklahoma State and was a longtime minor league coach. After growing up around the game, Vilade starred on the USA 15U and 18U national teams and won the home run derby at the Under Armor All-America Game at Wrigley Field. He was named the Oklahoma state player of the year as a senior and signed with the Rockies for $1,425,400 after they selected him with the 48th overall pick in the 2017 draft.

Vilade's offensive profile is what drives him. He has a strong frame and a quick bat that produces plus raw power, and he already has a knack for driving the ball in games. He makes adjustments quickly for his age and shows advanced instincts in the box. He recognizes and tracks pitches well and draws plenty of walks. Vilade is an average runner and there is some question whether he has the quick-twitch athleticism for shortstop defensively, but believers point to his above-average arm, soft hands and advanced instincts.

Vilade will play shortstop for now, but will also see time at third base and first base. It will be his bat that carries him regardless of position. Vilade is set to open his first full season at low Class A Asheville.

TODD BENNETT/GJ ROCKIES

BA GRADE
55 Risk: Extreme
HIT: 50. POW: 55.
SPD: 45. FLD: 50.
ARM: 60.

Year	Club (League)	Class	AVG	G	AB	R	H	2B	3B	HR	RBI	BB	SO	SB	CS	OBP	SLG
2017	Grand Junction (PIO)	R	.308	33	117	23	36	3	2	5	21	27	31	5	5	.438	.496
Minor League Totals			.308	33	117	23	36	3	2	5	21	27	31	5	5	.438	.496

10 TYLER NEVIN, 3B

Born: May 29, 1997. **B-T:** R-R. **Ht.:** 6-4. **Wt.:** 200. **Drafted:** HS—Poway, Calif., 2015 (1st round supplemental). **Signed by:** Jon Lukens.

Nevin grew up in a baseball environment as the son of 1992 No. 1 overall pick Phil Nevin. A severe hamstring injury limited Tyler to one game in 2016 and a right wrist/hand injury limited him the first half of 2017. He hit .336/.381/.523 for low Class A Asheville upon his return in the second half, showing the promise that made him a touted prep.

Two inches taller than his all-star father, Nevin's ticket will be his bat. He has bat speed, works counts and projects to hit for power as his body fills out and gets stronger. He shows all-fields power and drives the ball into the right-center gap frequently, just as his father loved to. Nevin grew up a third baseman but has increasingly seen time at first base, where he projects best. Scouts don't see the feet, agility or athleticism necessary for Nevin to handle third base on an everyday basis, and the Tommy John surgery he had as a junior in high school sapped some of his arm strength.

Evaluators generally see Nevin as a platoon corner power bat, but he has a chance to put up big offensive numbers at high Class A Lancaster in 2018 and prove he could be a potential everyday regular at the big league level sometime in the future. His health will bear watching as he tries to complete a full season for the first time, having never played more than 82 games in a professional season.

BA GRADE
50 Risk: High
HIT: 55. POW: 50.
SPD: 40. FLD: 50.
ARM: 50.

TONY FARLOW

Year	Club (League)	Class	AVG	G	AB	R	H	2B	3B	HR	RBI	BB	SO	SB	CS	OBP	SLG
2015	Grand Junction (PIO)	R	.265	53	189	29	50	15	1	2	18	29	42	3	7	.368	.386
2016	Boise (NWL)	SS	1.000	1	1	1	1	1	0	0	0	0	0	0	0	1.000	2.000
2017	Boise (NWL)	SS	.233	6	30	4	7	3	0	1	5	0	9	0	1	.233	.433
	Asheville (SAL)	LoA	.305	76	298	45	91	18	3	7	47	27	56	10	5	.364	.456
Minor League Totals			.288	136	518	79	149	37	4	10	70	56	107	13	13	.360	.432

11 SAM HOWARD, LHP

BA GRADE
45 Risk: Medium

Born: March 5, 1993. **B-T:** R-L. **Ht.:** 6-3. **Wt.:** 170. **Drafted:** Georgia Southern, 2014 (3rd round). **Signed by:** Alan Matthews.

Howard is an acquired taste. He isn't one of those guys who steps on the mound and overpowers. He is a pitcher, and he has proven since his high school days he can adjust over the course of a season. Howard doesn't back down from a challenge, which was evident his junior year in college when, after early season struggles, he moved into the No. 3 starter role and performed well enough to be the 82nd player selected in the 2014 draft out of Georgia Southern.

The Rockies worked to balance Howard's delivery after signing him and it has improved his command. It also was a factor in his fastball velocity jumping from the upper 80s to its present 91-94 mph with sink. Howard compliments his fastball with a back foot slider that has a promising late, hard break, and a usable changeup with fade. His ability to pitch inside to righthanded batters and also change speeds has allowed him to actually be more effective against righties than lefties, which is a tick in his favor for remaining a starter.

Having split the 2017 season between Double-A and Triple-A, the expectation is Howard will be ready to step in at the big league level sometime in 2018.

Year	Club (League)	Class	W	L	ERA	G	GS	CG	SV	IP	H	HR	BB	SO	K/9	WHIP	AVG
2015	Asheville (SAL)	LoA	11	9	3.43	25	25	1	0	134	131	8	32	122	8.2	1.22	.252
2016	Modesto (CAL)	HiA	4	3	2.47	11	11	0	0	66	43	3	24	73	10.0	1.02	.184
	Hartford (EL)	AA	5	6	3.99	16	16	0	0	90	113	11	28	67	6.7	1.56	.303
2017	Hartford (EL)	AA	1	4	2.33	9	9	1	0	46	31	5	10	40	7.8	0.88	.185
	Albuquerque (PCL)	AAA	4	4	3.89	15	14	0	0	81	82	6	33	64	7.1	1.42	.264
Minor League Totals			26	29	3.59	90	88	2	0	471	473	39	137	408	7.8	1.30	.259

12 TOM MURPHY, C

BA GRADE
45 Risk: Medium

Born: April 3, 1991. **B-T:** R-R. **Ht.:** 6-1. **Wt.:** 203. **Drafted:** Buffalo, 2012 (3rd round). **Signed by:** Ed Santa.

Murphy was in line to be the Rockies' starting catcher on Opening Day 2017, but on a throw to second base during a spring training game he hit the bat of Cubs' Anthony Rizzo and fractured his right forearm. He did not make his season debut with the Rockies until June 15, was sent down for more playing time at Triple-A two weeks later, and made only four appearances when he was called up in September with the Rockies riding Jonathan Lucroy down the stretch in their playoff run.

The only player ever drafted out of the University at Buffalo, Murphy remains the Rockies' top catching prospect. He had worked to soften his hands in receiving and made strides with his agility despite a muscular frame that has slowed him down at times. He has above-average arm strength and is continually working to improve. Murphy is mostly a threat at the plate, with above-average power with solid rhythm and timing in his swing that allows him to tap into his power.

With Lucroy leaving as a free agent, Murphy has a chance to claim the Rockies' starting catching job in 2018, just as he was expected to before he got hurt in 2017.

Year	Club (League)	Class	AVG	G	AB	R	H	2B	3B	HR	RBI	BB	SO	SB	CS	OBP	SLG
2015	New Britain (EL)	AA	.249	72	265	36	66	17	1	13	44	23	80	5	2	.320	.468
	Albuquerque (PCL)	AAA	.271	33	129	19	35	9	2	7	19	5	43	0	1	.301	.535
	Colorado (NL)	MAJ	.257	11	35	5	9	1	0	3	9	4	10	0	0	.333	.543
2016	Albuquerque (PCL)	AAA	.327	80	303	53	99	26	7	19	59	16	78	1	1	.361	.647
	Colorado (NL)	MAJ	.273	21	44	8	12	2	0	5	13	4	19	1	0	.347	.659
2017	Albuquerque (PCL)	AAA	.255	38	141	22	36	10	1	4	19	9	56	0	0	.312	.426
	Colorado (NL)	MAJ	.042	12	24	1	1	1	0	0	1	2	9	0	0	.115	.083
Major League Totals			.214	44	103	14	22	4	0	8	23	10	38	1	0	.289	.485
Minor League Totals			.280	405	1501	236	420	110	16	76	277	122	439	11	10	.344	.526

13 BRIAN MUNDELL, 1B

BA GRADE 50 Risk: High

Born: Feb. 28, 1994. **B-T:** R-R. **Ht.:** 6-3. **Wt.:** 230. **Drafted:** Cal Poly, 2015 (7th round). **Signed by:** Matt Hattabaugh.

Mundell moved around a bit in college—primarily used as a DH, but also catching a bit and playing some first base. Most of all, he hit. His bat caught the attention of the Rockies, and they made him the first college position player they drafted in 2015. They got more than they bargained for.

Mundell set a modern-day minor-league record with 59 doubles at low Class Asheville in 2016, and followed it up by hitting a combined .300 with 15 homers, 78 RBIs and an .857 OPS between at High-A Lancaster and Double-A Hartford in 2017. Mundell has power potential to go with what is a very disciplined approach, making hard contact and driving the ball the opposite way. Once he makes adjustments and starts to turn on pitches, more home runs figure to come. He has settled in at first base with soft hands and instincts, even though he had only limited time at the position before pro ball. Further, Mundell has provided a very strong clubhouse influence as a true leader.

Mundell will have to continue to hit as a first base-only prospect, but that's never been a problem. He has a chance to post huge numbers at Triple-A Albuquerque in 2017.

Year	Club (League)	Class	AVG	G	AB	R	H	2B	3B	HR	RBI	BB	SO	SB	CS	OBP	SLG
2015	Boise (NWL)	SS	.275	69	244	35	67	19	1	4	36	32	45	7	1	.355	.410
2016	Asheville (SAL)	LoA	.313	136	537	94	168	59	1	14	83	56	83	7	8	.383	.505
2017	Lancaster (CAL)	HiA	.295	67	264	44	78	16	1	12	59	35	44	0	1	.375	.500
	Hartford (EL)	AA	.302	52	172	30	52	12	0	3	19	25	26	1	1	.394	.424
Minor League Totals			.300	324	1217	203	365	106	3	33	197	148	198	15	11	.377	.473

14 SAM HILLIARD, OF

BA GRADE 50 Risk: High

Born: Feb. 21, 1994. **B-T:** L-L. **Ht.:** 6-5. **Wt.:** 225. **Drafted:** Wichita State, 2015 (15th round). **Signed by:** Brett Baldwin.

Hilliard has established himself as one of the top performers in the Rockies system since the day they drafted him. The physical 6-foot-5, 225-pound lefthanded hitter led the South Atlantic League in RBIs in 2016 and at high Class A Lancaster in 2017 he ranked among the top 10 in the California League in home runs (21), batting average (.300), RBIs (92) and stolen bases (37).

Hilliard shows flashes of all five tools but is still in search of consistency. He has the size, natural raw power, above-average speed and plus arm strength that scouts embrace. He squares up anything out over the plate and pulls the ball in the air with authority, with most of his home runs lined shots that carry over the right-field fence. However, his swing gets long at times and has resulted in a nearly 30 percent career strikeout rate. He struggles against lefties in particular and isn't especially adept at using the whole field. Hilliard is an efficient basestealer with his speed and plays an above-average right field, and can handle center field in a pinch.

Hilliard's tools and performance have scouts intrigued, but he'll have to make offensive adjustments to reach his everyday ceiling.

Year	Club (League)	Class	AVG	G	AB	R	H	2B	3B	HR	RBI	BB	SO	SB	CS	OBP	SLG
2015	Grand Junction (PIO)	R	.306	60	222	45	68	13	8	7	42	36	55	12	4	.397	.532
2016	Asheville (SAL)	LoA	.267	127	461	71	123	23	5	17	83	56	150	30	12	.348	.449
2017	Lancaster (CAL)	HiA	.300	133	536	95	161	23	7	21	92	50	154	37	17	.360	.487
Minor League Totals			.289	320	1219	211	352	59	20	45	217	142	359	79	33	.362	.481

15 JORDAN PATTERSON, OF/1B

BA GRADE
40 Risk: Low

Born: Feb. 12, 1992. **B-T:** L-L. **Ht.:** 6-4. **Wt.:** 215. **Drafted:** South Alabama, 2013 (4th round). **Signed by:** Alan Matthews.

After making his major league debut in 2016, Patterson was sent back to Triple-A in 2017 and struggled early. He hit .219 the first two months of the season but ultimately finished with a flourish, hitting .317 the final three months and posting career highs with 26 home runs and 92 RBIs.

A two-way player at South Alabama, Patterson had a big leg kick at the plate when he signed, but Rockies instructor Marv Foley worked with him to shorten up the stride, allowing him to stay on the ball longer and keep his head down. A middle of the field hitter, Patterson is still adjusting in order to pull the ball and improve his home run totals, but shows flashes of average to above power. Patterson originally played the corner outfield positions in pro ball and has plenty of arm for right field. However, he began working at first base the last two seasons at Albuquerque and adapted well.

Patterson didn't receive a September callup in 2017, because the Rockies were stocked at first base and outfield, but with a host of veterans departing, he has a chance to claim a role in 2018.

Year	Club (League)	Class	AVG	G	AB	R	H	2B	3B	HR	RBI	BB	SO	SB	CS	OBP	SLG
2015	Modesto (CAL)	HiA	.304	77	303	62	92	26	12	10	43	19	88	9	6	.378	.568
	New Britain (EL)	AA	.286	48	185	26	53	19	0	7	32	11	42	9	4	.342	.503
2016	Albuquerque (PCL)	AAA	.293	119	427	75	125	24	7	14	61	47	118	10	0	.376	.480
	Colorado (NL)	MAJ	.444	10	18	1	8	1	0	0	2	1	1	0	1	.474	.500
2017	Albuquerque (PCL)	AAA	.283	131	484	78	137	32	7	26	92	36	128	3	5	.348	.539
Major League Totals			.444	10	18	1	8	1	0	0	2	1	1	0	1	.474	.500
Minor League Totals			.288	560	2058	354	593	140	26	81	331	178	531	66	29	.364	.500

16 BREILING EUSEBIO, LHP

BA GRADE
50 Risk: V. High

Born: Nov. 21, 1996. **B-T:** L-L. **Ht.:** 6-1. **Wt.:** 175. **Signed:** Dominican Republic, 2013. **Signed by:** Rolando Fernandez/Martin Cabrera/Frank Roa.

Eusebio has come along slowly after signing out of the Dominican Republic for $100,000 in 2013. He needed two years in the Dominican Summer League and began 2017 in the short-season Northwest League for the second straight year. He delivered three dominant starts and was promoted to low Class A Asheville, where he made eight starts before going down with an oblique strain that ended his season in early August.

Eusebio packs premium stuff from the left side but is still searching for consistency. His lively fastball sits at 93-94 mph and touches 96, and he compliments it with a hard 78-80 mph curveball and a low-80s changeup he sells with the same arm action as his fastball. Both of his offspeed offerings flash plus. He has an easily repeatable, compact delivery that helps him maintain his command. Eusebio's fastball is so lively in all directions that he doesn't know where it's going, which gets him into trouble. His curveball also is wildly inconsistent and often ends up in the dirt. He made strides during a 24-inning stretch at Asheville where he allowed only five earned runs.

Eusebio has rotation upside but requires a lot fine-tuning. He may see high Class A Lancaster in 2018.

Year	Club (League)	Class	W	L	ERA	G	GS	CG	SV	IP	H	HR	BB	SO	K/9	WHIP	AVG
2014	Rockies (DSL)	R	1	2	3.72	11	5	0	0	29	29	2	11	33	10.2	1.38	.261
2015	Rockies (DSL)	R	4	4	1.88	14	14	0	0	72	59	1	16	76	9.5	1.04	.215
2016	Boise (NWL)	SS	2	5	5.26	13	13	0	0	63	78	6	30	42	6.0	1.71	.305
2017	Boise (NWL)	SS	3	0	1.59	3	3	0	0	17	10	0	4	22	11.6	0.82	.175
	Asheville (SAL)	LoA	3	3	4.46	8	8	0	0	40	44	3	16	31	6.9	1.49	.280
Minor League Totals			13	14	3.53	49	43	0	0	222	220	12	77	204	8.3	1.34	.257

17 JESUS TINOCO, RHP

BA GRADE
50 Risk: V. High

Born: April 30, 1995. **B-T:** R-R. **Ht.:** 6-4. **Wt.:** 190. **Signed:** Venezuela, 2011. **Signed by:** Marco Paddy/Rafael Moncada (Blue Jays).

Acquired along with fellow righthanders Jeff Hoffman and Miguel Castro from the Blue Jays as part of the package for Troy Tulowitzki at the 2015 trade deadline, Tinoco was considered the extra body in the deal. He always had a live arm, but the results weren't there. It all started to come together in 2017, when Tinoco at high Class A Lancaster went 11-4, 4.67 in one of the most hitter-friendly parks in the minors.

The Rockies reworked Tinoco's delivery and the confidence he had been lacking seemed to be adjusted, too. Tinoco features a live fastball that ranges from 93-96 mph and is complimented by a curveball and slider that both flash plus but lack consistency. His changeup further flashes above-average but is the least developed pitch in his arsenal. Tinoco's stuff is promising but he is still learning to how sequence it all in order to miss bats. He does generally throw strikes and keep the ball on the ground.

Tinoco will remain a starter for now, though some like the idea of him coming out of the bullpen in late innings with a fastball that could go up a few ticks. He should see time at Double-A Hartford in 2018.

Year	Club (League)	Class	W	L	ERA	G	GS	CG	SV	IP	H	HR	BB	SO	K/9	WHIP	AVG
2015	Lansing (MWL)	LoA	2	6	3.54	15	15	0	0	81	88	1	22	68	7.5	1.35	.271
	Asheville (SAL)	LoA	5	0	1.80	7	7	0	0	40	36	2	8	37	8.3	1.10	.243
2016	Modesto (CAL)	HiA	0	3	14.85	4	4	0	0	13	37	3	3	8	5.4	3.00	.536
	Asheville (SAL)	LoA	3	8	5.63	16	16	0	0	86	118	10	25	53	5.5	1.66	.324
2017	Lancaster (CAL)	HiA	11	4	4.67	24	24	0	0	141	157	19	50	107	6.8	1.47	.285
Minor League Totals			23	40	4.74	105	94	0	2	507	591	39	162	399	7.1	1.49	.291

18 FORREST WALL, 2B/OF

BA GRADE 45 Risk: High

Born: Nov. 20, 1995. **B-T:** L-R. **Ht.:** 6-0. **Wt.:** 176. **Drafted:** HS—Maitland, Fla., 2014 (1st round supplemental). **Signed by:** John Cedarburg.

The Rockies drafted Wall 35th overall in 2014, making him the highest drafted prep second baseman since the draft was consolidated into one phase in 1987. Wall's play at second base proved inadequate, however, and he began a transition to center field at high Class A Lancaster in 2017. The effort was cut short when he separated his left shoulder diving for a ball in May and missed the rest of the season.

Wall has struggled to live up to his draft pedigree as a gifted hitter. He has a solid feel for contact but little power and does not drive the ball. He has plus speed to make it work as a singles hitter with a lot of stolen bases, although the Rockies are optimistic he can grow into extra-base power as he gets stronger. Defensively, Wall was nearly unplayable at second base and labrum surgery on his right shoulder in high school sapped his arm strength.

Wall has hope to make it as a contact and speed-type, but now has major surgery on both shoulders to deal with and needs to find a defensive home. He is expected to be healthy for the start of 2018.

Year	Club (League)	Class	AVG	G	AB	R	H	2B	3B	HR	RBI	BB	SO	SB	CS	OBP	SLG
2015	Boise (NWL)	SS	.500	4	10	4	5	0	0	0	1	6	2	2	2	.647	.500
	Asheville (SAL)	LoA	.280	99	361	57	101	16	10	7	46	41	72	23	9	.355	.438
2016	Modesto (CAL)	HiA	.264	120	459	57	121	16	4	6	56	41	97	22	11	.329	.355
2017	Lancaster (CAL)	HiA	.299	22	87	17	26	4	1	3	16	9	16	5	3	.361	.471
Minor League Totals			.282	286	1074	183	303	42	21	19	143	124	219	70	30	.358	.413

19 WILL GADDIS, RHP

BA GRADE 50 Risk: Extreme

Born: March 12, 1996. **B-T:** R-R. **Ht.:** 6-1. **Wt.:** 185. **Drafted:** Furman, 2017 (3rd round). **Signed by:** Jordan Czarniecki.

Rockies scouting director Bill Schmidt saw Gaddis dominate in the Cape Cod League the summer between his sophomore and junior seasons at Furman, and had him among the players in consideration for one of the Rockies' two draft picks in the second round. Gaddis led the Southern Conference with nine wins and a 1.89 ERA in 2017, but his stuff was down a tick, sitting 88-92 mph, and he slipped to the third round, where the Rockies took him and signed him for $600,000.

Gaddis is a pitchability righthander who relies on his command. His fastball has just average velocity but plays up some with plus life when he gets on top of it and pitches downhill. Gaddis mixes in a curveball, changeup and cutter, all of which are usable but none draw rave reviews. His lack of plus stuff got him crushed in his pro debut, with 66 hits allowed in 44.1 innings at Rookie-level Grand Junction, but fatigue was a factor.

Gaddis is confident on the mound. His repeatable delivery, solid command, pitch mix and track record give him a chance to rise as a back-end starter if his stuff ticks back up.

Year	Club (League)	Class	W	L	ERA	G	GS	CG	SV	IP	H	HR	BB	SO	K/9	WHIP	AVG
2017	Grand Junction (PIO)	R	3	1	5.68	11	9	0	0	44	66	6	7	26	5.3	1.65	.353
Minor League Totals			3	1	5.68	11	9	0	0	44	66	6	7	26	5.3	1.65	.353

20 BEN BOWDEN, LHP

BA GRADE

45 Risk: High

Born: Oct. 21, 1994. **B-T:** L-L. **Ht.:** 6-4. **Wt.:** 235. **Drafted:** Vanderbilt, 2016 (2nd round). **Signed by:** Scott Corman.

Bowden missed the entire 2017 season with a pair of injuries, one traditional and one unusual. First, he suffered a severe hamstring strain in spring training that shelved him early on. Later, while helping an elderly lady put her bag into an overhead bin on airplane, he suffered a bulging disc in his back.

Bowden, who signed for $1.6 million as the 45th overall pick in 2016, was the closer for Vanderbilt's College World Series championship team in 2014. During his lone pro stint after signing in 2016, he showed that same closer's mentality, aggressively going after hitters with power stuff from the left side. Bowden's stands an imposing 6-foot-4, 235 pounds and features a power fastball that sits 93-95 mph with late life and downward plane. It can top out at 97. He shows promise with a changeup that has tumbling action as his main secondary. He also throws a slurvy breaking ball that varies between a curveball and slider, and that will be a focal point of his development moving forward.

Bowden has the stuff and pedigree to move quickly as a bullpen arm but has to show he's healthy.

Year	Club (League)	Class	W	L	ERA	G	GS	CG	SV	IP	H	HR	BB	SO	K/9	WHIP	AVG
2016	Asheville (SAL)	LoA	0	1	3.04	26	0	0	0	24	23	1	15	29	11.0	1.61	.261
2017	Did not play—Injured																
Minor League Totals			0	1	3.04	26	0	0	0	24	23	1	15	29	11.0	1.61	.261

21 MIKE NIKORAK, RHP

BA GRADE

50 Risk: Extreme

Born: Sept. 16, 1996. **B-T:** R-R. **Ht.:** 6-5. **Wt.:** 220. **Drafted:** HS—Stroudsburg, Pa., 2015 (1st round). **Signed by:** Mike Garlatti.

Nearly three years have passed since the Rockies drafted Nikorak with the 27th overall pick and signed him for $2.3 million to pass up a scholarship to Alabama. In that time he has made just 15 starts, worked 47 innings and has yet to advance past Rookie-level Grand Junction. Those totals won't get higher any time soon after he missed most of 2017 following Tommy John surgery.

Prior to surgery, Nikorak still showed intriguing stuff. His fastball gets up to 97 mph and he has a two-seamer he can use to induce ground balls. He also showed signs of progress with his changeup and low-80s curveball. Most important, he smoothed out his mechanics under the eye of pitching coaches Ryan Kibler and Bob Apodaca and was throwing significantly more strikes, shaving his walks rate from a disastrous 16.3 per nine innings to 5.8. His control was still poor, but at least it was moving in the right direction. Nikorak's stuff and control strides show promise, but he has to stay healthy.

The Rockies are tentatively planning to send Nikorak to an affiliate by midsummer.

Year	Club (League)	Class	W	L	ERA	G	GS	CG	SV	IP	H	HR	BB	SO	K/9	WHIP	AVG
2015	Grand Junction (PIO)	R	0	4	11.72	8	8	0	0	18	26	1	32	14	7.1	3.28	.347
2016	Grand Junction (PIO)	R	1	0	3.68	7	7	0	0	29	33	2	19	20	6.1	1.77	.287
2017	Did not play—Injured																
Minor League Totals			1	4	6.70	15	15	0	0	47	59	3	51	34	6.5	2.34	.311

22 HARRISON MUSGRAVE, LHP

BA GRADE

40 Risk: Medium

Born: March 3, 1992. **B-T:** L-L. **Ht.:** 6-1. **Wt.:** 205. **Drafted:** West Virginia, 2014 (8th round). **Signed by:** Ed Santa.

A product of West Virginia, Musgrave had Tommy John surgery in 2012 but returned to beat out Jon Gray for Big 12 Conference pitcher of the year honors in 2013.

Musgrave appeared to be on the fast track after making 19 starts at Triple-A in just his second full season, but he hit a detour in 2017. He struggled through 12 starts in 2017 before his season ended when he collided with his catcher and suffered a broken finger that required a pin. Musgrave doesn't overpower hitters. His fastball sits 89-90 mph and touches 93, but he makes it work because of solid command and deception from the left side. His out pitch is a solid-average changeup and he also has a fringy slider to give batters another look. Musgrave works aggressively, challenging hitters, and isn't afraid to throw inside despite his modest arsenal.

Musgrave will have a chance to see time in the big leagues as a long reliever in 2018.

Year	Club (League)	Class	W	L	ERA	G	GS	CG	SV	IP	H	HR	BB	SO	K/9	WHIP	AVG
2015	Modesto (CAL)	HiA	10	1	2.88	16	16	0	0	91	81	7	19	83	8.2	1.10	.240
	New Britain (EL)	AA	3	4	3.18	11	11	0	0	57	55	7	13	53	8.4	1.20	.255
2016	Hartford (EL)	AA	5	1	1.79	6	6	0	0	40	20	1	8	30	6.7	0.69	.145
	Albuquerque (PCL)	AAA	8	7	4.30	19	19	0	0	113	118	17	40	79	6.3	1.40	.271
2017	Albuquerque (PCL)	AAA	3	1	6.79	12	11	0	0	54	64	10	26	39	6.5	1.66	.301
Minor League Totals			31	18	4.04	77	74	0	0	403	398	52	120	334	7.5	1.29	.259

23 DANIEL MONTANO, OF

BA GRADE

50 Risk: Extreme

Born: March 31, 1999. **B-T:** L-R. **HT:** 6-1. **Wt.:** 170. **Signed:** Venezuela, 2015.
Signed by: Rolando Fernandez/Carlos Gomez/Orlando Medina.

Montano established himself as one of Venezuela's top teenaged prospects when he hit .375/.483/.542 at the 15U World Cup in 2014. The Rockies signed him for $2 million in 2015, which was the largest bonus the franchise has given to an international amateur. Montano spent his first two seasons in the Dominican Summer League, in part because the Rockies don't field a Rookie-level Arizona League team, and made noticeable improvements in his second season.

Montano features a compact, easy stroke from the left side, a disciplined approach and an advanced pitch recognition for his age. He currently has gap power but projects for possible average power as he fills out. Montano has played center field and right field in his two years in the DSL, but most likely will wind up in left field. He tracks the ball well and gets a good break, but as he physically matures will lose a step or two. He has slightly below average arm strength.

Montano will come to the U.S. in 2018, most likely debuting at Rookie-level Grand Junction.

Year	Club (League)	Class	AVG	G	AB	R	H	2B	3B	HR	RBI	BB	SO	SB	CS	OBP	SLG
2016	Rockies (DSL)	R	.228	65	241	41	55	17	2	9	32	31	65	8	3	.325	.427
2017	Rockies (DSL)	R	.270	52	189	32	51	14	3	3	39	24	39	9	7	.355	.423
Minor League Totals			.247	117	430	73	106	31	5	12	71	55	104	17	10	.338	.426

24 YONATHAN DAZA, OF

BA GRADE

45 Risk: High

Born: Feb. 28, 1994. **B-T:** R-R. **Ht.:** 6-2. **Wt.:** 190. **Signed:** Venezuela, 2010.
Signed by: Rolando Fernandez/Carlos Gomez/Orlando Medina.

Daza signed with the Rockies as a 16-year-old out of Venezuela in 2010 and spent his first three seasons in the Dominican Summer League. He came to the U.S. in 2014 and has made an impression ever since. He has hit a combined .328 in his four years stateside, including winning the California League batting title with a .341 average at high Class A Lancaster in 2017. He also was third in the league with 87 RBIs, second with 11 triples and fifth with 31 stolen bases.

Daza's game is built around making contact and using his above-average speed. He uses the middle of the field and has the alley power to pick up doubles and triples. He can manipulate the barrel and makes consistent hard, line drive contact, but doesn't have the strength or swing path for home runs. He primarily played center field at Lancaster but has experience at all three outfield positions. He gets good reads and jumps in center, although most scouts prefer him in a corner because he isn't a burner.

Most evaluators see Daza as an extra outfielder with contact ability and speed, but he could become an everyday regular if he keeps hitting the way he has.

Year	Club (League)	Class	AVG	G	AB	R	H	2B	3B	HR	RBI	BB	SO	SB	CS	OBP	SLG
2015	Boise (NWL)	SS	.418	16	67	18	28	7	2	2	14	4	11	4	3	.458	.672
	Asheville (SAL)	LoA	.301	70	259	27	78	13	4	1	39	6	36	6	11	.331	.394
2016	Asheville (SAL)	LoA	.307	119	475	63	146	35	2	3	58	23	78	2	7	.341	.408
	Modesto (CAL)	HiA	.242	8	33	1	8	2	0	0	3	1	7	1	1	.306	.303
2017	Lancaster (CAL)	HiA	.341	125	519	93	177	34	11	3	87	30	88	31	8	.376	.466
Minor League Totals			.310	540	2018	307	626	122	22	15	288	101	302	80	47	.353	.415

25 JOSH FUENTES, 3B

BA GRADE

40 Risk: Medium

Born: Feb. 19, 1993. **B-T:** R-R. **Ht.:** 6-2. **Wt.:** 215. **Signed:** Missouri Baptist, 2014 (NDFA). **Signed by:** Marc Gustafson.

Best known as the cousin of Rockies third baseman Nolan Arenado, Fuentes went undrafted despite hitting .365 his junior year at Missouri Baptist. He started to create his own legacy at Double-A Hartford in 2017, putting together a dominant final seven weeks to finish tied for second in the Eastern League with a .307 average and third with a .517 slugging percentage and .869 OPS.

Fuentes has always hit, putting together a career .287/.346/.456 slash line as a professional. His swing can get long at times and he doesn't walk much, but he maintained a compact approach during his hot stretch that shot him to new heights at Double-A. He gets to serviceable power too. Fuentes has the arm strength for third base and decent range, but began seeing time at first base playing for Culiacan in the Mexican Winter League in order to enhance his versatility.

Fuentes has beat the odds every step of his career. His bat and ability to play both infield corners give him a chance to rise to the big leagues, likely as a bench player.

Year	Club (League)	Class	AVG	G	AB	R	H	2B	3B	HR	RBI	BB	SO	SB	CS	OBP	SLG
2015	Asheville (SAL)	LoA	.252	93	337	45	85	24	1	6	42	29	64	7	6	.322	.383
2016	Asheville (SAL)	LoA	.398	28	93	18	37	14	0	4	20	4	22	2	4	.442	.677
	Modesto (CAL)	HiA	.278	77	291	44	81	15	4	9	44	16	54	1	1	.342	.450
2017	Hartford (EL)	AA	.307	122	414	48	127	28	7	15	72	24	92	8	5	.352	.517
Minor League Totals			.287	361	1285	175	369	88	12	35	194	86	271	24	18	.346	.456

26 REID HUMPHREYS, RHP

BA GRADE

45 Risk: High

Born: Nov. 21, 1994. **B-T:** R/R. **Ht.:** 6-1. **Wt.:** 205. **Drafted:** Mississippi State, 2016 (7th round). **Signed by:** Zack Zulli.

A two-way player in high school, Humphreys had Tommy John surgery his junior year. So, when he showed up to Mississippi State the decision was made for him to focus on hitting, initially as a DH and later at first base and the corner outfield spots. Humphreys hit .310 as a junior, but felt healthy his senior year and decided to return to the mound. He became Mississippi State's closer and wound up a seventh-round draft choice of the Rockies.

Humphreys saw limited time on the mound at Rookie-level Grand Junction in 2016, but stepped into the closer role at low Class A Asheville in 2017 and converted 13 of 14 save opportunities while posting a 47-to-6 strikeout to walk mark in 45.2 innings. Humphreys does most of his work with a four-seam fastball that sits 95-97 mph and reaches 99 and a cutter that ranges from 90-94 mph. He has a fringy but usable mid-80s slider and is working on a changeup. Most of all, he has the mentality of a closer and throws strikes consistently.

Humphreys will start 2018 at high Class A Lancaster with a chance to move up the system quickly.

Year	Club (League)	Class	W	L	ERA	G	GS	CG	SV	IP	H	HR	BB	SO	K/9	WHIP	AVG
2016	Grand Junction (PIO)	R	1	0	3.48	9	0	0	0	10	11	0	5	9	7.8	1.55	.250
2017	Asheville (SAL)	LoA	1	3	2.56	43	0	0	13	46	32	3	6	47	9.3	0.83	.194
Minor League Totals			2	3	2.73	52	0	0	13	56	43	3	11	56	9.0	0.96	.206

27 VINCE FERNANDEZ, OF

BA GRADE

45 Risk: High

Born: July 25, 1995, 210. **B-T:** L-R. **Ht.:** 6-3. **Wt.:** 210. **Drafted:** UC Riverside, 2016 (10th round). **Signed by:** Jon Lukens.

Fernandez led the Big West Conference in total bases and finished third in home runs in 2016 with UC Riverside before the Rockies drafted him in the 10th round. He has carried that pop into pro ball with 40 doubles and 21 home runs in 151 career games.

Fernandez has some tools, but evaluators mostly see a player whose entire package fits well together and who has great feel for the game. Offensively, Fernandez possesses a solid, consistent swing that generates above-average power to all fields. He hits with his hands, adjusts the barrel and still has some room to get stronger. He can get overly aggressive at times and run into contact issues, which showed up with 122 strikeouts in 100 games at low Class A Asheville. Defensively, Fernandez does the job in the outfield corners. He catches what needs to be caught, but isn't going to necessarily make the eye-popping catch. He is above-average arm strength and is best in left field, although he can slide to right.

Fernandez has a chance to keep putting up numbers at high Class A Lancaster in 2018 and could continue to rise as a lefthanded power bat.

Year	Club (League)	Class	AVG	G	AB	R	H	2B	3B	HR	RBI	BB	SO	SB	CS	OBP	SLG
2016	Grand Junction (PIO)	R	.310	51	203	36	63	17	6	5	31	20	61	6	2	.370	.527
2017	Asheville (SAL)	LoA	.269	100	375	57	101	23	1	16	59	44	122	12	8	.352	.464
Minor League Totals			.284	151	578	93	164	40	7	21	90	64	183	18	10	.358	.486

28 CHAD SPANBERGER, 1B

BA GRADE

45 Risk: High

Born: Nov. 1, 1995. **B-T:** L-R. **Ht.:** 6-3. **Wt.:** 235. **Drafted:** Arkansas, 2017 (6th round). **Signed by:** Jesse Retzlaf.

Spanberger finally settled in at first base his junior year at Arkansas, and made more starts (58) in 2017 than the previous two years combined (55). A catcher/third basemen in high school in Granite City, Ill., he saw limited time as a DH his freshman year at Arkansas and played some outfield his sophomore year. He finally became a regular as a first baseman in 2017, and responded by becoming the sixth player in Arkansas history to hit 20 home runs.

The Rockies drafted Spanberger in the sixth round in 2017, signed him for $260,200, and watched with glee as he hit 19 more home runs in 60 games at Rookie-level Grand Junction. Power is Spanberger's lone plus tool. He is physically imposing at 6-foot-3, 235 pounds and can turn around premium velocity and send it a long way. His below-average feel for hitting pushed him down draft boards despite his raw power, and that also showed up with 71 strikeouts in his pro debut.

Spanberger is a work in progress defensively at first, but has embraced the challenge. He will head to low Class A Asheville in 2018 and keep rising as long as he gets to his power.

Year	Club (League)	Class	AVG	G	AB	R	H	2B	3B	HR	RBI	BB	SO	SB	CS	OBP	SLG
2017	Grand Junction (PIO)	R	.294	60	235	49	69	15	2	19	51	27	71	2	0	.368	.617
Minor League Totals			.294	60	235	49	69	15	2	19	51	27	71	2	0	.368	.617

29 DOM NUNEZ, C

BA GRADE 40 Risk: High

Born: Jan. 17, 1995. **B-T:** L-R. **Ht.:** 6-1. **Wt.:** 202. **Drafted:** HS—Elk Grove, Calif., 2013 (6th round). **Signed by:** Gary Wilson.

Nunez played shortstop on an Elk Grove (Calif.) High team that featured future first-round picks Dylan Carlson (Cardinals) and Derek Hill (Tigers) as well as Astros third baseman J.D. Davis and Blue Jays prospect first baseman Rowdy Tellez. Nunez turned down a scholarship to UCLA after the Rockies selected him in the sixth round in 2013 and signed him for an over-slot $800,000 bonus.

Nunez played shortstop in Rookie ball in 2013 but returned to Grand Junction in 2014 and began the conversion to catcher. He has adapted to catching quickly. He has soft hands, quick feet and controls the game well. While his work behind the plate has drawn positive reviews, Nunez is an especially poor hitter who struggles to make adjustments. Opponents feed him pitches on the outer half of the plate that he can't do anything with, and the result has been steadily worse offensive production every year.

Nunez's average cratered with a .202 mark at Double-A Hartford in 2017. He needs to make significant offensive improvements to even be a backup, and a return to Double-A in 2018 will be telling.

Year	Club (League)	Class	AVG	G	AB	R	H	2B	3B	HR	RBI	BB	SO	SB	CS	OBP	SLG
2015	Asheville (SAL)	LoA	.282	104	373	61	105	23	0	13	53	53	55	7	7	.373	.448
2016	Modesto (CAL)	HiA	.241	105	390	44	94	13	2	10	51	49	91	8	1	.321	.362
2017	Hartford (EL)	AA	.202	95	297	37	60	10	1	11	28	53	83	7	1	.335	.354
Minor League Totals			.247	405	1431	196	353	71	4	45	195	194	291	38	24	.338	.396

30 RAYAN GONZALEZ, RHP

BA GRADE 40 Risk: High

Born: Oct. 18, 1990. **B-T:** R-R. **Ht.:** 6-4. **Wt.:** 231. **Drafted:** Bethune-Cookman, 2012 (21st round). **Signed by:** John Cedarburg.

Gonzalez was in position to make the Rockies' bullpen out of spring training in 2017, but arm problems eventually led to Tommy John surgery in mid-May and cost him the season.

Gonzalez overpowers hitters with a 96 mph cutter that has natural depth. It's complimented by a downer curveball that will play at altitude and he also throws a quality changeup. Given his limited experience—208.1 innings since signing with the Rockies as a 21st-round draft choice in 2012—the Rockies will be careful with him in the spring, and he most likely won't be ready to pitch competitively until midseason.

Coming off Tommy John surgery, combined with spending three stints on the disabled list with High-A Modesto in 2015, has the Rockies wanting to make sure Gonzalez has rebuilt his arm strength before getting him back in a competitive atmosphere.

Year	Club (League)	Class	W	L	ERA	G	GS	CG	SV	IP	H	HR	BB	SO	K/9	WHIP	AVG
2015	Modesto (CAL)	HiA	1	3	6.45	22	0	0	1	22	27	1	13	25	10.1	1.79	.307
2016	Hartford (EL)	AA	2	2	3.12	46	0	0	1	52	44	2	23	49	8.5	1.29	.242
2017	Did not play—Injured																
Minor League Totals			9	16	4.02	189	0	0	25	208	220	6	94	235	10.2	1.51	.271

Detroit Tigers

BY J.J. COOPER

For much of this decade, the Tigers were racing the clock. Detroit was trying to win a World Series for owner Mike Ilitch and no expense was spared.

Under Ilitch's leadership, Detroit signed a trio of players to $180 million-plus deals: Prince Fielder, Justin Verlander and Miguel Cabrera. Detroit won four straight American League Central titles from 2011-14, appeared in three consecutive AL Championship Series and the 2013 World Series.

But they never lifted the World Series trophy. And the team got farther from its goal in recent years as the core got older and more expensive.

Ilitch died before the 2017 season and the pressure for immediate success seemed to fade with his passing. Coincidentally or not, the Tigers have embarked on the team's first full rebuilding effort of this decade. Detroit had traded away Yoenis Cespedes and David Price during a fifth-place finish in 2015, but that was part of an attempt to retool on the fly. Much of that same roster bounced back to win 86 games in 2016.

After finishing with the worst record in baseball in 2017, there are no such expectations for 2018.

Justin Verlander, Justin Wilson, Justin Upton and J.D. Martinez all were dealt away during the 2017 season. Ian Kinsler joined the exodus in an offseason deal. The moves brought a much-needed infusion of prospects and also sped the Tigers' slide to the bottom. Detroit is following the plan spelled out by the Cubs and Astros in recent years—lose a lot and rebuild with high draft picks and the larger bonus pools that come with them.

The high-priced veterans who are still around are largely untradeable. Coming off the worst season of his career, 34-year-old Cabrera has at least six years left at more than $30 million a year. Righthander Jordan Zimmermann will make almost $25 million a year for the next three years.

But all around them, Detroit is getting much younger. The Tigers' Opening Day lineup should be as bad in 2018 as it has been since the team hit rock bottom in the early part of the 21st century. Most of the team's best prospects are still at least a year or two away. The team's lineup will be filled with players who will not be part of the team's next playoff contender.

That's an opportunity in itself. With at-bats and innings less valuable than they are for a playoff contender, the Tigers have the opportunity to find castoffs that may turn into contributors. They also can let their young starting pitchers work through struggles.

On the farm, Detroit now has an impressive wave of starting pitching prospects spread from

The lineup around Miguel Cabrera will get dramatically younger as the Tigers rebuild.

PROJECTED 2021 LINEUP

Catcher	Jake Rogers (25)
First Base	Jeimer Candelario (27)
Second Base	Isaac Paredes (22)
Third Base	Dawel Lugo (26)
Shortstop	Jose Iglesias (31)
Left Field	Christin Stewart (27)
Center Field	Daz Cameron (24)
Right Field	Nick Castellanos (29)
Designated Hitter	Miguel Cabrera (38)
No. 1 Starter	Michael Fulmer (28)
No. 2 Starter	Franklin Perez (23)
No. 3 Starter	Alex Faedo (25)
No. 4 Starter	Matt Manning (23)
No. 5 Starter	Daniel Norris (28)
Closer	Beau Burrows (24)

Double-A to low Class A. The Tigers have always developed hard-throwing relievers, and that hasn't changed.

The position player depth is less impressive and will need further reinforcements. Christin Stewart is the only Top 10 Prospect who projects as a significant power threat. Detroit has a number of potentially useful middle infielders and backup outfielders, but few hitters who project as sure-fire regulars.

That could become a problem in 2020 and beyond. But right now the renovation is just beginning. Detroit won't be catching Cleveland any time soon. But for the first time in a while patience is a part of the Tigers' plans.

DEPTH CHART

DETROIT TIGERS

TOP 2018 ROOKIE: Joe Jimenez, RHP. The Tigers have to hope that his brutal first taste of the big leagues will help him be better in his return to Detroit.

BREAKOUT PROSPECT: Sam McMillan, C. He needs to get stronger, but his outstanding batting eye will help him stay ahead of pitchers.

SLEEPER: Jose Azocar, OF. He struggled in his first time at high Class A Lakeland. He has to put together better at-bats, but he's as physically talented as almost anyone in the system.

SOURCE OF TOP 30 TALENT			
Homegrown	20	Acquired	10
College	8	Trade	9
Junior college	0	Rule 5 draft	1
High school	4	Independent league	0
Nondrafted free agent	2	Free agent/waivers	0
International	6		

LF
Christin Stewart (9)
Michael Gerber (14)
Victor Reyes (25)
Cam Gibson
Ro Coleman

CF
Daz Cameron (6)
Troy Montgomery (27)
Derek Hill (28)
Jacob Robson
Jhon Sandoval
Garrett McCain

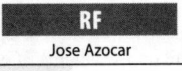

RF
Jose Azocar

3B
Kody Eaves

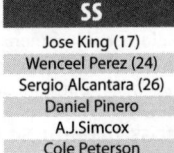

SS
Jose King (17)
Wenceel Perez (24)
Sergio Alcantara (26)
Daniel Pinero
A.J.Simcox
Cole Peterson

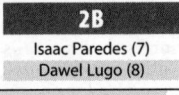

2B
Isaac Paredes (7)
Dawel Lugo (8)

1B
Reynaldo Rivera

C
Jake Rogers (5)
John McMillan (13)
Grayson Greiner (22)
Gresuan Silverio
Eliezer Alfonzo

LHP

LHSP	LHRP
Austin Sodders (29)	Gregory Soto (10)
Tyler Alexander	Matt Hall
Grayson Long	Evan Hill
Eudis Idrogo	Max Green

RHP

RHSP	RHRP
Franklin Perez (1)	Joe Jimenez (15)
Alex Faedo (2)	Bryan Garcia (16)
Matt Manning (3)	Gerson Moreno (18)
Beau Burrows (4)	Wilkel Hernandez (20)
Kyle Funkhouser (11)	Wladimir Pinto (21)
Spencer Turnbull (12)	Jason Foley (23)
Anthony Castro (19)	Sandy Baez (30)
Artie Lewicki	Mark Ecker
	Gio Arriera
	Zac Houston
	Garrett King
	Dane Myers
	John Schreiber
	Carson Lance
	Brad Bass
	Elvin Rodriguez
	Brandyn Sittinger

DRAFT ANALYSIS

2017

BEST PURE HITTER: C Sam McMillan (5) showed he was one of the most advanced hitters in the Rookie-level Gulf Coast League in his pro debut. His simple swing generates a lot of line-drive contact, but his most apparent tool is a very discerning batting eye. He walked more than he struck out in his pro debut and looks to be a solid defensive catcher with excellent on-base skills.

BEST POWER: 1B Reynaldo Rivera (2) faced questions from some amateur scouts about his bat speed, but few questioned his raw power. Rivera hit 20 home runs at Chipola (Fla.) JC this spring, although he looked tired and over-matched at short-season Connecticut, where he hit only two home runs in 52 games while slashing .187/.261/.280.

FASTEST RUNNER: OF Ro Coleman (34) is a double-plus runner who probably is the fastest Tigers draftee in a foot race. OF Luke Burch (9) is a plus runner and has a little more base-stealing savvy than Coleman. He swiped eight bases in nine tries in his pro debut.

BEST DEFENSIVE PLAYER: C Joey Morgan (3) turns in above-average pop times on his throws. He did allow seven passed balls in 34 pro games, but that's partly an artifact of catching wild young arms.

BEST FASTBALL: RHP Alex Faedo (1) saw his fastball velocity dip early in the spring of his junior season, but it bounced back to 92-94 mph by the postseason and he touches 98. His fastball is most notable for its excellent life that makes it hard to square up. The Tigers rested him after signing as he threw 123.2 innings while leading Florida to the national championship. LHP Max Green (8) and RHP Billy Lescher (17) will both touch 96 mph.

BEST SECONDARY PITCH: Faedo's 83-84 mph slider was one of the best in the draft. He has shown the ability to tone down its break to throw it for strikes or tighten up the break and bury it in

TOP DRAFT PICKS OF THE DECADE

Year	Player, Pos.	2017 Org
2008	Ryan Perry, RHP	Did not play
2009	Jacob Turner, RHP	Nationals
2010	Nick Castellanos, 3B (1st round supp.)	Tigers
2011	James McCann, C (2nd round)	Tigers
2012	Jake Thompson, RHP (2nd round)	Phillies
2013	Jonathon Crawford, RHP	Reds
2014	Derek Hill, OF	Tigers
2015	Beau Burrows, RHP	Tigers
2016	Matt Manning, RHP	Tigers
2017	Alex Faedo, RHP	Tigers

the dirt as a strikeout pitch.

BEST ATHLETE: RHP Dane Myers (6) was an infielder as well as pitcher for Rice who was a draftable prospect as a hitter in addition to being a top 10-round talent as a pitcher.

BEST PRO DEBUT: McMillan hit .288/.441/.432 with the GCL Tigers. RHP Drew Carlton (23) had a sparkling 1.08 ERA and a 29-3 strikeout-to-walk ratio in 25 innings between the GCL, New York-Penn and Midwest Leagues.

BEST LATE-ROUND PICK: After two seasons in the Florida State rotation, Carlton moved to the bullpen and had more success as he simplified to a low-90s fastball-cutter approach. Neither is a true plus pitch, but both are effective as he challenges hitters.

MOST INTRIGUING BACKGROUND: Lescher's father William is a Vice Admiral in the U.S. Navy; the former test pilot is a deputy chief of naval operations. 3B Colby Bortles (22) brother is the younger brother of Jacksonville Jaguars quarterback Blake Bortles.

THE ONE WHO GOT AWAY: It won't be a surprise to anyone if RHP Jack Leftwich (39) blossoms into a prominent draft prospect at Florida. He's already got a plus fastball but he has plenty of room to grow and develop as well.

—J.J. COOPER

2016

RHP Matt Manning (1) had an encouraging first full season and has plenty of raw tools to develop, though he remains far from the big leagues. RHP Kyle Funkhouser (4) started the year well, but an injury sidelined him late.

GRADE: C

2015

The Tigers had two first rounders in 2015 in RHP Beau Burrows (1) and OF Christin Stewart (1). Both have big raw tools, but are facing profile questions as they advance in the minor leagues.

GRADE: C

2014

Injuries limited many of the class' top players in 2017, including OF Derek Hill (1) and RHP Spencer Turnbull (2). RHP Artie Lewicki (8) reached Detroit, and C Grayson Greiner (3) and OF Mike Gerber (15) could soon follow.

GRADE: D

1 FRANKLIN PEREZ, RHP

Born: Dec. 6, 1997. **B-T:** R-R. **Ht.:** 6-3. **Wt.:** 197.
Signed: Venezuela, 2014.
Signed by: Oz Ocampo/Oscar Alvarado (Astros).

ROBERT GURGANUS

When he was training with Carlos Guillen as an amateur, Franklin Perez was a strong-armed third baseman. But in reality, he was a pitcher who just hadn't found his true home yet. When he moved to the mound, he quickly showed a delivery and an aptitude that seemed somewhat remarkable for a newly minted pitcher. He quickly surpassed many more experienced pitchers in the 2014 international amateur class as a clean delivery and ability to work in the strike zone made Perez stand out. He missed a month early the 2017 season with a knee injury but still reached Double-A before his 20th birthday. The Tigers made him the signature acquisition in the Justin Verlander trade, although the Aug. 31 deal came late enough in the season that Perez never got into a game with a Tigers club.

The Tigers have pitching prospects with higher ceilings than Perez, but none who combine stuff and feel like Perez does. For a young pitcher, Perez already understands many of the finer details of the craft. He responds quickly to instruction and shows an aptitude for adjustments. After working on a new grip for his slider in just one side session, he successfully took it into his next game. Perez generally sits 92-94 mph, although he can touch 95-96 at his best. There are some scouts who believe that he may end up throwing harder in his 20s because his delivery is clean and he has plenty of athleticism. What's most notable is he commands all four of his pitches. His 75-80 mph curveball is his best secondary pitch. He's long had an ability to spin it, with 12-to-6 break, and he's shown he can loosen it up as an early-count strike or tighten it as a swing-and-miss out pitch. His changeup is a potentially average pitch as well, with more deception than late fade. He's messed with a slider as well. It's hard (88-89 mph) with late movement. It could be described as almost a slutter, as it's in between a cutter and a bigger slider, but because of its power and late movement it's reasonably effective.

Perez doesn't blow hitters away like a future No. 1, but he also doesn't have all that much left to refine to be a future middle-of-the-rotation starter. He'll head to Double-A Erie, but could be only a year away from Detroit.

BA GRADE / SCOUTING GRADES

60 Risk: High

FB: 60. **CB:** 60 **SL:** 45.
CHG: 50. **CTL:** 60.
Projected future grades on 20-80 scouting scale

TOP PROSPECTS OF THE DECADE

Year	Player, Pos.	2017 Org
2008	Rick Porcello, RHP	Red Sox
2009	Rick Porcello, RHP	Red Sox
2010	Jacob Turner, RHP	Nationals
2011	Jacob Turner, RHP	Nationals
2012	Jacob Turner, RHP	Nationals
2013	Nick Castellanos ,3B/OF	Tigers
2014	Nick Castellanos, 3B/OF	Tigers
2015	Steven Moya, OF	Tigers
2016	Michael Fulmer, RHP	Tigers
2017	Matt Manning, RHP	Tigers

BEST TOOLS

Best Hitter For Average	Michael Gerber
Best Power Hitter	Christin Stewart
Best Strike-Zone Discipline	Sam McMillan
Fastest Baserunner	Derek Hill
Best Athlete	Derek Hill
Best Fastball	Beau Burrows
Best Curveball	Franklin Perez
Best Slider	Alex Faedo
Best Changeup	Sandy Baez
Best Control	John Schreiber
Best Defensive Catcher	Jake Rogers
Best Defensive Infielder	Sergio Alcantara
Best Infield Arm	Dawel Lugo
Best Defensive Outfielder	Derek Hill
Best Outfield Arm	Jose Azocar

Year	Club (League)	Class	W	L	ERA	G	GS	CG	SV	IP	H	HR	BB	SO	K/9	WHIP	AVG
2015	Astros Orange (DSL)	R	1	2	4.37	11	9	0	0	35	34	1	11	44	11.3	1.29	.250
	Astros (GCL)	R	0	2	4.80	5	1	0	0	15	19	0	3	17	10.2	1.47	.292
2016	Quad Cities (MWL)	LoA	3	3	2.84	15	10	0	1	67	63	1	19	75	10.1	1.23	.250
2017	Buies Creek (CAR)	HiA	4	2	2.98	12	10	1	2	54	38	4	16	53	8.8	0.99	.191
	Corpus Christi (TL)	AA	2	1	3.09	7	6	0	1	32	33	2	11	25	7.0	1.38	.266
Minor League Totals			10	10	3.33	50	36	1	4	203	187	8	60	214	9.5	1.22	.241x

2 ALEX FAEDO, RHP

Born: Nov. 12, 1995. **B-T:** R-R. **Ht.:** 6-5. **Wt.:** 225. **Drafted:** Florida, 2017 (1st round). **Signed by:** R.J. Burgess.

The Tigers understandably never imagined when the 2017 college season began that Faedo might be on the board when they picked. After knee surgery during the fall, Faedo got off to a slow start for the Gators and started sliding down draft boards (he'd been considered a likely top 10 pick). But just as teams lined up their preference lists, Faedo began to dominate again. He was the Most Outstanding Player of the College World Series after posting a 0.32 ERA with 44 strikeouts in 27.1 postseason innings to lead the Gators to the title.

The Tigers shut Faedo down when they signed him, as he already had thrown 123 innings during the college season. He will make his pro debut in 2018. At his best, Faedo has three plus pitches. He manipulates his 90-94 mph fastball as he can cut it, sink it or make it run. His low-80s slider was among the best in the college class as he can toy with its bite and depth depending on the situation. And his changeup falls off at the plate, giving him another swing-and-miss pitch. His stuff was not as firm early in the 2017 college season and he can get too reliant on his slider, but overall, it's a well-honed three-pitch package. While Faedo has a long arm action, he has average to above-average control. As an accomplished pitcher in the SEC, Faedo should move quickly, even if he's yet to make his pro debut.

The cold weather of West Michigan in April makes the case to push Faedo to high Class A Lakeland. He projects as a solid No. 3 starter.

BA GRADE
60 Risk: High

FB: 60. SL: 60.
CH: 60.
CTL: 55.

Year	Club (League)	Class	W	L	ERA	G	GS	CG	SV	IP	H	HR	BB	SO	K/9	WHIP	AVG
2017	Did not play																

3 MATT MANNING, RHP

Born: Jan. 28, 1998. **B-T:** R-R. **Ht.:** 6-6. **Wt.:** 190. **Drafted:** HS—Sacramento, 2016 (1st round). **Signed by:** Scott Cerny.

The son of an NBA player, Manning could have gone to Loyola Marymount to pitch and play forward on the basketball team. A $3.5 million signing bonus from the Tigers was a pretty convincing argument to give up basketball. Detroit held him back in extended spring training before sending him to the New York-Penn League.

Manning wavered between dominant efforts and struggles both in short-season Connecticut and in a late-season cameo in low Class A West Michigan. When he's synced up his mechanics, Manning can dominate. But so far, Manning has been out of sync a lot. His arm slot unintentionally varied in 2017 from over the top to more of a high three-quarters delivery. He also varied from being direct to the plate to throwing across his body. He struggled with location as a result. In each of his first two outings with West Michigan he failed to make it out of the second inning. But when he put it together, he showed a plus 92-93 mph fastball that touched 95-96. His fastball has riding life up in the zone, or he can gear it down to locate it down and away to a righthanded hitter. His 12-to-6 above-average curveball looks like a second future plus pitch. Right now it's a late-count weapon that he buries while hitters flail helplessly, but he doesn't consistently throw it for strikes early in the count. His changeup is below-average. He needs to refine and develop it. As a tall, if athletic, righthander, Manning will continually have to work on the consistency of his delivery and he has to pick an arm slot.

Ideally, Manning could develop into a front of the rotation ace, but if his control and changeup don't advance as expected he could also end up as a power reliever. He's ready to return to West Michigan for his first extended taste of full-season ball.

BA GRADE
60 Risk: V. High

FB: 60. CB: 60.
CH: 60.
CTL: 45.

Year	Club (League)	Class	W	L	ERA	G	GS	CG	SV	IP	H	HR	BB	SO	K/9	WHIP	AVG
2016	Tigers West (GCL)	R	0	2	3.99	10	10	0	0	29	27	2	7	46	14.1	1.16	.237
2017	Connecticut (NYP)	SS	2	2	1.89	9	9	0	0	33	27	0	14	36	9.7	1.23	.223
	West Michigan (MWL)	LoA	2	0	5.60	5	5	0	0	18	14	0	11	26	13.2	1.42	.209
Minor League Totals			4	4	3.47	24	24	0	0	80	68	2	32	108	12.1	1.24	.225

4 BEAU BURROWS, RHP

Born: Sept. 18, 1996. **B-T:** R-R. **Ht.:** 6-2. **Wt.:** 200. **Drafted:** HS—Weatherford, Texas, 2015. (1st round). **Signed by:** Chris Wimmer.

Burrows blitzed through the Florida State League, leaving plenty of helpless hitters in his wake as he earned a spot in the Futures Game, where he struck out a pair of hitters in a clean inning. Double-A hitters proved tougher, as Burrows' less-developed secondary offerings allowed hitters to look for his fastball.

Burrows has a better fastball than any of the Tigers' other top starting pitching prospects. He can blow hitters away with consistent 94-95 mph fastballs—he touched 98 in the Futures Game. Burrows has a high spin rate that makes it appear that his heater has a late hop, generating swings and misses. But if he's going to avoid eventually being moved to the bullpen, he'll need to improve his trio of below-average offspeed pitches. His below-average slider and curveball both are not consistent enough and they sometimes blend together, leading to the question of whether he'd be better off focusing on one or the other. His curve is a little ahead of his slider. It's loopy but it has 12-to-6 break. His changeup is further away and needs more separation and deception.

If Burrows were 25 years old, it would be time to move him to the pen and let him rely heavily on his excellent fastball. But he'll pitch the 2018 season as a 21-year-old, so there's plenty of time to let him continue to work on improving his offspeed pitches in Double-A Erie.

BA GRADE
50 Risk: Medium
FB: 70. CB: 45.
SL: 40. CH: 40.
CTL: 50.

Year	Club (League)	Class	W	L	ERA	G	GS	CG	SV	IP	H	HR	BB	SO	K/9	WHIP	AVG
2015	Tigers (GCL)	R	1	0	1.61	10	9	0	0	28	18	0	11	33	10.6	1.04	.184
2016	West Michigan (MWL)	LoA	6	4	3.15	21	20	0	0	97	87	2	30	67	6.2	1.21	.240
2017	Lakeland (FSL)	HiA	4	3	1.23	11	11	0	0	59	44	3	11	62	9.5	0.94	.221
	Erie (EL)	AA	6	4	4.72	15	15	1	0	76	79	5	33	75	8.8	1.47	.269
Minor League Totals			17	11	3.01	57	55	1	0	260	228	10	85	237	8.2	1.20	.239

5 JAKE ROGERS, C

Born: April 15, 1995. **B-T:** R-R. **Ht.:** 6-1. **Wt.:** 190. **Drafted:** Tulane, 2016 (3rd round). **Signed by:** Justin Cryer (Astros).

Rogers was seen as one of the best defensive catchers in the 2016 college draft class, but he also was an easy out at the plate for most of his Tulane career (.233 career hitter with seven home runs in three seasons). With many scouts seeing him as a glove-only catcher, he fell to the third round despite impeccable defensive credentials.

Rogers has proven a better hitter in pro ball and was a key part of the Justin Verlander trade. At the plate, Rogers is looking to drive the ball. He has a big leg kick to start his swing and takes a ferocious cut with a pull-heavy approach. When it works, he has the power to deposit pitches in the left field bleachers. When it doesn't he rolls over groundouts or hits a number of harmless pop outs. Evaluators generally see him as a below-average hitter with a lot of swings and misses and average bat speed. But his power-heavy approach also gives him a chance to hit 20-plus home runs. Combine that with his plus arm (he threw out 46 percent of base stealers) and his defensive skills and that could still be a valuable big leaguer. Rogers embraces the leadership role, moves well behind the plate and has a strong left hand, giving him chance to be an above-average receiver as well.

Rogers is at least a big league backup catcher and if he can make semi-consistent contact he has a solid chance to be an everyday regular. He'll jump to Double-A Erie in 2018 and with his defensive polish, isn't all that far from Detroit.

PAUL GIERHART

BA GRADE
50 Risk: High
HIT: 40. POW: 55.
SPD: 40. FLD: 55.
ARM: 55.

Year	Club (League)	Class	AVG	G	AB	R	H	2B	3B	HR	RBI	BB	SO	SB	CS	OBP	SLG
2016	Tri-City (NYP)	SS	.253	25	87	11	22	7	1	2	12	13	18	0	2	.369	.425
	Quad Cities (MWL)	LoA	.208	21	72	7	15	3	1	1	4	8	25	1	0	.305	.319
2017	Quad Cities (MWL)	LoA	.255	27	102	17	26	7	1	6	15	9	28	1	0	.336	.520
	Buies Creek (CAR)	HiA	.265	83	313	43	83	18	3	12	55	44	72	13	8	.357	.457
	Lakeland (FSL)	HiA	.143	2	7	0	1	0	0	0	0	1	2	0	0	.250	.143
Minor League Totals			.253	158	581	78	147	35	6	21	86	75	145	15	10	.348	.442

6 DAZ CAMERON, OF

Born: Jan. 15, 1997. **B-T:** R-R. **Ht.:** 6-2. **Wt.:** 189. **Drafted:** HS—McDonough, Ga., 2015 (1st round supplemental). **Signed by:** Gavin Dickey (Astros).

BA GRADE	
50	Risk: High
HIT: 45. POW: 50.	
SPD: 55. FLD: 55.	
ARM: 50.	

The son of longtime big league center fielder Mike Cameron, Daz slid in the 2015 draft because of his asking price. He landed a $4 million bonus that matched that of Astros first-round pick Kyle Tucker.

Cameron wasn't ready for the Midwest League in 2016, and a finger injury ended his season early. He was much better in his second try at full-season ball, impressing the Tigers enough to make sure he was included in the Justin Verlander trade. Cameron has a good understanding of the strike zone and recognizes pitches to hit, but early in his pro career he would fail to consistently square up hittable pitches, often fouling them off instead. His swing path proved to be too steep. Cameron has worked to keep the bat through the zone longer and it has paid off in better contact. Optimistic projections see Cameron as an average hitter, but that should be enough to be a regular as he has the strength and bat speed to hit 15-20 home runs in his prime. Cameron is an above-average defender in center field with an average arm and above-average speed.

Cameron lacks a truly exceptional tool, but he's a hard worker and he has a well-rounded skill set. He's ready for high Class A Lakeland.

Year	Club (League)	Class	AVG	G	AB	R	H	2B	3B	HR	RBI	BB	SO	SB	CS	OBP	SLG
2015	Astros (GCL)	R	.222	21	72	14	16	2	0	0	6	9	18	13	4	.326	.250
	Greeneville (APP)	R	.272	30	103	20	28	2	3	0	11	16	31	11	6	.372	.350
2016	Quad Cities (MWL)	LoA	.143	21	77	5	11	2	2	0	6	8	33	4	3	.221	.221
	Tri-City (NYP)	SS	.278	19	79	13	22	3	1	2	14	6	26	8	2	.352	.418
2017	Quad Cities (MWL)	LoA	.271	119	442	78	120	29	8	13	72	45	107	32	12	.350	.462
	West Michigan (MWL)	LoA	.250	3	8	1	2	0	0	0	1	3	4	0	1	.455	.250
Minor League Totals			.255	213	781	131	199	38	14	15	110	87	219	68	28	.340	.397

7 ISAAC PAREDES, SS/2B

Born: Feb. 18, 1999. **B-T:** R-R. **Ht.:** 5-11. **Wt.:** 175. **Signed:** Mexico, 2015. **Signed by:** Sergio Hernandez/Louie Eljaua (Cubs).

BA GRADE	
50	Risk: High
HIT: 55. POW: 50.	
SPD: 40. FLD: 50.	
ARM: 55.	

If not for Vladimir Guerrero Jr. or Fernando Tatis Jr.'s standout seasons, Paredes would have generated plenty of an attention as an 18-year-old shortstop who hit 11 home runs, drew walks and didn't strike out much. Along with Jeimer Candelario, he was acquired from the Cubs for lefthander Justin Wilson and catcher Alex Avila at the end of July.

Even if his stats don't fully indicate it, scouts saw him as one of the better pure hitters in the Midwest League. He showed a consistent ability to square up balls, while showing pitch recognition, a whole-field approach and the plate discipline of an older, more experienced hitter before wearing down in August. He should be at least an above-average hitter and he has a chance to hit 15-20 home runs a season. Defensively, there's much less consensus. Paredes' thick trunk draws comparisons to Jhonny Peralta, but more often, players with Paredes' build end up moving to second or third base. With an above-average arm, soft hands and good instincts, he should be able to stick at either spot if he stays on top of his conditioning. Paredes' ultimate ceiling depends on how his body develops.

If he doesn't get much thicker, Paredes could stick at a premium defensive position where his well-rounded offensive toolset will make him an asset. He should be one of the younger players in the Florida State League in 2018.

Year	Club (League)	Class	AVG	G	AB	R	H	2B	3B	HR	RBI	BB	SO	SB	CS	OBP	SLG
2016	Cubs (AZL)	R	.305	47	167	23	51	14	3	1	26	13	20	4	0	.359	.443
	South Bend (MWL)	LoA	.167	3	12	0	2	0	0	0	0	0	2	0	0	.231	.167
2017	South Bend (MWL)	LoA	.264	92	337	49	89	25	0	7	49	29	54	2	1	.343	.401
	West Michigan (MWL)	LoA	.217	32	115	16	25	3	0	4	21	13	13	0	0	.323	.348
Minor League Totals			.265	174	631	88	167	42	3	12	96	55	89	6	1	.341	.398

8 DAWEL LUGO, 3B/SS

Born: Dec. 31, 1994. **B-T:** R-R. **Ht.:** 6-0. **Wt:** 190. **Signed:** Dominican Republic, 2011.
Signed by: Marco Paddy/Hilario Soriano (Blue Jays).

One of the top signees in the Blue Jays' 2011 international class, Lugo has gotten used to the realities of pro baseball as he's been traded around the trade deadline twice in the past three seasons.

The first time he went to the Diamondbacks for Cliff Pennington and in 2017, the D-backs included him in the trade that also sent Jose King and Sergio Alcantara to the Tigers for J.D. Martinez. Lugo is trying to straddle a tricky paradox. He's a solid third baseman defensively, but he'll have to get to his power more often to really fit at third base. Scouts are less confident he can be an average defender at second base, where his above-average hit and average power would be a better fit. Lugo has plenty of bat speed and above-average hand-eye coordination. He recognizes pitches quickly out of the hand and has steadily turned himself into a very tough out. But that has come at the expense of power. He has above-average raw power, but he has a hit-first approach come game-time at the expense of power. Lugo has a plus arm which plays very well at third and good hands, but his first-step quickness is modest. He's a below-average runner.

Lugo isn't all that far away from competing for a big league job. The former shortstop could end up at second or third base depending on team need. He doesn't have exceptional upside, but he has a good chance at a solid big league career.

BA GRADE
45 Risk: Medium
HIT: 55. POW: 50.
SPD: 40. FLD: 50.
ARM: 60.

Year	Club (League)	Class	AVG	G	AB	R	H	2B	3B	HR	RBI	BB	SO	SB	CS	OBP	SLG
2015	Dunedin (FSL)	HiA	.219	67	260	16	57	9	2	2	21	9	49	1	3	.258	.292
	Lansing (MWL)	LoA	.336	31	122	15	41	6	1	2	23	5	24	3	1	.348	.451
	Kane County (MWL)	LoA	.333	22	81	12	27	1	1	0	3	4	13	2	2	.372	.370
2016	Visalia (CAL)	HiA	.314	79	315	61	99	14	5	13	42	15	41	2	1	.348	.514
	Mobile (SL)	AA	.306	48	173	24	53	9	2	4	20	4	15	1	1	.322	.451
2017	Jackson (SL)	AA	.282	88	341	40	96	21	4	7	43	21	51	1	0	.325	.428
	Erie (EL)	AA	.269	43	175	18	47	6	1	6	22	12	21	2	1	.314	.417
Minor League Totals			.276	609	2372	280	655	100	25	47	291	101	352	21	13	.309	.399

9 CHRISTIN STEWART, OF

Born: Dec. 10, 1993. **B-T:** L-R. **Ht.:** 6-0. **Wt.:** 205. **Drafted:** Tennessee, 2015 (1st round).
Signed by: Harold Zonder.

Stewart ranked among the top 10 in NCAA Division I in home run rate during his junior year of college and he's shown similar power with a wood bat. He's easily led the organization in home runs in each of his two full seasons and ranks second in the minors with 58 home runs over the past two years.

Like most power hitters in 2017, he strikes out, but not excessively. He is prone to chase out of the zone because he's looking to do damage whether early or late in counts. He does have some zone awareness and when he stays within himself, he can generate power from a relatively compact swing. Stewart is a little pull happy, but he has the ability to drive the ball out to all fields. Stewart is a below-average runner who is unlikely to be more than a below-average hitter, but with 25-30 home run power given regular at-bats. The concerns about Stewart revolve around when he's wearing an outfielder's glove. He has worked hard to improve his defense, and he has seen some improvement, but he's still well below-average. Most scouts say it's unrealistic to see him as anything better than a future 40 defensively on the 20-to-80 scouting scale. He's limited to left field by a well below-average arm. Stewart's best position is designated hitter, but few teams break in rookies at DH. To play left field regularly, he'll have to be a prodigious hitter to make up for his defensive limitations, which adds to his risk.

Stewart either is an everyday regular or a minor leaguer, but his swing gives him a chance to be a productive power hitter.

BA GRADE
50 Risk: High
HIT: 40. POW: 60.
SPD: 40. FLD: 40.
ARM: 30.

Year	Club (League)	Class	AVG	G	AB	R	H	2B	3B	HR	RBI	BB	SO	SB	CS	OBP	SLG
2015	Tigers (GCL)	R	.364	6	22	5	8	2	1	1	2	3	5	2	1	.462	.682
	Connecticut (NYP)	SS	.245	14	49	7	12	2	2	2	11	5	18	0	0	.322	.490
	West Michigan (MWL)	LoA	.286	51	185	29	53	9	4	7	31	18	45	3	2	.375	.492
2016	Lakeland (FSL)	HiA	.264	104	356	60	94	22	1	24	68	74	105	3	1	.403	.534
	Erie (EL)	AA	.218	24	87	17	19	2	0	6	19	12	26	0	0	.310	.448
2017	Erie (EL)	AA	.256	136	485	67	124	29	3	28	86	56	138	3	0	.335	.501
Minor League Totals			.262	335	1184	185	310	66	11	68	217	168	337	11	4	.363	.508

10 GREGORY SOTO, LHP

Born: Feb. 11, 1995. **B-T:** L-L. **Ht.:** 6-1. **Wt.:** 180. **Signed:** Dominican Republic, 2012. **Signed by:** Carlos Santana/Ramon Perez.

There's little question that Soto has a big league arm, but he's yet to do much to quiet the speculation that in the long run he'll end up pitching out of the bullpen. Soto has one of the best arms in the Tigers' farm system.

Soto sits 95-96 mph from the left side and his slider has enough power and shape to project as at least an above-average pitch as well. But Soto doesn't have a great idea of where the ball is going when it leaves his hand. His cross-body delivery helps contribute to his below-average control—he's walked 4.6 batters per nine inning over the past two seasons. Soto's changeup has a long way to go and its rudimentary nature leads more talk of relieving in the future. Soto has learned how to work out of trouble because he has had a lot of trouble he's worked out of already.

Soto most likely ends up as a valuable bullpen arm with two pitches that can eat up lefties and enough stuff to be able to face righthanders. But there are enough glimpses of more for the Tigers to keep working on developing him as a starter when he returns to Lakeland.

BA GRADE
50 Risk: High
FB: 60. SL: 55.
CH: 60.
CTL: 45.

Year	Club (League)	Class	W	L	ERA	G	GS	CG	SV	IP	H	HR	BB	SO	K/9	WHIP	AVG
2015	Connecticut (NYP)	SS	0	1	22.50	2	1	0	0	2	1	0	6	5	22.5	3.50	.143
	Tigers (GCL)	R	2	4	2.19	9	5	0	0	37	34	0	25	40	9.7	1.59	.250
2016	Connecticut (NYP)	SS	3	2	3.03	15	15	0	0	71	68	1	34	62	7.8	1.43	.256
2017	West Michigan (MWL)	LoA	10	1	2.25	18	18	0	0	96	70	3	54	116	10.9	1.29	.204
	Lakeland (FSL)	HiA	2	1	2.25	5	5	0	0	28	27	1	11	28	9.0	1.36	.267
Minor League Totals			23	14	2.99	81	66	0	0	322	270	6	191	359	10.0	1.43	.232

11 KYLE FUNKHOUSER, RHP

BA GRADE
50 Risk: High

Born: March 16, 1994. **B-T:** R-R. **Ht.:** 6-2. **Wt.:** 220. **Drafted:** Louisville, 2016 (4th round). **Signed by:** Harold Zonder.

Funkhouser had to wait longer than expected to become a pro. He was expected to be one of the best pitchers in the 2015 draft class, but his stuff took a step back and his control wavered as April turned to May. He slid to the back of the first round (35th overall) and turned down the Dodgers to return for his senior season. The same issues repeated as a senior and he slid to the fourth round.

Since signing he's looked more like first-round talent he'd showed earlier in his Louisville career, but the durability he's always shown deserted him in 2017. The Tigers shut him down with elbow soreness and say he's recovered well without surgery and expect him to be ready for 2018. Before he went on the DL, Funkhouser proved he could beat hitters with his 92-96 mph fastball that shows quality life. He uses his slider too much, but it is a plus pitch at its best and he has a fringy bigger curveball that works as a surprise early-count change of pace. His changeup is unlikely to ever be a weapon, but it can be average as it has enough separation and his fastball is good enough that hitters can't wait for the change.

Funkhouser's control is much better than it was late in his college career and he shows average command when he's really locked in. He should head back to Lakeland, but a midseason promotion could be in the offing if he performs as he has so far.

Year	Club (League)	Class	W	L	ERA	G	GS	CG	SV	IP	H	HR	BB	SO	K/9	WHIP	AVG
2016	Connecticut (NYP)	SS	0	2	2.65	13	13	0	0	37	34	0	8	34	8.2	1.13	.246
2017	West Michigan (MWL)	LoA	4	1	3.16	7	7	0	0	31	30	3	13	49	14.1	1.37	.254
	Lakeland (FSL)	HiA	1	1	1.72	5	5	1	0	31	23	1	6	34	9.8	0.93	.205
Minor League Totals			5	4	2.52	25	25	1	0	100	87	4	27	117	10.5	1.14	.236

12 SPENCER TURNBULL, RHP

BA GRADE
50 Risk: High

Born: Sept. 18, 1992. **B-T:** R-R. **Ht.:** 6-3. **Wt.:** 215. **Drafted:** Alabama, 2014 (2nd round). **Signed by:** Bryson Barber.

A workhorse at Alabama, Turnbull has not gotten the chance to serve a similar role in pro ball because of a variety of maladies. He's averaged less than 100 innings per year in his three pro seasons. After shoulder problems cost him significant time in 2016, Turnbull missed time in 2017 with elbow soreness. None of these injuries has required surgery.

When he's been on the mound, he's shown quality stuff with a 92-96 mph heavy fastball, an average high-80s power slider that has modest depth and a sporadic but promising 11-to-5 curveball that is at least average at its best. He can locate a get-me-over curve in early counts and also has a harder curve to try to finish off a batter. He could use his fringe-average changeup a little more often. Turnbull shows some ability to manipulate his fastball, as he can cut it in addition to sinking it.

Turnbull's command needs further improvement as he is wild in and out of the zone and nibbles a little too much. Turnbull has the stuff to be a back-end starter with a fallback option as a reliever with a blistering fastball. He'll head back to Double-A Erie in 2018 needing to prove he can stay healthy and further refine his command.

Year	Club (League)	Class	W	L	ERA	G	GS	CG	SV	IP	H	HR	BB	SO	K/9	WHIP	AVG
2015	West Michigan (MWL)	LoA	11	3	3.01	22	22	1	0	117	106	0	52	106	8.2	1.35	.242
2016	Tigers East (GCL)	R	0	0	7.36	2	2	0	0	4	4	2	1	5	12.3	1.36	.267
	Tigers West (GCL)	R	0	1	3.38	4	4	0	0	11	3	0	5	7	5.9	0.75	.091
	Lakeland (FSL)	HiA	1	1	3.00	6	6	0	0	30	24	1	10	27	8.1	1.13	.216
2017	Tigers West (GCL)	R	0	0	4.00	2	2	0	0	9	8	0	2	16	16.0	1.11	.242
	Lakeland (FSL)	HiA	7	3	3.05	15	15	0	0	83	68	3	25	64	7.0	1.13	.230
	Erie (EL)	AA	0	3	6.20	4	4	0	0	20	22	1	8	22	9.7	1.48	.272
Minor League Totals			19	13	3.46	67	67	1	0	304	268	9	118	270	8.0	1.27	.237

13 SAM McMILLAN, C

BA GRADE 50 Risk: High

Born: Dec. 1, 1998. **B-T:** R-R. **Ht.:** 6-1. **Wt.:** 195. **Drafted:** HS—Live Oak, Fla., 2017 (5th round). **Signed by:** R.J. Burress.

McMillan battled some very ill-timed tendinitis in his throwing shoulder during his senior season at Live Oak, Fla.'s Suwannee High. That led a number of teams to decide it would be better to let him head to Florida, but the Tigers stayed on him. They went far beyond slot value in the fifth round to sign him for $1 million.

McMillan responded by putting together one of the best seasons in the Gulf Coast League, although he fell a few plate appearances short of qualifying for league leaderboards. McMillan's approach was more advanced than the pitchers he faced. He spit at sliders off the plate, laughed at buried curveballs and connected consistently when pitchers did throw in the zone. He was equally happy to slap the ball around the field as he was to take a walk. Scouts are confident in McMillan's potentially plus hit tool, but they are much less confident in his ability to drive the ball. He needs to add strength as his power potential is well below-average. McMillan was considered more polished defensively than offensively in high school. He's an advanced receiver for his age and although his arm was only average in his pro debut, it could play up in the future as he puts the tendinitis in the rear-view mirror.

The Tigers' West Michigan manager in 2018 will be Lance Parrish, who would be a perfect mentor for the young catcher.

Year	Club (League)	Class	AVG	G	AB	R	H	2B	3B	HR	RBI	BB	SO	SB	CS	OBP	SLG
2017	Tigers West (GCL)	R	.288	37	111	24	32	5	1	3	25	19	17	1	1	.441	.432
Minor League Totals			.288	37	111	24	32	5	1	3	25	19	17	1	1	.441	.432

14 MIKE GERBER, OF

BA GRADE 45 Risk: Medium

Born: July 8, 1992. **B-T:** L-R. **Ht.:** 6-0. **Wt.:** 190. **Drafted:** Creighton, 2014 (15th round). **Signed by:** Marty Miller.

A four-year starter at Creighton, Gerber has proven an excellent 15th-round senior sign for the Tigers. He led the organization with a .304 batting average and was on the verge of a promotion to Triple-A when an oblique strain forced him to the DL for six weeks.

Gerber did make it up to Toledo for the final week of the season. Gerber is one of the purest hitters in the system. His bat comes through the strike zone on a level path, which leads to a lot of contact and more line drives than long flies. He's a plus hitter with 15-20 home run potential. If he were a little better in center field, he would profile as an everyday regular. But as a fringe-average defender in center, he is more likely to end up as a productive fourth outfielder who can play all three outfield spots with an above-average arm. He's an average runner. The Tigers added him to the 40-man roster to protect him from the Rule 5 draft.

Gerber will head to Toledo to start 2018, but he's a viable call-up option if the Tigers need an outfielder.

Year	Club (League)	Class	AVG	G	AB	R	H	2B	3B	HR	RBI	BB	SO	SB	CS	OBP	SLG
2015	West Michigan (MWL)	LoA	.292	135	513	74	150	31	10	13	76	49	97	16	4	.355	.468
2016	Lakeland (FSL)	HiA	.282	91	351	52	99	22	3	14	60	32	111	2	3	.343	.481
	Erie (EL)	AA	.261	41	153	17	40	8	3	4	20	20	41	6	0	.349	.431
2017	Lakeland (FSL)	HiA	.444	5	18	3	8	2	1	0	2	2	7	0	0	.500	.667
	Erie (EL)	AA	.289	92	350	62	101	22	2	13	45	39	85	10	6	.360	.474
	Toledo (IL)	AAA	.412	4	17	4	7	2	0	1	3	1	6	0	0	.444	.706
Minor League Totals			.290	433	1650	256	479	106	23	52	248	164	398	43	17	.357	.477

15 JOE JIMENEZ, RHP

BA GRADE

45 Risk: Medium

Born: Jan. 17, 1995. **B-T:** R-R. **Ht.:** 6-3. **Wt.:** 225. **Signed:** HS—Gurabo, P.R., 2013 (NDFA). **Signed by:** Rolando Casanova/German Geigel.

Jimenez was an effective reliever for Puerto Rico in the World Baseball Classic and he followed that up by making his big league debut just a week into the season. He went up and down between Triple-A and the major leagues with the exception of May when he went on the disabled list with a back injury.

Jimenez dominated with Triple-A Toledo largely on the basis of his fastball, but every time he returned to Detroit he found his wildness and lack of a consistent slider led to too many big innings. Jimenez's 94-96 mph plus fastball is effective but not good enough unless his inconsistent slider improves. Jimenez's slider flashes above-average, but too often it flattens out. He also has to prove it's more than just a chase pitch, because big league hitters laid off of it and waited for him to come back to the fastball. He will mix in a fringy changeup exclusively against lefthanded hitters. Jimenez's control is also below-average.

If Jimenez improves his control or refines his slider, he has the stuff to be a seventh/eighth-inning reliever, but he can't succeed long-term without doing one of the two. He's worked to get into better shape to prepare for a pivotal 2018 season.

Year	Club (League)	Class	W	L	ERA	G	GS	CG	SV	IP	H	HR	BB	SO	K/9	WHIP	AVG
2015	West Michigan (MWL)	LoA	5	1	1.47	40	0	0	17	43	23	2	11	61	12.8	0.79	.153
2016	Lakeland (FSL)	HiA	0	0	0.00	17	0	0	10	17	5	0	5	28	14.5	0.58	.089
	Erie (EL)	AA	3	2	2.18	21	0	0	12	21	12	0	8	34	14.8	0.97	.171
	Toledo (IL)	AAA	0	1	2.30	17	0	0	8	16	9	1	4	16	9.2	0.83	.164
2017	Lakeland (FSL)	HiA	0	0	0.00	1	1	0	0	1	1	0	0	1	9.0	1.00	.200
	Toledo (IL)	AAA	1	1	1.44	26	0	0	4	25	19	1	12	36	13.0	1.24	.214
	Detroit (AL)	MAJ	0	2	12.32	24	0	0	0	19	31	4	9	17	8.1	2.11	.356
Major League Totals			0	2	12.32	24	0	0	0	19	31	4	9	17	8.1	2.11	.356
Minor League Totals			15	7	1.56	153	1	0	56	167	100	5	52	241	13.0	0.91	.171

16 BRYAN GARCIA, RHP

BA GRADE

45 Risk: High

Born: April 19, 1995. **B-T:** R-R. **Ht.:** 6-1. **Wt.:** 205. **Drafted:** Miami, 2016 (6th round). **Signed by:** Nick Avila.

Garcia left his mark on the Miami record book, setting a school record and tying the ACC record with 43 saves. Some scouts saw him as a potential starter thanks to his three-pitch mix, but the Tigers liked his makeup and moxie in a lock-down back-of-the-bullpen role.

Garcia has lived up to those expectations by leaping through four minor league levels in his first full pro season. Garcia's delivery is a little long in the back and he finished into a stiff front leg, but he has shown an ability to repeat it. Garcia's 92-96 mph fastball is an effective above-average pitch, but it's his plus slider that makes hitters sweat. His changeup dives away from bats with late fade, giving him three average or better pitches.

Garcia seems to thrive on pressure. Triple-A was his first taste of anything less than dominance. He'll head back there to start 2018, but he could make it to Detroit this year.

Year	Club (League)	Class	W	L	ERA	G	GS	CG	SV	IP	H	HR	BB	SO	K/9	WHIP	AVG
2016	Connecticut (NYP)	SS	0	1	1.00	16	0	0	6	18	13	1	3	21	10.5	0.89	.194
	West Michigan (MWL)	LoA	0	1	40.50	1	0	0	0	1	3	0	0	1	13.5	4.50	.600
2017	West Michigan (MWL)	LoA	1	2	3.14	14	0	0	9	14	12	0	4	27	17.0	1.12	.218
	Lakeland (FSL)	HiA	2	0	0.00	7	0	0	9	7	0	2	15	15.6	1.04	.233
	Erie (EL)	AA	1	1	0.96	17	0	0	8	19	7	1	8	24	11.6	0.80	.115
	Toledo (IL)	AAA	1	0	4.05	14	0	0	0	13	10	1	8	12	8.1	1.35	.213
Minor League Totals			5	5	2.20	69	0	0	23	74	52	3	25	100	12.2	1.05	.196

17 JOSE KING, SS

BA GRADE

50 Risk: Extreme

Born: Jan. 16, 1999. **B-T:** L-R. **Ht.:** 6-0. **Wt.:** 160. **Signed:** Dominican Republic, 2015. **Signed by:** Junior Noboa (Diamondbacks).

One of the new trends in trades is the quest to dig deeper and deeper into farm system to find a gem that a team is willing to include in a deal. That explains why the Tigers asked for King on the basis of what he showed in less than 75 pro games. One of Baseball America's Top 20 Dominican Summer League prospects from 2016, he was one of three players the Tigers acquired in the trade that sent J.D. Martinez to the Diamondbacks.

King is skinny and physically undeveloped at this point and he knows it, which is why he slaps the ball and relies on his near top-of-the-scale speed. His swing has some length and modest bat control, but it's realistic to think that he'll improve it if he gets stronger. He doesn't have the strength yet to really manipulate the barrel and his plate discipline needs to improve. King has an average arm but he does need a longer release to generate that velocity, which leads a number of evaluators to say that in the long run he'll have to slide to second base or center field.

If he stays rail thin, King could end up as speedy, versatile utility infielder/outfielder able to play shortstop in a pinch. But if he fills out, he could end up as a top-of-the order table-setter with a plus hit tool and well below-average power.

Year	Club (League)	Class	AVG	G	AB	R	H	2B	3B	HR	RBI	BB	SO	SB	CS	OBP	SLG
2016	D-backs (DSL)	R	.350	61	240	51	84	7	4	0	27	21	36	21	3	.402	.413
2017	Diamondbacks (AZL)	R	.261	13	46	7	12	0	2	0	9	3	20	2	2	.333	.348
	Tigers West (GCL)	R	.321	28	112	18	36	3	1	0	6	6	29	8	9	.356	.366
Minor League Totals			.332	102	398	76	132	10	7	0	42	30	85	31	14	.382	.392

18 GERSON MORENO, RHP

BA GRADE
45 Risk: High

Born: Sept. 10, 1995. **B-T:** R-R. **Ht.:** 6-0. **Wt.:** 175. **Signed:** Dominican Republic, 2012. **Signed by:** Carlos Santana/Ramon Perez.

In a system that has plenty of high-velocity bullpen arms, Moreno has the best. Moreno sits in the high 90s and can get to 100 mph regularly. That velocity comes out of his hand easily with only modest effort. He can drive that fastball down in the zone with good plane or elevate it up in the zone.

After throwing a curveball earlier in his career, he's adopted a slider that has made steady improvement. It's fringe-average right now, but with the quality of his plus-plus fastball, if he can even get it to average it will be good enough. He has a below-average changeup to keep lefties honest, but he doesn't always maintain his arm speed with it so the deception is lacking. Moreno lands on a stiff front side in his delivery and finishes with some recoil. That helps explain why his control is well below-average. When Moreno throws strikes, he succeeds, but too often he is working from behind in the count.

Even with a less-than-ideal delivery, Moreno repeats it consistently enough to give hope that he can develop into a useful power reliever as he misses plenty of bats. But he'll get to that ceiling only with significant improvements.

Year	Club (League)	Class	W	L	ERA	G	GS	CG	SV	IP	H	HR	BB	SO	K/9	WHIP	AVG
2015	Connecticut (NYP)	SS	2	5	3.86	15	0	0	2	28	28	0	12	29	9.3	1.43	.259
	West Michigan (MWL)	LoA	0	0	0.00	5	0	0	1	9	3	0	3	9	8.7	0.64	.107
2016	West Michigan (MWL)	LoA	1	1	1.08	25	0	0	11	25	19	0	8	27	9.7	1.08	.209
	Lakeland (FSL)	HiA	0	3	6.93	21	0	0	3	25	22	4	20	27	9.9	1.70	.232
2017	Lakeland (FSL)	HiA	1	0	2.01	21	0	0	8	22	19	1	8	30	12.1	1.21	.226
	Erie (EL)	AA	0	3	6.43	20	0	0	0	28	23	4	17	36	11.6	1.43	.221
Minor League Totals			7	14	3.71	134	6	0	26	216	189	9	106	215	9.0	1.37	.234

19 ANTHONY CASTRO, RHP

BA GRADE
45 Risk: High

Born: April 13, 1995. **B-T:** R-R. **Ht.:** 6-2. **Wt.:** 165. **Signed:** Venezuela, 2011. **Signed by:** Oscar Garcia/Pedro Chavez.

Castro has been a slow developing prospect as he spent two years in the now-defunct Venezuelan Summer League and missed all of 2015 recovering from Tommy John surgery. He didn't make it to full-season ball until this year, but he showed promising stuff and some feel pitching for low Class A West Michigan.

There's an impressive fluidity to Castro's delivery as one part flows smoothly into the next. At his best, Castro has a 92-96 mph fastball with plenty of life. It shows cut and tail, and he can work it to both sides of the plate. He also has a hard curveball that has a chance to be at least above-average. There are some evaluators who see it as a future plus pitch.

Castro was left unprotected in the Rule 5 draft and went unpicked because he's still so far away. But he has the building blocks of a future back-end starter or useful reliever.

Year	Club (League)	Class	W	L	ERA	G	GS	CG	SV	IP	H	HR	BB	SO	K/9	WHIP	AVG
2015	Did not play—Injured																
2016	Tigers West (GCL)	R	3	3	4.26	11	10	0	0	51	52	0	16	54	9.6	1.34	.272
2017	West Michigan (MWL)	LoA	10	6	2.49	21	21	1	0	108	91	4	35	95	7.9	1.16	.226
Minor League Totals			22	16	3.24	71	67	1	0	328	281	9	128	300	8.2	1.25	.233

20 WILKEL HERNANDEZ, RHP

BA GRADE
50 Risk: Extreme

Born: April 13, 1999. **B-T:** R-R. **Ht.:** 6-3. **Wt.:** 180. **Signed:** Venezuela, 2015.
Signed by: Marlo Zerpa/Marlon Urdaneta (Angels).

The Tigers' rebuild hit full speed when Justin Verlander was dealt to the Astros. That helped make further decisions like trading away Ian Kinsler easier to make and Hernandez is a key part of that trade's return.

Hernandez, who signed as a 16-year-old for $125,000, put on about 20 pounds from the 2016 season, and the added weight and strength was reflected in his fastball velocity, which sat 93 mph with good movement and touched 96 mph in the Rookie-level Arizona League in 2017. Hernandez has a good feel for his changeup, which he can throw to lefthanded and righthanded batters as an average pitch. He has a nice, loose arm and impressed with his competitive nature and work ethic. Hernandez's primary focus coming out of his first full season in the U.S. is to improve his inconsistent curveball, which has good shape but is a little slow. The pitch, which Hernandez learned in the instructional league in 2017, was in the low 70s this season; it needs more arm speed and conviction.

It's too soon to determine whether Hernandez projects as a starter or a reliever. Hernandez doesn't turn 19 until after the start of the 2018 season, but may get a shot at full-season ball with low Class A West Michigan.

Year	Club (League)	Class	W	L	ERA	G	GS	CG	SV	IP	H	HR	BB	SO	K/9	WHIP	AVG
2016	Angels (DSL)	R	2	0	1.20	5	5	0	0	15	12	0	6	14	8.4	1.20	.231
2017	Angels (AZL)	R	3	1	2.61	11	7	0	0	41	23	1	20	42	9.1	1.04	.161
	Orem (PIO)	R	1	0	3.00	1	0	0	0	3	2	0	2	2	6.0	1.33	.222
Minor League Totals			6	1	2.28	17	12	0	0	59	37	1	28	58	8.8	1.10	.181

21 WLADIMIR PINTO, RHP

BA GRADE
50 Risk: Extreme

Born: Feb. 12, 1998. **B-T:** R-R. **Ht.:** 5-11. **Wt.:** 175. **Signed:** Venezuela, 2014.
Signed by: Delvis Pacheco.

A lat strain ruined Pinto's 2017 season. He had spent the first half of the year at extended spring training, but he dominated the New York-Penn League and earned a promotion to low Class A West Michigan after just eight excellent outings.

In his first appearance for West Michigan, he strained a lat muscle and was shut down for the rest of the season. Scouts who saw one of those rare Pinto appearances came away very impressed. He overpowered New York-Penn League hitters by working arm-side and glove-side with an overwhelming plus-plus 94-99 mph fastball. He has a slider that is already a 40-45 pitch on the 20-to-80 scouting scale because of his arm speed. Pinto's command is what's most notable. His fastball gets plenty of run but he still managed to locate it consistently. He progressed remarkably. Two years earlier, he walked more than a batter an inning and in his nine appearances in 2017, he didn't walk a batter and was rarely behind in counts. Pinto has to stay healthy and improve his breaking ball, but he has the stuff to finish off games one day. He's ready to head back to low Class A West Michigan.

With the friendly pitching environment of West Michigan and his stuff, he could earn a lot more attention in 2018.

Year	Club (League)	Class	W	L	ERA	G	GS	CG	SV	IP	H	HR	BB	SO	K/9	WHIP	AVG
2015	Tigers (VSL)	R	2	1	3.90	16	0	0	1	28	16	0	28	24	7.8	1.59	.167
2016	Tigers East (GCL)	R	1	1	2.66	16	0	0	1	24	11	0	10	32	12.2	0.89	.134
2017	Connecticut (NYP)	SS	1	0	0.00	8	0	0	4	10	2	0	0	18	16.8	0.21	.065
	West Michigan (MWL)	LoA	0	0	0.00	1	0	0	0	0	1	0	0	0	0.0	3.00	.500
Minor League Totals			4	2	2.79	41	0	0	6	61	30	0	38	74	10.9	1.11	.142

22 GRAYSON GREINER, C

BA GRADE
40 Risk: Medium

Born: Oct. 11, 1992. **B-T:** R-R. **Ht.:** 6-6. **Wt.:** 220. **Drafted:** South Carolina, 2014 (3rd round). **Signed by:** Grant Brittain.

Greiner is the biggest catcher in baseball. He's officially listed at 6-foot-6, which has long been considered by many to be too tall for a catcher—no one that height has ever had significant big league career as a catcher. Greiner has a good chance be the first.

Greiner is unlikely to ever be a big league regular, but he's also highly likely to have some sort of big league career as a catcher with some clear limitations. Despite his size, he's actually an average receiver thanks to excellent flexibility. His above-average arm plays as well, as he's long been able to slow down running games—he threw out 37 percent of base stealers in 2017. Greiner has a decent understanding of his strike zone, but it's a big zone that he struggles to fully cover. Also, he too often lets pitchers get ahead of him, and his approach isn't well suited for defensive two-strike swings.

When Greiner connects, he has average power, but he's a below-average hitter who will struggle to square balls up consistently. As one might expect, he's a below-average runner who goes base to base.

Year	Club (League)	Class	AVG	G	AB	R	H	2B	3B	HR	RBI	BB	SO	SB	CS	OBP	SLG
2015	Lakeland (FSL)	HiA	.183	89	312	24	57	12	0	3	21	27	90	0	0	.254	.250
2016	Lakeland (FSL)	HiA	.312	31	109	14	34	6	0	0	12	12	26	0	0	.385	.367
	Erie (EL)	AA	.288	59	208	20	60	9	3	7	30	10	55	1	0	.320	.462
	Toledo (IL)	AAA	.000	1	4	0	0	0	0	0	0	0	2	0	0	.000	.000
2017	Erie (EL)	AA	.241	98	328	34	79	20	1	14	42	38	72	0	0	.323	.436
	Toledo (IL)	AAA	.143	5	14	0	2	1	0	0	2	2	3	0	0	.235	.214
Minor League Totals			.245	309	1065	103	261	53	4	26	123	100	266	1	0	.313	.376

23 JASON FOLEY, RHP

BA GRADE 50 Risk: Extreme

Born: Nov. 1, 1995. **B-T:** R-R. **Ht.:** 6-4. **Wt.:** 215. **Signed:** Sacred Heart (NDFA), 2016. **Signed by:** Jim Bretz.

After impressing in the summer league Northeast Collegiate Baseball League in 2015, Foley struggled early and late in his junior season at Sacred Heart, which pretty much ruined his draft chances. But Tigers area scout Jim Bretz kept an eye on him in his return to the NECBL, where he showed better stuff in a relief role. Since he went undrafted as an eligible junior, he was free to sign as an undrafted free agent without having to wait to be drafted again.

Foley's stuff was even better in his first full season with the Tigers, as he started sitting 97-98 and touching 100-101 mph with a hard, above-average slider and a changeup that played as average (in part because hitters had to gear up for the fastball). Unfortunately for Foley, he blew out his elbow in early July. He'll miss more than half of 2018 as he rehabs from Tommy John surgery.

There have been studies that show that pitchers velocity sometimes jumps right before a significant elbow injury, so there's no surety that Foley will be tickling triple-digits again when he returns, but even if it diminished a little, he still would be one of the best relief prospects in the Tigers' organization.

Year	Club (League)	Class	W	L	ERA	G	GS	CG	SV	IP	H	HR	BB	SO	K/9	WHIP	AVG
2016	Tigers West (GCL)	R	0	0	0.00	1	0	0	1	1	1	0	0	1	9.0	1.00	.250
	Connecticut (NYP)	SS	0	0	4.26	5	0	0	0	6	6	0	7	6	8.5	2.05	.240
2017	West Michigan (MWL)	LoA	3	1	1.55	18	0	0	5	29	20	0	5	36	11.2	0.86	.189
	Lakeland (FSL)	HiA	0	2	6.14	6	0	0	1	7	8	1	2	5	6.1	1.36	.267
Minor League Totals			3	3	2.68	30	0	0	7	44	35	1	14	48	9.9	1.12	.212

24 WENCEEL PEREZ, SS

BA GRADE 50 Risk: Extreme

Born: Oct. 30, 1999. **B-T:** B-R. **Ht.:** 5-11. **Wt.:** 170. **Signed:** Dominican Republic, 2016. **Signed by:** Ramon Perez/Carlos Santana.

After signing for $550,000, Perez was the most promising prospect in the Tigers' 2016 international class, and he's exceeded those expectations so far.

He has some of Jose King's burst and athleticism, but with a chance to be a strong hitter with more gap power. He's already made strength gains since signing with more to come, and he uses his legs now in his swing. He's a hit-first prospect with good hand-eye coordination, hands and strong wrists to spray the ball around the field as a switch-hitter with a plan at the plate. He walked more than he struck out in his Dominican Summer League debut. Defensively he has a very good chance to stick at shortstop with a quick first step, hands that work, advanced feel and an average arm. He played some second base as well in his pro debut, but that's for versatility more than anything else.

Perez gets too aggressive at times right now and makes too many errors, but that's something he should refine as he gets more innings.

Year	Club (League)	Class	AVG	G	AB	R	H	2B	3B	HR	RBI	BB	SO	SB	CS	OBP	SLG
2017	Tigers (DSL)	R	.314	61	226	31	71	8	1	0	22	27	21	16	6	.387	.358
Minor League Totals			.314	61	226	31	71	8	1	0	22	27	21	16	6	.387	.358

25 VICTOR REYES, OF

BA GRADE 40 Risk: Medium

Born: Oct. 5, 1994. **B-T:** B-R. **Ht.:** 6-3. **Wt.:** 170. **Signed:** Venezuela, 2011. **Signed by:** Rolando Petit (Braves).

The Tigers picked Reyes with the top pick in the 2017 Rule 5 draft. It wasn't the first time he had been moved. The D-backs acquired Reyes from the Braves prior to the 2015 season as the second half of a two-part deal that sent Trevor Cahill to Atlanta. Reyes has tremendous hand-eye coordination and bat-to-ball skills that rival just about anyone in the organization. But those attributes sometimes work against him as his ability to make contact can sometimes lead to him swinging at—and putting in play—pitches out of the zone.

Reyes' biggest knock remains his lack of power; in four years at full-season levels he has yet to post a slugging percentage north of .416. Coaches believe he can tap into more power if he can become a more disciplined hitter but it might never be a big part of his game. He's a good competitor and puts together tough at-bats. He's an above-average runner and thrower, making him a solid defender in right field, and though he hasn't played much center field some scouts believe he's at least playable there. With the Tigers, Reyes likely has to prove he can slide to center in a pinch to stick all season as a backup outfielder.

Long-term, he and Michael Gerber fill a similar role and Gerber has more power, so he's got to keep developing to stick around.

Year	Club (League)	Class	AVG	G	AB	R	H	2B	3B	HR	RBI	BB	SO	SB	CS	OBP	SLG
2015	Kane County (MWL)	LoA	.311	121	424	57	132	17	5	2	59	22	58	13	4	.343	.389
2016	Visalia (CAL)	HiA	.303	124	469	62	142	11	12	6	54	33	78	20	8	.349	.416
2017	Jackson (SL)	AA	.293	126	478	59	140	29	5	4	51	27	80	18	9	.333	.400
Minor League Totals			.298	561	2058	284	614	84	23	12	256	152	342	80	35	.347	.379

26 SERGIO ALCANTARA, SS

BA GRADE

40 Risk: Medium

Born: July 10, 1996. **B-T:** B-R. **Ht.:** 5-9. **Wt.:** 151. **Signed:** Dominican Republic, 2012. **Signed by:** Junior Noboa (Diamondbacks).

The Tigers loaded up on shortstops in the J.D. Martinez trade. Of the three shortstops Detroit acquired, Alcantara is the best defensively but also has the least offensive potential.

Alcantara is a true shortstop who could be an above-average defender with an above-average arm. Alcantara isn't a speedster—he turns in fringe-average run times, but he has a quick first step, good hands and enough range. Alcantara can handle shortstop defensively, but he'll have to prove he can hit enough for it to matter. He has a contact-oriented approach, but his swing doesn't really use his legs. Alcantara is not a home run threat at all, but he needs to get to the point where outfielders at least worry about him hitting it over their head.

As a defense-first, light-hitting shortstop, Alcantara could develop into a second-division regular, but he's more likely to end up in a utility infielder role.

Year	Club (League)	Class	AVG	G	AB	R	H	2B	3B	HR	RBI	BB	SO	SB	CS	OBP	SLG
2015	Kane County (MWL)	LoA	.113	20	71	5	8	1	0	0	5	4	17	1	0	.169	.127
	Hillsboro (NWL)	SS	.253	71	257	34	65	12	2	1	23	24	46	6	0	.314	.327
2016	Diamondbacks (AZL)	R	.345	7	29	9	10	1	1	0	2	4	2	2	0	.424	.448
	Hillsboro (NWL)	SS	.319	15	47	12	15	2	0	0	8	10	10	4	2	.441	.362
	Kane County (MWL)	LoA	.267	53	180	15	48	6	1	1	16	14	26	3	2	.313	.328
	Visalia (CAL)	HiA	.267	4	15	2	4	1	0	0	0	3	2	0	1	.421	.333
2017	Visalia (CAL)	HiA	.279	86	340	44	95	15	2	3	28	34	57	11	10	.344	.362
	Lakeland (FSL)	HiA	.230	35	126	18	29	4	1	0	7	14	23	4	3	.307	.278
Minor League Totals			.253	409	1500	218	380	58	11	6	123	199	281	42	24	.340	.319

27 TROY MONTGOMERY, OF

BA GRADE

40 Risk: Medium

Born: Aug. 13, 1994. **B-T:** L-L. **Ht.:** 5-10 **Wt.:** 185. **Drafted:** Ohio State, 2016 (8th round). **Signed by:** John Burden (Angels).

Part of the return in the December trade that sent Ian Kinsler to the Angels, Montgomery has long impressed with his feel for the game and his ability to get the most out of his somewhat limited tools.

Montgomery's season was cut short by injury in early August, so the Angels sent him to the Arizona Fall League to get some more at-bats. A three-year starter at Ohio State who signed for $150,000, Montgomery is a gap-to-gap hitter with a tick below-average raw power and well above-average speed, though he does have a tendency to get a little reckless on the bases—he has been thrown out in 12 of 40 steal attempts in two seasons. Montgomery provides above-average defense at all three outfield spots with a solid-average arm in both strength and accuracy.

Montgomery projects as an extra outfielder in the big leagues whose defense and on-base skills could earn him a respectable amount of playing time.

Year	Club (League)	Class	AVG	G	AB	R	H	2B	3B	HR	RBI	BB	SO	SB	CS	OBP	SLG
2016	Orem (PIO)	R	.341	26	88	16	30	3	2	4	17	15	20	10	4	.453	.557
	Burlington (MWL)	LoA	.261	38	142	15	37	7	2	3	13	16	30	3	2	.340	.401
2017	Burlington (MWL)	LoA	.256	15	43	6	11	1	1	2	4	12	4	2	1	.418	.465
	Inland Empire (CAL)	HiA	.282	65	262	41	74	10	7	6	31	26	58	9	5	.348	.443
	Mobile (SL)	AA	.235	20	68	15	16	2	0	0	3	10	12	4	0	.350	.265
Minor League Totals			.279	164	603	93	168	23	12	15	68	79	124	28	12	.368	.431

28 DEREK HILL, OF

BA GRADE

40 Risk: Medium

Born: Dec. 30, 1995. **B-T:** R-R. **Ht.:** 6-2. **Wt.:** 195. **Drafted:** HS—Elk Grove, Calif., 2014 (1st round). **Signed by:** Scott Cerny.

As the son of long-time player and now scout Orsino Hill, Derek has grown up around the game, but injuries and inconsistency at the plate have hampered the Tigers' 2014 first-round pick. Hill missed time in 2014 with a back injury, half of 2015 with a nagging quadriceps injury and then was shut down in August of 2016 with an elbow injury that required Tommy John surgery.

Hill is a plus-plus defender with plus-plus speed who is confident and aggressive at running down balls in the gaps. That speed also plays on the basepaths, but that aggression doesn't translate to the plate. Hill has enough bat speed and his hands work well, but too often his hips open up too soon and he pulls off pitches. He's gaining strength, but his swing isn't geared toward driving the ball. At this point, his most likely path to the big leagues is as a useful backup outfielder who can play all three spots.

Hill will need to be added to the 40-man roster after the 2018 season, so this is a big test for him as he heads to Lakeland.

Year	Club (League)	Class	AVG	G	AB	R	H	2B	3B	HR	RBI	BB	SO	SB	CS	OBP	SLG
2015	West Michigan (MWL)	LoA	.238	53	210	33	50	6	5	0	16	20	44	25	7	.305	.314
2016	West Michigan (MWL)	LoA	.266	93	384	66	102	17	6	1	31	24	105	35	6	.312	.349
2017	Tigers West (GCL)	R	.163	14	49	11	8	1	1	1	7	10	15	7	0	.300	.286
	West Michigan (MWL)	LoA	.285	35	144	28	41	8	6	1	21	16	38	12	5	.367	.444
	Lakeland (FSL)	HiA	.194	9	31	3	6	1	0	0	2	5	10	10	0	.324	.226
Minor League Totals			.245	251	991	161	243	36	21	5	91	93	257	100	20	.316	.339

29 AUSTIN SODDERS, LHP

BA GRADE

45 Risk: High

Born: April 29, 1995. **B-T:** L-L. **Ht.:** 6-4. **Wt.:** 210. **Drafted:** UC Riverside, 2016 (7th round). **Signed by:** Steve Pack.

Sodders' father Mike was Baseball America's first College Player of the Year in 1981 and a first-round pick of the Twins that same year. The younger Sodders has consistently impressed more with his knack for pitching than any plus pitch.

Sodders' path to the big leagues is as a back-of-the-rotation lefty who has a fringe-average fastball (88-92 mph), average changeup and a fringe-average but improving slider. All of them play up because of plus control and his ability to throw all the pitches at any point in the count. Sodders has dominated lower-level hitters and he keeps the ball in the ballpark, which is vital for a touch-and-feel lefty. His strikeout rate plummeted after his promotion to high Class A and he doesn't currently have a true out pitch.

The jump to Double-A is going to be a big test for him, much like teammate Tyler Alexander found out in 2017.

Year	Club (League)	Class	W	L	ERA	G	GS	CG	SV	IP	H	HR	BB	SO	K/9	WHIP	AVG
2016	Connecticut (NYP)	SS	0	3	2.29	13	13	0	0	39	35	2	5	33	7.6	1.02	.230
2017	West Michigan (MWL)	LoA	7	0	1.40	11	11	0	0	64	49	2	13	65	9.1	0.96	.217
	Lakeland (FSL)	HiA	4	5	2.17	12	12	1	0	75	55	0	17	57	6.9	0.96	.203
Minor League Totals			11	8	1.92	36	36	1	0	178	139	4	35	155	7.8	0.98	.214

30 SANDY BAEZ, RHP

BA GRADE

45 Risk: High

Born: November 25, 1993. **B-T:** R-R. **Ht.:** 6-2. **Wt.:** 180. **Signed:** Dominican Republic, 2011. **Signed by:** Carlos Santana/Ramon Perez/Miguel Garcia.

Baez had the frame to add weight and a decent mid-to-high 80s fastball when he signed for just under $50,000. Since then he's developed as hoped.

Baez's broad-shouldered frame now is near ideal as he has size and strength. His delivery finishes with a little bit of recoil, but he repeats well. As he's filled out, his fastball has turned into a 94-96 mph above-average pitch. But Baez's biggest weapon is a fosh changeup. Not many pitchers have been able to master the fosh, which is like a split-change but with a different grip. Baez has mastered it, and it has both excellent separation and late dive like a splitter. His slider is below-average and needs to get better.

Baez's two present above-average pitches and fringe-average control give him a path to the big league bullpen, but he'll need to improve the slider significantly if he wants to remain a starter long-term.

Year	Club (League)	Class	W	L	ERA	G	GS	CG	SV	IP	H	HR	BB	SO	K/9	WHIP	AVG
2015	Connecticut (NYP)	SS	3	4	4.13	14	14	0	0	65	73	4	22	52	7.2	1.45	.289
2016	West Michigan (MWL)	LoA	7	9	3.81	21	21	0	0	113	125	7	28	88	7.0	1.35	.283
2017	Lakeland (FSL)	HiA	6	7	3.86	17	17	0	0	89	88	7	24	92	9.3	1.26	.257
	Erie (EL)	AA	0	1	4.50	2	2	0	0	10	9	3	5	13	11.7	1.40	.237
Minor League Totals			25	27	3.65	90	85	1	1	438	441	25	123	385	7.9	1.29	.262

Houston Astros

BY J.J. COOPER

The plan worked, right on schedule.

Ever since the day Jeff Luhnow arrived in Houston, he and his staff kept their eyes on a long-term goal of building a regular championship contender. Nothing else was allowed to interfere with that goal.

Putting together some of the worst teams of the 21st century in the early stages of the rebuild were a price the front office was willing to pay. Passing on signing No. 1 pick Brady Aiken because of concerns about his elbow brought plenty of criticism, but the Astros were willing to weather it.

When Houston arrived maybe a year early with a 2015 playoff spot, the front office didn't speed  up the process. The team sorted through homegrown options to fill its holes during a disappointing 2016 season. Only when those options failed did the Astros go out and acquire veterans through trades and free agency to bolster the roster for 2017.

All that planning paid off with a 2017 season that proved to be nearly perfect. Bolstered by acquisitions like Brian McCann and Josh Reddick, Houston ran away with the AL West crown from just after Opening Day. They had extended a double-digit lead in the division before June arrived. That lead never dipped below 10 games the rest of the season.

With a playoff spot assured, Houston appeared to be relatively comfortable standing pat with their lineup and rotation. The only move at the July 31 trade deadline was a modest one to add Francisco Liriano to the bullpen. But after the team struggled in August, Luhnow proved willing to spend big to acquire a difference maker. Acquired in the final seconds before the waiver-deadline on Aug. 31, righthander Justin Verlander cost three significant prospects (Franklin Perez, Jake Rogers and Daz Cameron). He was worth the price. Verlander proved to be just what Houston needed in the playoffs. With an ALCS and a World Series that went to seven games, it's fair to argue that without Verlander, Houston would not have won its first World Series title.

After an offseason of celebrations, Houston is situated to defend its crown. Houston managed to hold onto three of its top four prospects when making its trades. Forrest Whitley, Kyle Tucker and Yordan Alvarez give the team a trio of potential impact players who are not that far from Houston. The Astros' depth of hard-throwing righthanders is still impressive even after trading away Perez, Albert Abreu and Jorge Guzman in recent deals.

Houston's window of contention is still wide open. This team will start to get more expensive,

Jose Altuve weathered many losing seasons but emerged as a World Series champion.

PROJECTED 2021 LINEUP

Catcher	Garrett Stubbs (26)
First Base	Yordan Alvarez (24)
Second Base	Jose Altuve (31)
Third Base	Alex Bregman (27)
Shortstop	Carlos Correa (26)
Left Field	Derek Fisher (27)
Center Field	George Springer (31)
Right Field	Kyle Tucker (24)
No. 1 Starter	Forrest Whitley (23)
No. 2 Starter	Lance McCullers Jr. (27)
No. 3 Starter	Justin Verlander (38)
No. 4 Starter	Dallas Keuchel (33)
No. 5 Starter	J.B. Bukauskas (24)
Closer	Jorge Alcala (25)

but the big bills will not come due until 2020. George Springer is just reaching arbitration for the first time. Carlos Correa and Alex Bregman have not even reached arbitration yet. MVP Jose Altuve is under contract for two more years for a combined $13 million, which makes him one of the best bargains in sports. And while Justin Verlander will make $56 million combined over the next two seasons, his arrival gives the team a needed ace.

With a still solid farm system and a young core of big league stars, The Astros head into 2018 looking to turn a title into a dynasty. This team will already be remembered forever in Houston. A couple more titles would make them similarly remembered around the game.

DEPTH CHART

HOUSTON ASTROS

TOP 2018 ROOKIE: Forrest Whitley, RHP. He won't begin the season in the majors, but Whitley is the rare pitcher who could be big league ready as a 20-year-old.

BREAKOUT PROSPECT: Gilberto Celestino, OF. The Astros are suddenly thin at center field, but Celestino's well-rounded skill set gives him a chance to be a future regular.

SLEEPER: Luis Garcia, RHP. He has already added velocity since he signed. He's yet to pitch in the U.S., but he could quickly become a name to know.

SOURCE OF TOP 30 TALENT

Homegrown	26	**Acquired**	**4**
College	9	Trade	4
Junior college	2	Rule 5 draft	0
High school	4	Independent league	0
Nondrafted free agent	0	Free agent/waivers	0
International	12		

LF
Yordan Alvarez (3)
Ronnie Dawson (20)
J.J. Matijevic (25)
Jason Martin (26)
Drew Ferguson
Jon Kemmer
Carmen Benedetti

CF
Gilberto Celestino (19)
Ramiro Rodriguez
Jake Meyers

RF

Kyle Tucker (2)
Myles Straw (17)
Carlos Machado
Bryan de la Cruz
Corey Julks

3B
Colin Moran (9)
J.D. Davis (11)
Joe Perez (14)

SS
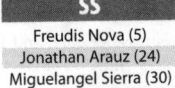
Freudis Nova (5)
Jonathan Arauz (24)
Miguelangel Sierra (30)

2B
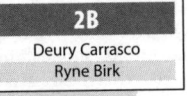
Deury Carrasco
Ryne Birk

1B
A.J. Reed (22)
Jake Adams
Abraham Toro-Hernandez

C
Garrett Stubbs (18)
Mike Papierski
Nathan Perry
Jamie Ritchie

LHP

LHSP	LHRP
Cionel Perez (12)	Framber Valdez (13)
Patrick Sandoval	Anthony Gose
	Brady Rodgers
	Brett Adcock

RHP

RHSP	RHRP
Forrest Whitley (1)	Jorge Alcala (8)
J.B. Bukauskas (4)	Corbin Martin (16)
Hector Perez (6)	Dean Deetz (21)
Jairo Solis (7)	Riley Ferrell (27)
David Paulino (10)	Jandel Gustave (28)
Rogelio Armenteros (15)	Elian Rodriguez (29)
Cristian Javier (23)	Trent Thornton
Heitor Tokar	Erasmo Pinales
Jose Betances	Luis Garcia
	Brandon Bielak
	Tyler Ivey
	Kyle Serrano
	Nick Hernandez

DRAFT ANALYSIS

2017

BEST PURE HITTER: OF J.J. Matijevic (2s) blossomed in his junior year at Arizona, hitting .383 after hitting .376 the summer before in the Cape Cod League. His emergence came after he simplified his swing, taking away a big leg kick and emphasizing an uphill bat path to develop loft. He impressed Astros scouts with his bat-to-ball skills and developing power. He got off to a slow start as a pro, but he has the potential to be a plus hitter.

BEST POWER HITTER: 1B Jake Adams (6) hit 10 home runs for short-season Tri-City after hitting 29 with Iowa last spring. Adams has 70 raw power on the 20-to-80 scouting scale, but he didn't alleviate the concerns about his athleticism by hitting .170 in his pro debut.

FASTEST RUNNER: The Astros valued bats over speed and athleticism, but OF Jake Meyers (13) is a plus runner and an efficient basestealer whose speed carries over to center field.

BEST DEFENSIVE PLAYER: C Mike Papierski (9) impressed Astros coaches with his ability to frame pitches, receive with a soft left hand and handle pitchers. He also has a solid arm.

BEST FASTBALL: RHP Kyle Serrano (10) showed a 97-98 mph fastball in short stints, although his command and control need refinement. RHP Corbin Martin (2) does a better job of locating his 90-96 mph fastball.

BEST SECONDARY PITCH: RHP J.B. Bukauskas (1) had arguably the best breaking ball in this draft, as his slider generates consistent 70 grades and was effective against lefties and righthanded hitters.

BEST PRO DEBUT: RHP Brandon Bielak (11) went 1-0, 0.92 as a piggyback starter with short-season Tri-City, striking out 37 and walking only four batters in 29.2 innings. He's a strong-bodied 6-foot-1, 210-pounder with three average pitches.

BEST ATHLETE: 3B Joe Perez (2) was a legitimate two-way star in high school, and many teams preferred him on the mound than at the plate. He had Tommy John surgery prior to the draft. OF Corey Julks (8) is a 6-foot, 200-pound outfielder with average speed, above-average raw power and present strength.

MOST INTRIGUING BACKGROUND: LHP Cole Watts (31) went to San Diego State as a student, but after two years, he opted to give baseball another try. He transferred to Skyline (Calif.) JC and led the conference in strikeout rate while showing a 92 mph fastball and funk and deception. Serrano played for his father Dave at Tennessee; the elder Serrano is now a pitching coach at West Virginia.

CLOSEST TO THE MAJORS: Bukauskas' collegiate experience and fastball/slider combo should allow him to make a quick trip through the minors.

BEST LATE-ROUND PICK: Senior-sign INF Josh Rojas (26) showed an ability to play third base, shortstop and second base while showing surprising pop. The Astros were impressed enough to give him a three-game emergency stint in Triple-A in his draft year.

THE ONE WHO GOT AWAY: Maryland OF Marty Costes (25) was going to be a difficult signing as an eligible sophomore, but he has a good, strong body with solid power. He hit .322 with 13 home runs at Maryland last spring.

—J.J. COOPER

TOP DRAFT PICKS OF THE DECADE

Year	Player, Pos.	2017 Org
2008	Jason Castro, C	Twins
2009	Jio Mier, SS	Mets
2010	Mike Foltynewicz, RHP	Braves
2011	George Springer, OF	Astros
2012	Carlos Correa, SS	Astros
2013	Mark Appel, RHP	Phillies
2014	*Brady Aiken, LHP	Indians
2015	Alex Bregman, SS	Astros
2016	Forrest Whitley, RHP	Astros
2017	J.B. Bukauskas, RHP	Astros

* Did not sign

2016

Prep RHP Forrest Whitley (1) exploded in his first full season, establishing himself as one of the top pitching prospects in the game. OF Ronnie Dawson (2) is off to a solid start and C Jake Rogers (3) was used in the Justin Verlander trade.

GRADE: B

2015

The Astros capatalized on having two top-five picks. 3B Alex Bregman (1) has become a fixture in Houston. OF Kyle Tucker (1) finished 2017 in Double-A. OF Daz Cameron (1s) and RHP Tom Eshelman (2) were used in key trades.

GRADE: A+

2014

Despite not signing No. 1 overall pick LHP Brady Aiken (1) and the inconsistency of 1B A.J. Reed (2), the Astros landed a solid class. Their top four signees have all reached the big leagues. OF Derek Fisher (1s) looks to be the best of the crop.

GRADE: B

1 FORREST WHITLEY, RHP

Born: Sept. 15, 1997. **B-T:** R-R. **Ht.:** 6-7. **Wt.:** 240.
Drafted: HS—San Antonio, 2016 (1st round).
Signed by: Noel Gonzales.

DAN ARNOLD

As a thick-bodied tall righthander, Whitley was considered one of the better prep prospects in the 2016 draft class. But during his senior season, he wowed scouts after he melted away 20-to-30 pounds, turning himself into a more athletic righthander with still excellent stuff. By the end of his senior year, he was touching 97 and breaking off 90 mph sliders. In his first full pro season, Whitley dominated three levels in 2017 and became only the fifth high school first round pick to pitch in Double-A in his first full season this century. The previous four were Chad Billingsley, Zack Greinke, Clayton Kershaw and Dylan Bundy.

There are few young pitchers as advanced as Whitley and few who can match the quality of his stuff. Whitley came into 2017 with four quality pitches and left it with five. All his pitches are at least average and a trio are already plus. Pitching from an over-the-top arm slot that emphasizes the downhill plane on his fastball, Whitley can blow hitters away with a 92-97 mph fastball. But he actually is even more comfortable toying with batters with his varied assortment of other pitches as he commands his breaking balls better than his fastball at this point in his career. His 84-87 mph plus slider has modest depth, but good tilt as it dances away from the bat-head as it nears the plate. His 78-82 mph curveball is also plus with a big 12-to-6 break. At times his changeup will also show otherworldly movement, as it dives down and away from lefthanders bats. And in 2017 he refined a 90-92 mph cutter that some scouts throw a plus grade on. With so many pitches, Whitley can stick one or two in his back pocket early in the game, then break them out the second time through the order. One of the few complaints raised is that he's a slow worker.

Scouts are understandably reticent to project almost anyone as a future No. 1 starter. But Whitley has a chance to be an ace with dominant stuff and advanced feel and control. It would surprise no one to see Whitley make his MLB debut later this season. Whitley doesn't require much projection. He's yet to throw even 100 innings in a season yet, so the Astros will likely be conservative in how much he's allowed to throw in 2018.

BA GRADE	SCOUTING GRADES
65 Risk: High	FB: 70. CB: 60. SL: 60. CHG: 55. CUT: 50. CTL: 55.

Projected future grades on 20-80 scouting scale

TOP PROSPECTS OF THE DECADE

Year	Player, Pos.	2017 Org
2008	J.R. Towles, C	Did not play
2009	Jason Castro, C	Twins
2010	Jason Castro, C	Twins
2011	Jordan Lyles, RHP	Padres
2012	Jonathan Singleton, 1B/OF	Astros
2013	Carlos Correa, SS	Astros
2014	Carlos Correa, SS	Astros
2015	Carlos Correa, SS	Astros
2016	A.J. Reed, 1B	Astros
2017	Francis Martes, RHP	Astros

BEST TOOLS

Best Pure Hitter	Kyle Tucker
Best Power Hitter	Yordan Alvarez
Fastest Baserunner	Myles Straw
Best Strike-Zone Discipline	Myles Straw
Best Athlete	Yordan Alvarez
Best Fastball	Jorge Alcala
Best Curveball	Framber Valdez
Best Slider	Forrest Whitley
Best Changeup	Forrest Whitley
Best Control	Rogelio Armenteros
Best Defensive Catcher	Garrett Stubbs
Best Defensive Infielder	Freudis Nova
Best Infield Arm	J.D. Davis
Best Defensive Outfielder	Gilberto Celestino
Best Outfield Arm	Myles Straw

Year	Club (League)	Class	W	L	ERA	G	GS	CG	SV	IP	H	HR	BB	SO	K/9	WHIP	AVG
2016	Astros (GCL)	R	1	1	7.36	4	2	0	0	7	8	0	3	13	16.0	1.50	.267
	Greeneville (APP)	R	0	1	3.18	4	4	0	0	11	11	0	3	13	10.3	1.24	.244
2017	Quad Cities (MWL)	LoA	2	3	2.91	12	10	0	0	46	42	2	21	67	13.0	1.36	.247
	Buies Creek (CAR)	HiA	3	1	3.16	7	6	0	0	31	28	2	9	50	14.4	1.18	.237
	Corpus Christi (TL)	AA	0	0	1.84	4	2	0	0	15	8	1	4	26	16.0	0.82	.157
Minor League Totals			6	6	3.16	31	24	0	0	111	97	5	40	169	13.7	1.23	.234

2 KYLE TUCKER, OF

Born: Jan. 17, 1997. **B-T:** L-R. **Ht.:** 6-4. **Wt.:** 189. **Drafted:** HS—Tampa, 2015 (1st round). **Signed by:** John Martin.

Baseball America's High School Player of the Year in 2015, Tucker broke his own brother (and ex-Astros outfielder) Preston's school home run record. In pro ball, he'd impressed with an advanced approach and hit tool in his first season and a half, but his power production took off in 2017, as he traded some additional strikeouts for a significant power increase.

Tucker's 25 home runs more than doubled his career total coming into the season. He wore down at the end of the season, hitting .196 in August and only .214 with no home runs in the Arizona Fall League. Tucker's swing has never been picture perfect. He begins his swing with the bat laid back over his shoulder, leading to a little bit of a sweepy beginning. He also has a tendency to drop his back knee in his swing at times, a la Adrian Beltre. But it's hard to argue with the results, as his excellent hand-eye coordination leads to ton of contact and as he's gotten stronger he's turned doubles into home runs. He makes consistently hard contact. Most young lefthanded hitters torch righties and struggle when they don't have the platoon advantages. Tucker is actually a better hitter against lefthanders, and a little too aggressive against righthanders who stay off the outer half. Tucker has played all three outfield spots for the Astros. Tucker isn't a true center fielder, but he has a chance to be fringe-average there while being above-average in the corners with an average arm that works in either spot. He's an average runner who has shown a knack for stealing bases, although it won't be a significant part of his game at the big league level.

Tucker's even-keeled approach turns off some scouts, who describe him as low energy. He has a half-season of Double-A experience under his belt before his 21st birthday so he may need a little more Double-A time, but a big league arrival by age 22 is a likelihood.

BA GRADE

60 Risk: Medium

HIT: 60. POW: 60.
SPD: 50. FLD: 55.
ARM: 50.

Year	Club (League)	Class	AVG	G	AB	R	H	2B	3B	HR	RBI	BB	SO	SB	CS	OBP	SLG
2015	Astros (GCL)	R	.208	33	120	19	25	3	2	2	13	9	14	4	2	.267	.317
	Greeneville (APP)	R	.286	30	112	11	32	9	0	1	20	7	15	14	2	.322	.393
2016	Quad Cities (MWL)	LoA	.276	101	373	43	103	19	5	6	56	40	75	31	9	.348	.402
	Lancaster (CAL)	HiA	.339	16	59	13	20	6	2	3	13	10	6	1	3	.435	.661
2017	Buies Creek (CAR)	HiA	.288	48	177	31	51	12	4	9	43	24	45	12	5	.379	.554
	Corpus Christi (TL)	AA	.265	72	287	39	76	21	1	16	47	22	64	8	4	.325	.512
Minor League Totals			.272	300	1128	156	307	70	14	37	192	112	219	70	25	.341	.457

3 YORDAN ALVAREZ, 1B/OF

Born: June 27, 1997. **B-T:** L-L. **Ht.:** 6-5. **Wt.:** 225. **Signed:** Cuba, 2016. **Signed by:** Ismael Cruz/Mike Tosar (Dodgers).

The Dodgers and Astros battled to sign Alvarez when he came to the States out of Cuba. The Dodgers won that battle, signing Alvarez on the last day of the 2015-2016 signing period for $2 million (which came with a penalty that doubled the total outlay for the team). But just 45 days later the Astros acquired Alvarez before he ever played a game for the Dodgers.

Alvarez earned a spot in the Futures Game in his first full pro season in the U.S. A wrist injury sapped his power in the second half of the season, but when healthy Alvarez showed some of the best power in the organization. He produces excellent exit velocities and has 25-plus home run potential. His swing is not really geared to power, but the ball carries thanks to leverage and bat speed. He's actually more of a pure hitter than a slugger. Alvarez uses a whole-field approach, and hit more home runs to left field than right last season. He has a big strike zone, but his ability to recognize breaking balls and lay off pitches out of the zone helps him cover the entire plate. Alvarez is an excellent athlete for his size. He is an above-average runner underway and is actually a better left fielder than first baseman, although he needs more reps at both positions. His fringe-average arm is his worst attribute.

Alvarez needs to continue to refine his game offensively and defensively, but he has an exceptionally high ceiling as a pure hitter with still developing plus power. He will be ready for Double-A Corpus Christi with a strong spring.

BA GRADE

60 Risk: High

HIT: 55. POW: 60.
SPD: 50. FLD: 50.
ARM: 45.

Year	Club (League)	Class	AVG	G	AB	R	H	2B	3B	HR	RBI	BB	SO	SB	CS	OBP	SLG
2016	Astros Orange (DSL)	R	.341	16	44	7	15	2	1	1	4	12	7	2	1	.474	.500
2017	Quad Cities (MWL)	LoA	.360	32	111	26	40	6	0	9	33	23	36	2	0	.468	.658
	Buies Creek (CAR)	HiA	.277	58	224	19	62	11	3	3	36	19	41	6	1	.329	.393
Minor League Totals			.309	106	379	52	117	19	4	13	73	54	84	10	2	.391	.483

4 J.B. BUKAUSKAS, RHP

Born: Oct. 11, 1996. **B-T:** R-R. **Ht.:** 6-0. **Wt.:** 196. **Drafted:** North Carolina, 2017 (1st round). **Signed by:** Tim Bittner.

A number of scouts saw Lance McCullers Jr. as a reliever when they watched the short righthander's breaking ball heavy-approach in high school. The Astros believed he could start and were rewarded when he helped pitch the Astros to a World Series title. Like McCullers, Bukauskas is a hard-throwing short righthander with an exceptional breaking ball whom some scouts see as a reliever, but whom the Astros believe can start. Bukauskas went 9-1, 2.53 with 116 strikeouts in 92.2 innings as North Carolina's ace as a junior.

Bukauskas had the best slider in the 2017 draft class. It's a 70 pitch on the 20-to-80 scouting scale. He relied on it too often in college—in some outings he threw more sliders than fastballs—but it's a pitch that requires no projection as it's already hard (85-87 mph) with sharp late bite and comes out of his hand looking like his 91-95 mph fastball. Bukauskas can touch 96 mph, but his velocity usually dips into the lower registers of his range as the game wears on. He has average command and control of that fastball and he has excellent command of his slider, and often succeeds with a largely two-pitch approach. His 84-86 mph changeup flashes average, but he didn't use it much in college with a few notable exceptions. Its development will be one of the keys to him remaining as a starter. Bukauskas graduated a year early to get to North Carolina, so he's a year younger than his draft contemporaries which leads some scouts to believe he has further refinement ahead of him.

Bukauskas has a very comfortable fall-back option as a closer-level reliever, but he also has a chance to be a Sonny Gray-esque starter. He could move quickly in his first full season.

BA GRADE	
55	**Risk:** High
FB: 60.	**SL:** 70.
CHG: 45.	
CTL: 50.	

Year	Club (League)	Class	W	L	ERA	G	GS	CG	SV	IP	H	HR	BB	SO	K/9	WHIP	AVG
2017	Astros (GCL)	R	0	0	0.00	1	1	0	0	4	3	0	1	3	6.8	1.00	.231
	Tri-City (NYP)	SS	0	0	4.50	2	2	0	0	6	4	0	4	6	9.0	1.33	.191
Minor League Totals			0	0	2.70	3	3	0	0	10	7	0	5	9	8.1	1.20	.206

5 FREUDIS NOVA, SS

Born: Jan. 12, 2000. **B-T:** R-R. **Ht.:** 6-1. **Wt.:** 170. **Signed:** Dominican Republic, 2016. **Signed by:** Oz Ocampo/Roman Ocumarez/Jose Lima.

Nova was expected to be the centerpiece of the Marlins' 2016 international signing class. A positive steroid test pushed the Marlins away. The Astros then signed him for $1.5 million. His bonus was then reduced further to $1.2 million after the medical report showed an issue with his elbow. That's a lot of dings before Nova ever got into a game professionally, but Nova has not had any other positive tests since, has stayed healthy so far and has shown the same athleticism and twitchiness he showed as an amateur.

Nova's earliest Houston ETA is sometime in the 2020s, but there are few prospects with more potential. He has a chance to be an impact bat who can stick at a middle-infield position. He's athletic with above-average bat speed, plus speed and a plus arm. Nova shows surprising power for a speedy teenager. Like your normal 17-year-old, he has to make strides in pitch recognition, but with his bat speed and bat-to-ball skills he has a chance to be an above-average hitter with average power. Defensively, everything is there for Nova to be a shortstop. His hands work well, he has the twitchiness for a quick first step and the arm to make plays in the hole. But he has to learn to slow the game down—he posted sub-.900 fielding percentages at both shortstop and third base in his pro debut and had one game where he made a trio of throwing errors. Right now he can get too quick and try to do too much, but his defensive issues are ones that usually go away with repetition.

Nova is ready to head to the States. As a teenager there's plenty of work ahead, but he has a chance to be an impact everyday shortstop.

COURTESY THE HOUSTON ASTROS

BA GRADE	
55	**Risk:** Extreme
HIT: 55.	**POW:** 50.
SPD: 60.	**FLD:** 55.
ARM: 60.	

Year	Club (League)	Class	AVG	G	AB	R	H	2B	3B	HR	RBI	BB	SO	SB	CS	OBP	SLG
2017	Astros Orange (DSL)	R	.247	47	166	30	41	6	0	4	16	15	33	8	3	.342	.355
Minor League Totals			.247	47	166	30	41	6	0	4	16	15	33	8	3	.342	.355

6 JAIRO SOLIS, RHP

Born: Dec. 22, 1999. **B-T:** R-R. **Ht.:** 6-2. **Wt.:** 160. **Signed:** Venezuela, 2016. **Signed by:** Oz Ocampo/Tom Shafer/Roman Ocumarez/Enrique Brito.

BILL MITCHELL

Solis was considered one of the better players in the Astros' 2016 international class and landed a $450,000 bonus that reflected it. The Astros liked how his arm worked and thought he had room to fill out. But since then, he's exceeded expectations.

Solis has put in a lot of work, improved his body and has seen his stuff jump up as well. When the Astros' signed him, Solis could touch 91 mph. Just a year later, he's touching 96 and sitting 90-94 mph and his fastball has late life. He's advanced for his age and has the makings of a big league starter with three promising pitches. Once Solis made his pro debut, it was hard to hold him back. He sped from the Dominican Summer League to the rookie-level Gulf Coast League to the rookie-level Appalachian League in the span of two months. He misses bats and shows advanced control for a teenager. Solis has a hard 76-78 mph slurvy slider that shows plenty of promise. He's also quickly picked up an 83-85 mph changeup that shows some late tumble. As much as the quality of his pitches stands out, the Astros are even more encouraged by his intelligence and aptitude.

The Astros have never been shy about moving pitchers quickly—Franklin Perez and Forrest Whitley reached Double-A as 19-year-olds. Solis could make it to low Class A Quad Cities in 2018 and with his feel, he may continue to move quickly.

BA GRADE
55 Risk: **Extreme**
FB: 55. SL: 55.
CHG: 50.
CTL: 55.

Year	Club (League)	Class	W	L	ERA	G	GS	CG	SV	IP	H	HR	BB	SO	K/9	WHIP	AVG
2017	Astros Orange (DSL)	R	1	1	2.73	6	4	0	0	26	20	2	8	28	9.6	1.06	.220
	Astros (GCL)	R	1	0	3.00	5	4	0	0	21	19	1	7	24	10.3	1.24	.229
	Greeneville (APP)	R	1	1	1.93	4	2	0	0	14	12	0	6	17	10.9	1.29	.226
Minor League Totals			3	2	2.64	15	10	0	0	61	51	3	21	69	10.1	1.17	.225

7 HECTOR PEREZ, RHP

Born: June 6, 1996. **B-T:** R-R. **Ht.:** 6-3. **Wt.:** 190. **Signed:** Dominican Republic, 2014. **Signed by:** Oz Ocampo/Roman Ocumarez/Leocadio Guevara.

When Hector Perez throws strikes, he dominates. Perez wasn't all that dominant in 2017 because he simply didn't throw enough strikes.

Perez is a fast-mover who has gone from the complex leagues to high Class A in two years, but his control problems have forced him to develop survival skills. There's nothing particularly ugly or problematic about Perez's delivery, but he has trouble keeping the timing of it in sync. His wildness has few patterns—he'll spike a ball into the ground after 55 feet and the next ball will be up and out of the zone—but Perez's arm is special. He sits 92-97 mph and touched 99 last season. When he can keep the fastball around the strike zone, it sets up his low-80s plus split-changeup that leaves hitters flailing. He can locate a potentially average slider at times but it and his 78-80 mph curveball can sometimes blend together.

BA GRADE
50 Risk: **High**
FB: 70. CB: 40.
SL: 45. CHG: 60.
CTL: 40.

Perez's control troubles lead some scouts to already say that the righthander would be better off moving to the bullpen, where he would likely touch 100 mph or better and his split-change would give him a second weapon. But Perez has a good frame and his delivery isn't awful so there's no reason to give up on starting just yet.

Year	Club (League)	Class	W	L	ERA	G	GS	CG	SV	IP	H	HR	BB	SO	K/9	WHIP	AVG
2015	Astros Blue (DSL)	R	1	0	2.12	7	7	0	0	30	20	0	6	32	9.7	0.88	.185
	Astros (GCL)	R	1	0	1.16	9	3	0	1	23	10	0	16	16	6.2	1.11	.135
	Greeneville (APP)	R	0	0	0.00	1	0	0	0	2	0	0	1	2	9.0	0.50	.000
2016	Tri-City (NYP)	SS	2	0	1.57	7	3	0	0	29	19	0	12	36	11.3	1.08	.181
	Quad Cities (MWL)	LoA	2	1	4.60	7	7	0	0	31	28	1	22	44	12.6	1.60	.246
2017	Quad Cities (MWL)	LoA	1	1	2.50	4	3	0	0	18	9	2	11	24	12.0	1.11	.150
	Buies Creek (CAR)	HiA	6	5	3.63	21	14	0	2	89	69	6	67	104	10.5	1.52	.218
Minor League Totals			13	7	2.91	56	37	0	3	222	155	9	135	258	10.4	1.30	.198

8 JORGE ALCALA, RHP

Born: July 28, 1995. **B-T:** R-R. **Ht.:** 6-3. **Wt.:** 180. **Signed:** Dominican Republic, 2014.
Signed by: Oz Ocampo/Roman Ocumarez/Leocadio Guevara.

The Astros signed Alcala as a late-blooming 18-year-old. He sat 90-92 at that point, but since then his velocity has improved by leaps and bounds, He's still making up for lost development time as the 22-year-old has less than 200 pro innings.

Alcala's fastball ranges from 93-99 mph. He generally sits in the mid-90s and has touched 100-102. His slider and changeup are both much less refined, but the quality of his fastball allows them to play up. His slurvy slider will flash average mainly because it's 88-90 mph and it has some modest late break. His below-average changeup doesn't move much, but when he maintains arm speed and throws it with conviction, hitters have a hard time gearing down from 100 to 87-88. Right now he just doesn't always maintain his arm speed. If Alcala could refine one of the two offspeed pitches into a two-strike weapon, he'd shorten his innings significantly, as right now he can't finish hitters off if they can foul off his fastball. Alcala's control needs to improve, but he did show strides improvement with that in 2017, especially when working out of the stretch.

Alcala is another flame-thrower in the Jorge Guzman/Albert Abreu mold—the Astros had success developing and then trading Guzman and Abreu in recent years. It's easy to see Alacala eventually ending up in the bullpen, but with physicality, athleticism and a delivery with no glaring issues, he'll keep trying to stick as a starter.

BA GRADE
50 Risk: High
FB: 80. **SL:** 40.
CHG: 40.
CTL: 40.

Year	Club (League)	Class	W	L	ERA	G	GS	CG	SV	IP	H	HR	BB	SO	K/9	WHIP	AVG
2015	Astros Blue (DSL)	R	2	0	3.06	12	2	0	1	32	27	0	19	20	5.6	1.42	.227
2016	Astros (GCL)	R	1	1	1.21	6	3	0	1	22	14	0	6	35	14.1	0.90	.175
	Greeneville (APP)	R	2	1	1.80	6	4	0	0	20	12	0	8	20	9.0	1.00	.174
	Tri-City (NYP)	SS	0	1	5.27	3	3	0	0	14	20	1	4	15	9.9	1.76	.345
2017	Quad Cities (MWL)	LoA	2	0	2.03	6	4	0	0	31	16	3	12	35	10.2	0.90	.155
	Buies Creek (CAR)	HiA	5	6	3.45	16	14	1	0	78	55	7	33	60	6.9	1.12	.200
Minor League Totals			12	9	2.87	49	30	1	2	198	144	11	82	185	8.4	1.14	.205

9 COLIN MORAN, 3B

Born: Oct. 1, 1992. **B-T:** L-R. **Ht.:** 6-4. **Wt.:** 204. **Drafted:** North Carolina, 2013 (1st round). **Signed by:** Joel Matthews (Marlins).

Moran made it to the majors, but he and the team realized his lack of power may keep him from sticking around. He completely retooled his swing in 2017, focusing on hitting the ball in the air more. From 2016 to 2017 he halved his ground ball rate, doubled his fly ball rate and nearly doubled his number of home runs. Moran is as much a success story of the fly ball revolution as more celebrated big league examples like Justin Turner.

Moran is more upright at the plate now with the bat laid on his shoulder at the start of his swing. He finishes his swing with more of an uppercut. He's long had the ability to make solid contact, but too often he drove the ball into the ground, where his below-average speed meant it was a single at best. Now he has a chance to be a 20-plus home run threat and he did so without doing anything to diminish his above-average hitting ability. Moran has to hit, as he's fringe-average at third base at best although his plus arm is an asset. His lack of range is less noticeable at first base.

Moran would have likely stuck around Houston in 2017 if not for a freak injury. He was hit in the face by his own foul ball and suffered facial fractures. He should be fully recovered for spring training. He may have to head back to Fresno because of the Astros' crowded roster, but he should contribute to the big league club at some point in 2018.

BA GRADE
45 Risk: Medium
HIT: 50. **POW:** 55.
SPD: 30. **FLD:** 45.
ARM: 60.

Year	Club (League)	Class	AVG	G	AB	R	H	2B	3B	HR	RBI	BB	SO	SB	CS	OBP	SLG
2015	Corpus Christi (TL)	AA	.306	96	366	47	112	25	2	9	67	43	79	1	0	.381	.459
2016	Fresno (PCL)	AAA	.259	117	459	50	119	18	1	10	69	47	124	3	2	.329	.368
	Houston (AL)	MAJ	.130	9	23	1	3	1	0	0	2	1	8	0	0	.200	.174
2017	Fresno (PCL)	AAA	.308	79	302	53	93	15	1	18	63	31	55	0	3	.373	.543
	Quad Cities (MWL)	LoA	.100	3	10	0	1	1	0	0	2	2	4	0	0	.250	.200
	Houston (AL)	MAJ	.364	7	11	3	4	0	1	1	3	1	1	0	0	.417	.818
Major League Totals			.206	16	34	4	7	1	1	1	5	2	9	0	0	.270	.382
Minor League Totals			.290	454	1764	215	511	94	5	48	279	175	363	6	8	.353	.430

10 DAVID PAULINO, RHP

Born: Feb. 6, 1994. **B-T:** R-R. **Ht.:** 6-7. **Wt.:** 214. **Signed:** Dominican Republic, 2010. **Signed by:** Carlos Santana/Ramon Perez/Miguel Garcia (Tigers).

Paulino only added to concerns about his durability in 2017. He missed the start of the season with a sore elbow and returned in May. But just a month later, he was suspended for 80 games after testing positive for a steroid.

Paulino came off the suspension on the final day of the season, but was immediately put on the 60-day disabled list (partly to clear roster space) because of surgery to remove bone chips in his pitching elbow. Paulino will be 24 when the 2018 season begins, but he's yet to prove he can hold up over a full season. Between Tommy John surgery and suspensions, he's yet to throw 100 innings in a season. When he's healthy, Paulino has a 91-94 mph fastball and a devastating, 82-84 mph plus curveball. The fastball wasn't as hard in 2017 as it's been in the past, but the curve retains its sharp 12-to-6 break and Paulino has the feel to manipulate it depending on the situation. He can make it bigger and slower or harder and sharper. His changeup also flashes plus.

Paulino still has the makings of a mid-rotation starter, but he is now one positive test away from a full-season ban and he has yet to demonstrate the durability to handle a full-season starting role.

BA GRADE
55 Risk: Extreme
FB: 60. CB: 60.
CHG: 55.
CTL: 45.

Year	Club (League)	Class	W	L	ERA	G	GS	CG	SV	IP	H	HR	BB	SO	K/9	WHIP	AVG
2015	Tri-City (NYP)	SS	1	0	0.00	2	2	0	0	9	4	0	2	10	9.6	0.64	.125
	Quad Cities (MWL)	LoA	3	2	1.57	5	5	0	0	29	21	0	7	32	10.0	0.98	.202
	Lancaster (CAL)	HiA	1	1	4.91	6	5	0	1	29	24	1	10	30	9.2	1.16	.220
2016	Astros (GCL)	R	0	0	0.75	3	3	0	0	12	9	0	2	14	10.5	0.92	.196
	Corpus Christi (TL)	AA	5	2	1.83	14	9	0	1	64	47	3	11	72	10.1	0.91	.204
	Fresno (PCL)	AAA	0	2	3.86	3	3	0	0	14	16	1	6	20	12.9	1.57	.267
	Houston (AL)	MAJ	0	1	5.14	3	1	0	0	7	6	0	3	2	2.6	1.29	.240
2017	Fresno (PCL)	AAA	0	1	4.50	3	3	0	0	14	11	3	9	13	8.4	1.43	.208
	Houston (AL)	MAJ	2	0	6.52	6	6	0	0	29	36	8	7	34	10.6	1.48	.300
Major League Totals			2	1	6.25	9	7	0	0	36	42	8	10	36	9.0	1.44	.290
Minor League Totals			13	10	2.35	51	42	0	2	210	157	9	59	232	9.9	1.03	.205

11 J.D. DAVIS, 3B

BA GRADE
45 Risk: Medium

Born: April 27, 1993. **B-T:** R-R. **Ht.:** 6-3. **Wt.:** 225. **Drafted:** Cal State Fullerton, 2014 (3rd round). **Signed by:** Brad Budzinski.

The Astros' depth at first and third base meant that Davis faced a tough-to-swallow assignment in 2017. Coming off of a productive full season at Double-A Corpus Christi and a strong spring training, he was sent back to the Hooks because Houston had Alex Bregman and Yuli Gurriel set in the majors and Colin Moran and A.J. Reed above him in Triple-A.

To Davis' credit, he didn't pout and was a little more productive in a second stay with the Hooks. He eventually made it to Triple-A and made his big league debut. Davis has some of the best raw power in the organization and one of the strongest arms. It will always come with a significant number of strikeouts and he's unlikely to hit better than .230-.240 albeit with decent on-base percentages because he draws some walks. While many Astros have embraced hitting more fly balls, Davis' swing leads to a lot of screaming ground balls. If he could get the ball into the air more he could hit 30+ home runs.

Davis is a fringe-average defender at third and is the same at first with limited range but good hands. He's also tried left field, where his arm is an asset, but his below-average speed is a detriment. Davis is an injury fill-in for the Astros for now, which may make him a trade asset eventually.

Year	Club (League)	Class	AVG	G	AB	R	H	2B	3B	HR	RBI	BB	SO	SB	CS	OBP	SLG
2015	Lancaster (CAL)	HiA	.289	120	485	93	140	28	3	26	101	54	157	5	2	.370	.520
2016	Corpus Christi (TL)	AA	.270	125	482	61	130	34	1	23	80	45	142	1	3	.336	.488
2017	Corpus Christi (TL)	AA	.279	87	351	49	98	18	0	21	60	31	90	5	2	.340	.510
	Fresno (PCL)	AAA	.295	16	61	10	18	5	0	5	18	9	18	0	0	.370	.623
	Houston (AL)	MAJ	.226	24	62	8	14	4	0	4	7	4	20	1	1	.279	.484
Major League Totals			.226	24	62	8	14	4	0	4	7	4	20	1	1	.279	.484
Minor League Totals			.282	421	1645	251	464	101	5	88	311	167	473	16	7	.354	.510

12 ROGELIO ARMENTEROS, RHP

BA GRADE
45 Risk: Medium

Born: June 30, 1994. **B-T:** R-R. **Ht.:** 6-1. **Wt.:** 215. **Signed:** Cuba, 2014. **Signed by:** Alex Jacobs.

As a crafty righthander, Armenteros was asked to throw for a Rusney Castillo workout but he impressed enough that the Astros signed him for a modest $40,000. That's proven to be a bargain.

Armenteros is still crafty, but now he's crafty while throwing 90-93 mph and touching 95. He will mix four-seamers up and away and two-seamers down in the zone. Even with increased velocity, he's still more sneaky than overpowering as hitters do not know what pitch is coming at any point in the count and he locates well with above-average control. Armenteros' plus changeup is his best pitch as he'll use it at any time and, thanks to its deception, trusts it enough to throw it back-to-back. His slider, curve and cutter are all more of fringe-average pitches, but all three can be effective.

Armenteros is ready to compete for a big league job and is a viable starting option if the Astros need a mid-season call-up. He's a durable back-of-the-rotation starter.

Year	Club (League)	Class	W	L	ERA	G	GS	CG	SV	IP	H	HR	BB	SO	K/9	WHIP	AVG
2015	Tri-City (NYP)	SS	2	2	4.09	12	9	0	0	44	44	3	17	40	8.2	1.39	.262
	Quad Cities (MWL)	LoA	1	0	2.65	3	3	0	0	17	9	1	7	21	11.1	0.94	.150
2016	Quad Cities (MWL)	LoA	1	0	1.93	4	3	0	0	19	12	0	3	20	9.6	0.80	.179
	Lancaster (CAL)	HiA	6	4	4.18	19	16	0	1	90	87	13	37	107	10.7	1.37	.251
	Corpus Christi (TL)	AA	2	0	1.96	3	3	0	0	18	17	1	4	13	6.4	1.15	.262
2017	Corpus Christi (TL)	AA	2	3	1.93	14	10	0	1	65	49	3	19	74	10.2	1.04	.207
	Fresno (PCL)	AAA	8	1	2.16	10	10	0	0	58	42	5	19	72	11.1	1.05	.203
Minor League Totals			21	12	2.97	65	54	0	2	312	260	26	106	347	10.0	1.17	.226

13 CIONEL PEREZ, LHP

BA GRADE

50 Risk: High

Born: April 21, 1996. **B-T:** L-L. **Ht.:** 5-11. **Wt.:** 170. **Signed:** Cuba, 2016. **Signed by:** Charlie Gonzalez/Oz Ocampo.

Perez was one of the most productive young pitchers in Cuba, pitching well for the 18U team and posted a Serie Nacional-best 2.08 ERA as an 18-year-old. The Astros originally signed him at $5.15 million, but reduced the bonus to $2 million after the team was concerned with an issue with his elbow.

Perez's fastball has gotten stronger and stronger. He touched 95 early on, but sits more in the 90-93 mph range generally. His slider has sharpened since he signed. Its depth and tilt is only average but he locates it well. He also throws a slow fringy curveball and a promising changeup that has above-average potential. Perez's stuff all plays up because he has above-average command and control. He had a rough, brief intro to Double-A at the end of the season but will return there in 2018. Perez had to be added to the Astros' 40-man roster because of his voided contract—he would have been Rule 5 eligible otherwise.

Perez's fastball/slider combo would work as a reliever, but he'll try to improve the changeup enough to stick as a starter.

Year	Club (League)	Class	W	L	ERA	G	GS	CG	SV	IP	H	HR	BB	SO	K/9	WHIP	AVG
2017	Quad Cities (MWL)	LoA	4	3	4.23	12	9	0	2	55	52	2	17	55	8.9	1.25	.254
	Buies Creek (CAR)	HiA	2	1	2.84	5	4	0	0	25	27	1	5	18	6.4	1.26	.276
	Corpus Christi (TL)	AA	0	0	5.54	4	3	0	0	13	15	1	5	10	6.9	1.54	.294
Minor League Totals			6	4	4.04	21	16	0	2	94	94	4	27	83	8.0	1.29	.266

14 FRAMBER VALDEZ, LHP

BA GRADE

50 Risk: High

Born: Nov. 19, 1993. **B-T:** L-L. **Ht.:** 5-11. **Wt.:** 216. **Signed:** Dominican Republic, 2015. **Signed by:** Oz Ocampo/Tom Shafer/Roman Ocumarez/David Brito.

When the Astros signed Valdez in 2015, he was the same age as many of the college draftees taken that year. That's positively ancient for a player signing his first contract out of the Dominican Republic, but Valdez has quickly made up for lost time and reached Double-A a little over two years after he signed.

Valdez's fastball actually took a step back last season as 92-95 mph downshifted to 92-93 on a consistent basis. But the improvement in his changeup and command made it a fair trade, as the overall quality of his stuff improved. He's relying more on his two-seam fastball, which shows quality sink. His four-seamer has excellent life as well. Valdez's breaking ball is an easy plus pitch. He trusts it no matter the situation. His changeup is still below-average, but it's a good bit further along than it was a year ago.

If Valdez isn't going to be forced to move to the bullpen he's going to have to tighten his command and control. He'll head back to Corpus Christi for a second try at Double-A.

Year	Club (League)	Class	W	L	ERA	G	GS	CG	SV	IP	H	HR	BB	SO	K/9	WHIP	AVG
2015	Astros Blue (DSL)	R	4	1	3.68	16	0	0	3	37	36	1	17	36	8.8	1.45	.259
2016	Greeneville (APP)	R	1	0	1.69	2	2	0	0	11	7	0	3	15	12.7	0.94	.179
	Tri-City (NYP)	SS	2	1	3.74	5	2	0	0	22	22	0	7	28	11.6	1.34	.259
	Quad Cities (MWL)	LoA	1	3	3.06	6	6	1	0	35	31	1	11	35	8.9	1.19	.244
	Lancaster (CAL)	HiA	0	1	4.76	1	1	0	0	6	8	0	2	1	1.6	1.76	.333
2017	Buies Creek (CAR)	HiA	2	3	2.79	13	9	0	1	61	41	3	29	73	10.7	1.14	.185
	Corpus Christi (TL)	AA	5	5	5.88	12	9	0	0	49	60	4	23	53	9.7	1.69	.306
Minor League Totals			15	14	3.76	55	29	1	4	220	205	9	92	241	9.8	1.35	.246

15 JOE PEREZ, 3B

BA GRADE
55 Risk: Extreme

Born: Aug. 12, 1999. **B-T:** R-R. **Ht.:** 6-3. **Wt.:** 210. **Drafted:** HS—Southwest Ranches, Fla., 2017 (2nd round). **Signed by:** Charlie Gonzalez.

For most of his high school career, Perez was a well-regarded third baseman with excellent power. But Perez quickly turned into one of the must-see pitching prospects in Florida thanks to a 95-98 mph fastball. Most teams quickly came to prefer Perez as a pitcher, but the Astros (and Perez) believed in his bat.

Perez hit a home run to finish hitting for the cycle in a playoff win, then was shut down with an elbow injury that eventually required Tommy John surgery. The Astros drafted him knowing that he would need to rehab the elbow injury. Perez has easy plus power to all fields although there's more debate over how much he's going to hit. The Astros are confident that he's going to hit for average as well as power while other scouts saw less bat-to-ball skills. When Perez does get back into the dirt, he has a plus-plus arm that makes up for some of his limitations in foot speed and range. He will have to work hard on his lateral agility to stay at third base. Perez will be able to hit again during spring training, although he'll need significantly more time before his arm is ready to handle playing third base again.

Perez always has a fallback option of going back to the mound if hitting doesn't work out, but the Astros are confident he's a slugging third baseman.

Year	Club (League)	Class	AVG	G	AB	R	H	2B	3B	HR	RBI	BB	SO	SB	CS	OBP	SLG
2017	Did not play																

16 CORBIN MARTIN, RHP

BA GRADE
50 Risk: High

Born: Dec. 28, 1995. **B-T:** R-R. **Ht.:** 6-2. **Wt.:** 200. **Drafted:** Texas A&M, 2017 (2nd round). **Signed by:** Noel Gonzalez.

Martin was a reliever in the Texas A&M bullpen for two and a half seasons, but in his junior year he moved into the rotation. He became the team's Saturday starter and while his fastball velocity dipped a little, the command and the quality of his breaking balls improved with more work.

The Astros signed Martin for $1 million as a second-round pick and used him in their tandem-starter system, something not all that unusual for Martin because of his multi-role background. Martin's 90-94 mph fastball has excellent glove-side life. He also throws an average slider that has bigger shape than most, with its break coming earlier than other sliders. His curve is a little behind the slider, and his changeup is generally below-average but it will flash above-average at times and could develop into a better weapon.

Martin may end up back in the pen in the long run—he has a quick arm but his delivery has some effort and a high back elbow. But he has the makings of four pitches and potentially average control, so there's no reason to not let him try to start.

Year	Club (League)	Class	W	L	ERA	G	GS	CG	SV	IP	H	HR	BB	SO	K/9	WHIP	AVG
2017	Astros (GCL)	R	0	0	0.00	2	1	0	0	5	0	0	1	5	9.0	0.20	.000
	Tri-City (NYP)	SS	0	1	2.60	8	3	0	1	28	20	1	8	38	12.4	1.01	.202
Minor League Totals			0	1	2.20	10	4	0	1	33	20	1	9	43	11.8	0.89	.174

17 MYLES STRAW, OF

BA GRADE
45 Risk: Medium

Born: Oct. 17, 1994. **B-T:** R-R. **Ht.:** 5-10. **Wt.:** 181. **Drafted:** St. John's River (Fla.) JC., 2015 (12th round). **Signed by:** John Martin.

When he was graduating high school, Straw didn't have many options to play college baseball. But St. John's River (Fla.) JC took a chance on him and once he was there Straw impressed Astros scout John Martin with his speed and bat control. He then went out and led the minors in batting (.358) in 2016.

Straw's approach is unique to say the least. A righthanded hitter, he peppers right field with an inside-out swing that leads to plenty of contact. Encouragingly, Straw showed a developing ability to yank the occasional pitch in 2017. In the outfield, Straw can be above-average at any of the three spots with a plus arm that fits in right field. His jumps and reads could use further refinement but his plus-plus speed helps him outrun any mistakes he makes. He has an excellent work ethic.

Straw is likely a useful backup outfielder in the big leagues, but his on-base ability, speed and defense give him a shot for a slightly larger role.

Year	Club (League)	Class	AVG	G	AB	R	H	2B	3B	HR	RBI	BB	SO	SB	CS	OBP	SLG
2015	Greeneville (APP)	R	.268	58	209	47	56	10	3	0	13	29	51	22	9	.355	.344
2016	Quad Cities (MWL)	LoA	.374	68	270	40	101	14	6	0	22	29	58	17	10	.432	.470
	Lancaster (CAL)	HiA	.303	19	76	21	23	4	0	1	5	11	17	4	2	.393	.395
2017	Buies Creek (CAR)	HiA	.295	114	437	81	129	17	7	1	41	87	70	36	9	.412	.373
	Corpus Christi (TL)	AA	.239	13	46	9	11	0	0	0	3	7	9	2	0	.340	.239
Minor League Totals			.308	272	1038	198	320	45	16	2	84	163	205	81	30	.401	.388

18 GARRETT STUBBS, C

BA GRADE
45 Risk: Medium

Born: May 26, 1993. **B-T:** L-R. **Ht.:** 5-10. **Wt.:** 175. **Drafted:** Southern California, 2015 (8th round). **Signed by:** Tim Costic.

Statistically, 2017 was the worst season Stubbs has had as a pro. A hamstring injury that sidelined him early in the season played a part, but his main issue is that his swing got a little bigger as he seemed to be trying to hit more home runs. That's not his game. At his best, he's an above-average line-drive hitter with very modest power.

Stubbs has always faced skepticism from scouts because of his small size. His frame is skinnier than almost any other pro catcher, which brings both advantages and disadvantages. He is extremely flexible and moves like a middle infielder in catcher's gear. He's an excellent pitch framer. But he battled nagging injuries while catching a career-high 83 games and showed signs of wearing down as the season dragged on, even with that modest workload. Stubbs' normally above-average arm didn't seem as strong in the second half of 2017 and he threw out only three of his final 19 base stealers.

With the trade of Jake Rogers, Stubbs is the Astros' most viable big league catching option in the minors. His size may limit him to a backup role, but as he heads back to Triple-A Fresno, he knows he'll have to hit to handle even that role.

Year	Club (League)	Class	AVG	G	AB	R	H	2B	3B	HR	RBI	BB	SO	SB	CS	OBP	SLG
2015	Tri-City (NYP)	SS	.235	11	34	5	8	0	0	0	2	7	3	2	0	.366	.235
	Quad Cities (MWL)	LoA	.274	25	84	15	23	5	0	0	5	14	2	1	0	.370	.333
2016	Lancaster (CAL)	HiA	.291	55	206	35	60	13	0	6	38	29	37	10	3	.385	.442
	Corpus Christi (TL)	AA	.325	31	120	23	39	9	1	4	16	14	11	5	0	.401	.517
2017	Corpus Christi (TL)	AA	.236	75	263	36	62	13	0	4	25	32	44	8	0	.324	.331
	Fresno (PCL)	AAA	.221	23	77	11	17	5	0	0	12	11	15	3	0	.341	.286
Minor League Totals			.267	220	784	125	209	45	1	14	98	107	112	29	3	.361	.380

19 JASON MARTIN, OF

BA GRADE
45 Risk: Medium

Born: Sept. 5, 1995. **B-T:** L-R. **Ht.:** 5-10. **Wt.:** 184. **Drafted:** HS—Orange, Calif., 2013 (8th round). **Signed by:** Brad Budzinski.

Martin hit 23 home runs in Lancaster in 2016, but his 18 home runs in 2017 were more significant, as he showed that he could hit for power outside of the launching pad of Lancaster (18 of those 23 home runs in 2016 came at Lancaster or High Desert).

A 20-20 man in 2016, Martin has surprising pop for his size. He gets excellent weight transfer and uses his lower half well, starting off his swing with a significant leg kick. It does leave him vulnerable to getting caught out front on offspeed pitches, but his hands work well enough to flick some of them to the opposite field. Ideally he'd be an everyday center fielder, but scouts don't see him as more than fringe-average there at best thanks to poor routes that negate his above-average speed. He primarily played left field at Double-A Corpus Christi. Martin runs a risk of ending up as a tweener without enough power or on-base ability to play in left field or enough defense to play in center.

The Astros left Martin unprotected in the Rule 5 draft and he went unpicked, so it's a fear other teams have as well. He is in position to move to Triple-A Fresno in 2018.

Year	Club (League)	Class	AVG	G	AB	R	H	2B	3B	HR	RBI	BB	SO	SB	CS	OBP	SLG
2015	Quad Cities (MWL)	LoA	.270	105	396	65	107	12	7	8	57	47	74	14	15	.346	.396
2016	Lancaster (CAL)	HiA	.270	110	400	74	108	22	7	23	75	55	108	20	12	.357	.533
2017	Buies Creek (CAR)	HiA	.287	46	174	34	50	11	2	7	29	20	42	9	5	.354	.494
	Corpus Christi (TL)	AA	.273	79	300	38	82	24	3	11	37	19	82	7	6	.319	.483
Minor League Totals			.269	453	1694	285	455	91	30	50	238	201	380	74	54	.345	.446

20 GILBERTO CELESTINO, OF

BA GRADE
50 Risk: High

Born: Feb. 13, 1999. **B-T:** R-L. **Ht.:** 6-0. **Wt.:** 170. **Signed:** Dominican Republic, 2015. **Signed by:** Oz Ocampo/Roman Ocumarez.

When the 2017 season began, Celestino had a massive number of center fielders ahead of him on the team's depth chart. But as 2018 begins, the Astros have traded away Teoscar Hernandez, Daz Cameron and Ramon Laureano, which cleared the long-term path ahead of him.

Celestino is the organization's best minor league center fielder defensively. He's already plus in center with great instincts and good reads and routes to go with above-average speed and an above-average arm. Offensively, he shortened his swing, reducing his load. He has plenty of bat speed, but he can get too noisy in his setup leading to a longer swing than he needs. A veteran of international baseball tournaments as an amateur, he has a pretty good understanding of the strike zone. He has a chance to end up as an average hitter with average power.

Celestino has the tools to eventually turn into an everyday regular, but he'll play all of the 2018 season as a 19-year-old, so that refinement may be a few years away. He's ready for low Class A Quad Cities.

Year	Club (League)	Class	AVG	G	AB	R	H	2B	3B	HR	RBI	BB	SO	SB	CS	OBP	SLG
2016	Astros Orange (DSL)	R	.279	38	136	22	38	9	3	2	17	25	23	9	2	.388	.434
	Astros (GCL)	R	.200	18	55	7	11	3	1	0	2	8	16	6	1	.308	.291
2017	Greeneville (APP)	R	.268	59	235	38	63	10	2	4	24	22	59	10	2	.331	.379
Minor League Totals			.263	115	426	67	112	22	6	6	43	55	98	25	5	.347	.385

21 RONNIE DAWSON, OF

BA GRADE
50 Risk: High

Born: May 19, 1995. **B-T:** L-R. **Ht.:** 6-2. **Wt.:** 225. **Drafted:** Ohio State, 2016 (2nd round). **Signed by:** Nick Venuto.

When Dawson was in high school, he served as a bat boy for the Columbus Clippers, working with future Indians stars like Trevor Bauer, Carlos Carrasco and Danny Salazar. A football/baseball star at Licking Heights High in Pataskala, Ohio, Dawson went on to be a three-year starter at Ohio State.

Dawson's introduction to pro ball in 2016 was a difficult one and he showed similar struggles in the first half of 2017. As of early June, he was struggling to stay above the Mendoza Line, but improved plate discipline and a tweaked swing path helped him take off. Dawson's strong enough that he can drive the ball even when he doesn't completely square pitches up. He hit over .330 in the second half of the season, but it's his power that has a chance to be plus. Like many lefthanded hitters, he's yet to figure out how to consistently stay in against lefties (he hit .210 against them). Dawson is an average runner who is a little better than that underway and he's shown some knack for basestealing, although it's unlikely he'll be a significant threat at the big league level.

Defensively he's limited to left field and will return to Buies Creek in 2018 and attempt to build on an excellent second half of the 2017 season.

Year	Club (League)	Class	AVG	G	AB	R	H	2B	3B	HR	RBI	BB	SO	SB	CS	OBP	SLG
2016	Tri-City (NYP)	SS	.225	70	244	41	55	13	1	7	36	41	66	12	6	.351	.373
2017	Quad Cities (MWL)	LoA	.272	115	434	80	118	23	4	13	60	55	99	17	8	.363	.433
	Buies Creek (CAR)	HiA	.327	13	52	7	17	3	1	0	5	4	9	1	3	.368	.423
Minor League Totals			.260	198	730	128	190	39	6	20	101	100	174	30	17	.359	.412

22 DEAN DEETZ, RHP

BA GRADE
40 Risk: Medium

Born: Nov. 29, 1993. **Ht.:** 6-1. **Wt.:** 198. **Drafted:** Northeast Oklahoma JC, 2014 (11th round). **Signed by:** Jim Stevenson.

The Astros have let Deetz work as one of their tandem starters since they drafted him out of Northeast Oklahoma JC, but a late-season move to an exclusively relief role showed his brighter future.

Pitching in shorter stints, Deetz's fastball jumped up to 95-98 mph and his slider improved as well. It's a dominating plus to plus-plus pitch at its best, with movement that seems almost like a Wiffle-ball. It's the big reason he struck out 23 in only 11 innings in the Arizona Fall League. His walk rate was almost as frightening as his slider in Fresno. Deetz has below-average control, but it's not as bad as his nearly walk per inning rate in Fresno would indicate. Deetz is more effective in shorter stints and his slider explains why he's much better against righthanded hitters.

Deetz was added to the 40-man roster in the offseason and will compete to pitch in the Astros' bullpen at some point in 2018.

Year	Club (League)	Class	W	L	ERA	G	GS	CG	SV	IP	H	HR	BB	SO	K/9	WHIP	AVG
2015	Tri-City (NYP)	SS	4	2	2.86	7	5	0	0	28	22	1	10	21	6.7	1.13	.208
	Quad Cities (MWL)	LoA	5	1	0.76	7	6	0	0	35	17	0	13	29	7.4	0.85	.136
2016	Lancaster (CAL)	HiA	6	5	4.24	23	16	0	1	93	86	9	45	86	8.3	1.40	.241
	Corpus Christi (TL)	AA	2	0	0.00	2	2	0	0	12	7	0	2	17	12.8	0.75	.175
2017	Corpus Christi (TL)	AA	4	2	1.82	8	6	0	0	40	27	3	9	42	9.5	0.91	.194
	Fresno (PCL)	AAA	3	4	6.40	17	10	0	0	45	46	5	41	55	11.0	1.93	.267
Minor League Totals			26	18	3.90	77	50	0	1	279	235	19	139	274	8.8	1.34	.226

23 JONATHAN ARAUZ, SS

BA GRADE
50 Risk: Extreme

Born: Aug. 3, 1998. **B-T:** L-R. **Ht.:** 6-0. **Wt.:** 150. **Signed:** Panama, 2014. **Signed by:** Norman Anciani (Phillies).

Understandably it was not the headline portion of the Ken Giles trade, but the Phillies and Astros pulled off an Arauz for Arauz swap, as the Phillies sent Jonathan Arauz, a shortstop, to Houston for Harold Arauz, a righthander. The Astros' Arauz acquisition has been a fast-mover, but he hit a pothole in 2017 as he was suspended 50 games after testing positive for a methamphetamine.

The Astros had him posted to their low Class A Quad Cities roster at the time of the suspension, which allowed him to get back into action in June instead of August. After posting low averages but generally holding his own with Quad Cities, he went down to short-season Tri-City, a better fit considering his age. The switch-hitter has a very good understanding of how to work counts for his age and draws his walks with excellent ability to make contact. There's some nascent power potential in the bat as well, which gives him a shot to hit for average with 10-15 home run power one day. Arauz is primarily a shortstop for now, but his limited range could eventually lead to a move to second or third base. He has a good understanding of game situations and a well-calibrated internal clock. He's an average runner with an average arm.

Arauz is ready for full-season ball. He's more solid than spectacular, but there's enough there to be a offensive middle infielder.

Year	Club (League)	Class	AVG	G	AB	R	H	2B	3B	HR	RBI	BB	SO	SB	CS	OBP	SLG
2015	Phillies (GCL)	R	.254	44	173	21	44	10	2	2	18	13	29	2	0	.309	.370
2016	Greeneville (APP)	R	.249	53	201	26	50	10	1	2	18	19	45	1	3	.323	.338
2017	Quad Cities (MWL)	LoA	.220	36	127	23	28	3	2	0	4	20	18	0	1	.331	.276
	Tri-City (NYP)	SS	.264	33	121	16	32	7	1	1	11	12	29	1	0	.341	.364
Minor League Totals			.248	166	622	86	154	30	6	5	51	64	121	4	4	.324	.339

24 A.J. REED, 1B

BA GRADE
45 Risk: High

Born: May 10, 1993. **B-T:** L-L. **Ht.:** 6-4. **Wt.:** 275. **Drafted:** Kentucky, 2014 (2nd round). **Signed by:** Nick Venuto.

For the second time in three seasons, Reed led the minors with 34 home runs. But this home run title isn't as encouraging as the last one. In 2015, Reed was a first baseman on his way up who was set to compete for the Astros' big league job in 2016. In 2017, he remained in Fresno for all but a two-game cameo and was not among the team's September callups, even though he is on the team's 40-man roster.

Reed's power has never been in doubt, and when he's locked in, he drives the ball to all fields, capably using left field. He adjusted his stance, moving up his hands and laying his bat over his shoulder in his setup, and it paid off as he slugged over .600 in July and August. But he's yet to show he can avoid chasing sliders off the plate and he's been an easy mark for lefthanders. Scouts have long thought Reed would be more nimble if he were 20-30 pounds lighter. His near bottom-of-the-scale speed limits him both on the basepaths and at first, although his plus arm is an asset.

It's hard to see Reed pushing aside Yuli Gurriel, and Colin Moran has passed him as a backup plan. He might need a change of scenery. Slugging first basemen/DH's don't land much in trade unless they've produced at the big league level, so for now, he's headed back to Triple-A.

Year	Club (League)	Class	AVG	G	AB	R	H	2B	3B	HR	RBI	BB	SO	SB	CS	OBP	SLG
2015	Lancaster (CAL)	HiA	.346	82	318	75	110	16	4	23	81	59	73	0	0	.449	.638
	Corpus Christi (TL)	AA	.332	53	205	38	68	14	1	11	46	27	49	0	0	.405	.571
2016	Fresno (PCL)	AAA	.291	70	261	42	76	22	1	15	50	32	67	0	0	.368	.556
	Houston (AL)	MAJ	.164	45	122	11	20	3	0	3	8	18	48	0	0	.270	.262
2017	Houston (AL)	MAJ	.000	2	6	0	0	0	0	0	0	0	1	0	0	.000	.000
	Fresno (PCL)	AAA	.261	127	476	89	124	24	0	34	104	72	146	0	0	.358	.525
Major League Totals			.156	47	128	11	20	3	0	3	8	18	49	0	0	.259	.250
Minor League Totals			.298	400	1509	287	450	96	7	95	335	220	389	2	0	.389	.560

25 CRISTIAN JAVIER, RHP

BA GRADE
45 Risk: High

Born: March 26, 1997. **Ht.:** 6-1. **Wt.:** 186. **Signed:** Dominican Republic, 2015. **Signed by:** Oz Ocampo/Roman Ocumarez/Johan Maya.

Javier's strengths as a pitcher weren't all that apparent when he was an amateur. At your typical amateur showcase event in the Dominican Republic, radar gun readings and an ability to spin a breaking ball are much more apparent than reading swings and mixing pitches. Javier signed for only $10,000, but getting a chance to face hitters in games has allowed him to demonstrate how well he can work with four average pitches.

Javier has gotten stronger as expected, and his fastball now sits at 88-92 mph. Hitters don't seem to get good swings against it, as it has some late life. Javier has always believed in his big, slow curveball and he's mastering a high-70s slider that is effective against same-side hitters. His changeup has developed over the past year into a fringe-average pitch. Javier has already climbed through five levels in just three seasons—his high Class A appearances were a pair of spot starts because the Astros felt comfortable he could handle the jump. He'll likely return to Buies Creek to start the 2018 season.

Without a plus pitch, Javier faces the challenge of proving he can continue to outthink more advanced hitters, but he's yet to find a challenge he can't handle.

Year	Club (League)	Class	W	L	ERA	G	GS	CG	SV	IP	H	HR	BB	SO	K/9	WHIP	AVG
2015	Astros Orange (DSL)	R	1	0	0.81	6	2	0	0	22	15	0	5	23	9.3	0.90	.185
	Astros Blue (DSL)	R	3	0	3.60	8	2	0	0	20	15	1	4	27	12.2	0.95	.203
2016	Astros (GCL)	R	3	1	2.84	6	2	0	1	25	19	1	8	37	13.1	1.07	.207
	Greeneville (APP)	R	1	1	1.75	7	4	0	0	26	15	1	10	29	10.2	0.97	.170
2017	Buies Creek (CAR)	HiA	1	0	0.00	2	0	0	0	6	2	0	3	9	14.3	0.88	.105
	Tri-City (NYP)	SS	0	0	2.70	4	2	0	0	17	11	0	9	24	13.0	1.20	.183
	Quad Cities (MWL)	LoA	2	0	2.39	8	7	0	1	38	25	3	15	47	11.2	1.06	.188
Minor League Totals			11	2	2.23	41	19	0	2	153	102	6	54	196	11.5	1.02	.186

26 J.J. MATIJEVIC, OF

BA GRADE
45 Risk: High

Born: Nov. 14, 1995. **B-T:** L-R. **Ht.:** 6-0. **Wt.:** 206. **Drafted:** Arizona, 2017 (2nd round supplemental). **Signed by:** Mark Ross.

In high school, Matijevic battled with Brendan McKay for the title of most promising prospect in the Pittsburgh area. Matijevic's first two seasons at Arizona were not particularly notable. He failed to hit .300 in either season and he showed little power. But after tweaking his approach and swing—changing a leg kick to a toe tap and finishing more uphill—Matijevic hit .387 as a junior while leading Division I with 30 doubles.

Matijevic is a pretty pure hitter, but he's long been comped to John Jaso as a first baseman with modest power. When the Astros drafted Matijevic, they announced him as a second baseman, a position he had practiced in the Cape Cod League. But Matijevic, a high school shortstop, played only left field and first base in his pro debut, and he's likely to focus on left field for now. He's unlikely to be more than a fringe-average defender in left thanks to below-average speed and slow feet, but if he hits like the Astros expect, that would be sufficient.

Matijevic let too many hittable pitches go early in counts in his pro debut, but his feel for the barrel should allow him to hit for average and get on base. He has enough strength and explosive bat speed to hit for at least average power as well.

Year	Club (League)	Class	AVG	G	AB	R	H	2B	3B	HR	RBI	BB	SO	SB	CS	OBP	SLG
2017	Tri-City (NYP)	SS	.240	53	200	34	48	14	0	6	27	18	60	11	3	.302	.400
	Quad Cities (MWL)	LoA	.125	6	24	2	3	0	0	1	4	1	9	0	1	.192	.250
Minor League Totals			.228	59	224	36	51	14	0	7	31	19	69	11	4	.290	.384

27 RILEY FERRELL, RHP

BA GRADE
45 Risk: High

Born: Oct. 18, 1993. **B-T:** R-R. **Ht.:** 6-2. **Wt.:** 200. **Drafted:** Texas Christian, 2015 (3rd round). **Signed by:** Jim Stevenson.

Ferrell also impressed in three years as Texas Christian's closer, but the success of the Horned Frogs meant he only logged 31.2 innings as a junior—the team didn't have many games close enough for Ferrell to finish out.

As a pro, Ferrell has put control troubles behind him, but his more frightening obstacle was an aneurysm in his shoulder. Doctors noticed it after a couple of Ferrell's fingers went numb early in the 2016 season. He missed the rest of the season. When he returned, he was much of the same guy as he had been before the surgery. He runs his fastball into the mid-90s, and while a plus pitch, it's more of a setup offering, as most of Ferrell's strikeouts come off of his monstrous slider that earns 70 grades on the 20-to-80 scale. It breaks enough that it rarely finishes in the strike zone, but that's yet to be a problem.

Ferrell profiles as a seventh/eighth-inning reliever because he has a swing-and-miss secondary. Time will tell if he has to figure out how to throw it for a strike or if it's just good enough that hitters can't lay off of it consistently.

Year	Club (League)	Class	W	L	ERA	G	GS	CG	SV	IP	H	HR	BB	SO	K/9	WHIP	AVG
2015	Quad Cities (MWL)	LoA	0	0	1.08	12	0	0	1	17	10	0	13	17	9.2	1.38	.175
2016	Lancaster (CAL)	HiA	0	1	1.80	8	0	0	4	10	9	1	2	14	12.6	1.10	.237
2017	Buies Creek (CAR)	HiA	0	0	0.00	2	0	0	2	2	0	0	0	5	22.5	0.00	.000
	Corpus Christi (TL)	AA	2	2	3.81	36	0	0	4	52	51	2	14	55	9.5	1.25	.263
Minor League Totals			2	3	2.90	58	0	0	11	81	70	3	29	91	10.2	1.23	.237

28 JANDEL GUSTAVE, RHP

Born: Oct. 12, 1992. **B-T:** R-R. **Ht.:** 6-2. **Wt.:** 209. **Signed:** Dominican Republic, 2010. **Signed by:** Felix Francisco/Rafael Belen.

BA GRADE

45 Risk: Extreme

When the Astros signed Gustave, they knew they were getting a special arm, and a long-term project.

In his first two seasons, Gustave walked 67 batters in only 45 innings. But he started to figure out how to repeat his delivery and get in the vicinity of the strike zone. Gustave had finally gotten to the point where he could help the Astros' big league bullpen—he'd earned a spot during the second half of 2016 and broke camp with the team in 2017. But only five outings into the season he was shut down with elbow soreness that led to Tommy John surgery in June 2017. He will likely not pitch significant innings again until 2019. If he comes back to his pre-injury form, his 95-100 mph plus-plus fastball with run and hard, cutting slider give him a pair of plus pitches. The slider is more of a weak-contact offering.

Gustave's control and command are still below-average, but his stuff is good enough that he has the ability to pitch in high leverage situations.

Year	Club (League)	Class	W	L	ERA	G	GS	CG	SV	IP	H	HR	BB	SO	K/9	WHIP	AVG
2015	Corpus Christi (TL)	AA	5	2	2.15	46	0	0	20	59	51	2	25	49	7.5	1.30	.235
2016	Fresno (PCL)	AAA	3	3	3.79	47	0	0	3	57	46	1	23	55	8.7	1.21	.219
	Houston (AL)	MAJ	1	0	3.52	14	0	0	0	15	13	2	4	16	9.4	1.11	.232
2017	Houston (AL)	MAJ	0	0	5.40	6	0	0	0	5	5	0	7	2	3.6	2.40	.278
Major League Totals			1	0	3.98	20	0	0	0	20	18	2	11	18	8.0	1.43	.243
Minor League Totals			17	23	4.70	164	34	0	25	312	301	10	194	303	8.7	1.59	.252

29 ELIAN RODRIGUEZ, RHP

Born: March 10, 1997. **B-T:** R-R. **Ht.:** 6-4. **Wt.:** 205. **Signed:** Cuba, 2017. **Signed by:** Charlie Gonzalez/Oz Ocampo.

BA GRADE

45 Risk: Extreme

Signed for $2 million in 2017, Rodriguez has about everything a team could look for in a young pitcher as far as pure stuff. He's strong, athletic and has long arms.

Rodriguez's fastball sits 92-95 and touches 97 and he pairs it with a hard mid-80s slider that has a chance to develop into a plus pitch. Generally, he's attacked hitters with power stuff, but he also has a slower mid-70s curveball and the beginnings of a potentially average changeup. What Rodriguez has not shown yet is the ability to throw strikes. In his first stint in the Dominican Summer League, he walked 10.6 batters per nine innings. It was a consistent problem—he walked more than a batter an inning in six of his nine outings.

Rodriguez has plenty of upside, but as he heads to the States in 2018, he's facing a lot of work and a lot of reps to tame his bottom-of-the-scale control.

Year	Club (League)	Class	W	L	ERA	G	GS	CG	SV	IP	H	HR	BB	SO	K/9	WHIP	AVG
2017	Astros Orange (DSL)	R	0	3	7.46	9	9	0	0	25	26	1	30	19	6.8	2.21	.313
Minor League Totals			0	3	7.46	9	9	0	0	25	26	1	30	19	6.8	2.21	.313

30 MIGUELANGEL SIERRA, SS

Born: Dec. 2, 1997. **B-T:** R-R. **Ht.:** 5-11. **Wt.:** 165. **Signed:** Venezuela, 2014. **Signed by:** Oz Ocampo/Oscar Alvarado/Jose Palacios.

BA GRADE

45 Risk: Extreme

There were few hotter hitters in baseball in 2016 than Sierra was during a month with rookie-level Greeneville. A $1 million signee in 2014, Sierra hit 11 home runs in only 31 games, which may have been the worst thing possible for his development.

That surprising power surge led Sierra to believe he was a power hitter, which led to bad habits. He hit .140 in a promotion to Tri-City, then hit an equally frightening .178 in his return there in 2017. The Astros have to hope that Sierra can shorten up his swing. Offensively, he has some bat-to-ball aptitude when he stays shorter to the ball. While he's unlikely to become an impact defender, Sierra has a chance to stay at the position as at least an average shortstop, with an average arm and fringe-average speed.

Sierra may eventually fill out to have 10-12 home run power, but only if he stays focused on being a contact hitter with gap power.

Year	Club (League)	Class	AVG	G	AB	R	H	2B	3B	HR	RBI	BB	SO	SB	CS	OBP	SLG
2015	Astros Orange (DSL)	R	.302	45	169	31	51	17	2	3	19	20	48	8	5	.406	.479
	Astros (GCL)	R	.160	24	75	6	12	2	1	0	1	8	33	4	3	.267	.213
2016	Greeneville (APP)	R	.289	31	121	23	35	3	2	11	19	12	40	6	6	.386	.620
	Tri-City (NYP)	SS	.140	25	93	6	13	2	1	0	5	7	34	0	3	.216	.183
2017	Tri-City (NYP)	SS	.178	57	185	15	33	8	1	4	13	17	62	6	1	.260	.297
Minor League Totals			.224	182	643	81	144	32	7	18	57	64	217	24	18	.318	.379

Kansas City Royals

BY BILL MITCHELL

The 2017 season was a crossroads campaign for the Royals. With the core of the 2014 and 2015 World Series teams all coming up for free agency after 2017, general manager Dayton Moore had to decide whether to go all in or start to rebuild a farm system in need of an infusion of talent. He chose the former.

The Royals overcame a slow start (7-16 in April) with a strong middle of the season in which they won 33 of 55 games during June and July.

The Royals didn't really go full bore on the trade market, instead making relatively smaller deals by acquiring outfielder Melky Cabrera from the White Sox and a trio of veteran relievers from the Padres. Instead, they thrived because of comeback seasons from center fielder Lorenzo Cain and third baseman Mike Moustakas—both of whom missed significant time in 2016 with injuries—and breakout performances by first baseman Eric Hosmer and scrappy second baseman Whit Merrifield.

Danny Duffy continued his ascension to the role of staff ace, though he missed eight starts with an injury during the middle part of the season. Veteran lefty Jason Vargas also turned in a surprising season with 18 wins, helping to fill the void caused by the untimely death of 25-year-old righthander Yordano Ventura in a January automobile accident in his native Dominican Republic.

The Royals came up short in their bid for the postseason, finishing with an 80-82 record, five games behind the Twins, who claimed the second American League wild card. It marked the end of an era for the Royals franchise. Core players Hosmer, Cain, Moustakas and shortstop Alcides Escobar all hit the free agent market after the season, and the franchise could lose all four.

The Royals hit pay dirt with 2007 second overall pick Moustakas and 2008 third overall pick Hosmer, and they scored both Cain and Escobar in the 2010 Zack Greinke trade. But now most of the Royals' better prospects are at the lower levels of the system. In other words, it's not going to be a quick rebuild.

The big league Royals didn't meet expectations in 2017, and the organization wasn't much more productive in the minor leagues. The seven domestic affiliates finished with a .466 winning percentage that ranked 25th in baseball.

The best stories from the system involved their top two picks, first baseman Nick Pratto and catcher M.J. Melendez, both high school products who turned in promising pro debuts in the Rookie-level Arizona League, and the improvement of teen outfielders Khalil Lee and Seuly

Shortstop Raul A. Mondesi is a key part of what will be a lengthy Royals rebuild.

PROJECTED 2021 LINEUP

Catcher	Salvador Perez (31)
First Base	Nick Pratto (22)
Second Base	Nicky Lopez (26)
Third Base	Cheslor Cuthbert (28)
Shortstop	Raul A. Mondesi (25)
Left Field	Seuly Matias (22)
Center Field	Khalil Lee (23)
Right Field	Jorge Bonifacio (28)
Designated Hitter	Hunter Dozier (28)
No. 1 Starter	Danny Duffy (32)
No. 2 Starter	Jake Junis (28)
No. 3 Starter	Josh Staumont (27)
No. 4 Starter	Eric Skoglund (28)
No. 5 Starter	Foster Griffin (25)
Closer	Kelvin Herrera (31)

Matias. Elsewhere, 2014 first-round lefthander Foster Griffin rebounded with a promising season.

On the other hand, the outlook for 2015 first-round righthanders Ashe Russell and Nolan Watson is not promising. Russell stepped away from the game after pitching only one inning in the last two years, and Watson struggled mightily for the second straight season. Kyle Zimmer, arguably the most talented pitcher in the system, continued to be plagued by injuries.

The trades made to bolster the 2017 playoff chances cost the Royals a few good prospects, namely lefthander Matt Strahm, righthander A.J. Puckett and exciting 18-year-old second baseman Esteury Ruiz.

KANSAS CITY ROYALS

TOP 2018 ROOKIE: Eric Skoglund, LHP. He got his first taste of the big leagues in 2017 and should be a rotation frontrunner in 2018.

BREAKOUT PROSPECT: Carlos Hernandez, RHP. Armed with an electric fastball approaching 100 mph, he is the guy to watch as he moves to full-season ball in 2018.

SLEEPER: Charlie Neuweiler, RHP. The 2017 fifth-round pick showed advanced pitchability and a diverse repertoire in his pro debut

SOURCE OF TOP 30 TALENT

Homegrown	26	Acquired	4
College	8	Trade	1
Junior college	3	Rule 5 draft	2
High school	7	Independent league	0
Nondrafted free agent	0	Free agent/waivers	1
International	8		

LF
- Brewer Hicklen
- Terrance Gore
- Alfredo Escalera

CF
- Khalil Lee (2)
- Michael Gigliotti (20)
- Donnie Dewees (23)
- Marten Gasparini
- Bubba Starling
- Raymond Lopez
- Juan Carlos Negret

RF
- Seuly Matias (3)
- Elier Hernandez
- Kort Peterson
- Anderson Miller

3B
- Hunter Dozier (8)
- Emmanuel Rivera (26)
- Travis Jones
- Oliver Nunez
- Dennicher Carrasco

SS
- Nicky Lopez (7)
- Humberto Arteaga
- Cristian Perez
- Jeison Guzman
- Julio Gonzalez
- Ricky Aracena

2B
- Gabriel Cancel
- D.J. Burt
- Tyler James

1B
- Nick Pratto (1)
- Samir Duenez (13)
- Ryan O'Hearn (15)
- Chris DeVito

C
- M.J. Melendez (6)
- Chase Vallot (12)
- Meibrys Viloria (24)
- Cam Gallagher (28)
- Sebastian Rivero
- Nick Dini
- Xavier Fernandez

LHP

LHSP	LHRP
Eric Skoglund (5)	Richard Lovelady (27)
Foster Griffin (9)	Eric Stout
Evan Steele (18)	Tim Hill
Daniel Tillo (19)	Sam Selman
Emilio Ogando	
Garrett Davila	
Marlin Willis	
Holden Capps	

RHP

RHSP	RHRP
Josh Staumont (4)	Burch Smith (21)
Scott Blewett (10)	Andrew Edwards
Miguel Almonte (11)	Pedro Fernandez
Yefri Del Rosario (14)	Franco Terrero
Gerson Garabito (16)	Yunior Marte
Carlos Hernandez (17)	
Brad Keller (22)	
Andres Machado (25)	
Scott Barlow (26)	
Kyle Zimmer (30)	
Janser Lara	
Charlie Neuweiler	
Zach Lovvorn	
Nolan Watson	
Ofreidy Gomez	
Jace Vines	
Bryar Johnson	
Collin Snider	
Tyler Zuber	
Sal Biasi	

DRAFT ANALYSIS

2017

BEST PURE HITTER: 1B Nick Pratto (1) was considered one of the most polished high school hitters in this draft class with a loose swing, excellent plate discipline and advanced timing and pitch recognition.

BEST POWER HITTER: C M.J. Melendez (2) and Pratto both have above-average power potential. Melendez uses a leg kick to get proper weight transfer to drive the ball and has shown above-average raw power.

FASTEST RUNNER: The Royals love to draft at least one speedster a year. OF Tyler James (25) is a top of the scale runner who stole 31 bases in 32 tries in his debut. He stole 46 bases last spring for NAIA William Carey (Miss.).

BEST DEFENSIVE PLAYER: The son of a long-time coach, Melendez has the feel for the game and all the tools to be an above-average catcher defensively. He has to shorten his arm stroke but he has a 70 arm. OF Michael Gigliotti (4) is the kind of speedy, rangy plus center fielder that the Royals love to have in center field in spacious Kauffman Stadium. Pratto is a nimble defender at first base.

BEST FASTBALL: LHP Daniel Tillo's (3) fastball sits at 92-94 mph and touches 96 mph with sink and some run. OF Isaiah Henry (14) touched 94-95 mph this spring as a pitcher. He's an outfielder, but pitching remains a long-term option if hitting doesn't work out.

BEST SECONDARY PITCH: RHP Charlie Neuwiler (5) throws a hard spike curveball with 12-to-6 shape and plenty of bite. It has plus potential but like many young pitchers who throw a spike curve, he has some trouble commanding it. LHP Evan Steele (2s) also throws an above-average true curve, it lacks Neuwiler's power and bite but he lands it consistently.

TOP DRAFT PICKS OF THE DECADE

Year	Player, Pos.	2017 Org
2008	Eric Hosmer, 1B	Royals
2009	Aaron Crow, RHP	Did not play
2010	Christian Colon, SS	Marlins
2011	Bubba Starling, OF	Royals
2012	Kyle Zimmer, RHP	Royals
2013	Hunter Dozier, SS	Royals
2014	Brandon Finnegan, LHP	Reds
2015	Ashe Russell, RHP	Royals
2016	A.J. Puckett, RHP (2nd round)	White Sox
2017	Nick Pratto, 1B	Royals

BEST ATHLETE: OF Brewer Hicklen (7) is a 70 runner on the 20-to-80 scouting scale and has above-average raw power that gives him a chance to develop into a power-speed threat, although he's less advanced than the average college hitter.

BEST PRO DEBUT: Gigliotti hit .329/.442/.477 with 15 steals in 20 attempts for Rookie-level Burlington. Neuwiler went 3-3, 1.76 in 41 innings in the Rookie-level Arizona League. OF Travis Jones (29) hit .335/.423/.537 for Rookie-level Idaho Falls and stole 20 bases in 23 attempts.

BEST LATE-ROUND PICK: Jones has some athleticism, strength and defensive versatility–he played left, right, first and third base in his debut.

MOST INTRIGUING BACKGROUND: Hicklen played wide receiver for Alabama-Birmingham's football team until the team was disbanded after the 2014 season. If he hadn't signed with the Royals, he would have played football for the now reinstated UAB football team this fall.

THE ONE WHO GOT AWAY: RHP Cason Sherrod (13) is a high-upside, still developing arm who emerged as a useful weapon out of the Texas A&M bullpen last year as a junior.

—J.J. COOPER

2016

The Royals didn't have a first round pick in 2016, making RHP A.J. Puckett (2) thier top pick. He was a part of their trade for Melky Cabrera this summer. OF Khalil Lee (3) has emerged as one of the top players in the system.

GRADE: C

2015

The class was topped by prep RHPs Ashe Russell (1) and Nolan Watson (1). Russell this summer took a leave of absence and Watson has struggled mightily as a pro. RHP Josh Staumont (2) has premium stuff, but is still learning to harness it.

GRADE: F

2014

LHP Brandon Finnegan (1) rocketed to the big leagues before being used in the Johnny Cueto trade. LHP Eric Skoglund (3) reached Kansas City in 2017; LHP Foster Griffin (1) and RHP Scott Blewett (2) are on track to join him in the rotation.

GRADE: B

1 NICK PRATTO, 1B

Born: Oct. 6, 1998. **B-T:** L-L. **Ht.:** 6-1. **Wt.:** 195.
Drafted: HS—Huntington Beach, Calif., 2017 (1st round).
Signed by: Rich Amaral.

The Royals used the 14th overall pick in the 2017 draft to select Southern California high school first baseman Pratto, nine years after taking Eric Hosmer third overall in 2008. Prep first basemen are a rare commodity in the first round, with only Josh Naylor (Marlins, 2015) and Dominic Smith (Mets, 2013) being other recent examples. Pratto first bust on the scene as part of the winning California team in the 2011 Little League World Series in which he delivered the game-winning hit against Japan. He played with Team USA's 18U national team for two summers, bringing home world championships in both 2015 and 2016. A two-way player throughout his amateur career, Pratto drew draft interest as a southpaw pitcher, and would have both pitched and hit had he honored his commitment to Southern California. Instead, he signed with the Royals for $3.45 million shortly after the draft and began his pro career in the Rookie-level Arizona League, where he ranked at that circuit's No. 9 prospect. He hit .247/.330/.414 in the AZL with four home runs, coming on strong in August when he cut down on strikeouts and put more balls in play.

Pratto profiles as a middle-of-the-order hitter thanks to a low-maintenance swing, above-average bat speed and the ability to use the whole field. His loose wrists and advanced approach allow Pratto to adjust to pitches late. He's still learning how to get to his power, but he drives balls to all fields and will add strength to an already powerful frame. Pratto is already a plus defender at first with good footwork and instincts. He's not flashy but knows how to play. His above-average arm and athleticism would allow him to handle a corner outfield position, but for now he's a first baseman. Pratto is a below-average runner but with good instincts that should get him double-digit steals at least early in his career. He takes a solid attitude and demeanor to the field, maintains an even keel and is competitive by nature.

Pratto has enough baseball savvy and experience for his age that he could likely handle a jump to full-season ball in 2018 with a possible assignment to low Class A Lexington. The Royals have a longer instructional league period than most other Arizona-based teams, so the extra work and experience against more advanced pitching will help Pratto make that next step. His upside is as a starting first baseman at the big league level.

BILL MITCHELL

BA GRADE	SCOUTING GRADES
55 Risk: Extreme	**HIT:** 60. **POW:** 55. **SPD:** 45. **FLD:** 60. **ARM:** 55.

Projected future grades on 20-80 scouting scale

TOP PROSPECTS OF THE DECADE

Year	Player, Pos.	2017 Org
2008	Mike Moustakas, SS	Royals
2009	Mike Moustakas, 3B	Royals
2010	Mike Montgomery, LHP	Cubs
2011	Eric Hosmer, 1B	Royals
2012	Mike Montgomery, LHP	Cubs
2013	Kyle Zimmer, RHP	Royals
2014	Kyle Zimmer, RHP	Royals
2015	Raul A. Mondesi, SS	Royals
2016	Raul A. Mondesi, SS	Royals
2017	Josh Staumont, RHP	Royals

BEST TOOLS

Best Hitter for Average	Emmanuel Rivera
Best Power Hitter	Chase Vallot
Best Strike-Zone Discipline	Nicky Lopez
Fastest Baserunner	Terrance Gore
Best Athlete	Khalil Lee
Best Fastball	Josh Staumont
Best Curveball	Josh Staumont
Best Slider	Richard Lovelady
Best Changeup	Foster Griffin
Best Control	Jace Vines
Best Defensive Catcher	Cam Gallagher
Best Defensive Infielder	Nicky Lopez
Best Infield Arm	Emmanuel Rivera
Best Defensive Outfielder	Bubba Starling
Best Outfield Arm	Seuly Matias

Year	Club (League)	Class	AVG	G	AB	R	H	2B	3B	HR	RBI	BB	SO	SB	CS	OBP	SLG
2017	Royals (AZL)	R	.247	52	198	25	49	15	3	4	34	24	58	10	4	.330	.414
Minor League Totals			.247	52	198	25	49	15	3	4	34	24	58	10	4	.330	.414

2 KHALIL LEE, OF

Born: June 26, 1998. **B-T:** L-L. **Ht.:** 5-10. **Wt.:** 192. **Drafted:** HS—Oakton, Va., 2016 (3rd round). **Signed by:** Jim Farr.

After a solid first pro season in 2016, Lee skipped a level by heading off to low Class A Lexington in 2017. It was an encouraging first full season for the Royals' 2016 third-round pick, despite the lower batting average and tendency to swing and miss.

Lee's high strikeout totals are less of a concern because of his advanced knowledge of the strike zone, which allowed him to walk in 12 percent of his plate appearances. He projects to be an average hitter with more power to emerge with experience and strength. There is a concern about how he sets up his hands at the plate and struggles to get his foot down, but his hands are lightning quick and give him plus bat speed and good barrel control. He has above-average raw power to all fields with a swing that helps him put the ball in the air. Lee could have also been drafted as a pitcher, so his plus arm strength is for real and will be more than enough for right field, and premium athleticism will let him handle center field. He moves well in the outfield and takes good routes. He's close to a plus runner now and will at least be above-average as he gets bigger.

Lee projects as a starting outfielder capable of handling all three positions. He'll head to high Class A Wilmington in 2018.

BA GRADE

50 Risk: High

HIT: 50. POW: 55.
SPD: 55. FLD: 60.
ARM: 60.

Year	Club (League)	Class	AVG	G	AB	R	H	2B	3B	HR	RBI	BB	SO	SB	CS	OBP	SLG
2016	Royals (AZL)	R	.269	49	182	43	49	9	6	6	29	33	57	8	4	.396	.484
2017	Lexington (SAL)	LoA	.237	121	451	71	107	24	6	17	61	65	171	20	18	.344	.430
Minor League Totals			.246	170	633	114	156	33	12	23	90	98	228	28	22	.360	.445

3 SEULY MATIAS, OF

Born: Sept. 4, 1998. **B-T:** R-R. **Ht.:** 6-3. **Wt.:** 204. **Signed:** Dominican Republic, 2015. **Signed by:** Fausto Morel.

Matias was the jewel of Kansas City's 2015 international class, signing for $2.25 million. Skipping over the Dominican Summer League, Matias made his pro debut in the Arizona League at 17 where he tied for the league lead in home runs and ranked as the league's eighth-best prospect.

After an extended spring training season in which reports of his long home runs and impressive exit speeds made the rounds among scouts, Matias headed to Burlington of the Appalachian League for his second pro season. The common statement about Matias is that he passes the eye test. He's an impressive physical specimen with twitchy athleticism and raw strength. He flashes explosive power to all fields with plus bat speed and a swing plane built for carry on fly balls. While still plenty raw at the plate, Matias improved in handling breaking balls this year and didn't chase as many pitches in the dirt. He still swings at fastballs up in the zone but has shown an ability to adjust. His plus arm makes Matias a natural fit for right field, his most likely position. He's an above-average runner but may slow down a tick as he ages.

While he'll still be a teenager next spring, Matias will likely break camp with low Class A Lexington, where he'll be challenged by better pitching. He's a prototypical right fielder with an explosive power bat.

BA GRADE

55 Risk: Extreme

HIT: 45. POW: 60.
SPD: 50. FLD: 55.
ARM: 60.

Year	Club (League)	Class	AVG	G	AB	R	H	2B	3B	HR	RBI	BB	SO	SB	CS	OBP	SLG
2016	Royals (DSL)	R	.125	7	24	2	3	1	0	0	2	2	13	0	0	.222	.167
	Royals (AZL)	R	.250	46	172	32	43	11	2	8	29	22	73	2	4	.348	.477
2017	Burlington (APP)	R	.243	57	222	27	54	13	3	7	36	16	72	2	1	.297	.423
Minor League Totals			.239	110	418	61	100	25	5	15	67	40	158	4	5	.314	.431

4 JOSH STAUMONT, RHP

Born: Dec. 21, 1993. **B-T:** R-R. **Ht.:** 6-3. **Wt.:** 200. **Drafted:** Azusa Pacific (Calif.), 2015 (2nd round). **Signed by:** Colin Gonzalez.

Ranked as the Royals' top prospect a year ago, Staumont continued to frustrate with his combination of premium velocity and the chance for two plus pitches playing down due to inconsistent command and control. He regularly strikes out well over a batter per inning, but his 7.6 walks per nine innings indicates that he's still got plenty of work to do.

BA GRADE

50 Risk: High

FB: 70. CB: 60.
CHG: 50.
CTL: 40.

The Royals' second-round pick in 2015, Staumont started the year with an aggressive assignment to Triple-A Omaha before heading back down to Double-A Northwest Arkansas in mid-July to work on using a more consistent release point. Staumont has top-of-the-rotation stuff, and he dominates hitters when he's repeating his delivery and commanding his pitches. It's very easy upper-90s velocity, a plus-plus four-seamer that touches triple digits. A power curveball is his out pitch, thrown from a high three-quarters slot at 78-82 mph with depth and 11-5 tilt; it's an above-average pitch now with the potential of being a plus offering. Rounding out his arsenal is a changeup that is developing into an average pitch as the Royals encourage him to use it more effectively.

The key to Staumont's success is developing consistency of his control and not trying to be too fine with his pitches. While some observers point to a future as an eighth-inning reliever, his stuff plays up as a starter and the Royals will keep him in that role for now.

Year	Club (League)	Class	W	L	ERA	G	GS	CG	SV	IP	H	HR	BB	SO	K/9	WHIP	AVG
2015	Royals (AZL)	R	0	0	0.00	4	3	0	0	9	3	0	8	7	7.3	1.27	.103
	Idaho Falls (PIO)	R	3	1	3.16	14	1	0	1	31	18	0	24	51	14.6	1.34	.168
2016	Wilmington (CAR)	HiA	2	10	5.05	18	15	0	0	73	62	3	67	94	11.6	1.77	.230
	NW Arkansas (TL)	AA	2	1	3.04	11	11	0	0	50	42	2	37	73	13.1	1.57	.232
2017	Omaha (PCL)	AAA	3	8	6.28	16	15	0	0	76	64	14	63	93	11.0	1.67	.227
	NW Arkansas (TL)	AA	3	4	4.44	10	10	0	0	49	42	2	34	45	8.3	1.56	.244
Minor League Totals			13	24	4.56	73	55	0	1	288	231	21	233	363	11.3	1.61	.222

5 ERIC SKOGLUND, LHP

Born: Oct. 26, 1992. **B-T:** L-L. **Ht.:** 6-7. **Wt.:** 200. **Drafted:** Central Florida, 2014 (3rd round). **Signed by:** Jim Buckley/Gregg Kilby.

Skoglund made his major league debut in Kansas City in just his third full season since being drafted in the third round in 2014 out of Central Florida, getting into seven games in two different stints with the Royals. The bulk of the lean, lanky southpaw's season was spent with Triple-A Omaha, where he put up a 4.11 ERA in the hitter-friendly Pacific Coast League while fanning just over one batter per inning.

BA GRADE

45 Risk: Medium

FB: 55. CB: 50.
SL: 45. CHG: 50.
CTL: 55.

Skoglund battled through a lat issue early in the season but showed no ill effects. He gets lots of leverage and good plane from his 6-foot-7 frame. An above-average 90-95 mph fastball, which he elevates with two strikes, gets good movement and plenty of swings and misses. The heater gets good four-seam ride and arm-side tail, coming in late on righthanded batters. A solid-average curveball with good shape delivered at 80 mph is his best secondary, followed by an 85 mph changeup with cut action he uses infrequently. Skoglund also mixes in an 87 mph slider that resembles a cutter, but it's still a work in progress. His stuff plays up because he commands it well.

Skoglund profiles as a No. 4 starter or better and will head to spring training looking to earn a shot in the Royals' 2018 rotation.

Year	Club (League)	Class	W	L	ERA	G	GS	CG	SV	IP	H	HR	BB	SO	K/9	WHIP	AVG
2015	Wilmington (CAR)	HiA	6	3	3.52	15	15	1	0	84	83	2	11	66	7.0	1.11	.260
2016	NW Arkansas (TL)	AA	7	10	3.45	27	27	0	0	156	135	19	38	134	7.7	1.11	.230
2017	NW Arkansas (TL)	AA	0	0	2.70	1	1	0	0	3	5	0	3	1	2.7	2.40	.385
	Omaha (PCL)	AAA	4	5	4.11	19	19	1	0	101	110	14	29	102	9.1	1.38	.274
	Kansas City (AL)	MAJ	1	2	9.50	7	5	0	0	18	30	2	12	14	7.0	2.33	.375
Major League Totals			1	2	9.50	7	5	0	0	18	30	2	12	14	7.0	2.33	.375
Minor League Totals			17	20	3.75	71	70	2	0	368	363	37	90	328	8.0	1.23	.257

6 M.J. MELENDEZ, C

Born: Nov. 29, 1998. **B-T:** L-R. **Ht.:** 6-1. **Wt.:** 185. **Drafted:** HS—Palmetto Bay, Fla., 2017 (2nd round). **Signed by:** Alex Mesa.

Melendez comes from a baseball family, with his father currently the head coach at Florida International. The Royals took him in the second round, knowing that it would take an over-slot bonus to lure him away from the chance of playing college ball for his dad.

After signing for $2,097,500, Melendez began his pro career in the Rookie-level Arizona League where he ranked as the 13th best prospect. Melendez brings a lot of tools and athleticism to the field, an advanced player for his age. At the plate, Melendez gets good carry off the bat with power to all fields, albeit with some swing and miss. He tends to get rotational in the batter's box with a deep barrel dip and gets his weight out in front, so improvements to his swing will help. He's an average or better runner now, which is good speed for a catcher. Melendez' calling card is his defense behind the plate. He's athletic with quick feet, good lateral mobility and good hands. Melendez is a smart game-caller and being bilingual gives him an edge in working with his pitchers. He's got at least a plus arm with sub-2.0 pop times, although some scouts put a plus-plus grade on his arm strength. He gets rid of the ball quickly and can throw from his knees, and while his arm stroke is a little long he makes up for it with arm strength and explosiveness from the crouch.

Melendez projects as a first-division regular catcher at the big league level. He may be advanced enough to tag along with draftmate Pratto, heading to low Class A Lexington to start the 2018 season.

BA GRADE	
55	**Risk:** Extreme

HIT: 50. **POW:** 55.
SPD: 50. **FLD:** 60.
ARM: 60.

Year	Club (League)	Class	AVG	G	AB	R	H	2B	3B	HR	RBI	BB	SO	SB	CS	OBP	SLG
2017	Royals (AZL)	R	.262	47	168	25	44	8	3	4	30	26	60	4	2	.374	.417
Minor League Totals			.262	47	168	25	44	8	3	4	30	26	60	4	2	.374	.417

7 NICKY LOPEZ, SS

Born: March 13, 1995. **B-T:** L-R. **Ht.:** 5-11. **Wt.:** 175. **Drafted:** Creighton, 2016 (5th round). **Signed by:** Matt Price.

The Royals were thrilled to get Lopez with their fifth-round pick in a 2016 draft that was weak in college shortstops, and their enthusiasm for the Creighton product showed when he made it to Double-A Northwest Arkansas by the middle of his first full year. Lopez was a Carolina League all-star in his first full pro season.

Lopez is an instinctive leader on the field with a high baseball IQ, a gamer with a lithe build and athleticism who will consistently play above his tools. He's a line-drive, base-hit type of hitter who takes good at-bats and gets on base with his good understanding of the strike zone and patient approach. He strokes balls gap-to-gap with a good feel for hitting, projecting as an above-average hitter but with well below-average power. He's a plus runner with good baserunning instincts. Lopez is an average defender now at both middle infield positions and could end up above-average at second. He's not flashy, but with good range and instincts Lopez gets to the ball and makes the plays. He has enough arm for shortstop and knows just how much to use to get runners out. It's at least an average arm now and projects to be above-average with added strength. Lopez has a high floor as a utility infielder but with the chance to grow into an everyday shortstop or second baseman. His lack of power does limit his ceiling, but he also knows he's not a power hitter and does a good job of getting on base and playing a small ball game.

Raul A. Mondesi, the heir apparent at shortstop now that Alcides Escobar has become a free agent, has much louder tools than Lopez. But Lopez has impressive feel and reliability that could work into a utility role in the not-too-distant future. And if Mondesi stumbles against offensively, he could move into an even larger role.

BA GRADE	
45	**Risk:** Medium

HIT: 55. **POW:** 30.
SPD: 60. **FLD:** 55.
ARM: 55.

Year	Club (League)	Class	AVG	G	AB	R	H	2B	3B	HR	RBI	BB	SO	SB	CS	OBP	SLG
2016	Burlington (APP)	R	.281	62	231	54	65	6	5	6	29	35	30	24	4	.393	.429
2017	Wilmington (CAR)	HiA	.295	70	285	42	84	12	7	2	27	36	23	14	8	.376	.407
	NW Arkansas (TL)	AA	.259	59	232	26	60	6	1	0	11	16	29	7	4	.312	.293
Minor League Totals			.279	191	748	122	209	24	13	8	67	87	82	45	16	.363	.378

8 HUNTER DOZIER, 3B/OF

Born: Aug. 22, 1991. **B-T:** R-R. **Ht.:** 6-4. **Wt.:** 220. **Drafted:** Stephen F. Austin State, 2013 (1st round). **Signed by:** Mitch Thompson.

After Dozier's prospect status began to dim with a subpar 2015 season at Double-A, he shortened his swing and improved his bat path to produce a strong 2016. After making his major league debut at the end of 2016, Dozier ranked as the Royals' No. 3 prospect. But 2017 turned out to be a lost season for Dozier. He was first sidelined early in the year with an oblique injury and then later missed two months with a broken hamate.

Dozier rounded back into form after returning to Triple-A Omaha in 2017. He compiled a strong August in which he hit .260/.351/.560, while building off swing improvements he made the previous season. He's a fringe-average defender who played as much in the outfield in 2017 as his more natural third base. He also saw time at first base. He may project best as a bat off the bench capable of filling in at all four corner positions. Dozier headed to the Mexican Pacific League after the 2017 season to make up for lost time, but he hit just .211/.298/.368 in a month of winter ball action before coming home.

With the Royals' 2018 lineup in a state of flux because of the free agency of several key regulars, Dozier has a good shot at earning at least a reserve role out of spring training.

BA GRADE

45 Risk: Medium

HIT: 55. POW: 55.
SPD: 50. FLD: 50.
ARM: 50.

Year	Club (League)	Class	AVG	G	AB	R	H	2B	3B	HR	RBI	BB	SO	SB	CS	OBP	SLG
2015	NW Arkansas (TL)	AA	.213	128	475	65	101	27	1	12	53	45	151	6	2	.281	.349
2016	NW Arkansas (TL)	AA	.305	26	95	14	29	8	0	8	21	14	23	4	0	.400	.642
	Omaha (PCL)	AAA	.294	103	391	65	115	36	1	15	54	40	100	3	1	.357	.506
	Kansas City (AL)	MAJ	.211	8	19	4	4	1	0	0	1	2	8	0	0	.286	.263
2017	Wilmington (CAR)	HiA	.364	3	11	1	4	1	0	0	1	1	5	0	0	.462	.455
	NW Arkansas (TL)	AA	.250	6	16	4	4	1	0	0	0	4	8	0	0	.400	.313
	Omaha (PCL)	AAA	.226	24	84	11	19	6	1	4	12	9	37	1	1	.313	.464
Major League Totals			.211	8	19	4	4	1	0	0	1	2	8	0	0	.286	.263
Minor League Totals			.261	489	1803	278	471	139	3	54	253	217	487	27	10	.343	.432

9 FOSTER GRIFFIN, LHP

Born: July 27, 1995. **B-T:** R-L. **Ht.:** 6-3. **Wt.:** 200. **Drafted:** HS—Orlando, 2014 (1st round). **Signed by:** Jim Buckley.

One of two first-round picks by Kansas City in 2014 when the Florida native was one of the top high school arms in that draft class, Griffin struggled in his first two full seasons coinciding with a drop in his velocity.

After finishing the 2016 season at high Class A Wilmington with a 6.23 ERA, Griffin returned the next year as a different pitcher. With an uptick in velocity and a more aggressive nature on the mound, Griffin pitched better off of his fastball, missed more bats and improved his breaking ball to post a 2.86 ERA in 10 starts back at Wilmington before moving up to Double-A Northwest Arkansas. His combined total of 15 wins was among the best in that category in the minor leagues. Griffin took more of a bulldog mentality to the mound in 2017, speeding up the game and getting better arm speed, which allowed him to make more quality pitches down in the zone. His fastball sits 88-92 mph, up a tick from before, and he located it better. His two-seamer has tail while his four-seam fastball has cut to it. He sharpened his 11-5 curveball, getting more shape to it and allowing him to be more aggressive with the pitch. Griffin uses his changeup to keep hitters off balance; it's a below-average pitch now but projects as an average or above-average offering. He sequences his pitches well and showed the ability to change speeds in and out. Griffin is credited with having good makeup and focus on the mound.

After 18 starts at Double-A, Griffin may be ready to move on to Triple-A Omaha although he'll still be only 22 in the spring. He has the upside of a No. 4 starter.

BA GRADE

50 Risk: High

FB: 50. CB: 55.
CHG: 55.
CTL: 55.

Year	Club (League)	Class	W	L	ERA	G	GS	CG	SV	IP	H	HR	BB	SO	K/9	WHIP	AVG
2015	Lexington (SAL)	LoA	4	6	5.44	22	22	0	0	103	123	8	35	71	6.2	1.54	.296
2016	Lexington (SAL)	LoA	1	4	3.38	7	7	0	0	37	35	3	9	29	7.0	1.18	.243
	Wilmington (CAR)	HiA	5	10	6.23	20	20	0	0	95	130	9	43	76	7.2	1.81	.330
2017	Wilmington (CAR)	HiA	4	2	2.86	10	10	0	0	57	43	2	20	60	9.5	1.11	.210
	NW Arkansas (TL)	AA	11	5	3.61	18	18	0	0	105	108	11	34	81	7.0	1.36	.271
Minor League Totals			25	29	4.49	88	88	0	0	425	458	35	153	336	7.1	1.44	.276

10 SCOTT BLEWETT, RHP

Born: April 10, 1996. **B-T:** R-R. **Ht.:** 6-6. **Wt.:** 210. **Drafted:** HS—Baldwinsville, N.Y., 2014 (2nd round). **Signed by:** Bobby Gandolfo.

Since being picked in the second round of the 2014 draft, Blewett's career has always been more about projection than production, and he continues trending in the right direction after a solid season with high Class A Wilmington at the age of 21.

It took him two years to get out of low Class A, but after a rough 2015 season, Blewett bounced back in 2016 when he regained some fluidity in his delivery and his velocity ticked upward. He continued that trend in 2017 with added strength and got better at attacking hitters. Blewett's fastball sits in the 92-93 mph range, touching 96 at its best. It's a relatively straight pitch but is a heavy fastball down in the zone that gets a lot of ground balls. He challenges batters with that fastball and throws it for strikes. Blewett's 75-77 mph curveball has good depth and was sharper in 2017; it is now an average pitch. His below-average changeup is still in development, with the Royals encouraging him to use it more often. It has good action but its mid-80s velocity doesn't provide enough separation from his fastball. It's an average pitch now but projects to be above-average in time.

Blewett will face his toughest challenge yet when he moves up to Double-A in 2018. If it all comes together for him, he projects as a mid-rotation starter.

BA GRADE
50 Risk: High
FB: 55. CB: 50. CHG: 55. CTL: 50.

Year	Club (League)	Class	W	L	ERA	G	GS	CG	SV	IP	H	HR	BB	SO	K/9	WHIP	AVG
2015	Lexington (SAL)	LoA	3	5	5.20	18	18	0	0	81	88	6	24	60	6.6	1.38	.272
2016	Lexington (SAL)	LoA	8	11	4.31	25	25	2	0	129	138	10	51	121	8.4	1.46	.275
2017	Wilmington (CAR)	HiA	7	10	4.07	27	27	1	0	153	153	16	52	129	7.6	1.34	.262
Minor League Totals			19	28	4.44	78	77	3	0	391	406	35	142	339	7.8	1.40	.268

11 MIGUEL ALMONTE, RHP

BA GRADE
45 Risk: Medium

Born: April 4, 1993. **B-T:** R-R. **Ht.:** 6-2. **Wt.:** 210. **Signed:** Dominican Republic, 2009. **Signed by:** Fausto Morel

Almonte got back on track in 2017 after a couple of rough years—at least when he was on the mound and not on the disabled list. He missed time due to arm discomfort but was impressive when he pitched, posting sub-2.00 ERAs in limited time at both Double-A Northwest Arkansas and Triple-A Omaha.

The gem of Almonte's arsenal is a fastball—both a two-seamer and four-seamer—with plus velocity that was up to 98 mph, sitting 93-97. The pitch has natural sinking action with arm-side run. His changeup is a plus pitch that at 90 mph is thrown hard, with slight arm-side fade and natural sink. His breaking ball has gotten better but doesn't have a lot of depth. He gets 12-6 movement from his curveball/slider hybrid, ranging from 83 for the curveball to 87 mph for the slider. He had more separation between the breaking balls this year, giving him four average or better pitches.

Almonte will go to spring training looking to break camp with the Royals. While some observers see him as more of a reliever, his diverse repertoire points to rotation potential for the Dominican righthander.

Year	Club (League)	Class	W	L	ERA	G	GS	CG	SV	IP	H	HR	BB	SO	K/9	WHIP	AVG
2015	NW Arkansas (TL)	AA	4	4	4.03	17	17	0	0	67	65	4	27	55	7.4	1.37	.255
	Omaha (PCL)	AAA	2	2	5.40	11	6	0	0	37	33	3	15	41	10.1	1.31	.244
	Kansas City (AL)	MAJ	0	2	6.23	9	0	0	0	9	7	4	7	10	10.4	1.62	.212
2016	Omaha (PCL)	AAA	3	7	5.55	21	12	0	0	60	63	5	42	57	8.6	1.75	.274
	NW Arkansas (TL)	AA	2	1	7.31	11	0	0	0	16	24	4	4	15	8.4	1.75	.348
2017	NW Arkansas (TL)	AA	1	0	1.86	7	6	0	0	29	22	2	6	35	10.9	0.97	.210
	Kansas City (AL)	MAJ	0	0	13.50	2	0	0	0	2	5	0	2	0	0.0	3.50	.556
	Omaha (PCL)	AAA	1	0	1.50	9	3	0	0	18	20	1	7	17	8.5	1.50	.299
Major League Totals			0	2	7.59	11	0	0	0	11	12	4	9	10	8.4	1.97	.286
Minor League Totals			32	34	3.77	145	104	1	0	556	516	36	189	536	8.7	1.27	.248

12 CHASE VALLOT, C

BA GRADE
50 Risk: High

Born: Aug. 21, 1996. **B-T:** R-R **Ht.:** 6-0. **Wt.:** 215. **Drafted:** HS—Lafayette, La., 2014 (1st round supplemental). **Signed by:** Travis Ezi.

Possessing as much raw power as anyone in the Royals system, Vallot is a bit of a polarizing prospect among observers. Some scouts don't believe the Louisiana native possesses the skills necessary to stay behind the plate nor the hit tool to go with his above-average power.

Vallot has missed valuable development time due to injury in each of the last two years in full-season ball, with his 2017 season ending on July 27 due to a low-back muscle strain. But he just turned 21 in August and has been young for every level at which he's played. Vallot will always hit for a lower batting average, but he's gotten better at handling offspeed pitches, knows the strike zone and consistently draws a fair share of walks. Vallot has the best raw power in the system. There's still plenty of swing and miss in his game, and he fanned in 36 percent of his at-bats in 2017 compared to 33 percent the previous year. Vallot is still a work in progress behind the plate, but his receiving has gotten better and he works well with pitchers. He has above-average arm strength, but inconsistent footwork affects the accuracy of his throw and he threw out just under 18 percent of base tealers at Wilmington.

Vallot won't turn 22 until August, so he may return to Wilmington to start the 2018 season before tackling Double-A.

Year	Club (League)	Class	AVG	G	AB	R	H	2B	3B	HR	RBI	BB	SO	SB	CS	OBP	SLG
2015	Lexington (SAL)	LoA	.219	80	279	46	61	13	3	13	40	41	105	1	0	.331	.427
2016	Royals (AZL)	R	.133	10	30	5	4	1	0	2	2	3	14	0	0	.257	.367
	Lexington (SAL)	LoA	.246	82	272	37	67	20	0	13	44	39	118	0	0	.367	.463
2017	Wilmington (CAR)	HiA	.231	89	281	34	65	22	0	12	37	64	127	0	0	.380	.438
Minor League Totals			.226	314	1048	151	237	70	3	47	150	173	445	1	1	.352	.433

13 SAMIR DUENEZ, 1B

BA GRADE

50 Risk: High

Born: June 11, 1996. **B-T:** L-R. **Ht.:** 6-1. **Wt.:** 195. **Signed:** Venezuela, 2012.
Signed by: Alberto Garcia/Richard Castro/Orlando Estevez.

Duenez has been one of the younger players in every league in which he's played since starting his pro career at 17 in the Arizona League. He spent the entire 2017 season with Double-A Northwest Arkansas despite not turning 21 until mid-season.

A career-high 17 home runs signaled the emergence of long-awaited power. Duenez projects to be an impact power bat from the left side as he continues to refine his approach, projecting to have above-average power to go with an above-average hit tool in time. He hits the ball with authority and a sharp line-drive plane, but he needs to manage the zone better. While his speed is a tick below average, Duenez is an opportunistic, instinctive baserunner who has recorded double-digit steals in each of his three full seasons.

After spending some time in the outfield in the past, he's now a full-time first baseman where he's an average defender. Duenez may be ready for Triple-A ball in 2018, where he'll again be one of the youngest players there, although he may return to Double-A if there's a logjam in the Omaha lineup.

Year	Club (League)	Class	AVG	G	AB	R	H	2B	3B	HR	RBI	BB	SO	SB	CS	OBP	SLG
2015	Lexington (SAL)	LoA	.266	101	361	47	96	13	4	1	37	24	33	11	5	.314	.332
2016	Lexington (SAL)	LoA	.272	68	265	30	72	15	3	6	49	15	40	14	2	.312	.419
	Wilmington (CAR)	HiA	.300	56	213	30	64	13	2	7	42	19	34	10	2	.363	.479
	NW Arkansas (TL)	AA	.278	14	54	4	15	5	0	0	9	5	12	2	0	.339	.370
2017	NW Arkansas (TL)	AA	.252	132	523	65	132	23	2	17	75	37	116	10	3	.304	.402
Minor League Totals			.270	498	1880	230	508	97	16	32	267	129	301	59	19	.319	.390

14 YEFRI DEL ROSARIO, RHP

BA GRADE

50 Risk: V. High

Born: Sept. 23, 1999. **B-T:** R-R. **Ht.:** 6-2. **Wt.:** 180. **Signed:** Dominican Republic, 2016. **Signed by:** Jonathan Cruz (Braves).

Del Rosario originally signed with the Braves for $1 million as part of that organization's deep 2016 international class. After making his pro debut in 2017, Del Rosario was declared a free agent as part of Major League Baseball's sanctions for the Braves circumvention of international signing rules from 2015 to 2017, and the Royals signed him for an additional $665,000.

One of the top pitchers in the 2016 international class, del Rosario's stock has risen as his velocity and stuff have gone up. After two games in the Dominican Summer League, del Rosario pitched for the Braves' Gulf Coast League affiliate where he ranked as the 16th best prospect. His fastball generates sink and arm-side run, sitting 89-92 mph and touching 95, and he projects to add more velocity because of his build and arm speed. He uses his potential plus curveball with sharp, late break to miss bats and doesn't hesitate to throw it in any count. Rounding out his repertoire is a solid changeup that should improve with experience. There's some concern that del Rosario's crossfire delivery with effort signals a bullpen future, but he's athletic and does a good job in getting himself back online to the plate with the ability to throw strikes.

With a cleaner delivery and increased strength, del Rosario has a future in the middle of a starting rotation.

Year	Club (League)	Class	W	L	ERA	G	GS	CG	SV	IP	H	HR	BB	SO	K/9	WHIP	AVG
2017	Braves (DSL)	R	0	0	1.80	2	2	0	0	5	1	0	4	7	12.6	1.00	.067
	Braves (GCL)	R	1	1	3.90	11	6	0	0	32	37	1	10	29	8.1	1.45	.285
Minor League Totals			1	1	3.62	13	8	0	0	37	38	1	14	36	8.7	1.39	.262

15 RYAN O'HEARN, 1B/OF

BA GRADE
45 Risk: Medium

Born: July 26, 1993. **B-T:** L-L. **Ht.:** 6-3. **Wt.:** 200. **Drafted:** Sam Houston State, 2014 (8th round). **Signed by:** Justin Lehr.

Being sent down a level during the season is usually looked at as a negative, but O'Hearn's move from Omaha after 114 games in Triple-A was done just to keep him getting consistent at-bats while making room for more experienced players at the Triple-A level.

Regardless, it was a solid year in which he hit 22 homeruns for the second straight season. His hand strength and average or better bat speed allow O'Hearn to get to his plus raw power in games, and he isn't baffled by lefthanded pitching. He gets too much weight transfer to his front side at times and struggles with his timing, and he needs to improve his consistency of contact to reach his projection of at least an average hitter. He's an adequate defender at first base, with average hands but below-average range. O'Hearn occasionally takes a turn in a corner outfield spot, but his well-below-average speed makes him a subpar defender there.

O'Hearn has a high floor as a big league power bat, but he was not added to the 40-man roster and went unpicked in the Rule 5 draft.

Year	Club (League)	Class	AVG	G	AB	R	H	2B	3B	HR	RBI	BB	SO	SB	CS	OBP	SLG
2015	Lexington (SAL)	LoA	.277	81	314	44	87	11	0	19	56	36	87	7	2	.351	.494
	Wilmington (CAR)	HiA	.236	46	161	14	38	10	0	8	21	19	54	0	0	.315	.447
2016	Wilmington (CAR)	HiA	.352	22	88	13	31	7	0	7	18	8	27	0	0	.408	.670
	NW Arkansas (TL)	AA	.258	112	414	49	107	25	2	15	60	48	131	3	5	.339	.437
2017	Omaha (PCL)	AAA	.252	114	413	48	104	26	1	18	53	45	119	1	0	.325	.450
	NW Arkansas (TL)	AA	.258	19	66	7	17	1	1	4	11	10	20	0	0	.355	.485
Minor League Totals			.278	458	1705	236	474	96	5	84	273	205	497	14	9	.356	.488

16 GERSON GARABITO, RHP

BA GRADE
50 Risk: High

Born: Aug. 19, 1995. **B-T:** R-R. **Ht.:** 6-0. **Wt.:** 202. **Signed:** Dominican Republic, 2012. **Signed by:** Edis Perez.

Garabito returned to low Class A Lexington for a second try there after a rocky 2016 season. He pitched much better in his return to the Legends rotation despite missing time to injury.

Garabito has a sturdy build for his size with some weight through his lower half. He pitches with deception and feel, delivering his 89-94 mph fastball with good arm speed and fade, distinct cut and sinking action. What stands out for Garabito is the plus command of his pitches coming from a smooth, online delivery. He has a larger arm swing, finishing firm and across the body. He locates a 76-79 mph curveball with good depth and action, and he has good feel for an improving 83-87 mph changeup. Garabito shows composure and good mound presence, and his athleticism allows him to make plays off the mound. He should be ready to move on to high Class A Wilmington in 2018.

Garabito's got the repertoire to remain in the rotation as a No. 4 or 5 starter, but his fastball/curveball combo could make him a solid bullpen piece in the future.

Year	Club (League)	Class	W	L	ERA	G	GS	CG	SV	IP	H	HR	BB	SO	K/9	WHIP	AVG
2015	Royals (AZL)	R	3	2	4.11	14	11	0	0	57	52	2	19	42	6.6	1.25	.242
2016	Lexington (SAL)	LoA	2	11	4.80	18	18	0	0	81	78	9	35	61	6.8	1.40	.256
2017	Royals (AZL)	R	0	0	6.00	2	2	0	0	3	4	1	1	2	6.0	1.67	.333
	Lexington (SAL)	LoA	4	5	2.81	15	15	0	0	77	52	8	19	72	8.4	0.92	.191
Minor League Totals			12	19	3.40	74	61	0	0	294	233	21	118	255	7.8	1.20	.219

17 CARLOS HERNANDEZ, RHP

BA GRADE
50 Risk: V. High

Born: March 11, 1997. **B-T:** R-R. **Ht.:** 6-4. **Wt.:** 200. **Signed:** Venezuela, 2016. **Signed by:** Richard Castro/Joelvis Gonzalez.

Most organizations have at least one pop-up prospect every year, that guy who no one knows about—at least not yet. Hernandez may be that player in the Royals organization. Signed for $15,000 in 2016 when he was already 19 years old, Hernandez made his pro debut in the Rookie-level Appalachian League.

Hernandez's numbers weren't anything special—a 5.49 ERA, albeit with a strikeout per inning—but Hernandez has as much upside as any pitcher in the system. Already flashing a plus fastball at 94-97 mph with late glove-side life and late cut showing heavy depth, Hernandez's large, meaty frame and whippy arm strength suggest that 100 mph velo is not far away. He has feel for a fringe-average 79-80 mph curveball with 11-5 two-plane depth, but his best secondary pitch is an average changeup from 84-87 that could develop into a plus offering. Improving his changeup was a priority during instructional league, and he made good progress with the pitch.

Hernandez has the upside of a mid- to top-of-the rotation starter, and at 21 will likely get his first crack at full-season ball in 2018.

Year	Club (League)	Class	W	L	ERA	G	GS	CG	SV	IP	H	HR	BB	SO	K/9	WHIP	AVG
2017	Burlington (APP)	R	1	4	5.49	12	11	0	0	62	64	6	27	62	9.0	1.46	.266
Minor League Totals			1	4	5.49	12	11	0	0	62	64	6	27	62	9.0	1.46	.266

18 EVAN STEELE, LHP

BA GRADE

50 Risk: V. High

Born: Nov. 14, 1996. **B-T:** R-L. **Ht.:** 6-5. **Wt.:** 210. **Drafted:** Chipola (Fla.) JC, 2017 (2nd round supplemental). **Signed by:** Jim Buckley.

Steele pitched infrequently at Vanderbilt in 2016 before heading to Chipola (Fla.) JC for his sophomore year, where he posted a 5-0, 2.01 record in 10 starts, striking out 58 in 40.1 innings.

Selected by the Royals with the 73rd overall pick in 2017, Steele saw limited innings in his pro debut, not getting on the mound in the Rookie-level Arizona League until mid-August. Steele has a good frame and squared shoulders, getting plenty of arm speed using an abbreviated windup from the first-base side of the rubber. He gets good plane and deception on his pitches, utilizing a 91-94 mph fastball with tail and arm-side sink. He has feel for an above-average changeup at 85-87 mph. While he didn't throw his breaking ball much in rookie ball or instructional league, he shows confidence in an 82-84 mph slider, backfooting it to righthanded hitters. His pitches play up because of the deception in his delivery.

Projecting as a No. 4 starter, Steele may get a low Class A assignment to start the 2018 season.

Year	Club (League)	Class	W	L	ERA	G	GS	CG	SV	IP	H	HR	BB	SO	K/9	WHIP	AVG
2017	Royals (AZL)	R	0	2	5.63	5	5	0	0	8	11	2	2	16	18.0	1.63	.306
Minor League Totals			0	2	5.63	5	5	0	0	8	11	2	2	16	18.0	1.63	.306

19 DANIEL TILLO, LHP

BA GRADE

50 Risk: V. High

Born: June 13, 1996. **B-T:** L-L. **Ht.:** 6-5. **Wt.:** 215. **Drafted:** Iowa Western JC, 2017 (3rd round). **Signed by:** Scott Melvin.

Tillo was first drafted by the Twins in 2015 in the 39th round from his Sioux City, Iowa high school where he was better known for his basketball exploits, having been named Iowa's Mr. Basketball in his senior year. He pitched briefly at Kentucky before heading to Iowa Western Community College. Tillo is a fresh-armed pitcher with little history on the mound but with a clean delivery and more pitchability than expected from his experience level.

Tillo got into 10 games in his first pro season split between the Rookie-level Arizona League and the Royals' Appalachian League affiliate in Burlington, N.C. Tillo has a sturdy body, using a compact delivery with a loose, easy arm. He delivers a 91-94 mph fastball to both sides of the plate with late tail and sink, and it bores in on lefthanded batters. His 82-85 mph slider is a below-average pitch now, but it's short, hard and has good three-quarters tilt. His changeup, working at 87-88 mph with moderate tumble, is a fringy pitch. Scouts got a limited look at Tillo during instructional league but gave favorable reports, projecting both his fastball and slider as plus pitches.

Tillo will likely join draftmate Evan Steele with an assignment to low Class A Lexington.

Year	Club (League)	Class	W	L	ERA	G	GS	CG	SV	IP	H	HR	BB	SO	K/9	WHIP	AVG
2017	Royals (AZL)	R	0	0	9.53	3	2	0	0	6	8	0	0	7	11.1	1.41	.333
	Burlington (APP)	R	3	2	3.48	7	7	0	0	31	35	1	6	25	7.3	1.32	.285
Minor League Totals			3	2	4.42	10	9	0	0	37	43	1	6	32	7.9	1.34	.293

20 MICHAEL GIGLIOTTI, OF

BA GRADE

50 Risk: V. High

Born: Feb. 14, 1996. **B-T:** L-L. **Ht.:** 6-1. **Wt.:** 180. **Drafted:** Lipscomb, 2017 (4th round). **Signed by:** Nick Hamilton.

A down year in his junior season at Lipscomb may have hurt Gigliotti's draft stock, with talent evaluators concerned that he had become a too patient hitter. The Royals grabbled the lefthanded hitting center fielder in the fourth round, signing him for $397,500 and assigning him to advanced-rookie Burlington to start his career.

Gigliotti made it to low Class A Lexington for the last month of the regular season, posting a combined slash line of .320/.420/.456 with 22 stolen bases. While his patient approach concerned amateur scouts, the Royals see his plate discipline as an elite tool, noting his advanced knowledge of the strike zone allows him to focus on contact and work counts. Gigliotti has a strong frame and quick hands, profiling as a top-of-the-order hitter with an efficient bat path and advanced feel at the plate but with below-average power. He's a plus-plus runner who gets good reads on fly balls, and his average arm is playable in center field.

With some time at low Class A behind him, Gigliotti may be able to jump right to high Class A Wilmington in 2018. He projects as a starting center fielder and leadoff hitter at the major league level.

Year	Club (League)	Class	AVG	G	AB	R	H	2B	3B	HR	RBI	BB	SO	SB	CS	OBP	SLG
2017	Burlington (APP)	R	.329	42	155	30	51	8	3	3	30	32	21	15	5	.442	.477
	Lexington (SAL)	LoA	.302	22	86	14	26	5	1	1	8	8	20	7	5	.378	.419
Minor League Totals			.320	64	241	44	77	13	4	4	38	40	41	22	10	.420	.456

21 BURCH SMITH, RHP

BA GRADE
45 Risk: High

Born: April 12, 1990. **B-T:** R-R. **Ht.:** 6-4. **Wt.:** 215. **Drafted:** Oklahoma, 2011 (14th round). **Signed by:** Lane Decker (Padres).

Smith made it to the big leagues with the Padres in 2013 in just his second full season after being drafted from Oklahoma in 2011 and signing for $250,000. Persistent injuries and eventually Tommy John surgery kept him out of action for much of the next three years.

During his time on the sidelines Smith was included in a late 2014 three-team deal to the Rays and didn't get back on the mound with Tampa Bay until 2017, when he pitched at three minor league levels. He wrapped up the year with a successful stint in the Arizona Fall League before the Royals picked him up in the 2017 Rule 5 draft, purchasing his rights from the Mets, who took him sixth overall. Smith has a starter's frame with a sturdy body and strong lower half, and he shows advanced command of all of his pitches and changes speeds well. His fastball sits 94-97 mph with some run and natural cut, and he complements his heater with an 11-to-5 curveball with two-plane depth that comes in at 74-76 mph. His best secondary pitch is a plus, swing-and-miss 79-81 mph changeup that has good tumble.

Smith could fill the role of back-end starter or seventh-inning reliever, with a move to the bullpen the more likely role because of his injury history.

Year	Club (League)	Class	W	L	ERA	G	GS	CG	SV	IP	H	HR	BB	SO	K/9	WHIP	AVG
2015	Did not play—Injured																
2016	Did not play—Injured																
2017	Rays (GCL)	R	0	1	6.00	1	1	0	0	3	4	0	0	4	12.0	1.33	.364
	Charlotte (FSL)	HiA	3	1	2.43	9	8	0	0	37	26	1	20	33	8.0	1.24	.200
	Durham (IL)	AAA	2	1	1.65	3	3	0	0	16	9	2	4	19	10.5	0.80	.161
Major League Totals			1	3	6.44	10	7	0	0	36	39	9	21	46	11.4	1.65	.269
Minor League Totals			20	14	3.45	61	58	0	1	285	255	21	80	302	9.5	1.18	.239

22 BRAD KELLER, RHP

BA GRADE
45 Risk: High

Born: July 27, 1995. **B-T:** R-R. **Ht.:** 6-5. **Wt.:** 234. **Drafted:** HS—Flowery Branch, Ga., 2013 (8th round). **Signed by:** T.R Lewis (Diamondbacks).

For the third consecutive season, Keller took the ball just about every fifth day and chewed up innings. By the end of 2017 he started producing the stuff and results that led some in the D-backs organization to believe a breakout might be on the horizon. The Royals apparently agreed, because they purchased the rights to the Rule 5 pick after the Reds selected him third overall in 2017.

Keller was a lightly-scouted eighth-round high school pick in 2013 who moved slowly but steadily through Arizona system. He commands his fastball well and has the ability to either cut or sink it. He is capable of filling the zone with strikes, though he did see his walk rate rise to 3.9 per nine innings in 2017. Regardless, Keller took a step forward late in the season, when his fastball suddenly jumped and he gained a better understanding of how to finish off hitters. Over his final month, Keller sat 93-94 mph and topped out at 97. He throws an average to above-average changeup and a slider that coaches said improved as the year progressed.

If his late-year run carries over to 2018, Keller could become a back-of-the-rotation starter. If not, he could wind up being a power arm out of the bullpen.

Year	Club (League)	Class	W	L	ERA	G	GS	CG	SV	IP	H	HR	BB	SO	K/9	WHIP	AVG
2015	Kane County (MWL)	LoA	8	9	2.60	26	25	0	0	142	128	3	37	109	6.9	1.16	.243
2016	Visalia (CAL)	HiA	9	7	4.47	24	24	0	0	135	147	13	26	99	6.6	1.28	.281
2017	Jackson (SL)	AA	10	9	4.68	26	26	0	0	131	142	7	57	111	7.6	1.52	.279
Minor League Totals			40	32	3.77	106	100	0	0	541	557	33	178	442	7.3	1.36	.269

23 DONNIE DEWEES, OF

BA GRADE
45 Risk: High

Born: Sept. 29, 1993. **B-T:** L-L. **Ht.:** 5-11. **Wt.:** 204. **Drafted:** North Florida, 2015 (2nd round). **Signed by:** Tom Clark (Cubs).

Dewees was acquired by the Royals prior to the start of the 2017 season in a straight-up swap for pitcher Alec Mills. The North Florida product was Chicago's second-round pick in 2015, rising to the high Class A level with his former organization.

Dewees is a high-energy gamer and a hard worker with a good feel for the game. He is a top-of-the-order hitter with above-average strike zone judgment, barreling balls with above-average bat speed. The biggest improvement from 2016 to 2017 was an increase in walk rate from 6.8 percent to 8.8 percent, and his strike-zone judgment grades as above-average. An above-average runner, he's already got 70 stolen bases in his two-and-a-half-year minor league career and became a more efficient baserunner as the 2017 season progressed. He takes good jumps and routes in the outfield, allowing him to stay in center, but a below-average arm will keep him out of right.

Dewees should head to Triple-A and looks to be a backup outfielder in Kansas City before long.

Year	Club (League)	Class	AVG	G	AB	R	H	2B	3B	HR	RBI	BB	SO	SB	CS	OBP	SLG
2015	Eugene (NWL)	SS	.266	66	282	42	75	14	1	5	30	14	54	19	7	.306	.376
2016	South Bend (MWL)	LoA	.282	94	365	65	103	15	12	3	54	29	51	17	5	.337	.414
	Myrtle Beach (CAR)	HiA	.289	35	149	25	43	10	2	1	19	10	36	14	0	.339	.423
2017	NW Arkansas (TL)	AA	.272	126	464	67	126	24	6	9	52	46	81	20	8	.340	.407
Minor League Totals			.275	321	1260	199	347	63	21	19	155	99	222	70	20	.332	.404

24 MEIBRYS VILORIA, C

BA GRADE 45 Risk: High

Born: Feb. 15, 1997. **B-T:** L-R. **Ht.:** 5-11. **Wt.:** 195. **Signed:** Colombia, 2013.
Signed by: Rafael Miranda.

In 2016, Viloria led the Pioneer League in hitting and earned MVP honors. The native Colombian didn't make the same kind of impact in the Sally League, but he registered a good season as one of the younger catchers in the league.

Viloria has a good feel for hitting, more of a gap-to-gap, line-drive hitter with plenty of bat speed. He should continue to gain strength, which will allow him to drive more balls out of the park–although perhaps not many more than the eight homers he hit with Lexington. He's an aggressive hitter who will need to improve his below-average plate discipline to get on base more often. Most concerning is that Viloria's walk rate has declined each year while his strikeouts jumped from 13.9 percent in 2016 to 19.8 percent. Viloria's real value comes from his ability to catch and handle a pitching staff. He plays with passion and energy, and speaks both English and Spanish. He frames well and moves adequately behind the plate, and while not always accurate, his plus arm allowed him to throw out nearly 40 percent of basestealers.

Most scouts see Viloria as a future MLB backup. He'll move on to high Class A in 2018.

Year	Club (League)	Class	AVG	G	AB	R	H	2B	3B	HR	RBI	BB	SO	SB	CS	OBP	SLG
2015	Burlington (APP)	R	.260	45	150	20	39	0	0	0	16	17	23	0	0	.335	.260
2016	Idaho Falls (PIO)	R	.376	58	226	54	85	28	3	6	55	20	36	1	1	.436	.606
2017	Lexington (SAL)	LoA	.259	101	363	42	94	25	0	8	52	25	79	4	3	.313	.394
Minor League Totals			.292	250	890	136	260	63	4	17	148	86	166	6	5	.361	.429

25 ANDRES MACHADO, RHP

BA GRADE 45 Risk: High

Born: April 22, 1993. **B-T:** R-R. **Ht.:** 6-0. **Wt.:** 175. **Signed:** Venezuela, 2010.
Signed by: Richard Castro.

It took Machado a long time to make it to full-season ball after signing with the Royals in 2010 for $13,000. The Venezuelan righthander spent five seasons in short-season plus one year on the sidelines recovering from Tommy John surgery, but he made it all the way to the major leagues by the end of his first full-season experience.

Machado flashes plus velocity with his four-seamer, ranging from 93 to 98 mph. It's a hard and heavy fastball with rising action that he locates well. His 88-89 mph changeup with some backspin is an above-average pitch now and could be plus before long. His third pitch is a slider at 83-86 with 12-6 movement. He throws with a long, full arm stroke from a three-quarters slot. Machado is still listed at his earlier weight of 175 pounds, but he now has a mature look with thickening in the middle of the body.

Machado will head to spring training in 2018 with a shot at the Kansas City rotation, but he more likely profiles best as a seventh-inning reliever.

Year	Club (League)	Class	W	L	ERA	G	GS	CG	SV	IP	H	HR	BB	SO	K/9	WHIP	AVG
2015	Did not play—Injured																
2016	Idaho Falls (PIO)	R	2	4	3.99	13	13	0	0	59	67	5	14	64	9.8	1.38	.283
2017	Wilmington (CAR)	HiA	6	7	5.03	21	9	0	2	73	88	8	14	72	8.8	1.39	.292
	NW Arkansas (TL)	AA	0	0	3.00	1	0	0	0	3	2	0	2	1	3.0	1.33	.182
	Omaha (PCL)	AAA	2	2	3.63	7	7	0	0	35	30	6	17	38	9.9	1.36	.233
	Kansas City (AL)	MAJ	0	0	22.09	2	0	0	0	4	10	2	3	1	2.5	3.55	.476
Major League Totals			0	0	22.09	2	0	0	0	4	10	2	3	1	2.5	3.55	.476
Minor League Totals			13	24	4.76	83	44	0	6	280	320	29	105	245	7.9	1.52	.286

26 SCOTT BARLOW, RHP

BA GRADE

45 Risk: High

Born: Dec. 18, 1992. **B-T:** R-R. **Ht.:** 6-3. **Wt.:** 215. **Drafted:** HS—Santa Clarita, Calif., 2011 (6th round). **Signed by:** Dennis Moeller (Dodgers).

Barlow has always had an enticing arsenal of pitches and solid pitcher's frame since being drafted by the Dodgers in the sixth round in 2011, but staying healthy has been his biggest challenge.

Barlow pitched just 1.2 innings combined in his first two pro seasons, recovering slowly from Tommy John surgery. He enjoyed a few solid seasons as a Dodgers farmhand, but wasn't perceived as valuable enough to avoid becoming a minor league free agent after the 2017 season. The Royals subsequently signed Barlow to a one-year major league contract with the Royals worth $900,000. He's coming off an outstanding season at Double-A Tulsa in which he posted a 3.29 ERA and stuck out 160 batters in 139.2 innings before struggling in seven starts at Triple-A Oklahoma City. Barlow thrives by mixing his pitches and locating them. His fastball sits 91-93 mph, touches 96, and plays up because of the elite extension he gets. His best secondary pitch is an average slider at 78-82 mph with cutting action and armside run, and he complements it with a slow 76-80 mph curveball that has a hump on it. Barlow gets good movement on a power 84-86 mph changeup that plays well off his fastball in going down in the other direction.

Barlow profiles as a back-end starter, but some observers believe his stuff could tick up in shorter stints in the bullpen.

Year	Club (League)	Class	W	L	ERA	G	GS	CG	SV	IP	H	HR	BB	SO	K/9	WHIP	AVG
2015	Dodgers (AZL)	R	0	1	4.00	3	3	0	0	9	8	1	4	11	11.0	1.33	.216
	Great Lakes (MWL)	LoA	0	1	5.79	1	1	0	0	5	8	2	1	1	1.9	1.93	.381
	R. Cucamonga (CAL)	HiA	8	3	2.52	14	13	0	0	71	61	4	32	64	8.1	1.30	.236
	Oklahoma City (PCL)	AAA	0	1	14.73	1	1	0	0	4	7	0	3	3	7.4	2.73	.438
2016	Tulsa (TL)	AA	4	7	3.98	24	23	0	0	124	125	9	52	102	7.4	1.42	.260
2017	Oklahoma City (PCL)	AAA	1	3	7.24	7	7	0	0	32	37	6	23	36	10.0	1.86	.276
	Tulsa (TL)	AA	6	3	2.18	19	19	0	0	107	60	9	37	124	10.4	0.90	.161
Minor League Totals			29	30	4.18	109	103	0	1	530	506	56	221	497	8.4	1.37	.250

27 EMMANUEL RIVERA, 3B

BA GRADE

45 Risk: High

Born: June 29, 1996. **B-T:** R-R. **Ht.:** 6-2. **Wt.:** 195. **Drafted:** Interamerican (P.R.) JC, 2015 (19th round). **Signed by:** Johnny Ramos.

One of the biggest improvements in the Royals system came from Rivera, who followed a .330/.393/.413 line and a rookie of the year performance in the Puerto Rican League by winning the South Atlantic League batting title in 2017. Kansas City's 19th-round pick in 2015 significantly improved his numbers in his first full season, batting .310 at low Class A Lexington after posting .174 and .249 averages in his first two seasons in rookie ball.

Rivera has a good feel for hitting and uses all fields but with some length in his swing. He has above-average raw power now and should get stronger, but he'll need to get more loft in his swing to tap into that power. It's not expected that any newfound power will come at the expense of batting average. He's a below-average runner. Rivera projects as an above-average defender at the hot corner with a plus arm.

After his fine low Class A season, Rivera will be ready for his next challenge with an assignment to high Class A Wilmington.

Year	Club (League)	Class	AVG	G	AB	R	H	2B	3B	HR	RBI	BB	SO	SB	CS	OBP	SLG
2015	Royals (AZL)	R	.174	38	115	13	20	5	0	0	14	23	32	9	4	.317	.217
2016	Burlington (APP)	R	.249	58	217	25	54	13	4	2	27	21	44	7	3	.317	.373
2017	Lexington (SAL)	LoA	.310	122	464	60	144	27	5	12	72	31	87	8	10	.364	.468
Minor League Totals			.274	218	796	98	218	45	9	14	113	75	163	24	17	.344	.406

28 RICHARD LOVELADY, LHP

BA GRADE

45 Risk: High

Born: July 7, 1995. **B-T:** L-L. **Ht.:** 6-0. **Wt.:** 175. **Drafted:** Kennesaw State, 2016 (10th round). **Signed by:** Sean Gibbs.

The most intriguing storyline among Royals prospects in 2017 was the development of Lovelady, the Royals' 10th pick from Kennesaw State just one year earlier. The lean southpaw with a funky delivery jumped a level with his first full-season assignment at high Class A Wilmington, and by mid-season he was bumped up to Double-A.

Lovelady possesses electric stuff, with a dominating plus fastball from 93-97 mph that he throws with deception and a lot of movement. The heater has hard tailing action with sink. He locates it well both arm-side and glove-side, but he needs to improve his command of the pitch. Because of the dominance of his fastball, Lovelady seldom needed to use his offspeed stuff, but when he did batters saw an average or better slider at 88 mph. He only occasionally went to his 88-90 mph changeup, which now is a below-average pitch. Lovelady is locked in and focused on the mound. He profiles as a setup man and not strictly as a left-on-left reliever.

It wouldn't be surprising to see Lovelady in the Royals bullpen in 2018, perhaps sooner rather than later.

Year	Club (League)	Class	W	L	ERA	G	GS	CG	SV	IP	H	HR	BB	SO	K/9	WHIP	AVG
2016	Royals (AZL)	R	2	0	1.74	8	0	0	3	10	4	0	2	14	12.2	0.58	.111
	Idaho Falls (PIO)	R	0	1	1.84	13	0	0	6	15	10	0	7	16	9.8	1.16	.200
2017	Wilmington (CAR)	HiA	1	0	1.08	21	0	0	7	33	18	0	4	41	11.1	0.66	.154
	NW Arkansas (TL)	AA	3	2	2.16	21	0	0	3	33	28	1	13	36	9.7	1.23	.228
Minor League Totals			6	3	1.67	63	0	0	19	92	60	1	26	107	10.5	0.94	.184

29 CAM GALLAGHER, C

BA GRADE

40 Risk: Medium

Born: Dec. 6, 1992. **B-T:** R-R. **Ht.:** 6-3. **Wt.:** 230. **Drafted:** HS—Lancaster, Pa., 2011 (2nd round). **Signed by:** Jim Farr.

Gallagher made it to the big leagues for 13 games six years after the Royals drafted the Pennsylvania native in the 2nd round. Since signing for a $750,000 bonus, Gallagher has moved steadily through the Royals system.

Profiling as at least a reliable second catcher, Gallagher has been blocked at the major league level by the presence of venerable catcher Salvador Perez and reliable backup Drew Butera. Gallagher is a gap-to-gap hitter who doesn't strike out that often (12 percent of plate appearances through his minor league career) with plate discipline that ranks among the best in the system. His bat has improved as he's progressed through the system and he has a very good approach at the plate. He doesn't get to his average raw power in games, with the six home runs Gallagher hit in 2017 marking his career high. He works well with pitchers, keeping them in the game, and his above-average, accurate arm threw out 33 percent of PCL runners in 2017.

Gallagher will head to spring training with a chance to earn a job with the parent club, but he most likely will be back in Omaha as a valuable insurance to the Royals' big league catching corps.

Year	Club (League)	Class	AVG	G	AB	R	H	2B	3B	HR	RBI	BB	SO	SB	CS	OBP	SLG
2015	Wilmington (CAR)	HiA	.245	76	249	24	61	15	0	5	22	28	34	0	0	.324	.365
2016	NW Arkansas (TL)	AA	.259	91	301	23	78	16	1	4	24	37	52	2	2	.348	.359
2017	Omaha (PCL)	AAA	.292	73	260	26	76	13	0	5	37	18	33	0	1	.336	.400
	Kansas City (AL)	MAJ	.250	13	24	2	6	1	0	1	5	3	4	0	0	.333	.417
Major League Totals			.250	13	24	2	6	1	0	1	5	3	4	0	0	.333	.417
Minor League Totals			.244	466	1579	137	385	87	1	26	159	164	220	4	6	.318	.350

30 KYLE ZIMMER, RHP

BA GRADE

55 Risk: Extreme

Born: Sept. 13, 1991. **B-T:** R-R. **Ht.:** 6-3. **Wt.:** 225. **Drafted:** San Francisco, 2012 (1st round). **Signed by:** Max Valencia.

Zimmer is unquestionably the best pitching prospect in the Royals organization—when he's healthy. The problem is that since being selected as the 5th overall pick in 2012 Zimmer has experienced a litany of injuries (labrum, thoracic outlet syndrome, arm fatigue) that have sapped his arm strength and put his career outlook in a fog as thick as nights in his native San Francisco.

Zimmer has pitched 100 innings just once in a season since turning pro and was limited to 36.2 innings in 2017. He worked mostly in a relief role with Triple-A Omaha, mostly to build up his innings. His fastball velocity was down earlier in the season, but later it was back up to 94-97 mph. When right, his fastball has natural sinking action, and he gets good bite and 12-6 movement on a 77 mph curveball that grades as plus.

But Zimmer's stuff generally hasn't been the same, and his consistency and ability to bounce back from appearances remains a big question. Expectations for 2018 and beyond are uncertain.

Year	Club (League)	Class	W	L	ERA	G	GS	CG	SV	IP	H	HR	BB	SO	K/9	WHIP	AVG
2015	Lexington (SAL)	LoA	1	0	1.13	9	0	0	0	16	11	1	6	21	11.8	1.06	.190
	NW Arkansas (TL)	AA	2	5	2.81	15	7	0	3	48	42	4	14	51	9.6	1.17	.235
2016	Wilmington (CAR)	HiA	0	1	1.93	2	2	0	0	5	3	0	4	9	17.4	1.50	.176
	NW Arkansas (TL)	AA	0	1	0.00	1	1	0	0	1	1	0	2	2	18.0	3.00	.250
2017	NW Arkansas (TL)	AA	0	0	2.25	1	1	0	0	4	6	0	0	6	13.5	1.50	.375
	Omaha (PCL)	AAA	0	0	5.79	20	2	0	3	33	35	4	16	34	9.4	1.56	.271
Minor League Totals			12	19	3.54	85	49	2	6	259	233	21	90	310	10.8	1.25	.239

Los Angeles Angels

BY MIKE DIGIOVANNA

The Angels have had the best player in baseball for six years and have zero playoff victories to show for it.

A Mike Trout-led club fought the good fight again in 2017, remaining in wild card contention until the final week of the season despite a dizzying array of injuries that decimated their pitching staff, but the playoffs went on without them. Again.

Since a decade-long run of dominance that included a 2002 World Series championship and five American League West titles from 2004 through 2009, the Angels have reached the postseason once, in 2014, when they won a major league-high 98 games and were swept by the Royals in the Division Series.

Now they're on the clock. Trout's six-year, $144.5 million contract expires in 2020, shortly after the star center fielder turns 29. If the Angels are unable to contend for a World Series title by then, the ultra-competitive Trout will probably look to sign with a team that can.

If the Angels aren't in playoff contention by the summer of 2019, they may have no choice but to explore trading Trout.

The good news: The Angels won the sweepstakes for touted Japanese righthander Shohei Ohtani during the offseason, bringing them both a No. 1-caliber pitcher and potential middle-of-the-order lefthanded power bat, both of which they desperately needed.

More good news: The organization's top prospect, center fielder Jo Adell, a dynamic five-tool player who was the 10th overall pick in 2017, could be ready for the big leagues faster than the typical high school talent.

The problem: The path to championship-caliber status is muddled. The Angels have been a decent major league team for several years, with several promising young pitchers, and Trout and dazzling shortstop Andrelton Simmons up the middle, but only once have they been good enough to reach the playoffs.

Their payroll will be saddled with Albert Pujols' 10-year, $240 million contract through 2021, and with the new contract given to Justin Upton, acquired from the Tigers in August, the Angels will have $101 million in payroll committed to just four players in 2020.

The Angels may not have the resources to sign multiple high-end free agents. And because of the slow progression of their farm system, most of their top prospects are years away from impacting the big league club. They're caught in a murky middle ground, neither perennial contenders nor in total rebuild mode.

Franchise icon Mike Trout will have support in 2018 after the Angels' busy offseason.

BOB LEVEY/GETTY IMAGES

PROJECTED 2021 LINEUP

Catcher	Taylor Ward (27)
First Base	Matt Thaiss (26)
Second Base	Leonardo Rivas (23)
Third Base	Kevin Maitan (21)
Shortstop	Andrelton Simmons (31)
Left Field	Jahmai Jones (23)
Center Field	Mike Trout (29)
Right Field	Jo Adell (22)
Designated Hitter	Justin Upton (33)
No. 1 Starter	Shohei Ohtani (26)
No. 2 Starter	Garrett Richards (33)
No. 3 Starter	Andrew Heaney (30)
No. 4 Starter	Tyler Skaggs (29)
No. 5 Starter	Jaime Barria (24)
Closer	Keynan Middleton (27)

The farm system is deep in outfield prospects, such as Adell, Jahmai Jones and Brandon Marsh, but very thin in pitchers that can help the Angels anytime soon.

That's a problem, given Garrett Richards, Andrew Heaney, Tyler Skaggs, Nick Tropeano and Matt Shoemaker have missed large chunks of the past two seasons because of injuries, and Alex Meyer will miss 2018 because of shoulder surgery.

The system is deeper after new scouting director Matt Swanson's first draft. The organization is slowly climbing out from the bottom of the prospect barrel, but it may not be fast enough to get the Angels to the playoffs before Trout's contract is up.

LOS ANGELES ANGELS

TOP 2018 ROOKIE: Shohei Ohtani, RHP/DH. Japanese superstar could be Angels' top pitcher from day one, as well as a provide needed lefthanded power from the order.

BREAKOUT PROSPECT: Jose Suarez, LHP. The polished 19-year-old lefty struck out 11.8 per nine innings at low Class A and already has a good feel for his changeup.

SLEEPER: Sam Fuller, RHP. The 15th-round Georgia prep throws a 93 mph fastball and reminds some of a young Tim Belcher because of his mature, businesslike approach.

SOURCE OF TOP 30 TALENT

Homegrown	27	Acquired	3
College	7	Trades	1
Junior college	0	Rule 5 draft	0
High school	9	Independent leagues	0
International	11	Free agents/waivers	2
Nondrafted free agents	0		

LF
Jahmai Jones (3)
Brennon Lund (18)
Jonah Todd (26)

CF
Jo Adell (2)
Trent Deveaux (17)
D'Shawn Knowles (21)
Torii Hunter Jr. (30)

RF
Brandon Marsh (5)
Michael Hermosillo (10)
Ryan Vega

3B
Nonie Williams (24)
Zach Houchins
Jose Rojas

SS
Kevin Maitan (4)
Leonardo Rivas (11)
Livan Soto (16)
Nolan Fontana
Connor Justus
Hutton Moyer

2B
David Fletcher (27)
Sherm Johnson
Jordan Zimmerman

1B
Matt Thaiss (8)
Jared Walsh

C
Taylor Ward (19)
Keinner Pina (29)
Jack Kruger

LHP

LHSP	LHRP
Jose Suarez (13)	Greg Mahle
Jerryel Rivera (22)	Jonah Wesely
Nate Smith	

RHP

RHSP	RHRP
Shohei Ohtani (1)	Jesus Castillo (12)
Jaime Barria (6)	Luis Pena (20)
Chris Rodriguez (7)	Jake Jewell (25)
Griffin Canning (9)	Joe Gatto (28)
Jose Soriano (14)	Luke Bard
Stiward Aquino (15)	Adam Hofacket
John Swanda (23)	Nathan Bates
Cole Duensing	Samil de los Santos
Troy Scribner	Justin Anderson
Osmer Morales	Daniel Procopio
Jose Rodriguez	Carlos Salazar
Alex Klonowski	Kida de la Cruz

DRAFT ANALYSIS

2017

BEST PURE HITTER: OF Jacob Pearson (3) has an above-average feel for hitting and a mature understanding of the strike zone for a high school product. OF Jonah Todd (6) has a very disciplined approach and a knack for putting the barrel on the ball.
BEST POWER HITTER: OF Jo Adell (1) was one of the toolsiest players in the draft, and his plus raw power was perhaps his most attractive asset. His size, strength and bat speed can produce prodigious home runs, and he has done a good job of getting to his power in games.
FASTEST RUNNER: OF Spencer Griffin (16) is a well above-average runner plucked out of the Texas junior college ranks. Adell and Todd are plus runners.
BEST DEFENSIVE PLAYER: C Harrison Wenson (24) was a two-year starter behind the plate at Michigan and is a solid defender. He is an excellent receiver and has above-average arm strength.
BEST FASTBALL: RHP Daniel Procopio (10) has only been pitching full time for two years, but already his elite arm strength stands out. He touched 100 mph this summer and consistently throws 96-97 mph. He is still learning the finer points of pitching, but his powerful arm gives him a chance in the bullpen.
BEST SECONDARY PITCH: Any of RHP Griffin Canning's (2) three offspeed offerings could earn the honor. His changeup, curveball and slider all flash plus, but his curveball was generally his go-to secondary pitch this spring at UCLA and earns consistent above-average to plus grades.
BEST PRO DEBUT: Adell made an easy transition from Kentucky's high school ranks to professional baseball, and earned a promotion form the Arizona League to the Pioneer League; he hit .325/.376/.532 overall. RHP Isaac Mattson (19) saved six games and struck out 40 batters in 26.2 innings to earn a spot on the Pioneer League all-

TOP DRAFT PICKS OF THE DECADE

Year	Player, Pos.	2017 Org
2008	Tyler Chatwood, RHP (2nd round)	Rockies
2009	Randal Grichuk, OF	Cardinals
2010	Cam Bedrosian, RHP	Angels
2011	C.J. Cron, 1B	Angels
2012	R.J. Alvarez, RHP (3rd round)	Rangers
2013	Hunter Green, LHP (2nd round)	Retired
2014	Sean Newcomb, LHP	Braves
2015	Taylor Ward, C	Angels
2016	Matt Thaiss, C	Angels
2017	Jo Adell, OF	Angels

star team.
BEST ATHLETE: Adell was one of the most athletic players in the draft class. He is solidly built at 6-foot-2, 195 pounds, has a 41-inch vertical leap and is a plus runner.
MOST INTRIGUING BACKGROUND: 1B David MacKinnon (32) pulled the rare baseball-soccer double at Hartford. He started at goalkeeper throughout his career and recorded 19 shutouts, second most in program history. On the diamond, he was the 2016 America East Conference player of the year.
CLOSEST TO THE MAJORS: Canning didn't pitch after signing due to his workload this spring, but he is the kind of mature, advanced college pitcher who should be able to make quick work of the minor leagues.
BEST LATE-ROUND PICK: LHP Jerryell Rivera (11), a native of Puerto Rico, offers plenty of upside. He has a projectable frame, repeats his delivery well and throws a lot of strikes. He mostly throws in the upper 80s now, but figures to add velocity as he physically matures.
THE ONE WHO GOT AWAY: RHP JoJo Booker (5) was a late riser last spring and ultimately upheld his commitment to South Alabama, becoming the second-highest drafted player not to sign.

—TEDDY CAHILL

2016

OF Brandon Marsh (2) and RHP Chris Rodriguez (4) have quickly risen from the prep ranks to become two of the system's top players. 1B Matt Thaiss (1) reached Double-A, but needs to hit for more power to become an impact player.
GRADE: C

2015

OF Jahmai Jones (2) is the class' prize and finished the year strong. Los Angeles capatalized on a solid season from RHP Grayson Long (3) by using him in the Justin Upton deal. C Taylor Ward (1) has a chance to help, but likely as a backup.
GRADE: D

2014

LHP Sean Newcomb (1) and RHP Chris Ellis (3) were used in the Andrelton Simmons trade. LHP Greg Mahle (15) made the big leagues in 2016, but RHP Joe Gatto (2) looks to be the class' best shot to give the Angels a homegrown contributor.
GRADE: C

1 SHOHEI OHTANI, RHP/DH

Born: July 5, 1994. **B-T:** L-R. **Ht.:** 6-3. **Wt.:** 189.
Signed: Japan, 2017.

No player since Bryce Harper has matched the mixture of hype and expectation as Ohtani. With a fastball clocked as high as 102 mph and a demonstrated ability to hit home runs 500 feet in Nippon Professional Baseball, Ohtani became the most sought-after free agent of the 2017 offseason. Ohtani's star progressively grew in NPB with the Nippon Ham Fighters and reached its high point in 2016, when he went 10-4, 1.86 with 174 strikeouts and 45 walks in 140 innings and, while serving as the designated hitter on days he wasn't pitching, hitting .322 with 22 home runs, 67 RBIs and a 1.004 OPS. A right ankle injury limited him to just five starts in 2017 and he had surgery in October. Ohtani jumped to the U.S and, with his signing bonus capped as an international amateur, nearly every team pursued him. He chose to sign with the Angels for $2.315 million in early December. Ohtani's physical revealed slight damage to his ulnar collateral ligament, but no more than other pitchers have.

Ohtani has been called the Japanese Babe Ruth, a gifted athlete so prolific as a hitter and pitcher he would be an All-Star at both. He can hold his fastball at 97-98 mph as a starter, and he dials it up and down from 93-100. His fastball doesn't have much life and is fairly straight, but when his command is on the raw velocity is enough to draw swings and misses. Ohtani's best pitch is his forkball. He throws it with the same arm speed and arm slot as his fastball, and the pitch dives two feet into the dirt after starting at the hitters thigh. Ohtani's slider is a third plus pitch but lacks consistency, and he also has a curveball and changeup. Ohtani has a No. 1 starter's arsenal, but pitches up in the zone too much at times and can fall in love with his breaking pitches, which leads to losing his feel and bouts of inconsistent command. As a hitter Ohtani packs massive raw power, and he pulverizes anything over the plate to center field or the opposite way to left. He rarely faced inside fastballs in Japan and will have to show he can adjust to them in the majors. Overall Ohtani is a disciplined hitter who knows the strike zone.

Ohtani will immediately slot into the Angels starting rotation, and on his off days will get at-bats as their designated hitter. If everything comes together, he can be a Cy Young Award contender who hits double-digit home runs.

ATSUSHI TOMIURA/GETTY IMAGES

BA GRADE	SCOUTING GRADES
75 Risk: Medium	FB: 80. SL: 60. SPLT: 70. CTL: 55. HIT: 50. POW: 60. SPD: 60.

Projected future grades on 20-80 scouting scale

TOP PROSPECTS OF THE DECADE

Year	Player, Pos.	2017 Org
2008	Brandon Wood, 3B/SS	Did not play
2009	Nick Adenhart, RHP	Deceased
2010	Hank Conger, C	Diamondbacks
2011	Mike Trout, OF	Angels
2012	Mike Trout, OF	Angels
2013	Kaleb Cowart, 3B	Angels
2014	Taylor Lindsey, 2B	Did not play
2015	Andrew Heaney, LHP	Angels
2016	Taylor Ward, C	Angels
2017	Jahmai Jones, OF	Angels

BEST TOOLS

Best Hitter for Average	Jahmai Jones
Best Power Hitter	Jo Adell
Best Strike-Zone Discipline	Matt Thaiss
Fastest Baserunner	Trent Deveaux
Best Athlete	Brandon Marsh
Best Fastball	Chris Rodriguez
Best Curveball	Joe Gatto
Best Slider	Chris Rodriguez
Best Changeup	Jose Suarez
Best Control	Jaime Barria
Best Defensive Catcher	Taylor Ward
Best Defensive Infielder	Leonardo Rivas
Best Infield Arm	Connor Justus
Best Defensive Outfielder	Torii Hunter Jr.
Best Outfield Arm	Brandon Marsh

Year	Club (League)	Class	W	L	ERA	G	GS	CG	SV	IP	H	HR	BB	SO	K/9	WHIP	AVG
2017	Nippon-Ham (NPB)	JPN	3	2	3.20	5	5	1	0	25	13	2	19	29	10.3	1.26	—
Japan Totals			42	15	2.52	85	82	13	0	543	384	24	200	624	10.3	1.08	—

Year	Club (League)	Class	AVG	G	AB	R	H	2B	3B	HR	RBI	BB	SO	SB	CS	OBP	SLG
2017	Nippon-Ham (NPB)	JPN	.332	65	202	24	67	16	1	8	31	24	63	0	1	.403	.540
Japan Totals			.266	403	1035	150	296	70	4	48	166	119	316	13	4	.358	.500

2 JO ADELL, OF

Born: April 8, 1999. **B-T:** R-R. **Ht.:** 6-3 **Wt.:** 200. **Drafted:** HS—Louisville, 2017 (1st round). **Signed by:** John Burden.

Adell's skills were raw on the showcase circuit before his junior and senior seasons at Louisville's Ballard High School, but he made adjustments to keep his bat through the zone longer and hit .562 with 25 homers, most in the nation, 61 RBIs, 53 runs, 22 stolen bases and only seven strikeouts as a senior. The Angels drafted him 10th overall and signed him for $4.377 million to pass up Louisville. Adell then went out and hit a combined .325 with a .908 OPS for rookie-league teams in Arizona and Orem.

BILL MITCHELL

BA GRADE	
60	**Risk:** Extreme
HIT: 60. POW: 70.	
SPD: 70. FLD: 55.	
ARM: 60.	

The Angels believed Adell possessed the best combination of power, speed and arm strength in the 2017 draft. He has run a 6.4-second 60-yard dash, 80-grade speed, has the strength to mash 450-foot home runs and the arm to make laser-like throws from the outfield. The broad-shouldered, muscular Adell stands out most for his quick-twitch athleticism, bat speed, raw power and ability to make consistent hard contact. His quick hands allow him to get to high pitches and he shows maturity in his at-bats and work ethic. He may not become an elite defender, but is solidly above-average with an arm good enough to play in center or right field. Adell's speed may not translate into stolen bases as he matures physically and adds muscle, but he should be a plus baserunner.

The dynamic Adell has the ability, makeup and intangibles to grow into an all-star-caliber outfielder. The degree to which he translates his physical gifts and attributes into baseball-specific skills will determine whether he becomes a superstar.

Year	Club (League)	Class	AVG	G	AB	R	H	2B	3B	HR	RBI	BB	SO	SB	CS	OBP	SLG
2017	Angels (AZL)	R	.288	31	118	18	34	6	6	4	21	10	32	5	0	.351	.542
	Orem (PIO)	R	.376	18	85	25	32	5	2	1	9	4	17	3	2	.411	.518
Minor League Totals			.325	49	203	43	66	11	8	5	30	14	49	8	2	.376	.532

3 JAHMAI JONES, OF

Born: Aug. 4, 1997. **B-T:** R-R. **Ht.:** 6-0. **Wt.:** 215. **Drafted:** HS—Norcross, Ga., 2015 (2nd round). **Signed by:** Todd Hogan.

The stiffer the competition, the better Jones performed last season. Pitchers exploited his tendency to swing at breaking balls out of the zone early and Jones got off to a sluggish start at low Class A Burlington, where he slashed .165/.211/.282 in his first 26 games.

But Jones, who signed for $1.1 million, rebounded so strongly he earned a July 20 promotion to high Class A Inland Empire, where he put up better numbers than he did at Burlington. Jones is an explosive athlete with NFL bloodlines—his father and two brothers played in the league. He makes consistent contact, sprays line drives all over the field, has plus speed and gap-to-gap power, and his defense is improving. Jones is thick and strong, and the ball jumps off his bat. Scouts like his makeup, work ethic and the adjustments he makes with two strikes, when he

PAUL GIERHART

BA GRADE	
55	**Risk:** High
HIT: 50. POW: 55.	
SPD: 60. FLD: 55.	
ARM: 50.	

widens his stance, chokes up and tries to put the ball in play. A short stroke and plus bat speed indicate that Jones could be an above-average hitter, but there are questions whether he'll be able to manage the strike zone at higher levels. He doesn't project as a home run hitter, and an adequate but not overwhelming arm could push him to left field.

If he maintains his speed and improves his plate discipline, Jones could be a solid big-league leadoff man. He should see Double-A Mobile in 2018.

Year	Club (League)	Class	AVG	G	AB	R	H	2B	3B	HR	RBI	BB	SO	SB	CS	OBP	SLG
2015	Angels (AZL)	R	.244	40	160	28	39	6	2	2	20	17	33	16	7	.330	.344
2016	Orem (PIO)	R	.321	48	196	49	63	12	3	3	20	21	29	19	6	.404	.459
	Burlington (MWL)	LoA	.242	16	62	8	15	1	0	1	10	5	13	1	0	.294	.306
2017	Burlington (MWL)	LoA	.272	86	346	54	94	18	4	9	30	32	63	18	7	.338	.425
	Inland Empire (CAL)	HiA	.302	41	172	32	52	11	3	5	17	13	43	9	6	.368	.488
Minor League Totals			.281	231	936	171	263	48	12	20	97	88	181	63	26	.353	.422

4 KEVIN MAITAN, SS

Born: Feb. 12, 2000. **B-T:** B-R. **Ht.:** 6-2. **Wt.:** 190. **Signed:** Venezuela, 2016. **Signed by:** Gordon Blakely/Mike Silvestri/Rolando Petit (Braves).

Evaluators universally considered Maitan the top prospect in the 2016 international class and the top hitter out of Latin America in years. The Venezuelan switch-hitter signed with the Braves for $4.25 million but had an underwhelming pro debut at the Rookie levels in 2017. After the season, Major League Baseball declared Maitan a free agent as part of the Braves' penalties for international signing violations.

BA GRADE
60 Risk: Extreme
HIT: 60. POW: 60.
SPD: 40. FLD: 45.
ARM: 60.

The Angels swooped in and signed him for $2.2 million in early December. Maitan's pro debut was worrisome. He gained significant weight in his lower half and few scouts now believe he will be able to stick at shortstop. His righthanded swing was quick and direct, but his lefthanded swing showed significant length and less bat speed. Maitain has plus power potential, but his approach will have to be refined to tap into what scouts have long seen as plus hitting ability. Maitan has good body control, a plus arm and soft hands, but his range was limited by his lack of speed and first-step quickness. Maitan slimmed down to 210 pounds for instructional league.

The Angels are expected to let Maitan stick at shortstop for now, but eventually most scouts believe he will end up moving off the position unless he cuts even more weight. Even with a probable eventual move to third base, he has the hitting ability to be an impact player. He will get a fresh start with the Angels in 2018 and could see low Class Burlington.

Year	Club (League)	Class	AVG	G	AB	R	H	2B	3B	HR	RBI	BB	SO	SB	CS	OBP	SLG
2017	Braves (GCL)	R	.314	9	35	5	11	3	0	0	3	2	10	1	0	.351	.400
	Danville (APP)	R	.220	33	127	10	28	5	1	2	15	9	39	1	0	.273	.323
Minor League Totals			.241	42	162	15	39	8	1	2	18	11	49	2	0	.290	.340

5 BRANDON MARSH, OF

Born: Dec. 18, 1997. **B-T:** L-R. **Ht.:** 6-3. **Wt.:** 210. **Drafted:** HS—Buford, Ga., 2016 (2nd round). **Signed by:** Todd Hogan.

Marsh, who signed for $1.073 million as the No. 60 overall pick in 2016, didn't play after his signing was delayed because of a medical exam found a stress reaction in his lower back.

Stronger after months of rehabilitation, Marsh flashed his five-tool potential as one of the best players in the Pioneer League in his pro debut in 2017, although he missed a month with a sprained thumb. A standout wide receiver who helped his high school team win Georgia AAAA state championships in 2013 and 2014, Marsh is an elite athlete with a strong frame, plus speed and plus arm strength. He looked a little raw offensively in instructional league last fall, but showed advanced plate discipline at Orem, sitting on pitches like a college hitter. Marsh has shown an ability to hit to all fields and could grow into more power as he matures physically. The way the ball comes off his bat leads some scouts to project above-average power in his future.

BA GRADE
55 Risk: Extreme
HIT: 55. POW: 55.
SPD: 60. FLD: 55.
ARM: 60.

The Angels believe Marsh has the speed and instincts to cover a lot of ground in center field, though he may eventually move to a corner spot. With a good, and healthy, first half at low Class A Burlington, Marsh could reach high Class A Inland Empire by the All-Star break.

Year	Club (League)	Class	AVG	G	AB	R	H	2B	3B	HR	RBI	BB	SO	SB	CS	OBP	SLG
2016	Did not play—Injured																
2017	Orem (PIO)	R	.350	39	177	47	62	13	5	4	44	9	35	10	2	.396	.548
Minor League Totals			.350	39	177	47	62	13	5	4	44	9	35	10	2	.396	.548

6 JAMIE BARRIA, RHP

Born: July 18, 1996. **B-T:** R-R. **Ht.:** 6-1. **Wt.:** 210. **Signed:** Panama, 2013. **Signed by:** Roman Ocumarea.

Barria has gained 30 pounds since he signed for $60,000 as a 16-year-old, and he continues to add velocity as he adds strength. Barria made a quantum leap in 2017, jumping from high Class A Inland Empire to Double-A Mobile to Triple-A Salt Lake in his age-20 season.

Barria combined to go 7-9, 2.80 with 117 strikeouts and 31 walks in 141.2 innings. Barria doesn't have electric stuff—he's about pitchability and racking up early-count outs—but his advanced feel for pitching, sneaky deception, pinpoint control and knack for turning up his intensity in jams pushed him to Triple-A. He works in and out, up and down with a fastball that sits in the 92-mph range. His best pitch is a changeup with fade at 77-80 mph that projects to be an above-aver-age-to-plus offering. His curveball, once loopier and slower, is thrown harder and shorter and sometimes with big depth and projects as a possible outpitch as well. Barria has the intangibles you'd expect in a major leaguer—good mound presence and demeanor, confidence in his repertoire and the ability to control the running game and field his position.

With his work ethic and progress Barria has cut a direct path to the big leagues, with the potential to be a No. 4 or 5 starter.

BA GRADE
50 Risk: High
FB: 50. CB: 50.
SL: 45. CHG: 60.
CTL: 55.

Year	Club (League)	Class	W	L	ERA	G	GS	CG	SV	IP	H	HR	BB	SO	K/9	WHIP	AVG
2015	Angels (AZL)	R	3	0	2.00	7	6	0	0	36	40	0	3	31	7.8	1.19	.280
	Orem (PIO)	R	2	4	6.21	8	8	0	0	33	45	4	7	30	8.1	1.56	.324
2016	Burlington (MWL)	LoA	8	6	3.85	25	25	0	0	117	133	6	21	78	6.0	1.32	.282
2017	Inland Empire (CAL)	HiA	4	3	2.48	11	11	0	0	65	48	6	13	57	7.9	0.93	.202
	Mobile (SL)	AA	1	6	3.21	12	12	1	0	62	62	8	15	47	6.9	1.25	.256
	Salt Lake (PCL)	AAA	2	0	2.45	3	3	0	0	15	11	0	3	13	8.0	0.95	.208
Minor League Totals			24	24	3.46	86	73	1	1	392	409	25	74	315	7.2	1.23	.266

7 CHRIS RODRIGUEZ, RHP

Born: July 20, 1998. **B-T:** R-R. **Ht.:** 6-2. **Wt.:** 185. **Drafted:** HS—Pace, Fla., 2016 (4th round). **Signed by:** Ralph Reyes.

Rodriguez, who signed for a well-above-slot $850,000 in 2016, is considered by some to be the most promising homegrown arm in the Angels system. But his 2017 results—he went a combined 5-3, 6.16 in 14 starts for Rookie-level Orem and low Class A Burlington, striking out 56 and walking 14 in 57 innings—didn't match his potential.

Rodriguez features a lively four-seam fastball that averages 95 mph, has touched 97 mph and sometimes cuts away from righthanded batters. He complements it with a sinking two-seamer that runs in to righties, making for an uncomfortable at-bat. He can throw his 83-86 mph changeup, his best secondary pitch, in any count, and it sometimes looks like a screwball the way the bottom drops out of it. He gets a hard, late break and good tilt on his 82-85 mph slider, and he's been throwing more of a 12-to-6 curveball. Rodriguez has an athletic, rhythmic delivery, but some scouts believe there's too much effort to his delivery, which he finishes with a big head whack. In part because of that, evaluators do not project Rodriguez to ever have more than average command.

Rodriguez is mature with a good work ethic. With polish and experience, he could develop into a mid-rotation starter.

BA GRADE
55 Risk: Extreme
FB: 60. CB: 50.
SL: 55. CHG: 60.
CTL: 50.

Year	Club (League)	Class	W	L	ERA	G	GS	CG	SV	IP	H	HR	BB	SO	K/9	WHIP	AVG
2016	Angels (AZL)	R	0	0	1.59	7	5	0	0	11	6	0	3	17	13.5	0.79	.154
2017	Orem (PIO)	R	4	1	6.40	8	8	0	0	32	35	1	7	32	8.9	1.30	.271
	Burlington (MWL)	LoA	1	2	5.84	6	6	0	0	25	32	1	7	24	8.8	1.58	.314
Minor League Totals			5	3	5.40	21	19	0	0	68	73	2	17	73	9.6	1.32	.270

8 MATT THAISS, 1B

Born: May 6, 1995. **B-T:** L-R. **Ht.:** 6-0. **Wt.:** 200. **Drafted:** Virginia, 2016 (1st round).
Signed by: Nick Gorneault.

Thaiss, who signed for $2.15 million, was a bat-first catcher in college. The Angels were sold on the bat, but not the glove so as soon as they drafted him, they announced that he was a full-time first baseman. He hasn't gotten behind the dish in two pro seasons.

Thaiss has carried the advanced plate discipline he showed in college to the minor leagues, where he has 141 strikeouts and 103 walks in 778 at-bats across four levels, but his power slipped after a July 11 promotion to Double-A Mobile, where he hit only one home run in 49 games. Thaiss has made considerable strides defensively at first base. He looked a little rigid and rough around the edges in his first instructional league, but his range, hands, and ability to pick balls in the dirt and complete the 3-1 play have improved to the point where he looks comfortable at his new position. Offensively, Thaiss controls the strike zone well and knows how to battle and spoil pitches. He has a good approach, doesn't chase bat pitches and isn't afraid to take a walk. He hits the ball hard but does not elevate it enough to clear the fence regularly.

BA GRADE

45 Risk: Medium

HIT: 55. POW: 45.
SPD: 30. FLD: 50.
ARM: 45.

Thaiss has solid gap-to-gap power, but until he learns how to turn on a ball and better punish mistakes, his ceiling will be that of a high on-base, 15-homer hitter and possible platoon player in the big leagues.

Year	Club (League)	Class	AVG	G	AB	R	H	2B	3B	HR	RBI	BB	SO	SB	CS	OBP	SLG
2016	Orem (PIO)	R	.338	15	65	16	22	7	1	2	12	4	4	2	4	.394	.569
	Burlington (MWL)	LoA	.276	52	199	24	55	12	3	4	31	22	28	1	0	.351	.427
2017	Inland Empire (CAL)	HiA	.265	84	336	46	89	13	4	8	48	40	59	4	3	.353	.399
	Mobile (SL)	AA	.292	49	178	29	52	14	0	1	25	37	50	4	3	.412	.388
Minor League Totals			.280	200	778	115	218	46	8	15	116	103	141	11	10	.370	.418

9 GRIFFIN CANNING, RHP

Born: May 11, 1996. **B-T:** R-R. **Ht.:** 6-2. **Wt.:** 180. **Signed:** UCLA, 2017 (2nd round).
Signed by: Ben Diggins.

A heavy workload as a junior at UCLA and a report of "potential issues" in a pre-draft MRI test didn't scare the Angels off Canning, a projected first-round pick who fell to the second round, No. 47 overall, and signed for $1.459 million.

The Angels were comfortable with Canning's medicals, but were still very careful with him. Canning spent the summer in Arizona working on strength and conditioning and didn't pitch for an affiliate—making him one of the few top 50 picks to not get into an official game. Canning's four-pitch mix includes a four-seam fastball between 90-94 mph with high spin rate that he commands, and a slider, curveball and changeup all flash ab0ve-average potential. His changeup was his go-to secondary pitch as a sophomore, but he threw more breaking balls as a junior, when he went 7-4, 2.34 in 119 innings over 17 starts, finishing second in the nation with

BA GRADE

55 Risk: Extreme

FB: 55. CB: 50.
SL: 50. CHG: 60.
CTL: 55.

140 strikeouts, walking 32 and holding opponents to a .213 average. He showed durability under a robust workload in 2017, throwing a 134-pitch shutout of rival Southern California in early May. Canning is a polished and advanced college pitcher who could move quickly through the system, but he needs to show he is healthy.

Canning will make his pro debut on Opening Day 2018 and projects as a mid-rotation starter.

Year	Club (League)	Class	W	L	ERA	G	GS	CG	SV	IP	H	HR	BB	SO	K/9	WHIP	AVG
2017	Did not play																

10 MICHAEL HERMOSILLO, OF

Born: Jan. 17, 1995. **B-T:** R-R. **Ht.:** 5-11. **Wt.:** 190. **Drafted:** HS—Ottawa, Ill., 2013 (28th round). **Signed by:** Joel Murrie.

A late-round pick who was committed to Illinois to play football out of high school, Hermosillo signed for $100,000 and certainly didn't come with a "can't-miss" label.

But after two so-so seasons to begin his career, Hermosillo blossomed at low Class A Burlington in 2016 and jumped from high Class A to Double-A to Triple-A in 2017, combining to hit .267/.366/.397 with 25 doubles, nine homers, 44 RBIs and 35 stolen bases. Hermosillo makes good contact and has shown solid plate discipline throughout his minor league career, though his strikeout-to-walk ratio dipped as he faced better pitching last season. A dead pull-hitter, Hermosillo needs a more balanced approach at the plate in order to use all fields. A limited launch angle prevents him from hitting more home runs. He has an above-average arm, allowing him to handle all three outfield positions. He has shown solid instincts in center, but is better coming in on balls than going back. His basestealing techniques, raw when he signed, have improved.

Hermosillo was invited to big-league camp in 2017, a testament to his steady progress, but unless he adds more power, his ceiling may be that of a fourth outfielder in the big leagues.

BA GRADE
45 Risk: **Medium**
HIT: 45. POW: 40.
SPD: 50. FLD: 50.
ARM: 55.

Year	Club (League)	Class	AVG	G	AB	R	H	2B	3B	HR	RBI	BB	SO	SB	CS	OBP	SLG
2015	Burlington (MWL)	LoA	.218	79	261	33	57	7	0	0	23	45	49	19	13	.340	.245
	Orem (PIO)	R	.294	14	51	9	15	3	0	0	2	6	10	5	3	.368	.353
2016	Burlington (MWL)	LoA	.326	37	138	22	45	8	1	2	22	18	22	4	3	.411	.442
	Inland Empire (CAL)	HiA	.309	40	149	36	46	7	4	4	17	16	30	6	7	.393	.490
2017	Inland Empire (CAL)	HiA	.321	13	53	5	17	6	0	0	2	9	15	5	2	.438	.434
	Mobile (SL)	AA	.248	77	278	40	69	13	2	4	26	40	73	21	9	.361	.353
	Salt Lake (PCL)	AAA	.287	30	115	20	33	6	1	5	16	7	28	9	2	.341	.487
Minor League Totals			.268	355	1241	204	332	60	12	18	131	171	278	80	43	.368	.379

11 LEONARDO RIVAS, SS

BA GRADE
50 Risk: **High**

Born: Oct. 10, 1997. **B-T:** B-R. **Ht.:** 5-10. **Wt.:** 150. **Signed:** Venezuela, 2014. **Signed by:** Carlos Ramirez/Lebi Ochoa.

Rivas signed with the Angels for $40,000 in 2014 as a 16-year-old and has worked his way up the system. The Venezuelan switch-hitter has a .278 career average and has shown advanced plate discipline at every level, with a .420 on-base percentage and nearly as many walks (132) as strikeouts (136) in 630 career at-bats.

Rivas has played all three infield positions and a little outfield, but focused primarily on shortstop in 2017. Rivas grows on you. He's not flashy in the field but makes all the plays, and he won't dazzle you at the plate but is competent from both sides and rarely swings at pitches out of the zone. Though small-framed, he has gotten stronger physically. He has an average to above-average arm, with good accuracy. His hands work well and he has solid range to both sides, but he's a little better going to his left. Rivas is athletic with a projectable build and good hand-eye coordination, is light on his feet with a loose arm, and is instinctive in the field and on the basepaths.

Scouts who watch Rivas over multiple games get a better appreciation for him. Though many project him as a utility player, he could develop into a starting middle infielder if he continues to hit and get on base.

Year	Club (League)	Class	AVG	G	AB	R	H	2B	3B	HR	RBI	BB	SO	SB	CS	OBP	SLG
2015	Angels (DSL)	R	.258	65	213	38	55	8	7	1	31	37	53	21	12	.401	.376
2016	Angels (DSL)	R	.323	33	99	26	32	3	3	0	15	20	23	20	5	.455	.414
	Angels (AZL)	R	.253	26	91	22	23	5	0	1	4	16	16	6	3	.364	.341
2017	Burlington (MWL)	LoA	.267	26	90	24	24	5	0	0	7	20	22	8	1	.412	.322
	Orem (PIO)	R	.299	35	137	37	41	6	4	2	29	39	22	11	0	.462	.445
Minor League Totals			.278	185	630	147	175	27	14	4	86	132	136	66	21	.420	.384

12 JESUS CASTILLO, RHP

BA GRADE
50 Risk: **High**

Born: Aug. 27, 1995. **B-T:** R-R. **Ht.:** 6-2. **Wt.:** 165. **Signed:** Venezuela, 2011. **Signed by:** Marlon Urdaneta (Diamondbacks).

What seemed like an innocuous deal at the 2016 trade deadline could pay huge dividends if Castillo, acquired from the Cubs for reliever Joe Smith, continues to develop as he did over the past year. After pitching to a 2.87 ERA in 2016, Castillo advanced from low Class A to high Class A to Double-A in

2017, recording a 3.32 ERA with 118 strikeouts and 26 walks in 124.2 innings.

Castillo has excellent command of a low-90s fastball with heavy sink that breaks a lot of bats and induces plenty of ground balls. Neither his mid-70s curveball nor his low-80s changeup are true swing-and-miss pitches, but he throws them for strikes consistently. Castillo has a very loose arm and is able to repeat a high-three-quarters delivery that has some deception. He has a great understanding of the need to attack hitters and get ahead in the count. The Angels believe Castillo can put on another 25 pounds, and with added size and strength, should come more velocity.

Castillo could remain in the rotation if his curveball becomes a go-to secondary pitch, but most scouts project him as a reliever. Out of the pen he could rely even more on his ground-ball inducing sinker. He'll start 2018 back at Double-A.

Year	Club (League)	Class	W	L	ERA	G	GS	CG	SV	IP	H	HR	BB	SO	K/9	WHIP	AVG
2015	Cubs (AZL)	R	1	2	4.58	11	0	0	0	20	26	1	9	17	7.8	1.78	.306
2016	Eugene (NWL)	SS	2	3	3.27	7	7	0	0	33	28	3	11	38	10.4	1.18	.224
	Burlington (MWL)	LoA	3	2	2.43	6	6	0	0	30	33	1	7	23	7.0	1.35	.295
2017	Burlington (MWL)	LoA	1	1	2.37	4	4	0	0	19	13	1	2	22	10.4	0.79	.191
	Inland Empire (CAL)	HiA	8	3	3.62	16	15	0	0	82	86	13	18	74	8.1	1.27	.270
	Mobile (SL)	AA	0	2	3.04	5	5	0	0	24	27	2	6	22	8.4	1.39	.287
Minor League Totals			18	19	3.62	79	53	0	0	303	318	24	89	274	8.1	1.34	.272

13 JOSE SUAREZ, LHP

BA GRADE
50 Risk: High

Born: Jan. 3, 1998. **B-T:** L-L. **Ht.:** 5-10. **Wt.:** 170. **Signed:** Venezuela, 2014.
Signed by: Carlos Ramirez/Mauro Zerpa/Lebi Ochoa.

Signed as a 16-year-old out of Venezuela for $300,000 in 2014, Suarez is still undersized but has an advanced feel for pitching.

Suarez's fastball velocity ticked up to 89-93 mph in 2017, he has an above-average changeup, and he's developing a curveball as a quality third pitch. The results can be seen in his strikeout rates, which have increased from 5.7 batters per nine innings in 2015 to 10.7 in 2016 to 11.8 in 2017, when he combined to go 6-1, 3.28 in 15 starts in the AZL and low Class A Burlington, striking out 90 and walking 22 in 68.2 innings. Suarez doesn't make many mistakes, having allowed only nine homers in 186 minor league innings. He has above-average pitchability and an easy, repeatable high-three quarters delivery with good direction to the plate. He should add velocity as he develops physically, but his changeup, which he can throw in any count, is his best pitch.

With advanced pitching smarts and above-average control, Suarez could reach high Class A and perhaps Double-A in 2018 at age 20.

Year	Club (League)	Class	W	L	ERA	G	GS	CG	SV	IP	H	HR	BB	SO	K/9	WHIP	AVG
2015	Angels (DSL)	R	2	2	2.13	11	11	0	0	55	43	0	8	34	5.6	0.93	.215
	Angels (AZL)	R	1	1	5.60	4	2	0	0	18	28	0	4	12	6.1	1.81	.364
2016	Angels (AZL)	R	1	3	5.36	11	5	0	0	40	48	1	13	46	10.3	1.51	.296
	Orem (PIO)	R	0	1	0.00	1	1	0	0	4	6	0	1	7	14.5	1.62	.300
2017	Angels (AZL)	R	1	0	1.93	3	3	0	0	14	10	1	4	19	12.2	1.00	.208
	Burlington (MWL)	LoA	5	1	3.62	12	12	0	0	55	49	7	18	71	11.7	1.23	.243
Minor League Totals			10	8	3.53	42	34	0	0	186	184	9	48	189	9.1	1.25	.260

14 JOSE SORIANO, RHP

BA GRADE
50 Risk: Extreme

Born: Oct. 20, 1998. **B-T:** R-R. **Ht.:** 6-3. **Wt.:** 170. **Signed:** Dominican Republic, 2016. **Signed by:** Domingo Garcia/Alfredo Ulloa.

It's easy to dream on the arm of Soriano, whose fastball at age 18 sat in the low-90s and touched 96 mph in 2017 pitching at the Rookie levels.

Though the pitch doesn't have a ton of movement, it has a little bit of late life. Soriano, who signed for $70,000, grew about three inches from 2016 to 2017, though he didn't add a lot of weight. It's not a leap to think that, with added size, strength and maturity, Soriano's fastball will hit 100 mph in a few years. He has an advanced feel for his curveball, which he throws between 80-85 mph, and has shown decent arm action and some feel for a mid-80s changeup, which is a developing pitch. Soriano has shown a good feel for pitching, but like most young, raw pitchers, he has struggled to gain consistency–he went 2-2 with a 2.92 ERA in 13 games in the AZL and Orem, but with his stuff, he should have struck out more than 39 batters in 52.1 innings.

Soriano had issues timing his delivery in 2016, but was more mechanically sound and more polished in 2017. Another leap of improvement could send him to low Class A Burlington in 2018.

Year	Club (League)	Class	W	L	ERA	G	GS	CG	SV	IP	H	HR	BB	SO	K/9	WHIP	AVG
2016	Angels (DSL)	R	3	5	1.58	14	14	0	0	57	37	2	30	45	7.1	1.18	.187
2017	Angels (AZL)	R	2	2	2.94	12	10	0	0	49	43	2	14	37	6.8	1.16	.234
	Orem (PIO)	R	0	0	2.70	1	1	0	0	3	4	0	4	2	5.4	2.40	.308
Minor League Totals			5	7	2.22	27	25	0	0	109	84	4	48	84	6.9	1.21	.213

15 STIWARD AQUINO, RHP

BA GRADE
50 Risk: Extreme

Born: June 20, 1999. **B-T:** R-R. **Ht.:** 6-6. **Wt.:** 170. **Signed:** Dominican Republic, 2016. **Signed by:** Domingo Garcia/Frankie Thon.

The Angels signed Aquino for $100,000 as a 17-year-old out of the Dominican Republic in 2016, intrigued by his projectable 6-foot-6 frame and impressive body control. He went out and had a solid professional debut in 2017, moving from the Dominican Summer League to the Rookie-level Arizona League and holding his own.

Aquino was labeled the "surprise" of instructs by Angels front office officials, who came away from the fall thinking Aquino might be the best of their collection of young Latin American arms. Aquino uses his long, lanky levers to his benefit, generating both downhill plane and velocity with extension. He works 93-95 mph with his fastball, spins 76-78 mph hammer curveball that projects, and throws them both for strikes consistently. The Angels believe there is even more velocity to come as he fills out his sizable frame. Aquino is still seeking a third pitch, but with two potential plus pitches, more velocity to come and solid strike-throwing ability, the Angels believe they have a diamond in the rough.

Aquino will likely start 2018 in extended spring training, with a chance to see Rookie-level Orem or low Class A Burlington during the year..

Year	Club (League)	Class	W	L	ERA	G	GS	CG	SV	IP	H	HR	BB	SO	K/9	WHIP	AVG
2017	Angels (DSL)	R	0	2	4.56	7	4	0	0	24	25	1	9	29	9.5	1.44	.272
	Angels (AZL	R	1	0	1.59	2	0	0	0	6	5	0	4	2	3.2	1.59	.250
Minor League Totals			1	3	3.99	9	4	0	0	29	30	1	13	31	9.5	1.47	.268

16 LIVAN SOTO, SS

BA GRADE
50 Risk: Extreme

Born: June 22, 2000. **B-T:** L-R. **Ht:** 6-0. **Wt:** 160. **Signed:** Venezuela, 2016. **Signed by:** Rolando Petit (Braves).

Soto signed with the Braves for $1 million as one of the top prospects during the 2016 international signing period. He made his pro debut the Rookie-level Gulf Coast League in 2017, but after the season was one the 12 Braves prospects declared free agents by Major League Baseball as punishment for violating international signing rules.

The Angels signed Soto the first day he was eligible sign with a new club for $850,000. Soto's 2017 stat line is ugly, with a .225 batting average and .586 OPS, but evaluators say the quality of his at-bats was better than his numbers indicate. He walked more than he struck out and showed an excellent understanding of the strike zone. There are scouts who believe Soto will end up as an above-average hitter with fringe-average power, but he has to add a lot of muscle and strength to get there. His swing is fundamentally sound with a line-drive approach and he's a good bunter. Soto mostly stands out at shortstop as a future plus defender with a plus arm. He has an excellent internal clock and possesses an advanced understanding of the nuances of the game.

Soto is an above-average runner and earns plaudits as a team leader. Soto has an everyday shortstop ceiling, but is a long way away.

Year	Club (League)	Class	AVG	G	AB	R	H	2B	3B	HR	RBI	BB	SO	SB	CS	OBP	SLG
2017	Braves (GCL)	R	.225	47	173	24	39	5	0	0	14	27	26	7	3	.332	.254
Minor League Totals			.225	47	173	24	39	5	0	0	14	27	26	7	3	.332	.254

17 TRENT DEVEAUX, OF

BA GRADE
50 Risk: Extreme

Born: May 4, 2000. **B-T:** R-R. **Ht.:** 6-3. **Wt.:** 185. **Signed:** Bahamas, 2017. **Signed by:** Carlos Gomez.

Finally freed from being restricted on the international market because of their $8 million signing of shortstop Roberto Baldoquin in 2014, the Angels made their first big splash in two years with their July 2 signing of the Deveaux for $1.2 million.

Deveaux, who moved from shortstop to the outfield last year, is an elite athlete and runner who has been clocked at 6.2 seconds in the 60-yard dash, an 80-grade time. He shows the makings of a premium defender in center field, with a solid arm, plus range and plus instincts to go with his elite speed. At the plate, Deveaux reminds some scouts of a young Dexter Fowler. He has a line-drive swing and a good understanding of the strike zone. Though his power is limited, he has a strong, lean, projectable frame.

There's quick burst in everything Deveaux does. He also showed an ability to make adjustments in 2017, closing off his upright, open stance to improve his balance, which helped him stay through the ball and use the middle of the field.

Deveau won't turn 18 until a month into the 2018 season and is set to spend the year at the Rookie levels, beginning in the Arizona League.

Year	Club (League)	Class	AVG	G	AB	R	H	2B	3B	HR	RBI	BB	SO	SB	CS	OBP	SLG
2017	Did not play—Signed 2018 contract																

18 BRENNON LUND, OF

BA GRADE
40 Risk: Medium

Born: Nov. 27, 1994. **B-T:** L-R. **Ht.:** 5-10. **Wt.:** 185. **Drafted:** Brigham Young, 2016 (11th round). **Signed by:** Chad Hermansen.

A prototypical leadoff hitter with above-average speed, good on-base skills and the ability to bunt, Lund jumped two levels in 2017, from low Class A Burlington to high Class A Inland Empire to Double-A Mobile, combining to slash .308/.373/.403 with 21 doubles, four triples, six homers, 47 RBIs and 20 stolen bases in 121 games.

Though he's a contact hitter with good hands and feel for the strike zone, Lund did have a tendency to chase pitches, striking out 100 times in 491 at-bats in 2017. Lund is athletic and strong for his size. He has a short, compact swing and is neither pull-dominant nor opposite-field dominant; he uses the whole field. When he finds the barrel, he has shown sneaky power. Lund is an instinctual defender with a slightly below-average arm who's working on jumps in the outfield. With his grit and baseball smarts, he reminds multiple scouts of veteran reserve outfielder Daniel Robertson.

Lund may not have enough bat for an every-day job in the big leagues, but he has the potential to be a fourth or fifth outfielder.

Year	Club (League)	Class	AVG	G	AB	R	H	2B	3B	HR	RBI	BB	SO	SB	CS	OBP	SLG
2016	Orem (PIO)	R	.397	18	73	15	29	3	0	2	11	7	11	7	2	.463	.521
	Burlington (MWL)	LoA	.271	45	181	19	49	9	2	1	19	12	33	8	1	.316	.359
2017	Burlington (MWL)	LoA	.306	46	173	25	53	7	4	2	18	24	26	14	3	.400	.428
	Inland Empire (CAL)	HiA	.321	46	196	26	63	11	0	3	23	16	41	5	4	.385	.423
	Mobile (SL)	AA	.287	29	122	17	35	3	0	1	6	3	33	1	2	.310	.336
Minor League Totals			.307	184	745	102	229	33	6	9	77	62	144	35	12	.368	.404

19 TAYLOR WARD, C

BA GRADE
40 Risk: Medium

Born: Dec. 14, 1993. **B-T:** R-R. **Ht.:** 6-1. **Wt.:** 200. **Drafted:** Fresno State, 2015 (1st round). **Signed by:** Scott Richardson.

Ward, who missed the first month of the season because of an oblique injury, stands out as a potentially above-average defender, with a plus arm that has allowed him to throw out 73 of 214 basestealers (34%) in 153 games over the past two seasons.

Ward is agile and athletic behind the plate, with good hands, and his receiving, blocking, game-calling and leadership skills have improved. After allowing 19 passed balls in 90 games in 2016, Ward allowed four passed balls in 63 games in 2017. But the more scouts watch Ward hit, the more surprised they are the Angels used a 26th overall pick and spent $1.67 million to sign him. He has shown good plate discipline, with almost as many walks (144) as strikeouts (164) in three seasons, but he doesn't have a consistent approach or setup at the plate or get enough load in his swing, which limits his power. He has also shown a tendency to give away at-bats. Ward slashed a combined .258/.368/.390 with nine homers, 14 doubles and 49 RBIs across two levels in 2017.

Most evaluators see Ward as a future backup at best, and only because of the dearth of catching they see in today's game.

Year	Club (League)	Class	AVG	G	AB	R	H	2B	3B	HR	RBI	BB	SO	SB	CS	OBP	SLG
2015	Orem (PIO)	R	.349	32	109	20	38	4	1	2	19	29	8	5	2	.489	.459
	Burlington (MWL)	LoA	.348	24	92	10	32	3	0	1	12	10	15	1	1	.412	.413
2016	Inland Empire (CAL)	HiA	.249	123	466	61	116	11	0	10	56	48	81	0	0	.323	.337
2017	Inland Empire (CAL)	HiA	.242	54	207	32	50	11	1	6	30	35	43	0	0	.348	.391
	Mobile (SL)	AA	.286	33	119	14	34	3	0	3	19	22	17	0	0	.400	.387
Minor League Totals			.272	266	993	137	270	32	2	22	136	144	164	6	3	.366	.375

20 LUIS PENA, RHP

BA GRADE

45 Risk: High

Born: Aug. 24, 1995. **B-T:** R-R. **Ht.:** 5-11. **Wt.:** 170. **Signed:** Dominican Republic, 2013. **Signed by:** Rene Rojas.

The Angels signed Pena for just $20,000 in 2013 and have seen him progress every year, topping out with a sterling second half in 2017 that ended in a promotion to Double-A Mobile.

Pena does some Johnny Cueto-like things with his delivery—he'll quick-pitch at times and hold his leg kick before driving toward the plate at others—that the Angels have so far refrained from changing, because Pena has been able to disrupt the timing of hitters and had success with it. Though his ERA (5.00) and walks (67) were high in 151.1 innings across 29 starts at two levels in 2017, Pena struck out 167 and held hitters to a .213 average in four Double-A starts. He relies primarily on a late-riding fastball that sits between 90-93 with life and late rise up through the zone. His hard, late-breaking slider that can be wipeout quality at times, inducing a lot of swings and misses. Pena's feel for his changeup has been sporadic, but the pitch has flashed above-average.

Pena pitched out of the bullpen his first two seasons and projects more as a reliever long-term, but if he continues to gain consistency with his changeup, he'll remain a starter.

Year	Club (League)	Class	W	L	ERA	G	GS	CG	SV	IP	H	HR	BB	SO	K/9	WHIP	AVG
2015	Angels (AZL)	R	1	0	1.80	7	0	0	2	10	7	0	1	12	10.8	0.80	.194
	Orem (PIO)	R	0	2	5.04	19	0	0	1	25	28	0	8	25	9.0	1.44	.280
2016	Burlington (MWL)	LoA	5	9	4.02	27	16	0	1	101	89	6	43	118	10.5	1.31	.239
2017	Inland Empire (CAL)	HiA	6	10	5.28	25	25	1	0	131	138	15	58	148	10.1	1.49	.267
	Mobile (SL)	AA	1	3	3.15	4	4	0	0	20	16	3	9	19	8.6	1.25	.213
Minor League Totals			14	24	4.33	92	45	1	6	303	285	24	122	334	9.9	1.34	.247

21 D'SHAWN KNOWLES, OF

BA GRADE

50 Risk: Extreme

Born: Jan. 16, 2001. **B-T:** B-R. **Ht.:** 5-11. **Wt.:** 165. **Signed:** Bahamas, 2017. **Signed by:** Carlos Gomez.

The Angels spent $850,000 to sign Knowles as their second big ticket signing of the 2016 international class along with fellow Bahamian Trent Deveaux. Knowles is a high-end athlete with borderline plus-plus speed, a solid arm and plus defensive instincts in center field, a position he has a natural feel for. Though several clubs felt that Knowles was raw as a hitter and lagged behind many of the other top players in the class, the Angels believe he has an advanced approach offensively, with good plate discipline, average-to-above power potential and a clean, compact, quiet swing from both sides of the plate. Some scouts had a difficult time gauging Knowles' hitting ability due to the lack of quality competition they saw him face. Knowles is mostly a line-drive hitter with gap-to-gap power that should increase as the slight 16-year-old gets bigger and stronger and gains more experience. The Angels were also impressed with the maturity, work ethic, enthusiasm, high energy and competitiveness Knowles showed in instructional league. "If he said he could tie his shoes faster than you," player development director Mike Gallego said, "he'd challenge you."

Year	Club (League)	Class	AVG	G	AB	R	H	2B	3B	HR	RBI	BB	SO	SB	CS	OBP	SLG
2017	Did not play—Signed 2018 contract																

22 JERRYEL RIVERA, LHP

BA GRADE

50 Risk: Extreme

Born: April 19, 1999. **B-T:** L-L. **Ht.:** 6-3. **Wt.:** 180. **Drafted:** HS—Florida, P.R., 2017 (11th round). **Signed by:** Ralph Reyes.

The Angels feel they got a steal with their 11th-round pick in Rivera, a lanky lefthander with a long, loose body, a smooth, athletic delivery and an advanced feel for his changeup that is rare for an 18-year-old. He was committed to Florida International before signing with the Angels for $450,000, fourth-round money.

Rivera's fastball is presently light, sitting 86-89 mph and occasionally touching the low 90s with some run but not much sink, but his velocity should improve with strength, physical maturity and experience. It's his changeup that has the Angels so excited. Rivera throws it with the arm speed and action of his fastball, and the pitch fades quite a bit in the zone as it approaches the hitter. Rivera's third pitch, which he calls a curveball but sometimes looks more like a slider, is a work in progress. He flashed his potential with a 1.64 ERA in eight Rookie League appearances after signing, striking out 11 and walking three in 11 innings.

With a delivery that requires little tinkering and a frame that could easily carry another 20-25 pounds, Rivera has a chance to blossom into a mid-rotation starter, although he is a long ways from getting there.

Year	Club (League)	Class	W	L	ERA	G	GS	CG	SV	IP	H	HR	BB	SO	K/9	WHIP	AVG
2017	Angels (AZL)	R	1	0	1.64	8	1	0	0	11	7	0	3	11	9.0	0.91	.175
Minor League Totals			1	0	1.64	8	1	0	0	11	7	0	3	11	9.0	0.91	.175

23 JOHN SWANDA, RHP

BA GRADE 50 Risk: Extreme

Born: March 18, 1999. **B-T:** R-R. **Ht.:** 6-2. **Wt.:** 185. **Drafted:** HS—Des Moines, 2017 (4th round). **Signed by:** Joel Murrie.

The Angels went well over slot to sign Swanda for $625,000 and get him to pass up a Nebraska scholarship. His numbers were not impressive in a brief seven-game stint in the Rookie-level Arizona League, and in late October the 18-year-old was arrested and charged in his native Iowa for operating a vehicle while intoxicated and possession of a fake I.D.

On the mound, Swanda throws a fastball between 89-91 mph and showed advanced feel for a low-80s changeup. He possesses an extremely clean delivery with good, loose arm action and a solid repertoire considering he played mostly shortstop in high school and didn't pitch much until about a month before the draft. The primary focus for Swanda in fall instructional league was the development of his breaking ball, which is slurvy right now and could wind up being more of a slider. But Swanda spins his breaking ball well, and the Angels see it being a solid-average pitch down the road. As a former infielder, Swanda fields his position well. He should add more velocity as he fills out physically, and he should improve as he gains more seasoning on the mound.

The Angels expect Swanda to have his legal issues resolved by the spring. He is slated to begin next season in extended spring training but should move up to Rookie-level Orem at some point.

Year	Club (League)	Class	W	L	ERA	G	GS	CG	SV	IP	H	HR	BB	SO	K/9	WHIP	AVG
2017	Angels (AZL)	R	1	2	9.31	7	1	0	0	10	13	1	6	6	5.6	1.97	.333
Minor League Totals			1	2	9.31	7	1	0	0	10	13	1	6	6	5.6	1.97	.333

24 NONIE WILLIAMS, SS

BA GRADE 50 Risk: Extreme

Born: May 22, 1998. **B-T:** R-R. **Ht.:** 6-2. **Wt.:** 200. **Drafted:** HS—Kansas City, Kan., 2016 (3rd round). **Signed by:** Drew Chadd.

It took an over-slot $950,000 to sign Williams away from Louisiana State in 2016. Williams was home-schooled but allowed to play at Turner High in the Kansas City area because he took one class there.

Williams started switch-hitting late in his high school career, but the Angels transitioned him back to hitting only from the right side this past summer, giving Williams the chance to see righthanded breaking balls as a righthanded hitter for the first time as a professional. He has explosive raw tools, with above-average bat speed and decent power potential, but he has a career .231/.284/.280 slash line and hit only one homer in 81 rookie league games. Williams has a plus arm, but his footwork and actions in the middle infield require polish. He's considered an average runner. Slowed by a sore arm last spring, he has gotten stronger since the draft, and the Angels plan to keep him at shortstop for now.

Some scouts already project Williams' size and lack of middle-infield instincts will necessitate a move to third base or a corner outfield spot, which puts additional pressure on him to show he can turn his raw tools into on-field skills and increase his offensive output.

Year	Club (League)	Class	AVG	G	AB	R	H	2B	3B	HR	RBI	BB	SO	SB	CS	OBP	SLG
2016	Angels (AZL)	R	.244	38	156	23	38	4	1	0	11	8	40	9	3	.280	.282
2017	Angels (AZL)	R	.220	43	168	22	37	3	2	1	15	14	53	11	3	.286	.280
Minor League Totals			.231	81	324	45	75	7	3	1	26	22	93	20	6	.284	.281

25 JAKE JEWELL, RHP

BA GRADE 40 Risk: Medium

Born: May 16, 1993. **B-T:** R-R. **Ht.:** 6-3. **Wt.:** 200. **Drafted:** Northeastern Oklahoma A&M JC, 2014 (5th round). **Signed by:** Drew Chadd.

Jewell bounced back from a brutal 2016 at high Class A Inland Empire to become an above-average strike thrower at Double-A in 2017. The difference was stark, as he became a pitcher who generates more swings and misses and weak contact and has lowered his walk rate with a more compact, smooth and repeatable delivery.

Jewell had a tendency to drop his arm slot and leave pitches in the upper part of the zone, where they were crushed, in 2015, but has made adjustments since then and added velocity as well. The average velocity of Jewell's fastball jumped from 91 mph in 2016 to 93 mph in 2017. He can ride his four-seam fastball, which sits at 94-95 mph, up to 98 mph with a natural cut and throws a sinking two-seamer in the low-90s. Jewell throws an average slider in the 86-89 mph range, a sweeping curveball in the low-80s and has mixed in an occasional cutter. His command has improved, but there's still room for growth.

Jewell, who has bounced back and forth between the rotation and bullpen throughout his career, projects better as a reliever. He'll take on the challenge of Triple-A Salt Lake in 2018.

Year	Club (League)	Class	W	L	ERA	G	GS	CG	SV	IP	H	HR	BB	SO	K/9	WHIP	AVG
2015	Burlington (MWL)	LoA	6	8	4.77	31	15	0	2	111	110	8	31	110	8.9	1.27	.263
2016	Inland Empire (CAL)	HiA	2	15	6.31	28	27	0	0	137	191	10	65	104	6.8	1.87	.334
2017	Inland Empire (CAL)	HiA	0	1	2.25	3	3	0	0	16	11	1	3	15	8.4	0.88	.183
	Mobile (SL)	AA	7	8	4.84	24	23	1	0	125	136	14	41	81	5.8	1.42	.284
Minor League Totals			16	34	5.07	98	77	1	2	432	493	34	156	345	7.2	1.50	.291

26 JONAH TODD, OF

BA GRADE
45 Risk: High

Born: Sept. 18, 1995. **B-T:** L-L. **Ht.:** 6-0. **Wt.:** 185. **Drafted:** Auburn, 2017 (6th round). **Signed by:** Chris McAlpin.

Persistence is a strength for Todd, who wasn't offered a single scholarship out of high school, attended a junior college in Alabama and made the team at Auburn as a walk-on, stocking shelves at a Walmart to earn enough money to cover his college expenses.

Todd won the Tigers starting center field job and blossomed into a star, slashing .376/.460/.471 with 13 doubles, five triples, 37 RBIs and only 28 strikeouts in 283 plate appearances over 63 games in 2017. Todd continued to show excellent plate discipline at rookie league Orem and low Class A Burlington, slashing .275/.373/.344. A prototypical leadoff man with plus speed, Todd shows the makings of a professional hitter who sprays the ball to all fields, doesn't swing at balls and is willing to take his walks.

Todd is an above-average defender with good instincts and an average but accurate arm in center field. The Angels love his grit and tenacity—Auburn coach Butch Thompson nicknamed him Joe Dirt.

Year	Club (League)	Class	AVG	G	AB	R	H	2B	3B	HR	RBI	BB	SO	SB	CS	OBP	SLG
2017	Orem (PIO)	R	.306	25	98	25	30	6	3	0	22	25	12	1	0	.440	.429
	Burlington (MWL)	LoA	.257	44	175	20	45	7	0	0	17	17	40	0	4	.330	.297
Minor League Totals			.275	69	273	45	75	13	3	0	39	42	52	1	4	.373	.344

27 DAVID FLETCHER, 2B/SS

BA GRADE
40 Risk: Medium

Born: May 31, 1994. **B-T:** R-R. **Ht.:** 5-10. **Wt.:** 175. **Drafted:** Loyola Marymount, 2015 (6th round). **Signed by:** Ben Diggins.

Fletcher's favorite player growing up in Orange County was David Eckstein, and the middle-infield prospect shares some traits with the shortstop and leadoff man.

Evaluators frequently label Fletcher an undersized "gamer" who consistently plays above his tools with good plate discipline and average speed but little power. He slashed .266/.316/.339 with 20 stolen bases in 111 Double-A and Triple-A games in 2017, with 55 strikeouts and 27 walks. Fletcher grinds out at-bats and has a solid approach with a line-drive stroke, but his added weight and muscle and lower body fat didn't translate into much power. Defensively, Fletcher has played mostly shortstop, but he projects as a second baseman or utility player in the big leagues. He's athletic with quick feet, soft hands, good instincts and solid range. What he lacks in arm strength he usually compensates for with good positioning, excellent footwork, a quick release and accurate throws.

Fletcher should make his MLB debut this season and could end up as the Angels go-to reserve infielder.

Year	Club (League)	Class	AVG	G	AB	R	H	2B	3B	HR	RBI	BB	SO	SB	CS	OBP	SLG
2015	Burlington (MWL)	LoA	.283	32	120	18	34	4	1	1	10	12	13	6	1	.358	.358
	Orem (PIO)	R	.331	37	160	28	53	12	4	0	30	16	9	11	4	.391	.456
2016	Inland Empire (CAL)	HiA	.275	78	324	42	89	12	1	3	31	22	43	15	3	.321	.346
	Arkansas (TL)	AA	.300	20	80	10	24	6	0	0	6	3	13	1	0	.325	.375
2017	Mobile (SL)	AA	.276	64	243	32	67	14	1	1	22	21	30	12	5	.341	.354
	Salt Lake (PCL)	AAA	.254	47	205	27	52	6	1	2	17	6	25	8	1	.285	.322
Minor League Totals			.282	278	1132	157	319	54	8	7	116	80	133	53	14	.334	.362

28 JOE GATTO, RHP

BA GRADE
45 Risk: V. High

Born: June 14, 1995. **B-T:** R-R. **Ht.:** 6-3. **Wt.:** 220. **Drafted:** HS—Richland, N.J., 2014 (2nd round). **Signed by:** Nick Gorneault.

Gatto threw so poorly at low Class A Burlington in 2016 he was sent back to the Angels complex in Arizona at midseason to rebuild his delivery. He returned to Burlington in 2017 and was visibly a different pitcher, throwing well enough to be promoted to high Class A Inland Empire in early August.

Gatto still flashes the best curveball in the system, a pitch with a sharp, late break, and a decent sinking, two-seam fastball that sits 90-93 mph mph. He's effective when he attacks the strike zone and trusts his stuff. Inland Empire pitching coach Mike Wuertz moved Gatto to the opposite side of the rubber last summer, and that allowed his two-seamer to work better. But Gatto is inconsistent with his fastball command—he struck out 101 and walked 59 in 128.2 innings in 2017—and he has been unable to develop his changeup into a serviceable third pitch. He throws too many non-competitive pitches, and some scouts question whether he has the makeup to reach the big leagues as a back-end starter.

Gatto may project more as a middle reliever, but still needs to significantly improve his control to get there. He'll start back at Inland Empire in 2018 and try to keep carrying his positive progress forward.

Year	Club (League)	Class	W	L	ERA	G	GS	CG	SV	IP	H	HR	BB	SO	K/9	WHIP	AVG
2015	Orem (PIO)	R	2	3	4.31	12	12	0	0	54	73	4	17	38	6.3	1.66	.340
2016	Burlington (MWL)	LoA	3	8	7.03	15	15	0	0	64	88	5	33	54	7.6	1.89	.321
2017	Burlington (MWL)	LoA	5	7	3.46	21	21	0	0	96	90	2	45	78	7.3	1.40	.247
	Inland Empire (CAL)	HiA	3	2	3.34	6	6	0	0	32	31	1	14	23	6.4	1.39	.258
Minor League Totals			15	21	4.63	65	61	0	0	274	318	14	118	209	6.9	1.59	.293

29 KEINNER PINA, C

Born: Feb. 12, 1997. **B-T:** R-R. **Ht.:** 5-10. **Wt.:** 165. **Signed:** Venezuela, 2013. **Signed by:** Carlos Ramirez/Lebi Ochoa.

BA GRADE 45 Risk: Extreme

The 20-year-old Pina's development has been slow—he spent most of his first two seasons in the Dominican Summer League, most of 2016 in the Arizona League and all of 2017 at Rookie-level Orem—but he has gradually matured into a stout defender and a favorite of the pitchers he works with because of his receiving skills, game-calling abilities and strong arm.

A natural leader, Pina has thrown out 95 of 240 basestealers (39.6 percent) and committed only 15 errors in 144 minor league games, earning plus grades as a defender from some evaluators. Offensively Pina makes consistent contact and has excellent plate discipline—he had more walks (23) than strikeouts (19) in 185 at-bats in 2017 and has almost as many walks (91) as strikeouts (114) in four minor league seasons—but he needs to get stronger physically just to develop into a gap hitter. Pina has no homers, 14 doubles and two triples in 652 at-bats in four seasons.

Pina will likely start at low-A Burlington in 2018. Because of his limited offensive potential, Pina projects as a backup catcher.

Year	Club (League)	Class	AVG	G	AB	R	H	2B	3B	HR	RBI	BB	SO	SB	CS	OBP	SLG
2015	Angels (DSL)	R	.246	35	122	15	30	2	1	0	13	21	21	7	4	.359	.279
	Angels (AZL)	R	.108	12	37	4	4	0	0	0	2	3	10	0	1	.171	.108
2016	Angels (AZL)	R	.296	37	142	19	42	4	1	0	17	12	26	5	2	.353	.338
	Orem (PIO)	R	.250	3	12	0	3	0	0	0	2	1	4	0	0	.308	.250
2017	Orem (PIO)	R	.292	48	185	34	54	7	0	0	33	23	19	1	0	.388	.330
Minor League Totals			.255	182	652	91	166	14	2	0	81	91	114	21	16	.357	.282

30 TORII HUNTER JR., OF

Born: June 7, 1995. **B-T:** R-R. **Ht.:** 6-2 **Wt.:** 180. **Drafted:** Notre Dame, 2016 (23rd round). **Signed by:** Jared Barnes.

BA GRADE 45 Risk: Extreme

The son of the former nine-time Gold Glove Award winner and five-time All-Star, Hunter passed up what would have been his senior season of football at Notre Dame—and a possible NFL career as a wide receiver—to sign with the Angels in 2016, even though he played baseball sparingly in college, hitting .182 in 11 at-bats and being used mostly as a pinch-runner in 18 games.

The Angels love Hunter's raw tools and athletic ability, and they saw that potential begin to emerge at Rookie-level Orem, where he hit .352 with a .432 on-base percentage in 52 games in 2017 and showed solid plate discipline, with 44 strikeouts and 23 walks in 213 at-bats. Hunter has regained his plus speed after a broken femur, suffered during a workout for the U.S. Army All-American Bowl his senior year of high school, sidelined him for two full baseball seasons.

Hunter needs to strengthen his arm, which is well-below average, and shorten his swing, but he has good raw strength and bat speed, which should translate to more power as he matures physically.

Year	Club (League)	Class	AVG	G	AB	R	H	2B	3B	HR	RBI	BB	SO	SB	CS	OBP	SLG
2017	Orem (PIO)	R	.352	52	213	48	75	10	3	1	28	23	44	13	2	.432	.441
Minor League Totals			.352	52	213	48	75	10	3	1	28	23	44	13	2	.432	.441

Los Angeles Dodgers

BY KYLE GLASER

The Dodgers experienced their best season in nearly three decades in 2017.

Now comes the even tougher task of carrying that success forward.

The Dodgers' 104 wins in 2017 were the franchise's most since relocating to Los Angeles from Brooklyn. They reached their first World Series since 1988 and came within one game of winning the title, ultimately falling in Game Seven at home to the Astros.

Merely getting to the World Series won't cut it again. The Dodgers roll into 2018 with the expectation of winning it.

The good news is they are in prime position to do so. The Dodgers top five hitters as measured by OPS are all slated to return in 2018. So are their top four starters and every key component of a bullpen that led the National League in ERA.

Though the Dodgers have made a concerted effort to trim baseball's highest payroll in recent years, they still have the financial might to make any move. What's more, they have a potent farm system with prospects ready to help.

The Dodgers led the majors in starter's ERA in 2017 and can expect reinforcements from top arms all age 23 or younger. Lefty Julio Urias is due back from his season-ending shoulder surgery and will still be just 21 years old on Opening Day. Walker Buehler, 23, got his first taste of the majors last year after shooting through the system and establishing himself as arguably the top pitching prospect in baseball. Mitchell White, 22, appears to be the latest in a line of productive draft picks made by the Dodgers. And international signees Yadier Alvarez and Dennis Santana finished the year in Double-A and can provide additional upper-90s heat at a moment's notice.

The position player side isn't as deep but it also doesn't need to be, with back-to-back Rookie of the Year winners Corey Seager and Cody Bellinger anchoring the infield and starters Austin Barnes, Chris Taylor, Yasiel Puig and Joc Pederson all still in their mid-20s. Even so, outfielder Alex Verdugo and catcher Keibert Ruiz lead a talented group of prospects awaiting a chance.

In fact, the only source of instability on the Dodgers comes in the front office. The team's success has led to other organizations poaching talented personnel. Assistant general manager Alex Anthopoulos left to become the Braves general manager, while farm director Gabe Kapler became the Phillies manager and highly regarded assistant farm director Jeremy Zoll was hired away to become the Twins farm director.

Still, Andrew Friedman, Farhan Zaidi and Josh

Corey Seager, 23, is just one of many talented young players in the Dodgers organization.

PROJECTED 2021 LINEUP

Catcher	Austin Barnes (31)
First Base	Cody Bellinger (25)
Second Base	Chris Taylor (30)
Third Base	Justin Turner (36)
Shortstop	Corey Seager (27)
Left Field	Joc Pederson (29)
Center Field	Alex Verdugo (25)
Right Field	Yasiel Puig (30)
No. 1 Starter	Clayton Kershaw (33)
No. 2 Starter	Walker Buehler (26)
No. 3 Starter	Julio Urias (24)
No. 4 Starter	Alex Wood (30)
No. 5 Starter	Mitchell White (26)
Closer	Kenley Jansen (33)

Byrnes remain in place, giving the Dodgers continuity at the top. The Dodgers have now won three consecutive NL West titles under the current regime (and five straight overall) and gotten one step further in the postseason each successive year: reaching the Division Series in 2015, the Championship Series in 2016 and the World Series in 2017.

Now it's a matter of taking that one final step and winning the franchise's first World Series since 1988. On the 30-year anniversary of Kirk Gibson, Orel Hershiser and the magical run that lives on in franchise lore, the Dodgers are in position to once again rise to the top. If they do, the parade down Vin Scully Boulevard will be a joyous one indeed.

LOS ANGELES DODGERS

TOP 2018 ROOKIE: Alex Verdugo, OF. He will have chance to earn immediate playing time and has the skills to take advantage of it.
BREAKOUT PROSPECT: Cristian Santana, 3B. The plus defender with power to all fields is beginning to show improved hitting ability.
SLEEPER: Tony Gonsolin, RHP. The two-way player in college is up to 99 mph out of bullpen with his full-time focus now on pitching.

SOURCE OF TOP 30 TALENT

Homegrown	28	Acquired	2
College	14	Trade	2
Junior college	1	Rule 5 draft	0
High school	6	Independent league	0
Nondrafted free agent	0	Free agent/waivers	0
International	7		

LF
Starling Heredia (17)
Luke Raley (26)
Cody Thomas

CF
Alex Verdugo (2)
Jeren Kendall (7)
Johan Mieses
Saige Jenco

RF
Yusniel Diaz (6)
D.J. Peters (8)
Carlos Rincon
Romer Cuadrado

3B
Cristian Santana (16)
Matt Beaty (21)
Rylan Bannon

SS
Gavin Lux (13)
Errol Robinson (28)
Drew Jackson (29)
Erick Mejia

2B
Tim Locastro (27)
Omar Estevez

1B
Edwin Rios (12)
Ibandel Isabel
Luis Paz

C
Keibert Ruiz (3)
Will Smith (9)
Connor Wong (18)
Kyle Farmer (23)

LHP

LHSP	LHRP
Caleb Ferguson (20)	Edward Paredes
Devin Smeltzer	Michael Johnson
Leonardo Crawford	Devin Hemmerich

RHP

RHSP	RHRP
Walker Buehler (1)	Josh Sborz (25)
Mitchell White (4)	Yaisel Sierra (30)
Yadier Alvarez (5)	Tony Gonsolin
Dennis Santana (10)	Corey Copping
Dustin May (11)	Parker Curry
Jordan Sheffield (14)	Andre Scrubb
Trevor Oaks (15)	Adam Bray
Morgan Cooper (19)	Chris Mathewson
Imani Abdullah (22)	Andrew Istler
James Marinan (24)	Shea Spitzbarth
Melvin Jimenez	
Andrew Spoko	
Riley Ottesen	
Jesus Vargas	

DRAFT ANALYSIS

2017

BEST PURE HITTER: C Connor Wong (3) hit .280/.372/.439 across three seasons with Houston before the Dodgers took him with the 100th overall pick, and he continued to hit well in his pro debut. Playing almost entirely in the low Class A Midwest League, he hit .276/.333/.490 while showing a solid use of the opposite field.

BEST POWER HITTER: While OF Jeren Kendall's (1) strikeout rate will continue to be a concern—he whiffed 27 percent of the time in 35 games in the Midwest League—he still has plus power, and the Dodgers like the progress they've seen with Kendall using his legs more in the batter's box.

FASTEST RUNNER: Kendall was arguably the most tooled-up college player in the 2017 class, partially thanks to his 80-grade running ability. He's still learning how to get the most of that natural speed on the bases (he went 5-for-13 on the bases in the Midwest League), but he also used it to rack up eight triples and six doubles.

BEST DEFENSIVE PLAYER: There's a reason Kendall was the Dodgers' first pick. He's already a plus defensive center fielder with plus speed and plus arm. His speed and defense give him survival tools, buying him time to improve at the plate.

BEST FASTBALL: RHP Zach Pop (7) pitches off a plus fastball that sits in the mid-90s and can get up to 98 mph. He left a game with Kentucky in mid-May with an arm injury and threw just five innings of relief for the Dodgers in the Rookie-level Arizona League this summer.

BEST SECONDARY PITCH: RHP Riley Ottesen (5) flashes plus with his slider, which remains inconsistent. He's athletic and has a quick arm, generating mid-to-upper 80s power. He's already striking out more batters in pro ball (9.7 K/9 between two levels) than he did during his last year at Utah (6.82 K/9).

BEST PRO DEBUT: A legitimate two-way prospect out of Boston College, Donovan Casey (20) was drafted as an outfielder, and he dominated at two Rookie-level stops. He he hit .396/.526/.533 with seven home runs in 33 games with Ogden

TOP DRAFT PICKS OF THE DECADE

Year	Player, Pos.	2017 Org
2008	Ethan Martin, RHP	Did not play
2009	Aaron Miller, LHP (1st round supp.)	Did not play
2010	Zach Lee, RHP	Padres
2011	Chris Reed, LHP	Retired
2012	Corey Seager, 3B	Dodgers
2013	Chris Anderson, RHP	Twins
2014	Grant Holmes, RHP	Athletics
2015	Walker Buehler, RHP	Dodgers
2016	Gavin Lux, SS	Dodgers
2017	Jeren Kendall, OF	Dodgers

in the Pioneer League after a 7-for-15 stint in the Arizona League, giving him a .403 average overall.

BEST ATHLETE: Arguably the most athletic player in the entire 2017 draft class, Kendall is the easy choice here.

MOST INTRIGUING BACKGROUND: Ottesen took two years off between high school and college, serving on a Mormon mission trip to Japan. He volunteered at a local school, where he helped out and taught younger baseball players. OF Zach Reks (10) started his college career at the Air Force Academy before leaving to attend Kentucky; when he didn't make the baseball team as a walk-on in his first try, he got a job at a local Toyota factory. He made the team after a second try. Unsigned C Logan White (39) is the son of ex-Dodgers scouting director Logan White, who now works in the Padres front office.

CLOSEST TO THE MAJORS: Reks signed for just $1,500 but hit .317/.394/.371 combined across the three leagues. He has speed and hitting ability to move quickly.

BEST LATE-ROUND PICK: Casey provides great value out of the 20th round and was ranked the No. 141 prospect on the BA500 draft ranking.

THE ONE WHO GOT AWAY: The Dodgers drafted Florida 2B Deacon Liput (29) as an eligible sophomore after he hit just .227 in an injury-plagued season. Liput returned to school after helping the Gators win the 2017 national title.

—CARLOS COLLAZO

2016

The early returns on the top picks in the class have been strong. C Will Smith (1) and RHP Mitchell White (2) carried momentum into pro ball and finished the year in Double-A. OF D.J. Peters (4) was named MVP of the California League.

GRADE: A

2015

The Dodgers' patience with RHP Walke Buehler (1) was rewarded, as he reached the big leagues he is now their top prospect. OF Willie Calhoun (4), used in the Yu Darvish trade, also reached the big leagues and is the Rangers' top prospect.

GRADE: A

2014

OF Alex Verdugo (2) and RHP Brock Stewart (6) have reached the big leagues, and Verdugo should be in line for a regular role soon. RHP Grant Holmes (1) is still figuring things out after being dealt to Oakland in 2016.

GRADE: B

1 WALKER BUEHLER, RHP

Born: July 28, 1994. **B-T:** R-R. **Ht.:** 6-2. **Wt.:** 175. **Drafted:** Vanderbilt, 2015 (1st round). **Signed by:** Marty Lamb.

JOHN WILLIAMSON

uehler's meteoric rise to top-prospect status in 2017 was just the latest chapter in a history of excellence. The Lexington, Ky., native was considered a top two-rounds talent out of high school but fell to the 14th round due to a strong Vanderbilt commitment. In college, he started a College World Series championship game as a sophomore and led the Commodores to a national title, pitched for Team USA and was co-MVP of the Cape Cod League. He pitched through elbow soreness as a junior to wrap up a decorated career, and the Dodgers drafted him 24th overall in 2015. An MRI later revealed he needed Tommy John surgery, which he had shortly after being drafted, and he missed virtually all of 2016. Buehler looked like a different pitcher in his first full season back in 2017. He returned sitting 96-99 mph, after previously living 91-96, and rocketed from high Class A Rancho Cucamonga to the majors.

Buehler is thin-framed, but that doesn't affect his stuff or the ability to hold it. His newly-enhanced fastball sits 97-98 mph deep into outings, reaching 100 and rarely dipping below 95. It jumps on hitters quickly out of his loose, athletic, elastic delivery, and he pounds the strike zone. The one shortcoming of his fastball is it doesn't have a ton of life, making it easier for hitters to square up when he misses his spot, a problem that was exposed during his September callup in the Dodgers bullpen. Buehler's slider and curveball are both plus pitches he locates well. His slider is a wipeout offering at 91-93 mph with tight spin and late tilt, and his north-to-south power curveball is equally dangerous at 81-84 mph. Buehler is still working on his changeup, with only about one in five he throws flashing average. He shows average to above command and control on all of his offerings. To top it off, he has a fearless mentality, exceptional makeup and a solid understanding of how to set hitters up.

Buehler's slight frame gives a few evaluators pause, but most see him as an elite pitching prospect with top-of-the-rotation potential. He has yet to pitch more then 95 innings in a season and will likely start 2018 back at Triple-A Oklahoma City in an effort to increase his durability.

BA GRADE	SCOUTING GRADES
65 Risk: Medium	**FB:** 70. **CB:** 60 **SL:** 60. **CHG:** 40. **CTL:** 55.

Projected future grades on 20-80 scouting scale

TOP PROSPECTS OF THE DECADE

Year	Player, Pos.	2017 Org
2008	Clayton Kershaw, LHP	Dodgers
2009	Andrew Lambo, OF	Atlantic League
2010	Dee Gordon, SS	Marlins
2011	Dee Gordon, SS	Marlins
2012	Zach Lee, RHP	Padres
2013	Hyun-Jin Ryu, LHP	Dodgers
2014	Joc Pederson, OF	Dodgers
2015	Corey Seager, SS	Dodgers
2016	Corey Seager, SS	Dodgers
2017	Cody Bellinger, 1B/OF	Dodgers

BEST TOOLS

Best Hitter For Average	Alex Verdugo
Best Power Hitter	D.J. Peters
Best Strike-Zone Discipline	Alex Verdugo
Fastest Baserunner	Tim Locastro
Best Athlete	Jeren Kendall
Best Fastball	Yadier Alvarez
Best Curveball	Walker Buehler
Best Slider	Mitchell White
Best Changeup	Imani Abdullah
Best Control	Dustin May
Best Defensive Catcher	Will Smith
Best Defensive Infielder	Errol Robinson
Best Infield Arm	Drew Jackson
Best Defensive Outfielder	Jeren Kendall
Best Outfield Arm	Alex Verdugo

Year	Club (League)	Class	W	L	ERA	G	GS	CG	SV	IP	H	HR	BB	SO	K/9	WHIP	AVG
2015	Did not play--Injured																
2016	Dodgers (AZL)	R	1	0	0.00	1	0	0	0	2	0	0	0	3	13.5	0.00	.000
	Great Lakes (MWL)	LoA	0	0	0.00	2	1	0	0	3	0	0	3	3	9.0	1.00	.000
2017	R. Cucamonga (CAL)	HiA	0	0	1.10	5	5	0	0	16	8	0	5	27	14.9	0.80	.143
	Tulsa (TL)	AA	2	2	3.49	11	11	0	0	49	40	5	15	64	11.8	1.12	.225
	Oklahoma City (PCL)	AAA	1	1	4.63	12	3	0	1	23	19	1	11	34	13.1	1.29	.216
	Los Angeles (NL)	MAJ	1	0	7.71	8	0	0	0	9	11	2	8	12	11.6	2.04	.306
Major League Totals			1	0	7.71	8	0	0	0	9	11	2	8	12	11.6	2.04	.306
Minor League Totals			4	3	3.17	31	20	0	1	94	67	6	34	131	12.6	1.08	.199

2 ALEX VERDUGO, OF

Born: May 15, 1996. **B-T:** L-L. **Ht.:** 6-0. **Wt.:** 205. **Drafted:** HS—Tucson, 2014 (2nd round). **Signed by:** Dustin Yount.

Most teams liked Verdugo as a pitcher coming out of high school in 2014, but the Dodgers went against the grain and drafted him as a hitter. It proved prescient. Verdugo's bat carried him all the way to Triple-A by age 21, when he earned a September callup in 2017.

Verdugo possesses a keen eye that led to more walks (52) than strikeouts (50) at Triple-A Oklahoma City, and he keeps it simple when he does get a pitch to hit. He has excellent rhythm and body control and a level, line-drive swing that allows him to drive the ball all over the field. He doesn't have much lift in his swing, but evaluators see enough strength and bat-to-ball skills to project about average power to go with a .290 or better average. Verdugo has average speed and it plays up in center field with good instincts and a quick first step. His best tool is his plus-plus, accurate arm. Verdugo's skills are undeniable, but criticisms of his effort level and maturity have plagued him since his amateur days and were again prevalent in 2017.

Verdugo will have a chance to win a roster spot in 2018, but he will have to improve his focus and motor to reach his above-average, everyday potential.

BA GRADE
55 Risk: Medium
HIT: 60. POW: 50.
SPD: 50. FLD: 55.
ARM: 70.

Year	Club (League)	Class	AVG	G	AB	R	H	2B	3B	HR	RBI	BB	SO	SB	CS	OBP	SLG
2015	Great Lakes (MWL)	LoA	.295	101	421	50	124	23	2	5	42	17	53	13	5	.325	.394
	R. Cucamonga (CAL)	HiA	.385	23	91	20	35	9	2	4	19	4	12	1	0	.406	.659
2016	Tulsa (TL)	AA	.273	126	477	58	130	23	1	13	63	44	67	2	6	.336	.407
2017	Oklahoma City (PCL)	AAA	.314	117	433	67	136	27	4	6	62	52	50	9	3	.389	.436
	Los Angeles (NL)	MAJ	.174	15	23	1	4	0	0	1	1	2	4	0	1	.240	.304
Major League Totals			.174	15	23	1	4	0	0	1	1	2	4	0	1	.240	.304
Minor League Totals			.305	421	1612	226	492	97	12	31	227	137	200	36	14	.362	.438

3 KEIBERT RUIZ, C

Born: July 20, 1998. **B-T:** B-R. **Ht.:** 6-0. **Wt.:** 200. **Signed:** Venezuela, 2014. **Signed by:** Francisco Cartaya/Pedro Avila.

The Dodgers signed Ruiz for $140,000 out of Venezuela when he turned 16, intrigued by his advanced defensive skills. They got an even better deal than they thought. Ruiz's offense has blossomed since signing. He hit .316 with an .813 OPS across both class A levels in 2017 and finished the year on Double-A Tulsa's post-season roster, all in his age-18 season.

Ruiz is a special switch-hitter with "a chance to be a star" in the words of one evaluator. He possesses superb timing, bat speed and ability to manipulate the barrel to all parts of the zone, and he began to learn to elevate for home runs toward the end of 2017. He makes solid contact from both sides but is much stronger lefthanded, though he is learning to take more aggressive swings righthanded. Behind the plate, Ruiz has good timing blocking balls and handles both good velocity and breaking stuff, but he loses focus at times and lets pitches to get away from him. He has average arm strength but an uncoordinated exchange and inconsistent footwork result in below-average pop times on throws down to second base.

Ruiz has to shore up his throwing and become a more consistent receiver. If he does, he has a chance to be an extraordinarily valuable switch-hitting, middle-of-the-order catcher.

BA GRADE
60 Risk: High
HIT: 60. POW: 45.
SPD: 40. FLD: 55.
ARM: 50.

Year	Club (League)	Class	AVG	G	AB	R	H	2B	3B	HR	RBI	BB	SO	SB	CS	OBP	SLG
2015	Dodgers (DSL)	R	.300	44	150	14	45	8	1	1	19	8	15	4	2	.340	.387
2016	Dodgers (AZL)	R	.485	8	33	5	16	4	1	0	15	3	4	0	0	.513	.667
	Ogden (PIO)	R	.354	48	189	28	67	18	2	2	33	12	23	0	0	.393	.503
2017	Great Lakes (MWL)	LoA	.317	63	227	34	72	16	1	2	24	18	30	0	0	.372	.423
	R. Cucamonga (CAL)	HiA	.315	38	149	24	47	7	1	6	27	7	23	0	0	.344	.497
Minor League Totals			.330	201	748	105	247	53	6	11	118	48	95	4	2	.372	.461

4 MITCHELL WHITE, RHP

Born: Dec. 28, 1994. **B-T:** R-R. **Ht.:** 6-4. **Wt.:** 207. **Drafted:** Santa Clara, 2016 (2nd round). **Signed by:** Tom Kunis.

White had Tommy John surgery in high school and took time to round into form in college. That finally happened his redshirt sophomore year, when his velocity spiked in Santa Clara's rotation and he flew up draft boards into the second round, where the Dodgers took him 65th overall. White's rapid ascent has extended to pro ball, where he overcame a broken toe that cost him six weeks to reach Double-A Tulsa in 2017.

No pitcher in the organization is harder to square up than White. His fastball sits 94-97 mph at its best, 92-93 at its worst, and that velocity is enhanced with late run and sink. His heater plays up even more with how he mixes it with his plus slider. He will manipulate break and depth of the pitch and use it to steal a strike before coming back with a nasty fastball that moves in the opposite direction. When he wants to go north-south he'll unleash an above-average curveball. His changeup is developing. White is a good athlete with a fluid delivery, but he loses his release point and direction in spurts, leading to bouts of wildness.

White has all the components to be a No. 2 or 3 starter. Improved control and health will be his biggest goals in 2018.

BA GRADE

60 Risk: High

FB: 60. CB: 55. SL: 60. CHG: 45. CTL: 50.

Year	Club (League)	Class	W	L	ERA	G	GS	CG	SV	IP	H	HR	BB	SO	K/9	WHIP	AVG
2016	Dodgers (AZL)	R	0	0	0.00	2	2	0	0	4	3	0	0	8	18.0	0.75	.200
	Great Lakes (MWL)	LoA	0	0	0.00	8	4	0	0	16	3	0	6	20	11.3	0.56	.058
	R. Cucamonga (CAL)	HiA	1	0	0.00	1	0	0	0	2	1	0	0	2	9.0	0.50	.167
2017	R. Cucamonga (CAL)	HiA	2	1	3.72	9	9	0	0	39	26	0	16	49	11.4	1.09	.187
	Dodgers (AZL)	R	0	0	0.00	3	3	0	0	7	2	0	2	8	10.3	0.57	.091
	Tulsa (TL)	AA	1	1	2.57	7	7	0	0	28	17	2	13	31	10.0	1.07	.168
Minor League Totals			4	2	2.26	30	25	0	0	96	52	2	37	118	11.1	0.93	.155

5 YADIER ALVAREZ, RHP

Born: March 7, 1996. **B-T:** R-R. **Ht.:** 6-3. **Wt.:** 175. **Signed:** Cuba, 2015. **Signed by:** Miguel Tosar/Patrick Guerrero/Bob Engle.

Alvarez had a big arm as a teenager in Cuba but failed to make the country's 18U national team because he was so wild. He popped up in the Dominican Republic throwing even harder, and the Dodgers signed him for an industry-stunning $16 million. After showing promise in his 2016 U.S. debut, his longstanding control problems resurfaced in 2017.

Alvarez is built like a scout's dream with a six-pack core, long limbs and comically easy velocity. He sits 95-99 mph as a starter with shockingly little effort, and his 86-88 mph slider shows plus movement and depth. The problem is both his fastball and slider play down to due to poor control and command. Lots of contact is made on Alvarez's fastball despite its velocity because he can't spot it, and he rarely lands his slider in the zone. He also lacks a third pitch with zero feel for an 87-90 mph changeup. The result was a 5.31 ERA at high Class A Rancho Cucamonga and 6.8 walks per nine innings at Double-A Tulsa.

Alvarez's youth and big velocity make him a big leaguer in evaluators eyes, but almost universally in the bullpen. He draws frequent comparisons with Neftali Feliz as someone too limited to be a starter, but electric enough to possibly be a first-division closer.

BA GRADE

55 Risk: High

FB: 70. SL: 55. CHG: 40. CTL: 40.

Year	Club (League)	Class	W	L	ERA	G	GS	CG	SV	IP	H	HR	BB	SO	K/9	WHIP	AVG
2016	Dodgers (AZL)	R	1	1	1.80	5	5	0	0	20	9	0	10	26	11.7	0.95	.127
	Great Lakes (MWL)	LoA	3	2	2.29	9	9	0	0	39	31	1	11	55	12.6	1.07	.214
2017	R. Cucamonga (CAL)	HiA	2	4	5.31	14	11	0	1	59	61	3	25	61	9.3	1.45	.263
	Tulsa (TL)	AA	2	2	3.55	7	7	0	0	33	29	1	25	36	9.8	1.64	.234
Minor League Totals			8	9	3.68	35	32	0	1	152	130	5	71	178	10.6	1.33	.227

6 YUSNIEL DIAZ, OF

Born: Oct. 7, 1996. **B-T:** R-R. **Ht.:** 6-1. **Wt.:** 195. **Signed:** Cuba, 2015. **Signed by:** Ismael Cruz/Miguel Tosar/Roman Barinas.

Diaz experienced great success in Cuba's junior leagues and major league before leaving the island. The Dodgers signed him for $15.5 million after the 2015 season and moved him aggressively, starting him at high Class A Rancho Cucamonga immediately and pushing him to Double-A Tulsa at age 21 in 2017.

Diaz is an alluring package of strength, tools and athleticism, and he began to translate his raw gifts into consistent skills in 2017. After toning down his pre-pitch movement and adjusting his hand position early in the year, Diaz's bat was much more explosive and on time through the zone, showing above-average to plus contact ability and big exit velocities. He tends to drive the ball on a line from gap to gap rather than in the air, limiting his power production. Diaz expands the zone at times but is improving. He is an average runner but above-average underway on the basepaths and in the outfield. He is capable of playing center field but his range is more suited to right, where he tracks back well and his plus arm plays.

Diaz is only beginning to turn his prolific tools into skills. He will start 2018 back at Double-A Tulsa with the chance for a quick move up to Triple-A.

BA GRADE

55 Risk: High

HIT: 55. POW: 50.
SPD: 50. FLD: 50.
ARM: 60.

Year	Club (League)	Class	AVG	G	AB	R	H	2B	3B	HR	RBI	BB	SO	SB	CS	OBP	SLG
2015	Did not play																
2016	Dodgers (AZL)	R	.143	3	14	2	2	0	0	1	3	0	3	0	0	.143	.357
	R. Cucamonga (CAL)	HiA	.272	82	316	47	86	8	7	8	54	29	71	7	8	.333	.418
2017	R. Cucamonga (CAL)	HiA	.278	83	331	42	92	15	3	8	39	35	73	7	9	.343	.414
	Tulsa (TL)	AA	.333	31	108	15	36	8	0	3	13	10	29	2	5	.390	.491
Minor League Totals			.281	199	769	106	216	31	10	20	109	74	176	16	22	.342	.425

7 JEREN KENDALL, OF

Born: Feb. 4, 1996. **B-T:** L-R. **Ht.:** 6-0. **Wt.:** 190. **Drafted:** Vanderbilt, 2017 (1st round). **Signed by:** Marty Lamb.

Kendall grew up in Wisconsin playing hockey and baseball and went on to Vanderbilt, where he started as a freshman on the 2015 national runner-up and blossomed into a top draft prospect. Kendall had top-10 pick helium entering his junior year, but a 25 percent strikeout rate dropped him to the Dodgers at 23rd overall, and he signed for an above-slot $2,897,500.

Kendall is a premium athlete capable of a highlight-reel play at any moment. He'll run down balls to the deepest parts of center field with his plus-plus speed, make leaping catches at the wall, throw out a runner on a line to or swipe a crucial bag. He shows a plus arm and is becoming a more efficient basestealer. The question is how much he'll hit. Opponents exploited the holes in his swing throughout college and at low Class A Great Lakes, deflating his average and nullifying his plus raw power. The Dodgers tweaked his setup and reworked his swing in instructional league to incorporate a more pronounced leg kick, and believe he can be an average hitter in time.

Kendall has all the tools to be an everyday player but has to prove he can hit. He'll try to do that at the Class A levels in 2018.

BA GRADE

55 Risk: V. High

HIT: 50. POW: 50.
SPD: 70. FLD: 70.
ARM: 60.

Year	Club (League)	Class	AVG	G	AB	R	H	2B	3B	HR	RBI	BB	SO	SB	CS	OBP	SLG
2017	Ogden (PIO)	R	.455	5	22	5	10	1	1	1	7	0	3	4	0	.455	.727
	Great Lakes (MWL)	LoA	.221	35	140	21	31	5	7	2	18	13	42	5	8	.290	.400
Minor League Totals			.253	40	162	26	41	6	8	3	25	13	45	9	8	.311	.444

8 D.J. PETERS, OF

Born: Dec. 12, 1995. **B-T:** R-R. **Ht.:** 6-6. **Wt.:** 225. **Drafted:** Western Nevada JC, 2016 (4th round). **Signed by:** Tom Kunis.

Peters grew up in Glendora, Calif., 30 miles east of Dodger Stadium, and joined his hometown team when the Dodgers drafted him in the fourth round out of Western Nevada JC in 2016. He signed for $247,500 and went on an immediate tear, winning MVP of the high Class A California League in 2017 after finishing third in home runs (27), second in walks (64) and first in slugging (.514)—but he also ranked second in strikeouts (189).

Peters is a tantalizing mix of size, power and athleticism. He is a muscular 6-foot-6 and a tick above average runner capable of playing center field. He carries his explosiveness into the batter's box. Peters' strength and long levers create tremendous impact, and he crushes anything left out over the plate with present plus power to all fields. He identifies pitches well and rarely chases, but he swings and misses through above-average velocity on the inner half and four-seamers up at an alarming rate. Peters projects as a right fielder, where he moves well side-to-side and his plus arm fits. He draws praise for his blue-collar work ethic and quiet leadership.

Peters' ability to reach his middle-of-the-order upside depends on whether he closes the holes in his swing. He will try with Double-A Tulsa in 2018.

BA GRADE
55 Risk: V. High
HIT: 45. POW: 60.
SPD: 50. FLD: 55.
ARM: 60.

Year	Club (League)	Class	AVG	G	AB	R	H	2B	3B	HR	RBI	BB	SO	SB	CS	OBP	SLG
2016	Ogden (PIO)	R	.351	66	262	63	92	24	3	13	48	35	66	5	3	.437	.615
2017	R. Cucamonga (CAL)	HiA	.276	132	504	91	139	29	5	27	82	64	189	3	3	.372	.514
Minor League Totals			.302	198	766	154	231	53	8	40	130	99	255	8	6	.394	.548

9 WILL SMITH, C

Born: March 28, 1995. **B-T:** R-R. **Ht.:** 6-0. **Wt.:** 195. **Drafted:** Louisville, 2016 (1st round). **Signed by:** Marty Lamb.

Smith caught scouts' attention as the catcher on Louisville teams loaded with pitching prospects, and the Dodgers drafted him 32nd overall in 2016 and signed him for $1,772,500. The best defensive catcher in the high Class A California League in 2017, he earned a bump to Double-A Tulsa, where a hit by pitch broke a bone in his right hand and ended his season.

Smith was a high school shortstop who converted to catcher in college, and that athleticism has translated brilliantly. As a result, he is an above-average runner with quick footwork and excellent flexibility and reflexes. He is an above-average receiver with soft hands that allows him to handle 100-mph arms, and he consistently posts pop times of sub-1.95 seconds on throws to second base because of a lightning-quick transfer. He further draws high praise for his leadership behind the plate. Offensively, Smith has excellent strike-zone discipline and showed sneaky power after making swing changes at the Dodgers' request, but his contact rate dropped as a result. He faces questions about his overall hitting and contact ability. Smith will head back to Double-A Tulsa in 2018.

The quality of Smith's defense can get him to the majors as a backup, while improved contact skills could make him an everyday option.

BA GRADE
50 Risk: High
HIT: 45. POW: 45.
SPD: 55. FLD: 60.
ARM: 60.

Year	Club (League)	Class	AVG	G	AB	R	H	2B	3B	HR	RBI	BB	SO	SB	CS	OBP	SLG
2016	Ogden (PIO)	R	.321	7	28	4	9	0	0	1	5	4	1	0	0	.394	.429
	Great Lakes (MWL)	LoA	.256	23	82	12	21	1	0	1	7	11	18	2	1	.371	.305
	R. Cucamonga (CAL)	HiA	.216	25	97	13	21	4	0	2	12	14	31	1	0	.330	.320
2017	R. Cucamonga (CAL)	HiA	.232	72	250	38	58	15	3	11	43	37	71	6	2	.355	.448
	Tulsa (TL)	AA	.000	1	1	0	0	0	0	0	0	0	1	1	0	.667	.000
Minor League Totals			.238	128	458	67	109	20	3	15	67	66	122	10	3	.357	.393

10 DENNIS SANTANA, RHP

Born: April 12, 1996. **B-T:** R-R. **Ht.:** 6-2. **Wt.:** 160. **Signed:** Dominican Republic, 2013. **Signed by:** Bob Engle/Patrick Guerrero/Elvio Jimenez

The Dodgers signed Santana for $170,000 as a shortstop out of the Dominican Republic in 2013, but they moved him to the mound after he hit .198 in the Dominican Summer League in his first year. Santana took time learning how to pitch but blossomed the last two seasons, earning all-star honors in both the Midwest and California leagues and reaching Double-A Tulsa by age 21.

Santana found his niche as a sinkerballer and has developed the pitch into a borderline plus-plus offering. He sits 94-95 mph and reaches 97 as a starter, frequently busting his catcher's thumbs with his life on the pitch. His late life often fools minor league umpires, too. Santana is still learning to harness the movement on his fastball, leading to an elevated walk rate. His slider is above-average but wasn't effective against lefthanders, so the improvement of his changeup in 2017 was critical. By the end of the year it was flashing average with increased consistency.

Santana has the loose arm and athleticism of a starter, but his arm slot and cross-body delivery more resemble a reliever. His improved changeup gives him a better chance to start.

BA GRADE
50 Risk: **High**
FB: 60. SL: 55. CHG: 50. CTL: 45.

Year	Club (League)	Class	W	L	ERA	G	GS	CG	SV	IP	H	HR	BB	SO	K/9	WHIP	AVG
2015	Ogden (PIO)	R	0	4	11.22	7	7	0	0	22	35	3	21	18	7.5	2.58	.361
	Dodgers (AZL)	R	2	1	2.42	6	4	1	0	26	13	1	17	34	11.8	1.15	.144
2016	Great Lakes (MWL)	LoA	5	9	3.07	25	14	0	0	111	84	2	56	124	10.0	1.26	.209
2017	R. Cucamonga (CAL)	HiA	5	6	3.57	17	14	0	0	86	87	5	22	92	9.7	1.27	.262
	Tulsa (TL)	AA	3	1	5.51	7	7	0	0	33	32	2	23	37	10.2	1.68	.256
Minor League Totals			17	22	3.75	82	47	1	4	312	270	14	154	343	9.9	1.36	.2310

11 DUSTIN MAY, RHP

BA GRADE
50 Risk: **High**

Born: Sept. 6, 1997. **B-T:** R-R. **Ht.:** 6-6. **Wt.:** 180. **Drafted:** HS—Justin, Texas (3rd round). **Signed by:** Josh Herzenberg.

May is best known for his big, bushy red hair and gangly 6-foot-6 frame. He is increasingly getting noticed for more than his looks, however. After the Dodgers drafted him in the third round in 2016 and signed him for $997,500, May finished in the top 10 in the Midwest League in wins (nine), ERA (3.88) and WHIP (1.20) in his first full season and ended the year strong after a promotion to high Class A.

May is a classic projectable righthander with excellent feel to pitch and velocity still to come. He presently sits 89-92 mph and will touch 94 with his high-spin rate fastball. While it's an average pitch, he attacks the zone and mixes it well with his above-average mid-80s slider, helping the pitches play up off each other. Both offerings could get to plus with added weight and strength. His changeup flashes average but is often too firm. Most importantly, May keeps his body and delivery in sync, no easy task with his long limbs. The result is true plus control that is best in the Dodgers system.

May proved durable after pitching 138 innings including the playoffs in 2017, but he'll need to continue to get stronger to add velocity. He will start 2018 back at high Class A Rancho Cucamonga.

Year	Club (League)	Class	W	L	ERA	G	GS	CG	SV	IP	H	HR	BB	SO	K/9	WHIP	AVG
2016	Dodgers (AZL)	R	0	1	3.86	10	6	0	1	30	37	0	4	34	10.1	1.35	.291
2017	Great Lakes (MWL)	LoA	9	6	3.88	23	23	0	0	123	121	8	26	113	8.3	1.20	.250
	R. Cucamonga (CAL)	HiA	0	0	0.82	2	1	0	0	11	6	0	1	15	12.3	0.64	.150
Minor League Totals			9	7	3.67	35	30	0	1	164	164	8	31	162	8.9	1.19	.252

12 EDWIN RIOS, 1B/3B

BA GRADE
45 Risk: **Medium**

Born: April 21, 1994. **B-T:** L-R. **Ht.:** 6-3. **Wt.:** 220. **Drafted:** Florida International, 2015 (6th round). **Signed by:** Adrian Casanova.

Rios started all three years at Florida International and grew into his power as a junior, bashing 18 home runs in 2015 to finish one shy of the national lead. The Dodgers drafted him in the sixth round and signed him for $222,500. Rios has continued mashing in pro ball, with 27 homers in his first full season and 34 doubles, 24 home runs and .533 slugging percentage across Double-A and Triple-A in 2017.

Rios is a big, physical lefthanded hitter with plus-plus raw power and the hittability to get to it. His swing gets long at times but he has electric hands and excellent timing, allowing his power to be a playable, carrying tool. Rios doesn't walk much but has good plate discipline and doesn't strike out much for a power hitter. Defensively he is below average at third base and has increasingly transitioned to first base, where he has a chance to eventually become average. He was also playable in left field in brief looks. Rios has the offensive impact to start, but with the Dodgers he seems limited to a bench option with Cody

Bellinger and Justin Turner already occupying the corners in Los Angeles.

Rios should be an appealing trade candidate, but for now will head back to Triple-A Oklahoma City.

Year	Club (League)	Class	AVG	G	AB	R	H	2B	3B	HR	RBI	BB	SO	SB	CS	OBP	SLG
2015	Dodgers (AZL)	R	.429	2	7	1	3	0	0	0	0	0	1	0	1	.429	.429
	Ogden (PIO)	R	.235	20	68	8	16	7	0	3	13	7	29	0	0	.307	.471
2016	Great Lakes (MWL)	LoA	.252	33	119	17	30	8	1	6	13	8	44	3	1	.305	.487
	R. Cucamonga (CAL)	HiA	.367	42	177	37	65	11	1	16	46	8	35	0	0	.394	.712
	Tulsa (TL)	AA	.254	33	122	14	31	7	0	5	17	8	31	0	0	.304	.434
2017	Tulsa (TL)	AA	.317	77	306	47	97	21	0	15	62	17	69	1	1	.358	.533
	Oklahoma City (PCL)	AAA	.296	51	169	23	50	13	0	9	29	18	42	0	1	.368	.533
Minor League Totals			.302	258	968	147	292	67	2	54	180	66	251	4	4	.350	.542

13 GAVIN LUX, SS/2B

BA GRADE

50 Risk: High

Born: Nov. 23, 1997. **B-T:** L-R. **Ht.:** 6-2. **Wt.:** 190. **Drafted:** HS—Kenosha, Wis., 2016 (1st round). **Signed by:** Trey Magnuson.

Lux's uncle Augie Schmidt was the No. 2 overall pick in 1982 after winning the Golden Spikes Award. Lux followed in his uncle's footsteps as a first-rounder when the Dodgers drafted him with the 20th overall pick in 2016 and signed him for $2,314,500. The Wisconsin native got off to a poor start in his first full season with low Class A Great Lakes, but rebounded to hit .260 with six of his seven home runs in the second half.

Lux recognizes pitches, controls the strike zone and manages at-bats well. His lefthanded stroke features good bat speed and more strength than expected, although he is too passive at times. Lefties give him trouble, holding him a .165/.250/.217 line. Lux is a plus runner with above-average arm strength, plus hands and solid instincts at shortstop. His tools play down, however, because he has trouble syncing his upper and lower body and lacks fluidity in his transfer and throwing motion. The result was 14 of his 24 errors were throwing, and evaluators are concerned his lack of fluidity will only get worse as he gets older.

Lux may have to move to second or third base, which puts extra pressure on his offense to improve. He will head to high Class A Rancho Cucamonga in 2018.

Year	Club (League)	Class	AVG	G	AB	R	H	2B	3B	HR	RBI	BB	SO	SB	CS	OBP	SLG
2016	Dodgers (AZL)	R	.281	48	192	34	54	10	5	0	18	25	43	1	0	.365	.385
	Ogden (PIO)	R	.387	8	31	7	12	3	0	0	3	3	8	1	0	.441	.484
2017	Great Lakes (MWL)	LoA	.244	111	434	68	106	14	8	7	39	56	88	27	10	.331	.362
Minor League Totals			.262	167	657	109	172	27	13	7	60	84	139	29	10	.346	.374

14 JORDAN SHEFFIELD, RHP

BA GRADE

50 Risk: High

Born: June 1, 1995. **B-T:** R-R. **Ht.:** 5-10. **Wt.:** 190. **Drafted:** Vanderbilt, 2016 (1st round). **Signed by:** Marty Lamb.

Sheffield had a chance to be the first prep righthander taken in the 2013 draft, but succumbed to Tommy John surgery midway through his senior year and went to Vanderbilt instead. He became the Commodores ace as a redshirt sophomore and was drafted by the Dodgers 36th overall in 2016, signing for $1,847,500.

Sheffield, whose younger brother Justus is a top pitching prospect for the Yankees, showed big velocity in his first full season but struggled mightily with his control (4.8 walks per nine innings) at the Class A levels. He sits 94-95 mph with his fastball and reaches 97 as a starter and 99 out of the bullpen. His fastball plays down because it is completely straight and he leaves it up, allowing hitters to barrel it or watch it rise out of the zone. He began experimenting with a two-seamer to try and give batters a different look. Sheffield's main secondary is an average-to-above slider and he also has a usable changeup, but he gets away from it too often.

Sheffield's injury history, limited control and thin frame have most projecting him to the bullpen. He will try to prove he can stay a starter at high Class A Rancho Cucamonga in 2018.

Year	Club (League)	Class	W	L	ERA	G	GS	CG	SV	IP	H	HR	BB	SO	K/9	WHIP	AVG
2016	Dodgers (AZL)	R	0	0	0.00	1	1	0	0	1	0	0	0	0	0.0	0.00	.000
	Great Lakes (MWL)	LoA	0	1	4.09	7	7	0	0	11	11	2	6	13	10.6	1.55	.275
2017	Great Lakes (MWL)	LoA	3	7	4.03	20	20	0	0	89	86	9	42	91	9.2	1.43	.255
	R. Cucamonga (CAL)	HiA	0	2	8.00	5	4	0	0	18	23	2	15	18	9.0	2.11	.307
Minor League Totals			3	10	4.60	33	32	0	0	119	120	13	63	122	9.2	1.53	.264

15 TREVOR OAKS, RHP

BA GRADE
45 Risk: Medium

Born: March 26, 1993. **B-T:** R-R. **Ht.:** 6-3. **Wt.:** 220. **Drafted:** California Baptist, 2014 (7th round). **Signed by:** Bobby Darwin.

Oaks overcame Tommy John surgery in high school and a transfer from NAIA Biola (Calif.) to become one of the top Division II players in the 2014 draft at California Baptist. The Dodgers drafted him in the seventh round and signed him for $161,600. Oaks shot through three levels in 2016 and was solid again at Triple-A in 2017 before going down with an oblique injury in July.

Oaks uses a heavy 92-96 mph sinker to do most of his damage. He generates downhill plane on the pitch and excels at avoiding barrels, helping draw consistent weak contact. He led the minors in double plays induced in 2016. Oaks' secondaries are limited, which cuts into his ability to miss bats. His changeup and cutter flash average, and he'll mix in a short slider and curveball to give batters a different look. He is efficient with plus control and has the physicality to eat innings.

The depth of the Dodgers' pitching staff means Oaks likely heads back to Triple-A in 2018. If injuries strike, he'll be one of the first starters called up.

Year	Club (League)	Class	W	L	ERA	G	GS	CG	SV	IP	H	HR	BB	SO	K/9	WHIP	AVG
2015	Great Lakes (MWL)	LoA	5	5	2.56	18	16	2	0	102	84	3	14	58	5.1	0.96	.221
	R. Cucamonga (CAL)	HiA	3	0	3.04	5	5	0	0	24	28	2	5	16	6.1	1.39	.292
2016	R. Cucamonga (CAL)	HiA	1	1	3.60	4	4	0	0	25	26	1	3	22	7.9	1.16	.280
	Tulsa (TL)	AA	8	1	2.14	10	10	0	0	63	56	1	9	38	5.4	1.03	.239
	Oklahoma City (PCL)	AAA	5	1	3.00	10	10	1	0	63	64	7	9	48	6.9	1.16	.262
2017	Oklahoma City (PCL)	AAA	4	3	3.64	16	15	0	0	84	87	5	18	72	7.7	1.25	.277
	Dodgers (AZL)	R	0	0	0.00	1	1	0	0	2	0	0	0	3	13.5	0.00	.000
	Ogden (PIO)	R	0	0	7.94	2	2	0	0	6	12	1	1	6	9.5	2.29	.429
Minor League Totals			31	13	3.27	80	66	3	0	404	398	22	72	292	6.5	1.16	.258

16 CRISTIAN SANTANA, 3B

BA GRADE
55 Risk: Extreme

Born: Feb, 24, 1997. **B-T:** R-R. **Ht.:** 6-2. **Wt.:** 175. **Signed:** Dominican Republic, 2014. **Signed by:** Bob Engle/Patrick Guerrero/Franklin Taveras.

The Dodgers signed Santana for $50,000 late in the 2013 signing period out of the Dominican Republic, an under-the-radar transaction that drew little notice at the time. He spent three seasons in Rookie ball before a breakout 2017. Santana hit .537 with five home runs in 10 games in the Pioneer League, and followed by hitting .322 with five more home runs in two months at low Class A Great Lakes.

Hitting ability had previously been the knock on Santana, but he made enormous strides in 2017. While he rarely walks, he has begun putting together consistent quality at-bats, and he has the bat speed and strength to punish the pitch he wants. He drives the ball to all fields and shows as much opposite-field power as pull power. Santana is a good athlete with the physicality to hit for power as he continues to grow. That athleticism also gives him a chance to be a plus defender with a plus arm at third base.

Santana's performance track record is limited, but he showed enough flashes to excite evaluators as a potential everyday third baseman. High Class A Rancho Cucamonga is his next stop.

Year	Club (League)	Class	AVG	G	AB	R	H	2B	3B	HR	RBI	BB	SO	SB	CS	OBP	SLG
2015	Dodgers (DSL)	R	.276	59	217	30	60	13	0	3	18	16	35	3	6	.329	.378
2016	Dodgers (AZL)	R	.256	42	172	26	44	6	2	8	24	5	46	0	1	.278	.453
2017	Ogden (PIO)	R	.537	10	41	18	22	2	1	5	16	6	6	0	0	.583	1.000
	Great Lakes (MWL)	LoA	.322	44	174	18	56	9	0	5	25	5	42	0	1	.339	.460
Minor League Totals			.285	193	722	99	206	37	4	21	94	38	158	5	10	.321	.435

17 STARLING HEREDIA, OF

BA GRADE
55 Risk: Extreme

Born: Feb. 6, 1999. **B-T:** R-R. **Ht.:** 6-2. **Wt.:** 200. **Signed:** Dominican Republic, 2015. **Signed by:** Bob Engle/Patrick Guerrero/Manaleik Pimentel.

Heredia finished as the runner-up at the Under Armour All-America Game home run derby in 2014, hitting balls out of Wrigley Field at age 15. The Dodgers signed him for $2.6 million out of the Dominican Republic the following summer. Heredia tore through Rookie ball in his U.S. debut in 2017, hitting .427 with a 1.221 OPS in the Pioneer League before finishing at low Class A Great Lakes.

Heredia is a physically mature specimen with plus power, thunderous hands and impressive speed for someone his size, routinely turning in average run times. He makes a tremendous amount of hard contact and can hit the ball out of any park on a line or in the air. He can be overly aggressive and breaking balls give him trouble, but he has shown the ability to make adjustments. Heredia's corner outfield play is wildly inconsistent, sometimes looking poor with a below-average arm and at other times looking solid-average with a plus arm. Nicknamed "Pit Bull", Heredia can get too aggressive and play too fast on both sides of the ball, and he wore himself out by the end of the year.

If Heredia can channel that aggressiveness, evaluators believe he could become a .240 hitter with 30 home runs. He will remain at the Class A levels in 2018.

Year	Club (League)	Class	AVG	G	AB	R	H	2B	3B	HR	RBI	BB	SO	SB	CS	OBP	SLG
2016	Dodgers2 (DSL)	R	.286	27	112	17	32	6	2	2	17	9	27	2	4	.339	.429
	Dodgers (DSL)	R	.234	37	128	25	30	7	2	3	23	15	24	8	2	.338	.391
2017	Dodgers (AZL)	R	.429	7	28	8	12	2	2	2	9	4	7	0	0	.500	.857
	Ogden (PIO)	R	.427	19	82	21	35	11	1	4	17	10	24	5	4	.489	.732
	Great Lakes (MWL)	LoA	.212	26	99	14	21	6	1	1	8	10	38	5	1	.291	.323
Minor League Totals			.290	116	449	85	130	32	8	12	74	48	120	20	11	.366	.477

18 CONNOR WONG, C

BA GRADE
50 Risk: High

Born: May 19, 1996. **B-T:** R-R. **Ht.:** 6-1. **Wt.:** 181. **Drafted:** Houston, 2017 (3rd round). **Signed by:** Clint Bowers.

Wong started at shortstop as a freshman at Houston but moved to catcher for his sophomore season. His progression in two years behind the plate and a solid junior season that included 12 homers and 26 stolen bases convinced the Dodgers to draft him in the third round and sign him for $547,500. Wong immediately went out to low Class A Great Lakes and took over as the Loons' starting catcher.

Wong is in the same vein as organization-mates Austin Barnes and Will Smith as plus athletes capable of catching or playing the middle infield. He is a plus runner with above-average-to-plus arm strength and the athleticism to become an above-average receiver, although he needs work to get there due of his lack of experience. He can fill in at shortstop, third base, or even the outfield as needed. Wong has sneaky power and good plate discipline, but his lack of noticeable bat speed limits his overall offensive potential.

The Dodgers believe Wong can become a plus defensive catcher as he gets more reps behind the plate, with enough bat to play everyday. He'll head to high Class A Rancho Cucamonga in 2018.

Year	Club (League)	Class	AVG	G	AB	R	H	2B	3B	HR	RBI	BB	SO	SB	CS	OBP	SLG
2017	Dodgers (AZL)	R	.000	1	1	0	0	0	0	0	0	0	1	0	0	.000	.000
	Great Lakes (MWL)	LoA	.278	27	97	19	27	6	0	5	18	7	26	1	1	.336	.495
Minor League Totals			.276	28	98	19	27	6	0	5	18	7	27	1	1	.333	.490

19 MORGAN COOPER, RHP

BA GRADE
50 Risk: Extreme

Born: Sept. 12, 1994. **B-T:** R-R. **Ht.:** 6-5. **Wt.:** 210. **Drafted:** Texas, 2017 (2nd round). **Signed by:** Clint Bowers.

Cooper had Tommy John surgery his sophomore year at Texas and took time to round back into form, but two years later emerged as the Longhorns' top starter in 2017 and finished second in the Big 12 Conference in strikeouts. The Dodgers drafted Cooper in the second round and signed him for $867,500.

Cooper battled shoulder tendinitis at the end of the college season, and the Dodgers shut him down to rest rather than send him out to an affiliate after signing. When healthy Cooper sits 92-95 mph with steep downhill angle on his fastball. He pounds the bottom of the zone and commands his heater well. A hard curveball was previously his main secondary, but he began to favor his slider as the spring went on. His slider now projects above-average to go with an average curveball and a changeup still to come. Cooper has at least average control, and the Dodgers had him as a plus strike-thrower in college.

Cooper has the potential to be a mid-rotation starter with a four-pitch power mix, but his injury record is concerning. He is tentatively ticketed for a Class A affiliate in 2018 pending his health.

Year	Club (League)	Class	W	L	ERA	G	GS	CG	SV	IP	H	HR	BB	SO	K/9	WHIP	AVG
2017	Did not play																

20 CALEB FERGUSON, LHP

BA GRADE
45 Risk: High

Born: July 2, 1996. **B-T:** R-L. **Ht.:** 6-3. **Wt.:** 215. **Drafted:** HS—West Jefferson, Ohio, 2014 (38th round). **Signed by:** Marty Lamb.

Ferguson had Tommy John surgery his senior year at West Jefferson (Ohio) High and intended to honor his commitment to West Virginia, but the Dodgers drafted him in the 38th round a few weeks after surgery and signed him for $100,000. Ferguson slowly worked his way back and pitched a full season in 2017 for the first time in four years. He led the high Class A California League in ERA (2.87) and finished third in strikeouts (140) at Rancho Cucamonga.

Ferguson is a physical lefthander who flashes intriguing stuff with a low-90s fastball that will touch 94 mph and a 12-to-6 curveball with bite in the mid-70s. The two pitches get him swings and misses, but he often nibbles with his fastball and his curveball feel comes and goes, resulting in a high walk rate (4.0 per nine innings). He also has a fledgling changeup that shows late action and fade. Ferguson's arm is late in his delivery and causes him trouble repeating his release point, leaving evaluators skeptical his control will get better.

Most see Ferguson as a future lefty specialist if he can improve the consistency of his curveball. He will remain a starter for now at Double-A Tulsa in 2018.

Year	Club (League)	Class	W	L	ERA	G	GS	CG	SV	IP	H	HR	BB	SO	K/9	WHIP	AVG
2015	Dodgers (AZL)	R	0	3	8.59	14	4	0	1	15	17	0	21	16	9.8	2.59	.298
2016	Dodgers (AZL)	R	1	0	1.50	2	0	0	0	6	4	0	0	11	16.5	0.67	.167
	Ogden (PIO)	R	1	0	0.90	2	2	0	0	10	4	0	2	11	9.9	0.60	.114
	Great Lakes (MWL)	LoA	1	4	2.68	10	10	0	0	50	49	3	3	41	7.3	1.03	.255
2017	R. Cucamonga (CAL)	HiA	9	4	2.87	25	24	0	0	122	113	6	55	140	10.3	1.37	.246
Minor League Totals			12	11	3.10	53	40	0	1	203	187	9	81	219	9.7	1.32	.243

21 MATT BEATY, 3B/1B

BA GRADE
40 Risk: Medium

Born: April 28, 1993. **B-T:** L-R. **Ht.:** 6-0. **Wt.:** 210. **Drafted:** Belmont, 2015 (12th round). **Signed by:** Marty Lamb.

Beaty delivered a decorated four-year career at Belmont, finishing in the top five in school history in hits, doubles, triples, RBIs and walks. The Dodgers then selected him in the 12th round in 2015 and signed him for $60,000, and he's kept on hitting in pro ball. The pinnacle came in 2017 when Beaty hit .326 with 15 homers at Double-A Tulsa and earned the Texas League MVP while also winning the batting title.

Beaty doesn't have the loudest tools but he seemingly does everything right. He has an advanced approach at the plate, rarely strikes out and consistently gets the barrel to the ball. He adjusts quickly and is rarely fooled. Beaty's power is mostly pull-side, but he has shwon the ability to line the ball to all fields, as well. Beaty is a solid-average defender at third base with an average arm and is adept at playing first base too. He recently began playing both corner outfield spots to enhance his defensive versatility.

Beaty has the approach, energy and grinder mentality to play above his tools, which should help him find a home on a big league bench in the future. He'll head to Triple-A Oklahoma City in 2018.

Year	Club (League)	Class	AVG	G	AB	R	H	2B	3B	HR	RBI	BB	SO	SB	CS	OBP	SLG
2015	Ogden (PIO)	R	.480	6	25	3	12	1	0	0	3	2	3	2	2	.519	.520
	Great Lakes (MWL)	LoA	.297	62	246	37	73	7	2	4	25	21	28	2	1	.353	.390
2016	R. Cucamonga (CAL)	HiA	.297	124	489	66	145	30	0	11	88	40	74	6	1	.352	.425
2017	Tulsa (TL)	AA	.326	116	438	61	143	31	1	15	69	35	54	3	3	.378	.505
Minor League Totals			.311	308	1198	167	373	69	3	30	185	98	159	13	7	.365	.449

22 IMANI ABDULLAH, RHP

BA GRADE
50 Risk: Extreme

Born: April 20, 1997. **B-T:** B-R. **Ht.:** 6-6. **Wt.:** 205. **Drafted:** HS—San Diego, 2015 (11th round). **Signed by:** Jeff Lachman.

Abdullah primarily played golf before pitching for the first time as a junior at San Diego's Madison High. He took to pitching immediately, and his projectable 6-foot-4 frame and fresh arm throwing 88-90 mph fastballs convinced the Dodgers to draft him in the 11th round in 2015. Abdullah signed for a well over-slot deal of $647,500, which was the equivalent of third-round money. In addition to the large money offer, Magic Johnson was the one who made the phone call telling Addullah he was drafted in hopes of further enticing him to sign with the Dodgers.

Since then, the organization has managed Abdullah carefully. The Dodgers held him back in extended spring training during the first half of the 2017 season on a strength and conditioning program, and then shut him down due to shoulder discomfort after only six starts at low Class A Great Lakes in the second half. When healthy, Abdullah features a 92-94 mph fastball and an advanced changeup that projects as a plus pitch. He is still trying to find a grip and feel for a breaking ball. Abdullah has sprouted to 6-foot-6 and is a good athlete with body control, but his lack of command due to inexperience has alternately led to too many home runs allowed and too many walks.

The Dodgers believe Abdullah possccsscs mid-rotation upside, but patience will be needed because he is still so raw in learning how to pitch.

Year	Club (League)	Class	W	L	ERA	G	GS	CG	SV	IP	H	HR	BB	SO	K/9	WHIP	AVG
2015	Dodgers (AZL)	R	0	1	4.85	6	3	0	0	13	9	0	5	13	9.0	1.08	.173
2016	Great Lakes (MWL)	LoA	4	4	3.61	16	16	0	0	72	70	10	12	59	7.3	1.13	.251
2017	Great Lakes (MWL)	LoA	0	2	5.11	6	6	0	0	12	12	1	7	13	9.5	1.54	.250
Minor League Totals			4	7	3.96	28	25	0	0	98	91	11	24	85	7.8	1.18	.240

23 KYLE FARMER, C

BA GRADE **40** Risk: Medium

Born: Aug. 17, 1990 **B-T:** R-R. **Ht.:** 6-0. **Wt.:** 214. **Drafted:** Georgia, 2013 (8th round). **Signed by:** Lon Joyce.

Farmer's big league debut in 2017 encapsulated the Dodgers' magical summer. He got his first big league at-bat when he entered as a pinch-hitter in the bottom of the 11th inning of a July game against the rival Giants. With the Dodgers trailing 2-1 and runners on first and second, Farmer lined a full-count fastball down the right field line for a walk-off, two-run double and was promptly mobbed by his new teammates at second base as Dodger Stadium shook with the noise of the crowd.

Farmer, who was college teammates at Georgia with Dodgers lefthander Alex Wood, is a former shortstop who converted to catching after the Dodgers drafted him. It took time, but he has developed into a solid defensive catcher with quick feet, a clean exchange and accurate throws, although his arm strength is just average. At the plate, Farmer has good knowledge of the strike zone and a compact, righthanded swing that produces a lot of line-drive contact. He began to elevate and hit a career-high 10 homers in 2017.

Farmer isn't flashy but has produced at every level. He is ready to be a big league backup catcher.

Year	Club (League)	Class	AVG	G	AB	R	H	2B	3B	HR	RBI	BB	SO	SB	CS	OBP	SLG
2015	R. Cucamonga (CAL)	HiA	.337	44	163	33	55	14	6	1	27	12	25	5	2	.396	.515
	Tulsa (TL)	AA	.272	76	283	25	77	26	1	2	39	14	55	0	1	.311	.392
2016	Dodgers (AZL)	R	.294	4	17	4	5	0	0	2	4	1	1	0	0	.333	.647
	Tulsa (TL)	AA	.256	74	266	31	68	18	2	5	31	25	44	2	0	.323	.395
2017	Tulsa (TL)	AA	.339	33	124	21	42	7	0	3	18	16	13	1	0	.411	.468
	Oklahoma City (PCL)	AAA	.305	59	223	32	68	16	1	7	38	13	36	0	4	.354	.480
	Los Angeles (NL)	MAJ	.300	20	20	1	6	1	0	0	2	0	3	0	0	.300	.350
Major League Totals			.300	20	20	1	6	1	0	0	2	0	3	0	0	.300	.350
Minor League Totals			.297	424	1602	216	475	121	15	26	243	113	247	20	11	.350	.439

24 JAMES MARINAN, RHP

BA GRADE **50** Risk: Extreme

Born: Oct. 10, 1998. **B-T:** R-R. **Ht.:** 6-5. **Wt.:** 220. **Drafted:** HS—Lake Worth, Fla., 2017 (4th round). **Signed by:** Adrian Casanova.

Marinan shot up draft boards after showing a velocity boost up to 96 mph as a senior at Park Vista Community High in Lake Worth, Fla. The Dodgers plucked the 6-foot-5 righthander in the fourth round in 2017 and signed him away from a Miami commitment for $822,500, more than double slot amount. Marinan showed promising tools in the rookie-level Arizona League after signing but also showed wildness, with as many walks as strikeouts (14) in 17 innings.

Marinan is a long-term project. He sits 90-93 mph with sink on his fastball, but his velocity drops off after the first inning. He is still trying to figure out if a curveball or slider works better for him, although he shows feel to spin in general. At times Marinan will show advanced feel for a changeup and at others none at all. He has a fluid delivery but loses direction in his stride, often going towards first base, which caused his high walk rate.

Marinan is physically well put together and a good competitor. The Dodgers believe added strength and mechanical fixes can help him become a three-pitch power starter. He will begin that process in extended spring training to begin 2018.

Year	Club (League)	Class	W	L	ERA	G	GS	CG	SV	IP	H	HR	BB	SO	K/9	WHIP	AVG
2017	Dodgers (AZL)	R	2	0	1.59	9	6	0	0	17	14	0	14	14	7.4	1.65	.250
Minor League Totals			2	0	1.59	9	6	0	0	17	14	0	14	14	7.4	1.65	.250

25 JOSH SBORZ, RHP

BA GRADE **40** Risk: Medium

Born: Dec. 17, 1993. **B-T:** R-R. **Ht.:** 6-3. **Wt.:** 225. **Drafted:** Virginia, 2015 (2nd round supplemental). **Signed by:** Clair Rierson.

Sborz carried Virginia to the 2015 national championship as the Cavaliers' relief ace and was named the College World Series' Most Outstanding Player. The Dodgers drafted him the supplemental second round, signed him for $722,500 and made him a starter, a role in which he pitched the entire season at Double-A Tulsa in 2017.

Sborz, whose older brother Jay pitched for the Tigers in 2010, lacks overwhelming stuff but keeps runs off the board. His fastball sits 92-94 mph with armside run, and his out pitch is an above-average slider with depth and late break. His fastball command isn't sharp, however, and his slider is inconsistent. As such, he struggled to the highest walk rate (4.3 per nine innings) and lowest strikeout rate (6.3) of his career in 2017. Sborz is an elite competitor with moxie and guile, though, and frequently pitched his way out of jams. He has a top-to-bottom curveball and changeup that flashes average, but neither are particularly reliable.

Sborz's lack of swing-and-miss stuff and shifty control prevent him from projecting as a major league starter, but his fastball gets up to 97 mph in relief and gives him a possible future there.

Year	Club (League)	Class	W	L	ERA	G	GS	CG	SV	IP	H	HR	BB	SO	K/9	WHIP	AVG
2015	Ogden (PIO)	R	0	1	4.50	2	1	0	0	4	2	0	4	4	9.0	1.50	.167
	Great Lakes (MWL)	LoA	0	1	2.84	2	2	0	0	6	5	2	2	9	12.8	1.11	.185
	R. Cucamonga (CAL)	HiA	0	0	1.50	9	0	0	2	12	12	1	3	12	9.0	1.25	.255
2016	R. Cucamonga (CAL)	HiA	8	4	2.66	20	19	0	0	108	82	8	30	108	9.0	1.03	.207
	Tulsa (TL)	AA	0	1	3.78	10	0	0	1	17	17	2	6	17	9.2	1.38	.258
2017	Tulsa (TL)	AA	8	8	3.86	24	24	0	0	117	106	8	56	81	6.2	1.39	.243
Minor League Totals			16	15	3.24	67	46	0	3	264	224	21	101	231	7.9	1.23	.227

26 LUKE RALEY, OF

BA GRADE

45 Risk: High

Born: Sept. 19, 1994. **B-T:** L-R. **Ht.:** 6-3. **Wt.:** 220. **Drafted:** Lake Erie (Ohio), 2016 (7th round). **Signed by:** Marty Lamb.

Raley hit .424/.528/.727 his junior season at Lake Erie (Ohio), and the Dodgers made him the highest Division II player taken in 2016 when they selected him in the seventh round. He signed for $147,500.

Raley made the jump from D-II competition to high Class A Rancho Cucamonga without a hitch in 2017, earning all-star honors in the California League and finishing with an .848 OPS. Raley is a physical, strong lefthanded hitter who wears cutoff T-shirts to show off his biceps. He packs legitimate above-average power and has the bat speed and swing path to get to it without sacrificing batting average. His power plays to all fields, and more could come as he learns to be more consistent in putting together quality at-bats, an area targeted for growth. Defensively, Raley is above-average in left field. He has good pre-pitch instincts, closes distance on ground balls exceptionally well, is quick getting the ball out of his glove and has an above-average, accurate arm that flashes plus. Raley further draws raves for his work ethic and competitiveness.

Scouts consider Raley a sleeper who could bust out if his power goes up one more tick. He will head to Double-A Tulsa in 2018.

Year	Club (League)	Class	AVG	G	AB	R	H	2B	3B	HR	RBI	BB	SO	SB	CS	OBP	SLG
2016	Dodgers (AZL)	R	.625	5	16	4	10	1	0	1	2	2	2	0	0	.684	.875
	Ogden (PIO)	R	.417	5	24	6	10	2	2	1	5	1	1	0	0	.440	.792
	Great Lakes (MWL)	LoA	.245	56	200	24	49	11	4	2	17	15	47	4	4	.319	.370
2017	R. Cucamonga (CAL)	HiA	.295	123	478	102	141	21	11	14	62	43	124	9	1	.375	.473
Minor League Totals			.292	189	718	136	210	35	17	18	86	61	174	13	5	.369	.464

27 TIM LOCASTRO, 2B/OF

BA GRADE

40 Risk: Medium

Born: July 14, 1992. **B-T:** R-R. **Ht.:** 6-1. **Wt.:** 200. **Drafted:** Ithaca (N.Y.), 2013 (13th round). **Signed by:** Jamie Lehman (Blue Jays).

The Blue Jays geared up to sign Vladimir Guerrero Jr. during the 2015 international signing period, but also craved enough pool space to only take one year of signing penalties instead of two. To that end, the Dodgers sent three international bonus slots totaling $1,071,300 to the Blue Jays and received Locastro and righthander Chase De Jong in return.

The speedy Locastro hit .308 and stole 34 bases at Double-A and Triple-A in 2017, and made his big league debut in September. His carrying tool is his plus-plus speed, so much so the Dodgers considered carrying him on their postseason roster solely as a pinch-runner. He is a quick-twitch athlete whose elite speed plays up with exceptional reads and jumps. He averaged 33 stolen bases at each of his full-season stops, and did it at a nearly 80 percent success rate. Locastro is also a solid contact hitter who gets out of the box quickly and posts a lot of doubles with his speed. His actions at second base and shortstop aren't particularly smooth, so he began playing center field, where is still not comfortable with his routes.

Locastro's speed and touch of hitting ability make him a utility candidate—a role he is ready to fill in the majors in 2018.

Year	Club (League)	Class	AVG	G	AB	R	H	2B	3B	HR	RBI	BB	SO	SB	CS	OBP	SLG
2015	Lansing (MWL)	LoA	.310	70	242	48	75	10	1	5	25	21	25	30	11	.409	.421
	R. Cucamonga (CAL)	HiA	.224	41	156	30	35	9	2	1	14	14	30	11	5	.328	.327
2016	R. Cucamonga (CAL)	HiA	.289	86	339	61	98	17	5	5	39	15	50	15	4	.347	.413
	Tulsa (TL)	AA	.277	45	191	27	53	8	1	1	13	8	16	9	2	.330	.346
2017	Tulsa (TL)	AA	.285	96	368	69	105	21	4	8	31	22	56	22	5	.366	.429
	Oklahoma City (PCL)	AAA	.388	31	103	18	40	10	0	2	9	6	12	12	2	.443	.544
	Los Angeles (NL)	MAJ	.000	3	1	0	0	0	0	0	0	0	1	0	0	.000	.000
Major League Totals			.000	3	1	0	0	0	0	0	0	0	1	0	0	.000	.000
Minor League Totals			.293	479	1793	330	525	91	16	24	171	111	224	143	35	.372	.402

28 ERROL ROBINSON, SS

BA GRADE
40 Risk: High

Born: Oct. 1, 1994. **B-T:** R-R. **Ht.:** 6-0. **Wt.:** 180. **Drafted:** Mississippi, 2016 (6th round). **Signed by:** Philip Stringer.

Robinson entered his junior year at Mississippi with top three-round expectations, but hit just .270 and dropped to the sixth round. Robinson rebounded to reach Double-A in his first full season in 2017 and earned wide praise as the best defensive infielder in the Dodgers system.

Robinson possesses special hands at shortstop that vacuum up even the toughest hops and make every play look smooth. He converts all the routine plays and then some, even though his range isn't exceptional. He slides over to second base effortlessly when needed, and evaluators believe he could play center field and third base, too. Robinson is an above-average runner with a grinder mentality that helps him excel anywhere on the field defensively. Offensively, Robinson is an aggressive sparkplug who brings energy and swagger to the top of an order, but power isn't his game and he is an average hitter at best.

Robinson lacks a carrying tool but has the aptitude to rise as a utility infielder. Triple-A awaits in 2018.

Year	Club (League)	Class	AVG	G	AB	R	H	2B	3B	HR	RBI	BB	SO	SB	CS	OBP	SLG
2016	Ogden (PIO)	R	.282	55	220	40	62	17	1	2	26	17	42	18	2	.336	.395
2017	Great Lakes (MWL)	LoA	.247	22	77	13	19	5	1	3	13	6	21	6	1	.291	.455
	R. Cucamonga (CAL)	HiA	.286	16	70	13	20	4	3	2	8	5	17	5	1	.342	.514
	Tulsa (TL)	AA	.273	57	227	35	62	8	2	2	14	29	50	11	3	.357	.352
Minor League Totals			.274	150	594	101	163	34	7	9	61	57	130	40	7	.339	.401

29 DREW JACKSON, SS

BA GRADE
40 Risk: High

Born: July 28, 1993. **B-T:** R-R. **Ht.:** 6-2. **Wt.:** 200. **Drafted:** Stanford, 2015 (5th round). **Signed by:** Stacey Pettis (Mariners).

Mariners general manager Jerry Dipoto went on a trading spree after the 2016 season and orchestrated two deals with the Dodgers, the second of which sent Jackson and reliever Aneurys Zabala to Los Angeles for righthander Chase De Jong as spring training opened. Jackson missed a month at high Class A Rancho Cucamonga after jamming his shoulder but returned to finish 2017 in Double-A.

Jackson is a plus-plus runner who flies out of the righthanded batter's box, and his arm strength from shortstop is easily plus-plus. While his tools are prolific, his hitting ability is limited. His feel for the barrel has been questioned since college. He gets out of his approach too easily and lacks natural rhythm and timing in his swing. His offensive profile further gets knocked for his timidity on the basepaths despite his elite speed, though he made strides in 2017.

Jackson's arm, glove and speed give him a chance as an utility infielder.

Year	Club (League)	Class	AVG	G	AB	R	H	2B	3B	HR	RBI	BB	SO	SB	CS	OBP	SLG
2015	Everett (NWL)	SS	.358	59	226	64	81	12	1	2	26	30	35	47	4	.432	.447
2016	Bakersfield (CAL)	HiA	.258	124	524	87	135	24	2	6	47	50	105	16	8	.332	.345
2017	Dodgers (AZL)	R	.200	3	10	1	2	0	2	0	4	1	4	0	0	.273	.600
	R. Cucamonga (CAL)	HiA	.254	66	252	48	64	16	2	8	30	34	67	14	6	.367	.429
	Tulsa (TL)	AA	.234	29	111	22	26	5	1	1	10	11	28	7	2	.346	.324
Minor League Totals			.274	281	1123	222	308	57	8	17	117	126	239	84	20	.361	.385

30 YAISEL SIERRA, RHP

BA GRADE
40 Risk: High

Born: June 5, 1991. **B-T:** R-R. **Ht.:** 6-1. **Wt.:** 180. **Signed:** Cuba, 2016. **Signed by:** Ismael Cruz/Roman Barinas/Miguel Tosar.

Sierra never experienced much success in Cuba despite premium stuff, but the Dodgers saw a powerful arm and shocked the industry when they gave him a six-year, $30 million contract in February 2016. Sierra got crushed in high Class A and was outrighted off the 40-man roster by July 4 of his first season.

Sierra pitched well in the bullpen at Double-A and Triple-A in 2017. He can run his fastball up to 97 mph and mixes in a slider that flashes average, but below-average command limits his effectiveness. His contract complicates his situation. Placing Sierra back on the 40-man puts the Dodgers even higher above the luxury tax threshold and increases their competitive balance tax bill. Sierra is likely stuck in the minors no matter how well he performs, similar to the situation with Red Sox outfielder Rusney Castillo.

Year	Club (League)	Class	W	L	ERA	G	GS	CG	SV	IP	H	HR	BB	SO	K/9	WHIP	AVG
2015	Did not play																
2016	R. Cucamonga (CAL)	HiA	5	5	6.20	20	13	0	0	74	87	9	25	65	7.9	1.51	.293
	Tulsa (TL)	AA	1	2	4.30	10	0	0	0	15	14	0	5	21	12.9	1.30	.237
2017	Tulsa (TL)	AA	5	0	2.54	26	0	0	4	50	47	1	16	64	11.6	1.27	.244
	Oklahoma City (PCL)	AAA	0	1	4.22	13	0	0	0	21	22	2	15	20	8.4	1.73	.268
Minor League Totals			11	8	4.62	69	13	0	4	160	170	12	61	170	9.6	1.45	.269

Miami Marlins

BY KEGAN LOWE

The lackluster on-field product paled in comparison to the drama surrounding the off-field headlines for the Marlins in 2017, despite the fact that right fielder Giancarlo Stanton hit a franchise-record 59 home runs, led the majors with 132 RBIs and won the first MVP award in the organization's quarter-century history.

In the team's first season since the tragic passing of Jose Fernandez, Miami sat three games above .500 and in the thick of the National League wild card race on Aug. 27. The Marlins then lost 16 of their next 18 games and eventually missed the postseason for an NL-worst 14th consecutive season.

The franchise's eighth straight losing season coincided with owner Jeffrey Loria finally selling the franchise after months of public speculation. Loria sold the team for $1.2 billion to a new ownership group led by venture capitalist Bruce Sherman and former Yankees shortstop Derek Jeter in early August. Jeter, who is now in charge of running the Marlins' front office, made several significant changes after taking over, including the dismissal of assistant general manager Mike Berger and farm director Marc DelPiano.

In addition to the front-office shakeup, Jeter was also charged with significantly cutting the team's payroll, which was just north of $111 million in 2017 and ranked 20th in the majors.

In an effort to reduce payroll and begin rebuilding a depleted farm system, Jeter made the controversial decision to trade Stanton, who signed a 13-year, $325 million contract with the club shortly after the 2014 season. Stanton, who had a full no-trade clause and rejected trades to the Cardinals and Giants, was sent to the Yankees for former all-star second baseman Starlin Castro, hard-throwing 21-year-old righthander Jorge Guzman and 18-year old Dominican shortstop Jose Devers.

Before trading Stanton and acquiring Castro, the Marlins traded an all-star second baseman of their own in Dee Gordon, who was sent to the Mariners for three prospects. Then, on the final day of the Winter Meetings, the Marlins continued their sell-off by trading outfielder Marcell Ozuna to the Cardinals for four prospects, including 22-year old righthander Sandy Alcantara, the system's new No. 1 prospect.

The Stanton, Gordon and Ozuna moves, in addition to saving the Marlins more than $300 million in future commitments, brought in eight prospects who now rank among the Marlins' top 30—six of whom rank as Top 10 Prospects.

Trading Giancarlo Stanton represented step one of the looming rebuild for the Marlins.

PROJECTED 2021 LINEUP

Catcher	J.T. Realmuto (30)
First Base	Brian Anderson (28)
Second Base	Riley Mahan (25)
Third Base	James Nelson (23)
Shortstop	Joe Dunand (25)
Left Field	Brian Miller (25)
Center Field	Magneuris Sierra (25)
Right Field	Christian Yelich (29)
No. 1 Starter	Sandy Alcantara (25)
No. 2 Starter	Jorge Guzman (25)
No. 3 Starter	Trevor Rogers (23)
No. 4 Starter	Braxton Garrett (23)
No. 5 Starter	Nick Neidert (24)
Closer	Tyler Kolek (25)

Miami saved additional money with the in-season trades of shortstop Adeiny Hechavarria (Rays) and righthanders David Phelps (Mariners) and A.J. Ramos (Mets).

The Marlins completed their farm system reboot with their 2017 draft class, which featured prep lefthander Trevor Rogers and college outfielder Brian Miller taken in the first 40 picks. All told, the Marlins acquired 19 of their Top 30 Prospects since June 2017.

That number is expected to increase as the Marlins continue to explore trade options to bolster a farm system that hadn't ranked inside the top 20 since the 2014 season.

DEPTH CHART

MIAMI MARLINS

TOP 2018 ROOKIE: Brian Anderson, 3B. After receiving a September callup, he has a chance to earn the everyday third base job in 2018.
BREAKOUT PROSPECT: Braxton Lee, OF. The speedy 5-foot-10 center fielder won the Southern League batting title in 2017 and hit .347 in the Arizona Fall League.
SLEEPER: John Norwood, OF. An undrafted

SOURCE OF TOP 30 TALENT			
Homegrown	16	Acquired	14
College	6	Trade	13
Junior college	1	Rule 5 draft	0
High school	6	Independent league	1
Nondrafted free agent	0	Free agent/waivers	0
International	3		

free agent out of Vanderbilt, Norwood profiles as a corner outfielder with some of the best raw power from any righthanded hitter in the organization. He led Double-A Jacksonville with 19 home runs in 2017.

LF	CF	RF
John Norwood	Magneuris Sierra (7)	Isael Soto (24)
Austin Dean	Brian Miller (12)	Albert Guaimaro
Stone Garrett	Brayan Hernandez (16)	John Silviano
Jhonny Santos	Braxton Lee (21)	Yeral Encarnacion
	Thomas Jones (27)	
	Corey Bird	
	Ricardo Céspedes	

3B	SS	2B	1B
Brian Anderson (4)	Chris Torres (9)	Riley Mahan (18)	Garrett Cooper
James Nelson (5)	Joe Dunand (14)	Sam Castro	Sean Reynolds
Brian Schales	Ynmanol Marinez (29)	Mason Davis	Colby Lusignan
	Jose Devers (30)	Gerardo Nunez	Lazaro Alonso
	Peter Mooney		
	Demetrius Sims		

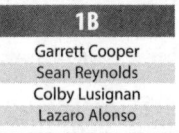

C
Chad Wallach
Roy Morales
Austin Nola
Rodrigo Vigil
Jarrett Rindfleisch

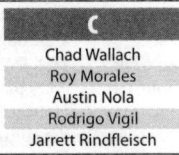

LHP		RHP	
LHSP	**LHRP**	**RHSP**	**RHRP**
Trevor Rogers (3)	Caleb Smith	Sandy Alcantara (1)	Colton Hock (20)
Braxton Garrett (4)	Miguel Del Pozo	Jorge Guzman (2)	Tayron Guerrero
Dillon Peters (11)	Jose Quijada	Nick Neidert (5)	Elieser Hernandez
Brett Lilek	Ben Holmes	Zac Gallen (10)	Brett Graves
Sean Guenther	Jeff Kinley	Edward Cabrera (13)	Severino Gonzalez
Manny Rodriguez	Dylan Lee	Merandy Gonzalez (15)	Andy Beltre
Dakota Bennett		Tyler Kolek (17)	Steven Farnworth
		Matt Givin (19)	Chad Smith
		Trevor Richards (22)	Michael Mertz
		Robert Dugger (23)	Kyle Keller
		Pablo Lopez (25)	
		Jordon Holloway (26)	
		Jeff Brigham (28)	
		Ryan Lillie	
		Taylor Braleyt	
		Cody Poteet	
		Brandon Miller	
		Sam Perez	

DRAFT ANALYSIS

2017

BEST PURE HITTER: CF Brian Miller (1s) hit .345 for his last two seasons at North Carolina and walked more than he struck out, then hit .322 while making consistent contact with low Class A Greensboro after signing. He has a line-drive swing path.

BEST POWER HITTER: SS/3B Joe Dunand (2) has a swing path that produces backspin and plenty of strength to earn plus raw power. He hit 18 home runs in the spring for North Carolina State, tied for 21st in Division I, and one in eight pro games in an injury-plagued debut.

FASTEST RUNNER: Miller turns in 70-grade times to first base at his best, and his speed has helped him become a capable defender in center field, which he's only played for two seasons.

BEST DEFENSIVE PLAYER: Dunand played shortstop the last two seasons and in his pro debut, but has the hands and arm strength to be a plus defender at third base.

BEST ATHLETE: A fourth-year junior, SS Demetrius Sims (14) is old for the class, but the 6-foot-2, 200-pounder moves well for his size and has a potential power-speed combination in an athletic, physical frame.

BEST FASTBALL: At 6-foot-5, 190 pounds, LHP Trevor Rogers (1) has the lean, lanky frame for projection and the current leverage in his delivery to pump 93-94 mph fastballs with ease, reaching as high as 95-97 at his best. His velocity and low three-quarters slot have evoked comparisons to Andrew Miller.

BEST SECONDARY PITCH: RHP Taylor Braley (6) starred as a two-way player at Southern Mississippi, but the Marlins wanted the burly 5-foot-11, 240-pounder for his plus changeup, which they grade as a 65/70 pitch on the 20-80 scale.

TOP DRAFT PICKS OF THE DECADE

Year	Player, Pos.	2017 Org
2008	Kyle Skipworth, C	Did not play
2009	Chad James, LHP	Did not play
2010	Christian Yelich, OF	Marlins
2011	Jose Fernandez, RHP	Deceased
2012	Andrew Heaney, LHP	Angels
2013	Colin Moran, 3B	Astros
2014	Tyler Kolek, RHP	Marlins
2015	Josh Naylor, 1B	Padres
2016	Braxton Garrett, LHP	Marlins
2017	Trevor Rogers, LHP	Marlins

BEST PRO DEBUT: Miller stole 21 bases in 27 tries in his .322/.384/.416 stint at low Class A Greensboro. RHP Matt Givin (20), a Colorado high school product, gave up only one earned run (four runs total) in seven short starts in the Rookie-level Gulf Coast League, turning in a 0.39 ERA.

MOST INTRIGUING BACKGROUND: Dunand's father is the half-brother of Alex Rodriguez, and Dunand has learned the game at the foot of his famous, 696-homer hitting uncle.

CLOSEST TO THE MAJORS: Miller, who went to North Carolina, and Dunand were friendly rivals in college and will have a friendly rivalry of who will get to the majors first.

BEST LATE-ROUND PICK: Givin signed for $458,000 as one of the Marlins' three above-slot signees after the 10th round. He has projection at 6-foot-2, 180 pounds, a clean arm and present 88-92 mph velocity to go with the ability to spin a breaking ball.

THE ONE WHO GOT AWAY: The Marlins signed every player through the first 25 rounds. LHP Tyler Holton (35) was a second-team All-American in the spring and returns to Florida State as a junior.

—JOHN MANUEL

2016

LHP Braxton Garrett (1) made just four starts in 2017 before requiring Tommy John surgery. OF Thomas Jones (2) has exceptional athleticism, but is still ultra raw. They are the class' top players, but both need much more developmental time.
GRADE: C

2015

1B Josh Naylor (1) and RHP Chris Paddack (8) were in 2016 dealt to the Padres in separate moves. Naylor faces profile questions and Paddack missed the season after Tommy John surgery. No other player from the class ranks in the handbook.
GRADE: D

2014

2B Brian Anderson (3) and LHP Dillon Peters (10) made their big league debuts in 2017. RHP Tyler Kolek (1) pitched only briefly as he returns from Tommy John surgery. How well he bounces back will likely determine the class' outcome.
GRADE: D

1 SANDY ALCANTARA, RHP

Born: Sept. 7, 1995. **B-T:** R-R. **Ht.:** 6-4. **Wt.:** 170.
Signed: Dominican Republic, 2013. **Signed by:**
Rodney Jimenez (Cardinals).

A long-time member of the Cardinals' stable of 100 mph Latin American arms, Alcantara had a breakout season in 2016 but experienced more of an up-and-down year in 2017, when his untamed arsenal yielded more hits and fewer strikeouts than his raw stuff would indicate. Even then, the 6-foot-4 righthander, who originally signed out of the Dominican Republic for $125,000 in 2013, earned a September callup and averaged 99 mph on his fastball in eight appearances as a reliever. Alcantara's big arm, tantalizing pure stuff and his proximity to the majors made him an intriguing, high-upside prospect for the Marlins to receive as the headliner in the return for outfielder Marcell Ozuna.

Alcantara packs big velocity but has yet to fully harness it. His fastball sits 96-97 mph as a starter, touches 100 and has been clocked as high as 102. It's a big pitch, but Alcantara's command and control are below-average, resulting in too many hittable fastballs over the plate or well off. His preferred pitch is an upper-90s sinker, but it's taken a backseat as he's focused on his four-seam fastball command. Alcantara complements his fastball with flashes of promising secondaries, but they have yet to become consistent. Both his curveball and slider tend to run together into an 83-88 mph power breaking ball, but he is learning to separate them, and they both project as average. His 90-92 mph changeup is wildly inconsistent and rarely used but flashes above-average potential.

Ultimately, Alcantara has the raw stuff to one day become a front-of-the-rotation starter, headlined by a fastball that is capable of sitting in the upper 90s for entire starts. He will, however, have to improve his command if he wants to reach that potential. If not—or if Alcantara never truly hones his breaking ball or changeup—then there is a chance the hard-throwing righthander will be forced to the role of a late-inning reliever. Despite receiving a handful of innings with the Cardinals in 2016, Alcantara will likely start in his first season with the Marlins at Triple-A New Orleans in 2018. If all goes well, Alcantara could be in the Marlins' rotation by season's end and for many years to come.

BILL MITCHELL

BA GRADE	SCOUTING GRADES
55 Risk: Medium	FB: 70. CB: 50 SL: 50. CHG: 40. CTL: 45.

Projected future grades on 20-80 scouting scale

TOP PROSPECTS OF THE DECADE

Year	Player, Pos.	2017 Org
2008	Cameron Maybin, OF	Astros
2009	Cameron Maybin, OF	Astros
2010	Giancarlo Stanton, OF	Marlins
2011	Matt Dominguez, 3B	Red Sox
2012	Christian Yelich, OF	Marlins
2013	Jose Fernandez, RHP	Deceased
2014	Andrew Heaney, LHP	Angels
2015	Tyler Kolek, RHP	Marlins
2016	Tyler Kolek, RHP	Marlins
2017	Braxton Garrett, LHP	Marlins

BEST TOOLS

Best Hitter for Average	Brian Miller
Best Power Hitter	Brian Anderson
Best Strike-Zone Discipline	Brian Miller
Fastest Baserunner	Magneuris Sierra
Best Athlete	Thomas Jones
Best Fastball	Jorge Guzman
Best Curveball	Braxton Garrett
Best Slider	Chad Smith
Best Changeup	Trevor Richards
Best Control	Ben Meyer
Best Defensive Catcher	Rodrigo Vigil
Best Defensive Infielder	Chris Torres
Best Infield Arm	Chris Torres
Best Defensive Outfielder	Magneuris Sierra
Best Outfield Arm	Albert Guaimaro

Year	Club (League)	Class	W	L	ERA	G	GS	CG	SV	IP	H	HR	BB	SO	K/9	WHIP	AVG
2015	Cardinals (GCL)	R	4	4	3.22	12	12	0	0	64	59	3	20	51	7.1	1.23	.244
2016	Peoria (MWL)	LoA	5	7	4.08	17	17	0	0	90	78	4	45	119	11.9	1.36	.228
	Palm Beach (FSL)	HiA	0	4	3.62	6	6	1	0	32	25	0	14	34	9.5	1.21	.216
2017	Springfield, MO (TL)	AA	7	5	4.31	25	22	0	0	125	125	13	54	106	7.6	1.43	.262
	St. Louis (NL)	MAJ	0	0	4.32	8	0	0	0	8	9	2	6	10	10.8	1.80	.273
Major League Totals			0	0	4.32	8	0	0	0	8	9	2	6	10	10.8	1.80	.273
Minor League Totals			17	29	3.95	72	68	2	0	369	343	21	152	365	8.9	1.34	.245

2 JORGE GUZMAN, RHP

Born: Jan. 28, 1996. **B-T:** R-R. **Ht.:** 6-2. **Wt.:** 182. **Signed:** Dominican Republic, 2014. **Signed by:** Oz Ocampo/Ramon Ocumarez/Francis Mojica (Astros).

The Astros signed Guzman out of the Dominican Republic in 2014 on the strength of his lightning-quick arm and projection for a massive fastball. He was then traded to the Yankees in December 2016 for Brian McCann before spending his 2017 season improving his walk rate at short-season Staten Island. The Marlins acquired Guzman in December 2017 as the headline prospect in the trade that sent Giancarlo Stanton to the Yankees, allowing the Marlins' new ownership to clear $265 million of the $295 left on Stanton's 10-year contract.

Just as the Astros hoped back in 2014, Guzman has developed a big-time fastball, exceeding even the highest of expectations. He averaged 99 mph with his four-seamer in 2017. To put that in perspective, Yankees righthander Luis Severino was the hardest throwing starter in the majors in 2017 with an average fastball velocity of 97.6 mph. Guzman paired his top-of-the-scale fastball—which has peaked at 103 mph—with a developing slider and a third-pitch changeup. Guzman's slider, which sits in the high-80s, can be inconsistent but has flashed above-average potential. His 90-93 mph changeup is seldom used but can show true fading action. Guzman has had trouble keeping his slider in the zone early in games before finding his feel later, but overall his walk rate of 2.4 per nine innings in 2017 suggests he has above-average control.

Guzman led the New York-Penn League with 88 strikeouts in 66.2 innings in 2017 and is ready for low Class A Greensboro in 2018. He could become a future No. 2 or No. 3 starter, though some Marlins officials believe he has front-of-the-rotation potential.

BA GRADE
60 Risk: V. High
FB: 80. SL: 50.
CHG: 50.
CTL: 50.

Year	Club (League)	Class	W	L	ERA	G	GS	CG	SV	IP	H	HR	BB	SO	K/9	WHIP	AVG
2015	Astros Orange (DSL)	R	0	2	7.43	4	4	0	0	13	19	1	8	8	5.4	2.03	.322
	Astros Blue (DSL)	R	2	1	4.91	9	7	0	0	33	36	1	15	19	5.2	1.55	.255
	Astros (GCL)	R	1	1	2.00	4	1	0	0	9	8	0	7	2	2.0	1.67	.258
2016	Astros (GCL)	R	1	1	3.12	7	4	0	0	17	4	0	10	25	13.0	0.81	.071
	Greeneville (APP)	R	2	3	4.76	6	4	0	0	23	25	1	7	29	11.5	1.41	.272
2017	Staten Island (NYP)	SS	5	3	2.30	13	13	1	0	67	51	4	18	88	11.9	1.04	.212
Minor League Totals			**11**	**11**	**3.67**	**43**	**33**	**1**	**0**	**162**	**143**	**7**	**65**	**171**	**9.5**	**1.28**	**.231**

3 TREVOR ROGERS, LHP

Born: Nov. 13, 1997. **B-T:** L-L. **Ht.:** 6-6. **Wt.:** 185. **Drafted:** HS—Carlsbad, N.M., 2017 (1st round). **Signed by:** Scott Stanley.

One of the oldest prep players in the 2017 draft class, Rogers was a top performer during the 2016 summer showcase circuit before producing inconsistent results as a senior against inferior New Mexico competition. Selected as the 13th overall pick, he signed with the Marlins for $3.4 million. Rogers, who is the cousin of former Marlins outfielder Cody Ross, did not pitch as a professional, though he did partake in several bullpen sessions.

The Marlins contend that Rogers is healthy and that he was simply suffering from a bit of fatigue after his senior season. He would have likely pitched in instructional league if not for Hurricane Irma canceling instructs altogether. Pitching from a lean, but projectable, 6-foot-6, 185-pound frame, Rogers uses a low three-quarters arm slot and can easily reach 95 mph with his fastball. Plus control allows his fastball, which routinely sits in the low 90s and has reportedly topped out at 97 mph in bullpens, to play up. A 10-to-4 slider gives Rogers a true above-average secondary offering, and though it can come across as sweepy at times, it has a chance to be an effective swing-and-miss pitch if he can find a bit more consistency. Rogers also flashes an average-or-better changeup with late fade, as well as a solid-average curveball that gives him a true four-pitch arsenal. As he gains experience, Rogers has the feel to develop plus command.

Rogers will get his first taste of pro action at the age of 20, nearly 10 months after being drafted. If the Marlins follow the same path they did with 2016 first-rounder Braxton Garrett, then Rogers could start at low Class A Greensboro in 2018.

BA GRADE
60 Risk: Extreme
FB: 60. CB: 45.
SL: 55. CHG: 45.
CTL: 50.

MIKE JANES

Year	Club (League)	Class	W	L	ERA	G	GS	CG	SV	IP	H	HR	BB	SO	K/9	WHIP	AVG
2017	Did not play																

4 BRAXTON GARRETT, LHP

Born: Aug. 5, 1997. **B-T:** L-L. **Ht.:** 6-3. **Wt.:** 190. **Drafted:** HS—Florence, Ala., 2016 (1st round). **Signed by:** Mark Willoughby.

The highest-drafted prep pitcher out of Alabama since righthander Rick James in 1965, Garrett went seventh overall in 2016 and signed for an above-slot deal worth $4,195,900 before the Marlins held him out for the rest of the year in anticipation for his pro-ball debut in 2017.

Garrett made four starts at low Class A Greensboro in 2017 before having Tommy John Surgery in June. When healthy, his best pitch is a true north-to-south curveball, which was considered one of the best offspeed offerings in the 2016 draft class and features a hard, tight break. He commands both his high-70s curveball and his low-90s fastball well, while his changeup is coming along as a third pitch with late fade. Advanced command should help each of Garrett's three offerings continue to play up.

Garrett will miss the entire 2018 season as he rehabs from surgery, which puts him on track to return in 2019, his age-21 season. Still, he projects to have three above-average or better pitches with above-average command, meaning, if he can return fully healthy, there still is a lot to recommend him as a potential No. 2 or 3 starter in the future.

BA GRADE
60 Risk: Extreme
FB: 55. CB: 60.
CHG: 50.
CTL: 60.

Year	Club (League)	Class	W	L	ERA	G	GS	CG	SV	IP	H	HR	BB	SO	K/9	WHIP	AVG
2016	Did not play																
2017	Greensboro (SAL)	LoA	1	0	2.93	4	4	0	0	15	13	3	6	16	9.4	1.24	.220
Minor League Totals			1	0	2.93	4	4	0	0	15	13	3	6	16	9.4	1.24	.220

5 NICK NEIDERT, RHP

Born: Nov. 20, 1993. **B-T:** R-R. **Ht.:** 6-1. **Wt.:** 180. **Drafted:** HS—Suwanee, Ga., 2015 (2nd round). **Signed by:** Dustin Evans (Mariners).

The Mariners' first selection in 2015, Neidert claimed California League pitcher of the year honors in 2017 after going 10-3, 2.76 at high Class A Modesto. The Marlins acquired Neidert, shortstop Chris Torres and righthander Robert Dugger after the 2017 season in the deal that sent Dee Gordon and international bonus pool money to Seattle.

Neidert advanced to Double-A Arkansas as a 20-year-old in 2017. He was adjusting to the level when he took a comebacker off his right forearm in mid-August, and he finished the year on the disabled list with a deep bone bruise. Neidert's aggressive approach allows him to excel. He goes right at hitters, has advanced feel for his secondary pitches and shows good poise on the mound. He effectively sequences his three pitches and throws strikes. Neidert's fastball sits 90-93 mph but plays up with carry through the zone due to a late hop in his delivery. Both of his secondary offerings—an average low-80s slider and future plus changeup at 78-81 mph with deception and fade—play up because of how well he commands them. He repeats his high three-quarters delivery, keeping hitters off balance. Neidert has a high aptitude for his craft with the ability to quickly make adjustments.

Some observers don't see a true out pitch in Neidert's arsenal, but he succeeds because of his competitive nature and advanced pitchabilty. He projects as a No. 4 starter and will likely return Double-A in 2018.

BA GRADE
50 Risk: High
FB: 55. SL: 50.
CHG: 60.
CTL: 60.

Year	Club (League)	Class	AVG	G	AB	R	H	2B	3B	HR	RBI	BB	SO	SB	CS	OBP	SLG
2015	Mariners (AZL)	R	0	2	1.53	11	11	0	0	35	25	1	9	23	5.9	0.96	.198
2016	Clinton (MWL)	LoA	7	3	2.57	19	19	0	0	91	75	7	13	69	6.8	0.97	.225
2017	Modesto (CAL)	HiA	10	3	2.76	19	19	0	0	104	95	7	17	109	9.4	1.07	.244
	Arkansas (TL)	AA	1	3	6.56	6	6	0	0	23	33	4	5	13	5.0	1.63	.324
Minor League Totals			18	11	2.87	55	55	0	0	254	228	19	44	214	7.6	1.07	.240

6 BRIAN ANDERSON, 3B

Born: May 19, 1993. **B-T:** R-R. **Ht.:** 6-3. **Wt.:** 185. **Drafted:** Arkansas, 2014 (3rd round). **Signed by:** Brian Kraft.

Anderson began to access his raw power more consistently in 2017, when he hit 22 home runs at Double-A Jacksonville and Triple-A New Orleans to earn a September callup. The Marlins like his solid righthanded swing and defensive versatility, though he has found a home at third base after playing first base, second base and outfield in the past.

Working from a strong, 6-foot-3 frame, Anderson has a smooth, line-drive swing and is able to go gap-to-gap with solid power. Though he shows plus power to his pull side in batting practice, he is at his best when he's spraying line drives to the right-center field gap. Defensively, Anderson possess a plus arm at third base, where his range has improved. He is excellent at coming in on the ball and making bare-handed plays. On the basepaths, Anderson shows above-average speed and instincts, but will never be known as a basestealer.

Anderson will turn 25 early in 2018 and will be looking to nail down the third base job out of spring training. Some observers believe he has the potential for 15-20 home runs.

BA GRADE

45 Risk: Medium

HIT: 45. POW: 50.
SPD: 50. FLD: 55.
ARM: 60.

Year	Club (League)	Class	AVG	G	AB	R	H	2B	3B	HR	RBI	BB	SO	SB	CS	OBP	SLG
2015	Jupiter (FSL)	HiA	.235	132	477	50	112	22	2	8	62	40	109	2	2	.304	.340
2016	Jupiter (FSL)	HiA	.302	49	182	27	55	12	2	3	25	22	38	3	0	.377	.440
	Jacksonville (SL)	AA	.243	86	301	38	73	9	1	8	40	36	59	0	0	.330	.359
2017	Jacksonville (SL)	AA	.251	87	311	53	78	14	3	14	55	36	71	1	1	.341	.450
	New Orleans (PCL)	AAA	.339	33	118	21	40	7	0	8	26	12	27	0	1	.416	.602
	Miami (NL)	MAJ	.262	25	84	11	22	7	1	0	8	10	28	0	0	.337	.369
Major League Totals			.262	25	84	11	22	7	1	0	8	10	28	0	0	.337	.369
Minor League Totals			.264	446	1619	227	427	74	9	52	257	165	343	7	5	.341	.417

7 MAGNEURIS SIERRA, OF

Born: April 7, 1996. **B-T:** L-L. **Ht.:** 5-11. **Wt.:** 160. **Signed:** Dominican Republic, 2012. **Signed by:** Rodney Jimenez/Angel Ovalles.

A touted international signing out of the Dominican Republic in 2012, Sierra slowly advanced before making the massive jump from high Class A straight to the majors in May 2017 when a rash of injuries left the Cardinals short of outfielders. He showed very well before returning to the minors at Double-A Springfield, and then rejoined the Cardinals in September. Sierra was then traded to the Marlins in December 2017, when he joined minor league righthanders Sandy Alcantara and Zac Gallen as headliners in the deal for outfielder Marcell Ozuna.

Sierra fits the mold of an old-school leadoff hitter. Lithe and athletic, he has a compact lefthanded swing and slaps the ball gap to gap. He excels playing small ball and using his plus-plus speed to beat out infield singles and put pressure on opposing defenses. His speed plays up even more with tight turns on the bases. Sierra is an aggressive hitter who doesn't walk much, but his improving pitch recognition has led to a reduction in strikeouts. He is adding strength but does not project to ever be a home run hitter. Center field is where Sierra shines defensively, with top-flight tracking ability, elite instincts, efficient routes and a plus, accurate arm.

Sierra's athleticism, elite speed and center field defense provide a solid baseline for a big league career, generally in the vein of a player like Jarrod Dyson.

BA GRADE

50 Risk: High

HIT: 50. POW: 30.
SPD: 70. FLD: 60.
ARM: 60.

Year	Club (League)	Class	AVG	G	AB	R	H	2B	3B	HR	RBI	BB	SO	SB	CS	OBP	SLG
2015	Peoria (MWL)	LoA	.191	51	178	19	34	1	3	1	7	7	52	4	5	.219	.247
	Johnson City (APP)	R	.315	53	216	38	68	8	0	3	15	19	42	15	2	.371	.394
2016	Peoria (MWL)	LoA	.307	122	524	78	161	29	4	3	60	22	97	31	17	.335	.395
2017	Palm Beach (FSL)	HiA	.268	20	82	16	22	3	4	0	9	7	15	3	5	.333	.402
	Springfield, MO (TL)	AA	.269	81	327	32	88	18	3	1	35	20	59	17	5	.313	.352
	St. Louis (NL)	MAJ	.317	22	60	10	19	0	0	0	5	4	14	2	2	.359	.317
Major League Totals			.317	22	60	10	19	0	0	0	5	4	14	2	2	.359	.317
Minor League Totals			.292	442	1741	269	508	77	20	11	177	120	328	98	44	.339	.378

8 JAMES NELSON, 3B

Born: Oct. 18, 1997. **B-T:** R-R. **Ht.:** 6-2. **Wt.:** 180. **Drafted:** Cisco (Texas) JC, 2016 (15th round). **Signed by:** Ryan Wardinsky.

An 18th-round pick out of high school by the Red Sox in 2015, Nelson didn't sign and instead went to Cisco (Texas) JC for one season before signing with the Marlins as a 15th-round pick in 2016. Nelson is the nephew of 2004 first-round pick and ex-big leaguer Chris Nelson and spent the entire 2017 season at low Class A Greensboro.

Nelson has tremendous bat speed and keeps his bat through the hitting zone, which has helped him hit an impressive 41 doubles in 145 career games. His approach at the plate is still evolving and needs maturing, but that is largely to be expected from a 19-year old in his first full season. His bat speed suggests above-average power, especially as he continues to fill out his 6-foot-2, 180-pound frame and those doubles should eventually turn into home runs. Nelson displays average

BA GRADE
50 Risk: High
HIT: 50. POW: 50.
SPD: 50. FLD: 55.
ARM: 60.

or better speed but isn't a stolen base threat. A shortstop in high school, Nelson made a smooth move to third base and showcases the tools necessary to be an above-average defender there. He has good range and at least above-average arm strength, but has been error-prone with a .907 fielding percentage.

Described as having an above-average baseball IQ, Nelson should continue his steady ascent at high Class A Jupiter. He profiles as an everyday third baseman in two or three years.

Year	Club (League)	Class	AVG	G	AB	R	H	2B	3B	HR	RBI	BB	SO	SB	CS	OBP	SLG
2016	Marlins (GCL)	R	.284	43	162	26	46	10	0	1	24	14	30	7	3	.344	.364
2017	Greensboro (SAL)	LoA	.309	102	395	41	122	31	3	7	59	26	106	6	2	.354	.456
Minor League Totals			.302	145	557	67	168	41	3	8	83	40	136	13	5	.351	.429

9 CHRIS TORRES, SS

Born: Feb. 6, 1998. **B-T:** S-R. **Ht.:** 5-11. **Wt.:** 170. **Signed:** Dominican Republic, 2014. **Signed by:** Tim Kissner/Eddy Toledo/Kelvin Dominguez (Mariners).

Signed by the Mariners in 2014 for $375,000, Torres started his pro career with promising seasons in the Dominican Summer League in 2015 and the Rookie-level Arizona League in 2016. An injury to Torres' non-throwing shoulder hampered him early in 2017, but he took off in the second half of the short-season Northwest League season with a .798 OPS. The Marlins acquired him after the 2017 season— along with Nick Neidert and Robert Dugger—for Dee Gordon.

Torres has a strong, physical frame and impressive athleticism. He has a solid approach at the plate and posted an 11 percent walk rate at short-season Everett. While his numbers so far don't support it, he projects to be an average hitter because of his pure swing and how well he uses his hands. He considered giving up switch-hitting and batting lefthanded only, but just needs to trust his righthanded swing.

BA GRADE
50 Risk: High
HIT: 50. POW: 45.
SPD: 60. FLD: 60.
ARM: 70.

Torre is a plus runner and projects to have fringe-average power as he grows, but his glove should carry him regardless. He has the potential to be a plus shortstop with a plus-plus arm, though he loses concentration at times and needs to learn better angles on his throws.

Torres is a long way from the majors, but could be an everyday shortstop with 15 home runs if everything comes together. Low Class A Greensboro likely awaits in 2018.

Year	Club (League)	Class	AVG	G	AB	R	H	2B	3B	HR	RBI	BB	SO	SB	CS	OBP	SLG
2015	Mariners2 (DSL)	R	.251	64	215	40	54	8	3	2	30	51	56	20	9	.399	.344
2016	Mariners (AZL)	R	.257	44	167	31	43	9	4	0	17	19	44	12	4	.337	.359
2017	Mariners (AZL)	R	.222	4	9	1	2	0	2	0	1	3	5	1	0	.417	.667
	Everett (NWL)	SS	.238	48	193	44	46	8	6	6	22	25	64	13	3	.324	.435
Minor League Totals			.248	160	584	116	145	25	15	8	70	98	169	46	16	.358	.384

10 ZAC GALLEN, RHP

CLIFF WELCH

Born: Aug. 3, 1995. **B-T:** R-R. **Ht.:** 6-2. **Wt.:** 191. **Drafted:** North Carolina, 2016 (3rd round). **Signed by:** Charles Peterson.

Gallen served as North Carolina's Friday starter for two years in a rotation that included future first-rounder J.B. Bukauskas. A cutter he picked up as a sophomore helped Gallen blossom into that role, and the Cardinals drafted him in the third round in 2016 and signed him for $563,100. Gallen provided instant value, zooming up three levels in his first full season and finishing 2017 at Triple-A Memphis. After the 2017 season, Gallen was traded to the Marlins with Sandy Alcantara, Magneuris Sierra and Daniel Castano for outfielder Marcell Ozuna.

Gallen's stuff is average across the board, but all four of his pitches play up with superb control and deception out of his slight crossfire delivery. He mows through lineups by attacking the strike zone with all of his offerings and getting early-count grounders for quick outs. He pounds the bottom of the zone with his 89-93 mph fastball, backs it up with an 86-88 mph cutter that stays low and on the black, and mixes in an 82-85 mph changeup to keep hitters off balance. He also has a 77-79 mph curveball, but it can get loopy and hang on him at times. Gallen is athletic and repeats his delivery, fields his position well and has top-flight makeup.

Gallen likely will start at Triple-A New Orleans in 2018 and fits as a potential back-end starter or swingman in the majors.

BA GRADE
45 Risk: Medium

FB: 50. CB: 50.
CT: 50. CHG: 50.
CTL: 55.

Year	Club (League)	Class	W	L	ERA	G	GS	CG	SV	IP	H	HR	BB	SO	K/9	WHIP	AVG
2016	Cardinals (GCL)	R	0	0	1.86	6	3	0	1	10	7	0	0	15	14.0	0.72	.194
2017	Palm Beach (FSL)	HiA	5	2	1.62	9	9	1	0	56	44	1	10	56	9.1	0.97	.215
	Springfield, MO (TL)	AA	4	5	3.79	13	13	0	0	71	76	8	19	42	5.3	1.33	.270
	Memphis (PCL)	AAA	1	1	3.48	4	4	0	0	21	18	2	6	23	10.0	1.16	.237
Minor League Totals			10	8	2.86	32	29	1	1	157	145	11	35	136	7.8	1.14	.242

11 DILLON PETERS, LHP

BA GRADE
45 Risk: Medium

Born: Aug. 31, 1992. **B-T:** L-L. **Ht.:** 5-9. **Wt.:** 195. **Drafted:** Texas, 2014 (10th round). **Signed by:** Ryan Wardinsky.

A highly-regarded prep lefthander out of Indianapolis in 2011, Peters turned down several big-money offers to pitch at Texas for three seasons. Listed at just 5-foot-9, Peters was highly successful at Texas, where he went 17-7, 2.26 in 50 appearances (38 starts). Despite a strong college pedigree, he fell to the 10th round in 2014 after he required Tommy John surgery.

Peters eventually signed with the Marlins for $175,000 and made 48 minor league starts over three years before making his big league debut as a September callup in 2017. Peters' height can be a bit deceiving, because he throws a lively fastball that can reach the mid-90s with sink. Pitching mostly in the 91-94 mph range, he maintains his velocity and his command was consistently praised in the minors. Peters' curveball has a tight rotation and can flash above-average at times, while his changeup has some depth and is considered at least average. His command allows his stuff to play up.

After making six starts for the Marlins in 2017, Peters will contend for a big league rotation spot in 2018. But with just 68 innings above high Class A, he could open the season at Triple-A New Orleans. He projects as a No. 4 starter.

Year	Club (League)	Class	W	L	ERA	G	GS	CG	SV	IP	H	HR	BB	SO	K/9	WHIP	AVG
2015	Marlins (GCL)	R	1	1	0.68	4	4	0	0	13	10	0	3	13	8.8	0.98	.217
	Batavia (NYP)	SS	0	3	4.83	7	7	0	0	32	40	2	10	27	7.7	1.58	.299
2016	Jupiter (FSL)	HiA	11	6	2.46	20	20	0	0	106	102	2	16	89	7.6	1.11	.253
	Jacksonville (SL)	AA	3	0	1.99	4	4	0	0	23	17	2	4	16	6.4	0.93	.205
2017	Marlins (GCL)	R	0	1	1.35	2	2	0	0	7	3	0	4	6	8.1	1.05	.130
	Jupiter (FSL)	HiA	1	0	0.00	2	2	0	0	11	5	0	2	9	7.6	0.66	.139
	Jacksonville (SL)	AA	6	2	1.97	9	9	0	0	46	33	1	11	40	7.9	0.96	.200
	Miami (NL)	MAJ	1	2	5.17	6	6	0	0	31	32	3	19	27	7.8	1.63	.271
Major League Totals			1	2	5.17	6	6	0	0	31	32	3	19	27	7.8	1.63	.271
Minor League Totals			22	13	2.40	48	48	0	0	237	210	7	50	200	7.6	1.10	.236

12 BRIAN MILLER, OF

BA GRADE
50 Risk: High

Born: Aug. 20, 1995. **B-T:** L-R. **Ht.:** 6-1. **Wt.:** 186. **Drafted:** North Carolina, 2017 (1st round supplemental). **Signed by:** Blake Newsome.

Miller started at North Carolina as a DH known for his plus speed but without any natural position. He moved to center field by his junior year and had a strong wood-bat track record, hitting .327 in the 2016 Cape Cod League, which led to him being the first hitter selected by the Marlins in 2017.

Miller spent his entire pro debut season with low Class A Greensboro. It was there that he showed off his natural feel for hitting by using his plus speed and strong contact ability, ending his 2017 season with the third-best average (.322) in the South Atlantic League from July 1 to season's end. With a slight 6-foot-1 frame, Miller projects to have fringe-average power at best. Defensively, he has shown improved range and instincts as he gets more time in center and projects as an above-average defender there, even if his arm strength may never be more than average.

After a successful pro debut, Miller should start 2018 at high Class A Jupiter, with a chance to move quickly. His makeup suggests he has a great chance to maximize his potential as a high-average, low-power, everyday center fielder.

Year	Club (League)	Class	AVG	G	AB	R	H	2B	3B	HR	RBI	BB	SO	SB	CS	OBP	SLG
2017	Greensboro (SAL)	LoA	.322	57	233	42	75	17	1	1	28	23	35	21	6	.384	.416
Minor League Totals			.322	57	233	42	75	17	1	1	28	23	35	21	6	.384	.416

13 EDWARD CABRERA, RHP

Born: April 13, 1998. **B-T:** R-R. **Ht.:** 6-4. **Wt.:** 175. **Signed:** Dominican Republic, 2015. **Signed by:** Albert Gonzalez/Sandy Nin/Domingo Ortega.

BA GRADE
55 Risk: Extreme

One of five international players the Marlins signed for $100,000 in 2015, Cabrera is on track to out-perform his signing bonus. At short-season Batavia in 2017, he stuck out 32 batters in 35.2 innings as an 18-year old. After throwing several innings in extended spring training, Cabrera pitched just 35 innings, which included several relief appearances to monitor his innings.

The tall, lean Cabrera reached the mid-90s in 2016, then took a big step forward in 2017, when he topped out at 101 mph. His typical fastball range is 94-96 mph as a starter. His plus fastball is paired with a hard slider that flashes plus at times and showcases good tilt. Cabrera has also been working on a changeup, which currently comes across a tad firm but shows the potential to be at least average. He shows above-average control.

In a system that has taken high school pitchers in the first round in recent years, it's Cabrera who might have the most upside. He should see his first action in full-season ball in 2018.

Year	Club (League)	Class	W	L	ERA	G	GS	CG	SV	IP	H	HR	BB	SO	K/9	WHIP	AVG
2016	Marlins (GCL)	R	2	6	4.21	11	7	0	0	47	54	1	10	28	5.4	1.36	.289
2017	Batavia (NYP)	SS	1	3	5.30	13	6	0	0	36	42	1	8	32	8.1	1.40	.286
Minor League Totals			3	9	4.68	24	13	0	0	83	96	2	18	60	6.5	1.38	.287

14 JOE DUNAND, SS

Born: Sept. 20, 1995. **B-T:** R-R. **Ht.:** 6-2. **Wt.:** 205. **Drafted:** North Carolina State, 2017 (2nd round). **Signed by:** Blake Newsome.

BA GRADE
50 Risk: V. High

Better known as Alex Rodriguez's nephew as an amateur, Dunand was a three-year starter at North Carolina State, where he played third base as a freshman before taking over at shortstop during his final two years. He hit .326 in the 2016 Cape Cod League.

Dunand's 6-foot-2, 205-pound frame would seemingly profile better at third base, but the Marlins intend to keep him at shortstop. Initial reports of his defense were encouraging, though he doesn't project to have much more than average range. Soft hands and an above-average arm will play at short or third, however, he has plus defensive potential at the hot corner. At the plate, Dunand's plus raw power grades well above his hit tool, but as long as he shrinks his strike zone and stays committed to using the whole field he could be projected as an above-average hitter. Dunand is an at least average runner.

Dealing with a finger injury in 2017, Dunand returned to play just eight pro games in 2017, and he should begin 2018 at high Class A Jupiter.

Year	Club (League)	Class	AVG	G	AB	R	H	2B	3B	HR	RBI	BB	SO	SB	CS	OBP	SLG
2017	Marlins (GCL)	R	.375	5	16	4	6	3	0	1	3	3	4	0	0	.476	.750
	Jupiter (FSL)	HiA	.364	3	11	1	4	2	0	0	1	2	4	0	1	.462	.545
Minor League Totals			.370	8	27	5	10	5	0	1	4	5	8	0	1	.471	.667

15 MERANDY GONZALEZ, RHP

Born: Oct. 9, 1995. **B-T:** R-R. **Ht.:** 6-0. **Wt.:** 216. **Signed:** Dominican Republic, 2013. **Signed by:** Daurys Nin/Gerardo Cabrera (Mets).

BA GRADE
50 Risk: V. High

Acquired from the Mets as part of the A.J. Ramos trade, Gonzalez produced a stellar season in 2017. At two Class A levels, he pitched to a 1.66 ERA that ranked second in the minors. His 0.97 WHIP ranked 10th.

Gonzalez is listed at just 6 feet, but he has a solid lower half and possesses a strong, yet high-effort delivery that helps him top out at 97 mph with his fastball. Working mostly in the 93-95 mph range, he also has an above-average curveball that will come across the plate hard with a tight, north-to-south spin in the high 70s or low 80s. He also has feel for a third-pitch changeup. Gonzalez's control has never been his strongest asset, but he took a step forward in 2017 by walking just 26 batters, against 103 strikeouts in a career-high 130 innings.

In his full-season debut Gonzalez proved durable and effective, though he still faces questions about his future role. Developing his command and changeup will be key to staying in the rotation. If he can't, his power repertoire should play as a high-leverage reliever.

Year	Club (League)	Class	W	L	ERA	G	GS	CG	SV	IP	H	HR	BB	SO	K/9	WHIP	AVG
2015	Mets (GCL)	R	2	1	2.05	4	2	1	0	22	9	1	3	25	10.2	0.55	.120
	Kingsport (APP)	R	2	2	2.82	9	7	0	0	45	40	1	19	39	7.9	1.32	.240
2016	Brooklyn (NYP)	SS	6	3	2.87	14	14	0	0	69	65	2	27	71	9.3	1.33	.254
2017	Columbia (SAL)	LoA	8	1	1.55	11	11	0	0	70	50	3	13	65	8.4	0.90	.200
	St. Lucie (FSL)	HiA	4	2	2.23	6	6	0	0	36	33	1	8	24	5.9	1.13	.232
	Jupiter (FSL)	HiA	1	0	1.11	5	3	0	1	24	18	0	5	14	5.2	0.95	.212
Minor League Totals			30	13	2.48	76	57	1	2	367	304	10	106	314	7.7	1.12	.226

16 BRAYAN HERNANDEZ, OF

BA GRADE
50 Risk: Extreme

Born: Sept. 11, 1997. **B-T:** R-R. **Ht.:** 6-2. **Wt.:** 175. **Signed:** Venezuela, 2014.
Signed by: Tim Kissner/Emilio Carrasquel/Illitch Salazar (Mariners).

Hernandez was one of the more sought-after international prospects in 2014, when he signed with the Mariners for $1.85 million. He struggled in the Dominican Summer League in 2015, which led the Mariners to end his switch-hitting experiment. Seattle traded him and three others to the Marlins in July 2017 for David Phelps.

A career .260 hitter with a 3-to-1 strikeout-to-walk ratio, Hernandez must continue to improve at the plate, especially when it comes to using the entire field and making solid contact against quality offspeed pitches. He has a level swing and generates solid bat speed with a knack for making contact, but he hasn't produced much power in his career. That power could still materialize for Hernandez, who is 20 years old and still has projection left in his athletic frame. He could become a plus defensive center fielder with a strong arm. He shows good natural defensive instincts, while his plus speed plays up in the outfield and on the basepaths.

Hernandez should get his first extended look in full-season ball in 2018, where he will flash all five tools but requires significant refinement.

Year	Club (League)	Class	AVG	G	AB	R	H	2B	3B	HR	RBI	BB	SO	SB	CS	OBP	SLG
2015	Mariners2 (DSL)	R	.224	50	174	32	39	8	2	2	22	18	44	9	6	.295	.328
2016	Mariners (DSL)	R	.278	31	133	30	37	6	2	5	15	10	23	12	2	.331	.466
	Mariners (AZL)	R	.285	33	130	13	37	8	2	1	19	7	36	9	3	.324	.400
2017	Tacoma (PCL)	AAA	.400	3	5	0	2	0	0	0	0	0	0	1	0	.400	.400
	Everett (NWL)	SS	.252	28	103	9	26	2	4	2	15	7	26	4	1	.306	.408
	Marlins (GCL)	R	.250	3	8	2	2	1	0	0	0	1	2	0	0	.333	.375
	Batavia (NYP)	SS	.271	15	59	9	16	2	3	0	3	2	14	0	0	.302	.407
Minor League Totals			.260	163	612	95	159	27	13	10	74	45	145	35	12	.313	.395

17 TYLER KOLEK, RHP

BA GRADE
50 Risk: Extreme

Born: Dec. 15, 1995. **B-T:** R-R. **Ht.:** 6-5. **Wt.:** 260. **Drafted:** HS—Shepherd, Texas, 2014 (1st round). **Signed by:** Ryan Wardinsky.

The No. 2 overall pick in 2014, Kolek signed for $6,000,000, which is the highest draft bonus in franchise history. After signing, he struggled for two seasons and then missed the entire 2016 season after having Tommy John surgery. He briefly returned in 2017, making five appearances in the Rookie-level Gulf Coast League, but he walked or hit 17 of the 31 batters he faced.

Kolek is a physically imposing righthander whose fastball can regularly sit between 96-98 mph. After routinely hitting triple digits as an amateur and topping out at 102 during his senior year, his fastball hasn't reached those levels as a pro, though it still plays as plus with heavy, downward tilt. During his only full season at low Class A Greensboro in 2015, Kolek's slider and changeup both showed below-average, which allowed hitters to sit fastball. More concerning than his lackluster offspeed offerings is Kolek's control, which is below-average. He has walked 5.9 per nine innings for his career.

Improving his slider and changeup would help Kolek realize his ceiling as a No. 3 starter. The Marlins worked with him during his rehab to refine his mechanics and improve his command, which at times went haywire because of a side-to-side, cross-arm delivery.

Year	Club (League)	Class	W	L	ERA	G	GS	CG	SV	IP	H	HR	BB	SO	K/9	WHIP	AVG
2015	Greensboro (SAL)	LoA	4	10	4.56	25	25	0	0	109	108	7	61	81	6.7	1.56	.258
2016	Did not play—Injured																
2017	Marlins (GCL)	R	0	0	29.45	5	4	0	0	4	4	0	14	1	2.5	4.91	.286
Minor League Totals			4	13	5.23	39	37	0	0	134	134	7	88	100	6.7	1.65	.262

18 RILEY MAHAN, 2B

Born: Dec. 31, 1995. **B-T:** L-R. **Ht.:** 6-3. **Wt.:** 185. **Drafted:** Kentucky, 2017 (3rd round). **Signed by:** Alex Smith.

Instead of signing with the Giants as a 40th-round pick out of high school in 2014, Mahan ended up at Kentucky, where he established himself as one of the most productive college bats in the 2017 draft. While his defensive ability has caused some concern, Mahan has continuously been lauded for his bat.

The 6-foot-3, 185-pound Mahan posseses a smooth lefthanded swing and shows good barrel control with the ability to use the entire field against both righthanders and lefthanders. Though his swing most often results in line drives, there is some untapped power in his frame that should continue to develop as he matures physically. Defensively, Mahan should be able to reach a ceiling of an at least average second baseman, though it will likely never be the strongest aspect of his game. Overall, Mahan is a good athlete and above-average runner, leading many to believe he could move to a corner outfield spot. He also possesses an above-average arm. Mahan will continue proving himself at second base for now, as his bat profiles better on the dirt.

Mahan played in just six games—all with low Class A Greensboro—after signing with the Marlins in 2017 and could start 2018 there. He has a chance to move up the Marlins system relatively quickly, due mostly to his pedigree as an advanced college bat.

Year	Club (League)	Class	AVG	G	AB	R	H	2B	3B	HR	RBI	BB	SO	SB	CS	OBP	SLG
2017	Greensboro (SAL)	LoA	.259	6	27	4	7	1	0	1	4	0	7	0	0	.259	.407
Minor League Totals			.259	6	27	4	7	1	0	1	4	0	7	0	0	.259	.407

19 MATT GIVIN, RHP

Born: June 17, 1999. **B-T:** R-R. **Ht.:** 6-3. **Wt.:** 180. **Drafted:** HS—Lone Tree, Colo., 2017 (20th round). **Signed by:** Scott Stanley.

Committed to play baseball at Xavier, where he would have joined his older brother Chris, Matt instead signed with the Marlins in 2017 as a 20th-round pick for an over-slot deal of $458,000. In fact, Givin's signing bonus was one of just six bonuses the Marlins handed out in 2017 that were $350,000 or higher.

Though Givin was regarded as a Colorado righthander with a short track record, he made seven successful starts in the Rookie-level Gulf Coast League in 2017, pitching to an 0.39 ERA and 0.94 WHIP in 23.1 innings. Working from a slim, 6-foot-3, 180-pound build, Givin has plenty of room to fill out his frame as he gets older, which is an encouraging sign considering the 18-year-old's fastball is already sitting in the low 90s. Though his fastball should add a tick or two as he matures, Givin's control already shows ahead of schedule, as seen by his 3-to-1 strikeout-to-walk ratio. Givin's changeup is currently ahead of his low-80s curveball, though both pitches have a chance to become above-average offerings with plus control in the future.

If Givin can continue to build on his first-year success in 2018 and beyond, then he would have a chance to be the Marlins' steal of the 2017 draft.

Year	Club (League)	Class	W	L	ERA	G	GS	CG	SV	IP	H	HR	BB	SO	K/9	WHIP	AVG
2017	Marlins (GCL)	R	0	0	0.39	7	7	0	0	23	16	0	6	19	7.3	0.94	.198
Minor League Totals			0	0	0.39	7	7	0	0	23	16	0	6	19	7.3	0.94	.198

20 COLTON HOCK, RHP

Born: March 15, 1996. **B-T:** R-R. **Ht.:** 6-4. **Wt.:** 220. **Drafted:** Stanford, 2017 (4th round). **Signed by:** John Hughes.

A standout reliever at Stanford for three years, Hock was the Marlins' fourth-round pick in 2017 and signed with the club for an above-slot $500,000. In college, he recorded a team-best 22 saves and an ERA just above 2.00 over his final two seasons. The Marlins selected Hock with the idea he could become a starter at the pro level, but that transition didn't go as smooth as hoped in 2017, when Hock recorded a 6.75 ERA in 26.2 innings.

At his best, Hock's mid-90s fastball features a late, heavy sink and pairs nicely with a tight, potentially plus curveball that gives him a dangerous one-two punch to attack opposing hitters. Improving his third-pitch changeup, which currently flashes fringe-average, would go a long way in boosting Hock's starter profile. Effort in his delivery would suggest a long-term role as a reliever. Hock showed plus control at Stanford, but his control wavered in pro ball with 6.1 walks per nine innings.

The Marlins are not giving up on the idea that Hock could still transition into a starter, though he has a fallback option of high-leverage reliever.

Year	Club (League)	Class	W	L	ERA	G	GS	CG	SV	IP	H	HR	BB	SO	K/9	WHIP	AVG
2017	Marlins (GCL)	R	0	1	7.00	4	1	0	0	9	8	1	0	10	10.0	0.89	.229
	Batavia (NYP)	SS	1	3	6.62	7	1	0	0	18	22	2	12	13	6.6	1.92	.324
Minor League Totals			1	4	6.75	11	2	0	0	27	30	3	12	23	7.8	1.58	.291

21 BRAXTON LEE, OF

BA GRADE

40 Risk: Medium

Born: Aug. 23, 1993. **B-T:** L-R. **Ht.:** 5-10. **Wt.:** 185. **Drafted:** Mississippi, 2014 (12th round). **Signed by:** Rickey Drexler (Rays).

A junior college transfer who spent one year at Mississippi, Lee was selected by the Rays in the 12th round in 2014. He then joined the Marlins organization in the June 2017 trade that sent shortstop Adeiny Hechavarria to Tampa Bay.

After a dismal 2016 in which Lee hit just .209 in the Double-A Southern League, Lee bounced back in a big way in 2017, winning the SL batting title with a .309 average. Standing at 5-foot-10, 185 pounds, Lee is a plus defender who can play all three outfield positions with plus-plus speed. Though center field is his natural position, and where his bat profiles best, Lee's arm is strong enough that he could also play the corners, giving him solid value as a fourth outfielder. He has a contact-first swing and possesses well below-average power. He still needs to work on his instincts on the basepaths, which helps explain his career stolen base success rate being barely north of 60 percent.

Lee will begin 2018 with his first taste of the Triple-A level. Lee's floor is a speedy, defense-first fourth outfielder, which could give him immediate value at the big league level.

Year	Club (League)	Class	AVG	G	AB	R	H	2B	3B	HR	RBI	BB	SO	SB	CS	OBP	SLG
2015	Charlotte, FL (FSL)	HiA	.281	115	374	48	105	7	1	6	24	36	67	23	13	.347	.305
2016	Montgomery (SL)	AA	.209	110	387	35	81	12	3	0	25	30	58	13	10	.269	.256
2017	Montgomery (SL)	AA	.317	67	262	47	83	9	3	2	16	29	56	12	11	.388	.397
	Jacksonville (SL)	AA	.294	60	214	34	63	12	0	1	21	36	48	8	2	.398	.364
Minor League Totals			.271	403	1439	200	390	47	8	3	99	150	262	68	45	.343	.321

22 TREVOR RICHARDS, RHP

BA GRADE

40 Risk: Medium

Born: May 15, 1993. **B-T:** R-R. **Ht.:** 6-2. **Wt.:** 190. **Signed:** Frontier League, 2016. **Signed by:** David Espinosa.

Undrafted out of Drury (Mo.), Richards spent nearly two seasons pitching for Gateway in the independent Frontier League before signing with the Marlins as a free agent in July 2016. Since joining the organization, Richards has proved he belongs. During the 2017 season he made 25 starts at high Class A Jupiter and Double-A Jacksonville and finished 12-11, 2.53 with 158 strikeouts in 146 innings. He claimed the organization's pitcher of the year award.

Line one with Richards is his stellar changeup, which at least one evaluator proclaimed to be a plus-plus pitch and the best in the organization. He can use his changeup as a true swing-and-miss pitch against both righthanded and lefthanded hitters, which has led him to a career strikeout rate of 9.5 per nine innings. Richards' fastball sits mostly 90-91 mph but can touch 94 at times. His fastball also plays up, in part due to the threat of his changeup, but also because of a deceptive delivery that can mess with hitters. Richards uses a fringe-average curveball as a third pitch. He shows above-average command, working his fastball to both sides of the plate and spotting his changeup down in the zone consistently.

Richards should see time at Triple-A New Orleans om 2018. He turns 25 in 2018, but if he can improve his curveball then he has a chance to become a back-of-the-rotation starter. If not, he could excel as a long reliever, relying on his fastball-changeup combination to navigate a big league lineup.

Year	Club (League)	Class	W	L	ERA	G	GS	CG	SV	IP	H	HR	BB	SO	K/9	WHIP	AVG
2015	Gateway (FRN)	IND	6	6	3.36	14	14	1	0	91	80	6	27	84	8.3	1.18	—
2016	Gateway (FRN)	IND	3	3	3.19	9	8	0	0	48	40	6	20	48	9.0	1.25	—
	Batavia (NYP)	SS	0	0	1.69	3	1	0	0	11	9	1	2	15	12.7	1.03	.225
	Greensboro (SAL)	LoA	2	3	2.68	8	8	0	0	44	29	3	14	38	7.8	0.98	.186
2017	Jupiter (FSL)	HiA	7	4	2.17	13	11	0	0	71	54	2	12	81	10.3	0.93	.204
	Jacksonville (SL)	AA	5	7	2.87	14	14	0	0	75	67	4	18	77	9.2	1.13	.231
Minor League Totals			14	14	2.52	38	34	0	0	200	159	10	46	211	9.5	1.02	.212

23 ROBERT DUGGER, RHP

BA GRADE
45 Risk: High

Born: July 3, 1995. **B-T:** R-R. **Ht.:** 6-2. **Wt.:** 180. **Drafted:** Texas Tech, 2016 (18th round). **Signed by:** Taylor Terrasas (Mariners).

Dugger relieved at both Cisco (Texas) JC and Texas Tech before the Mariners drafted him in the 18th round in 2016 and signed him for $70,000. He was largely just another nondescript minor league reliever until the Mariners shifted him to the rotation midway through 2017. The Marlins acquired him with Nick Neidert and Chris Torres in the trade of Dee Gordon after the 2017 season.

Dugger thrived in a starting role at low Class A Clinton, posting a 1.18 ERA as a starter compared to 3.42 out of the bullpen, and that continued with nine more starts at high Class A Modesto. Dugger comes at hitters with both a four-seam and two-seam fastball. His two-seamer sits 92-93 mph and touches 95 with sink, though he has started relying more on his slightly harder four-seamer. His best secondary is a 76-79 mph curveball that misses bats, and he also mixes in a low- to mid-80s slider and changeup. Dugger is athletic and works quickly, pounding the strike zone using a repeatable three-quarters delivery and a firm, but somewhat violent, cross-body finish.

Dugger's rapid ascent after moving to the rotation makes him an intriguing arm to watch in 2018 when he takes the next step to Double-A Jacksonville.

Year	Club (League)	Class	W	L	ERA	G	GS	CG	SV	IP	H	HR	BB	SO	K/9	WHIP	AVG
2016	Mariners (AZL)	R	0	0	1.04	4	0	0	2	9	6	0	1	9	9.3	0.81	.188
	Tacoma (PCL)	AAA	0	0	6.75	2	0	0	0	4	5	0	0	4	9.0	1.25	.294
	Everett (NWL)	SS	2	1	5.47	6	6	0	0	26	25	5	10	25	8.5	1.33	.250
2017	Clinton (MWL)	LoA	4	1	2.00	22	9	1	2	72	55	4	16	69	8.6	0.99	.206
	Modesto (CAL)	HiA	2	5	3.94	9	9	0	0	46	49	4	16	47	9.3	1.42	.272
Minor League Totals			8	7	3.22	43	24	1	4	157	140	13	43	154	8.8	1.17	.235

24 ISAEL SOTO, OF

BA GRADE
45 Risk: Extreme

Born: Nov. 2, 1996. **B-T:** L-L. **Ht.:** 6-0. **Wt.:** 190. **Signed:** Dominican Republic, 2013. **Signed by:** Albert Gonzalez/Sandy Nin/Domingo Ortega.

The second-highest paid player in the Marlins' 2013 international signing class, Soto signed for $310,000. He missed much of the 2015 season with a torn meniscus in his left knee and then—after hitting .261 in 113 games at low Class A Greensboro in 2016—he missed the entire 2017 season due to a fractured foot suffered during spring training.

The 6-foot Soto has some of the best raw power of any hitter in the Marlins organization, with short but strong arms that help produce above-average bat speed. A lefthanded hitter, Soto hit .262/.336/.434 against righthanders in 2016 but struggled against lefties, hitting .209 in 115 at-bats. If Soto can improve his pitch recognition and his platoon splits, he has the potential to be an above-average right fielder with a strong arm. Soto has never been much of a threat on the basepaths, stealing just four bases from 2014-16.

Soto resumed playing in the Dominican instructional league in 2107 and should be fully healthy for spring training. Assuming all goes well, an early-season assignment to high Class A Jupiter is likely.

Year	Club (League)	Class	AVG	G	AB	R	H	2B	3B	HR	RBI	BB	SO	SB	CS	OBP	SLG
2015	Greensboro (SAL)	LoA	.125	17	64	2	8	1	0	0	1	3	27	0	0	.164	.141
	Marlins (GCL)	R	.346	7	26	3	9	2	1	1	5	5	6	0	1	.438	.615
	Batavia (NYP)	SS	.095	5	21	1	2	0	0	0	0	1	10	0	0	.136	.095
2016	Greensboro (SAL)	LoA	.247	113	401	51	99	24	5	9	38	43	115	3	0	.320	.399
2017	Did not play—Injured																
Minor League Totals			.236	192	695	83	164	36	7	17	67	62	205	4	3	.301	.381

25 PABLO LOPEZ, RHP

BA GRADE
45 Risk: Extreme

Born: March 7, 1996 **B-T:** R-R. **Ht.:** 6-3. **Wt.:** 200. **Signed:** Venezuela, 2012. **Signed by:** Bob Engle/Emilo Carrasquel (Mariners).

Lopez signed as an international free agent with the Mariners in 2012 for $280,000 and was then traded to the Marlins in July 2017, along with Brayan Hernadnez and two others, for righthander David Phelps. Three years before the trade, Lopez had Tommy John surgery, missed the entire 2014 season and pitched just 37 innings in 2015.

Over the last two seasons Lopez has bounced back strong, throwing nearly 230 innings with an ERA of 3.41. He is not an overpowering pitcher, though his low-90s fastball can touch 95 mph and features heavy sink. Neither Lopez's slider nor changeup grade out as much more than average, though his plus command helps all three of his pitches play up. In 2017, he walked just 20 batters in more than 145 innings—good for a walk rate of 1.2 per nine innings. That would have led the Florida State League had he pitched enough innings to qualify.

Lopez will turn 22 in March and will likely be headed for Double-A Jacksonville. He needs either his slider or changeup to take a step forward if he wants to continue to succeed at the upper levels and reach his ceiling as a back-of-the-rotation starter thanks to plus command and strong competitive makeup.

Year	Club (League)	Class	W	L	ERA	G	GS	CG	SV	IP	H	HR	BB	SO	K/9	WHIP	AVG
2015	Mariners (AZL)	R	2	1	3.13	12	3	0	0	37	37	1	6	26	6.3	1.15	.248
2016	Clinton (MWL)	LoA	7	1	2.13	17	13	0	0	84	68	4	9	56	6.0	0.91	.219
2017	Modesto (CAL)	HiA	5	8	4.99	19	18	0	0	101	113	6	14	90	8.0	1.26	.279
	Jupiter (FSL)	HiA	0	3	2.18	8	6	0	0	45	42	0	7	32	6.4	1.08	.252
Minor League Totals			21	14	3.20	68	52	0	0	335	311	13	47	242	6.5	1.07	.244

26 JORDAN HOLLOWAY, RHP

BA GRADE
45 Risk: Extreme

Born: June 13, 1996. **B-T:** R-R. **Ht.:** 6-4. **Wt.:** 190. **Drafted:** HS—Arvada, Colo., 2014 (20th round). **Signed by:** Scott Stanley.

Holloway was a raw but projectable Colorado high school righthander in 2014 whom the Marlins took in the 20th round and signed to an over-slot deal. He signed for $400,000 but has since had an up-and-down career, despite having some of the best stuff in the organization.

Holloway had Tommy John surgery in June 2017, putting his 2018 season in doubt. When healthy, Holloway's electric stuff is highlighted by an upper-90s fastball that can touch 98 mph along with a hammer curveball that can flash plus. Holloway's changeup is still a work in progress, but it shows the velocity difference and movement necessary to be a potential above-average pitch down the road. Though he made just 11 starts in 2017, Holloway showed slightly improved command, but that is still the area of his game that needs the most polish.

At best, Holloway will make his mound return late in 2018, but even then his workload should be in a controlled environment. With that, Holloway's 2019 season becomes crucial to his development.

Year	Club (League)	Class	W	L	ERA	G	GS	CG	SV	IP	H	HR	BB	SO	K/9	WHIP	AVG
2015	Greensboro (SAL)	LoA	0	1	7.00	2	2	0	0	9	8	0	6	4	4.0	1.56	.250
	Batavia (NYP)	SS	5	6	2.91	14	14	0	0	68	60	0	36	40	5.3	1.41	.234
2016	Greensboro (SAL)	LoA	2	4	6.16	8	8	0	0	31	31	8	15	24	7.0	1.50	.261
	Batavia (NYP)	SS	0	3	6.23	5	5	0	0	17	21	0	13	17	8.8	1.96	.280
2017	Greensboro (SAL)	LoA	1	2	5.22	11	11	0	0	50	41	10	22	50	9.0	1.26	.220
Minor League Totals			9	19	4.91	50	46	0	0	202	199	18	100	143	6.4	1.48	.256

27 THOMAS JONES, OF

BA GRADE
45 Risk: Extreme

Born: Dec. 9, 1997. **B-T:** R-R. **Ht.:** 6-4. **Wt.:** 195. **Drafted:** HS—Laurens, S.C., 2016 (2nd round). **Signed by:** Blake Newsome.

After drawing interest from high-profile football programs such as Clemson, Notre Dame and South Carolina as a dual-sport star at Laurens (S.C.) High, Jones eventually committed to Vanderbilt's baseball program before the Marlins snagged him with the 84th overall pick in 2016. Jones signed with the Marlins for $1 million, but he hit just .181/.315/.282 in 68 games at short-season Batavia in 2017.

Jones is a tantalizing athlete with five-tool potential, but he remains very raw. It seems obvious that he is going to be a slow burner, especially at the plate where he struggles to make consistent contact. The bat speed is there, however. So is Jones' foot speed, which makes him a threat on the basepaths and gives him plus range in center field. He also has an above-average arm, which could also be said for his power potential if he ever hits enough to tap into the raw strength he possesses. Jones turned 20 in December, so there is still plenty of time for him to reach his potential.

Jones could see his first action in full-season ball at low Class A Greensboro in 2018, but it would not be surprising to see him receive more seasoning in extended spring training and short-season ball.

Year	Club (League)	Class	AVG	G	AB	R	H	2B	3B	HR	RBI	BB	SO	SB	CS	OBP	SLG
2016	Marlins (GCL)	R	.234	19	64	11	15	3	1	0	6	11	20	6	2	.380	.313
2017	Batavia (NYP)	SS	.181	68	238	31	43	10	4	2	21	34	94	7	6	.315	.282
Minor League Totals			.192	87	302	42	58	13	5	2	27	45	114	13	8	.329	.288

28 JEFF BRIGHAM, RHP

BA GRADE
45 Risk: Extreme

Born: Feb. 16, 1992. **B-T:** R-R. **Ht.:** 6-0. **Wt.:** 200. **Drafted:** Washington, 2014 (4th round). **Signed by:** Henry Jones (Dodgers).

Brigham was a fourth-round pick by the Dodgers in 2014, only a year after he missed his entire junior season at Washington recovering from Tommy John surgery. Brigham was eventually traded to the Marlins in July 2015, when righthanders Mat Latos and Michael Morse were sent to the Dodgers for Brigham and three other players.

The 6-foot Brigham struggled with lingering injuries in 2017, when he spent most of the season on the disabled list and made just 11 starts at high Class A Jupiter.

Brigham's best pitch is a mid- to upper-90s fastball that can touch 98 mph and also shows late armside run. He also uses a low-80s slider that flashes plus potential and shows feel for a changeup that's a clear third pitch. Brigham's control is just average, limiting his ceiling as a starter and making a switch to a relief role possible. Proving he can stay healthy will be vital for Brigham, who has experienced a shoulder injury, oblique strain and other relatively minor injuries throughout the last year.

Brigham will be 26 in 2018 and should begin the year at Double-A Jacksonville. If healthy, he could be pushed quickly and might make an early impact for the Marlins sooner rather than later.

Year	Club (League)	Class	W	L	ERA	G	GS	CG	SV	IP	H	HR	BB	SO	K/9	WHIP	AVG
2015	Great Lakes (MWL)	LoA	2	0	1.29	2	0	0	0	7	3	0	2	11	14.1	0.71	.125
	R. Cucamonga (CAL)	HiA	4	5	5.96	17	14	0	0	68	78	8	36	64	8.5	1.68	.286
	Jupiter (FSL)	HiA	2	2	1.87	6	5	0	0	34	34	0	9	22	5.9	1.28	.276
2016	Jupiter (FSL)	HiA	7	8	4.04	27	23	0	1	123	115	6	47	112	8.2	1.32	.246
2017	Jupiter (FSL)	HiA	4	2	2.90	11	11	0	0	59	49	2	20	53	8.1	1.17	.226
Minor League Totals			19	20	3.90	74	63	0	1	323	311	18	130	295	8.2	1.37	.254

29 YNMANOL MARINEZ, SS

BA GRADE 45 Risk: Extreme

Born: April 12, 2001. **B-T:** R-R. **Ht.:** 6-0. **Wt.:** 170. **Signed:** Dominican Republic, 2017. **Signed by:** Albert Gonzalez/Sandy Nin.

Marinez was the Marlins' biggest signee of the 2017 international free agent class. The native of the Dominican Republic signed with the club for $1.2 million.

At 6 feet and 170 pounds, Marinez isn't the biggest, but he has a thick lower half that could necessitate a move to third base in the future. He has soft hands and solid range that would play at either shortstop or third base. Though he doesn't have a quick first step, Marinez has a plus arm that gives him value as an above-average defender. He displays a compact swing and could develop above-average power as he matures, but his approach at the plate and ability to recognize offspeed pitches needs work. He projects as an average runner, at best.

Marinez will make his U.S. debut in 2018 in the Rookie-level Gulf Coast League.

Year	Club (League)	Class	AVG	G	AB	R	H	2B	3B	HR	RBI	BB	SO	SB	CS	OBP	SLG
2017	Did not play—Signed 2018 contract																

30 JOSE DEVERS, SS

BA GRADE 45 Risk: Extreme

Born: Dec. 7, 1999. **B-T:** L-R. **Ht.:** 6-0. **Wt.:** 160. **Signed:** Dominican Republic, 2016. **Signed by:** Juan Rosario (Yankees).

A talented prospect who signed with the Yankees out of the Dominican Republic for $250,000 in 2016, Devers is a much different prospect than his cousin, Red Sox third baseman Rafael Devers. Having just turned 18, Devers is a defense-first shortstop who was traded from the Yankees to the Marlins as the second of two prospects in the Giancarlo Stanton trade.

Before the trade, Devers ended his 2017 season in the Rookie-level Gulf Coast League, where he was ranked as the league's No. 19 prospect. He stood out for his defensive skills and athleticism. A wiry shortstop at 6 feet, 160 pounds, Devers showed above-average speed, good hands and good footwork while also showing an improved arm action and arm strength as a result of added strength. Devers' glove is clearly ahead of his bat, though he did hold his own against older competition in the GCL and flashed a sound swing and contact skills. Devers may never display above-average power, though that should improve as he continues to add strength.

Devers should see time at short-season Batavia in 2018.

Year	Club (League)	Class	AVG	G	AB	R	H	2B	3B	HR	RBI	BB	SO	SB	CS	OBP	SLG
2017	Yankees (DSL)	R	.239	11	46	4	11	2	1	0	7	0	16	1	0	.255	.326
	Yankees (GCL)	R	.246	42	138	17	34	7	2	1	9	18	21	15	3	.359	.348
Minor League Totals			.245	53	184	21	45	9	3	1	16	18	37	16	3	.336	.342

Milwaukee Brewers

BY TOM HAUDRICOURT

If the results on the field at the big league level meant anything in 2017, the Brewers' large-scale rebuilding process was ahead of schedule.

Not projected to be a contender, the Brewers led the National League Central for much of the first half before fading and finishing one game out of the second wild card with an 86-76 record, an improvement of 13 games from the previous season. Considering the relative inexperience of the club—there were 17 players making the minimum salary or thereabouts at the start of the season—it was an impressive showing.

Much of the credit went to general manager David Stearns for the offseason moves he made,  and to manager Craig Counsell for the positive culture he fostered, as well as his "no limits" challenge to his players in the spring. Several players took big steps forward from the previous season and put their names in the keeper category, preventing the Brewers from force-feeding prospects to the majors before they were ready.

Stearns continued his theme of "acquiring, developing and retaining young, controllable talent," both at the big league level and in the farm system. By acquiring third baseman Travis Shaw in a trade with Boston and signing first baseman Eric Thames after three years in Korea, Stearns secured those positions for the present and balanced his lineup with a pair of lefthanded power hitters.

The Brewers also formed a core of reliable starting pitchers to anchor their rotation in Zach Davies, Chase Anderson and Jimmy Nelson, though a September shoulder injury to Nelson required surgery that will sideline him at the outset of 2018. Righthander Brandon Woodruff, who rocketed into the upper echelon of a strengthened farm system, got his feet wet in the majors, in the heat of the playoff race, and has a good chance to open 2018 in the rotation.

The decision-makers were open-minded when it came to lefthander Josh Hader, generally considered their top starting prospect. Hader was promoted to the majors in June and placed in the bullpen, where he thrived and was a factor in many big victories down the stretch. Stearns said that he and Counsell would decide over the winter if Hader will remain in that role, where he can affect more games, or return to the rotation.

The Brewers have an interesting decision to make with their top prospect, center fielder Lewis Brinson, who spent a couple of short stints in the majors but was unavailable as a September call-up after suffering a hamstring strain at Triple-A Colorado Springs. With left fielder Ryan Braun having three more years on his contract and

Rookie lefthander Josh Hader morphed into a valuable bullpen arm for the 2017 Brewers.

PROJECTED 2021 LINEUP

Catcher	Manny Pina (34)
First Base	Travis Shaw (31)
Second Base	Keston Hiura (24)
Third Base	Lucas Erceg (26)
Shortstop	Orlando Arcia (26)
Left Field	Monte Harrison (25)
Center Field	Lewis Brinson (27)
Right Field	Domingo Santana (28)
No. 1 Starter	Brandon Woodruff (28)
No. 2 Starter	Corbin Burnes (26)
No. 3 Starter	Luis Ortiz (25)
No. 4 Starter	Zach Davies (28)
No. 5 Starter	Freddy Peralta (25)
Closer	Josh Hader (27)

Domingo Santana making huge strides in right field, center is the only outfield spot in question.

Keon Broxton was a 20-20 performer, but also a swing-and-miss hitter prone to long slumps. With Brinson out of the picture in September, another outfield prospect, Brett Phillips, filled the void nicely, and threw his hat into the ring for 2018.

The Brewers showed a willingness to think out of the box with 2017 first-round draft pick Keston Hiura, an accomplished hitter at UC Irvine who didn't play in the field in 2017 due to an elbow issue. The Brewers took Hiura anyway, and he got past that problem while showing signs of being an offensive prodigy in his pro debut by hitting .371/.422/.611 in his pro debut.

DEPTH CHART

MILWAUKEE BREWERS

TOP 2018 ROOKIE: Brandon Woodruff, RHP. He got his feet wet in the final weeks of 2017; now he'll get every chance in the spring to make the rotation.

BREAKOUT PROSPECT: Freddy Peralta, RHP. If he makes as big a leap in 2018 as he did last year, he'll be knocking on the door.

SLEEPER: Nate Orf, 2B/UTIL. His versatility makes him a natural fit for a National League club.

SOURCE OF TOP 30 TALENT

Homegrown	17	Acquired	13
College	8	Trade	12
Junior college	0	Rule 5 draft	0
High school	9	Independent league	0
Nondrafted free agent	0	Free agent/waivers	1
International	0		

LF
- Corey Ray (10)
- Troy Stokes
- Tyrone Taylor
- Ryan Aguilar
- Brandon Diaz

CF
- Lewis Brinson (1)
- Brett Phillips (7)
- Trent Grisham (15)
- Kyle Wren
- Johnny Davis

RF
- Monte Harrison (5)
- Tristen Lutz (11)
- Clint Coulter
- Demi Orimoloye
- Carlos Belonis

3B
- Lucas Erceg (8)
- Chad McClanahan (30)
- Gilbert Lara
- Dallas Carroll
- Kenny Corey

SS
- Mauricio Dubon (13)
- Antonio Pinero (29)
- Angel Ortega
- Luis Aviles
- Devon Hairston

2B
- Keston Hiura (4)
- Isan Diaz (9)
- Nate Orf
- Blake Allemand
- Javier Betancourt

1B
- Jake Gatewood (14)
- Dustin DeMuth
- Weston Wilson
- Ronnie Gideon

C
- K.J. Harrison (16)
- Mario Feliciano (20)
- Jacob Nottingham (23)
- Payton Henry (28)
- Tyler Heineman
- Dustin Houle

LHP

LHSP	LHRP
Kodi Medeiros (21)	Tyler Webb
Nathan Kirby (27)	Wei-Chung Wang
Brendan Murphy	Nick Ramirez
Drake Owenby	Quintin Torres-Costa
Cam Roegner	
Wilfred Salaman	

RHP

RHSP	RHRP
Brandon Woodruff (2)	Jorge Lopez
Corbin Burnes (3)	Taylor Williams
Luis Ortiz (6)	Tristan Archer
Freddy Peralta (12)	Jon Perrin
Phil Bickford (17)	Matt Ramsey
Cody Ponce (18)	Nate Griep
Josh Pennington (19)	
Marcos Diplan (22)	
Caden Lemons (24)	
Trey Supak (25)	
Carlos Herrera (26)	
Adrian Houser	
Aaron Wilkerson	
Bubba Derby	
Jordan Yamamoto	

DRAFT ANALYSIS

2017

BEST PURE HITTER: 2B Keston Hiura (1) has a long track record for hitting. He stays inside the ball, has a short, repeatable swing and controls the strike zone. That helped him lead Division I in batting (.442) and on-base percentage (.567). He destroyed pro pitching in his debut as well, batting .371.

BEST POWER: OF Tristen Lutz (1.5) had some of the best raw power in the draft class, thanks to his bat speed, present strength and leverage in his 6-foot-3, 210-pound frame. He then raked in his debut between two Rookie-level stops with nine home runs in 161 at-bats. Hiura doesn't hit them as far, but he hits them often, with power to right-center field.

FASTEST RUNNER: 3B Nick Egnatuk (5) gets the edge over Lutz here, as both are above-average runners. Lutz can play center field now but may outgrow the position and move to a corner.

BEST DEFENSIVE PLAYER: SS Devin Hairston (6) isn't twitchy, but he has excellent body control and hands to stick in the middle infield. His quick release mitigates his fringy arm strength, but he still may have to slide to second base long term if he's a regular.

BEST ATHLETE: Lutz is explosive, with tools across the board. He has a muscular frame that evokes a young Matt Holliday, runs and throws well, and has a chance to be average or better in all five tools.

BEST FASTBALL: RHP Caden Lemons (2) started to grown into his lanky 6-foot-6, 175-pound frame this spring, leaping up draft boards as his fastball reached 96 mph. He's raw but has 100 mph potential.

BEST SECONDARY PITCH: Another projectable, tall prep pick, LHP Karlos Morales (25) will need to add power but has the shape and spin on his

TOP DRAFT PICKS OF THE DECADE

Year	Player, Pos.	2017 Org
2008	Brett Lawrie, 3B	Did not play
2009	Eric Arnett, RHP	Did not play
2010	*Dylan Covey, RHP	White Sox
2011	Taylor Jungmann, RHP	Brewers
2012	Clint Coulter, C	Brewers
2013	Devin Williams, RHP (2nd round)	Brewers
2014	Kodi Medeiros, LHP	Brewers
2015	Trent Clark, OF	Brewers
2016	Corey Ray, OF	Brewers
2017	Keston Hiura, 2B	Brewers

*Did not sign.

curveball that could make it a weapon.

BEST PRO DEBUT: Hiura hit .371/.422/.611 overall in 167 at-bats, including hitting safely in 19 of his first 20 games at low Class A Wisconsin.

MOST INTRIGUING BACKGROUND: OF L.G. Castillo (17) was a three-sport athlete in high school, helping Lancaster (N.Y.) High to its first state football title since 1999. OF Je'Von Carrier-Ward (12) is the nephew of Mark Carrier, a three-time Pro Bowl NFL safety.

CLOSEST TO THE MAJORS: Hiura has to find a defensive home and is trying second base after an elbow injury relegated him to DH all spring and most of the summer. His bat will be big league ready soon.

BEST LATE-ROUND PICK: The Brewers signed Carrier-Ward and RHP Max Lazar (11) for $475,000 apiece, with high hopes for both. While raw, Castillo will challenge both.

THE ONE WHO GOT AWAY: SS Noah Campbell (19), the fastest player Milwaukee drafted, took his 70-grade speed to South Carolina, joining a recruiting class with athletic OF Kyle Jacobson (33).

— JOHN MANUEL

2016

It was a tough first full pro season for much of the class, including OF Corey Ray (1) and 3B Lucas Erceg (2), though both still have big raw tools. RHP Corbin Burnes (4), however, hit the ground running and ranks as one of the system's best arms.

GRADE: B

2015

RHP Cody Ponce (2) bounced back well after being limited by injury in 2016. LHP Nathan Kirby (1s), however, missed another season with elbow trouble. OFs Trent Grisham (1) and Demi Orimoloye (4) are still trying to get on track in pro ball.

GRADE: C

2014

The Brewers went for upside at the top of the draft and OF Monte Harrison (2) is beginning to deliver on his promise. RHP Brandon Woodruff (11) has risen to become the system's top arm and joined the Brewers' rotation down the stretch.

GRADE: B

1 LEWIS BRINSON, OF

Born: May 8, 1994. **B-T:** R-R. **Ht.:** 6-4. **Wt.:** 205.
Drafted: HS—Coral Springs, Fla., 2012 (1st round).
Signed by: Frankie Thon (Rangers).

MIKE JANES

Brinson had a disjointed 2017 season, beginning with a dislocation of his left pinkie finger on Opening Day at Triple-A Colorado Springs. He had two short stints with the Brewers, getting his first shot at the big leagues, but he didn't hit much and went back down. Slated for a September callup, he suffered a significant hamstring strain in August and was done for the season. Brinson performed for the Sky Sox when healthy (.962 OPS) and the Brewers designated him as the organization's player of the year despite seeing action in just 76 games. The Athletics tried to pry him away during trade negotiations for Sonny Gray, but the Brewers backed off rather than part with Brinson.

Brinson provides the rare combination of power and speed that every team seeks. He showed maturation as a hitter in 2017 by improving his plate discipline (.400 on-base percentage), with a better walk rate than the previous season and a lower strikeout rate. Part of that maturation was learning to lay off breaking balls off the plate and continuing to use the entire field, an improvement that began the previous year. While playing mostly in center field at Colorado Springs but also seeing some action in the corners, he worked on getting better jumps on the ball and taking better routes. Brinson has enough speed to play center in the majors but also has the arm and power to be a right fielder. Brinson hit barely .100 during his two stints with Milwaukee but didn't see regular action and pressed when he got a chance to play. He showed some pop with a couple of home runs, and his skill set bodes well once he gets a chance to be a regular at the top level. He has an even-keeled personality and a confident, but not cocky, approach to the game.

Brinson turns 24 in 2018 but will have to hit his way into the outfield picture. Left fielder Ryan Braun still has three years remaining on his contract and 25-year-old right fielder Domingo Santana is fresh off a breakthrough season. That leaves center field, where Keon Broxton and Brett Phillips have a foot in the door.

BA GRADE	SCOUTING GRADES
60 Risk: Medium	HIT: 55. POW: 60. SPD: 60. FLD: 55. ARM: 60.

Projected future grades on 20-80 scouting scale

TOP PROSPECTS OF THE DECADE

Year	Player, Pos.	2017 Org
2008	Matt LaPorta, OF	Did not play
2009	Alcides Escobar, SS	Royals
2010	Alcides Escobar, SS	Royals
2011	Jake Odorizzi, RHP	Rays
2012	Willy Peralta, RHP	Brewers
2013	Willy Peralta, RHP	Brewers
2014	Jimmy Nelson, RHP	Brewers
2015	Tyrone Taylor, OF	Brewers
2016	Orlando Arcia, SS	Brewers
2017	Lewis Brinson, OF	Brewers

BEST TOOLS

Best Hitter for Average	Keston Hiura
Best Power Hitter	Monte Harrison
Best Strike-Zone Discipline	Trent Clark
Fastest Baserunner	Johnny Davis
Best Athlete	Monte Harrison
Best Fastball	Josh Pennington
Best Curveball	Corbin Burnes
Best Slider	Brandon Woodruff
Best Changeup	Trey Supak
Best Control	Corbin Burnes
Best Defensive Catcher	Dustin Houle
Best Defensive Infielder	Antonio Pinero
Best Infield Arm	Lucas Erceg
Best Defensive Outfielder	Lewis Brinson
Best Outfield Arm	Brett Phillips

Year	Club (League)	Class	AVG	G	AB	R	H	2B	3B	HR	RBI	BB	SO	SB	CS	OBP	SLG
2015	High Desert (CAL)	HiA	.337	64	258	51	87	22	7	13	42	31	64	13	6	.416	.628
	Frisco (TL)	AA	.291	28	110	14	32	8	1	6	23	6	28	2	1	.328	.545
	Round Rock (PCL)	AAA	.433	8	30	9	13	1	0	1	4	7	6	3	0	.541	.567
2016	Rangers (AZL)	R	.231	4	13	3	3	1	0	0	1	2	2	2	0	.333	.308
	Frisco (TL)	AA	.237	77	304	46	72	14	6	11	40	17	64	11	4	.280	.431
	Colo. Springs (PCL)	AAA	.382	23	89	14	34	9	0	4	20	2	21	4	2	.387	.618
2017	Milwaukee (NL)	MAJ	.106	21	47	2	5	0	1	2	3	7	17	1	0	.236	.277
	Colo. Springs (PCL)	AAA	.331	76	299	66	99	22	4	13	48	32	62	11	5	.400	.562
Major League Totals			.106	21	47	2	5	0	1	2	3	7	17	1	0	.236	.277
Minor League Totals			.287	545	2134	374	613	133	29	89	322	199	608	96	36	.353	.502

2 BRANDON WOODRUFF, RHP

Born: Feb. 10, 1993. **B-T:** L-R. **Ht.:** 6-2. **Wt.:** 225. **Drafted:** Mississippi State, 2014 (11th round). **Signed by:** Scott Nichols.

Woodruff led the minors with 173 strikeouts in a breakthrough 2016 season, then reached the majors a year later. He pitched effectively at Triple-A Colorado Springs in 2017 to earn a mid-June callup, but a hamstring strain delayed his debut by another six weeks. He started hot but recorded a 4.81 ERA in eight starts overall.

When Woodruff is on top of his game, he pounds hard sinkers at hitters in the 93-95 mph range with good movement. He once had issues with tempo and rhythm but worked those out and his command improved markedly. Woodruff has an above-average slider he throws in the mid-80s and also mixes in an average changeup. He needs to work more on locating his changeup down in the zone, because he gets hit when he leaves the pitch up. A bulldog on the mound, he pitches with authority and confidence.

BA GRADE

55 Risk: Medium

FB: 55. SL: 55. CHG: 50. CTL: 60.

Woodruff did not change his game plan during a tough Pacific Coast League assignment. Thus the Brewers were confident starting him in the final weeks of 2017 while battling for a playoff spot. He will challenge for a big league rotation spot in 2018 and has No. 3 starter upside.

Year	Club (League)	Class	W	L	ERA	G	GS	CG	SV	IP	H	HR	BB	SO	K/9	WHIP	AVG
2015	Brevard County (FSL)	HiA	4	7	3.45	21	19	0	0	110	112	2	33	71	5.8	1.32	.270
2016	Brevard County (FSL)	HiA	4	1	1.83	8	8	0	0	44	33	2	10	49	9.9	0.97	.205
	Biloxi (SL)	AA	10	8	3.01	20	20	1	0	114	88	4	30	124	9.8	1.04	.211
2017	Brewers (AZL)	R	0	0	4.50	1	1	0	0	2	2	0	1	1	4.5	1.50	.250
	Colo. Springs (PCL)	AAA	6	5	4.30	16	16	0	0	75	78	8	25	70	8.4	1.37	.266
	Milwaukee (NL)	MAJ	2	3	4.81	8	8	0	0	43	43	5	14	32	6.7	1.33	.259
Major League Totals			2	3	4.81	8	8	0	0	43	43	5	14	32	6.7	1.33	.259
Minor League Totals			25	23	3.29	80	72	1	0	392	361	18	115	352	8.1	1.22	.244

3 CORBIN BURNES, RHP

Born: Oct. 22 1994. **B-T:** R-R. **Ht.:** 6-3. **Wt.:** 205. **Drafted:** St. Mary's, 2016 (4th round). **Signed by:** Joe Graham

No prospect made a bigger leap in the organization in 2017 than Burnes, who ranked second in the minors with a 1.67 ERA while working at high Class A Carolina and Double-A Biloxi. His meteoric rise left Burnes closer to the big leagues than the Brewers envisioned when making him a fourth-round pick in 2016.

Burnes pounds the strike zone with quality stuff and growing confidence. He modified his delivery in 2017 with the help of minor league pitching coordinator Rick Tomlin and Carolina pitching coach Dave Chavarria to square up to the plate and allow his lower half to drive forward. At Biloxi, he even switched to a traditional windup instead of a modified stretch. With quick arm action, Burnes throws a 92-95 mph fastball with natural cut. He has three secondary pitches—a 77-80 mph curveball, a mid-80s slider and a high-80s split changeup—none of which

BA GRADE

55 Risk: Medium

FB: 55. CB: 55. SL: 50. CHG: 50. CTL: 55.

grade much above average, but he commands all three. His curveball is his best secondary offering, but his slider is effective as well. Burnes maintains his stuff deep into starts with above-average control and can also be a groundball machine.

With an athletic, repeatable delivery and an aggressive demeanor, Burnes could help the Brewers in 2018 and has a No. 3 or 4 starter ceiling. His next test will be at hitter-friendly Triple-A Colorado Springs.

Year	Club (League)	Class	W	L	ERA	G	GS	CG	SV	IP	H	HR	BB	SO	K/9	WHIP	AVG
2016	Brewers (AZL)	R	0	0	1.29	3	1	0	0	7	3	0	2	10	12.9	0.71	.125
	Wisconsin (MWL)	LoA	3	0	2.20	9	5	0	0	29	20	1	16	31	9.7	1.26	.200
2017	Carolina (CAR)	HiA	5	0	1.05	10	10	0	0	60	37	1	16	56	8.4	0.88	.181
	Biloxi (SL)	AA	3	3	2.10	16	16	1	0	86	66	2	20	84	8.8	1.00	.212
Minor League Totals			11	3	1.74	38	32	1	0	181	126	4	54	181	9.0	0.99	.197

4 KESTON HIURA, 2B

Born: Aug. 2, 1996. **B-T:** R-R. **Ht.:** 5-11. **Wt.:** 190. **Drafted:** UC Irvine, 2017 (1st round). **Signed by:** Wynn Pelzer.

The Brewers selected Hiura ninth overall in 2017 despite the fact he didn't play an inning in the field as a college junior. A partial tear in his right elbow limited him to DH. One of the most productive college hitters of recent memory, he led Division I with a .442 average and signed for a below-slot $4 million. Hiura completed a throwing program while in the Rookie-level Arizona League, then hit .333 at low Class A Wisconsin following a promotion.

Hiura has a short, powerful stroke with tremendous bat speed and a good feel for the zone. He is explosive, strong hands with raw power that projects to be above-average. He will hit for average and show power to all fields. He is an average runner albeit not a basestealer. He played the outfield and second base in college, and some evaluators think he is destined for left field. The Brewers plan to give Hiura every chance to play second base, and barring any future elbow issues, he has the arm strength to play the position.

Hiura was throwing without problems by instructional league, and his advanced hitting ability should put him on the fast track to Milwaukee. He may begin 2018 at high Class A Carolina, but has a chance to go straight to Double-A.

BA GRADE
60 Risk: High
HIT: 60. POW: 55.
SPD: 45. FLD: 50.
ARM: 45.

Year	Club (League)	Class	AVG	G	AB	R	H	2B	3B	HR	RBI	BB	SO	SB	CS	OBP	SLG
2017	Brewers (AZL)	R	.435	15	62	18	27	3	5	4	18	6	13	0	2	.500	.839
	Wisconsin (MWL)	LoA	.333	27	105	14	35	11	2	0	15	7	24	2	0	.374	.476
Minor League Totals			.371	42	167	32	62	14	7	4	33	13	37	2	2	.422	.611

5 MONTE HARRISON, OF

Born: Aug. 10, 1995. **B-T:** R-R. **Ht.:** 6-3. **Wt.:** 220. **Drafted:** HS—Lee's Summit., Mo., 2014 (2nd round). **Signed by:** Drew Harrison.

The Brewers found out what Harrison could do if only he stayed healthy. In a breakthrough 2017 he reached high Class A Carolina, played in 122 games and demonstrated his power-speed potential with 21 home runs and 27 stolen bases. He had missed time in 2015 with a gruesome ankle injury and in 2016 with a broken left hamate. He appears to be back on track after having his mental toughness tested multiple times.

A strong, powerful athlete who could have played college football, Harrison has excellent bat speed with budding power. He sometimes gets long with his swing, resulting in big strikeout numbers, but overall has a good approach and is getting better at pitch recognition. Harrison has plus speed, making him a basestealing threat and also an above-average outfielder. He can handle center field but probably projects as a right fielder because of his physical frame. After missing so much time early in his career, Harrison merely needs at-bats to realize his impact potential.

Harrison appears destined for Double-A Biloxi in 2018. One of the more impressive athletes in the system, he requires only maturity and repetitions.

BA GRADE
60 Risk: V. High
HIT: 50. POW: 55.
SPD: 60. FLD: 55.
ARM: 60.

Year	Club (League)	Class	AVG	G	AB	R	H	2B	3B	HR	RBI	BB	SO	SB	CS	OBP	SLG
2015	Wisconsin (MWL)	LoA	.148	46	162	18	24	6	2	2	11	14	77	6	4	.246	.247
	Helena (PIO)	R	.299	28	97	20	29	4	2	3	13	14	23	14	2	.410	.474
2016	Brewers (AZL)	R	.211	5	19	4	4	1	1	0	1	4	4	0	0	.375	.368
	Wisconsin (MWL)	LoA	.221	75	267	34	59	11	1	6	37	20	97	8	3	.294	.337
2017	Wisconsin (MWL)	LoA	.265	63	223	32	59	12	1	11	32	29	70	10	3	.359	.475
	Carolina (CAR)	HiA	.278	59	230	41	64	16	1	10	35	14	69	16	1	.341	.487
Minor League Totals			.243	326	1178	186	286	57	10	33	149	126	388	86	15	.338	.392

6 LUIS ORTIZ, RHP

Born: Sept. 2, 1995. **B-T:** R-R. **Ht.:** 6-3. **Wt.:** 230. **Drafted:** HS—Sanger, Calif., 2014 (1st round). **Signed by:** Butch Metzger (Rangers)..

After acquiring Ortiz from the Rangers in the 2016 Jonathan Lucroy trade, the Brewers assigned him to Double-A Biloxi at age 21 and he recorded a 1.93 ERA in six starts. Sent back to Biloxi in 2017, he pitched effectively but missed time with a hamstring strain as well as an illness late in the year. Given Ortiz's large, hefty frame, conditioning has been an ongoing focus.

Ortiz's low-80s slider has a tight, late break that makes it look like a fastball initially. He throws his fastball in the mid-90s and maintains his velocity throughout his outings, a good sign in terms of remaining a starter. Ortiz continues to work on his changeup, an improving pitch that has a chance to be at least average. By working hard on repeating his delivery, he has become a consistent strike-thrower with a high ceiling. Ortiz still makes too many mistakes in the strike zone, so staying healthy to take regular turns is paramount.

If Ortiz proves he has a starter's stamina, he has No. 3 upside and could reach the majors in 2018. The Brewers will wrestle with the decision whether to send him to hitter-happy Triple-A Colorado Springs.

BA GRADE
55 Risk: High
FB: 60. **SL:** 60.
CHG: 50.
CTL: 50.

Year	Club (League)	Class	W	L	ERA	G	GS	CG	SV	IP	H	HR	BB	SO	K/9	WHIP	AVG
2015	Hickory (SAL)	LoA	4	1	1.80	13	13	0	0	50	45	1	9	46	8.3	1.08	.238
2016	High Desert (CAL)	HiA	3	2	2.60	7	6	0	0	28	23	4	6	28	9.1	1.05	.221
	Frisco (TL)	AA	1	4	4.08	9	8	0	1	40	47	3	7	34	7.7	1.36	.296
	Biloxi (SL)	AA	2	2	1.93	6	6	0	0	23	26	2	10	16	6.2	1.54	.280
2017	Biloxi (SL)	AA	4	7	4.01	22	20	1	0	94	79	12	37	79	7.5	1.23	.227
Minor League Totals			15	17	3.07	66	59	1	2	255	236	23	75	222	7.8	1.22	.244

7 BRETT PHILLIPS, OF

Born: May 30, 1994. **B-T:** L-R. **Ht.:** 6-0. **Wt.:** 175. **Drafted:** HS—Seminole, Fla., 2012 (6th round). **Signed by:** John Martin (Astros).

After Phillips had a disappointing season at Double-A Biloxi in 2016, the Brewers could have returned him to that club in 2017. Instead, they challenged him by promoting him to hitter-happy Triple-A Colorado Springs. Phillips met the challenge and earned his first big league callup in early June. By September he was playing regularly.

Phillips' swing tends to get long at times, but he produces hard contact when he keeps it compact. He was too pull-conscious in 2016 but got away from that in 2017. Phillips still strikes out frequently, but he became more consistent at hitting mistakes. He has plus speed, which plays on the bases and in center field. Phillips has a cannon for an arm and unleashed a Statcast-record 104 mph throw to the plate in September. His combination of power, speed and arm strength make him a candidate for regular action.

Beyond his physical tools, Phillips is a high-energy player with a desire to improve. He put himself in the Brewers' outfield picture for 2018, with a floor of fourth outfielder and ceiling as a regular contributor with room for growth.

BA GRADE
50 Risk: Medium
HIT: 50. **POW:** 50.
SPD: 60. **FLD:** 60.
ARM: 80.

Year	Club (League)	Class	AVG	G	AB	R	H	2B	3B	HR	RBI	BB	SO	SB	CS	OBP	SLG
2015	Lancaster (CAL)	HiA	.320	66	291	68	93	19	7	15	53	22	64	8	6	.379	.588
	Corpus Christi (TL)	AA	.321	31	134	22	43	8	4	1	18	8	26	7	2	.372	.463
	Biloxi (SL)	AA	.250	23	80	14	20	7	3	0	6	14	30	2	1	.361	.413
2016	Biloxi (SL)	AA	.229	124	441	60	101	14	6	16	62	67	154	12	7	.332	.397
2017	Colo. Springs (PCL)	AAA	.305	105	383	79	117	23	10	19	78	45	129	9	1	.377	.567
	Milwaukee (NL)	MAJ	.276	37	87	9	24	3	0	4	12	9	34	5	0	.351	.448
Major League Totals			.276	37	87	9	24	3	0	4	12	9	34	5	0	.351	.448
Minor League Totals			.283	574	2121	369	601	116	51	68	310	254	578	73	40	.363	.482

8 LUCAS ERCEG, 3B

Born: May 1, 1995. **B-T:** L-R. **Ht.:** 6-3. **Wt.:** 200. **Drafted:** Menlo, 2016 (2nd round). **Signed by:** Joe Graham.

The Brewers considered Erceg to be a second-round steal in 2016 after he transferred from California to NAIA Menlo College. He put together a strong first pro season in 2016 with an .894 OPS but struggled for much of 2017 at high Class A Carolina. at times looking too eager at the plate and getting himself out by swinging at bad pitches.

Erceg shows a broad set of tools, but his raw power probably tops the list. He can hit the ball a long way, with tremendous pull power evident when he crushes mistakes. He would benefit greatly by improving his plate discipline and thus his on-base percentage. He runs well for a third baseman, though stolen bases are not a big part of his game. He has good hands and feet at third base and a cannon for an arm (he pitched a little in college). The athletic Erceg has a strong work ethic, with the potential to be a complete player and difference-maker with the bat.

BA GRADE

55 Risk: V. High

HIT: 45. **POW:** 60. **SPD:** 50. **FLD:** 55. **ARM:** 60.

The Brewers have had trouble developing homegrown third basemen, but Erceg has a chance to put an end to that drought. He merely has to learn not to force things and let the game come to him. An assignment to Double-A Biloxi looms in 2018.

Year	Club (League)	Class	AVG	G	AB	R	H	2B	3B	HR	RBI	BB	SO	SB	CS	OBP	SLG
2016	Helena (PIO)	R	.400	26	105	17	42	8	1	2	22	8	16	8	1	.452	.552
	Wisconsin (MWL)	LoA	.281	42	167	17	47	9	3	7	29	12	38	1	3	.328	.497
2017	Carolina (CAR)	HiA	.256	127	496	66	127	33	1	15	81	35	95	2	3	.307	.417
	Colo. Springs (PCL)	AAA	.400	3	10	2	4	2	0	0	2	1	1	0	0	.455	.600
Minor League Totals			.283	198	778	102	220	52	5	24	134	56	150	11	7	.333	.455

9 ISAN DIAZ, 2B/SS

Born: May 27, 1996. **B-T:** L-R. **Ht.:** 5-10. **Wt.:** 185. **Drafted:** HS—Springfield, Mass., 2014 (2nd round supplemental). **Signed by:** Mike Serbalik (Diamondbacks).

The Brewers considered Diaz the key to the five-player trade that sent shortstop Jean Segura to Arizona after the 2015 season. After a big season at low Class A Wisconsin in 2016, Diaz joined high Class A Carolina in 2017 and was unable to repeat that success. His frustrations often showed, resulting in bad body language and failure to run balls out.

Diaz's lefthanded bat is what will carry him. He has plus bat speed and makes hard contact, driving the ball to all fields. He has impressive raw power, but with that comes an elevated strikeout rate. Diaz is aggressive at the plate, sometimes too much so, but also draws walks when being pitched around. He dealt with a broken right hamate for part of the season, which impacted his hitting. He is an average runner but has good instincts and gets decent jumps. The Brewers value versatility

BA GRADE

50 Risk: High

HIT: 45. **POW:** 55. **SPD:** 45. **FLD:** 50. **ARM:** 50.

in their system, so Diaz made 32 starts at shortstop, but his future is at second base, where his range and average arm will play. His hands and feel work well enough to be a good defender there. He remains an advanced hitter for his age and merely must improve his plate discipline and find an even keel on the field.

Diaz's ceiling as a power-hitting second baseman should carry him to Double-A Biloxi in 2018. At age 22, he has plenty of time to polish his rough edges.

Year	Club (League)	Class	AVG	G	AB	R	H	2B	3B	HR	RBI	BB	SO	SB	CS	OBP	SLG
2015	Missoula (PIO)	R	.360	68	272	58	98	25	6	13	51	34	65	12	7	.436	.640
2016	Wisconsin (MWL)	LoA	.264	135	507	71	134	34	5	20	75	72	148	11	8	.358	.469
2017	Carolina (CAR)	HiA	.222	110	383	59	85	20	0	13	54	62	121	9	3	.334	.376
Minor League Totals			.261	362	1344	210	351	86	16	49	201	193	390	38	23	.357	.458

10 COREY RAY, OF

Born: Sept. 22, 1994. **B-T:** L-L. **Ht.:** 5-11. **Wt.:** 185. **Drafted:** Louisville, 2016 (1st round).. **Signed by:** Jeff Simpson

BA GRADE
50 Risk: High
HIT: 40. POW: 50.
SPD: 60. FLD: 55.
ARM: 50.

When the Brewers tabbed Ray with the fifth overall pick in 2016 and signed him for a franchise-record $4.125 million, they assumed he would rise quickly through the system as an advanced college hitter. Instead he struggled badly at the plate at high Class A Carolina in 2017, looking nothing like the hitter he was at Louisville. He got a delayed start in 2017 after being held back in spring training to assure he was fully recovered from minor knee surgery.

Ray looked completely out of sorts for much of the season, showing signs of frustration. He swung at breaking balls off the plate, got jammed by inside pitches and generally did not make pitchers throw strikes. He had huge holes in his swing, displaying little of the bat speed and budding power he flashed in college. Ray also showed too much head movement at times and will need major mechanical adjustments to get back on track. Ray used his plus speed to chase down balls in center field and showed enough arm to remain there. He is a threat to steal when he reaches base, though he needs to improve his jumps.

The Brewers sent Ray to the Arizona Fall League with the hope of salvaging something from 2017, but he struggled badly there too. He might have to repeat the Carolina League to reestablish his plate discipline and hitting setup.

Year	Club (League)	Class	AVG	G	AB	R	H	2B	3B	HR	RBI	BB	SO	SB	CS	OBP	SLG
2016	Brevard County (FSL)	HiA	.247	57	231	24	57	13	2	5	17	20	54	9	5	.307	.385
	Wisconsin (MWL)	LoA	.083	3	12	2	1	0	0	0	0	3	4	1	1	.313	.083
2017	Carolina (CAR)	HiA	.241	112	449	56	108	30	4	7	48	48	156	24	10	.313	.372
Minor League Totals			.240	172	692	82	166	43	6	12	65	71	214	34	16	.311	.371

11 TRISTEN LUTZ, OF

Born: Aug. 22, 1998. **B-T:** R-R. **Ht.:** 6-3. **Wt.:** 210. **Drafted:** HS—Arlington, Texas, 2017 (1st round supplemental). **Signed by:** K.J. Hendricks.

BA GRADE
55 Risk: Extreme

The Brewers weren't going to let Lutz get away after taking him with the 34th pick of the 2017 draft. So with their last remaining bonus money that wouldn't result in losing a future draft pick, they signed him for $2,352,000, nearly $370,000 above the slot value, to lure him away from a commitment to Texas.

Lutz is considered to have a high ceiling as a righthanded power hitter. He has great bat speed and strength, which he immediately put on display by homering twice in his pro debut in the Rookie-level Arizona League. After tearing up that circuit for a few weeks, he was promoted to the Rookie-level Pioneer League, where he continued his offensive assault, with the ball jumping off his bat. With powerful wrists and a good feel for pitches he can handle, the athletic Lutz generates plenty of torque that results in hard contact. He's also an above-average runner, which is why he has handled center field well and been a factor on the bases, showing good instincts in both areas. As he matures and gets even stronger, he'll likely move to right field, where his strong, accurate arm will play. Lutz hits out of a crouch and might get even more leverage if he stands a bit taller in the box.

Beyond his power, Lutz shows natural hitting ability to all fields and recognizes pitches well for a young player. Low Class A Wisconsin awaits in 2018.

Year	Club (League)	Class	AVG	G	AB	R	H	2B	3B	HR	RBI	BB	SO	SB	CS	OBP	SLG
2017	Helena (PIO)	R	.333	24	93	23	31	1	1	6	16	12	21	2	4	.432	.559
	Brewers (AZL)	R	.279	16	68	12	19	4	3	3	11	4	21	1	0	.347	.559
Minor League Totals			.311	40	161	35	50	5	4	9	27	16	42	3	4	.398	.559

12 FREDDY PERALTA, RHP

Born: June 4, 1996. **B-T:** R-R. **Ht.:** 5-11. **Wt.:** 175. **Signed:** Dominican Republic, 2013. **Signed by:** Tim Kissner/Eddy Toledo/Kelvin Dominguez (Mariners).

BA GRADE
50 Risk: High

Acquired from the Mariners in the 2015 trade for Adam Lind, Peralta has long been knocked for being too undersized for a starting pitcher. He hardly let that get in his way in 2017 as he cruised through high Class A Carolina and Double-A Biloxi, posting a combined 2.63 ERA with 169 strikeouts in 120 innings. He led the minors with a .178 opponent average.

Peralta is confident and aggressive on the mound, challenging hitters with a fastball in the low to mid-90s, with good movement and improved command. He has deception with a bit of a crossfire delivery, and hitters have trouble picking up the ball, leading to plenty of swings and misses. Because of his "disappearing fastball," many have compared him with former Brewers starter Mike Fiers, who got the job done without an overpowering fastball because hitters picked up the ball so late. Peralta repeats his delivery well and mixes in a slider to keep opponents off his fastball. He also has an above-average changeup he throws for strikes with deceptive arm speed. Peralta strikes out opponents with seeming ease but still issues too many walks and must improve his control. He displays good mound presence and a feel for pitching, particularly given his youth. He's an intelligent pitcher with good instincts.

Despite concerns about Peralta's size, the Brewers believe he can be a mid-rotation starter because of his stuff and intangibles. He might be challenged with an assignment at Triple-A Colorado Springs.

Year	Club (League)	Class	W	L	ERA	G	GS	CG	SV	IP	H	HR	BB	SO	K/9	WHIP	AVG
2015	Mariners (AZL)	R	2	3	4.11	11	9	0	0	57	52	1	8	67	10.6	1.05	.242
2016	Wisconsin (MWL)	LoA	4	1	2.85	16	8	0	2	60	45	3	24	77	11.6	1.15	.202
	Brevard County (FSL)	HiA	0	3	5.73	8	2	0	0	22	27	4	12	20	8.2	1.77	.321
2017	Carolina (CAR)	HiA	1	3	3.04	12	8	0	0	56	39	6	31	78	12.5	1.24	.189
	Biloxi (SL)	AA	2	5	2.26	13	11	0	1	64	38	2	31	91	12.9	1.08	.167
Minor League Totals			13	24	3.28	85	60	1	3	365	294	19	145	424	10.4	1.20	.218

13 MAURICIO DUBON, SS/2B

BA GRADE

45 Risk: Medium

Born: July 19, 1994. **B-T:** R-R. **Ht.:** 6-0. **Wt.:** 170. **Drafted:** HS—Sacramento, 2013 (26th round). **Signed by:** Demond Smith (Red Sox).

The trade that sent reliever Tyler Thornburg to the Red Sox at the 2016 Winter Meetings should keep giving for years to come. Not only did the Brewers obtain major league third baseman Travis Shaw, they picked up Dubon, righthander Josh Pennington and 18-year-old shortstop Yeison Coca.

Dubon began the 2017 season at Double-A Biloxi and earned a Southern League all-star berth before being promoted to Triple-A Colorado Springs, where he continued to perform well while splitting time at shortstop and second base. The native of Honduras also represented the World Team in the Futures Game. Dubon is an athletic player who displays good instincts at the plate, in the field and on the bases. He has good hands and range in the field, and should be able to play either middle infield position in the majors. He makes solid contact, limits his strikeouts and has more pop than might be expected from his wiry frame. His arm strength, quick hands and feet play well on both sides of the bag. Dubon also has above-average speed, making him a threat to steal. He is a high-energy player and competes every day, showing leadership abilities and maturity on and off the field.

At the very least, Dubon should be able to find a niche as a utility player because of his athleticism and versatility.

Year	Club (League)	Class	AVG	G	AB	R	H	2B	3B	HR	RBI	BB	SO	SB	CS	OBP	SLG
2015	Greenville (SAL)	LoA	.301	58	236	43	71	12	3	4	29	18	34	18	4	.354	.428
	Salem (CAR)	HiA	.274	62	237	27	65	9	0	1	18	23	38	12	3	.343	.325
2016	Salem (CAR)	HiA	.306	62	235	53	72	11	3	0	29	33	25	24	4	.387	.379
	Portland (EL)	AA	.339	62	251	48	85	20	6	6	40	11	36	6	3	.371	.538
2017	Biloxi (SL)	AA	.272	71	268	34	73	14	0	2	24	25	42	31	9	.334	.347
	Colo. Springs (PCL)	AAA	.272	58	224	40	61	15	0	6	33	14	34	7	6	.320	.420
Minor League Totals			.297	459	1760	293	522	92	13	22	211	134	247	111	39	.348	.401

14 JAKE GATEWOOD, 1B/3B

BA GRADE

50 Risk: High

Born: Sept. 25, 1995. **B-T:** R-R. **Ht.:** 6-6. **Wt.:** 215. **Drafted:** HS—Clovis, Calif., 2014 (1st round supplemental). **Signed by:** Dan Huston.

Gatewood was drafted as a shortstop and later moved to third base, but he continued to grow, which ultimately landed him at first base in 2017.

With power being his main offensive tool, Gatewood profiles well at first base and got better in the field with each passing day. The Brewers knew when they signed Gatewood that he would swing-and-miss frequently, and that continued to be the case in his early pro years. But he got contact lenses to improve his vision and made big strides in all areas of his game at high Class A Carolina in 2017, earning Carolina League all-star honors and a promotion to Double-A Biloxi. In taking his biggest leap, Gatewood realized that he has opposite-field power and doesn't need to pull everything. Helped by his improved eyesight, he began chasing less and made pitchers come to him more often, improving his plate discipline and on-base percentage. Gatewood has good bat speed and is making more contact without sacrificing power. With good hands, range and footwork going back to his days at shortstop, he is an athletic, sure-handed first baseman.

Officially back on track and having reaffirmed his prospect status, Gatewood has a chance to move upward in a system with no real roadblocks at first base ahead of him.

Year	Club (League)	Class	AVG	G	AB	R	H	2B	3B	HR	RBI	BB	SO	SB	CS	OBP	SLG
2015	Helena (PIO)	R	.274	54	212	38	58	23	1	6	41	18	68	3	5	.331	.476
	Wisconsin (MWL)	LoA	.209	55	177	16	37	5	1	4	16	14	65	5	0	.275	.316
2016	Wisconsin (MWL)	LoA	.240	126	496	70	119	33	0	14	64	18	141	3	2	.268	.391
2017	Carolina (CAR)	HiA	.269	111	420	66	113	36	1	11	53	43	132	7	5	.340	.438
	Biloxi (SL)	AA	.239	23	92	9	22	4	2	4	9	8	29	3	0	.300	.457
Minor League Totals			.244	419	1601	218	391	107	5	42	215	114	506	28	20	.296	.396

15 TRENT GRISHAM, OF

BA GRADE

50 Risk: High

Born: Nov. 1, 1996. **B-T:** L-L. **Ht.:** 6-0. **Wt.:** 210. **Drafted:** HS—North Richland Hills, Texas, 2015 (1st round). **Signed by:** K.J. Hendricks.

Grisham, who was drafted as Trent Clark and took his mother's maiden name after the 2017 season, scuffled through an injury-plagued first full season and wasn't much better at high Class A Carolina in 2017, hitting .223 with a 708 OPS.

Grisham struggled to make consistent contact, striking out far too often with ugly swings and misses through hittable pitches in the strike zone. He did show a good eye at the plate, drawing 98 walks but had trouble getting comfortable while constantly tinkering with his batting stance. Grisham frequently pulls off the ball, nullifying his average raw power. It was obvious to many he was seeking a comfort zone, perhaps related to his switch from a golf-style grip to a more conventional grip of the bat. When he did get on base, he used his above-average speed to make things happen, with 37 steals in 42 attempts. That skill also helped in the outfield, where he handled all three positions while showing a fringe-average but accurate arm. Grisham's hitting mechanics have never been consistent, making him a shell of the player who was considered arguably top prep hitter in the 2015 draft.

Grisham likely will be sent back to Carolina in 2018 and is still young enough to get on a proper path to the majors.

Year	Club (League)	Class	AVG	G	AB	R	H	2B	3B	HR	RBI	BB	SO	SB	CS	OBP	SLG
2015	Brewers (AZL)	R	.309	43	165	34	51	7	6	1	16	30	36	20	5	.422	.442
	Helena (PIO)	R	.310	12	42	5	13	0	0	1	5	9	8	5	3	.431	.381
2016	Wisconsin (MWL)	LoA	.231	59	221	27	51	15	2	2	24	37	68	5	10	.346	.344
2017	Carolina (CAR)	HiA	.223	133	457	78	102	21	6	8	45	98	141	37	5	.360	.348
Minor League Totals			.245	247	884	144	217	43	14	12	90	174	252	67	23	.372	.367

16 K.J. HARRISON, C

BA GRADE

50 Risk: High

Born: Aug. 11, 1996. **B-T:** R-R. **Ht.:** 6-0. **Wt.:** 208. **Drafted:** Oregon State, 2017 (3rd round). **Signed by:** Shawn Whalen.

Harrison saw little time behind the plate during his junior year at Oregon State, mostly playing at first base and DH. That didn't stop the Brewers from announcing that they planned to play him primarily at catcher after they drafted him in the third round in 2017 and signed him for $667.000.

Few doubt Harrison's offensive ability. He opened eyes in the Rookie-level Pioneer League with easy power to all fields and a .546 slugging percentage. He showed good pull-side power but also took what pitchers gave him without over-swinging, the sign of an intelligent hitter. That approach should allow him to hit for average. Harrison needs considerable work behind the plate. He has a solid-average arm but a slow release affects his pop times on throws to second base. Nevertheless, he threw out 26 percent of basestealers in his pro debut. Harrison shows soft yet strong hands behind the plate, but he needs to clean up his mechanics, including his footwork. He has below-average speed but is smart on the bases and gets good jumps.

Being able to stay behind the plate would enhance Harrison's offensive profile but could also slow down his progress in the system. A position switch in the future, perhaps to first base, is in the cards.

Year	Club (League)	Class	AVG	G	AB	R	H	2B	3B	HR	RBI	BB	SO	SB	CS	OBP	SLG
2017	Helena (PIO)	R	.308	48	185	38	57	14	0	10	33	23	55	0	0	.388	.546
Minor League Totals			.308	48	185	38	57	14	0	10	33	23	55	0	0	.388	.546

17 PHIL BICKFORD, RHP

BA GRADE

50 Risk: High

Born: July 10, 1995. **B-T:** R-R. **Ht.:** 6-4. **Wt.:** 200. **Drafted:** JC of Southern Nevada, 2015 (1st round). **Signed by:** Chuck Fick (Giants).

The 2017 season was mostly a lost one for Bickford, who was acquired from the Giants in August 2016 with catcher Andrew Susac in the trade of reliever Will Smith. First he was suspended 50 games following a second positive drug test, believed to be for marijuana. Then, while pitching in extended spring training in preparation to return to action, he took a liner off his pitching hand, fracturing it.

Those setbacks resulted in Bickford pitching just 17 innings, all in the Rookie-level Arizona League. When on top of his game, he throws a four-seamer in the mid-90s and mixes in a low-90s two-seamer with sink that results in ground ball outs. His slider is a plus pitch when he stays on top of it, but gets slurvy at times when he loses his release point. A split-changeup gives him another pitch with above-average potential, which is why he should be able to remain a starter. Bickford is athletic on the mound, but also struggles at times with his mechanics, particularly dropping his arm slot. The Brewers need to be able count on him to remain clean and show he can remain focused to get the most out of his natural ability.

Some scouts believe that Bickford is destined to eventually move to the bullpen, where his stuff will play better in shorter bursts, but the Brewers' plan is to continue to develop him as a starter.

Year	Club (League)	Class	W	L	ERA	G	GS	CG	SV	IP	H	HR	BB	SO	K/9	WHIP	AVG
2015	Giants (AZL)	R	0	1	2.01	10	10	0	0	22	13	0	6	32	12.9	0.85	.169
2016	Augusta (SAL)	LoA	3	4	2.70	11	11	1	0	60	49	2	15	69	10.4	1.07	.220
	San Jose (CAL)	HiA	2	2	2.73	6	6	1	0	33	21	3	12	36	9.8	1.00	.186
	Brevard County (FSL)	HiA	2	1	3.67	6	5	0	0	27	26	1	15	30	10.0	1.52	.252
2017	Brewers (AZL)	R	1	0	2.12	6	5	0	0	17	14	0	10	16	8.5	1.41	.215
Minor League Totals			8	8	2.71	39	37	2	0	159	123	6	58	183	10.3	1.14	.212

18 CODY PONCE, RHP

BA GRADE 50 Risk: High

Born: April 25, 1994. **B-T:** R-R. **Ht.:** 6-6. **Wt.:** 240. **Drafted:** Cal Poly Pomona, 2015 (2nd round). **Signed by:** Josh Belovsky.

A right forearm strain delayed Ponce's first full season in 2016 for two months, and he scuffled in high Class A after being activated. He returned to the level in 2017 with Carolina and showed what he can do.

Ponce had his ups and downs with the Mudcats but still posted a 3.38 ERA before a late-season promotion to Double-A Biloxi, where he finished strong with three impressive starts. A big, physical pitcher, he attacks with a 90-93 mph fastball that can go a bit higher and a cutter he uses against lefthanded hitters. He has worked to tighten the spin on his curveball, but still has to improve his changeup, which he throws too hard at times. Ponce has worked to be more of a pitcher, and his strikeout rate has suffered as he dials back his fastball. But his goal has been to get quicker outs and command all of his pitches, not light up radar guns. He also has focused on pitching to both sides of the plate, and keeping his walk rate down. Ponce is athletic and uses his height to pound fastballs in the lower half of the strike zone.

The Brewers still believe Ponce has a future as a starter with a four-pitch mix and aggressive nature. He merely needs to sharpen his secondary pitches to continue moving forward.

Year	Club (League)	Class	W	L	ERA	G	GS	CG	SV	IP	H	HR	BB	SO	K/9	WHIP	AVG
2015	Helena (PIO)	R	0	0	3.60	2	2	0	0	5	4	0	0	4	7.2	0.80	.222
	Wisconsin (MWL)	LoA	2	1	2.15	12	7	0	3	46	43	1	9	36	7.0	1.13	.246
2016	Brevard County (FSL)	HiA	2	8	5.25	17	17	0	0	72	84	6	17	69	8.6	1.40	.285
2017	Carolina (CAR)	HiA	8	8	3.38	22	22	1	0	120	130	14	25	94	7.1	1.29	.274
	Biloxi (SL)	AA	2	1	1.53	3	3	0	0	18	10	0	5	9	4.6	0.85	.175
Minor League Totals			14	18	3.56	56	51	1	3	261	271	21	56	212	7.3	1.25	.266

19 JOSH PENNINGTON, RHP

BA GRADE 55 Risk: Extreme

Born: July 6, 1995. **B-T:** R-R. **Ht.:** 6-0. **Wt.:** 175. **Drafted:** HS—Cape May, N.J., 2014 (29th round). **Signed by:** Ray Fagnant (Red Sox).

The Brewers acquired Pennington and two others from the Red Sox after the 2016 season for Tyler Thornburg. Pennington had surgery to remove a bone chip from his elbow and was not be ready at the start of the 2017 season. That procedure was in addition to the Tommy John surgery he had as a high school senior that caused him to plummet to the 29th round in 2014.

Pennington had a setback in 2017 that delayed his return until late June, but after a brief outing in the Rookie-level Arizona League, he acquitted himself well with a 2.97 ERA in nine starts at low Class A Wisconsin. Pennington has a big fastball in the mid- to high 90s with solid command. An upper-70s curveball has the potential to be a plus secondary pitch, but he still needs to work on his changeup. Considering his physical setbacks, he showed better control than expected.

If Pennington improves his secondary pitches, he has a chance to remain a starter despite his slight frame, and the Brewers plan to keep him in that role. He is tentatively ticketed for high Class A Carolina.

Year	Club (League)	Class	W	L	ERA	G	GS	CG	SV	IP	H	HR	BB	SO	K/9	WHIP	AVG
2015	Red Sox (GCL)	R	2	1	0.82	7	6	0	0	22	17	0	13	22	9.0	1.36	.218
2016	Lowell (NYP)	SS	5	3	2.86	13	13	0	0	57	39	2	27	49	7.8	1.16	.200
2017	Brewers (AZL)	R	0	0	0.00	1	1	0	0	2	1	0	0	2	9.0	0.50	.167
	Wisconsin (MWL)	LoA	1	3	2.97	9	9	0	0	30	24	4	8	29	8.6	1.05	.211
Minor League Totals			8	7	2.43	30	29	0	0	111	81	6	48	102	8.3	1.16	.206

20 MARIO FELICIANO, C

BA GRADE
45 Risk: High

Born: Nov. 20, 1998. **B-T:** R-R. **Ht.:** 6-1. **Wt.:** 195. **Drafted:** HS—Florida, P.R., 2016 (2nd round supplemental). **Signed by:** Charlie Sullivan.

The Brewers knew Feliciano's offense was ahead of his defense when they drafted him 75th overall in 2016 but liked his tools enough to believe that he could develop into a solid defensive catcher. Feliciano made his full-season debut as an 18-year-old at low Class A Wisconsin in 2017, making him the youngest catcher in the Midwest League.

Feliciano got off to a strong start with a .778 OPS in April before running out of steam. Feliciano has a good idea of hitting, keeping his hands in the zone and showing some feel. He has hit only four home runs in his first 133 career games, but has the potential to develop more power as he matures and fills out. Feliciano did better at working counts after initially being too aggressive at times. He runs well, particularly for a catcher, and has athleticism behind the plate that should work in his favor. Feliciano has above-average arm strength but must work on his fundamentals, including a quicker transfer and release, to improve throwing out runners. Some question Feliciano's long-term future behind the plate, but the Brewers see no reason to make a change now, particularly at a position of need in the organization.

If he's able to stay behind the plate, Feliciano's potential as an offensive-minded catcher could pay off. He is still very young and raw however, and will be moved slowly.

Year	Club (League)	Class	AVG	G	AB	R	H	2B	3B	HR	RBI	BB	SO	SB	CS	OBP	SLG
2016	Brewers (AZL)	R	.265	29	117	16	31	5	3	0	16	7	19	2	2	.307	.359
2017	Wisconsin (MWL)	LoA	.251	104	402	47	101	16	2	4	36	34	72	10	2	.320	.331
Minor League Totals			.254	133	519	63	132	21	5	4	52	41	91	12	4	.317	.337

21 KODI MEDEIROS, LHP

BA GRADE
45 Risk: High

Born: May 25, 1996. **B-T:** L-L. **Ht.:** 6-2. **Wt.:** 180. **Drafted:** HS—Hilo, Hawaii, 2014 (1st round). **Signed by:** Josh Belovsky.

Ever since the Brewers took Medeiros in the first round of the 2014 draft, the same question has been asked: Is his future as a starting pitcher or a lefthanded specialist out of the bullpen? The Brewers have developed him as a starter, but Medeiros scuffled for a good portion of 2017 at high Class A Carolina, convincng most evaluators that his future is, indeed, in the bullpen.

With a funky delivery and low arm slot, he remains a big swing-and-miss pitcher, particularly against lefthanded hitters. Medeiros throws his fastball in the 92-95 mph range with great movement—too much, sometimes—and a plus slider he uses to put hitters away. His changeup has deception and fade, with a chance to be above-average. Medeiros is athletic, strong and mature for his age, but needs to sharpen his command to continue in a starting role. He has well below-average command and control, which resulted in 20 hit batters and 12 wild pitches in addition to a high walk rate in 2017. His low arm slot and high-effort delivery doesn't project for his command to improve much, but the Brewers think he has upside and can succeed as a starter with his three-pitch repertoire.

Medeiros has a bright future as a lefty specialist, if nothing else. He'll move to Double-A Biloxi in 2018.

Year	Club (League)	Class	W	L	ERA	G	GS	CG	SV	IP	H	HR	BB	SO	K/9	WHIP	AVG
2015	Wisconsin (MWL)	LoA	4	5	4.44	25	16	0	1	93	79	0	40	94	9.1	1.28	.228
2016	Brevard County (FSL)	HiA	4	12	5.93	23	22	0	0	85	102	4	63	64	6.8	1.94	.300
2017	Carolina (CAR)	HiA	8	9	4.98	27	18	0	1	128	114	7	53	121	8.5	1.30	.241
Minor League Totals			16	28	5.19	84	60	0	3	324	319	13	169	305	8.5	1.50	.257

22 MARCOS DIPLAN, RHP

BA GRADE
45 Risk: High

Born: Sept. 18, 1996. **B-T:** R-R. **Ht.:** 6-0. **Wt.:** 175. **Signed:** Dominican Republic, 2013. **Signed by:** Willie Espinal/Mike Daly (Rangers).

Diplan made tremendous strides during his first two seasons in the system, after being acquired in a trade with the Rangers before the 2015 season. Pitching the full year at advanced Class A Carolina at age 20, he finally struggled, in large part due to command issues (71 walks in 125.2 innings).

There were questions from the beginning if the undersized righty would be able to remain in a starting role, but Diplan has an electric arm and the Brewers certainly aren't going to give up on him after one tough season. He throws a fastball with late movement consistently in the mid-90s and complements it with a plus slider. Diplan also shows a good feel for his changeup, especially for a young pitcher. His main task is being more consistent with his delivery and therefore his command. His problems in that area led to high pitch counts and early exits from games. As his body has filled out a bit more, Diplan has had to make adjustments to repeat his delivery. When throwing strikes, he exhibits high swing-and-miss potential and generates lots of weak contact.

The Brewers believe that Diplan can be a dependable starting pitcher in the majors, but if he continues to struggle with pitch counts and getting deep into games, his future could be as a high-leverage reliever. Diplan has good makeup and takes coaching well, and at such a young age there's no reason to abandon the role of starting pitcher at this point.

Year	Club (League)	Class	W	L	ERA	G	GS	CG	SV	IP	H	HR	BB	SO	K/9	WHIP	AVG
2015	Helena (PIO)	R	2	2	3.75	13	7	0	2	50	47	4	21	54	9.7	1.35	.257
2016	Wisconsin (MWL)	LoA	6	2	1.80	17	11	0	1	70	49	3	32	89	11.4	1.16	.191
	Brevard County (FSL)	HiA	1	2	4.98	10	6	1	0	43	47	4	18	40	8.3	1.50	.276
2017	Carolina (CAR)	HiA	7	8	5.23	26	22	0	0	126	126	11	71	119	8.5	1.57	.266
Minor League Totals			23	16	3.64	79	59	1	3	354	301	24	178	359	9.1	1.35	.234

23 JACOB NOTTINGHAM, C

BA GRADE 45 Risk: High

Born: April 3, 1995. **B-T:** R-R. **Ht.:** 6-3. **Wt.:** 230. **Drafted:** HS—Redlands, Calif., 2013 (6th round). **Signed by:** Brad Budzinski (Astros).

When the Brewers sent slugger Khris Davis to Oakland before the 2016 season in a trade that netted Nottingham, the plan was to have a young prospect develop as their catcher of the future.

Davis hit 40-plus homers in each of his first two seasons with the Athletics, while Nottingham has stalled in Double-A. The raw Nottingham has worked hard to make strides defensively behind the plate, but his offense has suffered in the process. Back for a second season at Double-A Biloxi in 2017, the big, powerful Nottingham slugged just .369 and didn't reach 10 home runs. He has worked on cutting down his strikeouts but doesn't walk much, and needs to improve his general plate discipline. On defense he has improved his receiving, throwing accuracy, blocking and mobility behind the plate. He still has work to do, particularly in game calling, but is committed to the position and the Brewers plan to keep him there.

Nottingham will play the entire 2018 season at 23, so there's still time to get him on track, but he needs to rediscover his big power.

Year	Club (League)	Class	AVG	G	AB	R	H	2B	3B	HR	RBI	BB	SO	SB	CS	OBP	SLG
2015	Quad Cities (MWL)	LoA	.326	59	230	34	75	18	1	10	46	18	51	1	2	.387	.543
	Lancaster (CAL)	HiA	.324	17	71	14	23	6	1	4	14	3	10	0	0	.368	.606
	Stockton (CAL)	HiA	.299	43	164	25	49	9	0	3	22	12	38	1	0	.352	.409
2016	Biloxi (SL)	AA	.234	112	415	46	97	14	0	11	37	29	138	9	2	.295	.347
2017	Biloxi (SL)	AA	.209	101	325	37	68	21	2	9	48	37	87	7	3	.326	.369
Minor League Totals			.254	424	1525	204	388	88	7	43	215	138	416	25	11	.331	.406

24 CADEN LEMONS, RHP

BA GRADE 50 Risk: Extreme

Born: Dec. 2, 1998. **B-T:** R-R. **Ht.:** 6-6. **Wt.:** 275. **Drafted:** HS—Vestavia Hills, Ala., 2017 (2nd round). **Signed by:** Scott Nichols.

It's all about ceiling with Lemons, who figures to throw harder and get better as his long, lanky frame fills out. As it is, the righthander saw his draft stock soar as a high school senior in the spring when his fastball went from 89-91 mph to touching 96.

The Brewers drafted him 46th overall and paid him $1.45 million to forgo a scholarship to Mississippi. They were careful with Lemons afterward, allowing him to make only three short starts in rookie ball. With a three-quarters arm slot and a 6-foot-6 frame, Lemons gets good movement on his fastball but struggles to repeat his delivery and release point, making his secondary pitches erratic. He throws both a low-80s slider and a curveball, with the former showing more consistency. He has to continue to work on spinning the ball. Lemons also mixes in a changeup that needs work, but the potential of a four-pitch mix is intriguing for a young, raw pitcher who will need plenty of development.

Lemons showed some improvement with his balance and pitching mechanics in the spring, but that will be a constant focus as he fills out physically and learns his body as a pro. Lemons likely will spend the entire 2018 season at rookie ball as the Brewers ease him into a career with vast potential.

Year	Club (League)	Class	W	L	ERA	G	GS	CG	SV	IP	H	HR	BB	SO	K/9	WHIP	AVG
2017	Brewers (AZL)	R	0	1	6.75	3	3	0	0	3	2	1	0	1	3.4	0.75	.200
Minor League Totals			0	1	6.75	3	3	0	0	3	2	1	0	1	3.4	0.75	.200

25 TREY SUPAK, RHP

BA GRADE 45 Risk: High

Born: May 31, 1996. **B-T:** R-R. **Ht.:** 6-5. **Wt.:** 235. **Drafted:** HS—La Grange, Texas, 2014 (2nd round supplemental). **Signed by:** Trevor Haley (Pirates).

The Brewers already feel good about the December 2015 trade with the Pirates that brought center fielder Keon Broxton, a 20-home run, 20-stolen base player in 2017, to Milwaukee for infielder Jason

Rogers. But Supak also came in that trade, and if he makes it to the majors as well, that deal will become an even bigger steal.

Pittsburgh went over slot to sign Supak in 2014, giving him $1 million to forgo a commitment to Houston. He took a big step forward in 2017, pitching so well in eight outings for low Class A Wisconsin that he was promoted aggressively to high Class A Carolina. Supak's fastball sits in the low-90s, but he can reach 95 with late life. With a big, projectable frame, he has learned to throw downhill more and pound the bottom of the strike zone, inducing weak contact. Supak also features an above-average curveball and developing feel for a changeup with good fade. He induces many swings and misses, pitching ahead in the count and issuing few walks.

Supak is still young and should continue to improve, with a ceiling of being a back-end rotation starter and floor of a late-inning reliever. An assignment to Double-A Biloxi is likely to begin the 2018 season.

Year	Club (League)	Class	W	L	ERA	G	GS	CG	SV	IP	H	HR	BB	SO	K/9	WHIP	AVG
2015	Bristol (APP)	R	1	2	6.67	8	8	0	0	28	35	2	5	23	7.3	1.41	.304
2016	Helena (PIO)	R	1	1	1.29	4	2	0	0	14	10	0	1	11	7.1	0.79	.200
	Wisconsin (MWL)	LoA	2	3	3.86	11	6	0	1	44	48	3	17	40	8.1	1.47	.274
2017	Wisconsin (MWL)	LoA	2	2	1.76	8	7	0	0	41	21	1	10	53	11.6	0.76	.156
	Carolina (CAR)	HiA	3	4	4.60	15	11	0	1	72	65	12	28	57	7.1	1.29	.241
Minor League Totals			10	15	4.02	54	40	0	2	224	206	22	72	205	8.2	1.24	.246

26 CARLOS HERRERA, RHP

BA GRADE
45 Risk: High

Born: Oct. 26, 1997. **B-T:** R-R. **Ht.:** 6-2. **Wt.:** 150. **Signed:** Dominican Republic, 2014. **Signed by:** Eddy Toledo/Scott Hunter (Mariners).

One of three teenaged pitchers acquired from the Mariners in December 2015 in a trade for first baseman Adam Lind, Herrera was only 18, and coming off an impressive showing in the Dominican Summer League.

Herrera was assigned to the Rookie-level Arizona League the next season and led the circuit with 49 strikeouts. The Brewers knew Herrera was raw when they traded for him, but figured his lanky frame would fill out and he would add velocity to his fastball. He has continued to make progress, getting promoted after a couple of weeks in 2017 to low Class A Wisconsin, where he more than held opponents to a .180 average. Herrera's fastball sits in the low 90s, and he has a curveball that's above-average as well as an improving changeup. Not a big strikeout pitcher at this point, he still has command issues at times and needs to work on pitching more in the bottom of the strike zone, but the Brewers believe he'll continue to improve as he logs more innings and his body matures.

Herrera didn't turn 20 until after the season ended and has plenty of time to fill out.

Year	Club (League)	Class	W	L	ERA	G	GS	CG	SV	IP	H	HR	BB	SO	K/9	WHIP	AVG
2015	Mariners (DSL)	R	4	2	3.26	14	14	0	0	80	68	4	13	73	8.2	1.01	.228
2016	Brewers (AZL)	R	3	6	4.50	14	6	0	0	50	52	4	12	49	8.8	1.28	.271
2017	Helena (PIO)	R	2	0	4.29	4	4	0	0	21	16	5	5	26	11.1	1.00	.219
	Wisconsin (MWL)	LoA	3	2	3.79	9	5	1	0	38	24	4	17	26	6.2	1.08	.181
Minor League Totals			12	10	3.81	41	29	1	0	189	160	17	47	174	8.3	1.10	.230

27 NATHAN KIRBY, LHP

BA GRADE
50 Risk: Extreme

Born: Nov. 23, 1993. **B-T:** L-L. **Ht.:** 6-2. **Wt.:** 200. **Drafted:** Virginia, 2015 (1st round supplemental). **Signed by:** Dan Nellum.

It's easy to forget Kirby at this point, because he hasn't thrown a pitch in a real game since 2015.

Kirby had Tommy John surgery after throwing only 13 pitches that season, and was forced to sit out all of 2016. Then, just when it appeared that he was ready to return last spring, he began experiencing elbow discomfort again, and had another surgery to reposition the ulnar nerve. That procedure led to yet another full season of inactivity. He threw well in instructional league after the season with no issues. Kirby is far behind schedule, but as an advanced lefty, still has the chance to make an impact in the organization. He pitches in the low-90s with his fastball with good action and knows how to use both sides of the plate with it. His mid 80s slider is an above-average secondary pitch and he also shows a deceptive changeup that he throws with good arm speed. Add it all together and it's a three-pitch mix that should allow Kirby to remain a starter. He's a smart, athletic pitcher.

Health will be Kirby's biggest test, with an assignment to high Class A Carolina likely to begin 2018.

Year	Club (League)	Class	W	L	ERA	G	GS	CG	SV	IP	H	HR	BB	SO	K/9	WHIP	AVG
2015	Wisconsin (MWL)	LoA	0	1	5.68	5	2	0	0	13	15	0	7	7	5.0	1.74	.313
2016	Did not play—Injured																
2017	Did not play—Injured																
Minor League Totals			0	1	5.68	5	2	0	0	13	15	0	7	7	5.0	1.74	.313

28 PAYTON HENRY, C

Born: June 24, 1997. **B-T:** R-R. **Ht.:** 6-2. **Wt.:** 225. **Drafted:** HS—Pleasant Grove, Utah, 2016 (6th round). **Signed by:** Jeff Scholzen.

The Brewers liked Henry's potential enough to nearly double the recommended bonus for his slot, paying $550,600 for him to forgo a scholarship to Brigham Young.

Playing high school ball for his father, he was a two-time Gatorade player of the year in the state of Utah. Henry is a physical catcher with above-average power and good bat speed, and he flashed power potential with 17 doubles and seven home runs at Rookie-level Helena in 2017, although with considerable swing-and-miss and a 29 percent strikeout rate. Henry gets too pull-happy at times, and it affects his overall hitting ability. A below-average runner, he'll have no impact on the basepaths. Henry has a ways to go with his footwork behind the plate, but overall is a good defender with an above-average arm that produces sub-1.95 second pop times.

Henry showed progress in calling games and has the potential to be a solid catcher with a power bat. Henry should be ready for his first full-season assignment in 2018.

Year	Club (League)	Class	AVG	G	AB	R	H	2B	3B	HR	RBI	BB	SO	SB	CS	OBP	SLG
2016	Brewers (AZL)	R	.256	24	82	15	21	7	0	0	17	6	19	0	1	.333	.341
2017	Helena (PIO)	R	.242	55	207	38	50	17	1	7	33	30	69	1	0	.344	.435
Minor League Totals			.246	79	289	53	71	24	1	7	50	36	88	1	1	.341	.408

29 ANTONIO PINERO, SS

Born: March 15, 1999. **B-T:** B-R. **Ht.:** 6-1. **Wt.:** 155. **Signed:** Venezuela, 2016. **Signed by:** Fernando Veracierto.

Pinero originally signed with the Red Sox for $300,000 during the 2016 international signing period, but his contract was voided because of a rules violation and the Brewers got him for a mere $75,000. Coming out of the Dominican Summer League at age 18, he skipped the Rookie-level Arizona League.

What was obvious immediately was that Pinero had superior defensive skills. His arm is not particularly powerful but he has everything else you want at shortstop—range, soft hands, smooth actions around the bag. Still skinny and needing to gain strength, Pinero has the makings of a plus defender, turning in many highlight plays that drew attention. He was mostly overmatched offensively, basically swinging to make contact rather than work counts and make pitchers throw the ball over the plate. Scouts believe Pinero has the potential to hit because he has a short, compact swing and good hand-eye coordination. It's merely a matter of maturing, filling out and learning what pitchers are trying to do to him.

If Pinero hits at all, he'll advance because of his defensive skills. He set to see low Class A Wisconsin.

Year	Club (League)	Class	AVG	G	AB	R	H	2B	3B	HR	RBI	BB	SO	SB	CS	OBP	SLG
2016	Red Sox2 (DSL)	R	.198	22	81	12	16	0	0	0	6	7	10	7	1	.258	.198
	Brewers (DSL)	R	.235	28	98	15	23	2	0	0	7	9	20	7	0	.296	.255
2017	Helena (PIO)	R	.236	55	208	19	49	4	0	1	14	7	45	7	5	.258	.269
Minor League Totals			.227	105	387	46	88	6	0	1	27	23	75	21	6	.268	.251

30 CHAD McCLANAHAN, 3B/1B

Born: Dec. 22, 1997. **B-T:** L-R. **Ht.:** 6-5. **Wt.:** 200. **Drafted:** HS—Phoenix, 2016 (11th round). **Signed by:** Jeff Scholzen.

The physical tools are definitely there for McClanahan, but not everyone is convinced he can put them all together to maximize them.

The Brewers are banking on it, having paid far over slot value with a $1.2 million bonus as an 11th rounder in 2016. McClanahan homered in his first pro at-bat but has otherwise struggled, including a .234/.339/.315 slash line at Helena in the hitter-friendly Pioneer League in 2017.. A 6-foot-5, 200-pound specimen with big raw power, the fact his his power numbers never materialized were a major disappointment for a player of his size and potential. He's a below-average runner and has worked hard to improve his defense at third base, where he shows a strong-enough arm. But McClanahan also saw action at first base and eventually might move there on a permanent basis. He also has enough athleticism to move to an outfield corner, if it comes to that.

As McClanahan gets more at-bats and matures at hitter, the Brewers believe he'll get to his power more consistently. He didn't turn 20 until just before Christmas, so there's of time for McClanahan to make the most of his physical raw skills.

Year	Club (League)	Class	AVG	G	AB	R	H	2B	3B	HR	RBI	BB	SO	SB	CS	OBP	SLG
2016	Brewers (AZL)	R	.208	35	144	22	30	7	1	3	14	11	45	1	2	.277	.333
2017	Helena (PIO)	R	.234	63	235	33	55	8	1	3	30	39	78	5	5	.339	.315
Minor League Totals			.224	98	379	55	85	15	2	6	44	50	123	6	7	.317	.322

Minnesota Twins

BY MIKE BERARDINO

Back in 1987, moments after winning the first World Series title in Minnesota franchise history, Twins assistant general manager Bob Gebhard turned to young GM Andy MacPhail and uttered a line for the ages.

"We were just trying to get organized," Gebhard said as the Metrodome roared its approval, "and we ended up winning this thing!"

First-year Twins chief baseball officer Derek Falvey and GM Thad Levine didn't get to have the same exchange upon completion of the 2017 season, but they made history all the same. With a huge assist from the American League manager of the year Paul Molitor, rewarded with a new three-year contract at season's end, the Twins staged the biggest turnaround in major league history.

Not only did they improve by 26 wins, going from 59-103 to 85-77 one year after the revered Terry Ryan was fired as GM, but they became the first team to go from 98 or more losses to the postseason the following year. A disappointing Wild Card Game loss at Yankee Stadium couldn't possibly wipe out the unexpected gains of what in many ways was a transitional year for a proud franchise once more on the rise.

Barely seven months after their arrival from Cleveland and Texas, respectively, the Falvey-Levine combo oversaw the selection of the first overall pick in the draft. Picking 1-1 for just the third time, the Twins (under first-year scouting director Sean Johnson) surprised many by taking California high school shortstop Royce Lewis.

The hope is that Lewis will become the same sort of franchise player the Twins found the last time they picked first, grabbing hometown catcher Joe Mauer in 2001. Johnson and his amateur scouting staff wisely stretched their draft bonus pool and loaded up with impact players beyond Lewis. Mississippi State slugger Brent Rooker (taken 35th overall) and three other 2017 draftees also landed on this year's list of top 30 prospects.

Sticking to their vision of long-term, sustainable success, the so-called Falvine regime flipped Jaime Garcia after one start and dealt Brandon Kintzler at the July 31 trade deadline. In return they received two more pitchers (Zack Littell and Tyler Watson) that landed in the top 20.

Undeterred, a youthful Twins roster led by first-time Gold Glove winner Byron Buxton, first-time all-star Miguel Sano and breakout performers such as Jose Berrios, Jorge Polanco, Max Kepler and Eddie Rosario ripped off a 20-win August and went on to end a six-year postseason drought.

Success also spread through the minor league system, where Twins affiliates played to a com-

Highlight-reel center fielder Byron Buxton won his first of many Gold Gloves in 2017.

PROJECTED 2021 LINEUP

Catcher	Jason Castro (34)
First Base	Brent Rooker (26)
Second Base	Jorge Polanco (27)
Third Base	Wander Javier (22)
Shortstop	Royce Lewis (22)
Left Field	Eddie Rosario (29)
Center Field	Byron Buxton (27)
Right Field	Max Kepler (28)
Designated Hitter	Miguel Sano (28)
No. 1 Starter	Jose Berrios (27)
No. 2 Starter	Stephen Gonsalves (26)
No. 3 Starter	Brusdar Graterol (22)
No. 4 Starter	Fernando Romero (26)
No. 5 Starter	Adalberto Mejia (28)
Closer	Tyler Jay (27)

bined .581 winning percentage and came within a Triple-A tiebreaker of sending their top six clubs to the playoffs. On that note Brad Steil moved over to pro scouting director after five seasons running the farm system. Jeremy Zoll, 27, was hired away from the Dodgers as his replacement.

Daniel Adler, formerly of the commissioner's office and multiple NFL operations, was hired at 30 as director of baseball operations; and longtime Baseball America editor in chief John Manuel was hired after the season in a pro scouting role.

Key front-office departures during the year included former GM Bill Smith, former Reds GM Wayne Krivsky and international scouting director Howard Norsetter.

DEPTH CHART

MINNESOTA TWINS

TOP 2018 ROOKIE: Stephen Gonsalves, LHP. His steady rise finally lands him a spot in the big league rotation by midseason.

BREAKOUT PROSPECT: Aaron Whitefield, OF. The late-blooming Australian has come a long way from his competitive softball days.

SLEEPER: Derek Molina, RHP. Two-way player at Merced (Calif.) JC was up to 93 mph off the mound with potential as three-pitch starter after going in the 14th round.

SOURCE OF TOP 30 TALENT			
Homegrown	26	Acquired	4
College	6	Trades	4
Junior college	1	Rule 5 draft	0
High school	10	Independent leagues	0
Nondrafted free agents	0	Free agents/waivers	0
International	9		

LF
Akil Baddoo (11)
LaMonte Wade (17)
Jacob Pearson (22)
Trey Cabbage

CF
Aaron Whitefield (19)
Zack Granite (27)
Jean Carlos Arias
Tanner English

RF
Alex Kirilloff (3)
Jaylin Davis
Edgar Corcino

3B
Andrew Bechtold (25)
Wander Valdez
Chris Paul

SS
Royce Lewis (1)
Wander Javier (2)
Jermaine Palacios
Gorge Munoz
Ricky De La Torre
Sean Miller

2B
Nick Gordon (8)
Yunior Severino (14)
Luis Arraez (15)
Jose Miranda (24)
Travis Blankenhorn (29)

1B
Brent Rooker (7)
Lewin Diaz (26)
Zander Wiel

C
Mitch Garver (23)
David Banuelos (28)
Ben Rortvedt
Brian Navaretto
Caleb Hamilton

LHP

LHSP	LHRP
Stephen Gonsalves (4)	Tyler Jay (10)
Lewis Thorpe (16)	Gabriel Moya
Tyler Watson (20)	Alex Robinson
Lachlan Wells	Andrew Vasquez
Ryley Widell	Jovani Moran
Charlie Barnes	Mason Melotakis
Dietrich Enns	

RHP

RHSP	RHRP
Brusdar Graterol (5)	John Curtiss (21)
Fernando Romero (6)	Tyler Kinley
Blayne Enlow (9)	J.T. Chargois
Felix Jorge (12)	Alan Busenitz
Landon Leach (13)	Jake Reed
Zack Littell (18)	Tom Hackimer
Kohl Stewart (30)	Ryan Eades
Griffin Jax	Hector Lujan
Derek Molina	Eduardo Del Rosario
Aaron Slegers	Colton Davis
Tyler Wells	Bailey Ober
Sean Poppen	

DRAFT ANALYSIS

2017

BEST PURE HITTER: No. 1 overall pick Royce Lewis (1) had his doubters about his bat this spring, but he led USA Baseball's 18U national team in the 2016 Pan Am championships, hitting .500, then hit a robust .279/.381/.407 in his pro debut. He has the swing, approach, athleticism and makeup to continue to hit at higher levels.

BEST POWER: 1B/OF Brent Rooker (1s) has double-plus power and hit 18 homers between two levels in his debut, after hitting 23 to lead the Southeastern Conference in the spring. He slugged .552 in the high Class A Florida State League in 40 games; the league as a whole slugged .360.

FASTEST RUNNER: Lewis is a twitchy athlete who turns in some burner times but should settle in as a plus runner when he reaches the majors.

BEST DEFENSIVE PLAYER: Lewis made his greatest strides in 2017 as a shortstop. Many scouts saw him as a future center fielder entering the spring, but added reps prior to the draft and over the summer since signing have helped him improve significantly. Club officials now see him as a potentially plus defender at short, with range, arm strength and dynamic playmaking ability, once he hones his fielding mechanics and tightens his arm action.

BEST ATHLETE: Lewis ranked second on BA's Best Tools list for the draft among high school athletes, behind only Angels first-rounder Jo Adell. He's both fast-twitch and has body control and room to gain strength without becoming stiff.

BEST FASTBALL: The highest-drafted player out of Canada in 2017, RHP Landon Leach (2) was the Twins' third pick. His fastball isn't just hard, at 93-95 mph with a peak of 97, but it's heavy, with late sink.

BEST SECONDARY PITCH: RHP Blayne Enlow (3) signed for $2 million, with his lean frame and curveball the primary attractions. It's a plus pitch he can command, throwing it for strikes or as a chase pitch, and he manipulates the shape of it as

well. LHP Charlie Barnes (4) thrives with a plus changeup and command of his slider, curve and upper-80s fastball.

BEST PRO DEBUT: Lewis' .381 OBP impressed, but Rooker hit .281/.364/.566 with 18 homers overall between Rookie-level Elizabethton and Fort Myers in the FSL.

MOST INTRIGUING BACKGROUND: RHP Derek Molina (14) worked out for first-year area scout Michael Quesada as a pitcher after hitting .356 with a team-best five homers in the spring for Mercer (Calif.) JC. He pitched 28.1 innings in the spring as a reliever but impressed the Twins with his feel for spinning a breaking ball and 6-foot-3, 195-pound pitcher's body.

CLOSEST TO THE MAJORS: Rooker needs to find a defensive home, either in left field or his better spot, first base, but his bat looks ready to move quickly.

BEST LATE-ROUND PICK: RHP Bailey Ober (12) had an injury-plagued college career but is a tall (6-foot-8) command-oriented starter who posted a 35-3 strikeout-walk rate in his 28-inning pro debut.

THE ONE WHO GOT AWAY: Toolsy OF Gabriel Rodriguez (11) wanted more than the Twins had left in their bonus pool. He's attending Miami-Dade JC.

—JOHN MANUEL

TOP DRAFT PICKS OF THE DECADE

Year	Player, Pos.	2017 Org
2008	Aaron Hicks, OF	Yankees
2009	Kyle Gibson, RHP	Twins
2010	Alex Wimmers, RHP	Twins
2011	Levi Michael, SS	Twins
2012	Byron Buxton, OF	Twins
2013	Kohl Stewart, RHP	Twins
2014	Nick Gordon, SS	Twins
2015	Tyler Jay, LHP	Twins
2016	Alex Kirilloff ,OF	Twins
2017	Royce Lewis, SS	Twins.

2016

OF Alex Kirilloff (1) was off to a fast start to his career before Tommy John surgery sidelined him in 2017. SS Jose Miranda (1s) and OF Akil Baddoo (1s) showed well in their first full pro season, though they didn't advance past Rookie ball.
GRADE: C

2015

LHP Tyler Jay (1) was limited by neck and shoulder injuries and has returned to the bullpen. 3B Travis Blakenhorn has had mixed results and may end up at second base. OF LaMonte Wade (9) has come on strong and may be the class' first big leaguer.
GRADE: D

2014

RHP Trevor Hildenberger (22) found a role in the Twins' bullpen, but it will be up to SS Nick Gordon (1) to carry the class. He has been solid so far, but questions remain about his impact. RHP Nick Burdi (2) was selected in the Rule 5 Draft.
GRADE: C

1 ROYCE LEWIS, SS

Born: June 5, 1999. **B-T:** R-R. **Ht.:** 6-2. **Wt.:** 188.
Drafted: HS—San Juan Capistrano, Calif., 2017
(1st round). **Signed by:** John Leavitt.

PAUL GIERHART

Armed with the No. 1 overall draft pick for just the third time in club history, the Twins surprised many in the industry by passing on advanced college arms such as Brendan McKay and Kyle Wright along with high school phenom Hunter Greene. Instead, they took Lewis, a late-blooming gamer with outstanding makeup and the potential to become a five-tool, franchise-changing asset. Signed to a club-record draft bonus of $6.725 million, nearly a full million below slot value, Lewis became the first 1-1 selection for the Twins since hometown catcher Joe Mauer in 2001. Lewis' mother Cindy is a former softball first baseman and pitcher for San Jose State who once beat UCLA great Lisa Fernandez 1-0 at Westwood.

Pre-draft concerns about Lewis' hit tool proved unwarranted as he had no problem making the necessary adjustments for a smooth transition to pro ball. Hitting coordinator Rick Eckstein got him to use his hips and legs better, and that opened up the pull side for Lewis, who homered on a full count in his first pro plate appearance. With a high waist and wide shoulders, he showed excellent plate discipline and an all-fields approach that drew comps to Ian Desmond. Lewis has plus speed and advanced instincts on the bases, where he was caught stealing just three times in 21 attempts. In the field, after seeing time at third base and center field at JSerra Catholic High School, he was working hard to improve his range at shortstop with better positioning and pre-pitch anticipation. He flashed plus arm strength before the draft but saw that wane under the Florida heat and an increased workload. A separated left shoulder suffered in high school hasn't been an issue so far. Lewis' makeup and work ethic are off the charts, and his ability to connect with teammates, fans and media are reminiscent of Carlos Correa. After a week or so, Ramon Borrego, his GCL manager, was calling for Lewis to skip the Rookie-level Appalachian League and be promoted all the way to low Class A Cedar Rapids. That happened in early August.

Lewis figures to return to the Midwest League to start his first full pro season. If he dominates there the way Byron Buxton did in 2013, a promotion to high Class A Fort Myers could come by mid-season. He's given the Twins no reason to doubt his ability to stay at shortstop or their decision to invest the top overall pick in his vast potential.

BA GRADE	SCOUTING GRADES
65 Risk: V. High	HIT: 60. POW: 55. SPD: 60. FLD: 60. ARM: 55.

Projected future grades on 20-80 scouting scale

TOP PROSPECTS OF THE DECADE

Year	Player, Pos.	2017 Org
2008	Nick Blackburn, RHP	Did not play
2009	Aaron Hicks, OF	Yankees
2010	Aaron Hicks, OF	Yankees
2011	Kyle Gibson, RHP	Twins
2012	Miguel Sano ,3B/SS	Twins
2013	Miguel Sano, 3B	Twins
2014	Byron Buxton, OF	Twins
2015	Byron Buxton, OF	Twins
2016	Byron Buxton, OF	Twins
2017	Nick Gordon, SS	Twins

BEST TOOLS

Best Hitter for Average	Luis Arraez
Best Power Hitter	Brent Rooker
Best Strike-Zone Discipline	LaMonte Wade
Fastest Baserunner	Tanner English
Best Athlete	Royce Lewis
Best Fastball	Brusdar Graterol
Best Curveball	Blayne Enlow
Best Slider	Tyler Jay
Best Changeup	Stephen Gonsalves
Best Control	Felix Jorge
Best Defensive Catcher	Ben Rortvedt
Best Defensive Infielder	Royce Lewis
Best Infield Arm	Andrew Bechtold
Best Defensive Outfielder	Aaron Whitefield
Best Outfield Arm	Tanner English

Year	Club (League)	Class	AVG	G	AB	R	H	2B	3B	HR	RBI	BB	SO	SB	CS	OBP	SLG
2017	Twins (GCL)	R	.271	36	133	38	36	6	2	3	17	19	17	15	2	.390	.414
	Cedar Rapids (MWL)	LoA	.296	18	71	16	21	2	1	1	10	6	16	3	1	.363	.394
Minor League Totals			.279	54	204	54	57	8	3	4	27	25	33	18	3	.381	.407

2 WANDER JAVIER, SS

Born: Dec. 29, 1998. **B-T:** R-R. **Ht.:** 6-1. **Wt.:** 180. **Signed:** Dominican Republic, 2015. **Signed by:** Fred Guerrero.

The Twins liked Javier so much, they spent their entire 2015-16 international bonus allotment on him, even going 1.3 percent over their limit to secure him for $4 million. That's still an international amateur record for the organization, which saw five-tool potential in a player ranked No. 9 in his international class. Javier received the highest bonus among Dominican shortstops that year and was second only to Phillies outfielder Jhailyn Ortiz among all Dominican signees. Limited by hamstring issues to just 26 at-bats in his first pro summer, Javier surged forward in his first exposure to rookie-level Elizabethton.

Wiry, long-limbed and lanky upon signing, Javier has begun to add strength to his frame and could still be growing. Still fairly raw with limited game experience beyond the amateur showcase circuit, Javier worked with hitting coordinator Rick Eckstein and Elizabethton hitting coach Jeff Reed to better incorporate his lower half and improve his balance. Javier ditched his big leg kick and now has a simple setup and swing with quiet hands and a small lift of his front foot. While he still has a tendency to chase pitches out of the zone, the ball jumps off his bat and he shows gap-to-gap power with a willingness to stay up the middle with authority. A plus runner with plus athleticism, he shows plenty of range, plus-plus arm strength and should have no problem staying at shortstop as he advances through the system. He's also worked hard to improve his English and is acclimating well.

Low Class A Cedar Rapids should be the next logical step for Javier, but the Twins might need to start him at extended spring training in order to produce enough shortstop reps for both Royce Lewis and Javier. Swapping those two between shortstop and third base is another possible avenue.

BA GRADE
60 Risk: Extreme
HIT: 50. **POW:** 50.
SPD: 60. **FLD:** 55.
ARM: 70.

Year	Club (League)	Class	AVG	G	AB	R	H	2B	3B	HR	RBI	BB	SO	SB	CS	OBP	SLG
2016	Twins (DSL)	R	.308	9	26	7	8	3	0	2	6	4	5	0	0	.400	.654
2017	Elizabethton (APP)	R	.299	41	157	34	47	13	1	4	22	19	49	4	3	.383	.471
Minor League Totals			.301	50	183	41	55	16	1	6	28	23	54	4	3	.386	.497

3 ALEX KIRILLOFF, OF

Born: Nov. 9, 1997. **B-T:** L-L. **Ht.:** 6-2. **Wt.:** 195. **Drafted:** HS—Pittsburgh, 2016 (1st round). **Signed by:** Jay Weitzel.

Drafted 15th overall in 2016 and signed away from Liberty with a bonus of $2,817,100, the home-schooled prodigy raked his way to MVP honors in the Appalachian League after skipping the GCL in his first pro summer. Shut down late in the year with inflammation in his throwing elbow, he rehabbed all offseason but still had to have Tommy John surgery last March that wiped out his 2017 season.

Drawing comparisons to such corner outfielders as Max Kepler and Christian Yelich, Kirilloff has strong wrists, quick hands, excellent balance and a smooth lefthanded swing. The year off gave him a chance to strengthen his lower half and pack on close to 30 pounds of muscle, which should enable him to get to his 15- to 20-homer potential sooner. Using an all-fields approach, he has an advanced understanding of the strike zone, outstanding barrel awareness and the almost effortless ability to hit for average. An average runner who has played center field but likely fits better in right, Kirilloff also shows soft hands at first base. That could be a fallback option down the road and a way to take stress off his elbow post-surgery.

Kirilloff figures to open 2018 in extended spring training before heading up to the Midwest League, where it shouldn't take him long to make up for lost time.

BA GRADE
60 Risk: Extreme
HIT: 60. **POW:** 50.
SPD: 50. **FLD:** 50.
ARM: 50.

Year	Club (League)	Class	AVG	G	AB	R	H	2B	3B	HR	RBI	BB	SO	SB	CS	OBP	SLG
2016	Elizabethton (APP)	R	.306	55	216	33	66	9	1	7	33	11	32	0	1	.341	.454
2017	Did not play—Injured																
Minor League Totals			.306	55	216	33	66	9	1	7	33	11	32	0	1	.341	.454

4 STEPHEN GONSALVES, LHP

Born: July 8, 1994. **B-T:** L-L. **Ht.:** 6-5. **Wt.:** 213. **Drafted:** HS—San Diego, 2013 (4th round). **Signed by:** John Leavitt.

Given an above-slot bonus of $700,000 as a fourth-round steal, Gonsalves has justified the Twins' faith after he pitched just 48 innings as a high school senior. Makeup concerns had caused him to drop after he was suspended eight games after covering for a teammate's drug use during a national tournament.

A shoulder strain landed Gonsalves on the shelf at the 2016 Arizona Fall League and again last spring, when he missed the first six weeks of the Double-A season. Once he returned, it didn't take him long to show the same smooth repeatable delivery, feel for pitching and advanced command that pushed him up the prospect rankings. Tall with long levers, good mound presence and a three-quarters arm slot, he pitches at 88-91 mph and touches 94 mph with his fastball, which shows glove-side run and plays up due to deception and extension. He reads hitters well and works effectively at the top of the zone. He featured his 1-to-6 curveball more often in 2017, when it was a put-away pitch at times. His slurvy slider is just fringe-average with short tilt, but his changeup earns an above-average future grade due to its late fade and his ability to maintain arm speed. He throws slightly across his body, but his shoulder issues aren't traceable to his mechanics.

One of three starters added to the 40-man roster in November, Gonsalves figures to open the year back at Triple-A Rochester. If he continues to hone his command and cut his walk rate, which reached a career-best 2.37 per nine innings in his second crack at Double-A, it shouldn't be long before he is vying for a spot in the middle of the big league rotation.

BA GRADE
50 Risk: Medium
FB: 50. CB: 55.
SL: 45. CHG: 55.
CTL: 55.

Year	Club (League)	Class	W	L	ERA	G	GS	CG	SV	IP	H	HR	BB	SO	K/9	WHIP	AVG
2015	Cedar Rapids (MWL)	LoA	6	1	1.15	9	9	0	0	55	29	2	15	77	12.6	0.80	.154
	Fort Myers (FSL)	HiA	7	2	2.61	15	15	1	0	79	66	2	38	55	6.2	1.31	.225
2016	Fort Myers (FSL)	HiA	5	4	2.33	11	11	1	0	66	43	2	20	66	9.0	0.96	.188
	Chattanooga (SL)	AA	8	1	1.82	13	13	1	0	74	43	1	37	89	10.8	1.08	.171
2017	Chattanooga (SL)	AA	8	3	2.68	15	15	0	0	87	67	7	23	96	9.9	1.03	.207
	Rochester (IL)	AAA	1	2	5.56	5	4	0	0	23	27	4	8	22	8.7	1.54	.294
Minor League Totals			41	17	2.39	90	86	3	0	478	347	20	173	514	9.7	1.09	.202

5 BRUSDAR GRATEROL, RHP

Born: Aug. 26, 1998. **B-T:** R-R. **Ht.:** 6-1. **Wt.:** 225. **Signed:** Venezuela, 2014. **Signed by:** Jose Leon.

Signed out of Venezuela for $150,000, three days after his 16th birthday, Graterol was part of the Twins' 2014-15 international signing class headlined by fellow right-hander Huascar Ynoa out of the Dominican Republic. While the Twins shipped Ynoa to the Atlanta Braves last July in Part 1 of the Jaime Garcia flip process, Graterol returned from Tommy John surgery to rocket up the prospect charts while dominating at two levels. In his final outing of a season capped at 40 innings and 75 pitches in any individual outing, he struck out five in the first three innings of an elimination-game win that sent Rookie-level Elizabethton on its way to a four-game winning streak and the Appalachian League title.

After sitting at 87-88 mph with his fastball pre-surgery, Graterol used the rehabilitation process to completely remake his body and his repertoire. Now 6-foot-1 and 225 pounds after packing on nearly 60 pounds of good weight, most noticeably in his legs and hindquarters, he has boosted his fastball to 95-98 mph with flashes up to 101 mph. That enabled him to blow past Double-A righty Fernando Romero for ownership of the best fastball in the system. Graterol also has a late-breaking plus slider at 85-89 mph and a hard curve at 80-83 mph that has a chance to be above-average. His 86-89 mph changeup projects as at least average with good action and feel for his age. Graterol figures to open 2018 at low Class A Cedar Rapids, where he will continue to build up his innings and mound experience.

With outstanding work ethic and aptitude that point toward continued improvement, he has the highest ceiling of any Twins prospect, projecting rotation-topping potential.

BA GRADE
60 Risk: Extreme
FB: 70. CB: 55.
SL: 60. CHG: 50.
CTL: 50.

Year	Club (League)	Class	W	L	ERA	G	GS	CG	SV	IP	H	HR	BB	SO	K/9	WHIP	AVG
2015	Twins (DSL)	R	0	1	2.45	4	4	0	0	11	12	0	1	17	13.9	1.18	.273
2016	Did not play—Injured																
2017	Twins (GCL)	R	2	0	1.40	5	2	0	0	19	10	1	4	21	9.8	0.72	.152
	Elizabethton (APP)	R	2	1	3.92	5	5	0	0	21	16	1	9	24	10.5	1.21	.213
Minor League Totals			4	2	2.65	14	11	0	0	51	38	2	14	62	10.9	1.02	.205

6 FERNANDO ROMERO, RHP

Born: Dec. 24, 1994. **B-T:** R-R. **Ht.:** 6-0. **Wt.:** 215. **Signed:** Dominican Republic, 2011. **Signed by:** Fred Guerrero.

Signed less than two months from his 17th birthday, the late-blooming Romero was discovered at a select tournament in Jupiter, Fla. He signed for $200,000 after an unexpected bidding war broke out.

Rated the Twins' No. 12 prospect after his first Gulf Coast League season, Romero was limited to just three starts in 2014-15 due to Tommy John surgery and a knee injury suffered doing box jumps. He roared back onto the radar with a standout 2016 and mostly built on those gains last season, although he did fade late due in part to a shoulder impingement that landed him on the disabled list. Despite lacking leverage and an ideal pitcher's frame, Romero shows the potential for three above-average pitches. He touches 98 mph with his fastball and pitches at 92-96 mph with heavy sink, although his lack of elite arm speed and a max-effort delivery have raised concerns about his durability. Rated the No. 11 prospect in the Southern League, his high-80s slider shows sharp tilt when he stays on top, but it tends to flatten out when he drifts in his delivery. His command can be erratic, and some see him eventually turning into a Francisco Rodriguez-type late-inning piece. His changeup is just average, allowing lefties to post an OPS that was 116 points higher than righties could muster.

Added to the 40-man roster after the 2016 season, Romero twice was bypassed in favor of fellow Dominican righthander Felix Jorge when the Twins needed a spot start last summer. Ticketed for Triple-A Rochester to start the year, Romero should get his opportunity soon. He projects as a No. 2 or No. 3 starter if he can round out his third pitch.

BA GRADE

55 Risk: High

FB: 60. SL: 60.
CHG: 50.
CTL: 50.

Year	Club (League)	Class	W	L	ERA	G	GS	CG	SV	IP	H	HR	BB	SO	K/9	WHIP	AVG
2015	Did not play—Injured																
2016	Cedar Rapids (MWL)	LoA	4	1	1.93	5	5	0	0	28	18	0	5	25	8.0	0.82	.186
	Fort Myers (FSL)	HiA	5	2	1.88	11	11	0	0	62	48	1	10	65	9.4	0.93	.211
2017	Chattanooga (SL)	AA	11	9	3.53	24	23	1	0	125	124	4	45	120	8.6	1.35	.256
Minor League Totals			23	16	2.85	69	54	1	0	303	261	6	92	294	8.7	1.16	.231

7 BRENT ROOKER, OF/1B

Born: Nov. 1, 1994. **B-T:** R-R. **Ht.:** 6-4. **Wt.:** 220. **Drafted:** Mississippi State, 2017 (1st round supplemental). **Signed by:** Derrick Dunbar.

Drafted in successive years by the Twins, Rooker improved his stock considerably by going back to college. After nearly accepting a modest 38th-round bonus in 2016, the Memphis-area product signed for the full-slot figure of $1.935 million following a record-setting season at Mississippi State. He also earned his degree with a double major in business administration and management. Terry Rooker, his father, caught four seasons at the University of Memphis and younger brother Josh is a freshman catcher there now, but neither ever tried to convert Brent to the position. Lynne Oliver, his mother, played college tennis at Baylor and Memphis.

Rooker hit the ground running as expected, showing plus power and hitting 18 combined homers in just 62 games in the Appalachian and Florida State leagues. Having honed his power stroke and improved his contact rate in college, the powerfully built Rooker reminds some of former Twins left fielder Josh Willingham. Rooker still has some swing-and-miss in his game, especially on power breaking balls and soft stuff from lefties, but his walk rate should improve along with his pitch recognition. Primarily a first baseman in college, Rooker showed enough mobility and arm to be a tick below average in left. He is a smart baserunner despite below-average speed. After ranking second in Division I with an average exit velocity of 92 mph, Rooker matched that number in the FSL during his first pro summer.

Already on the fast track due to his advanced bat, Rooker should remain in left as he climbs the ladder. He projects as a middle-of-the-order weapon with power as a strong carrying tool.

BA GRADE

55 Risk: High

HIT: 50. POW: 60.
SPD: 40. FLD: 50.
ARM: 45.

Year	Club (League)	Class	AVG	G	AB	R	H	2B	3B	HR	RBI	BB	SO	SB	CS	OBP	SLG
2017	Elizabethton (APP)	R	.282	22	85	19	24	5	0	7	17	11	21	2	2	.364	.588
	Fort Myers (FSL)	HiA	.280	40	143	23	40	6	0	11	35	16	47	0	0	.364	.552
Minor League Totals			.281	62	228	42	64	11	0	18	52	27	68	2	2	.364	.566

8 NICK GORDON, SS/2B

Born: Oct. 24, 1995. **B-T:** L-R. **Ht.:** 6-0. **Wt.:** 170. **Drafted:** HS—Orlando, 2014 (1st round). **Signed by:** Brett Dowdy.

Bloodlines bode well for Gordon, son of 21-year big league pitcher Tom "Flash" Gordon and younger half-brother of Marlins second baseman Dee Gordon. Drafted fifth overall in 2014 after a standout prep career in Orlando, the Florida State signee received a $3.851 million signing bonus as the first high school position player drafted. He flashed a low-90s fastball and promising curveball on the summer showcase circuit, but his admiration of Derek Jeter and love of the daily grind led him to the middle of the diamond.

Voted the ninth-best prospect and best defensive shortstop in the Southern League, Gordon slashed his way to an appearance at the All-Star Futures Game, where he was the only Twins representative. He managed just 13 extra-base hits after June 18, and he hit .211 over his final 180 at-bats. Lefties have given him trouble at multiple levels, but overall his hit tool tops his list of attributes. Not a burner like his brother but an instinctive runner, Gordon shows advanced barrel awareness to go with sound plate discipline and a line-drive swing that produces gap power. His range is just average and he struggles at times with footwork, hop anticipation and throwing accuracy. His frame remains lean, and he has struggled to add visible muscle. Rival evaluators have their doubts about Gordon's ability to remain at shortstop, where he has averaged 20 errors in his three full seasons thanks in part to struggles with his throwing accuracy.

With Royce Lewis and Wander Javier coming up fast behind him in the system and Jorge Polanco handling himself well at shortstop in the majors, Gordon figures to see more time on both sides of the bag (and possibly left field) as he makes the climb to Triple-A.

BA GRADE
50 Risk: Medium

HIT: 50. POW: 45.
SPD: 50. FLD: 50.
ARM: 55.

Year	Club (League)	Class	AVG	G	AB	R	H	2B	3B	HR	RBI	BB	SO	SB	CS	OBP	SLG
2015	Cedar Rapids (MWL)	LoA	.277	120	481	79	133	23	7	1	58	39	88	25	8	.336	.360
2016	Fort Myers (FSL)	HiA	.291	116	461	56	134	23	6	3	52	23	87	19	13	.335	.386
2017	Chattanooga (SL)	AA	.270	122	519	80	140	29	8	9	66	53	134	13	7	.341	.408
Minor League Totals			.281	415	1696	261	476	81	25	14	204	126	354	68	35	.337	.383

9 BLAYNE ENLOW, RHP

Born: March 21, 1999. **B-T:** R-R. **Ht.:** 6-3. **Wt.:** 180. **Drafted:** HS—St. Amant, La., 2017 (3rd round). **Signed by:** Greg Runser.

Rated No. 33 overall before the 2017 draft, Enlow accepted $2 million (well above slot value of $755,500) to forego a commitment to his hometown Louisiana State. He suffered a broken ankle and pelvis in a car accident before his sophomore year of high school, but he made it back to pitch as a senior for Team USA's 18U team.

Enlow was rated the 13th-best prospect in the GCL, where his longest outing was 4.1 innings. With a long, lanky pitcher's frame and good arm speed, Enlow projects to add more velocity to a fastball that already touches 95 mph. He pitches at 88-93 mph out of a high three-quarters arm slot, but his best offering is a plus-plus curveball that rated as the best in the high school draft class. Enlow's curve, already the best in the Twins' system, reaches 82-84 mph with tight spin that produces plenty of swings and misses. His 79-80 mph changeup has potential, but he's reluctant to use it. At the Twins' urging he added an 87-88 mph cutter upon signing. He stays in his delivery well and has good mound presence.

Heading into his age-19 season, the Twins figure to expose Enlow to low Class A Cedar Rapids. After making just one start in his first pro summer, he will get a chance to adjust to an increased workload. He projects as a No. 2 or No. 3 starter.

BILL MITCHELL

BA GRADE
55 Risk: Extreme

FB: 55. CB: 70.
CHG: 45. CUT: 45.
CTL: 50.

Year	Club (League)	Class	W	L	ERA	G	GS	CG	SV	IP	H	HR	BB	SO	K/9	WHIP	AVG
2017	Twins (GCL)	R	3	0	1.33	6	1	0	0	20	10	1	4	19	8.4	0.69	.141
Minor League Totals			3	0	1.33	6	1	0	0	20	10	1	4	19	8.4	0.69	.141

10 TYLER JAY, LHP

LINWOOD FERGUSON

Born: April 19, 1995. **B-T:** L-L. **Ht.:** 6-1. **Wt.:** 185. **Drafted:** Illinois, 2015 (1st round). **Signed by:** Jeff Pohl.

Taken sixth overall in 2015, one pick ahead of Arkansas outfielder Andrew Benintendi and three picks ahead of Ian Happ, Jay received a $3,889,500 signing bonus and initially made a seemingly successful transition to a starting role after serving as an All-American closer at Illinois.

Upon reaching Double-A at midseason 2016, however, the slightly built Jay ran into neck, shoulder and fatigue issues. After Jay was worn down by the summer heat and a rotation burden that caused him to shed 20 pounds, a mutual decision was made to return him to the bullpen last spring. Instead, more neck and shoulder woes (that he blamed on poor mechanics) limited him to just two appearances over the first four months of the season and had him fearing surgery before he finally returned for good in mid-August. Sent to the Arizona Fall League, Jay mostly pitched in the low-90s with his four-seam fastball but did touch 95 mph in the Fall Stars Game. A hard, late-breaking slider that showed plus potential at 86-87 mph in his first two seasons remained erratic upon his return. Even in relief he continued to flash an above-average curveball at 78-80 mph and a show-me changeup just in case he's used in multi-inning roles.

The product of the Chicago suburbs has a football background and a competitive streak that should serve him well as he pushes for a spot in the big league bullpen at some point in 2018.

BA GRADE

50 Risk: High

FB: 55. SL: 55. CB: 55. CHG: 40. CTL: 55.

Year	Club (League)	Class	W	L	ERA	G	GS	CG	SV	IP	H	HR	BB	SO	K/9	WHIP	AVG
2015	Fort Myers (FSL)	HiA	0	1	3.93	19	0	0	1	18	18	0	8	22	10.8	1.42	.247
2016	Fort Myers (FSL)	HiA	5	5	2.84	13	13	0	0	70	64	5	21	68	8.8	1.22	.248
	Chattanooga (SL)	AA	0	0	5.79	5	2	0	0	14	13	2	5	9	5.8	1.29	.245
2017	Chattanooga (SL)	AA	0	0	4.50	2	0	0	0	2	1	1	3	2	9.0	2.00	.143
	Twins (GCL)	R	0	0	4.91	3	1	0	0	4	6	1	1	7	17.2	1.91	.353
	Fort Myers (FSL)	HiA	3	0	1.50	3	0	0	0	6	4	0	0	10	15.0	0.67	.182
Minor League Totals			8	6	3.40	45	16	0	1	114	106	9	38	118	9.3	1.27	.247

11 AKIL BADDOO, OF

BA GRADE

50 Risk: High

Born: Aug. 16, 1998. **B-T:** L-L. **Ht.:** 6-1. **Wt.:** 209. **Drafted:** HS—Conyers, Ga., 2016 (2nd round supplemental). **Signed by:** Jack Powell.

Baddoo received a $750,000 signing bonus to walk away from a commitment to the Wildcats. Former Kentucky assistant coach Rick Eckstein, now Twins minor league hitting coordinator, recruited Baddoo out of high school. After struggling mightily in his first pro summer, Baddoo grew two inches and added nearly 25 pounds of muscle to his frame. He came back in his first full season and wowed evaluators with his overall improvement.

Drawing comparisons to ex-Twins outfielders such as Matt Lawton and Ben Revere, Baddoo projects to show more gap power than Revere and runs better than Lawton did at the same stage. Despite adding muscle, Baddoo still gets down the line in sub 4.1 seconds. Baddoo has an average arm at best but has worked hard to improve his routes in center. His basestealing instincts are still being honed. His best tool is his hitting ability, augmented by advanced plate discipline that saw him walk more than he struck out in 2017. He had no trouble handling lefthanders, although his power production suffered against them. Promoted to Rookie-level Elizabethton in mid-July, he took his game to another level (1.057 OPS that was third in the league) in leading a talent-laden club to the Appalachian League title.

If he continues to fill out, Baddoo could easily slide over to left field and be a three-hole hitter down the road. His makeup and aptitude suggest nothing should be deemed out of his reach. He figures to open 2018 at low Class A Cedar Rapids.

Year	Club (League)	Class	AVG	G	AB	R	H	2B	3B	HR	RBI	BB	SO	SB	CS	OBP	SLG
2016	Twins (GCL)	R	.178	38	107	15	19	0	2	2	15	18	36	8	1	.299	.271
2017	Twins (GCL)	R	.267	20	75	18	20	4	3	1	10	9	13	4	0	.360	.440
	Elizabethton (APP)	R	.357	33	126	39	45	15	2	3	19	27	19	5	4	.478	.579
Minor League Totals			.273	91	308	72	84	19	7	6	44	54	68	17	5	.389	.438

12 FELIX JORGE, RHP

BA GRADE
45 Risk: Medium

Born: Jan. 2, 1994. **B-T:** R-R. **Ht.:** 6-2. **Wt.:** 175. **Signed:** Dominican Republic, 2011. **Signed by:** Fred Guerrero.

Signed late in the 2010-11 signing period, nearly two months after his 17th birthday, Jorge has more than justified his $400,000 signing bonus. Durable and long-limbed, Jorge has drawn comparisons to a young Ervin Santana with his smooth, deceptive delivery and unflappable mound demeanor.

Jorge's fastball carries a wide range, clocking in at anywhere from 88-94 mph with good arm-side run on his two-seamer. His changeup is his best secondary pitch, and he also features a late-breaking slider and a slow curveball. Added to the 40-man roster for the first time last winter, he dedicated his season to late friend and former teammate Yorman Landa, killed in an auto accident in December 2016. Jorge was given a pair of midseason spot starts in the majors before 44-year-old Bartolo Colon was signed as a stopgap. In five starts above Double-A, Jorge struggled to a 6.95 ERA and saw his strikeout rate drop noticeably. A good athlete, Jorge holds runners and fields his position well.

Jorge figures to open 2018 back at Triple-A Rochester, where he appeared to wear down last August and saw his command fade in and out. Once considered a future mid-rotation piece, he now projects as back-of-the-rotation starter.

Year	Club (League)	Class	W	L	ERA	G	GS	CG	SV	IP	H	HR	BB	SO	K/9	WHIP	AVG
2015	Cedar Rapids (MWL)	LoA	6	7	2.79	23	22	0	0	142	118	11	32	114	7.2	1.06	.225
2016	Fort Myers (FSL)	HiA	9	3	1.55	14	14	2	0	93	76	3	11	77	7.5	0.94	.226
	Chattanooga (SL)	AA	3	5	4.12	11	11	1	0	74	83	7	12	32	3.9	1.28	.290
2017	Minnesota (AL)	MAJ	1	0	10.57	2	2	0	0	8	14	4	2	4	4.7	2.09	.412
	Chattanooga (SL)	AA	10	3	3.54	22	22	0	0	135	142	11	37	99	6.6	1.33	.273
	Rochester (IL)	AAA	0	1	5.02	3	3	0	0	14	19	3	3	9	5.7	1.53	.339
Major League Totals			1	0	10.57	2	2	0	0	8	14	4	2	4	4.7	2.09	.412
Minor League Totals			38	32	3.28	130	116	5	2	686	658	48	168	550	7.2	1.20	.254

13 LANDON LEACH, RHP

BA GRADE
50 Risk: High

Born: July 12, 1999. **B-T:** R-R. **Ht.:** 6-4. **Wt.:** 205. **Drafted:** HS—Ajax, Ont., 2017 (2nd round). **Signed by:** Walt Burrows.

The first Canadian player taken in the 2017 draft, Leach is a converted catcher who caught the eye of Twins' scouts during the spring while touring Florida with the Canadian Junior National Team. That gave the Twins 10-plus looks at him as he grew two inches and packed on 25 pounds of muscle in the months leading up to the draft.

Used sporadically as a closer off the mound as a high school senior, Leach signed for $1.4 million as a second-round pick (slot was $1.85 million). With his frame and repertoire, he draws comparisons to countryman Mike Siroka, a 2015 first-round pick of the Braves. Leach pitches at 90-94 mph, touching 97 mph with his fastball. He also features a sharp-breaking 84-86 mph slider and a present-average curve he throws at 78-80 mph. Now a full-time starter still learning a professional pitcher's routine, he also shows a good feel for his changeup at 79-81 mph. Due to his conversion and cold-weather background, Leach carries a good bit of projection even after his growth spurt.

Fluent in French and serious and focused off the field, the former junior hockey player shows good mound presence and high-end competitiveness. He repeats his delivery well and has taken steps to correct some pre-draft lapses into drop-and-drive.

Year	Club (League)	Class	W	L	ERA	G	GS	CG	SV	IP	H	HR	BB	SO	K/9	WHIP	AVG
2017	Twins (GCL)	R	2	0	3.38	5	2	0	0	13	11	0	6	10	6.8	1.28	.220
Minor League Totals			2	0	3.38	5	2	0	0	13	11	0	6	10	6.8	1.28	.220

14 YUNIOR SEVERINO, 2B

BA GRADE
55 Risk: Extreme

Born: Oct. 3, 1999. **B-T:** B-R. **Ht.:** 6-1. **Wt.:** 180. **Signed:** Dominican Republic, 2016. **Signed by:** Jonathan Cruz (Braves).

When the Braves' 2016 international class was largely declared as free agents for violations of MLB signing rules, the Twins moved aggressively to sign Kevin Maitan. When Maitan opted to sign with the Angels, the Twins quickly followed up with an excellent Plan B, as they signed Severino for $2.5 million, which is $600,000 more than he received in his original contract with the Braves and $300,000 more than Maitan received from the Angels.

A shortstop as an amateur, Severino moved to second base immediately upon signing with the Braves. His below-average speed limits his range at second and he's working on reading the ball off the bat, but his hands and arm work well enough to remain at second. He projects as an offensive second baseman with plus power potential and plenty of bat speed thanks to strong hands and wrists. Unlike many teenagers, Severino has present strength, as he drives the ball even when he's just working to make two-strike contact.

The switch-hitting Severino was able to handle the aggressive move to the Gulf Coast League in his pro debut. He'll likely make his Twins debut with Rookie-level Elizabethton in 2018.

Year	Club (League)	Class	AVG	G	AB	R	H	2B	3B	HR	RBI	BB	SO	SB	CS	OBP	SLG
2017	DSL Braves (DSL)	R	.189	10	37	6	7	2	1	0	2	8	6	0	0	.348	.297
2017	GCL Braves (GCL)	R	.286	48	189	27	54	17	2	3	27	16	61	0	1	.345	.444
Minor League Totals			.270	58	226	33	61	19	3	3	29	24	67	0	1	.345	.420

15 LUIS ARRAEZ, 2B

BA GRADE **50** Risk: High

Born: April 9, 1997. **B-T:** L-R. **Ht.:** 5-10. **Wt.:** 184. **Signed:** Venezuela, 2013.
Signed by: Jose Leon.

Signed out of Venezuela for just $40,000, seven months after turning 16, Arraez has added 30 pounds since turning pro.

After leading the Midwest League in hitting and posting park-adjusted production that was 46 percent above league average in 2016, Arraez went down for the year with a torn ACL in his right knee when he awkwardly tripped over first base while beating out a double-play grounder. That came after hitting .335 as a teenager in the Venezuelan Winter League. His hand-eye coordination is off the charts, but he sometimes tries to force inside-out contact, which could give him trouble as he climbs the ladder and faces more back-foot sliders and late-moving cutters. He hits the ball to the opposite field nearly half the time but is learning to turn on pitches that leak over the inner half. His hit tool is easily his best feature, but he's more athletic than he appears and his feet work well around the bag. He also has good hands, an outgoing personality and leadership skills, which help offset below-average arm strength and speed.

Arraez should open back in the Florida State League, where his career 8-percent strikeout rate (including winter ball) will be tested anew.

Year	Club (League)	Class	AVG	G	AB	R	H	2B	3B	HR	RBI	BB	SO	SB	CS	OBP	SLG
2015	Twins (GCL)	R	.309	57	207	23	64	15	1	0	19	19	10	8	8	.377	.391
2016	Cedar Rapids (MWL)	LoA	.347	114	475	67	165	31	3	3	66	31	51	3	5	.386	.444
2017	Fort Myers (FSL)	HiA	.385	3	13	1	5	0	1	0	1	0	0	0	0	.385	.538
Minor League Totals			.338	205	810	114	274	52	5	3	101	66	70	21	16	.391	.426

16 LEWIS THORPE, LHP

BA GRADE **50** Risk: High

Born: Nov. 23, 1995. **B-T:** R-L. **Ht.:** 6-1. **Wt.:** 180. **Signed:** Australia, 2012.
Signed by: Howard Norsetter.

Having missed two full seasons following Tommy John surgery in April 2015 and a bout of mononucleosis in 2016, the burly Australian began to put his career back on track in 2017.

After adding two inches and 35 pounds in his first two years after signing, Thorpe hasn't quite reclaimed the velocity that once saw his fastball touch 96-97 mph regularly. He still works at 91-94 mph and did show decent command out of his three-quarters slot with his changeup, which has good sink and fade and projects as a second plus pitch. He also has a tight slider with good depth and a 12-to-6 curve he learned from countryman Travis Blackley. Both breaking pitches have the potential to at least be average, allowing him to hold lefties to a .280 OBP last season and average better than a strikeout per inning for his career.

After pushing his 2017 innings total close to 100, including extended spring training, Thorpe was added to the 40-man roster for the first time after being exposed to the Rule 5 draft the previous offseason. He projects as a back-end starter but must watch his conditioning and off-field habits.

Year	Club (League)	Class	W	L	ERA	G	GS	CG	SV	IP	H	HR	BB	SO	K/9	WHIP	AVG
2015	Did not play—Injured																
2016	Did not play—Injured																
2017	Chattanooga (SL)	AA	1	0	6.00	1	1	0	0	6	5	2	2	7	10.5	1.17	.217
	Fort Myers (FSL)	HiA	3	4	2.69	16	15	0	0	77	62	3	31	84	9.8	1.21	.226
Minor League Totals			11	7	2.94	45	40	0	0	199	161	14	75	235	10.6	1.19	.223

17 LAMONTE WADE, OF

BA GRADE **50** Risk: High

Born: Jan. 1, 1994. **B-T:** L-L. **Ht.:** 6-1. **Wt.:** 189. **Drafted:** Maryland, 2015 (9th round). **Signed by:** John Wilson.

Plagued by a broken hamate bone in his junior year at Maryland, Wade slipped all the way to the ninth round, even after a powerful display in an NCAA regional upset of top-ranked UCLA. Signed for $163,800, Wade has consistently shown advanced strike-zone discipline and a high-end hit tool.

For his pro career he has drawn 17 percent more walks than strikeouts, a trait that can be traced back to his college career. He reminds some of a young Garret Anderson with a high-contact, line-drive swing. He shows occasional pull-side power. Sturdily built with average speed and a fringe-average arm, Wade has handled center field well enough due to his athleticism but projects as a left fielder with the ability to play all three in a pinch. Wade hit just .238 but again showed outstanding plate discipline at the Arizona Fall League until a scary outfield collision with Cardinals' center fielder Oscar Mercado ended his assignment with a week to go.

Wade was diagnosed with a concussion but avoided additional injury. He should open 2018 at Triple-A and could push for a big league look soon.

Year	Club (League)	Class	AVG	G	AB	R	H	2B	3B	HR	RBI	BB	SO	SB	CS	OBP	SLG
2015	Elizabethton (APP)	R	.312	64	231	36	72	8	5	9	44	46	34	12	1	.428	.506
	Cedar Rapids (MWL)	LoA	.143	4	14	1	2	0	0	0	1	1	2	0	0	.250	.143
2016	Cedar Rapids (MWL)	LoA	.280	56	207	32	58	6	3	4	27	44	27	5	3	.410	.396
	Fort Myers (FSL)	HiA	.318	32	110	17	35	8	1	4	24	10	17	1	1	.386	.518
2017	Chattanooga (SL)	AA	.292	117	424	74	124	22	3	7	67	76	71	9	2	.397	.408
Minor League Totals			.295	273	986	160	291	44	12	24	163	177	151	27	7	.404	.437

18 ZACK LITTELL, RHP

BA GRADE
50 Risk: High

Born: Oct. 5, 1995. **B-T:** R-R. **Ht.:** 6-3. **Wt.:** 200. **Drafted:** HS—Mebane, N.C., 2013 (11th round). **Signed by:** Devitt Moore (Mariners).

Traded twice before his 22nd birthday, the former Mariners 11th-rounder just keeps improving. Signed for $100,000 out of a rural North Carolina high school, the former Appalachian State signee was shipped to the Yankees for lefty reliever James Pazos after the 2016 season. Eight and a half months later he was on the move again, this time to the Twins at the July trade deadline for veteran lefty Jaime Garcia.

Blessed with a sturdy pitcher's frame and a repeatable delivery, Littell has made improvements to his conditioning, command and pitchability. He pitches at 91-93 mph with his fastball, showing the ability to work effectively up in the zone due to his high spin rate. His sweeping curveball has good bite and depth and projects to be a plus pitch. His changeup can be at least average with swing-and-miss fade. Littell pushed his groundball rate as high as 54 percent in the Southern League while seeing his walk rate spike close to four per game after joining the Twins. He avoids the long ball.

Added to the 40-man roster after the season, Littell should open 2018 at Triple-A Rochester. He projects as a solid mid-rotation piece with the potential for a little more.

Year	Club (League)	Class	W	L	ERA	G	GS	CG	SV	IP	H	HR	BB	SO	K/9	WHIP	AVG
2015	Clinton (MWL)	LoA	3	6	3.78	20	20	0	0	112	119	4	28	83	6.7	1.31	.272
2016	Clinton (MWL)	LoA	5	5	2.76	16	16	0	0	98	94	5	21	95	8.8	1.18	.258
	Bakersfield (CAL)	HiA	8	1	2.51	12	11	0	0	68	64	3	13	61	8.1	1.13	.246
2017	Tampa (FSL)	HiA	9	1	1.64	13	11	2	0	71	64	4	15	57	7.2	1.11	.251
	Trenton (EL)	AA	5	0	2.05	7	7	0	0	44	37	3	8	52	10.6	1.02	.224
	Chattanooga (SL)	AA	5	0	2.81	7	7	0	0	42	33	1	18	33	7.1	1.22	.223
Minor League Totals			40	24	3.16	98	92	4	1	538	525	25	128	473	7.9	1.21	.258

19 AARON WHITEFIELD, OF

BA GRADE
50 Risk: V. High

Born: Sept. 2, 1996. **B-T:** R-R. **Ht.:** 6-4. **Wt.:** 200. **Signed:** Australia, 2015. **Signed by:** Howard Norsetter.

Signed out of Australia for $70,000, Whitefield comes from a family of athletes and continues to impress with his athleticism and production.

Already among the best defensive outfielders in the system, the big-bodied Whitefield is remarkably light on his feet as he covers ground with plus range in center. His arm is just average. He is an above-average runner who has been timed at sub-4.0 seconds to first from the right side. Still fairly raw after focusing on softball into his mid-teens, he squared up a drastically open stance early last year with the help of low Class A hitting coach Brian Dinkelman. That helped Whitefield with his pitch recognition during a standout first half, although he tailed off in August and struggled overall against lefties.

Whitefield projects to add another 20 pounds of muscle, which should only add to his above-average raw power as he improves his contact rate. Coachable and intense, he figures to open 2018 in the Florida State League.

Year	Club (League)	Class	AVG	G	AB	R	H	2B	3B	HR	RBI	BB	SO	SB	CS	OBP	SLG
2015	Twins (GCL)	R	.167	7	18	1	3	0	0	0	1	2	4	1	0	.250	.167
2016	Twins (GCL)	R	.298	51	191	30	57	7	0	2	17	19	47	31	9	.370	.366
2017	Cedar Rapids (MWL)	LoA	.262	116	413	66	108	18	6	11	57	31	118	32	9	.318	.414
Minor League Totals			.270	174	622	97	168	25	6	13	75	52	169	64	18	.332	.392

20 TYLER WATSON, LHP

Born: May 22, 1997. **B-T:** R-L. **Ht.:** 6-5. **Wt.:** 200. **Drafted:** HS—Gilbert, Ariz., 2015 (34th round). **Signed by:** Mitch Sokol (Nationals).

BA GRADE
45 Risk: High

Signed out of a Loyola Marymount commitment for $400,000 in 2015, Watson was climbing the Nationals' prospect list when he was sent to the Twins (along with $500,000 of international bonus money) for all-star closer Brandon Kintzler at the July 31 trade deadline.

Though hardly overpowering with a fastball at 88-91 mph, Watson does have a projectable frame and hides the ball well with the ability to locate. Watson initially struggled after the trade and saw his strike-out rate drop significantly. However, he rallied to fan seven in a quality start on the road in the playoffs. His 74-mph downer curveball grades out as the best offering of his four-pitch mix, and his changeup projects as future average. He held righties to a .298 on-base percentage, 51 points lower than lefties, with a 23-percent strikeout rate across two leagues. He reminds some of former Twins lefty Mark Redman.

A good athlete, Watson fields his position well but needs to improve his pickoff move. He figures to open 2018 at high Class A Fort Myers and projects as a mid-rotation starter if his changeup keeps improving.

Year	Club (League)	Class	W	L	ERA	G	GS	CG	SV	IP	H	HR	BB	SO	K/9	WHIP	AVG
2015	Nationals (GCL)	R	1	1	0.00	5	4	0	0	13	7	0	4	16	10.8	0.83	.149
2016	Auburn (NYP)	SS	1	2	1.88	9	9	0	0	43	30	1	9	48	10.0	0.91	.189
	Hagerstown (SAL)	LoA	1	1	4.80	3	3	0	0	15	16	0	6	16	9.6	1.47	.296
2017	Hagerstown (SAL)	LoA	6	4	4.35	18	17	0	0	93	92	7	24	98	9.5	1.25	.258
	Cedar Rapids (MWL)	LoA	1	3	4.28	5	5	0	0	27	28	4	8	18	5.9	1.32	.264
Minor League Totals			10	11	3.52	40	38	0	0	192	173	12	51	196	9.2	1.17	.240

21 JOHN CURTISS, RHP

Born: April 5, 1993. **B-T:** R-R. **Ht.:** 6-4. **Wt.:** 210. **Drafted:** Texas, 2014 (6th round). **Signed by:** Marty Esposito.

BA GRADE
45 Risk: High

Signed for $266,900 out of the sixth round in 2014, Curtiss had already worked his way back from UCL and thoracic-outlet syndrome surgeries in an eight-month span while at the University of Texas. Serving as closer on a Longhorns team that reached the College World Series, Curtiss caught the eye of Twins area scout Marty Esposito.

An academic all-America and aspiring country singer-songwriter who graduated in three years with an English degree, Curtiss suffered a freak concussion in 2015 and later missed two months with elbow pain that had him fearing a second Tommy John procedure. Since improving his overall conditioning, Curtiss has posted a 2.04 ERA, 24 saves and 12.5 strikeouts per nine innings at four minor league levels. His fastball tops out at 98 mph and sits at 94-96 mph, but it was a much-improved mid-80s slider that gave him a dominant two-strike weapon.

Upon reaching the majors Curtiss struggled to control his emotions and his mechanics. He figures to get more seasoning at Triple-A, but he should eventually fit as a back-end bullpen piece.

Year	Club (League)	Class	W	L	ERA	G	GS	CG	SV	IP	H	HR	BB	SO	K/9	WHIP	AVG
2015	Twins (GCL)	R	1	0	1.13	5	0	0	0	8	7	0	4	7	7.9	1.38	.233
	Cedar Rapids (MWL)	LoA	3	3	6.07	16	7	0	2	46	62	10	10	44	8.6	1.57	.323
2016	Cedar Rapids (MWL)	LoA	0	0	0.00	6	0	0	2	8	2	0	2	17	19.1	0.50	.077
	Fort Myers (FSL)	HiA	0	2	3.06	38	0	0	3	53	42	0	23	68	11.5	1.23	.220
2017	Chattanooga (SL)	AA	2	0	0.72	21	0	0	13	25	12	0	12	35	12.6	0.96	.140
	Rochester (IL)	AAA	0	0	1.85	18	0	0	6	24	11	0	10	33	12.2	0.86	.131
	Minnesota (AL)	MAJ	0	0	8.31	9	0	0	0	9	9	2	2	10	10.4	1.27	.257
Major League Totals			0	0	8.31	9	0	0	0	9	9	2	2	10	10.4	1.27	.257
Minor League Totals			8	6	2.99	113	13	0	26	196	169	11	68	245	11.3	1.21	.232

22 JACOB PEARSON, OF

Born: June 1, 1998. **B-T:** L-R. **Ht.:** 6-1. **Wt.:** 185. **Drafted:** HS—West Monroe, La., 2017 (3rd round). **Signed by:** J.T. Zink (Angels).

BA GRADE
50 Risk: Extreme

The Angels bought Pearson, the Louisiana Gatorade player of the year last spring, out of a Louisiana State commitment with a $1 million bonus after drafting him 85th overall. After batting .519 with 12 homers, 41 RBIs and 53 runs to lead his high school team to a 38-3 record, Pearson struggled in the Rookie-level Arizona League and was traded to the Twins in the offseason for $1 million in international bonus money, which the Angels used to pursue Shohei Ohtani.

Pearson is a pure hitter with plus speed—he regularly clocks 4.1 seconds from home to first—and an advanced approach at the plate. He has a strong, athletic build and is physically mature. He doesn't wow with tools, but he generates solid bat speed with a quiet swing that doesn't have a lot of moving parts. His speed allows him to beat out infield hits and turn doubles into triples, and his ability to barrel the ball and impart backspin on it gives him surprising power. Defensively Pearson has a slightly below-average but accurate arm, moves to the ball aggressively in the outfield and has good hands and sound fundamentals.

Pearson was an older high school draftee who will turn 20 next season, so he should begin his Twins career at low Class A Cedar Rapids in 2018.

Year	Club (League)	Class	AVG	G	AB	R	H	2B	3B	HR	RBI	BB	SO	SB	CS	OBP	SLG
2017	Angels (AZL)	R	.226	40	155	20	35	7	1	0	13	15	37	5	3	.302	.284
Minor League Totals			.226	40	155	20	35	7	1	0	13	15	37	5	3	.302	.284

23 MITCH GARVER, C

BA GRADE 40 Risk: Medium

Born: Jan. 15, 1991. **B-T:** R-R. **Ht.:** 6-1. **Wt.:** 220. **Drafted:** New Mexico, 2013 (9th round). **Signed by:** Ted Williams.

Signed as a senior draft out of New Mexico for $40,000, Garver has worked hard to become the Twins' best homegrown option at catcher.

Garver tries to elevate pitches he can handle until reaching two strikes, at which point he shortens his swing and reverts to an all-field, situational approach. Through hard work and constant drilling, Garver has defied doubters and turned himself into an average receiver and blocker who handles pitchers well. He shows an above-average arm with much-improved accuracy, as shown by his organization-leading 48-percent success rate against opposing basestealers in 2016. A good athlete who runs just slightly below average, Garver gamely tried left field and first base at Triple-A in order to increase his versatility.

The decision to outright Chris Gimenez clears a path for Garver to serve as Jason Castro's understudy.

Year	Club (League)	Class	AVG	G	AB	R	H	2B	3B	HR	RBI	BB	SO	SB	CS	OBP	SLG
2015	Fort Myers (FSL)	HiA	.245	127	433	46	106	24	1	4	58	69	82	5	3	.356	.333
2016	Chattanooga (SL)	AA	.257	95	358	44	92	25	0	11	66	43	86	1	3	.334	.419
	Rochester (IL)	AAA	.329	22	76	6	25	5	0	1	8	7	21	0	0	.381	.434
2017	Rochester (IL)	AAA	.291	88	320	56	93	29	0	17	45	50	85	2	0	.387	.541
	Minnesota (AL)	MAJ	.196	23	46	5	9	1	3	0	3	6	15	0	0	.288	.348
Major League Totals			.196	23	46	5	9	1	3	0	3	6	15	0	0	.288	.348
Minor League Totals			.271	508	1819	233	493	127	4	51	286	249	370	15	11	.364	.429

24 JOSE MIRANDA, 2B

BA GRADE 50 Risk: Extreme

Born: June 29, 1998. **B-T:** R-R. **Ht.:** 6-2. **Wt.:** 180. **Drafted:** HS—Guaynabo, P.R., 2016 (2nd round supplemental). **Signed by:** Freddie Thon.

The second Puerto Rican player taken in his draft class, behind only Cardinals first-rounder Delvin Perez, Miranda found his power stroke in his first full pro season. He tied for the Appalachian League lead in home runs while fanning less than 10 percent of the time.

Extremely athletic and still growing into his body, Miranda shows advanced plate discipline and projects to hit for both average and power as he climbs the ladder. He has good balance at the plate with quiet hands and a moderate load and stride, enabling him to use all fields with authority. An average runner with an above-average arm, he has more than enough mobility to handle second.

Miranda did make eight errors in 37 games, but some of that was due to his above-average range. Miranda's power potential and future frame could land him at third permanently. He figures to open 2018 at low Class A Cedar Rapids.

Year	Club (League)	Class	AVG	G	AB	R	H	2B	3B	HR	RBI	BB	SO	SB	CS	OBP	SLG
2016	Twins (GCL)	R	.227	55	185	14	42	7	1	1	20	19	36	4	5	.308	.292
2017	Elizabethton (APP)	R	.283	54	223	43	63	8	2	11	43	16	24	2	3	.340	.484
Minor League Totals			.257	109	408	57	105	15	3	12	63	35	60	6	8	.325	.397

25 ANDREW BECHTOLD, 3B

BA GRADE 50 Risk: Extreme

Born: April 18, 1996. **B-T:** R-R. **Ht.:** 6-1. **Wt.:** 195. **Drafted:** Chipola (Fla.) JC, 2017 (5th round). **Signed by:** Jack Powell.

One of four Twins prospects to make the Appalachian League Top 20, Bechtold quickly justified the Twins' decision to give him $600,000 (58 percent above slot) in the fifth round.

A product of the Philadelphia suburbs, like fellow Twins infield prospect Travis Blankenhorn, Bechtold spent two seasons at Maryland before transferring to tradition-rich Chipola JC, where he led a talented Indians club to the NJCAA Division 1 World Series title. Area scout Jack Powell did extensive work on Bechtold, who was drafted behind two of his Chipola teammates (second-rounders Rey Rivera and Evan Steele). Bechtold's father Scott played football at Syracuse and baseball at Delaware, so it's no surprise the younger Bechtold is extremely athletic with a mature mindset and approach. He has the potential to be a high-end defender at third, where his plus arm strength already rates at the top of the Twins' system, and could be tried in right field down the road. He has a compact swing with above-average bat speed, a high-contact, all-fields approach and the potential for future power.

Bechtold is a fringe-average runner with good instincts who should start at low Class A Cedar Rapids.

Year	Club (League)	Class	AVG	G	AB	R	H	2B	3B	HR	RBI	BB	SO	SB	CS	OBP	SLG
2017	Elizabethton (APP)	R	.299	43	144	33	43	10	1	2	19	27	40	0	0	.406	.424
Minor League Totals			.299	43	144	33	43	10	1	2	19	27	40	0	0	.406	.424

26 LEWIN DIAZ, 1B

BA GRADE

45 Risk: High

Born: Sept. 19, 1996. **B-T:** L-L. **Ht.:** 6-3. **Wt.:** 250. **Signed:** Dominican Republic, 2013. **Signed by:** Fred Guerrero.

Surprisingly left off the 40-man roster ahead of the Rule 5 draft, Diaz was signed for $1.4 million out of the Dominican Republic at the start of the 2013-14 international signing period.

Diaz' 70 raw power ranks a tick behind supplemental first-rounder Brent Rooker within the organization, and Diaz is gradually finding ways to get to that power during games. Most of his thump comes to the opposite field at this point as he learns he can shorten his swing and still do damage against both righties and lefties. Conditioning has been an issue after he packed on 40 pounds after signing, but he made significant strides last year at low Class A Cedar Rapids in improving his diet and cutting body fat. Those changes helped him maintain his strength throughout the season, and he saw his production improve in the second half. He has soft hands, smooth actions and surprisingly good mobility at first base, where he is an average to above-average defender. He has an above-average arm but lacks the wheels (below-average runner) to go back out to right field after some early career looks.

Friendly and coachable, Diaz has a personality that has evaluators waiting for him to make that next leap once everything clicks. He figures to open the year at high Class A Fort Myers.

Year	Club (League)	Class	AVG	G	AB	R	H	2B	3B	HR	RBI	BB	SO	SB	CS	OBP	SLG
2015	Twins (GCL)	R	.261	33	111	12	29	7	1	1	15	14	24	2	0	.354	.369
	Elizabethton (APP)	R	.167	14	48	7	8	1	0	3	5	3	17	0	0	.245	.375
2016	Elizabethton (APP)	R	.310	46	174	26	54	15	2	9	37	12	35	0	0	.353	.575
2017	Cedar Rapids (MWL)	LoA	.292	121	462	47	135	32	1	12	68	25	79	2	1	.329	.444
Minor League Totals			.280	257	939	109	263	68	4	30	152	80	179	4	1	.342	.457

27 ZACK GRANITE, OF

BA GRADE

40 Risk: Medium

Born: Sept. 17, 1992. **B-T:** L-L. **Ht.:** 5-11. **Wt.:** 167. **Drafted:** Seton Hall, 2013 (14th round). **Signed by:** John Wilson.

A classic undersized scrapper in the Brett Butler mold, the former 14th-round pick out of Seton Hall is a self-made prospect. A criminal justice major who hails from a family of educators, he is a 60 runner with the basestealing instincts to match.

Granite makes up for an average arm in center field with solid routes and jumps, and he showed the ability to play all three spots during a pair of big league callups in 2017. He stepped in ably for Byron Buxton during the latter's injury absence in late July, earning the trust of manager Paul Molitor with his situational hitting and bunting ability. Granite was named Twins minor league player of the year in 2016 after a breakout season at Double-A Chattanooga, where he credits manager Doug Mientkiewicz with teaching him to start his hands earlier and turn on more pitches on the inner half. Granite has well below-average power but shows a good approach, advanced plate discipline, a line-drive swing and enough strength to hit balls in the gaps.

Granite did have a couple of odd blips, throwing to an uncovered first base at Dodger Stadium and completely missing first base at Yankee Stadium on a close play in the wild-card game, but those figure to be footnotes to an unlikely big league career.

Year	Club (League)	Class	AVG	G	AB	R	H	2B	3B	HR	RBI	BB	SO	SB	CS	OBP	SLG
2015	Cedar Rapids (MWL)	LoA	.358	19	67	17	24	5	1	0	5	12	6	7	1	.463	.463
	Fort Myers (FSL)	HiA	.249	105	381	59	95	10	4	1	26	41	63	21	12	.328	.304
2016	Chattanooga (SL)	AA	.295	127	526	86	155	18	8	4	52	42	43	56	14	.347	.382
2017	Fort Myers (FSL)	HiA	.368	5	19	2	7	1	1	0	1	2	2	3	0	.429	.526
	Rochester (IL)	AAA	.338	71	284	46	96	16	4	5	29	24	34	15	6	.392	.475
	Minnesota (AL)	MAJ	.237	40	93	14	22	2	0	1	13	12	9	2	2	.321	.290
Major League Totals			.237	40	93	14	22	2	0	1	13	12	9	2	2	.321	.290
Minor League Totals			.293	413	1612	262	472	56	25	10	139	156	185	120	44	.357	.377

28 DAVID BANUELOS, C

BA GRADE

45 Risk: High

Born: Oct. 1, 1996. **B-T:** R-R. **Ht.:** 6-0. **Wt.:** 205. **Drafted:** Long Beach State, 2017 (5th round). **Signed by:** Gary Patchett (Mariners).

Few catchers in the 2017 draft class come close to Banuelos' elite defensive ability. He was traded from the Mariners to the Twins in exchange for $1 million in international bonus money.

Banuelos is a born leader with outstanding makeup, and the fact that he is bilingual and can easily communicate with his pitching staff is icing on the cake. His arm strength grades plus, with pop times to second base as quick as 1.9 seconds. In addition to his pure arm strength, Banuelos assesses situations well, picks up runners' tendencies quickly and makes firm throws. He has soft hands and blocks well, projecting to be an above-average-to-plus defender. Banueloos' biggest question is how much he'll hit at higher levels. He controls the barrel and has a patient approach, but projects as a fringe-average hitter at best for evaluators. There is an expectation his near-average power will play when he controls the zone better.

Banuelos projects as a backup catcher. He'll head to full-season ball in 2018.

Year	Club (League)	Class	AVG	G	AB	R	H	2B	3B	HR	RBI	BB	SO	SB	CS	OBP	SLG
2017	Everett (NWL)	SS	.236	36	127	24	30	8	0	4	26	16	40	1	1	.331	.394
Minor League Totals			.236	36	127	24	30	8	0	4	26	16	40	1	1	.331	.394

29 TRAVIS BLANKENHORN, 2B/3B

BA GRADE

45 Risk: High

Born: Aug. 3, 1996. **B-T:** L-R. **Ht.:** 6-2. **Wt.:** 208. **Drafted:** HS—Pottsville, Pa., 2015 (3rd round). **Signed by:** Jay Weitzel.

A Kentucky baseball commit who signed for $650,000 after earning all-state honors in Pennsylvania football and basketball, Blankenhorn missed 12 days with a strained lower back late in 2017. During his absence, Cedar Rapids manager Tommy Watkins had him chart whether the first three pitches to each batter were strikes or balls, driving home the importance of getting into offensive counts.

He homered five times in his first 11 games after coming off the disabled list and suddenly seemed to have unlocked himself against pitches on the inner half. Blankenhorn draws comparisons to a young Daniel Murphy. He flashes above-average as a runner, but his arm is average to a tick below. He spent most of the first half at third base before moving back to second base, where he moves well around the bag and shows better range to his left.

The ball gets on him in a hurry at third, so Blankenhorn's days at the hot corner seem numbered. Intense and streakier than most, he hangs in against lefties fairly well.

Year	Club (League)	Class	AVG	G	AB	R	H	2B	3B	HR	RBI	BB	SO	SB	CS	OBP	SLG
2015	Twins (GCL)	R	.245	14	49	6	12	4	2	0	3	7	11	2	0	.362	.408
	Elizabethton (APP)	R	.243	39	144	14	35	3	0	3	20	11	32	1	0	.306	.326
2016	Elizabethton (APP)	R	.297	34	138	30	41	7	1	9	29	8	33	3	0	.342	.558
	Cedar Rapids (MWL)	LoA	.286	25	91	11	26	5	2	1	12	8	28	2	1	.356	.418
2017	Cedar Rapids (MWL)	LoA	.251	117	438	68	110	22	11	13	69	46	119	13	2	.342	.441
Minor League Totals			.260	229	860	129	224	41	16	26	133	80	223	21	3	.339	.436

30 KOHL STEWART, RHP

BA GRADE

45 Risk: V. High

Born: Oct. 7, 1994. **B-T:** R-R. **Ht.:** 6-3. **Wt.:** 195. **Drafted:** HS—Houston, 2013 (1st round). **Signed by:** Greg Runser.

Amid another year of nagging injuries—issues with his left knee sent him to the disabled list twice in 2017—Stewart saw his once-bright star continue to fade. Left off the 40-man roster and unprotected and unpicked in the Rule 5 draft, the one-time Texas A&M quarterback signee struggled so far.

Even his trademark heavy sinker, which he throws at 91-92 mph, dropped off in terms of groundball rate (46.9 percent) in his second crack at the Southern League. A Type-1 diabetic, Stewart doesn't miss bats despite a hard 86-87 mph slider at and a 92-96 mph four-seamer. He also features a 12-to-6 curveball and a slow-developing changeup.

Now considered a back-end rotation piece at best, Stewart has struggled both to control his emotions and pick up the nuances of pitch sequencing.

Year	Club (League)	Class	W	L	ERA	G	GS	CG	SV	IP	H	HR	BB	SO	K/9	WHIP	AVG
2015	Fort Myers (FSL)	HiA	7	8	3.20	22	22	1	0	129	134	4	45	71	4.9	1.38	.273
2016	Fort Myers (FSL)	HiA	3	2	2.61	9	9	0	0	52	39	2	19	44	7.7	1.12	.207
	Chattanooga (SL)	AA	9	6	3.03	16	16	1	0	92	91	4	44	47	4.6	1.47	.265
2017	Rochester (IL)	AAA	1	0	7.20	1	1	0	0	5	7	1	1	5	9.0	1.60	.333
	Chattanooga (SL)	AA	5	6	4.09	16	16	0	0	77	72	4	45	52	6.1	1.52	.253
Minor League Totals			28	27	3.10	90	87	2	0	462	431	17	182	305	5.9	1.33	.249

New York Mets

BY MATT EDDY

The Mets began 2017 all-in but ended the year all-out after falling to seventh place in the National League wild card standings at the trade deadline. That triggered a sell-off that could benefit the 2018 team—but only if they can keep stars such as Noah Syndergaard, Yoenis Cespedes and Jeurys Familia healthy.

The Mets executed five trades in which they parted with pending free agents Jay Bruce, Lucas Duda, Curtis Granderson, Addison Reed and Neil Walker. In addition to shedding salary, the five trades yielded predictable consequences.

Minus those five veterans—and with starting pitchers Syndergaard, Steven Matz and Zack Wheeler on the disabled list—the Mets played .373 ball in August and September on their way to 92 losses. But those short-term defeats could contribute to long-term victories.

With their poor finish, the Mets snagged the No. 6 pick in the 2018 draft, while lowered expectations afforded playing time for top prospects such as shortstop Amed Rosario, first baseman Dominic Smith and outfielder Brandon Nimmo.

The 21-year-old Rosario ranked as the top prospect in the Triple-A Pacific Coast League and showed flashes of brilliance at the plate and in the field in Queens. Smith improved his power production by swatting 25 home runs between the minors and majors, while Nimmo compiled a .379 on-base percentage in the majors. Along with breakout star Michael Conforto, a first-time all-star in 2017, the quartet could form the core of the Mets' future lineup.

The farm system wasn't nearly so successful at patching holes on the pitching staff, and the team that rode young power pitchers to the 2015 World Series finished 2017 with a 5.01 ERA, third-worst in the majors. Rookie starters Robert Gsellman (5.19 ERA) and Chris Flexen (7.88) looked overmatched at times.

Overall, the Mets suffered from a lack of bullpen firepower—only the Twins had a lower reliever fastball velocity—because their inventory of hard-throwers has suffered from prospect graduations, injuries and trades of pitchers such as Michael Fulmer, Luis Cessa and Akeel Morris. To address the situation, the Mets targeted power relievers with every trade they made in 2017, including a deal with the Marlins for closer A.J. Ramos that cost them 21-year-old righthander Merandy Gonzalez, who ranked second in the minors with a 1.66 ERA.

In all, the Mets added seven young right-handed relievers to the system. Two of them, Jamie Callahan and Jacob Rhame, made their big

Amed Rosario showed flashes of offensive and defensive brilliance in his rookie season.

PROJECTED 2021 LINEUP

Catcher	Kevin Plawecki (30)
First Base	Dominic Smith (26)
Second Base	Andres Gimenez (22)
Third Base	Wilmer Flores (29)
Shortstop	Amed Rosario (25)
Left Field	Brandon Nimmo (28)
Center Field	Juan Lagares (32)
Right Field	Michael Conforto (28)
No. 1 Starter	Jacob deGrom (33)
No. 2 Starter	Noah Syndergaard (28)
No. 3 Starter	Steven Matz (30)
No. 4 Starter	David Peterson (25)
No. 5 Starter	Robert Gsellman (27)
Closer	Justin Dunn (25)

league debuts as September callups and averaged 95 mph. Meanwhile, Gerson Bautista hit 101 mph at high Class A and Drew Smith showed off a high-spin, swing-and-miss curveball at Double-A Binghamton. Though they are farther from the majors, Eric Hanhold, Steve Nogosek and Ryder Ryan all sit in the mid-90s with riding life on their fastballs and also throw power breaking pitches.

Following the graduation of blue-chip prospects Conforto, Matz, Rosario and Syndergaard in recent years, the upper levels of the Mets system is thin, with no impact prospects near the big league level. One bright spot could be Peter Alonso, who showcased big power as he finished his first full season in Double-A.

DEPTH CHART

NEW YORK METS

TOP 2018 ROOKIE: Marcos Molina, RHP. The physical, three-pitch starter will be next man up when the rotation needs reinforcing.

BREAKOUT PROSPECT: Christian James, RHP. The projectable Florida prep drafted in 2016 already throws a plus breaking ball and could blossom if he adds a tick to his velocity.

SLEEPER: Sebastian Espino, SS. He experienced a growth spurt just as the Mets signed him in 2016, and his Dominican Summer League-leading 27 extra-base hits in 2017 attest to his power.

SOURCE OF TOP 30 TALENT			
Homegrown	26	Acquired	4
College	8	Trade	4
Junior college	1	Rule 5 draft	0
High school	10	Independent league	0
Nondrafted free agent	0	Free agent/waivers	0
International	7		

LF
Quinn Brodey (22)
Jhoan Urena
Wagner LaGrange

CF
Desmond Lindsay (8)
Ranfy Adon
Champ Stuart
Anthony Dirocie

RF
Adrian Hernandez (28)
Wuilmer Becerra
Jose Miguel Medina

3B
Mark Vientos (6)
David Thompson (29)
Gregory Guerrero
Rigoberto Terrazas

SS
Andres Gimenez (1)
Luis Guillorme (10)
Ronny Mauricio (11)
Sebastian Espino
Colby Woodmansee
Dylan Snypes

2B
Gavin Cecchini (13)
Luis Carpio (26)
Phillip Evans

1B
Peter Alonso (4)
Dash Winningham
Jeremy Vasquez

C
Tomas Nido (12)
Patrick Mazeika (18)
Ali Sanchez (27)
Brandon Brosher
Juan Uriarte

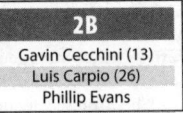

LHP

LHSP
David Peterson (2)
Thomas Szapucki (5)
Anthony Kay (14)

LHRP
P.J. Conlon (24)
Aaron Ford

RHP

RHSP
Justin Dunn (3)
Marcos Molina (7)
Chris Flexen (9)
Jordan Humphreys (15)
Corey Oswalt (16)
Christian James (30)
Harol Gonzalez
Tony Dibrell
Marcel Renteria
Tyler Pill
Ricky Knapp
Carlos Hernandez
Joey Cavallaro
Ezequiel Zabaleta
David Marcano
Junior Santos

RHRP
Jamie Callahan (17)
Ty Bashlor (19)
Drew Smith (20)
Adonis Uceta (21)
Jacob Rhame (23)
Gerson Bautista (25)
Steve Nogosek
Ryder Ryan
Eric Hanhold
Corey Taylor
Chasen Bradford
Kevin McGowan
Matt Blackham
Stephen Villines
Austin McGeorge
Joe Shaw
Alex Palsha
Josh Payne
Trey Cobb

DRAFT ANALYSIS

2017

BEST PURE HITTER: SS Mark Vientos (2) doesn't turn 18 until December but had no trouble adjusting to pro ball. After a slow start, he hit .305/.339/.467 in 115 August at-bats. He even launched four homers in the Rookie-level Gulf Coast League after hitting only one as a high school senior in Plantation, Fla. The Mets were on Vientos since February because of his plus bat speed, projectable 6-foot-4 frame and swing conducive to elevating the ball.

BEST POWER HITTER: Vientos has the highest power upside, but OF Quinn Brodey (3) has the most present power. He hit a career-high 11 homers as a Stanford junior and three in a pro debut spent mostly at short-season Brooklyn, a park notorious for suppressing lefthanded power.

FASTEST RUNNER: The Mets drafted few position players and targeted more bat-first players when they did. Brodey turns in times of 6.6 seconds in the 60-yard dash, while Oral Roberts SS Dylan Snypes (15) is a plus runner.

BEST DEFENSIVE PLAYER: Vientos has good hands and a strong arm at shortstop, but if he outgrows the position he can be a plus defender at third base.

BEST ATHLETE: Brodey also worked as a lefthanded pitcher in high school and as a college freshman.

BEST FASTBALL: RHP Marcel Renteria (6) hit 98 mph as a starter at New Mexico State. RHP Tony Dibrell (4) peaks at 95 mph but pitches with plus sinking life at about 93 as a starter.

BEST SECONDARY PITCH: LHP David Peterson (1) has the two best secondary pitches in the Mets' draft class. He shows advanced command of a plus slider that gives batters fits because of its unique angle and deceptive late drop. He wears out lefthanded batters with the pitch but also goes cross-corner to back foot righthanders. Peterson's changeup is another potential plus weapon that began to play when he improved his control as an

TOP DRAFT PICKS OF THE DECADE

Year	Player, Pos.	2017 Org
2008	Ike Davis, 1B	Dodgers
2009	Steven Matz, LHP (2nd round)	Mets
2010	Matt Harvey, RHP	Mets
2011	Brandon Nimmo, OF	Mets
2012	Gavin Cecchini, SS	Mets
2013	Dominic Smith, 1B	Mets
2014	Michael Conforto, OF	Mets
2015	Desmond Lindsay, OF (2nd round)	Mets
2016	Justin Dunn, RHP	Mets
2017	David Peterson, LHP	Mets

Oregon junior.

BEST PRO DEBUT: Sidearming Kansas RHP Stephen Villines (10) sits in the high 80s and can touch 90 mph to go with a slurvy breaking ball. In 27.1 innings as a reliever, mostly at Brooklyn, he recorded a 1.65 ERA with 41 strikeouts and only one walk.

MOST INTRIGUING BACKGROUND: Vientos' father was born in the Dominican Republic but grew up in New York and passed his Mets fandom on to his family. Peterson's father Doug, who passed away in 2004, worked as a thoroughbred horse trainer, notably for triple crown winner Seattle Slew.

CLOSEST TO THE MAJORS: Despite working just 3.2 innings at Brooklyn because he signed late and dealt with a toe injury, Peterson throws four pitches and is nearly fully developed. He simply needs to add polish to reach his ceiling as a workhorse mid-rotation starter.

BEST LATE-ROUND PICK: Nova Southeastern (Fla.) 1B Jeremy Vasquez (28) launched eight home runs and 15 doubles in 67 games at Rookie-level Kingsport and Brooklyn, while playing above-average defense at first base. West Texas A&M RHP Josh Payne (22) reached 96 mph while striking out 25 and walking four in 16.1 innings as a reliever at Kingsport

—MATT EDDY

2016

The advanced trio of RHP Justin Dunn (1), LHP Anthony Kay (1) and 1B Peter Alonso (2) has hit some early snags. Alonso has played the best, but has the most limited profile. Dunn struggled in 2017 and injury has sidelined Kay since the draft.

GRADE: C

2015

This class has big upside, but injuries threaten to derail it. OF Desmond Lindsay (2), LHP Thomas Szapucki (5) and RHP Jordan Humphreys (18) - all drafted from Florida's prep ranks - are promising, but are all coming back from elbow surgery.

GRADE: C

2014

The Mets are likely to only get OF Michael Conforto (1) out of this draft, but he alone makes it a success. No other player from the class made the handbook, though the Mets did deal SS Milton Ramos (3) for international bonus pool money.

GRADE: B

1 ANDRES GIMENEZ, SS

Born: Sept. 4, 1988. **B-T:** L-R. **Ht.:** 5-11. **Wt.:** 176.
Signed: Venezuela, 2015. **Signed by:** Robert Espejo/Hector Rincones.

The Mets acknowledged Gimenez's talent by signing him for $1.2 million in 2015, when he ranked as the No. 2 prospect on the international market, but they now hold his athleticism, maturity and work ethic in similarly high regard. After hitting .350 in his pro debut in 2016, when he led the Dominican Summer League with a .469 on-base percentage, he skipped domestic short-season ball entirely to make his U.S. debut at low Class A Columbia in late April 2017. As one of four 18-year-old regular position players in the South Atlantic League, Gimenez more than held his own, ranking 12th in the league with a .346 OBP and 11th with a 15.3 percent strikeout rate.

Described as a "ball of dynamite" by one Mets official, Gimenez has a shorter, thicker build than many shortstops but compensates with twitchy athleticism. Scouts expect him to impact the ball more frequently as his body matures in his 20s. Gimenez pushed his average to .289 on Aug. 2, but he closed the year in an 18-for-91 (.198) skid as he dealt with a jammed thumb and general fatigue. Nothing phases Gimenez at the plate, where he has the attributes to be an above-average hitter. His lefthanded swing is direct to the ball, and he identifies pitches well, doesn't swing and miss often and hangs in versus southpaws. Skeptics question his batting upside potential, however, because he has average present running speed, while his power projects to be below-average. Body control and quick actions serve Gimenez at shortstop, where he has above-average range, reliable hands and an arm that plays up to plus thanks to a quick release and accuracy. His instincts and feel for the game will keep him at shortstop—where he has plus defensive potential—as he climbs the ladder, while his arm and reliability would allow him to shift to second or third base as needed.

Given his youth and distance from the big leagues, Gimenez's future role has not yet come into focus. Some scouts fall short of giving him a single plus tool, which could make him a second-division regular or utility infielder, but those who see a plus middle-infield defender and above-average hitter envision a potential double-play partner for shortstop Amed Rosario in Queens. Gimenez has three more minor league levels to master before then, and that task begins at high Class A St. Lucie in 2018.

TOM PRIDDY

BA GRADE	SCOUTING GRADES
55 Risk: High	**HIT:** 55. **POW:** 40. **SPD:** 50. **FLD:** 60. **ARM:** 60.

Projected future grades on 20-80 scouting scale

TOP PROSPECTS OF THE DECADE

Year	Player, Pos.	2017 Org
2008	Fernando Martinez, OF	Did not play
2009	Fernando Martinez, OF	Did not play
2010	Jenrry Mejia, RHP	Permanently banned
2011	Jenrry Mejia, RHP	Permanently banned
2012	Zack Wheeler, RHP	Mets
2013	Zack Wheeler, RHP	Mets
2014	Noah Syndergaard, RHP	Mets
2015	Noah Syndergaard, RHP	Mets
2016	Steven Matz, LHP	Mets
2017	Amed Rosario, SS	Mets

BEST TOOLS

Best Hitter for Average	Andres Gimenez
Best Power Hitter	Pete Alonso
Best Strike-Zone Discipline	Desmond Lindsay
Fastest Baserunner	Champ Stuart
Best Athlete	Desmond Lindsay
Best Fastball	Ty Bashlor
Best Curveball	Chris Flexen
Best Slider	Thomas Szapucki
Best Changeup	Adonis Uceta
Best Control	Jordan Humphreys
Best Defensive Catcher	Ali Sanchez
Best Defensive Infielder	Luis Guillorme
Best Infield Arm	Andres Gimenez
Best Defensive Outfielder	Desmond Lindsay
Best Outfield Arm	Wagner Lagrange

Year	Club (League)	Class	AVG	G	AB	R	H	2B	3B	HR	RBI	BB	SO	SB	CS	OBP	SLG
2016	Mets2 (DSL)	R	.360	31	114	24	41	10	4	1	17	21	13	7	1	.461	.544
	Mets1 (DSL)	R	.340	31	100	28	34	10	0	2	21	25	9	6	7	.478	.500
2017	Columbia (SAL)	LoA	.265	92	347	50	92	9	4	4	31	28	61	14	8	.346	.349
Minor League Totals			.298	154	561	102	167	29	8	7	69	74	83	27	16	.397	.415

2 DAVID PETERSON, LHP

Born: Sept. 3, 1995. **B-T:** L-L. **Ht.:** 6-6. **Wt.:** 240. **Drafted:** Oregon, 2017 (1st round). **Signed by:** Jim Reeves.

An unsigned 28th-round pick out of high school, Peterson blossomed as an Oregon junior after he clicked with new pitching coach Jason Dietrich. He ranked sixth in Division I (and first in the Pacific-12 Conference) with 140 strikeouts. The Mets selected him 20th overall in 2017 and signed him for a tick less than $3 million.

Peterson walked 3.5 per nine innings in his first two college seasons before reducing that rate to 1.4 in 2017, when he showed the best control in his draft class. A physical, 6-foot-6 lefthanded starter, he has ordinary fastball velocity—he sits 90-91 mph and peaks at 95—but above-average sink and run to go with a wide repertoire. Peterson shows advanced command of an above-average, low-80s slider that flummoxes batters with its unique angle and deceptive late drop. It's an out pitch versus lefthanders and a back-foot weapon against righties. His fading changeup could develop into an above-average weapon now that he has sharpened his fastball command. He throws an occasional fringy curveball early in counts.

Peterson signed at deadline and then had surgery to remove an ingrown toenail, which inhibited his ability to walk or pitch, so he made just three abbreviated starts at short-season Brooklyn, none more than 39 pitches in duration. He notched 20- and 17-strikeout games at Oregon in 2017, but his repertoire suggests more of a durable, strike-throwing, groundball-oriented No. 3 or 4 starter.

BA GRADE
55 Risk: High
FB: 50. CB: 40.
SL: 55. CHG: 50.
CTL: 60.

Year	Club (League)	Class	W	L	ERA	G	GS	CG	SV	IP	H	HR	BB	SO	K/9	WHIP	AVG
2017	Brooklyn (NYP)	SS	0	0	2.45	3	3	0	0	4	4	0	1	6	14.7	1.36	.267
Minor League Totals			0	0	2.45	3	3	0	0	4	4	0	1	6	14.7	1.36	.267

3 JUSTIN DUNN, RHP

Born: Sept. 22, 1995. **B-T:** R-R. **Ht.:** 6-2. **Wt.:** 195. **Drafted:** Boston College, 2016 (1st round). **Signed by:** Michael Pesce.

Dunn worked primarily as a reliever at Boston College until moving to the rotation two months before the 2016 draft. He pitched well enough in eight starts to generate first-round attention, and the Mets selected him 19th overall. He shined at short-season Brooklyn in his debut but struggled with the jump to high Class A St. Lucie in 2017, where he ran up a 5.00 ERA.

As a starter with an athletic delivery, quick, loose arm and pitchability, Dunn could be in line for better days ahead. He flashes a plus fastball and slider, his primary weapons in college, but below-average control and command hampered his effectiveness. At his best, he ranges from 92-96 mph with above-average life on his fastball and breaks off a mid-80s slider with late three-quarters tilt. He even shows surprising command of a changeup given his bullpen background, but just as a platoon split plagued him in college, Dunn needs to find a way to retire lefthanded batters after they hit .345/.464/.462 against him in the Florida State League.

BA GRADE
55 Risk: V. High
FB: 60. SL: 60.
CHG: 45.
CTL: 50.

If he improves his fastball command, changeup and stamina, Dunn could profile as a No. 3 or 4 starter. If he doesn't, he should have no trouble reaching the big leagues as a high-leverage reliever. A key development year in which he should reach Double-A awaits.

Year	Club (League)	Class	W	L	ERA	G	GS	CG	SV	IP	H	HR	BB	SO	K/9	WHIP	AVG
2016	Brooklyn (NYP)	SS	1	1	1.50	11	8	0	0	30	25	1	10	35	10.5	1.17	.227
2017	St. Lucie (FSL)	HiA	5	6	5.00	20	16	0	0	95	101	5	48	75	7.1	1.56	.273
Minor League Totals			6	7	4.16	31	24	0	0	125	126	6	58	110	7.9	1.47	.263

4 PETER ALONSO, 1B

Born: Dec. 7, 1994. **B-T:** R-R. **Ht.:** 6-3. **Wt.:** 245. **Drafted:** Florida, 2016 (2nd round).
Signed by: Jon Updike.

Alonso's incredible righthanded power translated from Florida to pro ball. He launched a 421-foot home run to center field at the 2015 College World Series, and the blast still stands as the longest at Omaha's TD Ameritrade Park. In 2017 he walloped a Florida State League-leading 16 home runs at high Class A St. Lucie at the time the Mets promoted him to Double-A—despite missing six weeks with a broken hand.

BA GRADE

50 Risk: High

HIT: 50. POW: 60.
SPD: 30. FLD: 30.
ARM: 40.

Alonso generates by far the highest exit velocity and has the most power in the Mets system. He looks for pitches to elevate with his plus-plus raw power, and the ball carries to all fields when he connects. In addition to plus game power, Alonso has a chance for an average hit tool because he hits the ball hard with frequency and doesn't swing and miss as much as many sluggers. A well below-average runner and uncoordinated, slow-bodied defender, he committed 19 errors at first base in 2017, the majority of them fielding miscues and dropped catches. He requires a lot of work to be playable in the field.

Alonso has crushed lefthanders as a pro, compiling a 1.166 OPS, but he has hit a more modest .256/.316/.456 against same-side pitchers. Regardless, his power will play in the big leagues, perhaps in the second half of 2018, whether as a regular or a platoon masher.

Year	Club (League)	Class	AVG	G	AB	R	H	2B	3B	HR	RBI	BB	SO	SB	CS	OBP	SLG
2016	Brooklyn (NYP)	SS	.321	30	109	20	35	12	1	5	21	11	22	0	1	.382	.587
2017	St. Lucie (FSL)	HiA	.286	82	308	45	88	23	0	16	58	25	64	3	4	.361	.516
	Binghamton (EL)	AA	.311	11	45	7	14	4	1	2	5	2	7	0	0	.340	.578
Minor League Totals			.297	123	462	72	137	39	2	23	84	38	93	3	5	.364	.539

5 THOMAS SZAPUCKI, LHP

Born: June 12, 1996. **B-T:** R-L. **Ht.:** 6-2. **Wt.:** 181. **Drafted:** HS—Palm Beach Gardens, 2015 (5th round). **Signed by:** Cesar Aranguren.

One of the most promising pitchers in the Mets system, Szapucki looked sharp during his full-season debut at low Class A Columbia. He made just six starts, however, because he missed April and May while recovering from a shoulder impingement, then had Tommy John surgery in July that will cost him the 2018 season. His 2016 season also ended prematurely with back stiffness at short-season Brooklyn.

A physical 6-foot-2 lefthander, Szapucki when healthy delivers high-quality stuff from the left side out of a low three-quarters arm slot. He ranges from 90-96 mph and sits 93 with electric life on his plus fastball. He commands his big-breaking, low-80s slider and uses it as an out pitch. Szapucki even showed feel for a changeup he has developed in his three pro seasons, though it remains fringe-average. His control grades as below-average but can be improved with better direction to the plate.

BA GRADE

55 Risk: Extreme

FB: 60. CB: 50.
SL: 60. CHG: 45.
CTL: 45.

Szapucki might have ranked No. 1 in the system had he remained healthy—he has that kind of ceiling. If he recovers fully and proves his durability, he can develop into a No. 3 starter. He turns 23 in 2019, when he is targeted to return to the mound.

Year	Club (League)	Class	W	L	ERA	G	GS	CG	SV	IP	H	HR	BB	SO	K/9	WHIP	AVG
2015	Mets (GCL)	R	0	0	15.43	3	0	0	0	2	5	0	0	3	11.6	2.14	.455
2016	Kingsport (APP)	R	2	1	0.62	5	5	0	0	29	16	2	9	47	14.6	0.86	.157
	Brooklyn (NYP)	SS	2	2	2.35	4	4	0	0	23	10	0	11	39	15.3	0.91	.130
2017	Columbia (SAL)	LoA	1	2	2.79	6	6	0	0	29	24	0	10	27	8.4	1.17	.231
Minor League Totals			5	5	2.27	18	15	0	0	83	55	2	30	116	12.5	1.02	.187

6 MARK VIENTOS, SS/3B

Born: Dec. 11, 1999. **B-T:** R-R. **Ht.:** 6-4. **Wt.:** 185. **Drafted:** HS—Plantation, Fla., 2017 (2nd round). **Signed by:** Cesar Aranguren.

The youngest player selected in the top 10 rounds of the 2017 draft, Vientos didn't turn 18 until December of his draft year. His father was born in the Dominican Republic but grew up in New York a Mets fan and couldn't contain his excitement when New York selected Vientos in the second round and signed him for $1.5 million out of Florida prep power American Heritage.

The Mets zeroed in on Vientos early in the spring season, drawn to his fast, powerful swing, strong hands and projectable 6-foot-4 frame. He started slow in the Rookie-level Gulf Coast League but then hit .305/.339/.467 in 115 August at-bats. After hitting only one home run as a prep senior, Vientos clubbed four homers in the GCL, and the Mets believe his knack for elevating the ball will lead to plus power down the road. Though he is a well below-average runner, he has plus hands and an above-average arm at shortstop. Most scouts project him to third base because he's not as quick as a typical shortstop and his frame still has plenty of room to fill out.

BA GRADE
55 Risk: Extreme
HIT: 50. **POW:** 55.
SPD: 30. **FLD:** 50.
ARM: 55.

Vientos offers a promising blend of offensive upside and left-side-of-the-infield value, but he is four years or more away from the big leagues. With a good spring training, he could be on track for low Class A Columbia in 2018.

Year	Club (League)	Class	AVG	G	AB	R	H	2B	3B	HR	RBI	BB	SO	SB	CS	OBP	SLG
2017	Mets (GCL)	R	.259	47	174	22	45	12	0	4	24	14	42	0	2	.316	.397
	Kingsport (APP)	R	.294	4	17	1	5	2	0	0	2	1	4	0	0	.333	.412
Minor League Totals			.262	51	191	23	50	14	0	4	26	15	46	0	2	.318	.398

7 MARCOS MOLINA, RHP

Born: March 8, 1995. **B-T:** R-R. **Ht.:** 6-3. **Wt.:** 206. **Signed:** Dominican Republic, 2012. **Signed by:** Daurys Nin/Gerardo Cabrera.

Noted for his arm strength early in his career, Molina began to produce results and gain prospect helium at short-season Brooklyn in 2014. He lost momentum in 2015 and 2016 as he dealt with an elbow injury that required Tommy John surgery, but a convincing season at Double-A Binghamton in 2017, after recovering from a lat strain, restored his shine.

With a workhorse physique and easy, athletic delivery, Molina throws strikes and generates above-average life on all his pitches. He sat 94 mph in the Arizona Fall League in 2016, but his velocity dipped to 91 mph with a peak of 93 in 2017 as he focused on commanding and sinking the ball. He commands his high-spin two-seamer to both sides of the plate and hides the ball well. Molina's plus low-80s slider has late three-quarters tilt and depth to play against batters on both sides of the plate. His mid-80s changeup took a step forward in 2017 and projects as average.

BA GRADE
50 Risk: High
FB: 55. **SL:** 60.
CHG: 50.
CTL: 60.

Based on his pitch profile and sharp control, Molina has the attributes to be a No. 4 starter. If he rediscovers a few ticks of velocity, he could be better than that. He figures to be the next Mets starter to make his major league debut at some point in 2018.

Year	Club (League)	Class	W	L	ERA	G	GS	CG	SV	IP	H	HR	BB	SO	K/9	WHIP	AVG
2015	Mets (GCL)	R	0	0	0.00	1	1	0	0	3	0	0	0	3	9.0	0.00	.000
	St. Lucie (FSL)	HiA	1	5	4.57	8	7	0	0	41	49	1	11	36	7.8	1.45	.295
2016	Did not play—Injured																
2017	St. Lucie (FSL)	HiA	2	3	1.26	5	5	0	0	29	17	1	5	23	7.2	0.77	.174
	Binghamton (EL)	AA	3	7	3.92	13	12	2	0	78	77	5	21	63	7.3	1.26	.260
Minor League Totals			22	23	3.27	64	56	3	0	336	293	12	83	299	8.0	1.12	.233

8 DESMOND LINDSAY, OF

Born: Jan. 15, 1997. **B-T:** R-R. **Ht.:** 5-11. **Wt.:** 196. **Drafted:** HS—Sarasota, Fla., 2015 (2nd round). **Signed by:** Cesar Aranguren.

The Mets' top draft pick in 2015 after they sacrificed their first-rounder to sign free agent Michael Cuddyer, Lindsay has flashed impact potential in pro ball—but only in glimpses and only in between injuries. Hamstring trouble affected him in high school and in his first two pro seasons, then in 2017 he was plagued by elbow trouble that required season-ending surgery in late July to transpose his ulnar nerve.

At full strength, Lindsay has power-speed potential and a discerning batting eye. He struggled out of the gate in 2017 at low Class A Columbia and hit just .149 through his first 38 games, but an altered eyeglass prescription might have cued a late surge. In his final 27 games before surgery, he hit .300/.352/.560 with six of his eight home runs. Lindsay has plus raw power and impacts the ball to all fields when he connects, but he didn't do that often enough, with rates for walks (13 percent) and strikeouts (31 percent) that ranked among the highest in the South Atlantic League. A prep third baseman, Lindsay has used his above-average speed to develop into an average center fielder with an average arm.

A healthy season would go a long way toward determining Lindsay's future potential and timetable. Moving to a more hitter-friendly park at high Class A St. Lucie in 2018 could help.

BA GRADE
55 Risk: Extreme
HIT: 50. POW: 55.
SPD: 50. FLD: 50.
ARM: 50.

Year	Club (League)	Class	AVG	G	AB	R	H	2B	3B	HR	RBI	BB	SO	SB	CS	OBP	SLG
2015	Mets (GCL)	R	.304	21	69	10	21	4	2	1	6	11	21	3	2	.400	.464
	Brooklyn (NYP)	SS	.200	14	45	3	9	3	0	0	7	7	19	0	1	.308	.267
2016	Mets (GCL)	R	.364	5	11	3	4	1	0	0	0	5	5	0	0	.563	.455
	Brooklyn (NYP)	SS	.297	32	111	18	33	5	0	4	17	20	26	3	1	.418	.450
2017	Columbia (SAL)	LoA	.220	65	214	40	47	10	1	8	30	33	77	4	2	.327	.388
Minor League Totals			.253	137	450	74	114	23	3	13	60	76	148	10	6	.366	.404

9 CHRIS FLEXEN, RHP

Born: July 1, 1994. **B-T:** R-R. **Ht.:** 6-3. **Wt.:** 250. **Drafted:** HS—Newark, Calif., 2012 (14th round). **Signed by:** Jim Blueberg.

Flexen began the 2017 season on the disabled list after having surgery to remove a bone spur from his right knee. He ended it in the big leagues after a 10-start run through the minors that included his first seven turns at Double-A. Flexen missed time in 2014 and 2015 recovering from Tommy John surgery and wasn't ready for prime time as an emergency callup in 2017, as indicated by his 7.88 ERA in 48 innings.

Flexen added a few ticks to his fastball, threw more strikes and improved the effectiveness of his mid-70s curveball in 2017. In fact, he recorded the second-highest curveball spin rate on Mets' big league staff, finishing a (distant) second to Seth Lugo, owner of the highest-spin curve of the Statcast era. Flexen pitches at.92 mph and can reach 96, while adeptly adding sinking or riding life to his fastball by changing his grip. He made progress with his average changeup, but would benefit from developing his fringe-average slider into a chase pitch.

Flexen commands three pitches but lacks a knockout offering. Without an out pitch, he profiles as a No. 5 starter or reliever.

BA GRADE
45 Risk: Medium
FB: 50. CB: 55.
SL: 45. CHG: 50.
CTL: 50.

Year	Club (League)	Class	W	L	ERA	G	GS	CG	SV	IP	H	HR	BB	SO	K/9	WHIP	AVG
2015	Mets (GCL)	R	0	0	0.00	3	2	0	0	6	2	0	1	5	7.5	0.50	.100
	Brooklyn (NYP)	SS	0	2	5.11	3	2	0	0	12	15	0	8	13	9.5	1.86	.300
	Savannah (SAL)	LoA	4	0	1.87	6	5	0	0	34	28	0	7	33	8.8	1.04	.226
2016	St. Lucie (FSL)	HiA	10	9	3.56	25	25	1	0	134	125	6	51	95	6.4	1.31	.249
2017	St. Lucie (FSL)	HiA	0	0	2.13	3	3	0	0	13	12	1	3	13	9.2	1.18	.245
	Binghamton (EL)	AA	6	1	1.66	7	7	2	0	49	28	4	7	50	9.2	0.72	.165
	New York (NL)	MAJ	3	6	7.88	14	9	0	0	48	62	11	35	36	6.8	2.02	.321
Major League Totals			3	6	7.88	14	9	0	0	48	62	11	35	36	6.8	2.02	.321
Minor League Totals			32	21	3.28	78	74	5	0	417	376	24	140	343	7.4	1.24	.239

10 LUIS GUILLORME, 2B/SS

Born: Sept. 27, 1994. **B-T:** L-R. **Ht.:** 5-9. **Wt.:** 199. **Drafted:** HS—Coral Springs, Fla., 2013 (10th round). **Signed by:** Mike Silvestri.

Guillorme won the low Class A South Atlantic League MVP in 2015 despite not hitting a single home run. He continued his high-contact, low-watt production with a season of extremes at Double-A Binghamton in 2017. He ranked second in the Eastern League with 72 walks while turning in the EL's lowest strikeout rate (10 percent) and isolated power (.048).

Guillorme drew national attention during spring training 2017 when he nonchalantly barehanded a bat hurtling for the Mets dugout. Appropriately, his scouting report begins with lightning-quick hands and reflexes, which he parlays into plus defensive ability at shortstop and second base. He confidently makes difficult plays in the field with above-average range, a solid-average arm and a great internal clock. Guillorme hardly ever pulls the ball and has bottom-of-the-scale power, but he could develop an average hit tool because he works deep counts, hits the ball hard consistently and uses the whole field.

As a lefthanded batter who brings a plus glove to shortstop, second base or third base, Guillorme is a shoo-in for a utility infielder role. If his bat develops, he could be a second-division regular, possibly at second base for the Mets, where no long-term solution is apparent.

BA GRADE
45 Risk: Medium
HIT: 45. POW: 20.
SPD: 50. FLD: 70.
ARM: 55.

Year	Club (League)	Class	AVG	G	AB	R	H	2B	3B	HR	RBI	BB	SO	SB	CS	OBP	SLG
2015	Savannah (SAL)	LoA	.318	122	446	67	142	16	0	0	55	54	70	18	8	.391	.354
2016	St. Lucie (FSL)	HiA	.263	123	441	47	116	16	2	1	46	43	63	4	2	.332	.315
2017	Binghamton (EL)	AA	.283	128	481	70	136	20	0	1	43	72	55	4	3	.376	.331
Minor League Totals			.285	474	1774	246	505	66	2	2	172	204	233	38	21	.361	.328

11 RONNY MAURICIO, SS

BA GRADE
55 Risk: Extreme

Born: April 4, 2001. **B-T:** B-R. **Ht.:** 6-2. **Wt.:** 165. **Signed:** Dominican Republic, 2017. **Signed by:** Marciano Alvarez/Gerardo Cabrera.

Mets international scouts first set eyes on Mauricio at a Dominican Prospect League event. They stuck with him in the months leading up to the 2017 signing period, when the 16-year-old ranked as the No. 3 prospect on the international market but appeared fatigued at times as he showcased daily for teams. The Mets ultimately signed Mauricio for $2.1 million, a franchise record for an international amateur, surpassing Amed Rosario in 2012.

A switch-hitter from a young age with plenty of room to fill out his 6-foot-2 frame, Mauricio could develop into a power-hitting shortstop with the fluid actions to stick there. Direct to the ball despite long limbs, he projects for plus power once he fills out his skinny frame. His effortless stroke is compact, particularly from the left side, and he has good bat-to-ball skills. A below-average runner, Mauricio has smooth actions and good range at shortstop to go with a plus arm. He has solid body control and a strong internal clock, though some scouts project him to third base because of his size and lack of pure speed.

Mauricio will make his pro debut in 2018, possibly at a U.S. affiliate.

Year	Club (League)	Class	AVG	G	AB	R	H	2B	3B	HR	RBI	BB	SO	SB	CS	OBP	SLG
2017	Did not play—Signed 2018 contract																

12 TOMAS NIDO, C

BA GRADE
45 Risk: Medium

Born: April 12, 1994. **B-T:** R-R. **Ht.:** 6-0. **Wt.:** 210. **Drafted:** HS—Maitland, Fla., 2012 (8th round). **Signed by:** Mike Silvestri.

Nido moved to the Orlando area from Puerto Rico while in high school, then signed for $250,000 as an eighth-round pick rather than attend Florida State. A slow climb up the ladder brought him to Double-A Binghamton in 2017, his sixth pro season, prior to a September callup to New York, where he started a pair of games.

Nido offers above-average defensive ability at catcher but faces questions about his offensive potential. Despite winning a surprising batting title in the high Class A Florida State League in 2016, he's better known for his above-average raw power. He could tap that power more frequently with a more refined approach, but he focuses on making contact and tends to put the ball in play on the ground. Nido shines defensively with a plus arm that he used to throw out 45 percent of Eastern League basestealers to go with strong receiving and blocking skills. The Mets' internal metrics grade his pitch-framing favorably because he frequently steals strikes for his pitchers.

With a fringe bat and strong defensive acumen, Nido could make for an ideal backup catcher.

Year	Club (League)	Class	AVG	G	AB	R	H	2B	3B	HR	RBI	BB	SO	SB	CS	OBP	SLG
2015	Savannah (SAL)	LoA	.259	86	317	39	82	14	2	6	40	12	86	1	1	.284	.372
2016	St. Lucie (FSL)	HiA	.320	90	344	38	110	23	2	7	46	19	42	0	1	.357	.459
2017	Binghamton (EL)	AA	.232	102	367	41	85	19	1	8	60	30	63	0	0	.287	.354
	New York (NL)	MAJ	.300	5	10	0	3	1	0	0	3	0	2	0	0	.300	.400
Major League Totals			.300	5	10	0	3	1	0	0	3	0	2	0	0	.300	.400
Minor League Totals			.261	407	1459	156	381	74	6	25	193	91	276	4	5	.304	.371

13 GAVIN CECCHINI, 2B/SS

BA GRADE
45 Risk: Medium

Born: Dec. 22, 1993. **B-T:** R-R. **Ht.:** 6-2. **Wt.:** 196. **Drafted:** HS—Lake Charles, La., 2012 (1st round). **Signed by:** Tommy Jackson.

The 12th overall pick in 2012, Cecchini shined in the Triple-A Pacific Coast League in 2016, batting .325 with walks and gap power, but the hits did not fall at Las Vegas in 2017: He showed similar secondary skills but hit just .267. Undone by a poor first half, he watched fellow middle infielders T.J. Rivera and Matt Reynolds pass him on the organizational depth chart and gain a foothold in New York.

Cecchini received a late-season callup for the second year in a row, but now looks more like a utility option rather than a potential regular. He shows strong bat-to-ball skills but below-average power and speed to go with choppy infield actions. A good batting eye and a knack for hard contact give Cecchini a chance for an average hit tool, but a level swing plane and groundball batted-ball profile nets him below-average power. Cecchini teamed with shortstop Amed Rosario at Las Vegas in 2017, playing mostly second base for the first time in his career. His average arm with questionable accuracy fits best at second, where he shows average range and converts routine plays.

Cecchini probably faces more time at Triple-A because of the Mets' middle-infield depth.

Year	Club (League)	Class	AVG	G	AB	R	H	2B	3B	HR	RBI	BB	SO	SB	CS	OBP	SLG
2015	Binghamton (EL)	AA	.317	109	439	64	139	26	4	7	51	42	55	3	4	.377	.442
2016	Las Vegas (PCL)	AAA	.325	117	446	71	145	27	2	8	55	48	55	4	1	.390	.448
	New York (NL)	MAJ	.333	4	6	2	2	2	0	0	2	0	2	0	0	.429	.667
2017	Las Vegas (PCL)	AAA	.267	110	453	68	121	27	3	6	39	40	61	5	4	.329	.380
	New York (NL)	MAJ	.208	32	77	4	16	2	0	1	7	4	19	0	1	.256	.273
Major League Totals			.217	36	83	6	18	4	0	1	9	4	21	0	1	.270	.301
Minor League Totals			.283	571	2193	323	620	124	16	30	237	219	327	29	20	.348	.395

14 ANTHONY KAY, LHP

BA GRADE
55 Risk: Extreme

Born: March 21, 1995. **B-T:** L-L. **Ht.:** 6-0. **Wt.:** 190. **Drafted:** Connecticut, 2016 (1st round). **Signed by:** Michael Pesce.

Kay attended the same Long Island, N.Y., high school as Steven Matz, and joined the Mets as the 31st overall pick in the 2016 draft after three years at Connecticut. He had his bonus offer reduced to an under-slot $1.1 million after a physical turned up an elbow injury.

Kay had Tommy John surgery in October of his draft year, and returned to action at 2017 instructional league, where he threw bullpen sessions. In college, he drew praise for one of the best changeups in his draft class. The pitch features late fading action and could develop into a plus offering once he recovers his feel post-surgery. He pitches in the low 90s and topped out near 95 mph while in college. A high-spin curveball rounds out his repertoire.

Barring further setbacks, Kay should be ready to begin 2018 with a full-season club and log his first pro innings. A realistic ceiling for his workload should fall between 90 to 110 innings.

Year	Club (League)	Class	W	L	ERA	G	GS	CG	SV	IP	H	HR	BB	SO	K/9	WHIP	AVG
2016	Did not play—Injured																
2017	Did not play—Injured																

15 JORDAN HUMPHREYS, RHP

BA GRADE
50 Risk: High

Born: June 11, 1996. **B-T:** R-R. **Ht.:** 6-2. **Wt.:** 223. **Drafted:** HS—Crystal River, Fla., 2015 (18th round). **Signed by:** Jon Updike.

Under southeast regional supervisor Steve Barningham, the Mets have hit the state of Florida hard in recent drafts, both at the top of the board—second-round position players Pete Alonso, Desmond Lindsay and Mark Vientos—and with later-round high school pitchers. The 18th-rounder Humphreys fits in the latter group, along with righthanders such as John Gant (2011), Rob Whalen (2012) and Christian James (2016).

Humphreys began to emerge as a prospect in 2016, but didn't fully break through until 2017, when he went 10-1, 1.42 in 11 starts at low Class A Columbia to earn a mid-June promotion. He made just two starts at high Class A St. Lucie before going down with an elbow injury that required Tommy John surgery in August. Humphreys has all the ingredients to be a No. 4 starter. He throws strikes to both sides of the plate with plus fastball control (career walk rate of 1.6 per nine innings), he changes eye levels with a high-spin, high-70s curveball and has begun to develop feel for a solid-average changeup. He sat in the high 80s in high school before his body matured, but now pitches at 90-92 mph and tops out at 94. His fastball misses bats up in the zone with riding life.

Humphreys won't pitch in a game until 2019, but once healthy he could move quickly.

Year	Club (League)	Class	W	L	ERA	G	GS	CG	SV	IP	H	HR	BB	SO	K/9	WHIP	AVG
2015	Mets (GCL)	R	0	0	1.54	7	0	0	2	12	12	0	1	7	5.4	1.11	.255
2016	Kingsport (APP)	R	3	5	3.76	12	12	0	0	69	65	3	15	76	9.9	1.15	.247
	Brooklyn (NYP)	SS	0	1	1.50	1	1	0	0	6	7	0	1	9	13.5	1.33	.292
2017	Columbia (SAL)	LoA	10	1	1.42	11	11	2	0	70	41	2	9	80	10.3	0.72	.168
	St. Lucie (FSL)	HiA	0	0	4.09	2	2	0	0	11	17	1	3	3	2.5	1.82	.340
Minor League Totals			13	7	2.58	33	26	2	2	168	142	6	29	175	9.4	1.02	.226

16 COREY OSWALT, RHP

Born: Sept. 3, 1993. **B-T:** R-R. **Ht.:** 6-5. **Wt.:** 250. **Drafted:** HS—San Diego, 2012 (7th round). **Signed by:** Fred Mazuca.

BA GRADE
45 Risk: High

Intrigued by Oswalt's physical, 6-foot-5 frame and clean arm action in 2012, the Mets bought him out of a UC Santa Barbara commitment for $475,000. Because he converted to pitching as a high school senior, Oswalt (no relation to Roy) spent three seasons in short-season ball and another two at Class A.

Oswalt advanced to Double-A Binghamton in 2017 and claimed Eastern League pitcher of the year honors after leading the circuit in ERA (2.28) and ranking fourth in strikeout rate (8.0 per nine innings). He ranges from 90-94 mph and throws downhill with excellent plane and sink on his fastball. He allowed just nine home runs in 24 starts in 2017 and has always shown above-average control. A pair of solid-average secondary pitches paved the way for his breakthrough. His mid-80s split-changeup helps him neutralize lefthanders, while his 12-to-6 curveball with low-80s velocity has developed into a weapon.

Oswalt doesn't draw many plus grades, but he does enough things well to reach the majors in a No. 4 or 5 starter role, perhaps as early as 2018 after being added to the 40-man roster in November.

Year	Club (League)	Class	W	L	ERA	G	GS	CG	SV	IP	H	HR	BB	SO	K/9	WHIP	AVG
2015	Savannah (SAL)	LoA	11	5	3.36	23	23	0	0	129	153	6	21	99	6.9	1.35	.299
2016	Mets (GCL)	R	0	0	0.00	1	1	0	0	1	0	0	0	3	27.0	0.00	.000
	St. Lucie (FSL)	HiA	4	2	4.12	14	13	0	0	68	73	4	18	68	9.0	1.34	.271
2017	Binghamton (EL)	AA	12	5	2.28	24	24	2	0	134	118	9	40	119	8.0	1.18	.236
Minor League Totals			37	18	3.36	86	80	2	0	448	462	21	102	379	7.6	1.26	.266

17 JAMIE CALLAHAN, RHP

Born: Aug. 24, 1994. **B-T:** R-R. **Ht.:** 6-2. **Wt.:** 230. **Drafted:** HS—Dillon, S.C., 2012 (2nd round). **Signed by:** Quincy Boyd (Red Sox).

BA GRADE
45 Risk: High

The Red Sox drafted Callahan in the second round in 2012 out of high school. By 2015 they had made him a reliever, after he ran up a 6.96 ERA as a starter at low Class A the year before. He began to progress more rapidly beginning in 2016, and by the time the Mets acquired him in 2017, he had reached Triple-A. He joined New York along with fellow relievers Gerson Bautista and Stephen Nogosek in the trade that sent Addison Reed to Boston.

Callahan experienced a velocity spike at midsummer 2017 by going from 92-95 mph to 94-97 with a high of 99 and riding life above the barrel. The quality of his slider improved dramatically in 2017, especially when paired with a higher-octane fastball. His high-80s slider grades as above-average and generates myriad swinging strikes. He also has a splitter that the Mets have encouraged him to throw more often.

Callahan, who made his big league debut as a September callup, will play a vital role in boosting the velocity of the Mets' big league bullpen in 2018.

Year	Club (League)	Class	W	L	ERA	G	GS	CG	SV	IP	H	HR	BB	SO	K/9	WHIP	AVG
2015	Greenville (SAL)	LoA	7	6	4.53	31	6	0	3	89	94	4	33	94	9.5	1.42	.263
2016	Salem (CAR)	HiA	5	3	3.29	36	0	0	7	66	53	1	38	63	8.6	1.39	.218
2017	Portland (EL)	AA	4	1	1.38	10	0	0	2	13	8	0	0	20	13.8	0.62	.170
	Pawtucket (IL)	AAA	1	1	4.03	22	0	0	4	29	28	2	13	36	11.2	1.41	.250
	Las Vegas (PCL)	AAA	1	1	1.80	9	0	0	1	10	12	2	4	10	9.0	1.60	.293
	New York (NL)	MAJ	0	0	4.05	9	0	0	0	7	7	0	1	5	6.8	1.20	.250
Major League Totals			0	0	4.05	9	0	0	0	7	7	0	1	5	6.8	1.20	.250
Minor League Totals			27	26	4.71	151	47	0	17	384	388	25	174	373	8.7	1.46	.260

18 PATRICK MAZEIKA, C/1B

BA GRADE
45 Risk: High

Born: Oct. 14, 1993. **B-T:** L-R. **Ht.:** 6-3. **Wt.:** 208. **Drafted:** Stetson, 2015 (8th round). **Signed by:** Jon Updike.

Mazeika embellished his reputation as a professional hitter at high Class A St. Lucie in 2017, all while catching a career-high 77 games—but he still has work to do to profile as a regular for scouts. He hit .348 in three years at Stetson and has hit .311 in three pro seasons, thanks to a feel for the barrel and excellent strike-zone judgment.

Mazeika ranked third in the high Class A Florida State League with a .389 on-base percentage in 2017 and owns a career .411 mark, though with a focus on contact, his power production is limited mostly to line drives to the gaps. Mazeika shows aptitude for receiving the ball, but his ability to block pitches in the dirt is hampered by his slow-twitch actions, and his arm plays as below-average. A slow tempo with calling pitches turns off some scouts. Mazeika also plays first base, but his power doesn't fit the profile there, so his best path to a major league role is as a lefthanded-hitting catcher.

A full season at Double-A Binghamton will be a good test for Mazeika in 2018.

Year	Club (League)	Class	AVG	G	AB	R	H	2B	3B	HR	RBI	BB	SO	SB	CS	OBP	SLG
2015	Kingsport (APP)	R	.354	62	226	44	80	27	0	5	48	24	26	1	0	.451	.540
2016	Columbia (SAL)	LoA	.305	70	239	34	73	14	0	3	35	38	39	2	0	.414	.402
2017	St. Lucie (FSL)	HiA	.287	100	352	45	101	21	0	7	50	48	53	2	2	.389	.406
	Binghamton (EL)	AA	.333	6	21	3	7	5	0	0	5	2	6	0	0	.391	.571
Minor League Totals			.311	238	838	126	261	67	0	15	138	112	124	5	2	.413	.445

19 TYLER BASHLOR, RHP

BA GRADE
45 Risk: High

Born: April 16, 1993. **B-T:** R-R. **Ht.:** 6-0. **Wt.:** 197. **Drafted:** South Georgia JC, 2013 (11th round). **Signed by:** Jim Bryant.

Bashlor fights baseball's bias against short righthanders—he's closer to 5-foot-11 than his listed height—by throwing 100 mph and missing more bats than most. Working as a reliever, he struck out 15.2 batters per nine innings in 2017, which led all minor league pitchers with at least 40 innings.

Bashlor, an infielder in high school who moved to the mound in his second year at South Georgia JC, signed in 2013 but didn't jump on the prospect map until 2016, after he missed two full seasons due to Tommy John surgery. His velocity spiked in the second half of 2017 at Double-A Binghamton, where he sat 94-98 mph with a riding, high-spin fastball. He throws a slurvy breaking ball with depth but not the velocity of a typical slider. Bashlor needs to improve his control—he walked 4.5 per nine in 2017—which will be a challenge because of his high-effort delivery.

With a top-of-the-scale fastball and average breaking ball, however, Bashlor doesn't need to be too fine to find success in a big league bullpen.

Year	Club (League)	Class	W	L	ERA	G	GS	CG	SV	IP	H	HR	BB	SO	K/9	WHIP	AVG
2015	Did not play																
2016	St. Lucie (FSL)	HiA	0	1	5.06	4	0	0	0	5	4	0	2	5	8.4	1.13	.200
	Columbia (SAL)	LoA	4	2	2.50	34	0	0	3	50	35	2	28	68	12.2	1.25	.193
2017	St. Lucie (FSL)	HiA	2	2	4.89	34	0	0	10	35	32	1	21	61	15.7	1.51	.248
	Binghamton (EL)	AA	1	0	0.00	12	0	0	3	15	7	0	4	23	14.1	0.75	.143
Minor League Totals			7	6	3.42	97	0	0	16	121	92	4	67	175	13.0	1.31	.209

20 DREW SMITH, RHP

BA GRADE
45 Risk: High

Born: Sept. 24, 1993. **B-T:** R-R. **Ht.:** 6-2. **Wt.:** 190. **Drafted:** Dallas Baptist, 2015 (3rd round). **Signed by:** Chris Wimmer (Tigers).

Smith played at three levels and for three organizations in 2017 after being traded twice. The Tigers made the power reliever a third-round pick and the first of five Dallas Baptist pitchers drafted in 2015. He made 35 appearances at low Class A in 2016 as he worked around minor injuries to his shoulder, elbow and pectoral muscle. Detroit traded him to the Rays in April 2017 as the player to be named for outfielder Mikie Mahtook, and then Tampa Bay traded him to the Mets for first baseman Lucas Duda near the trade deadline.

Like all the relievers the Mets traded for in 2017, Smith throws a big fastball with riding life. He pitches at 96 mph and ranges from 94-98, but he differs from the group with his breaking ball of choice. He throws a high-spin, top-to-bottom curveball at 78-82 mph that can be a plus weapon. The spin rate on the pitch was measured by TrackMan at about 2,800 revolutions per minute, which would rank in the 90th percentile of all major league pitchers who threw a curve at least 25 times in 2017. Smith stayed off the disabled list in 2017, improved his control and threw a career-high 60 innings.

Smith finished 2017 at Double-A Binghamton in the Eastern League playoffs, and he will be a call away from New York at Triple-A Las Vegas in 2018.

Year	Club (League)	Class	W	L	ERA	G	GS	CG	SV	IP	H	HR	BB	SO	K/9	WHIP	AVG
2015	Tigers (GCL)	R	0	0	0.00	1	0	0	0	2	1	0	0	3	16.2	0.60	.167
	Connecticut (NYP)	SS	2	0	0.33	11	0	0	2	28	15	0	4	33	10.7	0.69	.155
	West Michigan (MWL)	LoA	1	0	0.00	1	0	0	0	2	1	0	1	2	10.8	1.20	.167
2016	West Michigan (MWL)	LoA	1	2	2.96	35	0	0	4	49	34	0	23	62	11.5	1.17	.205
2017	Lakeland (FSL)	HiA	1	0	0.77	7	0	0	0	12	4	0	4	12	9.3	0.69	.108
	Durham (IL)	AAA	0	0	0.00	1	0	0	0	1	1	0	0	0	0.0	1.00	.333
	Charlotte, FL (FSL)	HiA	0	2	2.20	20	0	0	7	29	26	1	5	28	8.8	1.08	.239
	Montgomery (SL)	AA	0	0	0.00	3	0	0	0	4	1	0	0	0	0.0	0.27	.091
	Binghamton (EL)	AA	3	2	1.80	11	0	0	0	15	8	1	5	17	10.2	0.87	.151
Minor League Totals			8	6	1.80	90	0	0	13	140	91	2	42	157	10.1	0.95	.186

21 ADONIS UCETA, RHP

BA GRADE

45 Risk: High

Born: May 10, 1994. **B-T:** R-R. **Ht.:** 6-1. **Wt.:** 228. **Signed:** Dominican Republic, 2013. **Signed by:** Alexis de la Cruz/Gerardo Cabrera.

After four seasons in Rookie ball, Uceta began 2017 at low Class A Columbia and ended at Double-A Binghamton after making a role change and experiencing a velocity spike.

A middling starter prior to 2017, Uceta moved to the bullpen and recorded a 1.51 ERA in 41 appearances while striking out 67 in 59.2 innings. He pitched at 92-94 mph at Columbia, but sat 96-99 by the end of the season. He pitches from a three-quarters arm slot and his ball features plus running action to his arm side. Uceta throws a sinking changeup with fade in the mid-80s that can be an above-average weapon. His workable slurvy breaking ball gives him a pitch to throw to his glove side, forcing batters to focus on both sides of the plate.

With a large frame, high-effort delivery and spotty rotation record, Uceta is now a full-time reliever. Some in the Mets organization liken him to big league reliever Hansel Robles.

Year	Club (League)	Class	W	L	ERA	G	GS	CG	SV	IP	H	HR	BB	SO	K/9	WHIP	AVG
2015	Mets (GCL)	R	4	3	3.08	12	9	0	0	61	67	1	9	46	6.8	1.24	.276
	Kingsport (APP)	R	1	0	3.00	1	1	0	0	6	6	0	2	6	9.0	1.33	.261
2016	Kingsport (APP)	R	3	6	4.99	12	11	0	0	61	77	5	16	63	9.2	1.52	.301
2017	Columbia (SAL)	LoA	4	0	1.26	29	0	0	11	43	23	0	16	47	9.8	0.91	.158
	St. Lucie (FSL)	HiA	0	0	0.84	8	0	0	2	11	5	1	3	15	12.7	0.75	.143
	Binghamton (EL)	AA	2	0	4.50	4	0	0	1	6	6	1	1	5	7.5	1.17	.250
Minor League Totals			20	13	3.49	94	35	0	15	301	289	15	84	270	8.1	1.24	.251

22 QUINN BRODEY, OF

BA GRADE

50 Risk: V. High

Born: Dec. 1, 1995. **B-T:** L-L. **Ht.:** 6-1. **Wt.:** 200. **Drafted:** Stanford, 2017 (3rd round). **Signed by:** Tyler Holmes.

The Nationals drafted Brodey as a lefthanded pitcher out of high school in the 37th round in 2014, but he opted to attend Stanford, where he played both ways as a freshman, both in Pacific-12 Conference play and in the summer-ball New England Collegiate League. Brodey focused on playing outfield beginning in 2016, and led the Cardinal in home runs as a sophomore and junior. The Mets made him a third-round pick in 2017 and signed him for a slightly below-slot $500,000.

Brodey didn't produce at short-season Brooklyn, a notoriously difficult park for lefthanded hitters, but began to unlock his solid-average raw power in a short trial at low Class A Columbia. He is an athletic lefthanded hitter with present strength and a chance for five average tools. The Mets value his performance in the Cape Cod League in 2016, when he finished fourth in batting average (.326) and slugging (.486). Brodey shows the ingredients to hit for average, but he may struggle to drive inside pitches because he bars his arm when he loads his swing.

If Brodey fails to develop a plus tool, as some scouts project, he could be an outfield tweener who doesn't defend well enough for center or produce enough power for a corner. He will advance to high Class A St. Lucie in 2018.

Year	Club (League)	Class	AVG	G	AB	R	H	2B	3B	HR	RBI	BB	SO	SB	CS	OBP	SLG
2017	Brooklyn (NYP)	SS	.257	54	210	20	54	9	2	2	30	14	49	10	3	.303	.348
	Columbia (SAL)	LoA	.229	9	35	4	8	1	1	1	7	4	14	0	0	.300	.400
Minor League Totals			.253	63	245	24	62	10	3	3	37	18	63	10	3	.302	.355

23 JACOB RHAME, RHP

BA GRADE
45 Risk: High

Born: March 16, 1993. **B-T:** R-R. **Ht.:** 6-1. **Wt.:** 215. **Drafted:** Grayson County (Texas) JC, 2013 (6th round). **Signed by:** Calvin Jones (Dodgers).

Though Rhame worked as a starter in junior college when the Dodgers drafted him in 2013, he had only one reliable pitch—a fastball—so Los Angeles developed him exclusively as a reliever. He first reached Triple-A in 2016 and remained there through most of 2017. The Dodgers traded him to the Mets for outfielder Curtis Granderson in late August, and he made his big league debut as a September callup.

Rhame pitches at 95 mph and tops out at 97 with late-riding life and high spin on a fastball that he uses to generate swings and misses at the top of the zone. The Mets saw improvement in the quality of his changeup in 2017. The pitch shows good fade to his arm side and good separation from his fastball—about 12 mph on average. He throws a mid-80s slider for early-count strikes, but it hasn't shown the necessary bite to be a true out pitch.

The Mets acquired Rhame to address their velocity-deficient bullpen, and pumping mid-90s fastballs is exactly what he'll be given a chance to do in 2018.

Year	Club (League)	Class	W	L	ERA	G	GS	CG	SV	IP	H	HR	BB	SO	K/9	WHIP	AVG
2015	R. Cucamonga (CAL)	HiA	0	0	0.00	5	0	0	1	7	2	0	1	13	16.7	0.43	.091
	Tulsa (TL)	AA	3	3	3.06	39	0	0	2	50	34	5	19	57	10.3	1.06	.192
2016	Oklahoma City (PCL)	AAA	1	7	3.29	54	0	0	7	63	53	5	28	70	10.0	1.29	.231
2017	Oklahoma City (PCL)	AAA	0	2	4.31	41	0	0	2	48	52	6	10	55	10.3	1.29	.274
	Las Vegas (PCL)	AAA	0	1	1.50	4	0	0	0	6	2	0	0	11	16.5	0.33	.100
	New York (NL)	MAJ	1	1	9.00	9	0	0	0	9	12	2	7	7	7.0	2.11	.333
Major League Totals			1	1	9.00	9	0	0	0	9	12	2	7	7	7.0	2.11	.333
Minor League Totals			10	19	3.07	214	0	0	29	261	210	21	81	317	10.9	1.11	.220

24 P.J. CONLON, LHP

BA GRADE
45 Risk: High

Born: Nov. 11, 1993. **B-T:** L-L. **Ht.:** 5-11. **Wt.:** 192. **Drafted:** San Diego, 2015 (13th round). **Signed by:** Fred Mazuca.

Conlon's ability to keep runs off the scoreboard despite not having big-time stuff continued in 2017. At Double-A Binghamton he ranked sixth in the Eastern League in ERA (3.38) and even tossed a trio of seven-inning shutouts. He previously logged 17 relief innings without allowing an earned run at short-season Brooklyn in 2015, his pro debut, then led all minor league starters with a 1.65 ERA at two Class A stops in 2016.

Conlon depends on command of a fringe-average fastball, plus changeup and plus control. He sits in the high 80s, scraping 90 mph, and relies on sinking his fastball and commanding it inside against righthanders. He sells an excellent changeup with arm speed and a deceptive delivery that prevents batters from easily picking up the ball out of his hand. Conlon will bounce his fringe curveball in the dirt as a chase pitch, but relies on his changeup when going offspeed. The Mets moved him to the bullpen in August, and they intend to keep him there after he allowed a .192 average and struck out 9.8 per nine innings in six relief appearances.

Conlon could see big league action in 2018, and has a ceiling similar to that of fellow lefty changeup artist Wade LeBlanc.

Year	Club (League)	Class	W	L	ERA	G	GS	CG	SV	IP	H	HR	BB	SO	K/9	WHIP	AVG
2015	Brooklyn (NYP)	SS	0	1	0.00	17	0	0	0	17	8	0	2	25	13.2	0.59	.136
2016	Columbia (SAL)	LoA	8	1	1.84	12	12	0	0	78	68	4	16	61	7.0	1.00	.233
	St. Lucie (FSL)	HiA	4	1	1.41	12	11	0	1	64	47	1	14	51	7.2	0.96	.203
2017	Binghamton (EL)	AA	8	9	3.38	28	22	3	1	136	130	14	38	108	7.1	1.24	.253
Minor League Totals			20	12	2.35	69	45	3	2	295	253	19	64	245	7.5	1.07	.231

25 GERSON BAUTISTA, RHP

BA GRADE
45 Risk: High

Born: May 31, 1995. **B-T:** R-R. **Ht.:** 6-2. **Wt.:** 170. **Signed:** Dominican Republic, 2013. **Signed by:** Manny Nanita (Red Sox).

Bautista signed with the Red Sox for $250,000 in 2013, just shy of his 18th birthday. He sat out that season, however, after being suspended 50 games for testing positive for the anabolic steroid stanozolol. Tall, gangly and quick-armed, Bautista worked as a starter in the complex Rookie leagues before shifting to the bullpen in 2016. He reached high Class A in 2017, when Boston shipped him and fellow relievers Jamie Callahan and Stephen Nogosek to the Mets for Addison Reed near the trade deadline.

Bautista owned the best fastball in the Red Sox system and came as advertised. He topped out at 101 mph and rarely threw a pitch slower than 95, as he struck out 11 batters per nine innings in 2017. He leans on his fastball, but he'll need to throw more strikes from a high-effort delivery that sees him open early, using a long arm action and dramatic recoil. His mid-80s slider could be a usable second pitch with continued improvement. He also throws a low-90s split-changeup that Mets closer Jeurys Familia complimented when he saw Bautista at high Class A St. Lucie while on a rehab assignment.

Bautista joined the 40-man roster in November and appears destined for Double-A Binghamton in 2018.

Year	Club (League)	Class	W	L	ERA	G	GS	CG	SV	IP	H	HR	BB	SO	K/9	WHIP	AVG
2015	Red Sox (GCL)	R	3	3	2.77	12	11	0	0	52	36	1	27	41	7.1	1.21	.196
2016	Lowell (NYP)	SS	0	0	0.87	8	0	0	5	10	5	0	2	13	11.3	0.68	.143
	Greenville (SAL)	LoA	1	4	3.24	15	0	0	1	25	20	3	11	23	8.3	1.24	.213
2017	Salem (CAR)	HiA	3	2	5.16	27	0	0	4	45	54	2	28	53	10.5	1.81	.292
	St. Lucie (FSL)	HiA	0	1	1.26	10	0	0	5	14	10	0	3	20	12.6	0.91	.204
Minor League Totals			9	11	2.64	85	23	0	15	208	162	7	92	182	7.9	1.22	.213

26 LUIS CARPIO, 2B/SS

Born: July 11, 1997. **B-T:** R-R. **Ht.:** 5-11. **Wt.:** 190. **Signed:** Venezuela, 2013.
Signed by: Carlos Perez/Hector Rincones.

BA GRADE
50 Risk: Extreme

Carpio first drew attention in 2015, when he hit .304 as a 17-year-old middle infielder in the Rookie-level Appalachian League. He tore the labrum in his right shoulder the following spring, and never played the field in 2016, though he did see limited action as a DH.

The rust showed at low Class A Columbia in 2017, when Carpio hit just .232 with three home runs and spent most of the season at second base rather than shortstop, partially in deference to system No. 1 prospect Andres Gimenez. His shoulder injury and long layoff affected his swing, but not his hitting approach—he continued to draw walks at a high rate and show bat-to-ball skills. He never has displayed much power and probably won't grade as even below-average until his body matures and adds strength. An average runner, Carpio shows solid-average range and arm strength at shortstop but is error-prone. His actions appear more confident at second base. Adding third base down the line is a distinct possibility if the Mets choose to groom him as a utility infielder.

Carpio sat out instructional league so that he could rest and work out as he prepares for the 2018 season.

Year	Club (League)	Class	AVG	G	AB	R	H	2B	3B	HR	RBI	BB	SO	SB	CS	OBP	SLG
2015	Kingsport (APP)	R	.304	45	181	31	55	10	0	0	22	17	34	9	7	.372	.359
2016	Mets (GCL)	R	.290	8	31	3	9	1	1	0	2	1	11	0	0	.353	.387
	Brooklyn (NYP)	SS	.140	12	43	4	6	2	0	0	1	8	10	0	0	.288	.186
2017	Columbia (SAL)	LoA	.232	125	474	53	110	18	3	3	36	53	95	17	5	.308	.302
Minor League Totals			.244	250	938	126	229	40	5	4	81	112	183	38	16	.330	.310

27 ALI SANCHEZ, C

Born: Jan. 20, 1997. **B-T:** R-R. **Ht.:** 6-1. **Wt.:** 196. **Signed:** Venezuela, 2013.
Signed by: Robert Espejo/Hector Rincones.

BA GRADE
50 Risk: Extreme

Sanchez has hit just .223 outside of the complex Rookie leagues, but his defensive tools are so tantalizing—and catchers tend to develop later than other position players—that he remains a prospect of interest.

At low Class A Columbia in 2017, Sanchez led all South Atlantic League catchers who caught at least 50 games by throwing out 48 percent of basestealers. He ranked second in the SAL in fewest steal attempts per game and fourth in fewest passed balls per game. TrackMan data estimates that Sanchez saved more than 20 runs with his ability to frame pitches as strikes; only Greenville's Roldani Baldwin saved more runs in the SAL. Sanchez has solid-average arm strength, a lightning-fast release and strong accuracy. Even at age 20, he shows advanced feel for calling a game. Sanchez shows some raw power in batting practice, but sticks to a contact-oriented, middle-of-the-field hitting approach in games. Even scouts who like him aren't convinced that he'll hit, and he lost hitting reps in 2017 when he broke the hamate bone in his left hand and missed August.

With even fringe-average hitting ability, Sanchez could be a big league backup catcher, but he's not there yet.

Year	Club (League)	Class	AVG	G	AB	R	H	2B	3B	HR	RBI	BB	SO	SB	CS	OBP	SLG
2015	Mets (GCL)	R	.278	46	162	20	45	6	0	0	17	12	26	2	0	.339	.315
	Kingsport (APP)	R	.182	3	11	2	2	0	0	0	3	0	2	0	0	.182	.182
2016	Brooklyn (NYP)	SS	.216	46	171	15	37	10	0	0	11	10	26	2	0	.260	.275
2017	Columbia (SAL)	LoA	.231	56	182	20	42	3	0	1	15	13	26	2	3	.288	.264
Minor League Totals			.255	201	701	78	179	26	0	4	70	62	111	12	9	.323	.310

28 ADRIAN HERNANDEZ, OF

BA GRADE

50 Risk: Extreme

Born: Feb. 8, 2001. **B-T:** R-R. **Ht.:** 6-0. **Wt.:** 185. **Signed:** Dominican Republic, 2017. **Signed by:** Fernando Encarnacion/Gerardo Cabrera.

Hernandez ranked as the No. 16 prospect in the 2017 international class before signing with the Mets for $1.5 million. Sporting a strong, compact build, he's more physically mature than the typical Mets international target.

Hernandez had never lifted weights prior to signing, so his power to his pull side and the middle of the field speaks to his present strength and bat speed. He shows the plus speed necessary to steal bases and man center field, but he needs to refine his instincts. Some scouts believe that with continued physical maturation he'll outgrow center and move to a corner, where an average arm could land him in left field. Below-average pitch recognition and an uphill swing path could limit Hernandez's ability to hit for a high average, but he works hard on all facets of his craft and has immense power-speed potential.

Regarded as a hard-nosed player, Hernandez will begin working to improve his defensive instincts, bat path and pitch recognition as he makes his pro debut in 2018.

Year	Club (League)	Class	AVG	G	AB	R	H	2B	3B	HR	RBI	BB	SO	SB	CS	OBP	SLG
2017	Did not play—Signed 2018 contract																

29 DAVID THOMPSON, 3B

BA GRADE

45 Risk: High

Born: Aug. 28, 1993. **B-T:** R-R. **Ht.:** 6-0. **Wt.:** 210. **Drafted:** Miami, 2015 (4th round). **Signed by:** Cesar Aranguren.

Injuries sidetracked Thompson in college—he had two shoulder surgeries and another for thoracic outlet syndrome—but he has remained healthy as a pro. He advanced to Double-A Binghamton in 2017, where he hit a career-high 16 home runs and ranked fourth in the Eastern League with 29 doubles.

After scuffling out of the gate by hitting .193 through May 15, Thompson hit .286/.350/.479 with 14 home runs in his final 102 games. He drives the ball for power to all fields, and his flyball-oriented swing and high exit velocities should translate to more home run power as he maximizes his launch angle. Thompson is a poor runner, but shows solid-average range and hands at third base. After multiple labrum injuries, his arm might be short for every-day play at third.

The Mets laud Thompson for his leadership ability, while his above-average power plays versus both righthanders and lefthanders. He will take the next step to Triple-A Las Vegas in 2018.

Year	Club (League)	Class	AVG	G	AB	R	H	2B	3B	HR	RBI	BB	SO	SB	CS	OBP	SLG
2015	Brooklyn (NYP)	SS	.218	59	206	22	45	10	1	3	22	11	44	3	0	.268	.320
2016	Columbia (SAL)	LoA	.294	61	228	45	67	22	2	5	58	14	49	3	0	.344	.474
	St. Lucie (FSL)	HiA	.265	55	204	29	54	12	0	6	37	15	41	3	0	.321	.412
2017	Binghamton (EL)	AA	.263	133	476	62	125	29	1	16	68	40	92	8	6	.325	.429
Minor League Totals			.261	308	1114	158	291	73	4	30	185	80	226	17	6	.318	.415

30 CHRISTIAN JAMES, RHP

BA GRADE

50 Risk: Extreme

Born: May 24, 1998. **B-T:** R-R. **Ht.:** 6-3. **Wt.:** 210. **Drafted:** HS—Tarpon Springs, Fla., 2016 (14th round). **Signed by:** Jon Updike.

After the 10th round of the draft, the Mets often look to the state of Florida for physical high school starting pitchers with a little room to fill out and potentially gain velocity. A 14th-round pick in 2016, James is the next in a line that includes John Gant, Rob Whalen and Jordan Humphreys.

Like the other Florida prep pitchers, James spent his second pro season, 2017, at Rookie-level Kingsport missing plenty of bats. In fact, he led all Appalachian League pitchers with at least 50 innings by striking out 10.1 batters per nine innings. James pitches at 89-91 mph and tops out at 93 with plus sinking action, and could add a few ticks of velocity as he matures. He already throws a strong curveball in the 78-84 mph range that could develop into an out pitch. He has begun to show feel for a mid-80s changeup that shows occasional average fading action.

James mixes pitches well and exudes mound presence, which are key components in his favor toward earning a full-season assignment to low Class A Columbia in 2018. He could develop into a No. 3 or 4 starter.

Year	Club (League)	Class	W	L	ERA	G	GS	CG	SV	IP	H	HR	BB	SO	K/9	WHIP	AVG
2016	Mets (GCL)	R	0	1	0.52	14	0	0	3	17	11	0	5	15	7.8	0.92	.177
2017	Kingsport (APP)	R	2	3	4.18	11	11	0	0	52	54	3	16	58	10.1	1.35	.267
Minor League Totals			2	4	3.26	25	11	0	3	69	65	3	21	73	9.5	1.25	.246

New York Yankees

BY JOSH NORRIS

After finishing 2017 a win away from the World Series, the Yankees made sure they went in to 2018 will a team that would be primed to contend for the franchise's 28th World Series title.

The first move, which came soon after the season concluded, was to switch managers. After a decade at the helm, Joe Girardi was out and Aaron Boone—the force behind one of the biggest home runs in team history—was in. General manager Brian Cashman selected Boone, who had never held a coaching or managing job in the minor leagues, on the strength of his communications skills and willingness to embrace analytics.

With that move crossed off, they were ready for their first big strike: A deal that sent reigning NL most valuable player Giancarlo Stanton to New York. The deal, with a Marlins club that featured all sorts of Yankees ties—including new owner Derek Jeter and vice president of player development and scouting Gary Denbo, was essentially a salary dump. The Yankees agreed to take on nearly all of the remaining $295 million on Stanton's contract, and in return the Marlins received second baseman Starlin Castro, righthander Jorge Guzman and shortstop Jose Devers.

With Stanton in tow, the Yankees' lineup suddenly went from formidable to downright frightening. The team that hit the most home runs in the majors (241) in 2017 was adding the player who hit the most home runs (59) in 2017. Put another way, the Yankees are now capable of rolling out three of the eight participants in the 2017 Home Run Derby—Stanton, Aaron Judge and Gary Sanchez—in the same lineup.

The surprising success the Yankees achieved was largely due to its new core of young talent taking significant steps forward. Judge, who struck out in 50 percent of his plate appearances in 2016, put together a stellar first full season. He hit an American League-best 52 home runs, won the AL rookie of the year unanimously and finished third in the league's MVP balloting.

The same went for catcher Gary Sanchez, who, despite defensive struggles, seemed to entrench himself as a franchise cornerstone. His 33 home runs set a Yankees record for longballs as a catcher and led the majors at the position as well.

New York also got a big boost in the rotation from Luis Severino, who rebounded from a rough 2016 season to emerge as the team's ace. He finished third in the AL Cy Young voting, and racked up 230 strikeouts, the third-most in franchise history.

Aaron Judge set rookie records for home runs (53), walks (127) and strikeouts (208).

PROJECTED 2021 LINEUP

Catcher	Gary Sanchez (28)
First Base	Greg Bird (28)
Second Base	Gleyber Torres (24)
Third Base	Miguel Andujar (26)
Shortstop	Didi Gregorius (31)
Left Field	Clint Frazier (26)
Center Field	Estevan Florial (23)
Right Field	Aaron Judge (29)
Designated Hitter	Giancarlo Stanton (32)
No. 1 Starter	Luis Severino (27)
No. 2 Starter	Justus Sheffield (25)
No. 3 Starter	Sonny Gray (31)
No. 4 Starter	Chance Adams (26)
No. 5 Starter	Albert Abreu (25)
Closer	Aroldis Chapman (33)

The team also made several trades at midseason that bolstered their roster for the 2017 playoff run and beyond. Most notably, they swung with the White Sox that netted them third baseman Todd Frazier and righthanded relievers David Robertson and Tommy Kahnle. Frazier was a free agent after 2017, but Robertson and Kahnle were still under control. They also sent a three-prospect package to the A's in exchange for righthander Sonny Gray, who won't reach free agency until 2020.

Entering 2018, the Yankees are sitting pretty. Their lineup and rotation are filled with a blend of young stars and talented veterans who should be able to lead them back to consistent championship contention.

DEPTH CHART

NEW YORK YANKEES

TOP 2018 ROOKIE: Gleyber Torres, SS. After finishing his rehab from Tommy John surgery, he'll push his way onto a talented roster.

BREAKOUT PROSPECT: Matt Sauer, RHP. Signed for double his slot value, Sauer shows electric stuff and high-level makeup.

SLEEPER: Nolan Martinez, RHP. He's been slowed by injuries, but the Yankees still love his potential.

SOURCE OF TOP 30 TALENT

Homegrown	21	Acquired	9
College	7	Trade	8
Junior college	0	Rule 5 draft	0
High school	2	Independent league	0
Nondrafted free agent	0	Free agent/waivers	1
International	12		

LF
Jake Cave
Canaan Smith

CF
Estevan Florial (2)
Jeff Hendrix

RF
Billy McKinney (23)
Isiah Gilliam
Jhalan Jackson
Everson Pereira

3B
Miguel Andujar (4)
Dermis Garcia (20)
Oswaldo Cabrera (26)
Andres Chaparro
Nelson Gomez

SS
Gleyber Torres (1)
Thairo Estrada (8)
Diego Castillo (27)
Kyle Holder
Ronny Rojas

2B
Nick Solak (12)
Tyler Wade (15)
Hoy Park
Abiatal Avelino

1B
Tyler Austin
Chris Gittens
Brandon Wagner
Ryan McBroom

C
Kyle Higashioka
Saul Torres
Donny Sands
Jason Lopez

LHP

LHSP
Justus Sheffield (3)
Daniel Camarena
Dalton Lehnen

LHRP
Stephen Tarpley
Caleb Frare
James Reeves
Andrew Schwaab
J.P. Sears

RHP

RHSP
Chance Adams (5)
Albert Abreu (6)
Luis Medina (7)
Domingo Acevedo (9)
Dillon Tate (10)
Matt Sauer (11)
Freicer Perez (13)
Clarke Schmidt (14)
Domingo German (16)
Juan Then (17)
Trevor Stephan (18)
Glenn Otto (19)
Juan De Paula (21)
Taylor Widener (22)
Deivi Garcia (24)
Jonathan Loaisiga (25)
Alexander Vargas (28)
Rony Garcia (29)
Nick Nelson
Nolan Martinez
Roancy Contreras
Jhonatan Munoz
Brian Keller

RHRP
Cody Carroll (30)
Ben Heller
J.P. Feyereisen
Raynel Espinal
Kaleb Ort
Cale Coshow

DRAFT ANALYSIS

2017

BEST PURE HITTER: The Yankees drafted one position player in the top 10 rounds and signed just six in the entire draft. OF Canaan Smith (4) has a very advanced batting eye. Smith walked 57 times as a high school senior, showing a willingness to take free pass after free pass. He then led the Rookie-level Gulf Coast League in walks. Smith has above-average bat speed and some power potential to go with his picky plate discipline.

BEST POWER HITTER: OF Steven Sensley (12) has 70 raw power on the 20-to-80 scouting scale. He hit 11 home runs for Louisiana-Lafayette this spring and had a number of 110+ mph exit velocities as measured by Trackman.

FASTEST RUNNER: Smith is an average runner. RHP Harold Cortijo (14) turned in plus times as a position player.

BEST DEFENSIVE PLAYER: SS/2B Ricky Surum (16) is stretched as a pro shortstop and is better as a second baseman, but he's the only shortstop/catcher/center fielder the Yankees' signed.

BEST FASTBALL: RHP Clarke Schmidt (1) is recovering from Tommy John surgery, but pre-injury he was locating a lively 92-94 mph fastball that touched 96-97. RHP Matt Sauer (2) has touched 97 as well and RHP Trevor Stephan (3) tickles 94-97 mph regularly.

BEST SECONDARY PITCH: Schmidt's slider was a plus pitch before his elbow injury. It's a mid-80s power slider with excellent tilt. Sauer's (2) low-80s slider has two-plane tilt and the potential to develop into a plus pitch.

BEST PRO DEBUT: Stephan was 1-1, 1.39 with 43 strikeouts in 32.1 innings with short-season Staten Island. His Staten Island teammate RHP Glenn Otto (5) was 3-0, 1.59 with 25 strikeouts in 17.2 innings.

BEST ATHLETE: The Yankees are developing Cortijo as a pitcher, but he was a prospect as a position player as well. He was an athletic center fielder with plus speed in high school and that athleticism is apparent on the mound as well.

MOST INTRIGUING BACKGROUND: Schmidt's brother Clate is a pitcher in the Tigers organization and cancer survivor, while their father Dwight is a colonel in the U.S. Marines. C Ryan Lidge (20) is a cousin of former Astros/Phillies righthander Brad Lidge.

CLOSEST TO THE MAJORS: Schmidt's recovery from Tommy John surgery will slow his development, but he's a polished college pitcher once he gets back on the mound. Stephan and Otto are a pair of power-arms that could climb quickly as relievers.

BEST LATE-ROUND PICK: Cortijo has potential as an athletic righthander. RHP Garrett Whitlock (18) has shown a plus fastball and performed in the Cape Cod League, but a back strain ruined his junior season at UAB. He bounced back as a pro, striking out 22 and walking no one in 14.1 pro innings.

THE ONE WHO GOT AWAY: RHPs Riley Thompson (25) and Tristan Beck (29) were never expected to sign once they lasted to day three, but both will be premium draft prospects in 2018.

—**J.J. COOPER**

TOP DRAFT PICKS OF THE DECADE

Year	Player, Pos.	2017 Org
2008	*Gerrit Cole, RHP	Pirates
2009	Slade Heathcott, OF	Giants
2010	Cito Culver, SS	Yankees
2011	Dante Bichette Jr., OF (1st round supp.)	Yankees
2012	Ty Hensley, RHP	Rays
2013	Eric Jagielo, 3B	Reds
2014	Jacob Lindgren, LHP (2nd round)	Braves
2015	James Kaprielian, RHP	Athletics
2016	Blake Rutherford, OF	White Sox
2017	Clarke Schmidt, RHP	Yankees
* Did not sign		

2016

OF Blake Rutherford (1) was off to a solid start in his first full pro season when the Yankees included him in their deadline deal with the White Sox. 2B Nick Solak (2) has lived up to his billing as an advanced bat, quickly reaching Double-A.

GRADE: C

2015

RHP James Kaprielian (1) has barely pitched as a pro, but the Yankees used him in their trade for Sonny Gray. RHP Chance Adams (5) has pitched his way to the cusp of the big leagues and RHP Cody Carroll (22) could be a valuable reliever.

GRADE: C

2014

From a pitching-heavy class, the Yankees have already gotten three big leaguers: LHP Jacob Lindgren (2), LHP Jordan Montgomery (4) and RHP Jonathan Holder (6). Montgomery looks to be the best of the trio.

GRADE: C

1 GLEYBER TORRES, SS/3B

Born: Dec. 13, 1996. **B-T:** R-R. **Ht.:** 6-1. **Wt.:** 175.
Signed: Venezuela, 2013.
Signed by: Louie Eljaua/Hector Ortega (Cubs).

Torres ranked as the No. 2 prospect available on the 2013 international market when the Cubs signed him for $1.7 million. Chicago traded Torres to the Yankees in July 2016 as part of the four-player package for closer Aroldis Chapman. Chapman returned to the Yankees as a free agent for 2017 on a five-year, $96 million deal, and Torres put together a torrid first three months of the season and looked like he could soon be in line to make his major league debut. Then, on one freak play, everything derailed. After a mid-June promotion from Double-A Trenton to Triple-A Scranton/Wilkes-Barre, Torres tore his left ulnar collateral ligament on a collision at home plate and required season-ending Tommy John surgery on his non-throwing elbow. He's expected to be ready for spring training.

When he was on the field, Torres was every bit of the player the Yankees expected when they acquired him. At the plate, he showed the ability to hit for a high average and power, as well a discerning knowledge of the strike zone. In particular, Torres' ability to make quick adjustments set him apart from other high-pedigree prospects. Coaches noted how quickly he would identify the way pitchers were working to get him out, then adjust and close those holes. Defensively, there's no reason Torres can't stick at shortstop, but the emergence of Didi Gregorius in New York necessitated that Torres learn other positions quickly. He shuffled around during his brief season, playing 15 games at third base and 10 more at second base before the injury. He has the above-average range and arm to play those positions or shortstop. If he were to land at third base, he would hit for enough power to profile there. The Yankees were working with Torres on the small things throughout the year. In particular, they were helping him find a consistent pre-set position in the field and getting him to chase fewer pitches out of the zone. He's an average runner, but needs to refine his basestealing technique to increase his efficiency.

Torres will likely return to Triple-A for more seasoning so he can be ready to fill a potential hole at second base or third base. Evaluators both inside and outside the organization see all-star potential.

BA GRADE	SCOUTING GRADES
65 Risk: Medium	HIT: 60. POW: 55. SPD: 40. FLD: 60. ARM: 60.

Projected future grades on 20-80 scouting scale

TOP PROSPECTS OF THE DECADE

Year	Player, Pos.	2017 Org
2008	Joba Chamberlain, RHP	Did not play
2009	Austin Jackson, OF	Indians
2010	Jesus Montero, C	Mexican League
2011	Jesus Montero, C	Mexican League
2012	Jesus Montero, C	Mexican League
2013	Mason Williams, OF	Yankees
2014	Gary Sanchez, C	Yankees
2015	Luis Severino, RHP	Yankees
2016	Jorge Mateo, SS	Athletics
2017	Gleyber Torres, SS	Yankees

BEST TOOLS

Best Hitter for Average	Nick Solak
Best Power Hitter	Dermis Garcia
Best Strike-Zone Discipline	Nick Solak
Fastest Baserunner	Estevan Florial
Best Athlete	Estevan Florial
Best Fastball	Luis Medina
Best Curveball	Luis Medina
Best Slider	Justus Sheffield
Best Changeup	Domingo Acevedo
Best Control	Adonis Rosa
Best Defensive Catcher	Kyle Higashioka
Best Defensive Infielder	Gleyber Torres
Best Infield Arm	Gleyber Torres
Best Defensive Outfielder	Estevan Florial
Best Outfield Arm	Estevan Florial

Year	Club (League)	Class	AVG	G	AB	R	H	2B	3B	HR	RBI	BB	SO	SB	CS	OBP	SLG
2015	South Bend (MWL)	LoA	.290	118	459	52	133	24	5	3	61	43	106	22	12	.350	.383
	Myrtle Beach (CAR)	HiA	.174	7	23	1	4	0	0	0	2	1	7	0	1	.208	.174
2016	Myrtle Beach (CAR)	HiA	.275	94	356	62	98	23	3	9	47	42	87	19	10	.359	.433
	Tampa (FSL)	HiA	.254	31	122	19	31	6	2	2	19	16	23	2	3	.341	.385
2017	Trenton (EL)	AA	.273	32	121	22	33	10	1	5	18	17	21	5	4	.367	.496
	Scranton/W-B (IL)	AAA	.309	23	81	9	25	4	1	2	16	13	26	2	2	.406	.457
Minor League Totals			.281	355	1344	202	378	75	18	23	196	161	310	60	39	.360	.415

2 ESTEVAN FLORIAL, OF

Born: Nov. 25, 1997. **B-T:** L-R. **Ht.:** 6-1. **Wt.:** 196. **Signed:** Haiti, 2015. **Signed by:**
Esteban Castillo.

The Yankees signed Florial out of Haiti for $200,000 when he was 17. They would have signed him a year earlier had he not been suspended by Major League Baseball after they discovered a discrepancy with his identification. He advanced from the Dominican Summer League to Rookie-level Pulaski in his first two pro seasons, showing hints of five-tool potential, before breaking out at low Class A Charleston and high Class A Tampa in 2017. Florial swings and misses frequently and racked up a 31 percent strikeout rate in 2017, but he impacts the ball when he connects. That's about the only ding on his card, however. Florial hit .298 and drew 50 walks in 2017 and projects to stick in center field, where he has a well above-average arm. He's got well above-average raw power that is beginning to play in games. A plus-plus runner, he regularly gets down the line to first base in fewer than four seconds. Florial got a taste of Double-A Trenton during the Eastern League playoffs and could return there to begin 2018 after six weeks in the Arizona Fall League. If he develops as the Yankees believe he will, Florial could be an all-star-caliber center fielder in the mold of early career Curtis Granderson.

BA GRADE
65 Risk:
V. High
HIT: 50. **POW:** 55.
SPD: 70. **FLD:** 60.
ARM: 70.

Year	Club (League)	Class	AVG	G	AB	R	H	2B	3B	HR	RBI	BB	SO	SB	CS	OBP	SLG
2015	Yankees1 (DSL)	R	.313	57	224	51	70	11	8	7	53	30	61	15	5	.394	.527
2016	Tampa (FSL)	HiA	.125	2	8	0	1	0	0	0	0	0	2	0	0	.125	.125
	Pulaski (APP)	R	.225	60	236	36	53	10	1	7	25	28	78	10	2	.315	.364
	Charleston, SC (SAL)	LoA	.300	5	20	4	6	0	1	1	5	2	5	0	0	.348	.550
2017	Charleston, SC (SAL)	LoA	.297	91	344	64	102	21	5	11	43	41	124	17	7	.373	.483
	Tampa (FSL)	HiA	.303	19	76	13	23	2	2	2	14	9	24	6	1	.368	.461
Minor League Totals			.281	234	908	168	255	44	17	28	140	110	294	48	15	.360	.459

3 JUSTUS SHEFFIELD, LHP

Born: May 13, 1996. **B-T:** L-L. **Ht.:** 5-10. **Wt.:** 203. **Drafted:** HS—Tullahoma, Tenn., 2014 (1st round). **Signed by:** Chuck Bartlett (Indians).

The older brother of Dodgers prospect Jordan Sheffield, Justus was a first-round pick of the Indians in 2014. He showed well in his pro debut but was arrested that offseason for criminal trespass in his hometown. Cleveland dealt Sheffield, Clint Frazier and two others to the Yankees in July 2016 as the freight for closer Andrew Miller. Despite standing just 5-foot-10, Sheffield packs lightning in his left arm. His fastball can sit in the mid-90s, and he has touched as high as 98 mph. Sheffield's fastball generates plenty of swings and misses thanks to intense riding life and a deceptive delivery. He couples the pitch with a slider and changeup that both project as above-average to plus. His slider, which sits in the mid-80s, ranks slightly ahead of his changeup, which sits in the high 80s. Sheffield missed a significant chunk of time in 2017 with a severely strained oblique muscle, so the Yankees sent him to the Arizona Fall League to make up innings. After a successful stint in the AFL, where he struck out 22 in 20 innings, Sheffield should move to Triple-A Scranton/Wilkes-Barre in 2018. If everything clicks, he has the ceiling of a No. 3 starter.

BA GRADE
60 Risk:
High
FB: 70. **SL:** 55.
CHG: 55.
CTRL: 50.

Year	Club (League)	Class	W	L	ERA	G	GS	CG	SV	IP	H	HR	BB	SO	K/9	WHIP	AVG
2015	Lake County (MWL)	LoA	9	4	3.31	26	26	0	0	128	135	8	38	138	9.7	1.36	.264
2016	Lynchburg (CAR)	HiA	7	5	3.59	19	19	0	0	95	91	6	40	93	8.8	1.37	.252
	Tampa (FSL)	HiA	3	1	1.73	5	5	0	0	26	14	0	10	27	9.3	0.92	.157
	Trenton (EL)	AA	0	0	0.00	1	1	0	0	4	2	0	3	9	20.3	1.25	.125
2017	Yankees2 (GCL)	R	0	1	1.93	2	2	0	0	5	4	0	1	6	11.6	1.07	.235
	Trenton (EL)	AA	7	6	3.18	17	17	1	0	93	94	14	33	82	7.9	1.36	.258
Minor League Totals			29	18	3.27	78	74	1	0	372	364	28	134	384	9.3	1.34	.252

4 CHANCE ADAMS, RHP

Born: May 13, 1996. **B-T:** R-R. **Ht.:** 6-0. **Wt.:** 215. **Drafted:** Dallas Baptist, 2015 (5th round). **Signed by:** Mike Leuzinger.

Adams moved back and forth between the rotation and bullpen during a collegiate career that saw him transfer from Yavapai (Ariz.) JC to Dallas Baptist after his sophomore season. The Yankees believed in Adams as a starter and took steps to establish him in that role after making him a 2015 fifth-round pick. He has excelled in that role as a pro. Returned to Double-A Trenton in 2018, Adams continued increasing his workload and earned a quick promotion to Triple-A Scranton/ Wilkes-Barre. He headlines a four-pitch arsenal with a 92-97 mph plus fastball and an plus slider. His fringe-average curveball and changeup rank third and fourth in his repertoire, and he spent time in 2017 working on refining his changeup. He already throws the pitch with the same conviction and arm speed as his fastball. A new two-seam fastball grip could lead to further improvement. Despite some of the best stuff in the system, Adams shows a tendency to nibble for the corners rather than attacking. With two plus pitches and above-average control, Adams profiles as a potential mid-rotation starter. He faces a probable return to Triple-A in 2018.

BA GRADE

55 Risk: Medium

FB: 60. CB: 45.
SL: 60. CHG: 45.
CTRL: 50.

Year	Club (League)	Class	W	L	ERA	G	GS	CG	SV	IP	H	HR	BB	SO	K/9	WHIP	AVG
2015	Staten Island (NYP)	SS	1	0	0.93	4	0	0	0	10	5	0	3	13	12.1	0.83	.147
	Charleston, SC (SAL)	LoA	1	1	3.09	5	0	0	0	12	7	0	4	16	12.3	0.94	.163
	Tampa (FSL)	HiA	1	0	1.29	5	0	0	0	14	12	0	2	16	10.3	1.00	.226
2016	Tampa (FSL)	HiA	5	0	2.65	12	12	0	0	58	41	4	15	73	11.4	0.97	.196
	Trenton (EL)	AA	8	1	2.07	13	12	0	0	70	35	5	24	71	9.2	0.85	.145
2017	Trenton (EL)	AA	4	0	1.03	6	6	0	0	35	23	2	15	32	8.2	1.09	.183
	Scranton/W-B (IL)	AAA	11	5	2.89	21	21	0	0	115	81	9	43	103	8.0	1.08	.197
Minor League Totals			31	7	2.33	66	51	0	0	313	204	20	106	324	9.3	0.99	.182

5 MIGUEL ANDUJAR, 3B

Born: March 2, 1995. **B-T:** R-R. **Ht.:** 6-0. **Wt.:** 215. **Signed:** Dominican Republic, 2011. **Signed by:** Coanabo Cosme/Victor Mata.

New York signed Andujar for $750,000 in 2011 out of the Dominican program run by Basilio Vizcaino, who also helped develop Gary Sanchez. The Yankees liked Andujar's overall mix of skills, particularly his power potential and athleticism. He has improved each year as a pro and made his big league debut with two separate callups in 2017. After correcting an issue with his stride early in the season with Double-A Trenton, Andujar made quick work of the Eastern League and continued to mash at Triple-A Scranton/Wilkes-Barre. There, the coaching staff worked with the free-swinger to refine his pitch selection, and Andujar responded with a career-high 16 home runs. Though his home run power plays exclusively to his pull side, he has shown the ability to pepper the whole field with doubles. Scouts are divided on Andujar's fielding ability. His arm strength is well above-average, but questionable footwork and hands might force him off third base. With Greg Bird at first base and Gleyber Torres potentially fitting best at third base, the Yankees don't necessarily have a position open for Andujar, who will return to Triple-A for more seasoning in 2018.

BA GRADE

55 Risk: Medium

HIT: 55. POW: 55.
SPD: 40. FLD: 50.
ARM: 60.

Year	Club (League)	Class	AVG	G	AB	R	H	2B	3B	HR	RBI	BB	SO	SB	CS	OBP	SLG
2015	Tampa (FSL)	HiA	.243	130	485	54	118	24	5	8	57	29	90	12	1	.288	.363
2016	Tampa (FSL)	HiA	.283	58	230	34	65	10	2	10	41	18	30	1	3	.343	.474
	Trenton (EL)	AA	.266	72	282	28	75	16	2	2	42	21	42	2	1	.323	.358
2017	Trenton (EL)	AA	.312	67	253	30	79	23	1	7	52	12	38	2	3	.342	.494
	Scranton/W-B (IL)	AAA	.317	58	227	36	72	13	1	9	30	17	33	3	0	.364	.502
	New York (AL)	MAJ	.571	5	7	0	4	2	0	0	4	1	0	1	0	.625	.857
Major League Totals			.571	5	7	0	4	2	0	0	4	1	0	1	0	.625	.857
Minor League Totals			.274	596	2271	296	622	131	15	51	336	152	374	30	13	.323	.412

6 ALBERT ABREU, RHP

MARK LOMOGLIO

Born: Sept. 25, 1995. **B-T:** R-R. **Ht.:** 6-2. **Wt.:** 198. **Signed:** Dominican Republic, 2013.
Signed by: Oz Ocampo/Rafael Belen/Francis Mojica (Astros).

When the Astros signed Abreu in 2013, they knew he had the potential for big-time stuff. They were proved right when he started hitting the mid-90s with his fastball when he got to low Class A. Houston dealt both Abreu and righthander Jorge Guzman to the Yankees for Brian McCann in December 2016 in a deal that worked out for both sides. Abreu dealt with right elbow inflammation at times in 2017, which he spent mostly at high Class A Tampa, but never had surgery. With another year under his belt, Abreu's fastball has ticked up even more. He now sits in the mid-90s with regularity and touches as high as 101 mph on occasion. He couples his fastball, which has average life, with a curveball and changeup that project to be at least average if not plus in the future. He still needs to refine his command, and some evaluators have seen more of a thrower than a pitcher at this point, but scouts inside and outside the organization see a pitcher with the upside of a No. 2 starter if everything develops. Abreu could be ready for Double-A to begin 2018, though a return to high Class A to begin the season is a likely option as well.

BA GRADE

60 Risk: High

FB: 70. CB: 60.
CHG: 55.
CTRL: 50.

Year	Club (League)	Class	W	L	ERA	G	GS	CG	SV	IP	H	HR	BB	SO	K/9	WHIP	AVG
2015	Greeneville (APP)	R	2	3	2.51	13	7	1	1	47	35	2	21	51	9.8	1.20	.206
2016	Quad Cities (MWL)	LoA	2	8	3.50	21	14	0	4	90	62	5	49	104	10.4	1.23	.193
	Lancaster (CAL)	HiA	1	0	5.40	3	2	0	0	12	12	2	9	11	8.5	1.80	.267
2017	Charleston, SC (SAL)	LoA	1	0	1.84	3	2	0	0	15	9	1	3	22	13.5	0.82	.180
	Yankees1 (GCL)	R	0	0	2.08	2	2	0	0	4	3	0	0	8	16.6	0.69	.177
	Tampa (FSL)	HiA	1	3	4.19	9	9	0	0	34	33	2	15	31	8.1	1.40	.252
Minor League Totals			10	16	3.20	65	50	1	5	270	202	13	126	281	9.4	1.22	.207

7 LUIS MEDINA, RHP

TOM DiPACE

Born: May 3, 1999. **B-T:** R-R. **Ht.:** 6-2. **Wt.:** 196. **Signed:** Dominican Republic, 2015.
Signed by: Juan Rosario.

When the Yankees signed Medina out of the Dominican Republic in 2015 for $280,000 he was already hitting the triple digits with his fastball. He has made tweaks to improve his delivery and allow himself to throw more strikes, but he's still a raw power arm first and foremost. Medina sits in the upper 90s and topped at 102 mph in 2017 in the Rookie-level Appalachian League. He couples his fastball with a high-spin curveball and a changeup. His curve is inconsistent but flashes the potential to be a true hammer that he can either land in the zone or bury for chases, and his changeup is above-average already with the potential to be plus as well. There are some in the organization who think Medina might be better served with a slider as his primary breaking ball. As would be expected with an 18-year-old, he needs to continue to refine his fastball command. Medina is talented enough to make the jump to low Class A Charleston in 2018, but he might be better served by starting in extended spring training before moving to short-season Staten Island. He's got the ceiling of a top-flight starter. In a pitching-rich system, Medina's ceiling is among the highest.

BA GRADE

60 Risk: Extreme

FB: 80. CB: 60.
CHG: 55.
CTRL: 45.

Year	Club (League)	Class	W	L	ERA	G	GS	CG	SV	IP	H	HR	BB	SO	K/9	WHIP	AVG
2016	Yankees1 (DSL)	R	0	0	1.93	3	3	0	0	5	2	0	4	4	7.7	1.29	.143
2017	Yankees1 (DSL)	R	1	1	5.74	4	3	0	0	16	17	0	10	17	9.8	1.72	.270
	Pulaski (APP)	R	1	1	5.09	6	6	0	0	23	14	1	14	22	8.6	1.22	.171
Minor League Totals			2	2	4.98	13	12	0	0	43	33	1	28	43	8.9	1.41	.208

8 THAIRO ESTRADA, SS/2B

Born: Feb. 22, 1996. **B-T:** R-R. **Ht.:** 5-9. **Wt.:** 184. **Signed:** Venezuela, 2012. **Signed by:** Alan Atacho/Ricardo Finol.

Overshadowed by Yankees prospects in his signing class like shortstop Jorge Mateo (now with the Athletics) and catcher Luis Torrens (Padres), Estrada has quietly risen to the ranks of the system's best prospects. He continued to show a knack for contact as he advanced to Double-A Trenton in 2017, when he took over at shortstop when Gleyber Torres was promoted to Triple-A. He was Trenton's most consistent player during its run to the Eastern League finals. None of Estrada's tools jump off the page, but he just keeps performing. As one of the Eastern League's youngest players in 2017, he finished among the top 10 in average (.301) and ranked second in the league with 149 hits. His quick hands and flat bat path allow him to make plenty of contact and spray line drives from gap to gap. Estrada proved that he could play shortstop with above-average range and a plus arm. He's got below-average power, and his smallish frame doesn't make it seem likely to change. He's an average runner on the bases. After a turn in the Arizona Fall League, Estrada will head to Triple-A Scranton/Wilkes-Barre, where he could split time again with Torres.

BA GRADE
50 Risk: High
HIT: 55. POW: 40.
SPD: 55. FLD: 60.
ARM: 60.

Year	Club (League)	Class	AVG	G	AB	R	H	2B	3B	HR	RBI	BB	SO	SB	CS	OBP	SLG
2015	Staten Island (NYP)	SS	.267	63	247	37	66	17	0	2	23	23	30	8	3	.338	.360
2016	Charleston, SC (SAL)	LoA	.286	35	140	11	40	3	1	5	19	8	21	11	3	.324	.429
	Tampa (FSL)	HiA	.292	83	315	52	92	15	1	3	30	29	46	7	5	.355	.375
2017	Trenton (EL)	AA	.301	122	495	72	149	19	4	6	48	34	56	8	11	.353	.392
Minor League Totals			.287	376	1454	213	418	68	11	18	143	113	194	49	28	.347	.387

9 DOMINGO ACEVEDO, RHP

Born: March 6, 1994. **B-T:** R-R. **Ht.:** 6-6. **Wt.:** 242. **Signed:** Dominican Republic, 2012. **Signed by:** Esteban Castillo.

When they signed Acevedo for a scant $7,500 in 2012, the Yankees saw a big man with a big arm. He dealt with injury issues early in his career, including blister issues that limited him to just 93 innings in 2016. Acevedo was fully healthy in 2017 and proved a valuable piece of the Double-A Trenton rotation until he reached his innings cap before the Eastern League playoffs. Aside from his massive frame, the first thing that jumps out about Acevedo is just how many strikes he throws— he rang up 142 strikeouts in 2017 against just 34 walks—in spite of a delivery that is littered with funkiness and moving parts. He starts his pitch package with a four-seam fastball in the mid- to high 90s and couples it with a high-80s slider that should develop into a plus pitch. He has enough confidence in his changeup to throw it to both sides of the plate and against both righthanders and lefthanders. The Yankees worked with Acevedo to help him gain more confidence in his offspeed pitches, including a fringe-average slider, by throwing them more often. Acevedo, who has the ceiling of a mid-rotation starter and a floor of a power reliever, will head to Triple-A Scranton/Wilkes-Barre in 2018

BA GRADE
50 Risk: High
FB: 70. SL: 50.
CHG: 60.
CTRL: 55.

Year	Club (League)	Class	W	L	ERA	G	GS	CG	SV	IP	H	HR	BB	SO	K/9	WHIP	AVG
2015	Charleston, SC (SAL)	LoA	0	0	5.40	1	1	0	0	2	2	0	1	1	5.4	1.80	.286
	Staten Island (NYP)	SS	3	0	1.69	11	11	0	0	48	37	2	15	53	9.9	1.08	.207
2016	Charleston, SC (SAL)	LoA	3	1	1.90	8	8	0	0	43	34	1	7	48	10.1	0.96	.221
	Tampa (FSL)	HiA	2	3	3.22	10	10	1	0	50	49	3	15	54	9.7	1.27	.261
2017	Tampa (FSL)	HiA	0	4	4.57	7	7	0	0	41	49	5	9	52	11.3	1.40	.290
	Scranton/W-B (IL)	AAA	1	1	4.38	2	2	0	0	12	12	0	8	8	5.8	1.62	.255
	Trenton (EL)	AA	5	1	2.38	14	14	1	0	79	65	8	17	82	9.3	1.03	.223
Minor League Totals			15	13	2.82	69	68	2	0	332	306	19	89	362	9.8	1.19	.243

10 DILLON TATE, RHP

Born: May 1, 1994. **B-T:** R-R. **Ht.:** 6-2. **Wt.:** 196. **Drafted:** UC Santa Barbara, 2015 (1st round). **Signed by:** Todd Guggiana (Rangers).

After being converted from a reliever to a starter in his junior season at UC Santa Barbara, Tate improved his draft stock immensely. The Rangers liked what they saw, drafted him with the fourth overall pick and signed him to a $4.2 million bonus. Hamstring issues limited his early innings in his first full season, and the Rangers dealt him to the Yankees as the headliner in the Carlos Beltran deal that summer. Tate's 2017 was delayed by lingering back and shoulder issues, but he was dynamite once he got on the field in late June. Between high Class A Tampa and Double-A Trenton, Tate showed off an impressive three-pitch combo led by a mid-90s fastball that topped out at 97 mph. He coupled the pitch with a slider and a changeup, both of which showed flashes of being plus once he's done developing. Scouts are still divided on whether Tate would be better served as a starter with a back-end rotation ceiling or as a power reliever late in games. With a high of 103.1 innings during his collegiate and pro careers, 2018 will be pivotal when it comes to determining Tate's future. He was originally slated to go to the Arizona Fall League, but the Yankees swapped him out in favor of Albert Abreu before the season began, opting instead to let Tate's work in the postseason with Trenton stand as part of the makeup for the time he missed in April and May. He's likely to return to Double-A to begin 2018.

BA GRADE
50 Risk: High
FB: 60. SL: 60.
CHG: 50.
CTRL: 50.

Year	Club (League)	Class	W	L	ERA	G	GS	CG	SV	IP	H	HR	BB	SO	K/9	WHIP	AVG
2015	Spokane (NWL)	SS	0	0	0.00	2	2	0	0	2	0	0	3	3	13.5	1.50	.000
	Hickory (SAL)	LoA	0	0	1.29	4	4	0	0	7	3	1	0	5	6.4	0.43	.130
2016	Hickory (SAL)	LoA	3	3	5.12	17	16	0	0	65	78	5	27	55	7.6	1.62	.311
	Charleston, SC (SAL)	LoA	1	0	3.12	7	0	0	0	17	21	1	6	15	7.8	1.56	.292
2017	Tampa (FSL)	HiA	6	0	2.62	9	9	0	0	58	48	4	15	46	7.1	1.08	.221
	Trenton (EL)	AA	1	2	3.24	4	4	1	0	25	23	3	9	17	6.1	1.28	.253
Minor League Totals			11	5	3.61	43	35	1	0	175	173	14	60	141	7.3	1.33	.263

11 MATT SAUER, RHP

BA GRADE
55 Risk: Extreme

Born: Jan. 21, 1999. **B-T:** R-R. **Ht.:** 6-4. **Wt.:** 201. **Drafted:** HS—Santa Maria, Calif., 2017 (2nd round). **Signed by:** Bobby DeJardin.

Many prospects these days have help constructing their offseason workout routines. Whether it's a local strength guru or a personal coach, there's no shortage of instruction available. Sauer, however, designed his own workout regimen and saw enough benefits to boost his fastball and his draft stock high enough after his senior season of high school that the Yankees popped him in the second round and signed him to a bonus of $2,497,500—more than double the slot for the 54th overall pick. Tall, athletic and project-able at 6-foot-4 and 201 pounds, Sauer has already given the Yankees plenty to be excited about. He's shown a fastball between 92-97 mph as well as a pair of breaking balls, though the team was using the instructional league to decide whether his slider or his curveball was a better fit for his delivery, as well as a changeup that he didn't need much in high school. Scouts leading up to the draft also saw a pitcher with a tendency to finish across his body as well as a head whack that could affect his control going forth. Given his size and present stuff, however, Sauer has the upside to pitch in the middle of a rotation when he's fully developed.

Year	Club (League)	Class	W	L	ERA	G	GS	CG	SV	IP	H	HR	BB	SO	K/9	WHIP	AVG
2017	Yankees2 (GCL)	R	0	2	5.40	6	6	0	0	12	13	0	8	12	9.3	1.80	.271
Minor League Totals			0	2	5.40	6	6	0	0	12	13	0	8	12	9.3	1.80	.271

12 NICK SOLAK, 2B

BA GRADE
50 Risk: High

Born: Jan. 11, 1995. **B-T:** R-R. **Ht.:** 5-10. **Wt.:** 180. **Drafted:** Louisville, 2016 (2nd round). **Signed by:** Mike Gibbons.

After an impressive Cape Cod League performance in 2016, Solak continued his standout performance in his junior season with Louisville. He hit .376/.470/.564 with the Cardinals and boosted his draft stock enough to earn a second-round selection and a $950,000 bonus. He was head and shoulders above the competition at short-season Staten Island and was skipped to high Class A Tampa to begin his pro career. With the T-Yanks, Solak continued solidifying his reputation as one of the more polished hitters in the system. He brings a short, quick line-drive stroke designed to spray line drives to all fields, though his spray chart this year suggests his hits skewed toward the opposite field. That's in line with a hole that scouts noticed in his swing on the inside part of the plate. There are also questions about his defense, specifically his stiff actions in the field. His entire profile leads to comparisons to former Yankee Rob Refsnyder, another bat-first second baseman with the outfield in his past and holes that got exposed once he saw the advanced pitching of the upper levels. He's neither a burner nor a clogger, but he'll never be more than an average runner. Solak was promoted to Double-A when Jorge Mateo was traded to Oakland in the Sonny Gray deal, and Solak provided the offensive production the Thunder needed to advance to the Eastern League Championship Series. He's likely to return to Trenton to begin 2018.

Year	Club (League)	Class	AVG	G	AB	R	H	2B	3B	HR	RBI	BB	SO	SB	CS	OBP	SLG
2016	Staten Island (NYP)	SS	.321	64	240	48	77	13	1	3	25	30	39	8	0	.412	.421
2017	Tampa (FSL)	HiA	.301	100	346	56	104	17	4	10	44	53	76	13	4	.397	.460
	Trenton (EL)	AA	.286	30	119	16	34	9	1	2	9	10	24	1	1	.344	.429
Minor League Totals			.305	194	705	120	215	39	6	15	78	93	139	22	5	.393	.441

13 FREICER PEREZ, RHP

BA GRADE
50 Risk: High

Born: March 14, 1996. **B-T:** R-R. **Ht.:** 6-8. **Wt.:** 240. **Signed:** Dominican Republic, 2014. **Signed by:** Arturo Pena.

When the Yankees signed Perez, they knew he was a project built on the projectability of the changeup he showed as a teenager. At 6-foot-8 and 190 pounds, Perez had plenty more room to add strength. He's added 50 pounds since then and has seen the corresponding velocity gains. Built like current Yankees reliever Dellin Betances, Perez can sit in the mid-90s with his fastball and has touched triple-digits. He spent all of 2017 at low Class A Charleston, where his 2.84 ERA and 117 strikeouts placed him among the league's top 10 in both categories. He's got a four-pitch package, with the changeup as the best of his three secondaries. His slider and curveball both vary in their consistency. On the right day, they might flash average, and some outside evaluators see them both becoming 55-grade offerings in the future. As would be expected for a man his size, Perez has some issues he needs to iron out in his delivery. In particular, he needs to work on staying on-line to home plate instead of getting side-to-side. He'll advance to high Class A Tampa this year, where he could work with pitching coach Tim Norton, who stands 6-foot-7 himself. If everything clicks, he has a chance to be a No. 3 starter. If not, he could be a fireballing reliever.

Year	Club (League)	Class	W	L	ERA	G	GS	CG	SV	IP	H	HR	BB	SO	K/9	WHIP	AVG
2015	Yankees1 (DSL)	R	7	3	3.23	15	15	0	0	70	66	4	17	68	8.8	1.19	.244
2016	Staten Island (NYP)	SS	2	4	4.47	13	13	0	0	52	51	3	25	49	8.4	1.45	.245
2017	Charleston, SC (SAL)	LoA	10	3	2.84	24	24	0	0	124	96	5	45	117	8.5	1.14	.213
Minor League Totals			19	10	3.30	52	52	0	0	246	213	12	87	234	8.6	1.22	.230

14 CLARKE SCHMIDT, RHP

BA GRADE
55 Risk: Extreme

Born: Feb. 20, 1996. **B-T:** R-R. **Ht.:** 6-1. **Wt.:** 205. **Drafted:** South Carolina, 2017 (1st round). **Signed by:** Billy Godwin.

Were he healthy, there was a good chance Schmidt would not have lasted until the 16th selection in this year's draft. Instead, he had Tommy John surgery during the season and fell to the Yankees, who were happy to snap him up and add him to their collection of hard-throwing righthanders for a below-slot bonus of $2,184,300. At his best, Schmidt, the brother of Tigers prospect Clate Schmidt, shows a low-90s fastball that routinely touched 95-96 during his junior year with the Gamecocks. He blended the four-seam fastball with a two-seamer, a slider that got plenty of swings and misses and a changeup that showed above-average potential as well. More than his stuff, the Yankees were wowed by makeup that made them buy in despite knowing he wouldn't get back on the mound until sometime in 2018. He had the surgery in early May, which would put him on track for a return during the summer. If his stuff returns in full, he has the potential to pitch in a big league rotation.

Year	Club (League)	Class	W	L	ERA	G	GS	CG	SV	IP	H	HR	BB	SO	K/9	WHIP	AVG
2017	Did not play—Injured																

15 TYLER WADE, SS/2B

BA GRADE
45 Risk: Medium

Born: Nov. 23, 1994. **B-T:** L-R. **Ht.:** 6-1. **Wt.:** 180. **Drafted:** HS—Murrieta, Calif., 2013 (4th round). **Signed by:** David Keith.

After a relatively quick rise through the minor leagues, Wade made his major league debut on June 27 and was quickly overmatched by major league pitching. Still just 22, he struck out in 19 of his 63 plate appearances and went just 9-for-58 in his big league time. With Triple-A Scranton/Wilkes-Barre, however, where he was still nearly five years younger than average in the International League, Wade thrived. He hit .310/.382/.460, the highest marks in all three categories in any of his four full minor league seasons. He showed up to spring training this year noticeably stronger and hit a career-best seven home runs as a result while seemingly sacrificing none of his well above-average speed. He doesn't show standout tools anywhere but on the basepaths, though he doesn't have any glaring deficiencies either. Didi Gregorius and Starlin Castro seem to have a lock on the middle-infield positions in the Bronx, and once he returns from Tommy John surgery top prospect Gleyber Torres will vault back to the top of the Yankees' infield prospects. Wade played outfield in the Arizona Fall League in 2016 and was used all over the diamond this past season in Scranton. With the extra versatility, Wade has the ceiling of a super-utility type of player.

Year	Club (League)	Class	AVG	G	AB	R	H	2B	3B	HR	RBI	BB	SO	SB	CS	OBP	SLG
2015	Tampa (FSL)	HiA	.280	98	368	51	103	11	5	2	28	39	65	31	15	.349	.353
	Trenton (EL)	AA	.204	29	113	6	23	4	0	1	3	2	24	2	1	.224	.265
2016	Trenton (EL)	AA	.259	133	505	90	131	16	7	5	27	66	103	27	8	.352	.349
2017	Scranton/W-B (IL)	AAA	.310	85	339	68	105	22	4	7	31	38	75	26	5	.382	.460
	New York (AL)	MAJ	.155	30	58	7	9	4	0	0	2	5	19	1	1	.222	.224
Major League Totals			.155	30	58	7	9	4	0	0	2	5	19	1	1	.222	.224
Minor League Totals			.275	524	2007	329	551	87	22	16	153	236	431	119	43	.355	.364

16 DOMINGO GERMAN, RHP

BA GRADE

50 Risk: High

Born: Aug. 4, 1992. **B-T:** R-R. **Ht.:** 6-2. **Wt.:** 175. **Signed:** Dominican Republic, 2009. **Signed by:** Albert Gonzalez/Sandy Nin/Alix Martinez (Marlins).

German first burst onto the national scene at the 2014 Futures Game in Minnesota. There, he pitched a scoreless inning that included strikeouts of two of the game's top prospects at the time—the Cubs' Kris Bryant and the Rangers' Joey Gallo. He was included in a trade with the Yankees that winter along with righthander Nate Eovaldi and infielder Garrett Jones in the deal that sent infielder Martin Prado and righthander David Phelps to the Marlins. He missed the 2015 season with Tommy John surgery but made up for lost time over the next two seasons and made his major league debut this June. He was dominant in the minor leagues this season, going 8-6, 2.88 with 119 strikeouts in 109.1 innings between Double-A Trenton and Triple-A Scranton/Wilkes-Barre. He boasts a three-pitch mix, starting with a fastball that sat between 92-96 this year and touched as high as 97 on occasion. German replaced his slider this year with a curveball that sat between 79-83 mph and a changeup in the 86-90 range. Both pitches flashed above-average potential, and he showed an ability in the minors to get lefties and righties out with near-equal aplomb. He's likely to head back to Triple-A to begin 2018.

Year	Club (League)	Class	W	L	ERA	G	GS	CG	SV	IP	H	HR	BB	SO	K/9	WHIP	AVG
2015	Did not play—Injured																
2016	Charleston, SC (SAL)	LoA	1	1	3.12	5	5	0	0	26	15	2	2	18	6.2	0.65	.167
	Tampa (FSL)	HiA	0	2	3.04	5	5	0	0	24	26	1	9	20	7.6	1.48	.283
2017	Trenton (EL)	AA	1	4	3.00	6	6	1	0	33	32	4	10	38	10.4	1.27	.248
	Scranton/W-B (IL)	AAA	7	2	2.83	14	13	0	0	76	59	5	22	81	9.6	1.06	.210
	New York (AL)	MAJ	0	1	3.14	7	0	0	0	14	11	1	9	18	11.3	1.40	.216
Major League Totals			0	1	3.14	7	0	0	0	14	11	1	9	18	11.3	1.40	.216
Minor League Totals			29	19	2.54	107	73	1	6	453	380	20	134	443	8.8	1.14	.227

17 JUAN THEN, RHP

BA GRADE

55 Risk: Extreme

Born: Feb. 7, 2000. **B-T:** R-R. **Ht.:** 6-1. **Wt.:** 155. **Signed:** Dominican Republic, 2016. **Signed by:** Eddy Toledo (Mariners).

Then was signed out of the Dominican Republic by the Mariners as a pitcher who, with a quick arm and a slight frame, had a good amount of projectability remaining. He was dealt to the Yankees in the 2017 offseason with lefthander J.P. Sears in exchange for righthanded reliever Nick Rumbelow as New York cleared space on its 40-man roster. He had a stellar opening season as a professional, allowing just 50 hits in 61.1 innings in the Dominican Summer League. He also experienced a velocity jump, moving into the low-90s with his fastball and touching as high as 94. He backs it up with a loose, 74-78 mph curveball that he needs to tighten and work to land in the strike zone more frequently. He also has an 81-86 changeup that's ahead of the curveball in both development and ability to throw the pitch for a strike. His delivery calls to mind Mariners closer Edwin Diaz, but he needs to gain strength to be able to repeat his motion. Added muscle will help him land on-line more often and keep from falling off the mound on every pitch. He's likely to start the year in extended spring training before heading to either one of the two Yankees half-season affiliates in mid-June.

Year	Club (League)	Class	W	L	ERA	G	GS	CG	SV	IP	H	HR	BB	SO	K/9	WHIP	AVG
2017	Mariners (DSL)	R	2	2	2.64	13	13	0	0	61.1	50	3	15	56	8.2	1.06	.220
Minor League Totals			2	2	2.64	13	13	0	0	61.1	50	3	15	56	8.2	1.06	.220

18 TREVOR STEPHAN, RHP

Born: Nov. 25, 1995. **B-T:** R-R. **Ht.:** 6-4. **Wt.:** 210. **Drafted:** Arkansas, 2017 (3rd round). **Signed by:** Matt Ranson.

BA GRADE
50 Risk: High

Stephan began his career at Hill (Texas) JC, where he pitched almost exclusively out of the bullpen. He transferred to Arkansas for this junior season and started in all 16 games in which he appeared. His use in the rotation, plus an uptick in stuff, raised his draft stock and led to the Yankees drafting him in the third round and sending him to short-season Staten Island to start his career. His fastball sits in the low-90s and can touch a tick higher. The pitch plays up because of the high, riding life—which the Yankees compare to the fastballs thrown by a pair of other SEC arms who became Yankees: David Robertson and Nick Goody—and the funkiness in Stephan's delivery. He couples the pitch primarily with a slider that developed throughout his college career into an offering that gets swings and misses. He has a changeup as well, but it's well below-average now and will need to be developed further if Stephan is to continue developing as a starter. He's likely to move to low Class A Charleston in 2018.

Year	Club (League)	Class	W	L	ERA	G	GS	CG	SV	IP	H	HR	BB	SO	K/9	WHIP	AVG
2017	Yankees1 (GCL)	R	0	0	0.00	1	1	0	0	2	0	0	0	1	4.5	0.00	.000
	Staten Island (NYP)	SS	1	1	1.39	10	9	0	0	32	20	0	6	43	12.0	0.80	.177
Minor League Totals			1	1	1.31	11	10	0	0	34	20	0	6	44	11.5	0.76	.168

19 GLENN OTTO, RHP

Born: March 11, 1996. **B-T:** R-R. **Ht.:** 6-5. **Wt.:** 241. **Drafted:** Rice, 2017 (5th round). **Signed by:** Brian Rhees.

BA GRADE
50 Risk: High

Much like they did with Chance Adams, the Yankees looked at Otto, who made just four starts in 84 appearances with Rice, and saw a pitcher with rotation potential. He dealt with a little bit of shoulder soreness early in his junior season but rebounded to strike out 81 in 59.2 innings with the Owls. That was enough for the Yankees to take him with their fifth-round pick. Once Otto got to pro ball, the Yankees used him on a starter's schedule, with five or six days coming between appearances. Those who saw him after he signed saw a potential horse, based on his massive size and fastball in the mid-90s with downhill plane. He coupled the fastball with an average or better 12-to-6 curveball that he used to ring up 30 strikeouts in his first 20 pro innings. He's still developing his changeup, and his fastball command will have to show continued refinement, but the Yankees like his upside as a rotation piece. If he falters in that role, he could easily move back to the bullpen and dominate. He's slated for the rotation with Charleston in 2018, where he would join an intriguing mix of high-end arms with varying backgrounds.

Year	Club (League)	Class	W	L	ERA	G	GS	CG	SV	IP	H	HR	BB	SO	K/9	WHIP	AVG
2017	Yankees1 (GCL)	R	0	0	0.00	1	1	0	0	2	1	0	0	3	13.5	0.50	.143
	Yankees2 (GCL)	R	0	0	0.00	1	1	0	0	1	0	0	0	2	18.0	0.00	.000
	Staten Island (NYP)	SS	3	0	1.59	7	2	0	0	17	12	0	5	25	13.2	1.00	.194
Minor League Totals			3	0	1.35	9	4	0	0	20	13	0	5	30	13.5	0.90	.181

20 DERMIS GARCIA, 3B

Born: Jan. 7, 1998. **B-T:** R-R. **Ht.:** 6-2. **Wt.:** 229. **Signed:** Dominican Republic, 2014. **Signed by:** Miguel Benitez.

BA GRADE
50 Risk: High

Signed for $3 million as part of the Yankees' massive international spending spree in 2014, Garcia's development has been slow but steady. There are serious questions as to whether he'll stay at third base in the long-term, but there are zero doubts about his massive power potential. Garcia was one of 25 players this season to hit 17 home runs, and he did it in 95 fewer at-bats than anybody else. As would be expected, however, those home runs came with significant swing-and-miss issues, as well. He struck out at a 33-percent clip during his time with low Class A Charleston over the season's last month, which was in line with the marks he's produced throughout his career. The 27.7 percent rate he produced with Rookie-level Pulaski to begin the season represented the best mark of his career. He's improved his footwork and agility at third base but has already begun seeing time at first base, which evaluators see as his potential home once he's fully developed. To avoid that fate, he'll need to keep up with his conditioning and continue working very hard to improve. Garcia needs to reduce his swing and miss, but his power makes him an incredibly intriguing prospect nonetheless. He should return to Charleston in 2018.

Year	Club (League)	Class	AVG	G	AB	R	H	2B	3B	HR	RBI	BB	SO	SB	CS	OBP	SLG
2015	Yankees2 (GCL)	R	.159	23	69	7	11	2	0	0	6	9	25	0	1	.256	.188
2016	Pulaski (APP)	R	.206	57	194	31	40	9	0	13	24	32	79	0	2	.326	.454
2017	Pulaski (APP)	R	.270	33	115	24	31	5	1	9	25	24	39	6	0	.397	.565
	Charleston, SC (SAL) LoA		.227	30	110	12	25	6	1	8	20	14	42	0	0	.312	.518
Minor League Totals			.219	143	488	74	107	22	2	30	75	79	185	6	3	.331	.457

21 JUAN DE PAULA, RHP

Born: Sept. 22, 1997. **B-T:** R-R. **Ht.:** 6-3. **Wt.:** 165. **Signed:** Dominican Republic, 2014. **Signed by:** Eddy Toledo/Tim Kissner (Mariners).

BA GRADE
50 Risk: High

De Paula was part of the two-pitcher package (along with fellow righthander Jio Orozco) that the Mariners sent the Yankees in exchange for outfielder Ben Gamel, who put together a fine season in Seattle after being given extended playing time. The Mariners originally signed De Paula for $175,000, and he rewarded them early by throwing a complete-game shutout in the Dominican Summer League. With short-season Staten Island this year, De Paula continued to show signs that he could be a future rotation piece. He attacked the zone with a low-90s fastball that got to 94-95 mph at times, and he coupled the pitch with an average changeup and a potentially average curveball, as well. With 25 walks in 62 innings, he'll need to continue to iron out his control as he moves up the ladder. The Yankees are encouraged, however, by the aggression he shows on the mound. He'll throw his fastball to all four quadrants of the strike zone, and he showed an ability to make big pitches when he needed to make them. He'll pitch all of 2018 at 20 years old, and he's likely shown enough to earn a spot at low Class A Charleston.

Year	Club (League)	Class	W	L	ERA	G	GS	CG	SV	IP	H	HR	BB	SO	K/9	WHIP	AVG
2015	Mariners2 (DSL)	R	5	4	2.32	14	14	1	0	78	62	1	15	68	7.9	0.99	.218
2016	Mariners (AZL)	R	1	2	3.07	11	7	0	0	41	41	2	11	53	11.6	1.27	.253
2017	Staten Island (NYP)	SS	5	5	2.90	12	11	0	0	62	42	0	25	53	7.7	1.08	.191
Minor League Totals			11	11	2.69	37	32	1	0	181	145	3	51	174	8.7	1.08	.218

22 TAYLOR WIDENER, RHP

Born: Oct. 24, 1994. **B-T:** R-R. **Ht.:** 6-0. **Wt.:** 195. **Drafted:** South Carolina, 2016 (12th round). **Signed by:** Billy Godwin.

BA GRADE
50 Risk: High

At South Carolina, Widener moved back and forth between the bullpen and the rotation before making nine starts in 17 appearances in his junior season. He ranked as BA's No. 2 prospect in the Coastal Plain League in 2015, just behind current Marlins prospect Brian Miller. Widener had ulnar transposition surgery in the fall between his sophomore and junior seasons and has also has dealt with injuries to his back and knee in the past. He spent all of the 2017 regular season with high Class A Tampa this year but was moved to Double-A Trenton for the postseason. He made history with the Thunder when he pitched the final five innings of the team's no-hitter in the Eastern League Division Series. His four-pitch arsenal includes a 92-97 mph fastball fired from a three-quarter arm slot. His go-to offspeed offering is his slider in the low-80s that gets swings and misses, but his 81-87 mph changeup, which features depth and fade, is catching up rapidly. His curveball is a distinct fourth pitch at this point. The Yankees have used Widener as a starter, but his future is more likely as a long reliever. He'll return to Trenton in 2018.

Year	Club (League)	Class	W	L	ERA	G	GS	CG	SV	IP	H	HR	BB	SO	K/9	WHIP	AVG
2016	Staten Island (NYP)	SS	2	0	0.00	6	1	0	1	15	2	0	4	25	14.7	0.39	.043
	Charleston, SC (SAL)	LoA	1	0	0.78	7	1	0	3	23	15	2	3	34	13.3	0.78	.188
2017	Tampa (FSL)	HiA	7	8	3.39	27	27	0	0	119	87	5	50	129	9.7	1.15	.206
Minor League Totals			10	8	2.68	40	29	0	4	158	104	7	57	188	10.7	1.02	.189

23 BILLY McKINNEY, OF/1B

Born: Aug. 23, 1994. **B-T:** L-L. **Ht.:** 6-1. **Wt.:** 205. **Drafted:** HS—Plano, Texas, 2013 (1st round). **Signed by:** Armann Brown (Athletics).

BA GRADE
45 Risk: Medium

No matter what happens in McKinney's career, he can always say he was part of a pair trades that helped the Cubs win their first World Series in 108 years. He was included with shortstop Addison Russell in the deal that sent Jeff Samardzija and Jason Hammel to Oakland, and he was then sent to New York in the trade that brought closer Aroldis Chapman in for the stretch run. Now with the Yankees, he's on the cusp of the major leagues. He was a late addition to big league spring training after Tyler Austin broke his foot in the early going, and he responded by going 10-for-25 with three home runs. Once he was assigned to Double-A Trenton, he went into a prolonged slump for the season's first two months. In June, however, he began to bust out and was excellent in the second half of the season with Triple-A. He worked extensively throughout the year to keep a strong base and be consistent with his timing. Despite the strong numbers, scouts who saw McKinney with Scranton saw a lower energy player who looked lost against pitchers with even an average breaking ball. He improved his throwing mechanics in the outfield this year, and he takes solid routes to balls despite not being an above-average runner. The Yankees had McKinney begin working at first base in the Arizona Fall League because the emergence of Aaron Judge in New York has put up a major roadblock in the outfield. He's likely to return to Triple-A in 2018.

Year	Club (League)	Class	AVG	G	AB	R	H	2B	3B	HR	RBI	BB	SO	SB	CS	OBP	SLG
2015	Myrtle Beach (CAR)	HiA	.340	29	103	19	35	5	2	4	25	17	13	0	2	.432	.544
	Tennessee (SL)	AA	.285	77	274	29	78	26	1	3	39	27	47	0	0	.346	.420
2016	Tennessee (SL)	AA	.252	88	298	37	75	12	3	1	31	47	68	2	4	.355	.322
	Trenton (EL)	AA	.234	35	128	15	30	7	1	3	13	12	29	2	2	.310	.375
2017	Trenton (EL)	AA	.250	69	232	34	58	16	4	6	29	30	45	2	1	.339	.431
	Scranton/W-B (IL)	AAA	.306	55	209	32	64	13	3	10	35	9	49	0	0	.336	.541
Minor League Totals			.277	534	1925	274	533	112	23	41	267	223	384	20	13	.355	.423

24 DEIVI GARCIA, RHP

BA GRADE 50 Risk: V. High

Born: May 19, 1999. **B-T:** R-R. **Ht.:** 5-10. **Wt.:** 163. **Signed:** Dominican Republic, 2015. **Signed by:** Ray Sanchez/Victor Mata.

When the Yankees signed Garcia in 2015 they did so because of the big-time arm speed they saw coming from his small frame. He opened his career with 61 strikeouts in 48.2 innings in the Dominican Summer League, then in 2017 shot from the DSL to the Gulf Coast League and finished the year at Rookie-level Pulaski. He's totaled 143 strikeouts in 101 career innings, good for nearly 13 strikeouts per nine innings. He produces a low-90s fastball that peaked this year at 93 mph, but his bread and butter is a curveball that registers a spin rate of better than 3,000 on StatCast. His fastball has a high spin rate, too, and comes with riding life in the zone. He's also got a fringe-average changeup with fade and sink in the low-80s as his third pitch. He obviously needs to gain strength if he wants to find a spot in a rotation. Still a teenager, he'll have plenty of time do that. He could begin next year in extended spring training before moving to short-season Staten Island in June.

Year	Club (League)	Class	W	L	ERA	G	GS	CG	SV	IP	H	HR	BB	SO	K/9	WHIP	AVG
2016	Yankees2 (DSL)	R	1	5	2.61	12	12	0	0	48	23	1	32	61	11.4	1.14	.149
2017	Yankees1 (DSL)	R	1	1	1.17	3	3	0	0	15	10	1	2	18	10.6	0.78	.196
	Yankees (GCL)	R	3	0	3.24	4	2	0	0	17	9	3	4	24	13.0	0.78	.155
	Pulaski (APP)	R	2	1	4.50	6	5	0	0	28	23	3	13	43	13.8	1.29	.232
Minor League Totals			7	7	2.99	25	22	0	0	108	65	8	51	146	12.1	1.07	.180

25 JONATHAN LOAISIGA, RHP

BA GRADE 50 Risk: V. High

Born: Nov. 22, 1994. **B-T:** R-R. **Ht.:** 5-10. **Wt.:** 175. **Signed:** Nicaragua, 2012. **Signed by:** Sandy Moreno (Giants).

Loaisiga originally signed with the Giants in 2012, but he was released after missing the 2014 and 2015 seasons with recurring injuries. The Yankees signed him out of a tryout camp in 2016. He pitched just 2.1 innings with low Class A Charleston before landing on the disabled list again with Tommy John surgery. This year, however, the Yankees finally saw the pitcher they signed when he blew away the competition at short-season Staten Island. He consistently sat in the mid-90s and touched as high as 98 mph with his fastball. He paired the pitch with an 11-to-5 curveball in the low-80s that showed plenty of depth and helped Loaisiga whiff 33 in 33.2 innings this year. He also throws an 87-88 mph changeup with sink, though he could stand to drive the pitch down in the zone better. If Loaisiga can stay healthy, his fastball and curveball combination give him a chance to pitch in the back of a big league bullpen. If he can show improvement with his changeup, however, he has an outside chance at a long-term spot in a rotation.

Year	Club (League)	Class	W	L	ERA	G	GS	CG	SV	IP	H	HR	BB	SO	K/9	WHIP	AVG
2015	Did not play																
2016	Charleston, SC (SAL)	LoA	0	0	7.71	1	1	0	0	2	2	1	1	2	7.7	1.29	.222
2017	Yankees2 (GCL)	R	0	0	0.00	1	1	0	0	2	0	0	0	0	0.0	0.00	.000
	Yankees1 (GCL)	R	0	1	2.63	6	6	0	0	14	10	1	2	15	9.9	0.88	.196
	Staten Island (NYP)	SS	1	0	0.53	4	4	0	0	17	7	0	1	18	9.5	0.47	.121
Minor League Totals			9	2	2.43	25	25	0	0	104	79	6	20	75	6.5	0.95	.211

26 OSWALDO CABRERA, SS/2B

BA GRADE 45 Risk: High

Born: March 1, 1999. **B-T:** S-R. **Ht.:** 6-0. **Wt.:** 193. **Signed:** Venezuela, 2015. **Signed by:** Borman Landaeta.

When the Yankees signed Cabrera out of Venezuela two Julys ago, he was extremely skinny at 5-foot-10 and 145 pounds. Since then he's grown two inches and added nearly 50 pounds, turning a frail frame into something slightly more imposing. The Yankees believe in his ability to hit and have assigned him aggressively throughout his short career. He spent just 26 combined games in complex-level leagues before moving to Rookie-level Pulaski, where he was one of just six 17-year-olds in the league and was just two weeks older than the league's youngest player, Vladimir Guerrero Jr. He opened this year with low Class A Charleston, where he was the youngest player, before moving to short-season Staten Island at midseason and then back to Charleston a few weeks later. He didn't tear the cover off the ball at either stop, but he made the strides the Yankees wanted to see. Specifically, he worked on improving his rhythm and timing at the plate and getting himself in a better position to hit. New York's hitting coaches worked with Cabrera to incorporate his hips more into his swing rather than trying to create with his hands and upper body. He moved around the infield all year and has the range and hands to play at second base and the arm to play at third base as well, though his below-average power would be more appropriate up the middle. He's also shown a quick release and a strong sense of timing in the field. He's a tick below-average on the bases now, and there are concerns about him slowing down as he gets older.

Year	Club (League)	Class	AVG	G	AB	R	H	2B	3B	HR	RBI	BB	SO	SB	CS	OBP	SLG
2016	Yankees2 (DSL)	R	.441	19	68	15	30	5	3	1	12	5	6	2	1	.487	.647
	Yankees1 (GCL)	R	.455	7	33	9	15	6	0	2	6	1	2	1	1	.471	.818
	Pulaski (APP)	R	.240	26	96	9	23	4	1	1	7	8	13	4	1	.305	.333
2017	Staten Island (NYP)	SS	.289	23	90	12	26	3	1	0	16	4	11	2	1	.337	.344
	Charleston, SC (SAL)	LoA	.241	89	319	37	77	11	0	4	37	26	46	6	0	.297	.313
Minor League Totals			.282	164	606	82	171	29	5	8	78	44	78	15	4	.335	.386

27 DIEGO CASTILLO, SS

BA GRADE
50 Risk: Extreme

Born: Oct. 28, 1997. **B-T:** R-R. **Ht.:** 6-0. **Wt.:** 170. **Signed:** Venezuela, 2014. **Signed by:** Roney Calderon.

Castillo was as fundamentally sound as shortstops come when he signed three years ago and has moved deliberately through the system. The Yankees thought enough of him this year to skip him past both half-season clubs—Pulaski and Staten Island—and place him among a pack of their youngest prospects at low Class A Charleston. Castillo is never going to be mistaken for a bopper, but he has impressive bat-to-ball skills. He's struck out just 101 times in 867 career at-bats, including just 51 in 463 trips this season. Part of the reason for such a successful contact rate involved his unwillingness to go deep in counts. The Yankees worked with him this year on learning to wait for pitches he could drive rather than swinging at the first hittable offering, which often produced weak contact. They also worked with him this year to become less of an exclusively pull-side hitter and let the ball get deeper in the zone. He's got impressive defensive instincts for someone his age as well as an average or better arm. He rotated between shortstop and second base this year because of the presence of Hoy Park and Oswaldo Cabrera on the roster. He's a project, but he could be a defensive-minded middle infielder in the major leagues if everything comes together. He'll head to Tampa in 2018.

Year	Club (League)	Class	AVG	G	AB	R	H	2B	3B	HR	RBI	BB	SO	SB	CS	OBP	SLG
2015	Yankees1 (DSL)	R	.331	56	239	43	79	11	8	0	40	16	29	5	1	.373	.444
2016	Yankees2 (GCL)	R	.267	44	165	14	44	7	0	1	8	14	21	5	3	.332	.327
2017	Charleston, SC (SAL)	LoA	.263	118	463	66	122	15	3	1	42	31	51	9	5	.310	.315
Minor League Totals			.283	218	867	123	245	33	11	2	90	61	101	19	9	.332	.353

28 ALEXANDER VARGAS, RHP

BA GRADE
45 Risk: High

Born: July 24, 1997. **B-T:** R-R. **Ht.:** 6-4. **Wt.:** 203. **Signed:** Dominican Republic, 2014. **Signed by:** Miguel Benitez.

When the Yankees signed Vargas for $10,000 in 2014, they did so because of the changeup he'd already developed and the projection they assumed would come as he matured. He missed 2016 with Tommy John surgery (check this) and was challenged this year with time at low Class A Charleston. He didn't overpower hitters there, but he certainly performed, with 34 strikeouts against just five walks in 48.1 innings. His changeup, which he throws in the mid-80s, is still his out pitch, and he uses it with confidence against both lefthanders and righthanders. He's still working on developing his slider, which shows potential but has more horizontal break than depth at this point. The major question with Vargas involves his projectability. Some see a 20-year-old who performed well this year at high Class A and could eventually add more strength to his 6-foot-4 frame, thus turning the low-90s fastball into something more in the mid-90s. Others see an already maxed-out body, which would severely limit his ceiling. If everything clicks, he could be a back-end type of starter because of his ability to fill up the zone.

Year	Club (League)	Class	W	L	ERA	G	GS	CG	SV	IP	H	HR	BB	SO	K/9	WHIP	AVG
2015	Yankees1 (GCL)	R	2	4	4.97	10	9	0	0	42	55	2	13	31	6.7	1.63	.318
2016	Did not play—Injured																
2017	Staten Island (NYP)	SS	4	0	1.88	4	4	0	0	24	20	0	3	14	5.3	0.96	.235
	Charleston, SC (SAL)	LoA	2	3	3.17	9	9	0	0	48	41	6	5	34	6.3	0.95	.229
Minor League Totals			8	7	3.40	28	27	0	0	127	130	8	27	92	6.5	1.24	.266

29 RONY GARCIA, RHP

Born: Dec. 19, 1997. **B-T:** R-R. **Ht.:** 6-3. **Wt.:** 200. **Signed:** Dominican Republic, 2015. **Signed by:** Ray Sanchez/Victor Mata.

BA GRADE
45 Risk: High

Yet another of the Yankees' low-dollar international signings that has begun to pay off, Garcia made his stateside debut in his first professional season before being moved to Rookie-level Pulaski this year to begin his season. When the rotation at low Class A Charleston ran thin, however, the Yankees challenged Garcia with a promotion and he spent the entire season thereafter with the RiverDogs. He starts his three-pitch arsenal with a low-90s fastball that touches the mid-90s regularly. The pitch shows both two-seam and cut life but will flatten when he rushes and leaves the ball up in the zone. He complements the fastball with a curveball that he can loosen and tighten as necessary and a changeup with split-finger diving action. Neither pitch is average at this point, though both could reach that level with time and repetitions. Scouts who like him see a pitcher who could fit in at the back of the rotation, while those who are more pessimistic see a swingman type of pitcher in the mold of a Brad Peacock. He's likely to begin 2018 in the rotation at high Class A Tampa.

Year	Club (League)	Class	W	L	ERA	G	GS	CG	SV	IP	H	HR	BB	SO	K/9	WHIP	AVG
2016	Yankees2 (DSL)	R	1	3	1.88	9	8	0	0	43	35	1	9	39	8.2	1.02	.208
	Yankees1 (GCL)	R	2	2	2.89	5	4	0	0	28	24	0	4	17	5.5	1.00	.238
2017	Pulaski (APP)	R	0	0	3.97	2	2	0	0	11	11	1	2	11	8.7	1.15	.262
	Charleston, SC (SAL)	LoA	2	3	2.24	11	11	0	0	64	52	3	15	45	6.3	1.04	.219
Minor League Totals			5	8	2.39	27	25	0	0	147	122	5	30	112	6.9	1.04	.222

30 CODY CARROLL, RHP

Born: Oct. 15, 1992. **B-T:** R-R. **Ht.:** 6-5. **Wt.:** 210. **Drafted:** Southern Mississippi, 2015 (22nd round). **Signed by:** Mike Wagner.

BA GRADE
45 Risk: High

It's no secret that the Yankees love to stockpile tall, hard-throwing righthanders as potential bullpen pieces. Carroll, the team's 22nd-round choice out of Southern Mississippi in 2015, certainly fits that bill. He had Tommy John surgery after his senior season of high school, then redshirted during his freshman year at SMU. The Yankees had a pack of prospects in that mold at their upper levels this year, but Carroll distanced himself from the others with his high-end velocity. His four-seam fastball sits in the mid-to-upper-90s and has touched triple-digits frequently. More impressively, he generates that velocity with relative ease. He couples the pitch with a low-80s slider and a mid-80s split-finger fastball that he uses as a changeup. His slider has improved greatly this season, and some scouts grade it as plus. There are still command and control issues to iron out, as shown by his 30 walks in 67.1 innings between high Class A Tampa and Double-A Trenton this year, but Carroll's stuff is tantalizing enough that he's put himself on the prospect map.

Year	Club (League)	Class	W	L	ERA	G	GS	CG	SV	IP	H	HR	BB	SO	K/9	WHIP	AVG
2015	Pulaski (APP)	R	1	1	1.75	14	0	0	3	26	16	0	14	26	9.1	1.17	.186
2016	Charleston, SC (SAL)	LoA	4	4	3.15	26	6	0	3	91	89	3	41	90	8.9	1.42	.259
2017	Tampa (FSL)	HiA	1	0	2.25	13	0	0	2	20	10	1	8	30	13.5	0.90	.141
	Trenton (EL)	AA	2	5	2.66	26	0	0	5	47	36	4	22	59	11.2	1.23	.212
Minor League Totals			8	10	2.73	79	6	0	13	184	151	8	85	205	10.0	1.28	.225

Oakland Athletics

BY STEVE KRONER

Though the Athletics finished last in the American League West for the third consecutive season in 2017, there is optimism in the East Bay, both about the team's short-term and long-term future.

The franchise's plan to build a ballpark near Oakland's Laney College, set to open in 2023, fell by the wayside in early December. Whether the A's and the Oakland city council can find and agree on another site in the city—perhaps at the Oakland Coliseum complex—for a new ballpark remains to be seen.

The prospect of leaving the much-maligned Coliseum was one major reason executive vice  president Billy Beane announced in July the organization planned to alter its philosophy on maintaining and upgrading its roster.

Instead of losing players via free agency or trades once those players earn much more than the major league minimum salary, Beane said that he expected to retain Oakland's core players over the next few years. The goal would be to carry an exciting, competitive and—crucial for fans—familiar team into a new ballpark.

The A's recently have added several promising position players from the minor leagues, though the organization hasn't enjoyed nearly the same success with its young pitchers in the majors.

Oakland brought up first baseman Ryon Healy in the middle of the 2016 season. He hit .271 with 25 homers in 2017 but spent much of his time as a designated hitter, which made him expendable. Oakland dealt him to the Mariners in November for young reliever Emilio Pagan and 17-year-old shortstop Alexander Campos.

The Healy deal came about in part because of the corner infielders who thrived as rookies.

Matt Chapman played a Gold Glove-level third base and hit 14 homers in 80 games. Though it took him six stints in the majors to stick, first baseman Matt Olson was a revelation, hitting 24 homers in 189 at-bats. Throw in power-hitting utilityman Chad Pinder, and the A's feel good about their rookie crop of position players.

However, the performances of righthanders Jharel Cotton (5.58 ERA) and Daniel Gossett (6.11) exemplified the problems the A's endured on the mound. Help could be coming from the system. Oakland appears to have solid options, thanks to the 2016 draft—when it took lefthander A.J. Puk and righthanders Daulton Jefferies and Logan Shore—and via trades over the past two seasons to acquire lefty Jesus Luzardo (from the Nationals) and righties James Kaprielian (Yankees)

Rookie third baseman Matt Chapman showed off Gold Glove potential and huge power.

PROJECTED 2021 LINEUP

Catcher	Sean Murphy (26)
First Base	Matt Olson (27)
Second Base	Franklin Barreto (25)
Shortstop	Jorge Mateo (26)
Third Base	Matt Chapman (28)
Left Field	Lazaro Armenteros (22)
Center Field	Dustin Fowler (26)
Right Field	Chad Pinder (29)
Designated Hitter	Khris Davis (33)
No. 1 Starter	A.J. Puk (26)
No. 2 Starter	Sean Manaea (29)
No. 3 Starter	Jesus Luzardo (23)
No. 4 Starter	James Kaprielian (27)
No. 5 Starter	Logan Shore (26)
Closer	Daulton Jefferies (25)

and Grant Holmes (Dodgers).

The A's also could use upgrades in the outfield, where they have Dustin Fowler, who might make his mark in 2018 depending on how he recovers from a serious knee injury.

The A's return second baseman Jed Lowrie and shortstop Marcus Semien in 2018, giving Oakland plenty of offense, and the A's have several middle-infield options knocking on the door, notably Franklin Barreto and Jorge Mateo.

Can the A's go from the cellar to the penthouse in the long-term? That and the ballpark issue are the storylines for the short- and long-term future. The answers have yet to come into focus, but could be coming very soon.

DEPTH CHART

OAKLAND ATHLETICS

TOP 2018 ROOKIE: Franklin Barreto, 2B. The middle infielder had two stints in the big leagues in 2017 and could stick in 2018.

BREAKOUT PLAYER: Sheldon Neuse, 3B/SS. The third baseman moved from low Class A to Double-A in 2017 and hit a combined .321 with 16 homers.

SLEEPER: Lou Trivino, RHP. The hard-thrower from Slippery Rock (Pa.) pitched for Double-A Midland and Triple-A Nashville in 2017. In a combined 68 innings, he struck out 65.

SOURCE OF TOP 30 TALENT			
Homegrown	19	Acquired	11
College	10	Trades	11
Junior College	1	Rule 5 draft	0
High School	4	Independent Leagues	0
Nondrafted free agents	0	Free agent/waivers	0
International	4		

LF
Lazaro Armenteros (9)
Tyler Ramirez (17)
B.J. Boyd (24)
Brett Siddall
Anthony Churlin

CF
Dustin Fowler (4)
Austin Beck (6)
Skye Bolt

RF
Greg Deichmann (11)
Ramon Laureano (30)
J.P. Sportman
Seth Brown

3B
Sheldon Neuse (14)
Will Toffey (19)
Mikey White

SS
Jorge Mateo (3)
Nick Allen (15)
Kevin Merrell (16)
Alexander Campos (22)
Richie Martin (23)
Yerdel Vargas (25)
Eli White

2B
Franklin Barreto (2)
Marcos Brito (28)

1B
Renato Nunez (20)
Viosergy Rosa
Sandber Pimentel

C
Sean Murphy (7)
Santis Sanchez
Beau Taylor
Collin Theroux

LHP
LHSP
A.J. Puk (1)
Jesus Luzardo (5)
Dalton Sawyer
Evan Manarino
Ivan Andueza

LHRP
Brandon Mann
Brandon Marsonek
Logan Salow

RHP
RHSP
James Kaprielian (8)
Logan Shore (10)
Grant Holmes (12)
Daulton Jefferies (13)
Heath Fillmyer (18)
James Naile (26)
Casey Meisner (27)
Dakota Chalmers (29)
Raul Alcantara
Norge Ruiz

RHRP
Frankie Montas (21)
Lou Trivino
Kyle Finnegan
Oscar Tovar
Nolan Blackwood
Sam Bragg

DRAFT ANALYSIS

2017

BEST PURE HITTER: SS Kevin Merrell (1s) shot up draft boards this spring thanks in large part to his ability to consistently put the bat on the ball with his compact swing. His fast hands and elite speed help his feel for hitting further.

BEST POWER HITTER: OF Austin Beck (1) had some of the best tools in the draft class, including his significant raw power that comes from his premium bat speed. OF Greg Deichmann (2) also has plus raw power and built a strong track record of getting to it in games with 27 homers between LSU in the spring and pro ball.

FASTEST RUNNER: Merrell is a top-of-the-scale runner and gets the most out of his speed. Beck is a plus runner.

BEST DEFENSIVE PLAYER: SS Nick Allen (3) is a gifted defender with an incredible feel to play shortstop. He doesn't stand out physically at 5-foot-9, 155 pounds, but he has excellent hands and infield actions, as well as an above-average arm.

BEST FASTBALL: After a pitcher-heavy 2016 class, the A's didn't take a pitcher until the sixth round this year and focused more on pitchability than power arms. LHP Logan Salow (6) runs his fastball up to 94 mph in short stints out of the bullpen.

BEST SECONDARY: RHP Wyatt Marks (13) earned All-America honors at Louisiana-Lafayette this spring and averaged 15.17 strikeouts per nine innings, best in the country, thanks in large part to his above-average power breaking ball. Salow's slider also grades out as above-average.

BEST PRO DEBUT: OF Logan Farrar (36) opened some eyes with his performance after signing. He tore up Rookie ball for nine games, earning a promotion to the short-season New York-Penn League, and hit .341/.413/.495 overall. He showed a good approach at the plate and has some strength

TOP DRAFT PICKS OF THE DECADE

Year	Player, Pos.	2017 Org
2008	Jemile Weeks, 2B	Cubs
2009	Grant Green, SS	Marlins
2010	Michael Choice, OF	Nexen (Korea)
2011	Sonny Gray, RHP	Yankees
2012	Addison Russell, SS	Cubs
2013	Billy McKinney, OF	Yankees
2014	Matt Chapman, 3B	Athletics
2015	Richie Martin, SS	Athletics
2016	A.J. Puk, LHP	Athletics
2017	Austin Beck, OF	Athletics

in his swing.

BEST ATHLETE: Beck stands out as much for his athleticism as for any of his raw tools. He is a plus runner, has impressive strength and is capable of making highlight reel plays in all aspects of the game.

MOST INTRIGUING BACKGROUND: It was a family affair at Washington for OF Jack Meggs (10). Lindsay Meggs, his father, was head coach, and Joe Meggs, his older brother, was the Huskies' director of operations. 3B Will Toffey (4) is the son of longtime baseball agent Jack Toffey.

CLOSEST TO THE MAJORS: Merrell, Deichmann and Toffey are all advanced college hitters who could advance quickly in the minor leagues.

BEST LATE-ROUND PICK: Farrar got off to a strong start this summer. SS Ryan Gridley (11) does a lot of things well on the diamond and fits in well to the A's class as an advanced college hitter. He likely profiles best as a utility player.

THE ONE WHO GOT AWAY: Oakland signed all but six of their draft picks. OF Garrett Mitchell (14) was the first (and best) player not to sign. His pure hitting ability is still developing, but he is a potential five-tool player who could develop into a star at UCLA.

—TEDDY CAHILL

2016

The Athletics used a college-heavy approach, and it has paid off handsomely. LHP A.J. Puk (1) has quickly become their top prospect. RHP Logan Shore (2) took a step forward and C Sean Murphy (3) got to Double-A thanks to his advanced defense.

GRADE: A

2015

Three players from the class made the handbook, and all three have grades of 40 High. SS Richie Martin (1) has yet to get on track. RHP Dakota Chalmers (3) remains a project, while RHP James Naile (20) likely will reach Oakland first.

GRADE: F

2014

3B Matt Chapman (1) and RHP Daniel Gossett (2) made their MLB debuts in 2017. Chapman showed off power and defensive skills that give him the potential to be a mainstay in Oakland. RHP Heath Fillyer (5) could also soon reach MLB.

GRADE: B

1 A.J. PUK, LHP

Born: April 25, 1995. **B-T:** L-L. **Ht.:** 6-7. **Wt.:** 220.
Drafted: Florida, 2016 (1st round). **Signed by:** Trevor Schaffer.

The lefthanded Puk, a native of Cedar Rapids, Iowa, struck out 251 hitters over 194 innings in his three seasons at Florida. As a junior, he held hitters to a .191 average. All that prompted the A's to take him with the sixth overall pick in 2016 and sign him for a $4.07 million bonus. Puk blossomed in 2017. In a combined 125 innings at high Class A Stockton and Double-A Midland, Puk racked up 184 punchouts and led all minor league starters with 13.2 strikeouts per nine. He gave up only three homers in those 125 innings after not allowing any with in his pro debut at short-season Vermont in 2016. Over his final seven starts with Midland (including one in the postseason), Puk struck out 61 hitters in 39.2 innings while amassing a 2.72 ERA. Moreover, Puk's walk rate in his junior year with the Gators was 4.6 per-nine innings.

Puk's raw stuff has never been in question as elite. His fastball resides comfortably at 93-96 and can reach 98 mph. His vicious side-to-side slider grades easily as plus and his changeup has developed into an potentially above-average pitch. Control has long been an issue, but Athletics minor league pitching instructor Gil Patterson helped Puk streamline his delivery, focusing mainly on his front leg. The altered motion produced a more consistent release point. With his height, Puk gets a pronounced downward angle in his delivery, which can make him both effective and intimidating. He gets a high percentage of swings and misses with all of his pitches. His stuff, competitiveness and pitching sense are all assets. So is his receptiveness to coaching. Over the past two years, the A's have arranged to have Randy Johnson and Al Leiter—two elite lefthanders in their day—give Puk advice.

Barring an offseason deal, the A's will have at least two, and perhaps three, spots open in their rotation in 2018. Puk has a shot at nailing down one of those by the end of the season. He's still only 22 and has fewer than 160 minor league innings under his belt, so a few months in Triple-A Nashville to begin the season are likely. In any event, Puk projects as a front-of-the-rotation starter as long as he keeps his newfound control intact. If he doesn't, he can serve the club as an elite reliever in the mold of Andrew Miller or Aroldis Chapman.

BILL MITCHELL

BA GRADE	SCOUTING GRADES
60 Risk: High	FB: 70. SL: 60. CHG: 50. CTL: 45.

Projected future grades on 20-80 scouting scale

TOP PROSPECTS OF THE DECADE

Year	Player, Pos.	2017 Org
2008	Daric Barton, 1B	Mexican League
2009	Brett Anderson, LHP	Blue Jays
2010	Chris Carter, OF/1B	Athletics
2011	Grant Green, SS	Marlins
2012	Jarrod Parker, RHP	Did not play
2013	Addison Russell, SS	Cubs
2014	Addison Russell, SS	Cubs
2015	Daniel Robertson, SS	Rays
2016	Franklin Barreto, SS	Athletics
2017	Franklin Barreto, SS/2B	Athletics

BEST TOOLS

Best Hitter For Average:	Sheldon Neuse
Best Power Hitter	Renato Nunez
Best Strike-Zone Discipline	Will Toffey
Fastest baserunner	Jorge Mateo
Best Athlete	Jorge Mateo
Best Fastball	Frankie Montas
Best Curveball	Grant Holmes
Best Slider	A.J. Puk
Best Changeup	Logan Shore
Best Control	Logan Shore
Best Defensive Catcher	Sean Murphy
Best Defensive Infielder	Nick Allen
Best Infield Arm	Eric Marinez
Best Defensive Outfielder	Tyler Ramirez
Best Outfield Arm	Skye Bolt

Year	Club (League)	Class	W	L	ERA	G	GS	CG	SV	IP	H	HR	BB	SO	K/9	WHIP	AVG
2016	Vermont (NYP)	SS	0	4	3.03	10	10	0	0	33	23	0	12	40	11.0	1.07	.185
2017	Stockton (CAL)	HiA	4	5	3.69	14	11	0	0	61	44	1	23	98	14.5	1.10	.196
	Midland (TL)	AA	2	5	4.36	13	13	0	0	64	64	2	25	86	12.1	1.39	.256
Minor League Totals			6	14	3.82	37	34	0	0	158	131	3	60	224	12.8	1.21	.219

2 FRANKLIN BARRETO, SS/2B

Born: Feb. 27, 1996. **B-T:** R-R. **Ht.:** 5-10. **Wt.:** 190. **Signed:** Venezuela, 2012. **Signed by:** Ismael Cruz/Luis Martinez (Blue Jays).

Acquired from the Blue Jays in the Josh Donaldson deal in November 2014, Barreto has steadily climbed the ladder of the Athletics organization. His .290/.339/.456 season at Triple-A Nashville in 2017 closely compares with his .292/.347/.463 career line in five minor league seasons.

Barreto had two stints in the majors in 2017 and went 14 for 71 (.197). Strikeouts have become an issue in the upper levels. He struck out 141 times in 510 plate appearances for Nashville and 33 times in 76 PAs for Oakland. Originally a shortstop, Barreto has spent time at second base in the minors and majors. He has the arm and range to play shortstop in the bigs, but is better suited for second because his arm at short can be a little erratic. As a hitter, he uses the whole field and has more power than you'd expect from someone his size. He needs to improve his plate discipline to get the most from his above-average bat and surprising power. His plus speed makes him a basestealing threat (92 career steals).

The A's will pick up the contract option on second baseman Jed Lowrie, which might mean that Barreto will begin the 2018 season back at Nashville. Oakland has several promising middle infielders in the organization, but Barreto remains at the top of the list. If he can become a bit more polished, he can be a first-division regular at second base.

BA GRADE
55 Risk: Medium
HIT: 60. POW: 50.
SPD: 55. FLD: 50.
ARM: 50.

Year	Club (League)	Class	AVG	G	AB	R	H	2B	3B	HR	RBI	BB	SO	SB	CS	OBP	SLG
2015	Stockton (CAL)	HiA	.302	90	338	50	102	22	3	13	47	15	67	8	3	.333	.500
2016	Midland (TL)	AA	.281	119	462	63	130	25	3	10	50	36	90	30	15	.340	.413
	Nashville (PCL)	AAA	.353	4	17	2	6	0	1	1	3	0	4	0	2	.389	.647
2017	Nashville (PCL)	AAA	.290	111	469	63	136	19	7	15	54	27	141	15	8	.339	.456
	Oakland (AL)	MAJ	.197	25	71	10	14	1	2	2	6	5	33	2	0	.250	.352
Major League Totals			.197	25	71	10	14	1	2	2	6	5	33	2	0	.250	.352
Minor League Totals			.292	456	1803	277	527	110	25	49	241	119	422	92	39	.347	.463

3 JORGE MATEO, SS

Born: June 23, 1995. **B-T:** R-R. **Ht.:** 6-0. **Wt.:** 190. **Signed:** Dominican Republic, 2012. **Signed by:** Juan Rosario (Yankees).

One of three highly regarded prospects the A's received from the Yankees in the trade-deadline deal that sent Sonny Gray to New York, Mateo's game is based on his top-of-the-line speed. He had a combined 52 stolen bases for three teams in 2017. He stole a combined 82 for two teams in 2015.

Mateo's development seemed to stall after he was sent back to high Class A Tampa in 2016. But a promotion to Double-A Trenton seemed to spur him to new heights and he was traded just a little bit more than a month later. Though the A's used Mateo exclusively as a shortstop in his stint with Double-A Midland, he did play some second base and center field in the Yankees' system. He's a disruptive force offensively. Infielders rush to make plays on his grounders, and pitchers can become distracted once he's on the bases. Mateo needs to make more consistent contact to best use his legs and sneaky power. He struck out 144 times in 584 plate appearances in 2017. Because Mateo hasn't played above Double-A in his six minor league seasons, he figures to begin 2018 at Triple-A Nashville.

Whether Mateo ultimately stays at shortstop or moves to second or the outfield, he has the speed and arm to thrive in any spot. If he can cut down his strikeout rate, he can become an above-average major leaguer with the potential to steal 40-plus bases and hit 15 homers per season.

BA GRADE
55 Risk: High
HIT: 50. POW: 45.
SPD: 80. FLD: 50.
ARM: 55.

Year	Club (League)	Class	AVG	G	AB	R	H	2B	3B	HR	RBI	BB	SO	SB	CS	OBP	SLG
2015	Charleston, SC (SAL)	LoA	.268	96	365	51	98	18	8	2	33	36	80	71	15	.338	.378
	Tampa (FSL)	HiA	.321	21	84	15	27	5	3	0	7	7	18	11	2	.374	.452
2016	Tampa (FSL)	HiA	.254	113	464	65	118	16	9	8	47	33	108	36	15	.306	.379
2017	Tampa (FSL)	HiA	.240	69	275	39	66	16	8	4	11	16	79	28	3	.288	.400
	Trenton (EL)	AA	.300	30	120	26	36	9	3	4	26	15	32	11	7	.381	.525
	Midland (TL)	AA	.292	30	137	25	40	5	7	4	20	9	33	13	3	.333	.518
Minor League Totals			.269	452	1816	300	489	85	46	30	179	169	430	234	57	.335	.416

4 DUSTIN FOWLER, OF

Born: Dec. 29, 1994. **B-T:** L-L. **Ht.:** 6-0. **Wt.:** 195. **Drafted:** HS—Dexter, Ga., 2013 (18th round). **Signed by:** Darryl Monroe (Yankees).

Another prospect the A's acquired from the Yankees in the Sonny Gray trade, Fowler endured an awful injury in his major league debut with New York on June 29: He ruptured the patellar tendon in his right knee when he crashed into the wall near the right field line in Chicago. He's since sued the White Sox for the placement of the unpadded electrical box that he ran into.

Fowler had made strong progress through the Yankees' system, including a Double-A season in 2016 with 30 doubles, 15 triples, 12 homers and 25 stolen bases. Fowler's combination of speed and power gives him a chance to become an impact player. He has played the corner outfield spots, but figures to stick in center given his range and solid arm. His plus speed makes him a basestealing threat with 74 steals in five minor league seasons, but he could improve his success rate. The A's tried several players in center field in 2017, including Rajai Davis, Jaycob Brugman and Boog Powell, without much success. Fowler's recovery went as planned through the fall, and he is expected to be ready for spring training.

Fowler should have every opportunity to become the A's starting center fielder in 2018, but how well he recovers will play a big factor. If he is deemed not quite healthy or ready, he will begin the season, and his Athletics career, at Triple-A Nashville.

BA GRADE

55 Risk: High

HIT: 55. POW: 55.
SPD: 60. FLD: 60.
ARM: 50.

Year	Club (League)	Class	AVG	G	AB	R	H	2B	3B	HR	RBI	BB	SO	SB	CS	OBP	SLG
2015	Charleston, SC (SAL)	LoA	.307	58	241	35	74	9	3	4	31	11	47	18	7	.340	.419
	Tampa (FSL)	HiA	.289	65	246	29	71	11	3	1	39	15	43	12	6	.328	.370
2016	Trenton (EL)	AA	.281	132	541	67	152	30	15	12	88	22	86	25	11	.311	.458
2017	Scranton/W-B (IL)	AAA	.293	70	297	49	87	19	8	13	43	15	63	13	5	.329	.542
	New York (AL)	MAJ	—	1	0	0	0	0	0	0	0	0	0	0	0	—	—
Major League Totals			—	1	0	0	0	0	0	0	0	0	0	0	0	—	—
Minor League Totals			.282	421	1694	221	477	90	39	39	251	80	315	74	32	.315	.450

5 JESUS LUZARDO, LHP

Born: Sept. 30, 1997. **B-T:** L-L. **Ht.:** 6-1. **Wt.:** 205. **Drafted:** HS—Parkland, Fla., 2016 (3rd round). **Signed by:** Alex Morales (Nationals).

Born in Peru and raised in South Florida, Luzardo was viewed by area scouts as a possible first-round pick in 2016 before he had Tommy John surgery that March. The Nationals are a team that has never shied away from draft talented pitchers who are recovering from Tommy John surgery. They drafted him in the third round and gave him a $1.4 million signing bonus.

Luzardo had pitched in only three Gulf Coast League games in 2017 before Washington sent him to the Athletics in the deal that brought Sean Doolittle and Ryan Madson to the Nats. Luzardo's abbreviated 2017 season with three teams was impressive: a combined 1.66 ERA in 43.1 innings, with 48 strikeouts and five walks. Poised, confident and smart are adjectives used to describe the lefthander, and his stuff is prodigious too. Luzardo can reach 97 mph with his fastball and has solid command of his curveball. He's developing a changeup that is already seen as above-average by some scouts. He has a simple arm stroke and a repeatable delivery. He appears to understand the art of pitching quite well for someone who's a mere 20 years old.

Considering Luzardo hasn't pitched above short-season, he remains many years away from the big league club. But also considering his tools and his refined skills at such a young age, he has the potential to rise to the level of a solid No. 3-or-better starter in the not-so-distant future.

BA GRADE

60 Risk: Extreme

FB: 60. CB: 55.
CHG: 60.
CTL: 55.

Year	Club (League)	Class	W	L	ERA	G	GS	CG	SV	IP	H	HR	BB	SO	K/9	WHIP	AVG
2016	Did not play—Injured																
2017	Nationals (GCL)	R	1	0	1.32	3	3	0	0	14	14	1	0	15	9.9	1.02	.259
	Athletics (AZL)	R	0	1	1.54	4	3	0	0	12	9	0	1	13	10.0	0.86	.205
	Vermont (NYP)	SS	1	0	2.00	5	5	0	0	18	12	1	4	20	10.0	0.89	.188
Minor League Totals			2	1	1.66	12	11	0	0	43	35	2	5	48	10.0	0.92	.216

6 AUSTIN BECK, OF

BRIAN WESTERHOLT

Born: Nov. 21, 1988. **B-T:** R-R. **Ht.:** 6-1. **Wt.:** 200. **Drafted:** HS—Lexington, N.C., 2017 (1st round). **Signed by:** Neil Avent.

Beck tore the ACL and meniscus in his left knee as a junior in high school, but rebounded with a brilliant senior year in which he hit .590 with 12 homers and 38 RBIs in 28 games. The A's drafted Beck with the sixth overall pick in June and signed him for $5.3 million to pass up a North Carolina commitment.

Beck didn't enjoy much success in the Rookie-level Arizona League after signing, hitting .211 with a 29 percent strikeout rate. Beck lacks polish at the plate, but the A's love his combination of bat speed and plus raw power. He can hit the ball out of any park to all fields. He has the plus speed to play center field and be a threat on the basepaths. His plus arm rounds out an enticing athletic profile. For all his tools, Beck's stint in the AZL revealed a tendency to chase pitches, and he needs to improve his plate discipline significantly as he moves through the system.

Still a teenager, Beck figures to begin 2018 in either extended spring training or low Class A Beloit depending on his camp performance. An explosive, strong athlete, Beck has the ability become a mainstay in the Oakland outfield in a few years, but only if he can lock in his plate discipline to fulfill his power potential.

BA GRADE

60 Risk: Extreme

HIT: 50. POW: 60.
SPD: 60. FLD: 55.
ARM: 60.

Year	Club (League)	Class	AVG	G	AB	R	H	2B	3B	HR	RBI	BB	SO	SB	CS	OBP	SLG
2017	Athletics (AZL)	R	.211	41	152	23	32	7	4	2	28	17	51	7	1	.293	.349
Minor League Totals			.211	41	152	23	32	7	4	2	28	17	51	7	1	.293	.349

7 SEAN MURPHY, C

Born: Oct. 10, 1994. **B-T:** R-R. **Ht.:** 6-3 **Wt.:** **215.** **Drafted:** Wright State, 2016 (3rd round). **Signed by:** Rich Sparks.

After enduring a painful 2016, Murphy blossomed in 2017. In 2016, a broken hamate bone forced Murphy to miss a considerable portion of his junior season at Wright State, then a staph infection cost him six weeks with short-season Vermont. Murphy made the jump from high Class A Stockton to Double-A Midland in 2017, although he still missed time with inflammation in his hand as a result of the scar tissue from his hammate surgery.

Murphy's mashed in the California League before his offensive numbers dipped when he got to the Texas League, but offense isn't his calling card. His defense is primarily what earned him his promotion, and defense will probably define him as he progresses through the system. Murphy's arm is universally plus-plus, with some calling it an "80" tool. He's thrown out 41 percent of runners in his pro career, and most teams simply stop running on him. He knows how to call game from behind the plate and is a plus receiver and blocker. Pitchers love throwing to him not only for his defense but also for his baseball intellect. At the plate Murphy has a simple swing with not much of a load, but he uses his considerable brute strength to bash the ball up the middle and to his pull side. He doesn't projects as much more than a fringe-average hitter, but his power coud improve as he learns to better incorporate his lower half.

Murphy is set to return to Double-A Midland in 2018, and he'll need to show he can stay healthy for a full season and make the necessary offensive adjustments. If he does, he'll be the Athletics' starting everyday catcher sooner rather than later.

BA GRADE

50 Risk: High

HIT: 40. POW: 50.
SPD: 30. FLD: 55.
ARM: 70.

Year	Club (League)	Class	AVG	G	AB	R	H	2B	3B	HR	RBI	BB	SO	SB	CS	OBP	SLG
2016	Athletics (AZL)	R	.000	1	3	1	0	0	0	0	0	0	0	0	0	.000	.000
	Vermont (NYP)	SS	.237	22	76	10	18	1	0	2	7	9	12	1	0	.318	.329
2017	Stockton (CAL)	HiA	.297	45	165	22	49	11	0	9	26	11	33	0	0	.343	.527
	Midland (TL)	AA	.209	53	191	25	40	7	0	4	22	21	34	0	0	.288	.309
Minor League Totals			.246	121	435	58	107	19	0	15	55	41	79	1	0	.312	.393

8 JAMES KAPRIELIAN, RHP

Born: March 2, 1994. **B-T:** R-R. **Ht.:** 6-4. **Wt.:** 200. **Drafted:** UCLA, 2015 (1st round). **Signed by:** Bobby DeJardin (Yankees).

The Athletics made sure to acquire Kaprielian from the Yankees in the Sonny Gray deal at the 2017 trade deadline, even knowing Kaprielian's alarming injury history.

A strained flexor tendon in Kaprielian's right arm limited his 2016 season to just three starts, and when arm problems arose again in 2017, Kaprielian had Tommy John surgery in April. Kaprielian's small-sample-size stats in the minors are impressive: 18 hits allowed in 29.1 innings, with 36 strikeouts and seven walks. He dominated hitters in his three seasons at UCLA (17-10, 2.06 ERA), serving as a freshman reliever on the Bruins' 2013 national championship team and as a starter the next two seasons. Considering he has missed the bulk of the past two seasons and probably won't be ready for the start of the 2018 season, a scouting report on Kaprielian should be taken with several grains of salt. When healthy, he employs a fastball that sits in the mid-90s and can reach the high-90s. He complements his heater with a deep arsenal of a curveball, slider and changeup that all flash above-average. He's not afraid to attack the strike zone.

Kaprielian is roughly targeting an early summer return to the mound and, once healthy, is in line to begin his Athletics career at Double-A Midland. His fastball, stuff and competitiveness give him a No. 3 starter projection, but staying healthy is the first step he needs to master.

BA GRADE
55 **Risk: Extreme**
FB: 60. **CB:** 60.
SL: 55. **CH:** 55.
CTL: 55.

Year	Club (League)	Class	W	L	ERA	G	GS	CG	SV	IP	H	HR	BB	SO	K/9	WHIP	AVG
2015	Yankees2 (GCL)	R	0	0	11.57	2	0	0	0	2	2	0	2	2	7.7	1.71	.250
	Staten Island (NYP)	SS	0	1	2.00	3	3	0	0	9	8	0	2	12	12.0	1.11	.229
2016	Tampa (FSL)	HiA	2	1	1.50	3	3	0	0	18	8	1	3	22	11.0	0.61	.136
2017	Did not play—Injured																
Minor League Totals			2	2	2.45	8	6	0	0	29	18	1	7	36	11.0	0.85	.176

9 LAZARO ARMENTEROS, OF

Born: May 22, 1999. **B-T:** R-R. **Ht.:** 6-0. **Wt.:** 182. **Signed:** Cuba, 2016. **Signed by:** Juan de la Cruz.

The A's invested heavily in the international market in 2016 and made Armenteros their marquee signing, getting the Cuban teenager for $3 million. He spent the bulk of his pro debut in the Rookie-level Arizona League in 2017 after only six games in the Dominican Summer League.

As an 18-year-old in the AZL Armenteros more than held his own, with a .288 average, 17 extra-base hits and 10 stolen bases in 41 games. One member of the A's organization likened Armenteros' body to that of a young Andre Dawson. Armenteros probably will fill out his body in the next couple of years. He shows feel to hit and his above-average power is real and could grow as his body does. Defensively he already plays a corner, and is limited to left because his well below-average arm strength leaves a lot to be desired. He is still learning some of the cultural nuances of pro ball in the U.S. Armenteros will probably begin the 2018 season at low Class A Beloit. His idol is former A's and current Mets outfielder Yoenis Cespedes.

If Armenteros progresses the way Oakland officials believe he can, he could have a big league career worthy of his idol, offensively at least.

BILL MITCHELL

BA GRADE
55 **Risk: Extreme**
HIT: 55. **POW:** 60.
SPD: 55. **FLD:** 50.
ARM: 40.

Year	Club (League)	Class	AVG	G	AB	R	H	2B	3B	HR	RBI	BB	SO	SB	CS	OBP	SLG
2017	Athletics (DSL)	R	.167	6	18	6	3	0	0	0	1	3	9	2	2	.385	.167
	Athletics (AZL)	R	.288	41	156	24	45	9	4	4	22	16	48	10	1	.376	.474
Minor League Totals			.276	47	174	30	48	9	4	4	23	19	57	12	3	.377	.443

10 LOGAN SHORE, RHP

Born: Dec. 28, 1994. **B-T:** R-R. **Ht.:** 6-2. **Wt.:** 215. **Drafted:** Florida, 2016 (2nd round). **Signed by:** Trevor Schaffer.

Shore was A.J. Puk's teammate at Florida, and Shore, not Puk, was the Gators' normal Friday starter. As a junior in 2016, Shore went 12-1, 2.31 and was drafted by the A's in the second round, one round after they took his teammate Puk.

After a solid showing for Vermont in the short-season New York-Penn League in 2016, Shore advanced to high Class A Stockton in 2017. A lat strain sidelined him for nearly two months. After Shore returned to the Ports, he struggled in his first four appearances before regaining his form for the final four outings. Shore's fastball sits in the average 92-94 mph range. What seperates him is a changeup that flashes plus and excellent control. How well Shore develops his fringy slider might determine how soon he can reach the big leagues, and how effective he'll be once he gets there. He will start 2018 at Double-A Midland.

BA GRADE
50 Risk: High
FB: 55. SL: 45.
CH: 60.
CONTROL: 60..

Shore doesn't have the upside of a lot pitchers in the A's system, but his polish and intensity give him a chance to rise as a back-end starter.

Year	Club (League)	Class	W	L	ERA	G	GS	CG	SV	IP	H	HR	BB	SO	K/9	WHIP	AVG
2016	Vermont (NYP)	SS	0	2	2.57	7	7	0	0	21	17	1	7	21	9.0	1.14	.207
2017	Athletics (AZL)	R	0	0	0.00	3	3	0	0	8	2	0	0	13	14.6	0.25	.077
	Stockton (CAL)	HiA	2	5	4.09	17	14	0	1	73	81	5	16	74	9.2	1.33	.277
Minor League Totals			2	7	3.45	27	24	0	1	102	100	6	23	108	9.6	1.21	.249

11 GREG DEICHMANN, OF

BA GRADE
50 Risk: High

Born: May 31, 1995. **B-T:** L-R. **Ht.:** 6-2. **Wt.:** 190. **Drafted:** Louisiana State, 2017 (2nd round). **Signed by:** Kelcey Mucker.

A shortstop in high school and a corner infielder as a sophomore at Louisiana State, Deichmann moved to right field as a junior in 2017 and found his niche. He hit 19 homers, earning him All-America honors and a second-round selection by the Athletics. He signed for $1.7 million.

The A's like Deichmann power stroke and his plate discipline. He had 28 walks and a .385 OBP in 195 plate appearances with Vermont in the short-season New York-Penn League. He's considered a mature player who knows his swing and what he needs to do to improve. With his inexperience in right field and merely average speed, Deichmann wouldn't rate as a plus defender at the moment, but his above-average arm gives him a chance to succeed at the position.

Deichmann profiles as a classic power-hitting corner outfielder. It's not hard to envision Deichmann becoming a consistent 25-home run hitter in the majors. He figures to begin 2018 at high Class A Stockton.

Year	Club (League)	Class	AVG	G	AB	R	H	2B	3B	HR	RBI	BB	SO	SB	CS	OBP	SLG
2017	Vermont (NYP)	SS	.274	46	164	31	45	10	4	8	30	28	40	4	1	.385	.530
Minor League Totals			.274	46	164	31	45	10	4	8	30	28	40	4	1	.385	.530

12 GRANT HOLMES, RHP

BA GRADE
50 Risk: High

Born: March 22, 1996. **B-T:** R-R. **Ht.:** 6-1. **Wt.:** 215. **Drafted:** HS—Conway, S.C., 2014 (1st round). **Signed by:** Lon Joyce (Dodgers).

One of three pitchers along with Jharel Cotton and Frankie Montas the A's acquired from the Dodgers in the Rich Hill-Josh Reddick trade at the 2016 deadline, Holmes spent all of 2017 as a 21-year-old at Double-A Midland.

Holmes has intriguing stuff with a 92-95 fastball that has riding life up in the zone, and a power curveball that draws plus grades. With that stuff he averaged more than a strikeout per inning with Midland, on par with his four-season average in the minors. What Holmes needs to improve and refine is his fastball command, not only to find the strike zone but to avoid throwing hittable fastballs across the middle of the plate as well. Back-to-back starts near the end of the regular season highlighted the "bad" and "good" Holmes. On Aug. 29 against San Antonio, he threw 94 pitches, courtesy of six walks, in five innings. On Sept. 3 against Frisco, he threw 94 pitches, with a one walk, in eight innings.

Holmes figures to begin 2018 at Triple-A Nashville. How quickly and effectively he can harness his command will go a long way toward determining when he might pitch for Oakland.

Year	Club (League)	Class	W	L	ERA	G	GS	CG	SV	IP	H	HR	BB	SO	K/9	WHIP	AVG
2015	Great Lakes (MWL)	LoA	6	4	3.14	24	24	0	0	103	86	6	54	117	10.2	1.35	.229
2016	R. Cucamonga (CAL)	HiA	8	4	4.02	20	18	0	1	105	103	6	43	100	8.5	1.39	.254
	Stockton (CAL)	HiA	3	3	6.91	6	5	0	0	29	44	4	10	24	7.5	1.88	.355
2017	Midland (TL)	AA	11	12	4.49	29	24	0	0	148	149	15	61	150	9.1	1.42	.262
Minor League Totals			30	26	4.13	90	81	0	1	434	421	34	181	449	9.3	1.39	.255

13 DAULTON JEFFERIES, RHP

BA GRADE
55 Risk: Extreme

Born: Aug. 2, 1995. **B-T:** L-R. **Ht.:** 6-0. **Wt.:** 180. **Drafted:** California, 2016 (1st round supplemental). **Signed by:** Jermaine Clark.

After two April starts at high Class A Stockton in 2017, Jefferies had Tommy John surgery. The righthander definitely has a high ceiling, but the caveat is his injury history. He missed a good chunk of his junior season at Cal because of shoulder injury, but still got drafted 37th overall and received a $1.6 million bonus.

When on the mound for the Golden Bears in 2016, Jefferies dealt. He went 7-0, 1.08 with 53 strikeouts and eight walks in 50 innings and limited hitters to a .185 average. Jefferies' fastball resides in the low- to mid-90s. He possesses superior command and an excellent changeup that has significant sink. Though their deliveries are much different, Jefferies, with his baby-face visage, slight build and all-around athletic ability, reminds some people of a young Tim Lincecum. Jefferies will still be rehabbing from his surgery at the outset of the 2018 season. When he does get cleared to pitch he'll likely head back to Stockton, about 60 miles from where he grew up in Atwater.

If he can remain fully healthy, Jefferies has a decent shot to move quickly up the system, possibly as a closer if durability remains a problem.

Year	Club (League)	Class	W	L	ERA	G	GS	CG	SV	IP	H	HR	BB	SO	K/9	WHIP	AVG
2016	Athletics (AZL)	R	0	0	2.38	5	5	0	0	11	11	0	2	17	13.5	1.15	.262
2017	Stockton (CAL)	HiA	0	0	2.57	2	1	0	0	7	7	0	1	6	7.7	1.14	.241
Minor League Totals			0	0	2.45	7	6	0	0	18	18	0	3	23	11.3	1.15	.254

14 SHELDON NEUSE, 3B

BA GRADE
50 Risk: High

Born: Dec. 10, 1994. **B-T:** R-R. **Ht.:** 6-0. **Wt.:** 195. **Drafted:** Oklahoma, 2016 (2nd round). **Signed by:** Ed Gustafson (Nationals).

The Nationals made Neuse the 58th overall pick in 2016 after a junior season at Oklahoma in which he hit .369 and slugged .646. One year later, the Athletics acquired Neuse from the Nationals in the July deal that sent Sean Doolittle and Ryan Madson to Washington.

Neuse was a shortstop in college and is a third baseman as a pro, but his main asset is his bat. He is a mature hitter with a high baseball IQ, a feel for the barrel and significant power in his thick, bulky frame. He shot through three levels in his 2017 pro debut and finsihed in Double-A, hitting a combined hitting a combined .321 with 26 doubles, 16 homers and 79 RBIs. He capped 2017 by going 6-for-14 in Midland's best-of-five Double-A championship series win over Tulsa. Neuse's bat and plus arm will play at third base, but he will have to watch his fitness with a thick midsection and lower half.

Matt Chapman appears ensconced as the A's third baseman of the future, but if Neuse keeps hitting, he'll find a place on Oakland's roster, maybe as soon as 2019. He'll open 2018 back at Double-A Midland.

Year	Club (League)	Class	AVG	G	AB	R	H	2B	3B	HR	RBI	BB	SO	SB	CS	OBP	SLG
2016	Auburn (NYP)	SS	.230	36	126	16	29	5	3	1	11	13	26	2	2	.305	.341
2017	Hagerstown (SAL)	LoA	.291	77	292	40	85	19	3	9	51	25	66	12	5	.349	.469
	Stockton (CAL)	HiA	.386	22	83	21	32	3	0	7	22	9	25	0	0	.457	.675
	Midland (TL)	AA	.373	18	67	9	25	4	0	0	6	6	21	0	0	.427	.433
Minor League Totals			.301	153	568	86	171	31	6	17	90	53	138	16	7	.365	.467

15 NICK ALLEN, SS

BA GRADE
50 Risk: Extreme

Born: Oct. 8, 1998. **B-T:** R-R. **Ht.:** 5-9. **Wt.:** 155. **Drafted:** HS—San Diego, 2017 (3rd round). **Signed by:** Anthony Aloisi.

Allen became known as a defensive wizard at San Diego's Francis Parker School and on the national showcase circuit, with evaluators considering him the top defensive shortstop in the 2017 draft class. A strong commitment to Southern California dropped him out of the first round, but the A's drafted him in the third round and signed him for $2 million, nearly triple slot value as the 81st overall pick.

In an organization brimming with promising middle infielders, Allen rates as the best defensive shortstop in the system. He has a plus arm and plus speed. Combine those assets with great hands, and his defense is plus-plus with ease. The main question about Allen is his size. He is generosuly listed at 5-foot-9 and extremely slight with little projection for strength. His bat is light and doesn't project to ever be much of a weapon, although his plus speed makes him a stolen base threat.

Some see Brendan Ryan as Allen's future, but even Ryan hit well in the minors. Allen will have to prove he can hit, even with his elite shortstop defense. He figures to begin 2018 at low Class A Beloit.

Year	Club (League)	Class	AVG	G	AB	R	H	2B	3B	HR	RBI	BB	SO	SB	CS	OBP	SLG
2017	Athletics (AZL)	R	.254	35	138	26	35	3	2	1	14	13	28	7	3	.322	.326
Minor League Totals			.254	35	138	26	35	3	2	1	14	13	28	7	3	.322	.326

16 KEVIN MERRELL, SS

Born: Dec. 14, 1995. **B-T:** L-R. **Ht.:** 6-1. **Wt.:** 180. **Drafted:** South Florida, 2017 (1st round supplemental). **Signed by:** Trevor Schaffer.

Merrell hit .384 with 19 stolen bases as a junior at South Florida in 2017 and earned second-team All-America honors. The Athletics selected him with the 33rd overall pick and signed him for a below-slot $1.8 million. Shoulder and foot injuries limited him to 31 games with Vermont in the New York-Penn League after signing, but he did manage to hit .320 and steal 10 bases.

Merrell is probably the fastest player in the organization not named Jorge Mateo. His plus-plus speed gives him the range to play shortstop, but his arm is considered only average. With Oakland's surplus of shortstops, Merrell could move to second base, which he played for most of his first two college seasons, or even center field at some point. His speed and lefthanded stroke draw comparisons to the Yankees' Brett Gardner.

Gardner has averaged 24 steals per season in his 10-year big-league career, and Merrell could be similarly productive on the basepaths. He figures to begin 2018 at low Class A Beloit.

Year	Club (League)	Class	AVG	G	AB	R	H	2B	3B	HR	RBI	BB	SO	SB	CS	OBP	SLG
2017	Vermont (NYP)	SS	.320	31	125	27	40	5	1	2	9	9	22	10	3	.362	.424
Minor League Totals			.320	31	125	27	40	5	1	2	9	9	22	10	3	.362	.424

17 TYLER RAMIREZ, OF

Born: Feb. 21, 1995. **B-T:** L-L. **Ht.:** 5-9. **Wt.:** 185. **Drafted:** North Carolina, 2016 (7th round). **Signed by:** Neil Avent.

Described as a "natural hitter" who can "flat-out hit," the lefthanded-batting outfielder put together a fine 2017 in which he owned a .304 average and 11 homers over stints with high Class A Stockton and Double-A Midland. Ramirez hit lefties (.297 in 111 at-bats) almost as well as he did righties (.306 in 376 ABs).

Ramirez possesses solid plate discipline. He walked (121) nearly as many times as he struck out (148) in his three seasons as a starter at North Carolina. His patience both helped (73 walks in 571 plate appearances) and hurt (133 strikeouts) him in 2017. Ramirez has played all three outfield spots in the minors, and seems to have found a home in left field. If necessary, he could play center at the big league level, but his lack of premium speed and first-step quickness make him better suited to left.

It's not certain whether Ramirez has the power for a prototypical corner outfielder. His patience, bat-to-ball skills and general maturity as a hitter from the left side give him a chance to keep rising.

Year	Club (League)	Class	AVG	G	AB	R	H	2B	3B	HR	RBI	BB	SO	SB	CS	OBP	SLG
2016	Athletics (AZL)	R	.286	8	28	5	8	3	2	0	8	1	10	1	0	.310	.536
	Vermont (NYP)	SS	.220	48	150	22	33	8	1	2	15	19	39	5	0	.324	.327
2017	Stockton (CAL)	HiA	.301	76	279	51	84	12	2	7	39	45	80	5	2	.399	.434
	Midland (TL)	AA	.308	58	208	29	64	11	1	4	24	28	53	3	3	.395	.428
Minor League Totals			.284	190	665	107	189	34	6	13	86	93	182	14	5	.378	.412

18 HEATH FILLMYER, RHP

Born: May 16, 1994. **B-T:** R-R. **Ht.:** 6-1. **Wt.:** 180. **Drafted:** Mercer County (N.J.) JC, 2014 (5th round). **Signed by:** Ron Vaughn.

Still relatively inexperienced on the mound, Fillmyer has made significant strides in understanding the art of pitching. Mainly a shortstop through high school and his first year in junior college, the righthander went to the mound full-time in his sophomore season, after which the A's drafted him. As a sophomore, he went 9-0 with an ERA under 1.00 as he helped Mercer County CC reached the Division II Junior College World Series.

Fillmyer's fastball sits in the low-90s, and he also throws a curveball and a changeup. Fillmyer doesn't have wipeout stuff, but he knows how to use both sides of the plate, change speeds and sequence pitches. He drops in a quick pitch every now and then, a la Johnny Cueto. Fillmyer capped his 2017 season by working five innings in Double-A Midland's 2-0 victory in Game 3 of the Texas League championship series. He has made steady progress in terms of innings pitched in the past three seasons, from 99 in 2015 to 134 in 2016 to 150 in 2017.

If Fillmyer keeps progressing in his adjustment to pitching, he could become a back-end starter in the next few years.

Year	Club (League)	Class	W	L	ERA	G	GS	CG	SV	IP	H	HR	BB	SO	K/9	WHIP	AVG
2014	Athletics (AZL)	R	1	0	2.79	6	0	0	0	10	5	0	5	10	9.3	1.03	.147
2015	Beloit (MWL)	LoA	3	13	4.98	23	22	0	0	99	112	10	56	77	7.0	1.69	.297
2016	Stockton (CAL)	HiA	5	6	3.60	18	16	0	0	95	101	4	31	89	8.4	1.39	.264
	Midland (TL)	AA	2	0	2.54	8	8	1	0	39	31	3	8	29	6.7	1.00	.223
2017	Midland (TL)	AA	11	5	3.49	29	29	0	0	150	158	19	51	115	6.9	1.40	.272
Minor League Totals			22	24	3.78	84	75	1	0	393	407	36	151	320	7.3	1.42	.269

19 WILL TOFFEY, 3B

BA GRADE

45 Risk: High

Born: Dec. 31, 1994. **B-T:** L-R. **Ht.:** 6-2. **Wt.:** 205. **Drafted:** Vanderbilt, 2017 (4th round). **Signed by:** Dillon Tung.

Known for his excellent plate discipline, Toffey walked 99 times and struck out 74 over his final two seasons at Vanderbilt. In 2017, Toffey led the Commodores' regulars in average (.354), on-base percentage (.475) and slugging percentage (.602). He also hit 12 homers.

The A's picked him in the fourth round and signed him for $482,600. Toffey comes from an athletic family: His father, Jack, is an agent. Will's brother, John, coached him in baseball and hockey at Salisbury (Conn.) Prep. Will was good enough in hockey to have Cornell, Harvard and Yale want him for that sport. Toffey's athleticism and mature approach help, but evaluators have questions about his ultimate offensive impact. With Vermont in the New York-Penn League after signing, Toffey exhibited his strike zone knowledge—38 walks and 45 strikeouts in 253 plate appearances—but managed only a .263 average and one home run. With his size and ability to wait for his pitch, Toffey could develop into more power. He is considered above average defensively at third base with a plus arm. His speed is fringe-average.

Members of the A's organization like Toffey for his approach and knowledge of the game. He figures to begin 2018 with low Class A Beloit.

Year	Club (League)	Class	AVG	G	AB	R	H	2B	3B	HR	RBI	BB	SO	SB	CS	OBP	SLG
2017	Vermont (NYP)	SS	.263	57	209	38	55	11	2	1	22	38	45	2	2	.377	.349
Minor League Totals			.263	57	209	38	55	11	2	1	22	38	45	2	2	.377	.349

20 RENATO NUNEZ, 3B/OF

40 Risk: Medium

Born: April 4, 1994. **B-T:** R-R. **Ht.:** 6-1. **Wt.:** 220. **Signed:** Venezuela, 2010. **Signed by:** Julio Franco.

Nunez hit 32 homers for Triple-A Nashville in 2017, and has hit no fewer than 18 in each of his past five minor league seasons. The problem is, Nunez doesn't get the bat on the ball enough to project to make a sizable impact at the major league level, even with his power, Nunez hit .249 with the Sounds in 2017 (after hitting .228 in 2016) and struck out 141 times.

Nunez rarely uses the opposite field. Though his arm is fine, Nunez doesn't have much speed, and is considered a below-average defensive player. He spent most of his first six minor league seasons as a third baseman, then split time between third and left field in 2017. He has also played a few games at first base. Nunez's power potential is real, but the time for him to make his mark in the majors is drawing near.

Nunez will have a shot at winning a bench spot on the Opening Day roster, but whether he can stick will depend on the strides he makes to control the strike zone and his aggressiveness.

Year	Club (League)	Class	AVG	G	AB	R	H	2B	3B	HR	RBI	BB	SO	SB	CS	OBP	SLG
2015	Midland (TL)	AA	.278	93	381	62	106	23	0	18	61	28	66	1	0	.332	.480
2016	Nashville (PCL)	AAA	.228	128	505	61	115	20	2	23	74	31	119	2	0	.278	.412
	Oakland (AL)	MAJ	.133	9	15	0	2	0	0	0	1	0	3	0	0	.133	.133
2017	Nashville (PCL)	AAA	.249	126	473	74	118	27	2	32	78	47	141	2	1	.319	.518
	Oakland (AL)	MAJ	.200	8	15	1	3	0	0	1	3	1	8	0	0	.250	.400
Major League Totals			.167	17	30	1	5	0	0	1	4	1	11	0	0	.194	.267
Minor League Totals			.262	694	2730	392	716	155	10	130	464	191	649	14	5	.317	.469

21 FRANKIE MONTAS, RHP

BA GRADE
40 Risk: Medium

Born: March 21, 1993. **B-T:** R-R. **Ht.:** 6-2. **Wt.:** 225. **Signed:** Dominican Republic, 2009. **Signed by:** Manny Nanita (Red Sox).

When your fastball consistently hits triple digits on the radar gun, teams will keep you in their plans for a while. Such is the case with Montas. He made Oakland's 25-man roster as a reliever out of spring training in 2017, but struggled mightily with a 6.91 ERA in 21 appearances and was optioned to Triple-A Nashville.

Montas got recalled by the A's in late July, and made two underwhelming appearances before returning to Triple-A for the rest of the season. Montas learned that at the big league level, hitters can get to 100-mph fastballs, especially if those fastballs lack major movement and aren't supplemented by at least one worthy secondary pitch. The A's like Montas' changeup, and want him to use it more. He has averaged more than a strikeout per inning in his pro career, but control can be a problem. He has pitched mainly as a starter in his minor league career, and made eight starts in his nine appearances with Nashville in 2017.

Montas' future in the big leagues is in the bullpen, but only if he can develop some semblance of control or a secondary.

Year	Club (League)	Class	W	L	ERA	G	GS	CG	SV	IP	H	HR	BB	SO	K/9	WHIP	AVG
2015	Birmingham (SL)	AA	5	5	2.97	23	23	1	0	112	89	3	48	108	8.7	1.22	.219
	Chicago (AL)	MAJ	0	2	4.80	7	2	0	0	15	14	1	9	20	12.0	1.53	.246
2016	Tulsa (TL)	AA	0	0	1.93	3	1	0	0	5	2	1	1	7	13.5	0.64	.133
	Oklahoma City (PCL)	AAA	0	0	2.38	4	3	0	0	11	12	0	2	15	11.9	1.24	.279
2017	Oakland (AL)	MAJ	1	1	7.03	23	0	0	0	32	39	10	20	36	10.1	1.84	.302
	Nashville (PCL)	AAA	0	2	5.22	9	8	0	0	29	25	4	7	37	11.4	1.09	.223
Major League Totals			1	3	6.32	30	2	0	0	47	53	11	29	56	10.7	1.74	.285
Minor League Totals			16	27	3.89	108	92	3	0	428	368	24	173	449	9.4	1.26	.231

22 ALEXANDER CAMPOS, SS

BA GRADE
50 Risk: Extreme

Born: Feb. 20, 2000. **B-T:** R-R. **Ht.:** 6-0. **Wt.:** 178. **Signed:** Venezuela, 2016. **Signed by:** Emilio Carrasquel/Scott Hunter (Mariners).

The Athletics acquired Campos and reliever Emilio Pagan in a November trade that sent first baseman Ryon Healy to the Mariners. Oakland had interest in Campos as an amateur before Seattle signed him in July 2016 for $575,000.

Campos is more highly regarded for his defensive skills—his arm rates as plus—than for his offense at this point, but he put up solid numbers in the Dominican Summer League in 2017, batting .290/.413/.367. Perhaps most impressive was the fact he drew more walks (41) than strikeouts (39) in 254 plate appearances. Campos doesn't project to have a ton of power, but he does hit the ball to all fields. He's considered a plus runner, but he stole just seven bases in 17 attempts in the DSL.

Oakland seems to have an abundance of promising shortstops—he's one of six included in the system's Top 30 Prospects—but his defense ought to be good enough to keep him at the position for the foreseeable future. He figures to begin 2018 in the Rookie-level Arizona League.

Year	Club (League)	Class	AVG	G	AB	R	H	2B	3B	HR	RBI	BB	SO	SB	CS	OBP	SLG
2017	Mariners (DSL)	R	.290	59	207	37	60	10	0	2	26	41	39	7	10	.413	.367
Minor League Totals			.290	59	207	37	60	10	0	2	26	41	39	7	10	.413	.367

23 RICHIE MARTIN, SS

BA GRADE
40 Risk: High

Born: Dec. 22, 1994. **B-T:** R-R. **Ht.:** 5-11. **Wt.:** 190. **Drafted:** Florida, 2015 (1st round). **Signed by:** Trevor Schaffer.

Injuries and a lack of offensive production have stunted Martin's progress in the Athletics' system since they made him the 20th overall pick in 2015. Surgery to repair a torn meniscus delayed his 2016 debut with high Class A Stockton until May 23. In 2017, he missed more than two weeks with Double-A Midland after getting hit in the face by a pitch on May 30.

When healthy, Martin hasn't excelled at the plate; he owns a .235 career average in three minor league seasons. After he batted .224 in 86 games with Midland in 2017, the A's sent Martin back to Stockton. His demotion coincided with Jorge Mateo joining Midland after the A's acquired him from the Yankees. Martin remains more than capable as a defensive shortstop. He has a plus arm and plus range. The problem is few believe he hit enough to allow him to display his defensive skills at the big league level. He's considered a good enough athlete to find a way to improve his offense and is still young enough to do so.

The A's think his problem is he doesn't get into a good position to hit, and that it can be rectified. Martin will try again at Double-A Midland in 2018.

Year	Club (League)	Class	AVG	G	AB	R	H	2B	3B	HR	RBI	BB	SO	SB	CS	OBP	SLG
2015	Vermont (NYP)	SS	.237	51	190	31	45	6	4	2	16	25	47	7	7	.353	.342
2016	Stockton (CAL)	HiA	.230	86	330	46	76	14	2	3	31	36	73	12	8	.322	.312
	Midland (TL)	AA	.333	5	15	1	5	1	1	0	7	3	2	2	1	.444	.533
2017	Midland (TL)	AA	.226	86	287	43	65	11	3	4	29	23	57	12	3	.306	.328
	Stockton (CAL)	HiA	.266	23	94	16	25	2	3	1	6	8	21	1	1	.330	.383
Minor League Totals			.236	251	916	137	216	34	13	10	89	95	200	34	20	.326	.334

24 B.J. BOYD, OF

BA GRADE

40 Risk: High

Born: July 16, 1993. **B-T:** L-R. **Ht.:** 5-11. **Wt.:** 230. **Drafted:** HS—Palo Alto, Calif., 2012 (4th round). **Signed by:** Jermaine Clark.

Boyd put together his best minor league season by far in 2017. With Double-A Midland, Boyd led the Texas League in hits (172) and finished third in average (.323). Boyd employs a compact stroke and is adept at hitting the ball to the opposite field.

Boyd knows how to make contact (74 strikeouts in 578 plate appearances in 2017). He has plus speed, but doesn't get great jumps on the bases. Boyd had alternated between center field and left for most of his pro career. He spent the bulk of 2017 in center, and his defense clearly improved. He doesn't possess a plus arm, so remaining in center could be problematic, but he doesn't have the power associated with many corner outfielders.

Some believe that his power could improve to the point that he might hit 10-15 homers per season in the big leagues. He'll likely begin 2018 with Triple-A Nashville.

Year	Club (League)	Class	AVG	G	AB	R	H	2B	3B	HR	RBI	BB	SO	SB	CS	OBP	SLG
2015	Stockton (CAL)	HiA	.277	132	458	67	127	20	8	5	52	41	89	18	5	.344	.389
2016	Stockton (CAL)	HiA	.288	101	413	48	119	14	3	8	58	34	74	8	6	.346	.395
	Nashville (PCL)	AAA	.267	7	30	2	8	0	0	0	1	2	3	0	0	.313	.267
2017	Midland (TL)	AA	.323	130	533	82	172	29	6	5	56	34	74	16	5	.366	.428
Minor League Totals			.282	605	2301	332	648	99	28	33	257	217	436	81	35	.347	.392

25 YERDEL VARGAS, SS/2B

BA GRADE

45 Risk: Extreme

Born: Feb. 17, 2000. **B-T:** R-R. **Ht.:** 6-0. **Wt.:** 170. **Drafted:** Dominican Republic, 2016. **Signed by:** Juan De La Cruz.

The A's signed Vargas as a 16-year-old from the Dominican Republic with a $1.5 million bonus in July 2016. After a 13-game stint in the Dominican Summer League in 2017, Vargas joined Oakland's Rookie-level Arizona League team.

Not surprisingly for a 17-year-old, Vargas had his troubles at the plate in Arizona, hitting .208 with no homers and a mere six walks in 157 plate appearances. The A's signed him as a shortstop, and then played him at short (15 starts), second base (15 starts) and third (nine starts) in the AZL. Vargas has the hands, arm and quick release necessary to play short, but as his body matures, he could become bigger than the prototypical shortstop. Also, with the Oakland system's wealth of promising shortstops a move to second base or third might make sense. Those in the organization like Vargas' body, makeup and baseball IQ.

As he'll be only 18 in 2018, Vargas is, in the words of one member of the A's organization, "miles and miles away" from big league consideration. A repeat in the AZL is possible in 2018.

Year	Club (League)	Class	AVG	G	AB	R	H	2B	3B	HR	RBI	BB	SO	SB	CS	OBP	SLG
2017	Athletics (DSL)	R	.173	13	52	6	9	0	0	0	6	0	15	1	0	.200	.173
	Athletics (AZL)	R	.208	39	144	13	30	6	4	0	13	6	36	3	4	.256	.306
Minor League Totals			.199	52	196	19	39	6	4	0	19	6	51	4	4	.242	.270

26 JAMES NAILE, RHP

BA GRADE

40 Risk: High

Born: Feb. 8, 1993. **B-T:** R-R. **Ht.:** 6-4. **Wt.:** 185. **Drafted:** Alabama-Birmingham, 2015 (20th round). **Signed by:** Kelcey Mucker.

Naile already owns a pretty cool distinction in his professional career: Pitching for Double-A Midland, he threw six shutout innings and got the victory in the deciding game of the 2016 Texas League championship series, and then threw six shutout innings and got the victory in the deciding game of the 2017 Texas League championship series as well.

Naile doesn't possess overpowering stuff, but his fastball jumped from sitting in the high 80s in 2016 to the low 90s in 2017. He gets excellent sink on his fastball, which runs in on righthanded hitters. He attacks the strike zone, with just 62 walks in 256 minor league innings. He also employs a slider, changeup and cutter. Naile won a minor league Gold Glove in 2016, when he handled 48 chances without an error at four different levels. Naile does have an injury history: He sat out the 2014 season at Alabama-Birmingham after Tommy John surgery, and he missed about two months of the 2017 season with an oblique strain.

People in the A's organization love his competitiveness. He figures to begin 2018 with Triple-A Nashville.

Year	Club (League)	Class	W	L	ERA	G	GS	CG	SV	IP	H	HR	BB	SO	K/9	WHIP	AVG
2015	Athletics (AZL)	R	0	0	0.00	2	0	0	0	2	0	0	0	1	4.5	0.00	.000
	Vermont (NYP)	SS	3	0	1.93	18	0	0	6	23	19	0	6	17	6.6	1.07	.218
2016	Nashville (PCL)	AAA	1	1	5.73	2	2	0	0	11	11	1	5	4	3.3	1.45	.256
	Beloit (MWL)	LoA	3	8	2.66	15	14	0	0	88	67	2	19	64	6.5	0.98	.211
	Stockton (CAL)	HiA	8	7	3.76	8	7	0	0	41	39	5	11	46	10.2	1.23	.257
	Midland (TL)	AA	1	1	4.76	3	3	0	0	17	20	1	3	11	5.8	1.35	.303
2017	Athletics (AZL)	R	0	0	1.80	2	2	0	0	5	4	1	0	11	19.8	0.80	.211
	Stockton (CAL)	HiA	0	0	5.14	2	2	0	0	7	9	0	1	4	5.1	1.43	.290
	Midland (TL)	AA	2	3	3.21	14	10	0	0	62	55	5	17	42	6.1	1.17	.239
Minor League Totals			14	14	3.20	66	40	0	6	256	224	15	62	200	7.0	1.12	.235

27 CASEY MEISNER, RHP

BA GRADE
40 Risk: High

Born: May 22, 1995. **B-T:** R-R. **Ht.:** 6-7. **Wt.:** 190. **Drafted:** HS—Cypress, Texas, 2013 (3rd round). **Signed by:** Ray Corbett (Mets).

Oakland acquired Meisner in the deal that sent reliever Tyler Clippard to the Mets at the trade deadline in 2015. Meisner thrived in his first three minor league seasons before a miserable 2016 at high Class A Stockton, but he rebounded in 2017 after some delivery changes to go 10-9, 4.04 for Stockton and Double-A Midland.

Meisner's fastball sits 90-92 mph and gets up to 95, and he flashes a plus changeup. He'll also mix in a slider, curveball and cutter to keep hitters guessing. While Meisner's arsenal is diverse, the A's would like him to be more aggressive in the strike zone. He showed some mental fortitude, not only bouncing back from a poor 2016 but finishing strong in Double-A after floundered initially after his promotion.

Still just 22 years old, the tall, lanky righthander figures to return to Midland to begin 2018.

Year	Club (League)	Class	W	L	ERA	G	GS	CG	SV	IP	H	HR	BB	SO	K/9	WHIP	AVG
2015	Savannah (SAL)	LoA	7	2	2.13	12	12	0	0	76	59	6	19	66	7.8	1.03	.213
	St. Lucie (FSL)	HiA	3	2	2.83	6	6	0	0	35	35	4	14	23	5.9	1.40	.259
	Stockton (CAL)	HiA	3	1	2.78	7	7	0	0	32	27	1	7	24	6.7	1.05	.220
2016	Stockton (CAL)	HiA	1	14	4.85	28	19	0	1	117	126	12	59	100	7.7	1.58	.275
2017	Stockton (CAL)	HiA	6	5	3.98	16	12	0	0	75	73	9	20	80	9.6	1.25	.254
	Midland (TL)	AA	4	4	4.12	12	12	0	0	59	55	4	27	37	5.6	1.39	.249
Minor League Totals			30	34	3.66	104	85	0	1	492	473	40	174	425	7.8	1.32	.252

28 MARCOS BRITO, 2B/SS

BA GRADE
45 Risk: Extreme

Born: March 6, 2000. **B-T:** B-R. **Ht.:** 6-0. **Wt.:** 160. **Signed:** Dominican Republic, 2016. **Signed by:** Juan Carlos de la Cruz

Signed for $1.1 million as a 16-year-old in July 2016 out of the Dominican Republic, Brito began his pro career in 2017 with a brief stint in the Dominican Summer League, followed by a longer stretch in the Rookie-level Arizona League.

Brito played 34 of his 44 games in Arizona at second base. He also played five games at shortstop and four at third. Errors were a problem. He committed eight at second base and five at short. It's not certain where on the infield he'll ultimately settle, but second base is the best guess for most evaluators. Brito is a switch-hitter who didn't display much power in Arizona. The A's know he needs to add strength to his frame, and considering his age, there's still plenty of time for him to do that.

Brito is slated to start 2018 in extended spring training, with a chance to get out to short-season Vermont if he progresses.

Year	Club (League)	Class	AVG	G	AB	R	H	2B	3B	HR	RBI	BB	SO	SB	CS	OBP	SLG
2017	Athletics (DSL)	R	.178	14	45	3	8	1	0	0	8	13	8	5	0	.339	.200
	Athletics (AZL)	R	.234	44	171	30	40	4	2	1	17	21	42	4	1	.320	.298
Minor League Totals			.222	58	216	33	48	5	2	1	25	34	50	9	1	.324	.278

29 RAMON LAUREANO, OF

BA GRADE
40 Risk: High

Born: July 15, 1994. **B-T:** R-R. **Ht.:** 5-11. **Wt.:** 185. **Drafted:** Northeast Oklahoma A&M JC, 2014 (16th round). **Signed by:** Jim Stevenson (Astros).

The Athletics acquired Laureano in a trade following the 2017 season, when they sent high Class A righthander Brandon Bailey to the Astros. Laureano required a spot on the 40-man roster to shield him from the Rule 5 draft. Houston was unwilling to make that move, but Oakland added him to its roster.

A native of the Dominican Republic, Laureano enjoyed a breakout 2016 season. Playing at high Class A Lancaster and Double-A Corpus Christi, he hit a combined .319/.428/.528 and led the minors in on-base percentage. His above-average speed and advanced instincts helped him steal 43 bases in 59 attempts. Laureano slumped decisively in a full season at Corpus Christi in 2017, althoug he still went 24-for-29 in stolen base attempts. Making contact can be problematic for Laureano. Given his well below-average power, his strikeout rate of 21 percent is too high. Laureano has played all three outfield positions in the minors. He spent most of 2017 in right field. He possesses a plus arm and racked up 16 assists. Laureano overcame a rough start to 2017, in which he hit .198 with three homers through June but rebounded to hit .262 with eight homers the rest of the way.

The A's figure to give him a third crack at Double-A in 2018, this time with Midland, to see if he can rediscover his batting stroke.

Year	Club (League)	Class	AVG	G	AB	R	H	2B	3B	HR	RBI	BB	SO	SB	CS	OBP	SLG
2015	Quad Cities (MWL)	LoA	.265	76	287	43	76	15	8	4	34	21	83	18	3	.323	.415
2016	Lancaster (CAL)	HiA	.317	80	293	69	93	19	5	10	60	50	86	33	11	.426	.519
	Corpus Christi (TL)	AA	.323	36	124	20	40	9	2	5	13	20	33	10	3	.432	.548
2017	Corpus Christi (TL)	AA	.225	123	463	65	104	21	6	11	55	40	110	24	5	.296	.367
Minor League Totals			.265	331	1220	205	323	64	21	31	164	138	328	89	22	.349	.428

30 DAKOTA CHALMERS, RHP

BA GRADE
40 Risk: High

Born: Oct. 8, 1996. **B-T:** R-R. **Ht.:** 6-3. **Wt.:** 175. **Drafted:** HS—Cumming, Ga., 2015 (3rd round). **Signed by:** Jemel Spearman.

One of the top high school arms in Georgia in 2015, Chalmers fell to the Athletics in the third round, where they signed him for $1.2 million, which was twice the slot amount.

Three numbers from Chalmers' 2017 season at low Class A Beloit illustrate his problems and potential: 29, 29 and 47. That is, 29 innings with 29 walks and 47 strikeouts. He also hit five batters. Control is a big issue for Chalmers, but his stuff is undeniable. In a four-inning relief appearance at Kane County on April 17, he struck out 10, walked none and allowed one hit. He throws a fastball in the 94-98 mph range and has what one member of the organization termed a wipeout breaking ball. He generates swings and misses with his curveball but seldom locates it for strikes. Chalmers left Beloit in late May for what was reported as a personal issue and did not return the rest of the regular season. During instructional league, the A's spent time with Chalmers trying to create a repeatable delivery.

Chalmers' youth and upside give the organization reasons to have patience with him. He could return to Beloit to begin 2018.

Year	Club (League)	Class	W	L	ERA	G	GS	CG	SV	IP	H	HR	BB	SO	K/9	WHIP	AVG
2015	Athletics (AZL)	R	0	1	2.66	11	11	0	0	20	15	0	17	18	8.0	1.57	.205
2016	Vermont (NYP)	SS	5	4	4.70	15	13	0	0	67	55	8	37	62	8.3	1.37	.217
2017	Beloit (MWL)	LoA	2	2	4.34	10	5	0	0	29	15	1	29	47	14.6	1.52	.155
Minor League Totals			7	7	4.26	36	29	0	0	116	85	9	83	127	9.8	1.44	.200

Philadelphia Phillies

BY BEN BADLER

For the fifth straight season, the Phillies finished with a losing record in 2017. Yet for the first time in their stretch of futility, the franchise began to show signs of hope for the future.

Rhys Hoskins arrived in Philadelphia in August and showed an outstanding combination of patience, power and contact skills, hitting 18 home runs in just 50 games while moving from first base to left field. Outfielder Nick Williams came up at the end of June and rebounded from a down year in 2016 to look like a core part of the team's future. Center fielder Odubel Herrera is another important young building block for the team's future, while Aaron Altherr was a pleasant surprise in right field during his age-26 season.

The Phillies' lineup is in good shape for the near future, with reinforcements coming in the infield. Shortstop J.P. Crawford flipped the switch in the second half of the 2017 season in Triple-A and should be a centerpiece player at shortstop on Opening Day. He and second baseman Scott Kingery are both candidates to hit at the top of the Phillies' lineup for years.

The rotation is where the Phillies need more help, with a lack of midrotation or frontline starters beyond Aaron Nola. The development of pitchers like Sixto Sanchez, JoJo Romero, Adonis Medina, Franklyn Kilome, Ranger Suarez and Seranthony Dominguez will be critical, but it's unlikely any of them will be contributing in Philadelphia until 2019.

Supplementing the pitching staff through trades or free agent signings seems likely. The Phillies have the money and deep prospect stash to do both, so making proper internal evaluations of their own talent will be key for the Phillies the next two years as they assess which players to hold and which ones to deal for major league help.

The Phillies have one of the game's deepest farm systems, one with few weaknesses. There is talent at all levels, including a slew of breakout candidates that have yet to reach full-season ball in outfielders Jhailyn Ortiz and Simon Muzziotti, righthander Francisco Morales and shortstop Jonathan Guzman. Much of that prospect depth has come from the team's Latin American pipeline, with the Phillies showing a particular knack for signing pitchers at bargain prices who take off in pro ball. Sanchez, Medina and Kilome are all Top 10 Prospects in the farm system signed for less than $100,000, while lefthander Ranger Suarez and righthander Seranthony Dominguez could both jump into that tier next year.

That depth has helped the Phillies absorb some

Rhys Hoskins bashed 18 home runs in 50 games during an outstanding rookie season.

PROJECTED 2021 LINEUP

Catcher	Jorge Alfaro (28)
First Base	Rhys Hoskins (28)
Second Base	Scott Kingery (27)
Third Base	Maikel Franco (28)
Shortstop	J.P. Crawford (26)
Left Field	Nick Williams (27)
Center Field	Odubel Herrera (29)
Right Field	Adam Haseley (25)
No. 1 Starter	Sixto Sanchez (22)
No. 2 Starter	Aaron Nola (28)
No. 3 Starter	Adonis Medina (24)
No. 4 Starter	Franklyn Kilome (26)
No. 5 Starter	Ranger Suarez (25)
Closer	Seranthony Dominguez (26)

disappointments from recent first-round picks. Outfielder Cornelius Randolph, the No. 10 overall pick in 2015, hasn't hit as well as the Phillies initially hoped, and Mickey Moniak, the No. 1 overall pick in 2016, remains in the team's Top 10 Prospects but has to show his sluggish first full season was an aberration instead of an arrow pointing in the wrong direction.

The Phillies should be a better team in 2018, but it's unlikely they will get to the postseason. The target for contention should be 2019, with the team well positioned to go on a stretch of playoff-caliber seasons from then on if they complement a promising young nucleus already in place with smart moves in trades and free agency.

DEPTH CHART

PHILADELPHIA PHILLIES

TOP 2018 ROOKIE: J.P. Crawford, SS. After going on a tear in the second half in Triple-A, he is positioned to carry that success over into a big rookie year at a premium position.

BREAKOUT PROSPECT: Simon Muzziotti, OF. He is a two-way threat who glides around center field with good speed while showing excellent contact skills at the plate.

SLEEPER: Nick Fanti, LHP. Fanti has outstanding control that should help him move quickly, especially if the Phillies can get him throwing harder, like they've done with several other prospects.

SOURCE OF TOP 30 TALENT			
Homegrown	25	Acquired	5
College	5	Trade	5
Junior college	0	Rule 5 draft	0
High school	5	Independent league	0
Nondrafted free agent	0	Free agent/waivers	0
International	15		

LF
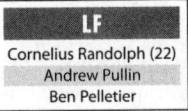
Cornelius Randolph (22)
Andrew Pullin
Ben Pelletier

CF
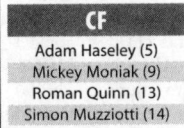
Adam Haseley (5)
Mickey Moniak (9)
Roman Quinn (13)
Simon Muzziotti (14)

RF

Jhailyn Ortiz (7)
Dylan Cozens
Jiandido Tromp

3B
Mitch Walding
Cole Stobbe

SS
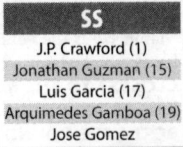
J.P. Crawford (1)
Jonathan Guzman (15)
Luis Garcia (17)
Arquimedes Gamboa (19)
Jose Gomez

2B
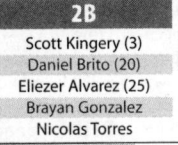
Scott Kingery (3)
Daniel Brito (20)
Eliezer Alvarez (25)
Brayan Gonzalez
Nicolas Torres

1B

Quincy Nieporte

C
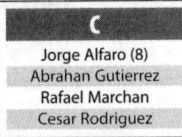
Jorge Alfaro (8)
Abrahan Gutierrez
Rafael Marchan
Cesar Rodriguez

LHP

LHSP
JoJo Romero (6)
Ranger Suarez (11)
Kyle Young (24)
Nick Fanti
Elniery Garcia
Manuel Silva
Brandon Leibrandt
Bailey Falter
Ethan Lindow
McKenzie Mills
Cole Irvin

LHRP
Jeff Singer

RHP

RHSP
Sixto Sanchez (2)
Adonis Medina (4)
Franklyn Kilome (10)
Seranthony Dominguez (12)
Francisco Morales (16)
Spencer Howard (18)
Jose Taveras (23)
Thomas Eshelman (27)
Edgar Garcia (28)
Jacob Waguespack (29)
Connor Seabold
Drew Anderson
Kevin Gowdy
Victor Vargas
Carlos Betancourt

RHRP
Victor Arano (21)
J.D. Hammer (26)
Mauricio Llovera (30)
Ricardo Pinto
Trevor Bettencourt
Luke Leftwich
Alberto Tirado

DRAFT ANALYSIS

2017

BEST PURE HITTER: OF Adam Haseley (1) hit .390 in the spring for Virginia and was one of the top hitters in the college class. The Phillies are all in on his above-average hitting ability and swing and expect him to improve now that he's giving up pitching.

BEST POWER HITTER: Haseley has above-average power that plays due to his feel for hitting. Righthanded-hitting 1B/OF Austin Listi (17) hit 24 home runs in the spring for Dallas Baptist and seven more as a pro.

FASTEST RUNNER: Haseley turns in plus times at his best and is a consistent above-average runner, giving him a slight edge on SS Jake Holmes (11).

BEST DEFENSIVE PLAYER: SS Dalton Guthrie (6) had throwing issues this spring due to injury, costing him some arm strength, but his internal clock, soft hands and fine footwork make him an asset in the infield.

BEST ATHLETE: Holmes likely will outgrow shortstop, with room to fill out his 6-foot-3, 195-pound frame while retaining his body control.

BEST FASTBALL: RHP Spencer Howard (2) was sitting 94-96 mph after signing with short-season Williamsport, and he gets swings and misses with it thanks in part to its late finish in the zone.

BEST SECONDARY PITCH: RHP Connor Seabold (3) has a tremendous "Bugs Bunny" changeup, the plus pitch in his arsenal that he uses well. It will be even more effective if he maintains the 90-93 mph velocity he flashed after signing.

BEST PRO DEBUT: LHP Jhordany Mezquita (8) fell about nine innings short of qualifying for the Rookie-level Gulf Coast League title but dominated in nine starts, going 3-0, 0.72 with 35 strikeouts in

TOP DRAFT PICKS OF THE DECADE

Year	Player, Pos.	2017 Org
2008	Anthony Hewitt, SS	Did not play
2009	Kelly Dugan, OF (2nd round)	D-backs
2010	Jesse Biddle, LHP	Braves
2011	Larry Greene, OF (1st round supp.)	Retired
2012	Shane Watson, RHP (1st round supp.)	Phillies
2013	J.P. Crawford, SS	Phillies
2014	Aaron Nola, RHP	Phillies
2015	Cornelius Randolph, SS	Phillies
2016	Mickey Moniak, OF	Phillies
2017	Adam Haseley, OF	Phillies.

37.2 innings. RHP Connor Brogdon (10), working in a relief role, struck out 45 in 34.2 innings while going 3-1, 2.34 for short-season Williamsport.

MOST INTRIGUING BACKGROUND: The Phillies tried to sign Mezquita out of the Dominican Republic, but he'd attended high school in Hazelton, Pa., and he was ruled ineligible as an international free agent. The Phillies drafted and signed him for $50,000 instead. Guthrie's father Mark made 765 appearances in a 15-year big league career, mostly as a reliever. SS/2B Nick Maton (7) is the younger brother of Padres righthander Phil Maton.

CLOSEST TO THE MAJORS: Haseley could beat 2016 No. 1 pick Mickey Moniak to Philadelphia.

BEST LATE-ROUND PICK: LHP Damon Jones (18), already 23, lacks command but has excellent arm strength, reaching 97 mph after signing and has good size at 6-foot-5, 225 pounds.

THE ONE WHO GOT AWAY: Loose-armed LHP Shane Drohan (23) took his pitchability, projection and fine secondary stuff to Florida State.

—JOHN MANUEL

2016

OF Mickey Moniak (1) was the top pick in the draft, but it's LHP JoJo Romero (4) who is now the class' top-ranked player. Moniak scuffled in his first full season and RHP Kevin Gowdy (2) had Tommy John surgery.
GRADE: C

2015

2B Scott Kingery (2) is on the cusp of the big leagues and is the class' bright spot. OF Cornelius Randolph (1) has been inconsistent offensively as a pro. No other player from the class ranks in the handbook.
GRADE: C

2014

RHP Aaron Nola (1) bounced back in the big leagues in 2017 and could be the Phillies' Opening Day starter. OF Rhys Hoskins (5) took the big leagues by storm, crushing 18 homers in the final two months.
GRADE: A

1 J.P. CRAWFORD, SS

Born: Jan. 11, 1995. **B-T:** L-R. **Ht.:** 6-2. **Wt.:** 185.
Drafted: HS—Lakewood, Calif., 2013 (1st round).
Signed by: Demerius Pittman.

ANDREW WOOLLEY

Crawford is the top prospect in the organization for the fourth straight season, but it hasn't been a smooth ride up the ladder. The No. 13 overall pick in 2013 made fast progress initially, reaching Double-A as a 20-year-old in 2015. Yet when Crawford spent most of 2016 in Triple-A Lehigh Valley, he struggled, and when he returned to the IronPigs in 2017 his poor performance continued. By June 10, his slash line had dropped to .194/.313/.252. He took the next nine days off to rest a nagging groin strain and take a mental break, and when he returned he looked like a different player. Crawford finished the season on a tear, batting .280/.381/.522 with 13 home runs in his final 71 games. He made his big league debut as a September callup.

Even when he struggles, Crawford stands out for his plate discipline. He's a patient, selective hitter who recognizes offspeed pitches, piles up walks and is a an on-base threat. At times, his strike-zone judgment was the only offensive attribute working for him. He got into a bad habit of pulling off the ball, causing his hips to fly open. That created a longer swing path, left him vulnerable to pitches on the outer third and cut into his ability to drive the ball. Crawford adjusted in the second half by setting up his hands closer to his body and keeping his lower half in his swing better. The changes improved his swing efficiency and helped him stay through the ball. Crawford's offensive game is still centered around hitting line drives, but he showed the potential for 15-plus home runs. Crawford struggled on defense early in the season, but by the end of the year he again looked like a true shortstop with good athleticism and range, quick hands, a smooth transfer and an accurate, above-average arm. He shifted to third base in August to get accustomed to the position with Freddy Galvis then at shortstop in Philadelphia.

Crawford's extended struggles in Triple-A can't simply be dismissed, but his turnaround showed he still has the talent to be a centerpiece player. With Galvis traded to the Padres, Crawford should step in as the Phillies' everyday shortstop and develop into an above-average player.

BA GRADE / SCOUTING GRADES

60 Risk: Medium

HIT: 60. **POW:** 45. **SPD:** 50.
FLD: 55. **ARM:** 60.

Projected future grades on 20-80 scouting scale

TOP PROSPECTS OF THE DECADE

Year	Player, Pos.	2017 Org
2008	Carlos Carrasco, RHP	Indians
2009	Domonic Brown, OF	Rockies
2010	Domonic Brown, OF	Rockies
2011	Domonic Brown, OF	Rockies
2012	Trevor May, RHP	Twins
2013	Jesse Biddle, LHP	Braves
2014	Maikel Franco, 3B	Phillies
2015	J.P. Crawford, SS	Phillies
2016	J.P. Crawford, SS	Phillies
2017	J.P. Crawford, SS	Phillies

BEST TOOLS

Best Hitter for Average	Scott Kingery
Best Power Hitter	Dylan Cozens
Best Strike-Zone Discipline	J.P. Crawford
Fastest Baserunner	Roman Quinn
Best Athlete	Roman Quinn
Best Fastball	Sixto Sanchez
Best Curveball	Franklyn Kilome
Best Slider	Edgar Garcia
Best Changeup	Jose Taveras
Best Control	Tom Eshelman
Best Defensive Catcher	Edgar Cabral
Best Defensive Infielder	J.P. Crawford
Best Infield Arm	J.P. Crawford
Best Defensive Outfielder	Roman Quinn
Best Outfield Arm	Jose Pujols

Year	Club (League)	Class	AVG	G	AB	R	H	2B	3B	HR	RBI	BB	SO	SB	CS	OBP	SLG
2015	Clearwater (FSL)	HiA	.392	21	79	15	31	1	0	1	8	14	9	5	2	.489	.443
	Reading (EL)	AA	.265	86	351	53	93	21	7	5	34	49	45	7	2	.354	.407
2016	Reading (EL)	AA	.265	36	136	23	36	8	0	3	13	30	21	5	3	.398	.390
	Lehigh Valley (IL)	AAA	.244	87	336	40	82	11	1	4	30	42	59	7	4	.328	.318
2017	Lehigh Valley (IL)	AAA	.243	127	474	75	115	20	6	15	63	79	97	5	4	.351	.405
	Philadelphia (NL)	MAJ	.214	23	70	8	15	4	1	0	6	16	22	1	0	.356	.300
Major League Totals			.214	23	70	8	15	4	1	0	6	16	22	1	0	.356	.300
Minor League Totals			.270	533	2034	309	549	93	17	40	217	311	340	67	35	.367	.391x

2 SIXTO SANCHEZ, RHP

Born: July 29, 1998. **B-T:** R-R. **Ht.:** 6-0. **Wt.:** 200. **Signed:** Dominican Republic, 2015. **Signed by:** Carlos Salas.

At a tryout for a Cuban catcher, it was Sanchez instead who grabbed the Phillies' attention. They quickly signed him for $35,000, and after a breakout 2016 season in the Rookie-level Gulf Coast League, he continued his ascension in 2017. He reached high Class A Clearwater in August as one of the best pitching prospects in the game.

Sanchez is one of the hardest-throwing starting pitchers in the minors, but you wouldn't know it from his delivery. He has easy, fluid mechanics that he repeats consistently, helping him command a lively fastball that sits in the mid-90s and touches 100 mph. Sanchez can overpower hitters with his fastball, though he's working to polish his secondary pitches to miss more bats. His changeup flashes plus with good sink and run, and it helps him thwart lefties, though he needs to do a better job of repeating the same arm slot as his fastball on the pitch. His slider is average now but could be above-average if he can add more power to that pitch.

BA GRADE

65 Risk: High

FB: 70. CB: 55.
CHG: 60.
CTL: 60.

Sanchez's fastball command should help him continue to move quickly, with a chance to join the big league rotation by 2019 and develop into a front-line starter along the lines of the Yankees' Luis Severino.

Year	Club (League)	Class	W	L	ERA	G	GS	CG	SV	IP	H	HR	BB	SO	K/9	WHIP	AVG
2015	Phillies (DSL)	R	1	2	4.56	11	2	0	0	26	32	0	6	18	6.3	1.48	.291
2016	Phillies (GCL)	R	5	0	0.50	11	11	0	0	54	33	0	8	44	7.3	0.76	.181
2017	Lakewood (SAL)	LoA	5	3	2.41	13	13	1	0	67	46	1	9	64	8.6	0.82	.191
	Clearwater (FSL)	HiA	0	4	4.55	5	5	1	0	28	27	1	9	20	6.5	1.30	.252
Minor League Totals			11	9	2.47	40	31	2	0	175	138	2	32	146	7.5	0.97	.216

3 SCOTT KINGERY, 2B

Born: April 29, 1994. **B-T:** R-R. **Ht.:** 5-10. **Wt.:** 180. **Drafted:** Arizona, 2015 (2nd round). **Signed by:** Brad Holland.

A walk-on at Arizona, Kingery played well in his first full season in 2016 before hitting a wall at Double-A Reading. Returning to the Eastern League in 2017, Kingery clobbered the competition and advanced to Triple-A Lehigh Valley, hitting a career-high 26 home runs after belting just five the previous season.

Kingery has a chance to develop into a plus hitter. He has a simple, efficient swing from the right side with good bat speed, balance and barrel control. He recognizes pitches well, stays back on offspeed pitches and covers the plate well, driving the ball with loft to all fields. Kingery has a medium build but strong forearms that help him generate solid-average power and a chance to hit 20 homers. A smart, instinctive player, he is a plus runner who gets good jumps stealing bases. He's also a plus defender at second base, where he has good range and turns the double play well with a fringe-average arm.

BA GRADE

60 Risk: Medium

HIT: 60. POW: 55.
SPD: 60. FLD: 60.
ARM: 50.

Kingery is a well-rounded player whose batting, baserunning and defensive value in the middle of the diamond could make him an above-average regular who hits toward the top of a lineup. He likely will open 2018 back in Triple-A, but he should be a key part of Philadelphia's big league club by the all-star break.

Year	Club (League)	Class	AVG	G	AB	R	H	2B	3B	HR	RBI	BB	SO	SB	CS	OBP	SLG
2015	Lakewood (SAL)	LoA	.250	66	252	43	63	9	2	3	21	18	43	11	1	.314	.337
2016	Clearwater (FSL)	HiA	.293	94	375	60	110	29	3	3	28	33	54	26	5	.360	.411
	Reading (EL)	AA	.250	37	156	16	39	7	0	2	18	5	36	4	2	.273	.333
2017	Reading (EL)	AA	.313	69	278	62	87	18	5	18	44	28	51	19	3	.379	.608
	Lehigh Valley (IL)	AAA	.294	63	265	41	78	11	3	8	21	13	58	10	2	.337	.449
Minor League Totals			.284	329	1326	222	377	74	13	34	132	97	242	70	13	.341	.437

4 ADONIS MEDINA, RHP

Born: Dec. 18, 1996. **B-T:** R-R. **Ht.:** 6-1. **Wt.:** 185. **Signed:** Dominican Republic, 2014. **Signed by:** Koby Perez/Carlos Salas.

The Phillies signed Medina for $70,000 when he was a 17-year-old with a loose arm action and a fastball that hit 90 mph. Now he's a power pitcher who took a big step forward at low Class A Lakewood in 2017 by improving his offspeed arsenal, which led to an increase in his strikeout rate.

Medina operates off a fastball that parks at 92-95 mph and touches 97. His fastball is his best pitch, and he combines plus velocity with late life and the ability to throw his heater for strikes. Over the past year, Medina altered his delivery to get more extension out front at his release point, which helps his fastball jump on hitters quicker than they expect. After striking out just 13 percent of batters in 2016, Medina doubled his strikeout rate to 26 percent in 2017. His changeup became a plus pitch and he introduced a slider that's a solid-average offering. Medina is a good athlete who controls the running game well.

The improvement of Medina's secondary stuff gives him an opportunity to develop into a mid-rotation starter. His next step will be high Class A Clearwater in 2018.

BA GRADE
55 Risk: High
FB: 60. SL: 55.
CHG: 60.
CTL: 55.

Year	Club (League)	Class	W	L	ERA	G	GS	CG	SV	IP	H	HR	BB	SO	K/9	WHIP	AVG
2015	Phillies (GCL)	R	3	2	2.98	10	8	0	0	45	42	1	12	35	6.9	1.19	.253
2016	Williamsport (NYP)	SS	5	3	2.92	13	13	0	0	65	47	5	24	34	4.7	1.10	.203
2017	Lakewood (SAL)	LoA	4	9	3.01	22	22	0	0	120	103	7	39	133	10.0	1.19	.227
Minor League Totals			14	17	2.81	56	45	0	1	256	214	13	79	224	7.9	1.14	.225

5 ADAM HASELEY, OF

Born: April 12, 1996. **B-T:** L-L. **Ht.:** 6-1. **Wt.:** 195. **Drafted:** Virginia, 2017 (1st round). **Signed by:** Paul Murphy.

In high school, Haseley earned attention from scouts for his bat and his arm. He took those skills to Virginia as a two-way player. The Phillies made him the eighth overall pick in 2017 as an outfielder and signed him for $5.1 million. Haseley looked run down in a pro debut that culminated with 18 games at low Class A Lakewood, which is understandable given he also threw 65 innings as a weekend starter in college.

Haseley doesn't have one loud 70 tool on the 20-80 scale, but he does a lot of things well. He's a potential above-average hitter with a good sense for the strike zone. He has an inside-out swing that leads him to use the opposite field frequently. He has average power, and once he learns which pitches he can turn on to drive with authority, his power numbers could spike, especially with his feel for hitting. Haseley isn't a burner, but his slightly above-average speed is enough to start his career in center field. He could stick there, though some scouts think he might rotate among all three outfield spots. He has an average, accurate arm.

Now that Haseley dropped pitching, the Phillies are optimistic that his bat will take off. He will open 2018 at one of their Class A affiliates, with a chance to develop into a solid-average regular.

BA GRADE
55 Risk: High
HIT: 55. POW: 50.
SPD: 55. FLD: 50.
ARM: 50.

Year	Club (League)	Class	AVG	G	AB	R	H	2B	3B	HR	RBI	BB	SO	SB	CS	OBP	SLG
2017	Phillies (GCL)	R	.583	3	12	3	7	1	1	0	4	2	3	1	1	.643	.833
	Williamsport (NYP)	SS	.270	37	137	18	37	9	0	2	18	14	28	5	3	.350	.380
	Lakewood (SAL)	LoA	.258	18	66	15	17	3	1	1	6	6	13	0	1	.315	.379
Minor League Totals			.284	58	215	36	61	13	2	3	28	22	44	6	5	.357	.405

6 JOJO ROMERO, LHP

Born: Sept. 6, 1996. **B-T:** L-L. **Ht.:** 6-0. **Wt.:** 190. **Drafted:** Yavapai (Ariz.) JC, **2016 (4th round). Signed by:** Brad Holland.

Romero was an athletic lefty with an average fastball and a four-pitch mix when the Phillies drafted him in the fourth round in 2016 and signed him for $800,000. In Romero's first full season, improved velocity helped his stock tick up as he cruised through two Class A levels.

After throwing 89-92 mph and touching 94 in college, Romero jumped to 91-94 in 2017 and topped out at 96. An excellent athlete, he repeats his delivery and locates his fastball well to both sides of the plate. Romero's changeup and curveball each earn 55-60 grades on the 20-80 scale, with his changeup the more consistently reliable weapon. He has a fringe-average slider that he mixes in as well to give hitters another look. Romero throws all of his pitches for strikes and is studious in his preparation. He does the little things well, too, with quick feet to hold runners close and field his position.

BA GRADE
55 Risk: High
FB: 55. CB: 55.
SL: 45. CHG: 55.
CTL: 60.

Romero's polish should help him continue to move quickly through the system, with a chance to crack the big league rotation by 2019 and develop into a No. 3 or 4 starter.

Year	Club (League)	Class	W	L	ERA	G	GS	CG	SV	IP	H	HR	BB	SO	K/9	WHIP	AVG
2016	Williamsport (NYP)	SS	2	2	2.56	10	10	1	0	46	44	2	11	31	6.1	1.20	.256
2017	Lakewood (SAL)	LoA	5	1	2.11	13	13	1	0	77	61	2	21	79	9.3	1.07	.223
	Clearwater (FSL)	HiA	5	2	2.24	10	10	0	0	52	43	2	15	49	8.4	1.11	.223
Minor League Totals			12	5	2.27	33	33	2	0	175	148	6	47	159	8.2	1.12	.232

7 JHAILYN ORTIZ, OF

Born: Nov. 18, 1998. **B-T:** R-R. **Ht.:** 6-3. **Wt.:** 250. **Signed:** Dominican Republic, 2015. **Signed by:** Carlos Salas/Franklin Felida.

When Ortiz signed with the Phillies for $4.01 million, he had humongous raw power, but his huge frame and struggles against live pitching concerned other clubs. He still is a big-bodied power hitter, but his improved feel for hitting helped him excel in 2017 as one of the youngest players in the short-season New York-Penn League.

Ortiz's calling card is his raw power, a 70 on the 20-80 scale. He has the bat speed and strength to launch balls deep out of the park to the pull side, but he uses the opposite field well to drive the ball out the other way with ease. Ortiz still gets his weight out too early on his front side at times and his power will always come with a high strikeout rate, but he made major strides with his approach in 2017. He can hammer fastballs, but he also did a better job recognizing offspeed pitches and

BA GRADE
55 Risk: V. High
HIT: 45. POW: 70.
SPD: 40. FLD: 40.
ARM: 60.

staying within the strike zone. Ortiz is built like a first baseman and there is risk he will move there, but moves surprisingly well for his size. His plus arm fits well in right field.

Ortiz is a potential 30-home run slugger who could become a middle-of-the-order hitter. Low Class A Lakewood is his next stop in 2018.

Year	Club (League)	Class	AVG	G	AB	R	H	2B	3B	HR	RBI	BB	SO	SB	CS	OBP	SLG
2016	Phillies (GCL)	R	.231	47	173	29	40	9	1	8	27	17	53	8	2	.325	.434
2017	Williamsport (NYP)	SS	.302	47	159	27	48	15	1	8	30	18	47	5	1	.401	.560
Minor League Totals			.265	94	332	56	88	24	2	16	57	35	100	13	3	.362	.494

8 JORGE ALFARO, C

Born: June 11, 1993. **B-T:** R-R. **Ht.:** 6-2. **Wt.:** 225. **Signed:** Colombia, 2010. **Signed by:** Rodolfo Rosario/Don Welke (Rangers).

Alfaro has tantalized scouts with his combination of power, arm strength and athleticism since signing with the Rangers for $1.3 million out of Colombia. Acquired from Texas at the 2015 trade deadline in the Cole Hamels deal, Alfaro has not put it all together yet. A disappointing 2017 season in Triple-A Lehigh Valley underscores that point, though he performed well once he reached the big leagues in August.

Alfaro's game is built around his strength. He has a fast bat and plus-plus raw power to go deep to any part of the park. He doesn't fully tap into his power in games, however, in part due to his free-swinging approach. Alfaro doesn't recognize offspeed pitches well and frequently expands the strike zone. His strikeout rate jumped to 32 percent in Triple-A and he rarely walks, so he will never be a high on-base threat. Alfaro has gotten bigger, and has below-average speed, but he still moves well for a catcher. His arm is well above-average, though his blocking and receiving need improvement.

Alfaro's power could carry him to an everyday role, but he must improve his pitch selectivity and clean up his receiving to get to that level.

BA GRADE
45 Risk: Medium
HIT: 40. POW: 70.
SPD: 40. FLD: 40.
ARM: 70.

Year	Club (League)	Class	AVG	G	AB	R	H	2B	3B	HR	RBI	BB	SO	SB	CS	OBP	SLG
2015	Frisco (TL)	AA	.253	49	190	22	48	15	2	5	21	9	61	2	1	.314	.432
	Phillies (GCL)	R	.500	3	4	0	2	1	0	0	1	0	0	0	0	.667	.750
2016	Reading (EL)	AA	.285	97	404	68	115	21	2	15	67	22	105	3	2	.325	.458
	Philadelphia (NL)	MAJ	.125	6	16	0	2	0	0	0	0	1	8	0	0	.176	.125
2017	Lehigh Valley (IL)	AAA	.241	84	324	34	78	13	2	7	43	16	113	1	1	.291	.358
	Philadelphia (NL)	MAJ	.318	29	107	12	34	6	0	5	14	3	33	0	0	.360	.514
Major League Totals			.293	35	123	12	36	6	0	5	14	4	41	0	0	.336	.463
Minor League Totals			.262	634	2416	347	634	135	20	74	360	133	710	39	19	.321	.427

9 MICKEY MONIAK, OF

Born: May 13, 1998. **B-T:** L-R. **Ht.:** 6-2. **Wt.:** 185. **Drafted:** HS—Carlsbad, Calif., 2016 (1st round). **Signed by:** Mike Garcia.

Moniak was the No. 1 overall pick in the 2016 draft and signed for $6.1 million. His first full season in pro ball was a disappointment, however. He held his own at low Class A Lakewood the first two months before going into a tailspin the rest of the year.

Moniak is a tricky player to project given his struggles. He still earns praise from scouts for his easy, simple swing that is direct to the ball with a good bat path. He got himself into trouble by getting away from a selective hitting approach and instead rolled over a lot of easy ground balls to the right side of the infield. Moniak will need to get stronger, both to handle the rigors of a full season and to add to his power, which for now is mostly limited to the gaps. An above-average runner, he drew mixed reviews for his defense in center field. He at times made good plays with a gliding stride and an above-average arm, though other scouts questioned his reads and routes.

Moniak's development will require more patience than originally anticipated, but his underlying talent suggests he can be an above-average big leaguer. There's just considerably higher risk of him tapping into that potential, so 2018 will be key for him to show that his full-season debut was more fluke than anything.

BA GRADE
50 Risk: High
HIT: 55. POW: 40.
SPD: 60. FLD: 50.
ARM: 60.

Year	Club (League)	Class	AVG	G	AB	R	H	2B	3B	HR	RBI	BB	SO	SB	CS	OBP	SLG
2016	Phillies (GCL)	R	.284	46	176	27	50	11	4	1	28	11	35	10	4	.340	.409
2017	Lakewood (SAL)	LoA	.236	123	466	53	110	22	6	5	44	28	109	11	7	.284	.341
Minor League Totals			.249	169	642	80	160	33	10	6	72	39	144	21	11	.300	.360

10 FRANKLYN KILOME, RHP

Born: June 25, 1995. **B-T:** R-R. **Ht.:** 6-6. **Wt.:** 220. **Signed:** Dominican Republic, 2013. **Signed by:** Koby Perez.

The Phillies signed Kilome for $40,000 when he was a tall, skinny 17-year-old with a fast arm. As he packed on weight and made mechanical changes, he grew into a power arm who finished 2017 in Double-A Reading after an August promotion.

Kilome's fastball gets on hitters quickly thanks to his extension, downhill plane and velocity that sits 93-96 mph and peaks at 99. He throws a power four-seam fastball, but he added a two-seamer to his repertoire in 2017 to help him induce weak, early-count contact to give him a chance to pitch deeper in games. One drawback was that Kilome's strikeout rate dropped from 26 percent in 2016 to 19 percent in 2017. He has a tick above-average curveball that he can use as a putaway pitch, but his struggles to coordinate the long levers in his delivery impacts his command and puts him in too many hitter's counts. He also throws a slider that tends to blend into his curveball. Kilome's changeup has shown progress with the Phillies forcing him to throw it more, but it's still a below-average pitch.

Kilome has the potential to be a No. 3 or 4 starter, but to reach that potential he will have to improve his fastball command, increase his swing-and-miss rate and develop his changeup into a more reliable third pitch. He should return to Double-A to start 2018.

BA GRADE
50 Risk: High
FB: 60. CB: 60.
SL: 40. CHG: 40.
CTL: 50.

Year	Club (League)	Class	W	L	ERA	G	GS	CG	SV	IP	H	HR	BB	SO	K/9	WHIP	AVG
2015	Williamsport (NYP)	SS	3	2	3.28	11	11	0	0	49	41	1	21	36	6.6	1.26	.230
2016	Lakewood (SAL)	LoA	5	8	3.85	23	23	0	0	115	113	6	50	130	10.2	1.42	.259
2017	Clearwater (FSL)	HiA	6	4	2.59	19	19	0	0	97	96	5	37	83	7.7	1.37	.265
	Reading (EL)	AA	1	3	3.64	5	5	0	0	30	25	2	15	20	6.1	1.35	.238
Minor League Totals			18	18	3.29	69	66	0	0	331	311	16	134	294	8.0	1.34	.252

11 RANGER SUAREZ, LHP

BA GRADE
50 Risk: High

Born: Aug. 26, 1995. **B-T:** L-L. **Ht.:** 6-1. **Wt.:** 190. **Signed:** Venezuela, 2012. **Signed by:** Jesus Mendez.

A $25,000 signing out of Venezuela as a 16-year-old, Suarez early became known for his control and pitchability, but looked like more of a smoke-and-mirrors pitcher with an upper-80s fastball. In 2017, his velocity jumped, his strikeout rate increased and he moved through two levels in his first year of full-season ball.

Suarez showed more zip on his fastball in 2017, sitting in the low 90s and touching 95 mph. He incorporated his legs more in his delivery, which helped him use his whole body to generate more power. He doesn't have a true out pitch among his secondary offerings, but they're all average or near-average across the board, with a slider or curveball that he goes to depending on what's working for him that night. His changeup also improved as he adjusted his hand position, which changed the movement on the pitch from cutting action to a more traditional sink and fade to run away from righthanded hitters. Suarez has control and pitching savvy beyond his years, with the ability to read swings, set hitters up and throw any pitch in any count. He's a good athlete who controls the running game well with a quick pickoff move.

Suarez should continue to move quickly and projects as a back-end starter.

Year	Club (League)	Class	W	L	ERA	G	GS	CG	SV	IP	H	HR	BB	SO	K/9	WHIP	AVG
2015	Phillies (GCL)	R	3	0	0.65	6	4	0	0	28	15	0	4	20	6.5	0.69	.158
2016	Williamsport (NYP)	SS	6	4	2.81	13	13	2	0	74	61	4	24	53	6.5	1.15	.223
2017	Lakewood (SAL)	LoA	6	2	1.59	14	14	1	0	85	52	4	24	90	9.5	0.89	.177
	Clearwater (FSL)	HiA	2	4	3.82	8	8	0	0	38	43	1	11	38	9.1	1.43	.293
Minor League Totals			22	14	2.09	66	54	3	3	327	258	13	67	296	8.2	0.99	.214

12 SERANTHONY DOMINGUEZ, RHP

BA GRADE
50 Risk: High

Born: Nov. 25, 1994. **B-T:** R-R. **Ht.:** 6-1. **Wt.:** 195. **Signed:** Dominican Republic, 2011. **Signed by:** Koby Perez.

On pure upside, Dominguez could rank higher on this list, but arm problems have slowed his progress and created more risk to his profile. He showed one of the most electric arms early in the high Class A Florida State League season in 2017, but in mid-May he went on the disabled list with shoulder tightness and missed two months. When he returned, some scouts thought he looked gassed, while others thought he looked tentative coming back from rehab.

At his best, Dominguez overpowers hitters with a fastball that sits at 94-96 mph with late movement and reaches 99. His fastball command improved in 2017 and he showed the ability to locate that pitch down in the strike zone early in the season. His slider took a step forward, and while it still flattens out on him at times, it's often an above-average pitch that misses bats. He's a four-pitch guy with an average curveball and a changeup that flashes as another above-average offering at times.

Dominguez has the stuff to be a midrotation starter, but he's 23 and his career-high workload is 76 innings, so his durability is a question mark and he could be a better fit as a late-inning reliever. Double-A Reading is his next step in 2018.

Year	Club (League)	Class	W	L	ERA	G	GS	CG	SV	IP	H	HR	BB	SO	K/9	WHIP	AVG
2015	Phillies (GCL)	R	1	1	2.35	2	1	0	0	8	6	1	7	9	10.6	1.70	.207
2016	Williamsport (NYP)	SS	1	1	2.12	3	3	0	0	17	8	0	4	15	7.9	0.71	.136
	Lakewood (SAL)	LoA	5	2	2.42	10	10	0	0	48	34	2	20	50	9.3	1.12	.202
2017	Phillies (GCL)	R	0	0	5.06	2	2	0	0	5	5	0	4	7	11.8	1.69	.250
	Clearwater (FSL)	HiA	4	4	3.61	15	13	0	0	62	51	6	30	75	10.8	1.30	.230
Minor League Totals			21	20	3.11	75	54	2	0	310	253	16	135	278	8.1	1.25	.225

13 ROMAN QUINN, OF

BA GRADE

45 Risk: Medium

Born: May 14, 1993. **B-T:** B-R. **Ht.:** 5-9. **Wt.:** 170. **Drafted:** HS—Port St. Joe, Fla., 2011 (2nd round). **Signed by:** Aaron Jersild.

Quinn's list of injuries could take up his full report. He's been one of the most frustrating prospects in the organization, because he's an outstanding athlete with premium speed in the middle of the diamond but struggles to stay on the field. In 2017, Quinn played through May 28, when he suffered a UCL injury to his left (non-throwing) elbow and missed the remainder of the season but didn't require surgery.

Wrist, leg and oblique injuries in previous seasons have prevented Quinn from ever playing more than 100 games in a season. When he's healthy, he's a 80 runner with excellent range and a plus arm in center field. Quinn's power is mostly to the gaps, but he has enough pop to sneak out 8-12 home runs per year. His strikeout rate has climbed at the upper levels, but he has solid enough contact skills with the speed to help him leg out extra hits.

Quinn has the upside to be an everyday center fielder, but his profile combined with his medical history make a fourth outfielder outcome more likely.

Year	Club (League)	Class	AVG	G	AB	R	H	2B	3B	HR	RBI	BB	SO	SB	CS	OBP	SLG
2015	Reading (EL)	AA	.306	58	232	44	71	6	6	4	15	18	42	29	10	.356	.435
2016	Phillies (GCL)	R	.500	6	22	6	11	2	0	0	0	1	3	5	1	.522	.591
	Reading (EL)	AA	.287	71	286	58	82	14	6	6	25	30	68	31	8	.361	.441
	Philadelphia (NL)	MAJ	.263	15	57	10	15	4	0	0	6	8	19	5	1	.373	.333
2017	Lehigh Valley (IL)	AAA	.274	45	175	24	48	8	3	2	13	18	49	10	4	.344	.389
Major League Totals			.263	15	57	10	15	4	0	0	6	8	19	5	1	.373	.333
Minor League Totals			.276	401	1569	276	433	56	32	25	133	158	367	169	50	.352	.400

14 SIMON MUZZIOTTI, OF

BA GRADE

55 Risk: Extreme

Born: Dec. 27, 1998. **B-T:** L-L. **Ht.:** 6-1. **Wt.:** 175. **Signed:** Venezuela, 2016. **Signed by:** Claudio Scerrato.

Muzziotti signed with the Red Sox for $300,000 in 2015 and played for their Dominican Summer League team the following year before Major League Baseball removed him and four other Venezuelan players from the organization as a penalty for the Red Sox signing players in package deals. He kept his original signing bonus and signed with the Phillies for $750,000 in 2016, then made a strong impression on scouts around the Rookie-level Gulf Coast League in 2017.

Muzziotti has outstanding hand-eye coordination and bat control, which enables him to square up pitches in all quadrants of the strike zone and leads to a high contact rate. He can put the bat to the ball even on pitches outside the zone, so a more selective approach will help him as he learns to swing at more pitches he can damage. He's a line-drive hitter who uses all fields but doesn't have much power yet. Muzziotti glides around center field with plus speed. He gets good jumps off the bat and ranges well to both sides and on balls over his head. He has a strong arm that has improved since an elbow injury hampered him as an amateur.

Muzziotti still needs to get stronger, but he has the upside to be an everyday center fielder with impact potential on both sides of the ball.

Year	Club (League)	Class	AVG	G	AB	R	H	2B	3B	HR	RBI	BB	SO	SB	CS	OBP	SLG
2016	Red Sox (DSL)	R	.317	17	60	9	19	2	1	0	10	4	6	1	1	.354	.383
	Phillies (DSL)	R	.231	37	143	12	33	4	1	0	12	11	10	7	3	.286	.273
2017	Clearwater (FSL)	HiA	.286	2	7	2	2	0	0	0	0	0	2	1	0	.286	.286
	Phillies (GCL)	R	.269	33	134	20	36	4	6	0	14	7	8	8	3	.305	.388
Minor League Totals			.262	89	344	43	90	10	8	0	36	22	26	17	7	.305	.337

15 JONATHAN GUZMAN, SS

BA GRADE
55 Risk: Extreme

Born: Aug. 17, 1999. **B-T:** R-R. **Ht.:** 6-0. **Wt.:** 160. **Signed:** Dominican Republic, 2015. **Signed by:** Carlos Salas.

After Guzman signed for $60,000 on his 16th birthday, the Phillies quickly realized they got a bargain. He hit well in his pro debut in the Dominican Summer League in 2016, then in 2017 hit well during extended spring training and was batting .319/.364/.458 in the Rookie-level Gulf Coast League in late July before fading down the stretch. He played most of the season as a 17-year-old.

Guzman is an instinctive shortstop with a high baseball IQ. He's an average runner who reads the ball well off the bat, has good range to both sides and charges in well on slow rollers with an above-average arm. He has soft hands at shortstop and also uses them well in the batter's box. He has good plate coverage, making frequent contact to put the ball in play at a high clip. He has shown a good approach at times, though by the end of the year he began chasing more pitches off the plate. Guzman has minimal power and probably won't ever hit many home runs, but he will need to get stronger after fatigue took a toll on his bat speed by the end of the year.

Guzman will play nearly all of 2018 as an 18-year-old, probably at short-season Williamsport.

Year	Club (League)	Class	AVG	G	AB	R	H	2B	3B	HR	RBI	BB	SO	SB	CS	OBP	SLG
2016	Phillies (DSL)	R	.300	64	240	27	72	11	0	0	13	21	25	13	13	.370	.346
2017	Clearwater (FSL)	HiA	.000	1	3	0	0	0	0	0	0	0	3	0	0	.000	.000
	Williamsport (NYP)	SS	.263	6	19	2	5	0	0	1	2	4	3	0	1	.391	.421
	Phillies (GCL)	R	.248	38	153	17	38	4	2	1	13	11	24	5	1	.299	.320
Minor League Totals			.277	109	415	46	115	15	2	2	28	36	55	18	15	.343	.337

16 FRANCISCO MORALES, RHP

BA GRADE
55 Risk: Extreme

Born: Oct. 27, 1999. **B-T:** R-R. **Ht.:** 6-5. **Wt.:** 220. **Signed:** Venezuela, 2016. **Signed by:** Jesus Mendez.

Morales was one of the top international amateur pitchers in 2016, when he signed with the Phillies for $720,000. The Phillies pushed him straight to the U.S. for his pro debut and he pitched well in the Rookie-level Gulf Coast League in 2017.

Morales has a huge frame with broad shoulders and long, lanky limbs, attacking hitters with downhill angle and good extension on a fastball that parks at 90-94 mph and touches 96. He offers physical projection, too, so he could continue to add velocity. His slider flashes as a plus pitch with late, sharp break. He has shown feel for a changeup that could become a reliable pitch once he throws it more frequently, so developing the changeup was a focal point for him during instructional league. Morales shows the ability to mix his pitches and set up hitters, though he will need to improve his fastball command.

Morales is ahead of where fellow big-bodied Phillies righthander Franklyn Kilome was at the same stage and has the stuff to develop into a mid-rotation starter, with a chance for more.

Year	Club (League)	Class	W	L	ERA	G	GS	CG	SV	IP	H	HR	BB	SO	K/9	WHIP	AVG
2017	Phillies (GCL)	R	3	2	3.05	10	9	0	0	41	34	1	20	44	9.6	1.31	.225
Minor League Totals			3	2	3.05	10	9	0	0	41	34	1	20	44	9.6	1.31	.225

17 LUIS GARCIA, SS

BA GRADE
55 Risk: Extreme

Born: Oct. 1, 2000. **B-T:** B-R. **Ht.:** 5-10. **Wt.:** 170. **Signed:** Dominican Republic, 2017. **Signed by:** Bernardo Perez.

Garcia stood out early in the scouting process as one of the top international prospects in the 2017 class, then signed with the Phillies for $2.5 million when the signing period opened on July 2.

Garcia is a smooth-fielding shortstop with slick defensive actions. His body is more compact than the typical wiry shortstops his age, but he was one of the best defensive shortstops in the 2017 class. A solid-average runner, he is light on his feet with quick, soft hands. He can make the flashy barehanded play but he's also a fundamentally sound player for his age and has a plus arm. Garcia's biggest believers saw him as a well-rounded player who could potentially hit toward the top of the lineup, though there was a split camp on his offensive upside. He's a switch-hitter whose stroke is better from the left side, but both swings are short and quick. He uses his hands well and hits to all fields, though he doesn't have much power and mostly puts the ball on the ground.

Garcia impressed Phillies coaches at the instructional league with his feel for the strike zone. He should make his pro debut in 2018 in the Rookie-level Gulf Coast League.

Year	Club (League)	Class	AVG	G	AB	R	H	2B	3B	HR	RBI	BB	SO	SB	CS	OBP	SLG
2017	Did not play—Signed 2018 contract																

18 SPENCER HOWARD, RHP

BA GRADE
50 Risk: High

Born: July 28, 1996. **B-T:** R-R. **Ht.:** 6-3. **Wt.:** 205. **Drafted:** Cal Poly, 2017 (2nd round). **Signed by:** Shane Bowers.

Howard was going to play club baseball at Cal Poly, but he made the varsity team as a walk-on after a fall tryout with a mid-80s fastball. He bulked up, added more zip to his fastball and moved from the bullpen to a starting role to develop into a second-round pick in 2017, signing for $1.15 million.

Howard attacks hitters inside aggressively with his fastball, which is his best pitch. He sits at 91-94 mph and touches 96, getting swinging strikes in the strike zone thanks to the late finish on the pitch. Howard has a solid-average slider with good depth that he can use to miss bats, along with a below-average changeup. He has a good delivery and threw a lot of strikes in college, though he was more erratic with his control in his pro debut.

Howard will go to one of the Phillies' Class A affiliates in 2018, likely low Class A Lakewood.

Year	Club (League)	Class	W	L	ERA	G	GS	CG	SV	IP	H	HR	BB	SO	K/9	WHIP	AVG
2017	Williamsport (NYP)	SS	1	1	4.45	9	9	0	0	28	22	0	18	40	12.7	1.41	.214
Minor League Totals			1	1	4.45	9	9	0	0	28	22	0	18	40	12.7	1.41	.214

19 VICTOR ARANO, RHP

BA GRADE
45 Risk: Medium

Born: Feb. 7, 1995. **B-T:** R-R. **Ht.:** 6-2. **Wt.:** 200. **Signed:** Mexico, 2013. **Signed by:** Mike Brito/Pat Kelly (Dodgers).

Arano signed with the Dodgers in 2013, then in August 2014 went to the Phillies along with second baseman Jesmuel Valentin in the trade for righthander Roberto Hernandez. The Phillies moved Arano to the bullpen in 2016 and he took off in that role. In 2017, elbow soreness kept Arano on the disabled list until the end of May, then he pitched well in his major league debut as a September callup.

Arano has a diverse repertoire from his days as a starter, but as a reliever he's mainly a two-pitch guy. His fastball sits at 93-95 mph and can touch 96. He mixes two-seamers and four-seamers with the ability to get swings and misses up in the zone. Arano leans heavily on his plus slider, throwing it even more frequently than his fastball when he got to the big leagues. It's an 83-85 mph pitch that he can bury down in the zone and get hitters to chase off the plate with sharp break and two-plane depth. He sprinkles in an occasional changeup and a rare curveball, but he mostly throws fastballs and sliders in relief.

Arano throws strikes and misses a lot of bats, which gives him a chance to pitch high-leverage innings. He should open 2018 in Philadelphia's bullpen, where he has a chance to be one of their best relievers.

Year	Club (League)	Class	W	L	ERA	G	GS	CG	SV	IP	H	HR	BB	SO	K/9	WHIP	AVG
2015	Clearwater (FSL)	HiA	4	12	4.72	24	22	1	0	124	131	7	26	69	5.0	1.27	.276
2016	Clearwater (FSL)	HiA	4	1	2.29	35	0	0	4	63	52	4	15	71	10.1	1.06	.222
	Reading (EL)	AA	1	1	2.16	11	0	0	1	17	11	2	4	24	13.0	0.90	.177
2017	Reading (EL)	AA	1	2	4.19	32	0	0	9	39	39	7	11	38	8.8	1.29	.264
	Philadelphia (NL)	MAJ	1	0	1.69	10	0	0	0	11	6	0	4	13	11.0	0.94	.158
Major League Totals			1	0	1.69	10	0	0	0	11	6	0	4	13	11.0	0.94	.158
Minor League Totals			17	25	3.93	137	45	1	17	378	373	35	89	334	8.0	1.22	.255

20 ARQUIMEDES GAMBOA, SS

BA GRADE
50 Risk: V. High

Born: Sept. 23, 1997. **B-T:** B-R. **Ht.:** 6-0. **Wt.:** 175. **Signed:** Venezuela, 2014. **Signed by:** Carlos Salas.

Gamboa was a big international prospect in 2014, when he signed with the Phillies for $900,000. Little went right for him on the field his first two seasons, but he showed signs of life in 2017 and played his best baseball at the end of the season, batting .327/.364/.531 at low Class A Lakewood from Aug. 1 to the end of the season, a span of 25 games.

Gamboa is an athletic shortstop who projects to stick at the position with a pair of plus tools in his speed and arm strength. He's a switch-hitter with a far more advanced swing from the left side, where he batted .274/.344/.416 with 25 walks and 29 strikeouts in 247 plate appearances compared to .227/.286/.284 in 98 plate appearances righthanded. His lefty swing has better rhythm, balance and timing than his righthanded stroke, though the Phillies plan to let him continue switch-hitting. Gamboa has more strength projection than some of the other young Phillies shortstops in the system, with enough power to occasionally sneak a ball out to his pull side, but he probably won't ever be a big power threat.

Gamboa flashed signals of breakout potential in 2017 and could carry that over into the 2018 season.

Year	Club (League)	Class	AVG	G	AB	R	H	2B	3B	HR	RBI	BB	SO	SB	CS	OBP	SLG
2015	Phillies (GCL)	R	.189	50	190	23	36	7	3	0	16	15	50	8	2	.252	.258
2016	Williamsport (NYP)	SS	.200	35	130	15	26	6	0	2	15	9	28	5	1	.254	.292
2017	Lakewood (SAL)	LoA	.261	79	307	44	80	12	3	6	29	33	52	8	0	.328	.378
Minor League Totals			.226	164	627	82	142	25	6	8	60	57	130	21	3	.290	.324

21 DANIEL BRITO, 2B

BA GRADE **50** Risk: V. High

Born: Jan. 23, 1998. **B-T:** L-R. **Ht.:** 6-1. **Wt.:** 165. **Signed:** Venezuela, 2014.
Signed by: Carlos Salas.

Signed for $650,000 as a 16-year-old in 2014, Brito looked like he was in the midst of a breakthrough season early in 2017. By the end of April at low Class A Lakewood, he was hitting .327/.377/.449, but his performance cratered the rest of the season.

Brito has the ingredients to be a good hitter. He uses his hands well at the plate with a loose, fluid stroke and good bat speed. He started to grow into more power in 2017, which may have gotten him into trouble as he got away from his usually sound approach in an attempt to show off that pop. Instead of keeping his weight back and using the whole field, Brito became more pull-conscious, trying to yank pitches on the outer third that led to a lot of ground outs to the right side. He could rebound if he gets back to his line-drive, all-fields approach. Brito is an average defender at second base with a chance to be a tick better. His speed and arm strength are both average tools and he does a good job turning double plays.

Repeating low Class A Lakewood is a possibility for Brito in 2018.

Year	Club (League)	Class	AVG	G	AB	R	H	2B	3B	HR	RBI	BB	SO	SB	CS	OBP	SLG
2015	Phillies (DSL)	R	.269	60	212	33	57	10	3	0	19	35	22	8	9	.383	.344
2016	Phillies (GCL)	R	.284	47	190	35	54	10	5	2	25	21	27	7	2	.355	.421
2017	Lakewood (SAL)	LoA	.239	112	447	54	107	15	1	6	32	33	95	12	9	.298	.318
Minor League Totals			.257	219	849	122	218	35	9	8	76	89	144	27	20	.333	.347

22 KYLE YOUNG, LHP

BA GRADE **50** Risk: V. High

Born: Dec. 2, 1997. **B-T:** L-L. **Ht.:** 6-10. **Wt.:** 223. **Drafted:** HS—Oyster Bay, N.Y., 2016 (22nd round). **Signed by:** Alex Agostino.

Young was going to pitch at Hofstra, but the Phillies signed him for $225,000 in the 22nd round of the 2016 draft. Young stayed back in extended spring training in 2017 before joining short-season Williamsport and was one of the best pitchers in the New York-Penn League.

At 6-foot-10, Young has the size of an NBA center but the body control of a point guard. It's often a struggle for pitchers as tall as Young to sync up the long levers in their deliveries, but he easily repeats his mechanics and throws strikes at a high rate. He commands his fastball well, though he sits at just 88-90 mph and touches 93 with a mix of four- and two-seamers. His fastball plays up because he gets great extension to releases the ball closer to the plate, and there's physical projection left for him to throw harder as he gets stronger. Young's slider improved to flash as an average pitch. It's still inconsistent, but he shows the ability to manipulate the shape of his slider to make it bigger or tighter depending on whether he wants to land it for a strike or use it as a chase pitch. He needs to improve his below-average changeup.

Young is ticketed for low Class A Lakewood in 2018 and could take a big step forward if he adds more power to his stuff.

Year	Club (League)	Class	W	L	ERA	G	GS	CG	SV	IP	H	HR	BB	SO	K/9	WHIP	AVG
2016	Phillies (GCL)	R	3	0	2.67	9	2	0	0	27	23	0	2	19	6.3	0.93	.228
2017	Williamsport (NYP)	SS	7	2	2.77	13	13	0	0	65	58	1	15	72	10.0	1.12	.237
Minor League Totals			10	2	2.74	22	15	0	0	92	81	1	17	91	8.9	1.07	.234

23 CORNELIUS RANDOLPH, OF

BA GRADE **45** Risk: High

Born: June 2, 1997. **B-T:** L-R. **Ht.:** 5-11. **Wt.:** 205. **Drafted:** HS—Griffin, Ga., 2015 (1st round). **Signed by:** Aaron Jersild.

The Phillies loved Randolph's bat when they drafted him with the 10th overall pick in 2015. While he's shown it in flashes, he hasn't quite put it all together yet to hit like they had hoped.

With a strong, stocky frame, Randolph entered pro ball with a hit-over-power profile. He stays inside the ball well with an approach geared toward going the opposite way. He has average raw power but didn't show it much in games, so he made an effort to get his contact point more out front in an attempt to pull the ball with more authority. Randolph did show more game power, though his strikeout rate jumped with it and his overall production was modest as he seemed caught in between with his approach. Randolph's lack of speed and arm strength limit him to left field, where his defense has improved but is

still below-average. Finding the right balance of contact and power will be key for Randolph to show he can produce at a high enough level to be an everyday left fielder.

Randolph is ticketed for Double-A Reading in 2018.

Year	Club (League)	Class	AVG	G	AB	R	H	2B	3B	HR	RBI	BB	SO	SB	CS	OBP	SLG
2015	Phillies (GCL)	R	.302	53	172	34	52	15	3	1	24	32	32	6	5	.425	.442
2016	Phillies (GCL)	R	.077	5	13	1	1	0	0	0	0	2	3	0	0	.200	.077
	Lakewood (SAL)	LoA	.274	63	241	33	66	12	1	2	27	26	57	5	4	.355	.357
2017	Clearwater (FSL)	HiA	.250	122	440	47	110	18	5	13	55	55	125	7	3	.338	.402
Minor League Totals			.264	243	866	115	229	45	9	16	106	115	217	18	12	.359	.393

23 JOSE TAVERAS, RHP

BA GRADE
40 Risk: Medium

Born: Nov. 6, 1993. **B-T:** R-R. **Ht.:** 6-4. **Wt.:** 210. **Signed:** Dominican Republic, 2013. **Signed by:** Koby Perez.

Shortly after he turned 20, Taveras signed with the Phillies for $5,000. He has proven to be a durable strike-thrower who has climbed through the system quickly, including a three-level rise up to Triple-A Lehigh Valley in 2017.

Taveras doesn't have the high-octane stuff to match some of the other electric young arms in the Phillies system, but he fills up the strike zone and messes with hitters' timing effectively. His fastball velocity is below-average at 88-92 mph, but it sneaks up on hitters because he generates tremendous extension and hides the ball well with the way he throws across his body. He locates his fastball well and mixes in a changeup that continues to improve, and it grades out as a plus pitch to get swinging strikes or weak contact by throwing hitters off balance. He will throw any pitch in any count, though his slider is just fringe-average. Taveras is a student of the game, so his intelligence and preparation help him get the most out of his stuff.

Taveras likely returns to Triple-A in 2018, but he should make his major league debut at some point during the season and could carve out a career as a back-end starter.

Year	Club (League)	Class	W	L	ERA	G	GS	CG	SV	IP	H	HR	BB	SO	K/9	WHIP	AVG
2015	Williamsport (NYP)	SS	7	4	3.88	13	13	0	0	63	63	3	21	59	8.5	1.34	.273
2016	Lakewood (SAL)	LoA	8	8	3.28	25	20	1	0	137	116	15	26	154	10.1	1.03	.229
2017	Clearwater (FSL)	HiA	6	4	2.38	16	16	1	0	102	86	13	23	92	8.1	1.07	.228
	Reading (EL)	AA	0	1	3.97	2	2	0	0	11	10	2	1	11	8.7	0.97	.233
	Lehigh Valley (IL)	AAA	3	1	1.32	7	7	0	0	41	26	5	15	37	8.1	1.00	.176
Minor League Totals			32	22	2.56	78	71	3	0	440	362	39	94	423	8.7	1.04	.225

25 ELIEZER ALVAREZ, 2B

BA GRADE
45 Risk: High

Born: Oct. 15, 1994. **B-T:** R-R. **Ht.:** 5-11. **Wt.:** 175. **Signed:** Dominican Republic, 2011. **Signed by:** Rene Rojas/Juan Mercado (Cardinals).

Alvarez broke through with a big year at the plate for the Cardinals in 2016 in the low Class A Midwest League, so he skipped a level and went straight to the Double-A Texas League in 2017. He struggled with the jump, and a high ankle sprain in mid-May kept him out for two months. After the Phillies claimed reliever Juan Nicasio on waivers from the Pirates on Aug. 31, they turned around a week later and flipped him to the Cardinals to get Alvarez.

While Alvarez's stock dropped in 2017, there's still promise he can return to his 2016 form. His strike-out rate jumped from 19 percent in 2016 to 27 percent in 2017, but he has an otherwise strong track record and a simple, balanced swing with an all-fields approach. Alvarez's swing isn't geared for power, so he projects to hit 8-12 home runs. Alvarez is an above-average runner, but his stolen bases were down in 2017 coming back from the ankle injury. Alvarez has a good arm but his hands and footwork need to improve for him to be better than a below-average defender.

Alvarez could make his Phillies system debut at Double-A Reading in 2018.

Year	Club (League)	Class	AVG	G	AB	R	H	2B	3B	HR	RBI	BB	SO	SB	CS	OBP	SLG
2015	Johnson City (APP)	R	.314	52	204	32	64	20	1	2	31	11	32	9	4	.353	.451
2016	Peoria (MWL)	LoA	.323	116	433	70	140	36	6	6	59	53	96	36	15	.404	.476
2017	Cardinals (GCL)	R	.250	7	24	4	6	2	0	1	2	2	3	1	0	.296	.458
	Springfield (TL)	AA	.247	54	186	29	46	11	1	4	26	16	56	8	3	.321	.382
Minor League Totals			.285	323	1158	191	330	82	18	17	155	119	243	73	32	.360	.431

26 J.D. HAMMER, RHP

BA GRADE

45 Risk: High

Born: July 12, 1994. **B-T:** R-R. **Ht.:** 6-3. **Wt.:** 215. **Drafted:** Marshall, 2016 (24th round). **Signed by:** Ed Santa (Rockies).

Hammer was a starter at Marshall but immediately became a reliever after signing with the Rockies for $1,000 as a 24th-round pick in 2016. The Phillies picked him up in 2017 at the trade deadline along with shortstop Jose Gomez and righthander Alejandro Requena for reliever Pat Neshek.

Hammer's move to the bullpen allows teams to play MC Hammer's "U Can't Touch This" when he enters a game, but more important, it helped him to throw harder in short stints. Hammer sits 94-96 mph and touches 99 with a lively, late-moving fastball. His fastball misses bats and so does his sharp slider in the mid-80s, which is why he struck out 38 percent of the batters he faced in 2017. Hammer had a brief spell where he didn't throw strikes in the extreme hitter's environment of high Class A Lancaster, but he's mostly shown good control.

After pitching in the Arizona Fall League in 2017, Hammer should be ready for an assignment to Double-A Reading in 2018.

Year	Club (League)	Class	W	L	ERA	G	GS	CG	SV	IP	H	HR	BB	SO	K/9	WHIP	AVG
2016	Grand Junction (PIO)	R	0	2	3.92	27	0	0	3	44	48	2	11	52	10.7	1.35	.274
2017	Asheville (SAL)	LoA	4	1	1.20	24	0	0	7	30	17	0	5	47	14.1	0.73	.164
	Lancaster (CAL)	HiA	0	1	5.25	12	0	0	6	12	10	0	9	18	13.5	1.58	.227
	Clearwater (FSL)	HiA	2	0	0.57	12	0	0	0	16	8	0	2	20	11.5	0.64	.154
Minor League Totals			6	4	2.75	75	0	0	16	101	83	2	27	137	12.2	1.09	.221

27 TOM ESHELMAN, RHP

BA GRADE

40 Risk: Medium

Born: June 20, 1994. **B-T:** R-R. **Ht.:** 6-3. **Wt.:** 210. **Drafted:** Cal State Fullerton, 2015 (2nd round). **Signed by:** Brad Buzinski (Astros).

The Astros drafted Eshelman with their second-round pick in 2015, then after the season they traded him to the Phillies as part of the return for Ken Giles. In 2017, Eshelman ranked second in the Triple-A International League with a 2.23 ERA.

Few pitchers in the minors can match Eshelman's pinpoint control. He walked just 1.1 batters per nine innings in 2017, because he commands his fastball with precise location to both sides of the plate. He is a finesse pitcher whose entire game is predicated on his ability to hit his spots, since his stuff—including an 87-91 mph fastball that touches 93, along with a curveball and changeup—is fringe-average across the board. His fastball plays better than the radar gun readings because of his ability to command the pitch away from hitters' hot zones, but he doesn't have the stuff to miss bats, which results in a low strikeout rate.

Eshelman bears similarities with former Twins righthander Kevin Slowey and could develop into a similar type of back-end starter. He should make his major league debut at some point in 2018.

Year	Club (League)	Class	W	L	ERA	G	GS	CG	SV	IP	H	HR	BB	SO	K/9	WHIP	AVG
2015	Astros (GCL)	R	0	1	4.50	2	2	0	0	4	3	0	2	3	6.8	1.25	.200
	Quad Cities (MWL)	LoA	0	0	4.26	2	2	0	0	6	9	0	3	5	7.1	1.89	.346
2016	Clearwater (FSL)	HiA	4	2	3.34	11	11	0	0	59	58	7	11	64	9.7	1.16	.251
	Reading (EL)	AA	5	5	5.14	13	13	0	0	61	79	4	17	55	8.1	1.57	.307
2017	Reading (EL)	AA	3	0	3.10	5	5	0	0	29	27	6	5	22	6.8	1.10	.257
	Lehigh Valley (IL)	AAA	10	3	2.23	18	18	3	0	121	101	8	13	80	6.0	0.94	.227
Minor League Totals			22	11	3.27	51	51	3	0	281	277	25	51	229	7.3	1.17	.257

28 EDGAR GARCIA, RHP

BA GRADE

45 Risk: High

Born: Oct. 4, 1996. **B-T:** R-R. **Ht.:** 6-1. **Wt.:** 195. **Signed:** Dominican Republic, 2014. **Signed by:** Carlos Salas.

Garcia rose through the system primarily as a reliever after signing for $30,000 in 2014. He opened 2017 in the high Class A Clearwater bullpen before moving to the rotation in mid-May.

Garcia could still end up in the bullpen, but the Phillies wanted to develop him as a starter to give him more opportunities to pitch off his fastball and develop his changeup. He is a good athlete whose two primary weapons are his fastball and slider. He throws his fastball in the low to mid-90s and finishes hitters with a plus slider. He leaned heavily on his slider in the bullpen, so moving to a starting role forced Garcia to throw his fastball more, and his command of that pitch needs to improve. He rarely threw his changeup in the bullpen, and while he used it more as a starter, it's still a below-average pitch.

Garcia has the stuff to miss bats, but he's still learning touch and feel and how to set up hitters. Double-A Reading is next for Garcia in 2018.

Year	Club (League)	Class	W	L	ERA	G	GS	CG	SV	IP	H	HR	BB	SO	K/9	WHIP	AVG
2015	Phillies (GCL)	R	1	2	3.31	12	2	0	2	33	27	1	8	34	9.4	1.07	.221
2016	Lakewood (SAL)	LoA	4	1	2.80	27	4	0	2	61	59	6	15	59	8.7	1.21	.249
2017	Clearwater (FSL)	HiA	3	4	4.47	27	15	0	0	89	95	10	31	89	9.0	1.42	.271
Minor League Totals			10	7	3.50	78	22	0	6	208	201	17	60	201	8.7	1.25	.249

29 JACOB WAGUESPACK, RHP

BA GRADE
40 Risk: High

Born: Nov. 5, 1993. **B-T:** R-R. **Ht.:** 6-6. **Wt.:** 225. **Signed:** Mississippi, 2015 (NDFA). **Signed by:** Mike Stauffer.

The Pirates drafted Waguespack out of high school in the 37th round in 2012, but instead of signing he went to college to pitch for Mississippi as a reliever. After his junior year, he signed with the Phillies for $25,000 as a nondrafted free agent.

Waguespack didn't do anything to distinguish himself as a prospect until 2017, when his fastball jumped multiple grades and he moved from the bullpen to the rotation at the end of May. He rose two levels during the season, then pitched for Triple-A Lehigh Valley in the playoffs. Coming into the year, Waguespack threw in the low 90s, but in 2017 he was sitting at 91-96 mph and had peaked at 98 mph. He has a huge 6-foot-6 frame but began throwing harder once he started using his legs more in his delivery. He has a variety of offspeed offerings that are below-average to fringe-average pitches, with a slider, cutter, curveball and changeup in his mix. He's a solid strike-thrower but will need to tighten his fastball command.

Waguespack could continue developing as a starter with a chance to pitch in the back of a rotation, and while he had success in that role in 2017, he still might end up back in the bullpen, with a chance to reach Philadelphia by the end of 2018.

Year	Club (League)	Class	W	L	ERA	G	GS	CG	SV	IP	H	HR	BB	SO	K/9	WHIP	AVG
2015	Phillies (GCL)	R	0	0	7.94	4	0	0	0	6	9	0	1	7	11.1	1.76	.375
	Williamsport (NYP)	SS	0	1	0.42	15	0	0	1	21	9	0	8	25	10.5	0.80	.132
2016	Lakewood (SAL)	LoA	4	2	3.52	43	0	0	6	72	75	1	29	72	9.0	1.45	.265
2017	Clearwater (FSL)	HiA	6	5	3.29	24	10	0	1	68	63	3	24	73	9.6	1.27	.245
	Reading (EL)	AA	3	2	3.65	7	6	0	0	37	37	2	16	35	8.5	1.43	.262
Minor League Totals			13	10	3.26	93	16	0	8	204	193	6	78	212	9.4	1.33	.250

30 MAURICIO LLOVERA, RHP

BA GRADE
40 Risk: High

Born: April 17, 1996. **B-T:** R-R. **Ht.:** 5-11. **Wt.:** 200. **Signed:** Venezuela, 2014. **Signed by:** Carlos Salas.

The Phillies have shown a knack for finding under-the-radar pitching prospects in Latin America. They signed Llovera for just $7,500 when he was an 18-year-old in Venezuela, and he's blossomed into one of the hardest throwers in the organization.

A starter his first two years in the minors, Llovera opened 2017 in the bullpen at low Class A Lakewood, usually throwing multi-inning stints. In July he moved to the rotation and continued to blow his high-octane fastballs past hitters, then in the winter pitched out of the bullpen in the Venezuelan League. Llovera has a smaller, compact frame and quick arm to generate fastballs that sit in the mid-90s and can reach 99 mph. He shows feel to spin his breaking pitches, with a hard slider that's an average pitch and a curveball and changeup that are fringe-average.

A lot of scouts think Llovera's future is in the bullpen, since he has a high-effort delivery and tends to overthrow, which costs him control, though the Phillies might keep developing him as a starter during 2018, when he will open with high Class A Clearwater.

Year	Club (League)	Class	W	L	ERA	G	GS	CG	SV	IP	H	HR	BB	SO	K/9	WHIP	AVG
2015	Phillies (VSL)	R	2	4	3.23	11	10	0	0	47	36	1	17	43	8.2	1.12	.209
2016	Phillies (GCL)	R	7	1	1.87	11	10	0	0	53	39	0	12	56	9.5	0.96	.205
2017	Lakewood (SAL)	LoA	2	4	3.35	30	10	0	0	86	81	2	33	94	9.8	1.33	.250
Minor League Totals			11	9	2.90	52	30	0	0	186	156	3	62	193	9.3	1.17	.227

Pittsburgh Pirates

BY DUSTIN DOPIRAK

Pirates general manager Neal Huntington said after the 2015 season that he expected 2016 to be a bridge year to 2017. He clarified later that he wasn't expecting a step back in performance, but simply acknowledging that the team was in the midst of altering its core. His hope and belief, he said, was that the new cast of characters, most of them homegrown, would be just as successful as the group that snapped the Pirates' record streak of 20 straight losing seasons with three straight playoff appearances and a combined 280 regular season wins from 2013 through 2015.

But the bridge year was bad, the season on the other side of the bridge was worse, and the future doesn't look nearly as bright for the new core as the Pirates hoped it would. After a 78-83 finish in 2016, the Pirates went 75-87 in a 2017 marred by injuries.

Despite the regression, the Pirates decided to stay the course with Huntington and manager Clint Hurdle, who both got four-year contract extensions through the 2021 season. Huntington has been with the organization since 2007 and Hurdle since 2011, so they were responsible for the franchise's rise, but are also culpable for its recent stumble.

It was a disappointing year for a number of homegrown players who were considered the pride of the player development system, and who the GM expected to make up the franchise's new core.

Chief among the disappointments was Tyler Glasnow, a 6-foot-8 righthander expected to be a centerpiece of the Pirates' future rotations. Glasnow earned the No. 5 spot in the rotation out of spring training, but was sent down in June with a 7.45 ERA. He dominated in Triple-A, but had the same control problems when he returned to the majors in September, allowing eight earned runs and walking 15 batters in 7.2 innings, raising more questions about his future with the club.

Austin Meadows, the Pirates' top prospect in 2017, started the year at Triple-A, but played just half a season due to injuries.

There were, however, important bright spots. First baseman Josh Bell's rookie season suggested that he's the middle-of-the-order bat that the Pirates will build their future around. He tied the franchise's rookie record with 26 home runs, led the team with 90 RBIs and finished second in slugging, putting together a campaign that might have been National League Rookie of the Year worthy if not for Cody Bellinger's dominance.

Trevor Williams, who entered the season as the Pirates' No. 14 prospect, provided a pleasant surprise, starting the year in the bullpen before win-

First baseman Josh Bell set a rookie record for switch-hitters by hitting 26 home runs.

PROJECTED 2021 LINEUP

Catcher	Elias Diaz (30)
First Base	Josh Bell (28)
Second Base	Cole Tucker (24)
Third Base	Ke'Bryan Hayes (24)
Shortstop	Kevin Newman (27)
Left Field	Austin Meadows (26)
Center Field	Starling Marte (32)
Right Field	Gregory Polanco (29)
No. 1 Starter	Jameson Taillon (29)
No. 2 Starter	Mitch Keller (25)
No. 3 Starter	Tyler Glasnow (27)
No. 4 Starter	Trevor Williams (29)
No. 5 Starter	Chad Kuhl (28)
Closer	Felipe Rivero (29)

ning a job in the rotation and becoming arguably the Pirates' most consistent starter.

Elias Diaz, the No. 10 prospect, hit just .223 but appears primed to be Pittsburgh's catcher of the future. Jose Osuna, last year's No. 26 prospect, became the team's first in-season callup after a strong spring training, and he slugged .428 off the bench to insert himself into the Pirates' future plans.

Triple-A Indianapolis reached the International League playoffs and Double-A Altoona won the Eastern League title, but the Pirates ended the season with just three prospects in the Top 100 Prospects. After back-to-back losing seasons, it's not easy to see where the Pirates' bridge is leading.

PITTSBURGH PIRATES

TOP 2018 ROOKIE: Jordan Luplow, OF: The Pirates went into 2017 without a true fourth outfielder. Luplow's quick maturation could allow him to fill that role.

BREAKOUT PROSPECT: Oneil Cruz, 3B. He's raw but has plenty of power and arm strength. The Pirates were ecstatic to acquire him in the Tony Watson trade with the Dodgers.

SLEEPER: Logan Hill, OF. The 25th-round pick from Troy in 2015 hit 18 home runs in 2017 and slugged .491.

SOURCE OF TOP 30 TALENT

Homegrown	28	Acquired	2
College	7	Trade	2
Junior college	0	Rule 5 draft	0
High school	15	Independent league	0
Nondrafted free agent	0	Free agent/waivers	0
International	6		

LF
Jordan Luplow (13)
Logan Hill
Barrett Barnes

CF
Austin Meadows (2)
Lolo Sanchez (10)
Conner Uselton (15)
Elvis Escobar
Casey Hughston

RF
Calvin Mitchell (14)
Jerrick Suiter
Jordan George
Kevin Krause

3B
Ke'Bryan Hayes (4)
Oneil Cruz (22)
Eric Wood
Dylan Busby

SS
Kevin Newman (5)
Cole Tucker (6)
Stephen Alemais (26)
Adrian Valerio
Alfredo Reyes

2B
Kevin Kramer (12)
Max Moroff (16)
Chris Bostick
Mitchel Tolman

1B
Mason Martin (18)
Will Craig (24)
Edwin Espinal
Carlos Munos

C
Jin-De Jhang
Jacob Stallings
Christian Kelley
Jason Delay

LHP

LHSP	LHRP
Taylor Hearn (9)	Jared Lakind
Brandon Waddell (19)	Blake Weimar
Braeden Ogle (20)	Sean Keselica
Domingo Robles	
Cody Dickson	
Ike Schlabach	
Austin Coley	
Cam Vieaux	

RHP

RHSP	RHRP
Mitch Keller (1)	Dovydas Neverauskas (17)
Shane Baz (3)	Edgar Santana (23)
Luis Escobar (7)	Nick Burdi (25)
Nick Kingham (8)	Yeudy Garcia (26)
Steven Jennings (11)	Jordan Milbrath
Clay Holmes (21)	Tate Scioneaux
Gage Hinsz (27)	Montana DuRupau
Tyler Eppler (29)	Miguel Rosario
Travis MacGregor	
Max Kranick	
J.T. Brubaker	
Tanner Anderson	
Alex McRae	
Pedro Vasquez	

DRAFT ANALYSIS

2017

BEST PURE HITTER: OF Calvin Mitchell (2) is a bat-first left fielder with a loose, fluid swing and an advanced ability to drive the ball to the opposite field. There are questions about his power potential, but he should hit for average and get on base.

BEST POWER HITTER: OF Conner Uselton (2s) has a significant load to his swing that may affect his hit tool, but it also helps him generate plus raw power. OF Mason Martin (17) also has raw power and showed productive power in his pro debut, hitting 11 home runs—four more than anyone else in the Rookie-level Gulf Coast League.

FASTEST RUNNER: OF Jared Oliva (7) is a plus runner. He swiped 15 bags in 19 attempts in his pro debut at short-season West Virginia.

BEST DEFENSIVE PLAYER: C Jason Delay (4) faces questions about his bat, but he's a very polished receiver who caught plenty of elite arms as Vanderbilt's catcher. He's a smooth receiver, excellent blocker and has an above-average arm.

BEST FASTBALL: RHP Shane Baz (1) had one of the best fastballs in this draft's prep pitching class. His arm is extremely quick and helps him fire 93-96 mph fastballs regularly, and he's touched 98.

BEST SECONDARY PITCH: Baz's slider or curveball both show plus potential. LHP Blake Weiman (8) has flashed a plus slider as well, as it played up in a move to the bullpen for Kansas and then short-season West Virginia.

BEST PRO DEBUT: Martin was the MVP of the GCL, leading the league in home runs (11), on-base percentage (.457) and slugging percentage (.637). 2B Tristan Gray (13) showed promising power as he hit .269/.329/.486 for short-season West Virginia and tied for the New York-Penn League lead with 25 extra-base hits.

BEST ATHLETE: Uselton was the quarterback for his high school team before giving up football to focus on baseball. His 6-foot-3, 185-pound frame portends future weight and strength gains, but he's

TOP DRAFT PICKS OF THE DECADE

Year	Player, Pos.	2017 Org
2008	Pedro Alvarez, 3B	Orioles
2009	Tony Sanchez, C	Braves
2010	Jameson Taillon, RHP	Pirates
2011	Gerrit Cole, RHP	Pirates
2012	*Mark Appel, RHP	Phillies
2013	Austin Meadows, OF	Pirates
2014	Cole Tucker, SS	Pirates
2015	Kevin Newman, SS	Pirates
2016	Will Craig, 3B	Pirates
2017	Shane Baz, RHP	Pirates

*Did not sign.

still an above-average runner with solid body control. Baz and RHP Steven Jennings (2), also a prep quarterback, are also excellent athletes.

MOST INTRIGUING BACKGROUND: Oliva didn't start for his high school team, but he walked on at Arizona and he turned himself into one of the better hitters in its lineup. C Deon Stafford (5), raised by his grandmother, has overcome a difficult childhood in which both parents were addicted to drugs and has become an ardent volunteer in cancer-related charities after the disease claimed his grandfather.

CLOSEST TO THE MAJORS: Weiman has above-average control that could allow him to move relatively quickly as a lefty reliever.

BEST LATE-ROUND PICK: The Pirates did a good job figuring out signability with Martin, who slid to the 17th round, but the promising high school hitter received $350,000, the sixth-highest bonus the club handed out. Gray seemed to blossom as a pro after he focused on one position; he'd played multiple spots at Rice. Scouts like his swing and see him as a useful middle infielder.

THE ONE WHO GOT AWAY: SS Hunter Wolfe (12) hit .393 at Walters State (Tenn.) JC as a redshirt freshman but opted to head to Tennessee instead. He has a chance to make an immediate impact as a middle infielder.

— J.J. COOPER

2016

1B Will Craig (1) has yet to tap into his power in pro ball, raising concerns after his first full season. LHP Braeden Ogle (4) has been encouraging in Rookie ball, while RHP Traivs MacGregor (2) struggled at the same level in 2017.

GRADE: C

2015

SS Kevin Newman (1) is closing in on the big leagues, but questions remain about how much impact he'll provide. 2B Kevin Kramer (2) isn't far behind Newman, and 3B Ke'Bryan Hayes (1) continues to offer upside.

GRADE: B

2014

RHP Mitch Keller (2) has become one of the top pitching prospects in baseball and is the pick of a strong class. SS Cole Tucker (1) made a jump offensively in 2017 and reached Double-A. OF Jordan Luplow (3) made his big league debut.

GRADE: A

1 MITCH KELLER, RHP

Born: April 4, 1996. **B-T:** R-R. **Ht.:** 6-3. **Wt.:** 195.
Drafted: HS—Cedar Rapids, Iowa, 2014 (2nd round).
Signed by: Matt Bimeal.

Keller, whose older brother Jon is a right-hander in the Rockies system, became a major draft prospect between his junior and senior years of high school when he added 10 mph and started hitting the mid-90s at showcase events. He struck out 91 batters in 69 innings as a senior and was committed to North Carolina, but the Pirates selected him in the second round in 2014 and got him on board with a $1 million bonus. Keller started out strong in the Rookie-level Gulf Coast League in 2014 but missed much of 2015 with forearm problems. However, his dominant 2016 campaign at low Class A West Virginia turned him into a priority prospect when he combined swing-and-miss stuff with outstanding command, striking out 131 batters and walking just 18. His rise accelerated in 2017 despite a lower-back injury that cost him several weeks and a shin injury that also cost him time. Keller began the season with high Class A Bradenton and was promoted to Double-A Altoona in August. He pitched a one-hit, 90-pitch shutout in the Eastern League playoffs against Bowie.

Keller has put on muscle to a rangy frame, which allows him to produce easy velocity without overly stressing his arm. His fastball sits 94-96 mph with late life, tilt and armside run. He can hit 99 when he rears back. His fastball command is improving, and he can throw it to all four quadrants against batters on either side of the plate. His heater sets up a big looping curveball with an 11-5 shape with hard downward bite. He still considers his fastball his best pitch, but the Pirates are trying to convince him to trust his curveball. Their next goal is to help him with a developing changeup, which is still an average pitch for him. It has armside run and sink, but he probably needs to take something off because it comes in too close to 90 mph.

Keller projects to be a mid- to top-of-the-rotation starter and could eventually mesh with a big league staff mostly comprised of young, tall righthanders with skill sets similar to his. He will most likely begin 2018 at Altoona, but could find his way to Triple-A Indianapolis by the end of the season. A big league debut in 2019 seems probable.

CLIFF WELCH

BA GRADE	SCOUTING GRADES
65 Risk: Medium	FB: 70. CB: 60. CHG: 50. CTL: 60.

Projected future grades on 20-80 scouting scale

TOP PROSPECTS OF THE DECADE

Year	Player, Pos.	2017 Org
2008	Andrew McCutchen, OF	Pirates
2009	Pedro Alvarez, 3B	Orioles
2010	Pedro Alvarez, 3B	Orioles
2011	Jameson Taillon, RHP	Pirates
2012	Gerrit Cole, RHP	Pirates
2013	Gerrit Cole, RHP	Pirates
2014	Gregory Polanco, OF	Pirates
2015	Tyler Glasnow, RHP	Pirates
2016	Tyler Glasnow, RHP	Pirates
2017	Austin Meadows, OF	Pirates

BEST TOOLS

Best Hitter for Average	Kevin Newman
Best Power Hitter	Jordan Luplow
Best Strike-Zone Discipline	Austin Meadows
Fastest Baserunner	Cole Tucker
Best Athlete	Austin Meadows
Best Fastball	Mitch Keller
Best Curveball	Mitch Keller
Best Slider	Edgar Santana
Best Changeup	Brandon Waddell
Best Control	Mitch Keller
Best Defensive Catcher	Christian Kelley
Best Defensive Infielder	Ke'Bryan Hayes
Best Infield Arm	Oneil Cruz
Best Defensive Outfielder	Casey Hughston
Best Outfield Arm	Jordan Luplow

Year	Club (League)	Class	W	L	ERA	G	GS	CG	SV	IP	H	HR	BB	SO	K/9	WHIP	AVG
2015	Bristol (APP)	R	0	3	5.49	6	6	0	0	20	25	1	16	25	11.4	2.08	.309
2016	West Virginia (SAL)	LoA	8	5	2.46	23	23	0	0	124	96	4	18	131	9.5	0.92	.211
	Bradenton (FSL)	HiA	1	0	0.00	1	1	0	0	6	5	0	1	7	10.5	1.00	.227
2017	West Virginia (NYP)	SS	0	0	0.00	2	2	0	0	4	2	0	1	7	15.8	0.75	.143
	Bradenton (FSL)	HiA	6	3	3.14	15	15	0	0	77	57	5	20	64	7.4	1.00	.207
	Altoona (EL)	AA	2	2	3.12	6	6	0	0	35	25	2	11	45	11.7	1.04	.197
Minor League Totals			17	13	2.79	62	61	0	0	293	229	12	80	308	9.5	1.05	.215

2 AUSTIN MEADOWS, OF

Born: May 3, 1995. **B-T:** L-L. **Ht.:** 6-3. **Wt.:** 200. **Drafted:** HS—Loganville, Ga., 2013 (1st round). **Signed by:** Jerry Jordan.

Meadows was considered one of the best high school bats in the 2013 draft. The Pirates took him No. 9 overall and signed him away from a Clemson commitment for $3,029,600. Meadows backed up his reputation all the way through Double-A, but he has struggled at Triple-A Indianapolis. He suffered through an injury-riddled 2017 season, playing just 81 games thanks to hamstring and oblique injuries. It's the third different season where hamstring injuries have hamstrung him.

Throughout his career, Meadows has shown a smooth swing, good feel for the barrel and the strike zone, so his struggles at Triple-A don't worry the Pirates. They trust that Meadows will be a plus hitter who will develop consistent home run power, even if it doesn't come early in his major league career. He is a plus runner with solid outfield instincts. His arm is his weakest tool, but it's still adequate enough to play all three outfield spots.

Meadows was widely expected to make his big league debut in 2017, but injuries prevented that from happening. There's a good chance he'll start 2018 at Indianapolis, especially if Andrew McCutchen remains with the team. Meadows has a chance of finally breaking through if he can stay healthy.

BA GRADE
60 Risk: High
HIT: 60. POW: 55.
SPD: 60. FLD: 60.
ARM: 50.

Year	Club (League)	Class	AVG	G	AB	R	H	2B	3B	HR	RBI	BB	SO	SB	CS	OBP	SLG
2015	Bradenton (FSL)	HiA	.307	121	508	72	156	22	4	7	54	41	79	20	7	.357	.407
	Altoona (EL)	AA	.360	6	25	5	9	2	3	0	1	2	5	1	0	.429	.680
2016	Altoona (EL)	AA	.311	45	167	33	52	16	8	6	23	16	32	9	3	.365	.611
	West Virginia (NYP)	SS	.200	5	15	0	3	2	0	0	0	2	1	0	0	.294	.333
	Indianapolis (IL)	AAA	.214	37	126	16	27	7	3	6	24	15	34	8	2	.297	.460
2017	Pirates (GCL)	R	.538	4	13	3	7	2	1	1	7	1	2	0	0	.571	1.077
	West Virginia (NYP)	SS	.238	5	21	2	5	1	0	0	3	3	3	0	0	.333	.286
	Indianapolis (IL)	AAA	.250	72	284	48	71	19	0	4	36	24	50	11	3	.311	.359
Minor League Totals			.292	388	1500	237	438	97	26	34	186	152	285	54	20	.359	.459

3 SHANE BAZ, RHP

Born: June 17, 1999. **B-T:** R-R. **Ht.:** 6-3. **Wt.:** 190. **Drafted:** HS—Tomball, Texas, 2017 (1st round). **Signed by:** Wayne Mathis.

Baz was a two-way star at Concordia Lutheran High, the same program that produced system-mate Ke'Bryan Hayes. As a senior, he played on USA Baseball's 18U National Team and recorded an 0.93 ERA and hit .431. The Pirates took him No. 12 overall in 2017 and gave him a slightly over-slot bonus of $4.1 million, buying him out of a commitment to Texas Christian. Baz finished the season strong in the Rookie-level Gulf Coast League, allowing only one run in nine innings in his final three starts.

Baz has a long athletic frame that can support additional weight. His double-plus fastball sits between 94-96 mph with late heavy life—both armside run and late sink that makes it exceptionally difficult on righthanded hitters. He's working with both a slider and a curveball, and both have bite, depth and plus potential. Baz's changeup isn't quite as developed but shows late fade. His control is advanced for his age.

Baz will require time to develop, but he has all the ingredients to eventually be a front-of-the-rotation starter. The Pirates haven't taken a prep pitcher in the first round since Jameson Taillon in 2010, and Taillon began at low Class A West Virginia in his first full season.

BA GRADE
60 Risk: Extreme
FB: 70. CB: 55.
SL: 55. CHG: 50.
CTL: 50.

Year	Club (League)	Class	W	L	ERA	G	GS	CG	SV	IP	H	HR	BB	SO	K/9	WHIP	AVG
2017	Pirates (GCL)	R	0	3	3.80	10	10	0	0	24	26	2	14	19	7.2	1.69	.289
Minor League Totals			0	3	3.80	10	10	0	0	24	26	2	14	19	7.2	1.69	.289

4 KE'BRYAN HAYES, 3B

Born: Jan. 28, 1997. **B-T:** R-R. **Ht.:** 6-1. **Wt.:** 210. **Drafted:** HS—Tomball, Texas, 2015 (1st round). **Signed by:** Tyler Stohr.

The Pirates took Hayes, whose father Charlie played 14 years in the big leagues, with the No. 32 pick in 2015, convincing him to turn down a commitment to Tennessee. After a strong performance in the Rookie-level Gulf Coast League in 2015, he played in just 65 games in 2016 thanks to a cracked rib. However, he still started 2017 in high Class A Bradenton and had his most complete season to date.

Hayes showed better feel for the strike zone, a compact swing and the ability to drive the ball to all fields in 2017. He hasn't shown a lot of home run power, but he could develop power similar to that of his father, who hit 144 home runs. Hayes continued to drop baby fat and add muscle in 2017. He's transformed from a poor baserunner into an above-average one. The conditioning also aided his range at third base. He has sure hands and a quick first step. He should be a defensive asset as a plus defender with a a plus arm.

BA GRADE
55 Risk: High
HIT: 60. **POW:** 45.
SPD: 50. **FLD:** 60.
ARM: 60.

Hayes will likely begin 2018 at Double-A Altoona despite being just 21 on Opening Day. While his statistics have been modest, scouts see him as a future above-average regular thanks to his hitting ability, work ethic and understanding of the game.

Year	Club (League)	Class	AVG	G	AB	R	H	2B	3B	HR	RBI	BB	SO	SB	CS	OBP	SLG
2015	Pirates (GCL)	R	.333	44	144	24	48	4	1	0	13	22	24	7	1	.434	.375
	West Virginia (NYP)	SS	.220	12	41	8	9	1	0	0	7	6	7	1	1	.320	.244
2016	West Virginia (SAL)	LoA	.263	65	247	27	65	12	1	6	37	16	51	6	5	.319	.393
	Pirates (GCL)	R	.400	2	5	0	2	1	0	0	0	1	1	0	0	.500	.600
2017	Bradenton (FSL)	HiA	.278	108	421	66	117	16	7	2	43	41	76	27	5	.345	.363
Minor League Totals			281	231	858	125	241	34	9	8	100	86	159	41	12	.353	.369

5 KEVIN NEWMAN, SS

Born: Aug. 4, 1993. **B-T:** R-R. **Ht.:** 6-1. **Wt.:** 180. **Drafted:** Arizona, 2015 (1st round). **Signed by:** Derrick Van Dusen.

Newman won the Cape Cod League batting title twice and hit .370 in his junior year at Arizona. He continued to build on his reputation as a pure hitter in his first two seasons as a professional, hitting a combined .320 in 2016.

Newman has a strong frame and outstanding feel for the strike zone and the barrel, so the Pirates have to fight the temptation to mess with his swing to try to produce more power. However, he has struggled any time his swing has become too big and has found his most success hitting line drives to the opposite field. He shows the potential for a plus hit tool, albeit with well below-average power. Newman has good speed on the basepaths and good athleticism, but his body is a bit stiff. He has average range and an average arm at shortstop. He's steady defensively, though and tends to make all the routine plays without issue, committing just 17 errors in the past two seasons.

BA GRADE
45 Risk: Medium
HIT: 60. **POW:** 30.
SPD: 55. **FLD:** 50.
ARM: 50.

Newman could still use some time at Triple-A Indianapolis. If he hits in 2018, he could earn a big league callup, particularly if Jordy Mercer is traded. He's a sure-fire big leaguer, but the question is how much impact he'll have.

Year	Club (League)	Class	AVG	G	AB	R	H	2B	3B	HR	RBI	BB	SO	SB	CS	OBP	SLG
2015	West Virginia (NYP)	SS	.226	38	159	25	36	10	1	2	9	10	22	7	1	.281	.340
	West Virginia (SAL)	LoA	.306	23	98	14	30	4	1	0	8	9	8	6	1	.376	.367
2016	Bradenton (FSL)	HiA	.366	41	164	24	60	10	1	3	24	17	12	4	1	.428	.494
	Altoona (EL)	AA	.288	61	233	41	67	11	2	2	28	26	24	6	3	.361	.378
2017	Altoona (EL)	AA	.259	82	343	42	89	18	2	4	30	22	40	4	2	.310	.359
	Indianapolis (IL)	AAA	.283	40	166	23	47	11	2	0	11	7	22	7	1	.314	.373
Minor League Totals			.283	285	1163	169	329	64	9	11	110	91	128	34	9	.340	.382

6 COLE TUCKER, SS

Born: July 3, 1996. **B-T:** R-R. **Ht.:** 6-3. **Wt.:** 185. **Drafted:** HS—Phoenix, 2014 (1st round). **Signed by:** Mike Steele.

The Pirates surprised many by taking Tucker in the first round in 2014 convincing him to pass up a commitment to Arizona. He missed time in 2015 as he recovered from labrum surgery to his right shoulder and the injury seemed to still limit him in 2016. Despite a broken left thumb, he had his best offensive season at high Class A Bradenton in 2017, when he led the Florida State League with 36 stolen bases, then helped Double-A Altoona to an Eastern League championship.

Tucker made drastic strides as a hitter in 2017, greatly improving his strike-zone awareness and overall approach. He has a loose swing and quick hands from both sides of the plate. Below-average power is still the weakest part of his game, but he has present gap power. His wiry frame suggests he can add strength as he ages. Tucker's long strides obscure his plus speed, his most impressive tool, and he drastically improved his intelligence on the basepaths in 2017. He is a fluid athlete with good range who projects as above-average at shortstop, and his above-average arm is back to full strength.

Tucker will likely start 2018 at Double-A Altoona but could eventually challenge Kevin Newman for a spot in the big leagues.

BA GRADE
50 Risk: High
HIT: 55. POW: 40.
SPD: 60. FLD: 55.
ARM: 55.

Year	Club (League)	Class	AVG	G	AB	R	H	2B	3B	HR	RBI	BB	SO	SB	CS	OBP	SLG
2015	West Virginia (SAL)	LoA	.293	73	300	46	88	13	3	2	25	16	49	25	6	.322	.377
2016	West Virginia (SAL)	LoA	.262	15	61	9	16	4	2	1	2	4	9	1	1	.308	.443
	Bradenton (FSL)	HiA	.238	65	269	36	64	12	1	1	25	29	62	5	6	.312	.301
2017	Bradenton (FSL)	HiA	.282	68	277	46	78	15	6	4	32	34	70	37	12	.361	.422
	Altoona (EL)	AA	.257	42	167	25	43	4	5	2	18	21	31	11	3	.349	.377
Minor League Totals			.269	311	1254	201	337	54	19	12	115	130	259	92	33	.339	.371

7 LUIS ESCOBAR, RHP

Born: May 30, 1996. **B-T:** R-R. **Ht.:** 6-1. **Wt.:** 200. **Signed:** Colombia, 2013. **Signed by:** Rene Gayo/Orlando Covo.

Pirates international scouts found Escobar as a 17-year-old in Cartagena, Colombia, and liked his live arm. They signed him for $150,000. He was just 155 pounds at the time and played third base, but the Pirates pushed him to pitch. Escobar has increased his velocity as he added weight and strength, and his breakthrough season in 2017 included a trip to the Futures Game. At low Class A West Virginia in 2017 he led the South Atlantic League with 168 strikeouts and a .200 opponent average, though he also ranked second with 60 walks.

Escobar throws a four-seam fastball with riding action that he can get up to 97 mph and usually sits in the 93-95 range. He can still be a little scattershot with his fastball, but he has made major control improvements in the past year. He pairs his heater with a sharp above-average 12-6 curveball with late drop. His changeup needs further development, but it generates fringe-average to average grades as well.

Escobar will likely begin 2018 at high Class A Bradenton. Some scouts see him as a future power reliever, but if his changeup and control keep developing he could stay in the rotation.

BA GRADE
50 Risk: High
FB: 60. CB: 55.
CHG: 45.
CTL: 45.

Year	Club (League)	Class	W	L	ERA	G	GS	CG	SV	IP	H	HR	BB	SO	K/P	WHIP	AVG
2015	Pirates (GCL)	R	2	1	3.54	11	11	0	0	41	29	1	13	37	8.2	1.03	.200
	West Virginia (NYP)	SS	0	0	5.68	2	2	0	0	6	7	0	4	5	7.1	1.74	.304
2016	West Virginia (NYP)	SS	6	5	2.93	15	12	0	0	68	50	4	28	61	8.1	1.15	.208
2017	West Virginia (SAL)	LoA	10	7	3.83	26	25	1	0	132	97	9	60	168	11.5	1.19	.200
Minor League Totals			20	17	3.79	67	63	1	0	301	233	16	136	305	9.1	1.22	.212

8 NICK KINGHAM, RHP

Born: Nov. 8, 1991. **B-T:** R-R. **Ht.:** 6-6. **Wt.:** 225. **Drafted:** HS—Las Vegas, 2010 (4th round). **Signed by:** Larry Broadway.

Kingham was one of several long-framed high school pitchers the Pirates went over slot to sign at the beginning of the decade. However, he has become a forgotten member of that group thanks to injury. He rose steadily through the organization until 2015, when he had Tommy John surgery while in his second season at Triple-A Indianapolis. That cost him most of that season and 2016, when he made just 10 starts. His 2017 campaign also got a late start thanks to a spring training ankle injury that kept him out until mid-May.

Kingham's average fastball generally sits around 92 mph, but his 6-foot-6 frame allows him to create downhill plane. He has an average hard curveball with three-quarters break and a plus changeup with sinking action. His control is a strength, but he can sometimes get hit hard by staying in the zone too much.

The Pirates consider Kingham one of 10 pitchers they would feel comfortable starting at the big league level, but the Pittsburgh rotation remained relatively injury free in 2017, and he was never called up. He will be in the rotation mix in 2018, but that's no guarantee that he'll be called up from Indianapolis.

BA GRADE
45 Risk: Medium
FB: 50. CB: 50.
CHG: 60.
CTL: 55.

Year	Club (League)	Class	W	L	ERA	G	GS	CG	SV	IP	H	HR	BB	SO	K/P	WHIP	AVG
2015	Indianapolis (IL)	AAA	1	2	4.31	6	6	0	0	31	34	3	7	32	9.2	1.31	.270
2016	Pirates (GCL)	R	0	4	3.00	6	6	0	0	24	23	0	1	16	6.0	1.00	.256
	Bradenton (FSL)	HiA	2	0	0.00	2	2	0	0	11	8	0	1	10	8.2	0.82	.211
	Altoona (EL)	AA	1	1	5.73	2	2	0	0	11	6	1	4	10	8.2	0.91	.162
2017	Bradenton (FSL)	HiA	1	0	0.00	1	1	0	0	5	1	0	0	0	0.0	0.20	.063
	Indianapolis (IL)	AAA	9	6	4.13	20	19	1	0	113	119	8	29	93	7.4	1.31	.271
Minor League Totals			41	40	3.42	134	129	1	0	699	638	48	189	590	7.6	1.18	.242

9 TAYLOR HEARN, LHP

Born: Aug. 30, 1994. **B-T:** L-L. **Ht.:** 6-5. **Wt.:** 210. **Drafted:** Oklahoma Baptist, 2015 (5th round). **Signed by:** Ed Gustafson (Nationals).

The Pirates acquired Hearn along with Felipe Rivero when they traded Mark Melancon to the Nationals in 2016. Rivero became the Pirates' closer in 2017 and was one of the most dominant relievers in baseball. Hearn has some of the same attributes as Rivero. He missed the final two months of 2017 at high Class A Bradenton thanks to a strained left oblique but still finished with 11 strikeouts per nine innings in a career-high 89 innings.

Hearn's near top-of-the-scale fastball plays in the 96-97 mph range, and he frequently hit 99 in games. On occasion he even topped triple digits. His below-average control is still an issue, and he is also working on secondary pitches. Hearn is making progress with his potentially average 84-86 mph changeup. It's tough on both righthanded and lefthanded hitters. He's working on his fringy slider, but he hasn't found a shape and velocity he feels comfortable with yet.

The central question for Hearn is whether or not he can remain a starter, and that might not be possible if his control and slider don't improve. He will likely move up to Double-A Altoona in 2018, but he could move to the bullpen there if it becomes clear that's his best bet to reach the majors.

BA GRADE
50 Risk: High
FB: 70. SL: 45.
CHG: 50.
CTL: 45.

Year	Club (League)	Class	W	L	ERA	G	GS	CG	SV	IP	H	HR	BB	SO	K/P	WHIP	AVG
2015	Nationals (GCL)	R	0	0	0.00	2	1	0	0	5	4	0	2	7	12.6	1.20	.250
	Auburn (NYP)	SS	1	5	3.98	10	10	0	0	43	49	2	13	38	8.0	1.44	.280
2016	Nationals (GCL)	R	0	0	1.42	2	2	0	0	6	2	1	6	8	11.4	1.26	.105
	Hagerstown (SAL)	LoA	1	0	3.18	8	2	0	0	23	25	3	7	31	12.3	1.41	.278
	West Virginia (SAL)	LoA	1	1	1.99	8	3	0	0	23	15	2	10	36	14.3	1.10	.183
2017	Bradenton (FSL)	HiA	4	6	4.12	18	17	0	0	87	65	8	37	106	10.9	1.17	.207
	Pirates (GCL)	R	0	0	0.00	1	1	0	0	2	0	0	0	3	13.5	0.00	.000
Minor League Totals			7	12	3.48	49	36	0	0	189	160	16	75	229	10.9	1.24	.228

10 LOLO SANCHEZ, OF

CLIFF WELCH

Born: April 23, 1999. **B-T:** R-R. **Ht.:** 6-0. **Wt.:** 150. **Signed:** Dominican Republic, 2015. **Signed by:** Rene Gayo.

The Pirates made Sanchez their big-ticket signing on the 2015 international market, coming to terms for $450,000. He showed impressive maturity for an 18-year-old in his first season in the U.S. in 2017, when he hit .284/.359/.417 in the Rookie-level Gulf Coast League with 21 walks against just 19 strikeouts and 14 stolen bases. He led the circuit with 42 runs and placed third with 85 total bases.

Sanchez showed excellent hand-eye coordination and plate control in the GCL. Even though his frame doesn't project for more than average power, his four home runs showed he is capable of running into a few because he's good at getting the barrel to the ball and his body possesses some twitchy athleticism. Sanchez's speed is a plus-plus tool, and he has good baserunning awareness for his age. He's also an above-average center fielder with an above-average arm. His display of all of those tools in the GCL have quickened his track significantly.

Sanchez may not start 2018 at low Class A West Virginia if the Pirates keep him in extended spring training, but he will almost certainly end up there at some point.

BA GRADE
55 Risk: Extreme
HIT: 60. POW: 40.
SPD: 60. FLD: 55.
ARM: 55.

Year	Club (League)	Class	AVG	G	AB	R	H	2B	3B	HR	RBI	BB	SO	SB	CS	OBP	SLG
2016	Pirates (DSL)	R	.235	45	153	19	36	4	1	0	10	24	18	4	8	.359	.275
2017	Pirates (GCL)	R	.284	51	204	42	58	11	2	4	20	21	19	14	7	.359	.417
Minor League Totals			.263	96	357	61	94	15	3	4	30	45	37	18	15	.359	.356

11 STEVEN JENNINGS, RHP

BA GRADE
55 Risk: Extreme

Born: Nov. 13, 1998. **B-T:** R-R. **Ht.:** 6-2. **Wt.:** 175. **Drafted:** HS—Smithville, Tenn., 2017 (2nd round). **Signed by:** Jerry Jordan.

Jennings didn't spend much time at showcases as a high schooler, in large part because he was the starting quarterback at DeKalb County High, ending his senior season early because of a torn anterior cruciate ligament in his knee. That probably helped the Pirates get him early in the second round with the No. 42 overall pick. Thin but athletic, Jennings posted a 0.52 ERA with 99 strikeouts in 51.2 innings as a prep senior, then signed for $1.9 million, passing up a commitment to Mississippi.

Jennings doesn't pitch with a ton of velocity yet, sitting around 90 mph in games, but the Pirates expect him to add velocity and be around 92-93 with armside run. He has an easy delivery and is good at repeating his arm action, which projects well long term. He's working on honing in on a breaking pitch, using several that fall somewhere on the spectrum between slider and curveball, and he has a changeup that could end up being a plus pitch. He shows control with everything he throws.

Jennings could be on the same track as 2017 first-rounder Shane Baz, which would mean he would start 2018 at low Class A West Virginia, but he could also be in a short-season league preceded by time at extended spring training.

Year	Club (League)	Class	W	L	ERA	G	GS	CG	SV	IP	H	HR	BB	SO	K/9	WHIP	AVG
2017	Pirates (GCL)	R	0	2	4.10	10	10	0	0	26	31	2	10	13	4.4	1.56	.282
Minor League Totals			0	2	4.10	10	10	0	0	26	31	2	10	13	4.4	1.56	.282

12 KEVIN KRAMER, 2B

BA GRADE
50 Risk: High

Born: Oct. 3, 1993. **B-T:** L-R. **Ht.:** 6-1. **Wt.:** 190. **Drafted:** UCLA, 2015 (2nd round). **Signed by:** Rick Allen.

Kramer was taken by the Pirates after his redshirt junior season at UCLA, having been a part of the 2013 national championship team before missing his third year with a torn labrum. He then hit .323 in 2015 for a Bruins team that entered the NCAA Tournament as the No. 1 overall seed.

Kramer has shown patience and the ability to hit for average at every level on the way up the Pirates' minor league ladder. He missed much of the 2017 season with a fractured hand but returned in time to help Double-A Altoona win the Eastern League title. Kramer reminds many in the system of former Pirates second baseman Neil Walker. He doesn't have great range or a great arm, but he has good hands and positions himself well, so he projects to be average at second base. He has hit just 10 minor league home runs, but his ability to drive the gaps suggests that he'll find below-average to fringe-average home run power in the major leagues.

Kramer might spend a little more time at Double-A in 2018, but he'll likely find himself at Triple-A Indianapolis at some point.

Year	Club (League)	Class	AVG	G	AB	R	H	2B	3B	HR	RBI	BB	SO	SB	CS	OBP	SLG
2015	West Virginia (NYP)	SS	.305	46	177	34	54	7	3	0	17	25	28	9	4	.390	.379
	West Virginia (SAL)	LoA	.240	12	50	9	12	2	1	0	3	5	8	3	0	.321	.320
2016	Bradenton (FSL)	HiA	.277	118	444	56	123	29	2	4	57	48	63	3	9	.352	.378
2017	Altoona (EL)	AA	.297	53	202	31	60	17	3	6	27	17	50	7	2	.380	.500
	Pirates (GCL)	R	.000	1	2	0	0	0	0	0	1	0	1	0	0	.000	.000
	West Virginia (NYP)	SS	.231	3	13	1	3	0	0	0	2	0	2	1	0	.286	.231
Minor League Totals			.284	233	888	131	252	55	9	10	107	95	152	23	15	.363	.400

13 JORDAN LUPLOW, OF

BA GRADE 45 Risk: Medium

Born: Sept. 26, 1993. **B-T:** R-R. **Ht.:** 6-1. **Wt.:** 195. **Drafted:** Fresno State, 2014 (3rd round). **Signed by:** Mike Sansoe.

Luplow was an afterthought heading into the 2017 season after a mediocre year at high Class A Bradenton. However, the former Mountain West Conference player of the year at Fresno State had the most successful offensive season among Pirates minor leaguers in 2017.

Luplow hit 23 home runs in 117 games at Double-A Altoona and Triple-A Indianapolis, helping both teams reach the postseason. He was then called up to the Pirates to shore up their outfield depth. Throughout the season, he showed power to all fields, good feel for the barrel, quick hands and good pitch recognition. His success at the plate also seemed to translate to improvements in the rest of his game. Luplow doesn't have great speed, but he's smart on the basepaths and quick to take extra bases when they're there. A converted third baseman, he doesn't have great range in right field, but it improved this year, and he also showed a plus arm with excellent accuracy.

Luplow has a good chance of starting 2018 with the Pirates as an extra outfielder.

Year	Club (League)	Class	AVG	G	AB	R	H	2B	3B	HR	RBI	BB	SO	SB	CS	OBP	SLG
2015	West Virginia (SAL)	LoA.	264	106	390	74	103	36	3	12	67	59	67	11	2	.366	.464
2016	Bradenton (FSL)	HiA	.254	104	354	63	90	23	3	10	54	60	78	6	2	.363	.421
2017	Altoona (EL)	AA	.287	73	254	45	73	15	0	16	37	29	45	1	3	.368	.535
	Indianapolis (IL)	AAA	.325	44	160	29	52	7	1	7	19	16	36	4	1	.401	.513
	Pittsburgh (NL)	MAJ	.205	27	78	6	16	3	1	3	11	6	22	0	1	.276	.385
Major League Totals			.205	27	78	6	16	3	1	3	11	6	22	0	1	.276	.385
Minor League Totals			.275	389	1378	242	379	93	8	51	207	191	270	32	14	.369	.465

14 CALVIN MITCHELL, OF

BA GRADE 55 Risk: Extreme

Born: March 8, 1999. **B-T:** L-L. **Ht.:** 6-0. **Wt.:** 190. **Drafted:** HS—San Diego, 2017 (2nd round). **Signed by:** Brian Tracy.

Mitchell was considered one of the best high school bats in the nation going into his senior year at Rancho Bernardo High in 2017. The year before he had finished second in the home run derby at the Perfect Game All-American Classic, and he helped Team USA win the Pan American Championships. He struggled early in his senior year, going through an 0-for-22 stretch at one point, which caused his stock to fall significantly.

Mitchell, however, found consistency late in his senior season and ended up hitting .369 with 11 home runs. He finished his first pro season in the Rookie-level Gulf Coast League with 12 hits in 36 at-bats in his last 10 games. The Pirates were never bothered by the slump and still considered Mitchell one of the best high school bats in the draft. He has a smooth lefthanded stroke, good command of the strike zone, and a quick enough bat to let the ball get deep and drive it to the opposite field. He has good power, and should be able to generate above-average home runs production more when he adds weight to a long frame. He has slightly below-average speed and average defensive tools, however, which means he profiles as a corner outfielder and will need his bat to play.

Mitchell should begin his full-season odyssey at low Class A West Virginia in 2018.

Year	Club (League)	Class	AVG	G	AB	R	H	2B	3B	HR	RBI	BB	SO	SB	CS	OBP	SLG
2017	Pirates (GCL)	R	.245	43	159	17	39	11	0	2	20	24	35	2	3	.351	.352
Minor League Totals			.245	43	159	17	39	11	0	2	20	24	35	2	3	.351	.352

15 CONNOR USELTON, OF

BA GRADE 55 Risk: Extreme

Born: May 20, 1998. **B-T:** R-R. **Ht.:** 6-3. **Wt.:** 185. **Drafted:** HS—Oklahoma City, 2017 (2nd round supplemental). **Signed by:** Phil Huttmann.

Uselton was a high school quarterback but gave up football in his sophomore year to pursue baseball. The move paid off when Uselton signed for $900,000 as the Pirates' supplemental second-round pick in 2017 after hitting .467 as a senior at Southmoore High.

Uselton played both ways in high school and hit 91 mph with his fastball, but he'll focus on the outfield as a pro. He went down with a hamstring injury in just his second game in the Rookie-level Gulf Coast League and never returned, but he went 3-for-5 in that game. Uselton's swing mechanics will need extensive work in the minor leagues. There's a lot of motion in the swing that doesn't need to be there, he's prone to too many strikeouts and he doesn't have a great feel for the barrel yet. However, he also has a lot of raw power, so when he does barrel the ball, it can go a long way. Uselton has a chance to start his career in center field because he has above-average athleticism, good instincts and a decent arm.

Uselton might eventually have to move to a corner outfield spot, but if he reaches his offensive ceiling, he may still fit well in PNC Park's spacious left field.

Year	Club (League)	Class	AVG	G	AB	R	H	2B	3B	HR	RBI	BB	SO	SB	CS	OBP	SLG
2017	Pirates (GCL)	R	.429	2	7	0	3	1	0	0	1	0	1	0	0	.429	.571
Minor League Totals			.429	2	7	0	3	1	0	0	1	0	1	0	0	.429	.571

16 MAX MOROFF, SS/2B

BA GRADE
45 Risk: Medium

Born: May 13, 1993. **B-T:** B-R. **Ht.:** 5-10. **Wt.:** 185. **Drafted:** HS—Winter Park, Fla., 2012 (16th round). **Signed by:** Nick Presto.

Five years after the Pirates convinced Moroff to pass up a commitment to Central Florida for a $300,000 signing bonus, he got extensive major league work in 2017.

Moroff never had more than eight home runs in a minor league season, but he hit 13 at Triple-A Indianapolis in 2017 in just 51 games, slugging a career-high .519. That earned him a spot in Pittsburgh as a utility infielder. He struggled with the bat for much of the season, but he drove in seven runs in the season's final two games. Moroff has good feel for the barrel and can create some leverage with the bat despite a lack of length. He's prone to high strikeout totals, but he also has high walk totals and can extend at-bats and make pitchers work. His defense at second base, third base and shortstop is about average. His arm can play at any of the three positions. His speed isn't what it was when he stole a combined 38 bases in 2014 and 2015, but he still has average speed.

Moroff could start in Indianapolis again in 2018, but he will have a chance to make the Pirates' Opening Day roster as a utility infielder.

Year	Club (League)	Class	AVG	G	AB	R	H	2B	3B	HR	RBI	BB	SO	SB	CS	OBP	SLG
2015	Altoona (EL)	AA	.293	136	523	79	153	28	6	7	51	70	111	17	13	.374	.409
2016	Pittsburgh (NL)	MAJ	.000	2	0	0	0	0	0	0	0	0	2	0	0	.000	.000
	Indianapolis (IL)	AAA	.230	133	421	61	97	18	4	8	45	90	129	9	7	.367	.349
2017	Indianapolis (IL)	AAA	.254	51	185	31	47	10	0	13	37	41	59	5	2	.390	.519
	Pittsburgh (NL)	MAJ	.200	56	120	19	24	4	1	3	21	16	43	0	1	.302	.325
Major League Totals			.197	58	122	19	24	4	1	3	21	16	45	0	1	.298	.320
Minor League Totals			.255	588	2092	320	534	107	19	38	238	337	541	67	48	.359	.379

17 DOVYDAS NEVERAUSKAS, RHP

BA GRADE
45 Risk: Medium

Born: Jan. 14, 1993. **B-T:** R-R. **Ht.:** 6-3. **Wt.:** 215. **Signed:** Lithuania, 2009. **Signed by:** Tom Randolph.

Neverauskas, who first drew the Pirates' attention at the European Academy in Italy as a 16-year-old, became the first Lithuanian player in major league history in 2017.

Neverauskas' career trajectory has spiked since he moved to the bullpen in 2015 after a rough season in at low Class A West Virginia, and he was dominant throughout the higher levels of the minors before breaking through and making 24 appearances in the majors in 2017. Neverauskas has long limbs, but he has an efficient delivery and can easily locate a four-seam fastball that averages 97 mph and tops out around 99. He also uses an average slider to keep the ball off the barrel.

The Pirates showed increased faith in Neverauskas throughout his big league appearances, and he could soon be part of their bridge to closer Felipe Rivero.

Year	Club (League)	Class	W	L	ERA	G	GS	CG	SV	IP	H	HR	BB	SO	K/9	WHIP	AVG
2015	West Virginia (NYP)	SS	1	0	3.86	1	0	0	0	2	4	1	3	2	7.7	3.00	.364
	West Virginia (SAL)	LoA	1	2	3.65	18	5	0	2	49	39	3	19	37	6.8	1.18	.214
	Bradenton (FSL)	HiA	0	0	1.62	12	0	0	4	17	15	0	5	10	5.4	1.20	.238
2016	Altoona (EL)	AA	1	0	2.57	22	0	0	1	28	12	0	11	32	10.3	0.82	.129
	Indianapolis (IL)	AAA	3	4	3.60	25	0	0	4	30	36	1	11	24	7.2	1.57	.308
2017	Indianapolis (IL)	AAA	1	2	2.86	40	0	0	13	50	47	1	21	46	8.2	1.35	.253
	Pittsburgh (NL)	MAJ	1	1	3.91	24	0	0	0	25	24	4	8	17	6.0	1.26	.253
Major League Totals			1	1	3.91	24	0	0	0	25	24	4	8	17	6.0	1.26	.253
Minor League Totals			22	26	4.05	187	58	1	24	435	434	32	186	335	6.9	1.42	.262

18 MASON MARTIN, 1B/OF

BA GRADE

50 Risk: Extreme

Born: June 2, 1999. **B-T:** L-R. **Ht.:** 6-0. **Wt.:** 201. **Drafted:** HS—Kennewick, Wash., 2017 (17th round). **Signed by:** Max Kwan.

Martin was the 508th overall pick in the 2017 draft and was committed to Gonzaga, but the Pirates offered $350,000 and acquired the player who had the most impressive summer of any of their 2017 draftees.

After hitting .507 as a high school senior, Martin slugged seven home runs in seven July games in the Rookie-level Gulf Coast League. He came back to earth, but then hit four home runs in the season's final nine games to win MVP honors in the GCL. He showed a simple, efficient lefthanded swing, good feel for the strike zone and the barrel. He also showed easy above-average power. He has wiry strength and could add more power as his body fills out. He doesn't have plus athleticism or speed, and he still has a lot to learn about the fundamentals of playing first base.

Because of those deficiencies, Martin may have to start 2018 with a short-season club to get work in extended spring training, but if he learns quickly, he could start the year at low Class A West Virginia.

Year	Club (League)	Class	AVG	G	AB	R	H	2B	3B	HR	RBI	BB	SO	SB	CS	OBP	SLG
2017	Pirates (GCL)	R	.307	39	127	37	39	8	0	11	22	32	41	2	2	.457	.630
Minor League Totals			.307	39	127	37	39	8	0	11	22	32	41	2	2	.457	.630

19 BRANDON WADDELL, LHP

BA GRADE

45 Risk: High

Born: June 3, 1994. **B-T:** L-L. **Ht.:** 6-3. **Wt.:** 180. **Drafted:** Virginia, 2015 (5th round). **Signed by:** Dan Radcliff.

Waddell was Virginia's go-to hurler in big games, and he went 6-1, 2.34 in 11 NCAA Tournament games. He won all five of his career starts in the College World Series, helping the Cavaliers to the 2015 national title. That convinced the Pirates to take him in the fifth round.

Waddell reached Double-A Altoona in his first full season in 2016. He didn't get a chance to move up in 2017, thanks in part to two left forearm strains that cost him close to a month, but he still became a stalwart for the Curve in their Eastern League championship run. He pitched six shutout innings in his start against Trenton in the championship series, continuing to be a go-to starter in big games. He gets most of his work done with the combination of a fastball that sits between 88-92 mph that he can locate to both sides of the plate and a changeup with fade that looks exactly like a fastball out of his hand. He's working on a breaking ball that's something in between a slider and a curveball, and he's trying to commit to one direction or another with it.

Waddell will join at backlog of pitchers at Triple-A Indianapolis in 2018 and has No. 5 starter potential.

Year	Club (League)	Class	W	L	ERA	G	GS	CG	SV	IP	H	HR	BB	SO	K/9	WHIP	AVG
2015	West Virginia (NYP)	SS	1	1	5.75	6	6	0	0	20	24	0	7	18	8.0	1.52	.276
2016	Bradenton (FSL)	HiA	4	0	0.93	5	5	0	0	29	13	1	2	26	8.1	0.52	.133
	Altoona (EL)	AA	7	9	4.12	22	20	0	0	118	122	9	61	94	7.2	1.55	.271
2017	Pirates (GCL)	R	1	0	0.00	1	0	0	0	3	1	0	0	4	12.0	0.33	.100
	West Virginia (NYP)	SS	1	0	1.00	2	2	0	0	9	5	1	3	11	11.0	0.89	.167
	Altoona (EL)	AA	3	3	3.55	15	15	0	0	66	60	3	27	56	7.6	1.32	.240
Minor League Totals			17	13	3.56	51	48	0	0	245	225	14	100	209	7.7	1.32	.243

20 BRAEDEN OGLE, LHP

BA GRADE

50 Risk: Extreme

Born: July 30, 1997. **B-T:** L-L. **Ht.:** 6-2. **Wt.:** 170. **Drafted:** HS—Jensen Beach, Fla., 2016 (4th round). **Signed by:** Nick Presto.

Ogle topped out at 96 mph in the first start of his senior season and struck out 59 batters in 35 innings at Jensen Beach High to draw a lot of college and pro attention. He ended up signing above slot for $800,000 with the Pirates, passing up a Florida commitment.

Ogle has spent his first two pro seasons in Rookie league, but he has shown good signs in 18 starts. He sits 94-96 mph with his fastball, with easy effort and a consistent delivery. The pitch has armside run, sometimes a little too much, but his overall command of it is better than expected at his age. He also has a sharp slider that runs between 83-86 mph and has some depth to it, and a changeup that matches the fastball well and has sink and armside run. Ogle's control of all three pitches is decent, and the Pirates hope he puts more faith in the secondary pitches.

After two seasons at the Rookie level, Ogle will most likely get a chance to experiment with all of his pitches in 2018 at low Class A West Virginia.

Year	Club (League)	Class	W	L	ERA	G	GS	CG	SV	IP	H	HR	BB	SO	K/9	WHIP	AVG
2016	Pirates (GCL)	R	0	2	2.60	8	8	0	0	28	18	2	11	20	6.5	1.05	.188
2017	Bristol (APP)	R	2	3	3.14	10	10	0	0	43	40	1	16	35	7.3	1.30	.242
Minor League Totals			2	5	2.93	18	18	0	0	71	58	3	27	55	7.0	1.20	.222

21 CLAY HOLMES, RHP

BA GRADE

40 Risk: Medium

Born: March 27, 1993. **B-T:** R-R. **Ht.:** 6-5. **Wt.:** 230. **Drafted:** HS—Slocomb, Ala., 2011 (9th round). **Signed by:** Darren Mazeroski.

Holmes still has the highest signing bonus ever given to a ninth-round pick at $1.2 million—which convinced the high school valedictorian and physics enthusiast not to go to Auburn. However, the Pirates haven't seen any return on that investment at the major league level yet, thanks in large part to his Tommy John surgery in 2014.

Holmes' 2016 and 2017 seasons show him coming much closer to making the leap, though, when he proved to be a durable starter with an average strikeout rate at Double-A Altoona and Triple-A Indianapolis. He has a heavy, two-seam fastball with which he usually pitches in the 94-96 mph range and a big, looping curveball that he struggles to control but could use as a chase pitch. He also throws a slider/cutter around 90 mph and keeps in the zone. His walk numbers remain a bit too high.

Holmes doesn't have a true out pitch, but he is an extreme groundball pitcher, which the Pirates favor. He has a chance to break into the majors in 2018, either as a starter if the Pirates deal with extensive injuries, or in long relief.

Year	Club (League)	Class	W	L	ERA	G	GS	CG	SV	IP	H	HR	BB	SO	K/9	WHIP	AVG
2015	Pirates (GCL)	R	1	0	2.03	3	3	0	0	13	13	0	1	10	6.8	1.05	.250
	Bradenton (FSL)	HiA	0	2	2.74	6	6	0	0	23	18	0	7	16	6.3	1.09	.222
2016	Altoona (EL)	AA	10	9	4.22	26	26	0	0	136	138	10	64	101	6.7	1.48	.272
2017	Indianapolis (IL)	AAA	10	5	3.36	25	24	0	0	113	96	4	59	99	7.9	1.38	.238
Minor League Totals			31	25	3.59	99	97	0	0	464	406	22	229	350	6.8	1.37	.241

22 ONEIL CRUZ, SS/3B

BA GRADE

50 Risk: Extreme

Born: Oct. 4, 1998. **B-T:** L-R. **Ht.:** 6-6. **Wt.:** 175. **Signed:** Dominican Republic, 2015. **Signed by:** Patrick Guerrero/Franklin Taveras/Bob Engle (Dodgers).

Cruz stood 6-foot-1 at age 15, but he had shot up to 6-foot-4 by the time he signed with the Dodgers for $950,000 as a 16-year-old. He now has grown to 6-foot-6. The extra length forced him to move from shortstop to third base, but it also helped him add power, which was a big reason why the Pirates were intrigued by him and took him as part of the trade that sent reliever Tony Watson to the Dodgers in July 2017.

Cruz hit a combined 10 home runs in his first season in the U.S., but he also struck out 132 times. He remains a fairly raw player but has two eye-opening tools—his power and throwing arm. His frame is still long and lean, but he shows power to all fields and can hit moonshots when he pulls the ball. He has a plus arm, good range at third base and good athleticism overall. He's still clearly growing into his body, and he isn't advanced as a hitter, but he shows signs of aptitude at the plate and can shorten his swing when needed.

Cruz will play the entire 2018 season as a 19-year-old and figures to center his effort at low Class A West Virginia.

Year	Club (League)	Class	AVG	G	AB	R	H	2B	3B	HR	RBI	BB	SO	SB	CS	OBP	SLG
2016	Dodgers (DSL)	R	.294	55	187	28	55	18	5	0	23	22	44	11	5	.367	.444
2017	Great Lakes (MWL)	LoA	.240	89	342	51	82	9	1	8	36	28	110	8	7	.293	.342
	West Virginia (SAL)	LoA	.218	16	55	9	12	2	1	2	8	8	22	0	0	.317	.400
Minor League Totals			.255	160	584	88	149	29	7	10	67	58	176	19	12	.319	.380

23 EDGAR SANTANA, RHP

BA GRADE

40 Risk: Medium

Born: Oct. 16, 1991. **B-T:** R-R. **Ht.:** 6-2. **Wt.:** 180. **Signed:** Dominican Republic, 2013. **Signed by:** Rene Gayo.

Santana didn't play much baseball growing up in the Dominican Republic, and he didn't start pitching until age 19 or sign until age 22. But just three years after signing, he found himself in the major leagues. He shot through the Pirates' system quickly, going from high Class A to Triple-A in 2016, then earning a callup in June 2017 after a dominant start at Triple-A Indianapolis.

Santana's fastball sits around 95 mph and is effective when it has downward plane, but he sometimes runs into trouble when it's flat. His slider is his go-to pitch, however. It has a lot of sharp, side-to-side break, but he can get it over for a strike just as easily as he can use it for a chase pitch.

Much like Dovydas Neverauskas, Santana has a chance to find his way to the Pirates' bullpen, but he also has the arm endurance to be used in multi-inning relief. The versatility should allow him much more opportunity to be part of the major league staff in some way in 2018.

Year	Club (League)	Class	W	L	ERA	G	GS	CG	SV	IP	H	HR	BB	SO	K/9	WHIP	AVG
2015	West Virginia (NYP)	SS	1	0	2.70	14	0	0	3	30	25	1	5	32	9.6	1.00	.219
	West Virginia (SAL)	LoA	0	0	4.38	8	0	0	1	12	12	3	4	16	11.7	1.30	.255
2016	Bradenton (FSL)	HiA	2	0	0.81	9	0	0	0	22	13	0	2	20	8.1	0.67	.169
	Altoona (EL)	AA	2	1	2.83	21	0	0	2	41	32	4	11	39	8.5	1.04	.216
	Indianapolis (IL)	AAA	0	0	5.06	13	0	0	1	16	22	1	6	12	6.8	1.75	.328
2017	Indianapolis (IL)	AAA	1	3	2.79	44	0	0	8	58	62	4	12	54	8.4	1.28	.281
	Pittsburgh (NL)	MAJ	0	0	3.50	19	0	0	0	18	16	2	12	20	10.0	1.56	.239
Major League Totals			0	0	3.50	19	0	0	0	18	16	2	12	20	10.0	1.56	.239
Minor League Totals			7	7	2.93	122	0	0	17	200	193	13	43	184	8.3	1.18	.256

24 WILL CRAIG, 1B

BA GRADE
45 Risk: High

Born: Nov. 16, 1994. **B-T:** R-R. **Ht.:** 6-3. **Wt.:** 212. **Drafted:** Wake Forest, 2016 (1st round). **Signed by:** Jerry Jordan.

Craig was taken in the 37th round by the Royals out of high school, but he improved his draft stock drastically at Wake Forest. He hit 37 career home runs with the Demon Deacons and also served as closer in his junior year. The Pirates took him with the No. 22 overall pick in 2016 and paid him just over $2.2 million, but they haven't seen the power show up yet in pro ball.

Craig hit 26 doubles in 2017 at high Class A Bradenton, but he has hit just eight home runs in 676 pro at-bats so far. He moved from third base to first base after committing 16 errors in 46 games at third in the short-season New York-Penn League in 2016. Craig had some issues with his hitting approach early in 2017, which led to 31 strikeouts in May, and he seemed to correct those, by hitting .354 in June, but then hit .198 in August. He showed good footwork around first base, and still has his arm as an above-average tool, but not much in the way of athleticism.

Craig likely will start 2018 at Double-A Altoona and will have a chance to get a jumpstart there.

Year	Club (League)	Class	AVG	G	AB	R	H	2B	3B	HR	RBI	BB	SO	SB	CS	OBP	SLG
2016	West Virginia (NYP)	SS	.280	63	218	28	61	12	0	2	23	41	37	2	0	.412	.362
2017	Bradenton (FSL)	HiA	.271	123	458	59	124	26	1	6	61	62	106	1	3	.373	.371
Minor League Totals			.274	186	676	87	185	38	1	8	84	103	143	3	3	.386	.368

25 NICK BURDI, RHP

BA GRADE
45 Risk: High

Born: Jan. 19, 1993 **B-T:** R-R. **Ht.:** 6-5. **Wt.:** 220 **Drafted:** Louisville, 2014 (2nd round, Twins). **Signed by:** Alan Sandberg (Twins).

Burdi was drafted in the 24th round by the Twins after a stellar Illinois prep career, then was taken again by Minnesota with the 46th overall pick in 2014 after a dominant career as Louisville's closer. The Pirates acquired the rights to Burdi at the 2017 Rule 5 draft by trading $500,000 in international bonus pool money to the Phillies, who had selected the reliever third overall. The Twins left him unprotected in the Rule 5 draft, possibly because he has pitched just 20 innings in the past two seasons and faces a long rehab.

Thanks to a fastball that sits in the upper 90s and can touch 100 mph—as well as a devastating slider in the 87-90 mph range and a decent changeup—Burdi continued to post high strikeout rates during his time with the Twins. He averaged more than 11.0 strikeouts per nine innings in each of his first two seasons. He missed most of the 2016 season with a bruised right humerus, however, pitching just three innings. In 2017, he drastically improved his control at Double-A Chattanooga by walking just four batters in 17 innings while striking out 20 and allowing only one run, but he tore the ulnar collateral ligament in his right elbow and needed Tommy John surgery in May.

Burdi will begin the season on the disabled list and likely won't be available until the second half. However, if he can return to form, the Pirates hope he can become a go-to high-leverage reliever.

Year	Club (League)	Class	W	L	ERA	G	GS	CG	SV	IP	H	HR	BB	SO	K/9	WHIP	AVG
2015	Fort Myers (FSL)	HiA	2	2	2.25	13	0	0	2	20	12	1	3	29	13.1	0.75	.179
	Chattanooga (SL)	AA	3	4	4.53	30	0	0	2	44	40	3	32	54	11.1	1.65	.242
2016	Chattanooga (SL)	AA	1	0	9.00	3	0	0	0	3	4	0	1	1	3.0	1.67	.308
2017	Chattanooga (SL)	AA	2	0	0.53	14	0	0	1	17	9	1	4	20	10.6	0.76	.161
Minor League Totals			10	6	3.20	80	0	0	10	104	78	5	50	142	12.3	1.23	.210

26 YEUDY GARCIA, RHP

Born: Oct. 6, 1992. **B-T:** R-R. **Ht.:** 6-2. **Wt.:** 203. **Signed:** Dominican Republic, 2013. **Signed by:** Rene Gayo/Juan Mercado.

Garcia was a late sign for a player from the Dominican Republic, not signing until he was 20. He moved quickly to high Class A Bradenton three years after he was signed, recording ERAs under 3.00 as a starter in 2015 at low Class A West Virginia and in 2016 with the Marauders.

Garcia's progress hit a speed bump early in 2017. He started 11 games and didn't make it through the sixth inning in any of them. However, he moved to the bullpen in late June and flourished. The change in roles had been expected at some point. After posting a 6.50 ERA as a starter, Garcia had a 3.25 ERA as a reliever. He still had well below-average control. The move allowed him to get more out of his fastball, which he was throwing at 92-93 mph as a starter. As a reliever, he typically sat 97 mph and hit 99 on occasion. He combined that with a wipeout power slider and a changeup that came in around 82 mph.

Garcia's move to the bullpen could put him on a much quicker path to the major leagues, and there's a chance he could start 2018 at Triple-A Indianapolis.

Year	Club (League)	Class	W	L	ERA	G	GS	CG	SV	IP	H	HR	BB	SO	K/9	WHIP	AVG
2015	West Virginia (SAL)	LoA	12	5	2.10	30	21	0	1	124	92	4	41	112	8.1	1.07	.204
2016	Bradenton (FSL)	HiA	6	8	2.76	26	25	1	1	127	122	7	54	127	9.0	1.38	.248
2017	Pirates (GCL)	R	1	0	0.00	2	0	0	0	3	1	0	2	4	12.0	1.00	.100
	Altoona (EL)	AA	4	7	5.25	29	11	0	5	72	76	8	46	67	8.4	1.69	.273
Minor League Totals			27	23	2.94	100	70	1	7	386	341	19	163	357	8.3	1.30	.235

27 GAGE HINSZ, RHP

Born: April 20, 1996. **B-T:** R-R. **Ht.:** 6-4. **Wt.:** 210. **Drafted:** HS—Billings, Mont., 2014 (11th round). **Signed by:** Max Kwan.

Hinsz was hard to scout because Montana doesn't have high school baseball, but the Pirates signed him based on what they saw from him playing American Legion baseball and with the Langley Blaze, a youth travel team based in British Columbia.

Hinsz's 2017 season at high Class A Bradenton provided the most obvious evidence so far that he's a project, as opponents hit just south of .300 against him. He continues to show flashes of elite stuff, including a fastball that can touch 97 mph and sits at 94-95, a sharp breaking ball with a three-quarters type break and a developing changeup. However, the Pirates minor league coaching staff is constantly working with Hinsz's mechanics, and he has issues with command. He doesn't have a problem throwing strikes, but he too often leaves pitches in problematic parts of the zone, which is a big part of the reason why his WHIP has been over 1.50 in three of his four minor league seasons.

The Pirates hope Hinsz can begin 2018 at Double-A Altoona, but he might have to stay behind in the Florida State League for more seasoning.

Year	Club (League)	Class	W	L	ERA	G	GS	CG	SV	IP	H	HR	BB	SO	K/9	WHIP	AVG
2015	Bristol (APP)	R	3	4	3.79	10	9	0	0	38	37	1	23	24	5.7	1.58	.252
2016	West Virginia (SAL)	LoA	6	8	3.66	17	17	0	0	93	93	8	25	67	6.5	1.26	.266
2017	Bradenton (FSL)	HiA	5	5	5.61	20	19	0	0	95	112	9	31	52	4.9	1.51	.296
Minor League Totals			14	17	4.46	50	47	0	0	234	250	18	83	150	5.8	1.42	.276

28 STEPHEN ALEMAIS, SS

Born: April 12, 1995. **B-T:** R-R. **Ht.:** 6-0. **Wt.:** 190. **Drafted:** Tulane, 2016 (3rd round). **Signed by:** Wayne Mathis.

Alemais' stock dropped in his junior year at Tulane despite the fact that his numbers were no different than they were his sophomore year. The former high school point guard's game has translated well to pro baseball, because he remains a very good defender and bat handler.

Alemais may be the smoothest, most fluid shortstop in the Pirates' system, with good hands and excellent footwork. His range and arm are both solid to above-average and he has the ability to make the position look easy. His offensive game is less reliable, but he hit .317 in 30 games at high Class A Bradenton in 2017 after missing extensive time with a hand injury. His hit tool is average and his well below-aveage power is occasional at best, but he rarely strikes out.

Alemais likely will have to start 2018 at Bradenton again, with Cole Tucker at Double-A Altoona and Kevin Newman at Triple-A Indianapolis, but he has a chance to move up if there's movement at the higher levels.

Year	Club (League)	Class	AVG	G	AB	R	H	2B	3B	HR	RBI	BB	SO	SB	CS	OBP	SLG
2016	West Virginia (NYP)	SS	.263	39	156	23	41	5	0	1	18	5	18	9	3	.297	.314
	West Virginia (SAL)	LoA	.189	11	37	2	7	1	1	0	2	2	11	1	3	.244	.270
2017	West Virginia (SAL)	LoA	.217	29	120	14	26	5	2	3	11	6	32	5	3	.266	.367
	Pirates (GCL)	R	.259	8	27	6	7	3	0	0	2	4	5	0	0	.355	.370
	Bradenton (FSL)	HiA	.317	30	101	10	32	6	0	1	20	14	14	5	2	.393	.406
Minor League Totals			.256	117	441	55	113	20	3	5	53	31	80	20	11	.311	.349

29 TYLER EPPLER, RHP

BA GRADE

40 Risk: Medium

Born: Jan. 5, 1993. **B-T:** R-R. **Ht.:** 6-6. **Wt.:** 220. **Drafted:** Sam Houston State, 2014 (6th round). **Signed by:** Trevor Haley.

The Pirates took Eppler in the sixth round in 2014 after he spent only one season at the Division I level and two years in junior college. Pittsburgh was intrigued by his big frame and decent velocity.

Eppler has moved up the minor league ladder steadily but not without difficulty. Opponents hit over .280 against him in 2016 and 2017, and he has allowed a combined 38 home runs in two-plus seasons at Double-A Altoona and Triple-A Indianapolis. Eppler's fastball sits in the 93-94 mph range, and he has a slider, cutter and curveball, but none of those secondary pitches are wipeout offerings and are generally used to draw contact. His changeup may be his best secondary pitch. He generally stays close to the zone with all of his pitches, but the Pirates are hoping he develops more ability to throw effective balls and get hitters to chase out of the zone.

Eppler will most likely begin 2018 at Triple-A and be on call if the major league staff has any problems.

Year	Club (League)	Class	W	L	ERA	G	GS	CG	SV	IP	H	HR	BB	SO	K/9	WHIP	AVG
2015	Bradenton (FSL)	HiA	6	1	2.58	14	12	1	1	66	58	1	14	46	6.2	1.09	.232
	Altoona (EL)	AA	0	1	10.13	1	1	0	0	5	4	1	3	3	5.1	1.31	.211
2016	Altoona (EL)	AA	9	10	3.99	27	27	1	0	162	176	14	33	106	5.9	1.29	.280
2017	Indianapolis (IL)	AAA	8	9	4.89	27	21	1	0	136	159	23	33	96	6.3	1.41	.292
Minor League Totals			26	23	3.90	83	75	3	1	439	451	45	94	300	6.2	1.24	.266

30 DARIO AGRAZAL, RHP

BA GRADE

45 Risk: High

Born: Dec. 28, 1994. **B-T:** R-R. **Ht.:** 6-3. **Wt.:** 216. **Signed:** Panama, 2012. **Signed by:** Rene Gayo.

Agrazal has put on substantial size since being signed out of Panama in 2012, which has allowed him to add more velocity. Though he missed much of the 2017 season with a right pectoral strain, he was still named a midseason all-star for the second time in three years, thanks to excellent work at high Class A Bradenton.

Agrazal's fastball is a four-seamer, but it has constant downhill angle and comes in around 96 mph, which leads to consistent ground balls. He also has an average slider and an average changeup with sinking action. All of those pitches usually lead to the ball staying on the ground, and he recorded nearly two ground out for every air out during his time in Bradenton. Agrazal also has excellent control and has never walked more than 18 batters in a season, striking out 65 against 12 walks in 2017.

Agrazal moved up to Double-A Altoona before his injury, so he'll likely start the 2018 season there.

Year	Club (League)	Class	W	L	ERA	G	GS	CG	SV	IP	H	HR	BB	SO	K/9	WHIP	AVG
2015	West Virginia (NYP)	SS	6	5	2.72	14	14	0	0	76	71	3	11	45	5.3	1.08	.245
2016	West Virginia (SAL)	LoA	8	12	4.20	27	27	0	0	150	173	18	18	88	5.3	1.27	.294
2017	Bradenton (FSL)	HiA	5	3	2.91	14	13	0	0	80	73	4	10	63	7.1	1.03	.243
	Altoona (EL)	AA	0	1	4.50	1	1	0	0	4	3	0	2	2	4.5	1.25	.231
Minor League Totals			28	25	3.44	81	79	0	0	426	442	30	63	264	5.6	1.19	.268

St. Louis Cardinals

BY KYLE GLASER

The year 2017 was not a particularly good one for the Cardinals.

They missed the playoffs for the second year in a row, the first time that's happened since 2007-08. They won just 83 games, their fewest in a decade. They were stripped of their first- and second-round draft picks, and fined $2 million, as the penalty for former scouting director Chris Correa's hacking of the Astros' computer system.

Calls for the firing of manager Mike Matheny were prominent—especially when the Cardinals began 3-9 and sat 33-40 in late June—and a year-long coaching shuffle ended with pitching coach Derek Lilliquist and bullpen coach Blaise Ilsley being let go at the end the season.

Pretty much, nothing went right.

The good news is things are looking up for 2018. Four of the Cardinals' top six prospects already have major league experience, and many helped the team go 16-12 in September, its best month of the season. Beyond them is another group of advanced, well-regarded prospects who led Triple-A Memphis to the Pacific Coast League championship.

To further enhance the Cardinals' outlook, they made a big splash at the Winter Meetings by acquiring all-star outfielder Marcell Ozuna from the Marlins in one of the offseason's biggest trades.

Strong campaigns by Paul DeJong, Luke Weaver and minor league Rule 5 pick John Brebbia represented the first group of rookie talent to cement spots on the major league roster, and a large group of 24-and-under players is set to compete for more in 2018.

That list includes Alex Reyes, the one-time No. 1 pitching prospect in the game who missed all of 2017 after having Tommy John surgery but is expected to be ready by spring.

The Cardinals' recent run of poor top picks continued with Delvin Perez struggling horribly and Dylan Carlson drawing mixed reviews in their first full seasons, but they've made up for it with later selections, including Dakota Hudson, Ryan Helsley and Andrew Knizner soaring to the upper minors in 2017.

The Cardinals are also seeing positive early returns from the team-record $20 million-plus they spent internationally during the 2016-17 signing period. Touted Cuban outfielders Randy Arozarena and Jose Adolis Garcia excelled in the upper minors in their first seasons stateside, while younger talents Johan Oviedo, Jonathan Machado and Ivan Herrera impressed at the lower levels. That success, as well as previous fruitful signings such as Reyes, Carlos Martinez and the since-

Paul DeJong learned shortstop after the 2016 season and excelled there as a rookie in 2017.

PROJECTED 2021 LINEUP

Catcher	Carson Kelly (26)
First Base	Matt Carpenter (35)
Second Base	Kolten Wong (30)
Third Base	Jedd Gyorko (32)
Shortstop	Paul DeJong (27)
Left Field	Marcell Ozuna (30)
Center Field	Tommy Pham (33)
Right Field	Tyler O'Neill (26)
No. 1 Starter	Carlos Martinez (29)
No. 2 Starter	Alex Reyes (26)
No. 3 Starter	Luke Weaver (27)
No. 4 Starter	Jack Flaherty (25)
No. 5 Starter	Michael Wacha (29)
Closer	Jordan Hicks (24)

traded Magneuris Sierra, led to the promotion of international director Moises Rodriguez to assistant general manager at the end of the year. It was the latest move of a front office restructuring that began when John Mozeliak moved to president of baseball operations and Michael Girsch was promoted to general manager on July 1.

The Cardinals had their troubles, but reinforcements are closer than they appeared to be entering the year. The addition of Ozuna provides badly needed thump to a lineup that was lacking it, and with pitching depth, impact power bats and versatile defenders all waiting in the upper levels, the Cardinals have valid reasons to believe they can return to the postseason soon.

DEPTH CHART

ST. LOUIS CARDINALS

TOP 2018 ROOKIE: Alex Reyes, RHP. After Tommy John wiped out 2017, he has the chance to show why he was once the game's No. 1 pitching prospect.

BREAKOUT PROSPECT: Jake Woodford, RHP. With advanced pitchability and command already, a velocity bump for the projectable righthander could send him soaring.

SLEEPER: Elehuris Montero, 3B. With a polished approach and plus raw power, the 18-year-old third baseman has promise if he can keep his big body in shape.

SOURCE OF TOP 30 TALENT			
Homegrown	27	**Acquired**	**3**
College	9	Trade	3
Junior college	0	Rule 5 draft	0
High school	7	Independent league	0
Nondrafted free agent	0	Free agent/waivers	0
International	11		

LF
Randy Arozarena (11)
Bryce Denton

CF
Harrison Bader (6)
Oscar Mercado (13)
Jonathan Machado (15)
Scott Hurst (25)
Wadye Ynfante (26)
Chase Pinder

RF
Tyler O'Neill (4)
Jose Adolis Garcia (9)
Dylan Carlson (24)
Victor Garcia (28)

3B
Patrick Wisdom
Evan Mendoza
Elehuris Montero

SS
Delvin Perez (12)
Yairo Munoz (17)
Tommy Edman (29)
Edmundo Sosa (30)
Alex Mejia
Kramer Robertson

2B
Max Schrock (19)
Breyvic Valera
Andy Young

1B
Luke Voit (16)
John Nogowski

C
Carson Kelly (3)
Andrew Knizner (10)
Ivan Herrera
Jeremy Martinez

LHP

LHSP	LHRP
Austin Gomber (14)	Ryan Sheriff
Evan Kruczynski	Jacob Evans
	Brett Seeburger

RHP

RHSP	RHRP
Alex Reyes (1)	Junior Fernandez (21)
Jack Flaherty (2)	Derian Gonzalez (28)
Jordan Hicks (5)	Josh Lucas
Dakota Hudson (7)	Artie Reyes
Ryan Helsley (8)	Chris Ellis
Jake Woodford (18)	Rowan Wick
Alvaro Seijas (21)	Daniel Poncedeleon
Connor Jones (22)	Will Latcham
Joahn Oviedo (23)	
Mike Mayers	
Mike O'Reilly	
Matt Pearce	

DRAFT ANALYSIS

2017

BEST PURE HITTER: St. Louis lacked picks in the first two rounds due to signing Dexter Fowler as a free agent and the hacking scandal of the Astros involving former scouting director Chris Correa. The Cardinals' first pick, OF Scott Hurst (3), got healthy this spring and broke out for Cal State Fullerton, showing the bat speed and feel for hitting he showed when he starred for USA Baseball's 18U team (2013) and was the top prospect in the Alaska League (2014). He swung and missed a lot in a productive (.282/.354/.432) debut.

BEST POWER HITTER: At 6-foot-4, 210 pounds, OF Terry Fuller (15) has size and plus-plus raw power from the left side. He's raw but athletic enough to play center field for now.

FASTEST RUNNER: 3B/OF Donivan Williams (14) received a $300,000 bonus in part due to his plus speed. Hurst is an above-average runner who has a chance to stick in center field.

BEST DEFENSIVE PLAYER: SS Kramer Robertson (4) succeeded Alex Bregman as Louisiana State's shortstop and has infield actions and hands. His arm strength, and whether he can improve it, will decide if he can remain at short. Hurst has a plus arm and could shine in right field if he doesn't stick in center.

BEST ATHLETE: Williams has some strength in his 6-foot, 190-pound frame to go with his speed. He could stick in the infield but played more outfield in his debut.

BEST FASTBALL: RHP Will Latcham (17) can sit 92-96 mph with his fastball. Two years ago he used it to rank fourth in NJCAA with 13.8 strikeouts per nine innings, and he averaged 12 K/9 in his debut.

BEST SECONDARY PITCH: LHP Jacob Patterson (10) already has played the lefty specialist role at Texas Tech and figures to do so as a pro thanks to his solid-average slider, which he commands

TOP DRAFT PICKS OF THE DECADE

Year	Player, Pos.	2017 Org
2008	Brett Wallace, 1B	Did not play
2009	Shelby Miller, RHP	D-backs
2010	Zack Cox, 3B	Tigers
2011	Kolten Wong, 2B	Cardinals
2012	Michael Wacha, RHP	Cardinals
2013	Marco Gonzales, LHP	Mariners
2014	Luke Weaver, RHP	Cardinals
2015	Nick Plummer, OF	Cardinals
2016	Delvin Perez, SS	Cardinals
2017	Scott Hurst, OF (3rd round)	Cardinals

fairly well.

BEST PRO DEBUT: 3B Evan Mendoza (11) hit just .262 in the spring for North Carolina State but won the short-season New York-Penn League batting title; he hit .370 in 41 games before a promotion to low Class A Peoria. He hit .339/.388/.508 overall with 20 doubles and has great hands at the plate and in the field.

MOST INTRIGUING BACKGROUND: OF Chase Pinder (7) is the younger brother of Athletics infielder Chad. Robertson's mother Kim Mulkey won women's basketball NCAA championships as a player at Louisiana Tech and as a coach at Baylor (2005, '12) and won an Olympic gold medal in 1984.

CLOSEST TO THE MAJORS: Patterson could shoot to the big leagues in a relief role.

BEST LATE-ROUND PICK: Fuller and Williams signed above-slot deals, helping them stand out as the Cardinals' primary high school picks. Primarily a position player in high school, RHP Alex Gallegos (35) excited the Cardinals with his 6-foot-3, 175-pound frame and fresh arm.

THE ONE WHO GOT AWAY: A smallish catcher with good athleticism, C Adam Kerner (37) opted to attend San Diego.

—JOHN MANUEL

2016

The Cardinals picked up a mix of upside and advanced players in this class RHP Dakota Hudson (1) finsihed the season in Triple-A and C Andrew Knizner (7) was a breakout performer in the Arizona Fall League. RHP Zac Gallen (3) was used in the Marcell Ozuna trade. SS Delvin Perez (1) struggled out of the gate, but still has exciting raw tools.

GRADE: B

2015

While the class' prep hitters—OF Nick Plummer (1) and 3B Bryce Denton (2)—have struggled, its college hitters—OF Harrison Bader (3) and SS Paul DeJong (4)—quickly reached St. Louis and impressed. DeJong especially surprised en route to a runner-up finish in the NL rookie of the year voting. RHP Jake Woodford (1s) won the Florida State League ERA title.

GRADE: B

2014

RHPs Luke Weaver (1) had a solid rookie season in the Cardinals' rotation. RHP Jack Flaherty (1) joined Weaver in St. Louis, making his big league debut. LHP Austin Gomber (4) remains on track to also get to the big leagues after a solid showing at Double-A. Those three pitchers are likely to be the Cardinals' haul from a pitching-heavy class.

GRADE: C

1 ALEX REYES, RHP

Born: Aug. 29, 1994. **B-T:** R-R. **Ht.:** 6-3. **Wt.:** 175.
Signed: Dominican Republic, 2012.
Signed By: Rodney Jimenez/Angel Ovalles.

Reyes grew up in Elizabeth, N.J., but after his junior year of high school, he moved to the Dominican Republic to live with his grandmother in the hope he could draw more attention as an international amateur. The move worked and the Cardinals signed him for $950,000. Reyes continually flashed power stuff after signing and asserted himself as one of the game's top prospects. He reached 100 mph as a 19-year-old at low Class A, was selected to two Futures Games and made his major league debut in August 2016. He flashed 101 mph heat and was expected to compete for a rotation spot in 2017, but he felt elbow soreness prior to spring training. An MRI revealed a complete rupture of his ulnar collateral ligament. He had Tommy John surgery on Feb. 16 and missed the season.

When Reyes is healthy, few pitchers can match his pure stuff. Strongly built with wide shoulders and thick, sturdy legs, he averages 97 mph with his fastball and touches triple digits with ease. He holds his velocity deep into his starts, blowing hitters away even when they know his fastball is coming. Reyes' command is imperfect, but he excels at elevating his fastball to get swings and misses. He backs up his top-of-the-scale fastball with knee-buckling hammer curveball at 78-81 mph, and his previously raw 88-91 mph changeup began increasingly playing as plus. He also began experimenting with an 83-86 mph short slider. Reyes struggles at times finding a rhythm for his delivery and the result has been below-average control his entire career. Reyes' track record of staying on the mound is also becoming increasingly spotty. He missed a month in 2015 with a sore shoulder, was suspended 50 games in 2016 after testing positive for marijuana in the Arizona Fall League and now has Tommy John surgery on his ledger. In response, he got noticeably stronger during his rehab, replacing fat with muscle and improving his eating habits to enhance his general fitness.

Reyes will spend the offseason continuing his rehab, and team officials expect him to be ready for spring training. If his stuff comes all the way back, he remains a front-of-the-rotation caliber pitcher.

JON DURR/GETTY IMAGES

BA GRADE	SCOUTING GRADES
70 Risk: High	**FB:** 80. **CB:** 70. **CHG:** 60. **CTL:** 50.

Projected future grades on 20-80 scouting scale

TOP PROSPECTS OF THE DECADE

Year	Player, Pos.	2017 Org
2008	Colby Rasmus, OF	Rays
2009	Colby Rasmus, OF	Rays
2010	Shelby Miller, RHP	D-backs
2011	Shelby Miller, RHP	D-backs
2012	Shelby Miller, RHP	D-backs
2013	Oscar Taveras, OF	Deceased
2014	Oscar Taveras, OF	Deceased
2015	Marco Gonzales, LHP	Mariners
2016	Alex Reyes, RHP	Cardinals
2017	Alex Reyes, RHP	Cardinals

BEST TOOLS

Best Hitter for Average	Jonathan Machado
Best Power Hitter	Tyler O'Neill
Best Strike-Zone Discipline	Nick Martini
Fastest Baserunner	Oscar Mercado
Best Athlete	Terry Fuller
Best Fastball	Alex Reyes
Best Curveball	Alex Reyes
Best Slider	Dakota Hudson
Best Changeup	Junior Fernandez
Best Control	Jack Flaherty
Best Defensive Catcher	Carson Kelly
Best Defensive Infielder	Alex Mejia
Best Infield Arm	Patrick Wisdom
Best Defensive Outfielder	Oscar Mercado
Best Outfield Arm	Jose Adolis Garcia

Year	Club (League)	Class	W	L	ERA	G	GS	CG	SV	IP	H	HR	BB	SO	K/9	WHIP	AVG
2015	Cardinals (GCL)	R	0	0	0.00	1	1	0	0	3	0	0	0	3	9.0	0.00	.000
	Palm Beach (FSL)	HiA	2	5	2.26	13	13	0	0	64	49	0	31	96	13.6	1.26	.216
	Springfield (TL)	AA	3	2	3.12	8	8	0	0	35	21	1	18	52	13.5	1.13	.174
2016	Memphis (PCL)	AAA	2	3	4.96	14	14	0	0	65	63	6	32	93	12.8	1.45	.252
	St. Louis (NL)	MAJ	4	1	1.57	12	5	0	1	46	33	1	23	52	10.2	1.22	.201
2017	Did not play—Injured																
Major League Totals			4	1	1.57	12	5	0	1	46	33	1	23	52	10.2	1.22	.201
Minor League Totals			20	21	3.50	69	69	1	0	334	269	14	170	449	12.1	1.31	.220

2 JACK FLAHERTY, RHP

Born: Oct. 15, 1995. **B-T:** 6-4. **Ht.:** 205. **Wt.:** 205. **Drafted:** HS—Los Angeles, 2014 (1st round). **Signed by:** Mike Garciaparra.

Flaherty was the definition of a projectable high school righthander when the Cardinals drafted him 34th overall in 2014. He possessed an alluring frame, polish and a feel for four pitches, but his velocity was yet to come. The velocity finally arrived in 2017 He filled out and began sitting 93-94 mph and touching 96 after previously working 90-92. The result was he missed more bats than ever, soared through the upper minors and made his big league debut on Sept. 1., joining former Harvard-Westlake High teammates Lucas Giolito and Max Fried as big leaguers.

Flaherty is extremely aggressive with his heavy fastball and uses it liberally. His pinpoint command and ability to add and subtract from it, combined with his velocity increase, make it a true plus pitch. His 83-86 mph slider leapt forward as well to become his primary secondary as an above-average pitch that generates swings and misses, and he has a 77-80 mph curveball to give batters a different look as well. Flaherty was projected to develop a plus changeup, but it is still an inconsistent pitch at 86-89 mph.

A rotation spot will be Flaherty's for the taking in 2018. As long as he maintains his velocity increase and fine-tunes his secondaries, he should settle into the middle of the rotation.

BA GRADE

55 Risk: Medium

FB: 60. CB: 50.
SL: 55. CHG: 50.
CTL: 55.

Year	Club (League)	Class	W	L	ERA	G	GS	CG	SV	IP	H	HR	BB	SO	K/9	WHIP	AVG
2015	Peoria (MWL)	LoA	9	3	2.84	18	18	0	0	95	92	2	31	97	9.2	1.29	.251
2016	Palm Beach (FSL)	HiA	5	9	3.56	24	23	0	0	134	129	8	45	126	8.5	1.30	.254
2017	Springfield (TL)	AA	7	2	1.42	10	10	0	0	63	47	2	11	62	8.8	0.92	.205
	Memphis (PCL)	AAA	7	2	2.74	15	15	0	0	85	73	10	24	85	9.0	1.14	.233
	St. Louis (NL)	MAJ	0	2	6.33	6	5	0	0	21	23	4	10	20	8.4	1.55	.284
Major League Totals			0	2	6.33	6	5	0	0	21	23	4	10	20	8.4	1.55	.284
Minor League Totals			29	17	2.77	75	72	0	0	400	359	23	115	398	8.9	1.18	.239

3 CARSON KELLY, C

Born: July 14, 1994. **B-T:** R-R. **Ht.:** 6-2. **Wt.:** 220. **Drafted:** HS—Portland, Ore., 2012 (2nd round). **Signed by:** Matt Swanson.

Kelly became the highest-drafted Oregon prep player since 1996 when the Cardinals selected him 86th overall in 2012 Drafted as a third baseman, Kelly converted to catcher after his first full season. He took to it with vigor, soaking up instruction from Mike Matheny and Yadier Molina and evolving into a premium defender. Kelly received a callup for the second straight season in 2017, and started seven of the Cardinals' final eight games.

Kelly remains a defense-first catcher, but the gap between his glove and his bat has shrunk. Behind the plate he shows soft hands, pristine footwork, good flexibility and a plus arm. He excels at game-calling and managing his staff, giving him the total package of a top-tier defensive backstop. Kelly's biggest development has come on offense. Early in his career he was overaggressive early in counts, but he has become more patient and better at hunting fastballs he can drive. The result was a career high for home runs and OPS and walk-to-strikeout ratio at Triple-A Memphis in 2017. He is still working on finding consistency in his load and timing but has a chance to be an average hitter with average power.

Molina is signed through 2020, but Kelly remains his heir. He will have a chance to make his first Opening Day roster in 2018 and serve as Molina's backup before taking over.

BA GRADE

50 Risk: Low

HIT: 50. POW: 50.
SPD: 20. FLD: 70.
ARM: 60.

Year	Club (League)	Class	AVG	G	AB	R	H	2B	3B	HR	RBI	BB	SO	SB	CS	OBP	SLG
2015	Palm Beach (FSL)	HiA	.219	108	389	30	85	18	1	8	51	22	64	0	0	.263	.332
2016	Springfield (TL)	AA	.287	64	216	29	62	7	0	6	18	14	46	0	1	.338	.403
	Memphis (PCL)	AAA	.292	32	113	14	33	10	0	0	14	11	17	0	0	.352	.381
	St. Louis (NL)	MAJ	.154	10	13	1	2	1	0	0	1	0	2	0	0	.214	.231
2017	Memphis (PCL)	AAA	.283	68	244	37	69	13	0	10	41	33	40	0	2	.375	.459
	St. Louis (NL)	MAJ	.174	34	69	5	12	3	0	0	6	5	11	0	0	.240	.217
Major League Totals			.171	44	82	6	14	4	0	0	7	5	13	0	0	.236	.220
Minor League Totals			.253	539	1955	228	494	97	6	45	243	160	310	2	3	.315	.377

4 TYLER O'NEILL, OF

Born: June 22, 1995. **B-T:** R-R. **Ht.:** 5-11. **Wt.:** 210. **Drafted:** HS—Maple Ridge, B.C., 2013 (3rd round). **Signed by:** Wayne Norton (Mariners).

O'Neill has has made a mockery of minor league pitchers with his titanic home runs the last three seasons. The son of a former Mr. Canada bodybuilder launched 56 homers in 2015-16 and, after a slow start that facilitated a July trade from the Mariners for Marco Gonzales, finished with 31 homers at Triple-A in 2017. He hit four more homers in the playoffs to lift Memphis to the Pacific Coast League title.

O'Neill is short in stature but jacked like a bodybuilder with bulging muscles in his arms, legs and backside. He leverages that massive strength with lightning-quick bat speed, producing massive home runs observers recount with disbelief. He packs double-plus power and knows it, which sometimes gets him in trouble when he gets too steep uphill in his swing plane. O'Neill swings and misses enough to not project as more than a fringe-average hitter, but when right he identifies pitches and draws a reasonable amount of walks. He tends to chase sliders and changeups out front in the dirt as opposed to ones too far inside or outside. Despite his bulk, O'Neill is a solid athlete who posts average run times, adequately plays all three outfield positions and packs an above-average arm. He is best in right field.

O'Neill's swing and approach are geared for power, so his strikeout totals will likely always be high and his average low, but he gets to his power enough to projects as en everyday, middle-of-the-order hitter. He should be big league ready at some point in 2018.

BA GRADE

50 Risk: Medium

HIT: 45. POW: 70.
SPD: 50. FLD: 50.
ARM: 55.

Year	Club (League)	Class	AVG	G	AB	R	H	2B	3B	HR	RBI	BB	SO	SB	CS	OBP	SLG
2015	Bakersfield (CAL)	HiA	.260	106	407	68	106	21	2	32	87	29	137	16	5	.316	.558
2016	Jackson (SL)	AA	.293	130	492	68	144	26	4	24	102	62	150	12	2	.374	.508
2017	Tacoma (PCL)	AAA	.244	93	349	54	85	21	2	19	56	44	108	9	2	.328	.479
	Memphis (PCL)	AAA	.253	37	146	23	37	5	1	12	39	10	43	5	0	.304	.548
Minor League Totals			.267	455	1725	258	461	89	12	101	339	178	550	49	13	.341	.508

5 JORDAN HICKS, RHP

Born: Sept. 6, 1996. **B-T:** R-R. **Ht.:** 6-2. **Wt.:** 185. **Drafted:** HS—Houston, 2015 (3rd round supplemental). **Signed by:** Ralph Garr Jr.

Shoulder inflammation delayed Hicks' debut after the Cardinals drafted him in 2015, but he's done nothing but impress since he's gotten on the mound. With an arsenal as electric as any in the system, Hicks excelled in short-season ball in 2016, was a Midwest League all-star in 2017 and finished with eight dominant appearances at high Class A Palm Beach.

Athletic, physical and aggressive, Hicks works 93-98 mph with his fastball, sits 95 and touches 101 in short bursts. He holds his velocity deep into his starts, and his fastball plays up further with armside life that handcuffs same-side batters. Hicks pairs his heater with a tight power curveball at 79-82 mph that draws plus-plus grades from evaluators and is his go-to swing-and-miss pitch. Hicks relies heavily on those two pitches, but he also has a firm changeup with depth that flashes average and an 83-85 mph slider he'll mix in. While Hicks' arsenal is nasty, his delivery has a lot of moving parts and causes below-average command and control. That hampered him the Arizona Fall League, where he got lit up for a 6.32 ERA and allowed 20 hits in 15.2 innings. Hicks has the athleticism to streamline and repeat his delivery but has yet to show he can.

Hicks has a chance to jump to Double-A Springfield in 2018, depending on his camp performance. How much he improves his command and control will determine if reaches his mid-rotation potential. In all likelihood he ends up a reliever, possibly as the Cardinals' closer of the future.

BA GRADE

55 Risk: V. High

FB: 70. CB: 70.
SL: 45. CHG: 50.
CTL: 40.

Year	Club (League)	Class	W	L	ERA	G	GS	CG	SV	IP	H	HR	BB	SO	K/9	WHIP	AVG
2015	Did not play																
2016	Johnson City (APP)	R	2	1	4.20	6	6	0	0	30	33	1	13	20	6.0	1.53	.292
	State College (NYP)	SS	4	1	1.76	6	6	0	0	31	25	0	16	22	6.5	1.34	.217
2017	Peoria (MWL)	LoA	8	2	3.46	14	14	0	0	78	75	3	39	63	7.3	1.46	.260
	Palm Beach (FSL)	HiA	0	1	1.00	8	5	0	1	27	21	0	6	32	10.7	1.00	.214
Minor League Totals			14	5	2.88	34	31	0	1	166	154	4	74	137	7.4	1.38	.250

6 HARRISON BADER, OF

Born: June 4, 1994. **B-T:** R-R. **Ht.:** 6-0. **Wt.:** 195. **Drafted:** Florida, 2015 (3rd round).
Signed by: Ty Boyles.

A decorated three-year starter at Florida, Bader hit his way up the minors and made his major league debut on July 25, barely two years after he was drafted. He returned for good in September and drew considerable playing time starting in center field.

Bader is, first and foremost, an eager and aggressive hitter who takes big hacks no no matter the count. His power output has progressively risen at each level with an ambush approach, and he has shown enough hitting ability to project for average power. Bader's overall hit tool is in question, however, because the gap between his strikeouts and walks widens at every level. He has yet to develop a two-strike approach and is particularly susceptible to curveballs. Bader is an above-average runner who shows solid range in center field with an average arm, and can slide over to left seamlessly.. His speed plays down on the bases and makes him an inefficient basestealer, with a low 58 percent success rate the last two seasons.

Bader's size, aggressiveness and power is similar to Cardinals teammate Randal Grichuk, with the same risks if he loses his strike-zone discipline or fails to develop a two-strike approach. He will get a shot to cement his spot in the Cardinals outfield in 2018.

BA GRADE

45 Risk: Medium

HIT: 45. POW: 50.
SPD: 55. FLD: 50.
ARM: 50.

Year	Club (League)	Class	AVG	G	AB	R	H	2B	3B	HR	RBI	BB	SO	SB	CS	OBP	SLG
2015	State College (NYP)	SS	.379	7	29	6	11	2	0	2	4	0	5	2	0	.400	.655
	Peoria (MWL)	LoA	.301	54	206	34	62	11	2	9	28	15	44	15	6	.364	.505
2016	Memphis (PCL)	AAA	.231	49	147	22	34	7	1	3	17	11	38	2	3	.298	.354
	Springfield (TL)	AA	.283	82	318	48	90	12	4	16	41	25	93	11	10	.351	.497
2017	Memphis (PCL)	AAA	.283	123	431	74	122	18	1	20	55	34	118	15	9	.347	.469
	St. Louis (NL)	MAJ	.235	32	85	10	20	3	0	3	10	5	24	2	1	.283	.376
Major League Totals			.235	32	85	10	20	3	0	3	10	5	24	2	1	.283	.376
Minor League Totals			.282	315	1131	184	319	50	8	50	145	85	298	45	28	.346	.473

7 DAKOTA HUDSON, RHP

Born: Sept. 15, 1994. **B-T:** R-R. **Ht.:** 6-5. **Wt.:** 215. **Drafted:** Mississippi State, 2016 (1st round). **Signed by:** Clint Brown.

Hudson surprisingly fell to the Cardinals at 34th overall in 2016 after a dominant junior season at Mississippi State. He signed for an above-slot $2 million and showed his draft-day slide was not representative of his ability, excelling at Double-A and reaching Triple-A in his first full season.

Hudson relies primarily on a fastball that sits at 94-95 mph and touches 97 and a plus short slider in the upper 80s. He previously worked mostly in and out with them but has made strides in 2017 at pitching vertically more effectively and changing eye levels at Double-A Springfield, where he was Texas League pitcher of the year. Hudson's curveball got progressively stronger throughout the season and began registering as an above-average to plus offering at 79-83 mph. He also mixes in an occasional changeup. While Hudson's stuff is quality, his fastball command is below-average, often elevating it too much, and as a result he doesn't miss many bats. His control is also inconsistent, especially on his secondary offerings.

BA GRADE

45 Risk: Medium

FB: 55. CB: 55.
SL: 60. CHG: 45.
CTL: 50..

Hudson has the stuff of a mid-rotation starter, but his limited fastball command may spell a future in the bullpen, where he won't have to be too fine. He is slated to begin 2018 at Triple-A Memphis and is in position to make his big league debut during the year.

Year	Club (League)	Class	W	L	ERA	G	GS	CG	SV	IP	H	HR	BB	SO	K/9	WHIP	AVG
2016	Cardinals (GCL)	R	1	0	0.00	4	1	0	0	4	4	0	0	9	20.3	1.00	.235
	Palm Beach (FSL)	HiA	1	1	0.96	8	0	0	3	9	6	0	7	10	9.6	1.39	.188
2017	Springfield (TL)	AA	9	4	2.53	18	18	1	0	114	111	5	34	77	6.1	1.27	.255
	Memphis (PCL)	AAA	1	1	4.42	7	7	0	0	39	36	2	15	19	4.4	1.32	.252
Minor League Totals			12	6	2.82	37	26	1	3	166	157	7	56	115	6.2	1.28	.250

8 RYAN HELSLEY, RHP

Born: July 18, 1994. **B-T:** R-R. **Ht.:** 6-1. **Wt.:** 195. **Drafted:** Northeastern State (Okla.), 2015 (5th round). **Signed by:** Aaron Looper.

Helsley grew up in the Cherokee Nation capital of Tahlequah, Okla., and often made the six-hour drive with his family to Busch Stadium to watch the Cardinals play as a child. His dream of playing for his favorite team was realized when the Cardinals drafted him in the fifth round in 2015 out of Division II Northeastern State. Helsley led the organization in wins in 2016 and shot from high Class A Palm Beach to Triple-A Memphis in 2017.

Helsley is a power pitcher through and through, with a 93-96 mph fastball that touches 98, a power curveball at 80-81 mph with hard, late drop, and an aggressive strike-throwing mentality. He also has a cutter at 87-89 mph and shows feel for an 84-86 mph changeup that flashes average. Helsley is strong and athletic in his 6-foot-1 frame with thick legs built to last. Like many power pitchers, his fastball command can get erratic at times, and his walk rate has increased every level he has climbed. Helsley has the arsenal to start, but late-inning relief would be an easy transition if his fastball command stalls.

Helsley reminds many of Cardinals closer Trevor Rosenthal. He will continue to develop as a starter at Triple-A in 2018.

BA GRADE

45 Risk: Medium

FB: 60. CB: 55. CT: 45. CHG: 50. CTL: 45..

Year	Club (League)	Class	W	L	ERA	G	GS	CG	SV	IP	H	HR	BB	SO	K/9	WHIP	AVG
2015	Johnson City (APP)	R	1	1	2.01	11	9	0	0	40	33	1	19	35	7.8	1.29	.221
2016	Peoria (MWL)	LoA	10	2	1.61	17	17	0	0	95	77	3	19	109	10.3	1.01	.216
2017	Palm Beach (FSL)	HiA	8	2	2.69	17	16	1	0	94	72	3	30	91	8.7	1.09	.213
	Springfield (TL)	AA	3	1	2.67	6	6	0	0	34	25	4	15	41	11.0	1.19	.200
	Memphis (PCL)	AAA	0	0	3.60	1	1	0	0	5	7	0	3	5	9.0	2.00	.350
Minor League Totals			22	6	2.22	52	49	1	0	268	214	11	86	281	9.4	1.12	.217

9 JOSE ADOLIS GARCIA, OF

Born: March 2, 1993. **B-T:** R-R. **Ht.:** 6-1. **Wt.:** 180. **Signed:** Cuba, 2017. **Signed by:** Matt Slater/Moises Rodriguez.

Garcia, the younger brother of Braves third baseman Adonis Garcia, long starred for Ciego de Avila in Cuba's major league and won MVP of the league in 2015-16. After a stint in Japan with the Yomiuri farm team that went poorly, he left Cuba and signed with the Cardinals for $2.5 million in February 2017.

The Cardinals signed Garcia for his explosive tools, but he showed better plate discipline and more polish than expected in his first season and blitzed through Double-A and Triple-A. Garcia's tools are widely evident. He is a plus runner and his arm is a borderline 80 tool from right field, with some managers calling it the strongest arm they've seen in years. His routes and reads need work, but could shore up with experience and make him an average defender. At the plate Garcia is an aggressive free swinger but shows solid pitch recognition, allowing him to drive hittable pitches with authority. He is more of a line-drive hitter into the gaps but shows above-average power potential as he learns to elevate.

Garcia's strong showing puts him in the Cardinals outfield mix for 2018. He has all the tools to start as long as he controls his aggressiveness.

BA GRADE

50 Risk: High

HIT: 50. POW: 55. SPD: 60. FLD: 50. ARM: 80.

Year	Club (League)	Class	AVG	G	AB	R	H	2B	3B	HR	RBI	BB	SO	SB	CS	OBP	SLG
2015	Ciego de Avila	CNS	.319	81	323	62	103	20	2	14	71	34	59	11	6	.399	.523
2016	Yomiuri	JPN	.000	4	7	0	0	0	0	0	0	0	3	0	0	.000	.000
2017	Springfield (TL)	AA	.285	84	309	43	88	23	0	12	55	26	77	12	8	.339	.476
	Memphis (PCL)	AAA	.301	40	136	21	41	11	2	3	10	7	31	3	1	.342	.478
Minor League Totals			.290	124	445	64	129	34	2	15	65	33	108	15	9	.340	.476

10 ANDREW KNIZNER, C

Born: Feb. 3, 1995. **B-T:** R-R. **Ht.:** 6-1. **Wt.:** 200. **Drafted:** North Carolina State, 2016 (7th round). **Signed by:** Charles Peterson.

Knizner started at third base as a freshman at North Carolina State and moved behind the plate as a sophomore, where his offense regressed as he focused on trying to learn the new position. The Cardinals saw enough to make Knizner a 2016 seventh-round pick and sign him for $185,300. His offense ticked back up in pro ball and has led to a quick rise.

Knizner reached Double-A Springfield in his first full season and hit .324 with an .833 OPS at that level. He followed up by hitting .358/.403/.537 in the Arizona Fall League. Knizner's bat is his carrying asset. He has solid bat speed and natural timing, recognizes pitches well and uses the whole field. Knizner's swing is geared mostly for line-drive contact, but he has the strength and approach to elevate for home runs to his pull side. He remains raw defensively, with his receiving, hands and blocking all works in progress, but he progressed and drew some average grades in the AFL. His arm strength is average.

Knizner works hard behind the plate for his pitchers and has a solid work ethic, giving evaluators faith he will eventually be a suitable defender back there. He is ticketed for Triple-A Memphis in 2018.

BA GRADE
50 Risk: High
HIT: 55. POW: 50.
SPD: 30. FLD: 50.
ARM: 50.

Year	Club (League)	Class	AVG	G	AB	R	H	2B	3B	HR	RBI	BB	SO	SB	CS	OBP	SLG
2016	Johnson City (APP)	R	.319	53	185	35	59	12	1	6	42	21	21	0	0	.423	.492
2017	Peoria (MWL)	LoA	.279	44	179	18	50	10	1	8	29	9	22	1	1	.325	.480
	Springfield (TL)	AA	.324	51	182	27	59	13	0	4	22	14	27	0	1	.371	.462
Minor League Totals			.308	148	546	80	168	35	2	18	93	44	70	1	2	.376	.478

11 RANDY AROZARENA, OF

BA GRADE
50 Risk: High

Born: Feb. 28, 1995 **B-T:** R-R. **Ht.:** 5-11. **Wt.:** 170. **Signed:** Cuba, 2016. **Signed by:** Ramon Garcia.

Arozarena starred in Cuba's junior leagues and on its 2013 18U national team, where he finished second behind only teammate Yoan Moncada in on-base percentage during tournament play in Taiwan. The Cardinals invested heavily in Cuban talent during the 2016-17 international signing period and signed Arozarena for $1.25 million.

Arozarena delivered a positive early return on that investment, finishing among the organization leaders in doubles (32), triples (four), and stolen bases (18) in 2017 while climbing to Double-A in his first season. He is wired for contact with a quick, simple righthanded stroke that stays in the hitting zone for a long time. He has a strong eye at the plate, doesn't chase, and uses the whole field. He has wiry strength and more juice in his bat than expected from his 5-foot-11, 170-pound frame, although his developing power is presently all pull-side. He enhances his offensive game as an above-average-to-plus runner who uses his speed efficiently to steal bases. Arozarena primarily played left field in his debut season, but is average to above in center field as well. He plays hard and with some flair on the field.

Arozarena's total package, with his line-drive ability and speed, fits atop a lineup.

Year	Club (League)	Class	AVG	G	AB	R	H	2B	3B	HR	RBI	BB	SO	SB	CS	OBP	SLG
2015	Did not play																
2016	Tijuana (MEX)	AAA	.100	5	20	3	2	1	0	0	0	2	3	0	0	.182	.150
2017	Palm Beach (FSL)	HiA	.275	70	265	38	73	22	3	8	40	13	53	10	4	.333	.472
	Springfield (TL)	AA	.252	51	163	34	41	10	1	3	9	27	34	8	3	.366	.380
Minor League Totals			.259	126	448	75	116	33	4	11	49	42	90	18	7	.339	.424

12 DELVIN PEREZ, SS

BA GRADE
55 Risk: Extreme

Born: Nov. 24, 1998. **B-T:** R-R. **Ht.:** 6-3. **Wt.:** 175. **Drafted:** HS—Celba, P.R., 2016 (1st round). **Signed by:** Mike Dibiase/Juan Ramos.

Teams considered Perez a potential top-10 pick in the 2016 draft, but he tested positive for an undisclosed performance-enhancing drug and fell to the Cardinals at No. 23 overall. He signed for $2,222,500. Nothing went right for Perez in 2017. He hit .194 at Rookie-level Johnson City and was demoted to the Gulf Coast League after 23 games. He struggled badly again in the GCL, and on Aug. 7 a hit-by-pitch broke a bone in his left hand and ended his season.

Perez's strength and ability to impact the ball have disappeared post-PED test. He has good bat speed and can work a count, but he is alarmingly slight physically and shows zero power, even in batting practice. He is fooled badly by breaking pitches away and lacks the strength to drive the ball when he does make contact. He will bunt for hits and beat out infield grounders with his double-plus speed. Defensively

Perez is a promising shortstop with exhilarating athleticism, above-average range, plus arm strength and smooth actions. He struggles playing under control at times but has improved.

Perez's shortstop defense, youth and athleticism work in his favor, but he has enormous strides to make as a hitter.

Year	Club (League)	Class	AVG	G	AB	R	H	2B	3B	HR	RBI	BB	SO	SB	CS	OBP	SLG
2016	Cardinals (GCL)	R	.294	43	163	19	48	8	4	0	19	12	28	12	1	.352	.393
2017	Cardinals (GCL)	R	.238	11	42	7	10	1	2	0	5	5	10	2	1	.320	.357
	Johnson City (APP)	R	.184	23	76	7	14	1	1	0	4	12	14	3	4	.311	.224
Minor League Totals			.256	77	281	33	72	10	7	0	28	29	52	17	6	.335	.342

13 OSCAR MERCADO, OF

BA GRADE **45** Risk: Medium

Born: Dec. 16, 1994. **B-T:** R-R. **Ht.:** 6-2. **Wt.:** 175. **Drafted:** HS—Tampa, 2013 (2nd round). **Signed by:** Charlie Gonzalez.

Mercado moved from Colombia with his family when he was 8 years old and became one of the top prep shortstops in the 2013 draft at Tampa's Gaither High. The Cardinals drafted Mercado in the second round and signed him for $1.5 million signing despite a poor senior season, but he struggled badly his first four pro seasons and fell off the prospect radar. A move to the center field changed that.

Mercado made the transition to center field at the end of 2016 and blossomed playing center everyday at Double-A Springfield in 2017, opening up confidence and an improved bat. He blew past his career-highs in nearly every offensive category and led the organization with 38 steals. Mercado is an above-average runner with excellent agility and body control, which translated to plus defense in center field. He has plus arm strength but is still learning how to access it from the outfield. Mercado shows good bat speed and wiry strength, but has work to do identifying pitches and using the whole field.

Overall fringy hitting ability has many evaluators projecting Mercado as an extra outfielder, but his bounceback season gives him momentum going up to Triple-A in 2018.

Year	Club (League)	Class	AVG	G	AB	R	H	2B	3B	HR	RBI	BB	SO	SB	CS	OBP	SLG
2015	Peoria (MWL)	LoA	.254	117	472	70	120	23	3	4	44	23	61	50	19	.297	.341
2016	Palm Beach (FSL)	HiA	.215	125	442	50	95	23	1	0	27	44	71	33	20	.296	.271
2017	Springfield (TL)	AA	.287	120	477	76	137	20	4	13	46	32	112	38	19	.341	.428
Minor League Totals			.245	464	1799	255	441	80	13	21	156	136	320	159	69	.309	.339

14 AUSTIN GOMBER, LHP

BA GRADE **45** Risk: Medium

Born: Nov. 23, 1993. **B-T:** L-L. **Ht.:** 6-5. **Wt.:** 215. **Drafted:** Florida Atlantic, 2014 (3rd round). **Signed by:** Charlie Gonzalez.

Gomber came out of Florida Atlantic a big-bodied lefthander with a fastball and changeup. The Cardinals implored him to develop a breaking ball early in his career, and the development of a curveball has elevated Gomber. After leading the system in ERA in 2016, the 6-foot-5, 230-pound southpaw finished second in the organization in strikeouts with a strong season at Double-A in 2017.

Gomber is an aggressive, confident pitcher who comes after hitters with three pitches and controls the tempo. He sits 89-92 mph with his fastball and complements it with an average changeup. His real bread and butter is his curve, a downward-diving pitch in the upper 70s that is consistently solid-average and draws plus grades at its best. Gomber controls that arsenal and complements it with a workhorse mentality. He pitched 143 innings in 2017 and saved his best for last, going 6-0, 0.96 over his final seven starts. Gomber is a flyball pitcher prone to giving up home runs when he doesn't spot his fastball precisely, and his lack of a second pitch better than average limits him.

Gomber will begin 2018 at Triple-A Memphis and projects as a possible lefthanded spot starter or swingman.

Year	Club (League)	Class	W	L	ERA	G	GS	CG	SV	IP	H	HR	BB	SO	K/9	WHIP	AVG
2015	Peoria (MWL)	LoA	15	3	2.67	22	22	1	0	135	97	10	34	140	9.3	0.97	.196
2016	Palm Beach (FSL)	HiA	6	8	2.93	17	17	1	0	108	91	5	24	101	8.4	1.07	.229
	Springfield (TL)	AA	1	0	1.40	4	4	0	0	19	11	0	9	15	7.0	1.03	.167
2017	Springfield (TL)	AA	10	7	3.34	26	26	0	0	143	116	17	51	140	8.8	1.17	.219
Minor League Totals			34	20	2.85	80	80	2	0	452	370	35	136	432	8.6	1.12	.221

15 JONATHAN MACHADO, OF

BA GRADE

55 Risk: Extreme

Born: Jan. 21, 1999. **B-T:** L-L. **Ht.:** 5-9. **Wt.:** 155. **Drafted:** Cuba, 2016. **Signed by:** Angel Ovalles.

The Cardinals made a large incursion into the international market in 2016-17, spending more than $20 million between their signing bonuses and overage tax payments. Machado was a marquee signing, reeling in $2.35 million in what was the largest international bonus the Cardinals had ever given out at the time.

Machado struggled to assimilate early in his first year in the U.S. in 2017 but eventually came into his own on the field. He increasingly recognized changeups—which he rarely saw in Cuba—and before long was barreling everything en route to a .323 average in the Gulf Cast League. Machado is a gifted natural hitter on par with any in the system. He is aggressive with his contact-oriented stroke but has excellent strike-zone awareness and rarely swings and misses. He recognizes all types of pitches and drives them gap-to-gap, and he enhances his offensive game with plus-plus speed. He projects as primarily a line-drive hitter, but has the natural ability to run into a few home runs as he gets stronger.

Machado is a bat-first player, but he plays a solid-average center field and moves into the gaps well. He is ticketed for Rookie-level Johnson City in 2018, and will move as quickly as his bat takes him.

Year	Club (League)	Class	AVG	G	AB	R	H	2B	3B	HR	RBI	BB	SO	SB	CS	OBP	SLG
2016	Cardinals (DSL)	R	.209	17	67	10	14	4	1	0	7	7	10	2	1	.284	.299
2017	Cardinals (GCL)	R	.323	35	124	27	40	8	0	2	20	8	13	8	2	.381	.435
Minor League Totals			.283	52	191	37	54	12	1	2	27	15	23	10	3	.347	.387

16 LUKE VOIT, 1B

BA GRADE

40 Risk: Low

Born: Feb. 13, 1991. **B-T:** R-R. **Ht.:** 6-3. **Wt.:** 225. **Drafted:** Missouri State, 2013 (22nd round). **Signed by:** Jared Odom.

Voit had a major league debut few could top in 2017. The St. Louis-area native and Missouri State product received a standing ovation at Busch Stadium when he entered as a pinch-hitter for his first big league at-bat on June 25. He was promptly hit by a pitch in the back and sustained a bruise, but beamed with a wide smile the entire length of his jog to first base. As the season went on, the 22nd-rounder in 2013 proved he was more than just a hometown novelty act.

Voit remained on the Cardinals' roster the rest of the season, drawing starts at first base and contributing as a righthanded power bat off the bench. He is a big, strong Midwestern thumper with an aggressive approach that yields big power and considerable swing-and-miss. He pounds anything with velocity—fastballs, sinkers and sliders—but is prone to slower offerings like changeups and curveballs. Voit is a converted catcher limited to first base, where he is above-average despite his size.

Voit, who will be 27 in 2018, doesn't offer versatility, but he makes enough contact for his power to play at the big league level and can serve as a valuable righthanded bench bat.

Year	Club (League)	Class	AVG	G	AB	R	H	2B	3B	HR	RBI	BB	SO	SB	CS	OBP	SLG
2015	Palm Beach (FSL)	HiA	.273	130	462	52	126	18	5	11	77	63	104	2	0	.360	.405
2016	Springfield (TL)	AA	.297	134	482	70	143	20	5	19	74	52	83	1	2	.372	.477
2017	Memphis (PCL)	AAA	.327	74	269	35	88	23	1	13	50	29	53	1	1	.407	.565
	St. Louis (NL)	MAJ	.246	62	114	18	28	9	0	4	18	7	31	0	0	.306	.430
Major League Totals			.246	62	114	18	28	9	0	4	18	7	31	0	0	.306	.430
Minor League Totals			.286	477	1713	228	490	89	16	54	268	197	348	6	4	.367	.451

17 YAIRO MUNOZ, SS/3B/OF

BA GRADE

45 Risk: Medium

Born: Jan. 23, 1995. **B-T:** R-R. **Ht.:** 6-1. **Wt.:** 165. **Signed:** Dominican Republic, 2012. **Signed by:** Amaurys Reyes (Athletics).

Munoz spent most of his first five seasons as a shortstop, but the Athletics seemed to be grooming him for a super-utility role in 2017 at Double-A Midland and Triple-A Nashville. The Cardinals acquired him and second baseman Max Schrock when they traded Stephen Piscotty to Oakland in December.

Munoz played all three outfield positions and every infield spot except first base in 2017. He needs some polish at the newer positions, but one thing is undeniable: He shows plus-plus arm strength. He put together a solid offensive season in 2017, hitting .300 with 13 homers at two levels. He also stole 22 bases in 27 attempts. Munoz doesn't have great speed, but has good instincts on the basepaths. He's an aggressive, early-in-the-count hitter (21 walks in 477 plate appearances in 2017). He needs to temper that approach just a bit without sacrificing the skills that helped him amass 43 extra-base hits in 2017.

Munoz will probably begin 2018 at Triple-A Memphis, but his bat and versatility could get him to the big leagues at some point in the season.

Year	Club (League)	Class	AVG	G	AB	R	H	2B	3B	HR	RBI	BB	SO	SB	CS	OBP	SLG
2015	Beloit (MWL)	LoA	.236	97	369	48	87	14	3	9	48	22	62	10	2	.278	.363
	Stockton (CAL)	HiA	.320	39	150	21	48	12	0	4	26	11	20	1	1	.372	.480
2016	Midland (TL)	AA	.240	102	387	44	93	16	3	9	39	23	76	6	7	.286	.367
2017	Midland (TL)	AA	.316	47	190	35	60	17	3	6	26	10	35	12	1	.348	.532
	Nashville (PCL)	AAA	.289	65	256	30	74	9	1	7	42	11	46	10	4	.316	.414
Minor League Totals			.267	473	1776	228	474	95	16	41	228	101	315	58	24	.308	.408

18 JAKE WOODFORD, RHP

BA GRADE

50 Risk: High

Born: Oct. 28, 1996. **B-T:** R-R. **Ht.:** 6-4. **Wt.:** 210. **Drafted:** HS—Tampa, 2015 (1st round supplemental). **Signed by:** Mike Dibiase.

Scouts flocked to Tampa's Plant High in 2015 to see outfielder Kyle Tucker, and Woodford took advantage of the eyes on his teammate. Tucker went fifth overall to the Astros, and the Cardinals drafted Woodford shortly after with the 39th overall pick and signed him for $1.8 million.

Woodford has slowly grown into his projectable frame and been increasingly durable at every level. His 3.10 ERA led the high Class A Florida State League in 2017, and he finished in the top 10 in innings and WHIP as well. Woodford's success is derived from his intelligence and pitchability as much as his stuff. He adds and subtracts from his fastball, sitting 91-92 mph but reaching for 94-96 when he needs it, and he manipulates the pitch to give it added sink or cut as needed. Woodford's changeup progressed to average and his slider is still a work in progress, although it will flash average. He ties it all together with excellent control.

Woodford's frame leaves room for a velocity bump, but even if it doesn't come evaluators still see enough for him to be a pitchability righthander in the vein of Jeff Suppan. A move to Double-A awaits in 2018.

Year	Club (League)	Class	W	L	ERA	G	GS	CG	SV	IP	H	HR	BB	SO	K/9	WHIP	AVG
2015	Cardinals (GCL)	R	1	0	2.39	8	5	0	1	26	26	1	7	21	7.2	1.25	.260
2016	Peoria (MWL)	LoA	5	5	3.31	21	21	0	0	109	104	7	37	82	6.8	1.30	.254
2017	Palm Beach (FSL)	HiA	7	6	3.10	23	21	0	0	119	128	7	39	72	5.4	1.40	.280
Minor League Totals			13	11	3.12	52	47	0	1	254	258	15	83	175	6.2	1.34	.267

19 MAX SCHROCK, 2B

BA GRADE

45 Risk: Medium

Born: Oct. 12, 1994. **B-T:** L-R. **Ht.:** 5-8. **Wt.:** 180. **Drafted:** South Carolina, 2015 (13th round). **Signed by:** Paul Faulk (Nationals).

Schrock has been traded twice in three pro seasons, first from the Nationals to the Athletics for Marc Rzepczynski in August 2016, then from Oakland to the Cardinals (along with shortstop Yairo Munoz) for Stephen Piscotty in December 2017. Schrock enjoyed another excellent offensive season at Double-A Midland in 2017.

The lefthanded-batting Schrock hit .321, just shy of his minor league career average of .324, while showing no platoon split in 2017. In 2016, he amassed a minor league-high 177 hits. He knows how to make contact consistently; he struck out a mere 42 times in 457 plate appearances in 2017. He's a solid-average runner, but after stealing a combined 22 bases for four years in 2016, his stolen base production dwindled to four in 2017. The knock on Schrock had been his fringe-average defense at second base. He worked diligently on improving his glove at Midland, and definitely made strides in terms of fielding percentage. Still, if he's going to reach the majors, it'll be because of his offense.

Having spent a season-plus at Double-A, Schrock figures to begin 2018 at Triple-A Memphis.

Year	Club (League)	Class	AVG	G	AB	R	H	2B	3B	HR	RBI	BB	SO	SB	CS	OBP	SLG
2015	Auburn (NYP)	SS	.308	46	172	31	53	10	4	2	14	13	16	2	1	.355	.448
2016	Hagerstown (SAL)	LoA	.326	67	270	46	88	20	2	4	39	22	20	15	3	.381	.459
	Potomac (CAR)	HiA	.341	54	232	30	79	11	0	5	29	9	22	7	2	.373	.453
	Stockton (CAL)	HiA	.111	2	9	0	1	0	0	0	0	0	0	0	0	.111	.111
	Midland (TL)	AA	.391	6	23	3	9	1	0	0	3	0	0	0	1	.375	.435
2017	Midland (TL)	AA	.324	106	417	55	135	20	1	6	44	35	42	4	2	.382	.420
Minor League Totals			.325	281	1123	165	365	62	7	17	129	79	100	28	9	.374	.438

20 JUNIOR FERNANDEZ, RHP

BA GRADE
50 Risk: V. High

Born: March 2, 1997. **B-T:** R-R. **Ht.:** 6-1. **Wt.:** 180. **Signed:** Dominican Republic, 2014. **Signed by:** Rodney Jimenez.

Fernandez played high school ball in the U.S. at Miami's Varela High before moving with his family to the Dominican Republic in 2013. He signed with the Cardinals for $400,000 as an international free agent one year later.

After a quick initial rise, Fernandez hit a speed bump in his development at high Class A. He had a middling performance in his third stint at the level in 2017, and was pulled from a July 26 start with arm soreness and did not return the rest of the season. Fernandez is yet another Latin American flamethrower in the Cardinals system. He comfortably sits 94-95 mph as a starter and can reach back for 99. However, Fernandez is more thrower than pitcher, with a violent delivery that yields poor control, and he doesn't have consistent secondaries to complement his fastball. Evaluators see his slider as a well below-average pitch, while his changeup flashes plus but he doesn't use it effectively.

Fernandez's future is in the bullpen, but the Cardinals will continue starting him to give him more innings to work on all the things he needs to. A move to Double-A Springfield is likely in 2018 if Fernandez is healthy.

Year	Club (League)	Class	W	L	ERA	G	GS	CG	SV	IP	H	HR	BB	SO	K/9	WHIP	AVG
2015	Cardinals (GCL)	R	3	2	3.88	11	9	0	0	51	54	0	15	58	10.2	1.35	.274
	Palm Beach (FSL)	HiA	0	0	1.35	2	1	0	0	7	8	0	2	5	6.8	1.50	.308
2016	Peoria (MWL)	LoA	6	5	3.33	14	14	0	0	78	71	3	34	63	7.2	1.34	.244
	Palm Beach (FSL)	HiA	2	2	5.36	10	6	0	0	44	48	4	20	25	5.2	1.56	.271
2017	Palm Beach (FSL)	HiA	5	3	3.69	16	16	1	0	90	82	5	39	58	5.8	1.34	.249
Minor League Totals			16	17	4.02	60	52	1	0	298	292	13	122	222	6.7	1.39	.260

21 ALVARO SEIJAS, RHP

BA GRADE
50 Risk: Extreme

Born: Oct. 10, 1998. **B-T:** R-R. **Ht.:** 6-1. **Wt.:** 175. **Signed:** Venezuela, 2015. **Signed by:** Jose Gonzalez Maestre.

The Cardinals signed Seijas for $762,500 as the headliner of the 2015 international class and watched with glee as he moved quickly, making his U.S. debut in his first season and holding his own at Rookie-level Johnson City in 2017.

Seijas sprouted from 5-foot-8 to 6-foot-1 and pitches with considerable stuff for an 18-year-old. His sinking fastball sits 92-94 mph with late life early in outings and he complements it with a curveball that flashes plus. Seijas' changeup is still raw and a focal point of his development, but it is usable off his fastball. Seijas doesn't hold his velocity well, dropping to 89-92 mph by the middle innings. His curveball is also inconsistent. Seijas throws strikes but is still learning how to get into pitchers counts quickly and set hitters up.

Seijas has starter traits, but has a ways to go in terms of durability, secondary development and pitch sequencing. He is in line for an assignment to low Class A Peoria in 2018.

Year	Club (League)	Class	W	L	ERA	G	GS	CG	SV	IP	H	HR	BB	SO	K/9	WHIP	AVG
2016	Cardinals (DSL)	R	2	0	4.19	4	4	0	0	19	20	0	6	22	10.2	1.34	.260
	Cardinals (GCL)	R	3	2	3.06	10	9	0	0	50	48	4	13	33	5.9	1.22	.249
2017	Johnson City (APP)	R	4	3	4.97	12	12	0	0	63	79	2	20	63	9.0	1.56	.306
Minor League Totals			9	5	4.14	26	25	0	0	133	147	6	39	118	8.0	1.40	.278

22 CONNOR JONES, RHP

BA GRADE
45 Risk: High

Born: Oct. 10, 1994. **B-T:** R-R. **Ht.:** 6-3. **Wt.:** 200. **Drafted:** Virginia, 2016 (2nd round). **Signed by:** Sean Moran.

Jones led Virginia to the 2015 national championship as the anchor of the Cavaliers rotation as a sophomore and was their Friday night starter as a junior. He finished his decorated college career 22-5, 2.86 and was drafted in the second round by the Cardinals in 2016, signing for $1.1 million. Expected to be a quick riser, Jones instead hit a speed bump in his first full season at high Class A Palm Beach.

Jones sits 92-93 mph and reaches 96 with his fastball and complements it with an above-average to plus breaking ball. However, his stuff plays down because he gets into his own head, nibbling too much and trying to do things he physically can't in terms of pitches he's trying to throw and spot. Jones has a mid-80s changeup with depth but doesn't have the confidence to use it, further complicating matters. The total result was a high walk rate, low strikeout rate, and .274 opponent average in the pitcher-friendly Florida State League.

Jones' two-pitch arsenal and tendency to overthink make him a future reliever for many evaluators, but he'll get the chance to self-correct as a starter at Double-A Springfield in 2018.

Year	Club (League)	Class	W	L	ERA	G	GS	CG	SV	IP	H	HR	BB	SO	K/9	WHIP	AVG
2016	Cardinals (GCL)	R	0	0	2.25	4	0	0	0	4	3	0	1	3	6.8	1.00	.231
	State College (NYP)	SS	0	0	4.22	7	0	0	1	11	15	0	2	8	6.8	1.59	.341
2017	Palm Beach (FSL)	HiA	8	5	3.97	24	21	0	1	113	120	3	49	76	6.0	1.49	.275
	Springfield (TL)	AA	1	0	2.70	1	1	0	0	7	6	1	3	2	2.7	1.35	.261
Minor League Totals			9	5	3.88	36	22	0	2	135	144	4	55	89	5.9	1.48	.279

23 JOHAN OVIEDO, RHP

BA GRADE

50 Risk: Extreme

Born: March 2, 1998. **B-T:** R-R. **Ht.:** 6-6. **Wt.:** 210. **Signed:** Cuba, 2016. **Signed by:** Angel Ovalles.

Oviedo joined Jonathan Machado, Randy Arozarena and Jose Adolis Garcia as big Cuban signings for the Cardinals in the 2016-17 international signing period. A late riser in the class who left the island and showed up in the Dominican Republic throwing five miles per hour harder than he did in Cuba, Oviedo signed with the Cardinals for $1.9 million.

Oviedo is huge physically at 6-foot-6, 210 pounds. That size and his mid-90s fastball helped him coast through Rookie-ball and reach short-season State College as a 19-year-old in his first full season. Oviedo sits 90-94 mph with his fastball, and it plays up with extension out of his large frame and slight cutting action. He is still learning to command the pitch, but generally keeps it in the strike zone and uses it effectively. Oviedo's secondaries are further behind. He'll flash an average curveball, but his slider and changeup project below-average and limit his ability to get through the order multiple times.

Oviedo's size is a blessing and a curse, in that he is well-built but lacks physical projection, leaving evaluators skeptical he can grow into more than a No. 5 starter. He'll try to show otherwise at low Class A Peoria in 2018.

Year	Club (League)	Class	W	L	ERA	G	GS	CG	SV	IP	H	HR	BB	SO	K/9	WHIP	AVG
2016	Cardinals (DSL)	R	0	1	1.66	7	7	0	0	22	19	0	6	29	12.0	1.15	.238
2017	Johnson City (APP)	R	2	1	4.88	6	6	0	0	28	22	0	18	31	10.1	1.45	.220
	State College (NYP)	SS	2	2	4.56	8	8	0	0	47	53	3	18	39	7.4	1.50	.285
Minor League Totals			4	4	4.00	21	21	0	0	97	94	3	42	99	9.2	1.41	.257

24 DYLAN CARLSON, OF

BA GRADE

45 Risk: High

Born: Oct. 23, 1998. **B-T:** B-L. **Ht.:** 6-3. **Wt.:** 195. **Drafted:** HS—Elk Grove, Calif. (1st round). **Signed by:** Zach Mortimer.

Carlson's father Jeff built a national prep baseball powerhouse as the coach at Elk Grove (Calif.) High just outside Sacramento, producing more than a dozen future draft picks including D-backs reliever David Hernandez and Astros third baseman J.D. Davis. Carlson became the programs' highest player ever drafted when the Cardinals took him 33rd overall in 2016 and signed him for $1.35 million.

One of the youngest players in the low Class A Midwest League on Opening Day, Carlson got off to a slow start in his first full season but performed better as the year went on, posting an .804 OPS in June and hitting .266 with a .358 on-base percentage his final 35 games. Carlson is a heady switch-hitter who is selective at the plate, shows above-average power potential from both sides and is a decent athlete with near-average run times and an average arm. Those attributes help him survive, but evaluators question his overall hitting ability and don't see a plus tool, which is especially problematic given Carlson will be limited to a corner outfield spot.

Some think a move to warmer weather will help, and Carlson will get that at high Class A Palm Beach in 2018.

Year	Club (League)	Class	AVG	G	AB	R	H	2B	3B	HR	RBI	BB	SO	SB	CS	OBP	SLG
2016	Cardinals (GCL)	R	.251	50	183	30	46	13	3	3	22	16	52	4	2	.313	.404
2017	Peoria (MWL)	LoA	.240	115	383	63	92	18	1	7	42	52	116	6	6	.342	.347
Minor League Totals			.244	165	566	93	138	31	4	10	64	68	168	10	8	.333	.366

25 SCOTT HURST, OF

BA GRADE

45 Risk: High

Born: March 25, 1996. **B-T:** L-R. **Ht.:** 5-10. **Wt.:** 175. **Drafted:** Cal State Fullerton, 2017 (3rd round). **Signed by:** Brock Ungricht.

The Cardinals were stripped of their first- and second-round picks in 2017 as the penalty for former scouting director Chris Correa's hacking of the Astros' internal database. Their first selection came in the third round and they used it on Hurst, who signed for $450,000. Hurst struggled with a back injury his first two years at Cal State Fullerton but blossomed as a junior, hitting .328 with 12 homers, 40 RBIs and a .994 OPS to lead the Titans to the College World Series.

Hurst stands just 5-foot-10, 175 pounds but is an excellent athlete. He's a solid defender in center field who tracks back well, shows excellent closing speed in the gaps, and flashes an above-average arm. He's an average runner but covers more ground than his speed might indiciate because of excellent instincts. Hurst has a good understanding of the strike zone and uses a short, compact swing to drive the ball from line-to-line. He'll flash average raw power but is more suited for doubles.

Hurst doesn't have the power for a corner and will have to prove he can stick in center despite just average speed. He'll get that shot at low Class A Peoria in 2018.

Year	Club (League)	Class	AVG	G	AB	R	H	2B	3B	HR	RBI	BB	SO	SB	CS	OBP	SLG
2017	State College (NYP)	SS	.282	55	213	36	60	11	6	3	21	22	58	6	4	.354	.432
Minor League Totals			.282	55	213	36	60	11	6	3	21	22	58	6	4	.354	.432

26 WADYE YNFANTE, OF

BA GRADE

50 Risk: Extreme

Born: Aug. 15, 1997. **B-T:** R-R. **Ht.:** 6-0. **Wt.:** 160. **Signed:** Dominican Republic, 2014. **Signed by:** Rodney Jimenez/Angel Ovalles.

The Cardinals signed Ynfante for $125,000 late in the 2013-14 international signing period. Signed as a shortstop, he has played the outfield exclusively since 2015 and settled into center field. Ynfante played his first full season in the U.S. in 2017 and flourished at Rookie-level Johnson City, finishing seventh in the Appalachian League in slugging percentage (.491) and ninth in OPS (.865).

Ynfante's bat has increasingly come around every year as he's grown into his body. He has solid bat speed, drives the ball to all fields and shows home run power both to his pullside and the opposite way. He enhances his offensive profile as a plus runner who stole 11 bases in 14 tries. Ynfante has a tendency to swing and miss due to a deep load, and his strikeout rate bears watching moving forward. He shows the raw tools to be an average center fielder, but his below-average arm could push him to left.

Ynfante intrigues with his skill set, but is also a 20-year-old who has never played above Rookie ball. He will try to show he can handle full-season competition at low Class A Peoria in 2018.

Year	Club (League)	Class	AVG	G	AB	R	H	2B	3B	HR	RBI	BB	SO	SB	CS	OBP	SLG
2015	Cardinals (DSL)	R	.311	49	212	32	66	16	3	3	34	16	42	4	5	.362	.458
2016	Cardinals (DSL)	R	.331	49	181	51	60	15	2	1	27	29	40	9	0	.429	.453
	Cardinals (GCL)	R	.059	6	17	1	1	0	0	0	0	1	4	0	1	.111	.059
2017	Johnson City (APP)	R	.299	43	167	27	50	11	0	7	23	17	51	11	3	.374	.491
Minor League Totals			.285	193	727	126	207	47	8	13	95	84	193	35	11	.365	.425

27 DERIAN GONZALEZ, RHP

BA GRADE

45 Risk: High

Born: Jan. 31, 1995. **B-T:** R-R. **Ht.:** 6-3. **Wt.:** 190. **Signed:** Dominican Republic, 2012. **Signed by:** Jose Gonzalez Maestre.

Gonzalez at one time had the helium to join Alex Reyes and Sandy Alcantara as Latin American flamethrowers rising quickly through the system, but it hasn't quite worked out that way. Various injuries have limited him every year, and the 79 innings he threw at high Class A Palm Beach in 2017 were a career high.

Gonzalez can bring the heat with a mid-90s fastball that touches 97 mph as a starter, and he has a swing-and-miss, above-average curveball he deploys as his main secondary. He has a good pitcher's body and is athletic, but he has struggled with below-average control at every stop. Gonzalez began relieving for the first time at the end of the 2017 season with Palm Beach and struck out eight in 3.1 innings.

Gonzalez's below-average control and lack of durability make the bullpen his likely future home. He will head to Double-A Springfield in 2018.

Year	Club (League)	Class	W	L	ERA	G	GS	CG	SV	IP	H	HR	BB	SO	K/9	WHIP	AVG
2015	Cardinals (GCL)	R	3	5	4.23	11	10	0	0	55	61	0	16	55	8.9	1.39	.274
2016	Peoria (MWL)	LoA	5	0	2.39	15	15	0	0	75	65	1	33	70	8.4	1.30	.236
	Palm Beach (FSL)	HiA	1	2	1.46	4	4	0	0	25	16	0	11	24	8.8	1.09	.182
2017	Cardinals (GCL)	R	0	0	3.00	2	2	0	0	3	5	0	0	6	18.0	1.67	.385
	Palm Beach (FSL)	HiA	4	7	4.33	18	15	1	0	79	78	5	30	72	8.2	1.37	.259
Minor League Totals			16	18	3.51	75	63	1	2	333	317	7	140	329	8.9	1.37	.250

28 VICTOR GARCIA, OF

BA GRADE

50 Risk: Extreme

Born: Sept. 16, 1999. **B-T:** R-R. **Ht.:** 6-3. **Wt.:** 235. **Signed:** Venezuela, 2016. **Signed by:** Estuar Ruiz.

Garcia put on power shows as a teenager in Venezuela that scouts talked about for weeks, and the Cardinals scouted him heavily before signing him for $1.5 million. A pair of hamstring injuries ruined his first pro season in 2017. He pulled one hamstring during extended spring training, then pulled the other in a Dominican Summer League game. He played just 28 games as a result.

Garcia is massive at 6-foot-3, 235 pounds and packs huge raw power he can tap into to all fields. He complements that pop with enough plate discipline and natural hitting ability to get to it, enough evaluators dream on him as a middle-of-the-order masher. Garcia hit only one homer in his pro debut because he was cautious with his lower half due to his hamstring injuries, which bear watching. Garcia is deceptively athletic but will have to work hard to keep his body in check. He has a feel for playing corner outfield but may head to first base if he gets bigger.

Garcia will get a do-over in Rookie ball in 2018 and try to show what he can do when healthy.

Year	Club (League)	Class	AVG	G	AB	R	H	2B	3B	HR	RBI	BB	SO	SB	CS	OBP	SLG
2017	Cardinals (DSL)	R	.250	28	92	11	23	5	0	1	15	8	16	0	0	.340	.337
Minor League Totals			.250	28	92	11	23	5	0	1	15	8	16	0	0	.340	.337

29 TOMMY EDMAN, SS

BA GRADE
40 Risk: Medium

Born: May, 9, 1995. **B-T:** S-R. **Ht.:** 5-10. **Wt.:** 180. **Signed:** Stanford, 2016 (6th round). **Signed by:** Zach Mortimer.

Edman started three years at Stanford and finished his junior year batting third for the Cardinal despite his 5-foot-10, 180-pound frame. An academic All-American who majored in math and computational science, Edman attracted the Cardinals with his smarts, makeup and performance track record and was drafted in the sixth round in 2016, signing for $236,400.

Edman's best asset is his defense at shortstop, and he rode that three levels to finish his first full season at Double-A Springfield. He is instinctive at shortstop and has solid tools as well, with soft hands, good actions, solid-average range and average arm strength. He is an average runner with the athleticism and mobility for the position. The switch-hitting Edman doesn't strike out much and makes contact at a solid rate from both sides of the plate, He shows the propensity to drive balls into the gaps and leg out doubles and triples, especially batting righthanded.

Lacking a plus tool, Edman profiles as a utility infielder but has a long track record of playing above expectations. He will either return to Double-A Springfield or open at Triple-A Memphis depending on his camp performance.

Year	Club (League)	Class	AVG	G	AB	R	H	2B	3B	HR	RBI	BB	SO	SB	CS	OBP	SLG
2016	State College (NYP)	SS	.286	66	255	61	73	14	5	4	33	48	29	19	3	.400	.427
2017	Peoria (MWL)	LoA	.284	38	155	24	44	8	5	2	18	15	19	8	2	.347	.439
	Palm Beach (FSL)	HiA	.257	18	70	7	18	2	1	1	11	7	18	0	1	.338	.357
	Springfield (TL)	AA	.247	63	219	20	54	12	2	2	26	16	34	5	2	.298	.347
Minor League Totals			.270	185	699	112	189	36	13	9	88	86	100	32	8	.352	.398

30 EDMUNDO SOSA, SS

BA GRADE
45 Risk: High

Born: March 6, 1996. **B-T:** R-R. **Ht.:** 5-11. **Wt.:** 170. **Signed:** Panama, 2012. **Signed by:** Arquimedes Nieto.

Sosa was a celebrated signing in the Cardinals' 2012 international class with Alex Reyes and Magneuris Sierra. While the other two have reached the majors, Sosa's climb has been slowed by injuries. Left wrist tendinitis injury ended his 2016 season a month early, and he played just 58 games in 2017, mostly at high Class A Palm Beach, after having hamate bone surgery.

When healthy, Sosa is a solid-average defensive shortstop with range, hands and an arm that are all above-average. However, he often plays too casually and often gives up on plays he should be able to make. Offensively Sosa shows solid bat-to-ball skills and he reined in his approach in 2017, staying within the strike zone and seeing his average and on-base percentage rise as a result. He has little power potential and doesn't steal bases despite above-average speed.

Evaluators generally see Sosa as future utility infielder, but his potential at shortstop and bat-to-ball skills give him a chance to be an everyday player at his peak. That will depend on Sosa's ability to stay healthy, which he hasn't for some time.

Year	Club (League)	Class	AVG	G	AB	R	H	2B	3B	HR	RBI	BB	SO	SB	CS	OBP	SLG
2015	Johnson City (APP)	R	.300	49	200	30	60	8	4	7	16	16	38	6	2	.369	.485
2016	Peoria (MWL)	LoA	.268	88	351	42	94	13	1	3	30	19	71	5	4	.307	.336
	Palm Beach (FSL)	HiA	.294	9	34	3	10	0	2	0	4	1	8	0	0	.314	.412
2017	Springfield (TL)	AA	.000	1	4	0	0	0	0	0	0	1	0	0	0	.200	.000
	Cardinals (GCL)	R	.364	6	22	7	8	1	0	1	2	1	2	0	0	.391	.545
	Palm Beach (FSL)	HiA	.285	51	193	25	55	10	1	0	14	12	34	3	0	.329	.347
Minor League Totals			.285	306	1185	177	338	48	16	15	116	90	199	29	16	.341	.391

San Diego Padres

BY KYLE GLASER

After a tumultuous 2016 that saw a full-on fire sale, the suspension of general manager A.J. Preller and the franchise's worst record since 2008, things finally began looking up for the Padres in 2017.

Their first wave of rookie talent arrived in San Diego. Outfielders Manuel Margot and Hunter Renfroe, righthander Dinelson Lamet, second baseman Carlos Asuaje and reliever Phil Maton all took on regular roles and showed promise, even with the inevitable rookie hiccups. Even while carrying that young talent—as well as three Rule 5 draft picks—the Padres managed to exceed expectations and avoid the National League West cellar.

While the first wave of prospect talent to arrive in the majors was promising, what happened on the farm was the franchise's primary source of excitement.

The more than $80 million the Padres spent on international signing bonuses and overage tax payments in 2016 bore fruit immediately. Cubans Michel Baez and Adrian Morejon showed their talent carried over to the U.S. and cemented themselves as two of baseball's top pitching prospects at low Class A Fort Wayne. Teenagers Gabriel Arias, Jordy Barley and Tirso Ornelas all had strong debuts in the Arizona League after signing bonuses of $1 million or more. Even the lighter performers, such as outfielder Jorge Ona and third baseman Luis Almanzar showed enough to project as possible regulars for evaluators.

While the international splash provided exciting depth to the system, two recent additions at the top give the franchise arguably its best 1-2 prospect duo since Sandy Alomar Jr. and Andy Benes in 1989. Fernando Tatis Jr., acquired for James Shields during the 2016 firesale, rewrote the Midwest League record book and skyrocketed to Double-A as an 18-year-old. MacKenzie Gore, the No. 3 overall pick in the draft and the Padres' reward for suffering through a disastrous 2016, immediately showed himself to be arguably the top lefthanded pitching prospect in baseball.

The next wave of Padres prospects is set to ascend to the majors in 2018 after Cal Quantrill, Eric Lauer, Joey Lucchesi and Jacob Nix finished the 2017 regular season in Double-A. The foursome is in position to inject desperately needed talent into the big league rotation.

With a promising group of largely position players entering the everyday lineup in 2017 and a core of starting pitchers primed to move in 2018, the future is beginning taking shape for the Padres.

The pressure for those young prospects to reach the majors and perform quickly is on after

Manuel Margot is one of many young players San Diego plans to build around in the future

ANDY HAYT/GETTY IMAGES

PROJECTED 2021 LINEUP

Catcher	Austin Hedges (28)
First Base	Wil Myers (30)
Second Base	Luis Urias (24)
Third Base	Yangervis Solarte (33)
Shortstop	Fernando Tatis Jr. (22)
Left Field	Franchy Cordero (26)
Center Field	Manuel Margot (26)
Right Field	Hunter Renfroe (29)
No. 1 Starter	MacKenzie Gore (22)
No. 2 Starter	Michel Baez (25)
No. 3 Starter	Cal Quantrill (26)
No. 4 Starter	Dinelson Lamet (28)
No. 5 Starter	Adrian Morejon (22)
Closer	Anderson Espinoza (23)

managing partner Peter Seidler repeatedly stated he expects the team to be in playoff contention in 2019. By that point Preller's regime will have been in place for four full seasons, and the Padres' playoff drought will have extended to 13 years.

Patience has been preached throughout this rebuild, and now the talent is in place at both the higher and lower levels of the system. More will be added as the Padres pick in the top 10 for the third straight draft with the No. 7 pick in 2018.

The time has arrived for the Padres to start turning their prospect depth into winning at the major league level as they aim for the promised 2019 playoff run. After seven straight losing seasons, it would be a welcome development for the fan base.

DEPTH CHART

SAN DIEGO PADRES

TOP 2018 ROOKIE: Franchy Cordero, OF. He got his first taste of the majors in 2017, and he's now ready for larger role with his speed, defense and improving bat leading the way.

BREAKOUT PROSPECT: Jeisson Rosario, OF. The toolsy center fielder keeps getting stronger, adding power potential to his plus speed, glove and plate discipline.

SLEEPER: Luis Patino, RHP. The 18-year-old Colombian is up to 95 mph with his fastball and routinely attacks the strike zone with an athletic delivery.

SOURCE OF TOP 30 TALENT			
Homegrown	22	Acquired	8
College	5	Trade	8
Junior college	0	Rule 5 draft	0
High school	7	Independent league	0
Nondrafted free agent	0	Free agent/waivers	0
International	10		

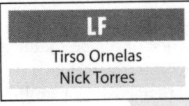

LF
Tirso Ornelas
Nick Torres

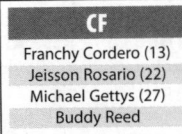

CF
Franchy Cordero (13)
Jeisson Rosario (22)
Michael Gettys (27)
Buddy Reed

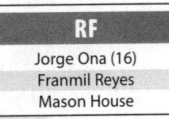

RF
Jorge Ona (16)
Franmil Reyes
Mason House

3B
Hudson Potts (17)
Luis Almanzar (24)
Ty France

SS
Fernando Tatis Jr. (1)
Gabriel Arias (10)
Jordy Barley (30)
Jose Rondon
Javier Guerra
Justin Lopez

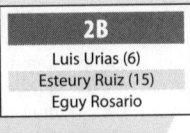

2B
Luis Urias (6)
Esteury Ruiz (15)
Eguy Rosario

1B
Josh Naylor (14)
Brad Zunica

C
Luis Campusano (20)
Austin Allen (29)
Blake Hunt
Luis Torrens
Marcus Greene

LHP

LHSP	LHRP
MacKenzie Gore (2)	Kyle McGrath
Adrian Morejon (5)	Brad Wieck
Logan Allen (8)	Jose Castillo
Joey Lucchesi (9)	Jerry Keel
Eric Lauer (12)	

RHP

RHSP	RHRP
Michel Baez (3)	Andres Munoz (19)
Cal Quantrill (4)	Trey Wingenter (23)
Anderson Espinoza (7)	Miguel Diaz
Jacob Nix (11)	David Bednar
Enyel De Los Santos (18)	Hansel Rodriguez
Chris Paddack (21)	Jose Ruiz
Mason Thompson (25)	T.J. Weir
Pedro Avila (26)	
Reggie Lawson (28)	
Brett Kennedy	
Walker Lockett	
Kyle Lloyd	
Henry Henry	
Chris Huffman	
Jesse Scholtens	
Luis Patino	

DRAFT ANALYSIS

2017

BEST PURE HITTER: C Luis Campusano (2) impressed scouts defensively and offensively prior to being taken with the 39th pick of the draft, and has hit well in his first stint with pro ball, to the tune of a .269/.344/.388 slash line in the Rookie-level Arizona League.

BEST POWER HITTER: OF Mason House (3) was one of the biggest late-rising prospects prior to the 2017 draft and has plus raw power. He managed just two home runs in 39 AZL games this summer, but he also had eight triples and six doubles, with a .171 isolated slugging.

FASTEST RUNNER: OF Robbie Podorsky (25) stole 39 bags and was caught just five times (an 88.6 percent success rate) during his spring season with McNeese State and has stolen 19 bags in 26 tries (76 percent) across two levels in pro ball. A legitimate 80-grade runner, Podorsky should become more efficient with more professional reps and is already a serious threat on the bases.

BEST DEFENSIVE PLAYER: Campusano put a lot of work into improving his body as a high school senior, and it's paid off for him behind the dish. While he caught just 14 percent of basestealers in the AZL this summer he has the tools to improve that mark going forward with average arm strength and improving receiving skills.

BEST FASTBALL: RHP Chandler Newman (11) was drafted out of high school in the 11th round and again in the 11th round out of college, both times for his arm strength. He can get his fastball up to 100 mph and sits in the mid-90s, but had serious control issues in his brief AZL stint.

BEST SECONDARY PITCH: LHP MacKenzie Gore (1) made a concerted effort to throw his changeup more frequently as a Whiteville (N.C.) High senior, and the Padres see the pitch as his best secondary offering—and the best of their 2017 class. His curveball and slider aren't far behind.

BEST PRO DEBUT: Gore debuted in the Arizona League and put together one of the best performances by a pitcher in the league's history and ranked as the circuit's No. 1 prospect. He allowed

TOP DRAFT PICKS OF THE DECADE

Year	Player, Pos.	2017 Org
2008	Allan Dykstra, 1B	Did not play
2009	Donavan Tate, OF	Did not play
2010	*Karsten Whitson, RHP	Did not play
2011	Cory Spangenberg, 2B	Padres
2012	Max Fried, LHP	Braves
2013	Hunter Renfroe, OF	Padres
2014	Trea Turner, SS	Nationals
2015	Austin Smith, RHP (2nd round)	Padres
2016	Cal Quantrill, RHP	Padres
2017	MacKenzie Gore, LHP	Padres

* Did not sign

just three earned runs in 21.1 innings (1.27 ERA) and struck out 40.5 percent of opposing hitters.

BEST ATHLETE: Gore was one of the best athletes in the draft. He could have been a real two-way player in college if he had attended East Carolina, with the ability to play a strong center field. As a pitcher, he uses his immense athleticism to repeat a high-leg-kick delivery and field his position well.

MOST INTRIGUING BACKGROUND: RHP Vijay Miller (14) is likely known more as a football player thanks to his role in Netflix's second season of "Last Chance U." Drafted out of East Mississippi JC, Miller was a backup quarterback for the famous school and started the first game of the season, where he was one of the focuses of the season's opening episode. RHP Cole Bellinger (15) is the younger brother of Dodgers first baseman Cody and son of ex-Yankees infielder Clay.

CLOSEST TO THE MAJORS: The Arizona League didn't provide Gore with much of a challenge, and he has the control, pitch mix and athleticism to move through the system quickly.

BEST LATE-ROUND PICK: Getting an elite tool in the 25th round is rare, but that's certainly what San Diego has in Podorsky's running ability.

THE ONE WHO GOT AWAY: OF Daniel Cabrera (26) was one of the most talented pure hitters in the 2017 high school class. Ranked as the 82nd overall prospect in the class, Cabrara figures to be an impact freshman for Louisiana State.

—CARLOS COLLAZO

2016

The Padres took advantage of their three first-round picks to and a strong class led by RHP Cal Quantrill (1). He and LHPs Eric Lauer (1) and Joey Lucchesi (4) all reached Double-A, while SS Hudson Potts (1) finished his first full season well.

GRADE: B

2015

RHP Austin Smith (2) was the Padres' top pick and has disappointed in pro ball. RHPs Jacob Nix (3) and Trey Wingenter (17) finished the year in Double-A. C Austin Allen (4) still has defensive questions, but slugged in high Class A in 2017.

GRADE: D

2014

With SS Trea Turner (1) starring in the big leagues for the Nationals, OF Michael Gettys (2) is left to carry the banner for the class in San Diego and he had a rough 2017 season. No other player from the class ranks in the handbook.

GRADE: B

1 FERNANDO TATIS JR., SS

Born: Jan. 2, 1999. **B-T:** R-R. **Ht:** 6-3. **Wt:** 185.
Signed: Dominican Republic, 2015.
Signed by: Miguel Peguero (White Sox).

PAUL GIERHART

orn in the Dominican Republic, Tatis nonetheless grew up around Major League Baseball. His father of the same name played 11 seasons as an MLB third baseman, and he often tagged along in clubhouses as a child. When it came time for Tatis Jr. to turn pro, he largely split evaluators because of a perceived weak physical frame and long swing. The White Sox were optimistic and signed him for $700,000. Tatis grew two inches and filled out after signing, and the Padres scouted him closely, ultimately trading James Shields to the White Sox in June 2016 and throwing in nearly $30 million to ensure they received Tatis. He has blossomed since. Playing at the same age as most high school seniors in 2017, Tatis became the first 18-year-old ever to hit 20 home runs and steal 20 bases in the low Class A Midwest League and was promoted to Double-A San Antonio in August

Early in 2017, Tatis would come to the plate without a plan and get caught swinging over breaking balls on the outer half, but he quickly adjusted and became a precocious mix of power and patience. He tracks pitches well and consistently drives hittable offerings with excellent extension and leverage through his swing. Balls jump off his bat from gap to gap, and he shows plus power with towering pull-side home runs. Tatis cut his strikeout rate each successive month at Fort Wayne, and at the time he was promoted, he led the Midwest League in walks. He enhances his offensive game with his basestealing ability. He is an average runner whose speed plays up on the bases with his instincts, reads and jumps. At shortstop, Tatis frequently makes highlight-reel plays and shows off a plus, accurate arm, but on a play-to-play basis, evaluators see fringy range and many project a move to third base if he grows bigger. Tatis will stay at shortstop for now and has the actions to stick there if he maintains his body. In addition to his physical talents, Tatis is a natural leader. He is nearly bilingual and an effective communicator with impressive self-awareness.

Tatis has all the components of a middle-of-the-order shortstop, and even if he has to move to third base has more than enough bat to flourish. His mix of talent, personality and bilingualism sets him up to become the face of the Padres franchise.

BA GRADE	SCOUTING GRADES
65 Risk: High	HIT: 60. POW: 60. SPD: 50. FLD: 50. ARM: 60.

Projected future grades on 20-80 scouting scale

TOP PROSPECTS OF THE DECADE

Year	Player, Pos.	2017 Org
2008	Chase Headley, 3B	Yankees
2009	Kyle Blanks, 1B	Mexican League
2010	Donavan Tate, OF	Did not play
2011	Casey Kelly, RHP	Giants
2012	Anthony Rizzo, 1B	Cubs
2013	Casey Kelly, RHP	Giants
2014	Austin Hedges, C	Padres
2015	Matt Wisler, RHP	Braves
2016	Javier Guerra, SS	Padres
2017	Anderson Espinoza, RHP	Padres

BEST TOOLS

Best Hitter For Average	Luis Urias
Best Power Hitter	Fernando Tatis Jr.
Best Strike-Zone Discipline	Luis Urias
Fastest Baserunner	Robbie Podorsky
Best Athlete	Jeisson Rosario
Best Fastball	Michel Baez
Best Curveball	Pedro Avila
Best Slider	MacKenzie Gore
Best Changeup	Cal Quantrill
Best Control	MacKenzie Gore
Best Defensive Catcher	Luis Campusano
Best Defensive Infielder	Justin Lopez
Best Infield Arm	Javier Guerra
Best Defensive Outfielder	Michael Gettys
Best Outfield Arm	Michael Gettys

Year	Club (League)	Class	AVG	G	AB	R	H	2B	3B	HR	RBI	BB	SO	SB	CS	OBP	SLG
2016	Padres (AZL)	R	.273	43	176	35	48	13	1	4	20	10	44	14	2	.312	.426
	Tri-City (NWL)	SS	.273	12	44	4	12	4	2	0	5	3	13	1	1	.306	.455
2017	Fort Wayne (MWL)	LoA	.281	117	431	78	121	26	7	21	69	75	124	29	15	.390	.520
	San Antonio (TL)	AA	.255	14	55	6	14	1	0	1	6	2	17	3	0	.281	.327
Minor League Totals			.276	186	706	123	195	44	10	26	100	90	198	47	18	.359	.477

2 MACKENZIE GORE, LHP

Born: Feb. 24, 1999. **B-T:** L-L. **Ht:** 6-3. **Wt:** 180. **Drafted:** HS—Whiteville, N.C., 2017 (1st round). **Signed by:** Nick Brannon.

Gore posted jaw-dropping numbers throughout his prep career, winning BA's High School Player of the Year award as a senior in 2017 after he went 11-0, 0.19 with 158 strikeouts and five walks in 74.1 innings for Whiteville (N.C.) High. Many clubs considered Gore the top prospect in the 2017 draft, even ahead of lauded righthander Hunter Greene, and the Padres took him with the No. 3 overall pick and signed him for $6.7 million to forgo a commitment to East Carolina.

An elite athlete with a sky-high leg kick in his delivery, Gore blends his supreme athleticism with an advanced four-pitch arsenal and top-notch competitive makeup. His fastball operates 92-95 mph, but plays up thanks to plus command and gets on hitters quickly with good extension out of his delivery. His mid-70s curveball with tight 1-to-7 snap is another plus pitch, and his tumbling 82-85 mph swing-and-miss changeup was even better than expected after signing. His low-80s short slider gives him another potential plus offering. With four pitches, command and deception, many evaluators who saw Gore in his pro debut called him one of the best pitching prospects in 30-year history of the Rookie-level Arizona League.

Gore shares physical similarities with Cole Hamels at the same age, with the potential stuff and control to match. He will head to low Class A Fort Wayne in 2018 as he tries to reach his top-of-the-rotation potential.

BA GRADE

65 Risk: Extreme

FB: 60. CB: 60.
SL: 55. CHG: 60.
CTL: 60.

Year	Club (League)	Class	W	L	ERA	G	GS	CG	SV	IP	H	HR	BB	SO	K/9	WHIP	AVG
2017	Padres (AZL)	R	0	1	1.27	7	7	0	0	21	14	0	7	34	14.3	0.98	.184
Minor League Totals			0	1	1.27	7	7	0	0	21	14	0	7	34	14.3	0.98	.184

3 MICHEL BAEZ, RHP

Born: Jan. 21, 1996. **B-T:** R-R. **Ht:** 6-8. **Wt:** 220. **Signed:** Cuba, 2016. **Signed by:** Trevor Schumm/Jake Koenig.

Teams scouted Baez as a teenager in Cuba but had limited interest because of his lack of control. He pitched in the island's national 18U league and in the major league, Serie Nacional, where he posted a 5.05 ERA with more walks (16) than strikeouts (14) pitching out of the bullpen in his lone season. Baez left for the Dominican Republic and the Padres had a front row seat to his development as he began working with the same trainer as Jorge Ona and Jordy Barley, both of whom the Padres signed for seven-figure bonuses early in the 2016 international signing period. They watched as Baez progressively added more fastball velocity and began demonstrating more control, and ultimately pulled the trigger and signed him for $3 million in December, beating out the Cardinals and Astros, among others.

BA GRADE

65 Risk: Extreme

FB: 70. CB: 55.
SL: 55. CHG: 60.
CTL: 60.

A trapezius injury held Baez back in extended spring training in 2017, but he made his low Class A Fort Wayne debut on July 4 and immediately became the talk of the low Class A Midwest League. He allowed only 19 hits and three runs in his first 36.2 innings, with 56 strikeouts and four walks. He eventually finished with a 2.04 ERA, 98 strikeouts and 10 walks in 70.2 innings including the MWL postseason. Baez's fastball is a head-turner out of his enormous 6-foot-8, 220-pound frame. He possesses a power arm and pounds the strike zone downhill out of his high three-quarters arm slot. He holds his fastball at 94-95 mph and frequently touches 98 to grade as a plus-plus pitch. His fastball comes out easy, teasing more velocity in the tank, and he hides the ball well behind his enormous frame to create deception. At times late in his outings Baez will get around his fastball and lose his downhill plane, but his velocity and deception are enough to get swings and misses up in the zone anyway. Baez's upper-80s slider flashes above-average and is his go-to secondary pitch, but isn't yet consistent. His mid-80s changeup flashes plus with fade away from lefthanders, and he flashes a hammer 11-to-5 curveball in the upper 70s with late action. Most importantly he repeats his delivery to throw frequent strikes, perhaps too many. He allowed as many home runs as walks (eight) in the MWL regular season.

Baez needs to fine-tune his fastball command and achieve a bit more consistency with his secondaries. If he does, he's a front-of-the-rotation starter.

Year	Club (League)	Class	W	L	ERA	G	GS	CG	SV	IP	H	HR	BB	SO	K/9	WHIP	AVG
2017	Padres (AZL)	R	1	0	3.60	1	1	0	0	5	2	1	2	7	12.6	0.80	.133
	Fort Wayne (MWL)	LoA	6	2	2.45	10	10	0	0	59	41	8	8	82	12.6	0.84	.192
Minor League Totals			7	2	2.54	11	11	0	0	64	43	9	10	89	12.6	0.83	.188

4 CAL QUANTRILL, RHP

Born: Feb. 10, 1995. **B-T:** L-R. **Ht:** 6-2. **Wt:** 165. **Drafted:** Stanford, 2016 (1st round).
Signed by: Sam Ray.

Quantrill, the son of former big league reliever Paul Quantrill, had Tommy John surgery three starts into his sophomore season at Stanford and missed all of his junior year, too. The Padres were impressed enough by his predraft bullpen sessions to draft him No. 7 overall in 2016 and sign him for just under $4 million. He delivered on that faith in 2017, cruising through the high Class A California League and reaching Double-A San Antonio.

BA GRADE
60 Risk: High
FB: 60. **CB:** 45.
SL: 50. **CHG:** 70.
CTL: 50.

The Padres streamlined Quantrill's mechanics to help his velocity come easier, and it did in 2017. He now sits comfortably at 93-95 mph and can reach back for 97. He holds that velocity, pitches downhill and commands his fastball, making it a plus pitch. His 81-83 mph changeup is his out pitch and one of the best in the minors. He sells it with identical arm speed as his fastball, and the pitch slows suddenly just in front of the plate, drawing lunging, off-balance swings. His 81-84 mph slider flashes above-average but lacks consistency, and the Padres are focused on developing his mid-70s curveball, which is currently a below-average pitch. Quantrill throws all his pitches for strikes and has above-average command, which could get to plus as he moves further away from surgery.

Quantrill's aggressiveness further helps his stuff play up, although he gets so competitive at times he lets his emotions get the best of him and he loses focus. Evaluators still see his competitive nature as a positive rather than a negative. Quantrill is a smart, self-aware individual who works hard and craves a challenge. His total package of stuff, command and mentality gives him a potential middle-to front-of-the-rotation future. Triple-A El Paso is next.

Year	Club (League)	Class	W	L	ERA	G	GS	CG	SV	IP	H	HR	BB	SO	K/9	WHIP	AVG
2016	Padres (AZL)	R	0	2	5.27	5	5	0	0	14	12	0	2	16	10.5	1.02	.231
	Tri-City (NWL)	SS	0	2	1.93	5	5	0	0	19	15	0	2	28	13.5	0.91	.205
	Fort Wayne (MWL)	LoA	0	1	17.36	2	2	0	0	5	12	1	4	2	3.9	3.43	.522
2017	Lake Elsinore (CAL)	HiA	6	5	3.67	14	14	0	0	74	78	5	24	76	9.3	1.38	.273
	San Antonio (TL)	AA	1	5	4.04	8	8	0	0	42	52	5	16	34	7.2	1.61	.296
Minor League Totals			7	15	4.12	34	34	0	0	153	169	11	48	156	9.2	1.42	.277

5 ADRIAN MOREJON, LHP

Born: Feb. 27, 1999. **B-T:** L-L. **Ht:** 6-1. **Wt:** 195. **Signed:** Cuba, 2016. **Signed by:** David Post/Trevor Schumm/Felix Feliz.

Morejon became a hot commodity after pitching Cuba to the gold medal at the 2015 15U World Cup in Mexico City, delivering a complete-game victory with 12 strikeouts against a United States lineup that included 2017 No. 1 overall pick Royce Lewis. The Padres signed Morejon for a franchise-record $11 million when he became eligible in July 2016, and he delivered a solid showing in his debut, finishing at low Class A Fort Wayne.

Morejon draws praise for his intangibles and poise as much as his stuff. He has an advanced understanding of how to set up hitters, mix his pitches and exploit weaknesses. His stuff isn't too shabby either. Morejon's fastball sits 91-93 mph and touches 95 in his starts and works 94-96 in short bursts. He throws two changeups that flash plus, one a diving knuckle-change and the other a traditional change with

BA GRADE
60 Risk: High
FB: 60. **CB:** 50.
CHG: 60.
CTL: 55..

sink and run. His curveball shows above-average spin and power, but he gets rotational and his arm drags at times when throwing it, peeling toward third base in his delivery and causing him to lose the strike zone. The same delivery flaw results in inconsistent fastball command.

Morejon is advanced for his age but still has work to do with his delivery and overall durability. He has never pitched more than 63 innings in a season and showed signs of fatigue at the end of his pro debut. He'll head to high Class A Lake Elsinore in 2018.

Year	Club (League)	Class	W	L	ERA	G	GS	CG	SV	IP	H	HR	BB	SO	K/9	WHIP	AVG
2017	Tri-City (NWL)	SS	2	2	3.57	7	7	0	0	35	37	2	3	35	8.9	1.13	.266
	Fort Wayne (MWL)	LoA	1	2	4.23	6	6	0	0	28	28	2	13	23	7.5	1.48	.264
Minor League Totals			3	4	3.86	13	13	0	0	63	65	4	16	58	8.3	1.29	.265

6 LUIS URIAS, 2B/SS

Born: June 3, 1997. **B-T:** R-R. **Ht:** 5-9. **Wt:** 160. **Signed:** Mexico, 2013. **Signed by:** Chad MacDonald/Robert Rowley.

The Padres purchased Urias' rights from the Mexican League's Mexico City franchise when he was 16 and got a better player than they even imagined. Urias hit .330 to win the high Class A California League batting title and MVP award in 2016 and parlayed that into a spot on Team Mexico in the 2017 World Baseball Classic as a 19-year-old. An ankle injury in late-July 2017 shelved him for three weeks and affected him when he returned, knocking him out of the Texas League batting title race, yet he still won the league's on-base percentage crown (.398) at age 20.

Urias rarely expands his strike zone, forcing pitchers to come to him. When they do he uses his elite hand-eye coordination and quick swing to drive all types of pitches on a line into the outfield. Though he doesn't elevate for home runs, he makes consistent hard contact with exit velocities in line with Yoan Moncada, Vladimir Guerrero Jr. and other top prospects. He rarely swings and misses, and projects as a true plus-plus hitter. Defensively, Urias is an athletic, plus second baseman with reliable hands, excellent footwork and an impressive vertical leap. He has an above-average arm. The Padres made Urias the starting shortstop at Double-A San Antonio the first half of the season and he progressively improved there, ultimately drawing a few plus grades from evaluators as a defender at short in the Arizona Fall League. His lateral range is better suited for second base.

Even so, it is Urias' special bat that separates him. He has a chance to win batting titles down the road and is the Padres' long-term second baseman of the future with Fernando Tatis Jr. ticketed for shortstop. Triple-A El Paso awaits Urias in 2018.

BA GRADE
55 Risk: Medium

HIT: 70. **POW:** 40.
SPD: 50. **FLD:** 60.
ARM: 55.

Year	Club (League)	Class	AVG	G	AB	R	H	2B	3B	HR	RBI	BB	SO	SB	CS	OBP	SLG
2015	Tri-City (NWL)	SS	.355	10	31	6	11	1	0	0	1	5	1	3	3	.487	.387
	Fort Wayne (MWL)	LoA	.290	51	193	28	56	5	1	0	16	16	18	5	10	.370	.326
2016	El Paso (PCL)	AAA	.444	3	9	6	4	0	0	1	3	5	1	1	0	.667	.778
	Lake Elsinore (CAL)	HiA	.330	120	466	71	154	26	5	5	52	40	36	7	13	.397	.440
2017	San Antonio (TL)	AA	.296	118	442	77	131	20	4	3	38	68	65	7	5	.398	.380
Minor League Totals			.310	347	1306	218	405	57	11	9	124	153	135	33	37	.396	.391

7 ANDERSON ESPINOZA, RHP

Born: March 9, 1998. **B-T:** R-R. **Ht:** 6-0. **Wt:** 160. **Signed:** Venezuela, 2014. **Signed by:** Eddie Romero/Manny Padron (Red Sox).

The Padres acquired the touted Espinoza from the Red Sox for Drew Pomeranz at the 2016 all-star break, and the deal carried repercussions. Major League Baseball later ruled the Padres did not properly disclose Pomeranz's medical history and suspended general manager A.J. Preller 30 days over the deal. In a twist of fate, Espinoza missed all of 2017 due to injury and projects to miss all of 2018 too. He began the year on the disabled list with forearm soreness, aborted two rehab attempts, and ultimately had Tommy John surgery in August.

When healthy, Espinoza is an undersized righthander with an electric arm who draws comparisons with the late Yordano Ventura. With an athletic delivery and a lightning-fast arm, Espinoza works 95-98 mph with his four-seam fastball with so much late tail it looks a two-seamer. He pitches to both sides of the plate and complements his heater with a dastardly mid-80s changeup. His upper-70s curveball had made strides and flashed plus with 11-to-5 movement. Durability is Espinoza's main concern after he visibly tired the second half of his 108-inning run in 2016, and he now will miss two full seasons with arm trouble.

Espinoza has front-of-the-rotation stuff, but it remains to be seen if it will come back post-surgery. He is scheduled to begin his throwing program in January, and his return to the mound is targeted for 2018 instructional league.

BA GRADE
65 Risk: Extreme

FB: 70. **CB:** 55.
CHG: 70.
CTL: 50.

Year	Club (League)	Class	W	L	ERA	G	GS	CG	SV	IP	H	HR	BB	SO	K/9	WHIP	AVG
2015	Red Sox2 (DSL)	R	0	0	1.20	4	4	0	0	15	13	0	3	21	12.6	1.07	.232
	Red Sox (GCL)	R	0	1	0.68	10	10	0	0	40	24	0	9	40	9.0	0.83	.170
	Greenville (SAL)	LoA	0	1	8.10	1	1	0	0	3	4	0	2	4	10.8	1.80	.267
2016	Greenville (SAL)	LoA	5	8	4.38	17	17	0	0	76	77	2	27	72	8.5	1.37	.269
	Fort Wayne (MWL)	LoA	1	3	4.73	8	7	0	0	32	38	1	8	28	7.8	1.42	.290
2017	Did not play—Injured																
Minor League Totals			6	13	3.35	40	39	0	0	167	156	3	49	165	8.9	1.23	.248

8 LOGAN ALLEN, LHP

Born: May 23, 1997. **B-T:** L-L. **Ht:** 6-3. **Wt:** 200. **Drafted:** HS—Bradenton, Fla., 2015 (8th round). **Signed by:** Stephen Hargett (Red Sox).

The Red Sox drafted Allen in the eighth round in 2015, and the Padres acquired him six months later as one of four players exchanged for Craig Kimbrel. Elbow soreness limited Allen in his first year in the Padres system in 2016, but he excelled in 2017 as he reached high Class A Lake Elsinore.

At his best, Allen sits 92-94 mph with his fastball and shows off a potential plus changeup and above-average curveball. At other times he's 89-91 mph with just average secondaries. He shows the poise and pitchability to succeed even when his stuff isn't at his best, however. Allen is aggressive with his fastball and establishes it early in games. He complements it with a "Vulcan" grip changeup he holds between his middle and ring finger that dives as it approaches the plate for a swing-and-miss offering. Allen still is trying to find a consistent release point on his hard, slurvy curveball, but he shows flashes of snapping it off. He throws all his pitches for strikes but can get wild in the zone.

Allen looks like a mid-rotation starter at his best, but he has to improve his consistency of stuff and iron out his command in the strike zone. He'll head to Double-A San Antonio in 2018.

BA GRADE
55 Risk: High
FB: 55. CB: 50.
CHG: 60.
CTL: 50..

Year	Club (League)	Class	W	L	ERA	G	GS	CG	SV	IP	H	HR	BB	SO	K/9	WHIP	AVG
2015	Red Sox (GCL)	R	0	0	0.90	7	7	0	0	20	12	0	1	24	10.8	0.65	.171
	Lowell (NYP)	SS	0	0	2.08	1	1	0	0	4	6	0	0	2	4.2	1.38	.300
2016	Padres (AZL)	R	0	0	3.00	3	3	0	0	6	5	0	1	8	12.0	1.00	.217
	Tri-City (NWL)	SS	0	1	7.71	1	1	0	0	2	4	0	1	4	15.4	2.14	.364
	Fort Wayne (MWL)	LoA	3	4	3.33	15	11	0	0	54	48	2	22	47	7.8	1.30	.242
2017	Fort Wayne (MWL)	LoA	5	4	2.11	13	13	0	0	68	49	1	26	85	11.2	1.10	.201
	Lake Elsinore (CAL)	HiA	2	5	3.97	11	10	0	0	57	60	2	18	57	9.1	1.38	.272
Minor League Totals			10	14	2.89	51	46	0	0	212	184	5	69	227	9.7	1.20	.234

9 JOEY LUCCHESI, LHP

Born: June 6, 1993. **B-T:** L-L. **Ht.:** 6-5. **Wt.:** 204. **Drafted:** Southeast Missouri State, 2016 (4th round). **Signed by:** Troy Hoerner.

Lucchesi led all of Division I in strikeouts as a senior in 2016 at Southeast Missouri State and signed with the Padres for $100,000 as a fourth-round pick. The funky 6-foot-5 lefty dominated both high Class A and Double-A in his first full season, leading the organization in ERA (2.20) and finishing second in strikeouts (148).

BA GRADE
50 Risk: Medium
FB: 55. CB: 55.
CHG: 55.
CTL: 55.

Lucchesi has a potent mix of deception and stuff. His unique windup features multiple stops and starts, unconventional hand positioning, a high leg kick and a slight turn to hide the ball. While hitters are simply trying to find the ball or time him up, he delivers the ball over the top and throws three above-average pitches for strikes. His fastball works 90-94 mph and is a swing-and-miss pitch with its location and downhill angle. His above-average 77-80 mph curveball features a hard, late drop and his 80-82 mph changeup looks like a breaking ball out of his hand before staying straight and drawing foolish swings. Lucchesi is athletic enough to repeat his complicated delivery, resulting in above-average command and control and a lot of called strikes. He is confident and self-assured on the mound. He also has one of the nastiest pickoff moves in the minors.

Lucchesi's No. 4 starter projection is a safe one he may surpass. Triple-A El Paso awaits in 2018.

Year	Club (League)	Class	W	L	ERA	G	GS	CG	SV	IP	H	HR	BB	SO	K/9	WHIP	AVG
2016	Tri-City (NWL)	SS	0	2	1.35	14	10	0	1	40	27	0	2	53	11.9	0.73	.189
	Fort Wayne (MWL)	LoA	0	0	0.00	1	0	0	0	2	4	0	1	3	13.5	2.50	.444
2017	Lake Elsinore (CAL)	HiA	6	4	2.52	14	14	0	0	79	56	9	19	95	10.9	0.95	.194
	San Antonio (TL)	AA	5	3	1.79	10	9	0	1	60	46	3	14	53	7.9	0.99	.208
Minor League Totals			11	9	1.99	39	33	0	2	181	133	12	36	204	10.1	0.93	.201

10 GABRIEL ARIAS, SS

Born: Feb. 27, 2000. **B-T:** R-R. **Ht.:** 6-1. **Wt.:** 185. **Signed:** Venezuela, 2016.
Signed by: Luis Prieto/Yfrain Linares/Trevor Schumm

Arias trained at the same program that produced Franklin Barreto and Gleyber Torres in Venezuela and was a starring member of the country's youth international teams. The Padres signed Arias for $1.9 million in 2016 and he proved worthy of his high profile, reaching low Class A Fort Wayne at age 17 and hitting .364 in the playoffs.

Arias is, first and foremost, a gifted defender who projects as a future plus shortstop. He is a lithe athlete with smooth actions and the range to make difficult plays look routine. His plus-plus, accurate arm can make throws from anywhere on the field. Arias' polished, reliable hands complement those skills to give him Gold Glove-potential in some evaluators' eyes. Offensively, Arias has developed faster than expected but still has a ways to go. He has plus bat speed and a short, controlled swing, but he gets pull-happy and is liable to chase pitches out of the zone. He shows average power in batting practice and is an average runner.

Arias' defense will carry him, and his offensive development will determine if he reaches his above-average everyday potential. He'll return to Fort Wayne to begin 2018.

BA GRADE
55 Risk: **Extreme**
HIT: 50. POW: 45.
SPD: 50. FLD: 60.
ARM: 70.

Year	Club (League)	Class	AVG	G	AB	R	H	2B	3B	HR	RBI	BB	SO	SB	CS	OBP	SLG
2017	Padres (AZL)	R	.275	37	153	18	42	6	3	0	13	10	51	4	6	.329	.353
	Fort Wayne (MWL)	LoA	.242	16	62	8	15	1	0	0	4	2	16	1	0	.266	.258
Minor League Totals			.265	53	215	26	57	7	3	0	17	12	67	5	6	.312	.326

11 JACOB NIX, RHP

Born: Jan. 9, 1996. **B-T:** R-R. **Ht.:** 6-3. **Wt.:** 200. **Drafted:** HS—Bradenton, Fla., 2015 (3rd round). **Signed by:** Chris Kelly.

BA GRADE
50 Risk: **High**

The Astros drafted Nix in the fifth round in 2014 but didn't sign him after they failed to agree with top overall pick Brady Aiken, costing them the bonus pool money needed to also sign Nix. The Padres redrafted Nix in the third round a year later out of post-grad IMG Academy. A groin strain shelved Nix for the first six weeks of the 2017 season, but he still rose through two levels and finished at Double-A San Antonio.

Nix is strongly-built at 6-foot-4, 220 pounds and maintains some of the highest average fastball velocity in the system at 93-96 mph. His plus power curveball is a hammer with depth in the low 80s, and his changeup shows above-average potential. Nix repeats his delivery and throws all of his pitches for strikes, but frequently catches too much of the plate. He also lacks deception and fastball life. As a result, he has allowed more than 10 hits per nine innings at every level and has a career strikeout rate of 7.5 per nine.

Nix has the pure stuff of a mid-rotation starter, but needs to improve his command and life to get there. He will try at Triple-A El Paso in 2018.

Year	Club (League)	Class	W	L	ERA	G	GS	CG	SV	IP	H	HR	BB	SO	K/9	WHIP	AVG
2015	Padres (AZL)	R	0	2	5.49	7	3	0	0	20	23	1	7	19	8.7	1.53	.284
2016	Fort Wayne (MWL)	LoA	3	7	3.93	25	25	0	0	105	115	5	20	90	7.7	1.28	.280
2017	Lake Elsinore (CAL)	HiA	4	3	4.32	11	10	1	0	67	78	5	10	51	6.9	1.32	.297
	San Antonio (TL)	AA	1	2	5.53	6	6	0	0	28	32	0	9	22	7.2	1.48	.281
Minor League Totals			8	14	4.39	49	44	1	0	219	248	11	46	182	7.5	1.34	.285

12 ERIC LAUER, LHP

Born: June 3, 1995. **B-T:** R-L. **Ht.:** 6-3. **Wt.:** 205. **Drafted:** Kent State, 2016 (1st round). **Signed by:** Matt Maloney.

BA GRADE
45 Risk: **Medium**

As Kent State junior, Lauer recorded an 0.68 ERA that was the lowest in Division I since 1979. The Padres drafted him that year with the last of their three first-round picks, No. 25 overall, and signed him for $2 million. Lauer battled through fatigue in his first full season, but still delivered 122.2 innings and finished strong at Double-A.

Lauer is a classic pitchability lefty who relies on mixing and locating his pitches. His fastball ranges from 87-94 mph and he sits 89-91, slowing it down and speeding it up depending on the situation. His fastball has some sneakiness to it and he isn't afraid to pitch inside, making for uncomfortable at-bats even with below-average velocity. Lauer's main secondary is an above-average 84-85 mph changeup he sells with identical arm speed. His fringy 82-86 mph slider lacks bite, but he places it effectively on the back foot of righthanded hitters for a usable third pitch. His below-average 75-76 mph curveball is loopy and rolls into the strike zone.

Lauer isn't flashy, but shows enough pitchability and control to potentially survive as a No. 5 starter. He'll head to Triple-A El Paso in 2018.

Year	Club (League)	Class	W	L	ERA	G	GS	CG	SV	IP	H	HR	BB	SO	K/9	WHIP	AVG
2016	Padres (AZL)	R	0	1	6.75	2	2	0	0	4	7	1	1	7	15.8	2.00	.368
	Tri-City (NWL)	SS	1	0	1.44	7	7	0	0	25	17	0	7	28	10.1	0.96	.191
	Fort Wayne (MWL)	LoA	0	0	0.00	1	1	0	0	2	0	0	1	2	9.0	0.50	.000
2017	Lake Elsinore (CAL)	HiA	2	5	2.79	12	12	0	0	68	65	4	19	84	11.2	1.24	.250
	San Antonio (TL)	AA	4	3	3.93	10	9	0	0	55	52	6	17	48	7.9	1.25	.251
Minor League Totals			7	9	3.05	32	31	0	0	154	141	11	45	169	9.9	1.21	.243

13 FRANCHY CORDERO, OF

BA GRADE 45 Risk: Medium

Born: Sept. 22, 1994. **B-T:** L-R. **Ht.:** 6-3. **Wt.:** 175. **Signed:** Dominican Republic, 2011. **Signed by:** Randy Smith/Felix Feliz/Martin Jose.

The Padres signed Cordero for $175,000 as a shortstop when he was 17, but moved him to center field after he made 126 errors in 165 games. The move unlocked increased confidence and a sharp uptick in production, as Cordero shot through three levels in 2016 and made his major league debut in 2017.

Cordero is a lithe athlete with exceptional first-step quickness and long strides. He is a plus-plus runner underway, finishing behind only Billy Hamilton, Byron Buxton and Bradley Zimmer among major league center fielders in sprint speed, as measured by Statcast. Cordero uses that speed to chase down long flies as an above-average defender in center field and make an impact on the bases. He tied for the minor-league lead with 18 triples and delivered his second straight season with at least 20 doubles, 10 triples, 10 home runs and 15 steals at Triple-A El Paso.

While he hits for impact and can fly, Cordero rarely walks and doesn't control the strike zone, limiting his overall offensive upside. He hits just enough, with his defense and speed, to be a second-division regular or oft-used extra outfielder. He'll get a shot at that role with the Padres in 2018.

Year	Club (League)	Class	AVG	G	AB	R	H	2B	3B	HR	RBI	BB	SO	SB	CS	OBP	SLG
2015	Fort Wayne (MWL)	LoA	.243	126	481	59	117	13	1	5	34	31	121	22	11	.293	.306
2016	Lake Elsinore (CAL)	HiA	.286	74	297	47	85	16	8	5	35	19	83	11	8	.339	.444
	San Antonio (TL)	AA	.306	59	245	31	75	8	8	6	19	17	67	12	6	.356	.478
	El Paso (PCL)	AAA	.077	4	13	1	1	0	0	0	0	3	4	0	0	.250	.077
2017	San Diego (NL)	MAJ	.228	30	92	15	21	3	3	3	9	6	44	1	1	.276	.424
	El Paso (PCL)	AAA	.326	93	390	68	127	21	18	17	64	23	118	15	4	.369	.603
Major League Totals			.228	30	92	15	21	3	3	3	9	6	44	1	1	.276	.424
Minor League Totals			.281	535	2122	313	597	81	52	46	251	158	610	101	41	.337	.434

14 JOSH NAYLOR, 1B

BA GRADE 50 Risk: High

Born: June 22, 1997. **B-T:** L-L. **Ht.:** 6-0. **Wt.:** 22. **Drafted:** HS—Mississauga, Ont. (1st round). **Signed by:** Steve Payne (Marlins).

The Marlins made Naylor the highest-drafted Canadian position player ever when they selected him 12th overall in 2015 and signed him for $2.2 million. One year later the Padres acquired him in the five-player trade that sent Andrew Cashner to Miami. Naylor started 2017 hot before a pickoff throw broke his right cheekbone and sapped his production after he returned, but he still made his second straight Futures Game and reached Double-A.

Naylor is stocky with a protruding belly, closer to 260 pounds than his listed 225, and limited to first base. He shows enormous raw power in batting practice but doesn't get to it in games, largely because he struggles picking out pitches he can drive and collapses hard on his front side. He has the bat speed and hand-eye coordination to project as an average hitter with above-average power if he improves in those areas. Naylor is a surprisingly good athlete for his girth, flashing average run times and good short-area quickness and hands defensively at first base.

Naylor needs to monitor his weight and make the adjustments to get to his power to reach his potential as a solid-average everyday first baseman. He'll start back at Double-A in 2018.

Year	Club (League)	Class	AVG	G	AB	R	H	2B	3B	HR	RBI	BB	SO	SB	CS	OBP	SLG
2015	Marlins (GCL)	R	.327	25	98	8	32	4	1	1	16	4	11	1	0	.352	.418
2016	Greensboro (SAL)	LoA	.269	89	342	42	92	24	2	9	54	22	62	10	3	.317	.430
	Lake Elsinore (CAL)	HiA	.252	33	139	17	35	5	0	3	21	3	22	1	1	.264	.353
2017	Lake Elsinore (CAL)	HiA	.297	72	283	41	84	16	2	8	45	27	48	7	1	.361	.452
	San Antonio (TL)	AA	.250	42	156	18	39	9	0	2	19	16	36	2	1	.320	.346
Minor League Totals			.277	261	1018	126	282	58	5	23	155	72	179	21	6	.326	.412

15 ESTEURY RUIZ, 2B

BA GRADE
55 Risk: Extreme

Born: Feb. 15, 1999. **B-T:** R-R. **Ht.:** 6-0. **Wt.:** 150. **Signed:** Dominican Republic, 2015. **Signed by:** Edys de Oleo (Royals).

Ruiz signed with the Royals for $100,000 in 2015 and is quickly proving a bargain. After a brilliant start in the Rookie-level Arizona League in 2017, Ruiz joined the Padres along with lefthanders Travis Wood and Matt Strahm in a July 24 trade for Trevor Cahill, Ryan Buchter and Brandon Maurer.

Ruiz performed as well after the trade as before it, and finished first in the AZL in hitting (.350), doubles (20) and triples (10) and was named MVP. Compared physically to a greyhound, Ruiz's wiry build belies his strong wrists, explosive hands and excellent bat speed. He produces frequent hard contact to all fields, and his long arms provide leverage to generate loft and in-game power. Ruiz will swing and miss and has some empty at-bats, but his overall package is enough to project a potential above-average hitter with above-average power as he gets stronger. Ruiz has average speed but is a prolific basestealer with his superb instincts and motor. He isn't particularly rangy and gets hard-handed at second base, leading some to believe a move to the outfield may be in store.

Ruiz's potent bat should carry him, regardless. He'll head to low Class A Fort Wayne in 2018.

Year	Club (League)	Class	AVG	G	AB	R	H	2B	3B	HR	RBI	BB	SO	SB	CS	OBP	SLG
2016	Royals (DSL)	R	.313	56	217	44	68	18	5	5	26	19	35	13	10	.378	.512
2017	Royals (AZL)	R	.419	21	86	22	36	10	6	3	23	4	20	9	0	.440	.779
	Padres (AZL)	R	.300	31	120	23	36	10	4	1	16	9	34	17	6	.364	.475
Minor League Totals			.331	108	423	89	140	38	15	9	65	32	89	39	16	.386	.556

16 JORGE ONA, OF

BA GRADE
50 Risk: High

Born: Dec. 31, 1996. **B-T:** R-R. **Ht.:** 6-0. **Wt.:** 220. **Signed:** Cuba, 2016. **Signed by:** Felix Felix/Trevor Schumm/Alvin Duran.

Ona jumped on scouts' radars when he hit .636 with four home runs in eight games playing for Cuba at the 2014 COPABE 18U Pan American Championships. The Padres kept tabs on Ona after he left to train in the Dominican Republic, and signed him for $7 million when he became eligible in July 2016.

Ona is a hulking physical specimen chiseled like a body-builder. He combines that brute strength with impressive bat speed to produce plus raw power, including the opposite way to right-center. However, Ona hit only 11 home runs and slugged just .405 at low Class A Fort Wayne because he is a free swinger who gets long and struggles to make adjustments, resulting in big holes and a below-average hit profile overall. He struck out almost a quarter of his plate appearances and nearly half of his batted balls were grounders. Defensively Ona is a liability in the outfield as a bulky, fringe-average runner who rakes poor routes. He has the above-average arm needed for right field if he improves.

Ona's ability to adjust to get to his plus power will determine if he reaches his everyday potential. He'll start at high Class A Lake Elsinore in 2018.

Year	Club (League)	Class	AVG	G	AB	R	H	2B	3B	HR	RBI	BB	SO	SB	CS	OBP	SLG
2017	Fort Wayne (MWL)	LoA	.277	107	415	54	115	18	1	11	64	40	115	8	2	.351	.405
Minor League Totals			.277	107	415	54	115	18	1	11	64	40	115	8	2	.351	.405

17 HUDSON POTTS, 3B

BA GRADE
50 Risk: High

Born: Oct. 28, 1998. **B-T:** R-R. **Ht.:** 6-2. **Wt.:** 180. **Drafted:** HS—Southlake, Texas, 2016 (1st round). **Signed by:** Matt Schaffner.

The Padres drafted Potts 24th overall in 2016 and signed him for a below-slot $1 million to pass up Texas A&M, saving the team money to go over-slot with later picks. Potts' first full season got off to a poor start when he hit just .226/.259/.360 in the first half at low Class A Fort Wayne, but he bounced back to hit .278/.325/.512 with 14 of his 20 home runs in the second half.

Potts is young but physically well put together with wiry strength and a pro body. He has a balanced swing and a sound bat path that produces above-average power, his primary asset. Though Potts rarely walks, he takes competitive at-bats, recognizes pitches and doesn't often expand the zone. He swings and misses in the zone enough, however, that most evaluators see him as a fringe-average hitter. Defensively Potts is new to third base after playing shortstop and is inconsistent, sometimes appearing solid-average with a plus arm and at others below-average with limited arm strength. He makes the plays he gets to, committing only nine errors all year in 2017.

Potts is a hard worker with exceptional makeup, giving him a foundation to adjust and improve as he did in his first full season. He'll begin at high Class A Lake Elsinore in 2018.

Year	Club (League)	Class	AVG	G	AB	R	H	2B	3B	HR	RBI	BB	SO	SB	CS	OBP	SLG
2016	Padres (AZL)	R	.295	43	183	35	54	12	2	1	21	9	34	8	4	.333	.399
	Tri-City (NWL)	SS	.233	16	60	7	14	0	1	0	6	9	13	2	1	.352	.267
2017	Fort Wayne (MWL)	LoA	.253	125	491	67	124	23	4	20	69	23	140	0	1	.293	.438
Minor League Totals			.262	184	734	109	192	35	7	21	96	41	187	10	6	.308	.414

18 ENYEL DE LOS SANTOS, RHP

BA GRADE 50 Risk: High

Born: Dec. 25, 1995. **B-T:** R-R. **Ht.:** 6-3. **Wt.:** 170. **Signed:** Dominican Republic, 2014. **Signed by:** Eddy Romero/Domingo Toribio (Mariners).

De los Santos signed with the Mariners for just $15,000 in 2014 and proved a bargain, jumping from 86-89 mph to reaching the mid-90s a year after signing. The Padres acquired him for Joaquin Benoit after the 2015 season. De los Santos has grown into one of the Padres' most reliable and intriguing arms, leading the organization in innings (150) while going 10-6, 3.78 at Double-A San Antonio in 2017

De los Santos has one of the better fastballs in the system, a 94-98 mph bullet he commands to both sides of the plate. His fastball has excellent carry through the zone, and his improved command has made it true weapon that draws swings-and-misses and weak ground-ball contact. De los Santos relies heavily on that fastball. His curveball flashes average but he lacks consistent feel for it, and he doesn't deploy his solid-average changeup at the right times.

De los Santos has to improve those secondaries to reach his starter potential. Even if he doesn't, his stuff will play in late relief. He'll head to Triple-A in 2018.

Year	Club (League)	Class	W	L	ERA	G	GS	CG	SV	IP	H	HR	BB	SO	K/9	WHIP	AVG
2015	Mariners (AZL)	R	3	0	2.55	5	5	0	0	25	24	1	5	29	10.6	1.18	.250
	Everett (NWL)	SS	3	0	4.06	8	8	0	0	38	37	2	13	42	10.0	1.33	.270
2016	Fort Wayne (MWL)	LoA	3	2	2.91	11	7	0	0	53	38	2	14	45	7.7	0.99	.199
	Lake Elsinore (CAL)	HiA	5	3	4.35	15	15	0	0	68	70	11	24	52	6.8	1.38	.267
2017	San Antonio (TL)	AA	10	6	3.78	26	24	0	0	150	131	12	48	138	8.3	1.19	.237
Minor League Totals			24	11	3.70	65	59	0	0	333	300	28	104	306	8.3	1.21	.242

19 ANDRES MUNOZ, RHP

BA GRADE 55 Risk: Extreme

Born: Jan. 16, 1999. **B-T:** R-R. **Ht.:** 6-2. **Wt.:** 165. **Signed:** Mexico, 2015. **Signed by:** Trevor Schumm.

The Padres signed Munoz from the Mexico City of the Mexican League for $700,000 in 2015, their top signing from that international period. The quick-armed righthander sat 88-92 mph when he signed, touched 95 the following spring and hasn't stopped adding velocity.

Munoz has grown into one of the hardest throwers in the minors, sitting 97-99 mph and touching 101 as an 18-year-old at low Class A Fort Wayne in 2017. He was the youngest player sent to the Arizona Fall League and allowed only one run while striking out 11 in 8.2 innings of relief. Munoz's fastball is close to an 80-grade pitch with its velocity and tremendous carry, and he excels pitching upstairs. He struggled badly to control it during the regular season, issuing 6.2 walks-per-nine innings, but made strides staying on line to the plate and throwing it for strikes in the fall. Munoz also fine-tuned his 84-86 mph slider, which shows good shape and he turns at the right time to flash average.

Evaluators love Munoz's stuff but not his arm action and are concerned with how much stress it puts on his shoulder. If Munoz can stay healthy and maintain his strides with his control, he has closer potential.

Year	Club (League)	Class	W	L	ERA	G	GS	CG	SV	IP	H	HR	BB	SO	K/9	WHIP	AVG
2016	Padres (AZL)	R	1	1	5.49	16	1	0	0	20	16	1	16	26	11.9	1.63	.213
2017	Tri-City (NWL)	SS	3	0	3.80	21	0	0	1	24	15	2	16	35	13.3	1.31	.177
	Fort Wayne (MWL)	LoA	0	0	3.86	3	0	0	0	2	2	0	2	3	11.6	1.71	.222
Minor League Totals			4	1	4.53	40	1	0	1	46	33	3	34	64	12.6	1.47	.195

20 LUIS CAMPUSANO, C

BA GRADE 55 Risk: Extreme

Born: Sept. 29, 1998. **B-T:** R-R. **Ht.:** 6-0. **Wt.:** 195. **Drafted:** HS—Augusta, Ga., 2017 (2nd round). **Signed by:** Tyler Stubblefield.

Campusano failed to make the USA Baseball 18U National Team after his junior year of high school and used it as motivation to get in better shape, trimming excess baby fat and growing significantly more muscular by the spring of his senior year. His power ticked up as a result and he became the top catcher selected in the 2017 draft when the Padres picked him 39th overall and signed him for $1.3 million to forgo a South Carolina commitment.

The newly-chiseled Campusano shows plus raw power, sometimes a tick above, and takes a strong swing in games to get to it. His overly aggressive approach prevents him from accessing that power consistently and his swing will get long, but he shows enough hitterish qualities to project as a possible average bat with usable pull-side power. Defensively Campusano receives well, has an above-average arm and has worked himself to make himself a solid blocker. He takes instruction well and is mature for his age.

Evaluators see a potential everyday catcher hitting .250 with 15-20 home runs and above-average defense in Campusano, but he is a ways from getting there. He has a chance to see full-season ball in 2018.

Year	Club (League)	Class	AVG	G	AB	R	H	2B	3B	HR	RBI	BB	SO	SB	CS	OBP	SLG
2017	Padres (AZL)	R	.278	24	90	3	25	4	0	1	13	6	14	0	1	.327	.356
	Padres (AZL)	R	.250	13	44	5	11	0	0	3	12	9	11	0	1	.377	.455
Minor League Totals			.269	37	134	8	36	4	0	4	25	15	25	0	2	.344	.388

21 CHRIS PADDACK, RHP

BA GRADE

55 Risk: Extreme

Born: Jan. 8, 1996. **B-T:** R-R. **Ht.:** 6-4. **Wt.:** 195. **Drafted:** HS—Cedar Park, Texas, 2015 (8th round). **Signed by:** Ryan Wardinsky (Marlins).

Paddack put up insane numbers to start his first full season in 2016, posting a 0.95 ERA with 48 strikeouts and two walks in 28.1 innings for the Marlins low Class A affiliate Greensboro. The Padres acquired him in a one-for-one trade for Fernando Rodney that June. Paddack was similarly dominant for three starts at low Class A Fort Wayne but succumbed to Tommy John surgery in July, ending his season and wiping out all of 2017 as well.

When healthy, Paddack excelled with a darting 90-95 mph fastball, a plus-plus mid-80s changeup and elite control. His fastball-changeup combination was his bread-and-butter, but his mid-70s curveball gradually improved to a usable pitch with decent depth as he became more consistent with his release point. Paddack got bigger and stronger during his rehab and showed hints of a velocity bump during bullpen sessions in instructional league, but shut down early with elbow tenderness.

Health is Paddack's biggest question mark. He missed six weeks with biceps tendinitis even before having Tommy John and has never thrown more than 45.1 innings in a season. He'll return to game action at the start of the 2018 season with a careful eye on his health and workload.

Year	Club (League)	Class	W	L	ERA	G	GS	CG	SV	IP	H	HR	BB	SO	K/9	WHIP	AVG
2015	Marlins (GCL)	R	4	3	2.18	11	7	0	0	45	37	1	7	39	7.7	0.97	.219
2016	Greensboro (SAL)	LoA	2	0	0.95	6	6	0	0	28	9	2	2	48	15.2	0.39	.098
	Fort Wayne (MWL)	LoA	0	0	0.64	3	3	0	0	14	11	0	3	23	14.8	1.00	.212
2017	Did not play—Injured																
Minor League Totals			6	3	1.54	20	16	0	0	88	57	3	12	110	11.3	0.79	.182

22 JEISSON ROSARIO, OF

BA GRADE

55 Risk: Extreme

Born: Oct. 22, 1999. **B-T:** L-L. **Ht.:** 6-1. **Wt.:** 175. **Signed:** Dominican Republic, 2016. **Signed by:** Felix Feliz/Ysrael Rojas/Alvin Duran.

The Padres signed Rosario for $1.85 million during their 2016 international spending spree, intrigued by his athleticism and balanced skillset. Rosario delivered in his first pro campaign, outperforming many of his peers in the Rookie-level Arizona League with a .299 average, nearly as many walks (33) as strikeouts (36) and growing tools.

Rosario is a top-tier athlete who can do standing backflips and runs a 6.5-second 60-yard dash, a plus-plus time. His speed plays more above-average to plus on the field. Rosario floats to balls in center field and projects to stay there with excellent closing speed, lateral quickness and an average arm. Offensively Rosario has some of the best plate discipline in the system and the bat-to-ball skills to project as an above-average hitter. His stroke is naturally geared to drive balls the opposite way into left-center, but he is adding strength and began showing the ability to turn on balls at the end of the year, including hitting five home runs during batting practice at Petco Park in the fall.

Rosario still has some maturing to do. He gets frustrated and overwhelmed at times and it affects his effort level. He'll take his promising tools and athleticism to low Class A Fort Wayne in 2018.

Year	Club (League)	Class	AVG	G	AB	R	H	2B	3B	HR	RBI	BB	SO	SB	CS	OBP	SLG
2017	Padres (AZL)	R	.299	52	187	31	56	10	0	1	24	33	36	8	6	.404	.369
Minor League Totals			.299	52	187	31	56	10	0	1	24	33	36	8	6	.404	.369

23 TREY WINGENTER, RHP

BA GRADE
45 Risk: Medium

Born: April 15, 1994. **B-T:** R-R. **Ht.:** 6-7. **Wt.:** 200. **Drafted:** Auburn, 2015 (17th round). **Signed by:** Steve Moritz.

A 36th-round pick by the Mariners out of high school, Wingenter progressively added velocity as he filled out his 6-foot-7 frame over the years and touched 100 mph for the first time in 2017. As the closer at Double-A San Antonio, he held opponents to a .193 average.

Previously 88-92 mph in high school and 92-94 in college at Auburn, Wingenter moved to the bull-pen full time in pro ball and added strength. He now sits 96-98 mph and touches triple digits, velocity that's compounded by a towering release point that produces steep downhill angle and makes his heater difficult to square up. As Wingenter's fastball has jumped, so has his slider. It now sits 84-86 mph with tilt and depth, giving him a viable above-average secondary. He excels in high-leverage spots and has no trouble entering with runners on. His long limbs cause some inconsistency with his control, but overall he limits his walks reasonably.

Wingenter's intimidating height, premium velocity and lock-down moxie has him primed for late-inning relief. He'll start 2018 at Triple-A El Paso and should break into the Padres bullpen during the year.

Year	Club (League)	Class	W	L	ERA	G	GS	CG	SV	IP	H	HR	BB	SO	K/9	WHIP	AVG
2015	Padres (AZL)	R	1	1	2.79	6	0	0	0	10	10	0	3	5	4.7	1.34	.250
	Tri-City (NWL)	SS	0	1	12.00	6	0	0	0	9	14	0	4	11	11.0	2.00	.350
2016	Fort Wayne (MWL)	LoA	1	0	0.82	8	0	0	4	11	6	0	2	14	11.5	0.73	.162
	San Antonio (TL)	AA	0	0	0.00	1	0	0	1	3	0	0	1	5	15.0	0.33	.000
	Lake Elsinore (CAL)	HiA	2	1	2.03	30	0	0	4	44	36	0	17	46	9.3	1.20	.229
2017	San Antonio (TL)	AA	2	1	2.45	49	0	0	20	48	33	6	19	64	12.1	1.09	.193
Minor League Totals			6	4	2.82	100	0	0	29	125	99	6	46	145	10.5	1.16	.218

24 LUIS ALMANZAR, 3B/SS

BA GRADE
55 Risk: Extreme

Born: Nov. 1, 1999. **B-T:** R-R. **Ht.:** 6-0. **Wt.:** 180. **Signed:** Dominican Republic, 2016. **Signed by:** Felix Feliz.

Almanzar played one year of high school baseball at American Heritage in Plantation, Fla., before moving back to the Dominican Republic and becoming one of the top prospects in the 2016 international class. The Padres fended off heavy interest and signed him for $4 million. The Padres challenged Almanzar with an assignment to the short-season Northwest League as a 17-year-old in his 2017 pro debut and he was overmatched against largely college players, hitting .230 with 30 percent strikeout rate.

Poor debut aside, Almanzar shows the ingredients of an above-average hitter with excellent bat speed, a direct path to the ball and a discerning eye. He still saw the ball well in his debut, but wasn't prepared for the quality of pitching he was facing. Some evaluators raised concerned with his open stride and note it opened the plate up for pitchers to attack him. Almanzar is trying to find a home defensively. Signed as a shortstop, Almanzar played nearly as much third base in his debut and projects better there long-term as an average runner with an above-average arm.

Almanzar is mature and relatively polished for his age. He will get another crack at short-season ball in 2018, where he will be more age-appropriate to let his skills show.

Year	Club (League)	Class	AVG	G	AB	R	H	2B	3B	HR	RBI	BB	SO	SB	CS	OBP	SLG
2017	Tri-City (NWL)	SS	.230	67	261	36	60	10	1	2	21	25	85	10	5	.299	.299
Minor League Totals			.230	67	261	36	60	10	1	2	21	25	85	10	5	.299	.299

25 MASON THOMPSON, RHP

BA GRADE
50 Risk: Extreme

Born: Feb. 20, 1998. **B-T:** R-R. **Ht.:** 6-7. **Wt.:** 186. **Drafted:** HS—Round Rock, Texas, 2016 (3rd round). **Signed by:** Matt Schaffner.

Evaluators considered Thompson a potential first-round talent as a prep underclassman, but Tommy John surgery wiped out his junior year of high school and limited him to one inning as a senior. The Padres were impressed enough by his workouts to draft him in the third round and sign him for an over-slot $1.75 million.

Injuries continued to plague Thompson in his first full season in 2017. He made just three starts at low Class A Fort Wayne before missing a month with biceps tendinitis, made four more appearances and then was shut down for good in July with shoulder inflammation. When healthy Thompson intrigues as a lanky, projectable righthander with a well-rounded arsenal and a feel to pitch. He'll sit 92-93 mph and touch 95 with his fastball, though his velocity drops off around the third inning, and he shows feel for an above-average 12-to-6 power curveball. His changeup is a potential plus pitch with fade and deception, and he commands his offerings down in the zone despite his 6-foot-7 frame and long levers.

Evaluators see the ingredients for a potential midrotation to back-end starter in Thompson, but his injury record is increasingly concerning. Staying healthy will be his primary goal in 2018.

Year	Club (League)	Class	W	L	ERA	G	GS	CG	SV	IP	H	HR	BB	SO	K/9	WHIP	AVG
2016	Padres (AZL)	R	0	0	2.25	5	5	0	0	12	8	0	5	12	9.0	1.08	.186
Minor League Totals			0	0	2.25	5	5	0	0	12	8	0	5	12	9.0	1.08	.186

26 PEDRO AVILA, RHP

BA GRADE 45 Risk: High

Born: Jan. 14, 1997. **B-T:** R-R. **Ht.:** 6-0. **Wt.:** 195. **Signed:** Venezuela, 2014. **Signed by:** German Robles (Nationals).

The Nationals signed Avila for $50,000 out of Venezuela in 2014 and traded him to the Padres for Derek Norris after the 2016 season. While Norris never played a game for the Nationals, Avila led the Padres system with 170 strikeouts in 2017, including an eight-inning, 17-strikeout night for low Class A Fort Wayne in August.

Avila has an average fastball that sits 92 mph and touches 94, but his plus curveball is a separator. It's a swing-and-miss pitch in the 73-77 mph range that he manipulates at will, adding and subtracting velocity while keeping the shape consistent. He can go to his curveball whenever he wants, although sometimes he falls in love with it and gets in trouble throwing it out of sequence. He also has a 82-83 mph changeup with above-average potential at his disposal.

Avila's command isn't great, which, combined with his average fastball, makes him a future swingman in evaluators' eyes. He's a good athlete with a clean delivery, so his command has the potential to jump forward and make him more of a rotation option. Avila will start at high Class A Lake Elsinore in 2018.

Year	Club (League)	Class	W	L	ERA	G	GS	CG	SV	IP	H	HR	BB	SO	K/9	WHIP	AVG
2015	Nationals (DSL)	R	6	3	2.26	13	13	0	0	60	46	1	17	87	13.1	1.06	.211
	Nationals (GCL)	R	1	0	0.00	1	0	0	0	4	1	0	1	5	11.3	0.50	.077
2016	Hagerstown (SAL)	LoA	7	7	3.48	20	20	0	0	93	86	10	38	92	8.9	1.33	.249
2017	Lake Elsinore (CAL)	HiA	1	4	4.98	10	9	0	0	43	50	2	18	53	11.0	1.57	.284
	Fort Wayne (MWL)	LoA	7	1	3.05	14	14	0	0	86	74	3	15	117	12.3	1.04	.231
Minor League Totals			22	15	3.28	58	56	0	0	286	257	16	89	354	11.2	1.21	.240

27 MICHAEL GETTYS, OF

BA GRADE 45 Risk: High

Born: Oct. 22, 1995. **B-T:** R-R. **Ht.:** 6-1. **Wt.:** 203. **Drafted:** HS—Gainesville, Ga., 2014 (2nd round). **Signed by:** Andrew Salvo.

Big tools and limited hitting ability have defined Gettys since his prep days. After appearing to shed that reputation with a breakthrough 2016, he regressed badly in 2017 with a California League-leading 191 strikeouts and a 37 percent strikeout rate at high Class A Lake Elsinore.

Gettys keeps evaluators intrigued with his athletic gifts. He is a plus defender who roams center field with ease as a plus runner and boasts a plus-plus arm that notched 24 assists the last two seasons. His plus speed plays on the basepaths and he can turn on the jets for extra bases when he drives balls into the gap. The problem with Gettys is he that doesn't make nearly enough contact. He lacks natural rhythm and timing in the box and is frequently caught lunging at pitches out front. He tried to increase his launch angle in 2017 and it only made things worse when opponents picked apart his uphill swing path. Lingering back stiffness didn't help.

A poor hitter overall, Gettys produced against Cal League lefthanders in 2017 (.318/.383/.553), which gives him a path as a platoon outfielder with his speed and defense. He'll be tested at Double-A in 2018.

Year	Club (League)	Class	AVG	G	AB	R	H	2B	3B	HR	RBI	BB	SO	SB	CS	OBP	SLG
2014	Padres (AZL)	R	.310	52	213	29	66	8	5	3	38	15	66	14	2	.353	.437
2015	Fort Wayne (MWL)	LoA	.231	122	494	62	114	27	6	6	44	28	162	20	10	.271	.346
2016	Fort Wayne (MWL)	LoA	.304	68	257	37	78	10	5	3	27	18	69	24	10	.369	.416
	Lake Elsinore (CAL)	HiA	.306	60	248	40	76	13	0	9	33	17	77	9	6	.356	.468
2017	Lake Elsinore (CAL)	HiA	.254	116	457	84	116	22	4	17	51	46	191	22	8	.329	.431
Minor League Totals			.270	418	1669	252	450	80	20	38	193	124	565	89	36	.325	.410

28 REGGIE LAWSON, RHP

BA GRADE 45 Risk: High

Born: Aug. 2, 1997. **B-T:** R-R. **Ht.:** 6-4. **Wt.:** 205. **Drafted:** HS—Victorville, Calif., 2016 (2nd round supplemental). **Signed by:** Jeff Stevens.

Lawson had first-round helium in the 2016 draft before a strained oblique limited him to six starts as a high school senior. The Padres grabbed him with the 71st overall pick and signed him for $1.9 million, more than double slot value.

Lawson posted a 5.30 ERA in his first full season at low Class A Fort Wayne, showing flashes of promise but struggling to put together consistent outings. Lawson intrigues as a loose, lean, long-armed athlete with a smooth delivery. He sits 91-94 mph with his lively fastball but he tends to leave it up in the zone where it flattens out, making it a hittable pitch. His 74-77 mph curveball has tight rotation but lacks consistent bite, and he rarely uses his raw, unrefined changeup. Locating his offspeed is a challenge for Lawson and contributed to his 4.2 walks-per-nine rate in his first full campaign.

When right, Lawson gets swings and misses on his fastball and shows a top-down, biting curveball, enough for evaluators to project a possible back-end starter. Fastball command, breaking ball consistency and third-pitch development will all be focal points in Lawson's development. He'll move to high Class A Lake Elsinore in 2018.

Year	Club (League)	Class	W	L	ERA	G	GS	CG	SV	IP	H	HR	BB	SO	K/9	WHIP	AVG
2016	Padres (AZL)	R	0	0	8.31	5	3	0	0	9	12	0	3	7	7.3	1.73	.316
2017	Fort Wayne (MWL)	LoA	4	6	5.30	17	17	0	0	73	65	8	35	89	11.0	1.37	.236
Minor League Totals			0	0	8.31	5	3	0	0	9	12	0	3	7	7.3	1.73	.316

29 AUSTIN ALLEN, C

BA GRADE
45 Risk: High

Born: Jan. 16, 1994. **B-T:** L-R. **Ht.:** 6-4. **Wt.:** 225. **Drafted:** Florida Tech, 2015 (4th round). **Signed by:** Willie Bosque.

The Padres made Allen the top Division II position player drafted in 2015 when they picked him in the fourth round and signed him for $484,000. The country-strong 6-foot-4, 225-pound lefthanded hitter showed off his plus power in 2017, finishing third in the California League in slugging (.497) and fourth in home runs (22) at high Class A Lake Elsinore.

Allen is an offensive catcher through-and-through. He uses his strength and leverage to launch balls deep to right-center, frequently clearing 400 feet. He pounds that gap for a large volume of doubles as well. His bat speed isn't ideal, but he makes up for it with good timing and a solid feel to hit for average. The same size and strength that helps Allen offensively hampers him defensively. He is a slow mover with limited range and flexibility, making him a liability in blocking. His hands in the strike zone are fine but he's an overall tick-below-average receiver. Allen has average arm strength but is sluggish out of the crouch and on his exchange, which led to 100 stolen bases in 126 attempts against him in 2017.

Allen's bat is enough to play everyday only if he can catch. He'll try to make needed defensive strides at Double-A in 2018.

Year	Club (League)	Class	AVG	G	AB	R	H	2B	3B	HR	RBI	BB	SO	SB	CS	OBP	SLG
2015	Tri-City (NWL)	SS	.240	53	196	23	47	10	1	2	34	21	38	1	2	.315	.332
2016	Fort Wayne (MWL)	LoA	.320	109	409	52	131	22	0	7	61	29	69	0	0	.364	.425
	San Antonio (TL)	AA	.273	3	11	1	3	0	0	1	1	0	0	0	0	.273	.545
2017	Lake Elsinore (CAL)	HiA	.283	121	463	71	131	31	1	22	81	44	109	0	1	.353	.497
Minor League Totals			.289	286	1079	147	312	63	2	32	177	94	216	1	3	.349	.440

30 JORDY BARLEY, SS

BA GRADE
50 Risk: Extreme

Born: Dec. 3, 1999. **B-T:** R-R. **Ht.:** 6-0. **Wt.:** 175. **Signed:** Dominican Republic, 2016. **Signed by:** Felix Felix/Jose Salado.

The Padres gave Barley $1 million during their 2016 international signing bonanza, a bonus well above industry consensus. He went out and showed himself to be arguably the top athlete in the entire Rookie-level Arizona League in 2017, flashing incredible quick-twitch, plus-plus speed and bouncy, freakish athleticism. That athleticism, however, has yet to translate into baseball skills.

Barley is wildly erratic defensively at shortstop. He closes on balls incredibly fast but rushes everything, sometimes botching grounders and at other times throwing the ball erratically, taking away from his plus arm strength. The end result was 30 errors in 43 games and a sense he will have to move to center field unless he learns to calm himself and play under control. Barley shows intriguing above-average power potential but again rushes everything, lacking timing at the plate and getting overaggressive. He wore himself out by the end of the season, hitting .183 with no home runs in August.

Barley's tools and athleticism shine, but he has a lot of growth ahead to make them play on the field. He may get a shot at low Class A Fort Wayne in 2018.

Year	Club (League)	Class	AVG	G	AB	R	H	2B	3B	HR	RBI	BB	SO	SB	CS	OBP	SLG
2017	Padres (AZL)	R	.242	49	182	34	44	11	6	4	28	11	65	7	2	.292	.434
Minor League Totals			.242	49	182	34	44	11	6	4	28	11	65	7	2	.292	.434

San Francisco Giants

BY J.J. COOPER

Stock market crashes often are obvious, but only in the rear-view mirror. Once the damage has been done, the cause is apparent.

The Giants experienced a crash in 2017 that, in hindsight, had some obvious causes.

For years, the Giants had exceeded expectations. Every year an Angel Pagan, Joe Panik or Matt Duffy would arrive and give an unexpected boost. And with Madison Bumgarner, Buster Posey and other stars providing October heroics, the Giants won three World Series titles in a five-year span.

But even when the Giants won it all in 2014, they were an 88-win, wild card team. They returned to the playoffs as an 87-win wild card in 2016. The Giants won with an airtight infield defense, a strong pitching staff and defenders who could cover AT&T Park's acres of outfield grass.

But in 2017, the bottom fell out in shocking ways. San Francisco finished with the worst record in the National League. Most embarrassingly, they finished seven games worse than the Padres—a team with a miniscule payroll that was focused on rebuilding with little emphasis placed on winning. San Francisco was significantly worse with a bloated payroll that forced it to pay the luxury tax.

The game has changed in ways that have emphasized San Francisco's weaknesses and minimized its strengths. While the rest of the league has embraced the home run, the Giants' lineup is still built around stringing together singles and doubles.

The 2017 Giants' offensive numbers don't look all that different than what they did in 2014, when they won the World Series. In 2014, the Giants hit 132 home runs and scored 4.1 runs per game.

In 2017, they hit 128 home runs and scored 3.9 runs per game. But the league went from scoring 3.9 runs per game in 2014 to 4.6 runs per game in 2017.

In 2017, the average major league team hit 204 home runs. The Giants' 128 home runs were not only worst in baseball, they were 23 fewer than any other team. They were also dead last in isolated slugging percentage. Brandon Belt led the team with 18 home runs, which ranked in a tie for 127th in baseball.

The Giants have a large, set payroll and an aging lineup that is largely 30 or older, which makes a quick turnaround difficult. With an established infield, the Giants' only way to add power is to upgrade their outfield and/or third base.

With the exception of Chris Shaw, the club's best upper-level prospects are better hitters than sluggers, which means a power boost will have to

Brandon Belt, the Giants' top slugger, ranked just 127th in baseball with 18 home runs.

PROJECTED 2021 LINEUP

Catcher	Buster Posey (34)
First Base	Brandon Belt (33)
Second Base	Joe Panik (30)
Third Base	Christian Arroyo (26)
Shortstop	Brandon Crawford (34)
Left Field	Chris Shaw (27)
Center Field	Heliot Ramos (21)
Right Field	Bryan Reynolds (26)
No. 1 Starter	Madison Bumgarner (31)
No. 2 Starter	Johnny Cueto (35)
No. 3 Starter	Jeff Samardzija (36)
No. 4 Starter	Tyler Beede (28)
No. 5 Starter	Garrett Williams (26)
Closer	Melvin Adon (27)

come from the outside, or the Giants will have to hope that baseball returns to a pitching-friendly environment similar to 2014.

The Giants farm system is thin on potential impact players, so it's going to be tough for the aging roster to get better quickly. They took one small step toward that by selecting 2017 first-rounder Heliot Ramos, a high school outfielder from Puerto Rico who led the Rookie-level Arizona League with a .645 slugging. San Francisco can add another high-ceiling talent when it picks second in the 2018 draft.

The Giants are going to need time to return to prominence. The climb back usually takes much longer than the crash.

SAN FRANCISCO GIANTS

TOP 2018 ROOKIE: Christian Arroyo, 3B. His 2017 season was ruined by injuries, but he could be a solid regular in 2018 thanks to his feel to hit.

BREAKOUT PROSPECT: Alexander Canario, OF. It wouldn't be a surprise to see the five-tool center fielder crack the top five next year.

SLEEPER: Garrett Cave, RHP. Like many recent Giants' draftees, Cave has to refine his control, but if he throws more strikes, he has two potentially plus pitches.

SOURCE OF TOP 30 TALENT

Homegrown	27	Acquired	3
College	14	Trade	3
Junior college	0	Rule 5 draft	0
High school	5	Independent league	0
Nondrafted free agent	0	Free agent/waivers	0
International	8		

LF
Chris Shaw (2)
Bryan Reynolds (5)
Austin Slater (17)
Heath Quinn
Logan Baldwin
Aaron Bond
Bryce Johnson

CF
Heliot Ramos (1)
Steven Duggar (8)
Alexander Canario (13)
Malique Ziegler
Ronnie Jebavy
Nick Hall

RF
Sandro Fabian (9)
Gio Brusa
Diego Rincones

3B
Christian Arroyo (4)
Jonah Arenado

SS
C.J. Hinojosa (30)
Manuel Geraldo
Brandon Van Horn

2B
Ryan Howard (16)
Miguel Gomez (23)
Jalen Miller
Kelvin Beltre

1B
Jacob Gonzalez (12)
Dylan Davis
Jose Vizcaino

C
Aramis Garcis (6)
Ricardo Genovese
Andres Angulo
Matt Winn

LHP

LHSP	LHRP
Garrett Williams (7)	Matt Krook (19)
Andrew Suarez (10)	Seth Corry (21)
Matt Gage	D.J. Snelten
Domenic Mazza	Mac Marshall
Conner Menez	Alex Bostic

RHP

RHSP	RHRP
Tyler Beede (3)	Melvin Adon (14)
Shaun Anderson (11)	Reyes Moronta (15)
Gregory Santos (20)	Kyle Crick (18)
Tyler Herb (27)	Joan Gregorio (22)
Jordan Johnson	Rodolfo Martinez (24)
Chase Johnson	Stephen Woods (25)
Jason Bahr	Tyler Cyr (26)
	Camilo Doval (28)
	Sam Coonrod (29)
	Julian Fernandez
	Garret Cave
	Roberto Gomez
	Logan Webb
	Cory Taylor
	John Russell
	Pierce Johnson
	C.J. Gettman
	Caleb Simpson
	Tyler Schimpf
	Jose Marte
	Patrick Ruotolo

DRAFT ANALYSIS

2017

BEST PURE HITTER: When scouting 3B Jacob Gonzalez (2), Giants scouts noticed how he worked counts and showed excellent balance. He has a direct swing path and should develop power as well. While some scouts worried about OF Heliot Ramos (1) ability to hit with wood, he ranked second in the Rookie-level Arizona League by hitting .348.

BEST POWER HITTER: Ramos hit some jaw-dropping home runs as an amateur. He's shown that his plus power potential has translated well to wood. He showed the ability to homer to left and right field in the Arizona League with impressive exit velocities and a league-best .645 slugging.

FASTEST RUNNER: OF Bryce Johnson (6) is a 70 runner on the 20-80 scouting scale and his speed plays both on the basepaths and in center field.

BEST DEFENSIVE PLAYER: Ramos has the highest ceiling of any position player the Giants have drafted since they picked Buster Posey in 2008. A big part of his ceiling is the projection that Ramos can be a plus defender in center field in addition to his power potential. He glides around center field, gobbling up acreage easily and showed the ability to track balls hit over his head.

BEST FASTBALL: RHP Garrett Cave (4) sits at 92-94 mph and touches 95 with a fastball that shows good life. LHP Seth Corry (3) could end up with an even better fastball when he matures. Corry's fastball sat at 91-94 mph as a pro after touching 96 at his best in high school this year.

BEST SECONDARY PITCH: Corry's command of his potentially plus curveball is ahead of his fastball command at this point. He showed an unusual ability to generate good break while pitching at high altitude in Utah. The break on his curve got even better once he was throwing at the lower altitude of the Arizona League.

BEST PRO DEBUT: Ramos hit .348/.404/.645 with six home runs and 10 steals in 35 games in the AZL. The only hiccup he faced was a stint on the DL for the concussion protocol after he was hit in the head by a pitch.

TOP DRAFT PICKS OF THE DECADE

Year	Player, Pos.	2017 Org
2008	Buster Posey, C	Giants
2009	Zack Wheeler, RHP	Mets
2010	Gary Brown, OF	Atlantic League
2011	Joe Panik, SS	Giants
2012	Chris Stratton, RHP	Giants
2013	Christian Arroyo, SS	Giants
2014	Tyler Beede, RHP	Giants
2015	Phil Bickford, RHP	Brewers
2016	Bryan Reynolds, OF (2nd round)	Giants
2017	Heliot Ramos, OF	Giants

BEST ATHLETE: Ramos was one of the younger players in this year's draft class, but he already has present power, strength and speed, giving him a chance to be a well-rounded impact player if the hit tool develops.

MOST INTRIGUING BACKGROUND: Gonzalez's father Luis was a five-time all-star outfielder for the D-backs who hit 354 homers in a 19-year career and had the game-winning hit in Game 7 of the 2001 World Series. SS Nico Giarratano (24) played for his father Nino at the University of San Francisco.

CLOSEST TO THE MAJORS: The Giants drafted high school players with their first three picks so this isn't an immediate impact draft but Cave could move quickly if he moved to the bullpen to be a power reliever.

BEST LATE-ROUND PICK: OF Aaron Bond (12) didn't play his way into being a regular in San Jacinto (Texas) JC's loaded lineup until April after many scouts had moved on. But scout James Mouton believed in the bat and was rewarded when Bond hit .306/.368/.565 in the AZL. OF Logan Baldwin (21) impressed with his speed and defense at Georgia Southern. If he can hit he has a chance to be a useful outfielder.

THE ONE WHO GOT AWAY: RHPs Blake Rivera (32) and Liam Jenkins (40) were a pair of large-framed, hard-throwing junior-college pitchers who could develop into useful arms. Jenkins is at Louisville; Rivera is back at Wallace State (Ala.) JC.

—J.J. COOPER

2016

The Giants didn't have a first-round pick in 2016, making OF Bryan Reynolds (2) their top pick. He had a solid first full pro season. LHP Garrett Williams (7) has emerged as the best of a handful of hard-throwing college pitchers in the class.

GRADE: C

2015

OFs Chris Shaw (1) and Steven Duggar (6) are on the cusp of the big leagues after finishing the season in Triple-A. RHP Phil Bickford (1) was dealt to the Brewers in 2016 and was slowed in 2017 by a drug suspension and hand injury.

GRADE: C

2014

OF Austin Slater (8) had taken over a spot in the Giants lineup in 2017 before injury ended his season. RHP Tyler Beede (1) was expected to join him in San Francisco, but scuffled in Triple-A and then also saw injury end his season early.

GRADE: C

1 HELIOT RAMOS, OF

Born: Sept. 7, 1999. **B-T:** R-R. **Ht.:** 6-2. **Wt.:** 185.
Drafted: HS—Guaynabo, P.R., 2017 (1st round).
Signed by: Junior Roman.

Ramos is the latest exceptional athlete from a family of them. His older brother Henry is a minor league outfielder who has reached Triple-A. His oldest brother Hector is a professional soccer player in the North American Soccer League and plays forward for Puerto Rico's national team. Heliot has a chance to be the best of the brood. He was a divisive prospect leading up to the draft. The teams who liked him, loved him while others worried about his hitting ability because he didn't have much of a track record with wood bats. Heliot (it's a silent "H" and his name is pronounced like Elliott) doesn't always put on a great batting practice, but he almost always performed in games as an amateur. He was the MVP of the Under Armour All-America game as he fell just a double short of the cycle. The Giants quickly locked in on him as their first-round pick and drafted him No. 17 overall, signing him for $3,101,700 to pass up a Florida International commitment.

Ramos is the most well-rounded and the toolsiest prospect to come through the Giants farm system this decade. In a system lacking in power, Ramos has the potential for 25-plus home runs, posting exit velocities that wouldn't look out of place in the middle of a big league lineup. He has already shown the ability to both yank the ball over the left field wall or drive it out with carry to right-center. Ramos' swing is relatively short and he has excellent bat speed, although pitchers found they could elevate and get the free-swinging Ramos to chase. He also has consistent plus speed, plus-plus at his best, although his thick trunk leads some to believe he will slow down as he matures. While Ramos' routes can be refined, he glides in the outfield and a majority of evaluators believe he can stay in center field long-term as an average to above-average defender. His above-average arm would also fit in right field, which is useful with how expansive AT&T Park is.

Scouts like Ramos' feel for hitting and he was among the best hitters in the Arizona League in his debut, but Ramos' overall future hitting ability remains his biggest question. His free-swinging tendencies are one major thing that could trip him up. Still, Ramos has speed, strength and a baseball-rat mentality, which should allow him to flourish in the low A Class South Atlantic League in 2018.

BILL MITCHELL

BA GRADE	SCOUTING GRADES
60 Risk: Extreme	HIT: 50. POW: 60. SPD: 60. FLD: 55. ARM: 55.

Projected future grades on 20-80 scouting scale

TOP PROSPECTS OF THE DECADE

Year	Player, Pos.	2017 Org
2008	Angel Villalona, 3B/1B	Did not play
2009	Madison Bumgarner, LHP	Giants
2010	Buster Posey, C	Giants
2011	Brandon Belt, 1B/OF	Giants
2012	Gary Brown, OF	Atlantic League
2013	Kyle Crick, RHP	Giants
2014	Kyle Crick, RHP	Giants
2015	Andrew Susac, C	Brewers
2016	Christian Arroyo, SS	Giants
2017	Tyler Beede, RHP	Giants

BEST TOOLS

Best Hitter For Average	Christian Arroyo
Best Power Hitter	Heliot Ramos
Best Strike-Zone Discipline	Steven Duggar
Fastest Baserunner	Malique Ziegler
Best Athlete	Heliot Ramos
Best Fastball	Melvin Adon
Best Curveball	Garrett Williams
Best Slider	Andrew Suarez
Best Changeup	Jordan Johnson
Best Control	Matt Gage
Best Defensive Catcher	Aramis Garcia
Best Defensive Infielder	Brandon Van Horn
Best Infield Arm	Manuel Geraldo
Best Defensive Outfielder	Ronnie Jebavy
Best Outfield Arm	Sandro Fabian

Year	Club (League)	Class	AVG	G	AB	R	H	2B	3B	HR	RBI	BB	SO	SB	CS	OBP	SLG
2017	Giants (AZL)	R	.348	35	138	33	48	11	6	6	27	10	48	10	2	.404	.645
Minor League Totals			.348	35	138	33	48	11	6	6	27	10	48	10	2	.404	.645

2 CHRIS SHAW, OF/1B

Born: Oct. 20, 1993. **B-T:** L-R. **Ht.:** 6-4. **Wt.:** 235. **Drafted:** Boston College, 2015 (1st round). **Signed by:** Mark O'Sullivan.

The Giants drafted Shaw 31st overall in 2015 because of his power potential, and he has lived up to those expectations. His 24 home runs between Double-A and Triple-A in 2017 were seven more than anyone else in the Giants system.

Shaw's plus power is his carrying tool, with scouts predicting he can hit 25-30 home runs a year in the majors. He has all-fields power with the strength to clear AT&T Park's high right field wall and power balls into McCovey Cove. Shaw doesn't sell out to get to his power and his swing is relatively short for a power hitter, allowing scouts to project him as a future .250-.260 hitter although like most power hitters, it will come with plenty of strikeouts. Shaw is going to have to hit because he's a below-average defender at first base and in left field. He is better-suited for the outfield because he is a better runner underway, although still below-average, and lacks short-area quickness. His average arm plays at both spots.

Shaw's power is desperately needed by the Giants. He has a chance to be an everyday slugger, but his lack of range will be noticeable in AT&T Park's expansive outfield.

BA GRADE
50 Risk: Medium
HIT: 50. POW: 60.
SPD: 40. FLD: 40.
ARM: 50.

Year	Club (League)	Class	AVG	G	AB	R	H	2B	3B	HR	RBI	BB	SO	SB	CS	OBP	SLG
2015	Salem-Keizer (NWL)	SS	.287	46	178	22	51	11	0	12	30	19	41	0	0	.360	.551
2016	San Jose (CAL)	HiA	.285	72	270	47	77	22	0	16	55	28	70	0	0	.357	.544
	Richmond (EL)	AA	.246	60	232	26	57	16	4	5	30	20	55	0	0	.309	.414
2017	Richmond (EL)	AA	.293	37	133	16	39	9	0	6	28	18	26	0	0	.383	.496
	Sacramento (PCL)	AAA	.289	88	336	42	97	25	1	18	50	20	106	0	0	.328	.530
Minor League Totals			.279	303	1149	153	321	83	5	57	193	105	298	0	0	.343	.509

3 TYLER BEEDE, RHP

Born: May 23, 1993. **B-T:** R-R. **Ht.:** 6-3. **Wt.:** 210. **Drafted:** Vanderbilt, 2014 (1st round). **Signed by:** Andrew Jefferson.

Beede appeared ready to compete for a job in the Giants rotation entering 2017. Instead, he scuffled through 19 starts at Triple-A Sacramento before a groin injury ended his season in late July. Beede's velocity dipped in 2017, as the plus fastball he previously pitched with became an average to above-average pitch, sitting 91-93 mph and touching 95. He uses both a two and four-seamer.

Beede's velocity has waxed and waned before, but his biggest hurdle to big league success is his subpar command, which has plagued him since college. Beede mixes in two average secondary offerings in a cutter and curveball and has a below-average changeup, but he doesn't land them consistently. His curve has flashed plus before, which leads scouts to think it could return to form in the future. However, there are concerns Beede uses too many pitches, which keeps him from developing a feel for any one pitch.

Beede's development has been full of hot streaks and setbacks, much like Chris Stratton, who broke into the Giants' rotation in 2017. A Stratton-esque leap is possible in 2018, but Beede doesn't miss many bats and now profiles as a possible No. 4 starter.

BA GRADE
50 Risk: High
FB: 55. CB: 50.
CHG: 40. CT: 50.
CTL: 45.

Year	Club (League)	Class	W	L	ERA	G	GS	CG	SV	IP	H	HR	BB	SO	K/9	WHIP	AVG
2015	San Jose (CAL)	HiA	2	2	2.24	9	9	0	0	52	51	2	9	37	6.4	1.15	.254
	Richmond (EL)	AA	3	8	5.23	13	13	0	0	72	62	4	35	49	6.1	1.34	.234
2016	Richmond (EL)	AA	8	7	2.81	24	24	1	0	147	136	9	53	135	8.2	1.28	.248
2017	Sacramento (PCL)	AAA	6	7	4.79	19	19	0	0	109	121	14	39	83	6.9	1.47	.282
Minor League Totals			19	25	3.72	71	71	1	0	396	386	29	143	322	7.3	1.33	.257

4 CHRISTIAN ARROYO, SS/3B

Born: May 30, 1995. **B-T:** R-R. **Ht.:** 6-1. **Wt.:** 180. **Drafted:** HS—Brooksville, Fla., 2013 (1st round). **Signed by:** Mike Metcalf.

Arroyo's 2017 season was as near-perfect analogy for the Giants' 2017 season, in that it's best forgotten. He made his major league debut in April, but his season went downhill quickly. He was hit by a pitch in mid-June and missed two weeks with a bruised left hand, returned and was plunked again, this time breaking a bone in the same hand and ending his season. He went to the Dominican Winter League, saw his injury flare up, and had surgery on the hand in November.

Arroyo's value as a regular depends on him being at least a plus hitter. Most scouts project a modest 10-12 home runs a year, but he's never reached double-digits in the minors. Arroyo got over-aggressive at the plate in his first big league stint, but normally he shows good timing and barrel control. He's a fringe-average defender at shortstop because of limited range, but is plus at second or third base with an average, accurate arm. He's a fringe-average runner and not a base-stealing threat.

BA GRADE

50 Risk: High

HIT: 60. POW: 40.
SPD: 45. FLD: 60.
ARM: 50.

The Giants have had success nurturing well-rounded infielders. The hand injuries have injected uncertainty into Arroyo's immediate future, but he could compete for the Giants third base job if healthy.

Year	Club (League)	Class	AVG	G	AB	R	H	2B	3B	HR	RBI	BB	SO	SB	CS	OBP	SLG
2015	San Jose (CAL)	HiA	.304	90	381	48	116	28	2	9	42	19	73	5	3	.344	.459
2016	Richmond (EL)	AA	.274	119	474	57	130	36	1	3	49	29	72	1	1	.316	.373
2017	San Francisco (NL)	MAJ	.192	34	125	9	24	5	0	3	14	8	32	1	2	.244	.304
	Sacramento (PCL)	AAA	.396	25	91	18	36	7	0	4	16	6	12	2	0	.461	.604
Major League Totals			.192	34	125	9	24	5	0	3	14	8	32	1	2	.244	.304
Minor League Totals			.300	368	1491	219	447	106	11	24	208	95	242	18	9	.345	.434

5 BRYAN REYNOLDS, OF

Born: Jan. 27, 1995. **B-T:** B-R. **Ht.:** 6-3. **Wt.:** 205. **Drafted:** Vanderbilt, 2016 (2nd round). **Signed by:** Jeff Wood.

Reynolds has always hit. He hit .329 in his three-year Vanderbilt career, hit .346 in the Cape Cod League and so far has hit .312 as a pro. That said, because he doesn't drive the ball as much as his raw size and strength might indicate he should, scouts have long pined for something more.

For a three-year starter at Vanderbilt who was a second-round pick, there's a surprisingly unfinished quality to Reynolds. The switch-hitter stays in control of his swings and frequently hits the ball on the ground. Scouts say he lacks the barrel control and pitch recognition of elite hitters, although he did cut his strikeout rate in 2017. Scouts have long thought Reynolds has above-average power potential or more, but it would take a significant change in his approach and swing to tap into it. Defensively, Reynolds plays a fringe-average center field because he lacks initial burst, but he is above-average in either corner. His average arm works everywhere.

BA GRADE

50 Risk: High

HIT: 55. POW: 45.
SPD: 50. FLD: 55.
ARM: 50.

Reynolds' strength and power potential give him upside, but his realistic ceiling is in question. He's likely to be a well-rounded big league outfielder with his current approach, but to be a long-term regular he'll need to unlock his power.

Year	Club (League)	Class	AVG	G	AB	R	H	2B	3B	HR	RBI	BB	SO	SB	CS	OBP	SLG
2016	Salem-Keizer (NWL)	SS	.312	40	154	28	48	12	1	5	30	11	41	2	0	.368	.500
	Augusta (SAL)	LoA	.317	16	63	11	20	5	0	1	8	3	20	1	0	.348	.444
2017	San Jose (CAL)	HiA	.312	121	491	72	153	26	9	10	63	37	106	5	3	.364	.462
Minor League Totals			.312	177	708	111	221	43	10	16	101	51	167	8	3	.363	.469

6 ARAMIS GARCIA, C

Born: Jan. 12, 1993. **B-T:** R-R. **Ht.:** 6-2. **Wt.:** 220. **Drafted:** Florida International, 2014 (2nd round). **Signed by:** Jose Alou.

Garcia missed two months in 2016 after surgery to repair facial fractures and he missed two more weeks in 2017 with a concussion. Because of those injuries, Garcia spent most of the year repeating high Class A San Jose, but earned a late-season promotion to Double-A Richmond and played in the Arizona Fall League's Fall Stars game.

Garcia checks off two catcher boxes with plus raw power potential and a plus arm. He finished second in the Giants system with 17 home runs and he should hit for at-least above-average power if he gets regular big league at-bats. But he's projected as a .230-.240 hitter because of undeveloped plate discipline and concerns about swing length. Defensively, Garcia has some stiffness behind the plate and evaluators are widely split on his receiving, noting his effort level isn't always there. At his best, Garcia shows the ability to be an average defender with a big arm.

BA GRADE

45 Risk: Medium

HIT: 40. **POW:** 55.
SPD: 40. **FLD:** 50.
ARM: 60.

Garcia has some of the best power in the organization, but if he can't catch, he doesn't have a clear fallback position defensively. His power numbers will likely be sapped by Double-A Richmond, but he is on track to eventually be Buster Posey's backup if he can stay healthy.

Year	Club (League)	Class	AVG	G	AB	R	H	2B	3B	HR	RBI	BB	SO	SB	CS	OBP	SLG
2015	Augusta (SAL)	LoA	.273	83	319	42	87	15	1	15	61	35	77	0	1	.350	.467
	San Jose (CAL)	HiA	.227	20	75	10	17	4	0	0	5	9	22	1	0	.310	.280
2016	Giants (AZL)	R	.227	6	22	1	5	1	0	0	4	0	1	0	0	.217	.273
	San Jose (CAL)	HiA	.257	41	144	20	37	6	0	2	20	14	42	1	0	.323	.340
2017	San Jose (CAL)	HiA	.272	81	324	43	88	20	1	17	65	15	73	0	0	.314	.497
	Richmond (EL)	AA	.282	22	78	11	22	12	0	0	8	9	21	0	0	.360	.436
Minor League Totals			.262	281	1064	138	279	64	2	36	178	92	261	2	1	.326	.428

7 GARRETT WILLIAMS, LHP

Born: Sept. 15, 1994. **B-T:** L-L. **Ht.:** 6-1. **Wt.:** 205. **Drafted:** Oklahoma State, 2016 (7th round). **Signed by:** Daniel Murray.

The Giants took a trio of hard-throwing but wild college pitchers in the 2016 draft. Matt Krook and Alex Bostic struggled in 2017, but taking Williams in the seventh round paid off handsomely. Williams responded well to steady work in his first full season, going 6-5, 2.32 in 97 innings at the Class A levels—more innings than he pitched in three seasons combined at Oklahoma State.

Williams has long had two plus pitches, but in college, he never threw enough strikes for it to matter. Pitching from a low three-quarter arm slot, his command is still well below average but he has begun repeating his delivery enough to stay around the strike zone. Williams' 91-94 mph fastball seems to find another gear at it nears the plate, generating swings and misses. His low-80s power curveball is hard with depth and some sweep thanks to his arm slot. He's also improved his still below-average changeup, but he doesn't use it much.

BA GRADE

55 Risk: Extreme

FB: 55. **CB:** 60.
CHG: 40.
CTL: 45.

Williams needs to refine his still fringy control, but he has some of the best pure stuff in the Giants system. After making massive strides in 2017, he's closer to his potential as a mid-rotation starter.

Year	Club (League)	Class	W	L	ERA	G	GS	CG	SV	IP	H	HR	BB	SO	K/9	WHIP	AVG
2016	Giants (AZL)	R	1	0	2.57	3	1	0	0	7	4	0	3	5	6.4	1.00	.174
	Salem-Keizer (NWL)	SS	1	2	5.68	7	7	0	0	25	28	1	14	22	7.8	1.66	.275
2017	Augusta (SAL)	LoA	4	3	2.25	12	11	0	0	64	59	0	25	58	8.2	1.31	.234
	San Jose (CAL)	HiA	2	2	2.45	6	5	0	0	33	28	3	10	38	10.4	1.15	.221
Minor League Totals			8	7	2.99	28	24	0	0	129	119	4	52	123	8.6	1.32	.236

8 STEVEN DUGGAR, OF

Born: Nov. 4, 1993. **B-T:** L-R. **Ht.:** 6-2. **Wt.:** 195. **Drafted:** Clemson, 2015 (6th round).
Signed by: Donnie Suttles.

Duggar slid to the sixth round in the 2015 draft because he was a solid but unspectacular hitter at Clemson despite impressive tools. After a breakthrough season in 2016, Duggar missed the first two and half months of 2017 with forearm and hamstring problems, but still reached Triple-A after a stint at high Class A San Jose and hit .263/.367/.421 in the Arizona Fall League.

Duggar has a discerning eye and sorts out pitches well, gets on base and stays within himself with a short stroke. He has natural strength, but he doesn't really use his legs to drive the ball consistently. He's a gap-to-gap hitter with more doubles than home run power. Defensively, Duggar is the Giants' best in-house option at center field. He has above-average speed and takes solid routes that give him a shot to be an above-average defender in center with an above-average arm. Duggar has improved his jumps to become a threat as a basestealer.

BA GRADE
45 Risk: Medium
HIT: 50. **POW:** 40.
SPD: 55. **FLD:** 55.
ARM: 55.

Duggar's on-base skills and defensive ability give him a shot at an everyday role, and his defensive ability to play all three outfield spots gives him a fallback option as a fourth outfielder.

Year	Club (League)	Class	AVG	G	AB	R	H	2B	3B	HR	RBI	BB	SO	SB	CS	OBP	SLG
2015	Salem-Keizer (NWL)	SS	.293	58	229	40	67	12	1	1	27	35	52	6	3	.390	.367
2016	San Jose (CAL)	HiA	.284	70	264	43	75	12	4	9	30	44	66	6	7	.386	.462
	Richmond (EL)	AA	.321	60	243	35	78	16	4	1	24	28	51	9	7	.391	.432
2017	Giants (AZL)	R	.000	2	3	0	0	0	0	0	0	2	0	0	0	.400	.000
	San Jose (CAL)	HiA	.270	29	115	22	31	11	0	4	20	17	42	7	0	.361	.470
	Sacramento (PCL)	AAA	.261	13	46	7	12	1	0	2	6	8	12	3	2	.370	.413
Minor League Totals			.292	232	900	147	263	52	9	17	107	134	223	31	19	.384	.427

9 SANDRO FABIAN, OF

Born: March 6, 1998. **B-T:** R-R. **Ht.:** 6-1. **Wt.:** 180. **Signed:** Dominican Republic, 2014.
Signed by: Pablo Peguero/Felix Peguero/Jonathan Bautista.

The Giants have been aggressive promoting Fabian because they trust in his feel for the game and hitting ability. Whenever he's been pushed, he's responded. He was the best player on their DSL team in 2015 and on the Rookie-level AZL Giants in 2016. Sent to low Class A Augusta as a 19-year-old in 2017, Fabian struggled in the first half but kept improving and hit .370/.382/.510 in August to finish the season.

Fabian impresses coaches with his ability to learn, adapt and adjust. Evaluators are generally confident he'll hit because he has a knack of putting bat to ball, even though that means he currently swings at pitches he should take. Scouts who like him see a future plus hitter with average power, which could work in right field because he's plus defender there with a plus, accurate arm. What he lacks is the typical right field power profile, as he's more a hitter than a slugger with 15-18 home run projections in his future once he matures.

BA GRADE
50 Risk: High
HIT: 55. **POW:** 50.
SPD: 40. **FLD:** 60.
ARM: 60.

Fabian's strong finish showed he's ready to jump to high Class A San Jose. He's going to have to become more selective about what pitches he swings at, but he's young enough to figure that out.

Year	Club (League)	Class	AVG	G	AB	R	H	2B	3B	HR	RBI	BB	SO	SB	CS	OBP	SLG
2015	Giants (DSL)	R	.269	65	242	47	65	10	2	3	37	15	47	2	0	.348	.364
2016	Giants (AZL)	R	.340	42	159	30	54	13	5	2	35	7	28	3	1	.364	.522
2017	Augusta (SAL)	LoA	.277	122	480	51	133	30	0	11	61	10	88	5	4	.297	.408
Minor League Totals			.286	229	881	128	252	53	7	16	133	32	163	10	5	.324	.417

10 ANDREW SUAREZ, LHP

Born: Sept. 11, 1992. **B-T:** L-L. **Ht.:** 6-2. **Wt.:** 205. **Drafted:** Miami, 2015 (2nd round). **Signed by:** Jose Alou.

Suarez was a reliable member of Miami's weekend rotation for three seasons and has been equally reliable as a pro. He is rarely sensational, but he's also rarely knocked out of a game early. He efficiently works his six to seven innings, keeps his team in the game and does it again five days later. He worked six or more innings 20 times in 2017 en route to a 10-10, 3.30 mark between Double-A and Triple-A.

Suarez succeeds as a lefty with plus control and a plus slider. His 90-93 mph fastball sets up his slider as he works it in and out. The slider eats up lefties, and he's equally adept at busting in or backdooring righthanders. He's toyed with a slower curveball as well, but so far it's only a sporadic diversion. He will throw a below-average changeup to keep righthanders honest, but against lefties, he generally sticks to a two-pitch approach.

BA GRADE

45 Risk: Medium

FB: 50. CB: 30.
SL: 60. CHG: 40.
CTL: 60.

Suarez could help the big league club soon in a variety of ways. He is a nearly ready back-of-the-rotation starter who could eat innings with his control and his slider. He also could become a two-pitch lefty out of the bullpen where his fastball would likely gain a tick. Either way, his big league debut should come in 2018.

Year	Club (League)	Class	W	L	ERA	G	GS	CG	SV	IP	H	HR	BB	SO	K/9	WHIP	AVG
2015	Giants (AZL)	R	0	0	1.80	3	0	0	0	5	2	0	1	6	10.8	0.60	.118
	Salem-Keizer (NWL)	SS	1	0	1.40	5	5	0	0	19	17	2	2	15	7.0	0.98	.236
	San Jose (CAL)	HiA	1	0	1.80	3	3	0	0	15	13	2	2	16	9.6	1.00	.236
2016	San Jose (CAL)	HiA	2	1	2.43	5	5	0	0	30	25	2	5	34	10.3	1.01	.225
	Richmond (EL)	AA	7	7	3.95	19	19	0	0	114	129	11	24	90	7.1	1.34	.292
2017	Richmond (EL)	AA	4	4	2.96	11	11	0	0	67	72	3	15	55	7.4	1.30	.276
	Sacramento (PCL)	AAA	6	6	3.55	15	13	0	0	89	94	7	27	80	8.1	1.36	.270
Minor League Totals			21	18	3.24	61	56	0	0	339	352	27	76	296	7.9	1.26	.270

11 SHAUN ANDERSON, RHP

BA GRADE

50 Risk: High

Born: Oct. 29, 1994. **B-T:** R-R. **Ht.:** 6-4. **Wt.:** 225. **Drafted:** Florida, 2016 (3rd round). **Signed by:** Stephen Hargett (Red Sox).

For a team that was on its way to a 64-win season, the Giants didn't exactly tear the big league team apart in a search for future help. But San Francisco did send third baseman Eduardo Nunez to the Red Sox for young pitchers, picking up Anderson and Dominican Summer League righthander Gregory Santos.

Anderson was the moment-of-truth reliever at Florida, but scouts saw all the traits of a starter, noting that he relieved because the team had a slew of first-round picks in the weekend rotation. He's lived up to those expectations as a pro, showing potential to be a back-of-the-rotation starter with above-average control and command. He attacks hitters with a 92-94 mph above-average fastball that touches 96 and a plus 87-88 mph slider. He also mixes in a fringe-average changeup and curveball that are effective enough because he can throw them for strikes and hitters have to look for the fastball since he can hit his spots.

Anderson's storied Gators career has proven he can also pitch in the bullpen, but there's nothing in his four-pitch mix, clean delivery and robust frame that should keep him from being a durable No. 4 starter.

Year	Club (League)	Class	W	L	ERA	G	GS	CG	SV	IP	H	HR	BB	SO	K/9	WHIP	AVG
2016	Lowell (NYP)	SS	0	0	30.38	2	2	0	0	3	12	1	0	4	13.5	4.50	.571
2017	Greenville (SAL)	LoA	3	0	2.33	7	7	0	0	39	30	1	11	37	8.6	1.06	.216
	Salem (CAR)	HiA	3	3	3.99	11	11	0	0	59	53	6	18	48	7.4	1.21	.236
	San Jose (CAL)	HiA	3	3	3.51	6	5	0	0	26	19	1	4	22	7.7	0.90	.198
Minor League Totals			9	6	3.94	26	25	0	0	126	114	9	33	111	7.9	1.17	.237

12 JACOB GONZALEZ, 3B

BA GRADE

55 Risk: Extreme

Born: June 26, 1998. **B-T:** R-R. **Ht.:** 6-3. **Wt.:** 190. **Drafted:** HS—Scottsdale, Ariz., 2017 (2nd round). **Signed by:** Chuck Hensley.

As the son of long-time big leaguer Luis Gonzalez, Jacob had a very good understanding of what pro ball entailed when the Giants drafted him. He's bigger and potentially stronger than his dad, who, despite a massive power spike in the early 2000s, generally hit 15-20 homers a season.

A mature hitting approach was evident in Gonzalez's strong debut in the Rookie-level Arizona League, where he proved to be among the tougher outs. In drafting Gonzalez, the Giants are betting on his bat. He was better at third base in his pro debut than amateur scouts would have expected, but he's a below-average runner who lacks range going side to side. He is better coming in on balls. He has an above-average arm, though he needs to improve his throwing accuracy. It's too early to give up on him sticking at third, but it's more likely he ends up as a left fielder or first baseman.

Gonzalez has legitimate plus power potential and he has a chance to hit for average as well thanks to bat speed and a discerning enough batting eye. After a strong pro debut, he's mature enough to make the jump to low Class A Augusta.

Year	Club (League)	Class	AVG	G	AB	R	H	2B	3B	HR	RBI	BB	SO	SB	CS	OBP	SLG
2017	Giants (AZL)	R	.339	46	168	23	57	15	1	1	21	16	23	0	1	.418	.458
Minor League Totals			.339	46	168	23	57	15	1	1	21	16	23	0	1	.418	.458

13 ALEXANDER CANARIO, OF

BA GRADE
55 Risk: **Extreme**

Born: May 7, 2000. **B-T:** R-R. **Ht.:** 6-1. **Wt.:** 165. **Signed:** Dominican Republic, 2016. **Signed by:** Ruddy Moreta.

Canario has yet to play a game in the U.S., but a pretty convincing case can be made that other than Heliot Ramos, he has the highest ceiling in the Giants' farm system. Canario signed for less than $100,000 in 2016, but he's already demonstrated a rare blend of speed, athleticism and feel to hit.

Canario hit five home runs in 2017 while his 18 other Dominican Summer League teammates combined to hit 10, and he was the MVP of the league's all-star game. His above-average bat speed is what allows him to drive the ball even though he hasn't filled out, but his plus speed, athletic frame and chance to stick in center field are equally notable. His swing will get long when he goes hunting for home runs, but when he's at his best, he's short to the ball and shows good pitch recognition for his age. He primarily played right field in the DSL (and had seven assists thanks to an above-average arm) but his long-term home is in center.

Canario is ready to come to the U.S. in 2018 and could rocket up this list in the next couple of years.

Year	Club (League)	Class	AVG	G	AB	R	H	2B	3B	HR	RBI	BB	SO	SB	CS	OBP	SLG
2017	Giants (DSL)	R	.294	66	235	42	69	17	4	5	45	33	40	18	10	.391	.464
Minor League Totals			.294	66	235	42	69	17	4	5	45	33	40	18	10	.391	.464

14 MELVIN ADON, RHP

BA GRADE
50 Risk: **High**

Born: June 9, 1994. **B-T:** R-R. **Ht.:** 6-3. **Wt.:** 195. **Signed:** Dominican Republic, 2015. **Signed by:** Pablo Peguero/Felix Peguero/Jesus Stephens.

The Giants have consistently searched the Dominican Republic for older prospects who were passed over. Adon is one of the prime examples of the payoffs for such scouting. He didn't sign with the Giants until he was 20 and didn't make his U.S. debut until he was 22. In 2017, he was arguably the hardest-throwing starting pitcher in the low Class A South Atlantic League.

Adon had a long way to go when he signed. For one thing, he couldn't effectively pitch out of the stretch. He still is far from a finished product but he has made significant progress. He has toned down his slinging, low three-quarters delivery, but even though he can carry top-shelf velocity throughout his starts, scouts are nearly unanimous that his energetic delivery and lower release point will eventually lead him to the bullpen. Adon's fastball is a top-of-the-scale pitch. He pitches at 95-100 mph as a starter with plenty of armside run on his fastball, and he touched 102 in relief stints. His slider will flash plus as well with downward break and exceptional power (88-91 mph). His less-developed changeup even flashes average, though he only uses it sporadically against lefties. Adon's control and command improved in 2017 but it was still well below-average. More importantly, he needs to sequence pitches better. He's predictable, which means hitters can sit on his fastball early in counts.

If Adon moved to the bullpen, he could move quickly as a pitcher with two potential standout pitches, but for now, there's no reason for San Francisco to give up on developing him as a starter.

Year	Club (League)	Class	W	L	ERA	G	GS	CG	SV	IP	H	HR	BB	SO	K/9	WHIP	AVG
2015	Giants (DSL)	R	4	0	2.48	14	14	0	0	69	57	2	21	54	7.0	1.13	.223
2016	Salem-Keizer (NWL)	SS	5	5	5.48	14	14	0	0	67	85	3	34	55	7.4	1.77	.317
2017	Augusta (SAL)	LoA	3	11	4.35	23	19	0	0	99	110	5	35	89	8.1	1.46	.277
Minor League Totals			12	16	4.12	51	47	0	0	236	252	10	90	198	7.6	1.45	.274

15 REYES MORONTA, RHP

BA GRADE
45 Risk: Medium

Born: Jan. 6, 1993. **B-T:** R-R. **Ht.:** 6-0. **Wt.:** 175. **Signed:** Dominican Republic, 2010. **Signed by:** Pablo Peguero/Felix Peguero/Jonathan Bautista.

Moronta is another late-blooming Latin American Giants pitching prospect. He didn't throw his first pro pitch until he was 18 and didn't reach full-season ball until he was 22—but just two years later he made his big league debut. A few weeks later, he was striking out Paul Goldschmidt and J.D. Martinez.

Moronta's listed weight of 175 pounds bears no relation to his actual size (which is probably closer to 230 pounds). He's a short, thick-bodied righthander with a mid- to upper-90s fastball and a plus slider he's comfortable throwing in any count. Moronta uses his fastball to get to the slider. His control has been fringy, but it's more that he nibbles trying to get hitters to chase rather than an inability to throw strikes. Moronta's fastball is a bit straight, so even at 96-98 it's more hittable than his low-80s slider, which has enough depth to at times look like a power curve.

Moronta has the stuff to pitch in high-leverage situations and seems intimidated by no one. He should be a part of the Giants' bullpen in 2018.

Year	Club (League)	Class	W	L	ERA	G	GS	CG	SV	IP	H	HR	BB	SO	K/9	WHIP	AVG
2015	Augusta (SAL)	LoA	1	7	5.73	42	0	0	12	49	56	1	23	64	11.8	1.62	.281
2016	San Jose (CAL)	HiA	0	3	2.59	60	0	0	14	59	43	7	20	93	14.2	1.07	.195
2017	Richmond (EL)	AA	0	1	4.00	19	0	0	5	18	15	1	12	26	13.0	1.50	.217
	Giants (AZL)	R	0	0	0.00	2	0	0	0	2	0	0	0	4	18.0	0.00	.000
	Sacramento (PCL)	AAA	3	0	2.12	13	0	0	0	17	13	1	8	17	9.0	1.24	.210
	San Francisco (NL)	MAJ	0	0	2.70	7	0	0	0	7	6	1	3	11	14.9	1.35	.231
Major League Totals			0	0	2.70	7	0	0	0	7	6	1	3	11	14.9	1.35	.231
Minor League Totals			10	15	3.59	193	6	0	42	246	213	18	104	310	11.4	1.29	.228

16 RYAN HOWARD, SS/3B

BA GRADE
45 Risk: Medium

Born: July 25, 1994. **B-T:** R-R. **Ht.:** 6-2. **Wt.:** 195. **Drafted:** Missouri, 2016 (5th round). **Signed by:** Daniel Murray.

The 2016 draft class was rather thin on college shortstops, but Howard had one of the longest track records of success. He was Team USA's shortstop and a three-year starter at Missouri. That experience has paid off in pro ball. He handled the jump to high Class A San Jose in 2017 with few issues.

Howard is one of a number of Giants middle infield prospects who does enough things adequately to have a big league career but lacks the carrying tools scouts look for in a future first-division regular. He's an average defender at shortstop with good instincts, but lacks the body control and quickness to ever be described as rangy. His above-average arm plays well at shortstop and he can handle third as well (where he played sporadically for San Jose). At the plate, Howard puts together professional at-bats and projects as a .250-.260 hitter, but with just 5-10 home runs a year.

Most scouts see Howard as a second-division regular or utility infielder. He's not going to unseat Brandon Crawford, but as he heads to Double-A, Howard has a good shot at a big league future.

Year	Club (League)	Class	AVG	G	AB	R	H	2B	3B	HR	RBI	BB	SO	SB	CS	OBP	SLG
2016	Giants (AZL)	R	.250	2	8	1	2	0	0	0	0	2	0	0	0	.400	.250
	Salem-Keizer (NWL)	SS	.272	59	224	33	61	10	0	4	31	13	24	2	2	.313	.371
2017	San Jose (CAL)	HiA	.306	127	526	59	161	21	0	9	50	23	81	7	2	.342	.397
Minor League Totals			.296	188	758	93	224	31	0	13	81	38	105	9	4	.334	.388

17 AUSTIN SLATER, OF

BA GRADE
45 Risk: Medium

Born: Dec. 13, 1992. **B-T:** R-R. **Ht.:** 6-2. **Wt.:** 205. **Drafted:** Stanford, 2014 (8th round). **Signed by:** Keith Snider.

Much like Christian Arroyo, Slater is only eligible for this list because of injury. Slater had largely assumed the Giants' left field job when he tore a thigh muscle off of his hip. He missed two months before returning in September.

Teams kept trying to find a defensive home for Slater, who is an excellent athlete. The Giants eventually let him move to left field and focus on hitting. Despite his speed, he's stretched in center field, though he's above-average in the corners. What Slater does best is mash lefthanders. Since 2016 began, he's hit .368/.442/.556 against lefties and a more modest but still useful .283/.357/.442 against righthanders. Slater has plus-plus raw power, which he demonstrated with a 461-foot home run against the Brewers that was the longest home run by any Giants hitter in 2017. Scouts see 15-20 home run potential as a regular.

Slater projects as a second-division regular, but is better suited as a useful backup on a championship team. If the Giants can't upgrade at left field for 2018, Slater could be a useful fallback option.

Year	Club (League)	Class	AVG	G	AB	R	H	2B	3B	HR	RBI	BB	SO	SB	CS	OBP	SLG
2015	San Jose (CAL)	HiA	.292	60	250	25	73	15	1	3	34	10	44	4	3	.321	.396
	Richmond (EL)	AA	.296	54	199	21	59	11	1	0	13	14	48	1	1	.350	.362
2016	Richmond (EL)	AA	.317	41	145	20	46	8	1	5	25	24	36	6	1	.413	.490
	Sacramento (PCL)	AAA	.298	68	245	36	73	12	0	13	42	33	53	2	6	.381	.506
2017	Sacramento (PCL)	AAA	.321	50	184	28	59	12	0	5	27	15	39	4	3	.377	.467
	San Francisco (NL)	MAJ	.282	34	117	15	33	3	1	3	16	8	29	0	0	.339	.402
Major League Totals			.282	34	117	15	33	3	1	3	16	8	29	0	0	.339	.402
Minor League Totals			.308	304	1150	153	354	64	4	28	166	106	239	24	15	.370	.443

18 KYLE CRICK, RHP

BA GRADE 45 Risk: Medium

Born: Nov. 30, 1992. **B-T:** L-R. **Ht.:** 6-4. **Wt.:** 220. **Drafted:** HS—Sherman, Texas, 2011 (1st round supplemental). **Signed by:** Todd Thomas.

One of the few bright spots in the brutal Giants season was Crick's return from the wilderness of wildness. Once the team's top prospect, Crick's control troubles got the best of his stuff for years and he had to gear down to try to throw strikes.

Crick moved full-time to the bullpen in 2017 and responded by reaching the big leagues. He hasn't fixed his control problems as much as he's tamed them just enough to be effective. He still battles bouts of wildness and struggles to get through innings cleanly, but his lively, plus 95-98 mph fastball is good enough to get swings and misses even if he's not dotting the corners. His starter's background allowed the Giants to feel comfortable using him for two innings or more out of the pen. His low-80s average slider is generally a chase pitch, and he will mix in a hard 88-90 mph fringe-average changeup to lefties.

Crick's stuff is big league caliber, and if he can continue to have even fringy control he could have a lengthy career as a setup man.

Year	Club (League)	Class	W	L	ERA	G	GS	CG	SV	IP	H	HR	BB	SO	K/9	WHIP	AVG
2015	Richmond (EL)	AA	3	4	3.29	36	11	0	0	63	47	2	66	73	10.4	1.79	.208
2016	Richmond (EL)	AA	4	11	5.04	23	23	0	0	109	110	8	67	86	7.1	1.62	.266
2017	Sacramento (PCL)	AAA	1	2	2.76	24	0	0	6	29	24	1	13	39	12.0	1.26	.220
	San Francisco (NL)	MAJ	0	0	3.06	30	0	0	0	32	22	2	17	28	7.8	1.21	.191
Major League Totals			0	0	3.06	30	0	0	0	32	22	2	17	28	7.8	1.21	.191
Minor League Totals			25	31	3.37	150	92	0	6	479	391	20	321	540	10.2	1.49	.225

19 MATT KROOK, LHP

BA GRADE 50 Risk: Extreme

Born: Oct. 21, 1994. **B-T:** L-L. **Ht.:** 6-4. **Wt.:** 195. **Drafted:** Oregon, 2016 (4th round). **Signed by:** Larry Casian.

Much like Kyle Crick, Krook was lost to control troubles as a starter, but found himself as a reliever. Still, Krook's stint as a reliever has not yet closed the door on him returning to the rotation. Krook was a supplemental first round pick of the Marlins out of high school, but the team opted not to sign him because of concerns about his elbow ligament. He did end up needing Tommy John surgery, which meant he missed all of his 2015 season at Oregon and was limited to 90 innings in 2016.

The Giants moved Krook to the bullpen in late July to limit his innings in 2017. After a brutal 2-11, 6.11 stint as a starter, he was more aggressive and threw more strikes in the pen, posting a 1.02 ERA and .121 opponent average as a reliever. In his last five relief appearances he struck out 17 and walked one in 10.2 innings. Krook's 90-94 mph fastball has extreme sink at its best, drawing comparisons with Zach Britton's sinker for its movement. As a starter, he too frequently failed to locate anything but his sinker in the zone. Once he moved to the pen, he regained the feel for his potentially plus slider. Krook's changeup hasn't developed as much.

The Giants haven't determined Krook's 2018 role, but power reliever seems to be his calling.

Year	Club (League)	Class	W	L	ERA	G	GS	CG	SV	IP	H	HR	BB	SO	K/9	WHIP	AVG
2016	Giants (AZL)	R	0	1	1.59	2	1	0	0	6	6	0	2	2	3.2	1.41	.261
	Salem-Keizer (NWL)	SS	1	3	6.17	11	10	0	0	35	35	2	33	39	10.0	1.94	.263
2017	San Jose (CAL)	HiA	4	9	5.12	25	17	0	0	91	75	4	66	105	10.3	1.54	.217
Minor League Totals			5	13	5.25	38	28	0	0	132	116	6	101	146	10.0	1.64	.232

20 GREGORY SANTOS, RHP

BA GRADE 50 Risk: Extreme

Born: Aug. 28, 1999. **B-T:** R-R. **Ht.:** 6-2. **Wt.:** 190. **Signed:** Dominican Republic, 2015. **Signed by:** Eddie Romero/Manny Nanita (Red Sox).

Acquired along with righthander Shaun Anderson in the trade that sent Eduardo Nunez to the Red Sox in July 2017, Santos signed for $275,000 in 2015 and quickly impressed because of his starter's frame, low- to mid-90s velocity (he touches 97) and promising breaking ball.

Santos is years from San Francisco, but he has the best combination of easy velocity, durability and repeatability of the Giants' rookie-ball pitchers. His arm works well and he generates plenty of angle with his fastball, which helps explain how he generated three ground outs for every air out in 2017. Santos' fastball and a developing curve are the building blocks of a mid-rotation starter, although at this point, it's equally likely he eventually ends up as a power reliever. Santos has a long way to go as far as developing his control, he'll have to continue sharpening his breaking ball and he needs to develop his changeup.

Santos is ready to come to the U.S., but he's likely still a year away from full-season ball.

Year	Club (League)	Class	W	L	ERA	G	GS	CG	SV	IP	H	HR	BB	SO	K/9	WHIP	AVG
2016	Red Sox2 (DSL)	R	3	3	4.17	16	10	0	1	41	40	1	26	25	5.5	1.61	.258
2017	Red Sox (DSL)	R	2	0	0.89	8	8	0	0	30	22	0	15	24	7.1	1.22	.206
	Giants (DSL)	R	1	0	1.93	4	4	0	0	19	21	2	5	17	8.2	1.39	.273
Minor League Totals			6	3	2.60	28	22	0	1	90	83	3	46	66	6.6	1.43	.245

21 SETH CORRY, LHP

BA GRADE
50 Risk: **Extreme**

Born: Nov. 3, 1998. **B-T:** L-L. **Ht.:** 6-2. **Wt.:** 195. **Drafted:** HS—Highland, Utah, 2017 (3rd round). **Signed by:** Chuck Hensley.

In 2016, the Giants spent the second day of the draft taking chances on college pitchers with excellent stuff but control problems. Garrett Williams' development rewarded that approach. In 2017, the Giants took an even bigger risk by drafting Corry. He had one of the best fastball/curveball combos in the draft class, but teams largely shied away because of his inability to command and control his fastball—something that became more evident when he walked eight batters per nine innings in his pro debut.

Corry is the highest-drafted prep pitcher out of Utah since Cubs first-rounder Mark Pawelek in 2005. Corry's control troubles largely stem from an effortful delivery. He has a head whack and is a little stiff in his finish, but his curveball is a true 12-to-6 hammer with easy plus potential. He also sits 92-94 mph with his lively fastball, giving himself a pair of weapons. He controls his curve better than his fastball.

The Giants are going to have to be patient with Corry and he'll need to work hard on his delivery, but he has worlds of potential, even if he's likely ticketed for extended spring training and short-season Salem-Keizer in 2018.

Year	Club (League)	Class	W	L	ERA	G	GS	CG	SV	IP	H	HR	BB	SO	K/9	WHIP	AVG
2017	Giants (AZL)	R	0	2	5.55	13	10	0	0	24	14	1	22	21	7.8	1.48	.163
Minor League Totals			0	2	5.55	13	10	0	0	24	14	1	22	21	7.8	1.48	.163

22 JOAN GREGORIO, RHP

BA GRADE
45 Risk: **High**

Born: Jan. 12, 1992. **B-T:** R-R. **Ht.:** 6-7. **Wt.:** 230. **Signed:** Dominican Republic, 2010. **Signed by:** Pablo Peguero.

Tall pitchers often take longer to develop, but Gregorio is running out of time to develop for the Giants. The Rookie-level Arizona League ERA leader in 2011 at the time drew comparisons with Ubaldo Jimenez because of his size and stuff. The 6-foot-7 Gregorio's development since then has been slowed by his struggles to maintain a consistent release point, which has led to a series of control struggles.

Gregorio also got in his own way in 2017 when he blew his chance at a September callup by being suspended for testing positive for a performance-enhancing steroid. He made up for lost time with a stint in the Arizona Fall League, where he was roughed up for 10 earned runs in 15.1 innings. Gregorio was granted a fourth option year, which gives him one more chance to develop his control and consistency in the minors. Gregorio still has a 91-95 mph above-average fastball and an above-average slider.

Time is running out for Gregorio as a starter, and considering his ticking minor league options clock, it wouldn't be surprising to see him try relieving at some point in 2018.

Year	Club (League)	Class	W	L	ERA	G	GS	CG	SV	IP	H	HR	BB	SO	K/9	WHIP	AVG
2015	Richmond (EL)	AA	3	2	3.09	37	9	0	1	79	64	6	32	72	8.2	1.22	.225
2016	Richmond (EL)	AA	0	2	2.33	5	5	0	0	27	15	1	6	30	10.0	0.78	.165
	Sacramento (PCL)	AAA	6	8	5.28	21	21	0	0	107	112	13	43	122	10.2	1.44	.267
2017	Sacramento (PCL)	AAA	4	4	3.04	13	13	0	0	74	63	9	35	61	7.4	1.32	.235
Minor League Totals			39	38	3.89	151	120	0	2	648	589	47	229	614	8.5	1.26	.243

23 MIGUEL GOMEZ, 2B

BA GRADE 40 Risk: Medium

Born: Dec. 17, 1992. **B-T:** B-R. **Ht.:** 5-10. **Wt.:** 185. **Signed:** Dominican Republic, 2011. **Signed by:** Pablo Peguero/Felix Peguero/Jonathan Bautista.

Other than Christian Arroyo, Gomez is the purest hitter in the Giants' farm system, which is why the switch-hitter was able to leap from low Class A Augusta to the big leagues in only a year.

Gomez projects as a plus hitter with average power thanks to excellent hand-eye coordination, but that may not be enough to ever win him a much larger role than the pinch-hitting fill-in he served as for a month before a disabled list stint ended his season thanks to a sore knee. His problem is he doesn't have a clear path to a regular job and even finding a roster spot as a backup role is hard. He's bounced around defensively from catcher to third base to second base. Second is his best spot, but he's below-average defensively thanks in part to his heavy feet, below-average speed and poor range.

Gomez is a hard worker whose work ethic impresses coaches, but he's a Lenny Harris type of professional pinch-hitter in a league context that no longer has many dedicated pinch-hitters.

Year	Club (League)	Class	AVG	G	AB	R	H	2B	3B	HR	RBI	BB	SO	SB	CS	OBP	SLG
2015	Salem-Keizer (NWL)	SS	.319	66	276	30	88	14	1	6	52	5	24	0	1	.331	.442
2016	Augusta (SAL)	LoA	.371	66	267	41	99	17	1	8	43	12	25	3	2	.401	.532
	San Jose (CAL)	HiA	.267	43	172	25	46	9	2	9	24	8	28	1	0	.302	.500
2017	Richmond (EL)	AA	.305	78	308	43	94	19	2	8	38	12	36	0	0	.330	.458
	San Francisco (NL)	MAJ	.242	22	33	3	8	2	0	0	2	0	6	0	0	.235	.303
Major League Totals			.242	22	33	3	8	2	0	0	2	0	6	0	0	.235	.303
Minor League Totals			.312	390	1513	207	472	95	10	39	257	75	202	10	4	.348	.465

24 RODOLFO MARTINEZ, RHP

BA GRADE 45 Risk: High

Born: April 4, 1994. **B-T:** R-R. **Ht.:** 6-2. **Wt.:** 178. **Signed:** Dominican Republic, 2013. **Signed by:** Pablo Peguero/Felix Peguero/Jesus Stephens.

Blessed with one of the best arms in baseball but with little idea yet of how to use it, Martinez needs plenty of innings. That makes the oblique injury that wiped out most of his 2017 season especially frustrating. That means Martinez he will enter 2018 no closer to realizing his potential.

Martinez didn't enter pro ball until he was 20. The late bloomer has touched 102 mph in the past, but was generally 94-98 mph when healthy in 2017—he never got fully stretched out enough to reach triple digits regularly. Martinez's fastball may be plus-plus at its best, but his below-average changeup and slider are hitters' best friends. He has started to throw his secondary pitches for strikes, but he still slows his arm to telegraph his changeup and his slider doesn't have much break. Martinez could develop into a useful big league reliever, but he needs time and innings to get there.

Martinez should head back to Double-A in 2018 as he continues to try to find a second pitch.

Year	Club (League)	Class	W	L	ERA	G	GS	CG	SV	IP	H	HR	BB	SO	K/9	WHIP	AVG
2015	Augusta (SAL)	LoA	1	2	2.54	35	0	0	0	46	41	1	14	44	8.6	1.20	.232
2016	San Jose (CAL)	HiA	1	1	0.88	32	0	0	21	31	23	1	10	33	9.7	1.08	.205
	Richmond (EL)	AA	0	3	6.65	25	0	0	3	23	29	1	15	17	6.7	1.91	.315
2017	Richmond (EL)	AA	0	0	5.63	8	0	0	0	8	12	0	5	5	5.6	2.13	.364
	Giants (AZL)	R	0	0	0.00	2	0	0	0	2	2	0	0	2	9.0	1.00	.250
	San Jose (CAL)	HiA	2	0	4.05	10	0	0	0	13	14	2	1	12	8.1	1.13	.269
Minor League Totals			5	11	4.24	127	7	0	24	151	166	6	61	148	8.8	1.51	.279

25 STEPHEN WOODS, RHP

BA GRADE 50 Risk: Extreme

Born: June 10, 1995. **B-T:** R-R. **Ht.:** 6-2. **Wt.:** 200. **Drafted:** Albany, 2016 (8th round). **Signed by:** Ray Callari.

Woods was another of the Giants' slew of 2016 draftees with big stuff and bigger control issues. It's hard to say that the Giants have tamed his wildness when he walked more than five batters per nine innings, but his fastball/curveball combo gives him survival skills while he works to become more efficient.

Woods' 90-96 mph fastball and his sharp 11-to-5 curveball proved hard for low Class A South Atlantic League hitters to square, even when they got ahead in counts. Both his fastball and curve have plus potential. He also throws a below-average slider that has little enough depth that at times it looks more like a cutter. Woods has to tone down some of the effort in his delivery if he's going to remain a starter and he'll have to repeat his motion much more consistently.

While Woods survived his first full-season test despite significant control issues, more advanced hitters will feast if he doesn't stay around the zone more often. He should start 2018 at high Class A San Jose.

Year	Club (League)	Class	W	L	ERA	G	GS	CG	SV	IP	H	HR	BB	SO	K/9	WHIP	AVG
2016	Giants (AZL)	R	0	2	2.67	10	8	0	0	27	25	0	17	25	8.3	1.56	.236
	Salem-Keizer (NWL)	SS	1	0	5.63	2	2	0	0	8	7	1	5	12	13.5	1.50	.233
2017	Augusta (SAL)	LoA	6	7	2.95	23	23	0	0	110	93	3	64	113	9.2	1.43	.226
Minor League Totals			7	9	3.04	35	33	0	0	145	125	4	86	150	9.3	1.46	.229

26 TYLER CYR, RHP

BA GRADE
40 Risk: Medium

Born: May 5, 1993. **B-T:** R-R. **Ht.:** 6-3. **Wt.:** 200. **Drafted:** Embry-Riddle (Fla.), 2015 (10th round). **Signed by:** James Gabella.

Anyone looking to become a pilot or an aeronautical engineer would struggle to find a better choice than attending Embry-Riddle Aeronautical University in Daytona Beach, Fla., home of a well-equipped fleet of airplanes. But it's not been a choice of players looking to make it to the majors. Cyr is in a race with Cardinals righthander Daniel Poncedeleon to become the first Eagles big leaguer.

Cyr joined the Giants' 40-man roster after the 2017 season and could figure into the Giants' 2018 plans. His success comes from plenty of movement on his 92-96 mph fastball and the deception his cross-body delivery brings. Lefthanded hitters don't pick up the ball until late in his delivery because they get a good look at the numbers on the back of his jersey. Cyr cuts and runs his fastball, with the above-average cutter and his delivery being the biggest reason he shut down lefties (who hit .179/.255/.221). Righthanded hitters actually pick the ball up better coming out of his hand. His below-average slurvy slider isn't nearly as effective which helps explain why righties hit .340/.413/.443 against him.

Cyr doesn't have a true plus pitch to use in high-leverage innings, but he could help the big league club as a low-cost, reliable reliever in the near future.

Year	Club (League)	Class	W	L	ERA	G	GS	CG	SV	IP	H	HR	BB	SO	K/9	WHIP	AVG
2015	Giants (AZL)	R	0	1	2.25	3	1	0	0	4	2	0	1	7	15.8	0.75	.133
	Augusta (SAL)	LoA	2	1	5.60	12	0	0	0	18	16	0	18	20	10.2	1.92	.242
2016	Augusta (SAL)	LoA	3	3	2.31	20	0	0	2	51	36	1	16	65	11.5	1.03	.201
	San Jose (CAL)	HiA	2	1	2.35	19	0	0	1	23	19	1	9	24	9.4	1.22	.232
2017	Richmond (EL)	AA	5	2	2.19	47	0	0	18	49	50	3	20	57	10.4	1.42	.260
Minor League Totals			12	8	2.68	101	1	0	21	145	123	5	64	173	10.8	1.29	.230

27 TYLER HERB, RHP

BA GRADE
40 Risk: Medium

Born: April 28, 1992. **B-T:** R-R. **Ht.:** 6-4. **Wt.:** 190. **Drafted:** Coastal Carolina, 2014 (29th round). **Signed by:** Devitt Moore (Mariners).

A senior sign of the Mariners out of Coastal Carolina in 2014, the Giants picked up Herb as the player to be named from the trade that sent Chris Heston to Seattle. That trade has already paid off for the Giants, when Heston was waived by the Mariners before Herb was even named in the trade.

The Mariners were willing in part to part with Herb because the 25-year-old would be Rule 5 eligible if not added to the 40-man roster in the offseason, but the Giants were impressed enough after his 10 starts with Double-A Richmond to add him. Herb impressed more with his consistency than his stuff. He has four pitches he can throw at seemingly any point in the count with above-average control, but he doesn't have a plus pitch. He sits at 90-92 mph with his sinking fastball that generates ground balls. He can touch 94-95 when he muscles up.

Herb has a little more trust in his slider than his changeup or curve, but all three get average grades at best and is a swingman starter.

Year	Club (League)	Class	W	L	ERA	G	GS	CG	SV	IP	H	HR	BB	SO	K/9	WHIP	AVG
2015	Clinton (MWL)	LoA	7	8	4.64	27	27	1	0	140	174	6	52	95	6.1	1.62	.305
2016	Bakersfield (CAL)	HiA	7	3	3.28	15	15	0	0	85	77	8	28	93	9.8	1.24	.241
	Jackson (SL)	AA	2	3	5.04	11	11	0	0	55	57	4	27	41	6.7	1.52	.268
2017	Arkansas (TL)	AA	6	4	3.31	16	16	0	0	98	97	5	30	88	8.1	1.30	.264
	Richmond (EL)	AA	2	3	2.76	10	10	1	0	65	61	5	18	48	6.6	1.21	.246
Minor League Totals			27	25	3.92	99	79	2	2	480	517	30	164	410	7.7	1.42	.275

28 CAMILO DOVAL, RHP

BA GRADE
45 Risk: Extreme

Born: July 4, 1997. **B-T:** R-R. **Ht.:** 6-2. **Wt.:** 180. **Signed:** Dominican Republic, 2015. **Signed by:** Gabriel Arias.

When the Giants signed Doval, he already had a fast arm that generated low-90s velocity. In the two years since then, he's added 3-5 additional mph, turning him into a flame-thrower. In his U.S. debut in 2017, Doval finished with the second-best strikeout ratio in the Rookie-level Arizona League (14.2 strikeouts per nine innings) because hitters couldn't catch up to his 93-97 mph fastball, which could eventually reach triple-digits.

Doval's arm is extremely fast, but his delivery ranges from being described as energetic to violent depending on how much the scout likes him. He throws across his body and finishes with some significant recoil, making it hard for hitters to pick up the ball, but also for Doval to consistently throw strikes. He relies almost entirely on his fastball, which he can cut or run, as well as the beginnings of a slider.

Doval is a reliever all the way and needs to improve his current near bottom-of-the-scale control, but he has the swing-and-miss stuff required of high-leverage relievers. He's a long way from that ceiling, but he could make it to full-season ball in 2018.

Year	Club (League)	Class	W	L	ERA	G	GS	CG	SV	IP	H	HR	BB	SO	K/9	WHIP	AVG
2016	Giants (DSL)	R	2	0	1.83	12	0	0	1	20	10	0	10	20	9.2	1.02	.159
2017	Giants (AZL)	R	1	2	3.90	17	0	0	1	32	23	0	13	51	14.2	1.11	.197
Minor League Totals			3	2	3.12	29	0	0	2	52	33	0	23	71	12.3	1.08	.191

29 SAM COONROD, RHP

BA GRADE | **45** Risk: **Extreme**

Born: Sept. 22, 1992. **B-T:** R-R. **Ht.:** 6-2. **Wt.:** 190. **Drafted:** Southern Illinois, 2014 (5th round). **Signed by:** James Gabella.

The Peter Principle suggests that workers are promoted until they fail, so eventually they reach one level above their actual level of ability. That principle may apply to Coonrod, who dominated Class A with a two-pitch approach, but has looked stretched in two seasons against Double-A competition as a starter because of the limitations of that same two-pitch approach.

Coonrod attacks hitters with a potentially above-average, heavy 92-95 mph fastball and a hard, above-average 85-89 mph slider. His below-average changeup fools no one and is easy for hitters to recognize. His struggles to develop his change and his high-effort delivery point to a future move to the bullpen, where his below-average command and control would be less of an issue. Coonrod injured his elbow late in the season and will miss all of 2018 after Tommy John surgery.

Coonrod was left off the 40-man roster thanks to the injury, but when he returns, the Giants will have to decide whether it's as a starter or as a reliever. Scouts for other teams would bet he ends up in the bullpen.

Year	Club (League)	Class	W	L	ERA	G	GS	CG	SV	IP	H	HR	BB	SO	K/9	WHIP	AVG
2015	Augusta (SAL)	LoA	7	5	3.14	23	22	0	0	112	103	3	34	114	9.2	1.23	.243
2016	San Jose (CAL)	HiA	5	3	1.98	11	11	0	0	64	46	3	22	42	5.9	1.07	.204
	Richmond (EL)	AA	4	3	3.03	13	13	0	0	77	59	7	38	52	6.1	1.25	.214
2017	Richmond (EL)	AA	4	11	4.69	24	18	0	0	104	96	7	42	94	8.2	1.33	.249
Minor League Totals			21	22	3.40	86	69	0	0	384	336	20	142	327	7.7	1.24	.237

30 C.J. HINOJOSA, SS

BA GRADE | **40** Risk: **V. High**

Born: July 15, 1994. **B-T:** R-R. **Ht.:** 5-10. **Wt.:** 180. **Drafted:** Texas, 2015 (11th round). **Signed by:** Todd Thomas.

Hinojosa was a College World Series star as a sophomore at Texas, but a poor junior season helped him slide to the 11th round in 2015. Since then he's looked more like the scrappy tough out he was earlier in his Longhorns career than the player who sacrificed contact for a modest power bump as a junior.

Hinojosa is the kind of player the Giants seem to collect in waves. He's best when he's spraying the ball around the field, and is especially pesky at poking line drives down the right-field line, but he has a lot of fringe-average to average tools and no real plus tool on his scouting report. He plays shortstop plausibly enough defensively to fill-in, but he lacks the range to play there everyday.

Hinojosa missed the start of the 2017 season with a quad strain, but when he returned he went right back to looking like a future big league utility infielder. Unfortunately, he tore his Achilles tendon at the end of the season and could miss time early in 2018.

Year	Club (League)	Class	AVG	G	AB	R	H	2B	3B	HR	RBI	BB	SO	SB	CS	OBP	SLG
2015	Salem-Keizer (NWL)	SS	.296	48	189	24	56	18	1	5	19	8	15	2	3	.328	.481
2016	San Jose (CAL)	HiA	.296	69	260	45	77	14	3	6	34	36	46	1	4	.378	.442
	Richmond (EL)	AA	.248	57	226	27	56	7	2	3	19	20	43	1	0	.312	.336
2017	Richmond (EL)	AA	.265	99	373	47	99	16	0	4	35	31	42	5	4	.321	.340
Minor League Totals			.275	273	1048	143	288	55	6	18	107	95	146	9	11	.335	.390

Seattle Mariners

BY BILL MITCHELL

On the heels of a strong 2016 season, the Mariners fell back to earth in 2017. Seattle finished seven games out of the American League wild card race with a disappointing 78-84 record. The poor season stretched the Mariners playoff drought to 16 years, longest in the majors.

It wasn't for lack of trying. General manager Jerry Dipoto continued to tinker with the Mariners' roster, primarily to help a pitching staff decimated by injuries. Seattle used a total of 40 pitchers in 2017, with no rotation member reaching 30 starts and just three starting more than 20.

While lefthander James Paxton had a breakout year, he took the mound just 24 times. Felix Hernandez was limited to 16 starts. Offseason acquisition Drew Smyly missed the entire season after having Tommy John surgery. Reliever David Phelps, obtained from the Marlins at for four prospects at the trade deadline, pitched just 10 games for Seattle before his season ended with an elbow injury.

The Mariners' minor league system looks significantly different than the previous year, in part because the major league team used 22 rookies in 2017. Eight players who ranked among the preseason Top 30 Prospects received enough major league time to no longer qualify for this year's list. Another nine of the Top 30 were subsequently traded.

Kyle Lewis repeats as the organization's No. 1 prospect, though concerns remain that he hasn't completely recovered from his knee injury suffered in 2016. He got back into action nearly a year after tearing his ACL, playing in 49 games, but had to leave the Arizona Fall League after just two games.

Dipoto traded last year's No. 2 prospect, outfielder Tyler O'Neill, to the Cardinals during the season for southpaw Marco Gonzales, who was ineffective in 10 games for Seattle. Last year's No. 3 prospect, lefthander Luiz Gohara, was sent off to the Braves just before the start of the 2017 season as part of a combination of deals that, in essence, netted Smyly from the Rays. Seattle non-tendered Smyly after the season and lost him to the Cubs.

Dipoto showed no signs of slowing down his transactional activity, whether it be trading, making waiver claims or Rule 5 draft selections.

Dipoto made the first trade following the 2017 season by acquiring first baseman Ryon Healy from the Athletics. He made a series of trades in November and December aimed at first adding and then divesting of international bonus pool money after Japanese star Shohei Ohtani decided to sign with the Angels. One such trade with the Marlins cost them righthander Nick Neidert, last year's No. 4 prospect.

Outfielder Mitch Haniger was one of eight Mariners rookies to lose prospect eligibility.

PROJECTED 2021 LINEUP

Catcher	Mike Zunino (30)
First Base	Evan White (25)
Second Base	Robinson Cano (38)
Third Base	Kyle Seager (33)
Shortstop	Jean Segura (31)
Left Field	Mitch Haniger (30)
Center Field	Dee Gordon (33)
Right Field	Kyle Lewis (25)
Designated Hitter	Ryon Healy (29)
No. 1 Starter	James Paxton (32)
No. 2 Starter	Felix Hernandez (35)
No. 3 Starter	Andrew Moore (27)
No. 4 Starter	Marco Gonzales (29)
No. 5 Starter	Max Povse (27)
Closer	Edwin Diaz (27)

Dipoto has established he is willing to trade prospects for big league assets, no matter how fringy. It's a philosophy that reflects the organization's desperation to return to the playoffs, as well as capitalize on the limited time they have left with veterans such as Hernandez, Nelson Cruz and Robinson Cano.

Because the Mariners' farm system has been thinned by trades, Seattle has few viable reinforcements left in the cupboard. Even the lower levels have been raided, putting the organization's future success in jeopardy.

All of that puts more pressure than ever on Dipoto and staff to turn in a winning product in 2018, Cruz's last year under contract with the club.

SEATTLE MARINERS

TOP 2018 ROOKIE: Rob Whalen, RHP. The Mariners don't have a lot of prospect depth at the upper levels of the organization, but with a return to health Whalen should be able to contribute to the pitching staff.

BREAKOUT PROSPECT: Joe Rizzo, 3B. Rizzo has a chance to build on a strong finish to 2017 with a return to the California League.

SOURCE OF TOP 30 TALENT			
Homegrown	23	Acquired	7
College	13	Trade	6
Junior college	2	Rule 5 draft	0
High school	3	Independent league	0
Nondrafted free agent	0	Free agent/waivers	1
International	5		

SLEEPER: Cesar Izturis Jr., 2B. With big league bloodlines, Izturis will make his U.S. debut and has the instincts and smarts to be one of the Rookie-level Arizona League's more interesting prospects.

LF	CF	RF
Eric Fila (14)	Kyle Lewis (1)	Julio Rodriguez (4)
Jansiel Rivera	Braden Bishop (5)	Ronald Rosario (29)
Greifer Andrade	Ian Miller (19)	Anthony Jimenez
	Luis Liberato (24)	
	DeAires Moses	

3B	SS	2B	1B
Joe Rizzo (9)	Juan Querecuto (10)	Joseph Rosa (25)	Evan White (2)
Johnny Adams (28)	Donnie Walton (23)	Bryson Brigman (27)	Dan Vogelbach (12)
Eugene Helder		Cesar Izturis Jr.	Mike Ford (22)
Nolan Perez		Chris Mariscal	

C
Joe DeCarlo
Geoandry Montilla
Ryan Scott

LHP		RHP	
LHSP	**LHRP**	**RHSP**	**RHRP**
Anthony Misiewicz (18)	Sam Moll (20)	Sam Carlson (3)	Matt Festa (7)
Oliver Jaskie (21)	Spencer Herrmann	Max Povse (6)	Art Warren (8)
Jorge Benitez (30)	Matt Clancy	Rob Whalen (15)	Wyatt Mills (11)
Max Roberts	Joe Pistorese	Chase De Jong (16)	Nick Rumbelow (13)
Nick Wells		Tommy Romero (26)	Seth Elledge (17)
Danny Garcia		Reggie McClain	Marvin Gorgas
		Andres Torres	Jamal Wade
		Darren McCaughan	Kyle Wilcox
		Nathan Bannister	Darin Gillies
		Ljay Newsome	

DRAFT ANALYSIS

2017

BEST PURE HITTER: 1B Evan White (1) established a long track record for hitting as an amateur and was a career .356 hitter at Kentucky. He has a mature, disciplined approach and sprays line drives to all fields.

BEST POWER HITTER: The biggest knock on White has long been his power, but he began to grow into it this year. He nearly doubled this spring his career extra-base hit total and has the tools to hit for at least average power. He consistently produces hard contact and he should be able to turn that into over-the-fence pop in time.

FASTEST RUNNER: OF Johnny Slater (28) was a senior sign out of Michigan, but has some intriguing tools, including plus speed. OF Billy Cooke (8) is nearly as fast and also turns in plus run times.

BEST DEFENSIVE PLAYER: Even as a first baseman, White was one of the best defenders in the draft class. He runs well enough to play the outfield, but his defensive value at first base, where he earns well above-average grades, has been good enough to keep him at the position. First-team All-American C David Banuelos (5) also earns praise for his defense.

BEST FASTBALL: RHP Seth Elledge (4) comes from a Dallas Baptist program known for producing power arms, and he can run his fastball up to 96-97 mph with a high spin rate that makes it a swing-and-miss pitch.

BEST SECONDARY: RHP Sam Carlson (2) saw his velocity tick up this spring, making his breaking ball into more of a true hard, mid-80s slider. Its short, late action makes it especially tough on hitters. His changeup also flashes plus potential.

BEST PRO DEBUT: LHP J.P. Sears (11) was an All-American this spring after leading the country in strikeouts in the regular season. He carried that performance over to pro ball, finishing the year in low Class A Clinton and averaging 16.6 strikeouts per nine innings this summer. Offensively, INF Johnny Adams (22) opened some eyes by hitting .316/.374/.445 in the Northwest League.

BEST ATHLETE: White doesn't fit the traditional profile of a plodding first baseman. He has above-average speed and shows impressive athleticism around first base, helping his defense.

MOST INTRIGUING BACKGROUND: RHP Jamal Wade (17) went to Maryland as a position player, like his older brother and former Terps teammate LaMonte, now in the Twins system. After struggling at the plate, the younger Wade moved to the mound following his sophomore season and has shown arm strength and feel for spinning a breaking ball.

CLOSEST TO THE MAJORS: RHP Wyatt Mills (3) has a side-winding delivery and built a strong track record for performance at the back of Gonzaga's bullpen. He throws harder than most sidearmers—his fastball reaches the mid-90s—and he fills up the strike zone. He could make quick work of the minor leagues.

BEST LATE-ROUND PICK: Sears is undersized (5-foot-11, 180 pounds) and not overpowering, but he gets swings and misses with his 88-92 mph fastball, which has an exceptional spin rate. With a pair of potentially average offspeed offerings, he is an intriguing weapon out of the bullpen.

THE ONE WHO GOT AWAY: OF Jesse Franklin (37) was a three-sport star at Seattle Prep HS and has an exciting set of raw tools. But instead of signing with his hometown club, he headlined Michigan's 10th-ranked recruiting class.

—TEDDY CAHILL

TOP DRAFT PICKS OF THE DECADE

Year	Player, Pos.	2017 Org
2008	Josh Fields, RHP	Dodgers
2009	Dustin Ackley, OF	Angels
2010	Taijuan Walker, RHP (1st round supp.)	D-backs
2011	Danny Hultzen, LHP	Did not play
2012	Mike Zunino, C	Mariners
2013	D.J. Peterson, 3B	Reds
2014	Alex Jackson, OF	Braves
2015	Nick Neidert, RHP (2nd round)	Mariners
2016	Kyle Lewis, OF	Mariners
2017	Evan White, 1B	Mariners

2016

The Mariners got great value with OF Kyle Lewis (1) falling to the 11th overall pick, but his progress has been slowed by knee injuries. RHP Matt Festa (7) had a breakout year. 3B Joe Rizzo (2) finished his first full pro season with a strong playoff performance in high Class A.

GRADE: C

2015

RHP Andrew Moore (2s) graduated to MLB, joining Seattle's rotation. RHP Nick Neidert (2) finished a solid season in Double-A and was then traded in the Dee Gordon deal. RHP Art Warren (23) is the breakout star of the group, as he took to a move to the bullpen.

GRADE: C

2014

OF Alex Jackson (1) found his footing in his first season in the Braves system, reaching Double-A. RHP Dan Altavilla (5) reached the big leagues and LHP Ryan Yarbrough (4) could soon get there with the Rays, but the rest of the class has not provided much.

GRADE: C

1 KYLE LEWIS, OF

Born: July 13, 1995. **B-T:** R-R. **Ht.:** 6-4. **Wt.:** 210. **Drafted:** Mercer, 2016 (1st round). **Signed by:** John Wiedenbauer.

BILL MITCHELL

L ewis' first full professional season was a trying one. The 2016 Baseball America College Player of the Year and Mariners first-rounder played just 49 games as he came back from a serious knee injury, with multiple stops and starts. Drafted 11th overall and signed for $3,286,700 in 2016, Lewis tore his anterior cruciate ligament and medial and lateral meniscus in his right knee a month into his career at short-season Everett in a grisly home plate collision. He spent the next 12 months rehabbing and finally returned to game action at high Class A Modesto in June 2017, only to bang his knee into the center field wall in his first game back and go back on the disabled list. He returned to Modesto in July and finished the season with a flourish, batting .429 in the California League playoffs to help the Nuts capture the league title. Lewis was assigned to the Arizona Fall League after the season but was shut down after two games because of discomfort in his surgically-repaired knee.

When healthy, Lewis has everything you want to see in a premier, middle-of-the-order outfielder. He plays the game hard and has the strong work ethic that allows him to make the most of his above-average tools. He has solid bat speed and a feel for the barrel, with plus raw power. It was obvious to scouts who saw him in the Cal League that he was not always in rhythm at the plate, with his upper half not syncing with the lower half, but he should get back in the groove when his knee is 100 percent healthy. His hands work well, and he's got a line-drive stroke with loft and home run power to all fields. Lewis speed hasn't come all the way back, but he should again be an average runner when healthy, perhaps a tick more underway. While Lewis has primarily been a center fielder, scouts don't see the instincts needed to stay there despite his ability to cover plenty of ground. An above-average arm makes him better suited for right field. He's primarily been a DH since returning from his knee injury out of caution.

Lewis aggressive by nature, so the Mariners will make sure he's 100 percent healthy before putting him back on the field. He is expected to be completely healthy by spring training and has a chance to see Double-A at the start of 2018. Lewis' above-average offensive potential makes him a future regular corner outfielder, potentially a first-division one if his power plays as plus in the major leagues.

BA GRADE / SCOUTING GRADES

BA GRADE	SCOUTING GRADES
60 Risk: V. High	HIT: 55. POW: 60. SPD: 50. FLD: 55. ARM: 55.

Projected future grades on 20-80 scouting scale

TOP PROSPECTS OF THE DECADE

Year	Player, Pos.	2017 Org
2008	Jeff Clement, C	Did not play
2009	Greg Halman, OF	Deceased
2010	Dustin Ackley, OF/1B	Angels
2011	Dustin Ackley, 2B	Angels
2012	Taijuan Walker, RHP	Diamondbacks
2013	Mike Zunino, C	Mariners
2014	Taijuan Walker, RHP	Diamondbacks
2015	Alex Jackson, OF	Braves
2016	Alex Jackson, OF	Braves
2017	Kyle Lewis, OF	Mariners

BEST TOOLS

Best Hitter for Average	Evan White
Best Power Hitter	Julio Rodriguez
Best Strike-Zone Discipline	Eric Filia
Fastest Baserunner	Ian Miller
Best Athlete	Kyle Lewis
Best Fastball	Art Warren
Best Curveball	Max Povse
Best Slider	Matt Festa
Best Changeup	Sam Carlson
Best Control	Robert Dugger
Best Defensive Catcher	Ryan Scott
Best Defensive Infielder	Bryson Brigman
Best Infield Arm	Juan Querecuto
Best Defensive Outfielder	Braden Bishop
Best Outfield Arm	Luis Liberato

Year	Club (League)	Class	AVG	G	AB	R	H	2B	3B	HR	RBI	BB	SO	SB	CS	OBP	SLG
2016	Everett (NWL)	SS	.299	30	117	26	35	8	5	3	26	16	22	3	0	.385	.530
2017	Mariners (AZL)	R	.263	11	38	9	10	2	1	1	7	4	14	1	0	.348	.447
	Modesto (CAL)	HiA	.255	38	149	20	38	4	0	6	24	15	38	2	1	.323	.403
Minor League Totals			.273	79	304	55	83	14	6	10	57	35	74	6	1	.351	.457

2 EVAN WHITE, 1B

Born: April 26, 1996. **B-T:** R-L. **Ht.:** 6-3. **Wt.:** 205. **Drafted:** Kentucky, 2017 (1st round). **Signed by:** Jackson Laumann.

White performed to first-round expectations his junior year at Kentucky, hitting .373 with 10 homers, 41 RBIs and 48 runs scored. The Mariners rewarded him by making him the 17th overall pick and signed him for $3.125 million.

White started strong after signing, but a quad injury cut his pro debut short after 14 games at short-season Everett. White is well-rounded and projects to be a plus hitter with average power. The Mariners are convinced his power will emerge because of the exit velocities he generates, and he has the athleticism and frame to add strength. White has a smooth, graceful righthanded swing, an outstanding eye and learns quickly from pitch to pitch. Defensively he is the rare example of a first baseman who is a plus runner with a plus arm. While he can handle either corner outfield spot, he's such an elite defender at first base, earning future 70 grades on the 20-80 scouting scale, that he'll likely stay in the dirt. His defensive ability has drawn comparisons to Dodgers first baseman Cody Bellinger, a similarly skilled athlete who is capable of playing in the outfield but is so good at first base that it seems foolish to take him out of the dirt. He's graceful around the bag, light on his feet and turns a pristine 3-6-3 double play.

White projects as a high-average hitter with 15-20 home run power and Gold Glove defense at first base. He'll get his first taste of full-season ball in 2018.

BA GRADE
55 Risk: High

HIT: 60. **POW:** 50.
SPD: 60. **FLD:** 70.
ARM: 60.

Year	Club (League)	Class	AVG	G	AB	R	H	2B	3B	HR	RBI	BB	SO	SB	CS	OBP	SLG
2017	Everett (NWL)	SS	.277	14	47	6	13	1	1	3	12	6	6	1	1	.345	.532
Minor League Totals			.277	14	47	6	13	1	1	3	12	6	6	1	1	.345	.532

3 SAM CARLSON, RHP

BILL MITCHELL

Born: Dec. 3, 1998. **B-T:** R-R. **Ht.:** 6-4. **Wt.:** 195. **Drafted:** HS—Burnsville, Minn., 2017 (2nd round). **Signed by:** Ben Collman.

Coming out of cold-weather Minnesota, Carlson was a late riser on 2017 draft boards before the Mariners popped him in the second round. It took a $2 million bonus to keep him from his commitment to Florida, and Carlson started his pro career with two short outings in the Rookie-level Arizona League before being shut down for the year as a precaution against some minor soreness. Carlson was a legitimate two-way player if he had gone to Florida, as he had line-drive gap power with decent speed.

Carlson was one of the best prospects to come out of Minnesota in years. Carlson sports a solid pitcher's frame with room for added strength. He drew a lot of comparisons to Florida Gators and now Athletics righthander Logan Shore as a fastball–changeup righthander. His heavy fastball with late action and natural sink was up to 96 mph in the AZL, consistent with the velocity during his final high school season when he consistently sat 91-95 mph. His mid-80s slider features late action and tilt and projects as a potentially above-average pitch. His changeup is especially advanced for a young, hard-throwing righthander. He didn't use it nearly as much during his senior season of high school, but it flashed plus consistently on the summer showcase circuit in the year before the date.

Carlson's delivery is easy and free-flowing out of a loose, quick arm. He participated in the Mariners' minor league strength camp in the fall to help prepare him for a pro workload. He will likely start 2018 in extended spring training in order to manage his innings, but he could get to low Class A Clinton before the end of the season.

BA GRADE
55 Risk: Extreme

FB: 60. **SL:** 55.
CHG: 60.
CTL: 55.

Year	Club (League)	Class	W	L	ERA	G	GS	CG	SV	IP	H	HR	BB	SO	K/9	WHIP	AVG
2017	Mariners (AZL)	R	0	0	3.00	2	2	0	0	3	4	0	0	3	9.0	1.33	.364
Minor League Totals			0	0	3.00	2	2	0	0	3	4	0	0	3	9.0	1.33	.364

4 JULIO RODRIGUEZ, OF

Born: Dec. 29, 2000. **B-T:** R-R. **Ht.:** 6-3. **Wt.:** 205. **Signed:** Dominican Republic, 2017.
Signed by: Eddy Toledo/Tim Kissner.

STACY JO GRANT

One of the premier international talents on the market in 2017 mainly because of his easy power and feel to hit, Rodriguez signed with the Mariners for $1.75 million. He has yet to play an official game with the Mariners, but already ranks as having the best power in the organization.

Rodriguez got his first taste of game action in the fall in Dominican instructional league, with positive reports coming from his performance there. While plus-plus raw power is Rodriguez's loudest tool, he is a quality hitter with the ability to retain information and make adjustments at the plate. He has quick hands and good bat speed, with a rhythmic righthanded swing that produces a solid bat path through the zone. He takes aggressive hacks at the plate and will have to learn to handle offspeed pitches. An average runner now, Rodriguez projects to slow down as he ages but still retain enough speed and baserunning acumen to take the extra base.

Rodriguez is athletic enough to handle any outfield position, but a plus arm profiles him for right field. Rodriguez will launch his pro career in the summer of 2018 at age 17, either in the Dominican Summer League or the Rookie-level Arizona League.

BA GRADE
55 Risk: Extreme
HIT: 55. POW: 55.
SPD: 45. FLD: 50.
ARM: 60.

Year	Club (League)	Class	AVG	G	AB	R	H	2B	3B	HR	RBI	BB	SO	SB	CS	OBP	SLG
2017	Did not play—Signed 2018 contract																

5 BRADEN BISHOP, OF

Born: Aug. 22, 1993 **B-T:** R-R. **Ht.:** 6-1. **Wt.:** 190. **Drafted:** Washington, 2015 (3rd round). **Signed by:** Jeff Sakamoto.

Bishop was very well scouted in high school because he played on the same team as 2011 first-round pick and future big leaguer Tyler Goeddel and 2015 first-round pick Alex Blandino. Bishop was a potential Division I wide receiver as well, but he opeted to attend Washington where he hit .292 over three seasons, albeit it with modest power.

Bishop is known for his 4MOM foundation that raises money for Alzheimer's disease in honor of his mother, but his performance on the field is earning increased notice, too. A premier athlete whose ability to hit was previously in question, Bishop hit .306 with a career-best 34 doubles and an .806 OPS across high Class A Modesto and Double-A Arkansas in 2017. He reworked his swing in offseason workouts with D-backs slugger Jake Lamb, a fellow University of Washington product. Bishop lowered his hands and became less jumpy in the batter's box, allowing him to stay in his legs more and introduce more drive into his swing to create more loft. He gets the barrel to the ball consistently, but questions remains whether he will develop enough upper-body strength to drive balls at the higher levels. He is a plus runner who upped his aggressiveness and stole 22 bases in 27 tries in 2017, and that speed helps him to be a plus-plus defender in center field with tremendous reads and reflexes. His average arm allows to handle any outfield spot.

Bishop's continued offensive progress will determine whether he meets his starting outfielder ceiling. If not, he can settle in for a career as a fourth outfielder.

BA GRADE
45 Risk: Medium
HIT: 50. POW: 40.
SPD: 60. FLD: 70.
ARM: 50.

Year	Club (League)	Class	AVG	G	AB	R	H	2B	3B	HR	RBI	BB	SO	SB	CS	OBP	SLG
2015	Everett (NWL)	SS	.320	56	219	34	70	8	1	2	22	5	33	13	3	.367	.393
2016	Clinton (MWL)	LoA	.290	63	248	38	72	5	1	1	21	25	48	6	1	.363	.331
	Bakersfield (CAL)	HiA	.247	41	166	19	41	6	0	2	22	11	39	2	0	.300	.319
2017	Modesto (CAL)	HiA	.296	88	355	71	105	25	3	2	32	45	65	16	5	.385	.400
	Arkansas (TL)	AA	.336	31	125	18	42	9	1	1	11	15	15	6	1	.417	.448
Minor League Totals			.296	279	1113	180	330	53	6	8	108	101	200	43	10	.368	.376

6 MAX POVSE, RHP

Born: Aug. 23, 1993 **B-T:** R-R. **Ht.:** 6-8. **Wt.:** 185. **Drafted:** UNC Greensboro, 2014 (3rd round). **Signed by:** Billy Best (Braves).

Acquired in the November 2016 trade that sent 2014 first-round pick Alex Jackson to the Braves, Povse made his major league debut with the Mariners in 2017 on June 22. He got into three big league games and split the rest of the year between Double-A Arkansas and Triple-A Tacoma.

Povse started strong in Arkansas' rotation before a hamstring injury put him out for a month. He struggled regaining his consistency after the injury while also taking on a new role as a long reliever. He got stronger and more coordinated in his 6-foot-8 frame in 2017, allowing him to better repeat his delivery. The velocity on his fastball increased from the low 90s to sitting 93-95 mph and touching 97. He also shows more downhill angle than pure life. He gets swings and misses from his high-70s downer curveball but needs to land it more to be effective against big league hitters. An firm upper-80s changeup with armside fade is his third pitch. He throws all his pitches for strikes, and his long levers provide deception in his delivery.

Povse's role for 2018 is still to be determined. He can win a rotation spot with a strong spring training or settle in as a long reliever.

BA GRADE

45 Risk: Medium

FB: 60. CB: 50.
CHG: 45.
CTL: 50.

Year	Club (League)	Class	W	L	ERA	G	GS	CG	SV	IP	H	HR	BB	SO	K/9	WHIP	AVG
2015	Rome (SAL)	LoA	4	2	2.56	12	12	0	0	60	50	2	16	50	7.5	1.11	.226
	Carolina (CAR)	HiA	1	3	9.33	5	5	0	0	18	24	0	7	10	4.9	1.69	.316
2016	Carolina (CAR)	HiA	5	5	3.71	15	15	0	0	87	89	5	17	91	9.4	1.21	.262
	Mississippi (SL)	AA	4	1	2.93	11	11	0	0	71	61	4	12	48	6.1	1.03	.236
2017	Arkansas (TL)	AA	3	2	3.46	9	8	0	0	39	34	1	14	32	7.4	1.23	.235
	Seattle (AL)	MAJ	0	0	7.36	3	0	0	0	4	9	1	1	2	4.9	2.73	.450
	Tacoma (PCL)	AAA	1	4	7.39	13	5	0	0	32	41	3	12	29	8.2	1.67	.315
Major League Totals			0	0	7.36	3	0	0	0	4	9	1	1	2	4.9	2.73	.450
Minor League Totals			22	19	3.92	77	67	0	0	354	341	16	89	297	7.6	1.21	.253

7 MATT FESTA, RHP

Born: March 11, 1993. **B-T:** R-R. **Ht.:** 6-2. **Wt.:** 195. **Drafted:** East Stroudsburg (Pa.), 2016 (7th round). **Signed by:** Ross Vecchio.

The Mariners drafted Festa in the seventh round in 2016 after he went 11-2, 2.35 for Division II East Stroudsburg (Pa.). Signed for just $5,000, Festa jumped from short-season Everett in 2016 to high Class A Modesto in 2017 and dominated at the end of games for the California League champions, posting a 99-to-19 strikeout-to-walk mark.

Festa's fastball velocity ticked up during the season, eventually sitting 94-96 mph at the top end with darting action, sink and run. He's very aggressive with the pitch and commands it well. Batters are frequently behind on his heater, and it draws an eye-opening amount of swings and misses from lefthanded batters. His wipeout slider in the 87-89 mph range earns plus grades, and he is developing an 87-90 mph cutter with armside action some evaluators like even more. He also has an 80-81 mph changeup and upper-70s curveball in his back pocket. Festa repeats his high three-quarters delivery with a loose arm and moderate effort, pounding the strike zone and frequently turning in 10-pitch innings.

Festa has the stuff, control and mentality to be a high-leverage reliever. He'll move up to Double-A to begin 2018.

BA GRADE

45 Risk: High

FB: 60. SL: 60.
CHG: 40. CUT: 55
CTL: 50.

Year	Club (League)	Class	W	L	ERA	G	GS	CG	SV	IP	H	HR	BB	SO	K/9	WHIP	AVG
2016	Everett (NWL)	SS	6	2	3.73	14	8	0	0	60	60	3	14	58	8.7	1.23	.259
2017	Modesto (CAL)	HiA	4	2	3.23	42	1	0	6	70	61	7	19	99	12.8	1.15	.229
Minor League Totals			10	4	3.46	56	9	0	6	130	121	10	33	157	10.9	1.18	.242

8 ART WARREN, RHP

Born: March 23, 1993. **B-T:** R-R. **Ht.:** 6-3. **Wt.:** 230. **Drafted:** Ashland (Ohio), 2015 (23rd round). **Signed by:** Jay Catalano/Devitt Moore.

Warren began his college career at Cincinnati before transferring to Division II Ashland (Ohio), where he had Tommy John surgery as a junior but rebounded to show plenty of stuff (52 strikeouts in 60 innings) but also plenty of wildness (47 walks) in his lone season on the mound for Ashland. The Mariners picked him in the 23rd round in 2015.

Warren excelled his first full year as a reliever in 2017, helping high Class A Modesto win the California League championship as the team's closer and emerged as a breakout talent in the Arizona Fall League with 11.1 scoreless innings as Peoria's closer. The gem of Warren's arsenal is a four-seam fastball that sits 92-97 mph and touches 99, getting ride and extension up in the zone. He has scattered command of his heater, but his velocity and movement produce a high rate of swinging strikes. His best secondary pitch is a plus 12-to-6 overhand curveball with depth and hard finish in the 80-84 mph range. He rounds out his arsenal with an 89-92 mph slider and below-average 85-88 mph changeup. He is physical and strong but not overly athletic, resulting in some wildness and an inconsistent release point.

Warren's stuff and gunfighter mentality give him a chance to be a late-inning reliever, but he'll have to fine-tune his release point and command. Double-A Arkansas is next in 2018.

BA GRADE
45 Risk: High
FB: 70. CB: 55.
CHG: 40.
CTL: 45.

Year	Club (League)	Class	W	L	ERA	G	GS	CG	SV	IP	H	HR	BB	SO	K/9	WHIP	AVG
2015	Mariners (AZL)	R	1	0	3.86	6	0	0	0	7	7	0	3	10	12.9	1.43	.269
2016	Clinton (MWL)	LoA	9	1	2.19	14	14	0	0	74	71	1	18	55	6.7	1.20	.253
	Bakersfield (CAL)	HiA	2	1	5.15	13	6	0	0	37	42	1	28	38	9.3	1.91	.284
2017	Modesto (CAL)	HiA	3	1	3.06	43	0	0	8	65	58	5	25	67	9.3	1.28	.247
Minor League Totals			15	3	3.16	76	20	0	8	182	178	7	74	170	8.4	1.38	.258

9 JOE RIZZO, 3B

Born: March 31, 1998. **B-T:** L-R. **Ht.:** 5-9. **Wt.:** 194. **Drafted:** HS—Vienna, Va., 2016 (2nd round). **Signed by:** Ross Vecchio.

Teams considered Rizzo one of the top high school hitters available in the 2016 draft, and the Mariners selected him 50th overall and signed him for $1.75 million. He made his full-season debut with 110 games at low Class A Clinton in 2017 before moving up to high Class A Modesto at the end of the year.

Though he struggled most of the regular season, Rizzo was named MVP of the California League championship series after batting 7-for-13 in the final round to help Modesto capture the crown. Rizzo is a polarizing prospect. He shows a feel for hitting and advanced plate discipline, but his supposed above-average raw power doesn't show up in batting practice or games and scouts say that you are betting very heavily on the bat because of his other limitations. Rizzo has to work on strength and conditioning to get the most out of his limited athleticism and physical skills. It's uncertain whether Rizzo has a future at third base. His tick above-average arm is enough for the position, but he needs to work on his thick lower half to stay quick enough for the hot corner. If he has to move off third base his short stature isn't an ideal fit at first base and his below-average speed doesn't work well in the outfield.

Rizzo's performance in the Cal League playoffs was encouraging, and he'll return to Modesto to start 2018. He needs to work hard on his conditioning, but has the work ethic and attitude to succeed.

PAUL GIERHART

BA GRADE
50 Risk: V. High
HIT: 55. POW: 55.
SPD: 40. FLD: 40.
ARM: 55.

Year	Club (League)	Class	AVG	G	AB	R	H	2B	3B	HR	RBI	BB	SO	SB	CS	OBP	SLG
2016	Mariners (AZL)	R	.291	39	148	21	43	7	1	2	21	17	36	2	1	.355	.392
2017	Clinton (MWL)	LoA	.254	110	410	47	104	17	0	7	50	63	113	3	1	.354	.346
	Modesto (CAL)	HiA	.200	5	20	1	4	0	1	0	1	1	8	0	0	.238	.300
Minor League Totals			.261	154	578	69	151	24	2	9	72	81	157	5	2	.351	.356

10 JUAN QUERECUTO, SS

Born: Sept. 21, 2000. **B-T:** B-R. **Ht.:** 6-3. **Wt.:** 175. **Signed:** Venezuela, 2017.
Signed by: Emilio Carrasquel/Tim Kissner.

The Mariners made Querecuto one of their top priorities in the 2017 international signing class and signed the 16-year-old Venezuelan for $1.225 million.

The switch-hitting shortstop comes from a baseball family. His father Juan played five years in the minors in the Blue Jays system, and his older brother Juniel is an infielder in the Giants system who reached the major leagues with the Rays in 2016. Querecuto doesn't flash any standout tools but has advanced instincts for his age and knows how to play the game. He's a gap-to-gap, situational hitter who does a good job of controlling the strike zone and uses the whole field. An average runner with an above-average to plus arm, he projects to be an above-average defender at shortstop with soft hands, a feel for where to position himself and the ability to slow the game down. While not a burner on the bases, Querecuto's baserunning acumen will allow his speed to play up. His makeup and instincts project to consistently allow him to play above his tools.

Querecuto will begin his pro career in 2018 along with fellow international classmate Julio Rodriguez, either in the Dominican Summer League or the Rookie-level Arizona League.

BA GRADE

50 Risk: Extreme

HIT: 55. POW: 40.
SPD: 50. FLD: 60.
ARM: 60.

Year	Club (League)	Class	AVG	G	AB	R	H	2B	3B	HR	RBI	BB	SO	SB	CS	OBP	SLG
2017	Did not play—Signed 2018 contract																

11 WYATT MILLS, RHP

Born: Jan. 25, 1995. **B-T:** R-R. **Ht.:** 6-3. **Wt.:** 175. **Drafted:** Gonzaga, 2017 (3rd round). **Signed by:** Alex Ross/Jeff Sakamoto.

BA GRADE

45 Risk: High

The Mariners' selection of Mills in the third round in 2017 sent draft analysts scurrying for information on the Gonzaga righthander. Mills signed for an under-slot $125,000 to give the Mariners extra bonus money to use on second-rounder rounder Sam Carlson.

After using an over-the-top delivery in high school, Mills walked on at Gonzaga and changed his delivery to a much lower slot after his freshman year. He worked exclusively as a setup reliever in college, recording a 1.79 ERA with a 58-to-4 strikeout-to-walk mark his senior year after he passed up an opportunity to turn pro when the Rays drafted him in the 17th round in 2016. Mills throws from a very low slot with the ball coming out of his hip—it's almost a submarine delivery that draws comparisons with Joe Smith and Steve Cishek. While Mills' velocity on his two-seam fastball was down in his pro debut split between short-season Everett and low Class A Clinton, he touched 95 mph in college with sink and deception, and he should get back to that velocity with an offseason of rest. He also uses a hard slider that projects as an average offering.

Mills could wind up pitching at multiple levels in 2018 and will be on a fast track to the big league bullpen.

Year	Club (League)	Class	W	L	ERA	G	GS	CG	SV	IP	H	HR	BB	SO	K/9	WHIP	AVG
2017	Everett (NWL)	SS	0	1	2.57	7	0	0	2	7	3	0	3	11	14.1	0.86	.120
	Clinton (MWL)	LoA	0	1	1.35	11	0	0	4	13	5	0	6	18	12.2	0.83	.111
Minor League Totals			0	2	1.77	18	0	0	6	20	8	0	9	29	12.8	0.84	.114

12 DAN VOGELBACH, 1B

Born: Dec. 17, 1992 **B-T:** L-R. **Ht.:** 6-0. **Wt.:** 250. **Drafted:** HS—Fort Myers, Fla., 2011 (2nd round). **Signed by:** Lukas McKnight (Cubs).

BA GRADE

40 Risk: Medium

A year after being acquired in a multi-player deal with the Cubs and coming off a strong season at Triple-A, Vogelbach went to spring training in 2017 with a chance to earn a major league platoon job at first base with Danny Valencia. Instead, he hit .228 in spring training and wound up at Triple-A Tacoma for most of the season.

A well below-average fielder and bottom-of-the-scale runner, the hefty Vogelbach has to mash to be a big leaguer. He has a good approach at the plate, uses the whole field and has some power, but evaluators aren't convinced it's enough to justify a regular lineup spot. He also struggles against lefthanders, making a platoon role his ceiling. While Vogelbach worked hard on improving his defense in 2017, he'll never have the range or mobility needed to be even close to an average defender. Most scouts say he's either a bottom-of-the-scale or at best a 30 defender at first base.

The ideal role for Vogelbach is as a platoon DH, provided he can get to more of his power. The Mariners acquired the Athletics' Ryon Healy after the 2017 season to handle first base moving forward. Vogelbach will come to spring training in 2018 with a shot to win a job as a platoon partner for Healy and DH Nelson Cruz, although the Mariners selection of Mike Ford in the Rule 5 draft creates further competition for Vogelbach.

Year	Club (League)	Class	AVG	G	AB	R	H	2B	3B	HR	RBI	BB	SO	SB	CS	OBP	SLG
2015	Cubs (AZL)	R	.455	5	11	4	5	2	0	0	0	6	1	0	0	.647	.636
	Tennessee (SL)	AA	.272	76	254	41	69	16	1	7	39	57	61	1	1	.403	.425
2016	Iowa (PCL)	AAA	.318	89	305	53	97	18	2	16	64	55	67	0	0	.425	.548
	Tacoma (PCL)	AAA	.240	44	154	26	37	7	0	7	32	42	34	0	0	.404	.422
	Seattle (AL)	MAJ	.083	8	12	0	1	0	0	0	0	1	6	0	0	.154	.083
2017	Tacoma (PCL)	AAA	.290	125	459	65	133	25	0	17	83	76	98	3	1	.388	.455
	Seattle (AL)	MAJ	.214	16	28	0	6	1	0	0	2	3	9	0	0	.290	.250
Major League Totals			.175	24	40	0	7	1	0	0	2	4	15	0	0	.250	.200
Minor League Totals			.287	669	2417	371	693	143	7	100	438	412	491	15	11	.390	.476

13 NICK RUMBELOW, RHP

BA GRADE 40 Risk: Medium

Born: Sept. 6, 1991. **B-T:** R-R. **Ht.:** 6-0. **Wt.:** 190. **Drafted:** Louisiana State, 2013 (7th round). **Signed by:** Andy Cannizaro (Yankees).

When the Yankees needed to clear space on their 40-man roster to protect new players in advance of the Rule 5 draft after the 2017 season, they traded Rumbelow to the Mariners for pitching prospects Juan Then and J.P. Sears.

Rumbelow made his major league debut in 2015, two years to the day after signing with the Yankees for $100,000 as a seventh-round pick out of Louisiana State. After missing virtually all of 2016 after having Tommy John surgery, Rumbelow returned in 2017 and recorded 45 strikeouts and 11 walks in 40.1 innings split between Double-A Trenton and Triple-A Scranton/Wilkes-Barre. He has a three-pitch mix consisting of a 92-94 mph four-seam fastball with armside run that touched 98 prior to surgery, a mid-80s changeup and an 81-84 mph solid-average curveball he lands for strikes. He repeats his high three-quarters to overhand delivery with a long, deep arm action.

The Mariners paid a relatively high price in prospect talent for Rumbelow, so he'll get every opportunity to earn a job in the Seattle bullpen in spring training.

Year	Club (League)	Class	W	L	ERA	G	GS	CG	SV	IP	H	HR	BB	SO	K/9	WHIP	AVG
2015	Scranton/W-B (IL)	AAA	2	3	4.27	37	0	0	8	53	47	4	13	57	9.7	1.14	.230
	New York (AL)	MAJ	1	1	4.02	17	0	0	0	16	16	2	5	15	8.6	1.34	.254
2016	Scranton/W-B (IL)	AAA	0	0	0.00	1	0	0	0	1	2	0	0	0	0.0	2.00	.400
2017	Trenton (EL)	AA	0	0	2.38	8	0	0	1	11	5	0	3	15	11.9	0.71	.128
	Scranton/W-B (IL)	AAA	5	1	0.62	17	0	0	5	29	16	0	8	30	9.3	0.83	.158
Major League Totals			1	1	4.02	17	0	0	0	16	16	2	5	15	8.6	1.34	.254
Minor League Totals			14	8	2.72	126	0	0	29	175	127	7	47	203	10.4	0.99	.197

14 ERIC FILIA, OF/1B

BA GRADE 45 Risk: High

Born: July 6, 1992. **B-T:** L-R. **Ht.:** 6-0. **Wt.:** 189. **Drafted:** UCLA, 2016 (20th round). **Signed by:** Ryan Holmes.

Filia led UCLA with a .444 batting average during the 2013 College World Series as a sophomore to lead the Bruins to their first national title. He expected to be a high pick in the 2014 draft, but instead missed the 2014 season after having labrum surgery. He was then suspended from the university the entire 2015 season after he plagiarized a philosophy paper. Filia took on multiple jobs during his suspension, including working as a butler at the Playboy Mansion.

Even after two years away, Filia never lost his feel to hit. He posted an .816 OPS in his return to UCLA in 2016, then hit .360 in his pro debut. He proceeded to hit .326 at high Class A Modesto in 2017 and led the California League with 65 walks and a .407 on-base percentage. He then led the Arizona Fall League with a .408 average and .483 OBP. Using an open stance with a shimmy routine that went viral on the internet, Filia takes professional at-bats and barrels up balls every time. He's an extreme contact hitter with excellent plate discipline who can handle breaking balls and doesn't get overpowered by velocity. He spoils pitches until he gets the one he wants and then drives it on a line. His stroke is flat and purely for hard line drives, without the loft to produce home run power.

Filia is a below-average runner and fielder at both corner outfield positions, complicating his profile. But if he continues to hit as he always has, he'll get a shot as at least a lefthanded bench bat.

Year	Club (League)	Class	AVG	G	AB	R	H	2B	3B	HR	RBI	BB	SO	SB	CS	OBP	SLG
2016	Everett (NWL)	SS	.362	68	246	43	89	19	1	4	46	39	19	10	5	.450	.496
	Tacoma (PCL)	AAA	.000	1	1	1	0	0	0	0	0	1	0	0	0	.500	.000
2017	Modesto (CAL)	HiA	.326	128	491	63	160	28	5	5	59	65	45	9	6	.407	.434
Minor League Totals			.337	197	738	107	249	47	6	9	105	105	64	19	11	.422	.454

15 ROB WHALEN, RHP

BA GRADE
40 Risk: Medium

Born: Jan. 31, 1994. **B-T:** R-R. **Ht.:** 6-2. **Wt.:** 220. **Drafted:** HS—Haines City, Fla., 2012 (12th round). **Signed by:** Mike Silvestri (Mets).

Whalen has been traded twice since being drafted by the Mets in the 12th round in 2012. He made his major league debut with the Braves in 2016 before being included with Max Povse in a trade for Alex Jackson. Whalen reached the big leagues the Mariners in 2017 but missed most of the season with leg and knee issues early and later a shoulder injury.

The sharpness of his secondary pitches suffered because of his leg problems, and Whalen became frustrated at not being healthy. He was mostly ineffective in 10 starts at Triple-A Tacoma in 2017. When he's right, Whalen has a lively 90-93 mph fastball with tail and heavy sinking action. His repertoire includes a low-80s slider with depth, a curveball with good downward movement and a changeup that is used infrequently. Whalen needs to work on holding runners and limiting damage with runners on base. He was often hurt by one bad inning in his subpar starts. None of Whalen's pitches grade above-average, but he has a diverse repertoire with different looks from both his fastball and curveball.

After a mostly lost season in 2017, Whalen will head back to spring training looking for a shot at the big league staff in 2018.

Year	Club (League)	Class	W	L	ERA	G	GS	CG	SV	IP	H	HR	BB	SO	K/9	WHIP	AVG
2015	St. Lucie (FSL)	HiA	4	5	3.36	15	14	0	0	83	72	4	34	61	6.6	1.28	.231
	Carolina (CAR)	HiA	1	2	3.29	3	3	0	0	14	11	2	4	7	4.6	1.10	.224
2016	Mississippi (SL)	AA	7	5	2.49	18	18	0	0	101	87	4	37	94	8.3	1.22	.232
	Gwinnett (IL)	AAA	0	1	1.93	3	3	0	0	19	12	0	7	18	8.7	1.02	.188
	Atlanta (NL)	MAJ	1	2	6.57	5	5	0	0	25	20	4	12	25	9.1	1.30	.217
2017	Seattle (AL)	MAJ	0	1	6.14	2	1	0	0	7	7	1	2	2	2.5	1.23	.259
	Tacoma (PCL)	AAA	0	7	6.58	10	10	1	0	53	61	9	20	43	7.3	1.52	.285
Major League Totals			1	3	6.47	7	6	0	0	32	27	5	14	27	7.6	1.28	.227
Minor League Totals			24	24	2.99	76	72	1	0	413	342	22	140	363	7.9	1.17	.222

16 CHASE DE JONG, RHP

BA GRADE
40 Risk: Medium

Born: Dec. 29, 1993. **B-T:** L-R. **Ht.:** 6-4. **Wt.:** 205. **Drafted:** HS—Long Beach, 2012 (2nd round). **Signed by:** Joey Aversa (Blue Jays).

De Jong won Dodgers minor league pitcher of the year honors in 2016 and was acquired by the Mariners that offseason for minor league shortstop Drew Jackson and righthander Aneurys Zabala. De Jong made the Mariners' Opening Day roster in 2017 because of injuries to other staff members, his first of multiple stints in the big leagues.

Despite three good outings out of his seven big league games, the rest of De Jong's season was shaky because he failed to regroup and get his footing at Triple-A Tacoma, where he posted a 6.00 ERA in 15 starts. He finished the year with five mostly ineffective starts at Double-A Arkansas. De Jong is a finesse righthander with average stuff who relies on pitching acumen and his ability to throw his four pitches for strikes. He's a flyball pitcher who needs to get the extension and rise he had in 2016 for his average 90-91 mph fastball to play up. He adds an average curveball and fringy changeup and slider, but his execution must be more precise in the strike zone.

De Jong will head to spring training with a chance to make up for a lackluster 2017 season. He has a chance to make it as a spot starter or swingman.

Year	Club (League)	Class	W	L	ERA	G	GS	CG	SV	IP	H	HR	BB	SO	K/9	WHIP	AVG
2015	Lansing (MWL)	LoA	7	4	3.13	14	14	1	0	86	75	9	18	77	8.0	1.08	.231
	R. Cucamonga (CAL)	HiA	4	3	3.96	11	10	0	0	50	44	6	15	52	9.4	1.18	.228
2016	Tulsa (TL)	AA	14	5	2.86	25	25	2	0	142	106	15	39	125	7.9	1.02	.207
	Oklahoma City (PCL)	AAA	1	0	1.69	1	1	0	0	5	6	0	1	8	13.5	1.31	.273
2017	Seattle (AL)	MAJ	0	3	6.35	7	4	0	0	28	31	5	13	13	4.1	1.55	.282
	Tacoma (PCL)	AAA	3	6	6.00	15	15	0	0	84	99	18	27	61	6.5	1.50	.291
	Arkansas (TL)	AA	1	3	5.97	5	5	0	0	29	32	3	10	18	5.7	1.47	.288
Major League Totals			0	3	6.35	7	4	0	0	28	31	5	13	13	4.1	1.55	.282
Minor League Totals			34	30	3.95	113	101	4	0	561	540	65	143	495	7.9	1.22	.251

17 SETH ELLEDGE, RHP

BA GRADE
45 Risk: High

Born: May 20, 1996. **B-T:** R-R. **Ht.:** 6-3. **Wt.:** 250. **Drafted:** Dallas Baptist, 2017 (4th round). **Signed by:** Ty Bowman.

After drafting Gonzaga reliever Wyatt Mills in the third round, the Mariners popped another college bullpen arm in Elledge one round later, signing the hard-throwing Dallas Baptist product for $400,000. After pitching in four games for short-season Everett, Elledge spent most of his first pro season with low Class A Clinton, saving five games and posting an outstanding 35-to-6 strikeout-to-walk mark in 21 innings.

Elledge's top pitch is a 92-95 mph fastball with a high spin rate and late life that gets plenty of swings and misses. He's also got a hard downer curveball at 78-83 mph, an average pitch that he throws to both sides of the plate and a changeup that he uses infrequently. While his deceptive delivery is high-energy and high-effort, Elledge repeats it well and commands all of his pitches. Considering the success in his first try at full-season ball, Elledge may be ready to start 2018 at high Class A Modesto with a move to Double-A later in the season.

As a robustly built reliever with a big fastball, Elledge could move quickly through the system.

Year	Club (League)	Class	W	L	ERA	G	GS	CG	SV	IP	H	HR	BB	SO	K/9	WHIP	AVG
2017	Everett (NWL)	SS	0	0	4.50	4	0	0	0	4	2	0	2	7	15.8	1.00	.154
	Clinton (MWL)	LoA	3	0	3.00	15	0	0	5	21	14	1	6	35	15.0	0.95	.182
Minor League Totals			3	0	3.24	19	0	0	5	25	16	1	8	42	15.1	0.96	.178

18 ANTHONY MISIEWICZ, LHP

BA GRADE
40 Risk: Medium

Born: Nov. 1, 1994. **B-T:** R-L. **Ht.:** 6-1. **Wt.:** 190. **Drafted:** Michigan State, 2015 (18th round). **Signed by:** Jay Catalano.

Originally drafted by the Mariners in 2015 out of Michigan State after a three-year college career spent mostly in the Wolverines' bullpen, Misiewicz reached Double-A before being packaged in a trade to the Rays midway through the 2017 season.

Tampa Bay then sent him back to Seattle for $1 million of international bonus pool money that the Mariners had accumulated prior to their unsuccessful attempt to sign Japanese superstar Shohei Ohtani. Misiewicz pitches above his mostly fringy stuff by throwing strikes, with his control being better than his command. He uses a four-seam fastball from 88-93 mph with average tail. He has feel for a firm mid-80s mph changeup with sink, which grades as a fringe-average pitch. Rounding out the arsenal is an average 79-82 mph downer curveball that slurves at times and doesn't get enough swings and misses from lefthanded hitters. He repeats a simple, deliberate high three-quarters delivery that doesn't provide a lot of deception.

Misiewicz profiles as an up-and-down back-end starter or swingman. He had some success at Double-A in 2017 and could be ready to move up to Triple-A in 2018.

Year	Club (League)	Class	W	L	ERA	G	GS	CG	SV	IP	H	HR	BB	SO	K/9	WHIP	AVG
2015	Everett (NWL)	SS	3	2	2.14	14	7	0	0	46	30	1	10	40	7.8	0.86	.189
2016	Bakersfield (CAL)	HiA	7	10	4.79	29	29	1	0	158	166	21	47	115	6.6	1.35	.272
2017	Modesto (CAL)	HiA	5	2	4.96	16	16	0	0	78	82	6	27	85	9.8	1.40	.265
	Arkansas (TL)	AA	3	3	4.35	7	7	0	0	41	40	4	11	32	7.0	1.23	.270
	Montgomery (SL)	AA	3	1	3.49	5	5	1	0	28	26	3	5	24	7.6	1.09	.239
Minor League Totals			21	18	4.33	71	64	2	0	352	344	35	100	296	7.6	1.26	.257

19 IAN MILLER, OF

BA GRADE
40 Risk: Medium

Born: Feb. 21, 1992. **B-T:** L-R. **Ht.:** 6-0. **Wt.:** 175. **Drafted:** Wagner, 2013 (14th round). **Signed by:** Brian Nichols.

The third time was the charm for Miller at Double-A, with much better results in 2017 after two previous tries at the level. He's always been an elite runner (averaging 47 steals his last three seasons) and played above-average defense, but an offseason working with hitting coordinator Brant Brown to re-invent his swing helped Miller get to more power and use the whole field.

After not posting an OPS above .700 since his debut year in 2013, Miller batted .326/.382/.430 with 30 stolen bases in 83 games at Double-A Arkansas. He finished the season at Triple-A Tacoma, where he looked more timid at the plate. Plus-plus speed and elite baserunning instincts are Miller's biggest strengths, but he needs to control the zone more against better pitching to draw more walks and take better advantage of his wheels. He played exclusively in center field at Double-A but got more time in left field with Tacoma, in preparation for his likely role as a reserve outfielder. Miller needs to improve in the corners, but his average arm is to handle all three outfield spots.

Miller has a ceiling as a fourth outfielder, but needs to continue to improve as a hitter to reach that projection.

Year	Club (League)	Class	AVG	G	AB	R	H	2B	3B	HR	RBI	BB	SO	SB	CS	OBP	SLG
2015	Bakersfield (CAL)	HiA	.296	39	159	20	47	5	2	0	6	10	34	21	5	.341	.352
	Jackson (SL)	AA	.254	87	347	40	88	13	5	0	23	29	53	29	13	.310	.320
2016	Jackson (SL)	AA	.253	114	430	64	109	8	7	0	28	45	54	49	3	.331	.305
2017	Arkansas (TL)	AA	.326	83	344	63	112	18	3	4	29	28	69	30	4	.382	.430
	Tacoma (PCL)	AAA	.268	41	168	22	45	4	2	0	6	5	33	13	1	.297	.315
Minor League Totals			.279	461	1811	279	506	58	23	5	119	153	313	175	35	.340	.345

20 SAM MOLL, LHP

BA GRADE
40 Risk: Medium

Born: Jan. 3, 1992. **B-T:** L-L. **Ht.:** 5-10. **Wt.:** 185. **Drafted:** Memphis, 2013 (3rd round). **Signed by:** Scott Corman (Rockies).

Moll reached the big leagues with 11 relief appearances for the Athletics in 2017 after nearly five seasons in the Rockies' minor league system. Colorado sold his contract to Oakland in August 2017. The Mariners claimed Moll on waivers in November.

While the short lefty had success in the Rockies organization as a reliever, Moll had been slowed at times with various injuries. He missed most of 2014 with bone chips and part of 2016 with elbow inflammation. What makes Moll an intriguing commodity is his mid-90s velocity from the left side with a max-effort delivery. His four-seam fastball touches 96 mph has sinking action. His fastball command suffers at the upper velocity range, and he's a much more effective strike thrower in his 90-91 mph comfort zone. He also throws a below-average slider in the mid-80s, but he doesn't always command the pitch. It has some two-plane movement. He rarely uses his changeup.

Moll hasn't started a game since his pro debut season, but the Mariners will give him a chance to earn a rotation job in spring training.

Year	Club (League)	Class	W	L	ERA	G	GS	CG	SV	IP	H	HR	BB	SO	K/9	WHIP	AVG
2015	Modesto (CAL)	HiA	0	1	3.02	25	0	0	2	54	40	7	12	57	9.6	0.97	.206
	New Britain (EL)	AA	0	0	1.23	13	0	0	0	15	7	0	4	17	10.4	0.75	.140
2016	Grand Junction (PIO)	R	0	0	0.00	2	0	0	0	2	0	0	0	5	22.5	0.00	.000
	Albuquerque (PCL)	AAA	3	5	4.94	42	0	0	2	47	55	5	19	39	7.4	1.56	.296
2017	Albuquerque (PCL)	AAA	3	2	4.18	44	0	0	0	47	56	4	18	39	7.4	1.56	.292
	Nashville (PCL)	AAA	0	0	0.00	6	0	0	0	7	5	0	1	8	10.3	0.86	.192
	Oakland (AL)	MAJ	0	0	10.80	11	0	0	0	7	13	2	3	7	9.5	2.40	.406
Major League Totals			0	0	10.80	11	0	0	0	7	13	2	3	7	9.5	2.40	.406
Minor League Totals			9	10	3.35	151	6	0	4	215	200	17	68	201	8.4	1.25	.245

21 OLIVER JASKIE, LHP

BA GRADE
45 Risk: High

Born: Nov. 17, 1995. **B-T:** L-L. **Ht.:** 6-3. **Wt.:** 210. **Drafted:** Michigan, 2017 (6th round). **Signed by:** Ross Vecchio.

Jaskie gained plenty of good weight and added 10 mph to his fastball between the time he arrived on campus at Michigan to the time he left. He finished 2017 in Ann Arbor as one of the Big Ten Conference's top starters with an 8-3, 3.77 mark and 11.5 strikeouts-per-nine innings.

Jaskie's fastball sat 87-90 mph during his pro debut at short-season Everett, down a couple of ticks due to a heavy workload at Michigan. He generally works inside to righthanded hitters with his fastball, setting up his changeup, which is his best secondary. Jaskie's changeup is an average pitch at 78-82 mph with late fade that he uses to get swings-and-misses. He also mixes in a fringy but usable slider at 79-83 mph. Jaskie has some funk that helps his stuff play up. His three-quarters delivery plays like a higher slot because of spinal tilt, and the effort in the delivery provides some deception. He is athletic for his size and has the mentality to remain in the rotation, but perhaps not the delivery to do so.

Jaskie will try to keep starting at low Class A Clinton in 2018.

Year	Club (League)	Class	W	L	ERA	G	GS	CG	SV	IP	H	HR	BB	SO	K/9	WHIP	AVG
2017	Everett (NWL)	SS	0	1	6.82	13	10	0	0	30	43	5	13	33	9.8	1.85	.333
Minor League Totals			0	1	6.82	13	10	0	0	30	43	5	13	33	9.8	1.85	.333

22 MIKE FORD, 1B

BA GRADE
40 Risk: High

Born: July 4, 1992. **B-T:** L-R. **Ht.:** 6-0. **Wt.:** 225. **Signed:** Princeton, 2013 (NDFA). **Signed by:** Damon Oppenheimer (Yankees).

After four strong years at Princeton, Ford was still passed over in the 2013 draft. But his strong Cape Cod League season in 2013, when he hit .407/.495/.663 with Cotuit, caught the eye of Yankees scouting director Damon Oppenheimer, who signed him as an undrafted free agent. The Mariners were in the bidding for his services that year, too, and acquired Ford four years later in the Rule 5 Draft.

With the Yankees, Ford was one of the system's most polished hitters, and his .410 on-base percentage led the Eastern League. He's posted OBPs of better than .400 in each of the past two seasons. He's got above-average power as well, and he tied for the system lead in home runs with 20 between Double-A Trenton and Triple-A Scranton/Wilkes-Barre. He knows the strike zone as well as anyone in the Mariners system. He's a below-average defender at first base, but he has improved his glovework some.

With the Yankees, he was blocked, and he'll face similar problems with Seattle, where Ryon Healy and Dan Vogelbach stand in his way. Still, the Mariners will give him a chance to win a spot on their roster come spring training.

Year	Club (League)	Class	AVG	G	AB	R	H	2B	3B	HR	RBI	BB	SO	SB	CS	OBP	SLG
2015	Tampa (FSL)	HiA	.260	123	435	62	113	23	3	6	55	60	75	1	0	.346	.368
2016	Tampa (FSL)	HiA	.371	10	35	3	13	1	0	2	14	5	4	0	1	.439	.571
	Staten Island (NYP)	SS	.167	4	12	2	2	1	0	1	3	2	0	0	0	.267	.500
	Trenton (EL)	AA	.280	42	143	21	40	10	0	5	26	34	25	0	0	.417	.455
2017	Scranton/W-B (IL)	AAA	.266	25	94	19	25	5	0	7	21	18	16	0	0	.383	.543
	Trenton (EL)	AA	.269	101	335	61	90	19	1	13	65	76	56	1	0	.408	.448
Minor League Totals			.272	443	1542	234	419	85	6	50	257	267	245	4	1	.379	.432

23 DONNIE WALTON, SS

BA GRADE 40 Risk: High

Born: May 25, 1994. **B-T:** B-R. **Ht.:** 5-10. **Wt.:** 184. **Drafted:** Oklahoma State, 2016 (5th round). **Signed by:** Ty Bowman.

Walton is the classic grinder ballplayer. A four-year starter at shortstop for Oklahoma State and the son of a coach, Walton has no plus tools and doesn't profile as a starting big league infielder.

However, he is capable of playing every position on the dirt and maximizes his skillset by doing a lot of things right on the field. Walton is exceptionally fundamentally strong and has an uncanny ability to slow the game down when he's on the field. Walton's 2017 batting line of .269/.349/.368 is a reasonable reflection of what he projects to do at the plate. He has a good approach and does all the little things to help the team, like bunting, advancing the runner and taking the extra base. He's a below-average runner but a capable basestealer with good instincts. Walton is a solid defender who positions himself well, and his tick above-average arm strength is enough for any infield spot.

Walton missed time in 2017 with a wrist injury, but may be advanced enough to head to Double-A Arkansas to start the 2018 season.

Year	Club (League)	Class	AVG	G	AB	R	H	2B	3B	HR	RBI	BB	SO	SB	CS	OBP	SLG
2016	Everett (NWL)	SS	.281	43	178	43	50	8	1	5	23	22	24	6	0	.361	.421
2017	Mariners (AZL)	R	.313	5	16	2	5	0	0	2	5	1	0	2	0	.353	.688
	Modesto (CAL)	HiA	.269	67	242	37	65	16	1	2	24	27	49	6	6	.349	.368
Minor League Totals			.275	115	436	82	120	24	2	9	52	50	73	14	6	.354	.401

24 LUIS LIBERATO, OF

BA GRADE 40 Risk: High

Born: Dec. 18, 1995. **B-T:** L-L. **Ht.:** 6-1. **Wt.:** 175. **Signed:** Dominican Republic, 2012. **Signed by:** Tim Kissner/Franklin Tavares Jr.

Since signing with the Mariners for $140,000 in 2012, Liberato has consistently flashed outstanding defensive tools and speed but never answered whether he can hit enough to be a major league contributor.

Liberato is streaky and inconsistent, and struggles mightily to hit lefthanded pitchers. That inconsistency comes from how he sets his hands at the plate, in that he locks them deep, sometimes up and sometimes down. He's also plagued by high strikeout totals, including a 26 percent mark in 2017. Liberato is a plus runner and better underway, but stole only 12 bases in 20 attempts. He uses his speed in the outfield and tracks balls well, and is good at going back on balls over his shoulder. He has an average arm with above-average accuracy.

Liberato's defense is promising, but he needs to improve his consistency at the plate and contact skills to be a backup outfielder. He will probably return to the Cal League in 2018 for more seasoning.

Year	Club (League)	Class	AVG	G	AB	R	H	2B	3B	HR	RBI	BB	SO	SB	CS	OBP	SLG
2015	Clinton (MWL)	LoA	.133	8	30	3	4	1	1	0	0	2	10	1	0	.188	.233
	Jackson (SL)	AA	.000	3	10	0	0	0	0	0	0	0	2	0	0	.000	.000
	Everett (NWL)	SS	.260	53	181	34	47	10	5	5	31	24	47	10	3	.341	.453
2016	Clinton (MWL)	LoA	.258	100	372	65	96	19	8	2	29	47	100	4	2	.340	.368
2017	Clinton (MWL)	LoA	.234	57	192	34	45	5	9	6	22	23	51	5	4	.312	.448
	Modesto (CAL)	HiA	.257	68	257	41	66	11	5	8	28	21	80	7	4	.314	.432
Minor League Totals			.244	395	1421	244	347	60	34	25	141	169	387	55	23	.325	.387

25 JOSEPH ROSA, 2B

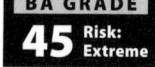

BA GRADE
45 Risk: Extreme

Born: March 6, 1997. **B-T:** B-R. **Ht.:** 5-10. **Wt.:** 165. **Signed:** Dominican Republic, 2014. **Signed by:** Eddy Toledo/Scott Hunter/Tim Kissner.

Rosa was born in New York and grew up in the U.S., but he moved to the Dominican Republic and signed with the Mariners for $30,000 in 2014. The diminutive switch-hitter spent most of his third professional season at short-season Everett, where he was named a Northwest League all-star.

Rosa has a sweet swing from both sides of the plate with better feel to hit from the left side, but needs to consistently trust himself and his instincts and not get into bad habits. While his size and speed indicate that he's more likely a gap-to-gap hitter, Rosa has some power as evidenced by the .235 isolated power he put up at Everett. He's a plus runner but was successful in only seven of 13 stolen base attempts in 2017. Rosa's best position is at second base because his average arm works better on that side of the bag, but he's capable of handling shortstop in a limited role.

Rosa finished 2017 with low Class A Clinton, and he'll head back there in 2018.

Year	Club (League)	Class	AVG	G	AB	R	H	2B	3B	HR	RBI	BB	SO	SB	CS	OBP	SLG
2015	Mariners (DSL)	R	.310	69	271	63	84	10	7	0	20	29	36	21	9	.390	.399
2016	Bakersfield (CAL)	HiA	.308	4	13	2	4	0	0	0	1	0	5	0	1	.357	.308
	Mariners (AZL)	R	.305	43	154	17	47	7	5	2	23	9	26	12	7	.345	.455
2017	Arkansas (TL)	AA	.286	2	7	0	2	0	0	0	0	1	2	0	0	.375	.286
	Tacoma (PCL)	AAA	.071	4	14	0	1	1	0	0	0	0	0	0	0	.071	.143
	Everett (NWL)	SS	.296	44	179	32	53	16	4	6	28	22	46	4	5	.374	.531
	Clinton (MWL)	LoA	.214	4	14	3	3	0	0	0	0	4	1	3	1	.389	.214
Minor League Totals			.298	170	652	117	194	34	16	8	72	65	116	40	23	.369	.436

26 TOMMY ROMERO, RHP

BA GRADE
45 Risk: Extreme

Born: July 8, 1997. **B-T:** L-R. **Ht.:** 6-2. **Wt.:** 225. **Drafted:** Eastern Florida State JC, 2017 (15th round). **Signed by:** Dan Rovetto.

Romero played two years of junior college ball in Florida, first at Polk State JC and then Eastern Florida State JC. He went 9-4, 1.55 at the latter but was fairly anonymous when the Mariners drafted him in the 15th round in 2017. The burly righthander has put himself on the radar with an outstanding pro debut in the Rookie-level Arizona League, going 5-1, 2.08 with 51 strikeouts and just 15 walks in 43.1 innings.

Romero stands out for his pitchability and fastball command, using a mechanically-sound delivery to pound the strike zone with downhill plane. He gets swings-and-misses with an average 88-92 mph fastball that has some cut to it, and a 74-77 mph curveball is his best secondary pitch. He also uses a 79-83 mph slider and an 80-83 mph changeup that are both below-average but play up off his fastball. There's not a lot of projection in Romero's body, but his pitching smarts should allow him to thrive in the lower levels of the system as he develops.

Romero may be advanced enough to jump to full-season ball to start the 2018 season.

Year	Club (League)	Class	W	L	ERA	G	GS	CG	SV	IP	H	HR	BB	SO	K/9	WHIP	AVG
2017	Mariners (AZL)	R	5	1	2.08	13	2	0	0	43	27	0	15	51	10.6	0.97	.188
Minor League Totals			5	1	2.08	13	2	0	0	43	27	0	15	51	10.6	0.97	.188

27 BRYSON BRIGMAN, 2B/SS

BA GRADE
40 Risk: High

Born: June 19, 1995. **B-T:** R-L. **Ht.:** 5-11. **Wt.:** 180. **Drafted:** San Diego, 2016 (3rd round). **Signed by:** Gary Patchett.

The Mariners picked Brigman as a draft-eligible sophomore in the third round in 2016 and signed him for $700,000.

Primarily a shortstop in college, Brigman has always been pegged for some type of super utility role in the pro game. That may now be the ceiling for Brigman since his bat has yet to come around. He has solid plate discipline but hasn't yet developed the strength to drive balls. Brigman's below-average arm strength isn't quite enough for shortstop, so he played more at second base in his first full year with low Class A Clinton. A plus runner and a good athlete, Brigman has stolen 33 bases as a pro but has also been thrown out 20 times. He needs to refine his technique to more effectively utilize his speed.

There are still plenty of question marks about Brigman's future, but the biggest one is whether he'll get strong enough to reach his ceiling as a utility bench bat.

Year	Club (League)	Class	AVG	G	AB	R	H	2B	3B	HR	RBI	BB	SO	SB	CS	OBP	SLG
2016	Everett (NWL)	SS	.260	68	265	51	69	6	1	0	19	41	43	17	12	.369	.291
2017	Clinton (MWL)	LoA	.235	120	463	55	109	14	4	2	36	44	74	16	8	.306	.296
Minor League Totals			.245	188	728	106	178	20	5	2	55	85	117	33	20	.330	.294

28 JOHNNY ADAMS, 3B/SS

BA GRADE

40 Risk: High

Born: Sept. 2, 1994. **B-T:** R-R. **Ht.:** 6-0. **Wt.:** 200. **Drafted:** Boston College, 2017 (22nd round). **Signed by:** Brian Nichols.

Adams went undrafted after his junior year at Boston College and a subpar senior year in which he posted a .603 OPS dropped him to the 22nd round in the 2017 draft. His bat came alive with short-season Everett when he hit .316/.381/.445 in a utility infield role for the AquaSox.

Adams possesses good baseball instincts and solid makeup, pre-requisites for the utility role that is his ceiling. He homered only three times in four college seasons, so the 12 doubles and five homers he hit in the Northwest League was surprising. Adams showed the strength to impact the ball in batting practice, although his actions at the plate are rigid. A shortstop in college, Adams doesn't have the range to play there on a regular basis but can be adequate in a utility role. His tick above-average arm is enough for the left side of the infield and he could also handle a corner outfield spot. He's a below-average runner but is smart and instinctual on the base paths. Adams will be right behind the very similar Donnie Walton on the Mariners depth chart, and at 23 years old could jump right to high Class A Modesto in 2018.

Year	Club (League)	Class	AVG	G	AB	R	H	2B	3B	HR	RBI	BB	SO	SB	CS	OBP	SLG
2017	Everett (NWL)	SS	.316	52	209	39	66	12	0	5	37	17	44	4	3	.374	.445
Minor League Totals			.316	52	209	39	66	12	0	5	37	17	44	4	3	.374	.445

29 RONALD ROSARIO, OF

BA GRADE

45 Risk: Extreme

Born: Feb. 8, 1997. **B-T:** L-L. **Ht.:** 6-3. **Wt.:** 185. **Signed:** Dominican Republic, 2013. **Signed by:** Eddy Toledo/Tim Kissner.

Rosario finally made it stateside in 2017 after three seasons in the Dominican Summer League. He originally signed in 2013 for $350,000, and early scouting reports had him as light on game skills but with tantalizing tools.

Four years later that's still the case with Rosario. He spent the early part of the season in the Arizona League before moving to short-season Everett after the trade that sent Brayan Hernandez to the Marlins. Rosario has some bat speed and makes hard contact, pulling balls on the inner half, but his actions at the plate are still very raw and he needs to learn to use all fields. He also needs to add strength to his lean, high-waisted frame. Rosario put up good numbers in the Northwest League, batting .275/.327/.478 with six home runs in 126 at-bats, but also had a 30 percent strikeout rate. He's got slightly above-average speed and can run down balls in the outfield, but is still a bit uncoordinated. Rosario's best tool is his plus-plus arm.

Rosario is still a lottery ticket, but the Mariners may have something if he gets stronger and learns to tap into his intriguing toolset.

Year	Club (League)	Class	AVG	G	AB	R	H	2B	3B	HR	RBI	BB	SO	SB	CS	OBP	SLG
2015	Mariners2 (DSL)	R	.208	53	168	13	35	8	1	0	16	16	34	2	8	.281	.268
2016	Mariners (DSL)	R	.292	52	171	29	50	13	4	1	31	13	33	6	4	.335	.433
2017	Mariners (AZL)	R	.232	13	56	5	13	6	0	1	8	2	19	0	1	.259	.393
	Everett (NWL)	SS	.294	40	126	22	37	6	2	6	17	11	40	1	0	.355	.516
Minor League Totals			.250	187	617	81	154	34	8	8	81	54	165	13	14	.310	.370

30 JORGE BENITEZ, LHP

BA GRADE

45 Risk: Extreme

Born: June 1, 1999. **B-T:** L-L. **Ht.:** 6-2. **Wt.:** 155. **Drafted:** HS—Gurabo, P.R., 2017 (9th round). **Signed by:** Rafael Santo Domingo/Dan Rovetto.

The Mariners went heavy on college players early in the 2017 draft, but found room on their draft board for an extreme projection play in Benitez.

Drafted in the ninth round from his high school in Puerto Rico, Benitez signed for $150,000 and began his pro career with an inconsistent performance in the Rookie-level Arizona League. The lean, lanky Benitez intrigues with a free and easy, whippy lefthanded delivery from a low-three-quarters arm slot. He got his fastball up to 91-92 mph by the end of the summer after earlier sitting in the upper 80s. Benitez's frame certainly has room to add strength, so more velocity is expected. He also shows an ability to spin his breaking ball. While Benitez shows two promising pitches, he was very wild in his pro debut.

Benitez is extremely raw and going to take a lot of time to develop. He needs at least one more full year, possibly two, before he'll be ready for full-season ball. He is slated to return to the AZL in 2018.

Year	Club (League)	Class	W	L	ERA	G	GS	CG	SV	IP	H	HR	BB	SO	K/9	WHIP	AVG
2017	Mariners (AZL)	R	1	0	7.82	13	10	0	0	25	28	1	20	24	8.5	1.89	.280
Minor League Totals			1	0	7.82	13	10	0	0	25	28	1	20	24	8.5	1.89	.280

Tampa Bay Rays

BY BILL BALLEW

After a disappointing 2016, the Rays proved again in 2017 why they're among the best in baseball at doing more with less.

The Rays' 2017 Opening Day payroll was a shade under $70 million, lower than every major league team other than the Brewers. It also was less than one-third of the Dodgers payroll, and slightly more than twice the salary of Clayton Kershaw.

Despite playing on a budget, the Rays made a 12-game improvement in 2017—trailing only the Twins (27) and Astros (17) for most in the American League—and remained in the playoff hunt until the final week of the season.

Third baseman Evan Longoria and righthander Chris Archer, the team's highest-paid players, rebounded from difficult 2016 campaigns to keep the Rays relevant. After getting questioned by observers near and far, the front office was rewarded for re-signing free agent Logan Morrison to a one-year deal when he contributed 38 home runs and 85 RBIs. The emergence of rookie righthander Jacob Faria filled a gap in the rotation, and the midseason acquisition of shortstop Adeiny Hechavarria aided a defense that lost Matt Duffy.

Those moves exemplified the Rays way. The front office uses analytics to project how players will perform, but also fully incorporates traditional scouting in making decisions. Tampa Bay has become among the most proficient teams in developing young players with minor league options, thereby making it easier to move players between Triple-A Durham and Tropicana Field based on immediate needs. The Rays are also adept at trading established big leaguers when their value is highest, and acquiring talent from other organizations who tend to blossom.

The Rays' formula generated success in 2017, when a prospect-laden Durham team won the International League title and the Triple-A national championship. Prospects such as righthander Brent Honeywell, shortstop Willy Adames and first baseman Jake Bauers benefited from being part of a championship environment while proving they're ready to elevate their game to the next level.

Winning and player development also went hand-in-hand at Double-A Montgomery, with the Biscuits reaching the Southern League finals, and at short-season Hudson Valley, which won the New York-Penn League title. In all, 15 Rays players were ranked among the top 20 prospects in their respective minor leagues.

The Rays' willingness to think outside the box is also evident in allowing 2017 first-round pick and BA College Player of the Year Brendan McKay, considered by some to be the best two-way player

Rookie Jacob Faria recorded a 3.43 ERA in 87 innings, putting him in the Rays' plans.

PROJECTED 2021 LINEUP

Catcher	Nick Ciuffo (26)
First Base	Jake Bauers (25)
Second Base	Lucius Fox (23)
Third Base	Evan Longoria (35)
Shortstop	Willy Adames (25)
Left Field	Jesus Sanchez (23)
Center Field	Kevin Kiermaier (31)
Right Field	Justin Williams (25)
Designated Hitter	Corey Dickerson (32)
No. 1 Starter	Chris Archer (32)
No. 2 Starter	Brent Honeywell (26)
No. 3 Starter	Blake Snell (28)
No. 4 Starter	Brendan McKay (25)
No. 5 Starter	Jake Odorizzi (31)
Closer	Alex Colome (32)

in college history, to pursue his desire to pitch as well as hit as a professional. Additional depth arrived in the draft with righthanders Michael Mercado, Drew Strotman and Riley O'Brien. The team's international efforts included a huge splash with the signing of Dominican shortstop Wander Franco, the top prospect in the 2017 class, for $3.825 million.

With revenue difficult to generate due to the Rays issues playing at Tropicana Field, the front office knows it must continue to be creative to get the most bang for its buck. The process worked in 2017, and it could lead to a playoff appearance with one of the game's youngest (and lowest-paid) rosters as soon as 2018.

DEPTH CHART

TAMPA BAY RAYS

TOP 2018 ROOKIE: Brent Honeywell, RHP. The Futures Game MVP helped guide Durham to the Triple-A national championship and is ready to make an impact in the rotation.
BREAKOUT PROSPECT: Ronaldo Hernandez, C. He made strides working with manager Danny Sheaffer at Rookie-level Princeton.
SLEEPER: Riley O'Brien, RHP. A former high school teammate of Blake Snell, the athletic righty has a solid repertoire and an impressive feel for pitching that could make the Rays' $7,500 investment in the College of Idaho product pay huge dividends.

SOURCE OF TOP 30 TALENT

Homegrown	22	Acquired	8
College	8	Trade	8
Junior college	1	Rule 5 draft	0
High school	5	Independent league	0
Nondrafted free agent	0	Free agent/waivers	0
International	8		

LF
Jesus Sanchez (5)
Nathan Lukes
Granden Goetzman
Bryce Brown

CF
Garrett Whitley (9)
Josh Lowe (11)
Ryan Boldt (18)
Jake Fraley
Michael Smith
Carl Chester

RF
Justin Williams (8)
Joe McCarthy (17)
Cade Gotta

3B
Grant Kay
Justin Bridgman
Kevin Padlo
Adrian Rondon

SS
Willy Adames (2)
Lucius Fox (7)
Taylor Walls
Zach Rutherford
Carlos Vargas
Andrew Velazquez

2B
Wander Franco (6)
Brandon Lowe (16)
Vidal Brujan (20)
Jake Cronenworth (22)
Riley Unroe

1B
Jake Bauers (4)
Dalton Kelly
Devin Davis

C
Ronaldo Hernandez (12)
Nick Ciuffo (21)
Zac Law
Chris Betts
Justin O'Connor
David Hernandez

LHP

LHSP	LHRP
Brendan McKay (3)	Adam Kolarek
Genesis Cabrera (14)	Kyle Bird
Resly Linares (24)	Jordan Harrison
Ryan Yarbrough (26)	Dalton Moats
Brock Burke	Jose Alvarado

RHP

RHSP	RHRP
Brent Honeywell (1)	Tobias Myers (15)
Austin Franklin (10)	Jose De Leon (25)
Michael Mercado (13)	Chih-Wei Hu (27)
Drew Strotman (19)	Jaime Schultz (28)
Yonny Chirinos (23)	Diego Castillo (29)
Riley O'Brien	Ian Gibaut (30)
Jose Mujica	Yoel Peguero
Mikey York	Ryne Stanek
Mike Franco	Hunter Wood
Greg Harris	Edwin Fierro
Taylor Guerrieri	Yoel Espinal
	Benton Moss

DRAFT ANALYSIS

2017

BEST PURE HITTER: 1B/LHP Brendan McKay (1) has a low-maintenance, pure and technically-sound swing. That's a necessity for a two-way player who doesn't get to spend as much time in the cage as the normal hitter. He uses the whole field well and has a track record of hitting for average.

BEST POWER HITTER: McKay is a hitter first, but his raw power portends 20-plus home run seasons in his future. His current swing is more geared for line drives than loft, but he has the strength and bat speed to drive the ball and could hit for more power if he tweaked his swing.

FASTEST RUNNER: The Rays drafted a trio of speedy outfielders in Carl Chester (12), Bryce Brown (15) and Michael Smith (18). All three are 70 runners on the 20-to-80 scouting scale with Smith the favorite to win a footrace.

BEST DEFENSIVE PLAYER: Chester played an excellent center field for short-season Hudson Valley. He's a plus defender in center. Neither SS Taylor Walls (3) nor Zach Rutherford (6) earns plus grades, but both are both noted for their reliability and steadiness.

BEST FASTBALL: McKay pitched at 92-95 mph for Hudson Valley on a once-a-week pitching schedule. He commands his fastball well and it has excellent late finish. RHP Drew Strotman (4) sat at 93-96 mph as a pro and touched 98.

BEST SECONDARY PITCH: McKay's breaking ball has morphed into different pitches throughout his Louisville career, but he always showed feel to spin it. It was more of a true curve as a sophomore and became a power slurve in 2017. He also added a cutter this year. Whatever it's shape, it's shown the potential to be a future plus pitch. LHP Josh Fleming (5) has a potentially plus changeup.

BEST PRO DEBUT: Strotman went 2-3, 1.78 for short-season Hudson Valley with an excellent 42-9 strikeout-to-walk ratio and only 29 hits allowed in 50.2 innings.

BEST ATHLETE: Chester, Smith and Brown are all quick-twitch athletes. Chester gets the nod because he has the most power to go with his speed. McKay's not quick twitch, but his baseball athleticism is notable because he is a legitimate pro prospect as a hitter and pitcher.

MOST INTRIGUING BACKGROUND: In addition to being the most decorated college player in BA history, McKay is the first first-round pick to try to play both ways as a pro since Casey Kelly a decade ago. RHP Riley O'Brien (8), a senior sign, was a high school teammate of Rays LHP Blake Snell at Shoreline (Wash.) High.

CLOSEST TO THE MAJORS: McKay's attempts to hit and pitch may slow his ascent, but he's a very polished lefthander/hitter with a long track record of college success.

BEST LATE-ROUND PICK: Chester often battled in the middle of Miami's lineup but he largely used a small-ball, get-on-base approach. He showed a more fluid swing as a pro and his approach fit well as a pro.

THE ONE WHO GOT AWAY: The Rays didn't sign RHP Drew Rasmussen (1s) after his post-draft medical exam raised concerns. Rasmussen has since had his second Tommy John surgery. RHP Justin Lewis (11) was one of the more talented sophomore-eligible pitchers in the draft. He should be a cornerstone of a very deep Kentucky weekend rotation this year.

—J.J. COOPER

TOP DRAFT PICKS OF THE DECADE

Year	Player, Pos.	2017 Org
2008	Tim Beckham, SS	Orioles
2009	*LeVon Washington, 2B	American Association
2010	Justin O'Conner, C	Rays
2011	Taylor Guerrieri, RHP	Rays
2012	Richie Shaffer, 3B	Indians
2013	Nick Ciuffo, C	Rays
2014	Casey Gillaspie, 1B	White Sox
2015	Garrett Whitley, OF	Rays
2016	Josh Lowe, 3B	Rays
2017	Brendan McKay, LHP/1B	Rays

* Did not sign

2016

OF Josh Lowe (1) overcame a slow start to put together a solid season, while OF Ryan Boldt (2) was one of the top hitters in the Florida State League. RHP Austin Franklin (3) is a project, but continues to impress.

GRADE: C

2015

Like teammate Josh Lowe, OF Garrett Whitley (1) rebounded after a slow start in low Class A. College bats 2B Brandon Lowe (3), OF Joe McCarthy (5) and SS Jake Cronenworth (7) all reached Double-A.

GRADE: C

2014

RHP Brent Honeywell (2s) was the MVP of the Futures Game and could soon join the Rays' rotation. It may be up to him to carry the class. 1B Casey Gillaspie (1) and OF Braxton Lee (12) were dealt away.

GRADE: C

1 BRENT HONEYWELL, RHP

Born: March 31, 1995. **B-T:** R-R. **Ht.:** 6-2. **Wt.:** 180.
Drafted: Walters State (Tenn.) JC, 2014 (2nd round supplemental). **Signed by:** Brian Hickman.

BRIAN WESTERHOLT

Honeywell displays the necessary arrogance to succeed in the major leagues. That confidence was evident in 2017, when he shined as the MVP of the Futures Game and helped guide Durham to the Triple-A national championship. Honeywell has had success at every level while posting a career 2.88 ERA in 79 minor league outings. After two dominant starts at Double-A Montgomery to open 2017, Honeywell made a seamless transition to Triple-A, becoming one of the youngest starters in the International League. He registered a 4.91 ERA in his first 12 starts before making adjustments and logging a 2.35 ERA in his final dozen starts. The lone negative was a four-game suspension imposed by the Rays in August for "disciplinary reasons."

Honeywell mixes five pitches with precision to keep hitters off balance. He works off his plus fastball that sits 93-94 mph and touches 97, and he features solid movement and above-average command. His best secondary pitch is a plus changeup, which coaxes hitters to chase outside the strike zone on occasion. He throws his above-average curveball primarily early in counts to set hitters up while altering their eye level. His above-average slider resides in the mid-80s and is developing into a plus pitch with improving sharp break. Honeywell also throws a screwball, which earned him some recognition early in his career. He pulls the plus offering out of his bag a few times a game, and more often than not, the results are devastating. Honeywell is a cerebral pitcher who knows how to get opponents out, and he's never afraid to challenge batters. A driven and determined young man, Honeywell understands the need to make adjustments. He did just that over the course of 2017, improving the consistency of his release point and generating better extension.

Even though Honeywell may have ruffled some feathers with a series of September tweets in which he referenced less-accomplished players who earned promotions to the big leagues while he remained with Durham, the fact is he would have already made his big league debut in many other organizations. The Rays, however, tend to move pitchers slowly. Many scouts project Honeywell as a No. 2 or No. 3 starter, while others envision him developing into a true ace.

BA GRADE	SCOUTING GRADES
65 Risk: Medium	FB: 60. CHG: 60. SCRW: 70. SL: 55. CB: 55. CTL: 60.

Projected future grades on 20-80 scouting scale

TOP PROSPECTS OF THE DECADE

Year	Player, Pos.	2017 Org
2008	Evan Longoria, 3B	Rays
2009	David Price, LHP	Red Sox
2010	Desmond Jennings, OF	Mets
2011	Jeremy Hellickson, RHP	Orioles
2012	Matt Moore, LHP	Giants
2013	Wil Myers, OF	Padres
2014	Jake Odorizzi, RHP	Rays
2015	Willy Adames, SS	Rays
2016	Blake Snell, LHP	Rays
2017	Willy Adames, SS	Rays

BEST TOOLS

Best Hitter for Average	Jesus Sanchez
Best Power Hitter	Brendan McKay
Best Strike-Zone Discipline	Joe McCarthy
Fastest Baserunner	Lucius Fox
Best Athlete	Josh Lowe
Best Fastball	Ryne Stanek
Best Curveball	Austin Franklin
Best Slider	Jaime Schultz
Best Changeup	Chih-Wei Hu
Best Control	Drew Strotman
Best Defensive Catcher	Nick Ciuffo
Best Defensive Infielder	Willy Adames
Best Infield Arm	Willy Adames
Best Defensive Outfielder	Jake Fraley
Best Outfield Arm	Josh Lowe

Year	Club (League)	Class	W	L	ERA	G	GS	CG	SV	IP	H	HR	BB	SO	K/9	WHIP	AVG
2015	Bowling Green (MWL)	LoA	4	4	2.91	12	12	0	0	65	53	3	12	76	10.5	1.00	.221
	Charlotte, FL (FSL)	HiA	5	2	3.44	12	12	1	0	65	57	2	15	53	7.3	1.10	.235
2016	Charlotte, FL (FSL)	HiA	4	1	2.41	10	10	0	0	56	43	5	11	64	10.3	0.96	.211
	Montgomery (SL)	AA	3	2	2.28	10	10	0	0	59	51	4	14	53	8.0	1.10	.231
2017	Montgomery (SL)	AA	1	1	2.08	2	2	0	0	13	4	1	4	20	13.8	0.62	.100
	Durham (IL)	AAA	12	8	3.64	24	24	0	0	124	130	11	31	152	11.1	1.30	.268
Minor League Totals			31	19	2.88	79	78	1	0	416	357	27	93	458	9.9	1.08	.230

2 WILLY ADAMES, SS

Born: Sept. 2, 1995. **B-T:** R-R. **Ht.:** 6-1. **Wt.:** 180. **Signed:** Dominican Republic, 2012. **Signed by:** Aldo Perez/Ramon Perez/Miguel Garcia (Tigers).

Adames made the jump to Triple-A Durham in 2017 and looked every bit the top prospect he showed at Double-A the year before. Ranked as the International League's fifth-best prospect, the Dominican shortstop struggled to a .230/.309/.344 slash through May before making a stance adjustment and rebounded to hit .303/.389/.455 over the final three months.

Adames has been considered a premier defensive shortstop since the Rays acquired him for his projectable body and mature approach in the David Price trade with the Tigers in 2014. His arm strength has increased over the past two seasons, and he displays excellent first-step quickness, plus range and soft hands. He's an ideal No. 2 hitter, and his bat has developed with his loose and easy swing. He narrowed his stance in 2017 to stay short to the ball and prevent over-striding. He has a solid feel for the strike zone, sees the ball early, and drives pitches consistently with some pop at the plate. Adames is an average runner with good instincts.

The Rays acquired Adeiny Hechavarria in 2017 as a placeholder because the organization did not want to rush Adames, who proceeded to win an International League title and the Triple-A Championship at Durham. With his tutelage nearly complete, Adames is in position to take over as the Rays starting shortstop in 2018.

BA GRADE	
60	**Risk:** Medium

HIT: 55. POW: 45.
SPD: 50. FLD: 60.
ARM: 60.

Year	Club (League)	Class	AVG	G	AB	R	H	2B	3B	HR	RBI	BB	SO	SB	CS	OBP	SLG
2015	Charlotte, FL (FSL)	HiA	.258	106	396	51	102	24	6	4	46	54	123	10	1	.342	.379
2016	Montgomery (SL)	AA	.274	132	486	89	133	31	6	11	57	74	121	13	6	.372	.430
2017	Durham (IL)	AAA	.277	130	506	74	140	30	5	10	62	65	132	11	5	.360	.415
Minor League Totals			.268	553	2038	317	546	116	36	34	247	303	546	49	30	.365	.410

3 BRENDAN McKAY, LHP/1B

Born: Dec. 18, 1995. **B-T:** L-L. **Ht.:** 6-2. **Wt.:** 212. **Drafted:** Louisville, 2017 (1st round). **Signed by:** James Bonnici.

A three-time All-American at Louisville and the 2017 BA College Player of the Year, McKay was drafted fourth overall and signed for $7.005 million. He promptly went out and ranked as the top prospect in the short-season New York-Penn League after signing.

The Rays envision the two-way standout pursuing both pitching and hitting for the foreseeable future. McKay has a simple, sound swing that generates live drives to all fields. He adds above-average raw power that could generate 20-plus home runs as he adds more loft to his swing. McKay worked on incorporating his lower half at the plate during instructional league to get to that power, which should help him generate even harder contact over time. While his footwork at first base is solid, he needs reps at the position. On the mound, McKay commands a fastball that sat 92-94 mph while pitching on Sundays at Hudson Valley. His heater has excellent late movement, making it difficult for batters to barrel. He mixes his fastball with a hard cutter that he developed late in college and a slurvy slider that complements and is his distinct third offering.

The Rays will allow McKay to play both ways until the dual responsibility becomes too much. McKay is determined to make the most of the rare opportunity to play both ways, and is supremely confident that he'll succeed. He will likely open 2018 at low Class A Bowling Green, but could move quickly once he starts building a foundation in pro ball.

BA GRADE	
60	**Risk:** High

HIT: 60. POW: 50.
SPD: 30. FLD: 55.
ARM: 60.
FB: 55. CB: 60.
CHG: 55. CTL: 55.

Year	Club (League)	Class	W	L	ERA	G	GS	CG	SV	IP	H	HR	BB	SO	K/9	WHIP	AVG
2017	Hudson Valley (NYP)	SS	1	0	1.80	6	6	0	0	20	10	3	5	21	9.5	0.75	.149
Minor League Totals			1	0	1.80	6	6	0	0	20	10	3	5	21	9.5	0.75	.149

Year	Club (League)	Class	AVG	G	AB	R	H	2B	3B	HR	RBI	BB	SO	SB	CS	OBP	SLG
2017	Hudson Valley (NYP)	SS	.232	36	125	16	29	4	1	4	22	21	33	2	0	.349	.376
Minor League Totals			.232	36	125	16	29	4	1	4	22	21	33	2	0	.349	.376

4 JAKE BAUERS, 1B/OF

Born: Oct. 6, 1995. **B-T:** L-L. **Ht.:** 6-1. **Wt.:** 195. **Drafted:** HS—Huntington Beach, Calif., 2013 (7th round). **Signed by:** Josh Emmerick (Padres).

Acquired from the Padres as part of the three-team deal that sent Wil Myers to the Padres, Bauers spent all of 2017 as one of the youngest players in Triple-A at age 21, and ranked as the IL's ninth-best prospect. He showed just fine against older competition, posting a .780 OPS.

Bauers has the makings of a younger version of Joey Votto. He has a pure stroke from the left side and an advanced approach that led to 78 walks in 2017, good for second in the International League. His willingness to wait for his pitch and ability to barrel the ball with his superior hand-eye coordination leads to a high on-base percentage. Bauers' solid-average bat speed generates raw power, but it has not shown consistently in game action. Scouts believe that he will generate plenty of extra-base hits to contribute as a first baseman in the big leagues. Bauers runs well and is intelligent on the bases. Despite seeing action as a corner outfielder, he's much more effective at first base, where he displays quick feet, soft hands and a solid overall feel for the position. Much like Willy Adames at shortstop, Bauers is the Rays' long-term answer at first base.

The organization traded Casey Gillaspie during the year and shifted Bauers back to his natural position, which is where he'll have a chance to earn the starting job at the big league level in 2018.

BA GRADE
55 Risk: Medium
HIT: 55. POW: 55.
SPD: 50. FLD: 55.
ARM: 45.

Year	Club (League)	Class	AVG	G	AB	R	H	2B	3B	HR	RBI	BB	SO	SB	CS	OBP	SLG
2015	Charlotte, FL (FSL)	HiA	.267	59	217	33	58	14	2	6	38	29	33	2	3	.357	.433
	Montgomery (SL)	AA	.276	69	257	36	71	18	0	5	36	21	41	6	3	.329	.405
2016	Montgomery (SL)	AA	.274	135	493	79	135	28	1	14	78	73	89	10	6	.370	.420
2017	Durham (IL)	AAA	.263	132	486	79	128	31	1	13	63	78	112	20	3	.368	.412
Minor League Totals			.276	554	2022	308	558	117	9	47	304	266	386	45	21	.362	.412

5 JESUS SANCHEZ, OF

Born: Oct. 7, 1997. **B-T:** L-R. **Ht.:** 6-2. **Wt.:** 190. **Signed:** Dominican Republic, 2014. **Signed by:** Danny Santana.

Sanchez continued his emergence by challenging for the low Class A Midwest League batting crown (.305), ranking as the league's seventh-best prospect, and receiving Bowling Green's player of the year award in 2017. Originally signed for $400,000 in 2014, Sanchez has shown the ability to perform every aspect of the game at a young age.

As a 19-year-old in the MWL, Sanchez displayed excellent hand-eye coordination that led to hard and consistent contact, while limiting his strikeout rate to 18 per-cent. He has a smooth and easy, whip-like swing from the left side and quick wrists that allow him to hit velocity and adjust to offspeed pitches. Most of his power has come when he pulls the ball, but given his age and raw strength, Sanchez should be a run producer at higher levels. His greatest need centers on gaining consistency with his leg kick so as not to drift on his front side. He also needs to improve his overall pitch selection to take full advantage of his high contact rate. Sanchez has a long running stride that generates above-average speed once he gets moving. He moved from center field to left in 2017 and has the range and arm strength to be above-average at the position.

BA GRADE
60 Risk: High
HIT: 60. POW: 55.
SPD: 55. FLD: 50.
ARM: 50.

The Rays believe that Sanchez has the ability to be a long-term solution in left field, but needs time to get there. He will make the jump to High A Charlotte in 2018.

Year	Club (League)	Class	AVG	G	AB	R	H	2B	3B	HR	RBI	BB	SO	SB	CS	OBP	SLG
2015	Rays (DSL)	R	.335	61	239	36	80	13	7	4	45	20	32	8	1	.382	.498
2016	Rays (GCL)	R	.323	42	164	25	53	6	8	4	31	6	31	1	5	.341	.530
	Princeton (APP)	R	.347	14	49	8	17	4	0	3	8	3	12	1	0	.385	.612
2017	Bowling Green (MWL)	LoA	.305	117	475	81	145	29	4	15	82	32	91	7	2	.348	.478
Minor League Totals			.318	234	927	150	295	52	19	26	166	61	166	17	8	.358	.499

6 WANDER FRANCO, SS

Born: March 1, 2001. **B-T:** B-R. **Ht.:** 5-10. **Wt.:** 170. **Signed:** Dominican Republic, 2017. **Signed by:** Danny Santana.

Franco's uncle is veteran big league shortstop Erick Aybar, and his two older brothers—both named Wander—play in the Royals and Astros systems. After training with Rudy Santin in the Dominican Republic, Franco, ranked the No. 1 international prospect for 2017, signed with the Rays for $3.825 million, which was the largest bonus in his signing class.

A switch-hitter with excellent bat speed from both sides, Franco has a short, pure stroke and keeps the barrel in the zone for an extended time. He shows good strike-zone discipline and advanced pitch recognition, and uses the entire field while making consistent contact. His raw power comes from his strong lower half, and he could generate impressive extra-base numbers as his body matures. Franco needs to learn the nuances of playing shortstop and hitting against premier pitching on a daily basis. Physically mature for his age, he possesses soft, quick hands and excellent first-step quickness. His arm is solid-average and could improve. He has the fluid actions that would allow him to play second base if his body or team needs necessitate a move.

Given his advanced feel and ability to drive the ball at a young age, Franco may leap to the Rookie-level Gulf Coast League in 2018. His bat could allow him to move faster through the system than most, but the Rays feel no need to rush him and want him to build a solid foundation at every level.

BA GRADE
60 Risk: Extreme
HIT: 55. **POW:** 55.
SPD: 50. **FLD:** 55.
ARM: 50.

BILL MITCHELL

Year	Club (League)	Class	AVG	G	AB	R	H	2B	3B	HR	RBI	BB	SO	SB	CS	OBP	SLG
2017	Did not play—Signed 2018 contract																

7 LUCIUS FOX, SS

Born: July 2, 1997. **B-T:** B-R. **Ht.:** 6-1. **Wt.:** 175. **Signed:** Bahamas, 2015. **Signed by:** Jose Alou/Joe Salermo (Giants).

A native of the Bahamas who played high school baseball in Florida, Fox returned to the island nation and was declared an international free agent in 2015. He signed with the Giants as an 18-year-old for $6 million, the largest bonus ever for a non-Cuban international amateur.

After a rough first season in the low Class A South Atlantic League in 2016, due in part to a foot injury, Fox was traded to the Rays in the Matt Moore deal. Fox is a natural athlete with plus-plus speed who is honing his all-around skills. He has a solid, line-drive swing from both sides of the plate, with the mindset to be a proto-typical leadoff man. He possesses decent raw power and can drive the ball on occasion, but his game is built on getting on base and creating havoc. Fox needs to stay short to the ball and improve his strike-zone judgment. He's learning to read pitchers to get better jumps when stealing bases. Fox has excellent range, quick hands and good arm strength at shortstop, but he needs to play lower and through the ball while increasing his release when needed.

Fox earned a late promotion to high Class A Charlotte in 2017 and will likely return to the Florida State League in 2018. He remains raw but has the tools to project as an everyday big leaguer.

BA GRADE
50 Risk: High
HIT: 50. **POW:** 40.
SPD: 70. **FLD:** 50.
ARM: 55.

Year	Club (League)	Class	AVG	G	AB	R	H	2B	3B	HR	RBI	BB	SO	SB	CS	OBP	SLG
2016	Augusta (SAL)	LoA	.207	75	285	46	59	6	4	2	16	37	76	25	7	.305	.277
2017	Bowling Green (MWL)	LoA	.275	77	302	45	83	13	3	2	27	33	80	27	10	.359	.358
	Charlotte, FL (FSL)	HiA	.235	30	115	19	27	3	0	1	12	12	33	3	3	.321	.287
Minor League Totals			.241	182	702	110	169	22	7	5	55	82	189	55	20	.330	.313

8 JUSTIN WILLIAMS, OF

Born: Aug. 20, 1995. **B-T:** L-R. **Ht.:** 6-2. **Wt.:** 215. **Drafted:** HS—Houma, La., 2013 (2nd round). **Signed by:** Rusty Pendergrass (D-backs).

BA GRADE
45 Risk: Medium
HIT: 55. POW: 50.
SPD: 45. FLD: 50.
ARM: 50.

The D-backs traded Williams to the Rays in the 2014 Jeremy Hellickson deal, and he's proven himself a potent hitter during his time in Tampa Bay's system. Williams spent all of the 2017 regular season in the Southern League, where he was tabbed the league's 16th-best prospect, despite battling minor injuries that led to him missing most of May. Despite his brief absence, Williams still finished among the league leaders in multiple offensive categories and was then called up to Triple-A Durham for the International League playoffs.

Williams has a line-drive stroke and uses the entire field, which helped him finish fourth in the SL batting race in 2017. He manages the strike zone well and makes consistent contact, thanks to improving pitch recognition. He hits lots of ground balls but has made progress in lofting the ball more often. Sanchez showed his above-average raw power late in 2017, when he hit eight homers in August, including three in one game. Williams turns on inside pitches well but struggles to cover the outside part of the plate. He has made strides as a defensive right fielder, particularly with his first step and reading balls off the bat. He's a fringe-average runner with solid-average arm strength featuring good accuracy and carry.

Williams is another potential solid piece to the Rays' youth movement at the major league level. Whether or not he continues to tap into his power will determine whether he can become a starting corner outfielder in the big leagues. Triple-A Durham awaits in 2018.

Year	Club (League)	Class	AVG	G	AB	R	H	2B	3B	HR	RBI	BB	SO	SB	CS	OBP	SLG
2015	Bowling Green (MWL)	LoA	.284	99	387	43	110	25	2	7	42	13	76	3	1	.308	.413
	Charlotte, FL (FSL)	HiA	.241	23	83	8	20	5	0	0	6	1	14	3	1	.250	.301
2016	Charlotte, FL (FSL)	HiA	.330	51	194	23	64	11	0	4	31	6	26	0	1	.350	.448
	Montgomery (SL)	AA	.250	39	148	20	37	7	2	6	28	5	30	0	1	.277	.446
2017	Montgomery (SL)	AA	.301	96	366	53	110	21	3	14	72	37	69	6	2	.364	.489
Minor League Totals			.308	433	1677	226	516	99	12	36	262	97	326	13	9	.348	.445

9 GARRETT WHITLEY, OF

Born: March 13, 1997. **B-T:** R-R. **Ht.:** 6-0. **Wt.:** 200. **Drafted:** HS—Niskayuna, N.Y., 2015 (1st round). **Signed by:** Tim Alexander.

BA GRADE
50 Risk: High
HIT: 50. POW: 55.
SPD: 60. FLD: 60.
ARM: 55.

The 13th overall pick in 2015, Whitley impressed the Rays with his tools, headlined by raw power and speed. Tampa Bay made him the highest high school pick out of New York state since the Indians took Manny Ramirez in 1991.

The organization expected his inexperience against top competition to affect his early progress, but they loved the way he rebounded from an 11-for-60 slow start at low Class A Bowling Green in 2017. After hitting .183 with one home run in April, Whitley batted .262 with an .827 OPS the rest of the way. Whitley possesses plus bat speed that led to 35 extra-base hits in his first taste of a full-season league. He feasts on fastballs and makes hard contact against premium velocity. Curveballs provide more of a challenge, with Whitley prone to getting fooled and chasing pitches outside the strike zone and creating a high swing-and-miss rate. He struck out 29 percent of the time in 2017, but scouts believe game experience will reduce that total. He's a plus-plus runner who was thrown out just four times in 25 steal attempts, even though he's still learning to read pitchers. He's a consistent defender in center field who covers the gaps well and has above-average arm strength.

Whitley is still a work in progress as he continues to improve his pitch recognition and pitch selection. His next challenge will come at high Class A Charlotte in the pitcher-friendly Florida State League to start 2018.

Year	Club (League)	Class	AVG	G	AB	R	H	2B	3B	HR	RBI	BB	SO	SB	CS	OBP	SLG
2015	Rays (GCL)	R	.188	30	96	12	18	4	2	3	13	16	25	5	4	.310	.365
	Hudson Valley (NYP)	SS	.143	12	42	3	6	0	1	0	4	5	12	3	1	.250	.190
2016	Hudson Valley (NYP)	SS	.266	65	256	38	68	12	7	1	31	30	75	21	5	.356	.379
2017	Bowling Green (MWL)	LoA	.249	104	358	65	89	18	4	13	61	57	122	21	4	.362	.430
Minor League Totals			.241	211	752	118	181	34	14	17	109	108	234	50	14	.347	.391

10 AUSTIN FRANKLIN, RHP

Born: Oct. 2, 1997. **B-T:** R-R. **Ht.:** 6-3. **Wt.:** 215. **Drafted:** HS—Paxton, Fla., 2016 (3rd round). **Signed by:** Brett Foley.

Franklin is one of the Rays' more underrated young pitchers with a high ceiling. He emerged as a high school senior in 2016 when he threw a pair of no-hitters and helped guide Paxton (Fla.) High to a district championship after his fastball velocity increased to the low 90s and touched 95 mph.

BA GRADE
55 Risk: Extreme
FB: 55. CB: 60.
CHG: 55.
CONTROL: 45.

The Rays drafted him in the third round and signed him for $597,500. Franklin bypassed Samford to sign with the Rays as a third-round pick, and has continued to hone his skills in pro ball while being moved conservatively through the system. He has a strong, athletic build and a short, easy arm action. He gets good downward trajectory with his heavy fastball that could add a little velocity as his body matures. While he works off his low-90s fastball, his best pitch is a hard, 11-to-5 curveball with a pronounced drop. His changeup has the potential to be above-average, and he's working on making the delivery of his offspeed pitches mirror that of his heater to create more deception. Franklin's greatest need centers on improving his fastball command and working ahead in the count.

Franklin has the makings of a mid-rotation starter and should graduate to the full-season ranks at low Class A Bowling Green in 2018.

Year	Club (League)	Class	W	L	ERA	G	GS	CG	SV	IP	H	HR	BB	SO	K/9	WHIP	AVG
2016	Rays (GCL)	R	1	2	2.70	11	9	0	1	43	30	0	16	40	8.3	1.06	.192
2017	Hudson Valley (NYP)	SS	4	2	2.21	13	13	0	0	69	51	4	31	71	9.2	1.18	.207
Minor League Totals			5	4	2.40	24	22	0	1	113	81	4	47	111	8.9	1.14	.201

11 JOSH LOWE, OF

BA GRADE
55 Risk: Extreme

Born: Feb. 2, 1998. **B-T:** L-R. **Ht.:** 6-4. **Wt.:** 190. **Drafted:** HS—Marietta, Ga., 2016 (1st round). **Signed by:** Milt Hill.

The Rays double-dipped with the Lowe family during the 2016 draft, taking Josh out of high school with the 13th overall pick and his older brother Nathan in the 13th round out of Mississippi State. A two-way player who was projected to pitch and hit at Florida State, Josh had a promising pro debut, ranking as the eighth-best prospect in the Gulf Coast League and the 11th-best in the Appalachian League in 2016.

Shaky defensively at third base, he moved to center field during instructional league and remained there in the low Class A Midwest League, where he struggled early before rebounding to hit .294/.355/.413 after the All-Star break. Lowe is an excellent all-around athlete who generates plus speed as a long-strider. He adjusted well in the outfield and possesses plus arm strength, but needs work on going back on balls hit over his head, as well as on the accuracy of his throws. He has excellent bat speed with quick hands and the potential to hit for power. He tends to swing and miss due to his long arms and needs to find a direct path to the ball while also improving his overall plate coverage.

Lowe is young and a work in progress. He'll move to high Class A Charlotte in 2018.

Year	Club (League)	Class	AVG	G	AB	R	H	2B	3B	HR	RBI	BB	SO	SB	CS	OBP	SLG
2016	Rays (GCL)	R	.258	28	93	14	24	6	1	2	15	20	27	1	1	.386	.409
	Princeton (APP)	R	.238	26	80	11	19	0	2	3	11	17	32	1	1	.360	.400
2017	Bowling Green (MWL)	LoA	.268	118	456	60	122	26	2	8	55	42	144	22	8	.326	.386
Minor League Totals			.262	172	629	85	165	32	5	13	81	79	203	24	10	.340	.391

12 RONALDO HERNANDEZ, C

BA GRADE
55 Risk: Extreme

Born: Nov. 11, 1997. **B-T:** R-R. **Ht.:** 6-1. **Wt.:** 190. **Signed:** Colombia, 2014. **Signed by:** Angel Contreras.

A former infielder who played on Colombia's 18U World Cup team as a 15-year-old in 2013, Hernandez signed for $225,000 and moved behind the plate with the Rays. He emerged as a legitimate dual-threat receiver in 2017 at Rookie-level Princeton after battling a groin injury for two years in the Dominican Summer League.

Hernandez ranked as the Appalachian League's fourth-best prospect and finished among the leaders in hits (third), doubles (second) and slugging percentage (fifth). He also paced the Rays system in batting average (.332). Hernandez has an easy swing and good barrel control despite possessing a bat wrap. He makes hard contact thanks to his quick wrists and strong forearms. Aggressive with above-average power potential, he needs to create a shorter path to inside pitches. Scouts are surprised to discover Hernandez's limited experience behind the dish based on his ability. He has plus-plus arm strength that led to him throwing out 57 percent of would-be basestealers last season. Hernandez does a solid job blocking balls in the dirt, but showed signs of tiring late in the season. He has made strides learning English.

Hernandez is on an upward trajectory that could see him emerge as one of the organization's premier prospects. He is in line to open 2018 as the starting catcher at low Class A Bowling Green.

Year	Club (League)	Class	AVG	G	AB	R	H	2B	3B	HR	RBI	BB	SO	SB	CS	OBP	SLG
2015	Rays (DSL)	R	.227	13	44	3	10	0	1	0	4	3	6	0	0	.320	.273
2016	Rays (DSL)	R	.340	54	206	34	70	12	0	6	35	20	12	3	5	.406	.485
2017	Princeton (APP)	R	.332	54	223	42	74	22	1	5	40	16	39	2	2	.382	.507
Minor League Totals			.326	121	473	79	154	34	2	11	79	39	57	5	7	.387	.476

13 MICHAEL MERCADO, RHP

BA GRADE 55 Risk: Extreme

Born: April 15, 1999. **B-T:** R-R. **Ht.:** 6-4. **Wt.:** 160. **Drafted:** HS—San Diego, 2017 (2nd round). **Signed by:** Jaime Jones.

Mercado was one of the most polished and projectable high school pitchers in the 2017 draft, signing for an above-slot $2.132 million bonus to pass up a commitment to Stanford as the 40th overall pick.

Scouts rave about Mercado's control for such a young pitcher. In high school, his four-seam fastball increased to the low 90s during his senior year and touched 94. His two-seam fastball sits in the 87-89 mph range and generates ground balls. He mixes in a sharp curveball that flashes plus potential, as well as a solid-average cutter/slider, and is working on adding a circle changeup that he still lacks confidence in. Tall, thin and gangly, Mercado is more coordinated than he would appear, and repeats his delivery well. He needs to keep building strength, which could increase his velocity. He also needs to incorporate his lower half more consistently, and finish each pitch to get as much movement as possible and reduce the chance of injury.

The Rays tend to move their high school pitchers slowly, and Mercado is a candidate for that track. A potential middle-of-the-rotation starter in the big leagues, Mercado could see low Class A Bowling Green at some point in 2018.

Year	Club (League)	Class	W	L	ERA	G	GS	CG	SV	IP	H	HR	BB	SO	K/9	WHIP	AVG
2017	Rays (GCL)	R	0	0	1.69	8	8	0	0	21	21	1	4	14	5.9	1.17	.256
Minor League Totals			0	0	1.69	8	8	0	0	21	21	1	4	14	5.9	1.17	.256

14 GENESIS CABRERA, LHP

BA GRADE 50 Risk: High

Born: Oct. 10, 1996. **B-T:** L-L. **Ht.:** 6-0. **Wt.:** 165. **Signed:** Dominican Republic, 2013. **Signed by:** Carlos Batista/Danny Santana.

In his four seasons with the Rays, Cabrera has made tremendous strides with his pitchability while maintaining one of the more electric arms in the organization. A 2016 all-star in the Midwest League at age 19, Cabrera made the jump from high Class A Charlotte to Double-A Montgomery midway through the 2017 campaign.

He opened the season trying to overpower hitters, and allowed 10 earned runs on seven hits and six walks in his first two starts, totaling five innings. His fastball touched 97 mph, but he had no command of the pitch. Tampa Bay's pitching coaches convinced the southpaw his heater had enough movement at a lower velocity, and he proceeded to rediscover his command while sitting in the 92-93 mph range. He also added a nasty cutter in the upper 80s, as well as a changeup with improving fade and depth, giving him the potential for three above-average offerings.

Cabrera could emerge as a starter or setup man once he adds more strength to his wiry frame.

Year	Club (League)	Class	W	L	ERA	G	GS	CG	SV	IP	H	HR	BB	SO	K/9	WHIP	AVG
2015	Princeton (APP)	R	0	0	3.18	5	2	0	0	17	16	0	4	19	10.1	1.18	.254
2016	Bowling Green (MWL)	LoA	11	5	3.88	23	22	2	0	116	110	9	48	96	7.4	1.36	.255
2017	Charlotte, FL (FSL)	HiA	4	5	2.84	13	12	0	0	70	45	3	25	60	7.8	1.00	.185
	Montgomery (SL)	AA	5	4	3.62	12	12	0	0	65	75	6	27	51	7.1	1.58	.292
Minor League Totals			22	15	3.40	67	49	2	0	297	266	18	107	252	7.6	1.26	.242

15 TOBIAS MYERS, RHP

BA GRADE 50 Risk: High

Born: Aug. 5, 1998. **B-T:** R-R. **Ht.:** 6-0. **Wt.:** 193. **Drafted:** HS—Winter Haven, Fla., 2016 (6th round). **Signed by:** Kelvin Colon (Orioles).

Some people were scratching their heads–including many in the Rays clubhouse–when at the trade deadline the Rays sent infielder Tim Beckham to the Orioles for a minor league pitcher who had yet to reach the full-season ranks.

Myers showed many of the traits that interested the Rays prior to the 2015 draft. A two-way player in high school who signed for $225,000 as a sixth-round pick, Myers is an excellent athlete with a loose and easy arm action. He understands how to pitch, possesses outstanding control, and has shown the ability to make quick adjustments during his short time in pro ball. His fastball now resides at 93-96 mph with solid movement, after sitting around 90 mph in high school. His plus curveball has a sharp drop, and he mixes it well with his fastball. He displays an impressive feel for his changeup, but needs to develop it more to remain a starter. The Rays are working with Myers to find a consistent alignment in his stride with his landing foot. He also needs to control the running game more effectively, which should occur as he gets his mechanics in order.

The Rays believe Myers has the ability to develop into a solid major league starter or a significant bullpen piece. He's expected to make the move to the full-season ranks at low Class A Bowling Green in 2018.

Year	Club (League)	Class	W	L	ERA	G	GS	CG	SV	IP	H	HR	BB	SO	K/9	WHIP	AVG
2016	Orioles (GCL)	R	0	0	4.70	3	3	0	0	8	10	1	2	4	4.7	1.57	.303
2017	Aberdeen (NYP)	SS	2	2	3.94	7	7	1	0	30	28	0	6	35	10.6	1.15	.235
	Hudson Valley (NYP)	SS	2	0	3.08	5	5	0	0	26	17	1	4	38	13.0	0.80	.181
Minor League Totals			4	2	3.68	15	15	1	0	64	55	2	12	77	10.9	1.05	.224

16 BRANDON LOWE, 2B

BA GRADE
45 Risk: Medium

Born: July 6, 1994. **B-T:** L-R. **Ht.:** 5-10. **Wt.:** 175. **Drafted:** Maryland, 2015 (3rd round). **Signed by:** Lou Wieben.

Lowe blossomed in 2017 when he was named the Florida State League most valuable player and the Rays' minor league player of the year. He led the FSL with a .524 slugging percentage and tied for first with 34 doubles despite spending the last month of the season in Double-A. He also established high Class A Charlotte's single-season franchise record for slugging and OPS.

An effective offensive player throughout his college career at Maryland due to his pitch recognition, disciplined approach and ability to work the count, Lowe increased his power in 2017 after shifting his hands away from his body during his setup. He has above-average bat speed with solid power and attacks pitches in the strike zone with his short, quick compact swing. An average runner who runs the bases intelligently, Lowe has cleaned up his pivot in turning double plays on defense, but needs to upgrade his footwork in order to improve his range. His arm strength is fringe-average, but shouldn't be a problem at the keystone.

With second base becoming more of an offensive position, Lowe fits the mold well. He'll likely open 2018 back at Montgomery, with an in-season promotion to Triple-A Durham a possibility.

Year	Club (League)	Class	AVG	G	AB	R	H	2B	3B	HR	RBI	BB	SO	SB	CS	OBP	SLG
2015	Did not play--Injured																
2016	Bowling Green (MWL)	LoA	.248	107	379	67	94	15	3	5	42	60	77	6	3	.357	.343
2017	Charlotte, FL (FSL)	HiA	.311	90	315	62	98	34	3	9	46	47	65	6	3	.403	.524
	Montgomery (SL)	AA	.253	24	95	8	24	5	1	2	12	2	26	1	1	.270	.389
Minor League Totals			.274	221	789	137	216	54	7	16	100	109	168	13	7	.366	.421

17 JOE McCARTHY, 1B/OF

BA GRADE
45 Risk: Medium

Born: Feb. 23, 1994. **B-T:** L-L. **Ht.:** 6-3. **Wt.:** 220. **Drafted:** Virginia, 2015 (5th round). **Signed by:** Lou Wieben.

McCarthy went undrafted out of his Pennsylvania high school but emerged as an offensive force during his first two years for a Virginia team that finished as the runner-up in the 2014 College World Series. A back injury that required surgery limited his effectiveness as a junior.

McCarthy led the Southern League in walks and triples, and was among the top four in on-base percentage, doubles and runs. McCarthy is an intelligent player with plus makeup and a tremendous eye at the plate who works the count, allowing him to get on base consistently. He has a compact swing with solid-average raw power to the pull side, but his game is centered more on hitting line drives while using the entire field. McCarthy has above-average speed and plays the outfield corners well, but his fringy arm strength is suited best for left. He also has seen time at first base.

McCarthy has the offensive game to be a starting outfielder in the big leagues but could settle into a utility role as well. He is scheduled to open 2018 at Triple-A Durham.

Year	Club (League)	Class	AVG	G	AB	R	H	2B	3B	HR	RBI	BB	SO	SB	CS	OBP	SLG
2015	Hudson Valley (NYP)	SS	.277	49	184	24	51	7	2	0	21	18	23	18	3	.362	.337
2016	Bowling Green (MWL)	LoA	.288	43	153	31	44	12	0	3	29	33	30	11	2	.425	.425
	Charlotte, FL (FSL)	HiA	.283	61	198	20	56	9	3	5	31	28	38	8	3	.376	.434
2017	Montgomery (SL)	AA	.284	127	454	76	129	31	8	7	56	90	94	20	5	.409	.434
Minor League Totals			.283	280	989	151	280	59	13	15	137	169	185	57	13	.396	.415

18 RYAN BOLDT, OF

Born: Nov. 22, 1994. **B-T:** L-R. **Ht.:** 6-2. **Wt.:** 210. **Drafted:** Nebraska, 2016 (2nd round). **Signed by:** Matt Alison.

Selected in the 22nd round by the Red Sox out of a Minnesota high school in 2013, Boldt instead spent three seasons at Nebraska and became the highest-drafted Cornhusker position player since Alex Gordon in 2005. He was drafted in the second round and skipped over low Class A in his first full season.

Boldt more than held his own, hitting .295 with 33 extra-base hits and 23 stolen bases despite missing 20 games. Boldt spent most of his time in right field in 2017, but has seen activity in all three outfield spots since signing with the Rays. He has a solid-average arm with good carry and above-average accuracy. Amazingly, he threw lefthanded prior to fracturing his left elbow on a throw at age 11 and now throws righthanded. Boldt has above-average speed that plays well in the field and on the basepaths. Some scouts suggest that he should hit for more power than he has due to his athletic and physical frame, but the Rays feel that his production will increase with experience. He employs a level swing and uses the entire field.

Given his solid all-around ability, Boldt could develop into a starter in the big leagues. He'll make the jump to Double-A Montgomery in 2018.

Year	Club (League)	Class	AVG	G	AB	R	H	2B	3B	HR	RBI	BB	SO	SB	CS	OBP	SLG
2016	Hudson Valley (NYP)	SS	.218	43	170	17	37	5	1	1	15	10	24	8	9	.280	.276
2017	Charlotte, FL (FSL)	HiA	.295	120	440	60	130	22	6	5	62	39	88	23	6	.358	.407
Minor League Totals			.274	163	610	77	167	27	7	6	77	49	112	31	15	.336	.370

19 DREW STROTMAN, RHP

Born: Sept. 3, 1996. **B-T:** R-R. **Ht.:** 6-3. **Wt.:** 195. **Drafted:** St. Mary's, 2017 (4th round). **Signed by:** Alan Hull.

Strotman was primarily a reliever at St. Mary's, but made seven of his 14 career starts in 2017 and overall went 6-1, 4.50, with a team-high 75 strikeouts in 67 innings. The Rays drafted him in the third round and signed him for $367,500. Strotman had one of the best pro debuts of any Rays pick.

Strotman has a lean, athletic frame and a fast arm. His four-seam fastball sits at 93-95 mph and touches 98. He has a sharp slider that flashes the ability to be a plus offering, but needs more consistency in finding the strike zone. Strotman also has the potential for a solid-average changeup, and is working on generating more depth while finding a comfortable grip. The righthander does an excellent job of working down in the strike zone, resulting in grounders on 58.6 percent of balls put in play. His delivery also possesses some deception, which led to 23 of his 51 strikeouts in West Coast Conference play coming on called third strikes.

Strotman's role at the major league level projects as a setup man, but the Rays will continue to get him innings as a starter in the Class A ranks in 2018.

Year	Club (League)	Class	W	L	ERA	G	GS	CG	SV	IP	H	HR	BB	SO	K/9	WHIP	AVG
2017	Hudson Valley (NYP)	SS	2	3	1.78	11	7	0	0	51	29	0	9	42	7.5	0.75	.168
Minor League Totals			2	3	1.78	11	7	0	0	51	29	0	9	42	7.5	0.75	.168

20 VIDAL BRUJAN, 2B

Born: Feb. 9, 1998. **B-T:** B-R. **Ht.:** 5-9. **Wt.:** 155. **Signed:** Dominican Republic, 2014. **Signed by:** Danny Santana.

Brujan hails from the forests of the Dominican Republic, and has blossomed quickly into a solid prospect with his quick-twitch athleticism. Signed for just $15,000, the switch-hitting Brujan is developing into the quintessential leadoff man. He led the short-season New York-Penn League in hits, runs and total bases, and ranked fifth in steals in 2017.

Brujan also served as a key ingredient in Hudson Valley's NYPL championship. Brujan possesses excellent pitch recognition, solid strike zone discipline, and superior hand-eye coordination. He ranked as the second-toughest player to strike out in the NYPL, whiffing once every 8.4 plate appearances, and had nearly as many walks (34) as strikeouts (36). Among the fastest runners in the organization, Brujan is efficient getting on base and creating havoc, but is working on improving his ability to read pitcher's moves in order to get better jumps. He also needs to improve his bunting technique to make his speed a greater weapon. The Rays also want him to work on his pre-pitch footwork to maintain proper balance at contact. He has excellent range at second base and solid instincts with average arm strength. The Rays feel that he could handle center field should the need arise.

After ranking as the fifth-best prospect in the NYPL in 2017, Brujan should continue to mature physically and emotionally as he moves up to low Class A Bowling Green.

Year	Club (League)	Class	AVG	G	AB	R	H	2B	3B	HR	RBI	BB	SO	SB	CS	OBP	SLG
2015	Rays (DSL)	R	.301	60	226	48	68	9	4	2	20	38	16	22	12	.411	.403
2016	Rays (GCL)	R	.282	49	202	41	57	12	5	1	8	14	15	8	5	.344	.406
	Hudson Valley (NYP)	SS	.000	2	8	1	0	0	0	0	0	1	1	2	0	.111	.000
2017	Hudson Valley (NYP)	SS	.285	67	260	51	74	15	5	3	20	34	36	16	8	.378	.415
Minor League Totals			.286	178	696	141	199	36	14	6	48	87	68	48	25	.377	.404

21 NICK CIUFFO, C

Born: March 7, 1995. **B-T:** L-R. **Ht.:** 6-1. **Wt.:** 205. **Drafted:** HS—Lexington, S.C., 2013 (1st round). **Signed by:** Brian Hickman.

BA GRADE
40 Risk: Medium

Ciuffo's steady and methodical climb through the minors since he was the 21st overall selection in the 2013 draft continued at Montgomery in 2017, his first season in Double-A. He has been named the organization's defensive player of the year in each of the past two seasons.

Ciuffo displays soft hands, moves well behind the plate, and works exceptionally well with pitchers. He threw out 38 percent of basestealers after nailing 59 percent in 2016. He has well-above-average arm strength with a quick release and accuracy. He also possesses above-average receiving skills, displaying good footwork with the ability to block pitches and frame the ball well. Drafted with an eye on his lefthanded bat, Ciuffo's offensive production has lagged behind his defense, but he continues to show power potential in batting practice with above-average bat speed. He uses an up-the-middle approach, and could hit for some power as he sharpens his ability to drive the ball.

Ciuffo was left off of the 40-man roster and went unpicked in the Rule 5 draft. He has a chance to be starting catcher in the big leagues if his bat develops. A full season at Triple-A Durham awaits in 2018.

Year	Club (League)	Class	AVG	G	AB	R	H	2B	3B	HR	RBI	BB	SO	SB	CS	OBP	SLG
2015	Bowling Green (MWL)	LoA	.258	94	356	30	92	21	0	1	32	7	55	2	3	.269	.326
2016	Rays (GCL)	R	.067	5	15	1	1	0	0	0	0	2	2	0	0	.176	.067
	Charlotte, FL (FSL)	HiA	.262	59	229	16	60	8	0	0	15	9	45	2	3	.288	.297
2017	Montgomery (SL)	AA	.245	102	371	42	91	29	1	7	42	42	95	2	0	.319	.385
Minor League Totals			.248	355	1322	125	328	71	3	12	134	86	282	8	7	.292	.334

22 JAKE CRONENWORTH, SS

Born: Jan. 21, 1994. **B-T:** L-R. **Ht.:** 5-10. **Wt.:** 170. **Drafted:** Michigan, 2015 (7th round). **Signed by:** James Bonnici.

BA GRADE
45 Risk: High

Players rarely develop the way Cronenworth has in his first three seasons in the Rays system. In college, he served as a closer and filled in as a starting pitcher for Michigan, in addition to playing first and second base. Many teams saw him as a reliever in pro ball, he has moved to shortstop.

An intense player who also excelled in hockey in high school, the smart and savvy Cronenworth is a natural leader with a grinder mentality. He bounced back from a tough second half of 2016 by opening 2017 with a 22-game hitting streak. His offense is ahead of his defense. He has an upright, smooth swing with a good eye at the plate, and he exudes confidence in the box with a sound approach. Cronenworth drives the ball well with his line-drive stroke, does a good job getting on base, and does the little things such as moving runners over. He also cleaned up his defense and improved his arm stroke while further distancing himself from pitching.

Cronenworth has the tool set to contribute in a variety of ways. He'll likely open the 2018 season back at Montgomery, but could see Triple-A Durham and even Tropicana Field later in the year.

Year	Club (League)	Class	AVG	G	AB	R	H	2B	3B	HR	RBI	BB	SO	SB	CS	OBP	SLG
2015	Hudson Valley (NYP)	SS	.291	51	196	31	57	12	3	1	16	31	59	12	7	.399	.398
2016	Charlotte, FL (FSL)	HiA	.171	35	111	15	19	3	1	1	9	13	26	2	1	.270	.243
	Bowling Green (MWL)	LoA	.322	81	314	66	101	15	6	3	48	54	57	12	7	.429	.436
2017	Charlotte, FL (FSL)	HiA	.268	87	328	58	88	16	5	2	29	47	69	12	5	.364	.366
	Montgomery (SL)	AA	.285	38	158	15	45	6	0	1	20	19	19	1	1	.363	.342
Minor League Totals			.280	292	1107	185	310	52	15	8	122	164	230	39	21	.380	.376

23 YONNY CHIRINOS, RHP

Born: Dec. 26, 1993. **B-T:** R-R. **Ht.:** 6-2. **Wt.:** 170. **Signed:** Venezuela, 2012. **Signed by:** Eucildes Vargas/Ronnie Blanco.

BA GRADE
40 Risk: Medium

After entering the 2017 campaign as one of the more unheralded hurlers in the Rays system, Chirinos was tabbed the organization's Minor League Pitcher of the Year after going a combined 13-5, 2.73

between Double-A Montgomery and Triple-A Durham.

Signed as an 18-year-old for just $10,000 out of Venezuela, Chirinos took a big step in 2015 by pitching at three levels in the minors, and continued his ascent over the last two years. He has learned to trust his stuff by pitching to contact, while pounding the lower half of the strike zone to generate ground balls. He throws four-seam and two-seam fastballs, with the former displaying excellent cutting action. His changeup has solid fade when he throws it correctly, but he can be inconsistent with his feel for the pitch. The biggest improvement has been Chirinos' low-to-mid 80s slider that resembles his fastball before tailing away to righthanded batters.

Chirinos is not a power pitcher like many of the organization's top prospects, but he has among the best command in the system. He could compete for a spot in the Rays' rotation as soon as the 2018 season. A swingman role is also a distinct possibility.

Year	Club (League)	Class	W	L	ERA	G	GS	CG	SV	IP	H	HR	BB	SO	K/9	WHIP	AVG
2015	Charlotte, FL (FSL)	HiA	0	0	0.00	2	0	0	0	3	2	0	0	3	9.0	0.67	.182
	Hudson Valley (NYP)	SS	1	0	0.60	3	3	0	0	15	10	1	3	14	8.4	0.87	.182
	Bowling Green (MWL)	LoA	4	5	2.20	10	10	0	0	61	59	3	7	47	6.9	1.08	.252
2016	Bowling Green (MWL)	LoA	1	0	2.31	4	2	0	0	12	8	0	1	9	6.9	0.77	.182
	Charlotte, FL (FSL)	HiA	6	1	2.15	11	7	0	0	50	47	5	3	31	5.5	0.99	.240
	Montgomery (SL)	AA	5	3	4.46	14	8	0	0	67	74	5	12	43	5.8	1.29	.276
2017	Montgomery (SL)	AA	1	0	2.63	4	4	0	0	27	22	5	4	21	6.9	0.95	.225
	Durham (IL)	AAA	12	5	2.74	23	22	1	0	141	116	10	22	120	7.7	0.98	.227
Minor League Totals			36	17	2.75	98	70	1	0	474	436	35	74	363	6.9	1.08	.244

24 RESLY LINARES, LHP

BA GRADE
50 Risk: Extreme

Born: Dec. 11, 1997. **B-T:** L-L. **Ht.:** 6-2. **Wt.:** 170. **Signed:** Dominican Republic, 2014. **Signed by:** Danny Santana.

Linares joins Austin Franklin as the top young Rays pitchers on the verge of taking their prospect status to another level. After the Rays uncharacteristically had him skip the Rookie-level Gulf Coast League in 2016, shortly after signing with Tampa Bay for $275,000 out of the Dominican Republic, Linares excelled in the short-season New York-Penn League last year, limiting hitters to a league-low .171 average.

Linares has a lightning-quick arm with clean mechanics and a repeatable delivery. Featuring an athletic build with plenty of room to add strength to his wiry frame, he possesses solid command of his 89-91 mph fastball and tight curveball that features a hard, late break. His changeup is promising, but he needs to soften the pitch by increasing the depth. Only 20, Linares is learning how to focus on every pitch while discovering how to break down hitters. Those traits should improve as he matures mentally and physically, which makes his potential so intriguing.

Linares is projected to graduate to the full-season ranks in 2018 at low Class A Bowling Green.

Year	Club (League)	Class	W	L	ERA	G	GS	CG	SV	IP	H	HR	BB	SO	K/9	WHIP	AVG
2015	Rays (DSL)	R	0	3	1.11	14	14	0	0	49	29	0	15	59	10.9	0.90	.178
2016	Princeton (APP)	R	2	3	5.34	8	7	0	0	32	40	6	8	30	8.4	1.50	.305
2017	Hudson Valley (NYP)	SS	3	3	2.35	13	12	0	0	61	36	2	23	60	8.8	0.96	.171
Minor League Totals			5	9	2.60	35	33	0	0	142	105	8	46	149	9.4	1.06	.208

25 JOSE DE LEON, RHP

BA GRADE
45 Risk: High

Born: Aug. 7, 1992. **B-T:** R-R. **Ht.:** 6-2. **Wt.:** 190. **Drafted:** Southern, 2013 (24th round). **Signed by:** Matthew Paul (Dodgers).

The baseball world believed that the Rays acquired a possible mid-rotation starter when they landed De Leon from the Dodgers for second baseman Logan Forsythe after the 2016 season. De Leon, however, struggled with injuries throughout the campaign, including three separate stints on the disabled list, beginning with a flexor issue in his right forearm and later a lat strain after being a late addition to Puerto Rico's WBC team.

Although he did throw 2.2 innings for Tampa Bay on May 29 when the big league team was short on pitching, De Leon bounced between Triple-A Durham as well as the Florida State and Gulf Coast leagues, accumulating only 38.1 innings in the process. His inability to get on track in 2017 overshadowed De Leon's potential. He possesses a swing-and-miss arsenal that includes a low-to-mid 90s fastball with late movement, but at times was down to 86-90 mph in 2017. He mixes his heater with a changeup that keeps hitters from both sides of the plate off-balance. His slider also flashes above-average potential, particularly against righthanded hitters. The Rays hope that De Leon is able to open the 2018 season in the Triple-A rotation.

Year	Club (League)	Class	W	L	ERA	G	GS	CG	SV	IP	H	HR	BB	SO	K/9	WHIP	AVG
2015	R. Cucamonga (CAL)	HiA	4	1	1.67	7	7	0	0	38	26	1	8	58	13.9	0.90	.193
	Tulsa (TL)	AA	2	6	3.64	16	16	1	0	77	61	11	29	105	12.3	1.17	.216
2016	Oklahoma City (PCL)	AAA	7	1	2.61	16	16	0	0	86	61	9	20	111	11.6	0.94	.194
	Los Angeles (NL)	MAJ	2	0	6.35	4	4	0	0	17	19	5	7	15	7.9	1.53	.288
2017	Tampa Bay (AL)	MAJ	1	0	10.13	1	0	0	0	3	4	1	3	2	6.8	2.63	.333
	Durham (IL)	AAA	0	2	6.75	3	3	0	0	12	14	1	6	14	10.5	1.67	.292
	Rays (GCL)	R	1	0	0.75	3	2	0	0	12	4	1	1	12	9.0	0.42	.103
	Charlotte, FL (FSL)	HiA	1	0	1.88	4	3	0	0	14	11	0	9	18	11.3	1.40	.216
Major League Totals			3	0	6.86	5	4	0	0	20	23	6	10	17	7.8	1.68	.295
Minor League Totals			25	15	3.32	77	72	1	0	369	302	32	115	490	12.0	1.13	.220

26 RYAN YARBROUGH, LHP

BA GRADE
40 Risk: Medium

Born: Dec. 31, 1992. **B-T:** R-L. **Ht.:** 6-5. **Wt.:** 205. **Drafted:** Old Dominion, 2014 (4th round). **Signed by:** Devitt Moore (Mariners).

A Mariners senior sign, Yarbrough was sent to the Rays in the Drew Smyly trade.

An intelligent pitcher who stays ahead in the count by commanding the strike zone, Yarbrough led the International League in strikeouts. He averaged 9.1 strikeouts per nine innings and walked 2.17 batters per nine, the fifth-best mark on the circuit. Yarbrough uses his 6-foot-5 frame to his advantage by throwing on a downhill plane to generate ground balls with his sinking 87-91 mph fastball. His plus changeup has outstanding deception. He continues to improve the consistency and bite of his slider while staying low in the zone. Yarbrough is tough on lefthanded hitters, limiting them to a .217/.278/.343 slash line.

Yabrough's knocking on the door of the big leagues, where he could contribute as a swingman or situational reliever in 2018.

Year	Club (League)	Class	W	L	ERA	G	GS	CG	SV	IP	H	HR	BB	SO	K/9	WHIP	AVG
2015	Mariners (AZL)	R	0	0	1.80	4	4	0	0	10	11	0	1	13	11.7	1.20	.282
	Clinton (MWL)	LoA	0	1	13.50	2	2	0	0	5	12	0	4	1	1.7	3.00	.462
	Bakersfield (CAL)	HiA	4	7	3.76	16	16	0	0	81	86	7	18	74	8.2	1.28	.266
2016	Jackson (SL)	AA	12	4	2.95	25	25	1	0	128	112	7	31	99	6.9	1.11	.232
2017	Durham (IL)	AAA	13	6	3.43	26	26	0	0	157	144	20	39	159	9.1	1.16	.243
Minor League Totals			29	19	3.22	87	83	1	1	425	391	35	98	404	8.6	1.15	.242

27 CHIH-WEI HU, RHP

BA GRADE
40 Risk: Medium

Born: Nov. 4, 1993. **B-T:** R-R. **Ht.:** 6-1. **Wt.:** 230. **Signed:** Taiwan, 2012. **Signed by:** Cary Broder (Twins).

After three early-season starts, Hu received his first taste of the big leagues in 2017 as a reliever, and remained in the bullpen for the rest of the season. The Rays have liked the resilient Taiwanese righthander since acquiring him from the Twins in 2015 in the Kevin Jepsen deal.

Hu sits 92-93 mph and can touch the mid 90s with his fastball in short stretches. He also features a deep repertoire that few bullpen arms can equal. His above-average changeup has outstanding late depth and is equally effective against righthanded and lefthanded hitters. He also mixes an overhand curveball, a cutter and a palmball that serves as a slower version of his changeup.

With a stocky build and the stamina and willingness to be a workhorse as a multi-inning reliever Hu can give the Rays' bullpen some consistency over the course of the season, beginning as soon as 2018.

Year	Club (League)	Class	W	L	ERA	G	GS	CG	SV	IP	H	HR	BB	SO	K/9	WHIP	AVG
2015	Rochester (IL)	AAA	1	0	1.50	1	1	0	0	6	2	0	4	6	9.0	1.00	.105
	Fort Myers (FSL)	HiA	5	3	2.44	15	15	0	0	85	79	5	19	73	7.8	1.16	.249
	Charlotte, FL (FSL)	HiA	0	3	7.36	5	4	0	1	18	23	1	8	20	9.8	1.69	.315
2016	Durham (IL)	AAA	0	1	7.71	1	1	0	0	5	7	1	2	7	13.5	1.93	.350
	Montgomery (SL)	AA	7	8	2.59	24	24	0	0	143	128	7	36	107	6.8	1.15	.241
2017	Durham (IL)	AAA	4	1	3.06	31	4	0	2	62	59	9	12	57	8.3	1.15	.251
	Tampa Bay (AL)	MAJ	1	1	2.70	6	0	0	0	10	5	2	4	9	8.1	0.90	.143
Major League Totals			1	1	2.70	6	0	0	0	10	5	2	4	9	8.1	0.90	.143
Minor League Totals			27	18	2.79	102	66	0	3	426	373	23	104	373	7.9	1.12	.235

28 JAIME SCHULTZ, RHP

BA GRADE
45 Risk: High

Born: June 20, 1991. **B-T:** R-R. **Ht.:** 5-10. **Wt.:** 200. **Drafted:** High Point, 2013 (14th round). **Signed by:** Brian Hickman.

Schultz was on the verge of contributing at the major league level in 2017 before a groin injury suffered in his initial outing of the regular season ruined his year.

Undersized for a righthander, Schultz generates pure power with a 94-95 mph fastball that flirts with the upper-90s and possesses hard armside run. He also has a plus swing-and-miss curveball that he throws from different arm slots while generating sharp, late movement. His changeup is solid average, and he uses it primarily as a show pitch.

Both command and control are Schultz's greatest shortcomings, although he displayed improvement in those areas when healthy. He projects favorably as a big league reliever who could possibly close if he continues to improve his control.

Year	Club (League)	Class	W	L	ERA	G	GS	CG	SV	IP	H	HR	BB	SO	K/9	WHIP	AVG
2015	Montgomery (SL)	AA	9	5	3.67	27	27	0	0	135	105	11	90	168	11.2	1.44	.218
2016	Durham (IL)	AAA	5	7	3.58	27	27	0	0	131	113	12	68	163	11.2	1.39	.236
2017	Rays (GCL)	R	0	0	0.00	3	1	0	0	4	3	0	0	4	9.8	0.82	.200
	Charlotte, FL (FSL)	HiA	0	1	6.23	3	0	0	1	4	4	1	2	7	14.5	1.38	.250
	Durham (IL)	AAA	1	0	3.86	13	0	0	0	12	10	1	4	21	16.2	1.20	.222
Minor League Totals			20	16	3.37	104	79	0	1	390	313	30	222	497	11.5	1.37	.222

29 DIEGO CASTILLO, RHP

Born: Jan. 18, 1994. **B-T:** R-R. **Ht.:** 6-3. **Wt.:** 195. **Signed:** Dominican Republic, 2014. **Signed by:** Braly Guzman/Danny Santana.

BA GRADE
40 Risk: Medium

Castillo has moved rapidly through the Rays organization since signing for $64,000 out of the Dominican Republic as a 20-year-old in 2014. He has received in-season promotions in each of the past three campaigns, and parlayed a strong performance in the Arizona Fall League in 2016 into stints at Double-A Montgomery and Triple-A Durham in 2017.

In 71.2 combined innings, the chunky, hard-throwing righthander went 15-for-18 in save opportunities, including saves in both the Governors' Cup-clinching victory and the Triple-A national championship game. Castillo is a classic fastball/slider, high-effort reliever who has touched 101 mph with his four-seamer. He generates a lot of ground balls but tends to give up a fair number of hits when hitters start making contact. Castillo has good overall control and command, but gets in trouble when he overthrows, reducing the movement on his pitches. Despite his late-season success as a closer, Castillo profiles better as a high-leverage reliever. He will compete for a job in the Rays bullpen in 2018.

Year	Club (League)	Class	W	L	ERA	G	GS	CG	SV	IP	H	HR	BB	SO	K/9	WHIP	AVG
2015	Hudson Valley (NYP)	SS	1	2	2.31	13	0	0	4	23	19	1	7	24	9.3	1.11	.216
	Bowling Green (MWL)	LoA	0	0	4.82	5	0	0	1	9	8	0	4	4	3.9	1.29	.229
2016	Bowling Green (MWL)	LoA	1	3	2.03	24	0	0	7	40	34	1	11	50	11.3	1.13	.221
	Charlotte, FL (FSL)	HiA	2	3	4.87	14	0	0	3	20	28	3	6	17	7.5	1.67	.326
2017	Montgomery (SL)	AA	1	3	1.86	21	0	0	8	29	20	1	7	32	9.9	0.93	.189
	Durham (IL)	AAA	3	2	3.38	30	1	0	7	43	38	2	13	58	12.2	1.20	.235
Minor League Totals			11	16	3.04	125	1	0	32	190	173	8	59	211	10.0	1.22	.238

30 IAN GIBAUT, RHP

Born: Nov. 11, 1993. **B-T:** R-R. **Ht.:** 6-3. **Wt.:** 235. **Drafted:** Tulane, 2015, (11th round). **Signed by:** Rickey Drexler.

BA GRADE
45 Risk: High

Gibaut spent the final four months of last year as a dominant force in Double-A Montgomery's bullpen. A closer throughout his three-year stint at Tulane, Gibaut saved 10 of 15 opportunities with the Biscuits, but profiles more as a setup man at the major league level.

Gibaut throws a fastball, slider and changeup, with his four-seamer sitting in the mid-90s and touching 97 mph. His power slider has a chance to be a difference-maker, but he's not consistent enough with the pitch to keep hitters from sitting on his fastball. His changeup, meanwhile, is nasty when he throws it correctly, and it works well in keeping hitters off-balance. Gibaut is equally dominant against righthanded and lefthanded batters, but lacks command and has struggled to find a consistent alignment in his stride with his landing foot. He also tends to leave pitches up in the strike zone.

Gibault will open 2018 at Triple-A Durham with a chance to make his big league debut during the year.

Year	Club (League)	Class	W	L	ERA	G	GS	CG	SV	IP	H	HR	BB	SO	K/9	WHIP	AVG
2015	Princeton (APP)	R	3	1	2.12	12	0	0	1	30	23	2	8	38	11.5	1.04	.213
2016	Bowling Green (MWL)	LoA	1	0	0.93	7	0	0	1	10	6	0	1	18	16.8	0.72	.171
	Charlotte, FL (FSL)	HiA	1	2	2.85	27	0	0	3	47	45	2	19	45	8.6	1.35	.253
2017	Charlotte, FL (FSL)	HiA	1	0	2.16	5	0	0	2	8	5	0	1	14	15.1	0.72	.172
	Montgomery (SL)	AA	6	1	2.22	43	0	0	10	53	33	6	26	63	10.8	1.12	.174
Minor League Totals			12	4	2.32	94	0	0	17	148	112	10	55	178	10.8	1.13	.207

Texas Rangers

BY BEN BADLER

Where do the Rangers go from here? Texas went to the playoffs five times in a seven-season stretch from 2010-16, including two World Series trips.

In 2017, the Rangers went backwards. They finished 78-84 and in fourth place in the American League West, just three games ahead of the last-place Athletics. And what was once a perennially robust farm system has thinned considerably. Some of that is due to graduations, while trades have sent former top prospects like outfielders Lewis Brinson to the Brewers and Nick Williams to the Phillies.

It is unclear if the Rangers are ready to rebound in 2018, or a larger rebuild is necessary. There is a core of young talent on the major league club. Shortstop Elvis Andrus is in his prime. Second baseman Rougned Odor regressed in 2017, but will still be just 24 in 2018. A breakthrough from Odor or 23-year-old right fielder Nomar Mazara would be huge, as would continued progress from 24-year-old Joey Gallo, who flashed star potential in the second half of 2017.

Adding No. 1 prospect Willie Calhoun to a lineup that includes Adrian Beltre, too, and the Rangers have reason to be optimistic about their 2018 offense.

Their pitching, however, remains dicey. Cole Hamels is 34 and looked more like a midrotation starter than the ace he had been in previous years. The rest of the pitching staff is full of back-end starters, and the farm system isn't going to deliver anyone with potential beyond that in 2018.

Lefthander Yohander Mendez should help, but the highest ceiling arms in the organization—2017 second-round righthander Hans Crouse and 2016 first-round lefthander Cole Ragans—are high school products who have yet to pitch in a full-season league. Righthander Kyle Cody, a 2016 sixth-rounder out of Kentucky, was one of best development stories in the system in 2017 but probably won't factor into the 2018 picture, while lefthander Joe Palumbo had an exciting start to the 2017 season but is still rehabbing from Tommy John surgery.

There aren't any strong signals of a rebuild in Texas yet. Beyond Calhoun, the most exciting talent in the system is still in the lower levels, starting with center fielder Leody Taveras. He is a dynamic talent with a chance for five average to plus tools, but like Crouse and Ragans, is still years away from the big leagues.

So are Texas' two first-round picks from 2017, high school shortstop Chris Seise and toolsy teenaged outfielder Bubba Thompson. The same

Joey Gallo blasted 41 home runs in 2017 and shined in the second half with a .929 OPS.

PROJECTED 2021 LINEUP

Catcher	Matt Whatley (25)
First Base	Ronald Guzman (26)
Second Base	Rougned Odor (27)
Third Base	Joey Gallo (27)
Shortstop	Elvis Andrus (32)
Left Field	Miguel Aparicio (22)
Center Field	Leody Taveras (22)
Right Field	Nomar Mazara (26)
Designated Hitter	Willie Calhoun (26)
No. 1 Starter	Hans Crouse (22)
No. 2 Starter	Cole Ragans (23)
No. 3 Starter	Cole Hamels (37)
No. 4 Starter	Yohander Mendez (26)
No. 5 Starter	Kyle Cody (26)
Closer	Keone Kela (28)

applies to Venezuelan outfielder Miguel Aparicio.

It puts the Rangers in a difficult spot. There isn't a need for them to go on a complete tear down. There are enough young hitters on the major league team to build around—both for 2018 and beyond—but a lot would have to break right for the club to return to the postseason in 2018.

So heading into the 2018 season, the Rangers don't have a clear direction. By July, that should change. There's a chance they can regroup from 2017, giving Beltre another postseason appearance at the end of his Hall of Fame career.

But if they're out of contention by midseason, the Rangers will have to take a step back to rebuild the minor league pipeline.

DEPTH CHART

TEXAS RANGERS

TOP 2018 ROOKIE: Willie Calhoun, OF. The Rangers will figure out where to play him—left field or DH—but he's a gifted hitter whose bat control and power should impact games.

BREAKOUT PROSPECT: Tyreque Reed, 1B. Reed annihilated pitchers in junior college and the Rookie-level Arizona League, with the swing and power combination to translate.

SLEEPER: Yohel Pozo, C. While his power is limited, but he's a catcher with an innate feel for putting the barrel to the baseball.

SOURCE OF TOP 30 TALENT			
Homegrown	26	Acquired	3
College	4	Trade	2
Junior college	5	Rule 5 draft	1
High school	7	Independent league	0
Nondrafted free agent	0	Free agent/waivers	0
International	11		

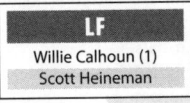

LF
Willie Calhoun (1)
Scott Heineman

CF
Leody Taveras (2)
Miguel Aparicio (8)
Bubba Thompson (9)
Carlos Tocci (13)
Pedro Gonzalez (24)
Jose Cardona
Eric Jenkins

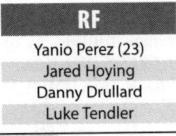

RF
Yanio Perez (23)
Jared Hoying
Danny Drullard
Luke Tendler

3B
Drew Robinson (14)
Isiah Kiner-Falefa
Brendon Davis
Luis Yander La O
Juremi Profar
Kole Enright
Yenci Pena

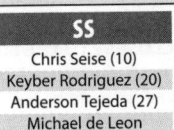

SS
Chris Seise (10)
Keyber Rodriguez (20)
Anderson Tejeda (27)
Michael de Leon

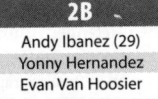

2B
Andy Ibanez (29)
Yonny Hernandez
Evan Van Hoosier

1B
Ronald Guzman (6)
Tyreque Reed (15)

C
Matt Whatley (12)
David Garcia (16)
Josh Morgan (22)
Jose Trevino (28)
Yohel Pozo
Melvin Novoa
Brett Nicholas
Carlos Garay

LHP

LHSP	**LHRP**
Cole Ragans (4)	C.D. Pelham (19)
Yohander Mendez (5)	Jeffrey Springs
Joe Palumbo (11)	
Brett Martin (18)	

RHP

RHSP	**RHRP**
Hans Crouse (3)	Nick Gardewine (21)
Kyle Cody (7)	Ricardo Rodriguez
Jonathan Hernandez (17)	Connor Sadzeck
A.J. Alexy (25)	Joe Kuzia
Alex Speas (26)	Jairo Beras
Michael Matuella (30)	
Ariel Jurado	
Ryan Dease	
Edgar Arredondo	
Collin Wiles	
Tyler Phillips	

DRAFT ANALYSIS

2017

BEST PURE HITTER: SS Chris Seise (1) dominated the Arizona League for 27 games to the tune of a .336/.395/.509 triple slash and earned a promotion to the Northwest League. He understandably struggled there but showed the ability to adjust, going 11-for-29 to finish the season.

BEST POWER HITTER: 1B/OF Tyreque Reed (8) dominated in the spring with Itawamba (Miss.) JC, slugging .943 and has 70-grade raw power that comes from a very short stroke out of a big, 6-foot-2, 260-pound frame. He's still learning to translate that power with wood but slugged .617 in his pro debut, impressing the Rangers with the average exit velocity of his contact.

FASTEST RUNNER: At least a 60-grade runner when healthy, OF Bubba Thompson (1) dealt with knee issues this summer, though anti-inflammatory drugs kept him in the lineup for 30 games. Texas never saw its top pick at full throttle, but when he's fully healthy has a chance to be a dangerous player on the bases and a talented defensive center fielder.

BEST DEFENSIVE PLAYER: C Matt Whatley (3) came as advertised as a polished defender behind the plate, throwing out 33 percent of base stealers during his pro debut. He's an above-average receiver, thrower and game-caller. His competitiveness and high energy should allow him to quickly pickup the nuances of pro ball quickly.

BEST FASTBALL: Used in two-inning stints in his pro debut, RHP Hans Crouse (2) showed off a fastball that routinely sat in the 96-99 mph range. Even in longer stints, it's easily a plus-plus offering already.

BEST SECONDARY PITCH: Crouse has above-average feel for his slider and manipulates the pitch, changing both its speed and shape to get more 12-to-6 movement at times and more of a sweep at others.

BEST PRO DEBUT: Crouse held opposing hitters to a .109 average while posting a 0.45 ERA and striking out 30 in 20 innings. His ultra-competitive mindset hasn't affected him in any negative

TOP DRAFT PICKS OF THE DECADE

Year	Player, Pos.	2017 Org
2008	Justin Smoak, 1B	Blue Jays
2009	*Matt Purke, LHP	White Sox
2010	Kellin Deglan, C	Yankees
2011	Kevin Matthews, LHP	Braves
2012	Lewis Brinson, OF	Brewers
2013	Chi Chi Gonzalez, RHP	Rangers
2014	Luis Ortiz, RHP	Brewers
2015	Dillon Tate, RHP	Yankees
2016	Cole Ragans, LHP	Rangers
2017	Bubba Thompson, OF	Rangers

* Did not sign

way off-the-field, with coaches and teammates alike loving him. Reed hit .350/.455/.617 with 20 extra-base hits in just 120 at-bats.

BEST ATHLETE: Crouse's athleticism gives him a decent argument, but Thompson gets the nod as one of the most athletic players in the draft class.

MOST INTRIGUING BACKGROUND: SS Myles McKisic (23) will never be faulted for lack of determination. The Florida prep product spent his free time coaching summer ball lessons to pay for his travel baseball expenses prior to getting drafted.

CLOSEST TO THE MAJORS: Crouse has a unique blend of power, strike throwing skills and finesse, and he could be fast-tracked if the Rangers decide they need him out of the bullpen. At the moment, the team is committed to developing him as a starter.

BEST LATE-ROUND PICK: RHP Ricky Vanasco (15) struck out 16 of the 41 batters he faced in the Rookie-level Arizona League. Signed for $200,000, he gets excellent extension that helps his four pitches—fastball, curveball, slider, changeup—none of which is consistently average, play up.

THE ONE WHO GOT AWAY: The Rangers knew they weren't going to sign Arkansas righthander Blaine Knight (29) but drafted him late anyways. Knight was rated as BA's No. 87 prospect prior to the 2017 draft and ranks No. 21 on BA's 2018 Top 100 College Prospects list.

—CARLOS COLLAZO

2016

LHP Cole Ragans (1) ranked as the top prospect in the Northwest League in his first full season of pro ball. RHP Kyle Cody (6) was one of the system's biggest success in 2017, while RHP Alex Speas (2) scuffled in short-season ball.

GRADE: C

2015

RHP Dillon Tate (1) has righted himself in the Yankees' system after being dealt in 2016. LHP C.D. Pelham (33) has emerged as a hard-throwing reliever, while RHP Michael Matuella (3) took a step forward with a healthy year.

GRADE: C

2014

RHP Luis Ortiz (1) was used in the Jonathan Lucroy trade and continues to progress in the Brewers' system. SS Josh Morgan (3) and LHP Brett Martin (4) continue to show flashes, but neither has put it all together yet.

GRADE: C

1 WILLIE CALHOUN, OF/2B

Born: Nov. 4, 1994. **B-T:** L-R. **Ht.:** 5-8. **Wt.:** 195. **Drafted:** Yavapai (Ariz) JC, 2015 (4th round). **Signed by:** Dustin Yount (Dodgers).

The Rays drafted Calhoun in the 17th round of the 2013 draft, but he opted to go to college instead. He played his freshman year at Arizona, then went to the Cape Cod League that summer. He returned to campus in the fall, but after being dismissed for academic reasons, Calhoun transferred to Yavapai (Ariz.) JC in 2015 and led all junior college hitters with 31 home runs. After the season, Calhoun signed with the Dodgers for $347,500 as a fourth-round pick and immediately showed his bat would translate. In 2017, Calhoun was continuing to rake at Triple-A when the Dodgers dealt him to the Rangers as the centerpiece of the Yu Darvish trade. He stayed in the Pacific Coast League after the trade, then made his big league debut as a September callup.

Calhoun has a smaller, stocky frame, but frequent reminders he's too small or too slow help fuel his motivation. Calhoun is one of the most talented hitting prospects in game, with an outstanding combination of barrel control and power. He has great rhythm and balance in the batter's box, quick hands and powerful hip rotation. He has good hand-eye coordination and a compact swing that stays on plane through the hitting zone for a long time. He has great plate coverage, with little problem handling premium velocity or barreling breaking pitches. He seldom swings and misses and struck out just 11 percent of the time at Triple-A. He hit 32 home runs in 2017 and could be a 35-plus home run threat in the big leagues. Calhoun's stature gives him a smaller strike zone to cover, and he doesn't expand it by chasing much. He tried playing second base with the Dodgers, but he's a well below-average runner with a below-average arm who didn't show much range at the position and often struggled to make routine plays. Calhoun showed some signs of progress in 2017, but in June the Dodgers started getting him work in left field. After joining the Rangers, Calhoun played left field almost exclusively.

The Rangers still plan to give Calhoun reps at second base, but Rougned Odor will force him to develop into an adequate left fielder. Calhoun will either DH or give away some runs with his defense, but he will create plenty of them with his bat. He's ready for an everyday job in Texas.

JOHN WILLIAMSON

BA GRADE	SCOUTING GRADES
55 Risk: Medium	HIT: 60. POW: 60. SPD: 30. FLD: 30. ARM: 40.

Projected future grades on 20-80 scouting scale

TOP PROSPECTS OF THE DECADE

Year	Player, Pos.	2017 Org
2008	Elvis Andrus, SS	Rangers
2009	Neftali Feliz, RHP	Royals
2010	Neftali Feliz, RHP	Royals
2011	Martin Perez, LHP	Rangers
2012	Jurickson Profar, SS	Rangers
2013	Jurickson Profar, SS/2B	Rangers
2014	Rougned Odor, 2B	Rangers
2015	Joey Gallo, 3B	Rangers
2016	Joey Gallo, 3B	Rangers
2017	Leody Taveras ,OF	Rangers

BEST TOOLS

Best Hitter for Average	Willie Calhoun
Best Power Hitter	Willie Calhoun
Best Strike-Zone Discipline	Drew Robinson
Fastest Baserunner	Bubba Thompson
Best Athlete	Bubba Thompson
Best Fastball	Hans Crouse
Best Curveball	A.J. Alexy
Best Slider	Kyle Cody
Best Changeup	Yohander Mendez
Best Control	Collin Wiles
Best Defensive Catcher	Jose Trevino
Best Defensive Infielder	Michael de Leon
Best Infield Arm	Anderson Tejeda
Best Defensive Outfielder	Leody Taveras
Best Outfield Arm	Leody Taveras

Year	Club (League)	Class	AVG	G	AB	R	H	2B	3B	HR	RBI	BB	SO	SB	CS	OBP	SLG
2015	Ogden (PIO)	R	.278	38	151	28	42	13	1	7	26	23	18	2	1	.371	.517
	Great Lakes (MWL)	LoA	.393	15	61	9	24	3	0	1	8	5	7	0	0	.439	.492
	R. Cucamonga (CAL)	HiA	.329	20	73	11	24	7	0	3	14	7	13	0	0	.390	.548
2016	Tulsa (TL)	AA	.254	132	503	75	128	25	1	27	88	45	65	0	0	.318	.469
2017	Oklahoma City (PCL)	AAA	.298	99	373	64	111	24	5	23	67	36	49	3	2	.357	.574
	Round Rock (PCL)	AAA	.310	29	113	16	35	3	1	8	26	6	12	1	0	.345	.566
	Texas (AL)	MAJ	.265	13	34	3	9	0	0	1	4	2	7	0	0	.324	.353
Major League Totals			**.265**	**13**	**34**	**3**	**9**	**0**	**0**	**1**	**4**	**2**	**7**	**0**	**0**	**.324**	**.353**
Minor League Totals			**.286**	**333**	**1274**	**203**	**364**	**75**	**8**	**69**	**229**	**122**	**164**	**6**	**3**	**.348**	**.520**

2 LEODY TAVERAS, OF

Born: Sept. 8, 1998. **B-T:** B-R. **Ht.:** 6-2. **Wt.:** 185. **Signed:** Dominican Republic, 2015. **Signed by:** Willy Espinal/Gil Kim/Thad Levine.

BA GRADE

60 Risk: V. High

HIT: 55. **POW:** 50. **SPD:** 60. **FLD:** 60. **ARM:** 60.

Taveras, a cousin of former big league center fielder Willy Taveras, signed for $2.1 million as a 16-year-old in 2015 and has shown the most upside of any prospect in the Rangers' system. Pushed to the low Class A South Atlantic League as an 18-year-old, Taveras' performance was modest but he still stood out as one of the league's premium prospects.

Taveras has a chance for five average to plus tools at a premium position. He has a simple, balanced swing from both sides, using his hands well to generate bat speed and a clean swing path. Taveras makes frequent contact and stays through the ball well, which allows him to use the whole field, and he could develop into a plus hitter. His strike-zone discipline continued to improve in 2017 and he started to flash more pop, with a lean, projectable frame that should help him develop average power. Taveras glides around center field with plus speed, good instincts and quick reads off the bat to go with a plus arm that's accurate.

Taveras has more risk than Willie Calhoun and is still a few years away, but if it all comes together he has a chance to be a cornerstone player and perennial all-star candidate. His aggressive path continues in 2018 at high Class A Down East.

Year	Club (League)	Class	AVG	G	AB	R	H	2B	3B	HR	RBI	BB	SO	SB	CS	OBP	SLG
2016	Rangers2 (DSL)	R	.385	11	39	6	15	2	2	0	9	6	5	4	3	.467	.538
	Rangers (AZL)	R	.278	33	144	22	40	6	3	1	15	11	24	11	4	.329	.382
	Spokane (NWL)	SS	.228	29	123	14	28	6	1	0	9	8	26	3	1	.271	.293
2017	Hickory (SAL)	LoA	.249	134	522	73	130	20	7	8	50	47	92	20	6	.312	.360
Minor League Totals			.257	207	828	115	213	34	13	9	83	72	147	38	14	.316	.362

3 HANS CROUSE, RHP

Born: Sept. 15, 1998. **B-T:** L-R. **Ht.:** 6-4. **Wt.:** 180. **Drafted:** HS—Dana Point, Calif., 2017 (2nd round). **Signed by:** Steve Flores.

BILL MITCHELL

BA GRADE

60 Risk: Extreme

FB: 70. **SL:** 60. **CHG:** 45. **CTL:** 60.

A fiery competitor who pitched for USA Baseball's 18U National Team in 2016, Crouse passed up a Southern California commitment and signed for $1.45 million as a second-round pick, No. 66 overall, in 2017. He completely overmatched Rookie-level Arizona League hitters in his pro debut after signing, allowing seven hits and one earned run in 20 innings while recording 30 strikeouts.

Crouse has the most upside of any pitcher in the Rangers organization. He has great arm speed on a power fastball that sits 93-96 mph and can reach 99, with Crouse cruising in that upper range in short stints in the AZL. His slider has tight spin, sharp bite and two-plane depth, giving him a putaway pitch. Crouse didn't throw his firm changeup much in high school so it's still below-average, but it shows promise with its late fading action. Crouse's delivery certainly isn't free and easy, with long arm action, a short stride and a violent finish across his body. However, Crouse repeats his arm slot well and is able to locate his fastball to both sides of the plate, with his long arms and legs flying at the hitter helping to enhance his deception.

Crouse has frontline starter potential, though he's at least a few years away from reaching the majors. Low Class A Hickory is next.

Year	Club (League)	Class	W	L	ERA	G	GS	CG	SV	IP	H	HR	BB	SO	K/9	WHIP	AVG
2017	Rangers (AZL)	R	0	0	0.45	10	6	0	0	20	7	1	7	30	13.5	0.70	.109
Minor League Totals			0	0	0.45	10	6	0	0	20	7	1	7	30	13.5	0.70	.109

4 COLE RAGANS, LHP

Born: Dec. 12, 1997. **B-T:** L-L. **Ht.:** 6-4. **Wt.:** 195. **Drafted:** HS—Tallahassee, Fla., 2016 (1st round). **Signed by:** Brett Campbell.

A first-round pick, No. 30 overall, in 2016, Ragans stayed back in extended spring training before pitching in the short-season Northwest League, where he ranked as the league's top prospect.

Hitters frequently find themselves off balance against Ragans, who throws off their timing with a promising fastball/changeup combination. Ragans throws his fastball at 89-93 mph and touches 95. It's solid velocity from the left side and plays up because of his fastball life, as its high spin rate allows him to get swings and misses when he elevates. Ragans fools batters with a plus changeup in the low-80s that has excellent separation off of his fastball. His curveball was more of a weapon in high school, but it's now a fringe-average pitch that's soft and sometimes loopy that he needs to tighten. Ragans creates good angle and hides the ball well in his delivery by keeping his front side closed, but he has to do a better job of repeating his mechanics because his control lags behind.

Ragans has the stuff to be a mid-rotation starter if he can throw more strikes. He's ready for his first full-season test with low Class A Hickory.

BA GRADE
55 Risk: V. High
FB: 55. CB: 50.
CHG: 60.
CTL: 50.

Year	Club (League)	Class	W	L	ERA	G	GS	CG	SV	IP	H	HR	BB	SO	K/9	WHIP	AVG
2016	Rangers (AZL)	R	0	0	4.70	4	2	0	0	8	11	0	6	9	10.6	2.22	.344
2017	Spokane (NWL)	SS	3	2	3.61	13	13	0	0	57	50	5	35	87	13.7	1.48	.234
Minor League Totals			**3**	**2**	**3.74**	**17**	**15**	**0**	**0**	**65**	**61**	**5**	**41**	**96**	**13.3**	**1.57**	**.248**

5 YOHANDER MENDEZ, LHP

Born: Jan. 17, 1995. **B-T:** L-L. **Ht.:** 6-5. **Wt.:** 200. **Signed:** Venezuela, 2011. **Signed by:** Rafic Saab/Pedro Avila/Mike Daly.

Mendez reached Triple-A in 2016 and pitched in two games out of the big league bullpen at the end of the season, but the Rangers sent him to Double-A Frisco in 2017 to have him focus on fastball command. He threw a career-high 150 innings, an important step for his durability given his previous injuries, and came back up to Texas as a September callup.

Mendez's bread-and-butter is his 80-84 changeup, a plus pitch he relies on heavily to catch hitters leaning out front for either a whiff or soft contact. For the first 10 starts of the season, the Rangers told Mendez he couldn't throw his changeup until he got to a two-strike count. Mendez already had good control, but the Rangers wanted to emphasize using his 90-95 fastball and hitting his spots with that pitch. The plan worked, as Mendez threw more strikes and missed even more bats in the second half. He throws a fringe-average slider and an occasional curveball that's below-average, but he mostly leans on his fastball/changeup combination.

Mendez showed promising signs that he can handle a starter's workload and the Rangers plan to keep him in that role. He should compete for a spot in Texas' rotation in 2018 and could settle in as a back-of-the-rotation starter.

BA GRADE
45 Risk: Medium
FB: 55. CB: 40.
SL: 45. CHG: 60.
CTL: 55.

Year	Club (League)	Class	W	L	ERA	G	GS	CG	SV	IP	H	HR	BB	SO	K/9	WHIP	AVG
2015	Hickory (SAL)	LoA	3	3	2.44	21	8	0	3	66	57	2	15	74	10.0	1.09	.230
2016	High Desert (CAL)	HiA	4	1	2.45	7	7	0	0	33	21	2	11	45	12.3	0.97	.176
	Frisco (TL)	AA	4	1	3.09	10	10	0	0	47	39	2	14	46	8.9	1.14	.228
	Round Rock (PCL)	AAA	4	1	0.57	7	4	0	0	31	12	0	16	22	6.3	0.89	.119
	Texas (AL)	MAJ	0	0	18.00	2	0	0	0	3	5	0	2	0	0.0	2.33	.333
2017	Frisco (TL)	AA	7	8	3.79	24	24	1	0	138	114	23	43	124	8.1	1.14	.229
	Texas (AL)	MAJ	0	1	5.11	7	0	0	0	12	13	3	3	7	5.1	1.30	.271
Major League Totals			**0**	**1**	**7.63**	**9**	**0**	**0**	**0**	**15**	**18**	**3**	**5**	**7**	**4.1**	**1.50**	**.286**
Minor League Totals			**28**	**18**	**2.89**	**101**	**83**	**1**	**3**	**430**	**344**	**38**	**133**	**404**	**8.4**	**1.11**	**.220**

6 RONALD GUZMAN, 1B

Born: Oct. 20, 1994. **B-T:** L-L. **Ht.:** 6-6. **Wt.:** 220. **Signed:** Dominican Republic, 2011. **Signed by:** Willy Espinal/Mike Daly.

It's the seventh Prospect Handbook appearance for Guzman, who signed for $3.45 million as a 16-year-old in 2011. Guzman spent all of 2017 with Triple-A Round Rock, where he set a career-high walk rate and cut down on his strikeout rate from 2016.

Guzman has a huge frame but a hit-over-power profile. Earlier in his career, Guzman got himself in trouble when he got away from his strengths and tried to yank the ball for power, but in 2017 he stayed with a balanced, all-fields approach. Gaining more hitting knowledge has helped and so has being able to learn how to keep his long limbs in sync to maintain a repeatable swing. Guzman has a big strike zone to cover but doesn't swing and miss much and has a sound eye for discerning balls and strikes. Guzman has average raw power, which is less than the traditional first-base profile, never topping more than 16 home runs in a minor league season. He has made significant defensive strides at first baseman, where he's a huge target and turns errant throws from his infielders into outs, but his range and mobility are limited.

The Rangers used Joey Gallo at first base down the stretch in 2017, so Guzman could end up starting 2018 back in Triple-A but should make his major league debut at some point this season.

BA GRADE

45 Risk: Medium

HIT: 55. POW: 50.
SPD: 30. FLD: 50.
ARM: 40.

Year	Club (League)	Class	AVG	G	AB	R	H	2B	3B	HR	RBI	BB	SO	SB	CS	OBP	SLG
2015	Hickory (SAL)	LoA	.309	24	97	10	30	3	0	3	14	6	15	2	0	.346	.433
	High Desert (CAL)	HiA	.277	107	422	54	117	25	7	9	73	27	101	3	0	.319	.434
2016	Frisco (TL)	AA	.288	102	375	51	108	16	5	15	56	33	82	2	1	.348	.477
	Round Rock (PCL)	AAA	.216	25	88	9	19	5	1	1	11	6	23	0	1	.266	.330
2017	Round Rock (PCL)	AAA	.298	125	470	78	140	22	3	12	62	47	85	4	1	.372	.434
Minor League Totals			.274	602	2282	294	626	126	19	51	338	186	482	24	7	.332	.413

7 KYLE CODY, RHP

Born: Aug. 9, 1994. **B-T:** R-R. **Ht.:** 6-7. **Wt.:** 245. **Drafted:** Kentucky, 2016 (6th round). **Signed by:** Mike Medici.

The Twins drafted Cody in the supplemental second round in 2015, but he returned to Kentucky instead for his senior season and went to the Rangers in the sixth round of the 2016 draft. Cody became one of the Rangers' biggest developmental success stories in 2017, pitching well at two Class A levels.

Cody has an extra-large frame at 6-foot-7, 245 pounds and drops the ball downhill with a lively fastball from 93-97 mph. He has a plus slider that comes out of his hand looking like a fastball until it snaps off at the end with late tilt and sharp action. Cody could lean heavily on his slider to get outs at the lower levels, but the Ranges instead forced him to pitch only with his fastball the first time through the order early in the season to help him improve his fastball command and learn how to attack hitters. They took off those restrictions in the second half, and Cody posted a 1.32 ERA with a 76-20 strikeout-to-walk mark over 61.1 innings in his final 10 starts. His changeup improved in 2017, but it's still a fringe-average pitch he needs to develop.

BA GRADE

50 Risk: High

FB: 60. SL: 60.
CHG: 45.
CTL: 50.

Cody has the stuff to become a No. 3 or 4 starter. He'll likely return to high Class A Down East to begin 2018, but he should be in the upper levels soon and be ready to help the major league club in 2019.

Year	Club (League)	Class	W	L	ERA	G	GS	CG	SV	IP	H	HR	BB	SO	K/9	WHIP	AVG
2016	Spokane (NWL)	SS	2	5	5.13	12	9	0	0	47	56	4	13	53	10.1	1.46	.293
2017	Hickory (SAL)	LoA	6	6	2.83	18	18	0	0	95	77	4	33	101	9.5	1.15	.218
	Down East (CAR)	HiA	3	0	2.05	5	5	0	0	31	25	0	10	35	10.3	1.14	.225
Minor League Totals			11	11	3.32	35	32	0	0	173	158	8	56	189	9.8	1.23	.241

8 MIGUEL APARICIO, OF

Born: March 7, 1999. **B-T:** L-L. **Ht.:** 6-0. **Wt.:** 180. **Signed:** Venezuela, 2015. **Signed by:** Jhonny Gomez/Rafic Saab.

Signed for $500,000 in 2015, Aparicio was just 18 in 2017, but he played so well in extended spring training the Rangers decided to push him to low Class A Hickory in May. He stumbled there but he looked comfortable when he went down to play at short-season Spokane in the college-heavy Northwest League.

Aparicio's all-around game awareness is well beyond his years. His speed and arm strength are both fringe-average, but even without explosive athleticism, he can handle center field because of his top-shelf instincts. Other center fielders have more closing speed, but Aparicio has a quick first step, gets excellent jumps off the bat and takes sharp routes to the ball. Aparicio is a high-contact hitter with good hand-eye coordination and a short, efficient swing. He gained more awareness of the timing with his leg kick as the season progressed and showed a line-drive, all-fields approach. His power mostly goes for doubles right now, with a chance to grow into 10-15 homers.

BA GRADE
50 Risk: High
HIT: 60. POW: 40.
SPD: 45. FLD: 55.
ARM: 45.

Aparicio is ready to return to Hickory in 2018. He could develop into an everyday center fielder along the lines of Gerardo Parra, albeit with less arm strength.

Year	Club (League)	Class	AVG	G	AB	R	H	2B	3B	HR	RBI	BB	SO	SB	CS	OBP	SLG
2016	Rangers2 (DSL)	R	.274	58	219	32	60	10	4	3	36	18	36	15	7	.337	.397
2017	Hickory (SAL)	LoA	.176	25	85	6	15	2	2	0	9	7	18	1	2	.255	.247
	Spokane (NWL)	SS	.293	70	294	47	86	12	3	4	33	16	39	2	8	.333	.395
Minor League Totals			.269	153	598	85	161	24	9	7	78	41	93	18	17	.324	.375

9 BUBBA THOMPSON, OF

Born: June 9, 1998. **B-T:** R-R. **Ht.:** 6-2. **Wt.:** 180. **Drafted:** HS—Mobile, Ala., 2017 (1st round). **Signed by:** Brian Morrison.

In a move that shouldn't surprise any Rangers fan, the team drafted a raw, premium athlete out of high school, selecting Thompson with one of their first-round picks, No. 26 overall, in 2017 and signing him for $2.1 million to pass up an Alabama commitment. At 19, Thompson was among of the oldest high school players drafted, and he held his own in his first taste of the Rookie-level Arizona League.

Thompson was a standout quarterback in high school who is now committed to baseball full-time. With broad shoulders and a high waist, Thompson is a plus-plus runner with a plus arm who projects as a center fielder, although his reads and routes off the bat need improvement. Thompson has plus bat speed and average raw power, but he has a lot of work to do to smooth things out at the plate. He has an aggressive approach and will swing and miss, though he kept that manageable in his pro debut.

BA GRADE
55 Risk: Extreme
HIT: 45. POW: 50.
SPD: 70. FLD: 60.
ARM: 60.

Thompson probably won't fly through the system, but he has some of the best tools in the system at a premium position if everything clicks. He has a chance to see low Class A Hickory in 2018.

Year	Club (League)	Class	AVG	G	AB	R	H	2B	3B	HR	RBI	BB	SO	SB	CS	OBP	SLG
2017	Rangers (AZL)	R	.257	30	113	23	29	7	2	3	12	6	28	5	5	.317	.434
Minor League Totals			.257	30	113	23	29	7	2	3	12	6	28	5	5	.317	.434

BILL MITCHELL

10 CHRIS SEISE, SS

Born: Jan. 6, 1999. **B-T:** B-R. **Ht.:** 6-2. **Wt.:** 185. **Drafted:** HS—Winter Garden, Fla., 2017 (1st round). **Signed by:** Brett Campbell.

After Seise made an impression on scouts in high school for his defensive prowess at shortstop, the Rangers selected him with the second of their two first-round picks, No. 29 overall, in the 2017 draft and signed him for $2 million to pass up a Central Florida commitment. Seise hit well in the Rookie-level Arizona League, then struggled when the Rangers aggressively promoted him to short-season Spokane.

Seise is a gifted defender with quick feet, soft hands and a plus arm. A tick above-average runner, Seise is an instinctive shortstop with a nose for the ball and good range to both sides. There is more risk in Seise's hitting ability, which he showed by striking out at a 26 percent clip in his pro debut. Seise has to improve his balance and timing at the plate to make more frequent contact, but he has good pop for the position. When he connects, it's usually loud contact, with average raw power that could tick up with physical maturity.

If Seise can keep his strikeout rate manageable, he could develop into an everyday shortstop with good defense and power. He should make his full-season debut in 2018 with low Class A Hickory.

BA GRADE
55 Risk: Extreme
HIT: 40. **POW:** 50.
SPD: 55. **FLD:** 60.
ARM: 60.

Year	Club (League)	Class	AVG	G	AB	R	H	2B	3B	HR	RBI	BB	SO	SB	CS	OBP	SLG
2017	Rangers (AZL)	R	.336	27	116	23	39	5	3	3	27	9	30	5	0	.395	.509
	Spokane (NWL)	SS	.222	24	99	10	22	3	1	0	9	4	30	1	1	.250	.273
Minor League Totals			.284	51	215	33	61	8	4	3	36	13	60	6	1	.330	.400

11 JOE PALUMBO, LHP

BA GRADE
55 Risk: Extreme

Born: Oct. 26, 1994. **B-T:** L-L. **Ht.:** 6-1. **Wt.:** 190. **Drafted:** HS—West Islip, N.Y., 2013 (30th round). **Signed by:** Takeshi Sakurayama.

Signed for $32,000 as a 30th-round pick from a Long Island high school, Palumbo did little to stand out in his first three seasons. That changed in 2016, as he moved from the low Class A Hickory bullpen to the starting rotation at midseason.

Palumbo was the talk of the high Class A Carolina League in April, but after just three starts he went down for the year with Tommy John surgery and isn't expected to return to game action until June 2018. Had Palumbo stayed healthy all season, he could have had a case as the organization's top pitching prospect. His fastball parks in the low-90s and reaches 96 mph, with his short arm stroke and crossfire delivery adding deception. Palumbo throws a lot of strikes with his fastball and misses a lot of bats with his curveball, a plus pitch with tight spin and sharp, late action. Palumbo's changeup is a fringe-average pitch with average potential, but he mostly has leaned on his fastball/curveball combination.

Palumbo looked like a potential midrotation starter early in the 2017 season, but the TJ clouds his status and he won't get a full season's workload until 2019 at the earliest.

Year	Club (League)	Class	W	L	ERA	G	GS	CG	SV	IP	H	HR	BB	SO	K/9	WHIP	AVG
2015	Spokane (NWL)	SS	3	3	2.82	12	9	0	0	54	52	3	22	42	7.0	1.36	.250
	Hickory (SAL)	LoA	0	0	6.23	1	0	0	0	4	5	0	3	1	2.1	1.85	.294
2016	Hickory (SAL)	LoA	7	5	2.24	33	7	0	8	96	71	5	36	122	11.4	1.11	.202
2017	Down East (CAR)	HiA	1	0	0.66	3	3	0	0	14	4	0	4	22	14.5	0.59	.087
Minor League Totals			16	13	2.61	76	26	0	8	231	180	8	94	258	10.1	1.19	.211

12 MATT WHATLEY, C

BA GRADE
50 Risk: High

Born: Jan. 7, 1996. **B-T:** R-R. **Ht.:** 5-10. **Wt.:** 200. **Drafted:** Oral Roberts, 2017 (3rd round). **Signed by:** Bobby Crook.

The Rangers already had one superlative defensive catcher in the system with Jose Trevino, their sixth-round pick in 2014. Three years later, the Rangers drafted Whatley, who won the Johnny Bench award as college baseball's top catcher, out of Oral Roberts in the third round and signed him for $517,100.

Whatley is a potential plus defender and one of the most polished defensive catchers in the 2017 draft. He's an advanced receiver with soft hands, with an above-average arm and quick feet that help him get rid of the ball quickly to control the running game. He earns praise for his game calling, leadership skills and high-energy style that should endear him to managers. Whatley's looked better than expected in the short-season Northwest League, where he put together consistent quality at-bats with a mature approach. He worked counts and gained a better understanding of how to control the timing of the pre-pitch movement in his swing to make frequent contact and drive the ball with fringe-average power.

Whatley's defense could carry him to a backup role, but has more offensive upside than Trevino and could develop into starter.

Year	Club (League)	Class	AVG	G	AB	R	H	2B	3B	HR	RBI	BB	SO	SB	CS	OBP	SLG
2017	Rangers (AZL)	R	.353	5	17	5	6	0	1	0	3	2	3	0	1	.421	.471
	Spokane (NWL)	SS	.289	39	149	23	43	6	0	6	25	16	28	3	4	.371	.450
Minor League Totals			.295	44	166	28	49	6	1	6	28	18	31	3	5	.376	.452

13 CARLOS TOCCI, OF

BA GRADE
45 Risk: Medium

Born: Aug. 23, 1995. **B-T:** R-R. **Ht.:** 6-2. **Wt.:** 180. **Signed:** Venezuela, 2011.
Signed by: Jesus Mendez (Phillies).

The Phillies signed Tocci for $759,000 on his 16th birthday in 2011. They left him off the 40-man roster after the 2016 season and he didn't get picked in the Rule 5 draft. They did the same thing after the 2017 season, but this time the White Sox picked him in the Rule 5 draft and traded him to the Rangers for cash considerations.

Since the time he's signed, Tocci has been an instinctive player with an extremely skinny frame. That's still the case, as Tocci has been slow to add strength, but he's a smooth center fielder who gets good jumps off the bat with average speed and arm strength. Tocci's swing is sound and he has good bat-to-balls skills, with an approach geared to hit the ball to the middle of the field and the opposite way. He would benefit from a more patient approach to draw more walks, especially since he has minimal power.

Tocci didn't play winter ball after the 2017 season, instead focusing on getting stronger, which remains the key for him taking the next step forward. The Rangers are counting on him stepping in as a fourth outfielder in 2018.

Year	Club (League)	Class	AVG	G	AB	R	H	2B	3B	HR	RBI	BB	SO	SB	CS	OBP	SLG
2015	Lakewood (SAL)	LoA	.321	59	234	35	75	14	2	2	25	20	31	14	2	.387	.423
	Clearwater (FSL)	HiA	.258	68	275	31	71	9	0	2	18	12	52	3	9	.296	.313
2016	Clearwater (FSL)	HiA	.284	127	500	66	142	26	2	3	50	34	76	13	6	.331	.362
2017	Reading (EL)	AA	.307	113	430	59	132	19	7	2	48	29	66	4	5	.362	.398
	Lehigh Valley (IL)	AAA	.189	17	53	2	10	0	0	1	4	1	11	0	0	.204	.245
Minor League Totals			.266	665	2497	305	663	105	19	12	210	149	427	59	42	.317	.337

14 DREW ROBINSON, 2B/3B/OF

BA GRADE
40 Risk: Low

Born: April 20, 1992. **B-T:** L-R. **Ht.:** 6-1. **Wt.:** 200. **Drafted:** HS—Las Vegas, 2010 (4th round). **Signed by:** Todd Guggiana.

Robinson signed with the Rangers out of high school in 2010 and would have been a minor league free agent after the 2016 season, but the Rangers added him to the 40-man roster. In his eighth season with the organization, Robinson made his major league debut in 2017 on April 5, went back down to Triple-A, then returned to Texas at the end of June.

Robinson is a versatile player who can play multiple positions and chips in value in different ways. He's a selective hitter who consistently walks at a high clip, including his 14 percent rate in Triple-A in 2017. His power is a tick above-average, with the ability to drive the ball in the air for home runs to all fields. His strikeout rate is high, a combination of his patience turning into passivity at times along with the swing-and-miss in his game. With average speed and arm strength, Robinson doesn't play shortstop but he does play steady defense just about everywhere else, including third, second and all three outfield spots, though he's stretched thin in center field.

Robinson's versatility should keep him around the big league club in 2018 as an offensive-oriented utility man with value as a lefthanded bat off the bench who can occasionally fill-in as a starter when needed.

Year	Club (League)	Class	AVG	G	AB	R	H	2B	3B	HR	RBI	BB	SO	SB	CS	OBP	SLG
2015	Frisco (TL)	AA	.231	126	432	78	100	23	5	21	64	83	139	14	8	.360	.454
	Round Rock (PCL)	AAA	.304	7	23	4	7	2	0	0	2	4	4	2	1	.407	.391
2016	Round Rock (PCL)	AAA	.257	125	467	76	120	24	10	20	67	66	148	17	5	.350	.480
2017	Round Rock (PCL)	AAA	.268	66	265	48	71	19	4	11	40	42	74	7	4	.369	.494
	Texas (AL)	MAJ	.224	48	107	11	24	5	0	6	13	14	42	0	2	.314	.439
Major League Totals			.224	48	107	11	24	5	0	6	13	14	42	0	2	.314	.439
Minor League Totals			.247	768	2692	437	665	148	37	89	396	450	835	82	37	.359	.429

15 TYREQUE REED, 1B

Born: June 6, 1995. **B-T:** R-R. **Ht.:** 6-2. **Wt.:** 260. **Drafted:** Itawamba (Miss.) JC, 2017 (8th round). **Signed by:** Brian Morrison.

BA GRADE
50 Risk: Extreme

Reed put up monster numbers in college, but those numbers came at Itawamba (Miss.) junior college. He led NJCAA Division II in batting average, slugging and on-base percentage in 2017, then signed with the Rangers for $135,000 as an 8th-round pick. He annihilated the Rookie-level Arizona League in his debut, with a 1.072 OPS that would have led the league had he had enough plate appearances to qualify.

Reed is a hulking righthanded power hitter, with some scouts giving him 70 raw power on the 20-80 scale. Reed can put on an impressive show during batting practice, but he also has a short swing that helps him make a lot of contact with good plate coverage in games. He's a patient hitter who walked in 15 percent of his plate appearances in the AZL. Reed is adept at driving the ball to the opposite field, and even more power should show up in games as he learns which pitches to turn on to his pull side. Reed has little speed and his defense is below-average.

Reed will head to low Class A Hickory in 2018, where he could have a breakout year.

Year	Club (League)	Class	AVG	G	AB	R	H	2B	3B	HR	RBI	BB	SO	SB	CS	OBP	SLG
2017	Rangers (AZL)	R	.350	35	120	35	42	13	2	5	29	22	26	3	1	.455	.617
Minor League Totals			.350	35	120	35	42	13	2	5	29	22	26	3	1	.455	.617

16 DAVID GARCIA, C

Born: Feb. 6, 2000. **B-T:** B-R. **Ht.:** 5-11. **Wt.:** 170. **Signed:** Venezuela, 2016. **Signed by:** Johnny Gomez.

BA GRADE
50 Risk: Extreme

Garcia was a small and slightly built as a 15-year-old, but over the next year he got stronger and improved on both sides of the ball to become a player several clubs considered the top catcher on the international market. He signed in 2016 for $800,000, and while he showed some positive signs in his pro debut especially during extended spring training, he mostly struggled while playing in the Dominican Summer League.

Garcia, who made the move from shortstop to catching full-time a year and a half before signing, threw out 41 percent of basestealers. He has an above-average, accurate arm with a clean throwing stroke and has quick feet to get rid of the ball quickly. He has soft hands and receives well. Garcia has the components to hit, with a simple stroke, solid contact skills and a mature, patient approach. Garcia doesn't have much power though and probably never will, but he will need to get stronger to do more damage on contact and become more than a singles hitter.

The Rookie-level Arizona League should be the next step for Garcia in 2018.

Year	Club (League)	Class	AVG	G	AB	R	H	2B	3B	HR	RBI	BB	SO	SB	CS	OBP	SLG
2017	Rangers2 (DSL)	R	.215	58	186	27	40	7	1	1	26	25	49	1	0	.321	.280
Minor League Totals			.215	58	186	27	40	7	1	1	26	25	49	1	0	.321	.280

17 JONATHAN HERNANDEZ, RHP

Born: July 6, 1996. **B-T:** R-R. **Ht.:** 6-2. **Wt.:** 185. **Signed:** Dominican Republic, 2013. **Signed by:** Willy Espinal/Mike Daly.

BA GRADE
45 Risk: High

Hernandez was born in Memphis, which is where his father, Fernando, pitched in Double-A in 1996 before making two big league relief appearances for Detroit the next year. Hernandez grew up in the Dominican Republic and signed for $300,000, with a fastball that has climbed since then.

Hernandez throws 92-95 mph and can reach 98 mph. His fastball has an effective combination of velocity and movement, with good armside run and a high spin rate that he took advantage of last year by elevating it to get swings-and-misses up in the zone, which helped his strikeout rate jump from 17 percent in 2016 to 23 percent in 2017. His slider is an average pitch and his changeup flashes average at times but it's less consistent. He can also flip over a curveball early in the count. Hernandez throws across his body, which creates deception, but can also impede his control. Some of that may stem from overthrowing, a habit he tends to get into when he's in a jam or goes through the order a second time.

Some scouts see Hernandez moving to the bullpen, though others see a potential back-end starter.

Year	Club (League)	Class	W	L	ERA	G	GS	CG	SV	IP	H	HR	BB	SO	K/9	WHIP	AVG
2015	Rangers (AZL)	R	1	1	3.00	11	9	0	0	45	45	0	12	33	6.6	1.27	.250
2016	Hickory (SAL)	LoA	10	9	4.56	24	22	1	0	116	110	14	49	85	6.6	1.37	.252
2017	Hickory (SAL)	LoA	2	5	4.86	9	9	0	0	46	55	5	13	46	8.9	1.47	.306
	Down East (CAR)	HiA	3	6	3.44	14	13	0	0	65	66	2	31	64	8.8	1.48	.271
Minor League Totals			24	24	3.52	85	75	1	0	393	376	29	144	323	7.4	1.32	.252

18 BRETT MARTIN, LHP

BA GRADE
45 Risk: High

Born: April 28, 1995. **B-T:** L-L. **Ht.:** 6-5. **Wt.:** 230. **Drafted:** Walters State (Tenn.) JC, 2014 (4th round). **Signed by:** Chris Kemp.

The Rangers continue to have high hopes for Martin, who has shown his potential in flashes, including seven scoreless, no-hit innings with 15 strikeouts in the high Class A California League playoffs in 2016.

Martin is yet to put it all together for a breakout season quite yet, though, some of which has been due to his health. Hip issues in 2015, a sprained elbow ligament in 2016 and an oblique injury that sidelined Martin for most of May and June in 2017 have prevented him from throwing more than 100 innings in a season. His fastball sits at 90-92 mph and can touch 95 with late riding life. His curveball is an above-average pitch with tight spin, good shape and power at 80-82 mph. He mixes a changeup that's still firm and below-average, along with an occasional slider/cutter. Aside from staying healthy, one of the keys for Martin's development will be his ability to sync up his delivery and find a consistent release point.

Martin has worked to get the arc out of the back of his motion to try to get his lower half into his mechanics more, but with his long limbs his delivery will always require some maintenance. Double-A Frisco is next for Martin, a potential No. 4 starter.

Year	Club (League)	Class	W	L	ERA	G	GS	CG	SV	IP	H	HR	BB	SO	K/9	WHIP	AVG
2015	Hickory (SAL)	LoA	5	6	3.49	20	18	0	0	95	92	6	26	72	6.8	1.24	.265
2016	Hickory (SAL)	LoA	2	3	4.53	9	9	0	0	44	58	3	14	48	9.9	1.65	.317
	Rangers (AZL)	R	0	0	3.86	2	2	0	0	2	3	0	0	6	23.1	1.29	.273
	High Desert (CAL)	HiA	2	1	4.24	6	6	0	0	23	24	3	7	16	6.2	1.33	.270
2017	Down East (CAR)	HiA	4	8	4.70	16	16	0	0	84	94	7	35	90	9.6	1.53	.287
Minor League Totals			14	22	4.31	68	57	0	1	284	307	22	94	271	8.6	1.41	.280

19 C.D. PELHAM, LHP

BA GRADE
45 Risk: High

Born: Feb. 21, 1995. **B-T:** L-L. **Ht.:** 6-6. **Wt.:** 245. **Drafted:** Spartanburg Methodist (S.C.) JC, 2015 (33rd round). **Signed by:** Jay Heafner.

The Rangers have had success identifying off-the-radar pitchers in South Carolina. They signed right-hander Carl Edwards with their 48th-round pick in 2011 and they got Pelham for $40,000 in the 33rd round in 2015.

Pelham was so raw that he walked more than a batter per inning in 2016, but in 2017 he moved to the bullpen full-time and took off, punctuating his season with a pair of shutout innings in the high Class A Carolina League playoffs where his fastball sat at 97 mph. Pelham has an extra-large frame and a huge fastball from the left side, parking at 95-96 mph and touching 99 with downhill angle and great extension out front. Pelham can blow his fastball by hitters and also gets a high swing-and-miss rate on his slider, which became a plus pitch last year. Pelham still needs to improve his location, but he already made huge strides with his control last year but cutting his walk rate from 22 percent in 2016 to 10 percent in 2017.

The arrows are pointing in the right direction for Pelham, who has the stuff to pitch high-leverage relief innings.

Year	Club (League)	Class	W	L	ERA	G	GS	CG	SV	IP	H	HR	BB	SO	K/9	WHIP	AVG
2015	Rangers (AZL)	R	4	0	5.40	16	0	0	0	18	15	1	13	24	11.8	1.53	.217
2016	Spokane (NWL)	SS	0	6	6.16	16	7	0	2	38	36	0	43	50	11.8	2.08	.243
2017	Hickory (SAL)	LoA	4	2	3.18	37	0	0	13	62	47	6	26	75	10.8	1.17	.204
Minor League Totals			8	8	4.47	69	7	0	15	119	98	7	82	149	11.3	1.52	.219

20 KEYBER RODRIGUEZ, SS

BA GRADE
50 Risk: Extreme

Born: Oct. 4, 2000. **B-T:** B-R. **Ht.:** 5-10. **Wt.:** 160. **Signed:** Venezuela, 2017. **Signed by:** Carlos Gonzalez.

Rodriguez was one of the top amateur prospects in Venezuela in the 2017 class, standing out more for his game savvy than his raw tools or physicality. Rodriguez has a small, wiry build and a good performance record in games.

Rodriguez is a switch-hitter with a quick, compact stroke, with high-contact skills to spray the ball all over the field without many strikeouts. Rodriguez has a good sense for the strike zone, with an offensive skill set tilted more toward getting on base than power, as he's mostly a singles hitter and probably won't ever be much of a home run threat. An above-average runner with basestealing savvy, Rodriguez is an athletic shortstop who fields his position well with a good internal clock. A lot of scouts expect Rodriguez to eventually slide over to second base due to his below-average arm and throwing mechanics.

The Rangers have been sending their top July 2 signings to the Dominican Summer League in recent years, with Rodriguez likely to follow that same path.

Year	Club (League)	Class	AVG	G	AB	R	H	2B	3B	HR	RBI	BB	SO	SB	CS	OBP	SLG
2017	Did not play—Signed 2018 contract																

21 NICK GARDEWINE, RHP

BA GRADE 40 Risk: Medium

Born: Aug. 15, 1993. **B-T:** R-R. **Ht.:** 6-1. **Wt.:** 185. **Drafted:** Kaskaskia (Ill.) JC, 2013 (7th round). **Signed by:** Derek Lee.

Gardewine was a starter who helped take his Kaskaskia team to the Junior College World Series in 2013, then signed with the Rangers for $162,300 as a seventh-round pick.

Gardewine remained a starter for the Rangers through 2015, then moved to the bullpen the next year. He broke through in 2017 with an excellent season for Double-A Frisco and jumped to the big league bullpen for his major league debut at the end of August. Gardewine has quick arm speed and a plus fastball at 93-96 mph. He's not tall, but he generates downhill plane and also has a high spin rate on his fastball to get swings-and-misses when he rides it up in the zone. His strikeout rate jumped from 28 percent in high Class A in 2016 to 34 percent in Double-A in 2017, and the key was his plus slider. It's a power slider Gardewine usually fires at 88-90 mph, but he can change speeds on that pitch too and often doubles up on it, landing it for a strike or using it as a chase pitch. He has a firm changeup but rarely throws it. Gardewine throws across his body and usually throws strikes, but got into trouble in the big leagues when his fastball control escaped him.

Gardewine should open 2018 in the big league bullpen, with the stuff to stick around as a middle reliever.

Year	Club (League)	Class	W	L	ERA	G	GS	CG	SV	IP	H	HR	BB	SO	K/9	WHIP	AVG
2015	Hickory (SAL)	LoA	6	8	4.31	22	17	0	1	96	111	11	23	80	7.5	1.40	.293
2016	High Desert (CAL)	HiA	5	1	2.47	29	0	0	7	55	39	5	14	60	9.9	0.97	.198
2017	Frisco (TL)	AA	1	2	2.21	33	0	0	6	37	35	2	12	53	13.0	1.28	.252
	Texas (AL)	MAJ	0	0	5.63	12	0	0	0	8	10	1	7	3	3.4	2.13	.303
Major League Totals			0	0	5.63	12	0	0	0	8	10	1	7	3	3.4	2.13	.303
Minor League Totals			21	17	3.61	113	38	0	15	306	281	26	92	290	8.5	1.22	.243

22 JOSH MORGAN, SS/C

BA GRADE 45 Risk: High

Born: Nov. 16, 1995. **B-T:** R-R. **Ht.:** 5-11. **Wt.:** 195. **Drafted:** HS—Orange, Calif., 2014 (3rd round). **Signed by:** Steve Flores.

Morgan repeated the high Class A level in 2017 at the Rangers' new Down East affiliate in the Carolina League, but he did so while having to learn a new position. Morgan had experimented with catching at instructional league in 2015 and 2016, and in 2017 the Rangers had him rotating between shortstop and catcher, with 36 games behind the plate but most of his time at shortstop.

Morgan missed a month in June with a tight hamstring but got extra work catching upper-level pitching after the season in the Arizona Fall League. It's been difficult for Morgan to learn catching while playing it only part time, but the Rangers like the versatility of having him at multiple positions. Morgan has a contact-oriented swing and a good eye for the strike zone, though he wasn't as selective with his approach as he has shown in the past. Morgan doesn't have much power but has enough to pull 8-12 home runs over the fence. Morgan doesn't have the range to stick at shortstop, but his hands, feet and slightly above-average arm would work well at second or third base. He's shown promising signs behind the plate, but he understandably has a ways to go to stick there.

Morgan is slated to move up to Double-A Frisco, where he will continue to work on his catching and bounce around the infield.

Year	Club (League)	Class	AVG	G	AB	R	H	2B	3B	HR	RBI	BB	SO	SB	CS	OBP	SLG
2015	Hickory (SAL)	LoA	.288	98	351	59	101	15	1	3	36	45	53	9	4	.385	.362
2016	High Desert (CAL)	HiA	.300	128	470	74	141	19	2	7	64	44	61	4	2	.367	.394
2017	Down East (CAR)	HiA	.270	106	408	56	110	21	3	6	45	26	54	3	0	.318	.380
Minor League Totals			.291	388	1431	226	417	58	7	16	164	144	191	19	9	.369	.375

23 YANIO PEREZ, 3B/OF/1B

BA GRADE
45 Risk: High

Born: Aug. 10, 1995. **B-T:** R-R. **Ht.:** 6-2. **Wt.:** 215. **Signed:** Cuba, 2016. **Signed by:** Jose Fernandez/Chu Halabe/Rafic Saab.

Perez hit well in Cuba's junior national leagues, earning a spot on the country's 18U World Cup team that played in Taiwan in 2013. Perez played briefly in Cuba's top league, Serie Nacional, before leaving the country and signing with the Rangers for $1.14 million in September 2016.

He hit well in his pro debut in the low Class A South Atlantic League, but he scuffled upon a promotion to high Class A Down East. Perez is a strong, physical player with plus raw power, and he uses the whole field and is adept at working the ball toward right-center. His strikeouts were manageable, but he has a power-over-hit profile and got into bad habits with his swing in the second half, possibly due to fatigue as he played more games in a season than he ever did in Cuba. A below-average runner, Perez split time between third base, first base and the outfield corners in 2017. The Rangers are optimistic he can handle third base, but he's not a natural defender at the position.

Perez moves well enough to play in the outfield with a solid-average arm that works in right field. He likely returns to Down East to start 2018.

Year	Club (League)	Class	AVG	G	AB	R	H	2B	3B	HR	RBI	BB	SO	SB	CS	OBP	SLG
2015	Did not play																
2016	Did not play																
2017	Hickory (SAL)	LoA	.322	49	180	27	58	9	1	9	30	18	34	3	0	.392	.533
	Down East (CAR)	HiA	.253	74	281	31	71	14	2	5	36	20	66	3	1	.311	.370
Minor League Totals			.280	123	461	58	129	23	3	14	66	38	100	6	1	.343	.434

24 PEDRO GONZALEZ, OF

BA GRADE
50 Risk: Extreme

Born: Oct. 27, 1997. **B-T:** R-R. **Ht.:** 6-5. **Wt.:** 210. **Signed:** Dominican Republic, 2015. **Signed by:** Rolando Fernandez/Jhonathan Leyba/Martin Cabrera (Rockies).

Gonzalez was one of the top international shortstop prospects in 2015, when he signed with the Rockies for $1.3 million. After signing, Gonzalez kept growing, to the point where the Rockies pushed him out to center field.

Gonzalez was hitting well in the Rookie-level Pioneer League last year when the Rangers acquired him on Aug. 23 as the player to be named later, completing the trade deadline deal for Jonathan Lucroy. Gonzalez is a smart player with good hitting actions, but it has and will continue to take time for him keep his long arms in sync and on time with his swing. He did a better job with his timing and getting into a better hitting position in 2017, dropping his Pioneer League strikeout rate from 32 percent in 2016 to 25 percent last year. Gonzalez has good bat speed and added significant bulk over the offseason, so there should be more thump coming than the mostly gap power he has shown so far. Gonzalez is huge for a center fielder, so whether he stays there long term is in question, but he has the tools to play there for now with slightly above-average speed and a plus arm.

Gonzalez is headed to low Class A Hickory next, where he might rotate around the outfield with Miguel Aparicio also there.

Year	Club (League)	Class	AVG	G	AB	R	H	2B	3B	HR	RBI	BB	SO	SB	CS	OBP	SLG
2015	Rockies (DSL)	R	.251	63	251	46	63	14	2	8	33	19	81	8	12	.318	.418
2016	Rockies (DSL)	R	.222	7	27	3	6	0	1	0	6	2	4	4	1	.300	.296
	Grand Junction (PIO)	R	.230	58	226	32	52	15	8	2	19	14	77	6	7	.290	.394
2017	Grand Junction (PIO)	R	.321	45	187	28	60	16	6	3	28	18	53	11	6	.388	.519
	Spokane (NWL)	SS	.000	6	17	2	0	0	0	0	0	2	8	0	0	.105	.000
Minor League Totals			.256	179	708	111	181	45	17	13	86	55	223	29	26	.322	.422

25 A.J. ALEXY, RHP

BA GRADE
45 Risk: High

Born: April 21, 1998. **B-T:** R-R. **Ht.:** 6-4. **Wt.:** 200. **Drafted:** HS—Elverson, Pa., 2016 (11th round). **Signed by:** Rich Delucia (Dodgers).

Alexy was committed to Radford, but the Dodgers lured him away with a $597,500 signing bonus as an 11th-round pick in 2016. The Dodgers kept a restrictive workload on Alexy, who threw more than five innings for them just once last season before they sent him to the Rangers at the trade deadline along with Willie Calhoun and infielder Brendon Davis in the Yu Darvish deal.

Alexy has a full windup with an aggressive, up-tempo delivery. It's made it difficult for him to repeat his mechanics and throw strikes, but he also misses a lot of bats with a 29 percent strikeout rate in 2017. Alexy isn't overpowering, but he can get swings-and-misses with a low-90s fastball and with his best pitch, a curveball that flashes plus. He shows feel for a changeup, though that's still below-average. Alexy is athletic and he's added 15 pounds since joining the Rangers, so the additional strength could potentially help him keep his delivery together more consistently.

Throwing more strikes will be key for Alexy, who should move up to high Class A Down East in 2018 and could eventually slot in to the back of a rotation.

Year	Club (League)	Class	W	L	ERA	G	GS	CG	SV	IP	H	HR	BB	SO	K/9	WHIP	AVG
2016	Dodgers (AZL)	R	1	0	4.61	7	3	0	0	14	17	2	3	12	7.9	1.46	.315
2017	Great Lakes (MWL)	LoA	2	6	3.67	19	19	0	0	74	46	3	37	86	10.5	1.13	.180
	Hickory (SAL)	LoA	1	1	3.05	5	5	0	0	21	13	3	15	27	11.8	1.35	.178
Minor League Totals			4	7	3.67	31	27	0	0	108	76	8	55	125	10.4	1.21	.199

26 ALEX SPEAS, RHP

BA GRADE
50 Risk: Extreme

Born: March 4, 1998. **B-T:** R-R. **Ht.:** 6-4. **Wt.:** 180. **Drafted:** HS—Powder Springs, Ga., 2016 (2nd round). **Signed by:** Derrick Tucker.

Speas checks off a lot of traditional scouting boxes, but he's still a raw project the Rangers are working to mold. In seven starts last year with short-season Spokane, Speas posted a 10.89 ERA with more walks (17) than strikeouts (16) in 19 innings. Once he moved to the bullpen, Speas was still wild but found far more success, throwing 14.2 scoreless innings with a 29-8 K-BB mark. The move to the bullpen isn't permanent—the Rangers will likely either start him or use him in a piggyback plan for their low Class A Hickory rotation in 2018—but it's a role that fit Speas well and could be in his future. Getting more innings as a starter will benefit Speas, an outstanding athlete with long arms and legs he's working to sync up in his delivery to throw more strikes. He has good arm action and has an explosive fastball from 93-97 mph. His slider is a fringe-average pitch but it played up out of the bullpen when he threw it with more power. Speas has a changeup too but it's still in its early stages.

Year	Club (League)	Class	W	L	ERA	G	GS	CG	SV	IP	H	HR	BB	SO	K/9	WHIP	AVG
2016	Rangers (AZL)	R	0	0	0.00	4	3	0	0	8	4	0	7	11	11.9	1.32	.138
2017	Spokane (NWL)	SS	1	6	6.15	16	7	0	1	34	29	5	25	45	12.0	1.60	.223
Minor League Totals			1	6	4.93	20	10	0	1	42	33	5	32	56	12.0	1.55	.208

27 ANDERSON TEJEDA, SS

BA GRADE
45 Risk: V. High

Born: May 1, 1998. **B-T:** L-R. **Ht.:** 5-11. **Wt.:** 185. **Signed:** Dominican Republic, 2014. **Signed by:** Rodolfo Rosario/Roberto Aquino.

After signing for $100,000 in 2014, Tejeda flashed breakout signals when the Rangers promoted him to short-season Spokane in 2016 and he smashed eight home runs in just 23 games.

Tejeda didn't carry that success over to low Class A Hickory in 2017, with a lot of swing-and-miss, especially early in the season. Tejeda's swing has a lot of moving parts and often gets long, but the Rangers emphasized the importance of trusting his hands and focusing on driving the ball to the middle of the field. Tejeda's strikeout rate dropped from 34 percent in the first half to 25 percent in the second half, and Tejeda finished the year by hitting .293/.350/.500 in August. He's an aggressive hitter who is still learning to recognize breaking pitches, but he can ambush a fastball and is a 20-homer threat. An average runner, Tejeda's plus arm is a weapon, but he's still cleaning up his footwork and first step, and his range is a touch short for what's ideal at the position.

Tejeda has a chance to stick there but could end up at second or third base. He will likely go to high Class A Down East to open 2018.

Year	Club (League)	Class	AVG	G	AB	R	H	2B	3B	HR	RBI	BB	SO	SB	CS	OBP	SLG
2015	Rangers1 (DSL)	R	.277	14	47	4	13	2	2	0	8	8	11	2	2	.382	.404
	Rangers2 (DSL)	R	.323	41	158	32	51	17	4	4	32	17	38	7	5	.397	.557
2016	Rangers1 (DSL)	R	.262	11	42	9	11	2	3	1	7	5	4	5	0	.340	.524
	Rangers (AZL)	R	.293	32	133	22	39	12	6	1	21	8	36	1	0	.331	.496
	Spokane (NWL)	SS	.277	23	94	15	26	0	1	8	19	5	33	1	0	.313	.553
2017	Hickory (SAL)	LoA	.247	115	401	68	99	24	9	8	53	36	132	10	7	.309	.411
Minor League Totals			.273	236	875	150	239	57	25	22	140	79	254	26	14	.335	.471

28 JOSE TREVINO, C

BA GRADE
40 Risk: High

Born: Nov. 28, 1992. **B-T:** R-R. **Ht.:** 5-11. **Wt.:** 210. **Drafted:** Oral Roberts, 2014 (6th round). **Signed by:** Bobby Crook.

Trevino is a potential plus-plus defender who is considered by scouts to be one of the best defenders in the minors. Trevino allowed just three passed balls in 99 games and threw out 41 percent of basestealers. Trevino doesn't have a cannon arm—it's slightly above-average—but it plays way up because his quick feet help him transfer and release the ball swiftly, with consistently on-target throws.

Pitchers and managers love Trevino for his game-calling, leadership skills and the way he handles a pitching staff. His blocking and receiving skills are both above-average too. Trevino's defense could help him carve out a decade-long career as a backup, but even in that role he will have to show more life at the plate. Trevino doesn't have a pure swing but he is a high-contact hitter who struck out in just 10 percent of his plate appearances. He has to become more selective, both to draw more walks and so that he's swinging at pitches he can drive instead of just putting the ball in play for weak contact. He's not a power hitter but has enough pop to his pull side to hit 10-15 home runs.

Added to the 40-man roster after the season, Trevino should go to Triple-A in 2018 and could make his major league debut by the end of the year.

Year	Club (League)	Class	AVG	G	AB	R	H	2B	3B	HR	RBI	BB	SO	SB	CS	OBP	SLG
2015	Hickory (SAL)	LoA	.262	112	424	62	111	19	2	14	63	18	60	1	4	.291	.415
2016	High Desert (CAL)	HiA	.303	109	433	67	131	30	0	9	68	26	49	2	1	.342	.434
2017	Frisco (TL)	AA	.241	105	402	39	97	12	0	7	42	19	44	1	2	.275	.323
Minor League Totals			.267	398	1547	226	413	83	5	39	222	86	203	6	7	.306	.403

29 ANDY IBANEZ, 2B/3B

BA GRADE 40 Risk: High

Born: April 3, 1993. **B-T:** R-R. **Ht.:** 5-10. **Wt.:** 180. **Drafted:** Cuba, 2015. **Signed by:** Jose Fernandez/Roberto Aquino/Gil Kim/Thad Levine.

Ibanez was the youngest player on Cuba's 2013 World Baseball Classic team, then signed with the Rangers two years later for $1.6 million. Ibanez spent most of his first season in 2016 with Double-A Frisco, but he repeated the Texas League in 2017 and didn't take the next step forward in his development at the plate. Ibanez is a steady player whose tool box has a lot of 40s and 50s on the 20-80 scouting scale. He's an offensive-minded prospect who puts together quality at-bats with a short swing and good bat-to-ball skills. He got away from his swing at times last year, causing him to get underneath too many balls for easy outs instead of staying with his line-drive approach. His power is below-average with a chance for 10-15 home runs. Ibanez is a below-average runner with a fringe-average arm who fits best at second base, where he can make the routine plays. Triple-A Round Rock is the next step for Ibanez.

Year	Club (League)	Class	AVG	G	AB	R	H	2B	3B	HR	RBI	BB	SO	SB	CS	OBP	SLG
2015	Did not play																
2016	Hickory (SAL)	LoA	.324	49	185	28	60	18	1	7	35	29	28	10	8	.413	.546
	Frisco (TL)	AA	.261	81	307	39	80	18	2	6	31	25	47	5	2	.318	.391
2017	Frisco (TL)	AA	.265	82	310	33	82	14	2	8	29	25	48	6	1	.323	.400
Minor League Totals			.277	212	802	100	222	50	5	21	95	79	123	21	11	.343	.430

30 MICHAEL MATUELLA, RHP

BA GRADE 45 Risk: Extreme

Born: June 3, 1994. **B-T:** R-R. **Ht.:** 6-6. **Wt.:** 220. **Drafted:** Duke, 2015 (3rd round). **Signed by:** Jay Heafner.

The 2017 season was a win for Matuella, simply because he stayed healthy all year. That has been an obstacle for Matuella, who was diagnosed with a chronic back condition while at Duke in the summer of 2014 and had Tommy John in April 2015.

Matuella never threw more than 60 innings in a season in college, but the Rangers signed him for $2 million as a third-round pick that year. Matuella rehabbed and pitched one game in 2016 with short-season Spokane, but he felt elbow pain and shut it down the rest of the year. So while Matuella's overall numbers were modest, he checked off the box for the organization's primary goal for him last year. The next step is to try to get all of his pitches working in the same start. His fastball ranged from 92-98 mph depending on the night. His curveball and changeup all flashed plus throughout the season, but rarely in the same outing and with a lot of inconsistency, no surprise given Matuella's multi-year layoff.

The Rangers want to keep Matuella as a starter, though given his medical history, a relief role seems like a better bet. The 2018 season will be a big step for Matuella, who's headed for High Class A Down East.

Year	Club (League)	Class	W	L	ERA	G	GS	CG	SV	IP	H	HR	BB	SO	K/9	WHIP	AVG
2015	Did not play--Injured																
2016	Spokane (NWL)	SS	0	0	0.00	1	1	0	0	3	1	0	2	1	3.0	1.00	.111
2017	Hickory (SAL)	LoA	4	6	4.08	21	20	0	0	75	88	6	23	60	7.2	1.48	.297
Minor League Totals			4	6	3.92	22	21	0	0	78	89	6	25	61	7.0	1.46	.292

Toronto Blue Jays

BY BEN BADLER

No team in baseball has a better prospect duo than the Blue Jays.

Third baseman Vladimir Guerrero Jr. and shortstop Bo Bichette moved up together as teenagers through two Class A levels in 2017 and overpowered their opponents. Guerrero is a prodigious hitter with impact power, driving all types of pitches in any part of the strike zone with authority, and with plate discipline rarely found in a hitter his age. He's one of the best prospects in Blue Jays franchise history, and that's saying something for an organization that has signed and developed players like Carlos Delgado, Shawn Green, Roy Halladay and John Olerud.

Bichette has more defensive value than Guerrero, and while there were questions about whether each player will remain at his position, their work with minor league infield coordinator Danny Solano has helped both of them exceed expectations defensively in 2017. Bichette is one of the most talented hitters in the minors, with an innate feel for the barrel, ferocious bat speed and big power.

Guerrero and Bichette could both be hitting in the middle of Toronto's lineup in 2019. Beyond them, though, the Blue Jays have a lot of holes to fill.

The Blue Jays are coming off a 76-86 season in 2017 in which they ranked 26th in baseball in runs scored. They don't project to be any better in 2018, with a major league roster heavy on players who are 30 and older.

Guerrero, Bichette and center fielder Anthony Alford should all factor into the 2019 picture, but after their top handful of prospects, the Blue Jays' farm system falls off quickly. Lefthander Ryan Borucki and catcher Danny Jansen elevated their statuses in 2017 with big years while reaching the upper levels, and the Blue Jays added a pair of exciting arms during the season with junior college righthander Nate Pearson in the first round of the draft and Brazilian righthander Eric Pardinho as their top international free agent signing.

However, several prospects the Blue Jays had been counting on struggled in 2017 in the upper levels, making it difficult to expect a next wave of prospect talent to push through in 2018. Figuring out a way to get those players back on track would be a huge boost for the club.

Where do the Blue Jays go from here? A rebuild makes sense. The Blue Jays don't need a complete teardown that involves multiple seasons of tanking, but they could greatly increase their chances of fielding a competitive team for 2019 and the years beyond through trades to boost a farm system that

Marcus Stroman is one of the few Blue Jays regulars who is younger than 30 years old.

PROJECTED 2021 LINEUP

Catcher	Danny Jansen (26)
First Base	Justin Smoak (34)
Second Base	Devon Travis (30)
Third Base	Vladimir Guerrero Jr. (22)
Shortstop	Bo Bichette (23)
Left Field	Anthony Alford (26)
Center Field	Kevin Pillar (32)
Right Field	Lourdes Gurriel (27)
Designated Hitter	Rowdy Tellez (26)
No. 1 Starter	Marcus Stroman (30)
No. 2 Starter	Aaron Sanchez (28)
No. 3 Starter	Nate Pearson (24)
No. 4 Starter	Ryan Borucki (27)
No. 5 Starter	Sean Reid-Foley (25)
Closer	Roberto Osuna (26)

needs help.

However, that doesn't seem to be the organization's plan. The Blue Jays instead have held steady, looking for options to improve their major league club for 2018.

There's a chance things break right for the Blue Jays in 2018 and they contend for a playoff spot, but if they don't, their timetable to get back to the postseason will only be on a longer delay.

Guerrero and Bichette are the jewels of the system, with perennial all-star potential and each with the upside to contend for an MVP award down the road. The young nucleus of the Blue Jays' future lineup is in terrific shape, but the organization needs to supplement that core with more talent.

DEPTH CHART

TORONTO BLUE JAYS

TOP 2018 ROOKIE: Ryan Borucki, LHP. After moving through three levels in 2017, he could step into the back of Toronto's rotation in 2018.
BREAKOUT PROSPECT: Ryan Noda, 1B/OF. The MVP of the Rookie-level Appalachian League in 2017, he could prove to be a late-round bargain out of the 15th round.
SLEEPER: Alejandro Melean, RHP. He was one of the top pitching prospects on the international market in 2017, showing a low-90s fastball, a curveball that misses bats and good feel for pitching for a 17-year-old.

SOURCE OF TOP 30 TALENT			
Homegrown	28	**Acquired**	**2**
College	9	Trade	2
Junior college	0	Rule 5 draft	0
High school	8	Independent league	0
Nondrafted free agent	0	Free agent/waivers	0
International	11		

LF
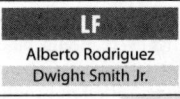
Alberto Rodriguez
Dwight Smith Jr.

CF

Anthony Alford (3)
Edward Olivares (14)
D.J. Davis
Jonathan Davis
Reggie Pruitt
Chavez Young
Roemon Fields

RF
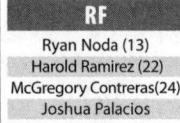
Ryan Noda (13)
Harold Ramirez (22)
McGregory Contreras(24)
Joshua Palacios

3B
Vladimir Guerrero Jr. (1)
Lourdes Gurriel (5)
Miguel Hiraldo (17)

SS

Bo Bichette (2)
Logan Warmoth (8)
Richard Urena (9)
Leonardo Jimenez (18)
Kevin Vicuna (25)
Kevin Smith (26)
Luis de los Santos
Yeltsin Gudino

2B

Cavan Biggio
Samad Taylor

1B

Rowdy Tellez (21)

C
Danny Jansen (7)
Reese McGuire (15)
Riley Adams (21)
Max Pentecost (23)
Hagen Danner (28)
Yorman Rodriguez

LHP

LHSP	LHRP
Ryan Borucki (10)	Tim Mayza
Tom Pannone	Kirby Snead
Randy Pondler	Tyler Saucedo
Naswell Paulino	

RHP

RHSP	RHRP
Nate Pearson (4)	Carlos Ramirez (19)
Eric Pardinho (6)	Emerson Jimenez
Sean Reid-Foley (11)	Chris Rowle
T.J. Zeuch (12)	
Conner Greene (16)	
Jordan Romano (27)	
Jon Harris (29)	
Yennsy Diaz (30)	
Maximo Castillo	
Alejandro Melean	
Zach Jackson	
Justin Maese	

DRAFT ANALYSIS

2017

BEST PURE HITTER: SS Logan Warmoth (1) has present strength, repeats his fairly simple swing and has a knack for finding the barrel. His pitch recognition and track record augur well for continued improvement, as he keeps improving his power numbers.

BEST POWER HITTER: OF/1B Ryan Noda (15) struggled in the spring with Cincinnati but feasted on younger competition with Rookie-level Bluefield, showing strength and leverage in his swing. His power-over-hit profile will be tested at higher levels.

FASTEST RUNNER: OF D.J. Neal (26) has size and speed, with 6.45-second times over 60 yards in workouts, translating to 70 grades. Canadian OF Tanner Kirwer (20) is a plus runner and accomplished basestealer (66-for-77 in three seasons at Niagara).

BEST DEFENSIVE PLAYER: SS Kevin Smith (4) was expected to be the first college shortstop drafted entering the season due to his glove and power. The glove held up in the spring at Maryland and in pro ball, as he showed body control, good footwork, above-average hands and arm strength. Warmoth has the tools for shortstop as well but could be a plus defender if he moves to second.

BEST ATHLETE: At 6-foot-3, 201 pounds, Neal looks and runs like a wide receiver, which he was for one season at South Carolina. Still just 20, his season at USC Sumter JC helped him catch up with much-needed at-bats, and he hit .297/.341/.426 in the Rookie-level Gulf Coast League in his debut.

BEST FASTBALL: RHP Nate Pearson (1) flashed 97-98 mph heat in the fall and during the spring, and by the time of an early June workout before the draft in Lakeland, Fla., he was hitting 102 mph with big-time life. It's a swing-and-miss fastball both at the bottom of the zone, with heavy life.

TOP DRAFT PICKS OF THE DECADE

Year	Player, Pos.	2017 Org
2008	David Cooper, 1B	Did not play
2009	Chad Jenkins, RHP	Did not play
2010	Deck McGuire, RHP	Reds
2011	*Tyler Beede, RHP	Giants
2012	D.J. Davis, OF	Blue Jays
2013	*Phil Bickford, RHP	Brewers
2014	Jeff Hoffman, RHP	Rockies
2015	Jon Harris, RHP	Blue Jays
2016	T.J. Zeuch, RHP	Blue Jays
2017	Logan Warmoth, SS	Blue Jays

* Did not sign

BEST SECONDARY PITCH: Pearson's slider and curve have flashed plus, as has his changeup, albeit less frequently. He's comfortable with the change and has power on his breaking balls, if not consistency, but it's an exciting four-pitch mix.

BEST PRO DEBUT: Including the short-season Northwest League playoffs, Pearson posted a 0.96 ERA and 40 strikeouts with 11 walks in 28 innings. Noda was MVP of the Appalachian League after hitting .364/.507/.575 with 59 walks and 60 strikeouts in 214 at-bats.

MOST INTRIGUING BACKGROUND: Neal's football background is rare, but so is being the son of former Blue Jay and seven-time Cy Young Award winner Roger Clemens, like 1B Kacy Clemens (8).

CLOSEST TO THE MAJORS: Warmoth has few holes in his game. Pearson would surpass him if he were to be moved to the bullpen.

BEST LATE-ROUND PICK: Neal and Noda will both be watched, with Neal's athleticism giving him an edge.

THE ONE WHO GOT AWAY: The Jays took several BA500 preps whom they couldn't sign once they hit their pool, led by LHP Sam Weatherly (27), who was part of a strong Clemson freshman class.

—JOHN MANUEL

2016

SS Bo Bichette (2) had a breakout year and won the minor league batting title. RHP T.J. Zeuch (1) was limited by injury, but was solid when he was able to get on the mound. They are the only players from the class to make the handbook, though OF J.B. Woodman (2) did bring back Aledmys Diaz in a December deal.

GRADE: B

2015

The Blue Jays failure to sign RHP Brady Singer (2), the early favorite to be the top pick in the 2018 draft, torpedoes this draft. RHP Jon Harris (1) is the class' lone member to appear in the handbook, and he is coming off a highly disappointing season in Double-A. OF Andrew Guillotte (32) provides some utility and reached Triple-A.

GRADE: F

2014

This class has been heavily utilized in trades, including RHP Jeff Hoffman (1), who was a part of the Troy Tulowitzki deal and has graduated to the big leagues. RHP Sean Reid-Foley (2) remains with the Blue Jays, but is coming off a poor season in Double-A. C Max Pentecost (1) is still working his way back from injury.

GRADE: C

1 VLADIMIR GUERRERO JR., 3B

Born: March 16, 1999. **B-T:** R-R. **Ht.:** 6-2. **Wt.:** 225.
Signed: Dominican Republic, 2015. **Signed by:** Ismael Cruz/Sandy Rosario/Luciano Del Rosario.

CLIFF WELCH

Vladimir Guerrero hit 449 home runs for his career, which included an American League MVP award in 2004. Vladdy Jr. followed his father around to big league ballparks but grew up in the Dominican Republic and trained with his uncle Wilton, also a former big leaguer. His bat stood out at an early age and he was the No. 1 international prospect when the Blue Jays signed him for $3.9 million in 2015. After dominating the Rookie-level Appalachian League in his pro debut in 2016, Guerrero was just 18 but looked like a man among boys by clobbering two Class A leagues in 2017. At an age when his peers in the U.S. were graduating from high school, Guerrero nearly led the minors in on-base percentage.

Guerrero is a prodigious offensive talent, with the combination of hitting ability, plate discipline and power in the mold of Manny Ramirez. Guerrero has high-end bat speed and outstanding bat control. With hitting mannerisms reminiscent of his father, Guerrero has a compact but aggressive swing. With his hand-eye coordination, he has excellent plate coverage, barreling premium velocity while also possessing the pitch recognition skills to square up all types offspeed pitches, too. He has plus raw power now, with 30-homer years likely in his future and a chance for 40. He drew more walks (76) than strikeouts (62) in 2017 and has the potential to contend for batting titles. A gifted offensive player, Guerrero did not inherit his father's speed or athleticism. He trained as an outfielder when he was an amateur and figured to be a left fielder at best, but after the Blue Jays signed him they put him at third base. He has surprised scouts with his play there, improving his arm strength to above-average and showing the hands to be a playable defender. However, Guerrero is already so big and stocky as a teenager that it's going to be a challenge for him to maintain his weight. Even if he moves to first base or possibly left field, his bat is good enough to be a premium player there too.

Guerrero has the upside to be one of the most best players in baseball. He likely will start 2018 at Double-A New Hampshire, and while the Blue Jays are conservative with promotions, Guerrero is in position to possibly make his major league debut by the end of the season as a 19-year-old.

BA GRADE	SCOUTING GRADES
75 Risk: High	HIT: 80. POW: 70. SPD: 40. FLD: 40. ARM: 55.

Projected future grades on 20-80 scouting scale

TOP PROSPECTS OF THE DECADE

Year	Player, Pos.	2017 Org
2008	Travis Snider, OF	Mets
2009	Travis Snider, OF	Mets
2010	Zach Stewart, RHP	Orioles
2011	Kyle Drabek, RHP	Atlantic League
2012	Travis d'Arnaud, C	Mets
2013	Travis d'Arnaud, C	Mets
2014	Aaron Sanchez, RHP	Blue Jays
2015	Daniel Norris, LHP	Tigers
2016	Anthony Alford, OF	Blue Jays
2017	Vladimir Guerrero Jr., 3B	Blue Jays

BEST TOOLS

Best Hitter For Average	Vladimir Guerrero Jr.
Best Power Hitter	Vladimir Guerrero Jr.
Best Strike-Zone Discipline	Vladimir Guerrero Jr.
Fastest Baserunner	Roemon Fields
Best Athlete	Anthony Alford
Best Fastball	Nate Pearson.
Best Curveball	Eric Pardinho
Best Slider	Nate Pearson
Best Changeup	Ryan Borucki
Best Control	Ryan Borucki
Best Defensive Catcher	Reese McGuire
Best Defensive Infielder	Kevin Smith
Best Infield Arm	Richard Urena
Best Defensive Outfielder	Anthony Alford
Best Outfield Arm	Reggie Pruitt

Year	Club (League)	Class	AVG	G	AB	R	H	2B	3B	HR	RBI	BB	SO	SB	CS	OBP	SLG
2016	Bluefield (APP)	R	.271	62	236	32	64	12	3	8	46	33	35	15	5	.359	.449
2017	Lansing (MWL)	LoA	.312	71	269	53	84	21	1	7	45	40	34	6	2	.406	.476
	Dunedin (FSL)	HiA	.333	48	168	31	56	7	1	6	31	36	28	2	2	.450	.494
Minor League Totals			.303	181	673	116	204	40	5	21	122	109	97	23	9	.401	.471

2 BO BICHETTE, SS/2B

Born: March 5, 1998. **B-T:** R-R. **Ht.:** 6-0. **Wt.:** 200. **Drafted:** HS—St. Petersburg, Fla., 2016 (2nd round). **Signed by:** Matt Bishoff.

Bichette's father Dante played 14 years in the big leagues, and his older brother Dante Jr. was a Yankees supplemental first-round pick in 2011. Bo went No. 66 overall in 2016 and quickly became the steal of the draft. He blasted his way through two levels in 2017 during his first full season, winning the low Class A Midwest League MVP and claiming the minor league batting title (.362).

Bichette loads his swing with an aggressive leg kick and unleashes a powerful swing with fierce bat speed. He's consistently on time and on plane through the hitting zone for a long time, which allows him to barrel balls at a high rate. Bichette has a good sense for the strike zone and uses the whole field, with above-average power and loft to go deep to all fields. He has a strong, compact frame and while some scouts think he's a future second or third baseman, he looked better than expected at shortstop in 2017. An average runner, Bichette lacks flash at shortstop and doesn't have the range or footwork many teams want at the position, but he's a fundamentally sound defender with a good internal clock and an above-average arm.

Bichette draws comparisons with Josh Donaldson, with a chance to be a middle-of-the-order hitter and has the potential to be one of the most talented offensive players in baseball. Double-A New Hampshire is his next step.

BA GRADE
65 Risk: High
HIT: 70. POW: 60.
SPD: 50. FLD: 45.
ARM: 60.

Year	Club (League)	Class	AVG	G	AB	R	H	2B	3B	HR	RBI	BB	SO	SB	CS	OBP	SLG
2016	Blue Jays (GCL)	R	.427	22	82	21	35	9	2	4	36	6	17	3	0	.451	.732
2017	Lansing (MWL)	LoA	.384	70	284	60	109	32	3	10	51	28	55	12	3	.448	.623
	Dunedin (FSL)	HiA	.323	40	164	28	53	9	1	4	23	14	26	10	4	.379	.463
Minor League Totals			.372	132	530	109	197	50	6	18	110	48	98	25	7	.427	.591

3 ANTHONY ALFORD, OF

Born: July 20, 1994. **B-T:** R-R. **Ht.:** 6-1. **Wt.:** 215. **Drafted:** HS—Petal, Miss., 2012 (3rd round). **Signed by:** Brian Johnston.

Alford was named Mississippi's Mr. Football and Mr. Baseball as a high school senior and signed a contract that allowed him to play college football, first at Southern Mississippi as a quarterback and then at Mississippi as a defensive back. He accumulated just 94 at bats over the first three seasons of his professional career before giving up football in the fall of 2014. Alford's stock jumped in 2015 with a breakthrough year, but in 2016 a knee injury and then a concussion slowed his progress. In 2017, he started in Double-A New Hampshire, made his big league debut on May 19 but broke his left wrist five days later, then returned to Double-A for the second half.

Alford is a premium athlete who glides around center field with plus speed. He has good anticipation off the bat, getting quick breaks with clean routes to give him above-average range, though with a below-average arm. Alford has a table setters offensive profile with his on-base skills and speed. His elevated strikeout rate in 2016 was an aberration, with Alford showing a patient approach, good bat-to-ball skills and the ability to use the opposite field in 2017. Alford has never cracked double-digit homers in a season, though more power could come once he learns which pitches he can turn on to drive and elevate to his pull side.

Alford finished 2017 in Triple-A and should return there to open 2018, though he should be back in Toronto soon. His ability to get on base and play plus defense at a premium position give him the potential to be an above-average regular.

BA GRADE
55 Risk: Medium
HIT: 60. POW: 50.
SPD: 60. FLD: 60.
ARM: 40.

Year	Club (League)	Class	AVG	G	AB	R	H	2B	3B	HR	RBI	BB	SO	SB	CS	OBP	SLG
2015	Lansing (MWL)	LoA	.293	50	188	49	55	14	1	1	16	39	60	12	1	.418	.394
	Dunedin (FSL)	HiA	.302	57	225	42	68	11	6	3	19	28	49	15	6	.380	.444
2016	Dunedin (FSL)	HiA	.236	92	339	53	80	17	2	9	44	53	117	18	6	.344	.378
2017	Toronto (AL)	MAJ	.125	4	8	0	1	1	0	0	0	0	3	0	0	.125	.250
	Dunedin (FSL)	HiA	.143	6	21	1	3	0	0	0	2	0	8	1	0	.182	.143
	New Hampshire (EL)	AA	.310	68	245	41	76	14	0	5	24	35	45	18	3	.406	.429
	Buffalo (IL)	AAA	.333	3	12	1	4	1	0	0	0	1	2	0	0	.385	.417
Major League Totals			.125	4	8	0	1	1	0	0	0	0	3	0	0	.125	.250
Minor League Totals			.274	301	1124	200	308	60	10	21	113	169	312	75	16	.375	.401

4 NATE PEARSON, RHP

Born: Aug. 20, 1996. **B-T:** R-R. **Ht.:** 6-6. **Wt.:** 245. **Drafted:** JC of Central Florida, 2017 (1st round). **Signed by:** Matt Bishoff.

After his freshman year at Florida International, Pearson transferred to the JC of Central Florida, where he elevated his stock to become the No. 28 overall pick in 2017 with a $2,452,900 bonus. The Blue Jays limited his workload after signing, but he blew away the competition when he was on the mound in the short-season Northwest League.

Pearson gives hitters an uncomfortable at-bat. He attacks them with downhill angle from his 6-foot-6 frame and pitches with a lively, heavy fastball that parked at 92-94 mph and touched 98 regularly in his college starts. In short bursts with the Blue Jays, Pearson sat in the mid- to upper 90s and touched 101 mph, with the fastball life to get swings-and-misses up and down in the zone. His secondary stuff is inconsistent but shows the makings of effective offspeed weapons. His changeup is an average pitch with late fade. He added power to his slider in pro ball, which took the pitch from a slurvy low-80s offering to a sharper breaking ball. It now reaches the mid- to upper 80s with late tilt, though he's still learning to land it for a strike. He throws a curveball but it's behind his other pitches.

Pearson should start 2018 at a Class A affiliate. If he can handle a starter's workload, he has a chance to develop into a mid-rotation arm.

BA GRADE

55 Risk: V. High

FB: 70. CB: 45.
SLD: 55. CHG: 50.
CTL: 45.

Year	Club (League)	Class	W	L	ERA	G	GS	CG	SV	IP	H	HR	BB	SO	K/9	WHIP	AVG
2017	Blue Jays (GCL)	R	0	0	0.00	1	1	0	0	1	1	0	0	2	18.0	1.00	.250
	Vancouver (NWL)	SS	0	0	0.95	7	7	0	0	19	6	0	5	24	11.4	0.58	.097
Minor League Totals			0	0	0.90	8	8	0	0	20	7	0	5	26	11.7	0.60	.106

5 LOURDES GURRIEL, SS/2B

Born: Oct. 19, 1993. **B-T:** R-R. **Ht.:** 6-3. **Wt.:** 190. **Signed:** Cuba, 2016. **Signed by:** Andrew Tinnish.

Gurriel, the younger brother of Astros first baseman Yuli Gurriel, signed a seven-year, $22 million contract with the Blue Jays in October 2016. He didn't play in 2016 as he worked in preparation to sign, and his debut in 2017 got off to a rocky start. Gurriel opened the year on the disabled list, played one game on April 19 and re-aggravated the injury, then finally returned two months later. He went to the Arizona Fall League after the season to make up for lost work.

A long layoff from competitive baseball combined with injury setbacks could explain some of Gurriel's 2017 struggles. At his best, he has shown good strike-zone discipline, though he got too aggressive in 2017, perhaps as he shook off rust and got used to facing better pitchers than he ever faced in Cuba. Gurriel is a long-armed hitter, so his swing will always have some length, but he doesn't strike out

BA GRADE

55 Risk: V. High

HIT: 55. POW: 60.
SPD: 55. FLD: 45.
ARM: 60.

excessively and has above-average raw power. In his final season in Cuba, Gurriel improved his speed to above-average, though the leg injury held him back in 2017. Gurriel's split time between shortstop and second base. His range might be stretched at shortstop, but he has a strong arm and could fit well at third base. He also has experience in the outfield.

While a lot of signs point to Gurriel's debut being a one-year blip that isn't in line with his true talent level, he will have to prove that on the field in 2018.

Year	Club (League)	Class	AVG	G	AB	R	H	2B	3B	HR	RBI	BB	SO	SB	CS	OBP	SLG
2015	La Habana (CNS)	CNS	.344	59	218	43	75	17	0	10	53	21	23	8	3	.407	.560
2016	Did not play																
2017	Dunedin (FSL)	HiA	.197	18	66	6	13	1	0	1	8	2	13	1	0	.217	.258
	New Hampshire (EL)	AA	.241	46	170	20	41	10	0	4	28	10	30	2	0	.286	.371
Minor League Totals			.229	64	236	26	54	11	0	5	36	12	43	3	0	.268	.339

6 ERIC PARDINHO, RHP

BILL MITCHELL

Born: Jan. 5, 2001. **B-T:** R-R. **Ht.:** 5-9. **Wt.:** 160. **Signed:** Brazil, 2017. **Signed by:** Andrew Tinnish/Sandy Rosario.

Pardinho struck out 14 batters in six innings against the Dominican Republic at the COPABE 16U Pan American Championship in July 2016, then two months later pitched out of the bullpen for Brazil in the World Baseball Classic qualifier as a 15-year-old.

After establishing himself as the top international pitching prospect in the 2017 class, Pardinho signed with the Blue Jays for $1.4 million. Pardinho has an outstanding combination of stuff and polish for his age, with his stuff continuing to tick up after signing. Prior to signing, his fastball sat 88-92 mph and reached 94. Now he's sitting regularly in the low 90s and has reached 97 mph. His curveball flashes plus with tight spin and sharp break to miss bats. The Blue Jays are teaching him a changeup that's still a new pitch for him. Pardinho throws with remarkable ease, showing smooth arm action and minimal-effort mechanics that he repeats consistently. His feel for pitching is well beyond his years and he throws strikes at a high rate. He has a small stature and his lower half is already strong, so several scouts had concerns about how much more velocity he would gain, but he's already seen a spike since becoming a professional.

Pardinho will likely make his pro debut as a 17-year-old in the Rookie-level Gulf Coast League. He's far away, but he has the talent to move quickly.

BA GRADE

55 Risk: Extreme

FB: 60. **CB:** 60.
CHG: 45.
CTL: 60.

Year	Club (League)	Class	W	L	ERA	G	GS	CG	SV	IP	H	HR	BB	SO	K/9	WHIP	AVG
2017	Did not play—Signed 2018 contract																

7 DANNY JANSEN, C

Born: April 15, 1995. **B-T:** R-R. **Ht.:** 6-2. **Wt.:** 225. **Drafted:** HS—Appleton, Wis., 2013 (16th round). **Signed by:** Wes Penick.

A broken left hand sidelined Jansen for three months in 2015 and a broken hamate bone in his left hand in 2016 put him out for two months that season. Healthy in 2017, Jansen broke through, hitting a combined .323/.400/.484 in a season he spent primarily at Double-A New Hampshire but finished at Triple-A Buffalo.

Jansen's success stems from excellent strike-zone judgment. He walked (41) more often than he struck out (40) because he tracks pitches well, has a disciplined approach and doesn't chase much off the plate, enabling himself to get into advantageous counts and draw walks to get on base. Jansen makes frequent contact with a pull-minded, line-drive approach and enough power to hit 10-15 home runs, with his value coming more from his on-base skills than his power. Behind the plate, Jansen blocks balls well, but his arm strength is fringe-average and he threw out just 24 percent of baserunners in 2017.

The Blue Jays added Jansen to the 40-man roster in November to protect him from the Rule 5 draft. He should return to Triple-A to start 2018 and could be up by midseason.

BA GRADE

50 Risk: High

HIT: 55. **POW:** 40.
SPD: 30. **FLD:** 45.
ARM: 50.

Year	Club (League)	Class	AVG	G	AB	R	H	2B	3B	HR	RBI	BB	SO	SB	CS	OBP	SLG
2015	Blue Jays (GCL)	R	.238	7	21	4	5	1	0	1	3	2	5	0	0	.304	.429
	Lansing (MWL)	LoA	.206	46	160	19	33	8	0	4	27	19	22	2	0	.299	.331
2016	Blue Jays (GCL)	R	.222	3	9	0	2	0	0	0	2	1	2	0	0	.364	.222
	Dunedin (FSL)	HiA	.218	54	188	18	41	7	0	1	23	22	40	7	1	.313	.271
2017	Dunedin (FSL)	HiA	.369	31	122	19	45	6	0	5	18	8	14	0	0	.422	.541
	New Hampshire (EL)	AA	.291	52	179	23	52	15	1	2	20	22	19	1	0	.378	.419
	Buffalo (IL)	AAA	.328	21	67	8	22	4	1	3	10	11	7	0	0	.423	.552
Minor League Totals			.267	288	984	132	263	55	2	21	138	122	136	12	2	.360	.391

8 LOGAN WARMOTH, SS

Born: Sept. 6, 1995. **B-T:** R-R. **Ht.:** 6-0. **Wt.:** 190. **Drafted:** North Carolina, 2017 (1st round). **Signed by:** Chris Kline.

A three-year starter at North Carolina, Warmoth was the first shortstop drafted in 2017, going No. 22 overall and signing for $2,820,200. He performed well in his pro debut in the short-season Northwest League.

Warmoth is a bucket full of 50-grade tools on the 20-80 scouting scale, with no one true calling card but a high overall baseball IQ and no glaring holes either. He's a steady hitter with quick bat speed, a good performance record and below-average power. While his hands tend to shoot out away from his body, he catches up to good velocity and uses the whole field. He has an aggressive approach and did get pull-happy early in his pro debut, though he adjusted as the season went on to better handle pitches on the outer third and drive them the opposite way.

An average runner with a solid-average, accurate arm and quick hands, Warmoth has a chance to stay at shortstop, though some scouts think he would fit better at second base. Warmoth is unlikely to develop into a star, but his skills in the middle of the diamond give him a chance to become a solid-average regular.

BA GRADE
50 Risk: High
HIT: 50. POW: 40.
SPD: 50. FLD: 50.
ARM: 55.

Year	Club (League)	Class	AVG	G	AB	R	H	2B	3B	HR	RBI	BB	SO	SB	CS	OBP	SLG
2017	Blue Jays (GCL)	R	.273	6	22	3	6	0	0	1	3	1	2	1	0	.304	.409
	Vancouver (NWL)	SS	.306	39	160	18	49	11	2	1	20	7	33	5	2	.356	.419
Minor League Totals			.302	45	182	21	55	11	2	2	23	8	35	6	2	.350	.418

9 RICHARD URENA, SS

Born: Feb. 26, 1996. **B-T:** B-R. **Ht.:** 6-0. **Wt.:** 185. **Signed:** Dominican Republic, 2012. **Signed by:** Ismael Cruz/Sandy Rosario/Luciano Del Rosario.

Urena signed for $725,000 as a 16-year-old in 2012 and made steady progress up through high Class A Dunedin. He reached Double-A New Hampshire at the end of 2016 and struggled there, then posted another sub-.300 OBP season with the Fisher Cats again in 2017.

Urena made his major league debut as a September callup. Urena was a 21-year-old shortstop in Double-A, so while he was one of the youngest players at the level, he seemed to hit an offensive wall. He has fast hands and has shown solid bat control throughout his career, but his overaggressive approach got him in trouble in 2017. He's not a total free-swinger, but he needs to develop a better plan to get into better counts and increase his OBP. Urena hasn't shown much power, though he has more extra-base sock from the left side. A below-average runner, his pure range is just adequate for shortstop, but he has good anticipation off the bat and can make acrobatic plays with a plus arm.

Urena has a chance to be a steady regular in the middle of the diamond, but his offensive performance will have to rebound to the levels he showed prior to 2017. He will head to Triple-A in 2018.

BA GRADE
45 Risk: Medium
HIT: 50. POW: 30.
SPD: 40. FLD: 50.
ARM: 60.

Year	Club (League)	Class	AVG	G	AB	R	H	2B	3B	HR	RBI	BB	SO	SB	CS	OBP	SLG
2015	Dunedin (FSL)	HiA	.250	30	124	9	31	3	1	1	8	3	26	3	1	.268	.315
	Lansing (MWL)	LoA	.266	91	384	62	102	13	4	15	58	13	84	5	5	.289	.438
2016	Dunedin (FSL)	HiA	.305	97	394	52	120	18	7	8	41	25	64	9	6	.351	.447
	New Hampshire (EL)	AA	.266	30	124	14	33	6	5	0	18	4	19	0	2	.282	.395
2017	New Hampshire (EL)	AA	.247	129	510	44	126	36	3	5	60	30	100	0	1	.286	.359
	Toronto (AL)	MAJ	.206	21	68	6	14	4	0	1	4	6	28	1	0	.270	.309
Major League Totals			.206	21	68	6	14	4	0	1	4	6	28	1	0	.270	.309
Minor League Totals			.277	510	2056	267	570	114	25	32	248	127	398	32	24	.320	.404

10 RYAN BORUCKI, LHP

Born: March 31, 1994. **B-T:** L-L. **Ht.:** 6-4. **Wt.:** 190. **Drafted:** HS—Mundelein Ill., 2012 (15th round). **Signed by:** Mike Medici.

Injuries have slowed Borucki's development. He had Tommy John surgery as a high school senior, then dealt with shoulder problems in 2013, 2014 and 2015. Borucki had pitched just six games above low Class A entering 2017, but he took off that season and finished the year at Triple-A Buffalo.

Borucki locates his fastball, gets ground balls and changes speeds effectively to keep hitters off balance. He's a strike-thrower who walked 2.2 per nine innings in 2017, with good command of a fastball that sits in the low 90s and scrapes 96 mph. He catches hitters leaning out front or swinging through his changeup, a plus pitch that he disguises well to look like a fastball out of his hand. Borucki's slider is a fringe-average pitch, so he mostly relies on his fastball/changeup combination. While arm problems have hampered him in the past, Borucki showed durability by throwing 150 innings in 2017.

Borucki's big leap forward put him in contention to compete for a rotation spot in Toronto in 2018, though most likely he begins back in Triple-A. He has the profile of a back-end starter.

BA GRADE
45 Risk: Medium
FB: 55. SL: 45.
CHG: 60.
CTL: 60.

Year	Club (League)	Class	W	L	ERA	G	GS	CG	SV	IP	H	HR	BB	SO	K/9	WHIP	AVG
2015	Blue Jays (GCL)	R	0	0	0.00	1	0	0	0	1	1	0	0	1	9.0	1.00	.250
	Vancouver (NWL)	SS	0	1	3.86	2	2	0	0	5	6	0	3	6	11.6	1.93	.300
2016	Dunedin (FSL)	HiA	1	4	14.40	6	6	0	0	20	40	10	12	10	4.5	2.60	.421
	Lansing (MWL)	LoA	10	4	2.41	20	20	1	0	116	105	1	26	107	8.3	1.13	.247
2017	Dunedin (FSL)	HiA	6	5	3.58	19	18	0	0	98	95	5	27	109	10.0	1.24	.255
	New Hampshire (EL)	AA	2	3	1.94	7	7	0	0	46	31	2	8	42	8.2	0.84	.187
	Buffalo (IL)	AAA	0	0	0.00	1	1	0	0	6	6	0	1	6	9.0	1.17	.273
Minor League Totals			23	19	3.32	73	64	1	1	355	327	22	86	343	8.7	1.16	.246

11 SEAN REID-FOLEY, RHP

BA GRADE
50 Risk: High

Born: Aug. 30, 1995. **B-T:** R-R. **Ht.:** 6-3. **Wt.:** 220. **Drafted:** HS—Jacksonville, 2014 (2nd round). **Signed by:** Matt Bishoff.

After Reid-Foley took a step forward in 2016, he struggled in 2017 in the Double-A Eastern League, where he struggled with fastball command, inconsistent stuff and gave up too much hard contact. Despite his struggles, Reid-Foley still flashes average to plus stuff across the board.

Reid-Foley's fastball parks at 91-94 mph with good movement and reaches 97. His best secondary pitch depends on the day. Usually either his curveball or slider are working for him. When they're right, they're average pitches, though they sometimes disappeared on him and contributed to his struggles. His changeup flashed average at times too. Reid-Foley must improve his fastball command, which is complicated because of his mechanics and arm action. That leads several scouts to think his future is in the bullpen, though the Blue Jays plan to keep Reid-Foley as a starter.

Reid-Foley has the repertoire to project as a back-end starter, though his stuff could tick up in short stints if he's moved to a relief role, with a chance to get to Toronto by the end of 2018.

Year	Club (League)	Class	W	L	ERA	G	GS	CG	SV	IP	H	HR	BB	SO	K/9	WHIP	AVG
2015	Dunedin (FSL)	HiA	1	5	5.23	8	8	0	0	33	25	1	24	35	9.6	1.50	.210
	Lansing (MWL)	LoA	3	5	3.69	17	17	0	0	63	57	3	43	90	12.8	1.58	.239
2016	Lansing (MWL)	LoA	4	3	2.95	11	11	0	0	58	43	2	22	59	9.2	1.12	.208
	Dunedin (FSL)	HiA	6	2	2.67	10	10	0	0	57	35	2	16	71	11.1	0.89	.172
2017	New Hampshire (EL)	AA	10	11	5.09	27	27	0	0	133	145	22	53	122	8.3	1.49	.278
Minor League Totals			25	28	4.12	82	79	0	0	367	326	30	168	402	9.9	1.35	.237

12 T.J. ZEUCH, RHP

BA GRADE
50 Risk: High

Born: Aug. 1, 1995. **B-T:** R-R. **Ht.:** 6-7. **Wt.:** 225. **Drafted:** Pittsburgh, 2016 (1st round). **Signed by:** Doug Witt.

The Blue Jays drafted Zeuch with the No. 21 overall pick in the 2016 draft, making him the highest draft pick from Pittsburgh's program.

In Zeuch's first full season, a lower back injury followed by another one to his hamstring caused Zeuch to miss June and July, limiting him to just 65.2 innings during the regular season before getting another 18.1 innings in the Arizona Fall League. Batters have a difficult time elevating the ball against Zeuch. He pounds the strike zone from a steep downhill angle with a heavy sinker at 92-94 mph and the ability to reach 97. That pitch helps him generate a high groundball rate, though he doesn't have a plus secondary pitch to consistently get swing-and-misses. His mid-80s slider and upper-70s curveball are both average pitches, while his changeup is a tick below-average.

Zeuch did a better job of incorporating his lower half into his delivery by the end of the season, and working to improve his strength and mobility will be priorities to help his durability.

Year	Club (League)	Class	W	L	ERA	G	GS	CG	SV	IP	H	HR	BB	SO	K/9	WHIP	AVG
2016	Blue Jays (GCL)	R	0	0	0.00	1	1	0	0	3	0	0	0	2	6.0	0.00	.000
	Vancouver (NWL)	SS	0	1	3.52	6	6	0	0	23	21	1	5	22	8.6	1.13	.247
	Lansing (MWL)	LoA	0	1	9.00	2	2	0	0	8	10	1	2	14	15.8	1.50	.294
2017	Blue Jays (GCL)	R	0	2	5.14	3	3	0	0	7	9	1	2	5	6.4	1.57	.321
	Dunedin (FSL)	HiA	3	4	3.38	12	11	0	0	59	63	3	17	46	7.1	1.36	.266
Minor League Totals			3	8	3.88	24	23	0	0	100	103	6	26	89	8.0	1.29	.262

13 RYAN NODA, 1B/OF

BA GRADE
50 Risk: V. High

Born: March 30, 1996. **B-T:** L-L. **Ht.:** 6-3. **Wt.:** 217. **Drafted:** Cincinnati, 2017 (15th round). **Signed by:** Coulson Barbiche.

Noda could have gone in the top three rounds of the 2017 draft, but he racked up a high strikeout rate during his junior year at Cincinnati and fell to the 15th round. He showed an exciting combination of patience and power after signing, winning the MVP award in the Rookie-level Appalachian League, where he led the circuit in batting average, on-base percentage and slugging.

Noda is a strong, physical hitter with quick wrists and plus power, who drives the ball with authority the opposite way. With an upright approach, Noda's swing can get stiff at times and he will have to prove he's more than a mistake hitter taking advantage of lower-level pitching, but he can hammer the ball out to all fields with natural loft in his stroke. He's an extremely patient hitter who walked at a 21 percent clip in his debut.

Noda is a below-average runner who spent most of his time in Bluefield at first base, but he has enough athleticism and arm strength to go to either corner outfield spot, and the Blue Jays plan to put him in the outfield in 2018.

Year	Club (League)	Class	AVG	G	AB	R	H	2B	3B	HR	RBI	BB	SO	SB	CS	OBP	SLG
2017	Bluefield (APP)	R	.364	66	214	62	78	18	3	7	39	59	60	7	4	.507	.575
Minor League Totals			.364	66	214	62	78	18	3	7	39	59	60	7	4	.507	.575

14 EDWARD OLIVARES, OF

BA GRADE
50 Risk: V. High

Born: March 6, 1996. **B-T:** R-R. **Ht.:** 6-2. **Wt.:** 190. **Signed:** Venezuela, 2014. **Signed by:** Ismael Cruz/Luis Marquez/Jose Contreras.

Olivares was one of Toronto's July 2 signings in 2014, though unlike the high-profile international prospects for big bonuses that day, Olivares received a $1,000 bonus. A broken left hamate bone limited Olivares to just 15 games in 2016, but he had a breakthrough season in 2017, albeit in the shadow of teammates Vladimir Guerrero Jr. and Bo Bichette.

Olivares has an array of plus tools. He's an athletic center fielder with plus speed and arm strength, recording 15 assists in 105 games in the outfield. At the plate he has quick hands, fast bat speed with solid-average raw power. Olivares doesn't strike out excessively, but he has an aggressive, pull-happy approach, so improving his plate discipline and being able to adjust his swing to drive pitches to the opposite field will be key as he faces better pitching.

Olivares will start 2018 in high Class A Dunedin.

Year	Club (League)	Class	AVG	G	AB	R	H	2B	3B	HR	RBI	BB	SO	SB	CS	OBP	SLG
2015	Blue Jays (GCL)	R	.198	38	116	21	23	8	1	3	10	11	27	14	2	.345	.362
2016	Bluefield (APP)	R	.273	15	55	8	15	3	1	1	6	5	12	1	2	.339	.418
2017	Lansing (MWL)	LoA	.277	101	426	82	118	26	9	17	65	22	82	18	7	.330	.500
	Dunedin (FSL)	HiA	.221	19	68	11	15	1	1	0	7	8	17	2	2	.312	.265
Minor League Totals			.267	213	805	153	215	43	15	22	110	66	161	47	16	.351	.440

15 REESE McGUIRE, C

BA GRADE
45 Risk: High

Born: March 2, 1995. **B-T:** L-R. **Ht.:** 5-11. **Wt.:** 215. **Drafted:** HS—Covington, Wash., 2013 (1st round). **Signed by:** Greg Hopkins (Pirates).

The Pirates used one of their two first-round picks in 2013 to draft McGuire at No. 13 overall. Three years later, they sent McGuire and outfielder Harold Ramirez to the Blue Jays along with Francisco Liriano in a trade for righthander Drew Hutchison.

McGuire repeated the Double-A Eastern League in 2017, though he didn't spend much time on the field due to a left oblique injury in early May, only returning to New Hampshire in August. He did make up for some lost time playing winter ball for the Aguilas in the Dominican League. Defense is McGuire's calling card. He's an above-average defender with high overall game awareness and thorough preparation, so pitchers like throwing to him. McGuire blocks and receives pitches well, and his average arm plays up because of his quick footwork to get rid of the ball. McGuire has a compact swing with good rhythm, a flat path and a sharp eye for the strike zone. His six home runs in 45 games in 2017 were a career high.

McGuire has a chance to be a starter if he can develop more power, but if not he should have just enough offensive skill to go with his defense to stick around for a long time as a backup.

Year	Club (League)	Class	AVG	G	AB	R	H	2B	3B	HR	RBI	BB	SO	SB	CS	OBP	SLG
2015	Bradenton (FSL)	HiA	.254	98	374	32	95	15	0	0	34	26	39	14	7	.301	.294
2016	Altoona (EL)	AA	.259	77	266	29	69	16	2	1	37	29	26	4	4	.337	.346
	New Hampshire (EL)	AA	.226	15	53	5	12	2	0	0	5	7	8	2	2	.328	.264
2017	Blue Jays (GCL)	R	.409	8	22	4	9	2	0	0	7	3	1	0	1	.462	.500
	Dunedin (FSL)	HiA	.250	3	12	1	3	1	0	0	1	1	2	0	0	.308	.333
	New Hampshire (EL)	AA	.278	34	115	19	32	5	1	6	20	16	19	2	1	.366	.496
Minor League Totals			.270	383	1423	169	384	63	7	10	170	122	158	35	18	.330	.345

16 CONNER GREENE, RHP

BA GRADE

45 Risk: High

Born: April 4, 1995. **B-T:** R-R. **Ht.:** 6-3. **Wt.:** 195. **Drafted:** HS—Santa Monica, Calif., 2013, (7th round). **Signed by:** Jim Lentine.

The arrows seemed to be pointing up for Greene after the 2015 season, when he finished the year in Double-A, was throwing strikes and was throwing harder than ever. Greene hit triple-digits on on the radar gun in 2017, but the rest of his numbers underwhelming.

Greene is an excellent athlete with a power arm, sitting in the mid-90s and reaching 101 mph. Despite that big velocity, hitters had little trouble squaring up Greene last year in Double-A. His fastball lacks great movement and he doesn't command it well yet, which led to a high walk rate. He also didn't miss many bats as he lacks a putaway secondary pitch. His 79-81 mph curveball and 86-88 mph changeup are fringe-average pitches, because he tends to slow his arm speed on when he throws them.

There are significant developmental jumps Greene will have to make to continue as a starter, and while the Blue Jays plan to keep him in that role, he has the type of stuff that could play well in short stints without having to get through a lineup multiple times.

Year	Club (League)	Class	W	L	ERA	G	GS	CG	SV	IP	H	HR	BB	SO	K/9	WHIP	AVG
2015	Lansing (MWL)	LoA	7	3	3.88	14	14	0	0	67	75	4	19	65	8.7	1.40	.285
	Dunedin (FSL)	HiA	2	3	2.25	7	7	0	0	40	36	1	8	35	7.9	1.10	.238
	New Hampshire (EL)	AA	3	1	4.68	5	5	0	0	25	25	1	12	15	5.4	1.48	.269
2016	Dunedin (FSL)	HiA	4	4	2.90	15	15	0	0	78	74	5	38	51	5.9	1.44	.252
	New Hampshire (EL)	AA	6	5	4.19	12	12	1	0	69	57	5	33	48	6.3	1.31	.224
2017	New Hampshire (EL)	AA	5	10	5.29	26	25	0	0	133	140	7	83	92	6.2	1.68	.275
Minor League Totals			31	31	4.04	103	91	1	0	501	495	27	226	377	6.8	1.44	.260

17 MIGUEL HIRALDO, SS

BA GRADE

50 Risk: Extreme

Born: Sept. 5, 2000. **B-T:** R-R. **Ht.:** 5-11. **Wt.:** 175. **Signed:** Dominican Republic, 2017. **Signed by:** Luciano del Rosario.

Several clubs had Hiraldo graded out as one of the top hitters available on the international amateur market in 2017, when Hiraldo signed with the Blue Jays for $750,000.

Hiraldo is built like a catcher with a strong, stocky frame with powerful legs and forearms. He has quick hands and a short, repeatable stroke. He swings hard and hammers fastballs for hard line drives with average raw power. Some scouts had questions about Hiraldo's ability to handle offspeed pitches and use the opposite field, with a swing that starts with his hands at his ears before coming straight down, but he frequently makes hard, quality contact in games. Hiraldo probably won't spend much time at shortstop. The Blue Jays plan to keep him there for now, though he probably fits better at third base.

Most of Hiraldo's focus as an amateur was on his hitting rather than his defense, so he will have to improve his defensive actions and smooth out a funky throwing stroke to stick in the dirt.

Year	Club (League)	Class	AVG	G	AB	R	H	2B	3B	HR	RBI	BB	SO	SB	CS	OBP	SLG
2017	Did not play—Signed 2018 contract																

18 LEONARDO JIMENEZ, SS

BA GRADE

50 Risk: Extreme

Born: May 17, 2001. **B-T:** R-R. **Ht.:** 6-0. **Wt.:** 165. **Signed:** Panama, 2017. **Signed by:** Alex Zapada.

Jimenez has a long track record of representing Panama at international youth tournaments, from the 12U World Cup in 2013 in Taiwan to the COPABE 14U Championship in 2015 in Venezuela to the COPABE 16U Championship in 2016 in Panama. He was the top prospect in Panama in 2017, when he signed with the Blue Jays for $825,000.

Jimenez stands out more for his baseball savvy and instincts than his raw tools or explosiveness. He's a smart all-around player with a good hitting approach, making frequent contact with a short swing. He stays through the middle of the field well, hitting a lot of line drives with gap power.

Jimenez is a fringe-average runner and doesn't have the quick first step a lot of scouts want to see in a shortstop, but he is an instinctive defender with a good internal clock, smooth hands, actions and good body control at the position.

Year	Club (League)	Class	AVG	G	AB	R	H	2B	3B	HR	RBI	BB	SO	SB	CS	OBP	SLG
2017	Did not play—Signed 2018 contract																

19 CARLOS RAMIREZ, RHP

BA GRADE

40 Risk: Medium

Born: April 24, 1991. **B-T:** R-R. **Ht.:** 6-5. **Wt.:** 205. **Signed:** Dominican Republic, 2009. **Signed by:** Hilario Soriano.

Ramirez signed with the Blue Jays in 2009 as a center fielder, then spent five seasons toiling around in rookie and short-season leagues. After struggling in low Class A Lansing in 2013, Ramirez went back to the Lugnuts to start 2014, but a month into the season he put away his bat and began the conversion to pitching at age 23.

Ramirez has only pitched out of the bullpen on his climb up the system, with his breakthrough season coming in 2017. Between Double-A New Hampshire and Triple-A Buffalo last year, Ramirez threw 37.2 innings without allowing an earned run, then continued to pitch well in his major league debut as a September callup. Ramirez has improved his control every season to become a prolific strike-thrower. He attacks hitters with an even mix of fastballs and sliders, getting a heavy dose of swing-and-miss both in and out of the strike zone. He can fill the strike zone with fastballs at 91-94 mph, then misses a lot of bats with a plus slider at 82-85 mph. Ramirez can land his slider for a strike or bury it away from righthanded hitters to get them to swing over the top of it as a chase pitch.

Ramirez should return to Toronto's bullpen on Opening Day and stick around for years as a middle reliever.

Year	Club (League)	Class	W	L	ERA	G	GS	CG	SV	IP	H	HR	BB	SO	K/9	WHIP	AVG
2015	Dunedin (FSL)	HiA	0	2	4.91	6	0	0	0	7	10	0	10	7	8.6	2.73	.313
	Lansing (MWL)	LoA	2	1	4.73	28	0	0	8	32	38	2	14	30	8.4	1.61	.295
2016	Dunedin (FSL)	HiA	3	0	2.20	30	0	0	9	41	32	2	21	41	9.0	1.29	.221
2017	New Hampshire (EL)	AA	2	0	0.00	18	0	0	3	24	10	0	7	29	11.0	0.72	.124
	Buffalo (IL)	AAA	1	0	0.00	7	0	0	0	14	6	0	3	16	10.3	0.64	.128
	Toronto (AL)	MAJ	0	0	2.70	12	0	0	0	17	6	3	3	14	7.6	0.54	.111
Major League Totals			0	0	2.70	12	0	0	0	17	6	3	3	14	7.6	0.54	.111
Minor League Totals			9	3	2.42	106	0	0	20	153	128	6	74	147	8.7	1.32	.227

20 RILEY ADAMS, C

BA GRADE

45 Risk: High

Born: June 26, 1996. **B-T:** R-R. **Ht.:** 6-4. **Wt.:** 225. **Drafted:** San Diego, 2017 (3rd round). **Signed by:** Jim Lentine.

Adams started at catcher for San Diego since his freshman year, then signed with the Blue Jays for $542,400 as a third-round pick in 2017 and hit well in his pro debut in the short-season Northwest League.

Adams immediately sticks out with an extra-large frame for a catcher. He has a plus arm and erased 40 percent of basestealers in the NWL. To remain behind the plate, he has work to do to improve his hands, receiving and blocking skills and avoid a move to either first base or the outfield. He already showed improvements in those areas since signing and looks like he could develop into an adequate defender..

Adams has a power-over-hit profile, with average raw power that comes with swing-and-miss because his swing tends to get big. He hit just three home runs in 52 games in pro ball, but he was playing home games in a park that suppresses power and looked fatigued by the end of the season.

Year	Club (League)	Class	AVG	G	AB	R	H	2B	3B	HR	RBI	BB	SO	SB	CS	OBP	SLG
2017	Vancouver (NWL)	SS	.305	52	203	26	62	16	1	3	35	18	50	1	1	.374	.438
Minor League Totals			.305	52	203	26	62	16	1	3	35	18	50	1	1	.374	.438

21 ROWDY TELLEZ, 1B

BA GRADE
40 Risk: Medium

Born: March 16, 1995. **B-T:** L-L. **Ht.:** 6-4. **Wt.:** 220. **Drafted:** HS—Elk Grove, Calif., 2013 (30th round). **Signed by:** Darold Brown.

Tellez's combination of patience and power led to strong numbers throughout the lower levels. His skill set started to translate when he got to the upper levels as well, as he ranked second in the Double-A Eastern League in on-base percentage and third in slugging in 2016. He hit a wall last year when he got to Triple-A, where he started slowly and never was able to climb out of the hole.

Tellez has a middle-opposite field approach, lift in his swing and above-average raw power. His bat speed is fair at best, though, and he looked out of rhythm and out of sync all season. Tellez has a heavy frame and isn't a great athlete, with below-average defense at first base. Tellez's track record up until Triple-A can't be ignored, so it's possible he could bounce back in 2018, although some scouts see him as more of a 4-A slugger.

The Blue Jays didn't want to risk losing him in the Rule 5 draft, so they protected him on the 40-man roster after the season. He will return to Triple-A in 2018.

Year	Club (League)	Class	AVG	G	AB	R	H	2B	3B	HR	RBI	BB	SO	SB	CS	OBP	SLG
2015	Lansing (MWL)	LoA	.296	68	270	36	80	19	0	7	49	24	56	2	2	.351	.444
	Dunedin (FSL)	HiA	.275	35	131	17	36	5	0	7	28	14	28	3	0	.338	.473
2016	New Hampshire (EL)	AA	.297	124	438	71	130	29	2	23	81	63	92	4	3	.387	.530
2017	Buffalo (IL)	AAA	.222	122	445	45	99	29	1	6	56	47	94	6	1	.295	.333
Minor League Totals			.271	448	1641	211	445	98	7	51	277	189	333	19	8	.346	.433

22 HAROLD RAMIREZ, OF

BA GRADE
40 Risk: Medium

Born: Sept. 6, 1994. **B-T:** R-R. **Ht.:** 5-10. **Wt.:** 220. **Signed:** Colombia, 2011. **Signed by:** Rene Gayo/Orlando Covo (Pirates).

The Pirates traded Francisco Lirano along with Ramirez and catcher Reese McGuire in 2016 in exchange for righthander Drew Hutchison. After spending all of 2016 in the Double-A Eastern League, Ramirez repeated the level in 2017 but didn't show many signs of progress and the Blue Jays outrighted him off the 40-man roster in November.

Ramirez is an unconventional player, starting with his compact frame. He ran well enough early in his career to play center field, though he's lost a step and now fits best in a corner. At the plate, Ramirez has a knack for putting the ball in play, with an approach geared toward using the middle of the field and shooting the ball the opposite way. He's strong and shows average raw power, but that doesn't translate into games, which is why his six home runs in 2017 were a career-high.

There's more power potential in there if Ramirez can adjust his swing plane to generate more loft and learns which pitches he should try to turn on to drive with authority to his pull side, but that would entail a significant offensive overhaul.

Year	Club (League)	Class	AVG	G	AB	R	H	2B	3B	HR	RBI	BB	SO	SB	CS	OBP	SLG
2015	Bradenton (FSL)	HiA	.337	80	306	45	103	13	6	4	47	25	48	22	15	.399	.458
2016	Altoona (EL)	AA	.306	98	379	58	116	16	7	2	49	21	66	7	10	.354	.401
	New Hampshire (EL)	AA	.750	1	4	2	3	1	0	0	1	1	0	0	0	.800	1.000
2017	New Hampshire (EL)	AA	.266	121	444	46	118	19	2	6	53	32	65	5	3	.320	.358
Minor League Totals			.296	459	1746	241	516	79	21	19	226	119	286	78	47	.353	.397

23 MAX PENTECOST, C/1B

BA GRADE
45 Risk: V. High

Born: March 10, 1993. **B-T:** R-R. **Ht.:** 6-2. **Wt.:** 195. **Drafted:** Kennesaw State, 2014 (1st round). **Signed by:** Mike Tidick.

Pentecost was the No. 11 overall pick in the 2014 draft, but since then he has three shoulder surgeries (on both shoulders), which is why he was still in high Class A Dunedin last year as a 24-year-old. Working with the organization's high performance staff, Pentecost mixed time at catcher, first base and DH, never catching on back-to-back days.

Pentecost caught just 19 games in Dunedin and another nine in the Arizona Fall League, but he showed a plus arm and looked advanced defensively. He threw out 7-of-15 basestealers (47 percent) and looked athletic behind the plate with good blocking, receiving and framing skills. Pentecost has a pull-heavy approach with above-average bat speed, solid bat-to-ball skills and average raw power. His bat would play well behind the plate, though with his durability in question, he could play more of a hybrid role, moving between catcher, first base and possibly the outfield.

The Blue Jays left Pentecost off the 40-man roster off the season but he didn't get picked in the Rule 5 draft. He's ticketed for Double-A New Hampshire in 2018.

Year	Club (League)	Class	AVG	G	AB	R	H	2B	3B	HR	RBI	BB	SO	SB	CS	OBP	SLG
2015	Did not play—Injured																
2016	Lansing (MWL)	LoA	.314	62	239	36	75	15	3	7	34	21	51	4	2	.375	.490
	Dunedin (FSL)	HiA	.245	12	49	6	12	2	0	3	7	3	17	1	1	.288	.469
2017	Blue Jays (GCL)	R	.000	1	2	0	0	0	0	0	0	0	0	0	0	.000	.000
	Dunedin (FSL)	HiA	.276	71	286	34	79	14	2	9	54	23	62	0	1	.332	.434
Minor League Totals			.294	171	681	93	200	35	8	19	107	49	151	7	6	.343	.452

24 McGREGORY CONTRERAS, OF

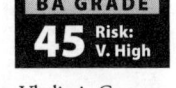

BA GRADE 45 Risk: V. High

Born: Aug. 30, 1998. **B-T:** R-R. **Ht.:** 6-1. **Wt.:** 180. **Signed:** Venezuela, 2015.
Signed by: Ismael Cruz/Luis Marquez/Jose Contreras.

When the Blue Jays went over their international bonus pool in 2015-16 to sign Vladimir Guerrero Jr., they exceeded their pool by a tick under 15 percent, which meant they were only subject to one year of being limited to international signings of $300,000 or less instead of two. The rest of their 2015-16 signings were for $10,000 or less (those are exempt from the bonus pools), and so far Contreras has been the best of that group.

Contreras hit well in his debut in the Dominican Summer League, so the Blue Jays skipped him over the Rookie-level Gulf Coast League with an assignment to the Rookie-level Appalachian League in 2017. Contreras showed plus bat speed and strong wrists, catching up to good velocity on the inner half. Contreras has near-average raw power that shows more in BP than it does in games, partly because his swing is geared to hit the ball on the ground instead of driving it for loft. He also needs to improve his ability to recognize offspeed pitches.

An average runner with an average arm, Contreras mostly played the outfield corners last year and probably fits best at one of those spots. Low Class A Lansing is next for him.

Year	Club (League)	Class	AVG	G	AB	R	H	2B	3B	HR	RBI	BB	SO	SB	CS	OBP	SLG
2016	Blue Jays (DSL)	R	.273	63	216	45	59	10	7	2	22	41	59	10	4	.408	.412
2017	Bluefield (APP)	R	.279	51	190	36	53	8	2	5	33	12	55	4	3	.335	.421
Minor League Totals			.276	114	406	81	112	18	9	7	55	53	114	14	7	.376	.416

25 KEVIN VICUNA, SS

BA GRADE 45 Risk: V. High

Born: Jan. 14, 1998. **B-T:** L-R. **Ht.:** 6-0. **Wt.:** 150. **Signed:** Venezuela, 2014.
Signed by: Ismael Cruz/Luis Marquez/Henry Sandoval.

Defense is where Vicuna shined when the Blue Jays signed him for $350,000 in 2014. His profile today is much the same as it was then, a slick-fielding shortstop with a slightly built frame.

Vicuna was reliable enough defensively that when the Blue Jays needed a fill-in with high Class A Dunedin near the end of April, they had Vicuna play there for a little more than a month before sending him to the short-season Northwest League which was more in line with his talent level. Vicuna is a smooth defender who is light on his feet with quick hands. His pure speed is below-average, but he has good anticipation and can make the flashy play, with an average arm that plays up because of his quick exchange.

Vicuna has solid bat-to-ball skills but it's mostly empty contact. He has 20 power, with no career home runs. His swing and approach lead to him mostly slapping the ball into the ground, so he will have to get stronger and figure out a way to cut back on all those easy groundouts. He should head to low Class A Lansing in 2018.

Year	Club (League)	Class	AVG	G	AB	R	H	2B	3B	HR	RBI	BB	SO	SB	CS	OBP	SLG
2015	Blue Jays (DSL)	R	.268	62	250	43	67	3	3	0	20	17	29	10	4	.354	.304
2016	Blue Jays (GCL)	R	.258	48	178	31	46	5	1	0	14	12	39	11	3	.343	.298
2017	Dunedin (FSL)	HiA	.202	26	84	10	17	1	1	0	4	3	19	0	0	.256	.238
	Vancouver (NWL)	SS	.280	46	189	34	53	3	1	0	17	11	36	14	7	.333	.307
	Lansing (MWL)	LoA	.340	12	50	6	17	1	1	0	4	2	13	3	2	.389	.400
Minor League Totals			.266	194	751	124	200	13	7	0	59	45	136	38	16	.338	.302

26 KEVIN SMITH, SS

BA GRADE

45 Risk: V. High

Born: July 4, 1996. **B-T:** R-R. **Ht.:** 6-1. **Wt.:** 188. **Drafted:** Maryland, 2017 (4th round). **Signed by:** Doug Witt.

Small and skinny in high school, Smith went to Maryland and seized the starting shortstop job as a freshman. He established himself as one of the top defensive shortstops in the nation when the Blue Jays signed him for $405,100.

Smith projects as a true shortstop with good range and body control and soft hands. His arm strength is above-average and he gets rid of the ball quickly with on-target throws. Smith is a fundamentally sound defender with a good internal clock, and while his pure speed is fringy, he gets quick jumps off the bat. Smith isn't just a light-hitting defender, as he flashes quick bat speed and solid-average raw power. That power comes with a high dose of swing-and-miss, however, with an uphill swing path that helps him lift the ball but also leaves him with holes pitchers can exploit.

Smith's defense should carry him, with a chance to be an everyday shortstop if he can keep his strikeout rate in check.

Year	Club (League)	Class	AVG	G	AB	R	H	2B	3B	HR	RBI	BB	SO	SB	CS	OBP	SLG
2017	Bluefield (APP)	R	.271	61	262	43	71	25	1	8	43	16	70	9	0	.312	.466
Minor League Totals			.271	61	262	43	71	25	1	8	43	16	70	9	0	.312	.466

27 JORDAN ROMANO, RHP

BA GRADE

40 Risk: High

Born: April 21, 1993. **B-T:** R-R. **Ht.:** 6-4. **Wt.:** 200. **Drafted:** Oral Roberts, 2014 (10th round). **Signed by:** Dallas Black.

Romano went from an Ontario high school to a pair of Oklahoma colleges—first Connors State JC, then Oral Roberts. Romano was a closer at Oral Roberts, then began his Blue Jays career as a reliever after signing for $25,000 in 2014.

Romano missed the entire 2015 season due to Tommy John surgery, and the Blue Jays made the unusual move of bringing him back as a starter. He proved surprisingly durable in 2017, though the injury has held back his timetable which is why he pitched last season as a 24-year-old in the high Class A Florida State League. Romano's tailing fastball sits at 91-94 mph and he can reach back for 96. Romano generates downhill plane but isn't a groundball pitcher, as he does a good job instead of getting swing-and-misses up in the zone. His go-to pitch is his slider, an above-average pitch that helped him strike out a batter per inning last year and makes him tough on righties, who batted .197./274/.260 with 81 strikeouts and 19 walks in 326 plate appearances against him in 2017. Better fastball command and improving his changeup will be key for Romano if he's going to stick as a starter, especially after lefties hit .352/.433/.452 in 268 plate appearances off him last season.

Romano will continue to develop as a starter, but he could ultimately fit best as a reliever whose fastball should tick up in short stints. Double-A New Hampshire is next for Romano.

Year	Club (League)	Class	W	L	ERA	G	GS	CG	SV	IP	H	HR	BB	SO	K/9	WHIP	AVG
2015	Did not play—Injured																
2016	Lansing (MWL)	LoA	3	2	2.11	15	14	1	0	73	49	3	27	72	8.9	1.05	.191
2017	Dunedin (FSL)	HiA	7	5	3.39	28	26	0	0	138	141	2	54	138	9.0	1.41	.263
Minor League Totals			11	8	2.83	56	40	1	0	239	211	5	94	244	9.2	1.28	.236

28 HAGEN DANNER, C

BA GRADE

45 Risk: Extreme

Born: Sept. 30, 1998. **B-T:** R-R. **Ht.:** 6-2. **Wt.:** 185. **Drafted:** HS—Huntington Beach, Calif., 2017 (2nd round). **Signed by:** Joey Aversa.

Danner played in the 2011 Little League World Series and went on to play for Huntington Beach High, one of the top high school programs in the country. He pitched for USA Baseball's 18U National Team twice and developed into a two-way prospect whom many scouts preferred on the mound, where he reached 95 mph and flashed a swing-and-miss curveball with tight spin.

The Blue Jays, though, signed Danner as a catcher for $1.5 million with their second-round pick. His pro debut was rocky, as Danner struggled in the Rookie-level Gulf Coast League. Danner has a high baseball IQ that helps him behind the plate. He may have been run down in the GCL, as he looked like he needed to improve his blocking and receiving skills and threw out just 21 percent of runners despite having a plus arm. Danner has solid-average raw power but will need time to develop as a hitter. His swing is built more around strength than bat speed, with an extreme pull approach that he will have to adjust to better handle pitches on the outer third.

Focusing full-time on catching should help Danner, though pitching could always be a fallback option down the road.

Year	Club (League)	Class	AVG	G	AB	R	H	2B	3B	HR	RBI	BB	SO	SB	CS	OBP	SLG
2017	Blue Jays (GCL)	R	.160	34	125	10	20	5	0	2	20	5	36	3	1	.207	.248
Minor League Totals			.160	34	125	10	20	5	0	2	20	5	36	3	1	.207	.248

29 JON HARRIS, RHP

BA GRADE 40 Risk: High

Born: Oct. 16, 1993. **B-T:** R-R. **Ht.:** 6-4. **Wt.:** 185. **Drafted:** Missouri State, 2015 (1st round). **Signed by:** Dallas Black.

Harris passed on signing with the Blue Jays out of high school as a 33rd-round pick to become a three-year starter at Missouri State, elevating his stock to become a first-round pick (No. 29 overall) of the Blue Jays in 2015.

Harris has proven to be durable but also very hittable, and he joined fellow righthanders Conner Greene and Sean Reid-Foley with their struggles last year in Double-A New Hampshire. Harris throws a lot of strikes but doesn't have the stuff to miss bats, either in or out of the strike zone. His fastball sits in the low-90s and he fills up the strike zone but made too many mistakes with his fastball command, which got him into trouble last year. Harris throws a curveball, slider and changeup that are all fringe-average pitches, flashing better at times but none of them was a reliable, consistent pitch for him in 2017.

If Harris can improve his fastball command and bring up at least one of his secondary pitches, he could reach the big leagues as a fifth starter.

Year	Club (League)	Class	W	L	ERA	G	GS	CG	SV	IP	H	HR	BB	SO	K/9	WHIP	AVG
2015	Vancouver (NWL)	SS	0	5	6.75	12	11	0	0	36	48	1	21	32	8.0	1.92	.318
2016	Lansing (MWL)	LoA	8	2	2.23	16	16	0	0	85	74	1	24	73	7.8	1.16	.232
	Dunedin (FSL)	HiA	3	2	3.60	8	8	1	0	45	37	2	14	26	5.2	1.13	.224
2017	New Hampshire (EL)	AA	7	11	5.41	26	26	0	0	143	169	20	47	113	7.1	1.51	.292
Minor League Totals			18	20	4.43	62	61	1	0	309	328	24	106	244	7.1	1.41	.270

30 YENNSY DIAZ, RHP

BA GRADE 40 Risk: V. High

Born: Nov. 15, 1996. **B-T:** R-R. **Ht.:** 6-1. **Wt.:** 190. **Signed:** Dominican Republic, 2014. **Signed by:** Ismael Cruz/Sandy Rosario/Luciano Del Rosario.

After signing with the Blue Jays for $70,000 in 2014, Diaz pitched well enough the next year in his pro debut in the Dominican Summer League that the Blue Jays jumped him to the United States later that season to pitch in the Rookie-level Gulf Coast League.

Diaz continued his ascent with by making his full-season debut with low Class A Lansing last year in June. An athletic pitcher with a quick arm, Diaz sits in the low-90s with his fastball with late riding life and he can gear up for 95 mph. His curveball and changeup are both a tick below-average pitches that will flash better at times, but he will need to continue to develop his secondary pitches. Better control and overall feel for pitching are also keys for Diaz, as he fell behind in too many counts last year and hitters were able to sit on his fastball.

High Class A Dunedin will be Diaz's next test.

Year	Club (League)	Class	W	L	ERA	G	GS	CG	SV	IP	H	HR	BB	SO	K/9	WHIP	AVG
2015	Blue Jays (DSL)	R	3	3	1.93	10	6	0	0	37	30	0	16	39	9.4	1.23	.217
	Blue Jays (GCL)	R	1	1	4.74	5	3	0	1	19	24	0	7	19	9.0	1.63	.316
2016	Bluefield (APP)	R	4	6	5.79	12	10	0	0	56	59	9	27	48	7.7	1.54	.267
2017	Lansing (MWL)	LoA	5	2	4.79	16	16	0	0	77	71	10	41	82	9.6	1.45	.249
Minor League Totals			13	12	4.52	43	35	0	1	189	184	19	91	188	8.9	1.45	.256

Washington Nationals

BY CARLOS COLLAZO

After winning the National League East in 2016 with a 95-67 record, the 2017 Nationals improved by two wins and took the division crown for the fourth time in the last six seasons.

However, while Washington has proven to be the class of the NL East for the last decade, playoff success remains elusive.

After losing the NL Division Series to the Dodgers three games to two in 2016, the Nationals again fell in the NLDS in 2017 to the Cubs by the same margin. Despite two years with 95 wins or more and back to back first-place finishes, the lack of postseason success cost manager Dusty Baker his job and continues to loom like a shadow over the Nationals fan base. Washington has played in four Division Series since 2012 but have yet to advance past the first round.

The pressure to play deeper into October will only mount in 2018, which is the last year that 25-year-old outfielder Bryce Harper will be under contract before hitting the free agent market for the first time—with a historic contract possible for the No. 1 overall pick from the 2010 draft.

Washington's run of success in recent seasons coincides with the start of Harper's big league career in 2012, which also marked Stephen Strasburg's first healthy big league season. During his Nationals tenure, Harper has won an NL Rookie of the Year award (2012), an MVP award (2015) and made five all-star teams (every year but 2014).

The good news is that the Nationals are positioned for success in 2018, with the Mets dealing with a plethora of injury questions, the Braves and Phillies continuing to work through rebuilds and the Marlins beginning another rebuild of their own under Derek Jeter and Co.'s new ownership.

The Nationals have one of the most enviable rotations in the game, headlined by Max Scherzer, Strasburg and Gio Gonzalez—each of whom posted an ERA below 3.00 in 2017—and consistent run producers around Harper such as Anthony Rendon and Daniel Murphy.

Scherzer won back-to-back NL Cy Young Awards in 2016 and 2017, becoming the 10th pitcher ever to claim three Cy Young trophies and also the 10th to win Cy Youngs in consecutive seasons. Strasburg finished third in the NL Cy Young voting and had the best season of his career at 28 years old.

The system's No. 1 prospect, 20-year-old outfielder Victor Robles, could be ready for an everyday major league role at some point in 2018 after

Homegrown third baseman Anthony Rendon turned in a career year at age 27 in 2017.

PROJECTED 2021 LINEUP

Catcher	Raudy Read (27)
First Base	Daniel Murphy (36)
Second Base	Wilmer Difo (29)
Third Base	Anthony Rendon (31)
Shortstop	Trea Turner (28)
Left Field	Adam Eaton (32)
Center Field	Victor Robles (24)
Right Field	Bryce Harper (28)
No. 1 Starter	Stephen Strasburg (32)
No. 2 Starter	Max Scherzer (36)
No. 3 Starter	Joe Ross (28)
No. 4 Starter	Erick Fedde (28)
No. 5 Starter	Wil Crowe (26)
Closer	Seth Romero (25)

showing enhanced power, earning a September callup and making the team's playoff roster. Other players from Washington's resurgent international program made strides in 2017, including No. 2 prospect Juan Soto, a 19-year-old outfielder who hit .360 through 23 games at low Class A Hagerstown before succumbing to injury.

Others such as shortstop Luis Garcia, catcher Raudy Reed and shortstop Yasel Antuna give the system a number of tantalizing prospects to replenish the major league team down the road, while a 2017 draft class heavy on college pitchers—including first-round lefthander Seth Romero and second-round righthander Wil Crowe—gave the system a needed influx of arms.

WASHINGTON NATIONALS

TOP 2018 ROOKIE: Victor Robles, OF. After playing his way onto the playoff roster in 2017, he should become a talented regular 2018.
BREAKOUT PROSPECT: Kelvin Gutierrez, 3B. If healthy, Gutierrez could put it all together and take another step offensively, for he was starting to leverage the ball more late in 2017.
SLEEPER: Gabe Klobosits, RHP. He dominated in his pro debut and has surprising strike-throwing ability for a pitcher of his stature at 6-foot-7.

SOURCE OF TOP 30 TALENT			
Homegrown	29	Acquired	1
College	9	Trade	1
Junior college	1	Rule 5 draft	0
High school	4	Independent league	0
Nondrafted free agent	0	Free agent/waivers	0
International	15		

LF
Telmito Agustin (25)
Justin Connell
Eric Senior

CF
Victor Robles (1)
Blake Perkins (11)
Andrew Stevenson (13)
Rafael Bautista (15)
Armond Upshaw

RF
Juan Soto (2)
Daniel Johnson (8)

3B
Kelvin Gutierrez (12)
Drew Ward (19)
Anderson Franco (28)
Adrian Sanchez

SS
Carter Kieboom (4)
Luis Garcia (6)
Yasel Antuna (10)
Jose Sanchez (23)
Osvaldo Abreu (30)
Edwin Lora

2B
Jake Noll
Cole Freeman
Bryan Mejia

1B
Jose Marmolejos (18)
Neftali Soto
Ian Sagdal

C
Raudy Reed (9)
Pedro Severino (14)
Taylor Gushue (20)
Jakson Reetz (29)
Spencer Kieboom
Anthony Peroni

LHP
LHSP	LHRP
Seth Romero (5)	Nick Raquet (20)
Matt Crownover	Alex Troop
	Jackson Stoeckinger
	Grant Borne

RHP
RHSP	RHRP
Erick Fedde (3)	Kyle Johnston (22)
Wil Crowe (7)	Jefry Rodriguez (24)
Jackson Tetreault (16)	Joan Baez (27)
Brigham Hill (17)	Gabe Klobosits
Austin Voth (26)	Wander Suero
Luis Reyes	A.J. Bogucki
Weston Davis	Jared Brasher
Jaron Long	Phillips Valdes
	Trey Turner

DRAFT ANALYSIS

2017

BEST PURE HITTER: 2B/OF Cole Freeman (4) was the only position player that the Nationals drafted in the first 10 rounds, where pitching was an obvious priority. While he has yet to get any at-bats in pro ball, he hit .321 in two seasons with Louisiana State and led the Cape Cod League in hitting (.376) in 2016.

BEST POWER HITTER: Jamori Blash (23) is the younger brother of Padres outfielder Jabari, but is a first base profile where his older brother can play the outfield. Blash has a ways to go in every facet of hitting at the pro level, but he has plus raw power in the bat.

FASTEST RUNNER: Freeman is the easy decision here with plus-plus speed. He's an aggressive basestealer who also looks to take extra bases.

BEST DEFENSIVE PLAYER: Freeman has the tools to develop into a solid to above-average defender at the keystone. His natural quickness should allow him to have good range, but he also has quick hands that allow him to turn the double play and a solid-average arm.

BEST FASTBALL: The Nationals have four legitimate candidates for best fastball, with LHP Seth Romero (1), RHP Will Crowe (2), LHP Nick Raquet (3) and RHP Jared Brasher (8). Each of Washington's first three picks can regularly get into the mid-90s, while Brasher—a senior out of Samford who signed for just $10,000—has been up to 97 this summer in short stints. Romero's combination of mid-90s velocity, command and life give him the best fastball of the class.

BEST SECONDARY PITCH: Romero has a sharp, hard-breaking slider that he's able to throw for strikes early in counts or use as a wipeout pitch to finish batters. The pitch is mostly in the mid-80s and is at least a plus offering.

BEST ATHLETE: OF Justin Connell (11) signed for $125,000 thanks to his aptitude and ability to play all three outfield positions, with a long-range chance to stick in center. He hit .323/.407./.365 in his debut.

BEST PRO DEBUT: After striking out 178 batters

TOP DRAFT PICKS OF THE DECADE

Year	Player, Pos.	2017 Org
2008	*Aaron Crow, RHP	Did not play
2009	Stephen Strasburg, RHP	Nationals
2010	Bryce Harper, OF	Nationals
2011	Anthony Rendon, 3B	Nationals
2012	Lucas Giolito, RHP	Nationals
2013	Jake Johansen, RHP (2nd round)	White Sox
2014	Erick Fedde, RHP	Nationals
2015	Andrew Stevenson, OF (2nd round)	Nationals
2016	Carter Kieboom, SS	Nationals
2017	Seth Romero, LHP	Nationals
*Did not sign		

in 182 innings at Auburn, 6-foot-7 RHP Gabe Klobosits (36) struck out 34 in 30.2 innings across three levels in 2017, starting in the Gulf Coast League before earning promotions to the New York-Penn and South Atlantic leagues in late August. Klobosits posted a 1.47 ERA across the three leagues. He uses his size to get great downhill angle on the ball, and his fastball ranges from the low 90s to a peak of 96. He also has a solid slider.

MOST INTRIGUING BACKGROUND: SS Darren Baker (27) is the son of former Nats manager Dusty, famous for being a Giants bat boy during the 2002 World Series. SS Jake Boone (38) is the son of ex-Mariner Bret while his uncle Aaron, grandfather Bob (who works for the Nats as vice president of player development) and great-grandfather Ray all played significant time in the majors. Neither Baker nor Boone signed.

CLOSEST TO THE MAJORS: Romero would be the most obvious choice here, but with real maturity questions left to be answered on that front, Crowe could beat him there and had the better pro start. Both are being developed as starters.

BEST LATE ROUND PICK: Klobosits over Connell.

THE ONE WHO GOT AWAY: RHP Bryce Montes de Oca (15) has tantalizing potential with a lively fastball out of a 6-foot-7 frame, but medical history and control concerns will always be a large question mark for scouts. He's returned to Missouri as a senior.

—CARLOS COLLAZO

2016

SS Carter Kieboom (1) and OF Daniel Johnson (5) are off to strong starts. The Nationals used three other top picks in trades, sending RHP Dane Dunning (1) to the White Sox, and 3B Sheldon Neuse (2) and LHP Jesus Luzardo (3) to Oakland.
GRADE: B

2015

OF Andrew Stevenson (2) was this class' top pick and made his MLB debut in 2017. RHP Koda Glover (8) has emerged as the best of several hard throwers and filled a key role in Washington's bullpen. OF Blake Perkins (2) offers plenty of upside.
GRADE: C

2014

RHP Erick Fedde (1) made his big league debut and could be in line to take a spot in Washington's rotation in 2018. C Jakson Reetz (3) is still trying to get on track offensively, but is the only other player from this draft to make the handbook.
GRADE: C

1 VICTOR ROBLES, OF

Born: May 19, 1997. **B-T:** R-R. **Ht:** 6-0. **Wt:** 185. **Signed:** Dominican Republic, 2013. **Signed by:** Modesto Ulloa.

Robles continues to speed through the minors, while making adjustments at every level on both sides of the ball, which makes his $225,000 signing bonus in 2013 a huge bargain. He started 2017 at high Class A Potomac and excelled before earning a promotion to Double-A Harrisburg, where he was one of just four 20-year-olds in the Eastern League. Robles has been one of the most impressive players in every minor league in which he has played. He handled the advanced pitchers in the EL with aplomb by lowering his strikeout rate to 14 percent while continuing hit for a high average. Robles impressed the Nationals enough to earn his first big league callup in September and made the postseason roster as well.

Robles' advanced understanding of the strike zone and ability to recognize pitches have helped his quick hands play in the batter's box. He is currently an average power hitter but with the strength and bat speed to project more power as he continues to develop physically. He was pitched backwards frequently in the Carolina League, which he countered by regularly using the entire field and showing the ability to drive the ball to the right-center field gap. Robles is fearless in the box and sets up very close to the plate. He led the Carolina league with 17 hit by pitches despite having just 338 plate appearances. He plays with great energy and aggression, which can hurt him at times, particularly on the bases where he needs to improve his decision-making and basestealing ability, though that might be the only part of his game to nitpick. Robles improved the most in 2017 in the outfield, where he has improved his jumps and routes. He also made strides with his throwing accuracy. He's always had the tools to develop into a premier defensive center fielder, with well above-average speed and a plus arm, and he's now taking the steps to become more efficient.

With current plus tools in every category except power—where he has a chance to become above-average—Robles has the chance to become a perennial all-star. While he may require a bit more minor league seasoning in 2018, he could quickly become an outfield fixture in Washington.

MITCHELL LAYTON/GETTY IMAGES

BA GRADE	SCOUTING GRADES
65 Risk: Medium	HIT: 60. POW: 50. SPD: 70. FLD: 60. ARM: 60.

Projected future grades on 20-80 scouting scale

TOP PROSPECTS OF THE DECADE

Year	Player, Pos.	2017 Org
2008	Chris Marrero, OF	Orix (Japan)
2009	Jordan Zimmermann, RHP	Tigers
2010	Stephen Strasburg, RHP	Nationals
2011	Bryce Harper, OF	Nationals
2012	Bryce Harper, OF	Nationals
2013	Anthony Rendon, 3B	Nationals
2014	Lucas Giolito, RHP	White Sox
2015	Lucas Giolito, RHP	White Sox
2016	Lucas Giolito, RHP	White Sox
2017	Victor Robles, OF	Nationals

BEST TOOLS

Best Hitter for Average	Victor Robles
Best Power Hitter:	Daniel Johnson
Best Strike-Zone Discipline	Juan Soto
Fastest Baserunner	Victor Robles
Best Athlete	Victor Robles
Best Fastball	Jefry Rodriguez
Best Curveball	Wil Crowe
Best Slider	Seth Romero
Best Changeup	Ryan Brinley
Best Control	Sterling Sharp
Best Defensive Catcher	Pedro Severino
Best Defensive Infielder	Jose Sanchez
Best Infield Arm	Kelvin Gutierrez
Best Defensive Outfielder	Blake Perkins
Best Outfield Arm	Daniel Johnson

Year	Club (League)	Class	AVG	G	AB	R	H	2B	3B	HR	RBI	BB	SO	SB	CS	OBP	SLG
2015	Nationals (GCL)	R	.370	23	73	19	27	6	1	2	11	10	12	12	1	.484	.562
	Auburn (NYP)	SS	.343	38	140	29	48	5	4	2	16	8	21	12	4	.424	.479
2016	Hagerstown (SAL)	LoA	.305	64	233	48	71	9	6	5	30	18	38	19	8	.405	.459
	Nationals (GCL)	R	.150	5	20	3	3	0	0	1	1	0	7	0	1	.190	.300
	Potomac (CAR)	HiA	.262	41	168	24	44	8	2	3	11	14	32	18	5	.354	.387
2017	Potomac (CAR)	HiA	.289	77	291	49	84	25	7	7	33	25	62	16	7	.377	.495
	Harrisburg (EL)	AA	.324	37	139	24	45	12	1	3	14	12	22	11	3	.394	.489
	Washington (NL)	MAJ	.250	13	24	2	6	1	2	0	4	0	6	0	1	.308	.458
Major League Totals			.250	13	24	2	6	1	2	0	4	0	6	0	1	.308	.458
Minor League Totals			.304	332	1246	242	379	79	25	26	141	103	220	110	38	.395	.470

2 JUAN SOTO, OF

Born: Oct. 25, 1998. **B-T:** L-L. **Ht.:** 6-1. **Wt.:** 185. **Signed:** Dominican Republic, 2015. **Signed by:** Modesto Ulloa.

Soto signed for $1.5 million in 2015, won the MVP award in the Rookie-level Gulf Coast League in 2016 and advanced to low Class A Hagerstown in 2017. He was limited to just 32 games, however, after fracturing his ankle, breaking a hamate bone and dealing with a hamstring injury late in the year.

Soto impressed evaluators with his advanced feel at the plate. He made adjustments within at-bats and displayed impressive hand-eye coordination that should allow him to be an above-average hitter. While he's still growing into it, Soto should have above-average power, and he has a chance to hit 20-plus homers a year thanks to strong hands and a simple swing. He is just an average runner, and profiles as a corner outfielder because of that, which limits his ceiling and will put additional pressure on his bat—his best tool. He currently has fringe-average arm strength that is better suited to left field than right, but he uses his legs efficiently on throws and is young enough to safely project an average arm as he continues to mature.

Soto is ready for high Class A Potomac in 2018, but given his injury-shortened 2017 season, Washington could opt to be conservative and start him in Hagerstown.

BA GRADE
60 Risk: V. High
HIT: 60. POW: 60.
SPD: 50. FLD: 55.
ARM: 50.

Year	Club (League)	Class	AVG	G	AB	R	H	2B	3B	HR	RBI	BB	SO	SB	CS	OBP	SLG
2016	Nationals (GCL)	R	.361	45	169	25	61	11	3	5	31	14	25	5	2	.410	.550
	Auburn (NYP)	SS	.429	6	21	3	9	3	0	0	1	3	4	0	0	.500	.571
2017	Hagerstown (SAL)	LoA	.360	23	86	15	31	5	0	3	13	10	8	1	2	.427	.523
	Nationals (GCL)	R	.320	9	25	3	8	1	1	0	4	2	1	0	0	.370	.440
Minor League Totals			.362	83	301	46	109	20	4	8	49	29	38	6	4	.418	.535

3 ERICK FEDDE, RHP

Born: Feb. 25, 1993. **B-T:** R-R. **Ht.:** 6-4. **Wt.:** 180. **Drafted:** Nevada-Las Vegas, 2014 (1st round). **Signed by:** Mitch Sokol.

The 2014 first-rounder had a roller-coaster season in 2017. He started off well in Double-A Harrisburg before being moved to the bullpen because the big league club needed for relievers.

Fedde's fastball ticked up to 96-97 mph out of the bullpen after he sat in the low 90s as a starter with excellent sinking action. After 16 appearances out of the pen and a promotion to Triple-A Syracuse, Fedde made four starts and posted a 6.94 ERA before making his big league debut, where he gave up seven earned runs in just four innings. Regardless, Washington still sees Fedde as a starter despite his mixed usage and was encouraged with the progress he made with his changeup, which he threw much more often. The pitch flashed plus at times and was occasionally was as much of an out pitch as his low-80s slider, which is still his go-to secondary and a true plus offering. Fedde can also drop in a below-average curveball.

Fedde has the repertoire and athleticism to turn into a mid- to back-of-the-rotation starter, and he has displayed no drop in velocity since having Tommy John surgery in May 2014 before being drafted.

BA GRADE
50 Risk: Medium
FB: 60. CB: 45.
SL: 60. CHG: 55.
CTL: 50.

Year	Club (League)	Class	W	L	ERA	G	GS	CG	SV	IP	H	HR	BB	SO	K/9	WHIP	AVG
2015	Auburn (NYP)	SS	4	1	2.57	8	8	0	0	35	38	1	8	36	9.3	1.31	.264
	Hagerstown (SAL)	LoA	1	2	4.34	6	6	0	0	29	24	1	8	23	7.1	1.10	.224
2016	Potomac (CAR)	HiA	6	4	2.85	18	17	0	0	92	85	7	19	95	9.3	1.13	.244
	Harrisburg (EL)	AA	2	1	3.99	5	5	1	0	29	33	1	10	28	8.6	1.47	.284
2017	Harrisburg (EL)	AA	3	3	3.04	17	7	0	0	56	45	4	18	54	8.6	1.12	.215
	Syracuse (IL)	AAA	2	4	4.76	12	6	0	0	34	37	3	5	25	6.6	1.24	.276
	Washington (NL)	MAJ	0	1	9.39	3	3	0	0	15	25	5	8	15	8.8	2.15	.385
Major League Totals			0	1	9.39	3	3	0	0	15	25	5	8	15	8.8	2.15	.385
Minor League Totals			17	13	3.37	66	49	1	0	275	262	17	68	261	8.5	1.20	.248

4 CARTER KIEBOOM, SS

Born: Sept. 3, 1997. **B-T:** R-R. **Ht.:** 6-2. **Wt.:** 190. **Drafted:** HS—Marietta, Ga., 2016 (1st round). **Signed by:** Eric Robinson.

The 28th overall pick in 2016, Kieboom had his full-season debut at low Class A Hagerstown shortened thanks to a hamstring injury, which forced him to the disabled list in mid-May and ended a torrid 29-game start in which he hit .333/.398/.586 with six home runs.

After rehabbing and making his way back to the South Atlantic League, Kieboom hit just .235 the rest of the way—though he managed to show the same selective approach by walking 18 times compared to 15 strikeouts. He has a chance to turn into a middle-of-the-order hitter, with impressive bat speed and a short swing. He shows the ability to drive the ball to all fields and could develop above-average power. Kieboom is an average defensive shortstop who projects to be more of a bat-first player. His high baseball IQ should help him in the field, where positioning and solid hands could be enough to make up for a lack of first-step quickness and an average arm. He showed improvement with his throwing in 2017, however.

Kieboom should be ready for an assignment to high Class A Potomac in 2018. Even if he slides to second base, he could become a big league regular.

BA GRADE
55 Risk: V. High
HIT: 55. POW: 55.
SPD: 50. FLD: 45.
ARM: 50.

Year	Club (League)	Class	AVG	G	AB	R	H	2B	3B	HR	RBI	BB	SO	SB	CS	OBP	SLG
2016	Nationals (GCL)	R	.244	36	135	22	33	8	4	4	25	12	43	1	2	.323	.452
2017	Nationals (GCL)	R	.417	6	12	1	5	3	0	0	5	3	0	0	0	.563	.667
	Auburn (NYP)	SS	.250	7	28	4	7	1	0	1	4	1	2	1	0	.276	.393
	Hagerstown (SAL)	LoA	.296	48	179	36	53	12	0	8	26	28	40	2	2	.400	.497
Minor League Totals			.277	97	354	63	98	24	4	13	60	44	85	4	4	.368	.477

5 SETH ROMERO, LHP

Born: April 19, 1996. **B-T:** L-L. **Ht.:** 6-3. **Wt.:** 240. **Drafted:** Houston, 2017 (1st round). **Signed by:** Tyler Wilt.

A top-10 talent in the 2017 draft on pure stuff, Romero slid to the Nationals with the No. 25 overall pick because he faced makeup questions after being kicked off the Houston baseball team in the spring. Houston also suspended Romero in 2016 and again in 2017 for violations that included failing a drug test, missing curfew and fighting with a teammate. He was removed from the roster only a week after being reinstated this spring.

Despite facing maturity questions, Romero has unquestionable talent. He has a mid-90s fastball that he can locate to both sides of the plate and a swing-and-miss slider that's already a plus pitch. Romero also throws a changeup that is close to average with a chance to become a third above-average offering. He has some funk to his delivery with a lot of moving parts, so being able to repeat his mechanics consistently while adjusting to pro hitters and a five-day pitching schedule will be a priority for him.

Romero's pro debut, spent primarily at short-season Auburn, wasn't terrific from a statistical standpoint, but he could move fairly quickly, especially if he's moved to the bullpen. For now, the Nationals are developing him as a starter with a No. 3 ceiling.

GLENN GASTON

BA GRADE
55 Risk: Extreme
FB: 60. SL: 60.
CHG: 50.
CTL: 55.

Year	Club (League)	Class	W	L	ERA	G	GS	CG	SV	IP	H	HR	BB	SO	K/9	WHIP	AVG
2017	Nationals (GCL)	R	0	0	0.00	1	1	0	0	2	0	0	2	3	13.5	1.00	.000
	Auburn (NYP)	SS	0	1	5.40	6	6	0	0	20	19	0	6	32	14.4	1.25	.244
Minor League Totals			0	1	4.91	7	7	0	0	22	19	0	8	35	14.3	1.23	.226

6 LUIS GARCIA, 2B/SS

Born: May 16, 2000. **B-T:** L-R. **Ht.:** 6-0. **Wt.:** 190. **Signed:** Dominican Republic, 2016. **Signed by:** Carlos Ulloa.

Garcia was Washington's top international target in a 2016 signing class that included three players ranked among the top 15. He commanded $1.3 million because of his impressive all-around set of tools and simple lefthanded swing geared for line drives. His father of the same name played shortstop for the Tigers in 1999.

Garcia lived up to his scouting report in his first season in 2017 in the Rookie-level Gulf Coast League. He used extremely quick hands and an advanced hitting approach to spray balls all over the field. He can rely on his hands a bit too much at the plate currently, and the next phase of his development will be getting his legs into his swing with more consistency. A plus-plus runner, Garcia gets down the line well and swiped 11 bases in 13 tries in his debut. Defensively, he has above-average arm strength, smooth actions and soft hands at shortstop, but he'll need a few years to continue honing the fundamentals and getting acclimated to the speed of the game.

Garcia will be just 18 for most of 2018, when he should find his way to short-season Auburn.

BA GRADE
55 Risk: Extreme
HIT: 55. POW: 40.
SPD: 70. FLD: 50.
ARM: 55.

Year	Club (League)	Class	AVG	G	AB	R	H	2B	3B	HR	RBI	BB	SO	SB	CS	OBP	SLG
2017	Nationals (GCL)	R	.302	49	199	25	60	8	3	1	22	9	32	11	2	.330	.387
Minor League Totals			.302	49	199	25	60	8	3	1	22	9	32	11	2	.330	.387

7 WIL CROWE, RHP

Born: Sept. 9, 1994. **B-T:** R-R. **Ht.:** 6-2. **Wt.:** 240. **Drafted:** South Carolina, 2017 (2nd round). **Signed by:** Paul Faulk.

The Nationals made Crowe their second selection in the 2017 draft and signed him for $946,500 after his bounce-back junior year at South Carolina. He had Tommy John surgery in 2015 that forced him to sit out the 2016 season.

Crowe served as the ace of South Carolina's staff as a freshman, posting a 2.75 ERA before his injury. He dominated early during his junior campaign in 2017 to show evaluators that he still had impact stuff. That translated to pro ball where Crowe posted a 2.96 ERA, mostly at short-season Auburn, while showing four average or better pitches. He has a fastball that sits in the low to mid-90s and has been up to 97 mph, a curveball and slider that are both average or slightly better, depending when you see him, and a low-80s changeup that's also an average pitch.

Washington will be cautious with Crowe given his medical history, but he's fairly polished and seems like a safe bet to be a No. 4 or 5 starter if he remains healthy. Washington could opt to challenge him with an assignment to high Class A Potomac in 2018 if he looks good in the spring.

BA GRADE
50 Risk: High
FB: 60. CB: 55.
SL: 55. CHG: 50.
CTL: 50.

Year	Club (League)	Class	W	L	ERA	G	GS	CG	SV	IP	H	HR	BB	SO	K/9	WHIP	AVG
2017	Nationals (GCL)	R	0	0	4.91	2	2	0	0	4	3	0	1	2	4.9	1.09	.250
	Auburn (NYP)	SS	0	0	2.61	7	7	0	0	21	18	3	3	15	6.5	1.02	.234
Minor League Totals			0	0	2.96	9	9	0	0	24	21	3	4	17	6.3	1.03	.236

8 DANIEL JOHNSON, OF

Born: July 11, 1995. **B-T:** L-L. **Ht.:** 5-10. **Wt.:** 185. **Drafted:** New Mexico State, 2016 (5th round). **Signed by:** Mitch Sokol.

Johnson was one of the toolsiest players in the Four Corners area for the 2016 draft, but many teams were concerned about the rawness of his game. The Nationals drafted him in the fifth round after his junior season at New Mexico State, where he hit 12 home runs and stole 29 bases.

After a mediocre pro debut in 2016 at short-season Auburn, Johnson began 2017 at low Class A Hagerstown and dominated. He finished second in the South Atlantic league in home runs (17) and fourth in slugging percentage (.529) despite moving to high Class A Potomac in late July. Johnson has quick hands and a whippy swing, with above-average raw power that he began to tap into thanks to better use of his legs. He also took a step forward with his pitch selection, lowering his strikeout rate after being promoted to the Carolina League. Johnson might be the strongest player in the system and is a plus runner with plus arm strength as well.

BA GRADE
50 Risk: High
HIT: 45. POW: 60.
SPD: 60. FLD: 50.
ARM: 60.

Johnson still has details to iron out, such as his baserunning, throwing accuracy and outfield jumps. He has the speed to handle center field but profiles best in right field with his strong arm.

Year	Club (League)	Class	AVG	G	AB	R	H	2B	3B	HR	RBI	BB	SO	SB	CS	OBP	SLG
2016	Auburn (NYP)	SS	.265	62	245	25	65	9	4	1	14	7	42	13	3	.312	.347
2017	Hagerstown (SAL)	LoA	.300	88	327	61	98	16	4	17	52	22	70	12	9	.361	.529
	Potomac (CAR)	HiA	.294	42	170	22	50	13	0	5	20	13	30	10	2	.346	.459
Minor League Totals			.287	192	742	108	213	38	8	23	86	42	142	35	14	.342	.453

9 RAUDY READ, C

Born: Oct. 29, 1993. **B-T:** R-R. **Ht.:** 6-0. **Wt.:** 170. **Signed:** Dominican Republic, 2011. **Signed by:** Modesto Ulloa.

Read has improved seemingly every year since signing with the Nationals in 2011, and he took strides on both sides of the ball in 2017. The best defensive catcher in the Carolina League in 2016, he improved his blocking technique in 2017 and reduced his passed ball count from 20 to 14. Read won the Nationals' Bob Boone award, which recognizes the minor leaguer who best displays professionalism, leadership and consistency

Read has an above-average arm and has improved his footwork. In previous seasons he tended to throw from his knees frequently, but that wasn't as much of an issue in 2017. Offensively, Read has potential for above-average power and held up well as the season progressed, hitting 10 of his 17 home runs during his final two months at Double-A Harrisburg before making his big league debut as a September callup. He occasionally loses balance in his lower half at the plate, but when he sits back and lets the ball travel, his power plays more consistently. Like most catchers, he's slow and doesn't hit for average.

Read has the tools to impact the game offensively and defensively, which is a rare commodity among major league catchers. He could earn a share of the big league catching job at some point in 2018.

Year	Club (League)	Class	AVG	G	AB	R	H	2B	3B	HR	RBI	BB	SO	SB	CS	OBP	SLG
2015	Hagerstown (SAL)	LoA	.244	82	295	38	72	20	1	5	36	25	50	4	3	.307	.369
	Potomac (CAR)	HiA	.389	5	18	1	7	2	0	0	5	2	3	0	0	.450	.500
2016	Potomac (CAR)	HiA	.262	101	386	54	101	30	1	9	51	31	53	6	3	.324	.415
2017	Harrisburg (EL)	AA	.265	108	411	44	109	25	1	17	61	27	79	2	0	.312	.455
	Washington (NL)	MAJ	.273	8	11	1	3	0	0	0	0	0	3	0	0	.273	.273
Major League Totals			.273	8	11	1	3	0	0	0	0	0	3	0	0	.273	.273
Minor League Totals			.253	497	1834	219	464	123	4	52	274	127	292	18	19	.309	.409

10 YASEL ANTUNA, SS/3B

BILL MITCHELL

Born: Oct. 26, 1999. **B-T:** B-R. **Ht.:** 6-0. **Wt.:** 170. **Signed:** Dominican Republic, 2016. **Signed by:** Pablo Arias.

Antuna ranked as the No. 14 international prospect in 2016, when he signed for $3.85 million and broke the Nationals' franchise record for an international amateur. He shows a calm hitting approach from both sides of the plate and the ability to man the left side of the infield.

Antuna has a line-drive approach and similar-looking swings whether batting lefthanded or right. However, he struck all but one of his 12 extra-base hits in the Rookie-level Gulf Coast League batting lefthanded, which is his natural side. Antuna has a projectable frame, long limbs and wide shoulders. That physicality allows evaluators to dream on his power potential, and he has a chance to be an impact hitter down the line thanks to his polished approach. At the same time, Antuna probably will outgrow shortstop and already is an unreliable defender who recorded a .815 fielding percentage in 2017. He frequently played third base in the GCL, in part because of Washington's glut of young shortstops at that level.

Antuna has enough arm for shortstop, so he will see more time there in 2018, possibly at low Class A Hagerstown, to improve his consistency.

Year	Club (League)	Class	AVG	G	AB	R	H	2B	3B	HR	RBI	BB	SO	SB	CS	OBP	SLG
	Nationals (GCL)	R	.301	48	173	25	52	8	3	1	17	23	29	5	5	.382	.399
Minor League Totals			.301	48	173	25	52	8	3	1	17	23	29	5	5	.382	.399

11 BLAKE PERKINS, OF

BA GRADE

50 Risk: High

Born: Sept. 10, 1996. **B-T:** B-R. **Ht.:** 6-1. **Wt.:** 165. **Drafted:** HS—Buckeye, Ariz., 2015 (2nd round). **Signed by:** Mitch Sokol.

During his first full season in the South Atlantic League, Perkins took strides offensively and has become more consistent at the plate. The Nationals are particularly excited about his progress out of the lefthanded batter's box, because the 21-year-old outfielder is a converted switch-hitter and natural from the right side.

Perkins' production was similar from both sides of the plate in 2017, but he showed much more in-game power from the left side, hitting all of his home runs and triples. There's still work to do, however. His strikeout rate from the left side is significantly higher than the right, but he's making the correct adjustments and should be seen as a legitimate switch-hitter at this point. Defensively, Perkins is the most instinctual outfielder in Washington's farm system and as a plus runner with good routes, and he should have no problems impacting the game with his glove. His arm is more average than plus at this point, but he flashes plus throws at times and improved his arm strength this season.

After a successful year at low Class A Hagerstown, Perkins' next challenge will be the advanced pitching of the high Class A Carolina League.

Year	Club (League)	Class	AVG	G	AB	R	H	2B	3B	HR	RBI	BB	SO	SB	CS	OBP	SLG
2015	Nationals (GCL)	R	.211	49	166	21	35	5	2	1	12	13	36	4	5	.265	.283
2016	Auburn (NYP)	SS	.233	56	210	31	49	5	1	1	16	25	39	10	3	.318	.281
	Hagerstown (SAL)	LoA	.200	7	25	4	5	0	0	0	2	5	6	0	1	.333	.200
2017	Hagerstown (SAL)	LoA	.255	129	482	105	123	27	4	8	48	72	118	31	8	.354	.378
Minor League Totals			.240	241	883	161	212	37	7	10	78	115	199	45	17	.329	.332

12 KELVIN GUTIERREZ, 3B

BA GRADE

50 Risk: High

Born: Aug. 28, 1994. **B-T:** R-R. **Ht.:** 6-3. **Wt.:** 185. **Signed:** Dominican Republic, 2013. **Signed by:** Modesto Ulloa.

Gutierrez's first complete year of full-season ball didn't materialize in 2017 because the 23-year-old missed parts of June and August and the entire month of July with an ankle injury.

Despite the highest strikeout rate of his career in the high Class A Carolina League, Gutierrez acquitted himself well offensively through 58 games with Potomac, where his quick hands played at the plate with a smooth, line-drive swing. More of a contact hitter, Gutierrez was beginning to leverage the ball more regularly before hitting the disabled list. With a 6-foot-3 frame, he has a chance to add in-game power. Gutierrez's strength continues to be his aptitude for the defensive side of the game, where his quick hands and plus arm are his best tools. He has arguably the best arm in Washington's system, and some evaluators said it was the best in the Carolina League. Despite his size, Gutierrez has smooth footwork and a quick first step that leads to solid range laterally and the ability to make plays on slow rollers in front of him.

Gutierrez will likely start 2018 in Potomac again and hope for good health.

Year	Club (League)	Class	AVG	G	AB	R	H	2B	3B	HR	RBI	BB	SO	SB	CS	OBP	SLG
2015	Auburn (NYP)	SS	.305	62	239	31	73	21	1	1	30	16	52	2	0	.358	.414
2016	Auburn (NYP)	SS	.323	9	31	5	10	3	0	0	6	3	5	4	0	.371	.419
	Hagerstown (SAL)	LoA	.300	96	377	58	113	19	6	3	48	29	65	19	7	.349	.406
	Potomac (CAR)	HiA	.237	10	38	7	9	1	0	1	2	3	5	2	2	.326	.342
2017	Potomac (CAR)	HiA	.288	58	222	34	64	10	6	2	16	19	59	3	0	.347	.414
	Nationals (GCL)	R	.212	10	33	6	7	3	1	0	1	4	7	2	0	.297	.364
Minor League Totals			.287	358	1340	203	384	76	19	7	151	120	258	45	17	.348	.387

13 ANDREW STEVENSON, OF

BA GRADE

45 Risk: Medium

Born: June 1, 1994. **B-T:** L-L. **Ht.:** 6-0. **Wt.:** 185. **Drafted:** Louisiana State, 2015 (2nd round). **Signed by:** Ed Gustafson.

After struggling in Double-A during his first trip to the Eastern League in 2016, Stevenson started the 2017 season with Harrisburg, where he posted an .866 OPS before being promoted to Triple-A and getting his first taste of the big leagues in late July.

Stevenson was overmatched at the plate in Triple-A and the majors, with elevated strikeout rates cutting into his production. He has shown the ability to adapt to higher levels in the past, but will likely never be an impact bat because his power is more of the doubles variety than over-the-fence. Stevenson is a strong athlete who takes good routes with above-average speed that leads to great range, giving him a chance to be an above-average defensive center fielder. His arm is below-average, which might make him a better fit for left, where his bat doesn't profile.

Given his speed and baserunning ability, Stevenson appears to be a safe bet as a fourth outfielder or second-division regular but will need more time to adjust to advanced pitching.

Year	Club (League)	Class	AVG	G	AB	R	H	2B	3B	HR	RBI	BB	SO	SB	CS	OBP	SLG
2015	Auburn (NYP)	SS	.361	18	72	11	26	1	2	0	9	7	12	7	3	.413	.431
	Nationals (GCL)	R	.200	2	5	1	1	0	0	0	0	1	2	0	0	.333	.200
	Hagerstown (SAL)	LoA	.285	35	137	28	39	3	2	1	16	8	16	16	4	.338	.358
2016	Potomac (CAR)	HiA	.304	68	273	37	83	12	8	1	18	24	44	27	9	.359	.418
	Harrisburg (EL)	AA	.246	65	256	38	63	11	2	2	16	20	51	12	5	.302	.328
2017	Harrisburg (EL)	AA	.350	20	80	14	28	5	1	0	12	11	19	1	3	.429	.438
	Syracuse (IL)	AAA	.252	79	309	38	78	7	4	2	26	19	72	10	1	.298	.320
	Washington (NL)	MAJ	.158	37	57	5	9	2	0	0	1	7	20	1	0	.250	.193
Major League Totals			.158	37	57	5	9	2	0	0	1	7	20	1	0	.250	.193
Minor League Totals			.281	287	1132	167	318	39	19	6	97	90	216	73	25	.336	.365

14 PEDRO SEVERINO, C

Born: July 20, 1993. **B-T:** R-R. **Ht.:** 6-0. **Wt.:** 215. **Signed:** Dominican Republic, 2010. **Signed by:** Moises de la Mota.

BA GRADE

45 Risk: Medium

Severino continued to live up to his reputation as an excellent defensive catcher in 2017, spending most of his time with Triple-A Syracuse, where he threw out 31 percent of basestealers.

Severino has plus arm strength and a quick release from behind the dish, as well as athleticism that allows him to block balls efficiently. He's a solid receiver behind the plate, with a chance to get better in that area with more time and focus on his framing ability. What continues to limit Severino's future potential is the offensive side of the game. He regularly gets into trouble by attempting to pull the ball, which was evident in a 2017 cup of coffee with the Nationals, where he was overmatched and struck out 32 percent of the time. Severino does have some strength but currently lacks the ability to get to it much in-game thanks to approach and hitting ability questions.

Until Severino makes an adjustment with his bat, he profiles as a defensive-oriented backup catcher.

Year	Club (League)	Class	AVG	G	AB	R	H	2B	3B	HR	RBI	BB	SO	SB	CS	OBP	SLG
2015	Harrisburg (EL)	AA	.246	91	329	33	81	13	0	5	34	19	51	1	2	.288	.331
	Washington (NL)	MAJ	.250	2	4	1	1	1	0	0	0	0	1	0	0	.250	.500
2016	Syracuse (IL)	AAA	.271	82	291	25	79	13	0	2	21	19	45	3	4	.316	.337
	Washington (NL)	MAJ	.321	16	28	6	9	2	0	2	4	5	3	0	0	.441	.607
2017	Auburn (NYP)	SS	.364	4	11	4	4	0	1	0	0	0	1	0	0	.417	.545
	Syracuse (IL)	AAA	.242	59	211	17	51	4	0	5	29	15	43	1	1	.291	.332
	Washington (NL)	MAJ	.172	17	29	0	5	1	0	0	3	2	10	0	0	.226	.207
Major League Totals			.246	35	61	7	15	4	0	2	7	7	14	0	0	.333	.410
Minor League Totals			.244	484	1639	173	400	71	6	24	182	106	287	8	7	.294	.339

15 RAFAEL BAUTISTA, OF

Born: March 8, 1993. **B-T:** R-R. **Ht.:** 6-2. **Wt.:** 165. **Signed:** Dominican Republic, 2012. **Signed by:** Pablo Arias.

BA GRADE

40 Risk: Medium

After stealing 56 bases in the Double-A Eastern League in 2016, injuries and the lowest on-base percentage of his career limited Bautista's steals total to just nine in 2017, with time between Triple-A Syracuse and the majors.

A premium runner, Bautista's speed is his carrying tool, so a hamstring injury that kept him out for two months clearly hurt his production. That's true at the plate, too, where he is a slap-and-dash hitter with just 11 home runs across six seasons and 608 games. Even while he was healthy, Bautista spent much of his time bouncing back and forth between Syracuse and the majors, where he started just four of 17 games and never got into any sort of offensive rhythm. His usage in 2017 is likely a good indicator of his future role on a first-division team, however. Bautista's bat doesn't profile as an everyday player. He could turn into a premium defender in center with fringe-average to average arm strength and elite speed.

Bautista likely will start 2018 back at Triple-A Syracuse, where his health will be worth watching considering his history and the nature of his 2017 injury.

Year	Club (League)	Class	AVG	G	AB	R	H	2B	3B	HR	RBI	BB	SO	SB	CS	OBP	SLG
2015	Nationals (GCL)	R	.313	6	16	3	5	0	0	1	2	0	1	0	0	.313	.500
	Auburn (NYP)	SS	.273	8	33	6	9	3	0	0	4	1	7	3	0	.294	.364
	Potomac (CAR)	HiA	.272	52	206	23	56	7	2	0	8	11	22	23	4	.318	.325
2016	Harrisburg (EL)	AA	.282	135	542	76	153	12	4	4	39	42	94	55	10	.341	.341
2017	Nationals (GCL)	R	.295	13	44	7	13	2	1	0	3	5	5	2	1	.404	.386
	Syracuse (IL)	AAA	.250	43	176	23	44	9	1	0	11	9	26	7	4	.290	.313
	Washington (NL)	MAJ	.160	17	25	2	4	0	0	0	0	2	5	0	0	.222	.160
Major League Totals			.160	17	25	2	4	0	0	0	0	2	5	0	0	.222	.160
Minor League Totals			.290	510	1916	317	555	68	18	11	173	146	300	232	48	.350	.361

16 JACKSON TETREAULT, RHP

BA GRADE

45 Risk: High

Born: June 3, 1996. **B-T:** R-R. **Ht.:** 6-5. **Wt.:** 170. **Drafted:** State JC of Florida, 2017 (7th round). **Signed by:** Buddy Hernandez.

A seventh-round pick in 2017, Tetreault signed for $300,000, which turned out to be the fourth-highest bonus of the Nationals' class. He managed to get that bonus after impressing in the State JC of Florida rotation along with Cubs first-round pick Brendon Little.

After spending one year at Cameron University in Lawton, Okla., and working mostly out of the bullpen, Tetreault transferred to the junior college ranks, where in 2017 he started 14 games and posted a 2.58 ERA with 105 strikeouts in 80.1 innings. He has an extremely thin, projectable body with a fast, whippy arm that allowed his fastball to touch 95 mph at times and is regularly in the low 90s. Tetreault throws a curveball and a changeup, and while the former is ahead of the latter, both pitches are works in progress. The Nationals like the 21-year-old's feel to spin the ball. Walks were an issue with Tetreault in college, and he'll need to improve his control significantly.

There's a lot left to be ironed out, but with increased weight and strength, Tetreault has the talent to turn into a starter prospect.

Year	Club (League)	Class	W	L	ERA	G	GS	CG	SV	IP	H	HR	BB	SO	K/9	WHIP	AVG
2017	Nationals (GCL)	R	0	0	4.50	1	0	0	0	2	1	1	1	2	9.0	1.00	.143
	Auburn (NYP)	SS	2	2	2.58	11	6	0	0	38	32	1	16	36	8.5	1.25	.216
Minor League Totals			2	2	2.68	12	6	0	0	40	33	2	17	38	8.5	1.24	.213

17 BRIGHAM HILL, RHP

BA GRADE

45 Risk: High

Born: July 8, 1995. **B-T:** R-R. **Ht.:** 6-0. **Wt.:** 185. **Drafted:** Texas A&M, 2017 (5th round). **Signed by:** Tyler Wilt.

Hill was first drafted in the 20th round in 2016 by the Athletics after a solid sophomore campaign at Texas A&M, but he returned for his junior year, where he threw 100 innings with 111 strikeouts. For that, the Nationals signed him for $291,200 as a fifth-rounder in 2017.

Hill pitches off of a low-90s sinking fastball and a plus changeup that has late tumbling action and often resembles a splitter. His changeup is his best offering, but he also has a curveball with downer shape and a chance to be a third average pitch. He's also experimented with a slider in the past. Aside from his changeup, pitchability and makeup are Hill's best attributes with coaches raving about his moxie on the mound and ability to attack different quadrants of the zone, with plus command in the future a possibility. His future in a rotation will likely depend on his ability to develop a consistently reliable breaking ball.

Without a reliable breaking ball, Hill's size and fastball/changeup mix could play better in the bullpen. Additionally, he has a Tommy John surgery on his résumé from 2012.

Year	Club (League)	Class	W	L	ERA	G	GS	CG	SV	IP	H	HR	BB	SO	K/9	WHIP	AVG
2017	Auburn (NYP)	SS	0	1	2.63	4	3	0	0	14	12	0	3	9	5.9	1.10	.214
	Hagerstown (SAL)	LoA	0	1	6.07	6	6	0	0	30	41	4	5	30	9.1	1.55	.318
Minor League Totals			0	2	4.98	10	9	0	0	43	53	4	8	39	8.1	1.41	.286

18 JOSE MARMOLEJOS, 1B/OF

BA GRADE

40 Risk: Medium

Born: Jan. 2, 1993. **B-T:** L-L. **Ht.:** 6-1. **Wt.:** 185. **Signed:** Dominican Republic, 2011. **Signed by:** Johnny DiPuglia.

Marmolejos has been remarkably consistent with his bat throughout his seven seasons in the Nationals organization and has one of the most mature and polished hitting approaches of any player in the system. After being named the Nationals' minor league player of the year in both 2015 and 2016, the 24-year-old put up solid numbers once again in his first full season at Double-A Harrisburg in 2017.

Marmolejos has an all-fields approach at the plate and handled lefthanders just fine with half of his 14 homers coming against same-side pitchers. His defensive profile and a lack of impact power cap Marmolejos' ceiling. He's more of a doubles hitter without much physical projection left and is at best a fringe-average defender at both first base and in the outfield. He's a below-average runner with a below-average arm and is still working on improving his footwork and routes in left field.

Marmolejos should be tested against Triple-A pitching in 2018 and doesn't have much left to prove offensively before getting a chance to serve as a big league pinch-hitter or as part of a platoon.

Year	Club (League)	Class	AVG	G	AB	R	H	2B	3B	HR	RBI	BB	SO	SB	CS	OBP	SLG
2015	Hagerstown (SAL)	LoA	.310	124	468	63	145	39	5	11	87	35	89	3	1	.363	.485
2016	Potomac (CAR)	HiA	.286	103	378	72	108	36	5	11	59	59	84	2	3	.381	.495
	Harrisburg (EL)	AA	.299	33	127	15	38	9	0	2	15	5	29	0	0	.333	.417
2017	Harrisburg (EL)	AA	.288	107	400	68	115	18	4	14	66	44	79	0	2	.361	.458
Minor League Totals			.288	598	2187	330	629	159	28	46	339	231	424	8	11	.359	.449

19 DREW WARD, 3B

BA GRADE
45 Risk: High

Born: Nov. 25, 1994. **B-T:** L-R. **Ht.:** 6-3. **Wt.:** 215. **Drafted:** HS—Leedey, Okla., 2013 (3rd round). **Signed by:** Ed Gustafson.

Ward completed his first full season at Double-A in 2017 after reaching Harrisburg for the first time in late June 2016. His second look in the league didn't improve his strikeout problem.

Ward struck out at a career-high rate of 27 percent in 2017, though he did walk more than the Eastern League average. He routinely failed to get into hitting position with good timing, which resulted in lots of swings and misses in the strike zone. Nationals evaluators think that his swing-and-miss issues are more timing-based than mechanics-based and when at his best, Ward showcases power to all fields. Defensively, he has limited range as a below-average runner but has solid hands and makes accurate throws with average to above-average arm strength. With a big, physical frame, first base might become his position down the line given his lack of quickness.

At first base, Ward's hit tool issues will become an even bigger question mark. A return to Double-A is a possibility for 2018.

Year	Club (League)	Class	AVG	G	AB	R	H	2B	3B	HR	RBI	BB	SO	SB	CS	OBP	SLG
2015	Nationals (GCL)	R	.154	4	13	2	2	0	0	1	2	3	8	0	0	.313	.385
	Potomac (CAR)	HiA	.249	111	377	47	94	19	2	6	47	39	110	2	1	.327	.358
2016	Potomac (CAR)	HiA	.278	64	230	36	64	16	0	11	32	34	70	0	1	.377	.491
	Harrisburg (EL)	AA	.219	53	178	19	39	7	0	3	24	22	51	0	1	.310	.309
2017	Harrisburg (EL)	AA	.235	121	413	47	97	20	0	10	53	55	131	0	0	.325	.356
Minor League Totals			.255	517	1810	220	461	101	5	42	259	220	535	6	9	.342	.386

20 TAYLOR GUSHUE, C

BA GRADE
45 Risk: High

Born: Dec. 19, 1993. **B-T:** B-R. **Ht.:** 6-1. **Wt.:** 215. **Drafted:** Florida, 2014 (4th round). **Signed by:** Darren Mazeroski (Pirates).

The Nationals acquired Gushue from the Pirates in September 2016 in a trade that sent prospect second baseman Chris Bostick to Pittsburgh.

Gushue has been a below-average hitter his entire pro career and didn't have a great track record with the bat in college either. Still, scouts have long admired his defensive potential and the raw power that translated into a career-high 18 home runs in 2017 at high Class A Potomac. Lauded for having a strong arm out of college, Gushue improved behind the dish, throwing out 32 percent of basestealers between the Carolina League and 25 innings of work in the Double-A Eastern League. He's a good receiver with soft hands and a strong lower half and also has a feel for calling games and handling his pitching staff. There's no indication that he'll ever be an average hitter at this point, but the switch-hitter's power from the left side (14 of 18 homers) and defensive ability give him a chance to impact a major league team.

A full season at Double-A Harrisburg in 2018 will be telling about Gushue's real offensive potential.

Year	Club (League)	Class	AVG	G	AB	R	H	2B	3B	HR	RBI	BB	SO	SB	CS	OBP	SLG
2015	West Virginia (SAL)	LoA	.231	99	360	35	83	17	4	5	47	25	79	1	2	.288	.342
2016	Bradenton (FSL)	HiA	.226	90	328	42	74	17	1	8	38	23	69	0	0	.282	.357
2017	Potomac (CAR)	HiA	.241	91	323	38	78	9	0	18	67	41	88	0	0	.327	.437
	Harrisburg (EL)	AA	.083	4	12	0	1	0	0	0	0	1	1	0	0	.154	.083
Minor League Totals			.232	338	1222	140	284	56	7	36	181	117	274	1	3	.304	.378

21 NICK RAQUET, LHP

BA GRADE
45 Risk: High

Born: Dec. 12, 1995. **B-T:** R-L. **Ht.:** 6-0. **Wt.:** 215. **Drafted:** William & Mary, 2017 (3rd round). **Signed by:** Bobby Myrick.

The Nationals made Raquet a 2017 third-rounder, signing him for $475,000 after a sophomore campaign at William & Mary that analytics departments might look at as mediocre at best. The 22-year-old southpaw transferred from North Carolina after a 2015 freshman season where he threw just 6.1 innings. He sat out a year, then pitched to a 4.66 ERA in 77.1 innings in the Colonial Athletic Association.

Raquet has a solid history in collegiate summer leagues—1.23 ERA in the Cal Ripken League; 2.23 ERA in the Northwoods League—and some exciting stuff with a mid-90s fastball that touched 96 mph in 2017. He also throws an above-average changeup and an upper-70s tweener curveball with above-average potential. He's most likely a reliever down the line but was solid in his pro debut in the short-season New York-Penn League in 12 starts. He's got a funky delivery that will be worth monitoring as far as repeating his mechanics goes, but he has the stuff to get both righties and lefties out.

Raquet has a small chance to be a starter, but the bullpen is a more likely outcome.

Year	Club (League)	Class	W	L	ERA	G	GS	CG	SV	IP	H	HR	BB	SO	K/9	WHIP	AVG
2017	Nationals (GCL)	R	0	0	0.00	1	1	0	0	2	2	0	2	2	9.0	1.00	.250
	Auburn (NYP)	SS	3	2	2.45	11	11	0	0	51	56	2	7	22	3.9	1.23	.283
Minor League Totals			3	2	2.36	12	12	0	0	53	58	2	7	24	4.1	1.22	.282

22 KYLE JOHNSTON, RHP

BA GRADE

45 Risk: High

Born: July 17, 1996. **B-T:** R-R. **Ht.:** 6-0. **Wt.:** 190. **Drafted:** Texas, 2017 (6th round). **Signed by:** Tyler Wilt.

The Nationals drafted Johnston in the sixth round in 2017 and signed him for $226,100 after a three-year career at Texas, where he started 57 games and posted a 3.31 ERA.

Prior to the draft, scouts were enamored of Johnston's plus fastball—which sits in the low to mid-90s with armside run—and a hard slider that flashed plus potential. He also throws a changeup, which is currently a work in progress. What evaluators were not as keen on was his lack of control. Johnston has never walked fewer than 4.6 batters per nine innings over more than 225 innings between Texas, the Rookie-level Gulf Coast League and the short-season New York-Penn League, and he has routinely had issues syncing up the timing between his arm and his lower half. Most scouts see him as a reliever down the road, and Washington has already split his usage between starting and relieving.

Johnston will likely continue to make starts in 2018, but there will be a priority on his innings and he could piggyback with a multi-inning reliever.

Year	Club (League)	Class	W	L	ERA	G	GS	CG	SV	IP	H	HR	BB	SO	K/9	WHIP	AVG
2017	Nationals (GCL)	R	0	0	0.00	1	0	0	0	2	0	0	2	1	4.5	1.00	.000
	Auburn (NYP)	SS	0	2	3.43	14	7	0	0	45	41	2	23	32	6.4	1.43	.241
Minor League Totals			0	2	3.28	15	7	0	0	47	41	2	25	33	6.4	1.41	.236

23 JOSE SANCHEZ, SS

BA GRADE

50 Risk: Extreme

Born: July 12, 2000. **B-T:** R-R. **Ht.:** 5-11. **Wt.:** 155. **Signed:** Venezuela, 2016. **Signed by:** German Robles.

The No. 9 prospect on the international market in 2016, Sanchez signed for $950,000, making him part of a bonus pool-busting international class that included fellow shortstops Luis Garcia and Yasel Antuna. Sanchez, a native of Venezuela, had the least impressive pro debut of the trio in 2017.

Nationals officials are high on Sanchez's defensive upside and consider him the most natural defender of the group, thanks to exceptional lateral mobility and quick footwork despite being just an average runner. He adds soft hands and plus arm strength. He's an extremely confident defender who has a tendency to get too flashy, but he has all the ingredients to turn into an above-average defensive shortstop with more time at the position. The Nationals' shortstop glut in the Rookie-level Gulf Coast League limited him to just 127 innings at the position in 2017. He also played second and third base. He has a raw, contact-oriented offensive approach and doesn't project for much offensive impact down the road, though he did add a significant amount of muscle this year and is currently more physical than his listed weight.

Sanchez could repeat the GCL in 2018 and play shortstop more regularly.

Year	Club (League)	Class	AVG	G	AB	R	H	2B	3B	HR	RBI	BB	SO	SB	CS	OBP	SLG
	Nationals (GCL)	R	.209	48	158	22	33	3	0	1	20	14	26	0	2	.280	.247
Minor League Totals			.209	48	158	22	33	3	0	1	20	14	26	0	2	.280	.247

24 JEFRY RODRIGUEZ, RHP

BA GRADE

50 Risk: Extreme

Born: July 26, 1993. **B-T:** R-R. **Ht.:** 6-5. **Wt.:** 185. **Signed:** Dominican Republic, 2012. **Signed by:** Pablo Arias.

Rodriguez has one of the more exciting arms in the Nationals' system, though his 2017 season was cut short by 80 games after he tested positive for a performance-enhancing substance on May 16. Prior to that, he posted a 3.51 ERA with 40 strikeouts and 11 walks at high Class A Potomac.

Rodriguez found success after his suspension, but his strikeout and walk totals were less impressive than the early season. The key to his success is a mid-90s fastball that can touch 97 mph with excellent plane and angle thanks to his 6-foot-5 frame and a lightning-quick arm. He can throw the pitch to both sides of the plate and also has a hammering, power curveball with downer action that flashes plus and has a chance to be an out pitch. Control issues are the big question mark for Rodriguez moving forward, as he's walked more than four batters per nine innings over six seasons and his strikeout rates aren't as impressive as one would assume, given his stuff. The Nationals have been working on shortening his arm action to keep him in the zone more regularly. He has a chance to be an impact reliever.

Year	Club (League)	Class	W	L	ERA	G	GS	CG	SV	IP	H	HR	BB	SO	K/9	WHIP	AVG
2015	Auburn (NYP)	SS	3	5	4.59	13	13	0	0	69	72	4	33	67	8.8	1.53	.277
	Hagerstown (SAL)	LoA	1	5	6.75	10	10	0	0	43	45	3	25	27	5.7	1.64	.276
2016	Hagerstown (SAL)	LoA	7	11	4.96	25	25	1	0	123	110	6	52	96	7.0	1.31	.240
2017	Potomac (CAR)	HiA	4	3	3.32	12	10	0	0	57	44	2	19	51	8.1	1.11	.220
Minor League Totals			19	28	4.35	89	86	1	0	416	382	18	191	339	7.3	1.38	.248

25 TELMITO AGUSTIN, OF

BA GRADE 45 Risk: V. High

Born: Oct. 9, 1996. **B-T:** L-L. **Ht.:** 5-10. **Wt.:** 160. **Signed:** Dominican Republic, 2013. **Signed by:** Virgilio DeLeon.

Agustin took a step back in 2017, his first complete year in full-season ball. He slumped to a .531 OPS at high Class A Potomac in 33 games before being sent back to the low Class A South Atlantic League for the remainder of the season.

Agustin improved offensively against the lesser competition, but there are new question marks about other areas of his game, including outfield defense and baserunning. Formerly a plus runner, Agustin has added weight and is now closer to an above-average runner. He takes solid routes defensively, but he profiles more as a corner outfielder than a center fielder because of his run-grade decline. He was also caught stealing six times in 18 attempts between the two leagues (66 percent). Agustin operates with a low motor and some in the organization have questioned his work ethic because of that.

The 21-year-old still has some tools and a chance to hit from the left side, but his ceiling is considerably lower now, with several questions—including minor injuries and conditioning issues—left to answer when he gets a second chance in high Class A in 2018.

Year	Club (League)	Class	AVG	G	AB	R	H	2B	3B	HR	RBI	BB	SO	SB	CS	OBP	SLG
2015	Nationals (GCL)	R	.331	38	130	13	43	8	2	1	18	9	17	9	2	.371	.446
	Auburn (NYP)	SS	.400	7	30	5	12	1	2	0	4	1	5	1	1	.419	.567
2016	Nationals (GCL)	R	.000	1	4	0	0	0	0	0	0	0	2	0	0	.000	.000
	Hagerstown (SAL)	LoA	.265	72	238	35	63	12	1	5	30	16	71	14	9	.309	.387
2017	Potomac (CAR)	HiA	.206	33	102	12	21	4	0	1	14	6	27	3	2	.257	.275
	Hagerstown (SAL)	LoA	.277	80	296	45	82	18	4	9	37	13	74	9	4	.308	.456
Minor League Totals			.281	291	1020	166	287	57	19	19	144	85	243	61	25	.338	.430

26 AUSTIN VOTH, RHP

BA GRADE 40 Risk: High

Born: June 26, 1992. **B-T:** R-R. **Ht.:** 6-2. **Wt.:** 215. **Drafted:** Washington, 2013 (5th round). **Signed by:** Fred Costello.

After leading the Nationals organization in strikeouts in 2015 and 2016 and reaching the cusp of the major leagues, Voth took a big step backward in 2017. He started the year at Triple-A Syracuse but was demoted to Double-A Harrisburg after 13 starts. At Triple-A, he recorded a 6.38 ERA and walked 4.6 batters per nine innings.

Voth dealt with mechanical issues that the Nationals tried to sort out by putting him back with Harrisburg pitching coach Chris Michalak, who has worked with him most often. His walk rate improved dramatically, but he still posted a 5.13 ERA as his arm strength has gone in the wrong direction. Voth was regularly in the upper 80s with his fastball rather than the low 90s he had reached before. His breaking ball is solid-average at times, and he's previously shown an above-average changeup, but Voth lacks a plus pitch and has a small margin for error that was exposed with both his drop in velocity and control issues.

Voth still has a chance to be a No. 5 starter, but 2017 was concerning.

Year	Club (League)	Class	W	L	ERA	G	GS	CG	SV	IP	H	HR	BB	SO	K/9	WHIP	AVG
2015	Harrisburg (EL)	AA	6	7	2.92	28	27	0	0	157	134	10	40	148	8.5	1.11	.230
2016	Syracuse (IL)	AAA	7	9	3.15	27	25	0	0	157	138	11	57	133	7.6	1.24	.232
2017	Syracuse (IL)	AAA	1	7	6.38	13	13	1	0	66	85	12	34	42	5.7	1.79	.310
	Auburn (NYP)	SS	0	1	13.50	1	1	0	0	2	4	0	1	2	9.0	2.50	.400
	Harrisburg (EL)	AA	3	4	5.13	10	10	0	0	54	63	8	13	44	7.3	1.40	.288
Minor League Totals			27	35	3.47	114	111	1	0	610	546	48	189	557	8.2	1.20	.237

27 JOAN BAEZ, RHP

BA GRADE 45 Risk: Extreme

Born: Dec. 26, 1994. **B-T:** R-R. **Ht.:** 6-3. **Wt.:** 190. **Signed:** Dominican Republic, 2014. **Signed by:** Modesto Ulloa.

Baez' first stint in high Class A Potomac didn't yield the control development that he and the Nationals were hoping for. In two different stretches in the Carolina League—sandwiching a short four-game stretch in the GCL—the flame-throwing righthander walked 7.5 batters per inning despite a respectable 3.87 ERA. That walk rate is the worst of Baez' career as he continued to struggle finding a consistent release point and couldn't get his lower half in line to the plate regularly. Making things worse, Baez tends to fall off the cliff when he fails on the mound, and he'll go through short dominant stretches only to have his outing fall apart after allowing a hit or a free pass. His stuff continues to make Baez exciting, however, as he has a mid-90s fastball that gets up to 96-97, a breaking ball that flashes plus and an improving changeup. He struggles to get on top of his curve regularly as his arm slot consistently drops on the pitch—another symptom of his mechanical struggles. He'll repeat the Carolina League in 2018 and try to figure out how to throw strikes.

Year	Club (League)	Class	W	L	ERA	G	GS	CG	SV	IP	H	HR	BB	SO	K/9	WHIP	AVG
2015	Hagerstown (SAL)	LoA	0	1	11.32	3	3	0	0	10	13	1	6	6	5.2	1.84	.295
	Nationals (GCL)	R	1	3	2.13	9	9	0	0	42	31	0	19	42	8.9	1.18	.211
	Auburn (NYP)	SS	2	2	7.13	5	5	0	0	18	21	0	14	17	8.7	1.98	.313
2016	Hagerstown (SAL)	LoA	9	7	3.94	27	27	0	0	126	120	5	64	119	8.5	1.46	.258
2017	Nationals (GCL)	R	2	0	1.47	4	3	0	0	18	9	0	5	23	11.3	0.76	.150
	Potomac (CAR)	HiA	4	8	3.87	17	17	1	0	79	64	3	66	65	7.4	1.65	.229
Minor League Totals			23	25	3.53	80	78	1	0	365	309	12	194	333	8.2	1.38	.233

28 ANDERSON FRANCO, 3B

BA GRADE
40 Risk: High

Born: Aug. 15, 1997. **B-T:** R-R. **Ht.:** 6-3. **Wt.:** 190. **Signed:** Dominican Republic, 2013. **Signed by:** Pablo Arias.

Franco didn't put up great numbers at low Class A Hagerstown in his first full season of pro ball, but given his health, age and the off-the-field development that he went through in 2017, the Nationals were pleased with the year he had.

Franco got married and had his first child at age 20 and became one of the team's leaders, and he also played 29 games at first base for the first time in his career. The Nationals see him as a third baseman in the future, with plus arm strength that might warrant a plus-plus grade, solid footwork and good hands. Franco played first base for a spell because the Nationals wanted him in Hagerstown, which they felt was best for his offensive development. He has plus raw power, which has gotten him into trouble with swings and misses thanks to a home run-seeking approach and a swing that tends to get long.

Franco hit 11 homers in 2017 despite a very poor overall season, but his walk rate jump and plus defensive actions are an encouraging sign for his development.

Year	Club (League)	Class	AVG	G	AB	R	H	2B	3B	HR	RBI	BB	SO	SB	CS	OBP	SLG
2015	Nationals (GCL)	R	.281	46	153	19	43	6	1	4	19	14	26	2	3	.347	.412
	Auburn (NYP)	SS	.225	11	40	0	9	1	1	0	4	7	2	0	0	.340	.300
2016	Nationals (GCL)	R	.277	24	83	9	23	3	0	1	9	4	11	1	0	.307	.349
2017	Hagerstown (SAL)	LoA	.201	120	408	57	82	23	2	11	63	41	100	3	1	.272	.348
Minor League Totals			.239	258	890	111	213	41	5	20	130	92	185	10	6	.309	.364

29 JAKSON REETZ, C

BA GRADE
40 Risk: High

Born: Jan. 3, 1996. **B-T:** R-R. **Ht.:** 6-1. **Wt.:** 195. **Drafted:** HS—Firth, Neb., 2014 (3rd round). **Signed by:** Ed Gustafson.

After missing the first month of 2017 with an injury, Reetz logged 37 games at low Class A Hagerstown before earning his first promotion to high Class A Potomac, where he threw out 39 percent of basestealers.

While Reetz has just average to solid-average arm strength, he has managed to consistently keep opponents' running games in check during the first few years of his pro career. Offensively, he hasn't managed to hit above .237 since his pro debut in the Rookie-level Gulf Coast League back in 2014 and is more of a gap-to-gap hitter, though he made adjustments with his lower half and has been driving the ball up the middle with more authority. Against Carolina League arms, Reetz struck out a career-high 31 percent of the time but managed a respectable walk rate (9 percent), as he has throughout his career.

Nationals evaluators rave about Reetz's makeup and work ethic, and while he doesn't have a single standout tool, he has an interesting package that could lead to a backup catcher role in the big leagues with continued offensive and game-calling development.

Year	Club (League)	Class	AVG	G	AB	R	H	2B	3B	HR	RBI	BB	SO	SB	CS	OBP	SLG
2015	Auburn (NYP)	SS	.212	36	113	18	24	4	0	0	5	13	37	3	0	.326	.248
2016	Hagerstown (SAL)	LoA	.230	88	283	41	65	24	0	4	38	38	79	4	1	.346	.357
2017	Hagerstown (SAL)	LoA	.238	37	122	16	29	7	0	2	11	15	41	1	2	.345	.344
	Potomac (CAR)	HiA	.236	26	89	8	21	6	0	2	11	9	32	2	1	.327	.371
Minor League Totals			.236	230	724	103	171	47	1	9	80	101	219	16	7	.355	.341

30 OSVALDO ABREU, SS

BA GRADE
40 Risk: High

Born: June 13, 1994. **B-T:** R-R. **Ht.:** 6-0. **Wt.:** 170. **Signed:** Dominican Republic, 2012. **Signed by:** Modesto Ulloa.

Abreu was challenged in 2017 with a full season at Double-A Harrisburg after a strong second half in 2016 in the Carolina and Arizona Fall leagues. The 23-year-old played exclusively shortstop for the second straight season, and while he struggled during the first half—hitting .237/.284/.325 from April through June—he improved in the second half and hit .258/.320/.352 from July through September.

Abreu has strong, quick hands at the plate and can turn on fastballs on the inner half, but he often gets too pull-happy and is still learning to hit the other way. The majority of his doubles were hit to the left side of the field. Despite another poor defensive year by Abreu, the Nationals think he can turn into a solid defender at shortstop, where he has a good arm but remains inconsistent. He has a tendency to carry his offensive struggles into the field, and vice versa.

Abreu will likely repeat in Double-A in 2018, and the Nationals will hope he can carry his late-season improvements over a full season and make strides in preventing his failures from snowballing into other areas of his game.

Year	Club (League)	Class	AVG	G	AB	R	H	2B	3B	HR	RBI	BB	SO	SB	CS	OBP	SLG
2015	Hagerstown (SAL)	LoA	.274	123	442	74	121	35	4	6	47	50	89	30	11	.357	.412
2016	Potomac (CAR)	HiA	.247	126	497	86	123	23	4	6	52	55	108	18	10	.328	.346
2017	Harrisburg (EL)	AA	.246	125	431	40	106	16	4	5	42	27	107	1	6	.299	.336
Minor League Totals			.257	535	1942	293	500	107	18	18	206	187	418	97	53	.333	.359

Baseball America senior writer Ben Badler reports on international players who were free agents as the Prospect Handbook went to press but are expected to sign with major league organizations for 2018.

JULIO PABLO MARTINEZ, OF

BA GRADE
60 Risk: High

Born: March 21, 1996. **B-T:** L-L. **Ht.:** 5-10. **Wt.:** 180.

Under the previous Collective Bargaining Agreement, teams were able to blast through their international bonus pools, which is how Cuban outfielder Luis Robert signed with the White Sox for a $26 million bonus in 2017. Martinez is subject to the new rules, which will curtail his earnings due to the hard cap on each club's international bonus pool. He had been one of the top players left in Cuba, having starred in the country's junior leagues and then in Cuba's top league, Serie Nacional, where in his final season he batted .333/.469/.498 in 264 plate appearances with 52 walks, 30 strikeouts, six home runs and 24 stolen bases in 29 attempts. Though he's not that big, Martinez has a promising combination of power and speed. He's a center fielder who is plus runner with an average arm. He has whippy bat speed, strong wrists and a tick above-average power. Martinez is a good low-ball hitter, and while his power comes with some swing-and-miss especially up in the zone, his strikeout rate should be manageable. His overall profile has similarities to a smaller version of Curtis Granderson. Based on his present talent level, Martinez should be ready for an assignment to a high Class A or Double-A affiliate.

RAIMFER SALINAS, OF

BA GRADE
55 Risk: Extreme

Born: Dec. 31, 2000. **B-T:** R-R. **Ht.:** 6-0. **Wt.:** 170.

Salinas has played for Venezuela at multiple international tournaments, often as one of the youngest players on his team. He made a big impression in front of scouts as a 14-year-old at the COPABE 15U Pan American Championship in Mexico in 2015, when he ranked among the tournament leaders in batting average (.457) and slugging (.686). He stood out as one of the toolsiest international prospects in the 2017 class. He has a lean, athletic build with plus speed, an easy stride and a plus arm, all of which should fit well in center field. During batting practice, Salinas shows good bat speed and a sound swing, hitting line drives to all fields. His raw power is a tick below-average, with a lot of doubles and triples that should turn into more home runs once he fills out. Salinas does have a good track record of hitting in games, though some scouts had concerns about his swing-and-miss tendencies. Some of them felt it may have been a pitch tracking issue that caused Salinas to chase pitches off the plate, while others thought he may have been pressing as July 2 approached. Though he didn't sign on July 2, Salinas continued to perform well in games in Venezuela over the winter.

ANTONIO CABELLO, C

BA GRADE
55 Risk: Extreme

Born: Nov. 1, 2000. **B-T:** R-R. **Ht.:** 5-11. **Wt.:** 185.

Cabello has an unusual skill set. He's an athletic catcher who is physically mature for his age and is also one of the fastest players in the 2017 international class. He doesn't have as much physical projection left as many of his peers because of his already strong, relatively filled out frame, but before July 2 he flashed plus or better speed, running the 60-yard dash as fast as 6.5 seconds. Given his build, he's likely to slow down considerably, but he's athletic enough for second base or the outfield to be backup plans. Cabello's game performance has been among the best in his class. His swing has little rhythm or separation, with his hands starting from a near standstill. He relies on his explosive hand speed, strength and a knack for consistently barreling the ball for quality contact. If he learns to load his swing more and generate more loft in his swing path, more power should come. He's already shown some signs of doing that in games this winter in Venezuela, where he has continued to perform well while showing a patient, disciplined approach that helps him draw walks. Cabello's quickness and athleticism should help him behind the plate, but he needs to improve his receiving skills. He has an average arm but needs to improve his transfer on throws to second.

JELFRY MARTE, SS

BA GRADE
50 Risk: Extreme

Born: March 27, 2001. **B-T:** R-R. **Ht.:** 5-11. **Wt.:** 175.

Marte originally signed with the Twins for $3 million on July 2, 2017, but the club voided the contract after it determined there was an issue with Marte's vision during his physical. Marte is a true shortstop who has grown an inch and added strength since then to his medium frame. He's a quick-burst athlete with plus speed who bounces around at shortstop. Marte is quick, agile and has good body control, ranging well to both sides and showing soft hands, slick actions and an above-average, accurate arm. Like a lot of young shortstops, Marte can get too flashy at times, but better decision-making at the position should come with experience. While there were scouts who thought Marte had the bat control to hit at the top of a lineup, many clubs projected him to hit toward the bottom of the order. He's not a pure hitter and he hasn't shown much power yet, as he's mostly a singles hitter with occasional doubles in the gap. Marte does wreak havoc on the bases, where he's an aggressive runner and a high stolen base threat with his speed.

2017 INTERNATIONAL TOP 50 PROSPECTS

Rk. Name	Pos.	Country	Team
1. Wander Franco	SS	Dominican Republic	Rays
2. Daniel Flores	C	Venezuela	*Red Sox
3. Ronny Mauricio	SS	Dominican Republic	Mets
4. Everson Pereira	OF	Venezuela	Yankees
5. George Valera	OF	Dominican Republic	Indians
6. Julio Rodriguez	OF	Dominican Republic	Mariners
7. Danny Diaz	SS	Venezuela	Red Sox
8. Carlos Rodriguez	OF	Venezuela	Brewers
9. Kristian Robinson	OF	Bahamas	D-backs
10. Raimer Salinas	OF	Venezuela	
11. Ronny Rojas	SS	Dominican Republic	Yankees
12. Luis Garcia	SS	Dominican Republic	Phillies
13. Jelfry Marte	SS	Dominican Republic	Rays
14. Eric Pardinho	RHP	Brazil	Blue Jays
15. Antonio Cabello	C	Venezuela	
16. Adrian Hernandez	OF	Dominican Republic	Mets
17. Aaron Bracho	SS	Venezuela	Indians
18. Ynmanol Marinez	SS	Dominican Republic	Marlins
19. Trent Deveaux	OF	Bahamas	Angels
20. Roberto Chirinos	SS	Venezuela	Yankees
21. Juan Querecuto	SS	Venezuela	Mariners
22. Ezequiel Tovar	SS	Venezuela	Rockies
23. Miguel Hiraldo	SS	Dominican Republic	Blue Jays
24. Keyber Rodriguez	SS	Venezuela	Rangers
25. Victor Vargas	RHP	Colombia	Phillies
26. Larry Ernesto	OF	Dominican Republic	Brewers
27. Wilderd Patino	OF	Venezuela	D-backs
28. Anthony Garica	OF	Dominican Republic	Yankees
29. Florencio Serrano	RHP	Mexico	Cubs
30. Carlos Aguiar	OF	Venezuela	Twins
31. Julio Machado	SS	Venezuela	Marlins
32. Alejandro Melean	RHP	Venezuela	Blue Jays
33. Fadriel Cruz	SS	Dominican Republic	Rockies
34. Mauro Bonifacio	OF	Dominican Republic	
35. Antoni Flores	SS	Venezuela	Red Sox
36. Leonardo Jimenez	SS	Panama	Blue Jays
37. D'Shawn Knowles	OF	Bahamas	Angels
38. Alberto Rodriguez	OF	Dominican Republic	Blue Jays
39. Alvaro Gonzalez	SS	Venezuela	Tigers
40. Stanly Consuegra	OF	Dominican Republic	Mets
41. Carlos Betancourt	RHP	Venezuela	Phillies
42. Cesar Rodriguez	C	Venezuela	Phillies
43. Carlos Irigoyen	SS	Venezuela	Tigers
44. Jorge Barrosa	OF	Venezuela	D-backs
45. Juan Pie	OF	Dominican Republic	Pirates
46. Osleivis Basabe	SS	Venezuela	
47. Luis Verdugo	SS	Mexico	Cubs
48. Karlo Seijas	RHP	Venezuela	Nationals
49. David Marcano	RHP	Venezuela	Mets
50. Heitor Tokar	RHP	Brazil	Astros

* Flores died on Nov. 8, 2017, from complications
from treatment for cancer.

Ronny Mauricio is an instinctive
shortstop with good range.

A true center fielder, Everson
Pereira has plus arm strength.

PHOTOS BY BILL MITCHELL

2017 RULE 5 DRAFT

The 2017 Rule 5 draft occurred on Nov. 14, 2017, our transactions deadline. A few of these players rank in their new organizations' Top 30 Prospects, but since all 15 will be in big league spring training camp in 2018, we provide thumbnail scouting reports for all of them in this space.

Pick	2018 Org	Player	Pos	2017 Org	BA Grade/Risk
1. Tigers		Victor Reyes	OF	D-backs	45/Medium

Reyes has always been able to hit and could fill a fourth outfielder option if he can prove he can play an adequate center field. He'll get that chance with a rebuilding Tigers club.

2. Giants   Julian Fernandez   RHP   Rockies   45/Extreme
The Giants love hard-throwing pitchers and few throw harder than Fernandez, who has touched 102 mph. He has to refine his secondary pitches and has no experience above low Class A. It will be hard for him to contribute productive innings in 2018, but he has long-term potential.

3. Pirates   Nick Burdi   RHP   Twins   45/High
The Pirates know that Burdi will spend much of the year rehabbing as he works his way back from Tommy John surgery. But pre-injury, he showed potential closer stuff with a high-90s fastball and a wipeout slider.

4. Rangers   Carlos Tocci   OF   Phillies   45/Medium
It's unlikely Tocci will ever gain enough strength to be a regular, but he demonstrated he can hit for average and play a solid center field, which makes him a viable fourth outfielder.

5. Royals   Brad Keller   RHP   D-backs   45/High
Keller ranked No. 8 in a thin D-backs system last year. A year later, he heads to Kansas City, where his heavy 92-94 mph fastball could fit in the bullpen or as a spot starter.

6. Royals   Burch Smith   RHP   Rays   45/High
Smith missed all of 2015 and 2016 recovering from Tommy John surgery. But he showed his stuff had fully recovered in a strong second half with the Rays. He's the rare Rule 5 pick who could actually start games in the big leagues.

7. Braves   Anyelo Gomez   RHP   Yankees   45/High
Gomez has a chance to contribute in the Braves' bullpen with a high-90s fastball and an excellent changeup. He also does a good job of keeping the ball in the park.

8. Pirates   Jordan Milbrath   RHP   Indians   45/Extreme
Milbrath dropped his arm slot without losing velocity. His high-90s fastball from a low arm slot makes it hard for righthanded hitters to pick up the ball.

9. Orioles   Nestor Cortes   LHP   Yankees   40/Medium
Cortes is more crafty than dominating. His fastball is average at best, but he mixes his pitches and locates well, which could fit in a low-leverage relief role.

10. Marlins   Elieser Hernandez   RHP   Astros   40/Medium
Hernandez doesn't wow with overpowering stuff, but he could help the Marlins with a good-enough changeup and curveball to keep hitters off balance. He has a low ceiling but is a relatively refined relief candidate.

11. Mariners   Mike Ford   1B   Yankees   40/High
Ford has a pretty lengthy track record for getting on base and hitting for average to above-average power. Sticking as a first baseman/DH in Seattle will be difficult since Nelson Cruz and Ryon Healy are already there.

12. Angels   Luke Bard   RHP   Twins   45/Very High
The younger brother of former Red Sox reliever Daniel Bard, Luke had a breakthrough season in 2017. He misses bats with a high-octane fastball.

13. Twins   Tyler Kinley   RHP   Marlins   45/Extreme
The Twins lost Nick Burdi and Luke Bard, a pair of hard-throwing relievers, om the Rule 5 draft, but they picked up Kinley, another hard-throwing reliever with a 95-100 mph fastball but control troubles.

14. D-backs   Albert Suarez   RHP   Giants   45/High
Arizona drafted a reliever with modest upside, but one who already has big league experience. The division-rival Giants had recently dropped Suarez from their 40-man roster, which made him Rule 5 eligible.

15. Astros   Anthony Gose   LHP   Rangers   45/Extreme
Gose may be the most interesting name in this year's Rule 5 class. A big league center fielder, he took up pitching and quickly showed a 95-100 mph fastball and a promising breaking ball, but he also has fewer than 10 pro innings.

16. Orioles   Pedro Araujo   RHP   Cubs   45/Extreme
Araujo's fastball/slider combo is good enough to pitch in the big leagues, but he'll be making a big jump because he has no experience above Class A.

17. Marlins   Brett Graves   RHP   Athletics   45/Extreme
Graves missed time in 2017 with a leg injury, but with the Marlins moving to a full rebuild, they will see if his fastball/slider pairing is good enough to fill innings.

18. Orioles   Jose Mesa Jr.   RHP   Yankees   45/High
The son of the long-time big leaguer closer of the same name, Mesa throws four usable pitches, including a 92-95 mph fastball. He will be battling with two other Orioles Rule 5 picks to stick on the roster.

SIGNING BONUSES

2017 DRAFT

FIRST ROUND

No. Team: Player, Pos.	Bonus
1. Twins: Royce Lewis, SS	$6,725,000
2. Reds: Hunter Greene, RHP	$7,230,000
3. Padres: MacKenzie Gore, LHP	$6,700,000
4. Rays: Brendan McKay, 1B	$7,005,000
5. Braves: Kyle Wright, RHP	$7,000,000
6. Athletics: Austin Beck, OF	$5,303,000
7. D-backs: Pavin Smith, 1B	$5,016,300
8. Phillies: Adam Haseley, OF	$5,100,000
9. Brewers: Keston Hiura, 2B	$4,000,000
10. Angels: Jo Adell, OF	$4,376,800
11. White Sox: Jake Burger, 3B	$3,700,000
12. Pirates: Shane Baz, RHP	$4,100,000
13. Marlins: Trevor Rogers, LHP	$3,400,000
14. Royals: Nick Pratto, 1B	$3,450,000
15. Astros: J.B. Bukauskas, RHP	$3,600,000
16. Yankees: Clarke Schmidt, RHP	$2,184,300
17. Mariners: Evan White, 1B	$3,125,000
18. Tigers: Alex Faedo, RHP	$3,500,000
19. Giants: Heliot Ramos, OF	$3,101,700
20. Mets: David Peterson, LHP	$2,994,500
21. Orioles: D.L. Hall, LHP	$3,000,000
22. Blue Jays: Logan Warmoth, SS	$2,820,200
23. Dodgers: Jeren Kendall, OF	$2,897,500
24. Red Sox: Tanner Houck, RHP	$2,614,500
25. Nationals: Seth Romero, LHP	$2,800,000
26. Rangers: Bubba Thompson, OF	$2,100,000
27. Cubs: Brendon Little, LHP	$2,200,000
28. Blue Jays: Nate Pearson, RHP	$2,452,900
29. Rangers: Chris Seise, SS	$2,000,000
30. Cubs: Alex Lange, RHP	$1,925,000

SUPPLEMENTAL FIRST ROUND

No. Team: Player, Pos.	Bonus
31. Rays: Drew Rasmussen, RHP	Did not sign
32. Reds: Jeter Downs, SS	$1,822,500
33. Athletics: Kevin Merrell, SS	$1,800,000
34. Brewers: Tristen Lutz, OF	$2,352,000
35. Twins: Brent Rooker, OF	$1,935,300
36. Marlins: Brian Miller, OF	$1,888,800

SECOND ROUND

No. Team: Player, Pos.	Bonus
37. Twins: Landon Leach, RHP	$1,400,000
38. Reds: Stuart Fairchild, OF	$1,800,300
39. Padres: Luis Campusano, C	$1,300,000
40. Rays: Michael Mercado, RHP	$2,132,400
41. Braves: Drew Waters, OF	$1,500,000
42. Pirates: Steven Jennings, RHP	$1,900,000
43. Athletics: Greg Deichmann, OF	$1,700,000
44. D-backs: Drew Ellis, 3B	$1,560,100
45. Phillies: Spencer Howard, RHP	$1,150,000
46. Brewers: Caden Lemons, RHP	$1,450,000
47. Angels: Griffin Canning, RHP	$1,459,200
48. Rockies: Ryan Vilade, 3B	$1,425,400
49. White Sox: Gavin Sheets, 1B	$2,000,000
50. Pirates: Calvin Mitchell, OF	$1,357,300
51. Marlins: Joe Dunand, 3B	$1,200,000
52. Royals: M.J. Melendez, C	$2,097,500
53. Astros: Joe Perez, 3B	$1,600,000
54. Yankees: Matt Sauer, RHP	$2,497,500
55. Mariners: Sam Carlson, RHP	$2,000,000
56. Astros: Corbin Martin, RHP	$1,000,000
57. Tigers: Rey Rivera, OF	$850,000
58. Giants: Jacob Gonzalez, 3B	$950,000
59. Mets: Mark Vientos, 3B	$1,500,000
60. Orioles: Adam Hall, SS	$1,300,000
61. Blue Jays: Hagen Danner, C	$1,500,000
62. Dodgers: Morgan Cooper	$867,500
63. Red Sox: Cole Brannen, OF	$1,300,000
64. Indians: Quentin Holmes	$988,970
65. Nationals: Wil Crowe, RHP	$946,500
66. Rangers: Hans Crouse, RHP	$1,450,000
67. Cubs: Cory Abbott, RHP	$901,900

SUPPLEMENTAL SECOND ROUND

No. Team: Player, Pos.	Bonus
68. D-backs: Daulton Varsho, C	$881,100
69. Padres: Blake Hunt, C	$1,600,000
70. Rockies: Tommy Doyle, RHP	$837,300
71. Indians: Tyler Freeman, SS	$816,500
72. Pirates: Conner Uselton, OF	$900,000
73. Royals: Evan Steele, LHP	$826,500
74. Orioles: Zac Lowther, LHP	$779,500
75. Astros: J.J. Matijevic, 2B	$700,000

THIRD ROUND

No. Team: Player, Pos.	Bonus
76. Twins: Blayne Enlow, RHP	$2,000,000
77. Reds: Jacob Heatherly, LHP	$1,047,500
78. Padres: Mason House, OF	$732,200
79. Rays: Taylor Walls, SS	$612,500
80. Braves: Freddy Tarnok, RHP	$1,445,000
81. Athletics: Nick Allen, SS	$2,000,000
82. D-backs: Matt Tabor, RHP	$1,000,000
83. Phillies: Connor Seabold, RHP	$525,000
84. Brewers: K.J. Harrison, C	$667,000
85. Angels: Jacob Pearson, OF	$1,000,000
86. Rockies: Will Gaddis, RHP	$600,000
87. White Sox: Luis Gonzalez, OF	$517,000
88. Pirates: Dylan Busby, 3B	$575,000
89. Marlins: Riley Mahan, 2B	$525,000
90. Royals: Daniel Tillo, LHP	$557,500
91. Astros: Tyler Ivey, RHP	$450,000
92. Yankees: Trevor Stephan, RHP	$797,500
93. Mariners: Wyatt Mills, RHP	$125,000
94. Cardinals: Scott Hurst, OF	$450,000
95. Tigers: Joey Morgan, C	$564,000
96. Giants: Seth Corry, LHP	$1,000,000
97. Mets: Quinn Brodey, OF	$500,000
98. Orioles: Mike Baumann, RHP	$500,000
99. Blue Jays: Riley Adams, C	$542,400
100. Dodgers: Connor Wong, C	$547,500

2016 DRAFT

FIRST ROUND

No. Team: Player, Pos.	Bonus
1. Phillies: Mickey Moniak, OF	$6,100,000
2. Reds: Nick Senzel, 3B	$6,200,000
3. Braves: Ian Anderson, RHP	$4,000,000
4. Rockies: Riley Pint, RHP	$4,800,000
5. Brewers: Corey Ray, OF	$4,125,000
6. Athletics: A.J. Puk, LHP	$4,069,200
7. Marlins: Braxton Garrett, LHP	$4,145,900
8. Padres: Cal Quantrill, RHP	$3,963,045
9. Tigers: Matt Manning, RHP	$3,505,800
10. White Sox: Zack Collins, C	$3,380,600
11. Mariners: Kyle Lewis, OF	$3,286,700
12. Red Sox: Jason Groome, LHP	$3,650,000
13. Rays: Josh Lowe, 3B	$2,597,500
14. Indians: Will Benson, OF	$2,500,000
15. Twins: Alex Kirilloff, OF	$2,817,100
16. Angels: Matt Thaiss, C	$2,150,000
17. Astros: Forrest Whitley, RHP	$3,148,000
18. Yankees: Blake Rutherford, OF	$3,282,000
19. Mets: Justin Dunn, RHP	$2,378,800
20. Dodgers: Gavin Lux, SS	$2,314,500
21. Blue Jays: T.J. Zeuch, RHP	$2,175,000
22. Pirates: Will Craig, 3B	$2,253,700
23. Cardinals: Delvin Perez, SS	$2,222,500
24. Padres: Hudson Potts, SS	$1,000,000
25. Padres: Eric Lauer, LHP	$2,000,000
26. White Sox: Zack Burdi, RHP	$2,128,500
27. Orioles: Cody Sedlock, RHP	$2,097,200
28. Nationals: Carter Kieboom, SS	$2,000,000
29. Nationals: Dane Dunning, RHP	$2,000,000
30. Rangers: Cole Ragans, LHP	$2,003,400
31. Mets: Anthony Kay, LHP	$1,100,000
32. Dodgers: Will Smith, C	$1,772,500
33. Cardinals: Dylan Carson, OF	$1,350,000
34. Cardinals: Dakota Hudson, RHP	$2,000,000

SUPPLEMENTAL FIRST ROUND

No. Team: Player, Pos.	Bonus
35. Reds: Taylor Trammell, OF	$3,200,000
36. Dodgers: Jordan Sheffield, RHP	$1,847,500
37. Athletics: Daulton Jefferies, RHP	$1,600,000
38. Rockies: Robert Tyler, RHP	$1,701,600
39. D-backs: Anfernee Grier, OF	$1,500,000
40. Braves: Joey Wentz, LHP	$3,050,000
41. Pirates: Nick Lodolo, LHP	Did not sign

SECOND ROUND

No. Team: Player, Pos.	Bonus
42. Phillies: Kevin Gowdy, RHP	$3,500,000
43. Reds: Chris Okey, C	$2,000,000
44. Braves: Kyle Muller, LHP	$2,500,000
45. Rockies: Ben Bowden, LHP	$1,600,000
46. Brewers: Lucas Erceg, 3B	$1,150,000
47. Athletics: Logan Shore, RHP	$1,500,000
48. Padres: Buddy Reed, OF	$1,075,000
49. White Sox: Alec Hansen, RHP	$1,284,500
50. Mariners: Joe Rizzo, 3B	$1,750,000

No. Team: Player, Pos.	Bonus
51. Red Sox: C.J. Chatham, SS	$1,100,000
52. D-backs: Andy Yerzy, C	$1,214,100
53. Rays: Ryan Boldt, OF	$997,500
54. Orioles: Keegan Akin, LHP	$1,177,200
55. Indians: Nolan Jones, SS	$2,250,000
56. Twins: Ben Rortvedt, C	$900,000
57. Blue Jays: J.B. Woodman, OF	$975,000
58. Nationals: Sheldon Neuse, 3B	$900,000
59. Giants: Bryan Reynolds, OF	$1,350,000
60. Angels: Brandon Marsh, OF	$1,073,300
61. Astros: Ronnie Dawson, OF	$1,056,800
62. Yankees: Nick Solak, 2B	$950,000
63. Rangers: Alex Speas, RHP	$1,024,900
64. Mets: Peter Alonso, 1B	$909,200
65. Dodgers: Mitchell White, RHP	$588,300
66. Blue Jays: Bo Bichette, SS	$1,100,000
67. Royals: A.J. Puckett, RHP	$1,200,000
68. Pirates: Travis MacGregor, RHP	$900,000
69. Orioles: Matthias Dietz, RHP	$1,300,000
70. Cardinals: Connor Jones, RHP	$1,100,000

SUPPLEMENTAL SECOND ROUND

No. Team: Player, Pos.	Bonus
71. Padres: Reggie Lawson, RHP	$1,900,000
72. Indians: Logan Ice, C	$850,000
73. Twins: Jose Miranda, SS	$775,000
74. Twins: Akil Baddoo, OF	$750,000
75. Brewers: Mario Feliciano, C	$800,000
76. Braves: Brett Cumberland, C	$1,500,000
77. Rays: Jake Fraley, OF	$797,500

THIRD ROUND

No. Team: Player, Pos.	Bonus
78. Phillies: Cole Stobbe, SS	$1,100,000
79. Reds: Nick Hanson, RHP	$925,000
80. Braves: Drew Harrington, LHP	$900,000
81. Rockies: Garrett Hampson, SS	$750,000
82. Brewers: Braden Webb, RHP	$700,000
83. Athletics: Sean Murphy, C	$753,100
84. Marlins: Thomas Jones, SS	$1,000,000
85. Padres: Mason Thompson, RHP	$1,750,000
86. White Sox: Alex Call, OF	$719,100
87. Mariners: Bryson Brigman, SS	$700,000
88. Red Sox: Shaun Anderson, RHP	$700,000
89. D-backs: Jon Duplantier, RHP	$686,600
90. Rays: Austin Franklin, RHP	$597,500
91. Orioles: Austin Hays, OF	$665,800
92. Indians: Aaron Civale, RHP	$625,000
93. Twins: Griffin Jax, RHP	$645,600
94. Nationals: Jesus Luzardo, LHP	$1,400,000
95. Giants: Heath Quinn, OF	$625,900
96. Angels: Nonnie Williams, SS	$950,000
97. Astros: Jake Rogers, C	$614,000
98. Yankees: Nolan Martinez, RHP	$1,150,000
99. Rangers: Kole Enright, 3B	$675,000
100. Mets: Blake Tiberi, 3B	$500,000

2015 DRAFT

TOP 100 PICKS

FIRST ROUND

No.	Pick Team: Player, Pos.	Bonus
1.	D-backs: Dansby Swanson, SS	$6,500,000
2.	Astros: Alex Bregman, SS	$5,900,000
3.	Rockies: Brendan Rodgers, SS	$5,500,000
4.	Rangers: Dillon Tate, RHP	$4,200,000
5.	Astros: Kyle Tucker, OF	$4,000,000
6.	Twins: Tyler Jay, LHP	$3,889,500
7.	Red Sox: Andrew Benintendi, OF	$3,590,400
8.	White Sox: Carson Fulmer, RHP	$3,470,600
9.	Cubs: Ian Happ, OF	$3,000,000
10.	Phillies: Cornelius Randolph, SS	$3,231,300
11.	Reds: Tyler Stephenson, C	$3,141,600
12.	Marlins: Josh Naylor, 1B	$2,200,000
13.	Rays: Garrett Whitley, OF	$2,959,600
14.	Braves: Kolby Allard, LHP	$3,042,400
15.	Brewers: Trent Clark, OF	$2,700,000
16.	Yankees: James Kaprielian, RHP	$2,650,000
17.	Indians: Brady Aiken, LHP	$2,513,280
18.	Giants: Phil Bickford, RHP	$2,333,800
19.	Pirates: Kevin Newman, SS	$2,175,000
20.	Athletics: Richie Martin, SS	$1,950,000
21.	Royals: Ashe Russell, RHP	$2,190,200
22.	Tigers: Beau Burrows, RHP	$2,154,200
23.	Cardinals: Nick Plummer, OF	$2,124,400
24.	Dodgers: Walker Buehler, RHP	$1,777,500
25.	Orioles: D.J. Stewart, OF	$2,064,500
26.	Angels: Taylor Ward, C	$1,670,000
27.	Rockies: Mike Nikorak, RHP	$2,300,000
28.	Braves: Mike Soroka, RHP	$1,974,700
29.	Blue Jays: Jon Harris, RHP	$1,944,800
30.	Yankees: Kyle Holder, SS	$1,800,000
31.	Giants: Chris Shaw, 1B	$1,400,000
32.	Pirates: Ke'Bryan Hayes, 3B	$1,855,000
33.	Royals: Nolan Watson, RHP	$1,825,200
34.	Tigers: Christin Stewart, OF	$1,795,100
35.	Dodgers: Kyle Funkhouser, RHP	Unsigned
36.	Orioles: Ryan Mountcastle, SS	$1,300,000

SUPPLEMENTAL FIRST ROUND

No.	Pick Team: Player, Pos.	Bonus
37.	Astros: Daz Cameron, OF	$4,000,000
38.	Rockies: Tyler Nevin, 3B	$2,000,000
39.	Cardinals: Jake Woodford, RHP	$1,800,000
40.	Brewers: Nathan Kirby, LHP	$1,250,000
41.	Braves: Austin Riley, 3B	$1,600,000
42.	Indians: Triston McKenzie, RHP	$2,302,500

SECOND ROUND

No.	Pick Team: Player, Pos.	Bonus
43.	D-backs, Alex Young, LHP	$1,431,400
44.	Rockies: Peter Lambert, LHP	$1,495,200
45.	Rangers: Eric Jenkins, OF	$2,000,000
46.	Astros: Tom Eshelman, RHP	$1,100,000
47.	Cubs: Donnie Dewees, OF	$1,700,000
48.	Phillies: Scott Kingery, 2B	$1,259,600
49.	Reds: Antonio Santillan, RHP	$1,350,000
50.	Marlins: Brett Lilek, LHP	$1,000,000

No.	Pick Team: Player, Pos.	Bonus
51.	Padres: Austin Smith, RHP	$1,200,000
52.	Rays: Chris Betts, C	$1,482,500
53.	Mets: Desmond Lindsay, OF	$1,142,700
54.	Braves: Lucas Herbert, C	$1,125,200
55.	Brewers: Cody Ponce, RHP	$1,108,000
56.	Blue Jays: Brady Singer, RHP	Unsigned
57.	Yankees: Jeff Degano, LHP	$650,000
58.	Nationals: Andrew Stevenson, OF	$750,000
59.	Indians: Juan Hillman, LHP	$825,000
60.	Mariners: Nick Neidert, RHP	$1,200,000
61.	Giants: Andrew Suarez, LHP	$1,010,100
62.	Pirates: Kevin Kramer, SS	$850,000
63.	Athletics: Mikey White, SS	$900,000
64.	Royals: Josh Staumont, RHP	$964,600
65.	Tigers: Tyler Alexander, LHP	$1,000,000
66.	Cardinals: Bryce Denton, 3B	$1,200,000
67.	Dodgers: Mitch Hansen, OF	$997,500
68.	Orioles: Jonathan Hughes, RHP	Unsigned
69.	Nationals: Blake Perkins, OF	$800,000
70.	Angels: Jahmai Jones, OF	$1,100,000

SUPPLEMENTAL SECOND ROUND

No.	Pick Team: Player, Pos.	Bonus
71.	Reds: Tanner Rainey, RHP	$432,950
72.	Mariners: Andrew Moore, RHP	$800,000
73.	Twins: Kyle Cody, RHP	Unsigned
74.	Dodgers: Josh Sborz, RHP	$722,500
75.	Braves: A.J. Minter, LHP	$814,300

THIRD ROUND

No.	Pick Team: Player, Pos.	Bonus
76.	D-backs: Taylor Clarke, RHP	$801,900
77.	Rockies: Javier Medina, RHP	$740,000
78.	Rangers: Michael Matuella, RHP	$2,000,000
79.	Astros: Riley Ferrell, RHP	$1,000,000
80.	Twins: Travis Blankenhorn, 3B	$650,000
81.	Red Sox: Austin Rei, C	$742,400
82.	Cubs: Bryan Hudson, LHP	$1,100,000
83.	Phillies: Lucas Williams, SS	$719,800
84.	Reds: Blake Trahan, SS	$708,900
85.	Marlins: Isaiah White, OF	$698,100
86.	Padres: Jacob Nix, RHP	$900,000
87.	Rays: Brandon Lowe, 2B	$697,500
88.	Mets: Max Wotell, LHP	$775,000
89.	Braves: Anthony Guardado, RHP	$550,000
90.	Brewers: Nash Walters, RHP	$800,000
91.	Blue Jays: Justin Maese, RHP	$300,000
92.	Yankees: Drew Finley, RHP	$950,000
93.	Indians: Mark Mathias, 2B	$550,000
94.	Mariners: Braden Bishop, OF	$607,700
95.	Padres: Jalen Miller, SS	$1,100,000
96.	Pirates: Casey Hughston, OF	$700,000
97.	Athletics: Dakota Chalmers, RHP	$1,200,000
98.	Royals: Anderson Miller, OF	$581,300
99.	Tigers: Drew Smith, RHP	$575,800
100.	Cardinals: Harrison Bader, OF	$400,000

TOP 20 PROSPECTS

FROM EVERY MINOR LEAGUE

TRIPLE-A

International League

1. Ronald Acuna, OF, Gwinnett (Braves)
2. Yoan Moncada, 2B, Charlotte (White Sox)
3. Rhys Hoskins, 1B/OF, Lehigh Valley (Phillies)
4. Brent Honeywell, RHP, Durham (Rays)
5. Willy Adames, SS, Durham (Rays)
6. Ozzie Albies, 2B/SS, Gwinnett (Braves)
7. Bradley Zimmer, OF, Columbus (Indians)
8. Scott Kingery, 2B, Lehigh Valley (Phillies)
9. Chance Adams, RHP, Scranton/W-B (Yankees)
10. J.P. Crawford, SS, Lehigh Valley (Phillies)
11. Sean Newcomb, LHP, Gwinnett (Braves)
12. Tyler Glasnow, RHP, Indianapolis (Pirates)
13. Lucas Giolito, RHP, Charlotte (White Sox)
14. Jacob Faria, RHP, Durham (Rays)
15. Miguel Andujar, 3B, Scranton/W-B (Yankees)
16. Clint Frazier, OF, Scranton/W-B (Yankees)
17. Dustin Fowler, OF, Scranton/W-B (Yankees)
18. Lucas Sims, RHP, Gwinnett (Braves)
19. Jake Bauers, OF/1B, Durham (Rays)
20. Chance Sisco, C, Norfolk (Orioles)

Pacific Coast League

1. Amed Rosario, SS, Las Vegas (Mets)
2. Lewis Brinson, OF, Colorado Springs (Brewers)
3. Derek Fisher, OF, Fresno (Astros)
4. Alex Verdugo, OF, Oklahoma City (Dodgers)
5. Paul DeJong, SS, Memphis (Cardinals)
6. Dominic Smith, 1B, Las Vegas (Mets)
7. Carson Kelly, C, Memphis (Cardinals)
8. Jack Flaherty, RHP, Memphis (Cardinals)
9. Ryan McMahon, 1B/2B, Albuquerque (Rockies)
10. Luke Weaver, RHP, Memphis (Cardinals)
11. Josh Hader, LHP, Colorado Springs (Brewers)
12. Chris Shaw, OF/1B, Sacramento (Giants)
13. Brandon Woodruff, RHP, Colorado Springs (Brewers)
14. Matt Chapman, 3B, Nashville (Athletics)
15. Willie Calhoun, 2B/OF, Round Rock (Rangers)
16. Matt Olson, 1B, Nashville (Athletics)
17. Franklin Barreto, SS/2B, Nashville (Athletics)
18. Victor Caratini, C/1B, Iowa (Cubs)
19. Harrison Bader, OF, Memphis (Cardinals)
20. Brett Phillips, OF, Colorado Springs (Brewers)

DOUBLE-A

Eastern League

1. Rafael Devers, 3B, Portland (Red Sox)
2. Victor Robles, OF, Harrisburg (Nationals)
3. Austin Hays, OF, Bowie (Orioles)
4. Brendan Rodgers, SS/2B, Hartford (Rockies)
5. Francisco Mejia, C, Akron (Indians)
6. Scott Kingery, 2B, Reading (Phillies)
7. Chris Shaw, OF/1B, Richmond (Giants)
8. Jorge Mateo, SS/OF, Trenton (Yankees)
9. Anthony Alford, OF, New Hampshire (Blue Jays)
10. Miguel Andujar, 3B, Trenton (Yankees)
11. Justus Sheffield, LHP, Trenton (Yankees)

12. Domingo Acevedo, RHP, Trenton (Yankees)
13. Michael Chavis, 3B, Portland (Red Sox)
14. Tanner Scott, LHP, Bowie (Orioles)
15. Ryan McMahon, 1B/2B, Hartford (Rockies)
16. D.J. Stewart, OF, Bowie (Orioles)
17. Erick Fedde, RHP, Harrisburg (Nationals)
18. Cedric Mullins, OF, Bowie (Orioles)
19. Beau Burrows, RHP, Erie (Tigers)
20. Christin Stewart, OF, Erie (Tigers)

Southern League

1. Ronald Acuna, OF, Mississippi (Braves)
2. Nick Senzel, 3B, Pensacola (Reds)
3. Michael Kopech, RHP, Birmingham (White Sox)
4. Mike Soroka, RHP, Mississippi (Braves)
5. Luiz Gohara, LHP, Mississippi (Braves)
6. Austin Riley, 3B, Mississippi (Braves)
7. Luis Castillo, RHP, Pensacola (Reds)
8. Corbin Burnes, RHP, Biloxi (Brewers)
9. Nick Gordon, SS/2B, Chattanooga (Twins)
10. Kolby Allard, LHP, Mississippi (Braves)
11. Fernando Romero, RHP, Chattanooga (Twins)
12. Luis Ortiz, RHP, Biloxi (Brewers)
13. Tyler Mahle, RHP, Pensacola (Reds)
14. Stephen Gonsalves, LHP, Chattanooga (Twins)
15. Jaime Barria, RHP, Mobile (Angels)
16. Justin Williams, OF, Montgomery (Rays)
17. Dawel Lugo, 3B/SS, Jackson (D-backs)
18. LaMonte Wade, OF, Chattanooga (Twins)
19. Max Fried, LHP, Mississippi (Braves)
20. Taylor Clarke, RHP, Jackson (Diamondbacks)

Texas League

1. Walker Buehler, RHP, Tulsa (Dodgers)
2. Kyle Tucker, OF, Corpus Christi (Astros)
3. A.J. Puk, LHP, Midland (Athletics)
4. Jack Flaherty, RHP, Springfield (Cardinals)
5. Luis Urias, 2B/SS, San Antonio (Padres)
6. Jorge Mateo, SS, Midland (Athletics)
7. Yohander Mendez, LHP, Frisco (Rangers)
8. Edwin Rios, 1B/3B, Tulsa (Dodgers)
9. Magneuris Sierra, OF, Springfield (Cardinals)
10. Dakota Hudson, RHP, Springfield (Cardinals)
11. Jose Adolis Garcia, OF, Springfield (Cardinals)
12. Rogelio Armenteros, RHP, Corpus Christi (Astros)
13. J.D. Davis, 3B, Corpus Christi (Astros)
14. Oscar Mercado, OF, Springfield (Cardinals)
15. Joey Lucchesi, LHP, San Antonio (Padres)
16. Eric Lauer, LHP, San Antonio (Padres)
17. Grant Holmes, RHP, Midland (Athletics)
18. Josh Naylor, 1B, San Antonio (Padres)
19. Foster Griffin, LHP, Northwest Arkansas (Royals)
20. Sandy Alcantara, RHP, Springfield (Cardinals)

HIGH CLASS A

California League

1. Brendan Rodgers, SS, Lancaster (Rockies)
2. A.J. Puk, LHP, Stockton (Athletics)
3. Cal Quantrill, RHP, Lake Elsinore (Padres)
4. Kyle Lewis, OF, Modesto (Mariners)

5. Keibert Ruiz, C, Rancho Cucamonga (Dodgers)
6. Jon Duplantier, RHP, Visalia (Diamondbacks)
7. Yadier Alvarez, RHP, Rancho Cucamonga (Dodgers)
8. Yusniel Diaz, OF, Rancho Cucamonga (Dodgers)
9. Jahmai Jones, OF, Inland Empire (Angels)
10. D.J. Peters, OF, Rancho Cucamonga (Dodgers)
11. Nick Neidert, RHP, Modesto (Mariners)
12. Peter Lambert, RHP, Lancaster (Rockies)
13. Sean Murphy, C, Stockon (Athletics)
14. Jaime Barria, RHP, Inland Empire (Angels)
15. Logan Allen, LHP, Lake Elsinore (Padres)
16. Joey Lucchesi, LHP, Lake Elsinore (Padres)
17. Will Smith, C, Rancho Cucamonga (Dodgers)
18. Josh Naylor, 1B, Lake Elsinore (Padres)
19. Bryan Reynolds, OF, San Jose (Giants)
20. Garrett Hampson, 2B/SS, Lancaster (Rockies)

Carolina League

1. Eloy Jimenez, OF, Winston-Salem (White Sox)
2. Victor Robles, OF, Potomac (Nationals)
3. Austin Hays, OF, Frederick (Orioles)
4. Kyle Tucker, OF, Buies Creek (Astros)
5. Franklin Perez, RHP, Buies Creek (Astros)
6. Trison McKenzie, RHP, Lynchburg (Indians)
7. Monte Harrison, OF, Carolina (Brewers)
8. Corbin Burnes, RHP, Carolina (Brewers)
9. Alec Hansen, RHP, Winston-Salem (White Sox)
10. Dane Dunning, RHP, Winston-Salem (White Sox)
11. Michael Chavis, 3B, Salem (Red Sox)
12. Willi Castro, SS, Lynchburg (Indians)
13. Zack Collins, C, Winston-Salem (White Sox)
14. Jake Gatewood, 1B, Carolina (Brewers)
15. Lucas Erceg, 3B, Carolina (Brewers)
16. Adbert Alzolay, RHP, Myrtle Beach (Cubs)
17. Ryan Mountcastle, SS, Frederick (Orioles)
18. Daniel Johnson, OF, Potomac (Nationals)
19. Jorge Alcala, RHP, Buies Creek (Astros)
20. Freddy Peralta, RHP, Carolina (Brewers)

Florida State League

1. Vladimir Guerrero Jr., OF, Dunedin (Blue Jays)
2. Bo Bichette, SS, Dunedin (Blue Jays)
3. Mitch Keller, RHP, Bradenton (Pirates)
4. Nick Senzel, 3B, Daytona (Reds)
5. Ke'Bryan Hayes, 3B, Bradenton (Pirates)
6. Austin Riley, 3B, Florida (Braves)
7. Dillon Tate, RHP, Tampa (Yankees)
8. Brent Rooker, OF/1B, Fort Myers (Twins)
9. Cole Tucker, SS, Bradenton (Pirates)
10. Ryan Helsley, RHP, Palm Beach (Cardinals)
11. Beau Burrows, RHP, Lakeland (Tigers)
12. Cornelius Randolph, OF, Clearwater (Phillies)
13. Seranthony Dominguez, RHP, Clearwater (Phillies)
14. Nick Solak, 2B, Tampa (Yankees)
15. JoJo Romero, LHP, Clearwater (Phillies)
16. Max Pentecost, C/1B, Dunedin (Blue Jays)
17. Franklyn Kilome, RHP, Clearwater (Phillies)
18. Ryan Boldt, OF, Charlotte (Rays)
19. Alex Jackson, C, Florida (Braves)
20. Brandon Lowe, 2B, Charlotte (Rays)

LOW CLASS A

Midwest League

1. Vladimir Guerrero Jr., 3B, Lansing (Blue Jays)
2. Fernando Tatis Jr., SS, Fort Wayne (Padres)
3. Bo Bichette, SS/2B, Lansing (Blue Jays)
4. Michel Baez, RHP, Fort Wayne (Padres)
5. Forrest Whitley, RHP, Quad Cities (Astros)
6. Taylor Trammell, OF, Dayton (Reds)
7. Jesus Sanchez, OF, Bowling Green (Rays)
8. Yordan Alvarez, 1B/OF, Quad Cities (Astros)
9. Isaac Paredes, SS, West Michigan (Tigers)
10. Marcus Wilson, OF, Kane County (D-backs)
11. Dylan Cease, RHP, South Bend (Cubs)
12. Jon Duplantier, RHP, Kane County (D-backs)
13. Jordan Hicks, RHP, Peoria (Cardinals)
14. Logan Allen, LHP, Fort Wayne (Padres)
15. Keibert Ruiz, C, Great Lakes (Dodgers)
16. Dustin May, RHP, Great Lakes (Dodgers)
17. Tyler Stephenson, C, Dayton (Reds)
18. Garrett Whitley, OF, Bowling Green (Rays)
19. Hudson Potts, 3B, Fort Wayne (Padres)
20. Daz Cameron, OF, West Michigan (Tigers)

South Atlantic League

1. Sixto Sanchez, RHP, Lakewood (Phillies)
2. Estevan Florial, OF, Charleston (Yankees)
3. Leody Taveras, OF, Hickory (Rangers)
4. Alec Hansen, RHP, Kannapolis (White Sox)
5. Cristian Pache, OF, Rome (Braves)
6. Ian Anderson, RHP, Rome (Braves)
7. Andres Gimenez, SS, Columbia (Mets)
8. Carter Kieboom, SS, Hagerstown (Nationals)
9. Colton Welker, 3B, Asheville (Rockies)
10. Adonis Medina, RHP, Lakewood (Phillies)
11. Bryse Wilson, RHP, Rome (Braves)
12. Micker Adolfo, OF, Kannapolis (White Sox)
13. Daniel Johnson, OF, Hagerstown (Nationals)
14. Joey Wentz, LHP, Rome (Braves)
15. Riley Pint, RHP, Asheville (Rockies)
16. Jake Burger, 3B, Kannapolis (White Sox)
17. Mickey Moniak, OF, Lakewood (Phillies)
18. Blake Rutherford, OF, Kannapolis (White Sox)
19. Sheldon Neuse, SS/3B, Hagerstown (Nationals)
20. Brian Miller, OF, Greensboro (Marlins)

SHORT-SEASON

New York-Penn League

1. Brendan McKay, 1B/LHP, Hudson Valley (Rays)
2. Jorge Guzman, RHP, Staten Island (Yankees)
3. Jhailyn Ortiz, OF, Williamsport (Phillies)
4. Matt Manning, RHP, Connecticut (Tigers)
5. Vidal Brujan, 2B, Hudson Valley (Rays)
6. Adam Haseley, OF, Williamsport (Phillies)
7. Greg Deichmann, OF, Vermont (Athletics)
8. Nolan Jones, 3B, Mahoning Valley (Indians)
9. Trevor Stephan, RHP, Staten Island (Yankees)
10. Will Benson, OF, Mahoning Valley (Indians)
11. Tobias Myers, RHP, Hudson Valley (Rays)
12. Evan Mendoza, 3B, State College (Cardinals)
13. Kyle Young, LHP, Williamsport (Phillies)

14. Juan De Paula, RHP, Staten Island (Yankees)
15. Samad Taylor, 2B, Mahoning Valley (Indians)
16. Oswaldo Cabrera, SS/2B, Staten Island (Yankees)
17. Cameron Bishop, LHP, Aberdeen (Orioles)
18. Michael Baumann, RHP, Aberdeen (Orioles)
19. Tristan Gray, SS/2B, West Virginia (Pirates)
20. Spencer Howard, RHP, Williamsport (Phillies)

Northwest League

1. Cole Ragans, LHP, Spokane (Rangers)
2. Pavin Smith, 1B, Hillsboro (D-backs)
3. Jhoan Duran, RHP, Hillsboro (D-backs)
4. Jose Albertos, RHP, Eugene (Cubs)
5. Adrian Morejon, LHP, Tri-City (Padres)
6. Logan Warmoth, SS, Vancouver (Blue Jays)
7. Drew Ellis, 3B, Hillsboro (D-backs)
8. Aramis Ademan, SS, Eugene (Cubs)
9. Javier Assad, RHP, Eugene (Cubs)
10. Daulton Varsho, C, Hillsboro (D-backs)
11. Riley Adams, C, Vancouver (Blue Jays)
12. Alex Speas, RHP, Spokane (Rangers)
13. Miguel Aparicio, OF, Spokane (Rangers)
14. Eudy Ramos, 3B/1B, Hillsboro (D-backs)
15. Matt Whatley, C, Spokane (Rangers)
16. Miguel Amaya, C, Eugene (Cubs)
17. Sean Bouchard, 1B, Boise (Rockies)
18. Malique Ziegler, OF, Salem-Keizer (Giants)
19. Kevin Vicuna, SS, Vancouver (Blue Jays)
20. Reggie Pruitt, OF, Vancouver (Blue Jays)

ROOKIE

Appalachian League

1. Kevin Maitan, SS, Danville (Braves)
2. Wander Javier, SS, Elizabethton (Twins)
3. Seuly Matias, OF, Burlington (Royals)
4. Ronaldo Hernandez, C, Princeton (Rays)
5. Brent Rooker, OF/1B, Elizabethton (Twins)
6. Luis Medina, RHP, Pulaski (Yankees)
7. Akil Baddoo, OF, Elizabethton (Twins)
8. Kyle Muller, LHP, Danville (Braves)
9. Drew Waters, OF, Danville (Braves)
10. William Contreras, C, Danville (Braves)
11. Gilberto Celestino, OF, Greeneville (Astros)
12. Ryan Noda, 1B/OF, Bluefield (Blue Jays)
13. Braeden Ogle, LHP, Bristol (Pirates)
14. Alvaro Seijas, RHP, Johnson City (Cardinals)
15. Deivi Garcia, RHP, Pulaski (Yankees)
16. Juan Uriarte, C, Kingsport (Mets)
17. Andrew Bechtold, 3B, Elizabethton (Twins)
18. Michael Gigliotti, OF, Burlington (Royals)
19. Mc Gregory Contreras, OF, Bluefield (Blue Jays)
20. Joel Peguero, RHP, Princeton (Rays)

Arizona League

1. MacKenzie Gore, LHP, Padres
2. Jo Adell, OF, Angels
3. Heliot Ramos, OF, Giants
4. Keston Hiura, DH, Brewers
5. Hans Crouse, RHP, Rangers
6. Bubba Thompson, OF, Rangers
7. Gabriel Arias, SS, Padres

8. Austin Beck, OF, Athletics
9. Nick Pratto, 1B, Royals
10. Esteury Ruiz, 2B, Padres
11. Tristen Luiz, OF, Brewers
12. Chris Seise, SS, Rangers
13. M.J. Melendez, C, Royals
14. Lazaro Armenteros, OF, Athletics
15. Jacob Gonzalez, 3B, Giants
16. Luis Campusano, C, Padres
17. Jordy Barley, SS, Padres
18. Jose Soriano, RHP, Angels
19. Nick Allen, SS, Athletics
20. Nelson Velazquez, OF, Cubs

Gulf Coast League

1. Royce Lewis, SS, Twins
2. Lolo Sanchez, OF, Pirates
3. Shane Baz, RHP, Pirates
4. Luis Garcia, 2B/SS, Nationals
5. Yasel Antuna, SS/3B, Nationals
6. Mason Martin, 1B/OF, Pirates
7. Simon Muzziotti, OF, Phillies
8. Jonathan Guzman, SS, Phillies
9. Elehuris Montero, 3B, Cardinals
10. Mark Vientos, SS/3B, Mets
11. Francisco Morales, RHP, Phillies
12. Jairo Solis, RHP, Astros
13. Blayne Enlow, RHP, Twins
14. Oswald Peraza, SS, Yankees
15. Yunior Severino, 2B, Braves
16. Yefri del Rosario, RHP, Braves
17. Michael Mercado, RHP, Rays
18. Jonathan Machado, OF, Cardinals
19. Jose Devers, SS, Yankees
20. Sam McMillan, C, Tigers

Pioneer League

1. Jo Adell, OF, Orem (Angels)
2. Chris Rodriguez, RHP, Orem (Angels)
3. Tristen Lutz, OF, Helena (Brewers)
4. Brandon Marsh, OF, Orem (Angels)
5. Starling Heredia, OF, Ogden (Dodgers)
6. Ryan Vilade, SS, Grand Junction (Rockies)
7. Pedro Gonzalez, OF, Grand Junction (Rockies)
8. K.J. Harrison, C, Helena (Brewers)
9. Leonardo Rivas, SS, Orem (Angels)
10. Jeter Downs, SS, Billings (Reds)
11. Eduardo Diaz, OF, Missoula (D-backs)
12. Andy Yerzy, C, Missoula (D-backs)
13. Stuart Fairchild, OF, Billings (Reds)
14. Janser Lara, RHP, Idaho Falls (Royals)
15. Packy Naughton, LHP, Billings (Reds)
16. Tommy Doyle, RHP, Grand Junction (Rockies)
17. Romer Cuadrado, OF, Ogden (Dodgers)
18. Payton Henry, C, Helena (Brewers)
19. Joey Rose, 3B, Missoula (D-backs)
20. Antonio Pinero, SS, Helena (Brewers)

INDEX

Diaz, Isan (Brewers) 265
Diaz, Lewin (Twins) 288
Diaz, Yennsy (Blue Jays) 481
Diaz, Yusniel (Dodgers) 232
Dietz, Matthias (Orioles) 63
Diplan, Marcos (Brewers) 270
Dominguez, Seranthony (Phillies) 346
Doval, Camilo (Giants) 416
Downs, Jeter (Reds) 122
Dozier, Hunter (Royals) 200
Dubon, Mauricio (Brewers) 267
Duenez, Samir (Royals) 203
Duggar, Steven (Giants) 409
Dugger, Robert (Marlins) 255
Dunand, Joe (Marlins) 251
Dunn, Justin (Mets) 294
Dunning, Dane (White Sox) 103
Duplantier, Jon (D-backs) 21
Duran, Jhoan (D-backs) 30

E

Edman, Tommy (Cardinals) 385
Elledge, Seth (Mariners) 429
Ellis, Drew (D-backs) 25
Encarnacion, Jean Carlos (Braves) 47
Enlow, Blayne (Twins) 281
Eppler, Tyler (Pirates) 369
Erceg, Lucas (Brewers) 265
Ervin, Phillip (Reds) 125
Escobar, Luis (Pirates) 360
Eshelman, Thomas (Phillies) 352
Espinoza, Anderson (Padres) 392
Esplin, Tyler (Red Sox) 81
Estrada, Thairo (Yankees) 313
Eusebio, Breiling (Rockies) 156
Eveld, Tommy (D-backs) 31

F

Fabian, Sandro (Giants) 409
Faedo, Alex (Tigers) 166
Fairchild, Stuart (Reds) 124
Farmer, Kyle (Dodgers) 239
Fedde, Erick (Nationals) 486
Feliciano, Mario (Brewers) 270
Fenter, Gray (Orioles) 64
Ferguson, Caleb (Dodgers) 237
Fernandez, Junior (Cardinals) 382
Fernandez, Vince (Rockies) 160
Ferrell, Riley (Astros) 192
Festa, Matt (Mariners) 424
Filia, Eric (Mariners) 427
Fillmyer, Heath (Athletics) 332
Flaherty, Jack (Cardinals) 374
Fletcher, David (Angels) 224
Flexen, Chris (Mets) 297
Flores, Antoni (Red Sox) 76
Flores, Bernardo (White Sox) 112
Florial, Estevan (Yankees) 310
Foley, Jason (Tigers) 175
Ford, Mike (Mariners) 430
Fowler, Dustin (Athletics) 327
Fox, Lucius (Rays) 440
Franco, Anderson (Nationals) 496
Franco, Wander (Rays) 440
Franklin, Austin (Rays) 442
Freeman, Tyler (Indians) 140
Fried, Max (Braves) 41
Friedl, T.J. (Reds) 124
Fuentes, Josh (Rockies) 159
Fulmer, Carson (White Sox) 107
Funkhouser, Kyle (Tigers) 170

G

Gaddis, Will (Rockies) 157
Gallagher, Cam (Royals) 209
Gallen, Zac (Marlins) 250
Gamboa, Arquimedes (Phillies) 349
Garabito, Gerson (Royals) 204
Garcia, Aramis (Giants) 408
Garcia, Bryan (Tigers) 172
Garcia, David (Rangers) 460
Garcia, Deivi (Yankees) 319
Garcia, Dermis (Yankees) 317
Garcia, Edgar (Phillies) 352
Garcia, Jose Adolis (Cardinals) 377
Garcia, Jose Israel (Reds) 122
Garcia, Luis (Nationals) 488
Garcia, Luis (Phillies) 348
Garcia, Rony (Yankees) 321
Garcia, Victor (Cardinals) 384
Garcia, Yeudy (Pirates) 368
Gardewine, Nick (Rangers) 461
Garrett, Braxton (Marlins) 247
Garver, Mitch (Twins) 287
Gatewood, Jake (Brewers) 267
Gatto, Joe (Angels) 224
Gerber, Mike (Tigers) 171
German, Domingo (Yankees) 316
Gettys, Michael (Padres) 400
Gibaut, Ian (Rays) 449
Gigliotti, Michael (Royals) 205
Gimenez, Andres (Mets) 293
Givin, Matt (Marlins) 253
Gohara, Luiz (Braves) 38
Gomber, Austin (Cardinals) 379
Gomez, Miguel (Giants) 414
Gonsalves, Stephen (Twins) 279
Gonzalez, Derian (Cardinals) 384
Gonzalez, Erik (Indians) 138
Gonzalez, Jacob (Giants) 410
Gonzalez, Luis (White Sox) 107
Gonzalez, Marcos (Indians) 145
Gonzalez, Merandy (Marlins) 251
Gonzalez, Oscar (Indians) 141
Gonzalez, Pedro (Rangers) 463
Gonzalez, Rayan (Rockies) 161
Gordon, Miles (Reds) 128
Gordon, Nick (Twins) 281
Gore, MacKenzie (Padres) 390
Graham, Josh (Braves) 49
Granite, Zack (Twins) 288
Graterol, Brusdar (Twins) 279
Greene, Conner (Blue Jays) 476
Greene, Hunter (Reds) 118
Gregorio, Joan (Giants) 414
Greiner, Grayson (Tigers) 174
Griffin, Foster (Royals) 201
Grisham, Trent (Brewers) 268
Groome, Jay (Red Sox) 69
Guerrero Jr., Vladimir (Blue Jays) 469
Guerrero, Jordan (White Sox) 111
Guillorme, Luis (Mets) 298
Gurriel, Lourdes (Blue Jays) 471
Gushue, Taylor (Nationals) 493
Gustave, Jandel (Astros) 193
Gutierrez, Kelvin (Nationals) 490
Gutierrez, Vladimir (Reds) 121
Guzman, Jonathan (Phillies) 348
Guzman, Jorge (Marlins) 246
Guzman, Ronald (Rangers) 456

H

Hall, Adam (Orioles) 61
Hall, D.L. (Orioles) 55

Hamilton, Ian (White Sox) 111
Hammer, J.D. (Phillies) 352
Hampson, Garrett (Rockies) 153
Hanifee, Brenan (Orioles) 61
Hansen, Alec (White Sox) 102
Hanson, Nick (Reds) 129
Harris, Jon (Blue Jays) 481
Harrison, K.J. (Brewers) 268
Harrison, Monte (Brewers) 263
Harvey, Hunter (Orioles) 55
Haseley, Adam (Phillies) 343
Hatch, Thomas (Cubs) 89
Hayes, Ke'Bryan (Pirates) 359
Hays, Austin (Orioles) 53
Hearn, Taylor (Pirates) 361
Heatherly, Jacob (Reds) 124
Helsley, Ryan (Cardinals) 377
Henry, Payton (Brewers) 273
Hentges, Sam (Indians) 141
Henzman, Lincoln (White Sox) 109
Herb, Tyler (Giants) 416
Heredia, Starling (Dodgers) 236
Herget, Jimmy (Reds) 125
Hermosillo, Michael (Angels) 218
Hernandez, Adrian (Mets) 305
Hernandez, Brayan (Marlins) 252
Hernandez, Carlos (Royals) 204
Hernandez, Darwinzon (Red Sox) 72
Hernandez, Johnathan (Rangers) 460
Hernandez, Marco (Red Sox) 74
Hernandez, Ronaldo (Rays) 442
Hernandez, Wilkel (Tigers) 174
Herrera, Carlos (Brewers) 272
Hess, David (Orioles) 59
Hicks, Jordan (Cardinals) 375
Hill, Brigham (Nationals) 492
Hill, Derek (Tigers) 177
Hilliard, Sam (Rockies) 155
Hinojosa, C.J. (Giants) 417
Hinsz, Gage (Pirates) 368
Hiraldo, Miguel (Blue Jays) 476
Hiura, Keston (Brewers) 263
Hock, Colton (Marlins) 253
Holloway, Jordan (Marlins) 256
Holmes, Clay (Pirates) 366
Holmes, Grant (Athletics) 330
Holmes, Quentin (Indians) 139
Honeywell, Brent (Rays) 437
Houck, Tanner (Red Sox) 70
Howard, Ryan (Giants) 412
Howard, Sam (Rockies) 154
Howard, Spencer (Phillies) 349
Hu, Chih-Wei (Rays) 448
Hudson, Bryan (Cubs) 91
Hudson, Dakota (Cardinals) 376
Humphreys, Jordan (Mets) 299
Humphreys, Reid (Rockies) 160
Hunter Jr., Torii (Angels) 225
Hurst, Scott (Cardinals) 383

I

Ibanez, Andy (Rangers) 465
Ice, Logan (Indians) 141

J

Jackson, Alex (Braves) 42
Jackson, Drew (Dodgers) 241
James, Christian (Mets) 305
Jansen, Danny (Blue Jays) 472
Jaskie, Oliver (Mariners) 430
Javier, Cristian (Astros) 191
Javier, Wander (Twins) 278

Jay, Tyler (Twins)	282	Lopez, Yoan (D-backs)	29	Miller, Jared (D-backs)	28
Jeffries, Daulton (Athletics)	331	Lovelady, Richard (Royals)	208	Mills, Alec (Cubs)	96
Jennings, Steven (Pirates)	362	Lowe, Brandon (Rays)	444	Mills, Wyatt (Mariners)	426
Jerez, Williams (Red Sox)	80	Lowe, Josh (Rays)	442	Minter, A.J. (Braves)	44
Jewell, Jake (Angels)	223	Lowther, Zac (Orioles)	60	Miranda, Jose (Twins)	287
Jimenez, Eloy (White Sox)	101	Lucchesi, Joey (Padres)	393	Misiewicz, Anthony (Mariners)	429
Jimenez, Joe (Tigers)	172	Luciano, Elvis (D-backs)	32	Mitchell, Calvin (Pirates)	363
Jimenez, Leonardo (Blue Jays)	477	Lugbauer, Drew (Braves)	48	Molina, Marcos (Mets)	296
Johnson, Brian (Red Sox)	79	Lugo, Dawel (Tigers)	169	Moll, Sam (Mariners)	430
Johnson, Daniel (Nationals)	489	Lund, Brennon (Angels)	221	Moniak, Mickey (Phillies)	345
Johnson, Tyler (White Sox)	111	Luplow, Jordan (Pirates)	363	Montano, Daniel (Rockies)	159
Johnston, Kyle (Nationals)	494	Lutz, Tristen (Brewers)	266	Montas, Frankie (Athletics)	334
Jones, Connor (Cardinals)	382	Lux, Gavin (Dodgers)	235	Montgomery, Troy (Tigers)	176
Jones, Jahmai (Angels)	214	Luzardo, Jesus (Athletics)	327	Morales, Francisco (Phillies)	348
Jones, Nolan (Indians)	135			Moran, Colin (Astros)	185
Jones, Thomas (Marlins)	256	**M**		Morejon, Adrian (Padres)	391
Jorge, Felix (Twins)	283	Machado, Andres (Royals)	207	Moreno, Gerson (Tigers)	173
		Machado, Jonathan (Cardinals)	380	Morgan, Eli (Indians)	145
K		Maciel, Gabriel (D-backs)	28	Morgan, Josh (Rangers)	462
Kaprielian, James (Athletics)	329	Maddox, Austin (Red Sox)	77	Moroff, Max (Pirates)	364
Kay, Anthony (Mets)	299	Mahan, Riley (Marlins)	253	Moronta, Reyes (Giants)	411
Keller, Brad (Royals)	206	Mahle, Tyler (Reds)	119	Moss, Scott (Reds)	129
Keller, Mitch (Pirates)	357	Maitan, Kevin (Angels)	215	Mountcastle, Ryan (Orioles)	54
Kelly, Carson (Cardinals)	374	Manning, Matt (Tigers)	166	Muller, Kyle (Braves)	45
Kendall, Jeren (Dodgers)	232	Maples, Dillon (Cubs)	91	Mullins, Cedric (Orioles)	57
Kennedy, Buddy (D-backs)	32	Marinan, James (Dodgers)	239	Mundell, Brian (Rockies)	155
Kieboom, Carter (Nationals)	487	Marinez, Ynmanol (Marlins)	257	Munoz, Andres (Padres)	397
Kilome, Franklyn (Phillies)	346	Marmolejos, Jose (Nationals)	493	Munoz, Yairo (Cardinals)	380
King, Jose (Tigers)	172	Marsh, Brandon (Angels)	215	Murphy, Sean (Athletics)	328
Kingery, Scott (Phillies)	342	Marte, Jelfry (Free Agent)	499	Murphy, Tom (Rockies)	154
Kingham, Nick (Pirates)	361	Martin, Brett (Rangers)	460	Musgrave, Harrison (Rockies)	158
Kirby, Nathan (Brewers)	272	Martin, Corbin (Astros)	188	Muzziotti, Simon (Phillies)	347
Kirilloff, Alex (Twins)	278	Martin, Jason (Astros)	189	Myers, Tobias (Rays)	443
Knizner, Andrew (Cardinals)	378	Martin, Mason (Pirates)	365		
Knowles, D'Shawn (Angels)	222	Martin, Richie (Athletics)	334	**N**	
Kolek, Tyler (Marlins)	252	Martinez, Joan (Red Sox)	79	Naile, James (Athletics)	335
Kopech, Michael (White Sox)	102	Martinez, Julio Pablo (Free Agent)	498	Naughton, Packy (Reds)	129
Kramer, Kevin (Pirates)	362	Martinez, Rodolfo (Giants)	415	Naylor, Josh (Padres)	395
Krieger, Tyler (Indians)	142	Mata, Bryan (Red Sox)	71	Neidert, Nick (Marlins)	247
Krook, Matt (Giants)	413	Mateo, Jorge (Athletics)	326	Nelson, James (Marlins)	249
		Mathias, Mark (Indians)	143	Netzer, Brett (Red Sox)	77
L		Matias, Seuly (Royals)	198	Neuse, Sheldon (Athletics)	331
Lakins, Travis (Red Sox)	78	Matijevic, J.J. (Astros)	192	Neverauskas, Dovydas (Pirates)	364
Lambert, Peter (Rockies)	151	Matuella, Michael (Rangers)	465	Nevin, Tyler (Rockies)	154
Lange, Alex (Cubs)	87	Mauricio, Ronny (Mets)	298	Newman, Kevin (Pirates)	359
Lauer, Eric (Padres)	394	May, Dustin (Dodgers)	234	Nido, Tomas (Mets)	298
Lauereano, Ramon (Athletics)	337	Mazeika, Patrick (Mets)	301	Nikorak, Mike (Rockies)	158
LaValley, Gavin (Reds)	126	McCarthy, Joe (Rays)	444	Nix, Jacob (Padres)	394
Lawson, Reggie (Padres)	400	McClanahan, Chad (Brewers)	273	Noda, Ryan (Blue Jays)	475
Leach, Landon (Twins)	283	McGuire, Reese (Blue Jays)	475	Nottingham, Jacob (Brewers)	271
Lee, Braxton (Marlins)	254	McKay, Brendan (Rays)	438	Nova, Freudis (Astros)	183
Lee, Chris (Orioles)	58	McKenzie, Triston (Indians)	134	Nunez, Dom (Rockies)	161
Lee, Khalil (Royals)	198	McKinney, Billy (Yankees)	318	Nunez, Renato (Athletics)	333
Lemons, Caden (Brewers)	271	McMahon, Ryan (Rockies)	150		
Lewis, Kyle (Mariners)	421	McMillan, John (Tigers)	171	**O**	
Lewis, Royce (Twins)	277	McWilliams, Sam (D-backs)	27	O'Neill, Tyler (Cardinals)	375
Leyba, Domingo (D-backs)	26	Meadows, Austin (Pirates)	358	O'Hearn, Ryan (Royals)	204
Liberato, Luis (Mariners)	431	Medeiros, Kodi (Brewers)	270	Oaks, Trevor (Dodgers)	236
Lin, Tzu-Wei (Red Sox)	78	Medina, Adonis (Phillies)	343	Ockimey, Josh (Red Sox)	74
Linares, Resly (Rays)	447	Medina, Luis (Yankees)	312	Ogle, Braeden (Pirates)	365
Lindsay, Desmond (Mets)	297	Meisner, Casey (Athletics)	336	Ohtani, Shohei (Angels)	213
Liranzo, Jesus (Orioles)	61	Mejia, Francisco (Indians)	133	Olivares, Edward (Blue Jays)	475
Littell, Zack (Twins)	285	Mekkes, Dakota (Cubs)	94	Ona, Jorge (Padres)	396
Little, Brendon (Cubs)	88	Melendez, M.J. (Royals)	200	Ortiz, Jhailyn (Phillies)	344
Llovera, Mauricio (Phillies)	353	Mella, Keury (Reds)	126	Ortiz, Luis (Brewers)	264
Loaisiga, Jonathan (Yankees)	319	Mendez, Yohander (Rangers)	455	Oswalt, Corey (Mets)	300
Locastro, Tim (Dodgers)	240	Mercado, Michael (Rays)	443	Otto, Glenn (Yankees)	317
Long, Shed (Reds)	121	Mercado, Oscar (Cardinals)	379	Oviedo, Johan (Cardinals)	383
Longhi, Nick (Reds)	127	Merrell, Kevin (Athletics)	332	Oviedo, Luis (Indians)	142
Lopez, Jose (Reds)	128	Merritt, Ryan (Indians)	144		
Lopez, Nicky (Royals)	202	Merryweather, Julian (Indians)	140		
Lopez, Pablo (Marlins)	255	Miller, Brian (Marlins)	250		
		Miller, Ian (Mariners)	429		

P

Pache, Cristian (Braves)	41
Paddack, Chris (Padres)	398
Palumbo, Joe (Rangers)	458
Pardinho, Eric (Blue Jays)	472
Paredes, Isaac (Tigers)	168
Patterson, Jordan (Rockies)	156
Paulino, David (Astros)	186
Pearson, Jacob (Twins)	286
Pearson, Nate (Blue Jays)	471
Pelham, C.D. (Rangers)	461
Pena, Keinner (Angels)	225
Pena, Luis (Angels)	222
Pennington, Josh (Brewers)	269
Pentecost, Max (Blue Jays)	478
Peralta, Freddy (Brewers)	266
Peralta, Ofelky (Orioles)	62
Perez, Cionel (Astros)	187
Perez, Delvin (Cardinals)	378
Perez, Franklin (Tigers)	165
Perez, Freicer (Yankees)	315
Perez, Hector (Astros)	184
Perez, Joe (Astros)	188
Perez, Michael (D-backs)	33
Perez, Wenceel (Tigers)	175
Perez, Yanio (Rangers)	462
Perkins, Blake (Nationals)	490
Peters, Dillon (Marlins)	250
Peters, DJ (Dodgers)	233
Peterson, David (Mets)	294
Peterson, Dustin (Braves)	46
Pfeifer, Phil (Braves)	49
Phillips, Brett (Brewers)	264
Pinero, Antonio (Brewers)	273
Pint, Riley (Rockies)	150
Pinto, Wladimir (Tigers)	174
Poche, Colin (D-backs)	33
Polo, Tito (White Sox)	112
Ponce, Cody (Brewers)	269
Potts, Hudson (Padres)	396
Povse, Max (Mariners)	424
Pratto, Nick (Royals)	197
Puckett, A.J. (White Sox)	108
Puk, A.J. (Athletics)	325

Q

Quantrill, Cal (Padres)	391
Querecuto, Juan (Mariners)	426
Quinn, Roman (Phillies)	347

R

Ragans, Cole (Rangers)	455
Rainey, Tanner (Reds)	126
Raley, Luke (Dodgers)	240
Ramirez, Carlos (Blue Jays)	477
Ramirez, Harold (Blue Jays)	478
Ramirez, Tyler (Athletics)	332
Ramirez, Yefry (Orioles)	63
Ramos, Heliot (Giants)	405
Ramos, Jeffrey (Braves)	48
Randolph, Cornelius (Phillies)	350
Raquet, Nick (Nationals)	494
Raudes, Roniel (Red Sox)	81
Ray, Corey (Brewers)	266
Read, Raudy (Nationals)	489
Reed, A.J. (Astros)	191
Reed, Tyreque (Rangers)	459
Reetz, Jakson (Nationals)	497
Reid-Foley, Sean (Blue Jays)	474
Reyes, Alex (Cardinals)	373
Reyes, Jomar (Orioles)	58
Reyes, Victor (Tigers)	175
Reynolds, Bryan (Giants)	407
Rhame, Jacob (Mets)	303
Richards, Trevor (Marlins)	254
Rifaela, Ademar (Orioles)	64
Riley, Austin (Braves)	40
Rios, Edwin (Dodgers)	234
Rivas, Leonardo (Angels)	218
Rivera, Emmanuel (Royals)	208
Rivera, Jerryel (Angels)	222
Rizzo, Joe (Mariners)	425
Robert, Luis (White Sox)	103
Robinson, Drew (Rangers)	459
Robinson, Errol (Dodgers)	241
Robinson, Kristian (D-backs)	26
Robles, Victor (Nationals)	485
Rodgers, Brendan (Rockies)	149
Rodriguez, Alfredo (Reds)	123
Rodriguez, Chris (Angels)	216
Rodriguez, Elian (Astros)	193
Rodriguez, Jefry (Nationals)	495
Rodriguez, Johnathan (Indians)	142
Rodriguez, Julio (Mariners)	423
Rodriguez, Keyber (Rangers)	461
Rogers, Jake (Tigers)	167
Rogers, Trevor (Marlins)	246
Romano, Jordan (Blue Jays)	480
Romero, Fernando (Twins)	280
Romero, Jojo (Phillies)	344
Romero, Seth (Nationals)	487
Romero, Tommy (Mariners)	432
Rooker, Brent (Twins)	280
Rosa, Joseph (Mariners)	432
Rosario, Jeisson (Padres)	398
Rosario, Ronald (Mariners)	433
Rose, Joey (D-backs)	30
Rucker, Michael (Cubs)	96
Ruiz, Esteury (Padres)	396
Ruiz, Keibert (Dodgers)	230
Rumbelow, Nick (Mariners)	427
Rutherford, Blake (White Sox)	105

S

Salinas, Raimfer (Free Agent)	498
Sanchez, Ali (Mets)	304
Sanchez, Jesus (Rays)	439
Sanchez, Jose (Nationals)	494
Sanchez, LoLo (Pirates)	362
Sanchez, Ricardo (Braves)	45
Sanchez, Sixto (Phillies)	342
Santana, Cristian (Dodgers)	236
Santana, Dennis (Dodgers)	234
Santana, Edgar (Pirates)	366
Santander, Anthony (Orioles)	57
Santillan, Tony (Reds)	120
Santos, Gregory (Giants)	413
Sauer, Matt (Yankees)	314
Sborz, Josh (Dodgers)	239
Scherff, Alex (Red Sox)	73
Schmidt, Clarke (Yankees)	315
Schrock, Max (Cardinals)	381
Schultz, Jaime (Rays)	448
Scott, Tanner (Orioles)	56
Sedlock, Cody (Orioles)	56
Seijas, Alvaro (Cardinals)	382
Seise, Chris (Rangers)	458
Senzel, Nick (Reds)	117
Severino, Pedro (Nationals)	491
Severino, Yunior (Twins)	283
Shaw, Chris (Giants)	406
Shawaryn, Mike (Red Sox)	73
Sheets, Gavin (White Sox)	105
Sheffield, Jordan (Dodgers)	235
Sheffield, Justus (Yankees)	310
Sherfy, Jimmie (D-backs)	27
Shore, Logan (Athletics)	330
Sierra, Jonathan (Cubs)	97
Sierra, Magneuris (Marlins)	248
Sierra, Miguelangel (Astros)	193
Sierra, Yaisel (Dodgers)	241
Siri, Jose (Reds)	120
Sisco, Chance (Orioles)	54
Skoglund, Eric (Royals)	199
Slater, Austin (Giants)	412
Smith, Burch (Royals)	206
Smith, Drew (Mets)	301
Smith, Kevin (Blue Jays)	480
Smith, Pavin (D-backs)	22
Smith, Will (Dodgers)	233
Sodders, Austin (Tigers)	177
Solak, Nick (Yankees)	314
Solis, Jairo (Astros)	184
Soriano, Jose (Angels)	219
Soroka, Mike (Braves)	38
Sosa, Edmundo (Cardinals)	385
Sosa, Lenyn (White Sox)	113
Soto, Gregory (Tigers)	170
Soto, Isael (Marlins)	255
Soto, Juan (Nationals)	486
Soto, Livan (Angels)	220
Spangberger, Chad (Rockies)	160
Sparks, Lamar (Orioles)	63
Speas, Alex (Rangers)	463
Staumont, Josh (Royals)	199
Steele, Evan (Royals)	205
Steele, Justin (Cubs)	93
Stephan, Trevor (Yankees)	317
Stephens, Jackson (Reds)	127
Stephens, Jordan (White Sox)	108
Stephenson, Tyler (Reds)	122
Stevenson, Andrew (Nationals)	491
Stewart, Christin (Tigers)	169
Stewart, D.J. (Orioles)	60
Stewart, Kohl (Twins)	289
Stinnett, Jake (Cubs)	97
Straw, Myles (Astros)	188
Strotman, Drew (Rays)	445
Stubbs, Garrett (Astros)	189
Suarez, Andrew (Giants)	410
Suarez, Jose (Angels)	219
Suarez, Kervin (Red Sox)	81
Suarez, Ranger (Phillies)	346
Supak, Trey (Brewers)	271
Swanda, John (Angels)	223
Szapucki, Thomas (Mets)	295

T

Tabor, Matt (D-backs)	26
Tarnok, Freddy (Braves)	47
Tate, Dillon (Yankees)	314
Tatis Jr., Fernando (Padres)	389
Taveras, Jose (Phillies)	351
Taveras, Leody (Rangers)	454
Tejeda, Anderson (Rangers)	464
Tellez, Rowdy (Blue Jays)	478
Tetrault, Jackson (Nationals)	492
Thaiss, Matt (Angels)	217
Then, Juan (Yankees)	316
Thompson, Bubba (Rangers)	457
Thompson, David (Mets)	305
Thompson, Jake (Red Sox)	75
Thompson, Keegan (Cubs)	91
Thompson, Mason (Padres)	399
Thorpe, Lewis (Twins)	284
Tillo, Daniel (Royals)	205

Tinoco, Jesus (Rockies)	156	Vicuna, Kevin (Blue Jays)	479	Whitley, Garrett (Rays)	441
Tocci, Carlos (Rangers)	459	Vieira, Thyago (White Sox)	109	Widener, Taylor (Yankees)	318
Todd, Jonah (Angels)	224	Vientos, Mark (Mets)	296	Wiliams, Garrett (Giants)	408
Toffey, Will (Athletics)	333	Vilade, Ryan (Rockies)	153	Wilkerson, Steve (Orioles)	65
Torres, Chris (Marlins)	249	Viloria, Meibrys (Royals)	207	Williams, Justin (Rays)	441
Torres, Gleyber (Yankees)	309	Vogelbach, Dan (Mariners)	426	Williams, Nonie (Angels)	223
Toussaint, Touki (Braves)	43	Voit, Luke (Cardinals)	380	Wilson, Bryse (Braves)	42
Trammell, Taylor (Reds)	118	Vosler, Jason (Cubs)	95	Wilson, D.J. (Cubs)	90
Travis, Sam (Red Sox)	72	Voth, Austin (Nationals)	496	Wilson, Israel (Braves)	46
Trevino, Jose (Rangers)	464			Wilson, Marcus (D-backs)	24
Tseng, Jen-Ho (Cubs)	89			Wingenter, Trey (Padres)	399
Tucker, Cole (Pirates)	360	**W**		Winker, Jesse (Reds)	119
Tucker, Kyle (Astros)	182	Waddell, Brandon (Pirates)	365	Wong, Connor (Dodgers)	237
Turnbull, Spencer (Tigers)	170	Wade, LaMonte (Twins)	284	Woodford, Jake (Cardinals)	381
		Wade, Tyler (Yankees)	315	Woodruff, Brandon (Brewers)	262
		Waguespack, Jacob (Phillies)	353	Woods, Stephen (Giants)	415
U		Walker, Christian (D-backs)	32	Wright, Kyle (Braves)	39
Uceta, Adonis (Mets)	302	Wall, Forrest (Rockies)	157	Wynns, Austin (Orioles)	65
Uelmen, Erich (Cubs)	96	Walsh, Connor (White Sox)	113		
Underwood, Duane (Cubs)	93	Walton, Donnie (Mariners)	431		
Urena, Richard (Blue Jays)	473	Ward, Drew (Nationals)	493	**Y**	
Urias, Luis (Padres)	392	Ward, Taylor (Angels)	221		
Uselton, Connor (Pirates)	363	Warmoth, Logan (Blue Jays)	473	Yacabonis, Jimmy (Orioles)	62
		Warren, Art (Mariners)	425	Yarbrough, Ryan (Rays)	448
		Waters, Drew (Braves)	44	Yerzy, Andy (D-backs)	28
V		Watson, Tyler (Twins)	286	Ynfante, Wadye (Cardinals)	384
Valdez, Framber (Astros)	187	Weigel, Patrick (Braves)	44	Ynoa, Huascar (Braves)	47
Valera, George (Indians)	137	Welker, Colton (Rockies)	151	Young, Kyle (Phillies)	350
Vallot, Chase (Royals)	202	Wells, Alex (Orioles)	59		
Vargas, Alexander (Yankees)	320	Wentz, Joey (Braves)	42	**Z**	
Vargas, Ildemaro (D-backs)	31	Whalen, Rob (Mariners)	428		
Vargas, Yerdel (Athletics)	335	Whatley, Matt (Rangers)	458	Zagunis, Mark (Cubs)	93
Varsho, Daulton (D-backs)	23	White, Evan (Mariners)	422	Zavala, Seby (White Sox)	113
Velazquez, Hector (Red Sox)	77	White, Mitchell (Dodgers)	231	Zeuch, T.J. (Blue Jays)	474
Velazquez, Nelson (Cubs)	90	Whitefield, Aaron (Twins)	285	Zimmer, Kyle (Royals)	209
Verdugo, Alex (Dodgers)	230	Whitley, Forrest (Astros)	181		